THE AMERICAN JOURNEY: 1865 TO THE PRESENT

Doug Baker
Susan Hutchins

SIMON & SCHUSTER
CUSTOM PUBLISHING

Cover Photos: Library of Congress; Department of Interior,
Office of Indian Affairs; Tania D'Avignon

Cover Illustration: Dennis Smith

Cover Design: Wing Ip Ngan

Printed in the United States of America

10 9 8 7 6 5 4 3 2 1

ISBN 0-536-59187-3
BA 1008

SIMON & SCHUSTER CUSTOM PUBLISHING
160 Gould Street/Needham Heights, MA 02194
Simon & Schuster Education Group

Table of Contents: Selected Topics

About the Authors

Doug Baker

Doug Baker received a Bachelor of Arts in history from Andrews University (in Michigan) and a Master of Arts degree in history from the University of Central Oklahoma. He also holds a Bachelor of Arts in religion, and is completing a Doctor of Ministry (D. Min.) degree. He is currently an assistant professor of history and the head of the Social Sciences Department at Oklahoma State University-Oklahoma City.

Susan Hutchins

Susan Hutchins received her Bachelor of Arts in social studies, secondary education and her Master of Arts degree in history from the University of Central Oklahoma. She is currently an instructor of history and American government at Oklahoma State University-Oklahoma City.

Foreword

When I had the pleasure of teaching Doug Baker and Susan Hutchins, I knew they would go on to make important contributions to teaching and to the history profession; with the publication of this text they have done just that. It is a clear presentation of the elements of American history from Reconstruction to the present.

While purposely listening to their students' cry for a no-nonsense presentation of the basics of American History since 1865, they have not sacrificed interest. Indeed, by concentrating on the "Why" of important events, they have provided a most interesting account that will both challenge and intrigue students.

In bemoaning the fact that students possess little knowledge of American history, Diane Ravitch has quoted a college professor who put the problem this way: "They have no furniture in their minds. You can assume nothing in the way of prior knowledge. Skills, yes; but not knowledge." Baker and Hutchins have provided students with the furniture in this text, and they have arranged it in an appealing setting.

James F. Baker, Ph.D.
Chair, Department of History/Geography
University of Central Oklahoma
Edmond, Oklahoma

Preface

Before beginning the task of actually organizing a textbook, we asked ourselves why colleges and universities needed another American history textbook. As teachers, and former students ourselves of course, we have reviewed many textbooks and not found one that we were completely satisfied with. This is not to say that there are not many good textbooks on the market, but we felt that we could write a book that would more closely meet the needs of our students. We wanted a book that was more "student friendly." We disliked the organization of many of the texts we had used, and there seemed to be too many questions left unanswered by most of them. It is true that the very nature of a survey course, which covers such a vast amount of material, demands that much detailed information be left out. It is also true that everything that has happened through the years of our nation's existence since the Civil War is not covered in this book. But we have tried to cover most events for a true understanding of not only what happened, but why it happened, what it lead to, and how it fit in with other events of the time, all without leaving out some of the interesting personal stories of the leaders who helped make that history. To put as much information as possible in the students' hands, we have included extensive appendices and numerous maps.

We chose the title *The American Journey* because that is one of our perspectives on history. It is the story of man's and woman's journey from past to present with a building of memories that must be recorded and remembered, or the lessons learned along the way will be wasted. In other words, the metaphor of a journey conveys the appropriate idea that events and attitudes do not occur or exist in a vacuum. The present is linked with both the past and the future.

There are at least three reasons why it is absolutely vital to study and understand history:

(1) *To learn from our mistakes*: Nations, like individuals, can mature. And an important part of the maturation process is to experience failures and then learn from our mistakes. Of course, if you don't think the United States has ever made any serious mistakes, then there is no point in studying our history. Our favorite American diplomatic historian, Thomas A. Bailey, put it this way:

> "Every generation of apes begins where the previous generation began, because apes can hand down no record of their experience. Man leaves a record; but how much better is he than the apes if he does not study it and heed its warnings?"—From *Woodrow Wilson and the Lost Peace*, p. v (Foreword).

(2) *To understand the present*: Everyone is influenced in some degree by the past whether he knows that past or not. Christianity, the Protestant Reformation, the Enlightenment, and other notable movements and events have had a profound impact on western civilization. Racism, slavery, the Civil War, and the

Reconstruction period all played vital roles in determining the nature and extent of racial problems in the United States today. What we are saying is that history gives us the perspective to judge the present. The present is full of the past. Or as the early twentieth-century American poet, T.S. Eliot, wrote:

> "The historical sense involves a perception, not only of the pastness of the past, but of its presence."

(3) *To see where we are headed*: History is not deterministic, but a clear understanding of our past and present will give us the direction that we are currently traveling. Then it is up to us collectively (which is the sum total of each citizen's contribution to thought) to determine whether we want to continue on that path or whether we wish to change the course of our American journey.

In order to learn from our past mistakes and to understand where we are presently and where we are headed, it is essential that the student be made aware of the facts, as well as differing viewpoints, of our past. In other words, a mere listing of events, names, dates, and places has little relevance, and it is no wonder that students are frequently turned off by that approach to history. Of course, paying attention to interpretations means making certain judgments, some of which are bound to conflict with some students' own personal views. But that is what the process of education is all about. The student should be aware that *The American Journey: 1865 to the Present* introduces the student to an in-depth examination of American history, including varying interpretive viewpoints of our past.

Will an American history course or text help a student to find a job? The answer is probably not, but it should increase his or her ability to question decisions that will affect the future of the nation with some knowledge of what questions to ask and why. Toward this goal, we humbly acknowledge our privilege to play a small part in imparting some of that necessary knowledge.

Doug Baker
Susan Hutchins

CHAPTER ONE

Reconstruction:
1865–1877

MAJOR EVENTS

1865   Abraham Lincoln Assassinated
Andrew Johnson begins Presidential Reconstruction
Thirteenth Amendment ratified
Freedmen's Codes enacted in southern states

1866   Congress approves Fourteenth Amendment
Civil Rights Act passed
Ku Klux Klan founded

1867   Reconstruction Acts, passed over President Johnson's veto, begin
Congressional Reconstruction
Tenure of Office Act
Southern states call constitutional conventions

1868   President Johnson impeached by the House, but aqcquitted in Senate
trial
Fourteenth Amendment ratified
Most southern states readmitted to Union
Ulysses S. Grant elected president

1869   Congress approves Fifteenth Amendment
National Woman Suffrage Association founded

1870   Ratification of Fifteenth Amendment

1871   Ku Klux Klan Act passed

1876   Disputed election between Samuel Tilden and Rutherford Hayes

1877   Electoral Commission elects Hayes president

INTRODUCTION

On April 9, 1865, General Robert E. Lee, Commander in Chief of the Confederate Army, surrendered to General Ulysses S. Grant, Commander of the Union Army. This surrender was the first of many that brought to a close 4 years of war. The Civil War, which had divided this country into North and South, was over, but the process of bringing unity to this country once again was just beginning. The process of reestablishing the correct and proper relationship between North and South was known as Reconstruction and included the following elements: (1) politically bringing the South back into its proper place in the Union; (2) physically re-

Historical Ruins of Charleston, South Carolina at the end of the Civil War. Credit: U. S. War Department

building the South; and (3) restructuring the South socially and economically to go forward without a slave system.

There were major stumbling blocks in the formulation of Reconstruction policies. First, the four years of bloody civil war—with approximately 620,000 killed and in excess of 400,000 wounded on both sides—left deep scars on the survivors of both sides. Second, the officials in control of the process did not have any precedents to follow. The United States had experienced neither civil war nor reconstruction before. Third, there was not a consensus in the nation nor in the government on the future role of the freed slaves in American society. And finally, opinion was divided within the government and the public concerning how Reconstruction should proceed. Should the president or Congress control Reconstruction? Should the South be punished for attempting to secede from the Union? What rights should the former slaves have? Should some Confederate officials face execution? These questions required answers, but a consensus among the leaders of the nation was difficult to reach.

Charles Sumner.
Credit: Dictionary of
American Portraits

Democrats favored a quick and easy Reconstruction because the South was their base of support. Thus, they pressed for quick restoration of the rights of Southern citizens and states and without punishment.

The Radical Republican faction in Congress, led by Senator Charles Sumner of Massachusetts, Senator Benjamin Wade of Ohio, and Representative Thaddeus Stevens of Pennsylvania, favored a long and harsh Reconstruction to punish the South for its rebellion. The Radicals believed the South should be treated as a conquered territory until the freedmen were protected from their former masters and the Republican Party controlled the politics of the South. Their programs to bring about radical changes in the South would take time.

The moderate Republicans, led by President Abraham Lincoln, favored a mild Reconstruction policy. They did not believe the South had left the Union. Because Lincoln and the moderates determined that secession had not occurred, the consequences for the South's actions should be mild. Lincoln's moderate views were hampered by ineffective moderate leadership in Congress.

This country faced serious problems immediately after the war. Although Union troops served as an occupation force in the South to protect the freed slaves and maintain law and order, thousands of Union soldiers had to be mustered out of the army. The federal government had to feed both whites and blacks in the South. The economy had to be placed on a peacetime footing as quickly as possible. Despite the immediate problems facing Congress, political reconstruction of the South was still a priority. Political rights for the Southerners and their state governments were invalidated at the end of the war. Government must exist in the South before social or economic reconstruction could begin. Deciding which branch of government would control Reconstruction became the next battlefield. President Lincoln, President Johnson, and Congress all wrote and attempted to implement a Reconstruction plan for the South.

PRESIDENT LINCOLN'S PLAN

Reconstruction plans began before the end of the war. As the Southern states were defeated by the Union armies, President Lincoln wanted to have a plan established so the states could take their proper place in the Union with speed and without punishment. Lincoln did not accept the notion that the Southern states had seceded legally because he believed that secession was not constitutionally possible. With this premise in mind, he could afford leniency to these wayward citizens. On December 8, 1863, President Lincoln issued a Proclamation of Amnesty and Reconstruction. Any rebel state could form a government and take its rightful place with the other states once they had met the conditions of Lincoln's 10 percent plan.

The Conditions of the 10 Percent Plan

There was a general amnesty and restoration of property to all who took an oath of future loyalty to the Constitution and the Union. Some groups were exempt from the general amnesty, such as senior Confederate officers, civilian and diplomatic officers, and judges and congressmen who had formerly served the Union. Those individuals among the exempt groups had to apply to the president directly for a pardon.

When the number of those taking the oath reached 10 percent of the number of those who had voted in the 1860 elections in that particular state, this 10 percent group could establish a state government. Lincoln believed that the loyalty of at least 10 percent of a state population was enough to begin reconstruction of a state.

State constitutional conventions would be called, delegates would be elected to the conventions, constitutions would be written, state governments would be established, and representatives would be elected to the national Congress. The new state constitutions would be required to abolish slavery.

By 1864, Tennessee, Arkansas, and Louisiana were under federal control and accepted the conditions of the 10 percent plan. These states organized new governments and elected representatives to the national Congress, but Congress refused to seat the members from the former Confederate states. President Lincoln strongly believed that his constitutional power to pardon gave him the authority to carry out his Reconstruction plan. But many in Congress, particularly the Radical Republicans, were resentful of the president's increased powers during the war and hostile to the Southern states, so they refused to seat the members from the newly reconstructed states. It was believed that the 10 percent plan was too lenient, considering the enormity of the South's transgressions.

The Wade-Davis Bill

The Wade-Davis Bill was passed by Congress on July 8, 1864, as the Radical Republican effort to replace the president's plan. The battle then commenced between the executive branch and the legislative branch to control the reconstruction conditions for the Southern states. The Wade-Davis Bill provided that (1) Congress, not the president, would administer Reconstruction; (2) a majority of a state's population must take an oath of future loyalty to the United States before a state government could be established; (3) a second oath, an "iron clad" oath, was required from Southern males in order to vote or become a delegate to a state constitutional convention; this "iron clad" oath was a vow that the person had not voluntarily supported the Confederate side in the war; (4) important Confederate officials and military leaders were disenfranchised and could only be restored with a Congressional pardon; (5) slavery was abolished in the Southern states; and (6) all Confederate debts were repudiated on the grounds that it was not fair for Southerners who had been loyal to the Union to help pay for the cost of a war which they had opposed. Lincoln pocket vetoed the Wade-Davis Bill so that it did not become law.

Congressional opposition to President Lincoln's plans was based on a variety of motivating factors. Behind much of the opposition lay the fact that if the former slaves were now citizens to be counted as whole persons rather than three-fifths of a person (as the original U.S. Constitution had mandated for slaves), the population of each Southern state would increase, and their representation in Congress would increase also. This meant the Southerners could control the political and economic life of the nation. The Republicans could not allow this.

President Abraham Lincoln's Assassination at Ford Theater. Credit: Library of Congress

Before the battle between Congress and Lincoln could be joined in earnest, Lincoln was assassinated on April 14, 1865, while attending a play at Ford's Theater in Washington D.C. John Wilkes Booth, an actor who sympathized with the South, shot and killed the president. Lincoln's strong desire to see his country reunited could possibly have made the peace after the war easier. His words held such promise.

> With malice toward none; with charity for all; with firmness in the right, as God gives us to see the right, let us strive on to finish the work we are in; to bind up the nation's wounds; to care for him who shall have borne the battle, and for his widow, and his orphans, to do all which may achieve and cherish a just and a lasting peace, among ourselves, and with all nations.
>
> Lincoln's Second Inaugural Address, March 1865

ANDREW JOHNSON BECOMES PRESIDENT

Vice-President Andrew Johnson became President with Lincoln's assassination. A skillful politician in his home state of Tennessee, Johnson did not have the political skills or power at the national level to carry out his own plan of Reconstruction, which closely resembled Lincoln's plan and defied the wishes of the powerful Radical Republican faction in Congress.

When Tennessee seceded from the Union, Andrew Johnson was serving in the United States Senate. Johnson did not believe that secession was constitutional and had stayed loyal to the Union, even though he was a Democrat from a Southern state. Lincoln later appointed him military Governor of Tennessee, once most of that state was in the hands of the Union army. In the 1864 election, Lincoln placed Johnson, a Southern Democrat, on the Republican ticket as his vice-presidential running mate. Technically, the Lincoln-Johnson ticket had been labeled the National Union Party, but that name and Johnson's association with Lincoln was clearly an attempt to appeal to national unity and win Democratic votes.

President Andrew Johnson. Credit: AP/Wide World Photos

Party leaders in 1864 did not truly consider what sort of president Johnson might make because Lincoln was in such good health. Andrew Johnson had many excellent political attributes, and under usual political circumstances, he probably would have been considered a fair president. After the Civil War, however, politics was not usual in Washington, D.C., and Johnson's political and personal failings soon came to overshadow his attributes. Johnson was a self-educated, intelligent man, devoted to duty and country. He was a good political speaker, but his style was suited to the politics of a rural state such as Tennessee.

Immediately after his ascendency to the presidency, the Radicals in Congress believed Andrew Johnson was a new ally in their desire to delay Reconstruction in the South until the South was contrite for the war, the freed slaves were protected, and the Republican Party had gained more control of the South. Johnson talked of the Southerners as traitors, and traitors must be punished. Within a few weeks of becoming president, he changed his mind and pushed for a quick and non-punishing Reconstruction policy. He did not have the political nor the personal finesse to maneuver Congress to agree with his ideas on Reconstruction. He referred to Reconstruction as restoration. Johnson was inflexible, a man to hold grudges, frequently petty, and he used colorful language publicly to describe all of his political opponents. He was his own worst enemy; the more he spoke about Reconstruction, the more supporters he pushed onto the side of the Radical Republicans.

Few presidents have been in as difficult a position as Johnson. He had to pull the country together after a war in which Americans had killed each other, not a common foe. Johnson governed in the shadow of a president who quickly took on the larger than life characteristics of a martyred leader. He did not have a political following in either the North or the South. Johnson had broken with the Democratic Party and was not accepted by the Republican Party. He was also a strict constitutionalist, which did not allow him much flexibility in his thoughts or plans. These difficulties do not excuse the president's poor judgement and failure to rise above his own personal failings. They merely are factors in understanding the whole story of the Johnson presidency.

PRESIDENT JOHNSON'S RECONSTRUCTION PLAN

Johnson put together his own plan based upon the moderate plan of Lincoln, with some modifications. Underlying Johnson's moderate plan was the theory that the Southern states had never been legally out of the Union, so constitutionally, their relationship to the federal government was intact. Federal control of each state would last until loyal governments were established in each state. In the meantime, the decision was made that there would be no trials for treason of former Confederate leaders. And provisional civilian governors were appointed, except in Louisiana, Arkansas, and Tennessee. Johnson considered these states to be reconstructed already, just as Lincoln had announced earlier.

Among other provisions of President Johnson's plans were his proposals on how to deal with individuals who had rebelled during the war. On May 29, 1865, Johnson proclaimed a general amnesty for all Southerners who took the oath of allegiance to the country and the Constitution. Their political rights would thus be restored. However, there were fourteen groups excluded from the general amnesty and required to request pardon from the president. Those who must ask for pardon included civil and diplomatic officers of the Confederacy, state governors, general officers of the Confederate Army, former U.S. army and naval officers, former United States Congressmen and judges who went to the Confederate side, those who fled to Mexico, and Confederates whose taxable wealth in 1860 was $20,000 or more. This was Johnson's punishment for the rich aristocrats, whom he blamed for causing the war. Eventually all Southerners who had held federal office before 1861 and who had afterwards entered the Confederate service or gave aid and comfort to the rebellion were added to the groups that must ask for a pardon to have their political rights restored.

The eight states which Johnson did not consider reconstructed must elect members to conventions for the purpose of writing new state constitutions. The constitutional conventions must invalidate their ordinances of secession, repudiate their state war debts, and declare slavery abolished by ratifying the proposed Thirteenth Amendment. The Thirteenth Amendment to the Constitution of the United States abolished slavery nationally upon its ratification on December 18, 1865. As to the issue of Confederate and state war debts, Johnson believed it would be unfair to use tax moneys from loyal Southerners to help pay debts accumulated by rebel governments which they had not supported. Specifically, this meant that war bonds issued to help finance the Confederate war cause would never be paid off; the loans to these governments would, in effect, become donations.

Elections were held in the Southern states after the conditions of the president's Reconstruction plan were basically met. By the fall of 1865, civil governments were functioning across the South, except in Texas, and congressmen and senators were elected to take their places in Washington, D.C.

Many in the North criticized Johnson's mild Reconstruction plans because many believed that (1) political Reconstruction should not occur until all problems between the North and the South had been resolved; (2) the South was not remorseful nor reconciled to defeat; and (3) the South still contained the spirit of rebellion. President Johnson sent observers into the South to determine if the above Northern objections were justified. He also received reports from Union military officers in the occupied South concerning the attitudes of the people. General Ulysses S. Grant, the Civil War hero for the Union, wrote these words to Johnson: "I am satisfied that the mass of thinking people in the South accept the situation of affairs in good faith." Other observers did not believe that the Southerners were repentant nor that they had accepted defeat. But Johnson accepted the reports of those who believed the South was contrite and eager to resume their old position in the Union.

Congress met on December 4, 1865, for the year's session. Representatives and senators from the Southern states were not officially recognized. Congress claimed that the status of these states was not yet decided because they had not been properly informed by the president of his plans nor had they approved their implementation. Therefore, the members from the Southern states could not take their seats. A Joint Committee of Fifteen was formed to determine the Congressional position on Reconstruction. The Committee decided that the Southern states had forfeited all rights due them under the Constitution and that their rights could only be restored by Congress. The states were intact, but their governments were not recognized as legitimate. Congress did not believe that the South was repentant; in fact, they seemed defiant.

Two situations in the South were particularly disturbing, and they were seen as signs that the war had not changed the attitudes in the South. Southern states had adopted Black Codes to control the freedmen, and many of the laws in the Codes seemed too much like a type of slavery. (See "Life in the South" in this chapter.) Also, Southerners sent former Confederate leaders as their representatives to Congress, including former Vice-President of the Confederate States of America, Alexander Stephens, from the state of Georgia. But it was the Black Codes that were the final straw that led Congress to attempt to take over Reconstruction policy.

Thus, the battle lines were now clearly drawn between Congress and the president. Both branches claimed the right to write and implement Reconstruction in the South. The spoils of the battle would be control over Southern Reconstruction. The president made the first move with his 1865 Reconstruction plan. The Radicals in Congress dismantled the Presidential Reconstruction Plan while also adopting measures to protect the freedmen in the South. Congressional Reconstruction would triumph over presidential Reconstruction, for better or for worse.

CONGRESSIONAL RECONSTRUCTION POLICIES

A series of confrontations between Congress and President Johnson began in early 1866. The confrontations dealt with the protection of the freed slaves in the South and political Reconstruction of the South.

Protection of the Former Slaves

Congress had originally created the Freedmen's Bureau in March 1865, to help former slaves in their movement from slavery to freedom. The Bureau fed the hungry, built schools for the uneducated freedmen, and stepped in to protect their new rights. Congress passed a bill in February 1866 to extend the life of the Freedmen's Bureau beyond the first year, but Johnson vetoed it. This veto was one of Johnson's last victories over Congress. The Radical Republicans would soon possess the power to override all of Johnson's vetoes. Indeed, Congress passed another Freedmen's Bureau Bill on July 16, 1866. When Johnson vetoed this one, Congress quickly passed it over his veto.

The Civil Rights Act of 1866 declared African-Americans to be United States citizens and, as such, were entitled to "equality before the law." Johnson vetoed this bill too, but Congress overrode the veto on April 9, 1866. This was the first time a major federal law had been passed over a presidential veto in American history!

In June 1866, Congress passed the Fourteenth Amendment on to the states for ratification. Congress decided a new constitutional amendment was needed to protect the rights of freedmen in the South. Congressional acts can be overturned by the Supreme Court as unconstitutional, and it was a real possibility that this might occur to the Civil Rights Act of 1866. The major provisions of the Fourteenth Amendment are discussed in the next three paragraphs.

All persons born or naturalized in the United States were citizens with full rights. States cannot deny anyone life, liberty, or property without due process of law. States must give everyone equal protection under the law.

If the right to vote was not granted to all males over the age of twenty-one (except for Indian males), that state would have its congressional representation reduced according to the percentage of potential voters who were denied their suffrage. In other words, if a state denied its African-American adult male population the right to vote, and African-American males made up 20 percent of that state's population, that state would lose 20 percent of its representation in the House of Representatives. It would also lose 20 percent of its electoral votes for presidential elections.

In other provisions of the amendment, anyone who had taken an oath to support the Constitution, and then supported the Southern rebellion, could not hold a political office until pardoned by Congress. Also, Southern states must cancel their war debts. And, of course, Congress could enforce this amendment with appropriate legislation.

President Johnson disagreed with the principles of the Fourteenth Amendment and worked against the ratification of the amendment by urging the Southern states not to ratify it. Ironically, Johnson's home state of Tennessee became the first state to ratify the amendment in July 1866, and it was readmitted to full standing in the Union. The ratification of the Fourteenth Amendment by Tennessee, Johnson's home state, was another blow to the president's ability to persuade and thereby govern effectively. The ten other former Confederate states refused to ratify the amendment, and Congress later made ratification of the Fourteenth Amendment a condition for readmittance into Congress. The Radical Republicans were gaining support for a harsher Reconstruction, but they did not have enough votes from the other factions in Congress, particularly the moderate Republicans. The moderates still hoped to come to a compromise with Johnson, but the events of the summer and fall of 1866 made compromise impossible.

The 1866 Congressional Elections

As the Congressional campaigns began in the summer of 1866, it was clear that Reconstruction would be a major issue for the Republican and Democratic parties. A small group of conservative Democrats and Republicans hoped to support Johnson with the founding of a new political party, the National Union Party. A convention was called to meet in Philadelphia in August of 1866. Johnson hoped the new party would bring Northern support for his policies and neutralize the power of Congress in areas of disagreement between the executive and legislative branches; it did not. Events came together in the summer of 1866 that put a stamp of approval on the Radical Republican Reconstruction program and disputed Johnson's claims that all was well in the South. The result was that Northerners sent Republicans to Congress with a 3 to 1 majority over the Democrats.

Among the crucial events in the middle of 1866 that helped the Radical Republican cause was rioting by whites in the South. In May 1866, a quarrel in Memphis, Tennessee between whites and demobilized African-American soldiers broke into a general riot. White mobs moved into black sections, and at least 46 people were killed before it was over, with many white policemen joining the mob. In New Orleans, Louisiana, in July 1866, a white mob moved against delegates to an African-American suffrage convention. Johnson had approved an order by the mayor of New Orleans to stop the delegates from meeting, but the commander of the Union forces decided the convention should meet and had sent troops to protect the delegates. When the troops arrived, the mob had already killed 37 blacks. Both of these events were used by Republicans as examples of the failure of Johnson's policies.

At the same time, the institution of the Black Codes in most of the former Confederate states (see "Life in South"), already alluded to, seemed too much like slavery. Furthermore, the repudiation of the Fourteenth Amendment by the Southern states was another indication that the South was not accepting a new place for the freedmen in Southern society. This was defiance of Congress that could not be tolerated. Were the Southerners defeated and willing to accept the freedmen as really free in their society? If nothing had changed in the South, then what had been the purpose of the war?

The actions of Andrew Johnson himself pushed people away from his policies. He campaigned against Republican candidates in his "swing around the circle," but his campaign tactics worked against him and his candidates and for those he opposed. He participated in shouting matches with hecklers; he traded insults with the crowds; he called the Radical Republicans traitors and other names. And he threw away his chances to convince the Northern Republicans he was right and Congress was wrong.

Congressional Political Reconstruction

The Radical Republicans gained the power to completely control Reconstruction with the Congressional elections of 1866. Thereafter, President Johnson's vetoes were simply overridden, as all hope of compromise between the two branches of government was gone. In terms of political Reconstruction, the Radical Republi-

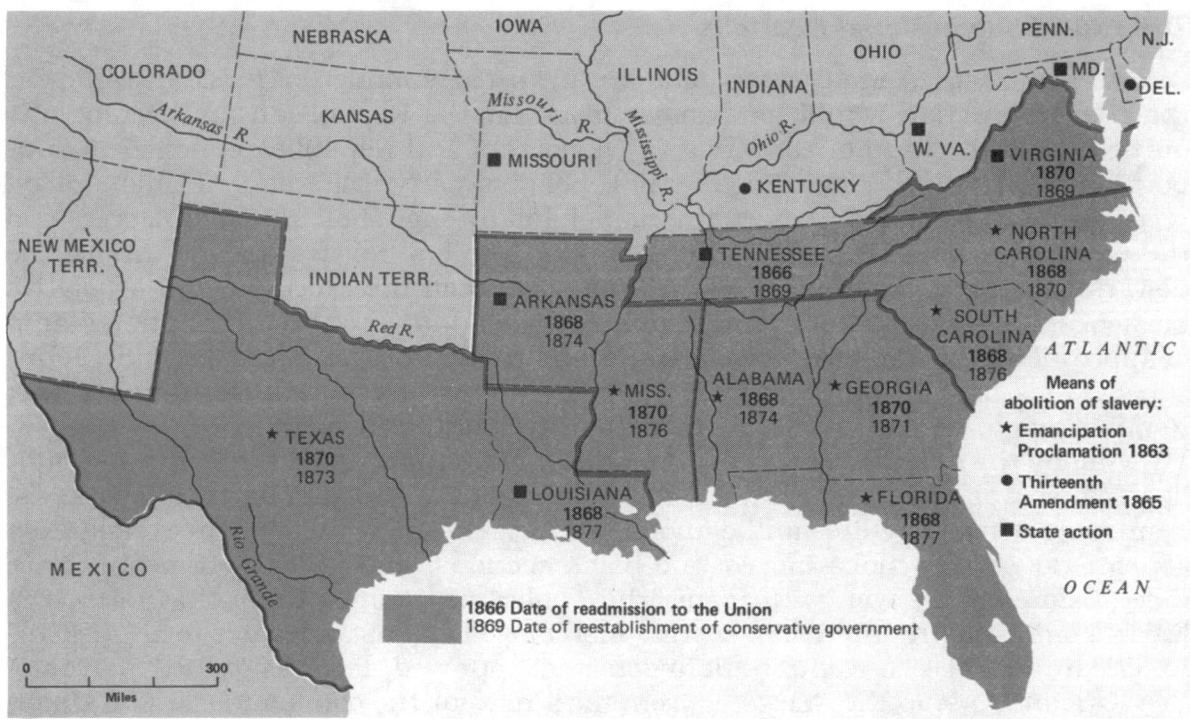

Reconstruction: Heavy lines indicate the military districts demanded by Congress. Credit: The United States: Combined Edition, by Winthrop D. Jordan and Leon F. Litwack, Prentice Hall, Inc., 1991.

cans pushed through 3 significant Reconstruction Acts, each over the president's veto, and passed on the Fifteenth Amendment to the states for ratification.

On March 2, 1867, Congress passed the First Reconstruction Act, also known as the Military Reconstruction Act, on its way to dominating Reconstruction policy after the congressional elections. The law dismantled Johnson's Reconstruction plan and substituted a congressional one in its place. While Tennessee was officially recognized as fully reconstructed, the other ten ex-Confederate states were not. Those ten states were to be divided into five military districts in order to protect all citizens and their property. A Union general was appointed to maintain law and order in each district, along with Union troops. The Fourteenth Amendment, granting suffrage to African-American males and other rights to all the freedmen, must be ratified by a state before its full readmittance into the Union. Eligible voters in each occupied state must elect delegates to a constitutional convention to rewrite that state's constitution; this new constitution must include black suffrage. The constitution must then go to a direct vote of the people and for final approval to Congress. Eligible voters included all adult males who were not banned by the Fourteenth Amendment. Only eligible voters could also serve as delegates to a state's constitutional convention, of course.

On March 23, 1867, Congress passed the Second Reconstruction Act, which ordered the 5 military governors to initiate voter registration and initiate the proceedings for the constitutional conventions. Then on July 19, 1867, with the Third

Reconstruction Act, Congress declared that a majority of the votes cast, not a majority of the registered voting population, would be suffficient to bring about ratification of the Fourteenth Amendment and readmission to the Union.

The Fourteenth Amendment was ratified nationally in July 1868, in time for the presidential election. Four ex-Confederate states still refused to ratify the amendment—Texas, Virginia, Mississippi, and Georgia. The final four Southern states delayed ratification long enough to have to ratify the new Fifteenth Amendment along with the Fourteenth in order to come back into their proper place in the Union. Georgia, the last state to ratify the Fourteenth Amendment, did so in July 1870.

In a final action to support Reconstruction policy, Congress passed the Fifteenth Amendment on to the states for ratification in February 1869. This amendment stated that states could not deny any adult male the right to vote because of race, color, or previous condition of servitude. Congress proposed the Fifteenth Amendment to the Constitution because it wanted to make sure that the vote was not denied to the freedmen at a future time. The Republicans also needed the freedmen's votes for the development of a national party, and the freedmen needed their right to vote guaranteed to protect their rights against white infringement once the South was returned to Southern rule. Congress also wanted to enfranchise Northern African-Americans, who were not brought the right to vote by the Fourteenth Amendment or the First Reconstruction Act of 1867. At the end of the Civil War, African-American men could vote in only five New England states. They could also vote in the state of New York, but only if they owned property. The Fifteenth Amendment was ratified in March 1870. After that, white Southerners began using poll taxes and literacy tests in an attempt to prevent African-American voters from exercising their suffrage rights (see Chapter Five).

ANDREW JOHNSON'S IMPEACHMENT

Congress was successful in checking presidential power in the area of Reconstruction. With these successes Congress decided to expand its power even further by taking away other rights of the president. In January of 1867, there was an impeachment investigation of the president. The moderates on the investigating committee established there was no evidence of treason, bribery, or other high crimes and misdemeanors required by Article II of the Constitution for the impeachment of a president. So on March 2, 1867, Congress took further actions which they knew the president could not accept quietly. A rider was added to an army appropriation bill requiring the president to issue all orders through the general of the army. General Ulysses S. Grant was the general of the army at the time, and he also disagreed with the president's reconstruction policy. On the same day Congress also passed the Tenure of Office Act, which required the president to receive consent from the Senate to fire any government official the Senate had previously confirmed.

On August 12, 1867, the president suspended Secretary of War, Edwin Stanton. Stanton was in agreement with the Radical Republicans on the issue of Reconstruction, and Johnson decided he could no longer tolerate this "traitor" on his cabinet. In response to the firing of Stanton without Senate approval, the House of Representatives in February 1868 established a committee to decide the charges to be brought against the president. Eight of the 11 impeachment charges made by the committee dealt with Johnson's violation of the Tenure of Office Act, an act that many doubt was constitutional in the first place. The full House of Representatives voted to impeach the president on February 24, 1868, by a vote of 126 to 47.

Impeachment, of course, is simply the bringing of formal charges against a political official; it is the political equivalent to the indictment in criminal proceedings. Impeachment, then, does not make anyone legally guilty. The Constitution provides that the House of Representatives may impeach a federal official like the president, but that the Senate must serve as the jury, with the Chief Justice of the United States Supreme Court acting as the presiding judge during the trial. The Senate began the trial of President Johnson on March 4, 1868, with Chief Justice Salmon P. Chase presiding. The trial lasted for almost 12 weeks before the final vote came. The Senate voted 35 to 19 for conviction, but that was one single vote short of the two-thirds majority that the Constitution requires for conviction. Andrew Johnson was therefore not removed from office, but he still stands as the only United States president to have ever been impeached.

One factor which may have played an important role in the legal acquittal of President Johnson concerned a personal feud between Chief Justice Chase and Senator Benjamin Wade. Both men were Ohio Republicans who had gotten in each other's way as they had climbed their way to power. Even former President Lincoln's appointment of Chase to the Supreme Court in 1864 did not lessen the hatred these two rivals had for each other. Under the laws then governing presidential succession in the event of the president's death, after the vice-president came the president pro tempore of the United States Senate. But after Johnson had ascended to the presidency upon the assassination of Lincoln, the office of vice-president remained vacant. Because Senator Benjamin Wade was the president pro tempore of the United States Senate in 1868, the conviction and removal of Andrew Johnson from the presidency would have automatically resulted in Benjamin Wade being sworn in as the

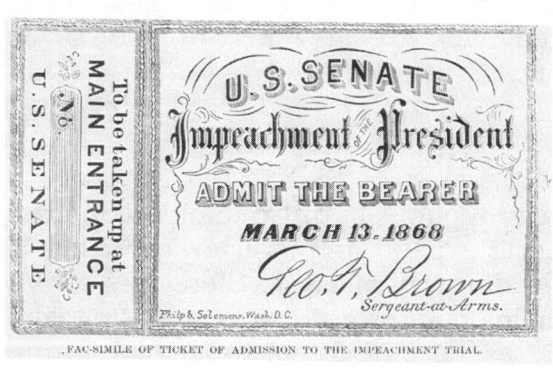

Ticket for President Andrew Johnson's Impeachment.

next president of the United States. This Chief Justice Chase could not tolerate for one moment. Therefore, Chase did everything he could in his statements and judicial rulings as the presiding judge in the trial of Andrew Johnson to place the president in the best light possible.

The story of Johnson's impeachment and trial illustrates human behavior on a collective scale. By 1868 the Radical Republican-dominated Congress was so angry at the president over what they perceived as obstructionism against their Reconstruction policies that the House of Representatives was determined to remove him from office. In all probability, the Tenure of Office Act was unconstitutional. Yet when Johnson fired Stanton because the latter supported Congressional Reconstruction, the House took its opportunity. They wanted a fight, and now they were going to force one. There are some historians who believe that President Johnson did not faithfully execute all aspects of Reconstruction law, which if true, might have been an impeachable offense. These historians believe that if the House had impeached him on these clearer constitutional grounds, Johnson may well have been convicted and removed from office. Of course, we will never know what the outcome would have been if different charges had been levied against the president.

What was left of President Johnson's influence was broken by his impeachment. He would not seek a place on the Republican ticket in the 1868 presidential election. The Republican Party searched for a different candidate and settled upon General Ulysses S. Grant. He was a leader of men and a war hero. What more could you ask for? General Grant won the election with the help of the votes of the freedmen. He was a great general, but he was not a great president. His two administrations would become known for their scandals. (See Chapter Four for a discussion of President Grant's administration.) However, he did get along well with Congress on the issue of Reconstruction. Radical Reconstruction was carried out by Congress during Grant's two terms.

While it may be hard to understand why an impeached president would want to retain the presidency, the fact is that Andrew Johnson hoped for the Democratic nomination in the election of 1868. The Democrats were not that ignorant of recent events, however. When Johnson failed to get the nomination, he returned home to Tennessee. There he unsuccessfully ran for Congress in 1869 and again in 1872. Persistence paid off, though, when the state legislature returned him to his old seat in the United States Senate in 1874. When he returned to Washington for the opening of the Congressional session in early 1875, Democrats controlled the House of Representatives for the first time since the Civil War. Johnson's feelings of personal vindication did not last long, for he died of a stroke on July 31, 1875.

LIFE IN THE SOUTH

The Civil War turned life in the South upside down for most Southerners. The African-American man and woman had to learn what freedom meant, and the Southern white man and woman had to learn how to adapt to a society without slaves and a society of temporary Northern dominance.

Freedom for the Slaves

Approximately 1 million slaves were freed as the Union armies defeated the individual Southern states. Then at the end of the war all were freed—approximately 3 million at this time. The Thirteenth Amendment to the Constitution legally and constitutionally ended all slavery in the United States in December of 1865. In the first months after the war, many of the freed slaves were not sure what to do with this gift of freedom, and their reactions to their new status were varied. Some stayed on with the old masters; some just took to the roads to sample life without dominance or to search for their families; and many moved to the cities. Black populations in many Southern cities doubled or tripled.

It was a time of instability and unrest. The former slaves, now known as freedmen, suffered in this unorganized manumission. Deaths occurred from starvation, disease, and violence. Frederick Douglass, an African-American leader, criticized the manner in which the government set the slaves free when he said that "the freedmen were free from the individual master but a slave of society. He had neither money, property, nor friends. He was free from the old plantation, but he had nothing but the dusty road under his feet. He was free from the old quarter that once gave him shelter, but a slave to the rains of summer and the frosts of winter. He was turned loose naked, hungry, and destitute to the open sky."

Movement of African-Americans to the cities brought concerns of increased crime and unemployment in Southern cities and a labor shortage in the rural areas. The South was strongly agricultural, and the freedmen were needed to plant the crops and repair the damage from the war. Many were not working but depending on the Freedmen's Bureau to supply their needs while they waited for their "forty acres and a mule" from the government.

In 1865–1866, in order to retain control over the former slaves and to insure a labor supply to plant the barren fields of the South, Black Codes were passed by the former Confederate States. These state laws legislated what the freedmen could and could not do in the South. The following are a few examples of the various codes in the states: (1) they could sue and be sued; (2) they could own and inherit property; (3) they could testify in a court of law; (4) they could not vote; (5) they could not serve on juries; (6) they had to have permission to meet after sundown; and (7) they had to work, and many had to sign employment contracts. If an African-American man could not show he was employed, he could be arrested as a vagrant and his labor sold to whomever could pay his fine. These vagrancy clauses in the Black Codes amounted to an attempt to reimpose a type of slavery on the former slaves.

The codes were dismantled by Congress and the Freedmen's Bureau. Southerners did not believe the freedmen would work unless forced to work. The fact that many freedmen were not working immediately after the war whites saw as confirmation of this long-held belief. Nor did they believe that African-American men had the intellectual capacity to make decisions without white control. Many in the South could not accept the sudden and complete freedom of those who had called them master a short time earlier. They would be forced to accept, for the time of occupation at least, many new roles for the freedmen.

To begin their new lives in the South, the freedmen knew they needed education and their own land. The Freedmen's Bureau helped to a certain degree with both, but it had greater success in the area of education.

The Freedmen's Bureau

Officially titled the Bureau of Refugees, Freedmen, and Abandoned Lands, the Freedmen's Bureau was established on March 3, 1865. It was a bridge between slavery and freedom, and it provided many vital services. The Bureau officially functioned until 1869, but its educational activities continued until 1872. The Bureau's services included the following: (1) feeding refugees from both races; (2) drafting and enforcing labor contracts; (3) settling thousands of freedmen on abandoned lands; (4) settling points of law between freedmen and white Southerners; (5) establishing hospitals; and (6) establishing schools.

The Commissioner of the Freedmen's Bureau was General Oliver O. Howard. An assistant commissioner was appointed for each former slave state, and 550 local agents were appointed to carry out the mission of the Bureau. Most of the local agents were junior army officers. However, civilian agents were appointed, and some of these agents were former slaves. The dollars to support the Bureau's assistance to the freedmen were supplied by a tax on cotton. By 1869, the cotton tax brought in $68 million.

When the South resisted dealing fairly with the freedmen, especially in the judicial system, General Howard asked Congress for permission to establish special courts. The Freedmen's Bureau Bill of July 1866 gave the Bureau the power to establish military tribunals until the Southern states were once again functioning in their proper roles. The courts functioned until 1868. Although the Southern whites criticized the Bureau for its interference in their daily lives, it brought assistance to the freedmen and helped stabilize them as a much needed workforce. The Bureau later fell into disrepute through corruption and its political activities in using the former slaves to build the Republican Party in the South.

Education for the Freedmen

Freedmen's aid societies were organized during the war to assist the newly freed slaves in a variety of ways as Southern states were defeated and then occupied by Union troops. One of their most important contributions was to begin a system of education for the African-American segment of Southern society. An estimated 200,000 African-Americans were taught at the freedmen's schools during the war.

The Freedmen's Bureau worked with these societies to promote education for the former slaves after the war was over. The Bureau built schools and brought teachers to the South. The teachers included both white Americans and African-Americans. It is estimated that up to 20 percent of the 4,000 teachers were African-American. One-third of the Bureau budget from 1865 to 1870 was spent on education. Young and old alike went to school. Some schools even had to turn away those who wanted to learn to read and write. Education had been denied to slaves, and the freedmen knew it took education for them and their children to function in a free world. Schools were so important that the freedmen would use their own limited resources to build and support schools in areas where other agencies did not.

Institutions of higher education were founded also. Howard, Atlanta, and Fisk Universities opened their doors in 1866–1867. Despite the promising advances in building schools, education for African-Americans lagged behind that of the whites. At the end of Reconstruction, at least 80 percent of the African-American population was still illiterate.

Land for the Freedmen

Most freedmen felt they must own title to their own land in order to achieve true freedom. There were those in the government, freedmen's aid societies, and the military who agreed. Several plans were formulated and a few implemented, but very little land was obtained by the freedmen.

The Confiscation Act of 1862, passed in July of that year, stated that those who actually participated in helping the Confederate cause would have their property confiscated. Such confiscated land was to be given to freed slaves. However, at President Lincoln's insistence, Congress later passed a resolution declaring that any surviving heirs would not have their property confiscated. Therefore, the land was only the freedmen's until the heirs of the offender could claim it. Lincoln's amnesty proclamation of 1863 restored what relatively little land had been confiscated back to Confederate owners who took an oath of allegiance to the United States.

In 1865, Indiana Representative George W. Julian and Senator Charles Sumner proposed to give the freedmen forty acres and a mule to begin careers as free farmers. The land would come from Confederate land taken under the Confiscation Act of 1862. However, their proposal was discarded for a system of rental property when the decision was made that heirs of Confederates could claim confiscated land. Confusion reigned about the alleged promise of 40 acres and a mule, and when the war was over, many former slaves refused to work for others because they were waiting for their 40 acres and a mule.

The Freedmen's Bureau was in control of some abandoned land on which some freedmen were settled. During the war, abandoned land had been seized, and land that the Southern owners had not paid their taxes on under the Direct Tax Act of 1861 was also confiscated. Land confiscated in the South Carolina Sea area was sold to freedmen, but this was the exception rather than the rule.

General William T. Sherman's Order No. 15 gave land along the coastal rivers in Georgia and South Carolina to freedmen, many of whom the Freedmen's Bureau had already placed upon the land. But President Johnson ordered the return of the land.

The Southern Homestead Act of 1866 was another attempt to give the freedmen the land that they so desperately needed. Forty-four million acres were set aside with the possibility to provide for individual grants of 80 acres to those who wanted them. Few took advantage of this program. Most of the land was of poor quality and most freedmen did not have the capital to come to the areas and begin farms. Fewer than 7,000 used the Homestead Act, and only 1,000 completed the terms for ownership.

Too few in government were really committed to land ownership for the freedmen. Most were willing to give them political and constitutional rights, but when it came to giving land with which they might make their freedom viable, they could not support it. This failure tied most of the freedmen, who knew nothing other than farming, to the land in another system called sharecropping. At the end of the war, there were thousands of whites with land and no one to work it, and thousands of freedmen who knew nothing other than agricultural work but had no money to buy land.

Group of Contrabands during Civil War. Credit: New York Public Library.

A variety of schemes were developed to provide workers for the land. There were some plantation owners who paid wages, but many wanted the freedmen to work in gangs under a boss. This was too much like their former work conditions under slavery and was therefore unacceptable. Some plantation owners paid cash for farm work, but there was not much cash in the South. Some freedmen did rent land from plantation owners, but too few had money. Therefore, a system of sharing tenancy was eventually worked out in the South. Share renting and sharecropping were eventually the most commonly used methods to get land to those who wanted to farm and workers for those who owned farmland. With share renting the landowner usually provided the land and house only, and the share tenant usually paid out one-fourth of the crop as rent. With sharecropping the tenant provided only his own labor and usually paid the land owner one-half of the crop in rent.

This system seemed to work out the problems of the agricultural South and get it back on its feet until cash and economic stability could be found. And for a while it did work. But the price of cotton dropped in the 1870s from the overproduction of this cash crop, and the country also went into an economic depression, produced by a number of other causes. This drove more farm workers, both freedmen and white, into sharecropping in order to make a living. By 1880, up to 80 percent of the land planted in cotton was farmed mostly by sharecroppers.

The rural South was also becoming a crop lien society, which increased the problems of the sharecroppers. Tenant farmers and sharecroppers placed liens on their crops to purchase necessary items from a local merchant until their crops were sold. The interest rate charged for the liens could run as high as 50 percent. Price gouging was also common. In the highly unlikely event that crops could be sold at a profit, the sharecropper had money left over after he paid the landowner and the local merchant (sometimes they were the same person) to save for his own small plot of land. If the crops could not be sold at a good profit, which was by far more common, the sharecropper owed more than he made. For many sharecroppers farming became a cycle of debt and poverty from which they could not escape. (See Chapter Five for more information on the state of African-Americans after slavery.)

GOVERNMENT IN THE SOUTHERN STATES

Governments in the Southern states during Congressional Reconstruction were originally controlled by the Republican Party. As the ex-Confederate Democrats regained their civil and political rights, they challenged and won control of state governments in the South again.

Republican Governments

Republican government in the South consisted of groups of carpetbaggers, scalawags, and freedmen. Carpetbaggers were northerners who came to the South to live. The reasons the northerners moved to the South were varied. Some came to buy inexpensive land or businesses and saw the South as a frontier, much as other Americans viewed the West. Union soldiers who had seen mild winters there during the war and the beautiful countryside came to live in a hospitable physical environment. Many others came to assist or teach the freedmen. And some did come to see what could be gained as a northerner in a South dominated by Reconstruction governments. Southerners gave most of these northern immigrants the unflattering nickname of "carpetbaggers" because some came with so few belongings that everything they owned could fit into a carpetbag (cloth suitcase). Northerners were particulary considered carpetbaggers if they became involved in politics or the advancement of the freedmen. Whatever the motives were for these northerners to journey south, they made new lives for themselves and began to participate in the government of their new communities. One out of every three offices in Southern Reconstruction governments were held by carpetbaggers.

Scalawags were white Southerners who approved of and participated in Republican governments in the South during Reconstruction. This group of people were considered traitors by Southern white Democrats. However, scalawags also had a variety of reasons for rejecting the Democratic Party and supporting the Republicans. Some had favored the Union cause throughout the war and continued to support the party that demanded the Union stay intact. Others were opportunists who saw a chance for personal gain through political office. Working within the party in control of Reconstruction was a way for others to control some aspects of Republican rule in the South. The character and the motives of both scalawags and carpetbaggers were frequently, although not always, misjudged.

Freedmen made up the remaining constituency of Republican governments in the South. The motives of the freedmen for supporting the Republican Party were not as multifaceted as the carpetbaggers and the scalawags. They supported the government and the party that had given them freedom and continued to support their advancement in Southern society. Freedmen were the backbone of the Republican votes in Southern elections, supplying about 80 percent of the party's votes in the South. Freedmen participated in the Southern constitutional conventions, often called "Black and Tan" conventions because they were dominated by freedmen and what the more aristocratic Southerners called lower class whites—small farmers who spent long hours in the hot sun and had developed significant tans. At one point, freedmen held almost 20 percent of the offices in Southern governments. They were elected to state legislatures and sent 14 African-American congressmen and 2 African-American senators to the national Congress. Participation by African-Americans in the political process was an anathema to most white Southerners and was seen as dominance by many. In actuality, whites dominated the Reconstruction governments. Carpetbaggers made up approximately 30 percent of the officeholders, with the scalawags providing the remaining 50 percent. Only in South Carolina did African-Americans have a majority in a state legislature.

It was devastating for the South to have to accept Congressional Reconstruction when they thought they would have the easy restoration of President Johnson. When conditions to regain their proper place in the Union were stiffened, and Republican rule was the result of Southern white disfranchisement, Southern Democrats would not rest until their states were redeemed from what they called the "interlopers."

Redemption of the South by the Democratic Party

Most white Southerners wanted to redeem their states from the clutches of the Republicans inside and outside of Southern governments. In order for redemption to occur—without another war, that is—the Democratic Party had to regain power in the South and then in the Congress of the United States. The Republicans dominated the present state of affairs in the nation and without a rebuilding of the Democratic Party there could be no challenge at the ballot box, which is the source of political power in a democratic republic. The ballot was the best hope for Southerners who wanted to resume controlling Southern destiny. Ex-confederate leaders regained their political rights with individual presidential and congressional pardons and with mass amnesty acts. In May 1872, the Amnesty Act of 1872 restored political rights to approximately 150,000 former Confederate officials, and left no more than 500 white Southern men still unable to vote or hold political office.

Once the right to vote was restored to virtually all white Southerners, these Democrats began challenging the Republicans. In 1869, three years before the Amnesty Act of 1872, the Democrats were once again in control of Virginia and Tennessee. In areas with white voter majorities, legal methods were sufficient to overthrow Republican rule in state after state. In areas with African-American voter majorities, the Republican Party was not easy to oust from control, and the white Southerners turned to illegal methods of intimidation, terror tactics, and in many instances, beatings or murder, to eliminate the Republican support by both races at the ballot box.

The Ku Klux Klan

The Ku Klux Klan, which later spread terror to achieve their goal of white supremacy in the South, began very quietly as a social club in Pulaski, Tennessee in 1866. Six young ex-Confederate veterans were bored and decided they needed to form a small club to bring some amusement to their lives. They met, decided upon a name derived from the Greek word for circle (Kyklos), added Klan for alliteration, and ran around the house in sheets that inspired their later white-robed uniforms.

Ku Klux Klan members. Credit: Historical Pictures Service.

At night they began prowling the area near their homes, pulling pranks and frightening anyone that happened to cross their path. Word of the antics of their group spread out to other areas and the club caught on. These clubs spread across the South under various names, including the Palefaces and the Knights of the White Camelia. Eventually the Klan had an organization that spread across the South, and the organized network became known as the "Invisible Empire."

The original group of young organizers tired quickly of aimless pranks and antics, and they began to find the intimidation of members of the African-American community particularly satisfying. The activities of the freedmen, such as owning land, going to school, voting, and running for office—in other words, attempting to gain true equality—was not to be tolerated. Vigilante groups rode at night to take back control of the South. They rode up to the cabins of freedmen in their ghostly white robes, maintaining that they were spirits of the dead. Some even cloaked their horses in white. Very few of the African-Americans believed these were visitors from the spirit world, but most were too afraid to let their intimidators know it.

Frightening African-Americans moved out of the realm of "fun" and into the realm of intimidation with a purpose by 1868. By this time, the former slaves were seen as a threat to the white supremacy of the South, and most Southern white males could not accept that the freedmen were out of their "proper" place. Freedmen and the white Republicans, particularly the Union League, who promoted racial equality, taught the freedmen to read, and pushed them to vote and run for public office, became the targets of the night-riding vigilante groups. Congress had dictated that the former slaves would have political and civil rights in the South, and the occupation forces were there to make sure that this policy was carried out.

The Klan, on the other hand, was intent on making sure that the Radical Republican plans for the South failed. Thousands of sympathizers of Reconstruction policy, people of both races, were beaten, mutilated, lynched, or murdered in other vicious ways by the Klan and other groups to stop Republican victories at the polls and to put the African-American man and woman back into their "proper" place in the South. That place was as a second-class citizen in subjugation to the white race.

The situation in the South became desperate. The activities of the Klan became so vicious that the leaders themselves attempted to disband the group in 1869. Republicans in the South begged the federal government to intervene and stop the night riders. President Grant pushed Congress to pass the Enforcement Acts to curb the vigilante groups, particularly the Ku Klux Klan, since it was so strong. Using the power given to them to enforce the Fourteenth and Fifteenth Amendments, Congress passed the first Enforcement Act on May 31, 1870. The act stated that interference with anyone's voting rights was a federal offense. The second Enforcement Act, passed on February 28, 1871, established that the federal government could organize supervision of registration and voting. The third Enforcement Act was passed on April 20, 1871, and was generally called the Ku Klux Klan Act. This third act gave the president the power to use the army to protect the civil rights of freedmen in the South, and to suspend the writ of habeas corpus where laws were not obeyed. With the Enforcement Acts, government infiltrators, and trials under federal jurisdiction, the federal government finally broke the organized power of the Klan, which disappeared "underground" until reemergence in the early twentieth century.

President Grant was reelected in 1872, with a decisive victory over his Democratic opponent Horace Greeley. (see Chapter Four.) His firm commitment to Reconstruction, even to the point of continuing the use of bayonet rule to carry out the dictates of Congress, was a positive factor in his campaign. Despite this fact, the importance of Reconstruction was already dwindling in the minds of many outside the South. By 1873, the country was moving into an economic depression. There were also problems in the West with the American Indian tribes, and many felt it was time to move on and let the freedmen take care of themselves. Most in the North felt they had done all they could do to guarantee the freedom of the former slaves. It was now up to them to find their own path in a new South. Most Americans were weary of the ongoing controversy and chose to escape with the proverbial burying of the head in the sand.

THE SUPREME COURT AND RECONSTRUCTION

The United States Supreme Court played an important role in the unraveling of Reconstruction. In its 1866 *Ex parte Milligan* decision, the Supreme Court ruled that military commissions could not try civilians in most places where civil courts existed. This ended the early practice of using military courts to enforce the Freedmen's Bureau Act. It also raised the question as to the legality of the entire Radical Reconstruction program. But in 1869, the Supreme Court, in *Texas v. White*, ruled that secession was impossible and that the Union had never been dissolved. The same decision, however, also stated that Reconstruction was constitutional because Congress had the power to protect the representative form of government in every state and to certify the legitimacy of any state government.

After the *White* decision, however, Supreme Court decisions in the 1870s contributed to the breakdown of Reconstruction by weakening the ability of the federal government to enforce Fourteenth Amendment "due process" rights and the Fifteenth Amendment's voting rights guarantees. (See Chapter Five for a more complete discussion of this process.)

ASSESSMENT OF RECONSTRUCTION: VARYING INTERPRETATIONS

With many historical events or movements, there have developed varying interpretations, or viewpoints, over time. Reconstruction is a case in point. Historians have looked back upon Reconstruction for decades with varying points of view. These points of view are basically divided into two schools of thought, the **Traditionalist** and the **Revisionist**. The **Traditionalists** dominated the scholarly interpretations of Reconstruction well into the twentieth century. Their viewpoint stated that the North was vindictive after the Civil War and that Reconstruction was a time when the North cruelly punished the South by plundering the area through political, social, and economic policies which benefited the North and humiliated the South. This is the basic assumption in the popular classic film *Gone With the Wind.*

Many twentieth century historians studied the **Traditionalist** views and the facts of Southern Reconstruction and developed a new perspective on the issue. Writing in the mid-1900s, these **Revisionists** (because they revised the older **Tradionalist** perspective) were able to distance themselves from the issue and write without many of the biases and judgments the **Traditionalists** were enmeshed in. The **Revisionist** studies of the issue developed a new perspective that Reconstruction was not nearly as heartless and punishing as the **Traditionalists** had portrayed it. **Revisionists** began to counter important **Traditionalist** views with strong arguments depicting a more honest and balanced analysis of issues in the South from 1865–1877, as the next few paragraphs discuss.

Traditionalists believed that state taxes and spending soared in the Southern states as the result of a plot by Republicans to place the South in a permanent role of submission. **Revisionists** agreed that taxes and spending did soar, but that there were very good reasons for the increases. Physical repairs to railroad tracks, roads, bridges, and public buildings were very costly to the Southern states after the war. State legislatures had to raise taxes to pay for these repairs. New Southern constitutions mandated public education for all children of both races. Public education was expensive, and the money had to be raised by the states. Before the war, only North Carolina had had any kind of public education system, and it was judged second best when compared to any education system in the North.

The lack of a public education system in the South can be explained by an understanding of pre-war Southern politics. The few larger plantation owners, along with their banking and business allies, dominated the political system in the region, and the wealthy elite could afford private tutors for their own children's education. Because property taxes would have to finance the greater share of any good public education system, the economic and political establishment were not inclined to raise their own taxes in order to educate other people's children. Besides, education has a way of creating a large middle class. This would be seen as a threat to the aristocratic Southern way of life, a view given to the South by its former system which revolved around slavery. Reconstruction had to fight against this ingrained Southern tradition. Therefore, when taxes were raised to cover the physical damage caused from fighting most of the war in the South, and attempting to raise the standard of living there to those in the North, tax levels were much higher than Southerners were used to. Taxes in some states increased sixfold and more. It is true that there was some corruption in Reconstruction governments and that several million dollars of taxpayer money were wasted. But this corruption was overblown by Reconstruction critics, and it certainly was not part of a plot to keep the South economically dependent.

Traditionalists charged that Northern occupation troops, and commanders with the support of the Republican Congress, were cruel and malicious toward the Southerners. **Revisionists** counter with the statement that the occupation troops were not always kind and gentle in their treatment of Southerners of either race; an occupation force usually isn't. However, the courts and the governments operating during Northern military rule of the South appear to have usually dispensed justice fairly. Only one person was executed after the Civil War. Major Henry Wirz, commander of the infamous Andersonville (Georgia) prisoner of war camp, was hanged for war crimes; his camp was the worst of all of the POW camps, none of which was very good on either side. The fact that only one execution resulted after the war was remarkable, considering the usual treatment afforded the vanquished in civil wars and revolutions in world history, where a bloodbath for the losers usually has followed. Most rebels regained all of their political rights, and Reconstruction would have been accomplished more quickly and with less force from the occupation troops if the South had not been so defiant on so many issues.

The **Traditionalist** view also alleged that Reconstruction forced political corruption upon the South, the governments of the South were controlled by freedmen, and that nothing of value was accomplished by these Reconstruction legislatures. **Revisionist** historians agree that corruption did exist, but maintain that the South was known for its political corruption almost from the early colonial times, especially when slavery had expanded greatly, and the large plantation owners began dominating Southern politics. Whenever a relatively small elite dominates the system, it is often manipulated by them for their benefit, with bribery, corruption, and collusion frequently occurring. Reconstruction was a period of time in American history in which corruption was the rule rather than the exception across the entire United States.

Revisionists have also demonstrated by factual evidence that governments in the South were not controlled by African-Americans. They did not serve in the office of governor in any state, and as it has been stated earlier, only held a majority in the South Carolina legislature. The Reconstruction legislatures passed laws that divided the tax burdens more equitably, provided for free public education, instituted charitable institutions, and advanced democracy, just to name a few of their accomplishments. These reforms must have had value because, when the Democrats regained control, they did not overturn most of these accomplishments by the Reconstruction legislatures.

Traditionalist and **Revisionist** historians generally agree that Reconstruction was ultimately a failure, but for very different reasons. **Traditionalists** say it was a failure because of what it did—namely, that it allegedly plundered the South economically, politically, and socially. **Revisionists**, on the other hand, say it was a failure because of what it did **not** do—namely, put the African-American family on a sound footing.

THE END OF RECONSTRUCTION

By 1875, only Mississippi, Louisiana, Florida, and South Carolina were under Republican rule. In the off-year elections of 1875, Mississippi Democrats adopted the Mississippi Plan to take back that state. In the Mississippi Plan, physical intimidation—men with guns at polling places—and economic intimidation—the threat of the loss of jobs, especially for freedmen who voted Republican—placed the Democrats back in control of Mississippi that year. In the 1876 presidential election, Florida, South Carolina, and Louisiana were the only Southern states still under Republican control.

In 1876, the Republican Party nominated Rutherford B. Hayes, the governor of Ohio. It was believed that the honest and upstanding Hayes would be the perfect candidate to counter the scandals of the Grant administration. The Democratic Party nominated Samuel J. Tilden, the reform governor of New York. When the votes were counted in November of 1876, Samuel Tilden claimed victory. However, there were disputes in the states of Louisiana, Florida, and South Carolina, with both parties claiming victory in these states. In those states, Democrats had adopted the tactics of the Mississippi Plan to attempt to win them, so the Republican-controlled election returning boards compensated by adjusting the vote count. Many historians believe that the Republicans would have carried the state if large numbers of voters had not been intimidated, and the Democrats would have won there if the votes that were cast had been accurately counted. There was also a dispute in the state of Oregon concerning the legality of one of that state's electors. A local postmaster was chosen an elector, although it was illegal for a federal employee to serve in that capacity. When that situation was made public in Oregon, the Democratic governor appointed a replacement; the other two electors, however, insisted that they had the legal right to name the third elector under those conditions. The disposition of twenty electoral votes was at stake in the election—Louisiana (8), South Carolina (7), Florida (4), and Oregon (1 of its 3). Excluding these twenty disputed electoral votes, Tilden possessed 184 electoral votes, one short of winning the White House. Hayes' total of 165 votes left him twenty short of victory.

Article II of the United States Constitution states that Congress shall count the electoral votes and declare the winner in a presidential race. But the House of Representatives was controlled by the Democrats, the Senate was under Republican control, and the whole country was extremely tense about the delicate situation. Rumors of violence, and even a return to civil war, circulated throughout the nation. Under these conditions, Congress attempted to cool the crisis by passing the Electoral Count Act in very early 1877. This law created the Electoral Commission to determine how to allocate the 20 disputed electoral votes. The Electoral Commission was to consist of 15 members: 5 from the House of Representatives (3 Democrats and 2 Republicans), 5 from the Senate (3 Republicans and 2 Democrats), and 5 Supreme Court justices. In the latter category, four justices were specifically named in the law; and these four would choose a fifth member among the court—one who was fairly independent politically. They chose Justice David Davis. This selection meant that there were 7 Democrats, 7 Republicans, and one independent on the commission, which, of course, would have given Davis the deciding vote if one assumed the others would vote on a strictly partisan basis.

Then an interesting twist of fate occurred. Davis wanted to be president of the United States. Unfortunately, the Supreme Court is not a place from which potential American presidents usually come. Therefore, David Davis resigned from the Supreme Court, and thus the Electoral Commission, in order to accept a seat in the United States Senate offered by his home state's (Illinois) legislature. With little choice left, the four justices on the commission appointed Joseph B. Bradley, a partisan Republican from New Jersey.

When the Electoral Commission finally got down to business, it gave all twenty of the disputed electoral votes to Republican Rutherford B. Hayes on a partisan 8–7 vote. This gave Hayes the presidency by the closest of all electoral margins, 185 to 184. It also resulted in the collapse of the Republican governments in the three Southern states with disputed electoral votes; there had briefly been great confusion there because each of two competing state governments attempted to claim it was the legitimate government. The Electoral Count Act stated that unless both houses of Congress overrode the Electoral Commission's decision, its verdict would prevail. By 4:00 a.m. on March 2, just two days before the presidential inauguration, Congress refused to vote to override.

Leaders of both parties wanted to avoid anything approaching civil war over this election. That proved to be the motivator for what history has termed the Compromise of 1877. Although many modern historians downplay the significance of this compromise, there was a behind-the-scenes agreement between Republican and Southern Democratic leaders. This so-called Compromise of 1877 consisted of agreements on the part of President Hayes to give land grants and loans to build railroads across the South, federal subsidies to make improvements in the South, a cabinet member appointed from the South, and a presidential promise to withdraw all federal troops from the South.

During President Hayes' administration, few of the agreements were effectively implemented. However, Hayes had even promised during the presidential campaign

1876	38	RUTHERFORD B. HAYES	Republican	4,036,572	185	48.0
		Samuel J. Tilden	Democrat	4,284,020	184	51,0

Electoral Votes in the Disputed 1876 Presidential Election.

that he would withdraw all federal troops from the South and end Reconstruction. (In this, Hayes and Tilden both agreed, so Reconstruction had not been a major issue in the campaign.) And this promise was kept by President Hayes when he ordered the withdrawal of the remaining few thousand troops in the South in April 1877, one month after his inauguration. Reconstruction was officially over for the South, although many of the problems of the era were not resolved.

ADDITIONAL READINGS

Michael Les Benedict, *The Impeachment and Trial of Andrew Johnson* (1973). The best history of the impeachment crisis.

Ellen Carol DuBois, *Feminism and Suffrage* (1978). Analyzes the emergence of an independent woman suffrage movement in the context of Reconstruction politics.

Michael W. Fitzgerald, *The Union League Movement in the Deep South* (1989). Uses the Union Lague as a lens through which to examine race relations and the close connections between politics and economic change in the post-Civil War South.

Eric Foner, *Reconstruction: America's Unfinished Revolution, 1863–1877* (1988). The most comprehensive and thoroughly researched overview of the Reconstruction era.

Steven Hahn, *The Roots of Southern Populism* (1983). Examines the deteriorating plight of poor white southern farmers after the Civil War and their efforts at political protest.

Jacqueline Jones, *Labor of Love, Labor of Sorrow* (1985). Includes excellent material on the work and family lives of African-American women in slavery and freedom.

Leon F. Litwack, *Been in the Storm So Long: The Aftermath of Slavery* (1979). A richly detailed analysis of the transition from slavery to freedom; excellent use of African-American sources.

Michael Perman, *Emancipation and Reconstruction* (1987). A short but very useful overview of Reconstruction politics emphasizing racial issues and the end of slavery.

Willie Lee Rose, *Rehearsal for Reconstruction: The Port Royal Experiment* (1964). A pioneering account of the transition from slavery to freedom on the Sea Island plantations during the Civil War.

Mark W. Summers, *Railroads, Reconstruction, and the Gospel of Prosperity* (1984). The best study of the economic and political importance of railroad building in this era.

Allen W. Trelease, *White Terror: The Ku Klux Klan Conspiracy and Southern Reconstruction* (1971). The most complete account of Klan activity and the efforts to suppress it.

CHAPTER TWO

Settling the West

MAJOR EVENTS

1848   Treaty of Guadalupe Hidalgo

1849–   California gold rush
1860s

1853   Gadsden Purchase

1858   Comstock Lode discovered

1862   Homestead Act
              Morrill Act

1865–67   "Red Cloud's War" or "Powder River War"

1866   Southern Homestead Act
              Texas cattle drive begins

1869   Golden spike struck for transcontinental railroad
              Board of Indian Commissioners created
              Edward Zane Carroll Judson's *Buffalo Bill, the King of the Border Men*,
              sets off "Wild West" publishing craze

1870s   Grasshopper attacks on the plains

1872   Yellowstone National Park created

1873   Timber Culture Act

1875   Sioux war in Black Hills of Dakotas

1876   Colorado statehood
              Custer's Last Stand

1877   Desert Land Act
Munn v. Illinois

1881   Helen Hunt Jackson, *A Century of Dishonor*

1882–83   Sante Fe, Southern Pacific, and Northern Pacific railroad link

1886   Bad winter in West ends cattle boom

1887   Dawes Severalty Act

1890   Sioux Ghost Dance movement
Massacre of Lakota Sioux at Wounded Knee
Wyoming and Idaho statehood
Census Bureau officially closes frontier

1896   Utah statehood

INTRODUCTION

During the post-Civil War era, Americans permanently settled the western half of the continent. In fact, perhaps the greatest internal westward migration in world history occurred from 1870 to 1900. From 1607, with the founding of the first permanent English settlement at Jamestown, to 1870, Americans occupied about 407 million acres in North America, with 189 million of those acres cultivated. But from 1870 to 1900, Americans settled on 430 million additional acres, with 225 million of them cultivated. That means that Americans occupied more new land in the last 30 years of the nineteenth century than they had in the first 263 years of their existence in North America.

Settlement patterns in the West, the area from the Mississippi valley to the Pacific Ocean, differed greatly from the settlement patterns of the East. American settlers from the time of the original colonies had moved west searching for land or adventure. The flow was a fairly constant movement west. This line of settlement stopped after the first row of states to the west of the Mississippi River, were formed—Minnesota, Iowa, Missouri, Arkansas, and Louisiana. Settlement to the west of this line occurred in random isolated areas, at greatly varying times, and for many different reasons. Continuous settlement stopped at the Great Plains, known as the "Great American Desert" for several decades. Explorers into the interior of the nation considered this dry area, from the ninety-eighth meridian to the Rocky Mountains, unfit for white settlement. It was considered fit for Native American Indian tribes only, either native inhabitants of the area or tribes removed from the East to the Indian Territory. While Americans later discovered the "Great American Desert" was not a true desert. When the demand for new territory grew after the Civil War, along with the capabilities to farm the dry plains, the dry interior of the nation, once called a desert, was opened to settlement.

Before and after the 1860s, Americans circumvented the inhospitable Great Plains and colonized isolated areas beyond. Settlement of the Great Plains would have to wait until circumstances for success came together. In the 1830s and 1840s, Americans came West for the land available in the Oregon Territory and the Mexican provinces of Texas, California, and New Mexico. Americans applied for land grants in the areas controlled by Mexico and were given thousands of acres for ranching and farming. After the American victory in the Mexican-American War of 1848, Americans came in greater numbers to the new western areas gained from the war in the Treaty of Guadalupe Hidalgo, signed on February 2, 1848. The United States gained 529,000 square miles from Mexico. The land ceded by Mexico later became the states of California, Nevada, and Utah, and also contributed portions to the states of Arizona, New Mexico, Colorado, and Wyoming.

Although the United States had increased its landholdings considerably, and its citizens were constantly pressuring for more land to settle, settlers did not flock in large numbers to the West at first. A journey of several thousand miles by wagon, with the possible dangers of Indian attacks, disease, the normal hardships of traveling in a wilderness area and leaving all that was familiar behind was daunting to most. (The reality was that, considering the number of travelers, very few faced Indian attacks.) However, in the 1840s, the opportunity to own land in the Oregon Territory brought thousands of American settlers west. Most of the

Group of Wagons. Credit: New Mexico Department of Development.

travelers to Oregon began their six month, two thousand mile journey by joining a wagon train at Independence, Missouri. The most common route used was the Oregon Trail, which had been marked by fur trappers in the 1820s and 1830s. A ten foot by four foot covered wagon, known as a "prairie schooner," was the mode of transportation for the travelers on the trail, and it was also used to transport all of their worldly possessions. The covered wagon was also known as the Conestoga wagon because it had first been manufactured in Conestoga, Pennsylvania. These large covered wagons traveled at a speed of one mile-per-hour, and on a good day they could cover 16 miles. Between 1843 and 1866, approximately 350,000 Americans traveled the trail to make a new beginning in the West.

In the 1840s, Mormons also traveled to the West to begin a new life free, they hoped, from persecution for their religious beliefs. The Church of Jesus Christ of Latter Day Saints, better known as the Mormon Church, was founded in the 1830s by Joseph Smith, Jr. This new religion studied *The Book of Mormon*, claimed by Smith as a divinely revealed new addition to the Bible. Smith claimed the book was his translation from certain gold plates an angel had shown him in upstate New York. The protestant denominations were suspicious and intolerant of this new religion, and they made life so difficult for Mormons in the East that they constantly moved west looking for sanctuary.

Members of the Mormon Church moved from New York to Ohio, next to Missouri, and finally to Illinois, where they chartered their own city, named Nauvoo. The Mormons built Nauvoo into a thriving community, but once again non-Mormons in the area were hostile to them. Joseph Smith was the law in Nauvoo. No Illinois law was valid in Nauvoo until he decided it was. Anyone using language disrespectful of the church was punished. He even asked Congress to elevate his city to a federal territory that would free it from state control. And he used his city's votes to gain concessions from both parties during elections. To the surrounding non-Mormon areas, the Mormons were becoming dangerous with their above-the-law attitude.

A split in the Mormon community occurred when Smith announced that polygamy, the practice of men having more than one wife, was desirable for church leaders. Many Mormons refused to accept this new order from the prophet. A newspaper was founded to print the opinions in opposition to Joseph Smith. But Smith ordered the paper closed and the press smashed. After that incident, the editors of the paper swore out a warrant for Smith's arrest in nearby Carthage. Smith and his brother surrendered and were put into the Carthage jail for protection against the hostile non-Mormons. On June 27, 1844, a mob broke into the jail and killed the two leaders. The citizens in the counties surrounding Nauvoo wanted the Mormons out of the area, or they promised more violence. The new leader of the church, Brigham Young, promised to take his people away. It was decided that the new home for the Mormon Church and its people would be in the Mexican territory of Utah, near the Great Salt Lake. Brigham Young and his followers reached their new homeland in July 1847. It was a barren wasteland, contrasting in every way with the beautiful descriptions Young had read. In a few short years, with hard work and irrigation, this barren desert began to bear fruit. In 1848, this territory was ceded to the United States, a disappointment to those who were attempting to escape from the control of the United States government.

Specific circumstances did account for settlement of the West. However, permanent widespread settlement was brought about by three groups—the miners, the cattle ranchers, and the farmers. These groups followed one after another when circumstances came together for their migrations to meet with success. One of the tragic outcomes of the movement west was war with the Indian inhabitants of the areas. The lands were not vacant, and many of the tribes fought to keep what was theirs. One explanation of American beliefs in their right to take land that was not theirs was the idea of "manifest destiny." In 1845, John L. O'Sullivan, editor of the *United States Magazine and Democratic Review*, stated that "our manifest destiny is to overspread the continent allotted by Providence for the free development of our yearly multiplying millions." The movement west grew from a trickle to a flood beginning with the discovery of gold in California.

THE MINING COMMUNITIES

Land and religious freedom pulled Americans west into unsettled territories, but the possibility of making a fortune from a discovery of gold or silver brought Americans by the tens of thousands. They spread across the mountainous areas of the West, moving from one mineral strike to another, colonizing while they prospected. While most individual prospectors were gradually replaced in the 1880s, when only large corporations from the East could afford the resources to mine the more difficult areas that remained, company miners continued the westward migration.

California

Gold was discovered in California at Sutter's Mill in January 1848. John Sutter, a Swiss settler, received a land grant from the Mexican government to build a settlement in what was the Mexican province of California in 1839. He built a small settlement, with a fort to protect the residents and the businesses that supplied travelers passing through to northern California. Sutter and a partner, James Marshall, decided the area needed a sawmill, and it was during the building of the mill that gold was discovered. Sutter swore his workers to secrecy in order to complete the mill and to gain clear title to the land which the mill stood upon. The United States Supreme Court later declared Sutter's land grant to have no legitimacy in the American state of California. The United States received California from its victory in the war with Mexico. Although the construction workers at the mill agreed to keep the gold strike a secret, the news leaked out. Sutter could not keep the secret himself. The rumors of gold, and then confirmation, brought in excess of 100,000 Americans to California in 1848 and 1849. The value of the gold miners took from California in 1848 has been calculated at approximately 10 million dollars, which in modern terms, would be closer to $200 million. Sutter was not involved in any other mineral finds, and he did not become wealthy from his involvement with the first important gold strike in this country's history. He was not a particularly good businessman and did not find a way to keep the gold found by his men. He later moved to Pennsylvania and lived in modest comfort.

By the mid 1850s, most of the areas containing gold in California were claimed. Miners turned to other areas in the West to look for their fortunes.

Nevada

A few prospectors on their way to California found small amounts of gold in the canyons to the east of the Sierra Nevada Mountains in 1849. These men were in a great hurry to reach California, where gold had been found in abundance, so they did not stay and mine an area that had not yet proven its value. In 1850 and 1851, Mormons farming in valleys not far from the mountains also discovered gold in the ravines and the ditches they dug for irrigation. This area later to become Nevada Territory was at this time in Utah Territory. The farmers began to mine the canyons, ravines, and mountainsides. Soon the mountainous areas to the east of California became the destinations of some of the prospectors who had not discovered gold in California. Gold miners in this new area were slowed in their mining by a blue substance that was frequently mixed in with their precious gold and had to be separated. This annoying blue substance, it was soon discovered, was silver and brought more wealth to the miners in Nevada than their discoveries of gold. In 1858 and 1859, Henry T. P. Comstock began to stake claims in a variety of locations near the Carson River valley. His claims contained rich veins of gold and silver that eventually yielded over $300 million worth of metal and was known as the Comstock Lode. The rumors of gold and silver finds brought thousands of prospectors to the area to stake their claims in 1860. By 1861, so many Americans were settling in the western portion of Utah Territory that Congress allowed the formation of the Nevada Territory. Nevada was then given statehood in 1864. Nevada's quick transformation from territory to statehood was the result of Republicans wanting the three electoral votes the new state would bring to President Lincoln.

Colorado

Gold seekers on their way to California in 1849 and 1850 also passed through the mountainous area which would later become Colorado. Some of them found small amounts of gold, but similar to the case of discovery in Nevada, the small finds did not deter their journey west. In 1858, rumors of travelers finding gold and the trading of gold nuggets by the Indians of the area, led some to believe that a thorough search for gold in this section of the Rocky Mountains was warranted. W.

Green Russell struck gold in the area near present-day Denver. It was not a large strike, but the rumors that flew back East exaggerated the amount of gold found, and the rush of the '59ers, also called the Pikes Peak Gold Rush, began.

Gold was difficult to find, and from the approximately 50,000 prospectors who came to seek their fortunes in the Pikes Peak area, more than 25,000 returned to the East in 1859. Many persevered in the streams and mountains of the area, and some found their fortunes in gold and later silver.

Idaho

Unsuccessful miners from the fields of California worked their way north and then east into the Rocky Mountain area of Idaho. Trading with the Nez Perce tribe in the northern Rockies led Elias Davidson Pierce to the discovery of gold in the area around the Clearwater River. A rush to the area commenced in 1861, after some of the gold prospected was brought back to Walla Walla, Washington. The Nez Perces agreed that whites could search for gold on their reservation land north of the Clearwater River only. The whites quickly violated this agreement and spread south looking for gold.

Montana

Traveling through Montana to reach Idaho, prospectors made the first major gold strike in the southwestern corner of Montana in July 1862. In 1863, at Alder Gulch, near present-day Virginia City, another rich strike was made. By 1864, there were from ten to fifteen thousand men looking for gold in the area. Prospectors moved to new areas finding gold, filing claims and establishing towns.

South Dakota

In the Treaty of Fort Laramie signed in 1868 by the United States government, the land of the present state of South Dakota was set aside as a reservation for the Sioux tribes. Within this reservation lay the Black Hills. In the 1860s and the 1870s, whites violated the terms of the Fort Laramie treaty by prospecting for gold in the Black Hills. The Sioux had known of the existence of the gold in the hills for some time and had kept it a secret so that the whites would not come to the area. The army attempted to keep the prospectors out of the area for a while. However, Lieutenant Colonel George Armstrong Custer was sent on an exploring expedition in 1874 to confirm for the government if the rumors of gold were true. Custer's official orders were to search for a likely site to build a new fort to protect the reservation from interlopers. Custer brought scientists, prospectors, and reporters with him, and they found gold. The find was reported in eastern newspapers, and gold seekers came to the Black Hills. There seemed to be no way to keep the Americans out of the region permanently. Knowing there would be trouble with the Sioux if whites were not kept out of this sacred region, the government attempted to buy the area from the tribes. The attempts to secure the Black Hills failed, and war between the Sioux and the Americans was the result of this gold discovery.

MINING CAMPS

The strikes and the settlements that developed had many elements in common. The miners who came to prospect for gold and silver usually faced difficult and dangerous journeys to reach their destinations. Their journeys were thousands of miles, either by land, across the interior of the nation, or by sea (either around South America or down to the Isthmus of Panama by ship, then across the Isthmus, and the final leg of the journey to California by ship once again). Another commonality was the fact that many of the prospectors met with failure and went home. But those who stayed, either as successful miners or moving into other en-

Coal Mine, 1895. Credit: The Bettmann Archive.

deavors, formed camps, then towns and cities. Perhaps the most famous of these mining towns was Deadwood, in the Dakota Territory (now South Dakota).

When a mining community began, the people had only themselves to create a system of justice and protection. The establishment of government in the mining areas of the West followed consistent patterns. When there were enough prospectors in an area to establish a fair-sized camp, there was usually a mass meeting held to establish laws for the camp. The laws usually concerned the size of the claims that could be staked and the punishment for crimes against the citizens of the camps. Law-breakers were brought before judges, who were elected by the members of the camp, and tried by juries of varying sizes. Trials were held only for serious crimes, such as theft, assault, and murder. Punishment depended on the nature of the crime and included banishment, lashes, and execution, usually by hanging.

If the system of justice established in each camp or mining town could not seem to handle the law-breakers, a group of miners or town members formed a vigilance committee to handle the troublemaker. This group worked in secret, tried the offender themselves, and carried out the sentence quickly. The sentence was usually an execution by lynching.

The miners and the other citizens who came to the mining areas and eventually formed small towns or large cities, were not satisfied for long with extralegal systems of justice and local governments only. As soon as populations were settled and their numbers large enough, petitions were sent to Congress for territorial status and later admission as full-fledged states of the Union. The protection and benefits of statehood were undeniable for most Americans in the West.

CONNECTING WEST TO EAST

The Stagecoach

The residents of the widely scattered communities in the West needed transportation routes to connect them to each other and the eastern half of the nation in order to trade goods and services and receive important news. In 1848, the government had arranged for mail delivery to California by ship on a semimonthly basis, but this was too infrequent to satisfy the Westerners. News frequently arrived too late to be useful. Californians wanted news from the other side of the continent to be sent daily, and they petitioned Congress in 1856 to develop an overland road. The Post Office Appropriation Act of 1857 authorized payment of a subsidy to a private company to develop an overland route and provide at least weekly mail service from a point on the Mississippi River to San Francisco.

John Butterfield and William Fargo received the government contract, along with the subsidy, and organized the Butterfield Overland Mail Company. In 1858, the red and green stagecoaches of the Butterfield Company began transporting the mail, along with a few passengers, along the southwest route from Missouri to California. Two stagecoaches left each week from each direction in order to provide fast service. The trip took approximately 25 days. Freight companies also marked overland routes to provide the goods which the western regions needed to purchase, and took back to the East goods they needed to sell.

The Pony Express

Hoping to gain a government contract for their stagecoach line to carry mail along a route through the center of the nation, the company of Russell, Majors and Waddell developed a faster way to deliver the mail from Missouri to California. Their new mail service was the Pony Express. By changing horses at stations every

10 miles and riders every 70 miles, letters arrived at their destinations in only ten days. This innovative method of mail delivery caught the attention of the country then and still lingers as a unique part of American history. The connection of East with West, through telegraph wires in October 1861, ended the need for the Pony Express.

The Transcontinental Railroad

Mail, passengers, and goods were transported across the dirt highways of the plains and through the mountain passes of the Rockies and the Sierra Nevadas in increasing numbers and speed in the late 1850s, but it was obvious that railroad transportation was needed to meet the needs of the growing West. This project was too large and profits too uncertain in this sparsely settled area for a private company to risk building a railway line to connect the West to the East without government assistance.

Government support for the transcontinental railroad project was delayed because of disagreements between northern and southern congressmen on the route. President Lincoln signed the first Pacific Railway Bill on July 1, 1862, during the Civil War, when the South had no say on the project, authorizing the building of the transcontinental railroad along a central route, with branches radiating north and south. The government subsidized the building of the first railroad in the West with contracts to the Union Pacific and the Central Pacific railroad companies. The Union Pacific was to begin building west from Council Bluff, Iowa, through the Rocky Mountains, near the South Pass in Wyoming and join the other line on the border between California and Nevada. The Central Pacific was to begin building east from Sacramento, California, and then across the rugged Sierra Nevada Mountains. Government loans were pledged to each company, ranging from 16,000 dollars to 48,000 dollars for every mile of track laid. The amount of money paid per mile of track depended on the difficulty of the terrain the company had to traverse. Federal land was also given to each company to entice the companies to bid upon the project. Each received a 400-foot right-of-way and 20 square miles of land alternating in 640-acre sections on either side of the tracks for each mile of track built. The land was to be sold to settlers that came west once the railroad was in operation. Some believed the government gave too much land to the railroad companies building the transcontinental railroad and later railroad lines. The builders of the first transcontinental line received a total of 335 million acres of public land. But the government knew that the growth of the country and the prosperity that would follow depended upon a good transportation system.

The Central Pacific was the first to begin building in 1863. A loan from the state of California gave the company the necessary capital to begin the work. Construction moved slowly for both companies. During the Civil War, workers and supplies were difficult to obtain. The labor problems for both companies, however, were alleviated by new immigrants. Chinese workers were a major labor source for the Central Pacific, and Irish laborers contributed greatly to the success of the Union Pacific. The labor problem was only one of many problems both companies had to overcome. The Central Pacific faced the task of going around, over, and sometimes through the mountain peaks of the Sierra Nevadas. Most of their loan money from

Thomas Hill's "Driving the Last Spike" depicts the ceremony completing the transcontinental railroad at Promontory Point, Utah on May 10, 1869. Credit: AP/Wide World Photos.

the federal government was in the $48,000 range, which was the amount given for difficult mountain terrain building.

The Union Pacific had the problems of bringing to their building sites all materials from great distances and fighting off hostile Indian tribes. Both railroad companies persevered and increased their building speed after the Civil War. Competition for the maximum amount of loan money and land from the federal government pushed both sides to increase their building speed. The construction crews of both companies laid rails parallel to each other for a distance in Utah in order to gain more money. The government finally ordered the two companies to meet at Promontory Point, Utah. The final spike, one made from gold, was put in place on May 10, 1869. Americans could now travel from the Atlantic Coast to the Pacific Coast by railroad. A journey that previously took months would now take approximately one week.

INDIAN WARS IN THE WEST

Mineral strikes and the transportation systems they spawned brought Americans in ever increasing numbers into western areas that had been controlled for centuries by Native American Indian tribes. As the mineral finds increased the wealth of the West, they also created the circumstances for the destruction of the Indian way of life in the West. For most Indian tribes, their existence depended upon hunting game in large areas where the animals were not disturbed by man. For the nomadic Plains tribes, their existence depended upon the buffalo thundering unimpeded across the Plains. The buffalo was called "a galloping department store" for the Plains Indians because it supplied them with so many essentials of life. They used the flesh for meat, the hides for blankets and robes, the sinew for bowstrings, the bones for tools and utensils, the hooves for glue, and the dung for fuel. (The latter were called buffalo "chips".) It is estimated that anywhere from 10 to 15 million bison roamed the western United States in the middle of the nineteenth century. That number would dramatically fall before the end of the century.

The horse had also come to be a valuable animal to the Plains Indians. The Spanish explorer, Cortez, had introduced horses into Mexico in the sixteenth century. These animals multiplied, and thousands of wild horses wandered north onto the Plains. By the nineteenth century, at least, the Plains tribes were using the horse in hunting the bison and in warfare. Many military historians, in fact, maintain that the Plains Indians of the mid-nineteenth century were equal to the military skill of Europe's finest cavalry divisions.

Relations between whites and Indians in the West repeated the same cycle of behavior followed from the beginning of white settlement on the North American continent. Whites moved into territory claimed by Indian tribes, and the tribes of the area fought to keep their land. The Indians were defeated and then forced to sign treaties giving up their traditional territories and to move into areas considered undesirable to whites. In 1830, Congress had passed the Indian Removal Act, establishing the government policy of moving all Indian tribes west of the Mississippi River and turning the Plains into one big reservation. Using this policy, the government removed the Five "Civilized" Tribes (Cherokee, Chickasaw, Creek, Choctaw, and Seminole) to land known as Indian Territory in present-day Oklahoma.

With the discovery of gold in California in 1848 and settlers moving into Kansas and Nebraska territory in the 1850s, the situation changed. Americans traveled across Indian lands in larger numbers, and some were attacked. The Fort Laramie Treaty of 1851 established the policy of setting boundaries on the lands the Indians claimed and gained protection for whites to pass through tribal territories. Tribes who agreed to limit themselves to smaller reservations were given gifts and annuities. This policy of constantly shrinking the areas claimed by the tribes was called the concentration policy. In each treaty, they were told they would have these lands forever. However, Americans came to the West to stay in greater numbers after the Civil War, and the Indians of the West fought their final battles for their lands. "Forever," in treaties with the United States government, meant until American citizens demanded what had been promised to the Indians.

There were at least 300,000 American Indians in the United States in the 1860s, and many went to war with the whites. The Indian wars began with the Indians of California, Washington, and Oregon, and moved eastward to the final arena on the northern and southern Plains and the Rocky Mountain areas. The wars with the Plains tribes pitched the United States armies against some of the fiercest fighters they would encounter. These wars had few large pitched battles and consisted mostly of cycles of attacks and counterattacks on both sides. From 1864 to 1890, the major tribes involved in warfare were the Sioux tribes, northern Cheyenne and northern Arapaho in the northern Plains area, the Nez Perce in the northern Rockies, the Comanche, Kiowa, southern Cheyenne, and southern Arapaho on the southern Plains, and the Apache in the Southwest. Misunderstandings and mistakes led to atrocities and innocent lives being taken on both sides. Not ascribing to the theories of the "noble red-man" nor the "evil whites," this period of time should be looked at from a balanced view as the clash between two cultures, with the stronger imposing its will on the weaker.

This last cycle of Indian wars began in 1862, when large numbers of federal troops were withdrawn from the West in order to assist the Union in Civil War fighting. There were earlier incidents, of course, some of which will be referred to in subsequent pages. After a general lull in fighting from late 1867 to mid-1868, fighting between Indians and settlers resumed. The announcement of the small reservation policy in 1867 fueled fears among the tribes that their entire way of life would be destroyed forever.

The event which made that destruction easier was the mass slaughter of buffalo, which nearly caused that animal to become extinct. The slaughter began in 1867 as a way to feed railroad workers laying part of the transcontinental track for the Union Pacific Railroad Company. William F. Cody, already a famous scout and Indian fighter, killed nearly 4,300 buffalo during 8 months in the 1867–1868 period. Eastern "sportsmen" next started coming to the West to shoot bison, often from the windows of trains. During this time, buffalo robes were in high demand in the East. Therefore, this economic incentive became another reason for the mass destruction of the buffalo. The United States Army then joined in the slaughter as an instrument of Indian policy in order to control the tribes through the destruction of this very important animal. At one time, someone remarked that you could walk on the Plains for several hundred miles on the carcasses of bison without ever touching the ground. By the 1880s, 10 to 15 million bison were reduced to a few thousand at best. Not coincidentally, the 1880s was also the decade in which the various Indian tribes were finally subdued permanently. Descriptions of just a few of the most important encounters—there were more than 1,000—gives insight into the final chapter of Indian conquest.

The Cheyenne-Arapaho

According to the Treaty of Fort Laramie (1851), the Cheyenne and Arapaho tribes held title to the land in the area of Colorado between the North Platte River and the Arkansas River. The discovery of gold brought thousands of Americans to dig for their fortunes in the hills and mountains which belonged to the Indian tribes. In 1861, Indian agents in Colorado tricked a few of the Cheyenne and Arapaho chiefs into signing a new treaty at Fort Lyon, limiting their reservation to a much smaller area in southeastern Colorado, between Sand Creek and the Arkansas River. Black Kettle, a Cheyenne chief known for his peaceful position, was one of the signers. It was important for the whites to negate the Forth Laramie Treaty because Americans were digging for gold, building businesses, and ranching in Colorado in 1859 and 1860 on land that did not belong to them. John Evans, governor of Colorado Territory, attempted to get all of the chiefs to sign the treaty, but they refused.

The whites came in greater numbers to Colorado in 1861, and the Cheyenne and Arapaho began raiding mining camps and attacking wagons and coaches on the trails to drive them from the area. Regular army units were pulled out of the West as more soldiers were needed to fight the Confederacy in the Civil War, so volunteer units were raised to protect settlers. Settlers in the West were particularly fearful after the 1862 uprising of the Santee Sioux in Minnesota. Colonel John M. Chivington was the commander of the Colorado Volunteers. Chivington, a former Methodist minister, believed that the way to solve the Indian problem in the West was to annihilate all of them. Chivington even advocated the murder of Indian children with his statement that "nits make lice." Many of his volunteers had the same harsh frontier attitude toward the Indians.

In the summer of 1864, Governor Evans ordered all Cheyenne and Arapaho to come in to Fort Lyon and proceed to the reservation assigned to them. All who did not come in would be considered enemies and would be killed. Black Kettle and other chiefs finally brought many from their tribes in and camped at Sand Creek, not far from the fort. On November 29, 1864, Colonel Chivington ordered 700 Colorado Volunteers to ride into the sleeping camp and kill all of the Indians there. There were approximately 600 Cheyenne and Arapaho at Sand Creek, and two-thirds were women and children. All thought they were under the protection of the army. The soldiers rode into the camp and confusion ensued. Many of the tribe members attempted to reach the teepee of Black Kettle. He had been given an American flag when he had visited President Lincoln, and he was told to fly the flag to keep his people safe from attack by the United States Army. The flag was flying, but still the soldiers attempted to kill everyone. About 200 men, women, and children were killed and scalped before the Chivington Massacre was finished. At hearings concerning the massacre, it was stated that not one body was left without mutilation. Colonel Chivington resigned from the militia, but his punishment for his deeds at Sand Creek was only a reprimand. The immediate result of the massacre was more raiding by the Indians, hoping to make the whites pay for Sand Creek. In October 1865, the Cheyenne and Arapaho conceded defeat and gave up their land in Colorado. Some went to join the northern Cheyenne and Arapaho, and others were settled in western Indian Territory. Black Kettle escaped death at Sand Creek only to face the repetition of the same circumstances at the Battle of the Washita in 1868. Once again his peaceful camp was attacked because of the actions of other Cheyennes and Arapahos, who were attacking whites. The story of retaliation by both sides against those who could be caught for the actions of those who could not was one of the tragedies of war between whites and Indians. Black Kettle was killed at the Battle of the Washita.

Sand Creek also served to enforce the resolve of many tribes in the West to fight the advancing whites. They were outraged by the treatment of the Indians under the supposed protection of the governor and the military. The American government later accepted responsibility for the massacre, and the widows and orphans of Sand Creek received recompence for the occurrences of that day on a Colorado creek bed.

The Sioux

In the 1700s, the Sioux had migrated into the northern Plains from the upper Mississippi River area, and the four major branches of the many tribes settled large areas of this land. They needed large areas of territory to support their nomadic lifestyle of following the buffalo and other game to supply their necessities. The Sioux tribes were among the fiercest of the Plains tribes. They were formidable foes because of their expert horsemanship and accuracy with bow and rifle. However, none of the Plains tribes stood much of a chance to win against the larger numbers and superior weaponry of the whites.

By 1862, the Santee Sioux had given up much of their land in treaties, and were living on reservation land on the Minnesota River, which the United States government had promised to them. In exchange for their land, the Santee were promised yearly supplies of goods, food, and cash. They also hunted for buffalo once a year to feed their people. In 1862, the Santee were suffering. Whites were encroaching on reservation land and driving away the game in their hunting areas, particularly the buffalo. There was food in the agency warehouses, but the white Indian agent would not distribute it until the tribe's money came from Washington, D.C. In August 1862, the Indians rose up and attacked their Indian agency, white settlements,

Sioux Indian Village, Fort Yates, North Dakota. Photo by Russell Reid, Bismarck, North Dakota.

isolated farms, trading posts, and Fort Ridgely. More than 500 white settlers were killed in the uprising before the warriors were defeated by the Minnesota militia. Thirty-eight Santee Sioux were hanged for their part in this war against the whites. Their reservation was taken from them. Many fled to other Sioux tribes to the west, some went to Canada, and a small group became farmers on a small reservation in northeastern Nebraska.

Red Cloud's War (or the Powder River War), which lasted from 1865–1867, was the next major engagement between whites and Sioux Indians. Red Cloud, a chief of the Oglala band, had many grievances against the whites. Whites had killed innocent Cheyenne and Arapaho at Sand Creek, taken away the territory of the Santee Sioux, and now they were invading treaty land with the building of the Bozeman Trail and military forts to protect its travellers. In 1862, John Bozeman found a more convenient route from Ft. Laramie, Wyoming to the Montana gold fields near

Bozeman. Some of the braves from the Sioux, northern Cheyenne, and northern Arapaho tribes had been sporadically raiding the trails in this area to avenge Sand Creek and stop the whites from coming to their area. But the army's decision to develop the Bozeman Trail into a road through their hunting lands and to build forts along this road brought a war to the area. The tribes joined in constant attacks on anyone connected with the endeavor. Captain William J. Fetterman and his 80 men were lured into an ambush and killed. Travellers were killed, and supplies were constantly taken from civilian and army wagon trains. The government finally gave in and agreed to stop building forts and the road to Bozeman. This was a great victory for the Indians, and Red Cloud was now a legend. A peace commission was sent to the Plains to sign agreements with the northern and the southern Plains tribes to persuade the tribes to give up their nomadic way of life and settle the Indians upon smaller reservations in areas that the whites would not want. Federal Indian policy had shifted from the old idea of placing the tribes on one big reservation in the West (beginning in 1830) to that of concentration (beginning in 1851), and eventually, to restricting them to fairly small reservations (beginning in 1867).

Two major reservations were set aside for the tribes. The Treaty of Fort Laramie of 1868 established that the western half of South Dakota and a small portion of North Dakota would be the permanent home of the Sioux. The Powder River country to the west, in present-day Montana, was "unceded Indian territory" forbidden to whites. However, there was a provision in the treaty for railroads and wagon roads to be built in the future. The reservation was so large that several agencies were required to pass out food and annuities. The most famous in the future were the Standing Rock agency in the north and the Red Cloud agency in the southwestern corner. Some members of the tribes settled close to the agencies, but the majority remained in the Powder River country, coming to the agencies for presents and winter camping only. There were also Sioux who never stepped foot on the reservations until physically forced to by American military victories.

The other large reservation was established for the southern tribes in Indian Territory. The Five "Civilized" Tribes had been forced to give up territory as punishment for their contributions to the Confederate cause in the Civil War. This land was in the western half of the territory and was divided among 22 tribes. The Treaty of Medicine Lodge Creek was signed by the Kiowa, Comanche, southern Cheyenne, and southern Arapaho in 1867, giving these tribes reservations in Indian Territory.

Federal commissioners then turned to the task of extending the small reservation policy to the tribes of the Rocky Mountains and to the Navaho and Apache of the southwest. The government optimistically announced that reservations were established for all of the tribes, and those who remained outside of the reservation system would be dealt with in the future. A basic problem with the treaties was that frequently only a few of the Indian leaders agreed to give up ancestral hunting grounds, and these leaders could not force their will on those who disagreed with the treaties. Assigning the Indians to the reservations was the easy aspect of the new Indian policy; placing those who did not want to go or keeping those on the reservation who did not want to stay was much more difficult. Many left the reservations to continue their old ways of raiding and hunting. Some left because the

Sitting Bull, Sioux Chief. Credit: Library of Congress.

conditions were not good on the reservation. The treaties made many promises that were not kept. Rations were frequently short or of very poor quality, such as moldy flour, spoiled meat, and moth-eaten blankets. They were supposed to farm, but many did not know how, the land was not good for farming, and the tools to farm were not sent. In 1868, the struggle continued between the Indians and the settlers for peace on the Plains. The southern Plains tribes were finally subdued after the Red River War in 1874.

The northern Plains tribes also faced their final defeat in the 1870s. The whites were on treaty land once again. Prospectors discovered gold in the Black Hills on the Sioux reservation. The army escorted intruders off the Sioux land only to have them return as soon as they rode out of sight. The government knew that a major conflict was inevitable in the Dakotas if both sides could not come to an agreement. The Sioux were asked to either sell the Black Hills or lease the mineral rights to the Americans. The Sioux tribes refused the offer. Not only did most not want to lose any more territory to the whites, but the Black Hills were sacred land to the Sioux. They believed that the Black Hills were the center of the universe. The Sioux would travel into the mountain area to commune with their God and refresh their spiritual selves.

The whites continued to enter the area, and the government ordered all Sioux back to the reservation in order to hopefully avoid trouble. Two major Sioux leaders, Sitting Bull and Crazy Horse, refused to go onto the reservation. In the summer of 1876, thousands of Indians gathered at the Rosebud River (in present-day Montana) for their annual sun dance. After one of the ceremonies, Sitting Bull, a medicine man, had a vision of soldiers falling into his camp. The Indians then moved their camp to the Little Big Horn River, also in present-day Montana.

In 1876, General Philip Sheridan was given the task of putting the hostile Indians on the reservation. He sent three columns into the Big Horn country to surround the Indians in their summer encampment. General George Crook came from the south, General Alfred Terry came from the east, and Colonel John Gibbon came from the west. General Terry ordered Colonel George A. Custer to track the Sioux to their camp and then circle around and position his troops to cut off any escape from the area. Custer was not new to Indian warfare; he had led troops in the Battle of the Washita in 1868. But Custer was his usual arrogant self, looking for glory, and would exceed his orders, thereby leading his men into an extremely dangerous situation from which many would die. He divided his 600 men of the Seventh Cavalry into three columns, with a fourth group to stay with the pack train of supplies and ammunition.

On June 25, 1876, he ordered the three columns to advance on the Indian encampment at the Little Big Horn River. Custer's column of 211 men was attacked by Crazy Horse and Gall and completely wiped out. It is estimated that anywhere from 1500 to 5,000 warriors were part of the attack. The other columns under the commands of Major Marcus Reno and Captain Fred Benteen, and the men assigned to the pack train, combined forces and fended off attacks on their positions. The Indians could have destroyed these forces, but decided to honor their dead and move on. General Terry arrived to assist the remaining troops on June 27. The Battle of the Little Big Horn, also known as Custer's Last Stand, shocked the nation. From the perspective of non-Indian Americans, it couldn't have come at a worst time. Nine days after Custer's defeat and annihilation, the United States celebrated its centennial Fourth of July, which was dampened by the event in southern Montana. It was hard to believe that the Indians were still strong enough to wipe out such a large number of trained soldiers. The victory of the Sioux was short-lived, however. The army was more determined, albeit more cautious, to bring in the tribes. One of the most effective strategies was the winter campaign. Riding into camps and destroying supplies and horses forced many of the remaining scattered bands onto the reservation. The buffalo was gone, so the food supplies were smaller as they went into winter encampments. Even Sitting Bull was forced to return from Canada in 1881 because he lacked supplies for his people. He had fled to Canada hoping to receive sanctuary and assistance from the Canadian government. The United States asked the Canadians to withold assistance to the Indians to force their return to the United States, which they did.

This was the end of the Sioux Indian wars and the end of major engagements in the West. There were still a few groups not subdued, and the infrequent breakouts from reservations to be dealt with.

The Nez Perce

This tribe in the far Northwest signed a treaty in 1855 to limit their territory to a ten thousand square mile area in Washington, Oregon, and Idaho. The Nez Perce had been on friendly terms with the whites for over 50 years, and it was believed that a concentration of the tribe would continue the peace. Then in 1863, the Nez Perce were asked to sign a treaty reducing their territory to 1,000 square miles in western Idaho. Whites had come to find gold in the area, and many stayed to farm when they could not find gold. The lower Nez Perce decided to stay on their land in the Wallowa Valley in northeastern Oregon. President Ulysses Grant set aside the Wallowa Valley as a reservation in 1873 only to reverse his decision in 1875 and allow white settlement in the valley belonging to the Nez Perce.

Young Chief Joseph, only one of many chiefs, advised his people to move to the reservation and avoid conflict with the whites. Before the move could be accomplished, however, a few young Indian men killed 4 white men. The murders were revenge for the murder of the father of one of the group, who had been killed by a white man. American troops were sent in to bring the hostile tribe members under control and force them to their new reservation home. This changed everything. The troops were defeated by the smaller Indian force. A larger force of troops was then sent to bring the tribe in. A meeting of the band leaders was called, and the majority decided to travel east to Montana and later into Canada. The 700 members of the Nez Perce tribe outmaneuvered and outfought American soldiers for seventeen hundred miles before they were finally defeated and forced to surrender within thirty miles of the Canadian border. Chief Joseph surrendered with approximately 400 of his followers after stating, "Our chiefs are killed. It is cold and we have no blankets. The little children are freezing to death. I am tired. My heart is sick and sad. From where the sun now stands, I will fight no more forever." The Nez Perce were sent to reservations, and one more tribe lost the land they had been promised.

The Apache

The Apache tribes of Arizona and New Mexico were the last and most difficult group to conquer. They were experienced guerilla fighters, very much at home in the harsh wilderness of their territory. They were used to wandering uninhibited over vast areas, raiding weaker groups—Mexican and other Indian tribes—for food and slaves. The Apache usually stayed away from Americans traveling the trails west that cut close to their territory, preferring to raid their old adversaries, the Mexicans. In the 1860s, however, relations between the Americans and Apaches broke down, and a cycle of attacks and counterattacks began that lasted until the last group of Chiricahua Apache, led by Geronimo, was put on the reservation for the final time. In the final campaign to bring in Geronimo and his 35 warriors, General Nelson Miles took to the field with approximately 5,000 troops. The group of Apaches surrendered on September 4, 1886, and they were sent to Florida for incarceration. Geronimo became a legend in his time, even to the extent that he was asked to participate in President Theodore Roosevelt's inaugural procession in 1905. When Geronimo died in 1909, he was a farmer on the reservation land of the Kiowa and Comanche near Ft. Sill, Oklahoma.

In the final Indian wars of the late nineteenth century, several advantages of the United States Army doomed the various Indian tribes to inevitable defeat. First, the army was better organized militarily. With rare exceptions, such as at Little Big Horn, the Indian tribes did not normally cooperate with one another very well. Most of the time, each tribe simply attacked settlers and other groups independent from what other tribes in the area were doing. Second, especially after the Civil War, American troops were experienced and battle-hardened; they knew how to fight and work together. Third, the growth of railroads in the West enabled troops to receive more supplies of food and ammunition than their Indian counterparts. Railroads were also used at times to coordinate troop movements from one area to another. Fourth, the telegraph that accompanied the growth of the railroads provided much better communications among army units—superior to the old ways the Indians still possessed to communicate with each other. And fifth, superior weapons simply made out-shooting the Indians a fairly simple task. The Colt repeating revolver, superior rifles, and the gatlin gun each played its role in overpowering Indian opponents. The Indians had some advantages. Certainly, they knew their own land better than the army did. The Plains Indians' superior horsemanship also enhanced their use of guerilla warfare. And American Indians were determined not to permit more encroachment upon their lands. These factors, plus the vastness of the West, made the last of the Indian wars so lengthy. But in the end, the American Indians were simply no match for the oncoming settlers and the army which had been sent to protect them and enforce federal Indian policy.

THE GHOST DANCE MOVEMENT

In 1888, a Paiute prophet named Wovoka began to spread a new religion based on his vision that the whites would be destroyed and a new world would emerge. In this new world, the Indians regained their land, the dead came back to life, the buffalo once again thundered across the Plains, and the whites were wiped out without the Indians going to war. In order to bring about the destruction of the whites, the tribes had to cleanse themselves, live honestly, pray, meditate, and dance. Whites named the special dance the Ghost Dance. The message of the Ghost Dance religion spread from the Nevada area to the reservations on the Plains, and the Sioux in particular grasped this last hope to rid their land of their white enemies. They danced, donned their special Ghost Dance shirts that they believed could repel bullets, and prayed that their old life would be restored soon.

White officials were disturbed by the dances. Fearing that the religious fervor of their charges would spill over into insurgency once again, the Ghost Dances were banned in November 1890. When the dances continued, the Indian leaders on the reservations were targeted for arrest. On December 15, 1890, Sitting Bull was killed during his arrest, by Indian policemen, on the Standing Rock reservation. This brought more tension to the situation because both sides feared the reaction of the other to the death of this revered man. The whites feared that the Indians might rise up to avenge the death of Sitting Bull, and the Indians feared that the death of Sitting Bull might be the beginning of a new cycle of punishment for acts of violence against whites.

The order to arrest Big Foot, another leader among the Ghost Dancers, led to the final engagement in the Indian wars. After the death of Sitting Bull, Big Foot began a journey to the Pine Ridge reservation area (in South Dakota) at the invitation of Red Cloud. Red Cloud had invited Big Foot to Pine Ridge in order to convince all participants in the dances to give up this final resistance to the domination of the whites. It was assumed by the military that Big Foot was dangerous and intent on causing trouble, so he and his followers were caught and taken into custody. This group of 230 women and children and 120 men were not inclined to resist. It was extremely cold, as it usually is in a Dakota winter, the Indians were outmanned and outgunned by the soldiers, and Big Foot was ill with pneumonia. All camped for the night at Wounded Knee Creek.

The next morning, December 29, 1890, the soldiers ordered their captives to relinquish all weapons. When they attempted to disarm a deaf Indian, his rifle discharged. It was probably an accident; the soldiers surrounding the camp began firing into the crowd of Indians and soldiers alike. Four Hotchkiss guns rained bullets into the encampment from their positions around the camp. At least 150 Indians, including Chief Big Foot, and 25 soldiers, were killed. The commanding officer at Wounded Knee, Colonel James Forsyth, was later charged with the killing of innocent men, women, and children, but he was exonerated. The irony was that the soldiers who massacred the Indians at Wounded Knee were part of the reorganized Seventh Cavalry, Custer's old unit. The massacre at Wounded Knee became a symbol for all the wrongs suffered by American Indians, and in 1973 there would be an uprising staged there by another generation of Sioux who were addressing both old and new grievances against the whites.

War was not the only factor that brought an end to the western Indian way of life. For example, whites brought several diseases that killed thousands of Indians. Smallpox was the most deadly for the native people, but the whites also brought measles, typhus, influenza, and venereal disease with them, to which there was no immunity and resistance. It is calculated that the losses among all of the tribes due to disease alone could run between twenty-five and fifty percent. Of course, the virtual extermination of the buffalo did irreparable damage to the nomadic lifestyle of those tribes.

ASSIMILATION

The second phase of policy to solve the dilemma concerning the place of Native Americans in the United States was assimilation into white society. It was not enough to place the Indians on reservations. They must also be "civilized" into accepting the ways of the whites. Missionaries went to the reservations to teach Christianity and open schools. The government sent Indian agents, along with farm tools and seed, to change the nomadic hunters into farmers. Richard Pratt founded the Carlisle Indian School in Pennsylvania to educate young Indian boys. This school was one of a number of boarding schools in the East established to reeducate the young Indian boys to adopt the skills and outlooks of the whites. These were assaults on the Indian way of life as effective as those of the army.

Many involved in the assimilation of the Indians were true humanitarians outraged by atrocities committed against the tribes in the West and the federal government's numerous broken promises to these same tribes. The general rule of thumb was that the closer to the western frontier one lived, the more likely he was to be hostile to Indians because he was likely to have experienced Indian attacks or at least know someone who had. And the farther east, and away from the frontier, that one lived, the more likely he was to be sympathetic to the plight of the American Indians. Such a sympathetic woman was Helen Hunt Jackson. In 1881, Jackson published a book entitled *A Century of Dishonor* to make the public aware of the dishonorable actions of its government toward the Indians.

Then in 1883, the Women's National Indian Rights Association was founded to take up the cause of fair and honest treatment for the tribes. Other reformers supported the plan of Senator Henry L. Dawes, who believed that the interests of the Indians would best be protected by breaking up the reservations into individually owned tracts of land. This would break tribal ties and firmly move them into mainstream America. The Dawes Severalty Act, named after Senator Henry Dawes, passed in 1887 and consisted of the following major provisions: (1) 160 acres of free government land was offered to heads of Indian families; 80 acres were offered to each single person over 18 and each orphan under 18; and 40 acres were to be made available to single persons under 18 then living or born before the president ordered individual allotment; (2) the government would purchase surplus land after all allotments were made, and make that land available to homesteaders; and (3) the government would hold the title of the land in trust for 25 years before the land owned by an Indian could be sold. This latter feature was designed to protect Indians from white land speculators. United States citizenship was also to be granted at the end of the twenty-five year period. The Burke Act, in 1906, revised this law by authorizing the Secretary of the Interior to reduce the 25-year period if he thought the Indian could handle his own affairs. Thus, the overall purpose of the Dawes Act was to "Americanize" the American Indian, meaning that he was encouraged to assimilate into the mainstream of the white man's world by leaving the reservation.

The Dawes Severalty Act did not benefit the Indians as much as it did the white land speculators who, along with the reformers, had also pressured Congress to pass the bill. In 1906, a boost was given to speculators when Senator Moses E. Clapp of Minnesota successfully obtained an amendment to an appropriations bill, which stated that all mixed-blood adult Indians were sufficiently "competent" to sell their land before the twenty-five year waiting period required by the Dawes Act. This resulted in huge land swindles being perpetuated against Indians, who were inexperienced in business dealings. Besides, among most Indians, the tribe had "owned" the land; actually, stewardship of the land by tribes on behalf of the Great Spirit is a better description of Indian attitudes toward land. The concept of individual ownership of land was therefore foreign to them. Most Indians, then, chose to remain on reservations and maintain their tribal customs. From 1887 to the 1920s, a substantial portion of the reservations was taken from the Indians, and the situation grew worse as land speculators got around the law and cheated Indians out of about 65 percent of the best land by 1934. Most of what was left was not suitable for farming, and most reservation Indians became dependent on federal aid. In 1924, Congress granted American citizenship to all Indians, largely as a reward for their service in the First World War.

Then in 1934, Congress reversed the federal policy of attempting to break up reservations when it passed the Wheeler-Howard Act (or the Indian Reorganization Act). This change of policy came about largely through the efforts of John Collier, the Indian Commissioner in the Franklin D. Roosevelt administration. The Wheeler-Howard Act sought to encourage tribal ownership of land and limited self-government in the following provisions: (1) if an Indian tribe voted against family allotments, the land was reverted to tribal ownership once again; (2) the federal government promised to purchase more land for landless Indians; (3) a $10 million fund was established for economic enterprises on the reservations; and (4) tribal constitutions were to be drawn up giving limited self-government to a tribal council. Oklahoma's Five "Civilized" Tribes were excluded because some of them had oil reserves or other financial holdings. The Navahos refused the offer. This meant that about twenty-five percent of all American Indians were not a part of the new Indian policy.

For an assessment of American treatment of the Indians, the words of President Rutherford B. Hayes, spoken in his first annual message in 1877, are indeed thought provoking. "The Indians were the original occupants of the land we now possess. They have been driven from place to place . . . . In many instances, when they had settled down upon lands assigned to them by compact and begun to support themselves by their own labor, they were rudely jostled off and thrust into the wilderness again. Many, if not most, of our Indian wars have had their origin in broken promises and acts of injustice on our part."

THE CATTLEMEN

The second wave of settlements in the West was brought about by the attempt of Americans to make their living from the cattle industry. There was a growing demand for meat in the cities east of the Mississippi River to feed the rapidly expanding industrial workforce at the end of the Civil War. Texas had an abundant supply of beef. There were millions of Texas longhorns, descendents of the long-horned cattle the Spaniards had introduced into Mexico in 1525 and mixed over the years with American breeds, roaming the plains of this southern state. The problem was how to get the cattle to the markets. The railroad did not extend into Texas yet, and it was too expensive and time consuming to send thousands of head of cattle to market by ship. The cattle drive, and later the cattle ranches, solved the problem of supplying the nation with beef. Driving the cattle to market was not a new practice, but the large numbers and great success of the long drives after the Civil War were unique.

Cowboys on the Cattle Drive Near Dickinson, North Dakota.

Cattle Drives

Cattle drives boomed in the southern Plains for about 20 years after the Civil War. The Texas cattle were rounded up and driven north in large herds, usually ranging from 1,000 to 2,500 head, to railroads in Kansas and Missouri. It took from sixteen to eighteen cowboys to move the typical sized herd to the railroad centers. Most cattle were then taken to either St. Louis, Missouri, or Chicago, Illinois, the two leading slaughterhouse and meatpacking centers of the country. In the spring of 1866, Texas longhorns were driven up the old Sedalia Trail to the railroad at Sedalia, Missouri for shipment to the East. The cattle drivers ran into numerous problems. The Indians whose land they crossed demanded payment for the cattle to graze. Missouri farmers demanded payment for the herds to cross their land, or forbade passage of the herds because of damage to farmland or fear that the longhorns carried the tick which caused Texas Fever and would infect Missouri cattle. Armed ruffians, known as Jayhawkers, also demanded payment to leave the herds alone. Driving the cattle on muddy trails, across swollen streams, and over wooded hills added to all of the other difficulties. It was a poor year for Texas cattle ranching, with only about 35,000 head reaching the railroad centers. Other major problems plagued the cattle drives in those days. Besides Indian raids and cattle rustlers, almost anything could set off a large herd of cattle and cause them to stampede out of control. The loud thunderclaps, for which the Great Plains is famous, were often enough to spook the cattle into stampeding. The obstacles were tough, but the profits that could be made were too enticing for these obstacles not to be surmounted. Steers could be purchased in Texas for $3 to $9 a head and sold at the end of the trail for up to $40.

Joseph McCoy, a young man from Illinois in the livestock and shipping business, envisioned large profits from the cattle industry if he could find a location to bring together Texas cattle, northern money from the packing houses, and a location for a stockyard on a railroad line. The cattle drives needed to move further west into areas that were not so thickly settled but had access to the railroad. McCoy built his stockyards at Abilene, Kansas, founded in 1867, which was located along the Kansas-Pacific Railroad line. When McCoy chose Abilene as a shipping site for Texas longhorns, he was violating the Kansas Quarantine Law. That law did not allow cattle from Texas in the eastern half of Kansas because of the disease-causing parasites they carried. However, the Abilene area was sparsely populated at this time, and no one protested. McCoy also improved Abilene's appeal by surveying and shortening the Chisholm Trail, which was a fairly straight and flat route from Texas to Kansas. The trail had received its name from Jesse Chisholm, who had marked an old buffalo and Indian trail in his trade with the Indians. The Chisholm Trail was only one of several cattle trails. The Western and the Goodnight-Loving were trails used to the west of the Chisholm. When the citizens of Abilene protested the crime and vice that the cowboys brought with them, and the destruction of the longhorns to fences or crops, other towns close to the railroad competed for their share of the prosperity from the cattle trade. Ellsworth, Newton, Dodge City, and others became famous cattle towns. Between 1867 and 1879, approximately four million steers from Texas were brought on the long drive to Kansas and shipped back East. By the end of the big cattle drives in the late 1880s, close to six million cattle had been driven by perhaps as many as 40,000 to 50,000 cowboys to railroad junctions and shipped eastward.

The Cowboys

America's hero, the cowboy, came from the ordinary group of young workers whose job was simply to take care of the cattle on the drives and on the ranches. The original cowboys were from Texas, or they were veterans of the Civil War, black men, or Mexicans. As ranching spread over the plains, cowboys came from all areas of the United States and many other professions. The typical cowboy was between the ages of 17 and 30, and about twenty-five percent were either Mexican or black. Most were uneducated and worked for only a year or two at low wages, usually about $30 per month, which was roughly equivalent to a common laborer's wage at the time. Cowboys worked long hours. When rounding up the cattle or driving them to a shipping point, a cowboy could spend from 16 to 20 hours a day in the saddle for weeks at a time. It was not surprising that when they arrived in any town after weeks on the trail they indulged in conduct that most of the townspeople found unacceptable. They drank, visited houses of prostitution, and were frequently involved in brawls.

Lawmen and Legends

Marshals hired by the cowtowns to control their rowdy visitors came from all walks of life. The marshals became famous heroes in spite of not always obeying the law themselves. James B. "Wild Bill" Hickok was a United States Marshal in Abilene, Kansas. He was so "wild" that in August 1876 he was shot to death at a poker table in Deadwood, Dakota Territory, by Jack McCall. Wyatt Earp was a member of the Peace Commission in Dodge City, Kansas and on the police force of Tombstone, Arizona; and William Barclay "Bat" Masterson served as a marshal in Dodge City, Kansas. Among the legends of the American West, the famous "gunfight at the OK Corral" stands out. Arizona's mining towns attracted many unsavory characters, including lawless gunmen, thieves, and gamblers. The Clantons, near Tombstone, were a well-known family involved with cattle rustling and other illegal activities. In 1881, Wyatt Earp and his four brothers, along with "Bat" Masterson and John Henry "Doc" Holliday, were themselves straddling the fence with the law. The Earp brothers and their associates became involved in a feud with the Clantons. And on October 26, 1881, a showdown gunfight at Tombstone resulted in the deaths of three Clantons and the serious injury of two of Wyatt Earp's brothers.

Women played a role in some aspects of the wild West. Martha Jane Canary, better known as "Calamity Jane," was one such legend. Calamity Jane worked in Wyoming and Dakota in the 1870s, driving wagons and serving as a scout. Jane dressed in men's clothes and was very skillful with a rifle. These unusual characteristics, coupled with a reputation for eccentric behavior, led later writers of fiction to enlarge her unusual exploits beyond their factual basis. She probably dressed as a man in order to obtain jobs usually reserved for men. And her behavior was more eccentric than really bad.

"Buffalo Bill's Wild West" traveling show also contributed to the enhanced mystery and legend of the American West. William F. Cody began his open-air Wild West show in 1883, and it toured the United States and Europe for the next thirty years. His show displayed fine horsemanship, staged cattle stampedes, sharpshooting, stagecoach robberies, and expert roping. Cody even employed Chief Sitting Bull for a time, paying him to sit very still and dignified on his horse. One of the most popular features in the show was the talented display of expert sharpshooter Annie Oakley. Oakley had been born Phoebe Anne Moses in 1860. While growing up, she learned to shoot by hunting game for the family table. As soon as she and her husband Frank Butler joined Cody's Wild West show in 1885, Annie Oakley became a star of the show. Perhaps her most brilliant act involved her husband. Butler would swing a glass ball at the end of a string. With her back turned to him, Annie used a mirror to site the ball and shot it with her gun pointed backwards over her shoulder.

Annie Oakley. Credit: AP/Wide World Photos.

Cattle Ranching

Cattle drives opened up the possibility of realizing large profits from the selling of beef, but it was cattle ranching that brought the industry into its boom period by the 1880s. The drives caused the steers to lose weight and diminished their value on the open market, so Texas longhorns were driven north, crossed with eastern cattle, and allowed to fatten up on the Great Plains before shipment back east. With the extermination of the buffalo herds, the placing of the Plains Indians on the reservations, and the advance of the railroads onto the plains, the area was opened up for cattle ranching. In the late 1860s, ranches multiplied in Kansas, Nebraska, and Colorado. In the 1870s, in spite of a national economic depression, cattle ranching extended into Wyoming, Montana, and even into Dakota Territory. Railroad construction crews and army posts were good markets in the be-

Buffalo Bill. Credit: The Bettmann Archive.

ginning for the beef of the plains ranchers. But as the quality of the beef improved along with the transportation system, and the country began to recover from the depression in 1877, demand for western beef increased in the eastern United States and in Europe also.

It seemed to many that it was impossible not to make money through raising cattle. The land used for grazing the cattle was free, and the government did not interfere with the industry. Most of the stock was purchased in Texas at a low price. As a result, by 1880 speculation in the cattle industry began to run rampant. Money from investors began flowing to western cattle concerns when dividends of some of the western companies were published. British capitalists also invested money when it was reported that thirty to forty percent profit might be had from their investment. The increased investments overstocked the plains and were a factor in the eventual downfall of the cattle kingdoms. Ranch owners organized stockbreeder's associations, hoping that cooperation would protect their investments from intruders, settle disputes between members, and establish a limit to the number of cattle grazing on the range. Several factors came together, however, and ended the cattle boom of the open range. First, the ranges were overstocked to the point that the grass could not support the cattle. Then severe blizzards in the winters of 1885–86 and 1886–87, with a severe drought in between (during the summer of 1886) caused the deaths of several million head of cattle. Cattle on the open range could only survive winter if they could dig through snow and ice to the grass below. Another factor which helped end the cattle boom of the open range were farmers and sheepherders who invaded cattle country. Farmers built miles of fences after Joseph Glidden invented "barbed wire." That shut off grazing areas that the cattlemen believed to be theirs by right of possession. Sheep destroyed the grassy areas where they grazed because of their propensity to leave the grass too short.

Settlers coming to farm the open range set off conflicts with the large ranchers that often erupted into bloody range wars. The most organized and brutal effort to stop the settlers occurred in Johnson County, in northern Wyoming. Wealthy cattlemen controlled the state of Wyoming by joining together in the Wyoming Stock Growers' Association and frequently bent the laws to suit themselves. Their attempts to drive out small farmers or ranchers, who put up fences on the range, began by charging them with stealing cattle. But juries would not convict most of the settlers. The next move was to persuade the Wyoming state legislature to pass the Maverick Bill, which made it a felony to brand a calf unless you were a member of the Stock Growers' Association. The Maverick Bill allowed the confiscation of thousands of head of cattle from the small farmers and ranchers who did not belong to the association. Settlers were also found lynched or shot to death with a note stating that they were cattle thieves. Their murderers were rarely brought to justice because a few powerful cattle men controlled the law. Gunmen were hired from Texas, and a group of men supported by the Stock Growers' Association, and calling themselves the Regulators, organized a reign of terror in the spring of 1892 to drive the settlers from the county. The settlers fought back, resulting in Wyoming Governor Barber asking President Benjamin Harrison to send in federal troops to rescue the Regulators. The president sent the troops, and the Regulators

Sod House on the Great Plains. Credit: Nebraska State Historical Society.

were rescued, with none of them going to trial for their crimes. This was the final effort to keep the range open.

Sometimes cattlemen could not get along with each other any better than they could with sheepmen or farmers. The most significant violent clash broke out in Lincoln County, New Mexico, in February 1878. Beginning as a dispute between two rivals, James J. Dolan and John H. Tunstall, over who could obtain a monopoly on big beef contracts with the government, the Lincoln County War became a very bitter and nasty affair. Both sides hired gunmen in an effort to blast the other one out of existence. One of Tunstall's hired ranch hands became the infamous outlaw Billy the Kid. Although most people believe his real name was William Bonney, the "Kid" had been born in 1859 as Henry McCarty. He also used the aliases of Henry, William, or Kid Antrim. After his mother died in 1874, Henry began a life on the edge of the law. He went over the edge when, at the age of 17, he killed a man in a saloon fight. During the Lincoln County War, Billy the Kid killed the county sheriff and his deputy. That resulted in him being constantly hunted by a later sheriff, Pat Garrett, who pursued him unceasingly. After escaping from Garrett's clutches in December 1880, Billy the Kid's luck finally ran out when a friend double-crossed him. On July 14, 1881, at Fort Sumner, New Mexico, Billy went to a friend's house to eat. Near midnight, Garrett, who had entered the house only minutes before Billy, shot him dead in a darkened room.

FARMING THE GREAT PLAINS

Between 1870 and 1900, the Great Plains was settled by farmers. Many areas were not settled before this because of the difficulties farmers soon discovered in their earlier attempts. The semiarid area could not be farmed successfully using the same methods and machinery that farmers used in the eastern half of the nation, where rain was much more constant. Farming on the plains required cheap fencing, improved farm machinery, scientific agriculture, and cheap land.

Fencing

Fields needed fences to keep out roaming steers, particularly from the cattle ranges. In the East, most farms used wood for their fencing material, but on the plains trees were fairly scarce. Lumber could be brought in, but the cost was prohibitive for most of the farmers. Then Joseph Glidden, a farmer in Illinois, patented and began producing an inexpensive wire fencing material in 1874. The material, known as "barbed wire," was in great demand by 1875, and it was a major factor in the decline of the open range and the big cattle drives.

Farm Machinery

Because of dry weather conditions—less than the twenty inches of rainfall required by most crops—farmers on the plains had to till more acres in order to produce the same amount as farmers in the more humid East. Without the development of labor-saving machinery in the 1870s and the 1880s, farming of the plains would have been prohibitive for most because of labor costs alone. Labor-saving farm machines were improved during the Civil War because of the need to replace the farm laborers who went to war. After the war, increased demand for grain in the United States and Europe encouraged inventors to continue their efforts to improve the efficiency of the farm machines to an even greater degree. So the demand after the Civil War for land, that brought the attention of so many to the harsh Great Plains, coincided with the technological advancement of the machinery to make farming the area feasible. The chilled steel plow allowed the farmers to cut into the heavy grasses of the plains. The twine binder cut and tied the grain in bundles, which saved an enormous amount of time. Grain drills allowed the farmers to seed their fields more quickly. Threshers, machines that separated the grain from the straw, were improved upon, especially in the 1880s, when a blower was added to force out the straw. Combines, which cut and threshed in the same operation, were used in the fields of California in the 1880s. These and other inventions cut the time to produce an acre of wheat from approximately 60 hours in 1860 to approximately three hours in 1890. The mechanization of farming led groups of speculators to attempt farming wheat on a grand scale in the areas of Minnesota and North Dakota. These large farms, known as "Bonanza farms," covered up to 15,000 acres and were factory-like organizations.

Scientific Agriculture

The use of science to improve agricultural output was not new to farmers in the 1860s. Virginia planters in the latter half of the eighteenth century, like George Washington and Thomas Jefferson, had adopted new methods and implements from England and had added a few of their own. However, the average farmer had not used scientific agriculture as long as there was an abundance of cheap land to move onto when the old land was no longer of use. Farmers have depended on the government for assistance in the United States.

In 1839, Congress appropriated one thousand dollars for agricultural research. In 1862, the Department of Agriculture was created and its commissioner raised to a cabinet secretary level in 1889. With the Morrill Land Grant Act of 1862, the federal government gave 30,000 acres of public land for each senator and representative in Congress to each state that established public agricultural and industrial colleges. Most states, in turn, sold much of the land to homesteaders, usually for $1.25 per acre. And the Hatch Act, in 1887, provided for the creation of agricultural experiment stations in every state.

Farmers on the Great Plains had to open up to new ideas. Because of the small amount of rainfall on the plains, farmers used irrigation where they could. Irrigation usually consisted of a system of windmills to reach subsurface water supplies. But few could use this method because of a lack of waterways on the plains and because it was too expensive for many small family farmers. Dry farming was another method employed. It consisted of plowing deeply to bring subsurface water to the roots of the plants and creating a dust mulch on the growing plants.

Federal Land Policy

An inexpensive system to provide land for farmers was essential to settling the plains. The United States government wanted the western half of the continent settled and contributed millions of acres of land to do so.

The Homestead Act of 1862 was the mainstay of federal land policy, and certainly the most famous of the land bills. Any adult citizen or alien who paid a ten dollar filing fee could claim 160 acres of public land. After he or she had "resided upon or cultivated the same for a term of five years immediately succeeding the time of filing," the final title was given to the resident. An option to buy the land, usually for $1.25 per acre, was extended to homesteaders after they had lived on the land for at least six months (lengthened to fourteen months in 1891). It is often stated that the Homestead Act was the great democratic land bill which was responsible for the successful settling of the West by ordinary American families. But, while the law intended to do just that, it was not very successful at achieving its goal. One of the reasons for this was the simple fact that relatively few American families could afford to move west and buy all the equipment necessary to farm the prairies. A farmer on the Great Plains needed much more land to farm or ranch successfully than he did in the East because of the dry, arid conditions. The 160 acres allowed under the law was simply not enough land in most areas of the West for farmers and ranchers to make a good living. About two-thirds of the individual homesteaders before 1890 failed and went back east. The law also did very little to prohibit land speculation. Speculators, including wealthy individuals and corporations, frequently hired people to file claims on land for them, and, at a later time, they would sell it for a profit. And, of course, there was the usual bribery of some land officials. It is estimated that in excess of one hundred million acres was obtained by speculators.

Recognizing that 160 acres was too little land to farm or ranch in most cases, Congress passed the Timber Culture Act in 1873. This new law provided an additional 160 acres to homesteaders if they planted at least one-fourth of the land in trees. But since laws are incapable of increasing annual rainfall amounts, the Timber Culture Act did very little to assist homesteading families. It is estimated that about ninety percent of those who filed for land never bothered to plant trees anyway. In a move to placate the cattle ranchers' lobbying efforts, Congress passed the Desert Land Act in 1877. Individuals could apply for tentative title to 640 acres in the Great Plains or Southwest by paying 20 cents an acre. If they irrigated a portion of the land within three years and paid another dollar an acre, the land became theirs permanently. Farmers would not attempt the arduous task of irrigating 640 acres, and the act did not state that the irrigation had to yield crops. The act was clearly intended to benefit ranchers, which it did quite well. Large cattle grazing companies and a few wealthy individual ranchers gobbled up the bulk of new public lands under the Desert Land Act. And about 95 percent of the proofs of irrigation were fraudulent. In 1878, the Timber and Stone Act applied to "lands unfit for cultivation" and "valuable chiefly for timber" or stone in California, Nevada, Oregon, and Washington. It allowed any citizen or new alien to buy such land up to 160 acres for $2.50 an acre. Fraud was rampant with this act also. Logging companies paid people to file a claim and then sign over the deeds to their land back to the company. The predictable result was that timber barons gobbled up vast forest areas in the West.

Under the Morrill Land Grant Act of 1862, states were granted 30,000 acres of western land for each of its senators and representatives in Congress. The states in return had to develop agricultural education programs. The states could choose land from the public domain anywhere in the West. The land was then resold to benefit the state.

In regard to Indian lands, when their holdings were reduced by the concentration policies, any surplus was either sold by the tribes or disposed of by the federal government. After the Dawes Severalty Act was put into place, surplus land was often illegally gained by white speculators. Finally, in the last big bastion of Indian Territory, present-day Oklahoma, 160 acres of free land was opened up to white homesteaders with a run for claims on April 22, 1889—an event known in history as the Oklahoma Land Run. The result of federal western land policy in the postwar era was that only about 80 million acres out of the 430 million new acres available went to homesteads. And not all of those people were legitimate homesteaders.

Another aspect of federal land policy concerned the railroad industry. In order to encourage private railroad companies to build rail lines, which would bring settlement to empty areas, government on the federal, state, and local level gave these companies millions of acres of land. Between 1850 and 1871, the federal government gave 130 million acres of land to the railroads. States gave an additional 50 million acres over the same time period. Land was given in checkerboard strips from five to forty miles on each side of future railroad tracks, for which a 100-yard right of way was reserved. The railroads in turn sold the land to settlers. The railroads advertised heavily for buyers in the United States and Europe. Agents were even sent to Europe to convince immigrants to come to the open areas of the Great Plains. Cheap land, free transportation to the new ranch or farm, low interest loans, and low-cost freight rates were all used to sell railroad land. The railroads demanded in return that the farmers plant a single crop that was guaranteed to bring in quick cash, such as wheat, corn, cotton, or tobacco. These crops brought in decent incomes when the crops were doing well on the market, but crop prices were subject to fluctuation and dependence on a single crop was very risky.

Besides free land, federal loans and state and local cash grants were also made available to many railroad companies. Most of the roughly $65 million in federal loans went to the Union Pacific and Central Pacific Railroad companies, which were building the transcontinental line across the middle of the country. Town leaders in the West knew that often the location of a railroad through or near their town might mean the difference between survival and ghost town status. Therefore, they were anxious to persuade railroad companies to lay track and build stations in their area. Railroad companies quickly learned how to exploit this railroad fever. Threats to by-pass towns often resulted in cash grants, tax exemptions, and other financial incentives for the companies to run through them. Towns and counties willingly competed with each other to attract the railroads. As a result, local governments in the West doled out about $300 million in cash grants, and states contributed another approximately $228 million in grants to railroads.

In 1861, the year the Civil War began, about 30,000 miles of railroad track existed in the United States, most of it between the Atlantic Ocean and the Mississippi River. But the railroad industry, the first nationwide industry (excluding banks) in American society, experienced a growth frenzy following the Civil War. By the turn of the century in 1900, the United States possessed about 193,000 miles of railroad track. This growth allowed western farmers and ranchers to get their commodities to a national market and to receive consumer goods from eastern cities and elsewhere. Not only did this go a long way toward settling the West, but it also provided a much improved transportation system for American industry. And while most people do not think of it, the rapid growth of the railroad industry in the post-war period also produced a construction materials boom in steel, iron and coal (to make steel), and lumber.

Problems of the Farmer

The role of the American farmer underwent drastic changes after the Civil War. Most farmers were no longer self-sufficient. Instead of growing all of their own food, they concentrated on producing a profitable cash crop and bought whatever else was needed at the local store. The manufactured goods needed by the farmers could be purchased in town or, beginning in 1872, ordered from the catalog of Aaron Montgomery Ward's new mail order business. Farmers became more dependent on bankers, railroads, and manufacturers; eventually, farmers came to believe that these groups were their enemies. Money was borrowed for the land and the machinery necessary to farm it. Railroads were the link between farmer and market, and the cost of transporting their crops could mean the difference between success and failure. The farmer in the Gilded Age (post-Civil War era) could not compete without the machinery of the manufacturer. The farmers of this time were also competing in a world market, not simply with other American farmers. If the farmer was not a good businessman, he quickly faced ruin in a new agricultural industry that had stripped away much of the individualism and freedom of farm life.

Problems of the farmer were many, including heavy taxes, attacks by insects, such as mile-wide swarms of grasshoppers, periods of drought followed by flooding, poor soil, and high prices for much of what they bought, from fertilizer to machinery. Low prices and a deflated currency were two major worries for the farmers. Debt remained static, but prices on crops changed, usually downward. Many factors drove prices of crops up or down, but it was increased output due to the increased efficiency of the industry that lowered the prices most consistently and was the most difficult for farmers to come to terms with. In fact, farmers never came to terms with overproduction until the government stepped in during the 1930s and paid farmers to produce less in order to raise crop prices. A deflated currency meant there was not enough money in circulation, and this forced prices for farm goods down. Many farmers entered into a vicious cycle of increasing production and debt, which led to lower prices, deeper debt, and bankruptcy. One result of this cycle was increased farm tenancy. In 1880, twenty-five percent of the land put to the plow in the United States was worked by tenants rather than owners. Another result was that many farmers united to solve their problems.

Farmers Unite

Oliver H. Kelley, a clerk in the Bureau of Agriculture, was sent to investigate the state of agriculture in the South in 1866. Kelley found that most farmers were poor, isolated, and uneducated. In 1867, Kelley and a group of government clerks founded the Patrons of Husbandry, which became known as the Grange. In the beginning, the Grange was an organization to promote social, educational, and fraternal activities. Farming was a lonely occupation for many, especially for the wives. The Grange sponsored picnics, nights of music and dance, and lectures on meeting the problems of farmers. The Grange also appealed to many with its rituals. There were passwords, secrecy, and a hierarchy of levels for men and women; men could move from Laborer to the ultimate Husbandman, and women from Maid to Matron. By 1875, the Grange had approximately 800,000 members.

The Grange eventually moved from merely social activities to politics and economics. After all, railroads and manufacturers organized for economic and political benefits for their industries; why not farmers? Farmers entered politics and elected candidates to office who were sympathetic to the problems of the farmers. They also worked for the passing of so-called Granger laws, which provided for state government intervention into unfair railroad and warehouse charges and abuses on individual small farmers. (See Chapter Four for a more detailed explanation of railroad abuses and the Interstate Commerce Act.) The federal government was finally pressured into passing the Interstate Commerce Act in 1887 in an attempt to bring some sort of regulation to the railroads to alleviate some of the abuses against farmers. It was not really used for the benefit of the farmer for some time.

Co-operative stores and ventures were established to eliminate the huge profits of the middle men. In these stores, profits were divided among the shareholders according to the volume of their purchases. The Grangers began co-operative warehouses, elevators, insurance companies, and even factories manufacturing farm machinery. Most of the co-operative enterprises failed for reasons of mismanagement, the independence of the farmers, or opposition by business or banking concerns. Membership in the Grange diminished when prosperity began returning to the farming industry in the late 1870s. The Grange still existed in farm areas but concerned itself with social issues once again.

Although the Grange diminished in numbers, many farmers continued to believe that the only possibility for resolving their common problems was to unite in organizations. The Farmers' Alliances, North and South, white and black, carried on what the Grange had begun. By 1890, there were one million members in various Alliance groups, many singing "Toilers Unite." The Alliances were not very effective, however. The farmers needed political power to insure that the government would implement solutions to problems crushing a major portion of the American population. The farmers began to form their own political party. The People's Party, better known as the Populists, came together as an ultimate protest movement in the early 1890s. It was a message to the Republican and Democratic Parties that they no longer met the needs of the farmers. In the elections of 1892, the Populists put together an impressive platform and ran a good race. (For more details, see Chapter Four.) Americans stuck with the traditional two party system, but most of the Populist platform was later implemented.

MYTHS OF THE WEST

Americans have always been fascinated with their western frontier. Even many Europeans became, in the late nineteenth and twentieth centuries, very interested in the old West. Many of the dime novels of the nineteenth century, so-called because for years they cost a dime, told stories of high adventure in the American West. These novelists and others often painted a distorted picture of the frontier, from exaggerating the number and role of outlaws and Indian raids to portraying the West as an idealistic, romantic paradise.

Two general myths emerged in time about the American western frontier. Chronologically, the first myth to surface was the myth of the innocent, virtuous hero. Daniel Boone, the eighteenth-century pioneer hero, epitomized this particular myth. Like Boone, the heroes of the West were portrayed as simple, honest folks who went west in order to escape the corruption of society in the East, especially the congestion, crime, and political corruption of the big cities. A second myth which emerged was the myth of the morality play. In this one, the western heroes were the good guys in the white hats, who brought social order out of chaos by rounding up the bad guys, fighting off Indians, and rescuing pretty women. A twentieth century fictional character, the Lone Ranger, seems to represent this myth the best. Like the morality play, the West was represented to be a large stage, in which the conflict between good and evil was played out. Good, of course, ultimately triumphed over evil, much as romance novelists always let the good guy win the girl and ride off into the sunset and live happily ever after. The dime novels of the 1860s and 1870s especially helped create this second myth. Edward Judson's (pen name Ned Buntline) *Buffalo Bill: King of the Border Men*, published in 1869, was a typical example of this viewpoint.

The myth of the innocent, virtuous hero and the myth of the morality play were inherently contradictory. The contradiction lay in the fact that in the first myth, the heroes left the corruption of civilization to find contentment in the wonderful world of nature; in the second myth, the heroes went west in order to bring the blessings of civilization to the frontier. Despite the inherent contradiction between the two myths, it appears that many, if not most, Americans clung to both at the same time. The "grass is always greener" syndrome played a major role in people's thinking about the West. And of course, during stressful times, most people have a tendency to remember with fondness only the good things in the past. This also assisted in producing a national, or collective, memory about the alleged "good old days" in the old West.

Theodore Roosevelt spent as much time as he could on his Dakota Badlands ranch in the 1880s. From his love affair with the great outdoors, he later wrote a four-volume book entitled *The Winning of the West* (1889–1896), which made its contribution to these myths as well. Perhaps the most significant writer who inadvertently portrayed life in the West inaccurately was Owen Wister. Wister impacted at least three different generations of Americans. In 1902, he published his novel, *The Virginian*. In 1929, Hollywood produced a Gary Cooper movie with the same title as the novel. Then "The Virginian" was a television series in the 1960s. In all three of these media, the transplanted Virginian heroes did very little actual work on their ranch. They were too busy fighting Indians, tracking down rustlers and other bad guys, and rescuing damsels in distress to do the mundane work of repairing fences, branding calves, and cleaning manure out of the barn. In other words, the myths of the West upheld the western cowboy hero as one who was disinterested in wealth, and who was primarily involved in upholding "truth, justice, and the American way."

Perhaps the myths make for more interesting reading or viewing, but the picture they have given many Americans and Europeans was at great variance from the reality. The cowboys, farmers, and miners of the West worked very long hours at hard, dirty, and mostly boring tasks for little pay. The typical westerner probably worked longer hours and received less income than most Americans in the East. And the dangers they faced were more numerous as well. Indian attacks were part of that reality, although not as frequent as legend dictates; they varied greatly in time and place according to specific and oftentimes local circumstances. For much of the time, prairie fires were probably a greater threat to the homesteader on the Great Plains. Carelessness or lightning could touch off such a fire, and the winds of the plains would send a wide path of terrible destruction sweeping across the prairie. A family was often lucky if they could escape with their lives; many died in such devastating prairie fires. If one word could accurately describe the human climate of the West, that word would probably be "greed." Serious problems, like limited water resources and open range versus farming interests, were too often "resolved" with personal violence. The use and allocation of natural resources, whether water, timber, stone, or precious metals, was a tragic story of greed, corruption, and violence. Of course, farming and ranching for the little guy were extremely risky ventures amid the arid climate and competition for the most productive land. While ordinary westerners deserve much credit for their courage and tenacity in the face of incredible odds, it is not quite true that everyone succeeded only by pulling themselves up by their own bootstraps. The fact is that without technological developments, including railroads, which were engineered mostly in the East, the West would not likely have been so settled or exploited.

THE SIGNIFICANCE OF THE WEST

The population census taken in 1890 suggested that the frontier had come to an end. With that generally accepted fact, a few Americans began giving thought to what the significance, or legacy, of the West had really been. Although myths die hard among the mass of citizens, American historians of the West led the way in the serious process of analyzing the contributions of the West to American history and society. In 1893, a historian by the name of Frederick Jackson Turner delivered a lecture on this subject that has been discussed ever since. Sometimes called the Turner Thesis in his honor, it is also known as the Frontier Thesis. Turner's Frontier Thesis is that the western frontier gave Americans their unique national characteristics of adaptability, hard work, inventiveness, and self-reliance; those are the characteristics that Americans generally refer to as rugged individualism. Many historians today find the Frontier Thesis too simplistic. They point out that the national characteristics usually attributed to Americans were already possessed by the early colonists and later immigrants to America. Indeed, that argument has much going for it. In other words, only persons with such characteristics would have dared make the long, dangerous trip across the Atlantic, especially in the earlier days of our history. After all, people who left England and other parts of Europe knew that there was little chance they would ever see their loved ones and friends who stayed behind in the Old World again. And they really didn't know what to expect when they got here. Then when the hardships of reality in America set in, survival itself depended upon using those skills of self-reliance and individual determination which they already possessed. Therefore, rather than producing the national characteristics in Americans, the western frontier afforded Americans the opportunity to display them. It reinforced, rather than produced, those characteristics by forcing each generation to bequeath them to their children.

If the Turner Thesis does not accurately reveal the real significance of the West, then what was its legacy to the American people? The answers to that question will vary somewhat from one historian to another, but the answers generally are less romantic than Turner's. On a generally accepted short list, it is of some value to state the obvious. First, the West certainly gave us an abundance of natural resources. Coal, timber, stone, precious metals, and oil are, or at least were, in large supply; water was the only resource the West has been short of. Without these available resources, the United States would have had to rely on trade with other nations to obtain them. And without them, this country would not have developed into the giant industrial power that it finally became. Second, the West also gave us the great "breadbasket" of the world. Grain production in much of the Great Plains, especially wheat, has supplied vital food for us and so much of the world. Third, despite the image of rugged individualism, the western frontier in our history has also promoted a sense of community. Ordinary individual farmers and ranchers, who were not wealthy, found that they needed each other in order to survive. House raisings are a part of American heritage that brought pioneers together and created social bonds that were happily made, both in building family shelters and in facing common dangers in the wilderness. Cooperation, as well as competition, is an important, albeit neglected, element in the American success story. On the negative side, the western frontier contributed to a careless attitude toward the environment. From the earliest colonial times, Americans cleared forests at will and wore out farmland, with little regard to the impact on the ecosystem. After all, if the land was ruined where they were, there was always more land to the west. For better or for worse, the West has left its mark on America's modern culture.

ADDITIONAL READINGS

Susan Armitage and Elizabeth Jameson, eds., *The Women's West* (1987). A collection of essays on women in western settlement. Stresses the varieties of experience among women of differing backgrounds, ethnic groups, and races.

Allen G. Bogue, *From Prairie to Corn Belt: Farming on the Illinois and Iowa Prairies in the Nineteenth Century* (1963). A close economic interpretation of the midwestern agricultural frontier. Examines the growth of farming from the pioneering homesteads to intensive, large-scale businesses and discusses the advantages enjoyed by the early settlers and their descendants over latercomers.

Anne M. Butler, *Daughters of Joy, Sisters of Misery: Prostitutes in the American West, 1865–1890* (1985). A study of ordinary prostitutes rather than the notorious and financially successful madams that fill western lore. Pays special attention to the women's background, age, health, and family status.

William Cronon, George Miles, and Jay Gitlin, eds., *Under an Open Sky: Rethinking America's Western Past* (1992). A useful collection of essays that reinterpret older evidence and add new data. The essays stress the bitter conflicts over territory, the racial and gender barriers to democratic community, and the tragic elements of western history.

Patricia Nelson Limerick, *The Legacy of Conquest: The Unbroken Past of the American West* (1987). A controversial and popular "revisionist" history of the West. Focused on conflict, Limerick's study shows the frontier most of all as a site of racial antagonism.

Frederick C. Luebke, ed., *Ethnicity on the Great Plains* (1980). Essays on Germans, Czechs, Russians, and other Europeans resettling in agricultural districts. The essays show that the immigrants, rather than assimilating, often sought to recreate their homeland communities within the United States.

John G. Neihardt, *Black Elk Speaks; Being the Life Story of a Holy Man of the Oglala Sioux* (1961). A classic as-told-to autobiographical account published originally in 1932. Black Elk recalls the tragedy of his tribe's destruction following the events involving General Custer and the Battle of the Little Bighorn.

Thomas E. Sheridan, *Los Tucsonenses: The Mexican Community in Tucson, 1854–1941* (1986). A highly readable account of Mexican American communities in the Southwest. Sheridan shows how a midcentury accommodation of Anglos and Mexicanos faded with the absorption of the region into the national economy, and with the steady displacement of the Mexicano community from its agricultrual landholdings.

Kevin Starr, *Americans and the California Dream, 1850–1915* (1973). A Study of California as the mythmaking "Golden State." Describes Americans' images of California's potential riches and natural beauty, and the ways the myths themselves became powerful conditions of immigration and development.

Jack Weston, *The Real American Cowboy* (1985). A lively account of the cowboy. Emphasizes the cowboy's identity as a low-paid, badly treated western agricultural laborer and cowboys' efforts to better their conditions.

Richard White, *"It's Your Misfortune and None of My Own": A History of the American West* (1991). A wide-ranging history that emphasizes cultural contact and the environment. Shows that conflicting cultures with little understanding of each other clashed tragically, with great losses to the environment and the ideal of a democratic American community.

CHAPTER THREE

Industrializing a Nation

MAJOR EVENTS

1843–84   "Old Immigration"

1866   National Labor Union founded

1869   Knights of Labor founded

1870   Standard Oil Company formed

1871   Chicago Fire

1873   Financial panic brings severe depression
Carnegie Steel founded

1879   Thomas Edison invents incandescent bulb
Depression ends

1882   Peak of German immigration to U. S. (1.2 million)
Standard Oil Trust founded

1885–1914   "New Immigration"

1886   Campaigns for eight-hour day
Haymarket episode
AFL founded

1890   Sherman Anti-Trust Act

1893   Stock market panic precipitates severe depression

1900   Carnegie, *The Gospel of Wealth*

1901   U. S. Steel Corporation formed

INTRODUCTION

From 1865 to 1900 the United States put back together a nation torn apart by war, conquered the western half of the continent, and passed through what is known as the Industrial Revolution. The revolution wrought by the explosive growth of industry established the economic path this nation would travel. Machines took the place of the hand craftsman as manufacturers of goods changed not only how American workers worked but also where they would work. The economy was transformed from a rural, agrarian society dominated by farmers into an urban, industrial society dominated increasingly by manufacturers and their factory workers. In 1890 the value of manufactured goods exceeded the value of agricultural products for the first time in our history. And by 1900, the value of manufactured goods was worth two times the value of our agricultural products.

Women assembling dolls at Shenhat Toy Company, Philadelphia. Credit: Forest Service.

Significant features of the changes brought by industrialization between the years 1860 and 1900 included increased capital investment in manufacturing from $1 billion to $10 billion; the number of workers in manufacturing increased from 1.3 million to 5.3 million; and the Gross National Product (GNP) increased from just under $2 million annually to more than $13 million. None of these facts should imply that the nation had no industries or factories before the Industrial Revolution. A small amount of manufacturing dates back to colonial times. But in the post-Civil War era, Americans experienced such a rapid growth in manufacturing and the factory system, with its accompanying profound changes in society, that it could only be called an Industrial Revolution. The United States moved from fourth place among manufacturing nations to first place by the end of the nineteenth century. In the Centennial Exhibition outside of Philadelphia in 1876, for example, 100 years of American ingenuity and progress were celebrated. The hall dedicated to displaying machinery seemed to capture the essence of the nation and the attention of those attending the exhibition. Industrial development was the path to American prosperity. Big business and industry came to dominate American society because they provided that prosperity.

FACTORS CONTRIBUTING TO AMERICA'S INDUSTRIAL REVOLUTION

Introduction

It is often believed that the Civil War was the principal cause of our Industrial Revolution. This belief is generally held by those who believe that wars in general are good for the economy. Actually, there are usually both positive and negative aspects of wars' effects on the economy. As far as the American Civil War is concerned, the war decade (1860s) experienced the lowest level of industrial growth during the period from 1840 to 1880.

Technology and Inventions

An explosion of mechanical inventions, both before and during the Industrial Revolution, paved the way for the industrializing of America. Inventors and industry applying new technology inspired each other to search for more efficient methods of manufacturing. Inventions provided products for the factories and also advanced the ability of the factories to mass produce, which in turn, increased output and lowered the price of products. This is what economists call productivity—the ability to produce a product with less time and effort. And this factor is still essential if a nation is to enjoy a relatively high standard of living. Especially in an increasingly global economy, it has become absolutely vital for the national economy to be on the cutting edge of new technologies.

During the Industrial Revolution period, a series of inventions brought about the rapid expansion of the American economy. Office work was greatly enhanced by Christopher Sholes' invention of the typewriter in 1867. While almost a relic from the past today, the typewriter did for the office then what computers have done in more modern times. The adding machine also assisted retail clerks and many other office workers after its introduction in 1888. The printing industry was given a boost when Otto Mergenthaler invented the linotype in 1867. Important to the railroad industry was the invention of the railway air brake by George Westinghouse in 1868, and the refrigerator railroad car by William Davis in 1875. The latter breakthrough eventually permitted the transport of fresh fruit and vegetables, although

New Products:
1. Early Telephone. Credit: A.T. & T. Company Photo Center.
2. Photoelectric cell converts light into electric impulses. Credit: Bell Telephone Laboratories.
3. Singer's Sewing Machine.

Thomas A. Edison in his laboratory. Credit: Keystone View Company.

Gustavus Swift first used the refrigerated cars on a large scale to ship dressed beef out of his Chicago meatpacking plants. In 1886 an alternating current electric power plant and transformer was invented. Related to the development of electric power was the invention of the alternating current (A-C) electric motor by a Hungarian-American, Nikola Tesla, in 1888. Then the telephone was invented by Alexander Graham Bell in 1876. The rise of the telephone industry revolutionized the communications business as nothing else had ever done before. Businesses and ordinary consumers profited from the convenience of voice communications.

The contributions of Thomas Alva Edison makes Edison America's premier inventor. He patented 1,093 inventions, including the phonograph in 1877 and the incandescent lamp in 1879. In 1876 he opened a laboratory, sometimes called the "invention factory," in the quiet setting of Menlo Park, New Jersey. Edison filled the laboratory with competent scientists and superb technicians, and operated it as an independent research and development center. It was here that most of his inventions were developed and that he came to be called "the Wizard of Menlo Park." Edison scoffed at the claims that he and other inventors were geniuses when he stated that "genius was one percent inspiration and ninety-nine percent perspiration." After the 1880s, Edison contributed few new inventions to the world, partly because he became bogged down attempting to manage whole new companies; his skills were definitely in tinkering and experimenting, not in management. Nevertheless, he did help develop motion picture projection technologies near the turn of the century, which paved the way for the rise of Hollywood. Thomas Edison's contributions are even more amazing when one realizes that he suffered from the learning disorder of dyslexia and that he had lost much of his hearing in his childhood.

Abundance of Natural Resources

Natural resources are the raw materials provided by nature which are necessary to manufacture products and develop a strong industrial economy. The United States contains an abundance of natural resources. Large amounts of lumber, coal, iron ore, oil, water, gold, silver, copper, zinc, and other elements have been found here. As iron replaced wood and then steel replaced iron as building materials, the United States could supply its own needs. Although modern Americans have become more conscious about the limited nature of these and other resources, most people probably still take them too much for granted. Although political and economic institutions cannot be ignored, many historians emphasize factors such as the abundance of natural resources in assessing the major reasons for the Industrial Revolution.

Transportation

Success in industry depends upon a good system of transportation. Raw materials are brought to the factories and molded into products that are then taken to markets. The numerous railroad lines built after the Civil War were invaluable in enlarging the market areas for manufactured goods in the United States. Foreign markets became more accessible to American products with the use of faster and more dependable steam-driven, iron ships.

Capital

Both foreign and domestic capital funded the American Industrial Revolution. Europeans, from England and Germany in particular, had already experienced their industrial revolutions and were looking for a good place to further invest their money. After our Civil War proved that the United States would remain united, European investors recognized that the best place to earn high rates of return on their investments was in the United States. Domestic capital came largely from companies and wealthy individuals who had earned excessive profits during the Civil War.

Labor

Workers for industry and the mineral fields to supply that industry came from the United States and from new immigrants from other nations. As machinery increased the efficiency of farming in the United States, fewer workers were needed in the agricultural sector. This brought both male and female workers from the farms to the factories. From 1870 to 1890, almost 4½ million Americans moved from the farm to the factory. In 1860 the percentage of workers engaged in farming or farm-related labor was about 80 percent; at the end of the century in 1900, only about 42 percent were working in the same fields. In other words, the number of Americans engaged in farming was virtually cut in half during the last forty years of the nineteenth century.

Between 1860 and 1900, 14 million immigrants arrived in the United States. They came to escape poverty, religious or racial persecution, military service, or lack of opportunities in their homelands. Shipping and railroad lines advertised that cheap land and economic opportunity were easy to obtain in a nation that had millions of acres of unsettled land for settlers and factories needing workers.

The "old immigrants" from Europe had been the first wave from the 1840s through the 1870s. Most came from Ireland, England, Germany, and the Scandinavian countries. Coming from northern and western Europe, they were fair skinned Anglo-Saxons, usually Protestant (except for the Irish Catholics and some German Catholics), usually literate, and familiar with constitutional government. Most of these immigrants fit into American society quite easily. Most came with money, except for the Irish, and they were able to move westward after reaching American shores.

Beginning in the 1880s, and intensifying during the next three decades, the second major wave of newcomers began arriving in large numbers from Southern and Eastern Europe. This group of Polish Jews, Italians, Slovaks, Greeks, Czechs, and others were known as the "new immigrants." This group had more difficulty assimilating because they were somewhat darker skinned, predominantly Roman Catholic, usually illiterate, unfamiliar with constitutional government, and usually arrived with little money. The new immigrants tended to group together in the large eastern cities, where they formed little foreign enclaves.

The internal migration to the cities, driven partly by increased agricultural productivity, and the large numbers of new immigrants, created an abundant labor supply to meet the demands of the rapidly expanding economy. In fact, a surplus of labor existed for much of this era, which had the effect of keeping wages depressed. In addition to the effect the labor surplus had on wages, most of the new immigrants came from such poor countries that they were usually better off in the United States. For this reason, they were willing to work for low wages. While bad for many of the industrial workers, relatively low wages did, in fact, keep manufacturing costs down and profits up, thus allowing more capital to be plowed back into the economy.

Government Policy

The industrializing of the United States was also greatly aided by a government that believed in a laissez faire (hands off) policy when it came to regulation of business. With no consumer or labor legislation and no effective regulatory commissions or laws, businessmen were able to concentrate on profits and expansion. Congress also helped industry through high tariff rates on foreign imports, which protected the fledgling industries from competition. Therefore, higher tariffs, or import taxes, were called protective tariffs. The protective tariff increased the cost of foreign products, thus making American products less expensive, although in many instances the American products were still quite expensive. The conservative monetary policy of "sound money" also aided business development by keeping the money supply relatively low compared to the population growth. With relatively fewer dollars in circulation that could purchase the nation's goods and services, prices tended to fall or at least remain stable. This created a deflationary economic climate in the country, which kept business costs down and enabled industries to expand.

The United States Supreme Court reinforced government support of business in 1886 with its ruling in the case of *Santa Clara County v. Southern Pacific Railway Company*. The Supreme Court ruled unanimously that corporations were legal "persons" under the Fourteenth Amendment and could not be deprived of profits or other property rights without due process of law. The Fourteenth Amendment had been adopted to protect the life, liberty, and property of the freedmen in the South from unfair treatment. It reads in part " . . . nor shall any state deprive any person of life, liberty, or property, without due process of law." By defining a corporation as a legal person the Supreme Court twisted the meaning of the Constitution and made it very difficult to regulate business. Indeed, after the *Santa Clara Case*, lower courts routinely issued injunctions on the basis of the Fourteenth Amendment that tied the hands of regulatory commissions.

ECONOMIC DEPRESSIONS

Although the United States experienced an Industrial Revolution during the late nineteenth century, the nation also suffered from two major economic depressions during that period. These depressions, in 1873–79 and 1893–97, had specific triggers that started them. (See Chapter Four for more details.) Ironically, some of the government policies which helped produce the Industrial Revolution were also largely responsible for the economic depressions. Conservative, or restrictive, monetary policies did help keep business costs down, but they eventually tightened credit and raised interest rates on borrowed money. Larger businesses, with their vast cash flow, could handle the higher interest rates, but many small businessmen were severely hurt by them. Furthermore, the low money supply devastated thousands of family farmers by shrinking farm prices and thus farm incomes. This, in turn, led to a serious drop in consumer demand for goods and services, which forced most businesses to cut back and drove others into bankruptcy.

INDUSTRY AND ITS TITANS

Railroads

Railroads led the way in the industrializing of America and were the first "big businesses." They carried raw materials to the factories to be molded into new products and then carried the products to new markets they had created. Railroad stops were transformed into towns and cities. They brought immigrants to this country to settle open areas, which provided more consumers for American products. Railroad building stimulated other industries to provide needed materials. The rails themselves were a product for the expanding steel industry. The railroads were the first modern companies to use effective management in a large industry. Early industries had been local, but railroads employed tens of thousands of men and covered thousands of miles of land. Other national industries would follow the big business organization of the railroads from its hierarchical management style to its use of an accounting system that kept detailed records of costs in order to set rates and predict profits. Finally, the railroads made some entrepreneurs enormously wealthy, and this new group of wealthy men were very instrumental in building a new industrial America.

With all of the benefits to be realized from railroad building it is not surprising that all levels of government gave land and loans to increase the railroad mileage throughout the nation. Following the success of the building of the first transcontinental railroad, Congress backed three other transcontinental railroad lines. The Northern Pacific was completed in 1883; the Atchison, Topeka and Santa Fe in 1883; and the Great Northern in 1893. Other railroad building projects brought the total mileage of railway track from 35,000 miles of track, mostly laid in the Northeast by 1865, to 193,000 miles of track throughout the nation by 1900.

Moving railroad train making a journey from Chama, New Mexico to Antonito, Colorado. Credit: New Mexico Department of Development.

Not only railway mileage increased after the Civil War, but efficiency was also increased with a series of technological advances. The use of steel instead of iron for the rails allowed the use of heavier locomotives and longer trains. The adoption of four standard time zones on November 18, 1883, decreased much of the confusion of traveling by rail. The use of George Westinghouse's air brake increased the safety of train travel. The introduction of George Pullman's sleeping, parlor, and dining cars led to more comfortable accommodations on the long or short train trip.

Great fortunes were made from the building of railroads and the other big businesses that generated the Industrial Revolution, and with that wealth came power and influence. There are differing views on the ethics and eventually the legality of the methods used by the railroad builders and other industrialists to increase the wealth of their companies. One view of the industrial titans was that they were captains of industry. While they used ruthless methods at times, including exploitation of workers or unethically undercutting competition, the nation benefitted from the industries they built. The industrialists provided jobs, higher wages for workers, and a higher standard of living for Americans. Another view is that these same entrepreneurs were robber barons who were only interested in making money, no matter what the cost to their workers, their nation, or their own industries. The truth was that most big business owners of the day were a mixture of both.

In railroads and other industries Jim Fisk, Jay Gould, and Daniel Drew made great fortunes with robber baron tactics. They manipulated stock market prices and ignored company policies in order to line their pockets. Cornelius (Commodore) Vanderbilt and his business methods represented an interesting mixture of both "captain of industry" and "robber baron." He was a man of vision, ruthless when necessary, and not above working just barely within the letter of the law. Vanderbilt began building his fortune with a lucrative steamboat business in the New York City area. He increased his fortune in the Civil War to more than $10 million, but he decided at that time that there was a great deal more money to be made in railroads than with ships. Therefore, he began investing in rival railroad companies, hoping to gain control of passenger and freight routes from New York to the Great Lakes. Gaining control of various companies through purchasing stock, he combined them into the New York Central and Hudson River Railroad System. The New York and Erie Railroad, controlled by Daniel Drew, James Fisk, and Jay Gould, was in competition with Vanderbilt's line. Vanderbilt, like most big businessmen at this time, wanted no competition in the area, because he wanted to control freight and passenger prices. He dropped his rates in an attempt to drive the Erie out of business. When this was not successful, he attempted to gain control of the Erie by purchasing a controlling interest in the company's stock. The owners of the Erie then simply offered more stock for sale, increasing the amount of watered stock (stocks sold beyond the true value of the business) to the point that even with his great fortune Vanderbilt would not acquire the railroad. The value of the railroad was ruined and the line went into bankruptcy in 1875. This destruction is an example of the robber baron mentality. The Erie was reorganized in 1894 by J. P. Morgan, who brought stability to the railroad. Vanderbilt continued to build his fortune and his raiload lines. By 1900 his New York Central system extended from New York to Boston, Cleveland, Detroit, Chicago, Baltimore, and Washington. Vanderbilt had passed away in 1877 as one of the richest men in America. His fortune was taken care of and expanded by his son William Henry. A statement attributed to William Vanderbilt summed up the attitude of many of the wealthy business owners, "The public be damned." Eventually, the public took measures to protect itself from attitudes such as that.

With the possibility of making fortunes from railroad building, the industry was overextended. Two-thirds of the railroad tracks were in the West and not profitable. The Panic of 1873 (see Chapter Four), and the depression that followed, began when the Northern Pacific defaulted on loans, and the bank that financed the venture, Jay Cooke and Company, had to close its doors. The depression ended in 1879, and the 1880s saw a resurgence in railroad investment and building. Consolidation of the lines into large corporations was the road to profitability in the railroad industry, as it came to so many other industries. John Pierpont (J.P.) Morgan and his partners in the firm of Drexel, Morgan and Company made a fortune bringing order to the web of competing and inefficient railroads. Morgan bought controlling interest in some companies and gained control of other railroad lines which were in financial jeopardy. The investment banks provided capital for the businesses and moved into a position to control many of the same businesses when they failed. Competition forced many companies out of business, and the depression beginning in 1893 forced more railroads into the hands of the investment houses or banks who had loaned money. Morgan, supported by other investment houses reorganized two-thirds of the railroad mileage into seven networks controlled by the bankers.

The success and failure of the railroad industry was repeated by other large scale businesses. Success brought many into a given industry, but overexpansion or depression spelled doom for the weak. The weak also faced the threat from the strong in their own industries who were wanting to dominate most of the manufacturing. Combinations which led to monopoly were the outgrowth of industrialization, which was good for some and bad for others.

Steel

Before the Civil War, steel was produced in small quantities because it was too expensive to manufacture on a large scale. Cast iron was used for railroad rails and other building projects because it was cheap and easy to manufacture. However, iron was a brittle metal and lacked malleability as a building material. The technology to produce steel efficiently and cheaply came from William Kelly, an American, and Henry Bessemer, an Englishman. It was discovered by both men that large quantities of iron ore could be converted into steel with a blast of cold air through the ore when it was in its molten liquid state. The air blew the impurities out of the hot iron ore and enabled steel manufacturers to make tons of steel in a few minutes, where formerly it had taken weeks to produce only pounds. The process became known as the Bessemer Process because it was Bessemer that developed the equipment and applied for patents first. In the United States, however, William Kelly received the first patent for the new process. The industrial world now had a cheap, all-purpose structural building material.

J.P. Morgan. Credit: Harris & Ewing, Washington, D.C

The manufacture of steel was on the rise and many businessmen saw the opportunities in the new industry. It was Andrew Carnegie, a self-educated immigrant from Scotland, who came to dominate this extremely important industry. The story of Carnegie's success was one of the few true rags to riches stories of an American business titan. Most of the wealthy and successful business owners were middle class and educated men. It was a misconception perpetuated repeatedly that the majority of the wealthy in America came from the poorest class of people. At the age of 12, Andrew emigrated from Scotland with his family. They settled in Allegheny City, Pennsylvania. The young Carnegie educated and trained himself as he moved up his career ladder from a bobbin boy in a Philadelphia textile mill to president of the Carnegie steel works. In between he worked as a Western Union messenger boy, a telegraph operator, secretary to the head of the Pennsylvania Railroad's western division, and eventually head of the western division himself. Carnegie invested his earnings in telegraph, sleeping-car, and bridge companies. His earnings from his investments were bringing in a yearly income of approximately $50,000 a year by 1865, when at the age of 29 he decided to retire. But Carnegie could not stay retired; there were simply too many opportunities to make more money. Vital to Carnegie's success, then and later, was his ability to cut costs, make quick and correct decisions, and his willingness to use the most up-to-date technology and innovations. He once stated that he would rather work with the "scientifically educated youth" than the "trained mechanic of the past because he has no prejudices, and goes on for the latest invention or newest method . . . ."

In 1872, Carnegie began his own steel company, Carnegie, McCandless and Company. As the country slid into a depression after the panic of 1873, Carnegie was securing the best men and equipment to make Bessemer steel rails. During the depression, he could buy cheap materials and make cheap investments. Many thought he was crazy to start a new business when so many were folding, but

Carnegie saw opportunity. He had met Henry Bessemer in London and saw the Bessemer converter in operation. His imagination was captured by the limitless possibilities to come from cheap steel production. He began to take over other steel mills, of which the Homestead Mills was the most famous. Homestead was built up as a model mill town, but the workers at the Homestead Mills had the same problems as other steel workers—low wages and the hostility of management toward union efforts to change circumstances for the workers. In 1892 they began a strike that has gone down in the pages of history. (See Chapter Four for coverage of that strike.)

Carnegie believed that the accumulation of wealth was important, but he also believed that the wealthy had an obligation to distribute much of that wealth to society. Carnegie's philanthropy included gifts of municipal libraries, Carnegie Hall in New York City for concerts, and his

Andrew Carnegie. Credit: Library of Congress

Endowment of International Peace. He donated more than $300 million to charitable projects. He explained his philosophies in magazine articles, printed under the title "The Gospel of Wealth." Carnegie defended monopoly in industry, which at the time was being challenged by the public, press, and government. He said that the concentration of business in the hands of a few had brought better and cheaper goods, a principle that was also promoted by one of his contemporaries in the oil refining business, John D. Rockefeller. In spite of the wealth of the corporation, Carnegie sold it all to J. Pierpont Morgan and associates for approximately $492 million in 1901. Carnegie Steel was merged with other companies into a new holding company, the United States Steel Corporation. This was the first American corporation capitalized at over $1 billion and the largest corporation in the world at the time.

Oil

Searching to increase the production of crude oil to refine into kerosene, Edwin Drake erected a wooden tower (derrick) and began drilling near Titusville in western Pennsylvania. Kerosene was burned in both lamps and stoves, and the de-

Lucas Well at Spindletop, Texas. Credit: Texas Mid-Continental Oil & Gas Association.

mand for it was constantly increasing. But crude oil, the source of the kerosene, was produced in very small quantities due to the fact that most oil was gathered by skimming it from ponds. In August 1859 Drake struck oil for his employer George Bissell, and opened up new and promising industries, from oil production to its refining into other products. The first well brought up approximately 8 to 10 barrels of crude oil a day. Drillers descended on Titusville and Oil City, Pennsylvania, and their wells brought oil gushing from the ground. The ground was covered with more than three thousand new barrels of oil a day. The new industry faced problems in its developmental stage, but the opportunity for wealth brought so many into production and refining that the price of a barrel of oil dropped from $10 to between 10 and 25 cents in a few months. The problems were storing the immense flow of oil, transporting it to refineries from areas that did not have railroads in the beginning, and restricting production to drive the prices back up. The problems were eventually solved, and over one thousand new companies were started to look for oil in Pennsylvania and surrounding areas.

John D. Rockefeller arose as the titan in the oil industry. At the age of 16 Rockefeller was a clerk in a wholesale firm, earning about $3.50 a week. At the age of 19, he was a partner in his own wholesale firm. When the oil boom began in Pennsylvania, Rockefeller, a bookkeeper at the time, traveled to the area to determine the advisability of investing in the boom. Deciding that the production sector of the business was messy and risky, Rockefeller decided that oil refining was his route to success. In 1863 Rockefeller invested in the company of Andrews, Clark, and Company which built a small refinery in Cleveland, Ohio. Cleveland and Pittsburgh, Pennsylvania were strongholds of refining because of their size and rail transportation availability. By 1865 the company owned two oil refineries. In 1870 the company and its various interests were reorganized as the Standard Oil Company of Ohio.

In the early days of refining, Rockefeller established practices that would allow him to build an extremely wealthy company. He examined the possibilities of controlling all aspects of the manufacturing process, from the barrels needed to transport the oil to the transportation on railroads or pipelines. Total control was not possible in the beginning, but it would come as his company grew. Waste from the refining process was sold or made into other products, such as gasoline and lubricating oils. Management was kept streamlined for efficiency also. Rockefeller's goal after forming Standard Oil was to bring order and more profit from oil refining. He would accomplish his goal by eliminating competition. From 1870 to 1878, Standard Oil grew from controlling about four percent of the oil refining business in the United States to controlling about 90 percent, which was a virtual monopoly. Acquiring control of the transportation upon which the oil traveled was Rockefeller's main tool in building his monopoly. Standard Oil grew so large that it could demand rebates and eventually drawbacks for the railroads. A rebate was a refund or a lower price for transporting your product. Rockefeller demanded cheaper freight rates to transport his oil. Railroads needed his business and agreed to the cheaper rates. With cheaper transportation costs, Rockefeller could cut his price and force competitors out of business. A drawback was the practice of receiving refunds from your competitors' shipments.

In order to protect his empire, which controlled businesses in states outside of Ohio, the Standard Oil Trust was formed in 1882. A corporation in one state could not hold stock in a corporation in another state, unless given permission by the

John D. Rockefeller (center) on his way to a Senate hearing in Washington. Credit: AP/Wide World Photos

state legislature. Rockefeller had used Standard Oil officers as trustees controlling the stock of individual companies out of state, but the trustee could act independently or perhaps have the bad grace to die. What would happen to the stock the individual trustee controlled? The problem was solved when nine trustees were appointed to give direction to the Standard companies through control of all stocks. Companies under control of the trustees received "trust certificates" in exchange for their company's stock.

The public and small businesses disliked the trusts that developed in big business. They were another device of monopoly and restricted free competition and trade. Pressure mounted for state and federal governments to regulate the corporations for the good of the public. In 1892 the Ohio state Supreme Court ordered Standard Oil to dissolve its trust status. The federal government had also stepped in by this time with the Sherman Antitrust Act in 1890 to control combinations that restrained trade. (see "The Gilded Age Presidents.") In 1899 Rockefeller and his associates regrouped under the title of Standard Oil Company of New Jersey, a holding company. Rockefeller retired as active head of Standard Oil in 1898, but he remained president of the New Jersey company until 1911—the year that the United States Supreme Court dissolved the Standard monopoly. Rockefeller's holdings reached more than $900 million at the time of his retirement, and he gave a great deal of it away in gifts to education and religious purposes.

BIG BUSINESS ATTEMPTS TO ELIMINATE COMPETITION

Industry flourished after the Civil War, which resulted in fierce competition in all areas of business, from railroads to sugar manufacturing. The large numbers of businesses kept prices low, and with profit as a driving force, this was not acceptable to the most competitive of the business titans. The drive for profit and order from the chaos in many businesses led a few in each industry to search for ways to eliminate competition through combining many companies into a few. The business pools, informal agreements between a few companies to set prices and quotas of production, were among the first efforts of cooperation to eliminate enough competition to increase profits of those in the pool. Railroads in particular used pools to drive out competitors. They were also used by the meat-packing companies of Armour, Swift, and Morris in Chicago to divide the areas that each would ship to each week. The pools were not particularly successful because not all involved in them abided by the arrangements. Then they were declared illegal by the Interstate Commerce Act of 1887.

Much more successful in limiting competition were the efforts of consolidating companies into large combinations. Using more efficient methods of production and vertical integration, companies cut costs and drove competitors under. Vertical integration was the practice of controlling all aspects of the manufacture of a product, including extracting the raw materials necessary, transporting the raw resources to the factory and the finished product from the factory, and selling the product to the consumer. This type of control was used very effectively by Andrew Carnegie and John D. Rockefeller to dominate their respective industries. Sometimes the big businesses bought out the competition; at other times they forced them out.

Horizontal integration was the practice of taking over the competition in the same industry. The trust arrangement was a tool of horizontal integration. The success of the Standard Oil Trust led to the development of trusts in many other industries. In the tobacco, sugar refining, meat-packing, steel manufacturing, and many others, a board of trustees controlled the majority of the business in one industry.

The Sherman Antitrust Act (1890), implemented to control big business and stop monopoly, was not a success. Presidents Harrison, Cleveland, and McKinley instituted a few suits against companies that appeared to violate the Sherman Act, but most of these were not even successful because of the rulings of the courts. An excellent example of the stand of the courts on regulation of business is the Supreme Court's ruling in the case of *E. C. Knight and Co. v. United States*. E.C. Knight was a sugar trust that controlled approximately eighty-five percent of the country's sugar refining. The Supreme Court declared that the company was involved in production and not commerce, and as such, the prohibition of trusts by the Sherman Antitrust Act did not apply. The United States government lost its case.

In deference to the Sherman Act, the trust was abandoned, and the use of the holding company established in its place. A holding company established technically independent companies controlled by either one board of directors or interlocking directorships, which then owned a controlling amount of stock in the company rather than complete ownership of the company. These giant combinations grew from twelve in 1893 to more than three hundred by 1904 and controlled two-fifths of the manufacturing of the nation. The fight against consolidation and monopoly continued in the Progressive Era with more success under the leadership of the Progressive presidents. Monopoly control was believed to violate the equal opportunity aspect of a democracy. However, the industrialists must be given their due. They built an industrial superpower, and the country grew and prospered. They must also accept their share of blame for the negative aspects of industrialization, which included the miserable lives of many of their workers.

LABOR ORGANIZES

Workers organizing into unions (originally known as associations or societies of workers) to improve their working conditions, was not a creation of the Industrial Revolution. However, the size, scope, and goals of the unions organized at this time took organized labor in a distinctly new direction. There had been a few craft associations of skilled artisans as early as the colonial period of American history. The first continuous organization consisting of workers only was formed by the shoemakers of Philadelphia in 1792. New York City printers founded a Typographical Society in 1794. In the 1790s and early 1800s the number of small local craft associations grew. The ranks of local organizations were enlarged by carpenters, painters, tailors, weavers, hatters, and many other skilled artisans. Factory workers organized in the 1820s, and they were the first to use the word "union" to dis-

Labor Strikes at Carnegie Steel Homestead Mill, 1892. Credit: Library of Congress.

tinguish their organizations from the journeymen's (skilled craftsmen working for daily wages) associations. The early craft associations and unions remained small and unorganized due to difficulties in organizing workers and economic downturns, which created unemployment. After the Civil War, however, the immense growth of industry brought millions of workers together in factories, and many of these factory workers were willing to organize and sacrifice in order to demand their fair share of the profits of their labor. The unions created during the Gilded Age worked for many of the same goals that unions created before had worked for—higher wages for the workers, an 8-hour work day, and safer work conditions. Three major national unions formed to garner for laborers some of the benefits the middle class and the industrial owners were enjoying from industrialization. Individual effort could not pressure large impersonal corporations to solve the problems faced by their employees. It would take the efforts of a large number of employees willing to resort to a strike in order make gains and win respect.

The National Labor Union

In 1866, William H. Sylvis and other union leaders called upon labor organizations to send representatives to Baltimore, Maryland to unify the various labor groups into an association to represent all workers. In particular the leaders who called the meeting wanted to organize to gain an eight-hour work day. The National Labor Union, a federation type organization, was the result. Sylvis, former head of the Iron Moulders' International Union, was the president of the new union and a driving force in its initial success. Skilled and unskilled workers were members of the unions under the NLU leadership. Sylvis also included working women in his new national union. Kate Mullaney, head of the Troy, New York union of collar laundresses, was a second vice-president in the NLU. Sylvis believed that black Americans should organize their own unions. As a result, black leaders organized a National Colored Labor Union in December 1869.

The National Labor Union worked toward a wide range of goals, including currency and banking reform, in order to free the economic system from the gold standard by inflating the currency supply with greenbacks; the end of convict labor; the formation of a federal department of labor; a restriction on immigration (immigrants worked for lower wages); and the formation of workers' cooperatives. Following the death of William Sylvis in 1869 and because of the increasing emphasis on political and social reforms, the approximately 300,000 member union declined quickly. In 1872 the NLU attempted to revive itself through a transformation into the National Labor Reform party. Its candidate for the presidency, Charles O'Connor, a member of New York City's Tammany Hall, pulled in only about 29,000 votes. The union was dead. Most of the NLU goals were not reached, but an 8-hour day for federal workers was passed by Congress in 1868.

The 1870s was a tumultuous decade for Americans, and the efforts to unionize were caught up in the storm. The panic of 1873 spiraled down into a nationwide depression with more than 20 percent of the workforce unemployed. The National Labor Union was one of 21 national unions that did not survive the economic downturn. Workers might not be in unions in great numbers, but they continued to show their discontent through demonstrations organized by the unemployed and strikes organized by exploited workers, often bringing about violence by both labor and management. On January 13, 1874, a squad of mounted police charged a crowd of unemployed workers marching in Tompkins Square in New York City. Hundreds of the demonstrators were injured and the police continued the violence throughout the East Side of New York. In 1877, railroad strikes led to the death of close to 100 people and approximately $5 million in damages when police and troops were called in to stop the strikes in Pennsylvania, Maryland, West Virginia, and Illinois. (See Chapter Four for more details.) The violence associated with workingmen gaining what they believed were fair wages and fair treatment turned public opinion against workers and their unions. Most of the strikes and the violence that followed were not directed by the unions but were mostly quickly planned incidents by individual groups of workers. Also, most were the result of a cut in wages or unbearable working conditions placed on them by business owners.

The violent activities of the Molly Maguires, a terrorist offshoot of the Irish Ancient Order of Hibernians, added to the public's poor opinion of labor organizations. This group was a secret society of Irish workers active in the anthracite mining fields of Pennsylvania from about 1854 to 1877. The original Molly Maguires had been a secret society in Ireland in the 1840s, whose members dressed in women's clothes and then attacked the British rent collectors. In America, a new group of Molly Maguires was formed to protect the Irish from abuse in the coal mining areas. When unionism failed to right the conditions for miners, and wages fell in 1871, a strike began that same year. Some of the Mollies turned to derailing mine cars, running strikebreakers out of the coal fields, burning equipment, and even to murdering mine superintendents and unpopular foremen.

The exact role played by the Mollies is uncertain, but it is clear that they were involved in terrorist activities. It was discovered later that mine managers were involved in some of the acts of violence to bring about the downfall of all union activity in the coal fields. Determined to destroy the Molly Maguires, the mine owners brought in the services of Allan Pinkerton's detective agency. James McParlan was chosen to infiltrate the organization, and he was so convincing in his role that he was made secretary of his district. He gathered evidence on crimes committed, and he also warned Pinkerton detectives so they could be on hand before crimes were committed. The leaders of the organization were arrested in 1875. Twenty-four members of the Molly Maguires were convicted and 10 hanged largely on the testimony of McParlan. Much of the evidence presented by McParlan was unsupported and some later believed it was manufactured. Nevertheless, the secret order was crushed and many of the miners without a union of their own drifted into the Knights of Labor.

The Knights of Labor

The Noble and Holy Order of the Knights of Labor was founded in 1869 in the city of Philadelphia by nine tailors. Uriah Stephens led the new organization and held the title of Master Workman. Keeping their organization a secret for some time, the new union set about recruiting members into one big union for all wage earners—male and female workers and skilled and unskilled workers, except "bankers, stockbrokers, professional gamblers, lawyers, and those who in any way derive their living from the manufacture or sale of intoxicating liquors." The Knights believed that secrecy was necessary to protect them from being fired by employers.

The Knights grew steadily in the 1870s, and by the 1880s they were the dominant labor organization with local and district assemblies across the nation in all areas of labor. In the midst of depression and violence occurring from strikes, the union promoted arbitration and boycotts as methods to deal with unfair labor practices of businesses. Their goals were modest and echoed by unions before and after their time. They included establishing bureaus of labor, setting up producers' and distributors' cooperatives, reserving public land for actual settlers, not railroads or speculators, establishing anti-child labor laws, implementing the eight-hour day, restricting immigration, and calling for equal pay for equal work for both sexes (a very radical idea for that time).

In 1879, Terence V. Powderly was elected to the position of Grand Master Workman. Powderly led the Knights during their years of greatest success. He was opposed to strikes, and yet it was the success of strikes that increased the membership roles to a peak in 1887 of close to 730,000 members. The success of a strike against Jay Gould's Wabash Railroad in 1885 contributed greatly to the increased membership of the union. The Knights of Labor turned their attention to politics, electing a few congressmen, mayors, and judges who believed in the goals of the organization. Destruction quickly followed success. In 1886 a series of unauthorized strikes failed, including one against Jay Gould, and many were disillusioned about the gains made by the union. The false connection of a few Knights of Labor with the Haymarket bombing incident (see Chapter Four) turned the public against the organization and caused many of the Knights to abandon their union. The union was dead, but the workers and the nation had glimpsed for a short time the potential power of unified action.

The American Federation of Labor

The American Federation of Labor (the AFL) replaced the Knights of Labor as the vanguard of the American labor movement. The AFL rejected the idea of one big union of all workers and put together a federation of individual craft unions. Local unions formed into national unions, and these national unions then joined the American Federation of Labor. Samuel Gompers and other union leaders believed that real strength in the union organizations lay in uniting workers according to craft, skill, or trade so that these members would have the same interests. Learning from the mistakes of the Knights of Labor and gaining their craft union membership, the AFL steered away from politics (the AFL would support candidates from time to time who had a favorable labor program, such as William Jennings Bryan in 1908 and Woodrow Wilson in 1912) and longterm reforms and worked for the concrete issues of higher wages, shorter workdays, job security, and an end to child labor (what Gompers called "unionism, pure and simple"). The leaders of the federation accepted capitalism and did not want to overturn the economic system. However, they demanded that the laborer receive his fair share, and were not hesitant to use the traditional methods of strikes and boycotts to achieve their goals.

Much of the success and longevity of the AFL can be attributed to Samuel Gompers, president of the AFL from 1886 to 1894 and again from 1896 to 1924. Gompers was an immigrant from England of mixed Hebrew and Flemish ancestry. He came to the United States in 1863, at the age of thirteen, and was soon a journeyman cigarmaker. He began his work in the labor movement as an active participant in the cigarmakers' union in New York City's Local No. 144. In 1881 he helped organize the Federation of Organized Trades and Labor Unions, which was reorganized in 1886 as the American Federation of Labor. Gompers held the AFL on a steady course of aggressive self interest. He frequently despaired from the lack of discipline in the American labor movement, but the AFL grew steadily with his dedicated leadership. There were more than 1 million members by 1903 and 2.5 million by 1917. The AFL made progress for the skilled workers, but approximately 90 percent of the workers in the United States were unskilled or semi-skilled and not represented by the federation. There was also hostility toward black workers and immigrants. Immigrants worked for low wages, which damaged a major goal of the unions, and the unskilled were seen as too undisciplined and easily replaced to be of great value to the AFL. These beliefs had merit, but to ignore such an overwhelming majority of the workers was not wise.

It is difficult to argue with success, and the AFL is still in existence today and has had much success. The members won the right to have closed shop industries (plants that hire only union workers) and the end of the yellow dog contracts (employer drawn contracts that forced workers to sign agreements not to join a union or participate in a strike as long as they work for the company). Workers in various AFL unions also gained better pay, shorter hours, and better working conditions.

KEEPING THE LABOR MOVEMENT WEAK

A number of basic factors in American society prevented the rise of a stronger labor movement. These factors contributed to the general weakness of the labor movement during the Gilded Age and beyond.

Rugged Individualism versus Collective Bargaining

Much of the psychological makeup of the American people included a strong belief in what is called rugged individualism. This is the idea that every individual stands on his own two feet, pulls himself up by his bootstraps, and needs no outside help to achieve his goals. Much of this had been part of the constitution of the men and women who first crossed the Atlantic and settled in colonial America. And, of course, the huge western frontier reinforced the prevailing philosophy that America was such a large land of opportunity, that people could make their own way by the sweat of their brow. Labor unions advocated a concept called collective bargaining. This means that representatives of the workers meet with management representatives and negotiate a legal contract about wages, hours, and other conditions that applies to everyone in the workplace. By definition, collective bargaining represented a different approach to labor-management relations that replaced the old system in which an individual worker simply had to accept the terms of employment as decreed by management. To most Americans, collective bargaining, then, seemed foreign and incompatible with the notion of rugged individualism. Understanding the philosophical clash of these two different concepts explains much of the opposition that organized labor had to face in the nineteenth and early twentieth centuries.

Fear of Labor Violence

The demands of organized labor were frequently moderate, but public opinion and the opinion of employers was so hostile to organized labor's views and goals that the workers achieved some of their goals only after a long period of strife. Between 1881 and 1900 there were more than 24,000 strikes. Middle-class Americans were especially fearful of labor-related violence, which did characterize much of labor-management relations during the Gilded Age. These Americans usually blamed the unions rather than company management for this violence. At least as much labor-related violence during this period was the result of management attempting to create middle class hostility to unions by perpetrating violence that could be blamed on union strikers. Such tactics usually worked very well. At the same time, there was certainly evidence that both sides were often guilty of fomenting violence.

Craft Union Arrogance

Some of the general weakness of organized labor during this period of the nation's history was the responsibility of the unions themselves. With the National Labor Union and the Knights of Labor as major exceptions, most labor organizations were craft unions, whose members belonged to the ranks of the skilled worker. The problem was that only about ten percent of the non-agricultural work-force were skilled workers, which meant that the unskilled majority could easily be replaced for union activity (including during strikes). Most labor unions added to this dilemma by intentionally ignoring about 90 percent of their potential members. That kind of arrogance was really counterproductive to a strong labor movement.

Management Opposition to Unions

Industry management vigorously opposed unions. The idea of workers organizing to control any aspect of business was threatening to owners and managers. Profit was usually the primary concern of any business, and merely the chance that profit might be negatively affected if the workers began to achieve their goals was enough to bring action against the formation of union groups. Union agitators were often blacklisted, which meant that managers of one company in a specific industry shared the names of union "agitators" with other companies in the same industry, preventing those workers from being rehired. The yellow dog contract was also used to intimidate workers. (See the earlier section entitled "The American Federation of Labor.") Paid agents (especially Pinkerton Detective Agents) were used to cause problems that could be blamed on the unions. Agents and paid strike-breakers were used to cross picket lines during strikes and commit violent acts against peaceful strikers. Immigrants were often used by companies to take the place of striking workers, which added to the hostility of unions toward immigrants. For new immigrants, low wages in the United States were usually an improvement on the wages they received in their homelands. Thus, they were willing to work for less and to be used as strikebreakers during major labor strikes.

Government Hostility to Unions

State and federal governments and the courts were also pro-business and anti-labor during the Gilded Age, although some progress was made by labor by the end of the 1890s. Governors, mayors, and even the president of the United States called out the state militia, the police, or troops to end strikes. (see Chapter Four.) Government might have had a laissez faire attitude toward business regulation during this time, but when it did intervene in disputes between business and labor, it was not sympathetic toward labor. The injunction, a court order to stop some action, was a new weapon given by the United States Supreme Court to employers in the case of *In Re Debs* (1895). The Supreme Court upheld the conviction of American Railway Union president Eugene Debs for ignoring an injunction to do nothing to prolong the Pullman strike in 1894. The Court based its decision on the Sherman Antitrust Act (1890), which forbid any "conspiracy in restraint of trade." The Court said that a strike could be considered an activity that restrained trade. And any interference with interstate commerce could bring in the federal courts or Congressional legislation. In 1902, the United Hatters of North America began a strike and nationwide boycott of the D.E. Lowe and Company of Danbury, Connecticut. When the boycott was challenged in the federal courts, the case made it all the way to the United States Supreme Court. In 1908, in the *Danbury Hatters Case*, the

Supreme Court expanded its anti-union decision *In Re Debs* by declaring that nearly all union boycotts also constituted a "conspiracy in restraint of trade," and thus were also violations of the Sherman Antitrust Act. These decisions made effective union action virtually impossible. Not until the 1930s would federal labor legislation bring effective relief to organized labor's efforts to have the fruits of the Industrial Revolution shared more equitably with workers.

Labor did make some gains with favorable state and federal laws in the late nineteenth century. In 1868, for example, public works laborers gained the eight-hour day. The federal government created the Bureau of Labor in 1884, and prohibited the importation of contract labor in 1885. The state of Massachusetts led the way with a ten-hour day for women and children in 1879. But each gain took monumental effort to achieve. At the end of the century big business controlled the affairs of the nation, but labor did not give up its fight for a fair share of the fruits of their labor. The struggle was continued in the Progressive Age and the decades thereafter.

ADDITIONAL READINGS

Alfred D. Chandler, Jr., *The Visible Hand: The Managerial Revolution in American Business* (1977). A highly acclaimed study of corporate management. Shows how the rapid growth in the scale of business, as well as the influence of business in public life, brought about a new type of executive armed with skills for national decison making and enjoying close links with others of his kind.

Herbert G. Gutman, *Work Culture and Society in Industrializing America: Essays in American Working-Class and Social History* (1977). Influential essays on the formation of working-class communities in the nineteenth century. Focuses on the role of immigrants in transforming the values and belief systems of working-class Americans undergoing the throes of industrialization.

Alice Kessler-Harris, *Out to Work: A History of Wage-Earning Women in the United States* (1982). A comprehensive survey of women's increasing participation in the labor force. Documents women's role in trade unions but also its impact on family patterns and on ideas about women's role in American society in general.

David Montgomery, *Workers Control in America: Studies in the History of Work, Technology and Labor Struggles* (1979). A detailed analysis of industrial change from the mid-nineteenth century to the early twentieth century, and a study of workers' responses to increased pace and loss of control.

David F. Noble, *America by Design: Science Technology and the Rise of Corporate Capitalism* (1977). A view of scientific advancement and its connections with the expanding economy. Shows how scientific breakthroughs were often created for, and especially adapted to, corporate purposes.

Dave Roediger and Franklin Rosemont, eds., *Haymarket Scrapbook* (1986). A large, beautifully illustrated book about the events and consequences of the Haymarket tragedy.

Alan Trachtenberg, *The Incorporation of America: Culture and Society in the Gilded Age* (1982). One of the best and most readable overviews of the post-Civil War era. Carefully describes how the corporation rose to become the defining institution of national life, and how culture was reoriented to reflect the tastes of the new middle classes employed by the corporation.

NEW YORK

1885-1889

1893-1897

Grover Cleveland

CHAPTER FOUR

The Gilded Age Presidents

MAJOR EVENTS

1867   Patrons of Husbandry (Grange) founded

1872   Liberal Republicans break with Grant and Radicals, nominate Horace
Greeley for president
Credit Mobilier scandal
Grant reelected president

1873   Financial panic and beginning of economic depression

1874   Democrats gain control of House for first time since 1856

1875   Species Resumption Act

1877   Rutherford B. Hayes elected president

1881   President James Garfield assassinated; Chester Arthur becomes president

1883   Pendleton Civil Service Reform Act

1884   Grover Cleveland elected president

1887   Interstate Commerce Act

1888   National Colored Farmers' Alliance and Cooperative Union formed
Benjamin Harrison elected president

1890   Populist (People's) party formed
Sherman Anti-Trust Act
Sherman Silver Purchase Act
McKinley Tariff
National American Woman Suffrage Association formed

1892   Grover Cleveland elected to second term as president
Homestead, Pennyslvania, strike

1893   World's Columbian Exhibition, Chicago
Financial panic and business recession begin

1894   "Coxey's Army" marches on Washington, D.C.
Pullman strike

1896   William McKinley defeats William Jennings Bryan for president

AN OVERVIEW OF POLITICS

An Uninspiring Record

The federal government during the Gilded Age was uninspiring partly because most Americans voiced support for laissez-faire, a philosophy advocating non-interference by government in the life of the nation. Thus, even during the two economic depressions of the period—in the 1870s and in the 1890s—the federal government basically did nothing except wait out the economic cycles.

Another reason for government's uninspiring record was the fact that because both major political parties were dominated by conservative factions which were content with the status quo, neither party challenged the country or the other party to expand its horizons or sharpen its vision of the future. Today Americans often complain that there's not a dime's worth of difference between the Democrats and the Republicans. Actually, at least since the 1930s, that has most definitely not been true. But in the Gilded Age, there truly was very little difference between them as far as most of the issues were concerned. The only issue, in fact, which tended to divide the two parties was the tariff issue. Democrats tended to favor a low, or revenue, tariff, while Republicans generally favored a high, protective tariff.

Congress was able to dominate the federal scene for two primary reasons. First, there was at that time a wide acceptance of the theory that the president should focus his attention on enforcing federal laws. And second, just in case a Gilded Age president had grand designs of real leadership, there was the painful memory of President Andrew Johnson's impeachment. Although the Senate had not convicted Johnson and removed him from office, the entire Congressional episode had a quieting effect on American presidents until the twentieth century.

The Nature of Political Campaigns

From the perspective of political campaigns, however, Gilded Age politics was nothing short of fascinating. It was here in the campaign arena that the major parties made up for their lack of significant differences on major issues. Republicans and Democrats ran their national campaigns with an eye to the recent past. Republicans, for example, habitually campaigned by "waving the bloody shirt," which means they constantly reminded voters that they should vote Republican because it had been those nasty Democrats who had been responsible for the recent American Civil War. For their part, Democrats tried to play to the consciences of Northern voters by reminding them of the alleged harshness of Reconstruction. Democrats, and a growing number of other Americans, developed the perception that Reconstruction had been a period in which carpetbaggers, scalawags, and the new freedmen had raped and plundered the South politically, economically, and socially. While attracting a number of votes outside the South, this tactic certainly solidified the region in the Democratic Party's camp. Whereas the South had been a strong Democratic base before the Civil War and Reconstruction eras, it became known as the "Solid South" for Democrats after those periods.

Political Corruption

Most American historians suggest that the Gilded Age was probably the worst era for political corruption in our history. It was a period of the big city and state political machines run by the most notorious and arrogant criminal politicians. The most famous corrupt city political organization was the Democratic machine in New York City, nicknamed Tammany Hall. Tammany Hall was led by William Marcy Tweed, whose infamous Tweed Ring robbed the city of about $200 million by padding bills the city owed to private contractors. It stole more money in one year than all the allegedly corrupt Republican Reconstruction governments "stole" during the entire Reconstruction period. At the state level of government, Marcus Hanna was the Republican Party boss in Ohio. Hanna ran a tight ship in accordance with the wishes of Standard Oil and other robber baron types of the period. During part of the Gilded Age many observers of the political scene in Ohio were convinced that Standard Oil actually controlled the state legislature.

Boss Tweed. Credit: The Bettmann Archive.

The Balance and Composition of the Political Parties

The two major political parties were quite evenly balanced in their ability to garner votes during the Gilded Age despite the fact that Republicans won 6 out of the 8 presidential elections. However, the close elections, in terms of the popular vote totals, meant a far closer balance between the Democrats and Republicans than the number of Republican presidential victories would ordinarily indicate. Furthermore, each party had clear control of the White House and both houses of Congress at the same time for only two years—the Republicans under President Benjamin Harrison in 1889-90 and the Democrats under President Grover Cleveland in 1893-94. Therefore, all these facts suggest that both major parties were evenly divided in their appeal to American voters. Ohio and New York were definitely the most politically influential states during the Gilded Age, both with large populations. In fact, not counting Johnson, only two presidents during the entire era did not claim either of those states as their home—Ulysses Grant, from Illinois, and Benjamin Harrison, from Indiana.

Republicans appealed to the majority of northern and northeastern business-men largely because Republicans championed themselves as supporters of economic growth and prosperity via their support for high tariffs, government assistance to the railroads, western expansion, and a gold standard. Northern and western farmers voted overwhelmingly for Republican candidates largely for the same reasons. Union Civil War veterans voted for Republican candidates at least partially because of their memory of Abraham Lincoln and their identification of Democrats with causing the Civil War. Their veterans' organization, the Grand Army of the Republic, was a very powerful lobby in Washington, D.C. and not much more than a wing of the Republican Party. Of course, African-American voters, when and where they were allowed to vote without intimidation, voted overwhelmingly for Republicans as the party which won the Civil War and ended slavery. Unlike modern political trends, most big cities outside the South were Republican strongholds. New York City and Boston were exceptions to this rule, with the immigrant voters keeping both cities heavily Democratic since the two major parties were Democrats and Republicans.

The Democrats possessed a firm political base in the "Solid South." Those northern bankers and merchants who did not benefit from high, protective tariffs also tended to vote Democratic. And most of the new immigrants were faithful to the Democratic Party. This allegiance of immigrants was due partly to the fact that most white Republicans envisioned the white, Anglo-Saxon, Protestant (WASP) virtues as being responsible for America's economic, political, and social strength. Many of the new immigrants of the Gilded Age, particularly from the 1890s onward, were Catholic and Jewish immigrants from southern and eastern Europe. This represented a new trend in the history of United States immigration. Their religious and cultural differences from northern and western Europeans alarmed many Americans. Of course, there were also the Irish immigrants whose Catholic religion and alleged propensity to drink caused many Americans to fear that old-fashioned values would eventually be destroyed. This reaction was known as Nativism, and most voters motivated by Nativism voted Republican. By contrast, their attitudes helped push new immigrants to the Democratic fold. Boston and New York City were the two main centers into which the millions of new immigrants entered the United States. The Democrats in those cities had powerful political machines. These highly organized Democrats welcomed the immigrants as they came off the boats and helped them find housing and even jobs. This was also a big reason that most immigrants returned their loyalty to the Democratic Party by voting for their candidates.

THE 1868 ELECTION

The year 1868 was a rough year for Americans to face a presidential election. Most of the first half of the year the nation's attention had been riveted on the impeachment proceedings and Senate trial of President Andrew Johnson. Just as that stressful event was coming to an end with the razor-thin acquital of Johnson, the major political parties were meeting in their national nominating conventions. It was a foregone conclusion that Johnson would not be nominated for president. Radical Republicans, who had just tried to oust him, controlled the Republican Party. Besides, Andrew Johnson was really an old Democrat from Tennessee. And the Democrats, for their part, were not sufficiently suicidal to nominate a humiliated president as their standard bearer.

Both parties attempted to persuade Civil War General Ulysses S. Grant to be their nominee. But his recent falling-out with President Johnson had moved him closer to the Radical Republicans, and in the end Grant became the unanimous nominee of that party. The Republican platform in 1868 endorsed Congressional Reconstruction policies and advocated the right to vote for African-American male adults. On economic matters, the Republicans passed a plank which called for the national debt to be paid in gold (more on this issue later in the chapter).

The Democrats had no outstanding national leader to nominate. Although he was not enthusiastic about the idea, Horatio Seymour, the governor of New York during the war, was eventually picked as the Democratic standard bearer that year. The Democratic platform differed from its Republican counterpart on both Reconstruction policy and the money question. The Democrats scathingly attacked the Republican Reconstruction policies by charging that they had been responsible for humiliating the South and carrying out the principle of "Negro supremacy." On the money question, the Democratic platform endorsed the so-called "Ohio idea," championed by Representative George H. Pendleton, which called for the repayment of national government bonds with greenbacks unless the bonds specifically mandated that they be paid in gold.

The November election gave the presidency to Ulysses Grant. Winning about 52.7 percent of the popular vote, Grant won a lopsided electoral victory with 214 electoral votes to just 80 for Seymour. While Seymour carried the major states of New York and New Jersey, the real margin of victory was provided by more than 500,000 black voters in the Southern states. The discussion of the Grant administration in this chapter will confine itself to the major issues other than Reconstruction. (See Chapter One for Grant's role in Reconstruction policy.)

THE MONEY QUESTION

The most important issue in Grant's first term revolved around the large question of money. During the Civil War, the federal government had issued about $447 million worth of new paper money called greenbacks as one method of financing the war effort. The Treasury Department had allowed the redemption of these greenbacks for gold dollars after the war. That means that a citizen could exchange his greenback dollars for gold dollars (coins) at his bank. Many farmers and others in considerable debt opposed the redemption of the greenbacks because it tended to limit the amount of greenbacks in circulation to the relatively low gold supply. They

1868	37	ULYSSES S. GRANT	Republican	3,013,421	214	52.7
		Horatio Seymour	Democrat	2,706,829	80	47.3

feared that such a reduction in the nation's money supply would result in a significant drop in crop prices—and thus, farm incomes—and that it would make it more difficult to pay their debts. Their expansionist idea concerning the money supply was known as the "soft money" position. The allies of this position in Congress were able to halt the Treasury Department's redemption policy in 1868. When Grant was sworn in as president in early March 1869, more than $350 million worth of these greenbacks were still in circulation.

Most bankers and business owners, however, were advocates of so-called "hard" or "sound" money policies, through which the amount of money in circulation was determined by the available supply of gold. These groups favored a gold standard as a means of keeping the money supply in check, fearing that a rapid increase in the money supply would create inflation. The theory behind this view is that more dollars in circulation compared with the relatively same amount of goods and services would create a consumer demand which suppliers could not keep up with; thus, goods and services would be "rationed" by a sharp increase in their prices.

As to the repayment of the national debt, President Grant kept his campaign promise when he signed the Public Credit Act in mid-March, 1869. This law laid the foundation for the payment of government bonds in gold. The next year Congress allowed the Treasury Department to replace the old Civil War bonds, which had promised 6 percent interest, with new bonds which varied between 4 percent and 5 percent. However, the difference was that the lower interest-yielding bonds would be paid on in gold dollars. These legislative steps concerning the repayment of the national debt pleased most business interests and other Americans who simply had more confidence in hard money.

Meanwhile, the larger question of the money supply continued to stir controversy over the greenbacks. Grant himself seemed uncertain of his own position in this area. This is best illustrated in the confusion of the U.S. Supreme Court over the so-called *Legal Tender Cases*. In 1870 the first of these, *Hepburn v. Griswold*, the Supreme Court declared that greenbacks were not legal tender for financial obligations made before greenbacks had been issued. This seemed to question the very constitutionality of the greenbacks. Before the next case was argued before the Court, Congress increased the number of Supreme Court justices from seven to nine, and the president appointed two justices who were favorable to greenbacks. Then in the *Knox v. Lee* decision, in 1871, the Court explicitly upheld the constitutionality of the greenbacks as full legal tender for all debts.

THE TARIFF ISSUE

High protective tariffs had been enacted during the Civil War as part of the war finance effort. It had been generally assumed that the average tariff rate would be reduced after the war. Instead, it was raised higher still in the late 1860s. While most Republicans wanted higher tariffs, many Republican voters in the West perceived these high tariffs, which raised consumer prices, as a threat to their standard of living. This in turn alarmed Republican leaders in the country who were already worried about corruption in the Grant administration possibly costing them the White House in 1872. The result was an election year tariff reduction of about 10 percent that year. Three years after the election, the Tariff of 1875 raised average tariffs to their Civil War levels.

INCOMPETENCE AND CORRUPTION

Ulysses Grant's inexperience in politics, his near worship of men who had made large fortunes, and his blind loyalty to friends all combined to rock the Grant presidency with incompetence and scandal. So many scandals wracked Grant's presidency that Grantism came to be a term synonymous with political corruption. Many of his political appointments were personal friends who simply were not competent to hold their positions. Others were given jobs based on the bad advice

Ulysses S. Grant, 18th President. Credit: AP/Wide World Photos.

of friends. Even Grant's appointments to the cabinet left much to be desired. Only his Secretary of State, Hamilton Fish, proved to be a really effective public official. Despite the many scandals in his administration, no evidence was ever found which implicated Grant in any of them. He made many mistakes in judgment, but Grant himself was a man of personal honesty and integrity. Even his alleged drinking problem, which is still commonly associated with the Grant presidency, is more myth than fact. In his pre-Civil War years Grant had had a problem with alcohol, which, at times, continued in the war. But there is no clear evidence that he ever allowed his drinking to interfere with his duties as soldier or president.

Gould and Fisk

The first major scandal of the Grant administration occurred in September of 1869. Two financial speculators, Jay Gould and James Fisk, schemed with the president's brother-in-law to corner the gold market. The plan was to buy as much gold from the Treasury Department as possible in order to drive the price of gold upward, then sell it for a huge profit. To have any hope of success, Gould, the architect of the scheme, attempted to persuade public officials that the federal government should stop selling gold on the money markets for awhile. Grant's brother-in-law used his connections to the president to advance the scheme. The argument they invented was that this would raise the price of gold and thereby somehow raise depressed farm prices. In September when Treasury withheld federal gold from sale to the public, Gould and Fisk began buying it in large quantities according to their arrangement with certain corrupt Treasury officials. The price of gold quickly rose from $132 to $163 an ounce. President Grant realized what was going on and ordered the Treasury Department to sell a large quantity of gold on September 24. That day became known as "Black Friday" because the price of gold dropped dramatically, hurting Gould, Fisk, and other gold speculators. The country, in fact, came close to an economic depression as a result of the entire affair.

The Credit Mobilier Scandal

During the election year in 1872 another major scandal was revealed. The Union Pacific Railroad Company had created the Credit Mobilier, a construction company that actually built the road for the transcontinental railroad project. Officials who controlled both companies then profited magnificently when extravagant contracts given to the Credit Mobilier by Union Pacific were used to line their pockets by overcharging on construction costs. The ordinary stockholders in the Union Pacific Railroad Company woke up to the realization that their company was nearly bankrupt. In order to cover up the fraud, these corporate swindlers used Massachussetts Republican Representative Oakes Ames to influence several key members of Congress, including prominent Republicans, by selling Credit Mobilier stock at less than market value. Former Speaker of the House Schuyler Colfax, now Grant's vice-president, and Representative James A. Garfield, a future president, were the most famous men implicated in the Credit Mobilier scandal. Although the fraud had been committed before Grant had been elected president in 1868, it nevertheless hurt the image of his administration and spurred the calls for civil service reform. The Credit Mobilier Scandal also forced Grant to dump Vice-President Colfax from the Republican ticket in 1872. And its long range significance lies in the fact that the public has been conscious of "conflict of interest" issues ever since Credit Mobilier.

CIVIL SERVICE REFORM

The president's mediocre appointments and administration scandals resulted in a partial split of the Republican Party. The first signs of serious trouble for the party came in 1870 when Carl Schurz, a German immigrant and war hero from Missouri, was elected by the Missouri legislature to the U.S. Senate as the result of a coalition between angry Republicans and many Democrats. This was the beginning of the Liberal Republicans, which bolted from the party in the 1872 presidential election.

Public pressure from Schurz and many others urged the government to follow the lead of some major European nations and create a system of competitive exams to bring qualified persons into many federal jobs. Grant signed a bill to establish a commission to study the issue in 1872. But that proved to be nothing more than good politics in an election year, for it was forgotten after Grant's reelection. However, the idea was implemented by a later administration.

THE 1872 ELECTION

In 1872 the Liberal Republicans, under the leadership of Senator Carl Schurz and others, made an open break with the regular Republican Party and the Grant administration by nominating its own candidate for president. At their national convention, the Liberal Republicans chose Horace Greeley, editor of the New York *Tribune*, as their candidate. The party platform called for civil service reform and criticized Radical Republican Reconstruction policy, but it avoided taking a stand on the tariff issue.

Greeley was considered an eccentric because of his support for nearly every reform movement in his lifetime, including vegetarianism. His support for the temperence movement—an anti-alcohol crusade—and high protective tariffs made him unacceptable to most Democrats. However, since the Democrats had no nationally known, popular candidate in 1872, they gave their nomination to Greeley as the only possible way of defeating Grant.

Despite the split in its ranks, the Republican Party nominated Ulysses Grant to run for re-election. His personal integrity and his status as a war hero was still quite high. The Republicans endorsed Radical Reconstruction policies, the high protective tariff, and gave lip service to civil service reform. Strong business support and recent Civil War memories combined against his rather eccentric opponent, and Grant won reelection by a wider margin than in his 1868 victory. The final results gave Grant about 55.6 percent of the popular vote and 286 out of 352 electoral votes. Greeley died shortly after the election and his 66 electors divided their votes among minor party candidates.

THE PANIC OF 1873

The reduction of the money supply produced by the earlier partial withdrawal of greenbacks had tightened credit and made it more difficult to borrow money. Several railroad companies had overexpanded in the post-Civil War era by moving into too many rural areas where financial profit was questionable at best. The railroad industry as a whole was already the most mismangaged industry in the country. It could ill afford to engage in much speculation. Before the summer had ended in 1873 all these factors had resulted in the bankruptcy of several railroads. Jay Cooke and Company, an investment banking firm, had tried to sell Northern Pacific Railroad bonds. When that had proved virtually impossible, the investment firm finally went bankrupt in September 1873. Its bankruptcy precipitated the Panic of 1873, in which investors in massive numbers sold their stocks. The stock market dropped so violently that it was actually closed down for ten days. The great loss of investor confidence led to a major economic depression that lasted between five and six years. Americans suffered the effects of very high unemployment and other

1872	37	ULYSSES S. GRANT	Republican	3,596,745	286	55.6
		Horace Greeley	Democrat	2,843,446	*	43.9

related economic problems for most of the decade before the depression ended in 1879.

THE RESUMPTION ACT AND ITS AFTERMATH

The greenback issue continued and essentially pitted agrarian interests against the banking and big business sectors of the country. However, farm groups had some allies in the small business community and, for a time, among working class Americans who worried about high interest rates for borrowed money. That coalition had been successful in getting the Treasury Department to halt the redemption of greenbacks in gold. But that setback for conservative monetarists was only temporary. President Grant vetoed a bill in 1874 which would have increased the money supply by providing for the issuance of new greenbacks. Then in January, 1875, allegedly in a compromise between those who wanted more greenbacks in circulation and those who wanted them completely withdrawn from circulation, Congress passed the Resumption Act. This law allowed the greenbacks already in circulation to continue as full legal tender for all debts. However, as of January 1, 1879, the Resumption Act stated that greenback dollars could be exchanged for gold dollars at full face value. In other words, at that time Americans could go to their bank and receive one gold dollar for every one greenback dollar which they turned in. The effect of this bill was to ensure that new greenbacks would not be issued by Treasury because the amount of greenbacks would be tied to the gold reserve. The political effect of the Resumption Act was to anger the "soft" or "cheap" money advocates. The National Greenback Party was created in the late 1870s, and it elected fourteen members to Congress in the offyear elections in 1878. But more significantly than the shortlived National Greenback Party was that soft money supporters began moving toward the new coining of silver as the method for increasing the money supply.

From the very beginning of the nation, the United States had been on a bimetallic standard. That means that the federal government purchased and coined all the gold and silver offered to it for sale. The amount of gold and silver varied in relationship to each other from year to year. But in 1834, reflecting the relative supply of silver and gold, Congress established a 16 to 1 ratio for purposes of coining the two metals. This was a way of reflecting the market price of gold and silver bullion (uncoined metal) and declaring that gold bullion was sixteen times more valuable than silver, or that silver bullion was only worth 1/16 the value of gold bullion. Not long after the 1834 ratio was set silver became more scarce relative to gold supplies, which raised the price of silver to gold in accordance with the law of supply and demand. The result was that it became more profitable to sell silver on the open market for commercial purposes than to sell it to the Treasury Department for coining. The Coinage Act of 1873 simply enacted into law what market prices had already done. Since very little silver was being offered to the federal government for sale, the Coinage Act forbid the coining of new silver coins. But later in the same decade large discoveries of silver, especially in Colorado and Nevada, lowered silver bullion's price to the point that the old 16 to 1 ratio would net big profits to owners of silver. By the late 1870s, then, agrarian interests and their allies began screaming about the Crime of '73. Thus began the political push for the "free and unlimited coinage of silver at 16 to 1"—the battle cry made so famous by the Populists in the 1890s. This free silver movement was the most controversial and emotional issue of the Gilded Age.

MORE SCANDALS

Grant's second administration suffered more than his first one from the revelation of more numerous political scandals. For example, a House of Representatives investigation uncovered the fact that Secretary of War William W. Belknap had taken bribes from agents at army posts in the West who traded with Indians. Belknap was impeached by the House but resigned before the Senate could try the case. In another case, the Treasury Department had hired John D. Sanborn to collect overdue taxes, from which he "earned" a 50 percent commission, which, by the time the scandal was revealed, was over $210,000. It was also revealed that the United States Postal Service had awarded contracts to carriers who paid kickbacks to corrupt officials.

Another of the Grant scandals was known as the Whiskey Ring Scandal. A group of whiskey distillers in St. Louis bribed a large number of Treasury officials in order to avoid paying excise taxes on their whiskey. When this scandal became public in 1875, due to Treasury Secretary Benjamin H. Bristow, the president's own personal secretary and close friend, Orville E. Babcock, was also implicated. Grant intervened on Babcock's behalf, resulting in charges against him being dropped.

INTRODUCTION TO THE HAYES ADMINISTRATION

Rutherford B. Hayes, the Republican governor from Ohio, was inaugurated as the nineteenth president of the United States on March 4, 1877. (For a discussion of the controversial election of 1876, see Chapter One.) Hayes quickly announced that he would serve only one term. A reform-minded politician who had fought corruption as governor of his home state, Hayes disagreed with the prevailing attitude that one who served his party well also served his country well. This personal conviction led to an executive order early in the Hayes' administration forbidding the collection of monetary assessments from federal employees for his own party's coffers. The order also prohibited political party officials from holding federal offices at the same time.

His cabinet nominations also demonstrated a commitment to increase the level of honesty in government. Ignoring the powerful Republican boss of New York, Senator Roscoe Conkling, Hayes chose William M. Evarts as his Attorney General. Evarts had been a defense attorney for President Andrew Johnson during his impeachment trial in the Senate. Carl Schurz, a reformer and critic of the Grant administration, was selected as the Secretary of the Interior. In a gesture to the Democrats, and the so-called Compromise of 1877, President Hayes appointed Democrat David M. Key as Postmaster General. And the influential, popular Republican leader from Ohio, John Sherman, was selected as the new Secretary of the Treasury; Sherman was the younger brother of the famed Union Civil War General William Tecumseh Sherman. The term "political fence-mending" originated with John Sherman, when as a member of Congress, he went back to Ohio frequently to meet with constituents. In an unrelated matter, it is noteworthy that Hayes became the first president to order that female attorneys could now address the Supreme Court. In 1879, Belva Lockwood became the first woman to do so.

THE UNITED STATES CUSTOMS HOUSE SCANDAL

The United States Customs House in New York City had been riddled with corruption for many years. New York Senator Roscoe Conkling operated a very powerful political party apparatus in the state, which he used to reward friends and punish enemies. Conkling was a master at using the spoils system—the custom of using government jobs as rewards for political favors. And Conkling's control over Republican affairs in the crucial political state of New York gave him a leading voice in national Republican Party politics. Despite this, however, Hayes appointed a commission in his first year of office (1877) to investigate the New York Customs Office because he was determined to bring about civil service reform at the federal level. The Jay Commission, headed by New York's John Jay, the grandson of the first Chief Justice of the Supreme Court, found widespread corruption and incompetence there. The three top political jobs at the customs office were the collector, who was the chief administrative officer, the naval officer, who supervised the clerks who computed the amount of import taxes on foreign goods, and the surveyor, the administrator who weighed and stored import goods. All three of the men who occupied these positions were implicated in the investigation. The most famous of these was Collector Chester A. Arthur, who ironically would later become president. When the three of them refused a presidential "request" to resign, President Hayes fired them. Senator Conkling was furious, and along with other defenders of the spoils system, he was able to block the confirmation of Hayes' appointed replacements for two of the three positions. Secretary of the Treasury John Sherman eventually negotiated an end to the dispute and a second replacement was finally approved by the Senate.

THE 1877 RAILROAD STRIKE

The depression triggered by the Panic of 1873 had taken its toll on Americans everywhere. High unemployment, drastically reduced wages and hours for many industrial workers, and a growing problem of homelessness frustrated the nation. In July 1877, during the depression, the Baltimore and Ohio (B&O) Railroad Company slashed its workers wages and precipitated a labor strike that quickly spread to shut down about two-thirds of the nation's railroads. Many of the railroads were mismanaged and overextended but wanted to keep profits high even during the depression. Workers are vulnerable to wage cuts during depressions, but some industrialists who wanted to maintain high profits during the depression of the 1870s took advantage of the workers' relative lack of power.

Strikers During the 1877 Railroad Strike. Credit: The Bettmann Archive.

The situation exploded into several violent clashes; about $5 million worth of property damage had been done by the end of the strike. Twenty strikers were killed in Pittsburgh, which resulted in a mob attempt to burn major railroad buildings in the city. Many of the railroads were being run by trustees (or receivers) appointed by federal courts because they were in the bankruptcy reorganization plan. Therefore, striking workers were declared to be in contempt of court when they refused to go back to work. This opened the door for more active federal action. President Hayes sent federal troops to several states (mostly in the East) in order to enforce the contempt of court order. He also allegedly acted to protect the United States mail service. Supported almost universally by the newspapers and the middle class, Hayes' use of federal troops proved popular and effective. The strikers respected the American military uniform and the first nationwide labor strike in American history was over by August 5. It had also been the first time that federal troops were used in a labor dispute. Overwhelmingly defeated, striking railroad workers were forced to accept the wage reductions.

THE BLAND-ALLISON ACT

Farmers and their monetary allies had been stung by the Coinage Act of 1873 and the Resumption Act in 1875. And as discussed earlier in the chapter, these groups turned to silver as the medium by which to increase the nation's money supply and thus raise farm prices and incomes. In February 1878, Missouri Democratic Representative Richard P. Bland and Iowa Republican Senator William B. Allison pushed through Congress the Bland-Allison Act over the veto of President Hayes. Bland-Allison required the Treasury Department to buy from $2 million up to $4 million of silver bullion each month and to coin it at the old 16 to 1 ratio in relationship to gold dollars. It was not the "free and unlimited coinage of silver" demanded by the silver advocates, but at first it looked like a partial victory. This bill saw the light of day largely because of Republican fears that many farmers in the Midwest and West would abandon, and therefore hurt, the Republican Party. However, the conservative monetarists still dominating the Treasury Department purchased only the minimum $2 million required by the law and then refused to actually place the new silver dollars into circulation. The result of the law, then, was to keep the monetary issue very much alive for the rest of the Gilded Age.

THE 1880 ELECTION

The Candidates

Because Rutherford B. Hayes had announced that he would not seek reelection, the Republican factions went after each other in an all-out convention fight in 1880. The two main factions had divided in the 1870s over the civil service reform issue. The Stalwarts were led by New York Senator Roscoe Conkling, the champion of the spoils system. Conkling was anxious to regain influence in a new administration after battling with Hayes for four years. Former Speaker of the House James G. Blaine of Maine and John Sherman of Ohio were leaders of the faction nicknamed the Half-Breeds. The Half-Breeds were not overly enthusiastic about civil service reform, but they did see a need for some reform in that area. At the Republican convention the Stalwarts backed former President Ulysses S. Grant, while the Half-Breeds split their support between Blaine and Sherman. The convention deadlocked for thirty-five ballots. On the thirty-sixth ballot, however, Ohio Representative James A. Garfield was nominated as the compromise candidate. Chester A. Arthur, of the New York Customs House Scandal fame, was selected as the vice-presidential running mate in a gesture designed to appease Conkling and the other Stalwarts.

The Democrats were hoping to get revenge for the controversial defeat of New York's Samuel J. Tilden in 1876 by nominating him again, but Tilden was indecisive about his intentions. There was also the matter of a scandal uncovered in 1878 that had implicated Tilden's nephew in a scheme to use bribery to get his uncle the necessary electoral votes back in '76. So they turned to a Civil War hero by nominating General Winfield Scott Hancock of Pennsylvania, who had fought bravely at the Battle of Gettysburg. Hancock had been edged out at the 1876 convention by

Samuel J. Tilden. Hancock's running mate was William H. English, an Indiana banker. English had been a pre-Civil War supporter of Kansas as a slave state.

The Platforms and Campaign

There was little difference in the party platforms in 1880. Both pledged their support for civil service reform, which by then was the popular thing to do. The one key difference in the campaign was the stand on tariffs. The Republicans continued their tradition of favoring high, protective tariffs, while the Democrats favored lower tariffs. The campaign was primarily a personality fight in which both candidates accused each other of corruption and using dirty tricks. Hancock tried to paint Garfield as a crook. And the fact was that Garfield had indeed been involved in a couple of public scandals. The investigation of the Credit Mobilier Scandal, for example, had implicated then Representative Garfield as a recipient of stocks in a railroad company, allegedly in order to prevent a Congressional investigation. Records showed that Garfield had received $329, but he denied the bribery charge by insisting that it had been a loan repayment. The matter died without any formal action being taken against him. Then when Garfield had been chairman of the House Appropriations Committee, he had represented a paving company that obtained a federal contract for a job in the nation's capitol. Again the conflict of interest complaint had not led to formal charges.

In the dirty tricks department, the Democrats fabricated a letter from Garfield to a fictitious labor leader supposedly in Lynn, Massachussetts, named H. L. Morey. In this infamous Morey Letter, Garfield had allegedly told Morey that he thought the United States should allow more Chinese immigrants to enter the country. This dirty trick was played, of course, in an attempt to win votes in the West and among industrial workers. Hancock had his own problems. Democrats were circulating the rumor that he had really been a coward at Gettysburg and elsewhere during the war. And at one point in the campaign Hancock referred to the tariff question as a local issue; his political inexperience was showing. For their turn, the Republicans' dirtiest trick of the campaign attempted to call public attention to Hancock's inexperience. They "published" a thick book about the Democratic candidate's political achievements, which was completely blank until the last page read "The End." The outcome of the election in 1880 was very close in terms of the popular vote. Garfield won the election with 214 electoral votes to Hancock's 155. The popular vote was much closer, however, with Garfield garnering less than 40,000 more votes than Hancock. James A. Garfield was thus elected as the twentieth president of the United States. However, he was not destined to remain president for very long.

1880	38	JAMES A. GARFIELD	Republican	4,453,295	214	48.5
		Winfield S. Hancock	Democrat	4,414,082	155	48.1
		James B. Weaver	Greenback-Labor	308,578		3.4

GARFIELD'S PRESIDENCY

James Garfield was a Latin scholar, a mathmetician, and a former college president. But those attainments, of course, could not help him avoid an almost immediate clash with Roscoe Conkling over patronage. Both New York senators—Conkling and "Me Too" Thomas Platt—were powerful bosses in Republican politics. And both urged Garfield to appoint some of their people to key federal jobs. Instead, President Garfield chose his own men. When the president appointed William A. Robertson, a Conkling enemy, to be the new collector at the New York Customs House both Conkling and Platt resigned their senate seats in protest. They immediately asked the New York legislature to reappoint them to the United States Senate in a move calculated to display their political pull in New York Republican politics. The plot ironically backfired, however, when the new collector turned out to have more political clout than people realized. Largely through Robertson's efforts, the legislature refused to reappoint them to their former senate seats. With his political influence severely damaged, Conkling's career was over.

Garfield's presidency was cut short when an eccentric lawyer and theological lecturer shot the president in the back on July 2, 1881, in the Washington, D.C. railway station. Garfield was on his way to Massachussetts at the time. Charles J. Guiteau, a disappointed office seeker, was arrested on the spot and proudly declared that he was a Stalwart who had just made Vice-President Arthur president. After Garfield died, Guiteau wrote a letter from jail to the White House, saying that the assassination had been a "sad necessity" to end the patronage fight and thereby unite the Republican Party in order to save the republic. Sadly, Guiteau himself received about one hundred letters in jail from Americans expressing support for the shooting of the president. Although he was almost certainly insane, the insanity defense failed, and Guiteau was hanged in 1882 in the nation's capitol.

President Garfield hung on to life until September 19, 1881. Cysts had developed around the bullet, which made the wound relatively harmless. But doctors were obsessed with removing the bullet anyway—except they weren't certain precisely where it was. During the operation to find and remove the bullet, doctors' hands and/or instruments left germs that caused internal bleeding and infection. If the doctors had left the bullet in his body, it is considered likely that James Garfield would have lived.

INTRODUCTION TO THE ARTHUR ADMINISTRATION

Chester Arthur was sworn into the presidency in September 1881. The new president had a tarnished image when he took his place as the nation's chief executive. He had been fired by President Hayes after being implicated in the New York Customs House Scandal in the 1870s. His placement on the Republican ticket in 1880 had been an effort to placate Roscoe Conkling. Now, as fate would have it, Chester A. Arthur found himself the twenty-first president of the United States by default. Arthur was a fashion conscious president who liked to entertain at the White House. Hayes had forbidden alcohol at the White House during his administration, but Arthur resumed serving it when he took over from Garfield. Arthur was also a well-read man of above average intellectual abilities who was determined to counteract his negative reputation. Almost instantly in 1881, he saw himself as a reformer who could attract support from all political areas. This perspective got him into trouble in 1882, when New York Republicans bowed to White House pressure and replaced their candidate for governor with President Arthur's choice. His choice, Charles A. Folger, was soundly defeated in November by Democrat Grover Cleveland—a position Cleveland used effectively four years later to become the next president after Arthur.

CIVIL SERVICE REFORM

With a new president in power, and Roscoe Conkling out of the way, the calls for real civil service reform were growing louder. Three events prepared the way. First, the death of Garfield was blamed on the spoils system as advocates exaggerated the late president's virtues and played on the emotions to build up meaningful momemtum for reform. Second, a new political scandal in the early '80s wracked the country. The United States Postal Service was hiring private contractors to deliver mail in many out-of-the-way rural areas in the West. The second Assistant Postmaster General had discretionary powers to give additional funds for improving rural mail delivery. This postal official, named Thomas A. Brady, and Arkansas Republican Senator Stephen W. Dorsey and at least 6 others were involved in a conspiracy to give rural contracts to friends and pocket federal money for improvements that were never made. The conspiracy was discovered when Brady asked for more money after $4 million in the discretionary fund were exhausted. The use of stars on U.S. Post Office literature identified specific private contractors who delivered the mail. That's why this scandal became known as the Star Route Scandal. Despite vigorous prosecution, however, the defendants were acquitted in 1883. The third event which made civil service reform possible was the return of a Democratic majority to the House of Representatives, as the staunchest opponents of reform were defeated.

The Pendleton Act

With a push from President Arthur, a sufficient number of both Republicans and Democrats got on the civil service reform bandwagon behind Ohio Democratic Senator George H. Pendleton's bill. And in January 1883, Congress passed the Pendleton Act, otherwise known as the Civil Service Reform Act. This law established the first regulatory commission at the federal level of government when it created the Civil Service Commission. Its three members were to be appointed by the president and confirmed by the Senate, with no more than two members from the same political party. This commission was empowered to create competitive exams for federal jobs that were classified as being under the Civil Service Commission's jurisdiction. Federal jobs were to be classified by the president via an executive order. The new system was phased in for classified jobs by allowing the current federal employee to keep his job without passing an exam; when he retired the position would be filled under the new format. An advantage to the federal employee under the civil service system was that he could not be fired for political reasons.

On the other hand, critics later accused the new system of making it difficult to fire lazy employees.

Presidents tended to classify many new jobs late in their terms in order to protect their appointments. President Arthur classified about 12 percent of all federal positions. Subsequent presidents expanded the classified list until 40 percent of all federal jobs had been classified by 1900 and about 60 percent by World War I. While Cabinet members, and a large number of other political positions in the federal government, are not subject to civil service regulations, the overwhelming percentage of federal jobs today are so covered. And it is the significance of the Pendleton Act that it paved the way for our present system.

THE TARIFF ISSUE

Tariffs, along with excise taxes on liquor and tobacco, had been the major source of revenue for the federal government since 1792. While the tariff rates varied over the years, they had been consistently very high since the Civil War tariff, with only a temporary 10 percent reduction in 1872. Beginning in 1880, the federal government was taking in a $100 million surplus each fiscal year. The problem with this surplus stemmed from the fact that federal moneys were kept in vaults rather than in banks in those days because there really was no national banking system. The annual surplus, then, was not being invested. This meant that each year the money supply (money in circulation) was being contracted, causing serious deflation. Deflation is the opposite of inflation and represents falling prices and incomes. Deflation is especially harmful to farmers, small businessmen, and other typically high-debt groups because these groups have less income to pay off their debts which do not get reduced.

While most government officials agreed that continued budget surpluses were bad, few options to resolve the situation were financially or politically feasible. A reduction in excise taxes was unacceptable to most Americans on moral grounds; those so-called "sin" taxes (modern term) were supported even by some Americans who used alcohol and tobacco. And business interests opposed any significant cuts in the tariff rates. Tinkering with tariffs, however, would not have necessarily resolved the budget surplus. A reduction in the tariff rates might have actually aggravated the situation. By encouraging Americans to buy more imported products, the federal government might have received more revenue from tariffs. Radical reform of the banking system to include a real national bank could have provided a safe place for federal dollars to be invested without the government playing favorites via "pet banks." But it would be more than 25 years before the nation's leaders recognized the need for such a system. Paying off the national debt was not a financially feasible way of getting rid of the budget surpluses either. Many of the government bonds had been purchased by so-called national banks. These banks issued their own bank notes (paper money) according to a formula based on the value of the government bonds they possessed. Therefore, if the government suddenly paid off the national debt, the money supply would be curtailed that much more. And, of course, Americans in the Gilded Age were not yet ready for the federal government to invest federal dollars in social programs.

With so many economic and political options considered unacceptable, President Arthur turned his attention to tariff reduction. In 1882 he appointed a Tariff Commission to study tariff rates and make recommendations. The idea of the "scientific tariff" was being discussed in the country then also. Some advocated that a "scientific tariff" could determine what the "right" tariff should be for a specific import by accounting for cost of production, market conditions, and other factors. When the Tariff Commission's work was completed it recommended that average tariff rates be reduced from the current 40 percent level to just 20 percent. But in 1883 Congress rejected the commission's recommendations and passed the Mongrel Tariff of 1883. The Mongrel Tariff bill contained some reductions and some increases but overall was very much a protectionist bill that was not much different from the Tariff of 1875. The next year the Democrats offered the Morrison Bill (1884) in order to implement the Tariff Commission's recommendations, but Republicans, who were dependent on big business support, defeated it.

IMMIGRATION RESTRICTION

The rise of industrial America in the post-Civil War era created a demand for millions of new industrial workers. This demand was being met by a surge in the number of immigrants coming to the United States from other countries. Many of these new immigrants brought new languages, music, and political and religious traditions. These cultural differences made many Americans uncomfortable and even hostile toward the immigrants. Human beings often fear those they do not understand. The Irish had long been viewed with suspicion in America because of their Roman Catholic religion and their acceptance of alcoholic beverages. Those from southern and eastern Europe, usually Catholic or Jewish, were treated similarly as the Irish. Still others, like the Chinese, looked different from other Americans and were neither Christian or Jewish in religious tradition. Many of these new immigrants added to their list of enemies by their willingness to work for lower wages and to act as strikebreakers during major strikes. This created a hostile relationship between immigrants and industrial workers in general, and labor unions in particular.

The Immigration Act of 1882

The growing nervousness and hostility toward immigrants in the Gilded Age led to public calls for legislation to restrict the type and/or numbers of immigrants allowed to come to the United States. Politicians in both parties partially heeded this public clamor. The Immigration Act of 1882 excluded convicted criminals and the insane. It also attempted to keep the very poor out of the country by requiring a 50-cent tax per person coming into the United States by water carrier; of course, in the days before air travel, that included everyone except immigrants from Canada or Mexico. Nevertheless, the Immigration Act of 1882 did not significantly reduce the flow of immigrants coming into the United States.

The Chinese Exclusion Act

More serious was the Chinese Exclusion Act passed in the same year. Based on racism and hostility toward cheap labor, that law prohibited all new Chinese immigration for ten years, except for Chinese merchants, teachers, students, and government officials, or any offspring of persons in those 4 categories. The significance of the Chinese Exclusion Act was that this was the first time that national origin was used to determine who could not migrate to the United States. The ten-year ban was renewed for another ten years in 1892. And in 1902 the ban on new Chinese immigrants was made permanent until its repeal in 1946. In the meantime, all Chinese and Chinese-Americans in the United States were required to carry identification papers with them at all times so that immigration agents could check their legal status. This law resulted in so-called paper families, in which Chinese emigrating to the United States forged papers "proving" they were closely related to someone in the four legally accepted categories. And that is the major reason why tracing the personal histories of many Chinese-Americans has been so difficult.

A BRIEF ASSESSMENT OF ARTHUR

The Arthur presidency proved mediocre at best. However, that was a fair accomplishment considering that so many expected it to be a total disaster. Historians generally give him high marks for his accomplishment of major civil service reform. IIis campaign to build up the Navy, which he began in 1883, is also praised as clearing the way for the modern navy that developed in the early twentieth century.

THE 1884 ELECTION

The Candidates

Chester Arthur sought the Republican Party's nomination to run for a second term in 1884. Arthur knew then that he had a serious kidney disease. Because no one else knew it at the time, this physical ailment did not affect the Republican nomination process that year. However, the disease eventually killed him. Arthur's attempt to win renomination was hampered by the fact that he had no strong, well-defined following. He was challenged at the 1884 Republican convention by James G. Blaine, a former House and Senate member from Maine. Blaine had been Garfield's Secretary of State, but Arthur had dumped him for his own replacement. This gave Blaine, who had always wanted to be president, another motive to defeat Arthur for the nomination. Illinois Senator John A. Logan, the first national head of the Grand Army of the Republic, also sought the nomination that year. Logan's political strengths included strong support from Union Civil War veterans. The Stalwarts in the party, who favored the old spoils system, also liked Logan. Blaine and Logan negotiated an agreement before the nominee was finally selected. If Blaine won the nomination he agreed to select Logan as his vice-presidential running mate. And if Logan won the nomination and the election, he promised to name Blaine as the country's Secretary of State. Blaine was nominated on the fourth ballot and promptly chose Logan as his running mate.

The Democrats smelled victory in 1884. The Solid South had clearly emerged by then as a Democratic strength. And the Republicans had done them a favor by denying the nomination to a president who had helped achieve meaningful civil service reform. This would enable the Democrats to paint the Republicans as the party of privilege and corruption. On the second ballot the Democrats chose Grover Cleveland, the popular governor of New York who had made himself famous for his reform measures. Cleveland had been the mayor of Buffalo, New York before that. His nomination had been helped when disgruntled reform-minded Republicans, led by Carl Schurz, told the Democrats that they would support a reform-minded Democratic candidate. Republican Stalwarts promptly labeled these reform Republicans Mugwumps, an Algonquin Indian word to describe a renegade chief. The support of the Mugwumps also virtually assured a Democratic victory in November. The Democrats picked the runner-up in the nomination race to be their vice-presidential candidate, Indiana Governor Thomas Hendricks.

The Campaign

For its time, the 1884 campaign was one of the most personally nasty presidential contests in American history. The Democrats played up the Republican reputation for corruption all they could, and in some ways the Republican Blaine helped them exploit that issue by his own past record and his campaign activities. Blaine's trouble went back to 1876 when, as House Speaker, he had helped an Arkansas railroad company obtain a federal land grant in exchange for company stock. Blaine then sold the stock for a handsome profit. The stockbroker who handled the transaction for Blaine had a bookkeeper named James Mulligan, who kept documents that led to an 1876 Congressional investigation of the Speaker. A House committee exonerated Blaine despite the fact that he had written "Burn this letter" on the bottom of one correspondence. Mulligan had kept extra documents on the case and he handed these Mulligan Letters to some Mugwumps during the presidential race in 1884. Blaine refused to respond to the charges during the campaign and did his best to ignore the issue. But there is no doubt that the Mulligan Letters went a long way toward connecting the Republican candidate to the general sleeze in the politics of the Gilded Age.

Then in October, not long before the election, Blaine committed a serious campaign blunder. He attended a campaign fundraising banquet in New York in which the Rev. Samuel Burchard labeled the Democratic Party as the party of "Rum, Romanism, and Rebellion." The reference to rum expressed hostility toward drinkers, many of whom were recent immigrants. The word "romanism," of course, echoed the nativist fear of Roman Catholics and a common Protestant fear that the pope wanted to rule America. The reference to rebellion was another example of the typical Republican practice of waving the bloody shirt, linking Democrats to the rebellion of the Civil War. When Blaine failed to repudiate Burchard's statement, the Cleveland campaign exploited his silence in a final appeal to voters. And newspapers generally portrayed Blaine's conduct as unseemly for a presidential candidate.

Grover Cleveland was not without his own problems in the election campaign. In late July a Buffalo newspaper accused Cleveland of having fathered an illegitimate child seven years earlier. In fact, he and a few of his pals had had sexual relations with a widow named Maria Halpin. When she became pregnant, Cleveland had accepted responsibility and agreed to help support the child. She eventually lost custody of her son on the grounds that she was an unfit mother. The circumstances of her pregnancy had been kept secret until Cleveland's run for the presidency. To his credit, the Democratic candidate responded to the public disclosure of his indiscretion by admitting his role in the sordid affair and explaining how he had tried to do the responsible thing afterward. But Republicans had a field day with the story. "Ma, Ma, where's my pa?" they mocked. Democrats responded with "Gone to the White House, ha, ha, ha!" Undoubtedly, this episode hurt Cleveland among middle class voters.

The Results

In the end, voter identification of Blaine with the rampant political corruption of the day, and the defection of the Mugwumps to Cleveland, cost the Republicans the election. Cleveland was elected president by a 219 to 182 electoral vote margin—the first Democrat elected to the White House since James Buchanan in 1856. His margin of victory, however, was extremely close, carrying his home state of New York by just over 1,100 votes. If the state had gone for Blaine, the Republicans would have carried the day.

INTRODUCTION TO THE CLEVELAND ADMINISTRATION

Grover Cleveland's own philosophical roots went back to the days of Andrew Jackson. Jacksonian Democrats had opposed the privileged class and championed the common man by advocating a hands-off, laissez-faire government approach to the economy. In those pre-Civil War days of the nineteenth century, the laissez-faire position had been the hallmark of American political liberalism. That was true for two primary reasons. First, conservative forces had advocated and used the power of the federal government to promote their vision of a manufacturing economy largely by policies which promoted the welfare of those already wealthy and powerful. Second, liberals in the early nineteenth century perceived that relatively small farmers and merchants were and would remain the dominant elements in the economy as long as the government left things alone.

But times had changed. The Industrial Revolution of the postwar era created huge enterprises which controlled whole manufacturing markets. While most businesses were still relatively small (they still are), the economic giants exercised a disproportionate degree of power and influence, not only economically but politically as well. Therefore, during the Gilded Age the old Jacksonian insistence on laissez-faire had become the conservative justification for unregulated economic power. Democrats in the Jacksonian tradition were very slow to recognize this fundamental change, which left the majority of both Democrats and Republicans endorsing

1884	38	GROVER CLEVELAND	Democrat	4,879,507	219	48.5
		James G. Blaine	Republican	4,850,293	182	48.2
		Benjamin F. Butler	Greenback-Labor	175,370		1.8
		John P. St. John	Prohibition	150,369		1.5

laissez-faire. Many, especially among Republicans, still upheld the conservative tradition of government assistance to business interests—especially big business. Grover Cleveland, on the other hand, was probably the most consistent advocate of a true laissez-faire philosophy in action during the entire Gilded Age.

THE HAYMARKET SQUARE BOMBING AND ORGANIZED LABOR

Beginning on May Day (May 1) 1886, a national strike on behalf of the eight-hour day had affected several cities. An already existing labor strike at the McCormick Harvester Company in Chicago led to serious violence that sent the middle class reeling. In early May, one striker had been killed by police in a clash. A protest rally was called for the next evening, May 4, at Chicago's

Grover Cleveland, 22nd and 24th President. Credit: AP/Wide World Photos.

Haymarket Square. The Haymarket Square rally had been peaceful and was breaking up when about 180 policemen began marching toward the demonstrators. Someone in the crowd threw a homemade bomb into the column of policemen, fatally wounding eight officers and wounding scores more. The police then began firing indiscriminately into the crowd, killing at least 4 demonstrators and injuring about 100 people, half of them fellow officers. Although no specific evidence was found linking anyone to the actual bombing incident, 8 well-known anarchists were eventually arrested and charged with conspiracy to incite murder. The middle class, already hostile to labor unions, demanded that justice—at least punishment—be brought against someone. In a very biased, shameful trial, all 8 were convicted; 7 of the defendants were sentenced to be hanged and one to a long prison term. Of the 7 sentenced to be executed, 1 hanged himself in his jail cell; Illinois Governor Richard J. Oglesby commuted the sentence of 2 others to life imprisonment; and the other 4 were executed before the end of the same year. Seven years later, in late June of 1893, another governor, John P. Altgeld, pardoned the other 3 convicts—a move praised by liberals sympathetic to the labor movement but soundly criticized by a majority of Illinois voters, who defeated him for reelection.

One of the significant results of the Haymarket Square episode was a speedy, sharp decline in the Knights of Labor. Although the Knights were not really involved with the McCormick Harvester strike, it was the largest labor union in the

Haymarket Bomb Explodes: Credit: The Bettmann Archive.

country at the time. Most Americans seemed to reason that if there had been no unions the strike and thus the violence would never have happened. Membership in the Knights of Labor fell precipitously as many workers did not want to suffer the stigma and other negative consequences associated with continued membership in that organization. The same incident helped pave the way for the rise of the American Federation of Labor, which quickly eclipsed the Knights in numbers and influence in the years to follow even though organized labor was not really well accepted in American society until the next century.

REMAINING CIVIL WAR ISSUES

During the Civil War, Congress had authorized the payment of disability pensions to Union soldiers and to widows and children of killed veterans. As a result of the political clout of the Grand Army of the Republic, veterans unable to obtain these pensions during the war were able to get them after the war by getting their congressman or senator to introduce a private bill on their behalf. A private bill is a proposed law that concerns one individual only. The result was that millions of dollars were being paid out in pensions, many to whom had not actually been disabled or who had become disabled after the war. Because the G.A.R. could deliver a crucial block of Republican votes, Republican presidents routinely signed every such private pension bill that Congress put on their desk. President Cleveland, however, actually read the bills and vetoed those he deemed undeserving (a few hundred) during his administration. The Republicans in Congress countered by passing a

Dependent Pension Bill (the Blair Bill) in January 1887. The Blair Bill would have authorized pensions to all disabled Union veterans regardless of when or how the disability had taken place, but Cleveland incurred the further wrath of the G.A.R. by vetoing the bill.

Another controversy involving Civil War memories brought emotional feelings to the surface. In 1887 house cleaning in the War Department resulted in the uncovering of nearly two hundred captured Confederate flags. In that same year President Cleveland issued an executive order to return the flags to their respective states in the South. Outrage from Northerners caused the president to revoke his own order. This seemed to prove that the country was not quite ready to put the war behind them. However, largely due to the healing and unifying effect of the Spanish-American War (1898), President Theodore Roosevelt was able to return the flags to the South in 1905 without serious controversy. In politics, timing is important.

THE INTERSTATE COMMERCE ACT

The railroad companies had really been America's first nationwide industry. While railroads played a crucial role in the settling of the West and in uniting the nation economically, many farmers saw themselves as victims of the industry. In fact, many of the railroad companies were discriminating against farmers and taking advantage of their need to get farm products to market in a timely manner. One of biggest complaints farmers made was the fairly common railroad practice of charging higher rates for short hauls than for longer ones on the same track. Another complaint concerned the practice of rebating a portion of the rate to major customers in order to keep their business. And some railroads were involved in collusion with competitors to fix freight prices.

Farm groups in heavy agricultural states began lobbying for state regulation of the railroads. The Grange was especially involved in this effort. Beginning in Illinois in 1871, so-called Granger laws to regulate the railroads and grain elevators were enacted in several farm states. In 1877 the Supreme Court upheld the constitutional right of states to regulate rates for storing and handling grain in *Munn v. Illinois*. The implication seemed to be that states could also regulate intrastate railroads (those that operated entirely within one state), although that was not made clear by the ruling. But in its 1886 *Wabash Railroad Case* (*Wabash, St. Louis, and Pacific Railway Company v. Illinois*), the Supreme Court ruled that states may not seek to regulate interstate railroads—railroads operating across state lines. The *Wabash Railroad Case* led to calls for federal regulation of the industry. In the U.S. Senate, Illinois Senator Shelby M. Cullom chaired a committee that investigated the entire railroad industry. The Cullom Committee concluded its hearings with the recommendation that the federal government should indeed regulate the railroads. The result was the passing of the Interstate Commerce Act in February 1887.

The Interstate Commerce Act established the Interstate Commerce Commission, a federal agency initially charged with the responsibility for regulating the railroads. The ICC consisted of 5 members appointed for 6-year terms by the president and confirmed by the Senate. No more than 3 commissioners could belong to the same political party. The law prohibited railroads from engaging in rate discrimination, short-haul abuse, collusion, and rebating, and it declared that rates must be "reasonable and just." The ICC was given authority to hold public hearings and issue "cease and desist" orders to railroad companies, but it was left to the federal courts to enforce ICC rulings. At first the ICC believed it had the authority to set rates in disputed cases. But a Supreme Court ruling in 1896, *Cincinnati, New Orleans, and Texas Pacific Railway Company v. ICC*, interpreted the law to mean that the Commission would have to either approve or disapprove a disputed rate. Indeed, from the law's inception in 1887 to the beginning of 1905, federal judges sided with the railroads in 15 of the 16 cases considered. This hostility from federal judges and Supreme Court justices made the Interstate Commerce Commission virtually impotent by the turn of the century. Thus, the Interstate Commerce Act was not significant for what it did but for its symbolic meaning as the federal government's first attempt to regulate a major industry.

THE TARIFF ISSUE UNDER CLEVELAND

The problem of the budget surplus was getting worse as the decade of the '80s continued. President Cleveland, being a traditional low-tariff Democrat, naturally saw the solution in a significant reduction of the tariff. In 1887 he made tariff reduction a major priority. He was confident that the House of Representatives would pass such a bill because the majority of the members were Democrats. And although he was certain that the Republican-controlled Senate would defeat it, this would give him an issue on which to run for reelection the next year. In December the House passed the Mills Bill in compliance with the president's request. After the Republican Senate offered its high tariff alternative measure—the Allison Bill—the conference committee was not able to iron out the differences between the two bills, and Cleveland got his campaign issue.

REMAINING ISSUES

President Cleveland enlarged the classified federal job list by over 12,000 during his administration. However, Cleveland finally caved in to Democratic officials who insisted that a large number of federal jobs be given to party workers. After all, they argued, Cleveland was the first Democrat in the White House since James Buchanan left it in early March of 1861. By the end of the Cleveland administration the president had appointed Democrats to about two-thirds of the nonclassified positions, bringing the wrath of civil service reformers upon him.

Under the Cleveland administration the Department of the Interior investigated reports of fraudulent land claims in the West. It turned out that several railroad companies, lumber interests, and cattlemen had obtained federal land illegally, and 81 million acres was returned to the government.

The Dawes Severalty Act (Dawes Act) changed the United States Indian policy by attempting to break up reservations into several land parcels which would be owned by individual Indian families. This was the first real effort to "Americanize" the American Indian. (For a complete discussion of postwar Indian policy see Chapter Two.)

THE 1888 ELECTION

The Candidates

President Grover Cleveland easily won the Democratic Party's nod to seek re-election. But Vice-President Thomas Hendricks had died in office in 1885, so a new running mate had to be selected. Against the wishes of most party leaders, Cleveland insisted on 75-year old Allen G. Thurman of Ohio, as Hendricks' replacement. There was general agreement among Republicans that James Blaine was a liability on a national ticket. He simply had been implicated in too many sordid political schemes to be a viable candidate for president. On the eighth ballot the Republicans finally settled on Indiana Senator Benjamin Harrison, the grandson of former President William Henry Harrison. New York banker Levi P. Morton was selected as Harrison's running mate.

The Campaign and Results

The major genuine issue in the campaign was the tariff question. The Republican Senate's frustration of President Cleveland's efforts to lower tariff rates had given Cleveland the political issue he had hoped for. Harrison countered with the familiar argument that tariffs must be kept high to protect American industries and jobs. Worried about a second Cleveland administration, business leaders raised $4 million for the Republican campaign war chest.

Most of the time the nation's voters were exposed to dirty politics, name-calling, and bribery schemes. In Harrison's home state capital of Indianapolis, several hundred voters were bribed to go to the polls for him. Harrison's campaign manager was Matthew S. Quay, a Pennsylvanian who was also the Republican National Committee Chairman. Quay had a well-deserved reputation as a political player who would win at any cost. As a collector of political dirt, Quay kept a blackmail file known as "Quay's Coffin" because of all the politicians he killed politically. In one of Quay's worst dirty tricks of the '88 campaign, he used a letter with a fictitious signature to discredit Cleveland among Irish-American voters, who had voted for the president in large numbers four years before. A California Republican leader, George Osgoodly, pretending to be a British-born naturalized citizen named Charles Murchison, wrote a letter to the British ambassador in Washington, D.C. (Sir Lionel Sackville West). In this "Murchison Letter," Osgoodly asked the ambassador whom he thought most Englishmen favored in the American election. When West replied in writing that most Englishmen preferred Cleveland, Quay released the letter to the press as an example of foreign interference in American politics. President Cleveland ordered the duped West out of the country, but the damage had already been done.

Cleveland's chances for reelection were also damaged by continuing bad relations between him and David Hill, the Democratic governor of New York, the president's home state. Hill was unpopular with reformers and therefore clashed with the president and his campaign officials in the state.

When the final votes were counted, Harrison had been elected president by a close margin. Cleveland actually received 60,000 or so more votes than Harrison. But Cleveland's home state of New York provided the electoral margin of victory for the Republicans. The electoral tally was 233 electoral votes for Harrison and 168 for Cleveland.

INTRODUCTION TO THE HARRISON ADMINISTRATION

The Republicans won not only the White House in 1888 but both houses of Congress by narrow margins. Speaker of the House, Thomas B. Reed of Maine, ruled that body with a partisan, iron hand, thus giving him the nickname of "Czar" Reed (after the Russian monarchs). Rhode Island Senator Nelson W. Aldrich was the majority leader in the Senate. The Harrison administration was unusually pro-business even for the Gilded Age. His cabinet was dubbed "the businessman's cabinet" because of some key appointments. Secretary of War Redfield Proctor, for example, was the marble stone king from Vermont. And John Wanamaker, the Postmaster-General, was a wealthy Pennsylvania merchant. James G. Blaine, by the way, became the nation's Secretary of State again; previously he had been appointed to that post by James Garfield.

The Republicans wasted no time in adding to their voting strength in Congress. The administration set a new record for the number of states added to the Union. The following 6 western states were admitted from November 1889 through July 1890 (in chronological order): North Dakota, South Dakota, Montana, Washington, Idaho, and Wyoming. These new states provided 12 new Republicans to the United States Senate. With firm control of the Congress and the White House, the Republicans proceeded to enact legislation which had been frustrated by the Cleveland administration.

THE DEPENDENT PENSIONS ACT

President Cleveland had vetoed a few hundred private pension bills for Civil War veterans during his term. Then when the Republicans in Congress had attempted to pass a comprehensive pensions bill to provide pensions to veterans regardless of when or under what circumstances they had become disabled, Cleveland had vetoed that also. The Grand Army of the Republic had been infuriated by these actions and vowed to defeat him in the upcoming elections. When their efforts proved successful, the Harrison administration acted to reward them. The result was that Congress passed the Dependent Pensions Act in June 1890. This bill was nearly identical to the one that Cleveland had vetoed three years earlier. The Dependent Pensions Act nearly doubled the number of pensioners from about 490,000 to 966,000. By 1911 the United States had spent about $4 billion on Civil War pensions alone—many times more than the cost of fighting the war. Along with subsidies to steamship lines and federally financed infrastructure projects, the

1888	38	BEJNAMIN HARRISON	Republican	5,447,129	233	47.9
		Grover Cleveland	Democrat	5,537,857	168	48.6
		Clinton B. Fisk	Prohibition	249,506		2.2
		Anson J. Streeter	Union Labor	146,935		1.3

Dependent Pensions Act dissolved the federal budget surplus. In fact, 1890 became the first year in American history that the federal budget appropriated over $1 billion in one fiscal year. As a result, the 1890 Congress was dubbed the "Billion Dollar Congress."

THE SHERMAN ANTITRUST ACT

A growing number of Americans in the late Gilded Age were becoming concerned about the size and power of big business monopolies and trusts. America had been built on the free market philosophy, with competition as the driving force for economic expansion and efficiency. That was part of the story, of course. But government had always played an important role also through its relatively high tariffs, federal financing of internal improvements (roads, canals, railroads, etc.), and other forms of assistance to industry. Nevertheless, new forms of business organization seemed to threaten the spirit of competition and free enterprise which pro-business groups touted with great enthusiasm. The most significant of these new organizations was the trust. A trust consisted of several companies giving control of their stock to an independent board of trustees, which in turn, ran all the companies under its umbrella. John D. Rockefeller formed the first trust when he organized the Standard Oil Trust in 1882. The oil trust then controlled about 90 percent of the country's oil refining business. Some argued that this was an inevitable result of competition and that it really increased business efficiency. But more Americans worried that their nation's economic heritage was threatened by these gigantic trusts and monopolies. Many states in the 1880s had passed antitrust laws, but many companies chartered in one state also operated in other states. Thus, individual states could not adequately regulate these big business combinations. Furthermore, the Supreme Court, in its 1886 *Santa Clara Case*, had ruled that corporations were legally "persons" under the Fourteenth Amendment and therefore entitled to due process before having restrictions placed on their property or property rights. This, of course, made it even more difficult to regulate or ban trusts.

Mounting public pressure finally succeeded in getting both political parties to give the appearance of consideration to federal antitrust legislation in their 1888 party platforms. At the same time, Republicans, least of all, really desired to do anything meaningful in the way of breaking up trusts. Therefore, the Harrison administration did the next best thing; it got Congress to pass a vague antitrust law with no enforcement teeth in it. This way the public might be satisfied that something was being done about the issue. The result was the Sherman Antitrust Act of July 1890. Named after popular Ohio Republican Senator John Sherman, the bill was actually written by someone else. The Sherman Antitrust Act prohibited business combinations in the form of trusts and monopolies and also made it illegal to engage in any conspiracy to restrain trade. The maximum penalty for violating the new federal law was $5,000 and/or one year in jail.

This act was not seen as radical, however, but merely an extension of what many states had attempted to do already. Unfortunately for reformers, the federal antitrust law was just as ineffective as the state laws. The act had no definition of its key words, such as "monopoly" and "trust," so its vagueness made enforcement difficult. No president was very interested in enforcing the law either, which they would have to do by instructing the Justice Department to file a lawsuit against an alleged violator. And, of course, the highly conservative federal courts demonstrated considerable hostility to the new law. Out of only 14 Justice Department suits filed under the act through 1900, just one conviction was obtained. That was the 1891 *U.S. v. Jellico Mountain Coal and Coke Company*, a supplier of raw materials to steel companies. In *U.S. v. E.C. Knight* (1895) a federal court ruled that the "Sugar Trust" was not a conspiracy in restraint of trade because the American Sugar Refining Company was engaged in manufacturing rather than trade. This decision allowed the company to maintain its control of about 98 percent of the sugar refining industry as a legal trust. It also slowed up the number of lawsuits against trusts and monopolies after that.

THE SHERMAN SILVER PURCHASE ACT

The Treasury Department's application of the Bland-Allison Act (1878) gave increasing momentum in the 1880s to another push for the free and unlimited coinage of silver. Farmers and their allies were relentless in this effort. Once again the Republican Party grew nervous about the possibility of losing votes among farmers in the West. In an attempt to both pacify its own silver wing and head off a free silver movement, Congress passed another monetary law dealing with the silver question. During the same month but after passing the Sherman Antitrust Act, Congress passed legislation called the Sherman Silver Purchase Act in July 1890. Another factor in the passage of the new bill was an exchange of votes between politicians wanting a higher tariff and those wanting a pro-silver bill. Repealing the Bland-Allison Act, the new law changed the rules completely. Instead of requiring a purchase of so many dollars of silver each month, Congress now required the Treasury Department to purchase 4.5 million ounces of silver per month at the market price. Instead of coining the silver, which it had not done anyway under Bland-Allison, the Treasury Department was required to pay for the silver with a new type of paper money called a "Coin Note." Coin notes could be redeemed in either gold or silver at the government's choice. Of course, conservative Treasury officials made the choice to redeem them in gold dollars.

As supplies of silver steadily increased due to discoveries in the West, silver bullion prices were dropping. Therefore, fewer and fewer coin notes were needed to purchase the mandated 4.5 million ounces of silver each month—which meant that the money supply did not expand sufficiently to raise farm prices and incomes. Exasperated, silver mine owners, farm groups, and their allies made the decision to enter electoral politics. The People's, or Populist, party emerged in time for the 1892 presidential election. In fact, the greatest legacy of the Sherman Silver Purchase Act was not a meaningful change in monetary policy, but the creation of the Populist Party.

THE MCKINLEY TARIFF ACT

The increased pension spending resulting from the Dependent Pensions Act would eventually help reduce the budget surplus. Meanwhile, Republicans turned their attention to the tariff question, partly with the same issue in mind. Lowering the average tariff rate was an anathema to Republicans, of course. Besides, it might just increase government revenues by encouraging imports on which tariffs were paid. At the same time a large number of Americans were becoming concerned about the nature of tariff bills as predominantly special interest legislation, which in fact it was. The prices of some consumer items were too high because of the high tariffs as well. The tariff question was always a difficult one, but these budget and political concerns made it much trickier in 1890. By a laborious process of negotiations among politicians and special interest lobbyists, Congress finally passed a tariff bill in October 1890.

Named after Ohio Republican Representative William McKinley, chairman of the powerful House Ways and Means Committee, the McKinley Tariff Act raised the average tariffs to an all-time high—an average of 49.5 percent. By increasing the protective nature of the tariff through the highest rates in history up to that time, McKinley's bill not only discouraged but virtually prohibited many imports. In this way, federal revenues from tariffs would decline. The bill placed tariffs on some agricultural products for the first time in a move to win support among farm belt states. Certain items, such as raw sugar, coffee, and tea, were placed on the duty-free list, meaning that no tariffs would be levied on them. This action was taken to placate consumers, for whom sugar was especially an important necessity. Making sugar duty free cut the costs of American sugar refiners and lowered the price of sugar. It also encouraged the importing of even more Cuban sugar cane. To compensate Louisiana sugar growers for the increased competition from Cuban sugar the bill provided a 2-cent bounty on each pound of United States sugar, which would be paid out of the federal treasury and thereby further reduce the budget surplus. For the first time the principle of reciprocity was applied to tariff policy, although in a manner unlike modern tariff reciprocity agreements. Aimed primarily at Latin American producers of coffee, tea, and other items, the president was authorized to impose tariffs on duty-free imports in retaliation for what he determined to be unjust tariff rates on American goods entering foreign markets. This reciprocity feature only caused resentment among Latin Americans.

The still higher tariffs on most imported goods angered Americans by increasing consumer prices further. That fact, along with the extravagant spending on veterans' pensions, led to dramatic Democratic gains in the House of Representatives during the Congressional elections that year. The newly created western states, however, allowed the Republicans to maintain control in that body.

THE HOMESTEAD STEEL STRIKE

A major violent strike in 1892 contributed to public animosity toward labor unions. The showdown occurred outside of Pittsburgh at the Homestead Works of the Carnegie Steel Company. Andrew Carnegie was a paternalistic owner who seemed to believe that he personally knew what was best for his "children" (workers). Although expressing sympathy for workingmen, Carnegie's paternalistic mindset did not sit well with many workers. Adding to the strained relations was Henry C.

Frick, Carnegie's right-hand man, who had basically run company operations since his arrival in 1889.

Matters came to a head when the labor contract with the Amalgamated Association of Iron and Steel Workers expired in June of 1892. The craft union of skilled workers only represented 325 employees at the Homestead Works, less than 10 percent of the total workforce. Carnegie left for an extended vacation in his native Scotland in May of that year, leaving Frick in complete charge of the negotiations and instructing him to break the union. Frick demanded a 25 percent wage cut, and when a new agreement with the union was not reached by June 29, he broke off all talks and announced that he would no longer deal with the union. When Frick ordered a lockout of all union workers at the plant the non-union employees all voted to join in a strike. Frick promptly fired the entire workforce on July 2. Three hundred Pinkerton

Homestead, Pennsylvania Steel Strike, 1892. Credit: Library of Congress.

security guards, hired even before negotiations had ended, came up the river by barge on July 6. Workers, already dug in, met them with force as the Pinkertons approached the plant. No one knows who fired the first shot, but the all-day battle resulted in several deaths and even more injuries (authorities vary the number killed anywhere from 9 to 16). The surviving Pinkertons surrendered and were forced to run a gauntlet through a crowd of townspeople, most of whom were relatives of the strikers.

The Pennsylvania governor then sent 8,000 state militiamen to the site on July 12. A veritable fortress was built around the Homestead Works, equipped with observation platforms and gunholes, and the militia enabled Frick to employ strikebreakers to keep the plant running. Feelings ran deep as the embittered workers continued their strike for several months. But public opinion had begun turning against them after news that an anarchist had shot and wounded Frick on the 23rd of July. The strike eventually collapsed in late November, when workers returned under management terms. Frick had broken the union, but it had taken the proverbial tank to kill the fly.

REMAINING ISSUES

In 1890 Massachussetts Republican Henry Cabot Lodge proposed a bill to counter the movement toward disenfranchisement of black voters in the South. Lodge's bill would have provided procedures for federal courts to investigate election irregularities. It passed the House of Representatives but was defeated by a broad-based coalition in the U.S. Senate. It was the last Republican attempt to carry out the ideals of Reconstruction by ensuring the integrity of black voting rights. There would not be another major attempt until the Voting Rights Act of 1965, 75 years later.

President Harrison's Secretary of the Interior, John Noble from Missouri, won approval from Congress of the Forest Reserves Act in 1891. The new law empowered the president to protect forest lands west of the Mississippi River.

THE 1892 ELECTION

The Candidates

Problems were plentiful as the 1892 presidential election approached. Many Americans were unhappy about higher prices produced by the McKinley Tariff Act. Labor unrest was still continuing at the Homestead steel plant near Pittsburgh. Farmers and silver interests were furious over what they considered to be a series of betrayals over the monetary question. And still others were worried that the strong socialist movement developing in Europe might cross to this side of the Atlantic.

As if the Republicans didn't have enough problems that year, strained relations between Secretary of State James G. Blaine and President Benjamin Harrison forced Blaine to resign before the election. Blaine challenged Harrison for the party's presidential nomination; even William McKinley was a candidate. But in the end the Republicans renominated Benjamin Harrison and selected former U.S. ambassador to France and *New York Tribune* editor, Whitelaw Reid, as his running mate.

Although opposed by New York Democratic Governor David Hill, the Democrats nominated former President Grover Cleveland as their standard-bearer for the third consecutive presidential election. The convention nominated Adlai E. Stevenson, from Illinois, as its vice-presidential candidate. Stevenson was the grandfather of the Adlai E. Stevenson who later ran for president on the Democratic ticket twice in the 1950s.

In response to the Sherman Silver Purchase Act, agrarian reformers organized the People's, or Populist, party and fielded a candidate in the presidential election. This new third party arose from Farmers' Alliances and included such key leaders as Tom Watson (Georgia), Mary Elizabeth Lease (Kansas), "Sockless Jerry" Simpson (Kansas), and Ignatius Donnelly (Minnesota). Donnelly, a political journalist, wrote the Populist Party platform that year. When the convention met in Omaha, Nebraska that summer, the platform, nicknamed the "Farmers' Declaration of Independence," was adopted on the 4th of July. The Populist platform included the following major proposals: (1) federal government ownership of the railroads, telegraph, and telephone systems; (2) a graduated, or progressive, federal income tax—based on the premise that higher income persons had a greater responsibility and should be taxed at a higher rate; (3) the direct election of United States senators (then selected by the state legislature in each state); (4) adoption of the secret ballot in federal elections; (5) a subtreasury system in which the federal government would loan money to farmers with crops stored in government warehouses to be used as collateral; (6) shorter working hours; (7) immigration restriction; and (8) the "free and unlimited coinage of silver at 16 to 1." The Populists nominated James B. Weaver, a former Republican Congressman from Iowa, as their presidential candidate. To appeal to Southern voters, the Populists chose James G. Field, an ex-Confederate general from Virginia, to be Weaver's running mate.

The Campaign and Results

The election that year featured two separate battles. Both Harrison and Cleveland did their best to ignore Weaver. In the contest between them, the two major party candidates mainly debated the tariff issue, which tended to help the Democrats this time. Weaver ran against both Harrison and Cleveland, accusing both men of ignoring the vital issues of the day. Of course, Weaver made the free silver question the number one issue of his campaign. The Populist appeal was mostly in the Middle West and the South, where agriculture was still the major industry. Southern Democratic leaders were near panic in their concern that many Democratic voters in that region might turn to the Populists. Therefore, they began an openly racist effort for Southern whites to stick with the Democratic Party, or else face the possibility that the Republicans might walk through the back door and repeat their "plunder" of the South, as they had allegedly done during Reconstruction. Unfortunately for the Populists, this racist logic worked well for the Democrats and actually spawned renewed efforts to restrict black voting rights in the South even more throughout the remaining years of the decade.

When the votes were counted that November, it appeared that the Populists had hurt the Republicans in the West more than the Democrats. Former President Grover Cleveland won the election with a plurality of the popular votes. The electoral vote tally was 277 for Cleveland, 145 for President Harrison, and 22 for Weaver. The Populists carried the states of Kansas, Colorado, Nevada, and Idaho; and Weaver received one electoral vote each from North Dakota and Oregon. With 22 electoral votes, and more than 1 million popular votes, the Populist Party was the most successful third party since the Civil War, and a sign of protest from groups ignored by the two major parties.

1892	44	GROVER CLEVELAND	Democrat	5,555,426	277	46.1
		Benjamin Harrison	Republican	5,182,690	145	43.0
		James B. Weaver	People's	1,029,846	22	8.5
		John Bidwell	Prohibition	264,133		2.2

INTRODUCTION TO THE CLEVELAND ADMINISTRATION

Grover Cleveland's election victory in 1892 gave him the distinction of being the only president ever elected to two non-consecutive terms—1884 and 1892—a record which he still holds to this day. Unfortunately for Cleveland, his second term in the White House was far more problem-riddled than his first one had been. Besides the depression that hit the country early in his administration, the president also had problems with an early appointment to the Supreme Court. Justice Samuel Blatchford had died in July 1893. Cleveland wanted to appoint a fellow New Yorker in his place, but New York Senator David Hill stood in his way. An old Senate tradition said that the president ought to clear a major appointment with the senators of the appointee's home state. Hill, the former governor of New York, had played an important role in defeating Cleveland's bid for a second term in the 1888 election by denying him their mutual home state of New York. The president was in no mood to deal with Hill. But when Cleveland ignored Hill and nominated Joseph Pulitzer's lawyer, William Butler Hornblower, to fill the Supreme Court vacancy, Senator Hill was able to defeat the nomination in the Senate. Stubbornly defying Hill, the president then nominated Wheeler H. Peckham without Hill's advice and consent. Once again the nomination was rejected by the Senate. Finally, President Cleveland submitted Senator Edward D. White's name, from Louisiana, and White was confirmed the same day.

THE PANIC OF 1893

Grover Cleveland had the unfortunate fate of being sworn into office just weeks before a financial panic triggered another major economic depression. This depression of the 1890s would be worse than the one in the '70s and would last from the spring of 1893 until early 1897. Many underlying factors contributed to the depression. Depressed farm prices and income had eventually led to a considerable decrease in consumer demand for industrial products. No economy can tolerate an important sector to be in poor shape for very long until it affects the entire economy. This was the reason for so much farmer discontent during the Gilded Age. But unfortunately for the agricultural sector, the giants of the Industrial Revolution had eclipsed the American farmers in political clout. Speculation and mismanagement, led by the railroad companies, also plagued important industrial sectors of the economy, leaving the country vulnerable to any financial panic that could trigger a prolonged depression. The panic came just weeks after Cleveland had taken office in the spring of 1893.

The United States gold reserve had been established in 1879 to redeem greenbacks in gold in accordance with the Resumption Act. During the 1880s financial experts had come to believe that American finances would be sound as long as the gold reserve did not dip below $100 million. This was a pyschological belief caused by traditional confidence in the gold standard. In fact, what makes any monetary system function well is the confidence which the people have in it. Because of its beautiful reflecting qualities, its inability to tarnish, and its relative scarcity, gold has historically been man's most cherished commodity. In other words, like anything else, gold's value is really determined by the demand or desire for it. The pyschological confidence in our basically conservative monetary system was underminded when the United States gold reserve fell below the "magic" $100 million level in early 1893.

At least three factors played important roles in diminishing the reserve. One factor was the Treasury Department's policy of insisting that the coin notes issued under the Sherman Silver Purchase Act be redeemed only in gold. Another factor contributing to the decline in the gold reserve was the Harrison administration's big spending via war pensions and its excessively high McKinley tariff. Import duties were paid in gold, and the McKinley tariffs were so high that with the significant drop in imports came an equivalent decline in tariff revenue. Third, severe economic problems in Europe during the the 1880s had caused foreign investors to withdraw large amounts of gold from the United States by selling American stocks and redeeming them for gold. When the gold reserve fell below $100 million, many American holders of coin notes and greenbacks feared that their money might become worthless and rushed to redeem them in gold. This run on the banks restricted the available credit supply to the country, and the resulting higher interest rates further added to the economic woes of the nation. In 1893 alone, about 16,000 businesses went into bankruptcy. And by the summer of 1894, 4 million Americans were unemployed.

Repeal of the Sherman Silver Purchase Act

President Cleveland typified the conventional wisdom of his day when he repeatedly warned Americans that government could do nothing to help suffering human beings; they must simply hang on for the ride. Instead, Cleveland saw his main task as protecting the financial condition of the federal government. But his failure to comprehend the complex causes of the depression allowed him to focus on the gold standard. He blamed the Sherman Silver Purchase Act for being the sole cause of hard times because of its provision to buy silver bullion with coin notes that were redeemable in gold. Therefore, he called Congress into special session in August 1893 and urged the repeal of the Sherman Silver Purchase Act. The House voted to repeal the law late that same month. But the Senate Finance Committee Chairman, Indiana Democratic Senator Daniel W. Voorhees, opposed the president's request and held up the Senate vote on the repeal measure. After Cleveland agreed to allow Senator Voorhees to handpick all new federal appointees in his home state, Voorhees changed his attitude and the Senate voted for the repeal at the end of October.

The repeal of the Sherman Silver Purchase Act did nothing to halt the continuing decline in the gold reserve. In fact, all it accomplished was to split the Democratic Party into two monetary factions—the Gold Democrats under Cleveland and the Silver Democrats. The existence of these factions would spell disaster for the Democrats in the next election. Meanwhile, the gold reserve stood at $65 million in January of 1894. The president then ordered the sale of $50 million in federal bonds which could only be bought with gold. When this tactic failed to raise the gold reserve sufficiently, the president issued another $50 million bond sale in November of that same year. But since other factors were not affected by these moves, they did little to resolve the perceived gold crisis. By early 1895, the reserve was well below $50 million. Almost desperate, President Cleveland worked out a deal with investment bankers John Pierpont Morgan and August Belmont. In 1895 the federal government sold an entire new issue of gold bonds worth more than $60 million at a discount to the J.P. Morgan and Belmont Banking Company. In return, the company was permitted to sell them later for a handsome profit. This deal with Wall Street did manage to restore public confidence that the quasi gold standard would be maintained. And when the government ordered a $100 million gold bond issue for public sale in January 1896, they were quickly sold. On the other hand, Cleveland's Wall Street maneuver antagonized the reform wing of his own party and fueled Populist hopes for better results in the election that November.

COXEY'S ARMY

While conventional wisdom was ruling in Washington, D.C. as usual, there were growing demands for federal action to combat the depression. The most significant of these demands came from an eccentric Ohio businessman, Jacob S. Coxey. In 1894 Coxey called for the federal government to print $500 million in new paper money in order to finance a large public works program. This money would not be backed by gold but simply be designated as "legal tender," just as our money is today. He demanded that the unemployed be hired for 8-hour days to repair public roads, bridges, and other parts of the country's infrastructure. Beginning in March 1894, Coxey led a March on Washington to build popular support for his ideas. Several hundred arrived in the nation's capital by late April. Police broke up the demonstration in Washington, which had no political effect on the government. Coxey himself paid a $5 fine and spent 20 days in jail for walking on the grass and carrying a sign without a permit. Coxey's reputation as an eccentric—he had named his son Legal Tender Coxey—helped cause most Americans to ignore his ideas. Of course, the dominance of economic conservative thinking was the major factor in the lack of a positive response. Actually, Coxey was just ahead of his time; in the Great Depression of the 1930s his basic ideas were behind the massive public works programs of the New Deal.

THE PULLMAN RAILROAD STRIKE

The Pullman Palace Car Company made the famous Pullman sleepers and diners for the railroad industry. Owner George Pullman had built what he called a model town just south of Chicago, Illinois, called Pullman. His workers rented living quarters from him, shopped at company town stores, and took care of virtually all their necessities within easy distance of the plant. Pullman held a paternalistic attitude toward his employees, believing that he personally knew what was best for them. At the same time, he employed a network of spies to keep everyone in line. This paternalism did not go over well with much of his workforce, some of whom had joined the newly created American Railway Union.

In 1894 the nation was in the depths of a depression. Pullman used this economic downturn as an excuse to lay off workers and reduce wages. At the same time, however, he did not reduce the rent or store prices which he charged his workers. Furthermore, the company had a surplus of some $25 million. The American Railway Union began a strike there in May of that year. When Pullman still refused to negotiate with the union, ARU president Eugene V. Debs called for a nationwide boycott of trains with Pullman cars. The strike spread as railroad workers who refused to handle Pullman cars in other parts of the country were fired. By summer the Pullman strike had become a national railroad strike affecting the western two-thirds of the nation.

The General Managers' Association (GMA), acting for the railroads, brought in unemployed workers from the eastern part of the country to be used as strikebreakers. Then it asked Illinois Governor John P. Altgeld to send in the state militia, allegedly to keep the peace. There had been considerable violence in the Chicago area, although much of it had been perpetrated by management so they could blame the union and win public support for their cause. Democratic Governor Altgeld was sympathetic to organized labor and refused the GMA request. At that point, the association went to United States Attorney-General Richard Olney, who had been an anti-union lawyer, and who was currently on several railroad companies' boards of directors, and asked him to secure a federal court injunction against the strikers for their alleged refusal to move the United States mail. The fact was that union strikers had volunteered to place cars carrying the mail on to trains that did not include Pullman cars. But the railroad companies refused to allow this exactly because they hoped to win sympathy by their own delay of the mail.

Olney had little trouble finding a federal judge willing to issue a labor injunction ordering the strikers back to work. The ruling was based on the "restraint of trade" clause in the 1890 Sherman Antitrust Act, which had forbidden conspiracies "in restraint of trade." Designed as a legal weapon against trusts and monopolies, the antitrust law was turned on its head and used against the strikers. The next year the Supreme Court upheld the lower court ruling in decision known as *In Re Debs*. This set a precedent for federal courts to issue labor injunctions virtually at will for almost the next forty years. In the meantime, Debs and the ARU refused to order its members back to work. That placed Debs in contempt of court, and he spent the next six months in jail. He came out of jail a confirmed socialist.

When strikers refused to obey the court order, Attorney-General Olney persuaded President Cleveland to send 2,000 federal troops to the Chicago area in early July to "protect" the mail. The president sent the troops despite the fact that the Constitution prohibits such an action unless a state governor or legislature requests it. After initial rioting, in which over 65 persons were killed or wounded, the presence of federal troops calmed the situation and ended the strike. By late July the Pullman strike was over. Once again the power of government was united with corporate efforts to bust a labor strike. It would be the next century before government and public attitudes toward labor disputes would alter significantly.

THE WILSON-GORMAN TARIFF ACT

Although the depression and the Pullman Railroad Strike had occupied a large amount of the president's time, Grover Cleveland did push Congress to lower the tariff rates. The depression had eliminated the earlier $100 million budget surplus and turned it into a $70 million deficit by 1894. If the McKinley tariff rates, which averaged about 49 percent, could be significantly reduced, the lower tariffs could actually result in more federal revenue by encouraging a sharp rise in foreign imports. That's why a lower tariff was sometimes called a revenue tariff. Under the leadership of Democratic Representative William L. Wilson of West Virginia, the House passed a tariff reduction bill much to the liking of President Cleveland.

In the Senate, however, protectionist Democrats led by Arthur P. Gorman of Maryland, passed a far different version. When the conference committee had completed ironing out the differences between the two versions, the resulting Wilson-Gorman Tariff Act (August 1894) provided for only a modest net reduction of about 10 percent. Cleveland was so unhappy that a Democratic Congress could not do a better job of reducing tariffs that he allowed the bill to become law without his signature. In a surprise reform move, however, the final bill included a small federal income tax of 2 percent on incomes over $4,000 per year. Few Americans earned such sums in the 1890s, but it was the first income tax since the equally insignificant one passed to help finance the Civil War (and which had been allowed to expire a few years after the war). But it was shortlived; in April of 1895, the Supreme Court ruled by a 5-4 vote, in *Pollock v. The Farmers' Loan and Trust Company* , that the income tax provision was unconstitutional on the grounds that the Constitution prohibited a "direct" tax on United States citizens. This decision created a national drive by reformers to adopt a constitutional amendment permitting a federal income tax. Such an amendment, the Sixteenth, would be added to the Constitution in 1913.

THE 1896 ELECTION

The Candidates

Large Republican gains in the 1894 Congressional elections had bolstered that party's chances to regain the White House in the 1896 presidential contest. The country was still suffering its worst economic depression up to that time. Although Cleveland could not accurately be blamed for the depression, the mass of voters always blame the party in the White House during such bad times. Certainly his actions concerning gold bonds and Wall Street dealing had hurt the president among the more liberal, populist wing of his party, as did his role in the Pullman strike. With a divided Democratic Party, the Republicans could have nominated almost anyone and carried the election.

Several prominent Republicans sought their party nomination at the Republican convention that summer. Former House Speaker "Czar" Thomas Reed, Pennsylvania boss Matthew Quay, former President Benjamin Harrison, and Ohio Governor William McKinley all hoped to win the nomination. Reed and Quay had made too many enemies with their politically ruthless tactics, and Harrison had the image of a loser since Cleveland had beaten him four years earlier. Besides, former President Harrison, age 62, had married a 37-year old woman earlier in the year. And that didn't go over very well. McKinley, the former Congressman of the McKinley tariff fame, was nominated partly because of his reputation for honesty and party activism. Of course, Ohio was still a very important state in electoral politics also. The convention selected Garret A. Hobart, a New Jersey corporation lawyer, as McKinley's running mate.

The Democrats put on quite a show at their national convention in 1896. Cleveland's "Gold" Democrats were challenged by the growing liberal, populist wing of the party. The early front runner was Richard Bland, the congressman from Missouri who had co-sponsored the Bland-Allison Act back in 1878. But William Jennings Bryan, a former Congressman from Nebraska, emerged at the convention as the undisputed leader of the populist Democrats. In fact, the Populist Party had already met and nominated Bryan as their candidate for president before the Democrats opened their convention. With the outcome still in doubt, Bryan delivered an electrifying speech that brought his supporters to their feet in a standing ovation. In his famous "Cross of Gold" Speech, Bryan attacked the conservative gold standard advocates with the following words: "You shall not press down upon the brow of labor this crown of thorns, you shall not crucify mankind upon a cross of gold." That speech is often credited as providing the emotional momentum that made Bryan the Democratic nominee. The Populists had nominated Tom Watson of Georgia as Bryan's running mate, but in a move that angered Populist Party leaders, the Democratic convention named Arthur Sewall, a Maine shipbuilder, as its vice-presidential candidate.

When the Democrats nominated Bryan, the "Gold," or Cleveland, Democrats walked out of the convention and nominated their own ticket. Illinois Senator John M. Palmer, a Cleveland supporter, was chosen by the renegade Democrats to be their standard-bearer. And a former Confederate general, Simon B. Buckner, was announced as Palmer's running mate. It was their desire to intentionally give the election to McKinley. The fact that party leaders loyal to Cleveland tried to defeat the regular Democratic nominee demonstrated the deep feelings that many people had about the money question in the Gilded Age.

The Campaign and Results

With Bryan as the candidate of two parties that year, the campaign was essentially a two-man race between Bryan and McKinley. The Republican platform defended the Republican high tariff policy as being beneficial to workers as well as industrialists. It blamed the Democratic Party as the party of economic depression and gave praise to civil service reform. Marcus Hanna, an Ohio industrialist and party leader, became the new chairman of the Republican National Committee and ran the McKinley campaign as his campaign manager. Hanna knew that McKinley was no match for Bryan's oratorical skills, so he had McKinley conduct a "front porch" campaign, in which newspapermen and others were brought to McKinley's home in Canton, Ohio, to hear the candidate issue formal statements. Hanna spent somewhere between $10 million and $15 million on campaign buttons, pamphlets, and other publicity activities—a stupendous sum in those days.

The Democratic platform in 1896 called for the "free and unlimited coinage of silver," lower tariffs, a progressive income tax, and an end to labor injunctions. William Jennings Bryan campaigned with Sewall as a Democrat, leaving Tom Watson with little formal campaigning to do. Bryan took advantage of his oratorical ability to capture huge crowds by becoming the first major presidential candidate to travel extensively throughout the country. With only a few hundred thousand dollars, Bryan traveled about 18,000 miles and delivered about 600 speeches dur-

William Jennings Bryan, July 3, 1908. Credit: Library of Congress.

ing the exhausting campaign. The irony was, that as a populist, Bryan did his cross-country traveling by railroad. Bryan was successful in making the "free silver" question the number one issue in the election. Presidential candidates who are successful in making their agenda the focus of the campaign usually win the election by putting their opponents on the defensive. But making "free silver" the most significant issue in this campaign did not help Bryan. The idea was simply too unpopular.

William McKinley won the election handily with 271 electoral votes. Bryan received 149 electoral votes as the Democratic candidate and 27 as the Populist candidate, for a total of 176 votes. Palmer, the "Gold" Democrat in the race, received a disappointing 135,000 popular votes and not a single electoral vote. McKinley had won the presidency, but the conservative Democrats could not take credit for his victory.

The 1896 election proved to be the most important presidential election since Abraham Lincoln's victory in 1860. It gave the Republicans such a clear popular majority that the party would dominate American politics, with the exception of just eight years, until the first election of Franklin D. Roosevelt in 1932. It also destroyed the Populist Party and pushed the Democrats back to their more conservative base in the South.

1896	45	WILLIAM MCKINLEY	Republican	7,102,246	271	51.5
		William J. Bryan	Democrat	6,492,559	176	47.7

ADDITIONAL READINGS

Ruth Bordin, *Women and Temperance: The Quest for Power and Liberty 1873-1900* (1981). Relates the history of the WCTU to other campaigns for women's emancipation in the late nineteenth century and highlights the leadership of Frances E. Willard. Demonstrates the central position of temperance in the political struggles of the era.

John G. Cawelti, *Apostles of the Self-made Man* (1965). Examines the popular cultural obsession with the idea of success. Analyzes the myths behind the notion of equal opportunity for all, and the methods of popularizing success in the various media of the time.

Lawrence Goodwyn, *Democratic Promise: The Populist Moment in America* (1976). The most detailed study of populism. Focuses on the economic cooperation and visionary schemes that preceded the Populist campaigns of the 1890s. Shows that populism was above all a movement aimed at turning back the monopolistic trend in the market economy and returning power to the nation's citizens.

William S. McFeely, *Grant: A Biography* (1981). The standard biography of this key Civil War general and Reconstruction era president.

Nell Irvin Painter, *Standing at Armageddon: The United States 1877–1919* (1987). Presents a broad overview of racial and industrial conflicts and the political movements that formed in their wake. Attempts to show that this period proved decisive to the future of the United States.

Thomas C. Reeves, *Gentleman Boss: The Life of Chester Alan Arthur* (1975). A detailed treatment of President Arthur as a product of a particular stage in the American political system. Analyzes the conflicts within the Republican party and the chaos of the Democratic party, which made Arthur's rise possible, and his brief presidency of lasting importance.

CHAPTER FIVE

Social History: 1870–1920

MAJOR EVENTS

1876   National League (baseball) formed

1879   Henry George, *Progress and Poverty*

1881   Tuskegee Institute founded

1883   Civil Rights Cases

1888   Edward Bellamy, *Looking Backward*

1889   Jane Addams founds Hull House in Chicago

1890   Jacob Riis, *How the Other Half Lives*

1895   Booker T. Washington addresses Cotton States Exposition in Atlanta
Lillian Wald establishes Henry Street Settlement in New York
Coney Island opens

1896   *Plessy v. Ferguson* opens the way for segregated public schools

1898   Florence Kelley becomes general secretary of National Consumers League

1909   Founding of the National Association for the Advancement of Colored People (NAACP)

1911   Triangle Shirtwaist Company fire kills 146 garment workers in New York City
The Masses magazine begun by socialist Max Eastman

1913   Margaret Sanger begins writing and speaking in support of birth control for women

INTRODUCTION

The late nineteenth century period of the Industrial Revolution had been dubbed the "Gilded Age" by authors Mark Twain and Charles Dudley Warner in their novel, *The Gilded Age*, published in 1873. It gradually came to be the accepted term for the entire period up to the turn of the century because it accurately described the period of time in which wealth and power obscured the reality of numerous pressing social problems. But as the nation moved toward the twentieth century, labor unrest, poverty, and the trend toward the elimination of competition by the captains of industry forced Americans to reevaluate their entire culture. A new chapter in American political thought was emerging by the turn of the century. It concerned a debate between those who favored the status quo and those who advocated that government should regulate big business on behalf of the public interest.

THE DOMINANT ECONOMIC AND POLITICAL PHILOSOPHY

Laissez-faire

In 1776, British political economist Adam Smith, in his book *The Wealth of Nations*, had argued for government to take a laissez-faire approach to the economy. Laissez-faire is a compound French word which, in the political-economic arena, has been defined as "hands off." In other words, government should keep its hands off economic activity. Smith argued that self-interest acted as an "invisible hand" in the marketplace, automatically regulating the fundamental law of supply and demand. The idea meant that government should provide for law and order and protect private property, but it should not become involved in business affairs.

In the late eighteenth and early nineteenth centuries, more politically liberal thinkers, such as Thomas Jefferson, James Madison, and Andrew Jackson had argued in favor of laissez-faire. Their reasoning was that American society was dominated by relatively small farmers, artisans, and merchants, and they wanted that to continue because they viewed this condition (of general equality for white males) as necessary for a healthy democracy. When more conservative leaders, like Alexander Hamilton, John Quincy Adams, and Henry Clay, pushed for an active central government to encourage more manufacturing, to establish a national bank, and to provide funding for internal improvements (roads, bridges, and canals), liberals reacted by asserting that these efforts would establish a powerful economic elite that would endanger democracy in the long run.

As the Industrial Revolution was beginning to change the face of the country, some farmers and other groups began to demand that states, then the federal government, regulate big business. Then industrialists and their allies, who tended to dominate the Republican Party, began using laissez-faire rhetoric to thwart those reform efforts. At the same time, Americans in the Jacksonian tradition (ie., Democrats) were slow to believe that the national government might be used to promote a more general state of equality. Therefore, the Jacksonian laissez-faire position ironically became a justification for unregulated power by the giants of industry. That is why liberal reformers were in the minority in both political parties during the Gilded Age, and why many of them turned to the Populist movement in the

Charles Darwin. Credit: Trustees of the British Museum (Natural History).

1890s. It was not until the public as a whole perceived dangers in unregulated economic power that progressive, or liberal, reformers took control of both parties in what history records as the Progressive Era (1901–1917).

To some degree, however, the federal government had always been involved in the economy, although minimally compared with modern times. Examples included relatively high tariff rates to protect American industries, land grants and loans to railroad companies, and conservative monetary policies. The rhetoric of most Americans continued to mouth the ideas of rugged individualism and laissez-faire, but the individual initiative of some Americans, for better or for worse, was assisted by the federal government. And although the Gilded Age is described as a time of laissez-faire, even minimal government assistance is not consistent with a strict definition of the term. In the Gilded Age, what most supporters of laissez-faire really meant was that government should not restrict, or regulate, business activity. Thus, a popular expression since the days of the Industrial Revolution has been, "The government of business is no part of the business of government."

Social Darwinism

Another argument picked up and employed by many conservatives in their struggle with reformers and other liberals became known as Social Darwinism. Charles Darwin, the British naturalist, had published his controversial book, *On the Origin of Species by Natural Selection*, in 1859. Few people actually read Darwin's work for themselves, but his theory of biological evolution became widely known through the writings of several popular authors. The most significant of these early popularizers of Darwin was a British social scientist named Herbert Spencer. In the book *First Principle*, published in 1864, Spencer coined the phrase "survival of the fittest" to describe the Darwinian view that in the natural world only the fittest of each species survives. Darwin had taught that this was a good thing because the healthiest would ensure the longrange survival of the species itself. Spencer, in his book, applied the "survival of the fittest" concept to social and economic life among human beings. Humans, he said, evolve psychologically and socially, and move inevitably toward perfection, which is measured in material terms. Therefore, if a person becomes wealthy and powerful, he is helping mankind move more quickly toward perfection.

William Graham Sumner, a professor of sociology at Yale University, was the foremost American intellectual champion of Social Darwinism. In a series of essays and in his book *What Social Classes Owe to Each Other* (1883), Sumner praised absolute competition as the only way for individuals to improve themselves. Wealthy individuals and big business tycoons had simply proven themselves to be the fittest. Such individuals were part of a natural aristocracy, which was good for the society as a whole. Any attempts to interfere with this natural selection process were doomed to fail because they would hurt society and ultimately harm the very individuals such reforms were intended to help.

Elbert Hubbard was a Social Darwinist who edited many popular magazines, such as *The Philistine*. In an 1899 essay entitled "The Message to Garcia," based on the Spanish-American War, Hubbard referred to a "natural aristocracy" of successful people, whom he identified as an elite to redeem the world. Such persons, wrote Hubbard, never ask for higher wages, never strike, and never complain. Everyone who was not part of this aristocracy was morally deformed, especially the reformers and preachers.

On the religious front, two of the most influential Protestant ministers took leading roles in advancing the Social Darwinist movement. Russell H. Conwell, a Baptist minister who founded Temple University in Philadelphia, became a popular lecturer in the Gilded Age. His most famous lecture, which he delivered some 6,000 times, was entitled "Acres of Diamonds." In an attempt to tell people how to become rich, Conwell declared that to make money honestly is to preach the gospel. At the same time, he said that personal wealth should be used for the public good.

The most influential Protestant minister in his day was the Reverend Henry Ward Beecher, a brother to Harriet Beecher Stowe (of *Uncle Tom's Cabin* fame) and pastor of the Plymouth Congregational Church in Brooklyn, New York. Beecher declared that it was everyone's divine duty to get as rich as possible. Those who were poor deserved to fail in life. Beecher vehemently opposed labor unions and urged that a reserve of immigrants be organized in order to be used as strikebreakers during major labor strikes. And Beecher also advocated the use of force to put down labor strikes. Naturally, he also opposed the movement for an eight-hour day as something which would encourage laziness on the part of industrial workers. Beecher wanted to become president of the United States. Therefore, he allowed his name to be used in advertising, such as for women's underwear, and he became involved in some of financier Jay Gould's schemes. A sex scandal involving the wife of one of his

Reverend Henry Ward Beecher. Credit: Ewing Galloway, New York.

own friends in his church resulted in a decline in Beecher's national standing and ruined whatever chances he might have had to become president.

Other prominent Social Darwinists included Harvard historian John Fiske, Johns Hopkins University History Department Chairman Herbert Baxter Adams, and University of Chicago anthropologist Frederick Starr.

SOCIAL REFORMERS

Among a new breed of thinkers, Lester Frank Ward led the intellectual assault on laissez-faire and Social Darwinism. Ward served as a geologist for the federal government until he accepted an invitation from Brown University in 1906 to serve as a professor of sociology. Some have even called him the father of American sociology. Ward was a Darwinist like William Graham Sumner, but unlike Sumner, Ward believed that human beings had the ability to direct their own evolutionary development. In his most influential book, *Dynamic Sociology*, published in 1883, Ward argued that natural law could be superceded by human will. He pointed to man's use of controlled breeding in cattle as a parallel to his possible use of government to regulate big business and help guide the societal evolutionary development. And in *Psychic Factors of Civilization* (1893), Ward again urged Americans to support the idea that government should use social planning to shape mankind's social evolution. Pointing out the hypocrisy among defenders of unregulated capitalism, Ward alleged that "those who dismiss state interference are the ones who most frequently and successfully invoke it."

Another prominent critic of the dominant Gilded Age philosophy was Henry George, a self-taught newspaper editor and writer who spent a number of years in San Francisco. George was concerned about the great inequality of wealth in the United States. In 1879 he wrote a book, *Progress and Poverty*, in which he blamed the inequality on the fact that a few land speculators could profit from rising land values and yet do nothing to develop the land. They simply took advantage of the rise of land prices resulting chiefly from climbing urban populations. So George argued for what he called the "single tax" idea, a steep tax on land sales that would put an end to most land speculation. This single tax, he wrote, would also eliminate the need for other taxes. And he claimed that an additional benefit would be the absence of a need for a heavy government intervention that would stifle individual initiative. Henry George's single tax idea became so popular in some areas that he only narrowly lost the race for mayor of New York City in 1886 on the Labor Party ticket.

Another newspaper editor and writer, Edward Bellamy from Massachussetts, influenced a number of Americans with a more visionary proposal of what human society should be like. In 1888 he published a novel called *Looking Backward: 2000-1887*, which described Boston and the entire country in the year 2000. The nation had evolved into a utopian society by that year, and Bellamy attributed this peaceful, orderliness to two factors—government ownership of all the means of production on behalf of everyone and a new religion of solidarity. Everyone shared equally in material rewards, and there were no lawyers, politicians, or class divisions left. Bellamy called his ideas "Nationalism." Within a short time after the publication of his book, almost 500 Nationalist clubs were formed all over the country. These Nationalist clubs pressed for civil service reform, government ownership of the railroads and public utilities, and other similar reforms. Bellamy's Nationalism looked a lot like socialism, but he himself avoided that term because he disliked Marxists and he knew that most Americans labeled socialism as communism or anarchism.

Thorstein Veblen, a Norwegian-American economist from Minnesota, added his voice to the intellectuals calling for major social reforms. In his book *The Theory of the Leisure* Class (1899), Veblen used much satire in characterizing the lives and values of the Gilded Age elite. In common with others calling for reform, Veblen also believed that man could shape his society by using scientific and technical expertise. Veblen's writings were too satiric to be widely read and understood, but many intellectuals did read them and were influenced to work to change the status quo.

Other major voices of protest included Richard T. Ely, Edward A. Ross, Charles and Mary Beard, and Herbert Croly. As an economist at John Hopkins University in the 1880s, Richard T. Ely had attacked laissez-faire ideas. Later, as president of the American Economic Association and at the University of Wisconsin, Ely actively supported the progressive Wisconsin governor, Robert M. LaFollette, in his efforts for reform legislation. Ely was also sympathetic to organized labor. Edward A. Ross was a sociologist at Stanford University who later moved to the University of Wisconsin. Ross attacked the tendency of Social Darwinists to compare the behavior of jungle animals with human industrial society.

Some historians also led the way for a new reform philosophy. Historian James H. Robinson, in *The New History*, published in 1912, encouraged historians to examine the events of history in order to determine the evolution of human society. Charles and his wife Mary Beard accepted the challenge given by Robinson and others. Mary Beard brought a new emphasis to women and labor unions in books such as *Woman's Work in Municipalities* (1915) and *A Short History of the American Labor Movement* (1920). However, her husband Charles contributed the most controversial work of historical interpretation when he wrote *An Economic Interpretation of the Constitution* in 1913. Although largely discredited among historians today, Beard's thesis was that the Founding Fathers at the Constitutional Convention in 1787 were primarily motivated by greed in their writing of the Constitution. They allegedly gave the young nation a Constitution which was designed to serve the interests of the economic elite. It is now widely believed that Beard was guilty of applying the economic and political philosophy of the Progressive Era to the Constitutional period in order to promote more progressive reforms in his own day.

Journalist Herbert Croly was an intellectual and philosophical ally of former President Theodore Roosevelt, who made a bid for the White House in 1912 as a third party candidate. Philosophically, Croly argued that a strong federal government needed to play an important role in regulating big business and in serving the needs of all Americans rather than just the wealthy industrialists. Croly stated his case most significantly in *The Promise of American Life*, which he wrote in 1909.

THE MUCKRAKERS

While intellectuals were undermining the status quo from a more philosophical approach, a large group of journalists and novelists took up the banner of reform. As early as 1894 Chicago journalist Henry Demarest Lloyd had attacked the monopoly power of the Standard Oil Company in his *Wealth Against Commonwealth*. This successful work paved the way for a new wave of journalistic exposes at the beginning of the twentieth century. Frank Norris, for example, hit the railroad industry in *The Octopus*, published in 1901. The door was then opened to a flood of exposes on corruption and abuse of power within both private industries and government.

These early twentieth century writers became known as muckrakers in 1906, when President Theodore Roosevelt gave them that nickname. Roosevelt sympathized with the need for major social reforms but was unhappy with the trend toward sensationalism which characterized much of these exposes. Remembering that John Bunyan's seventeenth century Christian classic, *Pilgrim's Progress*, had a character who enthusiastically dug up filth with his muckrake, Roosevelt coined the term "muckrakers" to describe these zealous reform-minded writers.

Historians generally date the beginning of the intense muckraking period to October 1902, when *McClure's Magazine*, published by S.S. McClure, printed an expose on corruption in several city governments. This expose, written by Lincoln Steffens and Claude H. Wetmore, was published in 1904 with the title *The Shame of the Cities*. Other magazines, such as *Collier's*, *Cosmopolitan*, and *Everybody's*, emerged as sources of muckraking exposes. Ida M. Tarbell, a female reporter for *McClure's Magazine*, wrote a series of articles that became the *History of the Standard Oil Company* in 1904. *Treason of the Senate*, written by David Graham Phillips, appeared in book form in 1906, as did Upton Sinclair's *The Jungle* in that same year. After President Roosevelt read *The Jungle*, he pushed Congress to pass the Meat Inspection Act. The irony is that Sinclair had meant to write an expose on the poor working conditions in Chicago's meatpacking plants. Instead, the country, like the president, focused on the quality of meat products being prepared and sold to American consumers.

Finley Peter Dunne was the best known newspaper political humorist of the late 1890s and early twentieth century. Dunne created a fictional character called Mr. Dooley, an Irish-American from Chicago. Mr. Dooley used humor and satire to call attention to specific issues that Dunne wanted to see reformed. Dunne's efforts to promote a reform spirit were a different but successful complement to the more straightforward serious approach of most muckrakers.

After 1910, muckraking declined sharply for a number of important reasons. For one thing, writers were actually running out of material to criticize. And of course, part of their decline can be attributed to their success in forcing several reforms in society. And lastly, the public had grown tired of reading about one corrupt crisis after another. When public demand had softened, the intense period of muckraking came to an end.

SOCIALIST REACTION

Most American reformers accepted the basic tenents of the capitalist economic system. They simply wanted to civilize it through a series of reforms. However, a relatively small group took a more radical approach to the problems resulting from industrialization. Their philosophical founder was the German writer Karl Marx, who lived from 1818 to 1883. Marx had expounded his views in such works as *The Communist Manifesto* (1844) and *Das Kapital* (1867). Marxism was founded on the principle that only the labor used to make a product was responsible for its true value. All profit made by capitalists, then, was "surplus value," which was stolen through the exploitation of their workers. Marx said that all history was the struggle between the haves and the have-nots, what he called the bourgeoisie and the proletariat, respectively. Under capitalism, Marx predicted that the economic and power gap between these two classes would eventually reach a crisis point in which the proletariat (workers) would overthrow the bourgeoisie (capitalists and their allies) and create a classless society where the workers controlled the means of production and distribution. The millennium of peace and prosperity would arrive when human nature had perfected itself and the necessity for government had gone. The state would then simply "wither away."

Marxism never did attract large numbers of American workers or intellectuals. Nevertheless, it did appeal to some disenchanted with the chaos and inequities created by the Industrial Revolution. Often these were new immigrants, primarily of German stock. Socialist political parties were formed in several major cities right after the end of the Civil War. The National Labor Reform Party was created on a national scale, but it drew less than 30,000 votes in the 1868 presidential election. In 1877 a decidedly Marxist organization, the Socialist Labor Party, was created. In its early days, the Socialist Labor Party avoided politics and tried to win control of labor unions. But most unions resisted the socialist movement, and the Socialist Labor Party was unsuccessful in these efforts. By 1890 the SLP had attracted only about 1,500 members.

In the early 1890s, Daniel DeLeon united the various SLP factions, for which he was nicknamed the "socialist pope." DeLeon steered the party toward electoral politics in the '90s, but those efforts went badly, partly because he was perceived to be closely aligned with the Russian communist Vladimir Lenin. Eugene V. Debs, the president of the American Railway Union who had led the famous Pullman strike in 1894 (see Chapter Four), formed a rival socialist group called the Social Democratic Party in 1897. The democratic socialists, which were more common than the more doctrinaire radicals, bolted from DeLeon's leadership in the Socialist Labor Party and united with Debs' Social Democratic Party to create the Socialist Party of America in 1901. Prominent leaders in the new organization included Eugene Debs, Morris Hillquit, a Russian-Jewish immigrant and labor organizer in New York City, and Victor Berger, the German-American leader of the democratic socialists in Milwaukee, Wisconsin. Debs was chosen to head the new party and was easily the most eloquent spokesman for democratic socialism in America until his death in 1926. Debs had become a socialist while in prison for contempt of court for failing to do anything to help end the Pullman strike in 1894. He was the Socialist Party candidate for president five different times between 1900 and 1920.

His best results came in the 1912 election, when he polled about 900,000 votes, which was about 6 percent of the popular vote. (He won a few thousand more popular votes in 1920, but they represented less of the votes percentage-wise.)

The Socialist Party advocated a reduction in the number of hours per work day, the creation of an unemployment insurance system, government ownership of the railroads, telegraphs, telephones, and other public utilities, and certain political reforms, such as the referendum, intiative, and recall. Many of these reform desires were shared by the progressives of the period, but the socialists denounced those reformers for what they said was only tinkering with the capitalist system.

In 1910 the Socialist Party in Milwaukee elected Emil Seidel as that city's mayor and Victor Berger as its Congressman in the House of Representatives. By 1912 thirty-three cities had Socialist mayors, including Butte, Montana, Berkeley, California, and Flint and Jackson, Michigan. The party owned 5 English daily newspapers, 8 foreign-language daily papers, and a host of weekly and monthly publications. Although most of its support came from workers and intellectuals in the big cities, the party did build coalitions with farmers and tenants in the Southwest. In the 1912 presidential election, Oklahoma gave Eugene Debs 16.5 percent of the popular vote, the highest he ever received from any state in the Union.

The year 1912 proved to be the peak year for the Socialist Party. The party was badly divided over the issue of United States participation in World War I. Then the successful Bolshevik Revolution in Russia in 1917, and the subsequently organized American Communist party, further divided the socialists. And the Socialist Party never recovered any electoral strength, partly also because Franklin D. Roosevelt's New Deal incorporated many of their reform ideas into federal law during the 1930s. That has been typical of American political history. One of the two major political parties eventually adopt ideas which were first advanced by more radical, third-party organizations. As for the Socialists, they eventually ended participation in electoral politics and transformed themselves into the Social Democratic Party, which today engages in educational efforts, often in coordination with labor and other left-of-center democratic institutions.

THE INDUSTRIAL WORKERS OF THE WORLD

The Industrial Workers of the World (IWW) represented a more violent-oriented reaction to the excesses of capitalism. Organized in Chicago in June 1905, the IWW had grown out of frustration among the miners and lumberers of the western states. The Western Federation of Miners, organized at Butte, Montana in 1893, had been involved in a number of violent clashes with mine owners, who had employed private armies of their own against the miners in states like Colorado and Idaho. Opposing the conservative craft unionism of the American Federation of Labor, western miners and several leading socialists formed the Industrial Workers of the World in 1905. Like the former Knights of Labor, the IWW advocated the organizing of all industrial workers, skilled, unskilled, men, women, and immigrants, into their one big union. But unlike the Knights of Labor, the Wobblies, as they came to be known, preached a violent class warfare and dreamed of a day in which all government would disappear and be replaced by one big union. How that one big union would govern was never really addressed. The Wobblies denounced reforms achieved through the political process and instead favored the use of the mass strike and acts of sabotage in order to achieve their goals. Despite this rhetoric and the actual use of some violence, the violent exploits that legend has attributed to the Wobblies has been exaggerated.

The Wobblies were led by William D. "Big Bill" Haywood, a former member of the Western Federation of Miners who, along with a partner, were acquitted in 1895 of charges of complicity in the assassination of the governor of Idaho. Haywood was a formidable man of over six feet tall, strong and muscular, who often wore an eyepatch over one eye to cover an old injury. Other colorful leaders in the IWW included "Mother" Jones, an Illinois coal mine union organizer, and Elizabeth Gurley Flynn, an Irish-American woman with a fiery rhetoric who once chained herself to a lamppost to delay her arrest during a labor strike. Then there was the Swedish-American Joe Hill, a labor organizer and songwriter who became the Wobblies' martyr when he was executed by a firing squad in Utah after a conviction for murder. Just before his death, Hill wrote his last words to "Big Bill" Haywood: "Goodbye, Bill. I die like a true blue rebel. Don't waste any time mourning. Organize."

The most significant victory for the IWW came in a textile strike at Lawrence, Massachusetts in 1912, in which Elizabeth Gurley Flynn played a major role. The strike resulted in a wage increase, overtime pay, and other significant benefits. But 1912 proved to be the peak year for the Wobblies. An internal debate over United States participation in World War I, as well as growing public fear and anger over labor violence, led to the IWW's massive problems. During the war, the federal government prosecuted several Wobblie leaders under the Sedition Act for their vocal opposition to the war. Estimates of IWW membership numbers vary widely, from 60,000 to 150,000 at any given time. Whatever the precise number, the Wobblies were never a significant factor after the war.

THE CHILD LABOR PROBLEM

Industrialization seemed to provide both blessings and curses. Technology was providing new products that made life more convenient at home. Developments in communications, transportation, and the new movie industry promised an exciting future even as these things were already changing the American lifestyle. And mass production techniques were lowering prices of many manufactured goods. At the same time, the average real income of industrial workers, adjusted for inflation, rose from $532 per year in the late nineteenth century to $687 per year in 1915. Despite these conditions, the typical industrial worker barely had sufficient funds to support his family. In addition to this unpleasant reality, the average worker in 1900 worked about 9 1/2 hours per day, despite repeated calls for an eight-hour day since the 1880s. And in some industries, such as the textile mills, workdays consisted of 12 or 13 hours.

Many families, especially among the new immigrants, felt compelled to send their children off to work in the mines or factories in order to make ends meet. Americans had a long tradition of their children working on the family farms. And from the employers' point of view, a child could be paid anywhere from one-third to

Children working in coal mines. Credit: International Museum of Photography at George Eastman House

three-fourths what an adult doing the same work would cost. As a result, the employment of children in the industrial sweatshops of the nation became a widespread practice, especially in the coal mines of Pennsylvania and the New England and Southern textile mills. Child-labor statistics are not very reliable, partly because many young girls were often classified in the census as "women workers." But in 1880, the number of children between the ages of 10 and 15 was at least 1.1 million, or about 16.8 percent of all children in that age group. In 1890 that percentage was 18.1 percent; in 1900 it was 18.2 percent; in 1910 it was 15 percent; and by 1920 it was down to 11.3 percent. The data from the 1920 census reflects the growing concern about the child-labor practice that was part of the early twentieth century progressive era. The 1900 census reflected both the highest percentage of children employed and the highest actual number of children, about 1.7 million.

Beginning in the 1890s, and then increasingly in the early twentieth century, many Americans were having second thoughts about the employment of children. Not only were most working conditions deplorable and unhealthy, but working children did not receive an education and were not allowed to be children. Many educators and other reformers began to push for the strict regulation of the employment of children.

One of the earliest states to take such a step was Illinois. Florence Kelley was an early pioneer in the fight against child labor. As a factory inspector for the state of Illinois, Kelley was particularly incensed at the use of young boys, ages 7 to 10, at the several glass-bottle factories in Alton, Illinois. Visiting many of them in the early 1890s, Kelley found young boys working even in the middle of the night. These boys were nicknamed "dogs." Such "dogs" were employed to carry trays of red-hot glass bottles to the cooling ovens. They were pushed to work so fast that many of them burned themselves and their clothes due to frequent accidents. The stuffy air in the factories also caused acute respiratory problems and other similar illnesses. Kelley's investigation revealed that city officials in nearby towns encouraged very poor families to move to Alton and send their boys to work in the glass-bottle factories in order to avoid providing public assistance to them.

Largely due to her efforts, the Illinois legislature passed a law in 1893 prohibiting the employment of children under the age of 14 in factories. However, many adults evaded this law by getting themselves appointed as legal guardians of orphan children. Then these adults lied about the ages of those who were really under 14 years and sent them to work in the glass-bottle factories. Kelley continued her work for a more effective child-labor law in Illinois, but she found that both the glass-bottle industry and the glassblowers' union to be formidable opponents. Finally, in 1903, the state legislature passed a law that prohibited children under the age of 16 from working at night. The new law allowed 14 and 15 year old children to work in the daytime, provided that both a parent and a teacher signed a statement declaring the child to be at least 14 years old and able to read and write. In 1905 Kelley wrote a book entitled *Some Ethical Gains Through Legislation*, which described several industries which exploited children. Through her work and writing, Florence Kelley aroused Americans in the twentieth century to address the child-labor problem and to allow children to be children.

The federal government responded to the progressive demand to end the exploitation of children in the nation's mines and factories when President Woodrow Wilson switched his position in 1916 and suddenly embraced a federal child-labor bill. (See Chapter Six for more details.) The result was the August 1916 Keating-Owen Act, sometimes referred to simply as the Child-Labor Act, which forbid the interstate commerce of goods made by children under the age of 14 (and under the age of 16 if working more than eight hours per day). But two years later the United States Supreme Court, in *Hammer v. Dagenhart* (1918), declared the law unconstitutional by insisting that only states had the authority to regulate the employment of children. The country would have to wait until 1938 before a new federal law, passed amidst a different legal climate, would effectively deal with the child-labor problem. (See Chapter Ten for more details.)

THE TRIANGLE SHIRTWAIST FIRE

The child-labor issue also helped highlight the hazardous environments of industrial workers regardless of age or gender. Industrialists, including many small manufacturers, cared very little about work safety for their employees. Like the wages they paid their workers, the cost of providing a safer work environment was viewed as an obstacle to higher profits. And, of course, the cultural climate of the country in the late nineteenth century, with its emphasis on rugged individualism and Social Darwinism, gave these businessmen the rationale and justification for their lack of action on this front.

On March 25, 1911, one of the worst industrial tragedies in United States history called attention to the work safety issue in the nation's mines and factories. On that date in New York City, 146 workers, consisting mostly of young women, were killed when a fire raged through the Triangle Shirtwaist Company. These workers performed low-paying piecework jobs for a company which lacked fire escapes and maintained a practice of locking all exits in order to prevent employees from taking breaks. When the fire was discovered, mass pandemonium broke out. Workers made a mad dash for the doors, only to discover that most of the ones which weren't locked opened inward (a violation of the city fire codes). Miraculously, some workers actually escaped death. One such example was a young woman, Pauline Grossman, who crawled on her hands and knees across three male workers who formed a human bridge between two buildings. Shortly after her successful escape, however, the weight of others broke the human bridge and sent the three crashing several stories to their heroic deaths. Still others desperately jumped to their deaths from windows in the frantic attempt to avoid the smoke and fire.

Triangle Shirtwaist Company Fire, New York, 1911.
Credit: AP/World Wide Photos.

The company's owners were indicted and tried on several charges. But when a jury acquitted them, public outrage grew even more furious. This outrage resulted in renewed efforts by the International Ladies

Garment Workers Union (ILGWU), created in 1900, to organize and fight for better working conditions in the garment industry. The state of New York established a commission to investigate the fire at the Triangle factory and to study the extent of hazardous working conditions in factories throughout the state. When the commission recommended major strengthening of city building codes and stricter standards for workplace safety in 1914, the legislature was reluctant to act. But pressure from Tammany Hall (the Democratic machine in New York City) and strong leadership from state Assemblyman Alfred E. Smith and state Senator Robert F. Wagner carried the day, and the tough new laws recommended by the commission were enacted.

TAYLORISM

The monotony of assembly-line work in the nation's factories was made more difficult by a management which generally viewed its workers as dispensable machines which could be worked until they dropped. Then, as if industrial workers didn't have enough problems on the job, management found a new trend that hoped and promised to speed up the factory work and thereby extract even more labor from their employees. Efficiency experts arose, claiming to conduct and interpret new time-and-motion experiments, which could revolutionize the efficiency and speed of factory life.

The father of this new trend was Frederick W. Taylor. Taylor had been a factory manager in a Philadelphia steel plant during the 1870s and had used his stopwatch to find ways to create more efficiency. In 1911, Taylor explained his methods for promoting efficiency in the workplace in his book, *Principles of Scientific Management*. It wasn't long before Taylorism was a synonym for efficiency.

THE STATE OF BLACK AMERICA

Economic State

Immediately after the Civil War, the ex-slaves had little cash in their pockets with which to purchase farms for their families. At the same time, many plantation owners did not have enough money to hire farm hands either. The result was the development of two related economic systems that the South became famous for long into the twentieth century—sharecropping and the crop-lien system. Sharecroppers were poor families, both white and African-American, who farmed someone else's land and paid a steep percentage of their crops in place of cash rent payments. Harvest time became the only "payday." Thus, sharecroppers were forced to rely on whatever merchant was willing to give them credit during the year. Of course, the southern economy was in poor shape after the war, so few merchants could afford to offer credit to their customers. In order to obtain what credit was available, merchants took a lien on the expected future harvest of crops. They also tended to charge exhorbitant interest rates. With farm prices generally depressed during the late nineteenth century, due at least partly to the conservative monetary policies, sharecroppers often failed to meet their debts. And that left very little for such families to meet their own personal needs.

Some African-Americans, as well as whites, became tenant farmers, which meant that they farmed on land which they actually rented. There were a number of skilled African-American men who had learned and performed most of the skilled labor on the plantations during the days of slavery. But after Reconstruction, many of them were denied the use of their skilled trades through racial discrimination and intimidation. Therefore, by 1880 nearly 90 percent of African-Americans in the South made their living in farming or domestic service. And by the turn of the century, nearly 70 percent of the nation's 10 million black Americans lived in the rural South as sharecroppers, tenant farmers, or domestic servants. In other words, the great majority of black families, especially in the South, were trapped in a cycle of poverty. Once born into this trap, it was extremely difficult for blacks to climb out onto level ground. This was true because of the harsh realities of racial discrimination, and also the psychology of poverty, which stripped the poor of their self-esteem and most of their hope.

Racial Segregation

Racial segregation and other forms of discrimination against African-Americans existed in both the South and the North. Even though most northerners had come to vigorously oppose slavery by the 1850s, the great majority of them never supported any concept of racial equality. In fact, racism was as rampant outside the South as it was in that region. However, in the years following the end of the Reconstruction period, a difference did assert itself between the two regions of the country. The difference was that racial discrimination in the North was generally by custom and in the South by law. Of course, the results were essentially the same no matter where someone lived and worked.

As early as 1873, the United States Supreme Court began handing down a series of decisions which chipped away the federal protections for the freedmen that had been written into the so-called Reconstruction amendments. In the *Slaughterhouse Cases* that year, the Supreme Court upheld a Louisiana state law which had granted a monopoly of the slaughtering business in the city of New Orleans to one company. The company's competitors sued the state on the basis of the Fourteenth Amendment. The lawsuit claimed that the amendment protected individual rights and that the state of Louisiana had violated their "due process" rights under the Constitution. One clause in the amendment reads as follows: "No state shall make or enforce any law which shall abridge the privileges or immunities of citizens of the United States." In its ruling against the plaintifs, the Supreme Court emphasized the difference between national and state citizenship and reduced the rights of national citizenship to things like the ability to freely travel from one state to another. It also declared that states still retained many rights under the federal system of government and that Louisiana had not violated the "due process" rights of the other butchers.

Three years later, involving a Louisiana case in which a group of whites had disrupted and attacked a meeting of African-Americans, the Supreme Court again diminished the application of the Fourteenth Amendment. In its decision, entitled *United States v. Cruikshank* (1876), the court declared that it was the obligation of the states, not the federal government, to protect citizens' rights. Then in a series of decisions known as the *Civil Rights Cases of 1883*, the court specifically ruled that (1) the Fourteenth Amendment protected individual rights only when trampled on by state government, and (2) the federal government had no authority over individuals or organizations that allegedly violated other people's civil rights.

The effect of the above Supreme Court decisions, especially the *Civil Rights Cases of 1883*, was to declare the Civil Rights Act of 1875 unconstitutional. That federal law, passed near the end of the Reconstruction period, had prohibited racial segregation in public facilities—places the general public was entitled to be during normal business hours, such as restaurants, railroad cars and depots, theaters, and other public places. When this law was struck down by the Supreme Court in 1883, southern states began passing laws segregating the races in nearly all facets of life. These Jim Crow laws were nicknamed after a white comedian, Thomas Dan Rice, who, in the 1830s, had blackened his face for a song and dance routine that made fun of black-skinned people. Rice had called his character "Jim Crow."

The trend toward legal segregation of the races in the South was intensified in the 1890s, curiously as the result of a perceived threat by the Populists. Tom Watson of Georgia, among other white southerners, was a key leader of the Populist Party in the South. The Populists in the South appealed to the farming class as it did elsewhere in the country. If the Populists were very successful at the ballot box they would be taking traditional Democratic votes from among white farmers. The Southern Democratic leaders leaped into action by launching an especially harsh racist campaign, arguing that "white supremacy" was being threatened and that any division among Democratic voters would open the door to Republican rule being restored in the South. The spectre of a return to anything like the Republican Reconstruction governments was enough to persuade most white voters sympathetic to the Populists to remain loyal to the Democratic Party instead. As a by-product of this racist white supremacy campaign, southern states increased its legal separation of the races.

Jim Crow laws were specifically upheld by the United States Supreme Court in the 1890s. When Louisiana segregated the races on railroad cars, the law was challenged in the federal courts. In 1896, in the landmark decision of *Plessy v. Ferguson*, the Supreme Court upheld the Louisiana law and proclaimed the new judicial doctrine of "separate but equal." The court said that states and communities could separate the races on the grounds that equal facilities existed for each race. This "separate but equal" doctrine was reaffirmed in *Cumming v. County Board of Education* (1899) specifically for public education. This "separate but equal" foundation for legal racial segregation throughout society was not overturned until the famous *Brown v. Board of Education of Topeka, Kansas* in May 1954.

Voting Rights

African-American male voters had been intimidated on a large scale in the South as early as the mid 1870s. Even the Radical Republicans had given up on enforcing black civil rights by then, and white southern Democrats took advantage in a successful attempt to wrest control back from the Republicans. (See Chapter One for more information.) In *United States v. Reese* (1876), the United States Supreme Court opened the doors for legally denying African-American voters the right to vote. The court ruled that the Fifteenth Amendment did not guarantee voting rights for anyone, but it only listed three specific reasons that such rights could not be denied to an adult male. Those factors are "race, color, or previous condition of servitude." Essentially, the decision allowed states to deny voting rights to any of its adult male population as long as the specific language of the Fifteenth Amendment was not employed to do so.

The *Reese* decision resulted in several southern states, beginning in the late 1870s, passing laws levying poll taxes, requiring literacy tests, or creating residency requirements in order to exercise the right to vote. Poll taxes are cash fees which the voter had to pay before he was allowed to vote. Some defended literacy tests as simply an expression of Thomas Jefferson's philosophy that educated voters are essential to a healthy democracy. But the literacy tests were blatantly used to discriminate against African-American voters. For example, the voting examiner at the polls might ask the potential voter to read a section of the state or national constitution. If the person obviously read it well, then he would often be asked to interpret what he read. The examiner could then simply say that his interpretation was incorrect and he couldn't vote this time. Such registration officials even declared African-American college graduates to be illiterate. In 1890 a new Mississippi Plan required all of the above factors in order to weed out African-American voters legally in that state.

The last federal attempt to carry out the ideals of Reconstruction to ensure black voting rights came in the year 1890. That year the Lodge Elections Bill, sponsored by Massachusetts Republican Representative Henry Cabot Lodge, was defeated. It would be seventy-five years later before Congress would actively seek to restore black voting rights. And the Voting Rights Act of 1965 would greatly resemble the Lodge Elections Bill. Meanwhile, the Supreme Court upheld the Mississippi Plan in the 1898 *Williams v. Mississippi* decision. Also in 1898, Louisiana became the first state to adopt the so-called "grandfather clause" in its voting laws. The "grandfather clause," placed in literacy, poll tax, and property qualifications provisions, exempted poor white voters from those requirements if they themselves or their fathers or grandfathers could vote before January 1, 1867. Thus, the legal means adopted to prevent black voting would not affect white voters. Other southern states followed the lead of Louisiana. But in 1915 the United States Supreme Court declared all such "grandfather clauses" unconstitutional. However, that decision had little impact on black voting rights. By 1900 only about 5 percent of the black adult male population in the South was able to exercise the right to vote, and there were no more black Congressmen from the region.

Lynchings

Some white southerners were not content with legal forms of discrimination against African-Americans. Physical intimidation had been used before to prevent them from voting, so it seemed logical to some that violence could be employed to keep them in their place. Therefore, black citizens who were judged as getting "uppity" sometimes found themselves literally hanged to the nearest tree. Such politically motivated hangings are known as lynchings. Lynch mobs sent a powerful psychological message to the entire African-American community to keep quiet and meekly stay in their second class status. And it was quite successful in accomplishing its intended purpose.

The 1890s was the peak decade for lynchings, with close to 2,000 of them. Lynchings occurred outside the South too, although most historians estimate that between 80 and 90 percent of all lynchings did happen in the South. Of course, that was the region where most African-Americans lived. Between 1900 and 1920 there were more than 1,300 lynchings in the country, an average of over 65 per year.

The audacity and openness of some of the lynchings is perhaps best illustrated in a Texas lynching which occurred in 1916. The mayor was most insistent that the hanging tree not be damaged since it was on city property.

A New Racism

Complicating the expected problems from traditional racism was the emergence of a new brand of racism in the late nineteenth and early twentieth centuries. Some European intellectuals in France, Germany, and England began to advocate racial theories that divided the races into white, black, and yellow categories, with the whites being judged as superior. The pseudo-science of phrenology was added to the mix of new ideas. Phrenology claimed that the size and shape of each human skull determined the character and worth of the human being. Culture, religion, and skin color had always been part of the racist equation, but the new racism added the new dimension of blood. The races could be ranked, according to the new theories, on the basis of the relative value of their blood. Since the white or Anglo-Saxon race was deemed to be at the top of the racial scale, it became vital that other races not be allowed to mix with it. To allow for the mixing of any colored race with the whites would allegedly contaminate the blood of the white race.

The German dictator, Adolf Hitler, would use these new racial theories and take them to their ultimate expression in the "final solution" effort to rid Europe of all Jews. Heinrich Himmler, the head of the Nazi Gestapo during the 1930s and part of the 1940s, claimed to be an expert in phrenology. Himmler had assembled hundreds of pictures of human heads. Himmler claimed these pictures proved the inferiority of the Jews. These concepts traveled across the Atlantic and influenced American intellectuals. Of course, Social Darwinism had already given new justifications for racism as well as a pseudo-scientific basis to believe it. Racism was accepted as being based on science, and it was taught in America's schools and universities. Harvard University historian John Fiske, who wrote *Excursions of an Evolutionist* in 1884, was just one of many American intellectuals who freely and openly taught racism. This remained true until the post-World War II period in our history. In fact, it was Hitler's use of racism in and before World War II which was largely responsible for racism becoming a dirty word. The world had seen what racism can lead to, and now only skinheads and other rednecks openly admit that they are racists. Of course, racism is still prevalent in the nation and in the world, but at least the word itself has become dirty in the post-war era.

Black Leaders Respond

The first significant African-American leader who emerged in the late nineteenth century was Booker T. Washington. Washington had been born in 1856 as a slave in the state of Virginia, the son of a slave woman and a white plantation owner. He was nine years old when the Civil War and slavery ended. At the age of sixteen, Washington walked considerable distance to attend the Hampton Institute, a school for freedmen established after the war in Hampton, Virginia. There he worked hard and applied himself diligently, earning respect and dignity. But Washington also had a dream for his people. Convinced that having good job skills was the ticket for other African-Americans to succeed in America, he founded Tuskegee Institute in Tuskegee, Alabama in 1881. Tuskegee Institute was a vocational school for African-Americans that won widespread praise and enjoyed the financial support of many northern whites.

In 1895, at the Cotton States and International Exposition in Atlanta, Georgia, Booker T. Washington made a speech that propelled him into the spotlight as the recognized national leader of the African-American community. The views he presented in that speech became known as the Atlanta Compromise, a term originally used by a black critic by the name of W.E.B. DuBois. Washington told the group that African-Americans should not demand political and social rights from society, but they should rather concentrate on getting the best vocational education possible. Then they should work hard in the workplace to prove their worthiness to have the full civil and political rights that come from citizenship. In this way, he said, white America will be forced someday to recognize their contributions and grant them their full civil rights. Most whites applauded the Atlanta Compromise because that played right into their plans to maintain the domination of the caucasian race. White Americans particularly enjoyed Washington's partial autobiography, *Up From Slavery*, published in 1901, because he credited the virtues of hard work and honesty for getting him where he was. This theme felt

Booker T. Washington. Credit: Boston Photo News Company

right to most Americans for it echoed the "rags to riches" stories of Horatio Alger and others.

Another African-American hero who endeared himself to both races was George Washington Carver. Carver was officially born a slave of the Carver family, who were successful farmers in Missouri, near the end of the Civil War. His mother disappeared when Carver was just an infant, apparently kidnapped by slave raiders. After that, Carver and his older brother were raised as sons by the childless Carver family. Although denied the opportunity to go to school as a child because of his skin color, Carver's curiosity about the natural world eventually led him to complete a master's degree in agriculture at Iowa State College in 1896. Again, denied opportunities to teach or engage in research at Iowa State College or other white institutions because of his color, Carver accepted an invitation from Booker T. Washington to head the agriculture department at Tuskegee Institute in Alabama, where he labored with Washington from 1896 until the latter's death in 1915.

Although Carver was not a good administrator, he did valuable work in encouraging African-American sharecroppers and tenant farmers to use the inexpensive resources already available to them rather than more expensive products. In place of expensive fertilizers, for example, Carver urged farmers to plant a variety of crops to enrich the soil in a more natural way. He became famous as the "Peanut Man" for his advocacy of peanuts as a less expensive source of protein. He developed more than 300 products from the peanut, as well as more than 100 from the sweet potato.

In the 1920s, Carver began to do less teaching and research and more public speaking, especially on white college campuses. Many white Americans lavished attention upon him because he, like Washington, did not advocate political efforts to undo the legal and social predicaments of his people. But unlike Washington, Carver did not actively promote a non-political approach; he simply avoided the subject most of the time and focused on agricultural and educational issues. This especially made him a symbol of African-American achievement that did not threaten the doctrine of white supremacy. On the other hand, many in his own racial community adored Carver because of his contributions to the poor sharecroppers among them. Indeed, at his death Carver left his life's savings for the creation of a foundation to assist African-American scientists.

Most southern Americans of color appeared to have supported Washington's Atlanta Compromise as much as whites did. But northern blacks increasingly tended to criticize him, calling his philosophy a convenient accomodationist viewpoint because it seemed to them a surrender without a fight. Publicly, Washington indeed seemed to endorse racial segregation and other forms of discrimination. Although few knew it at the time, Washington secretly worked behind the scenes, and through letters he signed with code names, to fight against segregation laws and lynchings. He simply felt that he was doing the only realistic thing he could do under the circumstances of the day. Other African-American leaders disagreed. One of Washington's bitter opponents in the black community was Ida Wells-Barnett, a Chicago editor who in the 1890s had moved from Memphis, Tennessee after her offices had been destroyed by racist vandals. Wells-Barnett was particu-

Dr. W.E.B. DuBois. Credit: Library of Congress.

larly incensed at what she said was Washington's silence about the scores of lynchings of African-Americans.

The most influential and well known opponent of Booker T. Washington's accomodationist views, however, was William E.B. DuBois. In 1895 DuBois became the first African-American in history to earn a Doctor of Philosophy (Ph.D.) degree. Having attended Harvard University and a few other schools, DuBois received his degree in history, although later he also earned a degree in sociology. DuBois represented the few African-Americans allowed to enter Harvard in those days. After his college days, DuBois taught at Atlanta University, a black institution, from 1896 to 1910. It was while at Atlanta University that Dr. DuBois wrote his classic book, *The Souls of Black Folk*, in 1903. In it DuBois sharply criticized Washington for his submissive attitude. DuBois declared that white Americans would never willingly bestow the full rights of citizenship upon African-Americans. He agreed that most should pursue a vocational education, but that the more capable should be allowed to enroll in any college or university of their choosing and pursue professional careers. In the meantime, African-Americans must agitate for their civil rights until they receive them. It was DuBois' dream that members of his race find a way "to be both a Negro and an American." This sentiment demonstrates the chief reason that DuBois also opposed Marcus Garvey, a Jamaican-born man who organized a group in 1916 to promote a "back to Africa" campaign. (See Chapter Nine for more information.)

From an organizational perspective, the Afro-American Council, founded in the 1890s, was initially the major civil rights organization for black Americans. Booker T. Washington won control of it about the turn of the century, but the divisions discussed above led to other organizations. In June 1905, a coalition of African-Americans led by DuBois, who broke away from the Afro-American Council, and supportive white Americans met in Niagara Falls, New York to discuss new strategies for the civil rights cause. From 1905 to 1908 the Niagara Movement, as it came to be called, met annually, although in a new place each year. From these annual strategy meetings came a new civil rights organization, the National Association for the Advancement of Colored People (NAACP), formed in February 1909.

Among the whites who helped form the NAACP was Oswald Garrison Villard, the grandson of the late famous abolitionist newspaper editor William Lloyd Garrison. Villard himself was a newspaper publisher also. Moorefield Storey, the first president of the NAACP, had been the secretary to the late abolitionist senator from Massachusetts, Charles Sumner. And DuBois himself was selected as the editor of the association's journal, *The Crisis*. These leaders gave as much credibility to the NAACP as possible, given the racist climate of the country. The NAACP tried to raise the consciousness of white and black Americans to the racial problems in the nation, and it emphasized legal action to fight segregation, lynchings, and other forms of racial discrimination.

Two years after the founding of the NAACP, in 1911 the National Urban League was founded with Washington's support. The National Urban League focused on social and economic conditions that African-Americans faced in the cities.

Whether by accomodation or by militant efforts, African-Americans were unsuccessful in achieving the goals of social justice and racial equality in the late nineteenth or early twentieth centuries. The cultural climate was simply not ready for most white Americans to accept the person of color on an equal basis with themselves. But the cultural climate would change. Major civil rights gains would have to wait until the 1960s, when Dr. Martin Luther King, Jr. would prove that DuBois' thesis about the necessity for agitation was correct.

IMMIGRATION

The largest flood of new immigrants in American history poured into the United States during the fifty years from 1870 to 1920. Over 26 million immigrants, mostly from Europe, came to this country for many of the same reasons that immigrants had always come here. New economic opportunities remained the most important reason that most of them came to America. Other factors included political or religious persecution and famine. On the economic front, much of Europe had already experienced its own industrial revolution. The industrialization of Europe had undercut the need for local crafts, such as weaving and shoemaking, which many farmers there had used to supplement their farm incomes. The competition from mass-produced goods greatly reduced this source of supplemental incomes for European farmers. Another consequence of the industrial revolution in Europe and elsewhere was the worldwide growth of cities, since the factories were largely located in them. This trend toward greater urbanization increased the demand for farm products, which in turn, encouraged more efficient, large-scale agriculture. The commercialization and specialization of agriculture made small family farms less profitable.

The enormous economic pressures, along with political turmoil, religious persecution, and local famines, gave great incentives for people to look longingly across the Atlantic. At the same time, new technology was making trans-Atlantic travel much faster and cheaper than ever before. After the Civil War, improved steamships reduced the Atlantic crossing time from about three months to between two and three weeks. This also created great competition among oceanliner compa-

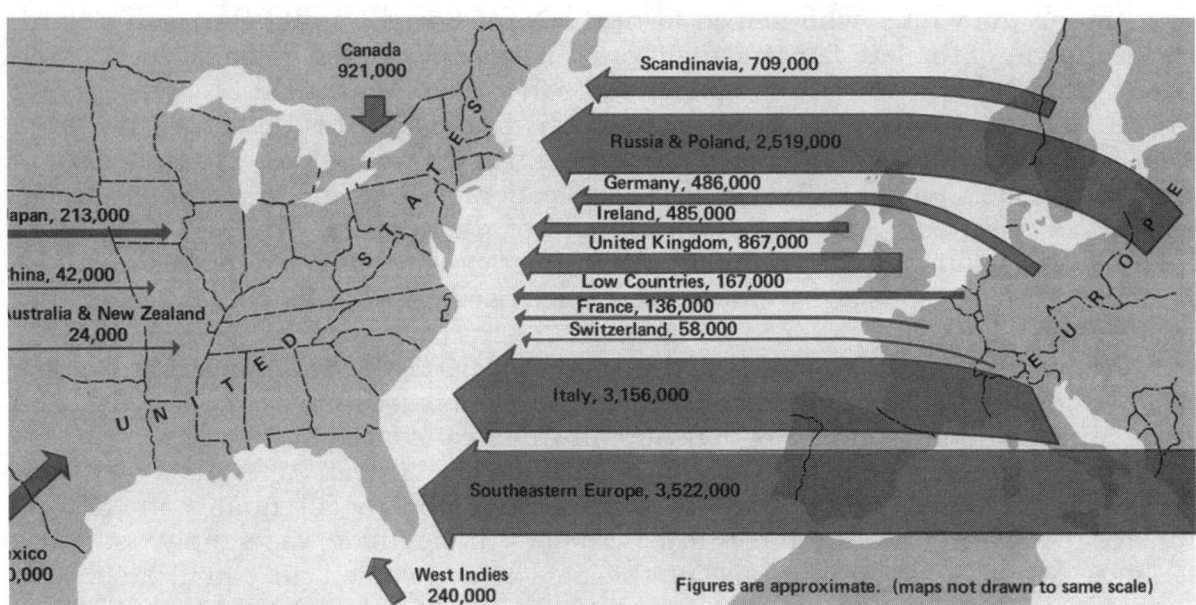

Immigration Trends during 1900-1920 period. Credit: The United States: Combined Edition, *by Winthrop D. Jordan and Leon F. Litwack, Prentice Hall, Inc., 1991.*

nies that further reduced the cost of the trip significantly. Therefore, both the demand and the opportunities to come to America expanded simultaneously to produce the largest period of immigration in American history.

Most of the European immigrants traveled great distances by train to a major port city, where they boarded ships bound for the United States. One of the most common routes was from Hamburg, Germany to New York City. The ships were usually over-crowded and had poor quality food for their passengers. Thus, many immigrants were sick by the time they arrived in America. Upon arrival, the first thing on the agenda was a physical examination of the passengers. (The wealthier passengers could obtain their physicals on board ship, thus avoiding the longest lines on shore.) Those who tested positive for venereal disease or other so-called "loathsome" diseases, like leprosy, were immediately deported at the steamship company's expense. For those who passed the exam, their names were recorded (and sometimes changed because the clerk did not know how to spell complicated last names), currencies exchanged, and train tickets sold to those headed for the American West. About 2 percent of the new arrivals were deported for some contagious disease, criminal record, or admission of being an anarchist.

As early as 1855, New York City established Castle Garden to receive immigrants coming off the ships. But charges of widespread fraud led to an investigation by the United States Congress. The investigation revealed that many immigrants were cheated in the currency exchanges. Baggage handlers sometimes blackmailed new arrivals into paying high fees to carry their luggage. And many others were overcharged for train tickets. As a result of this publicity, Castle Garden was closed in 1890, and the federal government's Bureau of Immigration was given the responsibility for processing the immigrants.

In 1892, the federal government opened new facilities on Ellis Island, which had been named for its late eighteenth century owner, Samuel Ellis. Located about one mile south of Manhattan off the New Jersey coast, the Ellis Island processing station sat only about 1,300 feet from the Statue of Liberty. Only a few years before, in 1886, France had given the statue in celebration of the Franco-American alliance during the Revolutionary War. Instead of reminding the world of that alliance, however, the Statue of Liberty quickly became a symbol of hope to the millions of immigrants who saw it as they approached Ellis Island. In fact, it was often the first thing new arrivals saw when entering the country through New York City. Chiseled into the base of this Lady Liberty were the following words written by the poet Emma Lazarus:

> Give me your tired, your poor,
> Your huddled masses yearning to breathe free,
> The wretched refuse of your teeming shore.
> Send these, the homeless, tempest-tossed to me,
> I lift my lamp beside the golden door!

Ellis Island was closed in 1954, but not before approximately 12 million immigrants had passed through it during its 62 years of operation. Other centers at Boston, Philadelphia, Baltimore, New Orleans, and Galveston processed immigrant arrivals too, but Ellis Island handled about 70 percent of all European immigrants that came into the country during those decades. The result is that Ellis Island has come to symbolize the American immigration story.

During the 1870-1920 period, immigrants came from other parts of the world also, but in few numbers relative to those from Europe. Canada, Mexico, and various countries in Asia were represented in the immigration explosion. It was for Asians that old-stock Americans reserved their greatest hostility. The Chinese had long been resented in this country despite the fact that they had provided much of the hard labor in building the longest railroad systems in the United

Immigrants at Ellis Island. Credit: Library of Congress.

States. After the great railroad systems had been built, many Chinese settled in the cities of the West, especially in California, where resentment was especially hostile. Their tendency to maintain important elements of their culture, which was so foreign to most Americans, led many to believe that the Chinese just couldn't fit in here. Obviously, they were of a different race, which played a major role in these hostile attitudes. But their language, religion, and dress (some men wore their hair back in one long braid) were additional factors that set them apart and made them targets of prejudice. In 1882, with support from President Chester A. Arthur, Congress passed the Chinese Exclusion Act, which prohibited most new Chinese immigration to the United States. In 1892, the Geary Act renewed the prohibition for another ten years. And in 1902, the law was amended to extend the prohibition indefinitely. It wasn't until Congress passed the Immigration Act of 1965 that this Chinese exclusion policy was lifted.

The first decade of the twentieth century had seen thousands of Japanese emigrating to the United States. Like the Chinese-Americans, most of them settled on the west coast, predominantly in California. The Japanese were not accepted any better than the Chinese, mostly for the same reasons. In 1905, the Oriental Exclusion League launched a major campaign in the West against Japanese immigrants, with support from many newspapers, such as the *San Francisco Chronicle*, and politicians like San Francisco Mayor Eugene Schmitz. When the San Francisco School Board ordered all Japanese students into a separate school in 1906, the government of Japan reacted negatively. Meanwhile, on April 18, 1906, a devastating earthquake shook the San Francisco area, leading to three days of fires and killing at least 2,000 people. Despite the anti-Japanese sentiment there, and because of a sizable Asian population, the government of Japan donated about $250,000 in relief funds, more than all other countries combined. However, the anti-Japanese campaign still continued on the west coast. American President Theodore Roosevelt intervened to calm the growing rift between the two nations. The result was a series of diplomatic messages that became known as the Gentlemen's Agreement in 1907. In that arrangement, Japan promised to prevent any more Japanese laborers from emigrating to the United States in return for an American pledge not to prohibit **all** Japanese immigration. The National Origins Act (1924) later violated the Gentlemen's Agreement by prohibiting all further immigration from east Asia.

As for European immigration patterns, they had historically come predominantly from northern and western Europe. England, Ireland, Scandinavia, and the German states were the most heavily represented among these immigrants. These so-called "old immigrants" had largely settled in the Mississippi Valley and Great Plains areas of the United States. Except for the Irish immigrants, who were resented chiefly for their Roman Catholic religion, these old immigrants were well accepted because of a similar cultural background with most Americans.

Beginning in the 1880s, however, southern and eastern Europeans began emigrating to the United States in larger numbers than in previous decades. That trend continued in the 1890s, when a majority of European immigrants came from places like Italy, Austria-Hungary, and Russia. And in the first decade of the twentieth century, about two-thirds of the European immigrants had come from the southern and eastern portions of that continent.

These so-called "new immigrants" were not easily accepted by other Americans. Many of them were poor and relatively unskilled, and like the Irish, they had to compete for the less desirable jobs in the beginning. Some of them were routinely used as strikebreakers during labor disputes, which created friction between organized labor and the new immigrants. Most of these new immigrants were Roman Catholic, while many others were Jewish immigrants from eastern Europe and Russia, where anti-semitism had run rampant for centuries. (Russia probably has the longest anti-semitic history of any country in the world.) These new religious groups "threatened" to end the domination of American society by white, Anglo-Saxon Protestants, and the old nativist feelings against foreigners from cultures markedly different from the American mainstream ran high in the early decades of the twentieth century. Among the Italian immigrants of the period there developed a popular saying that demonstrated the hostility that many new immigrants felt from other Americans: "I came to America because I heard the streets were paved with gold. When I got here, I found out three things: first, the streets weren't paved with gold; second, they weren't paved at all; and third, I was expected to pave them."

Overall, however, the social tensions were relatively mild compared to other parts of the world, where ethnic and religious differences has often led to large-scale bloodshed. One of the consequences of this new immigration was to transform American society from an overwhelmingly Protestant one to a pluralistic Protestant, Catholic, and Jewish society. This is generally regarded as a positive development because, as seen in our earlier history, the greater the mix of religions, the more religious toleration there has historically been here.

EUGENICS

Racism and bigotry of all kinds was given pseudo-scientific credibility in another way during the early twentieth century. (This is in addition to that described in "A New Racism" above.) The science of eugenics is the study of controlled reproduction in order to improve certain characteristics of plants or animals. In 1904, Carnegie Foundation grants helped fund a new research facility on Long Island, New York, to explore the possibilities of scientifically altering genetic characteristics. Charles B. Davenport, a respected zoologist, became the director of this center. Davenport was also a racist and an advocate of strict immigration restriction, particularly from Asia, Africa, and southern and eastern Europe. As a result of his work on Long Island, some states mandated the forced sterilization of sex offenders, criminals, and the mentally ill.

A progressive era author, Madison Grant, added to the voices of racism with the publication of his book *The Passing of the Great Race* in 1916. In the book, Grant used pseudo-scientific "facts" to prove the superiority of the white race and the inferiority of all others. Blacks, Jews, and southern and eastern Europeans bore the brunt of Grant's venomous assault. He even alleged that Jesus Christ had not been a Jew at all, but a white European he labeled as "Nordic." He argued for strict immigration restrictions, racial segregation, and the forced sterilization of what he called "unfit" and "worthless race types."

Thus, the eugenics movement added another element to racism and bigotry. The fruits of these racist ideas were seen in the revival of the Ku Klux Klan in 1915, the white-on-black racial violence of the 1920s and beyond, and the most restrictive immigration law in American history in 1924. (See Chapter Nine for more information.) Worse still, the entire world would witness the results of racism taken to its logical extreme during the Nazi holocaust years of the 1930s and '40s.

URBAN EXPANSION

The Industrial Revolution and its accompanying new technologies resulted in an explosive growth of American cities. Factories needed to operate near centers of transportation in order to efficiently receive raw materials and to ship out their finished goods. Of course, labor was concentrated in cities also. The growth in urban populations accompanied the Industrial Revolution in the United States just as it was doing in Europe and other parts of the world. From 1870 to 1920, the number of Americans living in urban areas increased from about 10 million to about 54 million persons. During the same period, the number of cities with populations over 100,000 increased from 15 to 68. The 1920 census reflected the fact that more Americans were living in cities than in rural areas for the first time in our history. Most of this urban growth was fueled by the flood of immigrants coming to America. But not only did many of the 26 million new immigrants settle in the eastern cities of the country, but rural Americans migrated to the cities in record numbers, looking for work, better education, and sources of entertainment.

The great surge in urban populations created a myriad of social problems for immigrants and old-stock inhabitants alike. Many of the nation's larger cities simply could not keep up with the growing demand for services such as garbage collection, sewage systems, safe drinking water, police and fire protection, schools, and health care. The crowded slum tenements, with their often unsafe and rat-infested structures, produced conditions that fostered enormous public health problems that the big cities could not adequately care for. The death rate in many immigrant areas of the big cities was approximately double the national average. Along with the increased numbers of people, the cities increasingly became bastions of criminal and immoral behavior. Con artists, pickpockets, and street gangs added to the dangers faced by urban Americans. Murder rates skyrocketed. To these scourges were added numerous new saloons, with their gambling, prostitution, and alcohol-driven brawls.

These urban problems were difficult enough to deal with under the best leadership, but corrupt city politicians and political machines often exacerbated the situation. Until the late 1890s most city police officers were controlled by the political bosses, who hired and fired them. Frequently, these law enforcement officials refused to enforce laws against gambling, prostitution, and other crimes in return for regular payoffs. A percentage of these bribes often went to the political bosses at city hall. But the movement to reform municipal government and law enforcement finally picked up steam in the 1890s. Reformers had long been striving to take police departments away from the jurisdiction of political machine-based patronage systems and to require more standard hiring procedures. Theodore Roosevelt was one such reformer who brought success to these efforts as the head of the New York City Board of Police Commissioners from 1895 to 1897. Nevertheless, the large percentage of immigrants in the cities often produced sympathy for the lax enforcement of laws which were perceived by many immigrants to be aimed at their social customs.

URBAN POVERTY AND SOCIAL REFORMERS

Most of the serious problems in the big cities could be reduced to the common denominator of poverty. A variety of approaches to fighting poverty were taken by a number of different social reformers. The social reform movements of the late nineteenth and early twentieth centuries was dominated by the growing middle class, although sometimes wealthy benefactors did contribute valuable financial resources to their efforts. One of the dominant approaches to poverty, especially before the turn of the century, was to assume that the personal habits of the poor were the cause of their poverty. This assumption led to a number of different reformers and organizations attempting to change individual behavior and mold it according to the middle class view of moral purity. Exposed by such public persons as *New York Evening Sun* reporter Jacob Riis, these reformers tended to ignore the fact that the unregulated desire for greater profits by industrialists and other investors had produced the uneven and unequal economic growth that had created much of the dislocation, crowded conditions, and poor health that had led to much of the urban poverty.

As early as 1853, reformer Charles L. Brace had formed the New York Children's Aid Society. Concerned that many young boys growing up in New York City would end up in street gangs or among other criminal elements, Brace created shelters where they could learn some practical skills and be relatively safe. When a boy had mastered some skill, Brace encouraged him to move out west, where he could apply his skill in a less corrupt environment. Before the turn of the century, Brace had assisted about 90,000 boys in being placed in foster homes in the midwest.

The Young Men's Christian Association (YMCA), which had been founded in England in 1841 and crossed the Atlantic in the early '50s, attempted to help young men from rural America make a sane shift to urban living. Both the YMCA and the later YWCA (Young Women's Christian Association) provided safe housing and recreational facilities for young people and maintained strict standards of personal conduct. Those who engaged in drinking or gambling, for example, were expelled from these organizations. While these youth-oriented organizations proved helpful to tens of thousands of young people over the years, they could not reach everyone.

Other reform groups that attempted to help the poor through the inculcation of middle class moral values included the Salvation Army and the New York Charity Organization Society. The Salvation Army had been founded in England in 1865 by a Methodist minister, "General" William Booth. In 1880 the Salvation Army established its work in the United States. Its strategy was to provide food and temporary housing and employment for the poor, and then train them in accordance with middle class, Christian values. The New York Charity Organization Society (COS) was founded in 1882 by Josephine Shaw Lowell, a well-known Bostonian widow. Everyone who requested assistance from the COS received one or more visists from the organization's representatives, who attempted to provide personal counseling so that the family might lift itself out of poverty. Reformers in other big cities adopted organizations very similar to the New York COS. Nevertheless, these groups were not very successful, partly because they were correctly perceived as condescending to those Americans who did not fit the white, Anglo-Saxon Protestant description.

A more extreme middle class reaction to poverty, although shared by many Americans, was represented by the writing and work of the Reverend Josiah Strong, pastor of the Cincinnati Central Congregational Church and secretary of the American Home Missionary Society. In 1885 Strong wrote a book entitled *Our Country: Its Possible Future and Its Present Crisis*. In this book and in other activities, Strong expressed a strong fear that the problems of urban America were threatening the very survival of our civilization. Typical of most Protestant leaders of the period, Strong shared the view that the values belonging to white, Anglo-Saxon Protestants (apparently exclusively to them), especially the Puritan work ethic, had been responsible for the greatness of the United States. Thus, he could not see those values expressed in people other than his own. Typically, then, Strong identified the two main culprits for this crisis as the recent immigrants and Roman Catholicism, and he exhorted Protestant Christians to work together to fight the saloons and dance halls, which he associated with both "culprits."

The Social Gospel

While most middle class anti-poverty reformers operated under the assumption that the poor were responsible for their own poverty, a different brand of Christian reformers focused most of their efforts against corporations and the prevailing philosophy of Social Darwinism. The Social Gospel movement, as it came to be called, arose in the 1870s from the leadership of George Washington Gladden, a Congregational minister in Columbus, Ohio. Frustrated by the apathy of most of his white middle class congregation, Gladden argued that true Christianity was one that fought social injustice and inequality as much as individual sins. During the great railroad strike of 1877, for example, he deplored the tendency of most ministers to side openly with the companies.

The Social Gospel movement attracted more support in the 1880s, when the minister of a New York City German Baptist church, Walter Rauschenbusch, began criticising the dogma of laissez-faire and Social Darwinism. In 1907, Rauschenbusch articulated his philosophy in his book *Christianity and the Social Crisis*. Essentially, Rauschenbusch defined the Social Gospel movement as the application of the teachings of Jesus to society and its institutions. He openly argued that all the Christian churches should unite to fight social injustice and work for world peace. Although the movement found some support among the progressives of the early twentieth century, relatively few Christian leaders were comfortable with its sharp criticism of the prevailing age.

Jane Addams and the Settlement-House Movement

In harmony with the proponents of the Social Gospel, but not overtly religious in context, was the settlement-house movement to fight urban poverty, led chiefly by Jane Addams. Addams had been the daughter of an Illinois businessman. After graduating from college in the early 1880s, Addams traveled to Europe with a personal friend named Ellen Gates Starr. While in London, England, the two women became enchanted with a charity workers' house located in a slum neighborhood. They became convinced that in order to really help the poor, one must live in their communities.

In 1889 Addams and Starr bought the old Charles J. Hull mansion in Chicago, Illinois, and turned it into a settlement-house known as Hull House. Soon Hull House became a famous center for Chicago's immigrant poor. It sponsored various programs for the poor, including classes in cooking, sewing, crafts, and English, as well as recreational activities and minimal legal and health care services. Hull House even operated an employment agency and provided a day nursery for the young children of working mothers. On the political front, Addams and her colleagues lobbied for better sanitation enforcement and housing conditions.

At least fifty settlement houses had been opened in various American cities by the mid 1890s, where they also served as good training grounds to provide energetic leaders to change the face of the future. Florence Kelley, who became Illinois' chief factory inspector in 1893, had worked at Hull House itself for awhile. But while settlement houses offered a sympathetic hand to the poor, their effectiveness was limited by the tendency to ignore the poor immigrants' own organizations and leaders. Thus, many of the very people they attempted to help resented their efforts as being given in a condescending context.

Jane Addams, Founder of Hull House in Chicago. Credit: Harris & Ewing, Washington, D.C.

OTHER URBAN ISSUES

At the same time that poverty was growing in the nation's cities, a revolution of sorts was transforming urban America—the rapid expansion of the largely native-born middle class. During the first twenty years of the new century, the number of "white collar" workers increased from 5.1 million to about 10.5 million. This was more than double the rate of the entire workforce as a whole. Teachers, lawyers, doctors, engineers, small businessmen, and big business bureaucrats dominated the middle class explosion. The old, familiar professional organizations, like the American Medical Association, the American Bar Association, and the National Education Association, exploded with members, as a new trend toward joining business and professional societies also skyrocketed. New organizations were added to the social landscape of America, like the United States Chamber of Commerce (1912), the American Association of University Professors (1915), and the National Association of Accountants (1919). Many members of these organizations obtained their sense of belonging from them rather than from their local community or political party affiliation.

In the 1890s, the electric streetcars, or trolleys, began making their appearance in American cities. Until then, the horse or horse-drawn cart or wagon had been the only real means of transportation in the cities, just as it had been in the rural areas. This new technology somewhat helped to relieve the stench and unsanitary conditions caused by piles of horse manure, that were both a nuisance and a health hazard in urban communities. It also encouraged the movement of city dwellers to more outlying areas.

During the same decade, the bicycle craze took the nation by storm. The modern version of the bicycle was then emerging. The best of these early bicycles cost about $150, which was comparable to the cost of an automobile for a few decades after World War II. Those were the days when $100 a month was considered a very high wage. While they never replaced the horse as a realistic means of transportation, bicycles almost immediately became the symbol of the "Gay '90s," as Americans frequently spent their life's savings just to show off the family "wheel." Of course, the rise of the automobile in the early decades of the twentieth century would quickly outdate the electric trolleys, and in time, would bring a serious pollution of a more chemical nature to the nation's cities.

RELIGION REACTS TO INDUSTRIALISM, DARWINISM, AND OTHER ASPECTS OF MODERN LIFE

The Issue of Industrialism

During the late nineteenth and early twentieth centuries, American Christians were confronted with the problems of industrialism, an issue which divided them. Henry Ward Beecher and Russell H. Conwell were leaders in the Protestant community who supported the status quo produced by the Industrial Revolution. (See "The Dominant Economic and Political Philosophy" earlier in this chapter.) Representing a minority viewpoint among Protestants, the advocates of the Social Gospel, churchmen like George Washington Gladden and Walter Rauschenbusch (discussed above under "The Social Gospel"), represented a politically liberal trend among some Protestants, favoring collective bargaining rights for workers and assistance for the urban poor.

Historically, the Catholic Church has identified with the established order as a practical means of surviving and flourishing. Thus, it has not often been in the forefront of great social reform movements. But in 1891, Pope Leo XIII issued a papal encyclical entitled *De Rerum Novarum* (ie., "of modern things"), which upheld some general rights of labor and gave Catholics permission to join labor unions for the first time. Partly, at least, this was a response to the reality that American Catholic workers had been joining unions in large numbers during the previous decade. There is a difference between granting official permission and championing a cause, a distinction that has not always been noted with regard to the 1891 encyclical. American Catholics have tended to be more politically liberal than either their church leaders or the country's population as a whole. This generalization is the result of the fact that historically (until the late 20th century), Catholics have experienced the suspicion and hostility that other minority groups have felt. Therefore, they have tended to be more sympathetic to most of the "underdogs" of American society. Catholic bishops and other clergy of that church in the United States are often found at the forefront of the fight for social justice today.

The Issue of Evolution

With regard to the issue of evolution, vast changes occurred among most Christians during the 1870-1920 period of our history. Various theories of biological evolution are nearly as old as human history, but until the nineteenth century, they almost always originated in the East, among the nations with large Hindu and Buddhist traditions. These religions place man at the center and teach that by human effort and meditation he can advance from a position of being out of harmony with the cosmos to one of absolute perfection, which is generally regarded as a place of harmonious nothingness called Nirvana. The individual has many chances to reach this perfection since he may be reincarnated several times. An individual person may be reincarnated as a cow, a rock, or some other part of nature until he finally arrives. In this way, someday everyone and everything will have arrived at a state of perfect harmony with all else in nature. In brief, this was the context for most theories of biological evolution, predicated as they were on gradual improvement toward perfection.

But in 1859, a British naturalist named Charles Darwin rocked the foundations of western civilization with the publication of his book, *On the Origin of Species by Natural Selection.* (See above, under "The Dominant Economic and Political Philosophy.") Darwin claimed that he had found evidence that could support the theory that simple organisms had evolved over millions of years into more complex organisms. When a particular species evolved into a more complex form, it was almost always an improvement over the earlier version. Therefore, given enough time, all life forms on this planet could have evolved to their present form, including man himself. Darwin himself did not rule out the possibility that a supernatural being (God) may have begun the evolutionary process. Neither was he quite as emphatic about the certainty of his ideas as his publicists and other westerners came to be. There is even the disputed story that Darwin himself abandoned his evolutionary ideas shortly before his death.

The most amazing revolution in Christian history took place in reaction to the teachings of Charles Darwin. By the turn of the century—no more than forty years—a large number of Protestants apparently had accepted Darwin's basic premises. For example, the Reverend Henry Ward Beecher, the most famous Protestant minister of the period, embraced Darwinism in 1885 in his book entitled *Evolution and Religion.* The reasons for this are undoubtedly complex, but the major factors seem clear. Despite the Civil War, most of the nineteenth century had been a time of great optimism in this country. Romanticism of the intellectual world and the Second Great Awakening of the religious world had both dominated most of the first half of the century, with their emphasis on the perfectability of human nature and his inevitable progress. Most of the great social reform movements of the 1830s and '40s had been generated by people who believed they were helping to usher in the earthly millennium of peace and prosperity in America and eventually the world. The only significant movement to challenge these optimistic concepts had been the Millerite movement of the 1830s and '40s, and it had been discredited in the minds of the overwhelming majority of Americans when Christ did not return in 1844 as it had predicted. Therefore, nothing of any significance remained to detract people from their optimistic belief in inevitable progress.

The Civil War might have been expected to crush this belief into oblivion, but it was immediately followed by the Industrial Revolution, which seemed to promise that new technologies and mass-produced prosperity would accelerate the nation and the world toward the millennial goal. Americans had a long historical conviction, going back to the Puritans' "city on a hill" dream, that we Americans were going to show the world how to create a truly remarkable human society. Europeans were less affected by the progress of the new industrialism, but the fact that since the defeat of Napoleon and the subsequent Congress of Vienna (1815), that continent enjoyed a century of relative peace (until that was shattered in 1914 with the coming of what became World WarI), did cause some Europeans to hope for a coming millennium.

Therefore, when Charles Darwin and his prolific publicists spoke openly about evolutionary progress toward perfection, the concept rung remarkably familiar to Americans who saw themselves as fulfilling a kind of predetermined destiny. The fact that it did not ring true to traditional Christianity did not seem to bother most people who were caught up with themselves and their national destiny; perhaps it says something about the entire nineteenth century's optimistic outlook being out of step with Christianity as it had been handed down through the centuries. Even the normally staunch Roman Catholic Church gave a qualified nod of approval to Darwinism. Its major insistence to the contrary was that God creates a new soul in every human being at conception. In this way, centuries of Christian tradition about creationism were radically ended.

The adoption of the theory of biological evolution by most leaders of the Protestant churches was quickly followed by an open questioning of other parts of the Scriptures. After all, if the book of Genesis was not accurate about a literal seven-day creation week, then how accurate could the Bible be about other scientific matters, including the reports of numerous miracles within its pages? Thus, many church-goers began denying most of the miracles, and religious modernism was born among professed Christians. Higher criticism, with its "cut and paste" or "pick and choose" approach to the interpretation of the Bible, demolished the traditional perspective among Christians that the book had been inspired by God. This new view also became widely accepted in many Protestant circles, even more so in the twentieth century.

There were Protestants who reacted against the Darwinian view and the modernist trend among many churches. These more traditional Christians maintained belief in a literal interpretation of the Bible and tenaciously advocated what they called the fundamentals of the Christian faith. Such Christians became known as fundamentalists because of their emphasis on traditionally accepted beliefs. The fundamentalists were strongest in the South and in the rural parts of the country. Their geographical location in rural areas helped make traveling evangelists popular among fundamentalists. Among such evangelists who preached the "old time religion," the Reverend William A. "Billy" Sunday was the best known and most loved. As a result of the decline in the number of Americans engaged in farming and the increasing numbers migrating to the cities, there would be a greater clash of urban versus rural values during the 1920s. (See Chapter Nine for evidence of this clash.)

A Split Within Judaism

Until the last quarter of the nineteenth century, most Jewish immigrants had been Germans who established themselves successfully in America. By the end of the century, most of these old-stock American Jews had developed a branch of Judaism that became known as Reform Judaism. Led by Rabbi Isaac Mayer Wise, Reform Judaism kept the core values of their ancient religion, but abandoned many of their old traditions and rituals. More than 2 million additional Jewish immigrants came into the United States between 1880 and 1920, most of them from eastern Europe (especially Poland) and Russia. The persecution they experienced in those places caused these Jews to tenaciously hold on to what was called Orthodox Judaism, with its strict codes of conduct and traditional rituals.

A number of American Jews during the early twentieth century found themselves uncomfortable with both the Reform Jews and the Orthodox Jews. These Jews created a third branch of Judaism, known as Conservative Judaism, which held onto many of the old traditions while still trying to adapt to the modern world. Thus it was that the social tensions produced by massive changes in American society during the late nineteenth and early twentieth centuries also split American Judaism. Of the three groups, the Orthodox Jews clearly represent the smallest faction within American Judaism today.

The Sunday Law Movement

Many American Protestant leaders during the late nineteenth century launched a major campaign to prohibit most labor and recreational activities on Sunday. The origins of this Sunday law movement can be traced back to the middle of the Civil War. The National Reform Association (NRA), founded in February 1863 by several prominent ministers, argued that God was angry with the United States because the nation had not officially acknowledged the lordship of Jesus Christ by enforcing His moral law. By 1879, the NRA was calling for a national Sunday law in order to appease God and recognize His sovereignty in America. Another Protestant organization which joined the Sunday law movement was the American Sabbath Union. In addition to these overtly religious groups, the Woman's Christian Temperence Union (WCTU) also participated in the crusade for stricter Sunday observance. Frances E. Willard, who headed the WCTU, was also one of the vice-presidents of the National Reform Association. The anti-alcohol, or temperence, movement had historically close ties to most of the Protestant churches, and had linked the drinking habit with non-attendance at churches.

The push for a national Sunday law was almost exclusively a Protestant movement, with support coming from most denominations, although Congregationalists, Methodists, and Presbyterians were most prominent in the effort. Despite the end of the Civil War, there were a number of other reasons which motivated the movement. As discussed earlier in this chapter, a mighty wave of "new immigrants" was threatening to change America's religious face, and many Protestants perceived that their period of religious domination was coming to an end. Specifically, many believed that the work ethic, and other character virtues which had made the country great, were exclusively Protestant values. The fact that many Catholic immigrants did not observe Sunday as strictly as other Christian groups added fuel to Protestant demands to legally enforce stricter Sunday observance. In addition to Catholics, the influx of Jewish and atheist immigrants further strengthened fears that perhaps Christians would not even remain the dominant religious voice in the nation. At the same time, new religious groups had emerged during the nineteenth century, such as the Mormons and Seventh-day Adventists, which were winning new converts from the mainstream Protestant denominations. This phenomenon also increased the perception among many Protestant leaders that their religious and moral values were losing ground in society.

Another motivation declared by many of the Sunday law advocates was their alleged concern that many working class Americans would be condemned to a seven-day work week of drudgery without a national Sunday law to protect them. This argument was used to win union support for the movement, especially among retail clerks and journeymen barbers. But this argument was not altogether an honest one because nearly all the religious crusaders for Sunday legislation were opposed to the labor movement and the issues it was fighting for. Even the editor of the *Western Christian Advocate* conceded this hypocrisy when he admitted, "I have not as much interest in the laboring man on the six days as I have on the Sabbath day."

The leaders of the Sunday law movement adopted the "Christian nation" argument, which maintains that the Founding Fathers established a nation based on Christian values and principles. According to this view, the First Amendment's "establishment" clause was never designed to erect a wall of separation of church and state, but only to prevent the establishment of a tax-supported church. Although there are numerous examples of references to a deity among the nation's early leaders, many of them held a view of God as One who started human beings into motion and then left them to their own devising. Thus, the Bible to them was interesting as a literary collection, but not as an authoritative source for morality. In any case, constitutional experts can be found on both sides of the controversy about the First Amendment. However, a strong tendency exists among American historians to interpret the "establishment" clause as indeed creating some type of wall separating church and state—meaning that government should not show preference for one religion over another, whether that be for a particular Christian church, Christianity itself, Judaism, Buddhism, or any other religious perspective.

The national Sunday law proponents made major efforts in 1888 to pass a law that would have prohibited most secular work and recreation on Sunday in areas directly under the jurisdiction of the federal government. The chief sponsor of the bill, New Hampshire Republican Senator Henry W. Blair, declared, "Only a homogeneous people can be great. No nation can exist with more than one religion." Despite their best efforts, the Blair Bill was defeated.

The movement was much more successful at the state and local level in the late nineteenth century, although such laws were sporadically enforced. Great prejudice was displayed against people belonging to unpopular religions, including Catholics, Jews, Chinese Buddhists, Seventh Day Baptists, and Seventh-day Adventists. (Jews, in varying degrees, Seventh Day Baptists, and Seventh-day Adventists observed the seventh-day Saturday as the Sabbath.) State Sunday laws provided many occasions for neighbors to take revenge on those they didn't like. Hundreds of people were arrested for a wide variety of activities performed on Sunday, including hoeing in their own gardens, riding bikes, cutting firewood during the winter, and even helping neighbors repair weather-damaged houses. Eventually, the vindictiveness against observers of the Saturday Sabbath, and a growing flood of more Catholic and Jewish immigrants in the early twentieth century, produced a backlash against the groups pushing for Sunday legislation. The strong, organized cry for a national Sunday law faded into the past, and even state laws were less enforced during the next several decades.

THE TEMPERENCE MOVEMENT

From colonial times, Americans have experienced a serious alcohol problem. Since women, in their capacity as wives and mothers, bore the brunt of this problem from husbands and fathers, it naturally followed that they became the leading spokespersons in the temperence crusades against alcohol. The period after the Civil War was no exception to this general rule.

The leading female temperence fighter in the late nineteenth century was Frances E. Willard. Willard resigned her position as the dean of women and professor of English at Northwestern University in 1874 to devote her energies fulltime in the temperence movement. Five years later, in 1879, Willard was elected president of the Woman's Christian Temperence Union (WCTU), a post she held until 1898. As discussed under "The Sunday Law Movement" above, Willard was also a vice-president of the National Reform Association. This led her to place the WCTU in the forefront of the drive for Sunday closing legislation. Willard also broadened the role

Frances Willard, Female Temperance Leader. Credit: Sophia Smith Collection.

of the WCTU to work for other causes, including the right of women to vote, prison reform, and welfare work. By 1890, the WCTU numbered 150,000 members, making it the first mass organization of women in American history.

The temperence movement in general, and the WCTU in particular, claimed a victory when President Rutherford B. Hayes banned alcohol from the White House in the late 1870s. His wife, nicknamed "Lemonade Lucy" for her active support of the WCTU, influenced her husband, who himself was a moderate drinker. Ulysses S. Grant had been Hayes' immediate predecessor, and although Grant's reputation as a heavy drinker was somewhat unfair (at least during his presidency), it made Hayes' decision to ban alcohol seem like a great victory for the temperence movement.

Although several states had gone "dry" during the 1850s as the result of pressure from temperence societies, the main focus of the early nineteenth century had been on education and persuading people to take the temperence pledge never to touch alcoholic beverages. In the post-Civil War era, momentum toward legally prohibiting alcohol picked up steam, however. This trend was especially strengthened with the founding of the Ohio Anti-Saloon League in 1893, which grew into the National Anti-Saloon League by 1895. The saloon had become the symbol to many Americans of a threat to stable families, public health, law and order, and worker efficiency. By the late nineteenth century, it had also become a symbol of working-class culture, particularly of the new immigrants. Thus, nativist hostility toward the newer immigrants (see the section labeled "Immigration" above) was added to the concerns for public health and safety, family values, Sunday church attendance, and other reasons given by advocates for legal prohibition.

Saloons became a favorite target of female temperence workers. Women often visited saloons and taverns in order to persuade customers to give up the drinking habit and owners to close the establishment. Most of these women were conscious of the expected role of women in the Victorian age as nurturing wives and mothers inside the family unit. That awareness led most of them to be quiet and humble; some even prayed right in the saloons. This behavior served its intended purpose by making it more difficult for most saloon owners to throw the temperence ladies out. The most famous, or infamous, exception to this rule of very proper decorum was the activity of Carrie Nation. Beginning her work in Kansas, Carrie Nation began walking into saloons with a hatchet, which she used to destroy tables, chairs, liquor bottles, and other saloon property. This brought shock to the owners and customers, but it did little to persuade them to reform their ways.

The Anti-Saloon League especially worked for municipal "local-option" elections as a means of closing saloons and prohibiting alcohol altogether in urban areas. As expected, this often put middle and upper middle class Americans into further conflict with recent immigrants and other working-class citizens.

The National Prohibition Party had been organized as early as 1869 at the impetus of John Russell, who is often regarded as the "Father of the Prohibition Party." Although it fielded presidential candidates for several national elections, the Prohibition Party was never a significant political force, managing to elect just one member of Congress (in 1914). Nevertheless, this third party did add another voice to the movement to legally prohibit the manufacture and use of alcoholic beverages.

Continuing the early nineteenth century trend, most Protestant church leaders actively supported the temperence movement, at least partly out of a desire to increase church attendance on Sundays. The momentum for prohibition increased in the early twentieth century during the Progressive Era. Most progressives shared the general optimism, so pervasive at the time, that human beings could engineer the coming millennium of peace and prosperity by their own actions. This basic concept had propelled the country into the great social reform era almost a century before. But unlike earlier social reformers, the progressives saw government as a potential ally in this evolutionary struggle toward perfection. Thus, progressives were heavily inclined to seek legislation to alleviate the social problems of the day.

Since alcohol was a clearly perceived social problem, then the way to "fix" things was to legally prohibit it nationally.

Although all of the above-mentioned forces were slowly leading the nation toward prohibition, it was World War I that succeeded in putting it over the top. When war broke out in Europe in 1914, the Allies found it impossible to continue agricultural production at levels that would meet their own needs. American farmers were asked to fill in the gap and help feed the Allies. That meant that grain could not be turned into beer or whiskey. Also, beer became associated with the dreaded German "Huns" because most breweries were German-American businesses. Congress passed the Eighteenth Amendment (over President Woodrow Wilson's veto), legally prohibiting the manufacture and use of alcoholic beverages, and sent it on to the states for ratification in December 1917. Ratification was achieved by January 1919 and went into effect the following January. At the time that Congress passed the Prohibition amendment, more than half of the states in the union had already legally prohibited alcohol, and at least two-thirds of Americans lived in "dry" areas, either by state or local law.

EDUCATION

In the late nineteenth century there was a growing recognition that the home and church were failing to provide adequate educations for young people. The era was bringing great social and economic changes that in turn made public education more important than ever before. Many people saw public schools as an important tool to use in the assimilation of new immigrants into the American culture, not only to teach the English language but also to impart democratic values. At the same time, millions of new immigrants also looked to the public schools as the source of hope and inspiration for a brighter future for their own children. Indeed, America's public education system did accomplish just that for millions of second generation immigrants.

The result of this perceived need was an explosion in the nation's public education system at all levels. The number of public school students increased from 6.9 million in 1870 to more than 23 million by 1920. Elementary education had been the most established element of the public education system. But in the late nineteenth and early twentieth centuries, the number of public high schools multiplied more than twenty times, to well over 10,000, with about 2 million students, by 1920. The number of colleges and universities approximately doubled by 1920, with their student populations more than doubling to 530,000 by the same year. Even enrollment in graduate schools multiplied more than five times to more than 2,500 by 1920. Along with the increased enrollments in public education, the literacy rate went from about 80 percent in 1870 to the mid 90s by 1920. Of course, as usual, teachers were poorly paid; the average salary in 1900 was about $42 per month, which was less than the wage of a day laborer.

Not only did the number of public schools and their students multiply rapidly around the turn of the century, but so did the changes in educational methods and philosophy. During the nineteenth century, school children had been taught almost exclusively to use rote memorization to master academic material. To do this, a very quiet atmosphere, with little or no movement away from the student's desk, was enforced. But a new educational trend began to promise a change to all that. Francis Wayland Parker, the superintendent of schools in Quincy, Massachusetts, created a more open atmosphere in that city's elementary classrooms. Parker implemented curriculum changes that made knowledge more practical. Language study focused more on real communication than on memorization of long lists of verb tenses and modes. He also brought a number of arts and crafts into the classroom and supplemented science instruction with field trips for students to gain firsthand knowledge of many things in the natural world.

But it was educational philosopher John Dewey who made the biggest impact across the entire nation in support of Parker's home state experiments. John Dewey, who was a professor first at the University of Chicago and then (after 1904) at Columbia University, turned the educational world upside down with his new theories. The basis for Dewey's ideas about education were found in his more fundamental philosophy that he himself called "instrumentalism." Essentially, instrumentalism is the concept that intelligence could be a powerful tool for reform if it applied the scientific method to solving social problems. Public schools, said Dewey, should be instruments of reform by actually becoming a cooperative community of inquiry and learning in a more open environment. In this way, he argued, democracy and other enlightened values could be experienced, not simply taught. On the education front, this philosophy became known as progressive education. Its two most important elements were an emphasis on the school children as opposed to the subject material per se and an emphasis on "learning by doing." The heart of John Dewey's philosophy was expressed in his best known books, *The School and Society* (1899) and *Democracy and Education* (1916).

The new trends in educational philosophy translated into major changes in the curriculum. In the twentieth century, high schools began offering courses outside the traditional college preparatory curriculum, such as home economics and vocational technology classes. Colleges and universities began altering the traditional fixed curriculum to allow for more elective classes. The old emphasis on the classics was also partially replaced with courses in psychology, sociology, political science, and social work. The idea in all these changes was to encourage schools and students to apply knowledge toward improving the nation's social problems. Another important trend in higher education was the gradual development of the junior or community college system as an intermediate step between high school and the regular four-year institution. And a movement toward establishing academic standards through an accreditation system was also pushing forward in the very early twentieth century.

THE CHAUTAUQUA MOVEMENT

An informal approach that offered educational advantages to adults unable or unwilling to attend universities was the Chautauqua movement. In the 1870s, the Methodist Church was conducting summer institutes for Sunday school teachers at Lake Chautauqua in southwestern New York. Methodist Bishop John H. Vincent suggested that secular educational classes be added to the program each summer.

The result was that, beginning in 1874, the Chautauqua Assembly was opened to the public as a kind of outdoor university that attempted to provide for the spiritual and intellectual development of adults. Based on the philosophy that adults should improve their lives through educational self-help during their leisure time, the Chautauqua Assembly attracted between 50,000 and 75,000 visitors each summer for most of the last two decades of the nineteenth century. Through means of lectures, public readings, and concerts, classes were offered in religion, art, science, foreign languages, and the humanities in general.

Recreational facilities were provided for the students as well. The lake itself, a baseball field, and tennis courts, all in a rural outdoor setting of 165 acres, made the eight-week summer sessions very enjoyable for the middle and upper middle class Americans who could afford the time and expense to go there. Seven United States presidents lectured at Lake Chautauqua, beginning with Ulysses S. Grant. Other famous speakers included William Jennings Bryan, Harvard philosopher William James, and inventor Thomas A. Edison.

The Chautauqua movement spread across the nation when William R. Harper (a later president of the University of Chicago) adopted a home reading course in 1878. And in the early twentieth century, various lecture bureaus sent out whole Chautauqua troupes, equipped with tents, which offered entertainment and lectures on various subjects in town after town. But the entire movement suffered a serious blow after World War I, when people in general lost confidence in the ability of human nature to inevitably reach perfection. By the early 1920s, the Chautauqua movement, as such, came to an end, although assemblies at Lake Chautauqua itself continued with much fewer visitors for many years after.

SCIENCE AND THE NEW MORALITY

From the 1890s to the 1920s a revolution in the way Americans thought about moral values and established traditions was taking place. Changes resulting from the Industrial Revolution—mass production and mass marketing, urbanization, and monumental numbers of new immigrants—formed the background for a new intellectual movement which eventually damaged the old value systems. Just as the Enlightenment had given way to Romananticism with the turn of the previous century, Romanticism (or whatever was left of it) was giving way to the age of pragmatism, or relativism, with the dawn of the twentieth century. The key difference, however, was that the new way of thinking did not offer a new set of truths to replace the old ones. Instead, the door was opening for everyone to fashion truth according to his own liking.

What had become known as the Victorian world view, named after British Queen Victoria, had emerged in the 1830s on both sides of the Atlantic. Related to, and developing during, the age of Romanticism, the Victorian perspective had featured an optimistic view of human nature and belief in the inevitable progress of man and his society. Such progress, however, depended upon a great deal of human effort. This had formed the background so essential to the social reform movements of the early nineteenth century. Along with this reform spirit, the Victorian age also produced a hostility toward pleasure and nearly all kinds of individual self-indulgence because these were perceived as opposites of the virtues, like hard work and conservative lifestyles, that had made important people successful. Its unwritten but strict moral code had confined women to the home or at least to a subordinate role to men, heavily clothed women in public, made public discussions of sex taboo, and generally used social pressure to attempt to enforce prevailing Protestant Christian values in literature, art, and other parts of American culture. In other words, it attempted to do nearly everything that the earlier Puritans have been accused of doing. Of course, the upper classes often hypocritically ignored the Victorian restraints on seeking pleasure for themselves while singing its praises to the socioeconomic classes "beneath" them. It was not surprising, then, that this "do as we say not as we do" approach to social control was sometimes limited in its success. But despite that, the vast majority of Americans in the nineteenth century at least gave lip service to most Victorian principles.

By the turn of the century, however, the Victorian era was showing signs of old age. Change always produces stress, and the dizzying changes resulting, directly and indirectly, from the Industrial Revolution, produced much unmanageable stress. Such stress became reflected in profound changes in the way Americans began to think about themselves and the natural world around them. While new technologies, economic expansion, millions of new immigrants, and the strains of urbanization provided the background for the end of the Victorian world, new theories in the fields of psychology and physics contributed more to a changed perception of reality and truth than any other specific disciplines.

In the area of psychology, William James and Sigmund Freud contributed more than any others to laying the foundation for the view that truth and reality is subjectively understood, not objectively found. William James, older brother to the famous novelist Henry James, studied an intense variety of subjects, including zoology, physiology, anatomy, psychology, and philosophy. He also read widely in religion and psychic phenomena, among other things. In 1890, James published *The Principles of Psychology*, arguing that knowledge about man's nature must be acquired by scientific means. And in 1907 he wrote *Pragmatism*, which expressed his views on the nature of truth. Truth, he said, cannot be understood from either fixed, absolute laws or from abstract reasoning divorced from the real world. Instead, truth is pragmatic; it is what actually works. And since what works is subject to frequent alterations due to changes in society, then truth is relative, not absolute. This, of course, hit at centuries of traditional Christian thinking. If there is no absolute truth, then, there can be no moral absolutes, no fixed standard by which men and women can judge their behavior. Ironically, much of the Protestant world had just been prepared for this new philosophy by its general acceptance of Darwinist evolution and higher criticism of the Bible.

Austrian-born Sigmund Freud's views on psychology did not directly reach the masses in America until the 1920s. But through American intellectuals, Freudian psychology was indirectly being introduced before that decade. Freud taught that human behavior and even human reasoning were beyond man's direct control because they were led by his unconscious urges. Furthermore, if one tried to repress his natural urges in order to obey some absolute standard of behavior, the results might take the form of some kind of dangerous behavior. According to Freud, sexual repression is one of the worst forms of psychological repression that exists among human beings. Needless to say, Freud's influence, coupled with James', helped produce something of a sexual revolution in the 1920s.

Physics also played a major role in the emerging values revolution in the early twentieth century. German-born Albert Einstein first published his theory of relativity in the fall of 1905. This was the document that declared that matter's energy is equal to its mass times the square of the speed of light; this concept is represented in the famous $E = mc^2$ equation. This announcement by Einstein laid the theoretical basis for the splitting of the atom, which first occurred in the explosion of an atomic bomb in the summer of 1945.

During the second decade of the twentieth century, the scientific work of men like Max Planck, Niels Bohr, and Lord Rutherford laid the foundation for our present understanding of atoms and their structure. Matter, or substance, was theorized to be a complex arrangement of electrical relationships within a much larger area of empty space. The effect of the new physics was to make reality, or substance, appear so small as to have no meaning for ordinary people. If reality was that tenuous, then perhaps there was no stable foundation on which to build an absolute standard of anything, including morality. Thus, new theories in psychology and physics prepared Americans for a new era in which many of the old standards were exchanged for a more individualistic approach to morality. And when a century of relative peace in western civilization was shattered in the horribly disillusioning World War I, the Victorian era came to a crashing halt.

CONVENIENT HOME PRODUCTS

One of the important elements that pushed America into its Industrial Revolution was the development of inventions and new technologies. (See Chapter Three for more on this factor, and for a discussion of some of the more significant inventions.) The mass production techniques of that economic revolution often resulted in the manufacturing of too many products. In order to sell the surpluses, the advertising industry had to create a higher consumer demand. In 1865, American businesses spent about $9.5 million in advertising. In 1900, that figure had increased ten-fold to about $95 million. And by 1920, American advertisers were spending close to $500 million annually to sell the nation's goods and services. To facilitate this advertising boom, Congress enacted the first federal trademark law in 1881, which provided for the registration of brand names in order to protect them from being copied by competitors. Until the 1920s, when commercial radio blossomed, the newspaper was the most important medium for advertising. Brand loyalty was increasingly displayed by consumers, as names such as Borden milk, Heinz catsup, Campbell's soup, and Proctor and Gamble's Ivory soap became fixed into the American culture.

Many of the newly available products made life more convenient for the entire family, especially the woman of the house. For example, ice had long been necessary to refrigerate perishable food items. But many families in the cities were forced to do food shopping nearly everyday because ice was expensive or even sometimes unavailable. But after an easier and cheaper method of making ice commercially was invented in the 1870s, the use of home iceboxes dramatically increased. And by the 1890s, railroad refrigerator cars had been invented and were being used first by meatpackers and then by marketers of other perishable foods. Increasingly after 1880, commercial use of tin cans made store-bought canned vegetables and soups available to people. Women had historically spent many long hours each day using wood stoves to cook the family meals. But the invention of the gas burner in the 1890s meant that most urban women were cooking on gas stoves by the turn of the century.

Breakfast was made a lot easier and faster by the development of the dry breakfast cereal industry in the late 1870s. The father of the new industry was John Harvey Kellogg, a Seventh-day Adventist physician from Battle Creek, Michigan who put his church's emphasis on healthful living into marketable action. In 1878, Kellogg began selling his Granola, a dry cereal containing wheat, corn, and oats. Over the next several years, Kellogg introduced a variety of other dry cereals, including wheat flakes and the now famous Kellogg's Corn Flakes. Another pioneer who became one of Kellogg's competitors was Charles W. Post, who became most famous for his Grape Nuts Flakes. Post also offered Americans a healthier alternative to coffee, a grain beverage he called Postum.

By the turn of the century, other convenient products and services were making life more pleasant, especially for Americans living in the cities. Many, for example, had electricity in their homes. (However, it would be the end of the 1920s before the overwhelming majority of urban dwellers would have access to it, and the end of the 1950s before nearly all rural Americans would have it.) Most urban families also enjoyed the benefits of indoor flush toilets and telephones, and nearly all Americans could afford store-bought clothing by 1900.

In the retail store business between 1865 and 1900, spacious and fancy department stores, like Macy's in New York City and Marshall Field's in Chicago, made shopping more attractive and fun. For less affluent customers, F.W. Woolworth opened his first "Five and Ten Cent Store" in Utica, New York in 1879. The old general store had always offered a limited variety of products at relatively high prices. But the trend toward the department store saw the adoption of the mass production mentality of manufacturers. Through buying large quantities of merchandise at lower cost and doing whatever was necessary to sell their inventories, the department stores could sell the latest version of almost every household item available conveniently under one roof. While several successful merchants expanded into a department chain, with stores across the country, the Great Atlantic and Pacific Tea Company (better known as A&P) had reorganized in 1869 to become the first chain-store system in the United States and, of course, the first chain grocery store.

The rise of the mail-order catalog companies transformed shopping and inadvertently helped to standardize urban middle class consumer tastes across the country by giving isolated rural families access to nearly all the consumer goods available to people in the cities. A traveling salesman named Aaron Montgomery Ward established the first mail-order business in history in 1872. Like the department stores, mail-order companies bought in huge quantities directly from the manufacturer, which enabled them to undercut the local general store in most small towns. The rapidly expanding railroads afforded the companies an extensive transportation network that helped keep mail service costs relatively low. By 1884, the Montgomery Ward catalog contained almost 10,000 consumer items, ranging from clothing to furniture, medicines, and tools.

Ward's chief rival in the mail-order business soon turned out to be Richard W. Sears. Sears moved from Minnesota to Chicago in 1887, where he shortly entered the business with his partner, A.C. Roebuck, a watch repairman. For many years both the Montgomery Ward's and Sears, Roebuck and Company's catalogs were available in the German and Swedish languages as well as English. This was successfully done to appeal to many midwestern German and Swedish immigrants. Although Ward's had been the first mail-order company, Sears quickly overtook him and became the leader in the field. In 1900, Sears sold about $10 million in merchandise through his catalogs. By 1920, the company was selling at least $200 million annually. Their success led several other competitors into the mail-order business. But declining sales, due largely to the rise of the automobile and improved roads, forced both Montgomery Ward and Sears, Roebuck into creating a chain of retail stores in the early decades of the twentieth century.

OTHER MODERN TECHNOLOGIES

Other modern technologies that were first being developed around the turn of the twentieth century radically altered not only American but world transportation, communications, and entertainment industries. The major inventions included the automobile, the airplane, radio, and motion pictures. For a discussion about the motion picture industry, see the section entitled "The Motion Picture Industry" in this chapter. For discussions on the origins of automobiles, airplanes, and commercial radio, see the chapter entitled "The Roaring Twenties to the Great Depression."

MEDICINE AND PUBLIC HEALTH

During most of the nineteenth century, the leading causes of death were infectious diseases like cholera, malaria, yellow fever, and diphtheria. The state of the nation's health was poor primarily because there was no consensus on the causes or treatments of disease. So Americans were forced to select among a variety of conflicting perspectives on disease and treatment, whose different advocates often engaged in bitter public disputes. It is little wonder that most citizens had no idea about what to believe or who to see for treatment when they became ill. This confusion also explains why hundreds of patent medicines were so popular. Such inexpensive "remedies," consisting of different chemical compounds and often a high alcohol content, promised a cure for whatever ailed you. Hundreds of traveling salesmen made their living selling miracle cures in the West, where cheap access to these products appealed to many people.

Among the groups offering conflicting medical advice were three major ones—"heroic therapy," homeopathy, and hydropathy. The advocates of "heroic therapy" believed that the number of illnesses known as "fevers" were caused by the buildup of too much tension in the vascular system (ie., primarily the blood circulation system). "Heroic therapy" physicians prescribed bleeding and vomiting in an alleged effort to relax the vascular system. It was this school of thought that had been responsible for bleeding George Washington to death in 1799. Waning in popularity around the middle of the nineteenth century, "heroic therapy" really died out after the end of the Civil War.

Advocates of the homeopathic approach to health argued that tiny amounts of drugs that produced symptoms of a disease in a healthy person would cure a sick person with those same symptoms. This idea was based on the so-called law of similars and on the belief that the smaller the amount of medicine the more potent that medicine was. Whereas "heroic therapy" was based on pure ignorance and was therefore harmful to the patient, homeopathy has some evidence to support part of its claims. But like most unorthodox health systems, homeopaths have historically exaggerated the benefits of their approach and have thereby turned people away from investigating it for themselves.

Hydropaths, as the name suggests, emphasized the application of water treatment, both cold and hot water, upon the body. They also criticized the use of drugs in any proportion. Proclaiming the natural way to health, physicians and other health reformers who favored hydropathy also tried to educate people to drink plenty of fresh water, experience an abundance of fresh air, get enough exercise, and eat a varied and proper diet of vegetables, fruits, and whole grains. Most of the advice of hydropaths, including the water treatments, is based on sound principles of health. Medical science in the late twentieth century has even corroborated the non-flesh food diet which many health reformers in and out of the hydropathic movement, beginning with early nineteenth century reformer Sylvester Graham, have advocated. Unfortunately, the marvels of modern, scientific medicine and sophisticated medical technologies has led most doctors in the twentieth century to largely ignore the benefits of water treatments.

It was not until the germ theory was widely accepted that scientific medicine finally built medical practice on a relatively firm foundation. Nineteenth century French chemist Louis Pasteur championed, but did not originate, the germ theory, which said that certain microorganisms can cause disease in humans and animals. Joseph Lister, the British surgeon of the same century for whom Listerine mouthwash was later named, introduced an antiseptic approach to surgery. Septic refers to decay, so an antiseptic is that which prevents or stops the multiplication of microorganisms that cause decay and thus disease. While it was later replaced by an aseptic method for surgery, Pasteur and Lister were giants who finally got most physicians to accept the germ theory of disease. Pasteur also contributed to the science of bacteriology. Bacteria are microorganisms that can chemically affect the host they live in. To prevent harmful bacteria from affecting beverages, Pasteur developed a process called pasteurization that destroys bacteria in beverages such as milk. At least as significant, Pasteur also pioneered a new approach to immunization, which was later applied to and was successful in preventing a large number of diseases.

The gradual acceptance of the germ theory of disease in the late nineteenth century resulted in major cleanliness campaigns both in and out of the circle of medical practitioners beginning in the 1870s. Physicians and surgeons, and their public health allies, began a major effort to get doctors to wash their hands before touching their patients and to use only sterilized instruments. Hospitals had long been places which provided free medical care for the poor and elderly, while other social classes avoided them because of the greatly increased risk of infections there—which, as a group, was called "hospitalism." The cleanliness effort was so successful that by the 1890s the general public was accepting and using the services of hospitals, which propelled them into the central role they have played in medical practice in the twentieth century.

About the same time that physicians and hospitals were literally cleaning themselves up, public health concerns about the crowded conditions in the big cities were leading to loud calls for improved sanitation services there. The vast influx of new immigrants, along with the growing internal migration to the cities, created crowded and unhealthy conditions in many of America's urban areas, especially in the eastern half of the nation. More than any one other individual, Colonel George E. Waring led the fight for urban sanitation programs. After a yellow fever epidemic killed about 5,000 people in Memphis, Tennessee in 1878, Waring persuaded the city to build a complete, modern sewer system. Other cities followed the lead of Memphis in perfecting their sewer systems. Precautions were also taken in a number of areas to preserve safe drinking water supplies and to pursue regular street cleaning programs. States and municipalities also began establishing health departments to enforce the tougher public health standards.

The more accurate, scientific approach to health care being gradually adopted in the closing decades of the nineteenth century, left many of the nation's medical schools woefully behind. The Carnegie Foundation for the Advancement of Teaching commissioned Abraham Flexner in the early twentieth century to study the quality of education in medical schools. When the Flexner report was released in 1910, it was sharply critical of the institutions charged with the training of physicians. As a result, about 50 percent of them closed their doors, and most of the others were forced to raise their standards.

While advancements in medical knowledge and improvements in public sanitation were taking place even before the turn of the twentieth century, the personal health habits of more Americans were also contributing to the increased health of the nation. Frequent bathing had long been advocated, but it wasn't until the middle of the century that it became an accepted practice to the majority of Americans. Actually, it had not been the health benefits as much as the improved body odor that convinced most Americans of the wisdom of bathing. As the twentieth century drew nearer, more and more people were paying closer attention to other aspects of personal hygiene as well.

Advances in food preservation were also made in the late nineteenth century. For example, when commercial ice began to be more cheaply available in the 1870s, this had led to increased use of home iceboxes. The rise of the canning industry during the next decade also resulted in better preservation of food and in a greater variety becoming available to urban Americans.

All of these developments in personal health habits and food preservation paid huge dividends and were probably at least as responsible for the lower death rates and higher life expectancy numbers as the advancements in medical science. In 1830, for example, the average life expectancy in the United States was about 35 years. By 1915, it was 54.5 years. The infant mortality rate also declined dramatically. During the post-Civil War era, every year approximately 150 infant deaths occurred per 1,000 live births. In 1915, that figure was down to about 100 deaths per 1,000 live births, a drop of about one-third. And the total annual national death rate declined from 17.7 per 1,000 Americans in 1900 to only 13.1 deaths per 1,000 by 1920. The medical theories and treatments of diseases which had literally plagued mankind during the previous centuries of world history were revolutionized every bit as much as the Industrial Revolution had impacted economic production and consumption in the late nineteenth and early twentieth centuries. The continued advancement of medical knowledge and equipment in the twentieth century would even further reduce the death rates of Americans and the people of other industrialized nations.

THE WOMEN'S MOVEMENT

The Job Picture

Traditionally, the woman's place was in the home, where she nurtured and cared for her family in a supportive and behind-the-scenes manner. Men overwhelmingly believed that women were not suitable for most jobs outside the home, with the exceptions of teaching, nursing, and secretarial work preferably only if a woman was single. Even most nineteenth century women agreed with men about what their proper role was in American society. But the increasing demand for labor resulting from the Industrial Revolution began to change things significantly, even if temporarily, in the early decades of the new century. World War I created the demand for more wartime production jobs than men, many of whom had been drafted, could fill. This was an important factor in the employment of women also. In 1900, about 1.3 million women worked outside the home, but by 1920 that figure was around 8.5 million.

Of course, even when women did work in outside jobs, they were still expected to maintain the same responsibilities at home. Husbands and fathers were not ready to do the cooking, laundry, and cleaning chores. As to wages, women who did the same work as men could only expect to receive about half the pay. Female factory workers usually worked at least ten hours per day for six days a week and received an average of just $10 a week. African-American women not only experienced gender discrimination in the job market, but their color also kept them out of most decent jobs, to say nothing about careers. Most working black women were confined to domestic service, where they made less than half the pay of most white female factory workers while working nearly twice the number of hours each week.

Changing Female Roles

Even before the job market for women improved slightly in the early twentieth century, the entire place and role of women in American society was changing.

Women were beginning to view themselves as just as intelligent as men and therefore capable of providing social, economic, and political leadership to their country. Probably the single most significant factor contributing to this change was education. Oberlin College, in Ohio, had been the first college in the country to admit female students. This, of course, provided a precedent for other institutions of higher education to follow. In the post-Civil War era, dozens of other colleges and universities opened their doors to women in the Midwest, while some big name universities in the East—Columbia, Brown, and Harvard, for example—created separate institutions for female students. Between 1880 and 1900, the number of colleges and universities admitting female students increased dramatically from 30 percent to 71 percent, and women made up more than one-third of the college student population. The almost inevitable effect that education has on people is to build their self-confidence, open their horizons, and raise their expectations that dreams can be fulfilled. And this was exactly the effect that higher education had upon most of the women who attended colleges and universities. Furthermore, the participation in student and other voluntary organizations gave women the same leadership skills that men had historically reserved for themselves.

Denied the right to vote nearly everywhere in the country, women turned to voluntary organizations in order to fine tune newly acquired leadership tools. This they had done earlier in the century, when women had dominated the temperance movement and played a large role in the anti-slavery and prison reform movements. Increasingly educated, late nineteenth and early twentieth century American women greatly expanded their involvement in a number of causes. Some of them, like Jane Addams, Florence Kelley, and Margaret Sanger, were pioneer reformers in their fields. (See the following sections within this chapter for more information about each of these women: "Jane Addams and the Settlement-House Movement," "The Child Labor Problem" for Florence Kelley, and "Margaret Sanger and the Birth Control Movement.") In the 1890s, several national women's organizations were founded to encourage greater female participation in the affairs of the nation. The more significant ones included the General Federation of Women's Clubs, the National Council of Jewish Women, and the National Association of Colored Women. In addition to her efforts in Illinois to eliminate the use of child labor, Florence Kelley became the general secretary of the National Consumers' League in 1899, an organization newly established to use publicity and other public pressure to improve working conditions in factories. Education and liberal amounts of leisure time were generally prerequisites for heavy involvement in community problems. Therefore, because higher income families could alone provide the education and leisure time necessary, the involvement and leadership in the expanding women's movement was primarily a middle and upper middle class phenomena.

If more education and community involvement set the stage for the emergence of the new women's movement, it was the bicycle craze in the 1890s that allowed the modern woman to express her independence from the Victorian role for women. (See the section "Other Urban Issues" within this chapter for more information on the bicycle craze.) Traditionally, respectable women did not exercise in public. They also usually wore as much clothes as humanly possible in order to cover nearly every part of the female body. But when the better bicycles became available in the

'90s, modern women took advantage of the opportunity to make a statement for independence by riding them frequently. In order to ride a bicycle successfully, women could not be weighed down with so much clothing. So discarding their tight corsets (which weren't healthy anyway) and padded clothing, female bikers told the world that they were riding into a new and expanding era for women.

Two women during this era who agitated for an expanding role for women were Emma Goldman and Charlotte Perkins Gilman. Goldman was an anarchist who coedited *Mother Earth*, a radical monthly publication, and became an active lecturer on feminism and politics around the country. Charlotte Perkins Gilman undoubtedly had a great influence on the women's movement because she is considered by social historians to be the most prominent feminist intellectual of her day. Gilman was a divorcee who was, interestingly, related to the famous Harriet Beecher Stowe. In 1898, Gilman wrote a book called *Women and Economics*, in which she chronicled the history of gender casting and sex discrimination. Concluding that women had been kept out of the public sphere because of their historical dependence on men for financial support, Gilman urged women to seek economic independence from men. Not only was education vital to achieve this independence, but equal access to traditionally male jobs and equal pay for equal work would also be necessary.

As might be expected, tensions between men and some women increased because of the changes in gender behavior that threatened people's comfort zone and challenged the Victorian norms. Many husbands found themselves married to someone they professed not to "know" anymore. And when their wives demanded respect for their new-found lifestyles and help with the chores around the house, the resulting friction often ended in divorce. The national divorce rate almost doubled from 1880 to 1900, from one in every twenty-one marriages to one in twelve by the end of the century. Surprisingly, many traditional male judges sided with women who filed for divorce and granted them alimony for the support of them and their children. Of course, conservative groups, and others opposed to the new trends, viewed the rising divorce rate as proof that women belonged in the proverbial "barefoot and pregnant" state.

Margaret Sanger and the Birth Control Movement

One of the most controversial aspects of the women's movement was the birth control movement that arose in the 1910s. Margaret Sanger almost single-handedly engineered this effort and has become known as the founder of the birth control movement, even coining the term birth control. Margaret was one of eleven children born into a New York family. Her mother died at the age of 49, a fact which she later attributed to bearing too many children. Sanger used education to find her independence and became a nurse who worked among New York City's poor in the 1910s. Sanger, a mother of three children herself, loathed the poverty and medical problems of the urban poor and placed most of the blame on unwanted pregnancies.

In 1914, Margaret Sanger launched a campaign to disseminate information about contraception in order to alleviate the suffering of poor women and to provide all women with control over their own reproductive systems. She also began editing

The Woman Rebel to spread the word about birth control. In that same year (1914), Sanger produced a pamphlet called *Family Limitation*, which gave explicit instructions for contraception. Such activity was very controversial in those days, and Sanger had to flee to Europe in order to avoid prosecution on obscenity charges. She returned to the United States the following year, and the charges were dropped. Then in 1916, Sanger opened the first birth control clinic in history in Brooklyn, New York. Although the very existence of her clinic was illegal (it was closed and she was arrested), other birth control clinics defiantly opened across the country, and women flocked to them by the thousands.

Also in 1916, Sanger took the lead in creating the New York Birth Control League to lobby for the doctors' right to advise women about contraception, which at the time was also illegal. Five years later, in 1921, she helped organize the American Birth Control League, with its monthly publication *Birth Control Review*, to coordinate national efforts. This was the origin of the Planned Parenthood Federation of America, which took the new name in 1942.

Margaret Sanger's birth control efforts angered many religious groups and others who worried that open talk about sexual matters and the practice of birth control by women would lead to sexual promiscuity and general moral looseness. But in the more permissive era of the 1920s, Margaret Sanger became something of a feminist heroine. Between the 1920s and the 1960s, several states legalized contraception and the dissemination of information about it. Of course, the development of the birth control pill and its availability in the mid-1950s would bring effective reproductive control to most women.

The Women's Suffrage Movement

When Wyoming was granted statehood in 1890, it became the first state in the nation to allow women the right to vote. The value of women on the western frontier had been recognized for several decades because it took everyone working together just to survive in most parts of the West. Nevertheless, and despite a renewed drive to win the right to vote for women in the post-Civil War era, only three other states had joined Wyoming as late as 1910—Utah, Idaho, and Colorado.

During the Reconstruction period, former abolitionists Elizabeth Cady Stanton and Susan B. Anthony left the black struggle for justice when Radical Republicans had ignored their efforts to include women's suffrage rights in the fourteenth and fifteenth amendments to the United States Constitution. And in May 1869, the two women became the driving force in the creation of the National Woman Suffrage Association. The NWSA not only campaigned for women suffrage but also for other reforms, including the unionization of women workers. The group also endorsed politicians who advocated women's suffrage and were reformist on certain other issues. But when political candidates refused to endorse women's right to vote, even though they were supportive of reforms in general, the NWSA would not work for them.

Other women rights leaders disagreed with the NWSA policy of working to achieve several social reforms, declaring that such a broad interest only served to dilute the effort for women suffrage. Dominating the New England Woman Suffrage Association, which had just been formed in 1868, these women transformed it into

Suffrage Parade March, New York, May 3, 1913. Credit: Sophia Smith Collection.

a national organization called the American Woman Suffrage Association. The AWSA worked exclusively to achieve the goal of women suffrage and were tied to the Republican Party. Its main leaders included well-known former abolitionist and women's rights fighters Lucy Stone and Julia Ward Howe.

As the women's movement in general was picking up steam, the differences between the NWSA and the AWSA slowly disappeared. The two organizations merged in 1890 to form the National American Woman Suffrage Association. Susan B. Anthony served as its first president until her retirement in 1900, although she continued to labor for the cause until her death in 1906. The NAWSA succeeded in winning the right to vote on certain local issues, such as in school board elections, in several parts of the country, but it achieved no really major successes during its first several years in existence. However, from 1900 to 1904, and then again after 1915, the very capable Carrie Chapman Catt served as the NAWSA president. Under her leadership, the organization adopted a strong grassroots base coupled with tight central control from the national office. They organized parades, distributed literature, and lobbied members of state legislatures. The highly organized effort paid off as several key states in the West and Midwest granted at least partial women's suffrage. While many states gave full voting rights to women, like Wyoming, Utah, Idaho, and Colorado before them, others allowed them to vote only in presidential elections. Suffrage victories in New York in 1917 and Michigan in 1918 were particularly helpful in eventually achieving the goal of total, national women suffrage.

True to history, some of the most severe critics of the women's movement—especially the suffrage effort—were other women. The opposition was led by Josephine Dodge, a wealthy New York City widow, who formed the National Association Opposed to Women Suffrage in 1911. It argued that since women already had great influence behind-the-scenes, female voting and other political rights would reduce women's supportive role and thus their indirect influence on society.

Despite the opposition, of course, the suffrage movement was nearing total victory when World War I broke out in Europe. Unlike most other social reform issues, the women's suffrage movement was actually helped by the war. At the very time that many men were drafted and sent to Europe with General John J. Pershing's army in 1917, the demand for war materials was exploding. Women successfully filled the gap as wartime factory workers without disastrous results. The recognition of their support in helping achieve the Allied victory was the proverbial straw that broke the camel's back. Congress narrowly passed the Nineteenth Amendment in June 1919 and sent in on to the states for ratification. The women's suffrage amendment was ratified by August 1920, just in time for the presidential election that November. A very long struggle by women's groups finally was over.

LITERATURE

For much of the nineteenth century, the dime novel dominated the book reading of the masses. Its sentimentalism and proverbial happy endings offered an escape from the hard life of most Americans by portraying life as people dreamed it might be. After the Civil War, reaction against the cheap enterntainment of the dime novel attempted to end its influence but with little success. By 1910 or so, however, it was being replaced by popular pulp magazines like *Argosy* (founded in 1915), which featured unrealistic, hero-worshipping stories in its pages each month.

Negative reaction to the cheap, sentimentality of the dime novel after the Civil War resulted in a concerted effort to reestablish high Victorian standards in literature and other areas of American culture. This campaign was led by high brow, genteel magazines, such as *The Nation*, edited by E.L. Godkin, *The Century*, edited by Richard W. Gilder, and *The Atlantic Monthly*, edited by William Dean Howells. All slang, sexual references, and criticisms of Christianity were voluntarily removed from those magazines by their own editors. Both in and out of those magazines, and with the support of others in the artistic community, especially in New York and Boston, this cultural elite attempted to mold the preferences of the masses according to its own standards by telling them what they should like and purchase.

Late in the nineteenth century, new publications like *Cosmopolitan*, the *Ladies' Home Journal*, and *McClure's Magazine* slashed their prices in order to compete with the elite magazines. Instead of relying heavily on the price for their incomes by charging 25 to 35 cents a copy, as the more elite publications did, these new magazines reduced their prices to 10 or 15 cents a copy and relied more on advertising. This move opened the door for writers who were repulsed by the elitism of Howells and others but still wanted to write about life in a more realistic way to reach vast audiences of readers.

This trend toward realism in literature during the late nineteenth and early twentieth centuries was reflected in the authors of books as well. Henry James became recognized as the most influential of the realists. Although born in New York City and had his first essay published in the *North American Review* (considered another elitist journal), James moved to England at the age of thirty-eight in the early 1880s, where he eventually became a British citizen in 1915, the year before he died. There he became a first-class novelist, ably writing about American and European life. James was a prolific writer, but some of his best-known novels include *The Portrait of a Lady* (1881), *The Turn of the Screw* (1898), *The Ambassadors* (1903), and *The Golden Bowl* (1904). Another famous realist of the period was Henry James' friend Edith Wharton. In *The House of Mirth* (1905) and *The Age of Innocence* (1920), Wharton portrayed the aristocratic life as devoid of joy and meaning.

Some of the realists became known as regionalists because they wrote so intimately about the specific regions they lived in. Perhaps the best known of these regionalists was Willa Cather. Cather managed to capture the spirit of adventure and hard work experienced by the immigrant families on the Great Plains in her novels *O Pioneers* (1913) and *My Antonia* (1918).

Related to realism, but taking its readers into the harsher aspects of life, was a school of literary thought known as naturalism. Stephen Crane is generally given credit for introducing naturalism into American literature. His first novel, *Maggie: A Girl of the Streets*, was published in 1893 and based on his own sketches of slum life in New York City. His character Maggie is a young woman who eventually commits suicide to escape the hopelessness of life in the slums. Two years later, in 1895, he wrote *The Red Badge of Courage*, a sad and morbid story of a Civil War soldier. Crane's own life seemed to mirror the harshness of his own stories. In January 1897 he survived the sinking of the *Commodore* while enroute as a journalist to cover the Cuban revolution against Spain. After a brief recovery, he went abroad to cover the Greco-Turkish War in-

Mark Twain (Samuel L. Clemens). Credit: Bettman Archive.

stead, before finally ending up in Cuba to cover what had turned into the Spanish-American War. There he apparently contracted tuberculosis, which he tragically died from in 1900 at the age of twenty-nine.

Other well-known authors, variously categorized as realists and naturalists, include Samuel Langhorne Clemens, Theodore Dreiser, and Jack London. Clemens was better known by his pen name, Mark Twain, which he derived from the boatman's term which meant that the depth of the river was two fathoms. Clemens learned this in his younger days on a Mississippi River steamboat. He began his career as a journalist, but he traveled extensively and often wrote from his own experiences. Mark Twain became the leading literary critic of the social order of his day. After co-authoring *The Gilded Age* in 1873 with Charles Dudley Warner, he went on to fame, although, as often is the case, he has been celebrated more since his death than when he lived. His two most famous works are viewed as children's books today, but they really embodied his social criticism of American society before the turn of the century. *The Adventures of Tom Sawyer*, published in 1876, and *Adventures of Huckleberry Finn* in 1884, were largely drawn from his childhood days growing up in Hannibal, Missouri, and from his days on the Mississippi River. The more caustic of the two, *Adventures of Hucklebery Finn*, tells the fictional story of a runaway slave named Jim and a runaway white boy named Huck. In it, Twain attacks racial prejudice as Huck gradually comes to bond with Jim when he sees him as another human being like himself. Given the prevalence and respectability of racism in his day, it is no wonder that the book was scathingly attacked.

While Stephen Crane may have introduced naturalism to American literature, many literary experts credit Theodore Dreiser with being the most significant naturalist of his era. Dreiser was born in Terre Haute, Indiana and, like Mark Twain, began his career as a newspaper reporter. Also like Twain, Dreiser traveled widely and learned about the greed and corruption of his time by experiencing it up close. This too gave him most of his material for his writing. Three of his finest novels were *Sister Carrie* (1900), *The Financier* (1912), and *An American Tragedy* (1925). In the first one, heroine Carrie Meeber left her rural Wisconsin home to find work in the big city of Chicago. There she moves in with a married man, falls victim to the fast, expensive lifestyle of the rich, moves with her live-in man to New York City, and eventually leaves him to pursue an acting career in the theater. *The Financier* is the fictional account of a financial robber baron in the late nineteenth century. In *An American Tragedy*, Dreiser conveys his own belief, through the story of a man compelled to seek riches and social position, that some people are so trapped by their circumstances that they are incapable of exercising their will.

Another naturalist who borrowed material for his novels from his own experiences as a world traveler was Jack London. Born in abject poverty in San Francisco, London held several jobs at an early age, including working as a cannery worker and as a seaman. His early, and most famous, works were based on his experiences in the Klondike during the Alaskan gold rush of 1897-1898. In *The Call of the Wild* (1903) and *White Fang* (1906), Jack London captured the essence of the bestiality of human nature when greed takes hold of men in the environment of the harsh north country.

Other notable authors of the period include Horatio Alger, Lewis Wallace, Frank Baum, and Zane Grey. Alger was an unsuccessful nineteenth century Unitarian clergyman who left the ministry after charges surfaced that he was a child molester. Beginning in 1867 with *Ragged Dick*, Alger went on to write well more than one hundred novels for young readers before his death in 1899. Horatio Alger's hero almost always started out as a young boy, who through honesty and hard work, ended up a multi-millionaire tycoon. Of course, he usually placed his hero in unlikely and lucky situations where some important man would find him and give him a start on the road to wealth. Alger epitomized the wild confidence that middle class Americans possessed about the land of opportunity. And the expression "rags to riches" has been identified with Horatio Alger ever since.

Lewis Wallace wrote about a young Jewish lad who was adopted by a powerful Roman official during the days of the Roman Empire in his novel *Ben-Hur* in 1880. Frank Baum wrote *The Wizard of Oz* in 1900, which became a Judy Garland movie in 1939. While most people picture the movie only as a children's fantasy story, Baum actually wrote his book as a Populist, pro-silver satire of the monetary question. In his book, the various wicked witches represented different institutions, like the banks, that Populists and many farmers viewed as their enemies. His main character's slippers were silver, representing that metal as the medium of exchange favored by farm interests. (Judy Garland's slippers were ruby red because the producers wanted to show off the color; the movie version was the first color movie made.) A dentist from Zanesville, Ohio, named Zane Grey, became one of the country's greatest novelists of the American West. Beginning with *Riders of the Purple Sage* in 1912, Grey went on to write about thirty western novels depicting both the hard life and the exciting adventures that were part of the great conflicts on the western frontier.

ART AND ARCHITECTURE

Painting and Sculpting

The literary giant Henry James had once written that "it is art that *makes* life. . . ." This view was reflected in a movement of art for art's sake beginning in the late nineteenth century, which said that it was more important how an artist portrayed his subject than what he portrayed. James A. McNeill Whistler did much to promote this movement also. His most famous painting was a portrait in 1871 entitled *Arrangement in Gray and Black, No. 1*, better known as *Whistler's Mother*.

Much of the art world was also influenced by the same new trend toward realism and naturalism that literature was experiencing during the late nineteenth and early twentieth centuries. The two most significant and influential realist painters of the period were Winslow Homer and Thomas Eakins. Homer had worked as artist for *Harper's Weekly* during the Civil War. Summarizing the realists' view of art, he once wrote, "If a man wants to be an artist, he should never look at paintings." Artists should draw their material from the real world. In the 1880s, Homer moved to Maine, where he became recognized as the foremost painter of the sea by the end of that decade. He also frequently lived in the Caribbean area during the winter months. Some of his better known sea paintings include *The Life Line*

(1884), *Eight Bells* (1886), and *Lost on the Grand Banks* (1886). Perhaps his most famous painting, however, was *The Gulf Stream* (1899), which depicts a black man in a boat after he has just survived a harrowing storm.

Thomas Eakins studied anatomy at a medical school in order to make his paintings of human beings very realistic. Like Homer, Eakins also was famous for depicting human struggle and physical endurance in his paintings. *Champion Single Sculls*, painted in 1871, is representative of this motif in Eakins' work. When he painted *The Gross Clinic* in 1875, depicting an exhausted surgeon simply standing with blood-stained hands beside his patient in the middle of an operation, he ruined his artistic reputation. Americans were then too easily reminded of the horrors of surgery during the Civil War to appreciate his work. He once wrote that his "honors are misunderstanding, persecution and neglect." Later generations, however, would respect him as one of the greatest painters of his period.

In the opening decade of the new century, the so-called Ashcan school of art developed among a group of New York painters, led by men like Robert Henri, Arthur B. Davies, and John Sloan. These artists avoided the genteel landscape paintings so popular in the nineteenth century and concentrated on the seamier side of life in the cities. Sometimes their art has been labeled naturalist because of the extremely realistic portrayal of some of the more negative sides of American life. In 1913, Robert Henri and a group of other like-minded artists, including Ashcan latecomer George Bellows, organized the International Exhibition of Modern Art in New York City. And four years later, in 1917, they were instrumental in creating the Society of Independent Artists.

The foremost sculptor of the early twentieth century was Augustus Saint-Gaudens, whose sculptures of people were extremely realistic and lifelike. Another American sculptor whose representation of human beings was remarkably realistic was Daniel Chester French. Although he created many sculptures, his most famous work was the impressive figure of Abraham Lincoln, completed in 1922, which is part of the Lincoln Memorial in Washington, D.C.

Architecture

American architecture also departed from many traditional norms during the late nineteenth and early twentieth centuries. Clearly, the two most important architects who fostered change during this period were Louis H. Sullivan and Frank Lloyd Wright. A natural catastrophe, the infamous Chicago fire, destroyed more than 60,000 buildings and made almost 100,000 people homeless in October 1871. But out of this disaster came a great opportunity to rebuild that big city's business district in a new architectural style. For the next two decades, architects designed and put back the city of Chicago partly by using relatively new technologies. The earlier development of steam-driven and electrical elevators, fireproof materials, and steel frames made possible the rise of the skyscraper. But it was Louis Sullivan and others who refined these materials and combined them in new designs that actually created the skyscrapers. Sullivan had propounded the theory that "form follows function," which meant that buildings should be constructed in accordance with their specific purpose for existing. By following that motto, he and other architects completed the very first skyscraper in Chicago in 1884. Their success led to

Frank Lloyd Wright's "Robie House." Credit: Chicago Photo.

the building of skyscrapers in the nation's big cities that came to characterize the twentieth century.

Frank Lloyd Wright was another Chicago architect who, for a few years, worked closely with Louis Sullivan until the latter fired him in 1893 for violating his contract's provision not to take any commissions for himself. In the 1890s, Wright developed a maverick reputation by designing what he called the "prairie house," the first one being built in the Chicago suburb of Oak Park, Illinois. This residential design, sometimes also called the "prairie-school" house, featured longer and lower horizontal lines in harmony with the flatter horizons of the Midwest and Middle West, and more open, connected rooms to provide the illusion of spaciousness. Wright's personal life was filled with tragedy, with the divorce from his first wife, the murder of his live-in lover and her children, numerous other love affairs and marriages, lawsuits, and bankruptcy. He recovered briefly during the 1910s with a few design commissions and then did more writing and lecturing than anything else until his miraculous architectural comeback in 1935. Frank Lloyd Wright left no consistent style or pattern to copy, but his numerous innovations and maverick stubbornness to make his own way in his field left him as perhaps the most important architect in American history.

THE WORLD OF MUSIC

Music in the late nineteenth and early twentieth centuries reflected a wide cultural gap between the middle and upper middle classes on the one hand and the working class on the other.

Orchestra Music and the Opera

The middle and upper middle classes were more attracted to orchestras and operas than the working class was. The New York Philharmonic Symphony Orchestra had been established back in 1842 to provide music for the refined, sophisticated tastes of society's elite. In 1881, both the Boston Symphony Orchestra and the Philadelphia Orchestra were added the nation's fine orchestras. The Boston Symphony Orchestra was especially regarded highly for the wonderfully acoustic building in which it performed its music. Most of the serious music composers and conductors of the period were Europeans rather than Americans. However, the United States did have a few outstanding composers. Two of the most important American composers of the period were Edward MacDowell and Charles Ives.

The best-loved operatic company in the United States was clearly the Metropolitan Opera House established in New York City in 1883. The famous Italian tenor Enrico Caruso made his debut there in 1903 and remained its most famous opera star until his death in 1921.

Vaudeville and Musical Theater

America's working classes did not frequent orchestra concerts or operas but were attracted to lighter musical tunes which also served as a diversion from the stress of everyday life. The tunes from the musical theater were more to their liking. Musical theater was heavily influenced by the vaudeville shows. Vaudeville itself had originated from the early nineteenth century minstrel shows, which had featured white comedians with blackened faces performing song and dance routines as well as mini-comic scenes. The vaudeville shows contained a great deal of variety in order to appeal to the masses. Typically, a show consisted of a dance routine, a music show, comic skits (often satirizing the problems of urban life, immigrant accents, and ethnic stereotypes), magician and/or ventriloquist acts, and gymnastic feats. Vaudeville became very popular by the 1880s as an escape from the dull urban working class life.

George M. Cohan, a former vaudevillian, was one of the most talented figures in the early twentieth century musical theater business. Cohan often wrote all the songs and words for a performance as well as starring and directing in it. Some of his most famous musical compositions include "Give My Regards to Broadway" (1904) and "Over There." (Written in 1917, the last song became the most popular song of World War I.)

Another brilliant producer of theatrical musicals in the early twentieth century was Florenz Ziegfeld. In 1907, he first introduced the nation to the Ziegfeld Follies, a lavish show of detailed sets, beautiful costumes, and outstanding comedians. The

Ziegfeld Follies became an annual musical event for just over twenty years. The spectacular nature of his shows, in which he spared no expense, also attracted some of the country's social elite, including the Rockefellers and the Vanderbilts. The Follies featured a number of American favorites, including Al Jolson, Eddie Cantor, Fanny Brice, Will Rogers, W.C. Fields, and the black vaudeville entertainer Bert Williams.

Ragtime

Coming out of the tradition of African-American spirituals and secular songs from the days of slavery was a new kind of music in the post-Civil War era. Ragtime employed the elements of syncopation, a heavier bass rhythm, and the musical structures of marching band music to create a lively but carefree style of its own. Ragtime began among black musicians in the 1880s, but after it was introduced to the general public in the '90s, it became quite popular. The upper classes, however, scorned ragtime because they viewed it as wild and sensual music that fit the stereotype of African-Americans in that generation. By far the most popular ragtime composer was Scott Joplin, an African-American piano player from St. Louis, Missouri. His most famous composition, "Maple Leaf Rag," gave Joplin national recognition when he wrote it in 1899.

Band Music

A form of music which generally cut across social lines in its appeal was band music. Many small towns all over the country organized bands with volunteer musicians who often performed in local parks during the summer months. Such local bands gave virtually anyone able to play an instrument the opportunity to publicly perform as a musician. But it was the professional bands of the period, many of which gave national tours, that really gave a large number of Americans the chance to hear highly skilled musicians perform live music. As an allusion to the military origin of bands, these groups often played marches. But they also played theater tunes and even orchestra numbers. The best known band leader of the day was John Philip Sousa, who composed as well as conducted band music. Among his approximately one hundred compositions is the premiere marching band hit, "The Stars and Stripes Forever," which he wrote in 1897. Concert band music declined sharply in popularity after World War I, when Americans were increasingly attracted to the more complex rhythms of the dance bands.

THE MOTION PICTURE INDUSTRY

Nothing would come as close to dominating the artistic world in the twentieth century as the movies. This new miracle technology fascinated people and drew them by the millions to watch whatever the young industry was producing. Of course, as with all significant inventions, this entertainment revolution did not occur overnight. Several inventors played important roles in the development of this new technology. As early as 1870, Henry Heyl used what he called his Pharmatrope to rapidly display pictures in order to give the illusion of motion. In the 1890s, motion picture technology was improved, although primitive by modern standards. George Eastman had developed celluloid film for still cameras in the previous decade. In the '90s, an associate of Thomas Edison by the name of W.K.L. Dickson perfected a movie camera called the Kinetograph, which allowed a single viewer to watch "movies" of thirty seconds duration or shorter. Dickson also built the nation's first film studio at Edison's facilities in West Orange, New Jersey in 1893. Edison himself quickly realized that there was no mass market for single-viewer machines, so he purchased the rights to several emerging projection systems and perfected them with his Vitascope in the mid 1890s. In April 1896, Edison showed the first motion pictures ever projected on a screen to an American audience in New York City. It included part of a boxing match and pictures of dancing. Meanwhile, European inventors, especially in France, were already showing motion pictures to audiences in parts of that continent.

The development of a screen projection system quickly outdated the private Kinetograph mode of seeing motion pictures, and continual, rapid progress was made in the perfection of the new approach. The most important early film director was Edwin S. Porter, who produced the first movie with a complete storyline in 1903—*The Great Train Robbery*. With the rise of longer, more expensive narrative films, middlemen came along who purchased films from producers and then charged an admission price to show them to audiences. In this way, the the first of the "nickelodeons" opened in the Pittsburgh, Pennsylvania area in 1905. These earliest American movie theaters were so nicknamed because the admission price charged to viewing customers was a nickel. Within three years, there were over 8,000 nickelodeons operating in the United States, attracting more than 25 million viewers a week. Of course, the motion pictures of this early era were silent movies with subtitles on the screen to show what the actors were saying. They also tended to show motion in an uneven, or jerky, manner compared with modern technical standards.

After nearly a decade of legal fighting in the courts over patent rights, most of the litigants decided to come together; they formed the Motion Picture Patents Company in 1908. Thomas Edison's group held much power in this new company and tried to use it to win monopoly control over the entire industry. However, even before the courts found the company guilty of violating the Sherman Antitrust Act in 1915, independent movie producers were already undercutting its power. When Florence Lawrence left one of the company's affiliated producers to join an independent company in 1910, she became the first movie celebrity to win name recognition. (The producers affiliated with the Motion Picture Patents Company had refused to give actors and actresses any billing.) The door now open, dozens of other actors and actresses became almost overnight celebrities also. Mary Pickford, known as "America's Sweetheart," Charlie Chaplin, and the dean of the early cowboys, William S. Hart, were all stars before the dawn of the 1920s.

Early in the new century, movie production companies moved from the East coast to the West. The rural area just outside Los Angeles, California, known as Hollywood, became the focal point for the young industry. Attracted there by the presence of vast amounts of sunshine for outdoor filming throughout the year, Hollywood became the movie capital of the world by 1920. And names such as Samuel Goldwyn and Louis B. Mayer became dominate Hollywood producers in those early years. Among the Hollywood directors, Mack Sennett and D.W. (David Wark) Griffith were the most influential. Sennett introduced slapstick comedy to the movies. The best known of the early comedic actors was Charlie Chaplin, the "king of comedy," who made his movie acting debut in 1914. D.W. Griffith perfected and employed several new techniques, such as the fade-out, the close-up, and panning, in the first technically well produced film, *The Birth of a Nation*, in 1915. Unfortunately, this technical achievement was accomplished on a film which reinforced racism. Based on Thomas Dixon's book, *The Clansman*, Griffith's movie portrayed the Reconstruction era from an openly racist point of view, making the Ku Klux Klan members the heroes of that period. Ironically, and perhaps not entirely coincidental, 1915 was the very year that the KKK was reorganized and went on to become an influential political force in the 1920s. (See Chapter Nine for more information on the KKK and race relations during that decade.)

THE RISE OF PROFESSIONAL SPORTS

During the late nineteenth and early twentieth centuries, the rise of professional sports provided another kind of diversion that especially appealed to the urban working classes. After a long, hard day at the factory, workers and their families could vicariously experience renewed energy and strength through the organized play of other adults. Baseball, football, and boxing all became professionalized during the period. And basketball, although not really going professional until the 1920s, was invented during this era as well.

Baseball

A crude form of the game we call baseball had been played by children in England as long ago as the seventeenth century. It had been played under various names, such as rounders, one o'cat, and base. American children played it in this country too in the decades before the Civil War. But in 1845 a group of young adult men in New York City organized the first real baseball team, known as the New York Knickerbockers. The Knickerbockers helped standardize the rules of the game, which grew in enormous popularity over the next twenty years, with New York City as the capital of the baseball world. In other words, the alleged invention of baseball by Abner Doubleday in Cooperstown, New York, in 1839 is a myth of American history.

Then in 1869, the Cincinnati Red Stockings became the first regular professional baseball team, with its players under contract. Its national tour that year, which ended in an undefeated season, did much to persuade other organizations to form professional clubs to compete with each other. And in 1876, the National League was established with several teams. By the 1890s, baseball had emerged as America's favorite sport, its "national pastime." Some of the early greats among the players were Honus Wagner, Ty Cobb, and Christy Mathewson.

The National League was controlled by the owners of the clubs and operated much as the business world did. When other leagues arose to compete for the better players, the National League used its growing political and economic influence in the big cities to run them out or simply incorporate them into their own league. One rival league that survived these baseball wars was the American League (originally, the American Association). Established in 1901, this new league became successful because it took measures to appeal to immigrants and other working class Americans. For example, the National League teams had kept beer out of their ballparks and refused to schedule any games on Sunday. Not only did American League teams sell beer and play Sunday games, but they also undercut the older league by charging only about half the price for their tickets. In these ways, the American League ensured their survival in the baseball world. In 1903, just two years after the introduction of the American League, the two leagues played the first World Series championship in which the best team in both leagues played for the bragging rights as the very best baseball team in the world. The American League's Boston Red Socks beat the Pittsburgh Pirates in that first ever World Series.

Football

The origins of American football extend back to medieval times, when players carried, threw, and kicked a ball from one small town to another. This crude game developed into the European sport of soccer and the English game of rugby in the nineteenth century. Although it is often said that the first intercollegiate "football" game was played in 1869, between Princeton and Rutgers, it was really a soccer game. (Rutgers defeated Princeton by a score of 6 to 4.) The modern game of football as we know it was largely the result of Walter C. Camp, the famous football coach at Yale University. Camp brought a number of innovations into the crude game and literally wrote the first real rule book.

Intercollegiate football was a very dangerous game in the late nineteenth century. In 1905, eighteen players died from injuries and more than one hundred fifty others were seriously injured. That season prompted President Theodore Roosevelt to call a special conference at the White House to discuss ways to tame the game and make it much safer. The result of this conference was the creation of the Intercollegiate Athletic Association in 1906, renamed as the National College Athletic Association (NCAA) in 1910, to oversee the game by enacting and enforcing rules to make it safer.

Professional football teams were established in the 1890s, but it was not until the National Football League (NFL) was formed in 1920, under the main leadership of George Halas, that professional football really became a major spectator sport.

Boxing

During the nineteenth century, boxing was illegal in most states. However, that did not prevent a number of British boxers from touring the United States by the middle of that century and taking on all comers. After the Civil War, big city ethnic groups on the East coast began forming their own clubs in which to hold boxing matches. These often served to reinforce the feeling of superiority of each ethnic group. As would be expected with this kind of origin, such amateur boxing appealed to young working-class males, especially among the recent immigrants.

Even amateur boxers usually fought for a cash prize—thus, the term prize fighter. That is why the line between amateur and professional boxing was often blurry. Boxing gained some respectability when the British-developed Marquis of Queensbury rules were introduced into the United States. This code provided for the wearing of gloves, outlawed wrestling holds, and reduced the count time for an official knockout from thirty to ten seconds. The introduction of these rules into the United States is often regarded as the beginning of professional boxing in America. The first match to use these rules occurred between James J. "Gentleman Jim" Corbett and John L. Sullivan, the "Boston strong boy," in September 1892. Although Corbett won that fight, Sullivan's personal popularity and extremely macho style made him the single most popular sports hero of the entire nineteenth century.

James J. Jeffries was the first heavyweight champion of the twentieth century. But when John Arthur "Jack" Johnson won that title in 1908, he became the first black American to ever do so—a title he held until 1915.

Basketball

The game of basketball has an interesting origin. Although the Mayan civilization had a game similar to it, there was no direct, or intentional, link between the Mayans and the American who invented modern basketball.

In late 1891, the head of the physical training staff of the Young Men's Christian Association (YMCA) office in Springfield, Massachusetts, was worried about the lack of attendance during the winter months. So he approached Dr. James A. Naismith, a YMCA physical education instructor, about the need for more competitive sports during the winter to attract more people. That winter (1891), Naismith invented the game of basketball as an indoor sport. Relying on a round ball and two peach baskets on opposite ends of a large room, he established rules for two teams whose goal was to get the ball into their appropriate basket. Originally, the game was played with seven players on each team; the number was increased to nine before eventually being reduced to five. Most of the rules established by Naismith have remained unchanged through the years.

Basketball quickly grew popular because of the simplicity of the game, and in 1896 the first intercolliegate game was played. The NCAA gave the game official sanction in 1908, and high schools and colleges attracted large crowds to watch after that. A professional league was formed on the East coast in 1898, but it ended after just a couple of seasons. Professional basketball had to wait for the 1920s, when the American Basketball League was created (1925).

CONCLUSION

Enormous changes in the late nineteenth and early twentieth centuries had significantly altered American society. The United States had emerged at the turn of the century as the most productive industrial nation in the world. New ideas in the areas of science, religion, education, psychology, and sociology were already beginning to transform the nation, and to impact the entire world. By the twentieth century, in fact, most of the really big new ideas and trends no longer originated somewhere else and were transplanted in the United States. Instead, they began here and crossed both oceans on their way to impacting other countries. But change was just beginning, for the decade following the First World War would be appropriately termed the "Roaring Twenties."

ADDITIONAL READINGS

Ellen Chesler, *Woman of Valor: The Life of Margaret Sanger* (1992). The definitive biography of the birth control pioneer.

Allen F. Davis, *Spearheads of Reform: The Social Settlements and the Progressive Movement,* 1890-1914. Focuses on the influence of the settlement house movement on progressive reform.

Allen F. Davis, *American Heroine: The Life and Legend of Jane Addams* (1973). The standard biography of this central figure of the Progressive era.

Leslie Fishbein, *Rebels in Bohemia* (1982). Surveys the people and causes clustered around *The Masses* magazine and Greenwich Village.

Louis Harlan, *Booker T. Washington: The Wizard of Tuskegee 1901–1915* (1983). The most comprehensive analysis of Washington's thought, leadership, and influence

John F. Kasson, *Amusing the Million: Coney Island at the Turn of the Century* (1978). A heavily illustrated account of America's favorite amusement park. Sees Coney Island as the meeting point for shrewd entrepreneurs and pleasure-seeking immigrants, its amusements and architectural styles emblematic of a special era in American history.

Kenneth L. Kusmer, *A Ghetto Takes Shape: Black Cleveland 1870–1930* (1976). A keen analysis of a long-standing African American community. Shows how black workers suffered downward mobility and increased segregation as their skilled jobs and small-business opportunities were given to European immigrants.

Lawrence H. Larsen, *The Rise of the Urban South* (1985). In Larsen's view, the true "New South" was the city, for relatively few had lived there before the late nineteenth century. But rural values remained vital, especially in religious life and voting patterns.

Kathy Peiss, *Cheap Amusements: Working Women and Leisure in Turn-of-the-Century New York* (1986). Explores how working-class women both shaped and were shaped by new forms of commercial leisure.

Howard N. Rabinowitz, *Race Relations in the Urban South 1865–1890* (1978). A detailed account of black-white social and political relations in southern cities.

Roy Rosenzweig, *Eight Hours for What We Will: Workers and Leisure in an Industrial City 1870–1920* (1983). Treats the city park as the arena for conflict over whether public community life should be uplifting (devoted to nature walks and concerts) or entertaining (allowing drinking, courting, and amusement).

Nancy Woloch, *Women and the American Experience* (1984). Includes excellent material on women's crucial contributions to progressive reform, as well as an analysis of the larger changes in women's public and private lives during this period.

C. Vann Woodward, *The Strange Career of Jim Crow*, 3rd rev. ed. (1974). The classic study of southern segregation. Shows how racist laws and customs tightened in the South and in many parts of the North in the last decades of the nineteenth century, and how the ideologies of the society encouraged the rise of Jim Crow legislation.

CHAPTER SIX

McKinley and the Progressive Era Presidents

MAJOR EVENTS

1897   Dingley Tariff

1900   Currency Act commits U.S. to gold standard
McKinley reelected
Robert M. La Follette elected governor of Wisconsin

1901   Theodore Roosevelt succeeds the assassinated William McKinley as president

1902   Lincoln Steffens, *The Shame of the Cities*

1905   President Roosevelt creates U.S. Forest Service and names Gifford Pinchot head

1906   Upton Sinclair, *The Jungle*
Congress passes Pure Food and Drug Act and Meat Inspection Act and establishes Food and Drug Administration (FDA)

1908   In *Muller v. Oregon* Supreme Court upholds a state law limiting maximum hours for working women

1912   Democrat Woodrow Wilson wins presidency, defeating Republican William H. Taft, Progressive Theodore Roosevelt and Socialist Eugene V. Debs

1913   Sixteenth Amendment, legalizing a graduated income tax, is ratified

1914   Passage of Clayton Anti-Trust Act
Establishment of the Federal Trade Commission (FTC)

1917   Congress passes Eighteenth Amendment, prohibiting the manufacture and sale of alcoholic beverages

1919   Eighteenth Amendment (Prohibition) ratified

1920   Nineteenth Amendment (woman suffrage) ratified

INTRODUCTION TO THE MCKINLEY ADMINISTRATION

Ohio Republican William McKinley was elected the nation's twenty-fifth president in 1896. (See Chapter Four for an analysis of the 1896 election.) This marked the beginning of Republican rule, in the Congress as well as the White House, that would not end until after the collapse of the national economy in 1929. Only Democrat Woodrow Wilson would interrupt the Republican control of the White House (1913-1921) from McKinley's inauguration on March 4, 1897, to Franklin D. Roosevelt's inauguration on March 4, 1933—a period of thirty-six years.

President McKinley's most important cabinet positions initially included John Sherman as Secretary of State, who was appointed to get him out of the Senate so that the Ohio legislature could elect another Ohio Republican, National Republican Committee Chairman and McKinley's presidential campaign manager Marc Hanna, to the Senate. Sherman, a fellow Ohio Republican, had been one of the most popular members of Congress, allowing his name to be attached to several key pieces of legislation, including the Sherman Antitrust Act and the Sherman Silver Purchase Act. (See Chapter Four for more information on these laws.) Although William R. Day initially replaced him in 1898 as Secretary of State, John Hay served in that capacity longer than the previous two, from 1898 through Theodore Roosevelt's first complete term, which ended in early March 1905. Other major cabinet members in his first term included Lyman J. Gage as Secretary of the Treasury and Elihu Root as Secretary of War. Root, who joined the cabinet in 1899, went on to serve as Theodore Roosevelt's Secretary of War during his first term (1901-1905) and his Secretary of State during the second Roosevelt term (1905-1909).

The McKinley administration was mostly occupied with foreign policy concerns, especially the Spanish-American War in 1898. In this chapter, however, the focus will be on his domestic accomplishments. In fact, the focus of this entire chapter for all four American presidents—McKinley, Roosevelt, Taft, and Wilson—will be on the domestic political and economic issues which they faced. (See Chapter Seven for the foreign policy history of the United States under these four presidents.)

THE DINGLEY TARIFF ACT

Although the Democrats had only modestly lowered the average tariff rate in the August 1894 Wilson-Gorman Tariff Act (see Chapter Four), the Republican penchant for raising tariffs in allegiance to big business leaders was revived in a new tariff law. Sponsored by Maine Republican Representative Nelson Dingley, Jr., the Dingley Tariff Act was passed by Congress in July 1897. The Dingley Tariff raised the average tariff rate to about 52 percent (some authorities say 57 percent), which raised them beyond the 1890 McKinley Tariff Act to a new all-time record. The law also expanded the reciprocity provisions in the tariff system. In the Dingley Tariff Act, the president now had the authority to negotiate trade agreements with other nations to reduce rates up to 20 percent in return for certain American trade advantages. These agreements took the form of treaties, which meant that a two-thirds vote in the United States Senate was necessary for ratification and adoption.

During the life of the Dingley Tariff, all 11 such tariff reduction treaties were rejected by the Senate. The president also was given authority to proclaim lower tariffs on luxury items, without need for Congressional approval, in return for concessions from another country.

THE REFUSE ACT

With the vast growth in factories during the Industrial Revolution, there was a growing concern about the pollutants being dumped into the nation's rivers and waterways. So in 1899, Congress passed the Refuse Act as one of the nation's first federal anti-pollution laws. The new law forbid the dumping of refuse into navigable rivers or tributaries without permission from the United States Army Corps of Engineers. The penalty for violating the law ranged from $500 to $2,500 in fines and up to one year in jail. Half of the fines were to go to informants. The approval of the Army Corps of Engineers proved to be a leaking sieve in the law, which was not very effective. A major environmental movement focusing on water and air pollution would have to wait for the 1960s and 1970s.

GOLD AND THE GOLDEN AGE OF AGRICULTURE

When gold was discovered in the Klondike region of western Canada in August 1896, the Klondike Gold Rush ushered in another period of gold fever from 1897 to 1898. Thousands of Americans crowded onto boats in the Puget Sound near Seattle, Washington, or at San Francisco, bound for the Klondike River area. Most entered Canada via the Lynn Canal and the port of Skagway, Alaska, while others used Valdez, Alaska as a gateway to the gold fields. Supply towns grew up almost overnight in order to meet the needs of those who risked their lives in search of quick riches. As with all gold rushes, the few who got there early obtained the lion's share of the gold, but the majority who came later faced incredible hardships that did not result in the obtaining of wealth. Hundreds died in the extremely cold winters. Scurvy and other diseases killed many others, as did avalanches, other accidents, and greed-motivated murders. Prices for supplies were exhorbitantly high, but people paid them in the desperate hope that they would strike it rich beyond their wildest dreams. Gambling and prostitution were rampant too. Increasingly tough law enforcement by the Canadian Mounted Police ("Mounties"), stiff Canadian requirements that prospectors bring large, expensive supplies of food and other provisions with them into Canada, high customs duties, men joining to fight in the popular Spanish-American War, and the discovery of gold in Nome, Alaska in 1899, all contributed to a sharp drop in American prospecting activity in the Canadian Klondike before the turn of the century. That was immediately followed by the Alaskan Gold Rush, properly speaking. By the middle of 1900, an estimated 10,000 Americans were in the Nome area seeking the precious metal.

The economic result of the new supply of gold was a rapid increase in the nation's money supply, which in turn, helped to both end the economic depression (since the Panic of 1893; see Chapter Four) and raise farm prices significantly. Although William Jennings Bryan never appeared ready to abandon the silver question (See Chapter Four for information on the monetary issue in general, and the silver movement in particular.), the Klondike and Alaskan Gold Rushes effectively ended the silver movement. And in March 1900, the federal government put the country officially on a full gold standard with the passage of the Gold Standard Act. This meant that all forms of American money were then redeemable in gold, and that gold was **the** monetary standard. The irony in all this was that gold, the bastion of conservative monetarists, proved the Populists essentially correct when they had complained that a basic problem in causing farm prices to remain depressed was the very low money supply in the American economy during the Gilded Age. (Farmers failed to recognize overproduction as their most important problem, but they were still correct that the low money supply had significantly hurt farm prices.) In a fluke of history, gold, not silver, became the financial ally of the nation's farmers. By the turn of the new century, American agriculture was entering its golden age, which lasted until 1920.

Factors other than the gold discoveries in the north country also assisted in the development of the golden age of American agriculture. The closing of the western frontier, officially announced in the results of the census of 1890, meant that fewer new farms were being added to drive crop and farmland prices downward. At the same time, the urbanization trend and America's bulging cities increased the demand for farm products. Technological advances also provided farmers with better farm equipment, providing greater productivity on their land. And even before the United States entered World War I, those early war years saw huge increases in American farm exports to parts of Europe in order to help feed the Allies, whose major portion of their workforce had been drafted into the military or diverted to wartime production efforts. The early twentieth century was the most successful era for American farmers.

THE 1900 ELECTION

With the end of the depression, a return to prosperity, and the successful conclusion of the Spanish-American War during his first term, William McKinley was virtually assured reelection in 1900. The only real maneuvering left for the Republican convention concerned the vice-presidential nomination. The main player in the politicking for McKinley's running mate was the powerful New York Republican boss and senator, Thomas C. Platt. Platt's choice for the vice-presidential nominee was Theodore Roosevelt, who was then the popular governor of New York. Platt, in fact, had been instrumental in getting Roosevelt the Republican nomination for governor in 1898. But Roosevelt, although popular with the voters, had angered Platt by fighting the corrupt New York Superintendent of Insurance, Lou Payn. It was during this political struggle that Governor Roosevelt had first publicly used the West African proverb, "Walk softly and carry a big stick." Therefore, Platt worked tirelessly to get Roosevelt the second place on the national ticket in 1900 because he wanted to get him out of New York. And, indeed, Vice-President Garret A. Hobart was replaced by Theodore Roosevelt on the national Republican ticket that year, illustrating the power and influence wielded by major political party bosses in those days.

The Democrats nominated William Jennings Bryan for president again in 1900, despite his heavy loss to McKinley 4 years earlier. Former Vice-President Adlai Stevenson from Illinois, who had served in that capacity during Grover Cleveland's second term in office (from 1893 to 1897), became Bryan's running mate this time. During the campaign, Bryan tried to make his anti-imperialism stance the most important issue, although the Democratic platform had once again endorsed free silver. But on both issues, the Republicans held the upper hand. The growing movement for imperialistic policies had been strengthened by the Spanish-American War. And as already stated, the silver movement was really dead; Bryan just didn't realize it yet. In fact, Bryan's talk about silver during the election drove more conservative Democrats (the so-called Gold Democrats) to the Republican camp. Marc Hanna ran the McKinley campaign again in 1900, on a "Full Dinner Pail" slogan that emphasized the return of economic prosperity.

The very two issues which the Democrats emphasized during the campaign ensured McKinley's reelection victory because the majority of Americans had simply agreed with the Republicans in those areas. When the votes were counted, McKinley won with the largest electoral majority to that date, garnering 292 votes to just 155 for Bryan. A third party candidate, John C. Wooley of the Prohibition Party, received just less than 209,000 popular votes and no electoral votes.

THE ASSASSINATION OF MCKINLEY

On September 6, 1901, while attending the Pan-American Exposition in Buffalo, New York, President William McKinley became the third American president to be assassinated. He was shot at point-blank range by Leon Czolgosz, a fanatical anarchist, who had hidden a handgun in his bandaged hand. At first, it appeared that the president would survive his wound, so Vice-President Roosevelt continued with his plans to hike and hunt in the Adirondack Mountains of upstate New York. Several days later, a messenger caught up with Roosevelt to inform the vice-president that McKinley's condition was worsening. Traveling all night by horse and wagon, Roosevelt then boarded a train that took him to Buffalo. President McKinley, who had yielded to pressure and taken the country into the Spanish-American War (1898) primarily because he wanted to be reelected (See Chapter Eight for more details.), ironically died on September 12, only 6 months into his second term. And on September 14, 1901, Theodore Roosevelt was sworn in as the twenty-sixth president of the United States.

1900	45	WILLIAM MCKINLEY	Republican	7,218,491	292	51.7
		William J. Bryan	Democrat: Populist	6,356,734	155	45.5
		John C. Woolley	Prohibition	208,914		1.5

AN OVERVIEW OF THE PROGRESSIVE ERA

The unexpected inauguration of Theodore Roosevelt launched the nation into what historians call the Progressive Era, a time of great social and political change (1901–1917) that stretched into Woodrow Wilson's second term and ended only with the entrance of the United States into World War I. Three different presidents occupied the White House and contributed to the progressive winds of change, each with his own unique approach and personality—Theodore Roosevelt, William Howard Taft, and Woodrow Wilson.

A Definition of Progressivism

A precise definition of progressivism is difficult because it was an American reaction to a number of social and economic problems that faced the country, most of them directly or indirectly as the result of the Industrial Revolution. Opinions and solutions varied greatly among the progressives, but each of them sought ways and means to level the playing field between the haves and the have-nots, whether it was on the issue of child labor, the power of corporations, or concern about the lack of economic competition in general. Perhaps the best definition that gets to the heart of the progressive soul is this: it was a moral reaction to the feared effects of the concentration of wealth and power, principally its effect on democratic government and on corruption in both business and government. It was a conservative movement in the sense that progressives wished to restore the old-fashioned values of real competition, hard work, and fair play. But it was liberal, in the twentieth century sense of that term, because progressives saw the need for a federal government role to preserve capitalism and protect it from the growing numbers choosing socialism or communism, which at least seemed to threaten the American way of life.

In other words, progressivism did not offer a set of inflexible, doctrinaire solutions to the country's ills. Rather, it expressed an anxiety that the nation badly needed some changes before some groups decided to overthrow the present system. To the progressive, nothing less than fairness, integrity, and the American dream were at stake. Because of their middle course between traditional political conservatism, which had always championed the rich and powerful, and radical leftism, progressives tended to shy away from general solutions and offer piecemeal plans for specific problems. Emphasizing the moral part of their reaction to problems, progressives tended to view social problems in simplistic terms. That is to say, many progressives looked at corrupt or inefficient leaders in business or government as the main source of problems, and felt that if they could get rid of the "bad" people, everything would eventually turn out quite well. Progressives have been properly criticized for this naive view because they often forgot that good, honest, and efficient people pursuing bad policies still end up producing negative results.

Progressives and Populists

It is tempting to view the progressives of the early twentieth century simply as an extension of the populists of the 1890s, but that would be misleading. There were both similarities and differences between these two groups. Both groups were certainly concerned about certain abuses of economic power. In this sense, both populists and progressives were reformers who recognized that government should not be simply a tool of the economic elite but an agency of all the people. The demographics of these two groups, however, was as stark as the difference between night and day. The populists of the 1890s had basically been rural, agrarian Americans, both white and black, with less formal education than the average citizen. Early twentieth century progressives, by contrast, were typically white, middle class urban Americans, with more formal education than the average citizen. The populists had been more radical in their approach to problems, calling for government ownership of the railroads and utilities, for example, and advocating the so-called "cheap" money, or inflationary, view of the money supply. And most populists distrusted urban dwellers in general, especially if they lived in the Northeast, and of bankers and railroad executives, whom they viewed as villains.

Progressives, on the other hand, were really not radical at all. They tended to view monopoly and corruption as the villains rather than specific people groups, and they opposed government ownership of the railroads, while advocating the so-called "sound" money policy of conservative monetarists. Despite the very different backgrounds between the two groups (which basically did not exist simultaneously), progressives supported nearly every populist program except government ownership of the railroads and free silver. The irony is that the populist movement was crushed by a smashing conservative Republican victory in the 1896 presidential election because it was perceived as too radical, but the more "respectable" progressives managed to accomplish almost every major populist reform within the first 16 years of the new century, more often than not with Republican votes in Congress and under mostly Republican presidents.

Progressivism at the Local Level

Progressives began efforts to reform government at the city level. Two of the nation's most effective and popular progressive mayors of the early twentieth century were Democrat Tom L. Johnson of Cleveland, Ohio, and Republican Samuel M. "Golden Rule" Jones of Toledo, Ohio. Both mayors were honest men, but Johnson was generally considered to have been the most competent mayor of a major city in American history up to that time. Among Mayor Jones' accomplishments were the establishment of a minimum wage and an 8-hour day for city employees.

The traditional mayor-city council system of local government encouraging political corruption was one of the first targets for change. Under that form of local government, the city was divided into special districts, usually called wards, each of which would elect one member to sit on the city council. Powerful political party machines often gained control over a city for decades by making deals with different ethnic groups and favoring certain business interests with municipal contracts and other shady, if not illegal, methods. New York City's Democratic organization,

Tammany Hall, was only the most notorious of these powerful machines. This prompted many progressives to advocate alternatives to the mayor-city council system.

The two most well-known alternatives to the traditional form of municipal government were the city manager and the city-commission plans. The city-manager plan was based on the premise that a city could and should be run something like a company, which reflected the progressive tendency to believe that efficiency and order would always produce the best results. A group of elected commissioners would act like a company board of directors and select a nonpolitical professional to serve as the city manager. Staunton, Virginia became the first city to adopt the city-manager plan in 1908, although Dayton, Ohio seemed to have more national influence on other cities after it adopted the plan in 1914. But while some cities experienced positive results from it, a basic problem remaining was that cities simply are not businesses, and this system did not work as well as expected to bring efficiency and end corruption at the municipal level.

In the city-commission form of government, the main board, or legislative body, consisted of a small group (usually 5) of members elected on a city-wide basis, with no districts or wards. Each commissioner managed a particular department in city government and was responsible for its operation. This board selects one of their members to act as the chairperson for the group, but the real power lay with the commission as a body. After a devastating hurricane, Galveston, Texas became the first city to adopt the city-commission form of government in 1901. By 1914, more than 400 smaller towns and cities across the country had adopted similar plans. But as with the city-manager system, this one did not prove to be a panacea for urban problems either, and many cities eventually abandoned the concept.

Progressivism at the State Level

Progressives were generally more successful at the state level in achieving meaningful reforms than they were at the municipal level. Wisconsin led the way by electing the nation's first progressive governor, Republican Robert M. "Fighting Bob" LaFollette, in 1900. LaFollette, who served three consecutive terms as governor before being elected to the United States Senate in 1906, developed a collection of programs which became known as the "Wisconsin Idea." Progressive reforms in that state included the adoption of the direct primary in 1903 (the first state to do so) and closer state regulation of railroads, banks, and insurance companies. Wisconsin also reduced the number of working hours per week for women and children and adopted several measures aimed at conserving the state's many natural resources.

The second most notable progressive governor of the period was Charles Evans Hughes, the Republican governor of New York. Hughes had worked as a lawyer for the Congressional Armstrong Committee in 1905, which had investigated corrupt practices in the insurance industry. One year later, in 1906, Hughes defeated the newspaper tycoon, William Randolph Hearst, in a successful bid for the governorship of New York. As governor, Hughes tightened the reins on New York's insurance companies and increased the power of the state to investigate corruption in city and county governments.

Other notable progressive state leaders included California Republican Governor Hiram W. Johnson, who ended the political domination of that state by the Southern Pacific Railroad Company, and New Jersey Democratic Governor Woodrow Wilson, who later became a two-term president of the United States. And although the South, as a region, was least affected by the progressive movement, it also produced a few important progressive governors who favored limiting the power of corporations. Among these were Alabama Governor Jeff Davis, Georgia Governor Hoke Smith, and Texas Governor James Hogg.

Believing that state legislatures were too often the pawns of special interest groups, especially powerful corporations and business lobbies, progressives pushed hard for more direct forms of democracy at the state level. These efforts resulted in several states adopting the direct primary, the recall, the initiative, and the referendum. As already noted above, Wisconsin was the first state to adopt the direct primary in 1903. The direct primary is an election in which the voters directly select the candidates of the political parties that will run in the regular election. By 1933, the direct primary was being used in all but 6 states in the country.

The recall was first implemented in 1903 in the city of Los Angeles and then spread to cover statewide officials in a number of states. If a specific minimum percentage of registered voters, usually 25 percent, signed a recall petition to remove an officeholder before his term expired, then a special election would be held to determine the fate of the official. The initiative was first adopted in South Dakota in 1898, allowing voters to force a vote on a proposed state law by collecting signatures of a certain percentage of registered voters, usually about 10 percent. The referendum, like the initiative, was first adopted in South Dakota in 1898. The referendum usually requires the same percentage of signatures as the initiative, but allows the people to directly approve or reject a law that has passed the state legislature. In some states, the legislature itself may call for a referendum on a bill it has adopted. The state's voters in a referendum (and initiative) have the final determination on whether a proposed law is enacted or defeated.

Progressivism at the Federal Level

Progressive efforts at the federal level of government are probably best illustrated by a series of progressive amendments to the Constitution, officially proposed and finally ratified between 1909 and 1920. The so-called progressive amendments are the four amendments from the sixteenth through the nineteenth.

Amendment	Proposed by Congress	Ratified
Sixteenth—Income Tax	1909	1913
Seventeenth—Direct Election of United States Senators	1912	1913
Eighteenth—Prohibition	1917	1919
Nineteenth—Women's Suffrage	1919	1920

Progressives, like the populists before them, favored a federal income tax as one method of leveling the vast extremes of income. They also viewed it as a simple matter of fairness; those who possessed greater financial rewards should also bear greater responsibility to society. Thus, the idea of the progressive, or graduated, income tax was that the higher the income, the higher the percentage of the tax. During the Civil War, Congress did enact an income tax as just one small way to help finance the Union war effort, but it was allowed to die a few years after the war had ended. Then after the United States Supreme Court declared the federal income tax provisions of the Wilson-Gorman Tariff Act (1894) unconstitutional in 1895, on grounds that it was a forbidden direct tax, reformers worked to enact a constitutional amendment to override the decision. In August 1909, Congress officially proposed such an amendment as part of the Payne-Aldrich Tariff Act. And in 1913 the Sixteenth Amendment was ratified, granting Congress the constitutional permission to enact a federal income tax, which they did almost immediately.

The direct election of senators had long been an objective of reformers, who were suspicious that too many backroom deals had placed political cronies in the Senate. In 1912, in the context of the Progressive Era, Congress proposed via the Seventeenth Amendment that voters directly elect each state's two senators. This very popular measure was quickly ratified by the next year (1913) and was seen by the progressive leaders themselves as their finest accomplishment in the political reform arena.

(See Chapter Five for more information on the Eighteenth and Nineteenth Amendments to the Constitution. And see the remainder of this chapter for legislative and other actions taken by the progressives at the federal level.)

A BIOGRAPHICAL SKETCH OF THEODORE ROOSEVELT

The first progressive president, Theodore Roosevelt, was born in 1858 to a wealthy upstate New York family. As a young boy, Roosevelt was in poor health, especially suffering from bad eyes and asthma. For this reason, he received his early education from private tutors. He later attended Harvard University, where he learned boxing and further improved his physical health and stamina. He graduated from Harvard in 1880, briefly studied law at Columbia University, and wrote *The Naval War of 1812* in 1882. With the precedence of a politically active family heritage, mostly in state Republican politics, the young Roosevelt entered into a political career in his home state as a Republican. Devoted to reform issues in the New York State Assembly, Roosevelt was not always popular. But he did help write civil service reform legislation for his state government.

On Valentine's Day 1884, both his mother and first wife died in unrelated incidents. Emotionally crushed, Roosevelt left New York and established two ranches in the Dakota Territory, where he became a deputy sheriff and something of a cowboy. But he was a terrible manager of money, and his ranches were a financial disaster; he survived as an amateur historian by writing books on a contract basis. In 1886 he returned to New York, where he lost a race for the mayor of New York City. To defeat the Labor Party candidate, Henry George, many traditional Republicans voted for the Democratic candidate, Abram S. Hewitt. He returned to writing with

President Theodore Roosevelt on his historic visit to the Redwood Grove at Santa Cruz in May, 1903.

the publication of *The Life of Thomas Hart Benton* in 1887 and *Governor Morris* in 1888. Roosevelt also had remarried in 1887.

Roosevelt moved to the national political level with an appointment from President Benjamin Harrison to the federal Civil Service Commission in 1889, where he earned a reputation as a maverick reformer. For that reason, Democratic President Grover Cleveland kept him on the commission until he resigned in 1895 to become one of three members of the New York City Police Commission. Becoming its president, Roosevelt insisted on strict enforcement of all regulations, especially the hours reserved for serving liquor. This latter effort angered many New Yorkers, so he left the job in 1897. With the influence of his personal friend, Senator Henry Cabot Lodge, Roosevelt was appointed the Assistant Secretary of the Navy by President McKinley. In this capacity, he vigorously supported the building of a strong navy. He resigned in 1898 to become a Lieutenant-Colonel and second in command of a voluntary cavalry unit known as the "Rough Riders" during the Spanish-American War. After the war, Roosevelt wrote about his experiences in *The Rough Riders* (1899). His war hero status helped elect him governor of New York in 1898. In 1900 he accepted the vice-presidential nomination with reluctance, and in a twist of irony, he became president upon the assassination of President McKinley.

INTRODUCTION TO THE ROOSEVELT ADMINISTRATION

With the swearing in of Theodore Roosevelt as president, most professional Republican politicians and their big business allies were frightened by what National Republican Committee Chairman Marc Hanna called "that damn cowboy." Two well-established tendencies in the new president especially worried them—his reputation for doing things his own way and his many reform-minded ideas. Roosevelt tried to allay their fears by immediately announcing that he would continue the same policies that McKinley had followed. Nevertheless, in his first State of the Union message sent to Congress in December 1901 (presidents did not personally deliver such addresses in those days), President Roosevelt outlined a progressive agenda for the country. The federal government would have to exert greater control over the overwhelming power of corporations. Roosevelt also proposed to strengthen the ability of the Interstate Commerce Commission to more effectively regulate the railroad industry. Roosevelt proposed to develop a systematic approach to the conservation of the nation's natural resources.

Many professional politicians were worried about the president, but the general public was ready for meaningful reforms, and they saw in Roosevelt a man who could lead them into the twentieth century. Over the years he so endeared himself to the American people that his admirers affectionately referred to him as "Teddy." No president had ever been so energetic as Roosevelt. He bubbled with enthusiasm and at times he boiled with frustration and anger. But mostly he was the buoyant, aggressive president that the common man could understand. Roosevelt enhanced his image with ordinary Americans by obviously enjoying the great outdoors and hunting whenever possible. On a hunting expedition while president, Roosevelt refused to shoot a bear cub. Picking up on the story, a toy manufacturer introduced children to the now-famous "Teddy" bear.

Theodore Roosevelt became the first president in peacetime to really mold the presidency into a powerful center for change. He saw that position as the focal point for initiating legislation as well as the main public forum for the president to express the will of the people. Thus, he sought to expand his power constantly. Besides his controversial foreign policy achievements, this was Roosevelt's most significant contribution to American history. Fundamental to understanding the Roosevelt presidency is to recognize that his greed for power was tempered by his strong convictions in favor of hard work, duty, and order. Roosevelt saw power as the means to impose order, which was absolutely necessary for morality to exist. That is why he emphasized sound administration, change primarily within the existing institutional framework of society, and individual integrity as the basis for institutional morality. Thus, Roosevelt's obsession with order and stability motivated him to seek reforms in the business world, not because he saw the bigness of corporations as bad, but to ensure that honesty and integrity existed as a dominant force in the system. Furthermore, he saw federal power as sometimes necessary to change the system in order to prevent revolt and disorder by those Americans at the bottom of the socioeconomic ladder. This helps explain, for example, his unconstitutional threat to take over the mines during the 1902 coal strike.

ROOSEVELT'S ANTITRUST ACTIONS

In February 1902, beginning his program to regulate big business, President Roosevelt directed Attorney-General Philander C. Knox to sue the Northern Securities Corporation for violating the Sherman Antitrust Act of 1890. The Northern Securities Company was a holding company created in 1901 to resolve major conflicts in the Northwest among the various railroad companies there. Its creation had meant that it held a virtual monopoly of that industry in the Northwest. With several unpopular financiers involved, such as J.P. Morgan and James J. Hill, most Americans cheered the news of the impending government suit. Wall Street, however, was alarmed and predicted that capitalism itself was under siege. The following year a federal court agreed with the government and ordered the company to dissolve. Upon appeals, the United States Supreme Court heard the case of the *United States v. Northern Securities Company* in 1904 and upheld the lower court's order to dissolve the company for being in violation of the Sherman Antitrust Act.

President Theodore Roosevelt's view of the Harvester Trust as a "good trust." Credit: Brown Brothers.

In a tour of New England and the Midwest in August 1902, Roosevelt gave a theme to his presidency when he called for a "square deal" for the American people, which meant that he would enforce the antitrust law and work for closer regulation of corporate power. Roosevelt never thought of himself as a great trust-buster, but that is what his reputation has been through the years. The main reason for this reputation was the clear fact that he did revitalize the use of the Sherman Antitrust Act, instituting more than 40 antitrust suits during his nearly 7½ years in the White House. However, he had repeatedly gone out of his way to emphasize his belief that the growing size of business was an inevitable part of progress which could not and should not be stopped. He had the Department of Justice bring suits against alleged trusts and monopolies that he felt endangered the virtues of honesty and integrity, virtues he believed to be vital to the public morality of the American society. Thus, he made a distinction between what he called good trusts and bad trusts, although the distinction was never clearly outlined by the president's words or by consistent action. Instead, he called for more government regulation of corporations in order to promote the best interests of every citizen, which was also in the national interest. When he didn't get all that he wanted from Congress, he resorted to using antitrust suits to wield presidential power.

In February 1903, Congress passed the Expedition Act, which made the federal courts give precedence to cases involving both the Sherman Antitrust Act and the Interstate Commerce Act. In the same month, Congress also created the Department of Commerce and Labor, with a Bureau of Corporations to investigate corporations engaged in interstate commerce. The Bureau could recommend antitrust suits to the Justice Department, but it generally operated to advise companies on possible law violations so that costly court battles would be unnecessary. Use of the Sherman Antitrust Act by the government, however, was like treading water. Even when the Supreme Court ordered a trust to dissolve, it was generally in response to the government's civil suit, so corporate executives or financiers were not held personally responsible for the actions of their companies. Executives involved often would informally, via so-called "gentlemen's agreements," continue to do what they had formally done when the trust had actually existed.

THE CONSERVATION MOVEMENT AND THEODORE ROOSEVELT

During the Gilded Age, many Americans were growing concerned about the squandering of natural resources. This had led to a movement to conserve natural resources like water, forests, minerals, and soils for future generations. In 1891, for example, Secretary of the Interior John Noble received permission from the Forest Reserves Act to protect forest lands west of the Mississippi by declaring them national forests and thus, off limits to private developers. Major objectives of the Interior Department included the building of dams for irrigation, flood control, and hydroelectric power, and the restoration of fish and game for hunting and fishing. Secondarily, but during the same period, support for setting apart large amounts of federal land, especially in the West, as state and national parks for the protection of the natural environment and beauty, also became an objective of the conservation movement. Yellowstone National Park, in the northwest corner of Wyoming, became the first national park in our history when it was established in 1872. Several more such parks were created during the next four or five decades so that Congress created the National Park Service in 1916 to oversee them.

Progressives in the early twentieth century were more successful in their conservation goals than in any other single area of public policy, and the conservation movement was greatly accelerated during this time. President Roosevelt, an outdoor enthusiast and sportsman, did more to champion the conservation movement than any previous president, and perhaps more than any to date. After an agreement in principle among several leading members of Congress from the West the year before, Congress finally passed the National Reclamation Act in the summer of 1902. It is often called the Newlands Reclamation Act in honor of Nevada Democratic Senator Francis G. Newlands, the chief sponsor of the bill in Congress. The law stipulated that money from the sale of federal lands in the West would be used to finance irrigation projects that would benefit farmers and ranchers in that part of the country. Those farmers and ranchers who used the federal water would pay a user's fee, the proceeds from which would be placed in a revolving fund that would finance further irrigation projects. The law also established the Bureau of Reclamation, which proceeded to construct a series of dams in the West. Two of the most famous were the Boulder Dam (later renamed the Hoover Dam in honor of President Herbert Hoover), on the Nevada-Arizona line, and the Roosevelt Dam, on the Salt River in Arizona. Former President Theodore Roosevelt himself dedicated the dam named after him in March 1911.

While Roosevelt was the number one cheerleader for conservation, his own Forest Service Director, Gifford Pinchot, did most of the actual organizational work needed to actually protect large areas of federal lands. Under Roosevelt and Pinchot, the federal government set aside more than 200 million acres of public lands as national forests, mineral reserves, and possible water power sites from 1901 to 1909. In 1908, the Roosevelt White House hosted a conference of governors to discuss the broad strategies of the conservation effort. The result of that meeting was the creation of the National Conservation Commission, chaired by Pinchot, to coordinate plans with state conservation commissions, which were also created in three-fourths of the states as a result of the White House conference.

THE 1902 COAL STRIKE

The anthracite coal areas of eastern Pennsylvania were worked by miners who had tried unsuccessfully for years to improve their standard of living along with their working conditions. Coal mine owners had refused to discuss the issues of higher pay, fewer work hours, and official recognition of the union. In May 1902, after the owners turned down a request for a third party to arbitrate the issues, the growing discontent resulted in a major coal strike, which included miners in West Virginia too. The Mine Workers' Union, led by John Mitchell, demanded a 20 percent wage increase, a reduction in workday hours from 10 to 9 and official union recognition. The coal owners' association, led by George F. Baer, president of the Reading Railroad Company, refused to talk to union representatives and stubbornly prepared for a long strike. Baer echoed the dominant Gilded Age philosophy of Social Darwinism when he arrogantly announced: "The rights and interests of the laboring man will be protected and cared for, not by the labor agitators, but by the Christian men to whom God in his infinite wisdom has given control of the property interests of the country." Those words probably did as much as anything to win sympathy for the striking miners.

President Roosevelt grew more concerned as the strike lingered on for several months. The anthracite coal supply affected by the strike was the main source of heating fuel for homes by the turn of the century. Fearful that winter might arrive before the strike had been settled, and that he might be blamed for the cold homes even by the Republican voters in New England and the Midwest, the president called both sides to the White House on October 3 in an effort to mediate an end to the dispute. During the entire meeting, the coal owners refused to talk to Mitchell or any of the other union representatives, either directly or indirectly. Union officials at the meeting repeated their long-standing offer to either negotiate their differences with the owners or submit them to binding arbitration. When Roosevelt asked if the owners were willing to do either, they maintained their refusal and demanded that the president send in federal troops, if necessary, to put down the strike, just as had been done 8 years earlier in the famous Pullman strike. The intransigence of the owners angered Roosevelt, and he made certain they knew it. Later he said that he wanted to pick up George Baer and personally throw him out the White House window.

After the White House meeting ended in an impasse, the president told close advisors that he was prepared to send troops to take over the mines. That action would have been highly questionable from a constitutional point of view since previous judicial decisions had never given the slightest indication that this would be judged as an acceptable use of presidential power. The president had the right to use federal troops anywhere in American territory if required to exercise federal authority. And a president could also send troops to a state if the governor or state legislature requested them to restore or maintain the peace. But the idea that federal troops could seize and operate private property was almost certainly unconstitutional. However, President Roosevelt used Pennsylvania Republican Senator Matthew Quay to arrange for the governor of that state to request the use of federal troops there. Meanwhile, Roosevelt also sent Secretary of War Elihu Root to New York to meet secretly with J.P. Morgan for the purpose of getting him to pressure the coal operators to compromise.

All these maneuvers worked to produce a compromise by the middle of October. The miners agreed to return to work, and the president would appoint an arbitration panel to hear and decide the issues; both sides agreed to abide by the arbitration commission's decisions. At the last minute, the operators refused to accept a union official on the panel, so Roosevelt promptly changed his title to an "eminent sociologist." Not wanting further trouble, the operators caved in, and the strike ended before the month was over.

President Roosevelt was satisfied that both the companies and the mine workers had received a square deal out of the compromise. The 1902 coal strike was certainly significant for several reasons. For the first time, it represented the typically progressive political attitude that government interventions in labor disputes, when necessary, should no longer occur for the purpose of imposing management's will, but as an even-handed action to promote the national interest. It was the first time the president of the United States had called both sides in a labor dispute into the White House for the purpose of attempting to mediate the conflict. It was also the first time a president had appointed a panel to arbitrate the issues in a labor-management dispute, and the first time that a president threatened to use federal troops to take over and operate a major industry. In March 1903, the arbitration commission handed down a mixed decision. The miners received an average 10 percent wage increase and a workday of 9 hours (some classification of miners even got an eight-hour day), but no official union recognition as an agent for collective bargaining, which was a major disappointment.

THE ELKINS ACT

In February 1903, Congress passed the Elkins Act in response to pleas from President Roosevelt to strengthen the Interstate Commerce Act. Passed in 1887, the Interstate Commerce Act had made it illegal for railroads to give rebates to companies in return for their shipping business. This practice had given huge advantages to the larger, more powerful railroads, as well as to the businesses receiving the rebates. But the practice had continued underground with the use of secret rebates, which were more difficult to trace. Therefore, the Elkins Act, sponsored by West Virginia Senator Stephen B. Elkins, also made it illegal to receive (as opposed to give) shipping rebates. The practice of rebating had alarmed many railroads, who feared it was leading to bankruptcies. Therefore, in an effort to protect themselves from unscrupulous railroad companies, most of the railroad industry itself supported the prohibitions of the Elkins Act, and it passed with both liberal and conservative support in Congress. Its effectiveness was still doubtful, however, because so-called "smokeless" rebates were untouched by the new law. These were rebates that were granted in indirect ways, such as the Santa Fe Railroad Company "renting" a useless one-mile stretch of railroad track from a Kansas salt company in return for its shipping business.

THE 1904 ELECTION

After serving nearly all of McKinley's second term in the White House, Theodore Roosevelt wanted to be elected president in his own right. Despite his willingness to use the antitrust suit against large business combinations, and his impulsive intervention in the 1902 coal strike, most business leaders would rather support Roosevelt than to see a Democrat elected. The populist wing of the Democrats had taken over the party and had nominated William Jennings Bryan in the last two presidential campaigns. Besides, most business leaders and party professionals had supported the president's imperialistic policies in putting down the Filipino Insurrection, in acquiring the Panama Canal, and in his issuance of the Roosevelt Corollary to the Monroe Doctrine. (See "Chapter Seven for Roosevelt's handling of foreign affairs.) In any case, his popularity with the American people meant that the Republicans really had no choice but to nominate Roosevelt. Roosevelt's running mate in 1904 was Indiana Senator Charles W. Fairbanks.

The Democrats were tired of losing, and looked away from William Jennings Bryan to find their standard bearer. (Their weariness was only temporary, however, for Bryan would be their nominee again in 1908.) Instead, the Democrats nominated Alton B. Parker, a former law partner with former President Grover Cleveland and the New York State Supreme Court Chief Justice. Henry G. Davis, a West Virginia banker and former senator, was selected as the Democratic nominee for vice-president in 1904.

There were very few issues discussed during the political campaign. The Democrats curiously tried to label Parker as the conservative in the race despite the popularity of the growing progressive movement in the nation. Actually, Parker was not all that conservative, although his support for the gold standard was certainly a conservative monetary position; but monetary policy was not an issue in the country in 1904. As Chief Justice in New York, Parker had supported organized labor's position on the closed shop and the right of the state to limit the hours of work, which hardly made him a card-carrying conservative. During the campaign, Parker pledged to actively pursue the prosecution of antitrust cases, but Roosevelt already had the upper hand on that issue. It has generally been difficult in American history to unseat a president who is seeking a second term. But when the opposition candidate cannot find a hot political issue to attract voters to seriously consider his candidacy, then the incumbent is all but assured of the victory. Such was the impotent position of Alton B. Parker in the 1904 presidential campaign.

Theodore Roosevelt won a landslide victory with 336 electoral votes compared to Parker's 140. The Democratic candidate carried only the Solid South of the former Confederacy and the two border states of Maryland and Kentucky. The popular vote margin was equally as impressive, a Republican advantage of about 7.6 million votes to about 5.1 million for the Democrat. Socialist candidate Eugene V. Debs, 10 years after he led the unsuccessful Pullman strike, received about 400,000 votes, and Prohibition candidate Silas C. Swallow won only 259,000 votes. Neither of the latter two candidates carried any states or received any electoral votes.

THE HEPBURN ACT

While the Elkins Act in 1903 (see above) had attempted to do more to end the practice of rebating in the railroad industry, there had been no comprehensive strengthening of the original Interstate Commerce Act since its passage in 1887. And railroad companies were still perceived as the most notorious abusers of the public interest. After his election victory in 1904, President Roosevelt stepped up his rhetoric and political maneuvering in order to get Congress to pass a tougher railroad regulation bill. The House of Representatives satisfied the president with the Hepburn Bill in early 1905, but the more conservative Senate, still elected by state legislatures often dominated by big business interests, held up action on the proposal.

The major sticking point concerned Roosevelt's insistence that a new law give the Interstate Commerce Commission the right to set railroad rates. The ICC had originally interpreted the Interstate Commerce Act as granting them the authority to set "reasonable and just" rates, but the United States Supreme Court ruled in

1904	45	THEODORE ROOSEVELT	Republican	7,628,461	336	57.4
		Alton B. Parker	Democrat	5,084,223	140	37.6
		Eugene V. Debs	Socialist	402,283		3.0
		Silas C. Swallow	Prohibition	258,536		1.9

1896 that the ICC could only approve or disapprove a rate that had been challenged. (See Chapter Four for a thorough discussion of the early efforts to regulate the railroads.) The railroads and their conservative allies in the Senate predictably reacted with great vigor to denounce Roosevelt's proposal as an intrusion into their sacred property rights guaranteed by the Constitution. Nevertheless, public pressure for a tough regulation bill forced the railroads and their political friends in Washington to compromise.

The final version of the Hepburn Act passed Congress in June 1906. On the question of rate setting, the new law did explicitly allow the ICC to set some rates for the first time, but with serious limitations. The Commission could only set a new rate if they agreed with a shipper who had challenged the current one as unreasonable and unjust. And then the new rate was subject to federal court review, which could still throw it out. On other matters of railroad regulation, the Hepburn Act was more palatable to the president and his progressive supporters. For example, the law expanded the jurisdiction of the ICC to include storage and terminal areas. It also mandated new, uniform accounting procedures in the industry and gave the ICC the right to inspect the financial records. The new law also forbade railroads to hand out free railroad passes to non-railroad employees, and in a measure to curtail the monopolistic tendency of some of the larger railroad companies, the railroads were required to divest themselves of all coal companies and other businesses whose goods they shipped by rail.

Most progressives considered the two chief weaknesses of the bill to be (1) the lack of a limit on the power of judicial review that often overturned ICC rates, and (2) the continued lack of a way to ascertain the real assets and worth of a railroad company other than relying on a company's own capitalization figures. But it was a major step forward in the effort to regulate the industry, which had virtually been able to ignore the ICC for almost twenty years.

CONSUMER PROTECTION LEGISLATION

For several years, the chief chemist in the Department of Agriculture, Dr. Harvey W. Wiley, had been agitating about unsafe foods sold in the nation. Wiley had virtually conducted a one-man crusade for a pure-food bill, which, despite support from the American Medical Association and several muckraking magazines, had been held up in Congress. Again, the culprit was the Senate, where conservatives usually maintained political control. At the same time, Indiana Senator Albert J. Beveridge had been attempting to win approval from the Senate for a federal meat inspection bill.

The stalement ended quickly with the publication of Upton Sinclair's *The Jungle* in 1906. Sinclair had written the book to expose the unsafe working conditions for workers in the Chicago meatpacking plants. But most Americans who read the book focused on the issue of the quality of meat offered for sale in the country instead. As Sinclair later declared, "I aimed at the nation's heart, but hit it in the stomach." When President Roosevelt read the book, he ordered a reinvestigation of the industry by the Department of Agriculture, and this time the report painted a bleak picture of the poor quality of the meat being prepared for American consumers. As Congress continued to stall, the president released part of the damaging report and threatened to release the remainder if it failed to pass the proposed bill in a timely fashion. This action also helped build public anger at both the "packing trust" and its allies in Congress. Concerted opposition ended, and in June 1906 Congress passed both the Meat Inspection Act and the Pure Food and Drug Act. The former set minimum sanitary standards in the meatpacking industry and created the federal meat inspection program. The latter bill made it illegal to make, sell, or transport bad or poisoned food or drugs, and it required labeling on certain foods and medicines. Relatively weak enforcement machinery in both laws left conditions still fairly bad.

THE SUPREME COURT AND WORKER PROTECTION

As noted in Chapter Four, the federal courts of the late nineteenth century were conservative and therefore hostile to nearly all government attempts to regulate the power of big business. Since federal judges are appointed for life under the constitutional system, that conservative domination did not soon end. However, a moderating trend did develop early in the twentieth century, at least with regard to the regulation of working hours. In 1896, the United States Supreme Court, in *Holden v. Hardy*, had upheld a state law regulating the hours of miners on the grounds that mining was dangerous work. This "dangerous work" principle was indirectly upheld in the 1905 *Lochner v. New York* case, when the Supreme Court struck down a New York state law limiting the hours of bakery workers to a 10-hour hour day and a 60-hour week. The Court ruled that baking was not dangerous work and thus, the law violated the Fourteenth Amendment's right of persons to make contracts by abolishing their "due process" rights. Progressives were outraged, but as the Supreme Court has often done, it did eventually respond to growing public demands for worker protection.

Evidence of this response came in 1908, when the Supreme Court handed down its decision in *Muller v. Oregon*. In this case, the Court set aside the *Lochner* decision by declaring that economic and sociological factors justified the Oregon law that had limited women laundry workers to 10-hour work days. This made the regulation of their working hours in the "public interest." Arguing the case for the state of Oregon was a bright Jewish-American attorney from Boston named Louis D. Brandeis, who was later appointed by President Woodrow Wilson to the Supreme Court in 1916. Although this new "public interest" rationale was progressive by definition, this particular Supreme Court decision did serve to keep women out of traditionally male jobs where longer, or nighttime, hours were required, such as the transportation and printing industries.

THE PANIC OF 1907

In October 1907, the Knickerbocker Trust Company collapsed from notoriously bad management. This led to the bankruptcies of several other New York City banks and some railroad companies as well during the late fall and early winter. The chain reaction precipitated by this Panic of 1907 led to deep wage cuts and lay-offs in major industries, from which the country did not recover until 1909. Conservatives blamed progressive laws and trust-busting activities and warned that socialism was threatening to destroy free enterprise, but the real causes were over-speculation in the railroads and trusts and the inelastic nature of the money supply system. Many railroads continued their old practice of overselling stocks ("watered" stocks) well beyond the total net worth of their companies. This created a condition resembling a pyramid scheme in which investors' confidence eventually collapses. The economy was more complicated than it had ever been before, and the rather severe limits on banks printing paper money meant that new moneys were increasingly not available precisely when they were needed for the expanding economy. So-called national banks could print money only on the basis of United States bonds they possessed.

Despite the public gestures and finger-pointing from all sides, the president maneuvered behind the scenes with powerful financiers to restore investor confidence and public confidence in their banks. And the panic ended when J.P. Morgan got the federal Treasury Department to place large sums of federal money in certain national banks, which then loaned to other financial institutions, stopping the run on the nation's banks. The short but severe recession did not end, however, until 1909.

The Panic of 1907 was a wake-up call to Roosevelt and other progressives. It persuaded them that prohibitions of certain economic activities were not the simple solutions they thought they would be. The complexities of the economy required a more sophisticated approach to promoting the national interest through government action. In the months following the outbreak of the financial panic, President Roosevelt also worked for legislation which would provide more elasticity in the money supply. As a result, Congress finally passed the Aldrich-Vreeland Act in May 1908, whose main Senate sponsor was Rhode Island Republican Senator Nelson W. Aldrich. The bill allowed national banks to issue currency not only on the basis of federal government bonds they had but also on the state and local bonds and commercial notes (debtors' notes) in their possession. It also created the National Monetary Commission, chaired by Senator Aldrich himself, to study and recommend reforms in the banking industry as a whole. It was this commission's 4-year study that resulted in the federal reserve system being established in late 1913. The Aldrich-Vreeland Act turned out to be the last significant legislation passed during the Roosevelt presidency.

THEODORE ROOSEVELT AND THE RACE QUESTION

Southern Patronage Policy

In October 1901, barely a month after assuming the presidency, Roosevelt invited the African-American educator Booker T. Washington to the White House for a luncheon. The hue and cry from newspapers and most politicians in the South was almost deafening in its protest. The president was accused of everything ranging from committing a horrible "outrage" to "treason" against the so-called decency of southern society. The incident made Roosevelt appear to be an ardent defender of African-American rights. The reality was that, like most progressives of the period, the president was a moderate racist for his time. He opposed the crime of lynching and other expressions of racial hatred, and he hoped for economic improvement for African-Americans, but he did not believe in racial equality or in enforcing black suffrage.

Actually, Washington had been invited to the White House to discuss federal job appointments (patronage) in the South. Roosevelt was already thinking of election in his own right in 1904, and he realized that his chief rival might well be Senator Marcus Hanna, the chairman of the National Republican Committee. Hanna had helped McKinley win the Republican nomination in 1896 by weakening former President Benjamin Harrison's powerful influence in the party's "black and tan" organizations in the South. (See Chapter One for background information on these political machines.) Hanna had succeeded in replacing most of them with "lily white" Republicans. Thus, if Roosevelt wanted to weaken Hanna's chances of winning the nomination in 1904, he would be forced to reverse the process by appointing many of the "black and tan" party members to federal jobs in the South. And that meant that at least some of them would be loyal African-American party members. Washington knew many southern blacks and educated whites, and that was the reason for his invitation to see the president. Therefore, both his southern patronage policy and his specific White House invitation to Booker T. Washington were motivated more by politics than by racial concerns.

The Brownsville Affair

More evidence of Roosevelt's true racial feelings was provided by his handling of an incident in Brownsville, Texas during his second term. On the night of August 3, 1906, at least a dozen African-American soldiers of the Twenty-fifth United States Infantry, stationed at Fort Brown, went on a 10-minute shooting spree in Brownsville in retaliation for racist treatment by the townspeople. One local citizen was killed, but the soldiers all returned to the base before any of them could be identified or captured. When none of the soldiers in the 3 black companies at Fort Brown (at least 160 total) came forth with information on who might have been involved in the incident, President Roosevelt ordered all of them dishonorably discharged from the service, which included 6 recipients of the prestigious Medal of Honor award. He took this action on November 5, just one day before the congressional elections that year.

While Democrats were almost universal in their praise of the president, African-Americans and most Republican politicians severely criticized Roosevelt for adopting a guilt by association philosophy in the case, and the incident caused great strain between Congress and the president for the rest of his term. At the annual Gridiron Club dinner on January 26, 1908, Ohio Senator Joseph B. Foraker, an announced candidate for the Republican presidential nomination, fiercely responded to Roosevelt's stern lecture about his congressional critics' need to respect the office of the presidency by denouncing the president and demanding that he

Picture of Presidents William Howard Taft and Woodrow Wilson at the White House. Credit: Library of Congress.

have "equal respect for the chosen representatives in the Senate of the Sovereign States of the Union." After Roosevelt denied any lack of such respect for his critics, the president promptly walked out of the banquet.

In 1972, the Secretary of the Army cleared the soldiers of guilt and posthumously revoked President Roosevelt's orders by changing their dishonorable discharges to honorable ones.

THE 1908 ELECTION

Theodore Roosevelt had earlier announced that he would respect the precedent set by George Washington by not running for what would, in effect, be a third consecutive term. That left the Republican nomination open. Ohio Senator Joseph B. Foraker had already announced his candidacy several months earlier, but Foraker was hurt by revelations that he had been on the payroll of the Standard Oil Company during his years in the Congress. Roosevelt himself preferred William Howard Taft, who had served as the Secretary of War during his second term. Taft had been generally supportive of Roosevelt's progressive agenda, but his more conservative temperament made him somewhat attractive to the "Old Guard" conservatives in the party. Relieved that they would at last be getting rid of Roosevelt, the conservatives accepted Taft, who became the nominee. Roosevelt and his supporters at the convention hoped to nominate a progressive for the vice-presidential spot on the ticket too, but conservatives won that fight when the delegates selected James S. Sherman, a New York conservative.

In 1908, the Democrats returned to their populist heritage by nominating William Jennings Bryan for the last time. John W. Kern, an Indiana attorney and progressive state legislator, was selected to be his running mate. The Democratic platform once again endorsed free silver and lower tariffs, while also calling for a federal income tax amendment and an end to labor injunctions.

Newspaper heavyweight William Randolph Hearst, frustrated in his efforts to become president and unusually hostile to the Standard Oil Company, formed his own third party. Calling it the National Independence Party, its major platform statement blasted the continued existence of monopolies. The new party nominated Thomas L. Hisgen of Massachusetts for president and John T. Graves of Georgia for vice-president. It had been Hearst, in an effort to gain publicity for his party in 1908, who used the stolen bribery file of John D. Archbold (John D. Rockefeller's right-arm man) to make speeches implicating Foraker (see above). Other minor party presidential candidates included perennial Socialist Eugene V. Debs, Prohibition candidate Eugene W. Chafin, and Populist Tom Watson of Georgia. This was the last time the Populist Party fielded a presidential candidate.

Democrat Bryan ignored advice and made free silver an active issue during the campaign. By calling for an end to labor injunctions, the Democratic candidate received the endorsement of the American Federation of Labor. This was the first time that the AFL had endorsed a presidential candidate because of its preference for what Gompers called "pure and simple unionism," but it did Bryan little good. Taft and the Republicans skirted the tariff issue but did endorse conservation. Of course, nearly everyone ignored the minor party candidates.

When the ballots had been counted and the electoral votes tabulated, the Republican Taft won a major victory with 321 electoral votes to Bryan's 162. The minor party candidates' combined popular vote totals added up to less than one million, with none of them receiving any electoral votes whatsoever. The Republican domination of the White House continued.

1908	46	WILLIAM H. TAFT	Republican	7,675,320	321	51.6
		William J. Bryan	Democrat	6,412,294	162	43.1
		Eugene V. Debs	Socialist	420,793		2.8
		Eugene W. Chafin	Prohibition	253,840		1.7

TAFT'S ANTITRUST ACTIONS

Although Roosevelt had the reputation for being a trust-buster, President William Howard Taft actually instituted at least 80 antitrust suits against alleged monopolies. This meant that Taft instigated approximately twice the number of suits in four years that Roosevelt had begun in 7½ years in the White House. The reason for this increased antitrust activity under the Taft administration was the president's unshakable belief that government could employ the Sherman Antitrust Act to successfully restore real competition in the marketplace. He believed that there was no middle approach between competition and socialism, and that to avoid the latter, the country must find a way to get back to effective economic competition. And the Sherman Antitrust Act seemed just the method to get the job done.

Taft failed to get the credit, not only for his antitrust suits but for other progressive efforts as well, primarily because of his personality. The first thing to say about his personality was that he was no Theodore Roosevelt. Taft simply didn't have the energy and vitality that Roosevelt possessed. And by contrast to the popular Roosevelt, Taft's placid nature made it virtually impossible for him to carry the progressive banner in the aggressive way that his predecessor had done. Psychologically, he was more inclined to try to hold back the more aggressive reformers than to lead the charge to win moderates or conservatives in Congress to progressive legislation. Part of his motivation for this was his tendency to interpret the Constitution in a strict sense. While he was definitely conservative in some areas, Taft was not the "Old Guard" conservative of his historical reputation.

The most famous Supreme Court decision involving an antitrust case during the Taft administration had nothing directly to do with the president. In 1907, then President Roosevelt had ordered the Justice Department to file suit in federal court against the Standard Oil Company for its alleged violation as an illegal trust. After a few years in the lower courts, the Supreme Court finally agreed to review the case and handed down its judgment in 1911. In *United States v. Standard Oil Company*, the court ordered the Standard Oil trust dissolved. However, in the majority opinion, the court used the "rule of reason" for the first time, saying that bigness was not necessarily bad nor did it automatically constitute a restraint of trade, or at least not an unreasonable restraint of trade. By its "rule of reason," the Supreme Court, in effect, changed the Sherman Antitrust Act from a law which outlawed all interstate business combinations that restrained trade to one that allowed "reasonable" restrainers of trade to operate. The Supreme Court would be the final determiner of what was "reasonable" and what was "unreasonable."

THE PAYNE-ALDRICH TARIFF ACT

Another major hassle over tariff reform occurred during the Taft administration. When the dust had settled, Congress passed the Payne-Aldrich Tariff Act in August 1909, sponsored by New York Republican Representative Sereno E. Payne and Rhode Island Republican Senator Nelson W. Aldrich. The House of Representatives had earlier passed a genuine reform tariff that would have significantly lowered the average tariff on imports. But the Senate was besieged by special interests, and as senators were still elected by state legislatures (often heavily influenced by special business interest groups), its version was far different. The final version that made it out of conference committee and into the Payne-Aldrich Tariff Act produced little effect on over-all rates. But what it did do was dramatically increase tariffs on manufactured goods while placing most raw materials either on the duty-free list or with only token rates. The economic effect of Payne-Aldrich was to greatly benefit the manufacturers in the eastern half of the nation and leave most of the producers of raw materials in the West and South unprotected—and angry. The bill also created a Tariff Commission to study rates in the hope that the mythical "scientific" tariff could someday take the political and emotional trauma out of the tariff issue. And in a gesture to the more progressive members of Congress (although they still voted overwhelmingly against the final bill), the bill also included a 2 percent corporate income tax on net earnings and a federal income tax amendment that would go on to the states for eventual ratification as the Sixteenth Amendment.

The political effect of the Payne-Aldrich bill was to geographically and philosophically polarize the Republican Party by pitting more liberal, long-time progressives, including Roosevelt, against the Republican president. In Iowa, a special "progressive Republican" convention was called for the purpose of discussing and devising strategies to reorganize the national party and throw out the eastern party leaders who were accused of being servants of the trusts. Realizing that his party and his presidency were both in trouble, President Taft was persuaded to make a national speaking tour in the fall (1909) to bolster his image. The problem with that strategy, however, was that Taft hated and even feared making speeches. Uncertain of what he would say when he began the tour, President Taft badly blundered on his second stop, in Winona, Minnesota. There he specifically praised those members of Congress who had supported the Payne-Aldrich Tariff and attacked those who didn't; he even called it the "best tariff" bill ever passed. Having begun this course in his speeches, the president continued along similar lines throughout his speaking tour. What the president's role in support of Payne-Aldrich had begun, Taft personally intensified in his speaking trip. His Republican Party was showing signs of falling apart.

THE PROGRESSIVE REVOLT IN THE HOUSE OF REPRESENTATIVES

The number of Republican and Democratic progressives was far greater in the House of Representatives than in the United States Senate, so more progressive-minded Republicans chose to pick a fight with their party's conservative forces in the House in early 1910. Their specific target was the powerful Speaker of the House, Congressman Joseph G. "Uncle Joe" Cannon of Illinois. As Speaker, Cannon both served on and appointed all the members of the Committee on Rules. This was the important committee which set the basic rules and procedures for conducting business in the House. He also personally approved every member of all other standing, or permanent, committees in the House and selected each chairman as well. In his powerful capacity, "Uncle Joe" Cannon used his influence on behalf of conservative measures. In the Payne-Aldrich Tariff fight, for example, he had used his influence with the House members of the conference committee so that the final report looked more like the conservative Senate bill than the House version. He then supported Taft's efforts to approve the final version of the bill.

In March 1910 the progressive revolt against House Speaker Cannon began. Progressive Republicans, led by Nebraska Representative George W. Norris, put together a coalition with the Democrats, who were the minority party in the House at the time. This coalition then succeeded in getting the House of Representatives to change its rules so that Speaker Cannon was forbidden to serve on the Rules Committee or appoint any members to it. The split in the Republican Party led to Democratic gains in Congress in the off-year elections in 1910. And when the new House convened after those elections, the Democrats held a majority of seats. As a result of Democratic and progressive Republican cooperation in 1911, the House of Representatives passed a resolution which took away the Speaker's right to appoint standing committees. In these efforts to reform the power of the Speaker of the House, President Taft further weakened his position with the progressives of his own party by supporting Cannon.

THE BALLINGER-PINCHOT CONTROVERSY

Taft's political bungling of the Payne-Aldrich Tariff Act was not the only issue over which he hurt himself badly with the progressive wing of his party. Inept handling of a conservation dispute that became known as the Ballinger-Pinchot Controversy further strained the relations between the administration and the more liberal elements. Taft's Secretary of the Interior, Richard A. Ballinger, was a politically conservative lawyer from Seattle, Washington, who was sensitive to the fact that many westerners regarded conservation measures as a hindrance to economic development and growth. Ballinger also believed that former President Roosevelt had acted well beyond his legal authority in setting aside more than one million acres of western water power sites technically as ranger stations. Therefore, Ballinger opened up these areas to private developers.

Back in 1907, when Ballinger had briefly served as head of the General Land Office, he had ruled favorably on some controversial land claims among Alaska's coal area that a group of Seattle businessmen had made. An investigator for the General Land Office, Louis R. Glavis, found evidence that suggested these Cunningham claims were illegal because the participants had engaged in collusion. Furthermore, they intended to commit more violations by selling at least part of the claims, once they were validated by the General Land Office, to a newly organized financial syndicate, the Morgan-Guggenheim Syndicate. As a result of Glavis' investigation, Interior Secretary James R. Garfield overruled the Ballinger decision and ordered further investigations. Ballinger left his government post a short time later, and as an attorney, he agreed to legally represent the Seattle group, some of whom were his personal friends, against the Department of Interior.

When President Taft replaced Garfield by appointing Ballinger as his Secretary of the Interior in March 1909, Ballinger promptly removed Glavis from the investigation of the Cunningham claims. At that point, Glavis complained to Gifford Pinchot, whom Taft had kept on as the head of the United States Forest Service (in the Department of Agriculture). Shortly after Pinchot took the matter to the president, Taft fired Glavis in September 1909, whereupon Pinchot became enraged and made the matter a public dispute in the muckraking magazines and in Congress itself. The disgusted president believed he had no choice, so he fired Pinchot in January 1910. A Congressional committee exonerated Ballinger of all wrongdoing later that same year, but the damage had been done. Most of the American people seemed to side against Ballinger and for Glavis and Pinchot, an apparent fact that even Taft acknowledged. The stream of protests from conservationists kept the issue alive and made Ballinger a political liability for the president. As a result, he resigned his cabinet position in 1911.

Was Taft really retreating from the conservation policies of Roosevelt, as most progressives charged? The answer is almost certainly "no." For one thing, Taft replaced Ballinger with Walter Fisher, a friend of Pinchot whose conservation credentials were beyond reproach. Then under the Appalachian Forest Reserve Act (1911), the Taft administration created large amounts of national forest land in the eastern part of the country by purchasing it, as the new law allowed. And like the antitrust suits, Taft actually gave federal protection to more public lands in four years than Roosevelt had given in 7 and 1/2 Once again, Taft's poor political judgment had pushed him into a position which made him appear to be less progressive than he really was. It also contributed to his reputation then, and later, as a traditional conservative president, when in fact he was a moderate progressive with a cautious personality and a real talent for bungling political challenges. As usual, people are more complex than simplistic labels often make them out to be.

THE MANN-ELKINS ACT

In 1910 Taft managed to support a tougher railroad regulation bill and alienate the progressives in Congress both at the same time. In January of that year, the administration's proposals were introduced in the House of Representatives as the Mann bill. The bill allowed the Interstate Commerce Commission to set railroad rates on its own intiative (without waiting for a complaint from a shipper), provided for a special Commerce Court to hear appeals of ICC decisions, and exempted railroads from some antitrust requirements. Progressives immediately attacked the bill in the House, suspicious because the antitrust exemption had been placed in the bill at the last moment after an administration meeting with railroad industry officials earlier that same month. They also objected to the broad powers of the Commerce Court and the lack of any provision for physical evaluations to more accurately assess the assets of a company (and thus provide a sounder basis for determining a "reasonable" rate). When progressives finished with the bill in the House, they had barely kept the Commerce Court in it while removing the antitrust exemption and adding a physical evaluation provision. They also expanded the jurisdiction of the ICC to include telegraph and telephone companies.

The fight in the Senate was even rougher, with more than two hundred amendments being offered by progressives there. But in the end, Republican Senator Nelson Aldrich made a deal with a large group of Democrats to support the admission of New Mexico and Arizona as states (presumably they would be Democratic) in return for their votes to approve a rewritten version of the railroad bill. When the final version, known as the Mann-Elkins Act, finally passed Congress in 1910, it went a long way toward providing effective regulation of the railroad industry. Its main features were: (1) the ICC was given authority to set rates on its own initiative without waiting for a shipper's challenge; (2) the burden of proof for what was a "reasonable" rate was specifically shifted from the ICC to the railroad; (3) a special Court of Commerce was created to hear appeals of ICC decisions; (4) telegraph and telephone companies were placed under the jurisdiction of the ICC; and (5) prohibitions on short haul rate abuses were strengthened. Aldrich kept his end of the bargain he had made with the Democrats, and New Mexico and Arizona did come into the Union 2 years later, in 1912. And indeed, for many years, these states were dominated by the Democratic Party.

About the only thing that the Mann-Elkins Act didn't do was corrected in the Physical Valuation Act, passed just 3 days before Taft left office, on March 1, 1913. It made use of more objective means, including physical inspections, to measure the real assets of a company more accurately; before this bill, the ICC had been force to rely on a railroad's own capitalization figures. As far as the Commerce Court was concerned, when one of its judges, Robert W. Archbald, was impeached for reaping financial profits from inside information in 1912, the court was discredited. And in 1913, Congress abolished it after only three years of existence.

REMAINING ISSUES

The progressive tendency to look at social problems from a moralistic perspective was reflected in 1910, when Congress passed the Mann Act, or sometimes known as the White Slave Traffic Act. The Mann Act prohibited the interstate transportation of women for immoral purposes. It was designed to end prostitution on a national scale by putting interstate prostitution rings out of business, but even teenage girls who crossed state lines and were raped were sometimes also prosecuted. Professional boxer Jack Johnson was one of the more famous Americans of that era who was prosecuted under the Mann Act. Following the lead of the federal government, nearly every state had outlawed brothels and solicitation for sexual favors by 1915.

Other notable progressive measures, such as the Postal Savings Bank Act, were enacted with the recommendation and support of President Taft in 1910. Congress created the postal savings bank system, which permitted certain post offices to collect deposited funds and pay interest on them. The idea for a postal savings bank system had been endorsed by the Populist Party platforms of the 1890s as a way to allow small depositors to bank and save money. The Roosevelt administration had favored such a system too but was unable to get it established. During the Taft administration, Democrats in Congress began demanding that the federal government guarantee bank accounts, but Taft and the conservative Republicans opposed that as "socialistic." For that reason, they had established the postal savings bank system to appease the Democratic proposal.

In other government reorganization moves, the Federal Bureau of Mines, operating within the Department of the Interior, was established in 1910. It was designed to promote mine safety through regular inspections and the enforcement of safety regulations. And the Federal Children's Bureau was established as part of the Department of Labor in 1912. Its task was to study the effects of industrialization on women and children. President Taft appointed Julia Lathrop to head this agency. Lathrop, who had earlier been associated with Jane Addams at Chicago's Hull House (see "Social History: 1870–1920") and then was the first woman member of the Illinois Board of Charities, then became the first woman in American history to head a federal agency (1912). Then on Taft's last day in office in March 1913, Congress separated the Department of Commerce and Labor and replaced it with two separate departments.

One other federal reform measure undertaken by Congress during the Taft presidency was the passage of the White Phosphorus Match Act in 1912. White phosphorus was cheaper to use in the making of matches than red phosphorus, and for that reason, it was predominantly used by the match industry. But a condition known as Phossy Jaw disease, which tended to rot away the jaw, had become a chronic problem among workers in that industry. To encourage the use of red phosphorus instead, the White Phosphorus Match Act levied a tax of 2 cents per 100 matches on all white phosphorus matches and created a number of reporting and registering requirements by those companies using the white phosphorus. The new law was successful in getting the match industry to transfer entirely to red phosphorus shortly after it was signed into law.

THE 1912 ELECTION

The Republicans

The Republican National Convention opened in Chicago in June 1912 and promised to be a very rancorous affair. The split between President Taft and the progressive wing of the party was far beyond repair by this time, with most progressive leaders vowing not to support the president even if he were renominated. Instead, most of them originally pinned their hopes on Wisconsin Senator Robert M. La Follette. La Follette had been the most consistent, articulate, and ardent promoter of the progressive movement, even surpassing Theodore Roosevelt in this respect. But supporters of the former president convinced Roosevelt to announce his candidacy for the nomination because they believed that La Follette was too radical to defeat Taft. Finally persuaded, Roosevelt declared himself a candidate for the Republican nomination in February (1912) and set out with a vengeance to unseat the man he had been largely responsible for placing in the White House in the first place.

In the 13 states where delegates to the convention were elected by voters, Roosevelt had a commanding lead of 278, compared to 48 for Taft and 36 for La Follette. The former president even carried Ohio, Taft's home state, in a bitter primary fight that both sides poured huge amounts of resources into. In the remaining states, however, Taft's control of the political patronage (federal jobs) and his support from most of the party bosses, enabled him to win the nomination easily. The Republicans also renominated Vice-President James S. Sherman, but Sherman died before the November election. The Republican National Committee then replaced the deceased Sherman with Columbia University president Nicholas M. Butler.

The Progressives

After Taft won the nomination fight at the Republican convention, the followers of Roosevelt and La Follette walked out. The split became official when the Progressive Party, newly organized at Roosevelt's urging, opened its first convention in August. In a contest between Roosevelt and La Follette, even most of those who were inclined to support La Follette conceded that Roosevelt had a far better chance to be elected in November. So Roosevelt won the nomination for president, with California Republican Governor Hiram W. Johnson being selected as his running mate. The Progressive Party was nicknamed the "Bull Moose" Party because Roosevelt had often used the term to describe persons, like himself, who were energetic and strong.

The Progressive Party platform was as important to the future of the American progressive tradition as the Populist platform of 1892 had been to the Progressive Era of the early twentieth century in that both accurately predicted the future political trend. It called for the prohibition of child labor and the enactment of workmen's compensation, social insurance, and a federal trade commission to exercise broad authority in the regulation of interstate commerce beyond the railroad and communications industries.

The Democrats

The Democrats smelled the freshness of victory in the air in 1912. Their only candidate in the White House since James Buchanan in the late 1850s had been Grover Cleveland (elected in 1884 and 1892). But with the Republicans badly divided, an almost certain Democratic victory awaited them in November. As a result, three candidates entered the race for the nomination. William Jennings Bryan, however, was not one of them. Bryan made it known that he did not want a fourth nomination. Now nearly everyone in the party recognized that they had an opportunity to get themselves reorganized under brand new leadership, which would probably determine the party's destiny for the forseeable future.

The progressive governor of New Jersey, Woodrow Wilson (a Virginian by birth), had begun campaigning the year before (1911). But despite his head start, by the opening of the Democratic convention in late June 1912, Wilson was trailing the new Speaker of the House, Bennett Champ Clark of Missouri. Champ Clark had the support of the Bryan Democrats, William Randolph Hearst and his newspaper chain, and most party professionals. Clark had had a consistent progressive record since coming to Congress in the 1890s, but he had not demonstrated any real political courage, and many careful watchers of the Democrats believed a Clark nomination would bring disaster to the party. Congressman Oscar W. Underwood, chairman of the powerful House Ways and Means Committee, had cut into Wilson's strength in the South as the third significant candidate.

But developments at the convention itself that summer were to turn the tide in favor of Wilson. For about a century, from the 1830s to the 1930s, the Democratic Party rules required a presidential nominee to collect at least two-thirds of the voting delegates. In 1912, this enabled the Wilson and Underwood camps to agree to hold firmly against Clark in hopes that the momentum would shift to one of them. Although Bryan announced his switch from Clark to Wilson on the fourteenth ballot, most Bryanites remained loyal to Clark. More significant was the behind-the-scenes efforts to win the party boss-controlled state delegations over to Wilson. The first major break came when the Illinois boss, Roger Sullivan, delivered his delegates to Wilson on the forty-second ballot. The tide was shifting, and when most of the Underwood delegates saw that Wilson was clearly now their best chance to defeat Clark, Woodrow Wilson captured the necessary two-thirds vote on the forty-sixth ballot and was nominated. Indiana Governor Thomas R. Marshall, a conservative, was placed on the ticket as the vice-presidential candidate of the party. Marshall became famous for his statement, "What this country needs is a good five-cent cigar."

The Campaign

Even before the official post-convention campaigns began, President Taft realized that his defeat was imminent. "I think I might as well give up so far as being a candidate is concerned," he wrote in late July. "There are so many people in the country who don't like me." As a man who hated speeches anyway, Taft delivered none after his obligatory acceptance speech at the Republican convention. And the race settled into a two-man affair between Woodrow Wilson the Democrat and former President Theodore Roosevelt the Progressive.

The Roosevelt campaign almost met a tragic end in October. On the fourteenth of that month, Roosevelt was leaving his hotel in Milwaukee, Wisconsin to make a speech at an auditorium. Before he climbed into the waiting car, a fanatical man shouted something about no third term and shot Roosevelt in the chest. The bullet went through his coat, a case for his eyeglasses, and his copy of the folded speech he was about to deliver, before it fractured a rib and stopped just below his right lung. The macho Roosevelt insisted on delivering his speech despite his wound. With his characteristic flare for dramatics, the former president showed his audience the blood on his shirt and the written speech with a hole in it and then defiantly declared, "It takes more than this to kill a bull moose." Doctors removed the bullet after he delivered his speech. And the presidential campaign continued as normal.

New Nationalism Versus the New Freedom

While both Roosevelt and Wilson were progressives, they each represented very different approaches within the movement. During the 1912 presidential campaign, Roosevelt began calling his brand of progressivism New Nationalism. Echoing his earlier actions, although not reputation, Roosevelt's New Nationalism emphasized the inevitability of large combinations of business organizations. Fearing that a wholesale effort to trust-bust businesses to smaller sizes might well destroy economic efficiency and ruin the nation, Roosevelt instead urged that the power of the federal government be used to regulate the behavior of corporations and thus become a vehicle for social and economic justice. Historians disagree about who influenced whom, but all acknowledge some kind of parallel relationship between Roosevelt and journalist Herbert Croly. Croly had written *The Promise of American Life* in 1909 with the same basic philosophy that Roosevelt was now calling New Nationalism. The bottom line was that bigness, in business or government, was not inherently bad. But the expanding power of the federal government should be employed to regulate the economy in everyone's interest, or the national interest. Roosevelt had pretty much said the same thing when he had used the term "square deal" earlier as president.

Woodrow Wilson's progressive philosophy became known as the New Freedom. Wilson was influenced in his ideas by Louis D. Brandeis, the attorney who had successfully argued before the Supreme Court in the *Muller* case back in 1908 (see earlier in the chapter). Brandeis and Wilson charged that bigness was inherently inefficient and dangerous to personal rights. Therefore, the federal government should use its power to reduce and keep limits on the size of businesses so that the good old days of real competition could be restored. Beyond that, the federal government should largely defer to the states. In other words, the New Freedom emphasized that small businesses should be protected, competition restored, and the powers of the states preserved. Wilson's approach to progressivism was in harmony with the historical roots of the modern Democratic Party, the party of Thomas Jefferson and Andrew Jackson, who had attacked special privilege, championed the common man, and de-emphasized federal power most of the time. And similarly as the earlier generation of Democratic leaders did not know how to stop the trend toward an industrialized society, with its wider gaps between rich and poor, the Wilsonian Democrats of the New Freedom could not clearly state exactly how the government would determine that a corporation was too big or what the real effect on economic efficiency and technological growth would be.

While Wilson's New Freedom still advocated the use of Jeffersonian means (tendency to focus on states' rights more than a powerful federal government) to achieve Jeffersonian ends, Roosevelt's New Nationalism favored the use of Hamiltonian means (emphasis on a strong, active federal government) to achieve Jeffersonian ends. This debate would have far-reaching consequences, for the ultimate winner would determine the nature and role of American liberalism in the twentieth century and perhaps beyond. And although Wilson won the presidency, in one of history's many ironies, even he later switched to Roosevelt's approach (see later in this chapter). The election of 1912 belonged to the New Freedom, but twentieth century liberalism would soon belong to New Nationalism.

The Results

Despite Roosevelt's valiant efforts, the serious division within the ranks of Republicans produced a landslide Democratic victory in 1912. Woodrow Wilson carried 40 of the 48 states, winning 435 electoral votes and about 6.3 million popular votes. For the first time ever—and the only time thus far—a third party presidential candidate finished in second place. Roosevelt carried 6 states with about 4.1 million popular votes and 88 electoral votes. Not only did Taft make history as a major party candidate by coming in third, but as a sitting president of the United States, his electoral vote total of 8 was kept in single digits. President Taft even failed to carry his home state of Ohio (Wilson carried it); only Vermont and Utah gave him their votes. Socialist candidate Eugene V. Debs polled just over 900,000 popular votes compared to Prohibitionist Eugene W. Chafin's 206,000. Neither of the last two candidates carried any states nor won any electoral votes. William Howard Taft was later appointed by President Warren G. Harding in 1921 as the Chief Justice of the United States Supreme Court, a position he held until his death in 1930.

The election of 1912 was significant in a variety of ways. First, it brought the Democrats real national power for the first time since before the Civil War. In the congressional races held at the same time, Democrats regained effective control of both the House and the Senate. While they had, on average, held their own in one or both houses of Congress since the war, for only the first two years of Grover Cleveland's second term (1893-1895) did they control both houses of Congress and the White House at the same time. Second, by bringing the Democrats back to national power, southerners were also restored to the national political scene. And finally, the election that year marked a turning point for the Republican Party. Although it nominated a moderate progressive in 1916, the party machinery would remain in conservative hands for an indefinite period of time—where it still is today. The next generation of progressives found a champion in Franklin Delano Roosevelt, the Democratic fifth cousin of Teddy. And with a relative handful of exceptions, after 1932, progressives found themselves far more comfortable in the Democratic Party.

A BIOGRAPHICAL SKETCH OF WOODROW WILSON

Thomas Woodrow Wilson was born in Staunton, Virginia in 1856, and grew up in Georgia and the Carolinas during the Civil War and Reconstruction period. The son of a devout Presbyterian minister, the younger Wilson developed a strong sense of morality that sometimes gave him an inflexible attitude. After completing an undergraduate degree at Princeton University in 1879, Wilson obtained a law degree at the University of Virginia and spent one unhappy year practicing law in Atlanta, Georgia. From Atlanta, he went to John Hopkins University in Baltimore, Maryland, where he studied history and political science. In 1885, he wrote a book entitled *Congressional Government: A Study in American Politics* in lieu of a regular dissertation. Wilson admired the parliamentary system of Britain, so in his book he

1912	48	WOODROW WILSON	Democrat	6,296,547	435	41.9
		Theodore Roosevelt	Progressive	4,118,571	88	27.4
		William H. Taft	Republican	3,486,720	8	23.2
		Eugene V. Debs	Socialist	900,672		6.0
		Euguen W. Chafin	Prohibition	206,275		1.4

argued for a stronger presidency which would actively pursue legislative goals rather than simply enforce the laws of the nation. The next year (1886) Wilson received his Ph.D. in political science, which meant that when he was later elected to the White House, he became the first—and thus far only—president to possess an earned academic doctorate.

With his advanced degree in hand, Wilson taught elsewhere at the college level until he returned to Princeton in 1890. There he earned an outstanding reputation as a public speaker and writer, so much so that he was unanimously elected president of the university in 1902. While president of Princeton University, Woodrow Wilson set out to institute a number of reforms, including the raising of academic standards and the enlargement of the curriculum and faculty. But when he attempted to fully integrate the graduate school within the total institution, the dean of the graduate school (Andrew F. West) successfully defeated him with the board of trustees in 1910.

Wilson then resigned his position in September of that year in order to become the Democratic candidate for governor of the state (New Jersey). New York magazine publisher George Harvey and New Jersey's Democratic Party boss James Smith, Jr. were successful in getting Wilson the nomination. Harvey saw Wilson as a conservative who might be able to lure the party away from the Bryanites. Actually, Wilson did want to defeat the Bryanites in the party, but he himself had moderated his earlier conservatism by then. And the corrupt Smith, a former United States senator, believed Wilson would give the party in New Jersey a good respectable image.

After his election, Governor Wilson asserted his independence from Smith, including blocking Smith's attempts to get the state legislature to return him to the United States Senate, and achieved several important reforms in the state. Among the reforms he instituted were the adoption of a workmen's compensation system, regulation of public utilities, a direct primary, and tighter regulations on corporate chartering practices. In a state with a reputation for corruption, and knicknamed the "home of the trusts," such reforms were an impressive accomplishment indeed, and they put Woodrow Wilson in the national spotlight within just two years with a nomination for president. Few men had ever politically risen so high in such a short period of time.

THE UNDERWOOD-SIMMONS TARIFF ACT

The election of 1912 had given the Democrats control of both houses of Congress and the White House. And as Wilson had campaigned for lower tariffs as a traditional Democrat, the entire country expected tariff reform within the first year of his administration. Indeed, the new president wasted no time on the issue. Calling Congress into special session in early April 1913, President Wilson became the first president to address that body personally since John Adams. In his speech, Wilson asked Congress for a meaningful tariff reform bill he could sign.

Led by the Ways and Means Committee Chairman Oscar W. Underwood, Wilson's southern opponent at the previous year's national party convention, the House of Representatives quickly passed a major tariff reform bill. The more conservative, and less responsive Senate, however, was besieged by hundreds of special interest lobbyists that threatened to conduct business as usual and transform an initial reform bill into a confusing mess, as it had done on earlier occasions. At that point, the president went over their heads to the American people and turned up the heat on the Senate through speeches and statements made to the press. The strategy worked, and Wilson signed the Underwood-Simmons Tariff Act into law in early October. (North Carolina Democratic Senator Furnifold M. Simmons led the fight for the president in the Senate.)

The Underwood-Simmons Tariff Act represented the first substantial tariff reform law since the Civil War. Of the roughly 1,700 itemized products dealt with by the bill, the tariff rate was reduced on almost 1,000 of them, while the rate went up on fewer than 100 items. The general affect was to reduce the average tariff rate from over 37 percent to about 29 percent. The duty-free list was expanded from roughly 200 to 300 products, including sugar, iron ore, steel, wool, coal, and many agricultural products. To make up for the expected loss of revenue to the federal government, the bill also imposed a progressive, or graduated, income tax which the recently ratified Sixteenth Amendment had explicitly permitted. A tax of just 1 percent was levied on incomes between $4,000 and $20,000 on married couples filing a joint return, and a graduated surtax, ranging from an additional 1 percent on incomes around $20,000 up to 6 percent on incomes over $500,000 per year, was also enacted. Those low rates meant that no one really felt pinched, even when the Revenue Act of 1916 raised the minimum rate from 1 percent to 2 percent and the maximum surtax from 6 percent to 13 percent. But a permanent federal income tax was adopted, fulfilling yet another of the original goals of the populists. The political significance of the Underwood-Simmons Tariff was not lost on anyone; President Wilson was confirmed as the national leader of his party and as a president whom Congress could not ignore.

In 1916, a new Tariff Commission was established to study the entire tariff issue again in the context of changing world economic conditions. And in 1918, Congress passed the Webb-Pomerene Act to exempt certain international marketing associations (exporters) from antitrust suits. This was done in order to facilitate greater American exports in an increasingly worldwide economy.

THE FEDERAL RESERVE ACT

After the Panic of 1907, nearly everyone agreed that the nation's decentralized banking system needed much reform. The current system relied too heavily on the health and leadership of several major New York City banks, which often made it difficult for other parts of the country to obtain the credit they needed in a timely fashion. The inability of the monetary system to respond to nationwide demand spurts for huge increases in the money supply was also recognized as a deficiency. Somehow a national system had to be devised that would provide for more efficient access to credit and a more flexible money supply. The country had not even had a real national bank system since President Andrew Jackson had killed the Second Bank of the United States back in 1836.

When the National Monetary Commission, created as part of the Aldrich-Vreeland Act in 1908, released its recommendations in 1912, the national debate began. The Commission had recommended the creation of a private central, or national, bank called the National Reserve Association with 15 branches across the country. President Wilson urged Congress in 1913 to give the nation a truly national system with a central governing board, but beyond that he initially left himself free to listen and compromise. To traditional progressive Democrats, the Commission proposal seemed too much like the old, hated Bank of the United States, which had been 80 percent controlled by private investors. Virginia Democratic Representative Carter Glass, an opponent of the central bank idea, drew up a counterproposal that would have created a decentralized reserve system with several independent regional banks. Wilson tentatively agreed with the Glass idea but insisted that he modify his proposals to include some type of central supervisory board.

On the other side of the spectrum, the Bryan wing of the party, with the support of William Jennings Bryan himself, who was Wilson's Secretary of State, rejected the Glass-Wilson concept and insisted on a centralized national banking system that would be entirely controlled by the federal government. Any other arrangement, they feared, would simply lead to a government-supported group of a privileged economic elite, who would only strengthen their hold on the nation's banking and monetary system. Wilson held, or at least expressed, no firm conviction on the question of private or public control of the reserve system. But to maintain his standing as the real leader of his party, as well as the nation, he had to find a way to reach a compromise and get a bill passed. Toward this end, he called his good friend and intellectual ally Louis D. Brandeis to the White House in June. After Brandeis told him that the Bryanites were correct in their insistence that private interests should not control a national reserve banking system, Wilson arranged several meetings with congressional leaders and finally convinced Glass and other leading members that a bill must provide for government control of a central board. It was also the only way, he said (undoubtedly he was right), to get the Bryan Democrats to support the bill and to get any reserve bill through Congress. Glass finally agreed, and by the end of June, he and Oklahoma Democratic Senator Robert L. Owen had introduced identical bills in the House and Senate.

A group of southern and western progressives held out for additional amendments to the Glass bill, including one that would make interlocking business arrangements among the banks illegal. When William Jennings Bryan assured them that Wilson had promised to prohibit interlocking directorates in a forthcoming bill to reform the antitrust laws, their opposition faded. The House of Representatives passed the Glass bill in August. Howls of protests from the banking industry, charging that the bill was socialistic and ruinous of business affairs, forced lengthy hearings in the Senate, however, until late November, when public outcry against the special interests led to debates on the floor itself.

Just before Christmas in December 1913, Congress finally passed the conference committee bill, known as the Glass-Owen Act or the Federal Reserve Act. It created the federal reserve system with 12 privately owned regional banks operating under the umbrella of the Federal Reserve Board (headquartered in Washington, D.C.), whose 9 members consisted of the secretary of the treasury, the comptroller of the currency, and 7 others appointed by the president (and confirmed by the Senate) for 14-year terms. Thus, it was a blend of private ownership at the regional level and public control at the national level. The 14-year terms for 7 of the 9 members on the Board ensured a great deal of independence from politically-motivated pressure for quick fixes in the monetary supply, much like the United States Supreme Court justices are able to be somewhat insulated from immediate public demands.

Each regional Federal Reserve bank would act as a bankers' bank, not dealing directly with business and individual account holders. These banks would not only serve as holders of federal funds but as depositors of member banks' cash reserves. By its very nature, the new system created a broad network of pooled money, which would make it easier to meet the expanding credit needs anywhere in the country. The Federal Reserve banks were authorized to print a new kind of paper money called Federal Reserve Notes (most of our paper money today). In this way, they could control interest rates by loaning money to member banks and setting an interest (or rediscount) rate that the banks would have to pay them. Thus, when the Federal Reserve System raises the rediscount rate, commercial banks are generally forced to raise the rates they charge their business and individual customers. Or when the rediscount rate is lowered, commercial banks then have an incentive (along with competition from other banks) to lower their interest rates too. This established a way to tighten or loosen interest rates and the money supply to meet the particular financial needs of the economy at any given moment. As such, it really represented a modification, but not an abandonment, of the gold standard.

For the first time in more than 75 years, the United States had a truly national banking system, although conservative appointments to the Federal Reserve Board left each of the regional banks free to pursue their own monetary policies until that was corrected in 1934 under the Franklin Roosevelt administration. The Federal Reserve Act was clearly the most significant piece of legislation passed during the Wilson presidency.

WILSON AND THE ANTITRUST LAWS

During the election campaign in 1912, Woodrow Wilson had outlined in his New Freedom the solution for the continued growth of huge business combinations, which both he and Roosevelt agreed were restricting competition. That solution was to corrrect the vague language in the Sherman Antitrust Act (1890) by specifying the business practices which constituted "restraint of trade," and then to go after the violators in court with antitrust suits. Roosevelt, on the other hand, had argued that it would be impossible to list all the possible unfair business practices by law and that what was needed was a strong federal trade commission armed with broad powers that could determine whether an alleged practice constituted a restraint of trade. His proposal was for an agency similar to the strengthened Interstate Commerce Commission, which investigated, held public hearings, and issued "cease and desist" orders against unreasonable railroad rates.

As the fight over the Federal Reserve Act was winding down in late 1913, President Wilson started soliciting recommendations for amendments to the Sherman Antitrust Act from members of Congress. By the end of the year, it was clear that the two different approaches taken by Wilson and Roosevelt during the election campaign the year before were also reflected in Congress. Most Democrats sided with their president, but a minority within his own party, and nearly all progressive Republicans, favored a strong federal trade commission along the lines that Roosevelt had proposed. Alabama Democratic Representative Henry D. Clayton, of the House Judiciary Committee, submitted two separate bills for consideration. The one known as the Clayton bill enumerated a long list of unfair trade practices and outlawed interlocking directorates, something the president had promised the Bryan Democrats during the long struggle over the Federal Reserve Act. The other one, co-sponsored with him by three of his House colleagues, created a federal trade commission to replace the Bureau of Corporations, an agency which had been established under the Roosevelt administration. The federal trade commission would not have broad powers but would essentially provide information and assistance to the Justice Department in antitrust cases. The Clayton bills represented Wilson's antitrust views perfectly. And after a compromise over language which stopped short of explicitly granting labor unions exemption from antitrust laws, the House of Representatives overwhelmingly approved both bills in early June 1914.

The Federal Trade Commission Act

Within one week of the House action, while the Senate was still giving consideration to antitrust legislation, President Wilson reversed himself and began lobbying for a stronger federal trade commission. At least two factors seemed prominent in Wilson's change of heart. First, a number of small business groups, including the United States Chamber of Commerce, had stepped up their campaign for a powerful trade commission. Small business groups resented the unethical practices that their larger competitors could afford to engage in, such as selling at a loss in order to drive others out of business. And these groups tended to favor a federal agency which would have the power required to protect them from these bigger companies. And second, Wilson's trusted friend and advisor Louis D. Brandeis worked on the president to persuade him to change his position. Earlier in the spring, Brandeis had persuaded Democratic Representative Raymond B. Stevens of New Hampshire to introduce his plan in the House, but the Clayton version passed instead. Now the president swung into action in support of the Stevens bill, which was then introduced in the Senate after a White House conference in June. The Senate passed the Stevens version in August and the House of Representatives agreed in early September.

On September 10, President Wilson signed the Federal Trade Commission Act. As a replacement for the Bureau of Corporations, the Federal Trade Commission was established with 5 commissioners who would be appointed by the president and confirmed by the Senate for 7-year terms. The FTC was authorized to investigate and publicize complaints of unfair interstate business practices (excepting railroads and banks, which had the ICC and the Federal Reserve System respectively) and issue "cease and desist" orders against violating companies. Despite Wilson's conversion to a tougher federal trade commission, he hoped to appeal to the better nature of businessmen in general. Therefore, because he appointed more business-oriented men to the commission, the FTC was not an effective regulatory agency for several years.

The Clayton Antitrust Act

With the enactment of the strong Federal Trade Commission Act a reality, President Wilson nearly lost interest in the Clayton antitrust bill which the House had also passed in early June. He seemed to place all his faith in the new trade commission instead. Largely as a result, conservatives in the Senate so watered the Clayton bill down that Missouri Senator James A. Reed called it an "apology to the trusts." The main weapon in the conservative arsenal was vague language, which seemed to qualify every prohibition in the bill. Instead of simply outlawing interlocking directorates or other illegal combinations, the Senate version usually added the words "where the effect may be to substantially lessen competition or tend to create a monopoly in any line of commerce," or other similar language. In other words, the Supreme Court's "rule of reason," which it had adopted in the 1911 *Standard Oil* decision, was placed into federal antitrust law.

With a disinterested president and an adamant Senate, the House conferees essentially accepted the Senate's amendments, and the Clayton Antitrust Act was adopted in October 1914, one month after the Federal Trade Commission Act had passed. The Clayton Antitrust Act, despite its vague language, did list several specific unfair business practices for the FTC to use in its work. The prohibitions included interlocking directorates, selling at a loss, corporate purchases of stock in competing companies, and price discrimination (where different customers are charged different prices for the same product), among many others. Officials of companies were made personally liable for their company's violations of the antitrust laws, and those who suffered from certain unfair business practices could sue for three times the amount of damages they had incurred.

On the issue of labor union exemption from antitrust action, the final version mirrored the original House bill in that unions were not specifically exempted by the new law. The bill did, however, declare that labor was not a commodity and therefore, labor unions were not in themselves illegal combinations or conspiracies in restraint of trade per se. And in a weak attempt to limit the use of federal court injunctions to end strikes, the law stated that labor injunctions could not be issued to stop a strike "unless necessary to prevent irreparable injury to property, or to a property right." That latter clause, especially the words "property right," allowed the courts to get around the restriction and uphold traditional property rights dogma by issuing labor injunctions at will. As to the legality of labor organizations, the Clayton Antitrust Act didn't say anything that state and federal courts hadn't been consistently saying since the Massachusetts state Supreme Court upheld the existence of unions in the 1842 *Commonwealth v. Hunt* decision. American Federation of Labor president Samuel Gompers initially hailed the Clayton Antitrust Act as labor's "Magna Carta" (a document limiting the powers of the king that English nobles forced King John to sign back in 1215). But that exclamation proved to be premature indeed.

WILSON SHIFTS TO THE LEFT

In November 1914, one month after the enactment of the Clayton Antitrust Act, President Wilson announced that his major goals had been accomplished and the New Freedom was now completed. Besides this announcement, Wilson continued to oppose a woman's suffrage amendment, federal child labor bill, workmen's compensation, farm credits, and other social and economic legislation that progressives wanted. Progressives, in and out of his Democratic Party, were confused as to the president's true colors, and tensions between them and Wilson were rising throughout the year 1915. These tensions had risen to crisis proportions by early 1916 because of Wilson's efforts to strengthen the military might of the nation in the event that we could not stay out of the European war, which had begun in August 1914. Bryan and the other progressive Democrats bitterly opposed Wilson on the war preparedness issue, and it appeared that the party might fracture itself, thus allowing the Republicans to win the White House that November in the same way that the Democrats had won it four years earlier. (See Chapter Eight for a discussion of the origins of that war and the war preparedness controversy.) In fact, with the virtual return of Roosevelt to the fold, the Republican split of 1912 had almost completely healed by 1916.

As Wilson surveyed the political landscape that year, he realized that disaster awaited his party unless he could attract the firm loyalty of the more liberal progressives. And with a firm conviction that the Democratic Party remained the best hope for progressivism in the nation, Woodrow Wilson suddenly shifted his philosophy to the left. Embracing the ideology of Roosevelt's New Nationalism, the president reversed himself on a host of social and economic legislation, which the progressives in Congress quickly passed. He also helped his cause with the Bryan Democrats when he nominated Louis D. Brandeis for the Supreme Court in January (1916). Brandeis became the first Jewish-American to sit on the Supreme Court after opponents lost a bitter confirmation battle in the Senate.

Wilson's shift to the left did, as planned, hold the Democratic Party together and managed to get him reelected in November 1916. But then progressivism was forced to take a back seat when the United States entered World War I the next April. (See Chapter Eight for a discussion of the 1916 election and the entire story of how the United States became involved in the war.) The war did not kill progressivism as such, but it did end what historians call the Progressive Era. Following the war, the "dollar decade" of material acquisition would further restrain progressive efforts. But the legacy begun by the Republican Roosevelt and enhanced by Wilson would be cemented in American liberalism and society by Democrat Franklin Roosevelt in the 1930s.

Progressive Labor Legislation

Even before Wilson's political shift to the left in 1916, he had signed the La Follette Seamen's Act. Sponsored by Senator Robert M. La Follette and argued persuasively by the president of the Seamen's Union, the La Follette Seamen's Act of March 1915 set higher standards for sanitation and safety for the sailors working on commercial ships. It also mandated regular payments of wages and generally reduced the previously dictatorial power of ship captains.

The use of child labor in the nation's factories and mines had been recognized by educators, women's groups, and other reformers as having detrimental health, educational, and psychological affects on the children for many years. (For a discussion of the child labor problem, see Chapter Five.) When President Wilson suddenly announced his intention to support a federal child labor bill, Congress passed the Child Labor Act, or the Keating-Owen Act in August 1916 (named after chief sponsors, Colorado Representative Edward Keating and Oklahoma Senator Robert L. Owen). The Keating-Owen Act forbid the interstate transportation of goods manufactured by children under the age of 14, of the products of mines and quarries brought out by children under 16, and of all products made by children under the age of 16 if they worked more than eight hours a day. In *Hammer v. Dagenhart* (1918), the United States Supreme Court declared the Keating-Owen Act unconstitutional, ruling that only states could regulate the employment of children. It would be 20 years after that court decision before another child labor law would be enacted, one that would stand as written. (See Chapter Ten for more information on the Fair Labor Standards Act.)

Congress under the Wilson administration adopted two other significant labor laws in 1916. In August, Congress passed the Workmen's Compensation Act, also known as the Kern-McGillicuddy Act, which provided a model compensation system for job injuries among federal employees. And in September of that year, Congress passed a railroad labor bill sponsored by Representative William C. Adamson, Democrat of Georgia, in response to a threatened nationwide railroad strike over wages and working hours, and only after the president had called in both sides into the White House and became irritated at the adamant position of the railroad companies. The law provided an 8-hour workday (with same pay as at 10 hours) and time and a half for overtime for interstate railroad workers. It also created a commission to study the special problems of labor in that industry.

Farm and Related Progressive Legislation

In July 1916 the Federal Farm Loan Act was passed in response to the hopes and demands of smaller western and southern farmers that dated back to the heyday of the Alliances and the old Populists. Borrowing a page from the new Federal Reserve System, this bill created a system of 12 regional Federal Farm Loan Banks in order to provide longterm loans (from 5 to 40 years in duration) to farmers at low interest. And the Warehouse Act of 1916 helped farmers get short-term bank loans by providing for federal licensing of produce warehouses; this made the stored farm produce easier for banks to accept as collateral.

Then in a series of laws especially benefiting farmers, the dollar matching concept—where the federal government matches state funds—was originated under the Wilson administration. The first of these was the Smith-Lever Act, passed in 1914, which made federal grants available for farm demonstration agents under the direction of land-grant colleges. This was the beginning of the agricultural extension programs within the Department of Agriculture. In the Smith-Hughes Act of 1917, vocational education of both an agricultural and mechanical nature was offered through federal matching dollars. And even the Federal Highways Act, or the Bankhead Good Roads Act of 1916, benefited farmers and rural Americans disproportionately by providing matching federal dollars for the construction of numbered highways across the nation, more efficiently linking rural and urban areas of the country. (Do not confuse this program directly with the major interstate highway network, which became an important legacy of the Dwight D. Eisenhower presidency in the 1950s.)

A BRIEF ASSESSMENT OF PROGRESSIVISM

One of the ironies of the progressive movement in the first two decades of the twentieth century was that while it sought diligently to bring more people into the political process, it ignored three significant groups in society—the poor, new immigrants, and African-Americans. It is true that individual progressives, like Jane Addams, sought to reach the urban poor, but they usually did so in a condescending manner that failed to empower and motivate them sufficiently to get them out of poverty. (See Chapter Five for more information on Jane Addams and others interested in the problems of urban poverty.) Progressivism was basically a white, middle class movement, and therefore, it generally shared the same views that conservatives did about the alleged superiority of white, Anglo-Saxon Protestantism (WASP). Thus, most progressives feared the influx of Catholic and Jewish immigrants from southern and eastern Europe and the so-called "yellow peril" associated with Chinese and Japanese immigrants. Most white Americans, regardless of political philosophy, held racist views at that time, including most progressives. So when Roosevelt had reached the "gentlemen's agreement" with Japan to exclude new Japanese laborers (See Chapter Five), and Wilson allowed for the systematic reduction of African-American federal job-holders, almost no one among the ranks of progressive leaders sounded an alarm.

On the issue of government regulation of corporate power, business leaders often took the very practical view that since the demanding public was going to get regulatory laws anyway, they and their friends in Washington would simply help write them as vaguely as possible so as to make them largely ineffective. Big business was indeed often successful in these efforts, and that was all that conservative-dominated federal courts needed to further reduce the effectiveness of government regulation in the public interest.

The most significant effect of the Progressive Era was to change the way many Americans felt about the role of government in the economic and social life of the nation. In this area at least, progressivism expanded the meaning of democracy and challenged the cynical view that government was and should be only a tool of the economic elite. This represented a radical departure from the liberalism of the nineteenth century and laid the foundation for additional reforms that would come in response to the Great Depression.

ADDITIONAL READINGS

Paul M. Boyer, *Urban Masses and Moral Order in America 1820–1920* (1978). Contains useful material on the social control side of progressivism.

John D. Buenker, *Urban Liberalism and Progressive Reform* (1973). Explores the contributions of urban ethnic voters and machine-based politicians to the progressive movement.

John D. Buenker, John C. Burnham, and Robert M. Crunden, *Progressivism?* (1977). Reviews the large scholarly output on the subject and emphasizes the diversity within progressivism.

John M. Cooper, Jr., *The Pivotal Decades: The United States 1900–1920* (1990). A good overview focusing on American political history of the era, with special attention to the national scene.

Robert M. Crunden, *Ministers of Reform: The Progressives' Achievement in American Civilization 1889–1920* (1982). Emphasizes the moral and religious traditions of middle-class Protestants as the core of the progressive ethos.

Melvyn Dubofsky, *We Shall Be All: A History of the Industrial Workers of the World* (1969). The best overview of this radical labor group.

Louis Filler, *The Muckrakers* (rev. ed., 1980). Offers a useful synthesis of these influential journalists.

Susan A. Glenn, *Daughters of the Shtetl: Life and Labor in the Immigrant Generation* (1990). A sensitive analysis of the experiences of immigrant Jewish women in the garment trades.

Lewis Gould, *The Presidency of William McKinley* (1980). A biography and political study of the president who in several key ways represented a new kind of national leader. Gould presents McKinley as a model Republican, a product of "machine" politics, but also, in his own eyes, an enlightened and modern administrator.

Dewey Grantham, *Southern Progressivism: The Reconciliation of Progress and Tradition* (1983). Examines the contradictions within the southern progressive tradition.

James R. Green, *The World of the Worker: Labor in Twentieth-Century America* (1980). Includes a fine overview of life and work in company towns and urban ghettos in the early twentieth century.

Arthur Link and Richard L. McCormick, *Progressivism* (1983). The best recent overview of progressivism and electoral politics.

Roderick Nash, *Wilderness and the American Mind* (1967). Contains good material on John Muir, the Hetch Hetchy controversy, and the intellectual origins of environmentalism.

David W. Noble, ed., *The Progressive Mind* (rev. ed., 1981). A compendium of important strains in progressive thought.

Ruth Rosen, *The Lost Sisterhood: Prostitutes in America 1900–1918* (1982). Examines prostitution from the perspectives of both prostitutes and reformers.

Nick Salvatore, *Eugene V. Debs: Citizen and Socialist* (1982). The best biography of America's most important socialist leader.

David P. Thelen, *Robert M. La Follette and the Insurgent Spirit* (1976). The best analysis of this pivotal midwestern progressive leader.

James Weinstein, *The Corporate Ideal in the Liberal State 1900–1918* (1969). Emphasizes the important role of business leaders in various reform movements.

Richard White, *"It's Your Misfortune and None of My Own": A History of the American West* (1991). Contains excellent material on progressive politics in the West.

Robert Wiebe, *The Search for Order 1877–1920* (1967). A pathbreaking study of how the professional middle classes responded to the upheavals of industrialism and urbanization.

CHAPTER SEVEN

An Expanding Foreign Policy

MAJOR EVENTS

1898   Hawaii becomes a U. S. possession
War declared against Spain; Cuba and Philippines seized

1903   U. S. obtains canal rights in Panama

1904   Roosevelt Corollary to Monroe Doctrine

1905   Theodore Roosevelt mediates peace treaty between Japan and Russia at Portsmouth Conference

1911   Mexican Revolution begins

1912   U.S. troops intervene in Cuba and Nicaragua

1914   U.S. forces invade Mexico
Panama Canal opens

INTRODUCTION

Foreign policy is not an attitude or a philosophy about international relations, but a nation's plan of action to deal with an international situation in order to achieve an important national goal. The most important national goal for any nation should be that which promotes its national interest. That makes foreign policy the means and the national interest the ultimate goal. National interest loosely refers to any condition which promotes the country's economic health and political influence. In world history, as well as our own, many nations have frequently not acted in a manner that promoted their national interest in the long run. Of course, the identification of what policies are genuinely successful and which are counterproductive in the long run is what makes for a national foreign policy debate.

American foreign policy was fairly simple from the time of George Washington to the Spanish-American War. President Washington had warned the young nation in his farewell address to stay free from "entangling alliances," particularly with European nations. American policy makers believed that their nation must remain above the greedy and self-serving foreign policies of Europe. There was a new destiny to be fulfilled with the idea of "the city on the hill" to which all peoples of the world could admire. As a result, an isolationist foreign policy developed. However, this isolationism did not prevent the nation from expanding its continental territory (frequently at the expense of European nations), expanding trade in the Pacific, or from enlarging American interests in the affairs of the nations south of the borders of the United States. In other words, American actions were inconsistent with its language of isolationism.

As the country grew and developed into an industrial nation after the Civil War, the areas of and reasons for expansionism grew and changed also. One of the most important of these was the expansion of trade necessitated by an excess of goods. The realities of economic advancement, security considerations, and idealistic humanitarian intentions altered foreign policies. As the world moved into the last decade of the nineteenth century and into the first decade of the twentieth century, America was a participant in imperialistic policies for which they had criticized European nations. Imperialism is the act of dominating a foreign nation to the point that the citizens of that nation have little or no control concerning their own national policies.

Not always accepting the negative label of imperialism, Americans called their domination of foreign territory expansionism. American imperialism was somewhat different from European; the United States usually wanted economic domination rather than overseas colonies with its imperialism. Thus, we called our overseas possessions territories rather than colonies. And as long as the native people in those "territories" helped produce economic benefits for the United States, we were generally content. This was evident in the few territories taken and the few that were kept. A foreign policy developed slowly and sporadically for the young nation. Essentially isolationist only toward Europe, in the late nineteenth and early twentieth centuries the United States gradually adopted policies toward some other parts of the world that led to interference, intervention, and even to war. In spite of the differences between the United States and the great European powers with regard to imperialism, the young nation was essentially following their example.

FOREIGN POLICY DURING THE RECONSTRUCTION PERIOD

Immediately after the Civil War, the United States significantly reduced its army and navy. Tired of war, Americans focused most of their attention on expanding the economy and in settling the West. Nevertheless, President Andrew Johnson's Secretary of State, William H. Seward, pursued an expansionist foreign policy. Seward persuaded Napoleon III to withdraw French forces from Mexico and abandon his dream of a Mexican empire in 1867. (The French puppet, the so-called Emperor Maximilian, was killed by the Mexican people.) This American diplomatic success gave some credibility to the Monroe Doctrine, which had been issued by President James Monroe in 1823 to warn Europeans not to interfere in the western hemisphere.

Also in 1867, despite being mocked, Seward persuaded the United States Senate to ratify a treaty which provided for the American purchase of Alaska from Russia for $7.2 million. Seward not only wanted Russia out of North America, but he was one of the earliest government officials who actively sought to push the United States into expanding in the Pacific area. The deal for Alaska was called "Seward's Folly" and "Seward's Icebox," among other things. But Seward's expansionist drive had given the United States its best investment in land since the Louisiana Pur-

Cartoon depicting territorial appetite. Credit: Library of Congress.

chase in 1803. Gold was later discovered there in huge quantities, resulting in the Klondike Gold Rush of 1897–1898. Alaska has paid for itself many times over in its gold reserves. Twentieth century discovery of vast oil fields there again proved the region's extreme financial value. And, of course, during the Cold War era after World War II, the earlier purchase of Alaska meant that at least the Soviets were not sitting on our back porch.

Seward also persuaded the Congress to annex the small Midway Islands west of Hawaii in 1867. But his attempt to push American expansion into the Caribbean proved futile when a treaty with Denmark to purchase the Virgin Islands was rejected early in the Grant administration.

Problems with Britain

The Grant administration, in sharp contrast to its uncertain leadership in domestic affairs, proved far more successful at foreign policy. Secretary of State, Hamilton Fish, is given most of the credit for successes in foreign policy. And while Fish deserves most of the credit, it must be acknowledged that Grant generally gave him a free hand in foreign affairs. The most serious issues facing Fish were part of a complex series of disputes with England. During the Civil War, the United States had accused the British of violating international law by building several warships that were used by the Confederates to inflict heavy damage on United States shipping. The *Alabama* and the *Florida* were the most infamous of these warships. After the war, the United States demanded reparations for damage done by the warships; these claims became known as the "Alabama claims." At the same time, the British insisted on payment for destruction of cotton bought from the Confederacy and for damage inflicted upon British ships carrying Southern cotton.

Then there were the Irish-American radicals, called Fenians, who illegally raised small armies and invaded Canada several times during the Johnson and Grant presidencies. The Fenians vainly hoped to hold Canada hostage in order to secure the independence of Ireland. The British held the United States government responsible for these violations of international law and demanded reparations for the damages incurred by British Canada.

The Johnson-Clarendon Convention, in early 1869, would have submitted the disputed questions between the British and the Americans to arbitration by a third party. However, when Grant took office in early March that year, the Senate rejected the treaty by a vote of 54 to 1. In the debate, Massachusetts Republican Senator Charles Sumner expanded the "Alabama claims" by declaring that the British action had delayed the end of the Civil War by two years. Britain, he charged, should also pay for those so-called indirect costs, which he estimated to be about $2 billion. Most Americans undoubtedly agreed with Sumner and seemed ready to accept Canada as a substitute for the proposed $2 billion. Of course, Britain was not about to offer Canada to the United States, so any possible resolution to the problem was postponed.

In 1871 the United States and Britain signed the Treaty of Washington, which provided for the arbitration of the major disputes between them. The results of this treaty included the decision by a panel of arbitrators appointed by five countries to award the United States $15.5 million for the "Alabama claims." Another arbitration panel awarded Britain almost $2 million for damages suffered during the American Civil War. The greatest significance of this treaty and Fish's handling of these Anglo-American disputes was that the two nations continued the tradition of settling their differences peacefully—a tradition which had begun with the 1818 Anglo-American Convention, which had provided for joint occupation of the Oregon Territory for several years.

The Caribbean

In the late 1860s, Secretary Fish used his great diplomatic skill to prevent war in the Caribbean when a revolt against Spanish rule in Cuba broke out in 1868. Many Americans, including President Grant himself, favored the Cuban revolutionaries, but Fish finally persuaded the president and the Congress that the United States should remain neutral. President Grant went sofar as to recognize the rights of the revolutionaries to revolt, but Secretary Fish filed the document away to avoid trouble with Spain. These efforts were almost dashed to pieces when the Spanish captured and executed 53 Cuban crew members of a vessel (the *Virginius*) that was flying the United States flag with doubtful legality to do so. The ship was allegedly carrying arms to the rebels in Cuba. Due to Fish's efforts, however, the crisis calmed when Spain returned the ship and paid an indemnity to the victims' families.

The one foreign policy endeavor which President Grant undertook without the full approval of Hamilton Fish concerned the Dominican Republic (called Santo Domingo in those days), in the Caribbean Sea. Like William Seward, President Grant longed for United States influence in the Caribbean. The rulers of Santo Domingo desired annexation because the island's economic problems made their political status shaky at best. Therefore, in 1870 Grant sent his own personal secretary to the Caribbean to negotiate an annexation treaty. The resulting treaty was rejected by the United States Senate in the same year. Senator Charles Sumner led the successful opposition as chairman of the powerful Senate Committee on Foreign Relations, shortly after which the president used his influence to have his chairmanship removed from him.

Except for the attempted annexation of Santo Domingo, the Johnson-Grant years proved successful in the arena of foreign affairs. This was especially beneficial to the United States even in the short term because the country was in no condition to become involved in another war so recently after its own bloody Civil War.

EARLY EXAMPLES OF EXPANSIONISM

White settlement of what eventually became the United States began with 13 small colonies along the Atlantic coast. Through wars, purchases, or merely moving into uninhabited areas, the nation expanded to its present size. Imperialism and expansionism actually began with the conquest of the lands of the Native Americans. Domination of these tribes continued until all were effectively controlled by 1890. America also gained a large area of territory from war with Mexico in 1848. (See Chapter Two for more information.)

Purchase of land also added vast areas to the new nation. The Louisiana Purchase from France in 1803 added approximately 827,000 square miles to the United States, roughly doubling the size of the young nation overnight. The Gadsden Purchase from Mexico in 1853 (ratified in 1854) added almost 30,000 square miles to the nation, completing the present-day size of the continental United States. And the purchase of Alaska from Russia in 1867 added another 589,000 square miles to the United States.

INTEREST IN THE PACIFIC GROWS

China

Americans involved in the whaling industry, the China trade, and Christian missionary efforts in the late 1700s and early 1800s initiated contact with an area of the world that would later have great importance to a then small and struggling new nation. In May 1785, Captain John Greene, commander of the *Empress of China*, returned from China with a cargo of tea and silks. Impressed by the possibilities of huge profits from these exotic trade goods, American merchants began outfitting ships in larger numbers to sail to the ancient shores of China. In 1844, the first treaty between the United States and China, the Treaty of Wang Hiya, opened 5 ports for trading by American merchants and gave special rights to Americans living in China, including the right to remain subject to American law. As exemplified in China, private enterprise frequently precedes government action of some sort and brings about changes in the nation's foreign interests and formal foreign policy positions. China also drew the attention of several American Protestant churches and remained an important field for missionary work well into the twentieth century.

Japan

Commodore Matthew C. Perry was given the mission of opening up relations with the isolated islands of Japan. Japan had allowed only limited contact with the other nations of the world since the 1620s. Only the port of Nagasaki received foreign visitors, and the numbers allowed in the country were very small. Washington's concern with the fate of shipwrecked sailors in Japanese waters, who were not allowed to leave, and increasing East Asian trade, led to the Perry expedition in July 1853. Perry sailed into the port of Yokohama with 4 warships. Initial negotiations were brief, with the United States asking Japan to open up its ports to Western trade and allow shipwrecked sailors to leave the islands.

In 1854, Perry returned to Japan bearing gifts of a miniature railroad and telegraph, examples of the advanced culture of the Western world. Perry was also accompanied on this trip by 7 ships to intimidate the Japanese. The United States wanted to impress upon this isolated nation its determination to open up the islands. The Treaty of Kanagawa, signed on March 31, 1854, opened the ports of Shimoda and Hakodate for trade. Japan also agreed to the opening of an American consulate and to proper treatment of castaways. Japan's isolation was thereby broken. This nation, once so committed to strict isolationism, and to shunning all things foreign, eventually moved into an imperialism of its own in Asia that would clash with the policies of the United States, and war in the 1940s would be the result.

Hawaiian Islands

The sea routes to the shores of Asia brought American ships into contact with islands in the Pacific which were used as layover or resupply stations for the ships and their crews. The most important of these were the Hawaiian Islands and the islands of Samoa.

Captain James Cook is credited with the discovery of the Hawaiian Islands in 1778. Hawaii is an archipelago of 8 principal islands and numerous islets in the central Pacific. King Kamehameha I united the various kingdoms on the islands under his leadership, with advice and firearms provided by foreign visitors to the islands. Initial American contact with the islands came from missionaries, whaling vessels, and trading ships stopping in Hawaii on their way to Asian ports of call. Not certain of the role Hawaii might play in future American plans, President John Tyler stated in a message to Congress in 1842 that the United States would not approve of any nation taking control of the islands. The American population on the islands grew, and both Secretary of State William Marcy in the 1850s and William Seward in the 1860s tried to move the United States to annex Hawaii, but both of those efforts failed. The Reciprocity Treaty of 1875 tied Hawaii and the United States closer together. Sugar and other products could enter the United States duty free in return for a pledge from King Kalakaua that the islands would not give up their independence to any other nation. Another aspect of American influence on Hawaii was the leasing of land at Pearl Harbor in 1884 for an American naval base.

The treaties between the United States and Hawaii brought more Americans and American investment to the islands. Sugar, from the vast sugar cane fields, was the primary product. By 1881, Secretary of State James G. Blaine declared that the Hawaiian Islands were part of the American system, which was borne out by the fact that by 1890 99 percent of all Hawaiian exports were bound for the United States. Blaine was one of the first post-Civil War politicians who realized that the United States needed specific foreign policy goals.

By the 1890s, Hawaii was dominated by Americans both economically and politically, when two events finally brought an end to Hawaiian independence. The booming Hawaiian sugar trade was indirectly damaged by the McKinley Tariff of 1890, which put all sugar on the free list and compensated American sugar growers with a bounty of 2 cents per pound. Annexation with the United States would bring all of the privileges of American growers to the planters in Hawaii. This was not desired by all cane planters there because annexation would probably bring to the islands the contract-labor laws of the United States, restricting or cutting off the supply of cheap Asian labor.

More important to growing American discontent on Hawaii were the actions of the native ruler, Queen Liluokalani, or Queen Lil as she was nicknamed by Americans. Queen Lil ascended to the throne in 1891, and was soon attempting to eliminate American influence, reestablish the autocracy of the monarchy, and drive foreigners from her kingdom. In January 1893, when she attempted to establish a new constitution by royal edict that would give her the autonomy she wanted, the white planters on the islands staged a revolution to overthrow the queen. John L. Stevens, the United States government representative in Honolulu and an annexationist himself, aided the revolution with his summons to a nearby American warship for armed men to protect American lives and property. Queen Lil did not have the resources to resist the planters and the soldiers. The leader of the planters was Sanford Dole, of Dole pineapple fame, who helped establish a provisional government. Stevens promptly extended formal recognition to the new government without authorization from Washington.

President Grover Cleveland replaced President Benjamin Harrison before a treaty of annexation could be acted upon by the Senate. Cleveland, an avowed anti-imperialist, withdrew the treaty and ordered an investigation of the affair and the future desires of the Hawaiian people. The investigators discovered that the majority of the Hawaiians did not want annexation and that the revolution probably would not have succeeded without the assistance of Stevens, Dole, and American marines. There would be no annexation at this time. President Cleveland also attempted to persuade the provisional government to step down, but Dole and his American supporters refused. Cleveland was forced to recognize the new Republic of Hawaii under the leadership of President Sanford Dole. Annexation finally came by a joint resolution of Congress on July 7, 1898, during the Spanish-American War and under President William McKinley's administration. Hawaii was a valuable recoaling and supply station between the United States and East Asia. It could also present a first line of defense for the United States in the Pacific Ocean. In 1900 Hawaii was officially organized as the Territory of Hawaii, and it became the fiftieth state in the Union in 1959.

The Samoan Islands

Early American interest in the Samoan Islands developed along the same lines as those of Hawaii, beginning with missionaries in the 1830s, but developments in the 1880s brought a different destiny for Samoa. In 1872, a United States Navy officer, Richard W. Meade, negotiated a treaty with a Samoan chief that gave the United States the outstanding harbor of Pago Pago (pronounced Pango Pango) on the island of Tutuila for a naval base, but the Senate took no action on the treaty. After an American agent for President Grant proclaimed himself the prime minister of Samoa and was quickly overthrown and sent home via a British ship, new talks eventually ensued. Finally, in 1878, another treaty was negotiated and ratified by the Senate. This one presented the United States with the harbor of Pago Pago, but also provided for increased trade relations and the right of Americans living there to remain under American law. Britain and Germany then promptly negotiated their own deals concerning other islands in the group in the following year.

Talk of annexing the islands in the 1880s developed when it became noticeable that Germany and Great Britain were also interested in annexing the islands. An 1887 civil war in Samoa resulted in the Germans installing a Samoan ruler of their choice on the throne. Thus, in 1889, with tensions between the 3 nations at such a pitch concerning control of the islands, naval vessels from all three nations were in the harbor of Pago Pago to guarantee that their nation would get its fair share of any division. Before the threatened battle could commence a hurricane severely damaged the fleets. This event gave the 3 nations time to cool off, and that same year they all entered into a tripartite protectorate over the Samoan Islands. The significance of this new arrangement was that this was the first entangling alliance that the United States had entered into with European powers. A long standing policy was changing, with regards to the Pacific at least. In 1899, Great Britain stepped out of the protectorate, and the islands were divided between Germany and the United States.

UNITED STATES POLICY IN LATIN AMERICA

The Monroe Doctrine

By the 1820s, most of the European colonies in Latin America, south of the United States, had wrested their independence from these nations. Contrary to its isolationist policies toward events in Europe, the United States was greatly concerned with what transpired in the western hemisphere. President James Monroe appeared before Congress in December 1823 and presented to the world an American foreign policy decision that would be used to the present day. Constructed by Secretary of State John Quincy Adams, the statement known as the Monroe Doctrine warned European nations that new colonization efforts in this hemisphere would not be tolerated, nor would the United States accept interference in the independence of former colonies. In return, the United States pledged not to interfere in European affairs or the affairs of existing European colonies in Latin America.

This was a strong statement of policy for a new nation still expanding its own boundaries and without the naval or military strength to enforce such a policy. It is ironic that the policy was backed by the interests of Great Britain. Great Britain had approached the United States to consider a joint statement to the powers of Europe to stay out of this hemisphere, but the United States did not want an entanglement of this sort and issued its own policy. The policy matched the goals of Britain to keep others from interfering with their hold on the Atlantic trade. However, it was Great Britain, not the United States, who had the naval strength to enforce such a policy and did so.

Pan Americanism

Until the late 1870s, the Monroe Doctrine was interpreted as a barrier to keep European nations from meddling in the western hemisphere. The interpretation then began to undergo a revision to secure for the United States special interests and domination, both economically and at times politically, in Latin America. The United States demonstrated its new policy beginning with the mediation of problems between neighboring countries. Border disputes between Argentina and Paraguay in 1876 and between Mexico and Guatemala in 1881 were both mediated by the United States.

The promotion of Pan Americanism was another step in the change in American foreign policy. The policy was mostly economic in nature, as was most of American foreign policy at this time. In 1889, Secretary of State James G. Blaine hosted

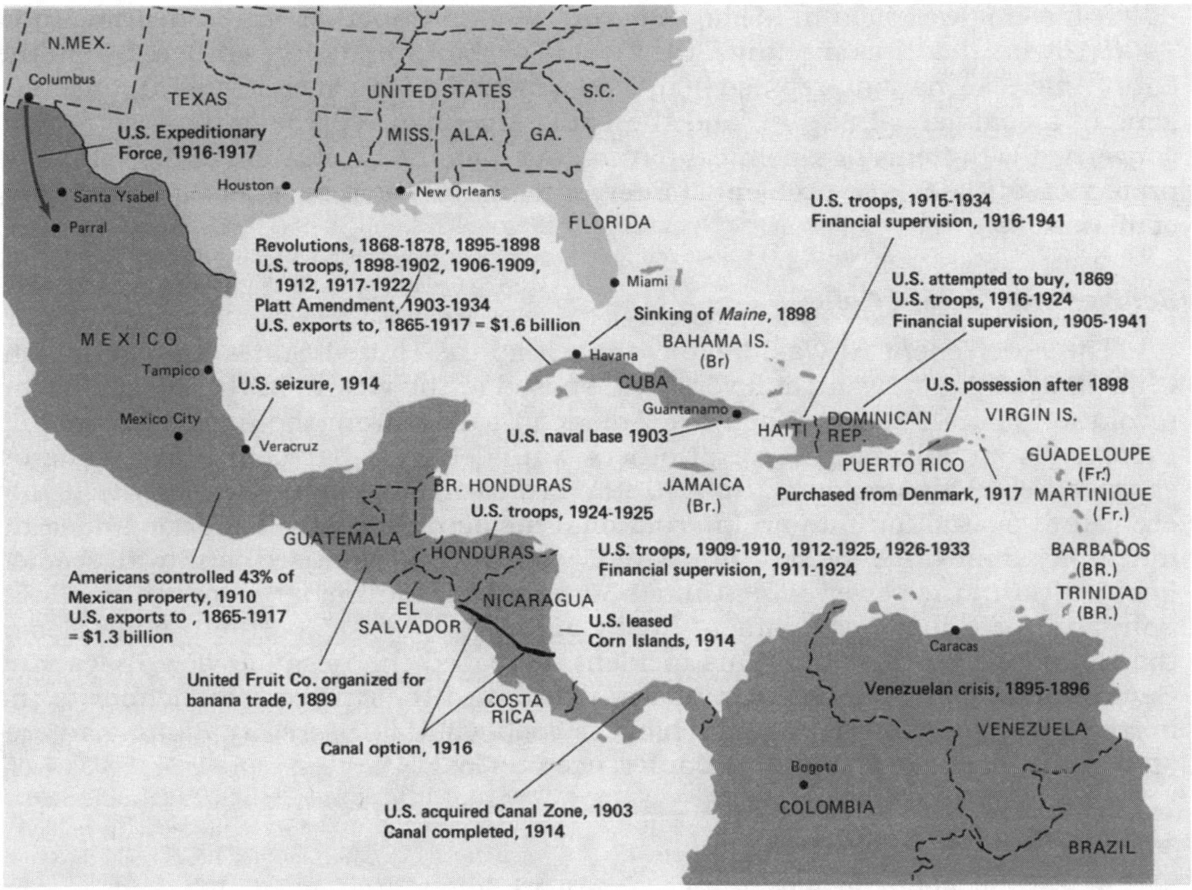
N.MEX.
Columbus
TEXAS
UNITED STATES
S.C.
MISS.
ALA.
GA.
LA.
U.S. Expeditionary Force, 1916-1917
Santa Ysabel
Parral
Houston
New Orleans
FLORIDA
U.S. troops, 1915-1934
Financial supervision, 1916-1941
Revolutions, 1868-1878, 1895-1898
U.S. troops, 1898-1902, 1906-1909, 1912, 1917-1922
Platt Amendment, 1903-1934
U.S. exports to, 1865-1917 = $1.6 billion
Miami
U.S. attempted to buy, 1869
U.S. troops, 1916-1924
Financial supervision, 1905-1941
Sinking of Maine, 1898
MEXICO
BAHAMA IS. (Br)
Havana
Tampico
CUBA
U.S. seizure, 1914
U.S. possession after 1898
Guantanamo
Mexico City
DOMINICAN REP.
VIRGIN IS.
HAITI
Veracruz
U.S. naval base 1903
GUADELOUPE (Fr.)
PUERTO RICO
BR. HONDURAS
JAMAICA (Br.)
Purchased from Denmark, 1917
MARTINIQUE (Fr.)
U.S. troops, 1924-1925
GUATEMALA
HONDURAS
U.S. troops, 1909-1910, 1912-1925, 1926-1933
Financial supervision, 1911-1924
BARBADOS (BR.)
Americans controlled 43% of Mexican property, 1910
U.S. exports to, 1865-1917 = $1.3 billion
EL SALVADOR
NICARAGUA
TRINIDAD (BR.)
U.S. leased Corn Islands, 1914
Caracas
United Fruit Co. organized for banana trade, 1899
COSTA RICA
Venezuelan crisis, 1895-1896
VENEZUELA
Canal option, 1916
Bogota
U.S. acquired Canal Zone, 1903
Canal completed, 1914
COLOMBIA
BRAZIL

The United States and America. Credit: The United States: Combined Edition, by Winthrop D. Jordan and Leon F. Litwack, Prentice Hall, Inc., 1991.

the First Pan American Conference in Washington, D.C. Previously there had been small regional conferences called by various groups of countries to deal with common defense, and Blaine had called for a conference in 1881, which did not take place because of the death of President Garfield. So the 1889 conference was the first meeting encompassing most of the nations of the western hemisphere.

The delegates from 18 countries came together and were met with a proposal from Blaine for a customs union and the establishment of a system of arbitration to settle disagreements and disputes. Most of the exports from these nations came into the United States duty free, but Blaine wanted a larger share of the import market into these countries for the United States. The countries did not establish the customs union, nor was Blaine's proposal for an arbitration system accepted. The nations were too suspicious of the motives of the United States to agree to many recommendations. The results of the conference were the organization of the Pan-American Union to act as a clearing house for commercial information, establishing a climate for future economic cooperation that eventually included reciprocal tariff reductions, and an agreement that future meetings could be beneficial.

A meeting was held in Mexico City in 1901 and another in Rio de Janeiro in 1906. During the three meetings, the agenda of the United States differed from the Latin American nations represented. The United States concentrated upon problems of a commercial nature, and the Latin American representatives were more concerned with items of a political nature, such as the arbitration of disputes, the protection of aliens, the problem of intervention, and the respect of the sovereignty of all nations.

Belligerence toward Chile

The government in Washington, as well as the United States ambassador to Chile, Patrick Egan, was not favorably disposed to the victors in the latest Chilean revolution of 1890–1891. When two American sailors from the American warship *Baltimore* were killed and several others wounded in a barroom brawl while on shore leave in Valparaiso in October 1891, President Benjamin Harrison decided to escalate the situation into an international incident. The president demanded an indemnity from Chile for the "murdered" victims. Chile refused, and war seemed imminent. But the power of the United States was too intimidating to the small nation, and the Chilean government finally agreed to pay $75,000 to the families of the wounded and the slain. This incident increased the negative view that many Central and South American countries had toward their powerful neighbor to the north as being too interfering. Much of the good will that Secretary Blaine had created at the recent Pan American Conference was lost.

The Alaskan Seal Controversy

A growing willingness to protect American domination of this hemisphere and to demand the recognition of this right were evident in two confrontations with Great Britain. Seals were the problem between the two nations during the 1880s. The Pribilof Islands, acquired with Alaska, were the breeding grounds for millions of fur-bearing seals. A profitable fur trade brought Canadian poachers to lay in wait outside the 3-mile limit, where they slaughtered the animals indiscriminately as they swam out to sea. In order to prevent the extermination of the seals, American revenue vessels began seizing Canadian ships. Great Britain protested, and both nations agreed to arbitration of the matter in 1891. In 1893, the arbitration commission established a 60-mile protection zone for the seals. This was a defeat for the United States because it wanted the Canadians completely stopped, but the decision was a victory for international arbitration.

The Venezuelan Boundary Dispute

When gold was discovered in the interior of Venezuela and British Guiana, it led to the flare up once again of a long standing boundary dispute between the two countries in the early 1890s. Great Britain refused to submit the question to arbitration, basically snubbing Secretary of State Richard Olney's original reminder of the Monroe Doctrine. Believing the Secretary's position to be more political posturing to gain Irish-American votes for the Democratic Party than a real threat to the number one naval power in the world, Britain was slow to answer, but then answered in the negative. An angry President Cleveland sent a special message to Congress in December 1895, proposing that the United States run the boundary line between the two South American countries and stand behind the new border with all of the power of the United States. Congress supported the stand of the president, and war seemed imminent. Considering that the United States navy was 6 times smaller in battleship strength than Great Britain's and the boundary dispute was not concerned with American territory, the belligerence of Cleveland and his Secretary of State was puzzling to some then and later. However, Cleveland was suspicious of British intentions in Latin America, and if the issue was not resolved soon, Venezuela might declare war on Great Britain, with American intervention a possibility.

Luckily, neither country wanted war. Britain was closely watching the growing strength of Germany and developing problems in South Africa that would lead to the first Boer War. So the dispute went to arbitration in 1897, which included the United States, and the special commission drew the boundary line close to the original British claim. Secretary Olney explained the belligerent language and American demands later on the grounds that "in English eyes the United States was then so completely a negligible quantity that it was believed only words the equivalent of blows would be really effective." United States action over the Venezuelan boundary dispute illustrated a growing tendency by the 1890s that it, not the British, were now ready to enforce the Monroe Doctrine. At the same time, it also demonstrated a relatively new American attitude that its own law was "practically sovereign" in the western hemisphere.

AMERICAN IMPERIALISM IN THE 1890S

End of the Frontier

From the Civil War to the 1890s, the United States had relatively little interest in foreign affairs, with a few exceptions. Domestic concerns controlled the attention of government and populace, but there was a growing number of government leaders who wanted to expand American foreign interests, even to the point of gaining American territory overseas. But settling the interior of the nation and building an industrial society was the focus for most. As the country moved into the final decade of the century, however, interest in areas outside the continental United States increased. Many factors came together at this particular time to bring most Americans to accept intervention and imperialism in lands far from the borders of this country. In 1890, the United States Census Bureau declared an end to the frontier. This was a cultural shock to a nation that had thrived on opening up new frontiers throughout its entire history up to that point. Frederick Jackson Turner, the historian, prophetically declared in the 1890s that frontier expansion would continue but on an international scale. A new "manifest destiny" clutched at the United States, but this one would lead the country off of its continent, primarily in two directions—the Caribbean and the Pacific.

Leading Imperialists and Their Arguments

Imperialists advanced very powerful arguments for the expansion of American interests. The economic argument was that the United States needed guaranteed foreign markets for the excess of goods that industry was now able to produce, and the United States must get into these markets in the Pacific quickly before the great powers of Europe controlled all of the trade of the area with their own imperialism. There was a large increase in the 1890s of European countries searching for overseas territory. A depression in the 1890s opened the door further to the acceptance of expansionism overseas as a necessity. New areas in which to sell manufactured goods must be secured in order to increase orders at the factories and put people back to work.

The writings of Alfred T. Mahan promoted the cause of imperialism by providing a strategic argument for its justification. In his 1890 book, *The Influence of Sea Power Upon History, 1660–1783*, Mahan argued that the national greatness and wealth of all former great powers had flowed from their strong navies. A powerful nation must build a strong navy and merchant marine to engage in foreign commerce and gain control of overseas territories to advance this commerce and provide bases for the ships. This was also seen as an action which would counter the major European nations that were also so inclined; in other words, if the United States didn't take over and dominate certain areas, then someone else will. In the 1830s, the government had begun to modernize the navy with steel and steam. By 1893, the United States had the fifth strongest navy in the world. Theodore Roosevelt and Massachusetts Republican Senator Henry Cabot Lodge were two very influential followers of the imperialistic ideas of Captain Mahan.

A religious justification for American imperialism was provided by the missionary elements of the churches in the country. Missionaries were one of the first groups of Americans to venture outside the country in order to carry the Christian religion to the continent of Asia and the islands in the Pacific. Apparently, it did not bother many such Americans that, in effect, the native peoples of other lands would be converted at the end of a gun barrel; the point seemed to be that they would be converted, for their own good, of course. The Reverend Josiah Strong, in his book *Our Country*, published in 1885, added more arguments for imperialism from a religious perspective. Strong claimed that the Anglo Saxon race was superior to all others, and it was the duty of the United States to extend its superior civilization to "backward" people everywhere. In fact, he openly declared that these foreign areas must come under the control of the United States for their own good. Strong's writings also expressed the views of the Social Darwinists, who believed that the "survival of the fittest" concept belonged to nations of the world as well as to the animal kingdom, and racists who believed that the people of color could not rule themselves.

Other imperialists used still different rationale to support aggressive American action and domination in parts of the world. Some argued that American imperialism was needed to bring the blessings of democracy to other peoples. The historical experience, however, suggests that democracy is not something which can be exported in the same way that bananas and truck parts can be. Americans developed a thriving democracy in relative ease, so many have thought that other nations should simply copy its political institutions and create a flourishing democracy. It is considered the best political system that human beings have ever devised, but it must grow slowly and with great care if it is to be strong and effective. American democracy began with the establishment of the first 13 colonies; possessed the wealth of democratic experience and special (and largely beneficial) economic blessings from "Mother England;" was protected by its geographic isolation (someone said we were surrounded by weak neighbors on the north and south, fish to the east and fish to the west) and the world's superpower with the number one navy; and was inadvertently "allowed" to develop some of its own democratic institutions for more than 150 years (1607–1775) before Americans achieved their independence. Many historians suggest Americans remember those great advantages before expecting to export democracy as a "quick fix" for other nations' problems.

The humanitarian argument for imperialism promised to free people from poverty and disease. With the growth in scientific medicine near the turn of the twentieth century, the United States could, and did indeed, provide the kind and level of medical care that was so desperately needed in other parts of the world. But our economic imperialism, coupled with a condescending attitude mixed with racism for the people we said we wanted to help, usually failed to bring long-lasting relief to the impoverishment of other peoples. And then there were Americans, like Theodore Roosevelt, who used national pride to justify imperialistic policies. The United States is the greatest nation on earth, the argument went, so it needed to prove it by dominating weaker nations.

The major, heavier industries, such as transportation, oil, and steel, generally gave their support to imperialistic foreign policies. Many political conservatives also tended to be imperialistically minded, although Theodore Roosevelt, the leading progressive in the early twentieth century, was also the number one imperialist of the same period. More Republicans and more Americans outside the West than in that region were imperialists as well.

Anti-Imperialists and Their Arguments

Although swimming against the tide, there were those among the American people who opposed imperialism for a variety of reasons. Anti-imperialists drew most of their support from the majority of progressives and other reform-minded Americans. Social reformers, by definition, are supportive of the proverbial "underdog," and it was only natural that they would likely support less powerful foreign nations too. Many leaders among the smaller businesses, who often could not take advantage of foreign economic opportunities created by such policies, saw imperialism as the use of the nation's political and military power by their larger economic competitors to gain an even bigger advantage. Most labor unions, more Democrats, and more people living in the West tended to oppose most imperialistic ventures.

Anti-imperialists offered a number of reasons for their opposition to imperialism. Some used the historical argument, maintaining that imperialism violates American ideals which have been historically advocated, such as the Declaration of Independence's assertion that "all men are created equal." Americans, they urged, should remember their own historical beginnings as 13 colonies themselves, and then they would see imperialism as an exercise in hypocrisy.

Those using the constitutional argument claimed that the president had no constitutional authority to take over and dominate other countries. Such action was, they claimed, contrary to international law, even though nations had almost always violated those standards.

Those using the civil liberties argument claimed that if the United States government became accustomed to violating the individual rights of foreign peoples with great ease, then eventually it would turn on its own population at home. This argument possessed shades of prophetic truth, for German-Americans during World War I, Japanese-Americans during World War II, and official surveillance and harrassment of many anti-Vietnam War groups in the late 1960s and early '70s became victims of a federal government (with much popular support) that had gotten used to doing just that in parts of southeast Asia and especially in Latin America.

Other reasons given by the anti-imperialists to justify their opposition to imperialism included the financial, economic, and racist arguments. Those who employed the financial argument claimed that the price of imperialism's efforts to defeat and dominate many foreign peoples was too high in terms of blood and money. This is related in a similar way to the later anti-Vietnam War opinion which wondered whether or not some extreme advocates of that war really supported a policy of destroying Vietnam in order to save it; that seemed a bit ludicrous to them. Labor unions, in their use of the economic argument, exclaimed that one effect of imperialism would be to bring job competition from low-paid and otherwise exploited foreign labor with American workers. This cheap labor argument won many converts among the working classes and the poor. And finally, there were racists who opposed imperialism just as there were those who supported it. The anti-imperialist racists feared that such policies would inevitably increase the number of people of color, which in turn would increase the intermingling and intermarrying of the races. This would then allegedly dilute and pollute the "purity" of the white race.

THE SPANISH-AMERICAN WAR

Historical Background

Since 1512, the island of Cuba had belonged to the Spanish Empire in the New World of the western hemisphere. Cuba was important because her strategic location placed her in the position of a gateway to the Empire in the Caribbean and South and Central America. When the other Latin American Spanish colonies were fighting for their freedom in the early 1800s, Cuba remained loyal. However, there were later attempts by Cuban patriots to rid the colony of its Spanish rulers, and many of these involved American citizens acting without the sanction of the United States government. American involvement in the long road to Cuban independence grew to the point that America finally declared war on Spain to accomplish this goal.

In the 1840s, individual Americans were involved in assisting Cuban rebels in their revolutionary efforts with supplies and with men to fight for the freedom of

Cuba. President Zachary Taylor forbade Americans from making these so-called filibustering trips into Cuba on August 11, 1849. President Taylor did not want problems with Spain because of unofficial American assistance in the rebellion of one of its colonies. In 1851, General Narciso Lopez, a Cuban refugee, ignored President Fillmore's proclamation against filibustering and led a group of Americans to Cuba to participate in a revolt against Spanish rule. Fifty of the American volunteers, along with General Lopez, were captured and executed in Cuba. In 1868, the Ten Years' War began in Cuba, and once again private American assistance was forthcoming. President Grant himself attempted to issue a statement supportive of the Cuban rebels. And he apparently escaped war only by the diplomatic efforts of Secretary of State Hamilton Fish over the *Virginius* affair.

Presidents from the time of Thomas Jefferson had expressed interest in the island. President James K. Polk was willing to pay $100 million to purchase Cuba from Spain in 1848, and President Franklin Pierce renewed the effort in 1854 without success. Just before the Civil War, there was also talk in the Senate of annexing Cuba at some time in the future. Southerners looked longingly at Cuba as another future potential slave state. The government of the United States also realized Cuba's strategic importance. In spite of this long standing interest in Cuba, the United States did not seize the opportunity to bring the island under domination during the Ten Years' War (1868–1878), when the timing appeared opportune because of Spanish offenses. Circumstances would not come together for the freeing of Cuba from Spanish rule until the 1890s, when yet another revolution pulled the United States into the problems of this Spanish colony, and the United States was prepared for a new step in its alleged destiny.

Jose Marti, a Cuban exile residing in the United States and known as the "George Washington" of Cuba, founded the Cuban Revolutionary party in 1892 in Tampa, Florida. Marti had led the revolt begun in 1868 and had fled to the United States in the late 1870s when the revolution had failed. He gathered American money, arms, and men for the Cuban revolution that erupted in February 1895. Returning to Cuba to lead the rebellion, Marti was killed in battle in 1895. A Cuban "junta" continued to orchestrate the revolution from New York. They spread propaganda, sold bonds, and encouraged filibustering expeditions to their homeland.

The United States bore a great deal of responsibility for the beginning of this final revolution. Economic conditions, which had been bad for the island, were worsened by the passage of the Wilson-Gorman Tariff Act in 1894, which imposed a duty charge on Cuban sugar, which had been entering the United States duty free under the McKinley Tariff Act (1890). This duty taxed sugar at a 40 percent rate, and because the United States was a major buyer of Cuban sugar, it ruined the Cuban sugar market, a major source of employment, which had increased production after the McKinley Tariff Act had put sugar on the duty free list. In this time of crisis, the rebels struck to rid Cuba of Spanish political oppression and economic exploitation. They burned sugar-cane fields and sugar mills to further destroy the economy to the point that the Spanish would leave or the United States would intervene. The people of Cuba suffered terribly in this guerrilla war from the actions of both sides.

American Intervention

America had remained neutral in the Ten Years' War, but would not remain so in the revolution of 1895. Why? By the 1890s, American interests had changed. The nation was interested in new areas to carry forth the philosophy of "manifest destiny." Acceptance that the nation could not remain isolated and continue to prosper had increased in the government and with the general public. Large numbers of Americans believed the United States should actively search for land, markets, and influence in the Pacific and Latin America. Specifically, American economic interest in Cuba had increased over the years since the Civil War to the point that, when these economic interests were threatened by this new revolution, the United States was concerned. In 1895, American investments there totaled $50 million, and trade with the island was $100 million annually. Finally, the American public was so inundated with stories from the newspapers that the cry for American intervention to free the island from Spanish rule was almost impossible to be ignored by a government accountable to its citizens.

Events in Cuba provided material that newspaper owners must surely dream about. High drama and the cruel suffering of an oppressed people were daily on the front pages of America's most important newspapers. Stories of young women jailed for resisting the advances of Spanish officers or stripped and searched on the deck of ships bound for American ports brought an outcry from American women and men who believed in the old tradition of fighting for the honor of women. The outrage concerning the plight of young and seemingly innocent women led to letter campaigns appealing to the Queen Regent of Spain, the American Congress, and even the Pope to end the suffering of the unfortunate Cubans and the outrages committed against women.

Competing with each other, the newspapers printed the truth, half truths, and sometimes even lies to increase circulation. Sensationalizing the events in Cuba and appealing to the readers' emotions rather than their good judgement in order to sell papers became known as "yellow journalism." The name came from the "Yellow Kid" comic strip of the *New York Journal*. William Randolph Hearst, the owner of the *New York Journal*, and Joseph Pulitzer, the owner of the *New York World*, surged into the forefront in perpetuating this type of journalism. Hearst is supposed to have said it cost him $3 million dollars to bring about a war between the United States and Spain. The press was important in whipping up high emotions and thereby bringing pressure from the public, but it would be a mistake to assume that the press created public support for war. Most Americans appear to have supported armed intervention in Cuba anyway, and other subsequent events finally brought about war.

President Cleveland had managed to keep the United States out of war with Spain, but President McKinley was unable to convince the American public that a war was not in the best interest of the country. In 1896, General Valeriano Weyler, the Spanish military governor of Cuba, had begun a policy of reconcentration of the civilians from outlying areas into barbed wire enclosures in order to cut off their support to the Cuban revolutionaries and to determine who the rebels actually were. Without proper food and hygiene, the inmates in the camps died in large numbers. It is estimated that perhaps as many as 200,000 died in the camps, and the general earned the title of "Butcher" Weyler in the press. In September of 1897, President McKinley offered the assistance of the United States to restore peace in Cuba, but Spain rejected the offer. A new more liberal Spanish government did institute reforms, hoping to resolve problems in Cuba and end the rebellion before the United States intervened. General Weyler was recalled, the reconcentration policy was changed, Cubans were to be given the same political rights as Spaniards, and a proposal for eventual home rule (not complete independence) for Cuba was initiated. But the rebels would accept nothing less than complete independence. President McKinley asked the American people, in his annual message of December 1897, to allow Spain the time to implement their new policies toward Cuba.

Two events occurred in February 1898 that took the decision for war virtually out of the president's control. On February 9, 1898, the *New York Journal* printed a letter written by the Spanish Ambassador Dupuy de Lome, which had been stolen from the Havana post office by a Cuban rebel. In the letter, de Lome criticized the president's annual message of 1897. He said the message proved that "McKinley is weak and a bidder for the admiration of the crowd, besides being a would be politician who tries to leave a door open behind himself while keeping on good terms with the jingoes of his party." De Lome and Spain were put in an extremely awkward situation, and the ambassador resigned at once. The American public was not satisfied with a mere resignation, however. They were outraged by this insult to their president. It was ironic that many Americans were guilty of insulting their president also. One of his nicknames in the press was "Wobbly Willie," and Undersecretary of the Navy, Theodore Roosevelt, had commented to friends that McKinley had "no more backbone than a chocolate eclair." Of course, the difference between the comments was that de Lome's was from a Spanish official and made public, while the comment from Roosevelt was kept private, and the American press had a right to create nicknames for the president, especially when many Americans agreed.

The second event that finally brought war with Spain was the sinking of the American battleship *Maine* in Havana harbor on the night of February 15, 1898, with the loss of at least 260 lives. The *Maine* had been sent to Cuba in January after riots protesting Cuban autonomy broke out in the capitol city of Havana. The ship was on an officially friendly call, but it would be available to assist Americans if their safety were threatened. A naval court of inquiry reported that the cause of the explosion was an external submarine mine. Spain conducted its own investigation and theorized that a boiler on the ship had exploded and caused the deaths. Later inquiries have theorized that the explosion aboard the *Maine* was caused by an internal accidental explosion probably caused by a small fire on board igniting the stored ammunition. In 1976, an American navy review of all available evidence concluded that Spain's version of the event had probably been the correct one. Of course, that was 78 years after the fact. Most Americans at the time clearly believed that Spain had intentionally blown up the ship and must pay the consequences. It is important to interject in the study of the causes of the war that Spain was attempting to avoid a war, not begin one. In spite of Spain's attempts until the last minute to avoid war, the battle cry for the war was established in February 1898,

"Remember the Maine." And Congress appropriated $50 million for national defense as the country moved toward war.

President McKinley was no anti-imperialist, but neither was he anxious to go to war over the situation in Cuba because he recognized that Spain was attempting to do all it could to pacify American public opinion. In the end, McKinley too sought to pacify public opinion. His own view of presidential leadership was to essentially take whatever actions the people wanted him to take. If he were going to get the nomination of his own Republican Party and win reelection in 1900, McKinley knew he must be careful not to alienate public opinion against him. Therefore, he sent his final ultimatum to the Spanish government on March 27, 1898, demanding an end to the reconcentration policy, an acceptance of the United States offer to arbitrate the dispute, and an immediate armistice. A demand for Cuban independence was implied in the message. Ambassador Woodford received the last proposals from the Spanish government, and on April 10 the McKinley administration was informed that Spain had agreed to all his specific demands. In addition, they proposed to assume reparations for the *Maine*, the amount to be determined by submitting the matter to arbitration. In the meantime, they announced that an autonomist Cuban government would decide the question of permanent peace. Although independence for Cuba was not mentioned, the American ambassador believed it could be gained shortly.

Fearing that peace negotiations at this point would split the Republican Party, damage his chances for reelection, and not being sure he could trust Spain to follow through with its promises, McKinley asked Congress for the power to use force to free Cuba from Spain on April 11. The Senate seemed nearly ready to force the president to accept such a resolution by that time. McKinley mentioned, almost as an afterthought, that Spain had agreed to satisfy most of America's demands. At this point, the public wanted war or Cuban independence. Events began to move quickly from this time forward. On April 20, Congress adopted a joint resolution calling for the removal of Spanish troops from Cuba, complete Cuban independence from Spain, and authorizing the use of force to ensure those steps if necessary. Added to the resolution was the Teller Amendment, sponsored by Colorado Senator Henry M. Teller, which stated that the United States would not exercise sovereignty over the island of Cuba and would leave the control of the island to its people once it was pacified.

Congress increased the size of the army and passed the Volunteer Army Act on April 22, which called for an organization of a First Volunteer Cavalry. This volunteer cavalry unit received from the press the nickname the "Rough Riders," and it was commanded by Colonel Leonard Wood and Lt. Colonel Theodore Roosevelt (one of the heroes to emerge from the war). Roosevelt resigned his post as Assistant Secretary of the Navy to pull together his "cowboy soldiers" from polo clubs to western ranches. On the same day, the United States Navy began a partial blockade of Cuban ports, which is considered an act of war according to international law. Feeling cornered and humiliated, Spain declared war on the United States on April 24. To show contempt for Spain, Congress officially declared war on Spain the next day (April 25) and made its declaration retroactive to April 21 in order to say that the United States had declared war first (which, in effect, it had anyway via its use-of-force resolution).

Fighting the War

While the army prepared for the invasion of Cuba, the first battle of the war was a naval action in Manila Bay, Philippines, a Spanish colony in the Pacific. In February, Theodore Roosevelt, then still Assistant Secretary of the Navy, ordered Commodore George Dewey to take his squadron of ships to Hong Kong and, if war broke out, to attack the Spanish in the Philippines. On May 1, Commodore Dewey led his Asiatic squadron of four cruisers, two gunboats, and a revenue cutter to victory in battle against an old and decrepit Spanish squadron of only one modern cruiser and ten old cruisers and gunboats. The amazing success of Dewey's forces—no Americans killed and only eight wounded—increased the war fever of Americans. His order, "You may fire when ready, Gridley," would be placed on the list of famous Americans' quotations. The American Navy could not take the entire Philippine Islands from the Spanish because they did not have the proper forces with them. However, the United States did persuade Emilio Aguinaldo, a former Filipino revolutionary, to return to his homeland and take up the fight once again to free his country from Spanish rule. On May 25, the first American troop ships departed for the Philippines.

American troops, commanded by General William Shafter, began the invasion of Cuba by landing a small force of marines at Guantanamo Bay on June 10. The Cuban rebel army was basically ignored once the United States took over the war in Cuba. The United States was not ready for war, but raising and equipping an army was accomplished quickly, although the troops were poorly equipped and poorly trained. This was an extremely popular war, and no military draft was needed or instituted. The young men lined up quickly to join up for their adventure in Cuba. There were approximately 63,000 regular troops and 200,000 volunteers in the army.

The regular troops were supplied with modern rifles, but many of the volunteers carried old fashioned single shot rifles. Thousands fought in hot woolen uniforms. (Khaki cloth was not available in the United States at that time.) The Commissary Department bought thousands of pounds of bad meat from private companies and passed it on to the soldiers. Sanitation in many of the camps was poor, and soldiers died from dysentery before leaving American soil. Transportation to the beaches of Cuba was appallingly confusing and bungled. The ships were overcrowded, and there was a lack of adequate railroad connections between the city of Tampa and the main departure point of Port Tampa. Once the troops reached Cuba, they had to be rowed from the ships to the beaches east of the main target, the city of Santiago, which put them in a very vulnerable position. And unfortunately for the Rough Riders, most of their horses were left behind, and they became known as "Wood's Weary Walkers." The War Department faced an investigation by Congress after the war.

In spite of the bungling and the hardships, by July 1, the American forces were prepared to advance on their major objective, the city of Santiago de Cuba. Attacking the city of El Caney, to the north of Santiago de Cuba, and Kettle Hill and San

Juan Hill (fortified hills protecting the eastern approach to the city), the American forces took heavy casualties from the Spanish firing from entrenched positions. It was quickly discovered that a balloon sent up by the American forces to observe Spanish troop placement was giving the Spanish gunners a perfect target. So the balloon was taken down, but the Spanish did not need it for long because the soldiers themselves were soon in sight as they began the trek up the hills. The soldiers faced gunfire raining down upon them, and confusion, terror, and delayed orders were costing lives. Colonel Theodore Roosevelt rushed to the forefront of the advance up Kettle Hill, brandishing his weapons and shouting for his men to follow. Thanks to the assistance of the Tenth Black Cavalry unit and the renewed efforts of the other units, the hill was taken. Once Kettle Hill was secured, the American forces there marched over to San Juan Hill and assisted the efforts there. However, Roosevelt did not lead the charge up San Juan Hill, as the mythical legend has it; he came late to help other forces at that site. On July 3, the Spanish fleet bottled up in Santiago Harbor attempted to break out of the harbor past the American blockade. The fleet, commanded by Admiral Cervera, was quickly demolished by 5 American cruisers and 2 armed yachts under the command of Commodore Winfield Scott Schley. Realizing the situation was hopeless, Santiago surrendered on July 17.

On July 26, the French ambassador in Washington, acting at the request of the Spanish government, approached the American government for their peace terms. The American terms were as follows: (1) independence for Cuba; (2) American control of Puerto Rico and an island in the Ladrones; and (3) the United States would occupy Manila until further negotiations. President McKinley's terms were accepted on August 9 by the Spanish. Fighting ceased on Puerto Rico on August 16, and the American expeditionary force, with the support of Aquinaldo's forces, took the city of Manila on August 13. The peace protocol, or armistice, was signed by Spain and the United States on August 12, 1898. The war, lasting less than 4 months, was dubbed "a splendid little war" war by soon-to-be Secretary of State John Hay.

The Treaty of Paris

The Spanish-American War officially ended with the signing of the Treaty of Paris on December 10, 1898, four months after the armistice had begun. The main reason for the delay was that negotiations bogged down over the fate of the Philippines. Not bound by the Teller Amendment to free the Pacific islands (it had guaranteed Cuban independence only), the president found himself bombarded on all sides to both keep and let the islands go. Between August and December of 1898, McKinley, faithful to his leadership philosophy, attempted to discover what the American people truly wanted. He traveled around the country to listen and speak to the public concerning the issue of annexing the Philippines. He read thousands of letters and telegrams, and he listened to advice from friends and officials. What he discovered was that most Americans wanted the fruits of military victory—territory conquered by the American forces. Businessmen wanted the markets on the islands and in other areas of Asia. (Reluctant for the United States to enter into a war, many businesses soon saw the benefits.) Missionaries wanted to Christianize the Filipinos because it was the "white man's burden." Most were not aware that the Spanish had converted many on the islands to Catholicism, but of course, many in the United States did not see this as true Christianity. And policy makers insisted that if the United States did not keep the Philippines, Germany or Japan would take control of a new independent and vulnerable nation. McKinley finally notified the peace negotiators to demand the Philippines in return for $20 million dollars paid to Spain.

The Treaty of Paris gave the United States control of Cuba until the latter was ready for independence. (See the section in this chapter entitled "Administering Cuba" for more details of the American relationship with Cuba.) The treaty also granted official permission for the United States to annex Puerto Rico, Guam, and the Philippines. In return, it was agreed to pay Spain $20 million in compensation, allegedly for public works projects.

The treaty was then sent to the United States Senate for ratification. Conflict arose between imperialist and anti-imperialist schools of thought concerning annexation of the Philippines. The imperialists were led by Senator Albert Beveridge of Indiana and Senator Henry Cabot Lodge of Massachusetts. These senators stressed the commercial and strategic value of the islands, and Lodge in particular stressed that it would damage the political power of the presidency to have the treaty he negotiated turned down. The opposition formed the Anti-Imperialist League, but the group was very diverse in its reasons for opposing imperialism and an effective campaign was difficult to organize. It did not help the anti-imperialist cause that the most powerful critic of an overseas empire, William Jennings Bryan, agreed that the peace treaty with its possessions should be ratified. Bryan believed that once the peace was official, both Cuban and Philippine independence would be closer to a reality; the details could be worked out after the treaty was ratified. The treaty was ratified on February 6, 1899 by more than a 2 to 1 margin, 57-27.

Results of the Spanish-American War

There were 5,462 American deaths in the war, but only 379 were battle deaths. Bad meat sold by the Armour Company may have led to non-battlefield deaths, but the rest were due to disease, particularly yellow fever and malaria.

Hawaii was annexed during the war in July 1898 because it was believed to be vital as a refueling and supply station between the United States and the Philippines once Manila Bay was controlled by Commodore Dewey. The United States emerged from the war with an overseas empire in possession of Puerto Rico, Guam, and the Philippines. The nation, which had begun as 13 colonies, now had acquired colonies of its own for the first time. The war had not begun with a territorial expansion goal in mind. The original goals included humanitarian assistance for the Cubans and protection of American trade and business interests, but once the country gained control of overseas lands, most were reluctant to let them go. Gaining the Philippines in the treaty with Spain, however, led to war between the United States and the Filipinos, who did not want to trade one colonial power for another.

The Spanish-American War did much to reunite the country following the divisiveness of the Civil War by giving Americans in both the North and the South a sense of national unity and purpose. This healing aspect of the war was well illustrated when troops from Massachusetts were cheered in Baltimore, Maryland, on their way to Cuba in 1898; this was in sharp contrast to the reception given to Union soldiers from that same state in 1861, who were attacked by a mob with rocks. Massachusetts Senator Henry Cabot Lodge later exclaimed, "The war of 1861 was over at last and the great country for which so many died was one again." The United States would now play a much larger role in events outside of its borders. Actions to protect its Pacific territory and domination of Latin America expanded the foreign policy of a nation which had not often had a need previously for such policies.

WAR IN THE PHILIPPINES

The anti-imperialist forces did not give up the fight to free the Philippines after the ratification of the treaty. A crusade developed with support from the different political parties, vocations, and schools of thought. Anti-imperialism tended to draw supporters from reform-minded Americans, labor unions, small business leaders (Andrew Carnegie was an exception), and more from the Democratic Party than the Republican. An impressive group was arrayed—Massachusetts Republican Senator George F. Hoar, American Federation of Labor president Samuel Gompers, Andrew Carnegie (Mr. Carnegie paid most of the bills for the group), Jane Addams, and Mark Twain, to name a few. Their arguments were varied. It was observed that government without the consent of the governed violated the historical foundation of the United States and violated the concepts of the Declaration of Independence. It was argued that constitutionally the president did not have the right to acquire extraterritorial possessions without the consent of the alien peoples.

The price of conquest, defense, and administration of the Philippines would cost more than they would ever be worth. Labor unions objected to the inclusion of a cheap labor pool in areas owned now by the United States. The objections of the anti-imperialists were valid, and many came to pass. Democratic presidential candidate William Jennings Bryan and the Democratic Party took up the cause of the anti-imperialists in their platform during the election campaign of 1900. For most Americans, however, the economic progress engineered by McKinley and the Republican Party was too compelling to lose the incumbent the election with a foreign policy issue, and McKinley easily won reelection.

Brought back to the Philippines by the United States, Emilio Aguinaldo and his guerilla forces had fought the Spanish on land while Commodore Dewey blockaded Manila Bay and waited for American troops to arrive and complete the defeat of the Spanish forces on the islands. On June 12, 1898, Aguinaldo declared the independence of the Philippine Republic. A Congress of lawyers and other elite groups of Filipinos soon met, and this revolutionary regime began administering a large portion of the islands. The United States had not formulated plans to keep the Philippines during the Spanish-American War, and all parties went forward with an assumption of independence for the area. But when the American troops arrived, the Filipinos were not allowed to participate in the taking of the capital city of Manila nor its occupation. The United States wanted to control the surrender of Spain and the peace terms.

By the time it was decided to deny the islands their immediate independence, the United States would have to deal with a large number of Filipinos who had already developed a sense of nationhood and would fight for their country's independence. Aguinaldo claimed that the American consul in Singapore, E. Spencer Pratt, and later Commodore Dewey, had promised that the Philippines would be independent when the war with Spain was won. But both Dewey and Pratt denied this. Witnesses to the meeting between Pratt and Aguinaldo concurred with General Aguinaldo's account. It certainly should have been obvious that Aguinaldo would not have exchanged one colonial master for another. Shortly after the treaty ending the Spanish-American War had been ratified by the Senate in early February 1899, a move to grant the Philippines independence once a stable government was established there was narrowly defeated. Pushed by William Jennings Bryan (who was not in Congress then), that move took the form of the Bacon Amendment, which Vice-President Garret A. Hobart cast the tie-breaking "no" vote. The Philippines came close to independence, but they would have to wait 47 more years for their dream to come to fruition. Meanwhile, more lives would be lost in another war in the Philippines.

On February 4, 1899, open conflict erupted between Filipino nationalists and American troops. The Philippine-American war, sometimes called the Filipino Insurrection, was fought in two phases. The first phase was a conventional war that lasted from February 1899 to November 1899. Aguinaldo commanded an army and engaged American forces under the command of General Elwell Otis in battle until the increasing number of American reinforcements forced him into the second phase of the war, a guerilla war.

During the first phase of the war, President McKinley appointed a special commission, headed by the president of Cornell University, Jacob Gould Schurman, to go to the Philippines and determine the social and political state on the islands and the measures that should be instituted to bring order and provide for the welfare of the people. The commission promised the Philippine people limited autonomy with civil liberties and fair administration of the laws. However, Aguinaldo and other revolutionary leaders did not believe the commission and wanted only independence and the right to govern themselves. In November, Aguinaldo dispersed his troops and began a querilla war that lasted until the last group of insurgents laid down their weapons in May 1902.

There was nothing "splendid" about this war. Atrocities and acts of barbarism were perpetrated by both sides against civilians as well as soldiers. The guerilla fighters tortured, starved, and killed American prisoners, frequently mutilating the bodies. They also tortured and murdered Filipino collaborators. For their part, American soldiers tortured and sometimes killed guerilla captives also. One of the most common methods of torture to gain information from captives was the "water cure." The victim had a large amount of water forced down his throat, which extended the abdomen severely. The interrogator would then stand or jump up and down on the tortured victim's abdomen until he decided to talk or until he died. It was true that much of the brutal treatment of captives was left to Filipinos attached to American units. However, the actions of American soldiers sank to a level of brutality that most Americans believed impossible for citizens of a civilized nation. In warfare, treatment in kind is certainly not unusual. Secretary of War, Elihu Root, was called to answer questions concerning the conduct of the Philippine War. Root admitted that some American troops had acted in an unacceptable manner, but it was to be expected that some soldiers would react irresponsibly in the heat of battle and especially when fighting an enemy who behaved in an uncivilized manner. Many Americans accepted this explanation.

The policy of reconcentrating civilians, however, could not be denied by military and civilian officials. Philippine civilians in areas where insurgent activity was heavy were gathered into fenced, guarded compounds in order to separate friend from foe. Disease visited these camps and thousands died. There was a roar of criticism in the United States from anti-imperialists, newspapers, and the public against this policy that we had found so abhorrent when used by the Spanish in Cuba. But the practice continued.

The capture of Emilio Aguinaldo was an early objective for the Americans, but he continued to elude them to the point that some believed he might already have died. In early 1901, however a message was intercepted from Aguinaldo to his brother. The messenger was persuaded to divulge the location of the Filipino general. Colonel Frederick Funston plotted to ambush Aguinaldo. He disguised a squadron of Macabebe scouts as insurgent reinforcements, and he and 4 Americans were portrayed as prisoners of the false insurgent group. The Macabebes entered the camp with their false prisoners hiding behind them and opened fire on Aguinaldo's guards. Aquinaldo was taken to the coast and placed upon an awaiting American warship before his troops could regroup and stop the capture. On April 1, 1901, the guerilla commander swore an oath of allegiance to the American government, and a short time later he called for his followers to lay down their arms. The war ended in May 1902 with 4,234 Americans having lost their lives and more than 200,000 Filipino soldiers and civilians dead.

GOVERNING THE PHILIPPINES

In July 1901, the Second Commission, headed by William Howard Taft, established a civil government in the Philippines. Taft was the first governor-general, and the commission acted as the legislature and cabinet. The commission was instructed to reconstruct the government on the islands along the same lines as that of the United States and improve the standard of living. But what were the rights of the Filipinos? Did the Constitution extend to dependencies? These were complicated questions that the United States Supreme Court dealt with in a series of cases known as the Insular Cases of 1901. The Supreme Court decision in *Downes v. Bidwell*—a case from Puerto Rico to decide if Congress had the right to impose special import taxes on goods from this American territory—was that the Constitution did not automatically apply to all new lands, and it was to be extended only when Congress decided it should be. The Organic Act of July 1, 1902, recognized the islands as unincorporated territory of the United States. The inhabitants were citizens of the Philippine Islands, not the United States, but entitled to the protection of the United States. The islanders would eventually create their own bicameral legislature with the lower house elected by popular vote. This was a time for the

United States to tutor the Filipinos in democracy, with the understanding that at some point in the future the Philippines would be prepared for independence. The United States never planned on integrating these far away islands of alien non-white people as a state of the union.

Conditions on the islands improved dramatically. Schools, hospitals, and roads were built; sanitation was implemented in the cities; a native police force was trained; and even baseball was played by the Filipinos. The United States purchased land from the Roman Catholic religious orders and sold it in small holdings to the peasant farmers. In spite of all the benefits as a possession of the United States, the Filipinos continued to work for independence. The Jones Act, sponsored by Virginia Representative William A. Jones, was passed in May 1916, formally announcing the intention of the United States to withdraw from the Philippines "as soon as a stable government can be established therein." The law also abolished the Commission, provided for a two-house legislature elected by popular vote, and gave the legislature the authority to reorganize the government.

President Woodrow Wilson reminded Congress as he was leaving office that the time had come to give the Philippines their independence. The Republicans who followed in the 1920s, however, were not inclined to release the islands. A new Commission was sent to the Philippines, dominated by General Leonard Wood (the Rough Rider), and Wood reported the islands were not ready for independence. Finally in 1934, the Tydings-McDuffie Bill stated that the Philippines would be given independence after a 10-year probationary period. There were several motivating factors in this final approval of Philippine independence. States that grew sugar cane and sugar beets did not want the competition from Philippine products, which had been duty free since 1913. The increased trade that businessmen had expected from the Philippines and China had not materialized. (Business interests often fail to realize that for other peoples to buy American products, they have to be financially able to buy them.) Naval experts agreed that the islands could not be defended, and if war came with Japan, they would be a liability. With all of these negative aspects apparent, Americans were glad to rid themselves from the responsibility of ownership. War came with the Japanese before the islands could be granted their independence, but on July 4, 1946, the Philippines were finally given charge of their own destiny. However, American ties with the islands would not be completely broken.

THE OPEN DOOR POLICY

A long standing American interest in trade with China increased with the acquisition of the Philippines. Hoping to use the Philippines as a jumping off point to enlarge trade with China, America was ready to demand her share of the markets and goods that other European nations controlled in China. After Japan's defeat of the Chinese in the Sino-Japanese War of 1894–1895, the nation was weak and vulnerable. Japan gained Chinese territory after the war and so did Russia, Germany, Great Britain, and France. Each of these nations gained control of areas along China's coastline, including leases on ports and the railway concessions within these areas. With this intense domination of these important trading areas, the European powers controlled most of the internal trade of China, which had been known as the "Sick Man of Asia" in the nineteenth century.

The United States refused to be denied access to this trade, especially since it would reduce the potential value of the Philippines. On September 6, 1899, Secretary of State John Hay notified the European nations with spheres of interest in China and the Japanese that the United States desired equal trading access to these areas. This equal trade policy became known as the Open Door Policy and Hay's diplomatic letters as the Open Door Notes. The Open Door Notes requested that each power in its respective sphere maintain the Chinese custom tariffs and charge equal harbor fees and railway rates to all traders. All of the powers except Russia agreed to accept but with the condition that all others accept it unconditionally. Despite Russia's refusal to go along, the United States proclaimed that the new policy was official. Invigorated from success in the Spanish-American War and the responsibility of an overseas empire, American foreign policy makers were prepared to venture further afield in the politics and power plays of Asia and Latin America.

Involvement with the China trade pulled the United States into a joint action with the European trading nations to put down the "Boxer Rebellion." The secret Chinese society of the Harmonious Righteous Fists (or the I Ho Ch'uan), known as the "Boxers" by Europeans, was organized in 1899 to drive the "foreign devils" from China. Resentful of foreign "invaders" and Christian missionaries, the rebellion broke out in the late spring of 1900, and by June 1900, the Boxers had occupied Peking (Beijing), the capital of China, and killed more than 200 foreigners. In August 1900, the United States contributed about 2,500 soldiers to an international army which then totaled over 17,000 to put down the rebellion and free the Europeans who had taken refuge in the British legation compound in Peking. The rebellion was quickly crushed.

The successful and vindictive European nations quickly issued the Boxer Protocol, demanding about $333 million from a prostrate China. The United States returned $18 million of its $25 million to China, which used it to help educate Chinese youth in American colleges and universities. The Protocol also insisted on severe punishment of the Boxers and a 5-year moratorium on arms shipments to China. The Chinese government promptly did as it was told. Meanwhile, in July (during the rebellion), fearing that the European nations would turn China into a group of European colonies, Secretary Hay sent another round of notes to the parties involved. This second group of Open Door Notes reaffirmed the principle of equal trade in China and added that the territorial integrity and sovereignty of this nation was to be preserved. The European powers did not appreciate the American effort, but mutual distrust of each other and the unwillingness to risk a world war among themselves did at least maintain the status quo in China for several years. The charitable attitude of American policy makers toward China at the turn of the century was not motivated so much by generosity as by the need to protect American economic and national interests in that country.

Boxer Rebellion in China, 1900. Credit: The Bettmann Archive.

ADMINISTERING CUBA

In 1899 on the island of Cuba, the United States implemented the first of many protectorates in the Caribbean area. The government of the islands was in the hands of the American military until a Cuban constitution could be written and implemented because the government of the Cuban revolution movement was not acceptable. It was determined that a democracy was to be established in Cuba friendly to the economic and security goals of the United States. American dollars and effort built up the island's education, sanitation, public works, and judicial system, and prepared Cuba for self government under the umbrella leadership of General John R. Brooks and his successor, General Leonard Wood.

One of the first goals of the occupation was to put an end to some of the diseases that took the lives of American soldiers during the war and continued to threaten the well-being of occupation forces and the island population afterward. The work of Dr. Walter Reed and the Yellow Fever Commission confirmed the theory of the Cuban physician Carlos Finlay that yellow fever was carried by a particular mosquito. Members of the Commission allowed themselves to be used as human guinea pigs, and two doctors, Dr. Lazear and Dr. Carroll, both died from yellow fever carried by a mosquito. Proof of the cause of this deadly disease led to its eradication in Cuba and also in Panama, where it had taken a great toll on canal workers in the past, and in the future would delay the successful construction of a canal until the breeding grounds of the mosquito carrying the disease were destroyed.

The Cuban people demanded their own government. Elections were held for delegates to attend a constitutional convention. The delegates were instructed by General Wood that the convention should "provide for and agree with the Government of the United States upon the relations to exist between that Government and the Government of Cuba." But the convention ignored the demands of the United States. Secretary of War Elihu Root then urged Congress to legislate the future relationship between the two countries and state the conditions under which the President would terminate military occupation. Written and introduced by Senator Orville Platt of Connecticut, the Platt Amendment outlined the formal boundaries of the relationship between the two nations. The key points of the amendment were number 3, which allowed the United States to intervene to preserve Cuban independence and ensure a Cuban government able to protect the citizens of Cuba, and number 7, which required that Cuba sell or lease land necessary for an American coaling or naval station. An American naval base was built at Guantanamo Bay, which is still there today. The Cubans added the amendment to their constitution under duress, and the Cuban Republic was inaugurated on May 20, 1902.

A reciprocity treaty decreased the tariffs on Cuban goods sold in the United States, and American goods sold in Cuba greatly increased the trade between the nations. But trade was only one source of American and Cuban ties. From 1906 to 1909, the United States occupied the island to restore order to the islands and put into place again a Cuban government. In 1917 the United States once again intervened in Cuba by sending troops to restore calm to the islands and maintain President Menocal in power. Cuba continued to suffer from political and social disorder, but the United States intervened in non-military ways after that. The protectorate status of Cuba came to an end with President Franklin Roosevelt's good neighbor policy in the 1930s.

THEODORE ROOSEVELT'S FOREIGN POLICY GOALS

A priority for President Theodore Roosevelt, who took office in September 1901 following the assassination of McKinley, was for the United States to take its position among the recognized great powers of the world. His foreign policies were a mixture of bullying to promote American interests beyond their continental borders and diplomacy to make the world a safer haven to promote those same interests. "Speak softly and carry a big stick and you will go far" was a favorite West African proverb that Roosevelt used to justify a major portion of his views concerning foreign policy. Roosevelt meant that a nation must build up its naval and military strength to the point that it could be an influential factor in any foreign policy endeavor. Roosevelt prevailed upon Congress to finance the building of at least two battleships a year to give power to his "big stick" policy. Building up military preparedness along with the building of an inter-ocean canal were Roosevelt's first goals.

THE PANAMA CANAL

The idea of a canal in Central America was as old as the sixteenth century Spanish Conquistadors. Thomas Jefferson had recommended one early in the nineteenth century. For centuries, passage across the narrow Isthmus of Panama joining North and South America had been available to small vessels for two-thirds of the journey and the rest by pack mule, but a route for large ships was not available. In 1848 the United States ratified the Bidlack Treaty with New Grenada (later renamed Colombia) guaranteeing a right of way across its territory in the Isthmus of Panama for the United States "upon any modes of communication that now exist, or that may be . . . constructed." Concerned with a shorter journey then and for the future, the United States wanted to guarantee American influence across the isthmus on whatever mode of transportation might develop to shorten the travel time between the two oceans. In return, the United States guaranteed to keep the right of way neutral and protect the sovereignty of New Grenada over its territory.

Americans moving west in the late 1840s for land or gold greatly increased American interest in the transit across Panama. In 1849, New Grenada granted a concession to the American-owned Panama Railroad Company to build a line across the narrow neck of its Panamanian possession. The line opened in 1855. Although American ships and troops were dispatched on 6 different ocassions (4 times at the request of the Colombian government) to keep the railroad line open in times of disorder, the United States did nothing to open a transocean passageway until after the Spanish-American War.

The journey of the battleship *Oregon* from San Francisco to Cuba, during the Spanish-American War, brought to the forefront once again the necessity for a shorter route between the Atlantic and Pacific oceans. It took 68 days for the ship to make its way down the Pacific coast, around Cape Horn, and up the Atlantic coast of South America before reaching its destination. Following the Spanish-American War, overseas interests of the United States had increased. Puerto Rico was an American possession, Cuba was under occupation, and the power and mobility of the United States navy must be increased to protect new American interests from the Philippines to the Caribbean.

American Fleet, 1899. Credit: The Bettmann Archive.

In order to ensure the viability of the American navy to protect the country's overseas possessions, a canal must be built and controlled by the United States exclusively. But in order to build the canal exclusively, the United States must rid itself of the Clayton-Bulwer Treaty signed with Britain in 1850 to reduce tensions between the two nations concerning aspirations in the Caribbean. The treaty provided that neither nation would exclusively build or control a canal across the Isthmus, erect fortifications, or exercise sovereignty over any Central American area. The second Hay-Pauncefote Treaty, ratified in 1901 between the two great powers, provided that a canal could be built and controlled by the United States with equal terms to be extended to vessels of all nations, and fortifications could be built and controlled by the United States.

The next step was to select a route and gain the rights to build a canal. The Walker Commission, originally organized by President McKinley in 1899, studied Panama and Nicaragua as possible sights. The Commission leaned toward the Panama location, which was a shorter distance from shore to shore. There was also the beginning of a canal already underway in Panama. The French Panama Canal Company, under the direction of Ferdinand de Lesseps, the builder of the Suez Canal, had attempted but failed to finish the project and went into bankruptcy. The New Panama Canal Company took over the debts and the concessions of the canal project and proposed to sell their rights to the United States for $109 million. But the Walker Commission believed this price was too high and in 1901 recommended Nicaragua for the building site instead. There had also been strong support for this route from the beginning.

In January 1902, the House of Representatives passed the Hepburn Bill to appropriate funds for a canal through Nicaragua. But before the Senate could make a decision on the bill, new elements were added to the situation. The New Panama Canal Company reduced its asking price to $40 million, and Philippe Bunau-Varilla, an engineer from the old Panama Canal Company and now a representative of the new company, and William Cromwell, a New York attorney hired to promote the American purchase of the canal rights of the New Panama Canal Company, lobbied hard for the Panama route and against the Hepburn Bill. Bunau-Varilla wined and dined senators, along with their wives and staff. Cromwell had been working for the Panama route before the Walker Commission had reached its decision. He made sure a $60,000 campaign contribution had been made to the Republican campaign fund in 1900, and now he was instrumental in persuading Ohio Republican Senator Mark Hanna to carry the fight for the Panama route to the Senate floor. The Panama route was the shorter and less expensive of the routes, and President Roosevelt eventually favored this location. Add to the Nicaragua route the negative aspect of volcanic activity, and the Panama location was back once again as a possibility. Therefore, the Spooner Act (technically an amendment to the Hepburn Bill) passed both the House and Senate on June 28, 1902, proposing that if the New Panama Canal Company sold its concession for the cheaper price, and Colombia agreed to grant the United States the right to build a canal in its territory, the canal would be dug in Panama. If all transactions could not be concluded quickly, Nicaragua would be the location.

Secretary of State John Hay negotiated the Hay-Herran Treaty in January, 1903. The United States was to lease a 6-mile-wide strip across Panama with the right to construct a canal, in return for $10 million dollars and $250,000 a year to the nation of Colombia. The New Panama Canal Company was to receive $40 million for its concession. But the Colombian Senate unanimously rejected the treaty that August because it wanted more money for the project, either from the United States or from the canal company, and more control of the canal zone than the treaty had included. President Roosevelt was outraged by Colombia's decision. He was determined to build the canal in Panama but not to pay more money. Meanwhile, Bunau-Varilla and Cromwell continued their lobbying efforts for the Panama location.

A revolution was planned for Panamanian independence, and negotiations with the United States for a canal without Colombian interference continued. The revolution was planned by a small group in Panama (there had been previous attempts at revolution) from the hotel room of Bunau-Varilla at the Waldorf-Astoria in New York City, and from the New York office of William Cromwell. Bunau-Varilla even sent a declaration of independence, military orders, a flag, and a constitution to Panama with the representative from the revolutionary junta, Dr. Manuel Amador, all worked on in his New York hotel room. This was one more tie between the United States and the revolution in Panama, even though these efforts were rejected in Panama. Bunau-Varilla was under a deadline, and he worked fervently to determine the role the United States would play in a revolution. Roosevelt and his administrators did not plan the revolution nor support it financially (Bunau-Varilla financed the revolution), but the conspirators were encouraged to continue their plans when it was determined that the overthrow of Colombia would meet with favor and that American warships had been ordered to the area. The warships were ordered there ostensibly to keep the railroad line open and to prevent the landing of armed forces from either side of the revolution if it seemed conflict would follow. Colombia also knew that a revolution was close at hand from information given to them from a knowledgeable source, and it was sending troops to Panama to fight.

The revolt in Panama began on November 3, 1903, when the Panama City fire brigade began distributing weapons to crowds in the streets. There was basically no violence since the Colombian army detachment in Panama City had sold its services to the revolution, and reinforcements could not reach the city. Only an innocent Chinese merchant and a donkey were killed when a Colombian gunboat fired on the city. America recognized the new Republic of Panama on November 6, 1903, and within two weeks had signed a treaty for a canal in Panama (November 18). The treaty was officially brought to Washington by Philippe Bunau-Varilla, who was appointed as a special envoy from Panama. The Hay-Bunau-Varrilla Treaty gave the United States the right to build a canal across a 10-mile wide Canal Zone, over which Panama was sovereign, but the United States could act as if it were sovereign there (like renting someone's house; it doesn't technically belong to you, but you can treat it more or less as if it does). The United States agreed to pay Panama a one-time fee of $10 million and $250,000 per year in rent. The treaty also authorized the United States to interfere in the internal affairs of Panama, but only if

Construction of the Panama Canal. Credit: AP/ Wide World Photos.

necessary to keep the canal open and protected. Contrary to American popular opinion, the treaty never actually gave the United States the Panama Canal.

President Roosevelt was criticized by Colombia, some Americans, and other nations for the self-serving role the United States played in the revolution of Panama. The president denied that he had any part in the revolt and justified his decision to send American warships to the area on the terms of the Bidlack Treaty. In later years, however, Roosevelt claimed that "I took the Canal Zone and let Congress debate." Roosevelt is known to have a tendency to exaggerate some of his accomplishments, but whatever the extent of his involvement in the Panamanian revolution, it is considered by many to be a negative action in the conduct of his foreign policy. Later, President Woodrow Wilson tried to get Congress to vote an official apology and monies to Colombia because of Roosevelt's questionable role in the revolution, but Congress rebuffed his efforts. However, after Roosevelt's death in 1919, the 1921 Thomson-Urrutia Treaty gave Colombia $25 million in return for certain oil concessions to American oil companies, a generous amount that indirectly represented an apology to Colombia.

Construction on the Panama Canal began in 1906, and it took 8 years to complete the 50 mile canal, which was a monument to modern engineering. The construction cost more than $700 million and hundreds of workers' lives. The canal could not have been built without the leadership of Lieutenant Colonel George Goethals, an army engineer, and the implementation of sanitation and health conditions by Colonel William Gorgas of the Army Medical Corps. Gorgas practically eradicated yellow fever in Havana and the Canal Zone by eliminating the breeding grounds of the mosquito carriers. The canal was completed in January 1914 and officially opened to traffic on August 15, 1914. An ocean voyage from the Atlantic coast of the United States to the Pacific coast was now 7,000 miles shorter in distance.

THE ROOSEVELT COROLLARY STRENGTHENS BUT CHANGES THE MONROE DOCTRINE

With possessions in the Caribbean and negotiations for and building of a canal in Panama, the United States increased its interests and concern with protection of those interests in Latin America. In 1902, Britain and Germany sent warships to Venezuela to collect debts owed to creditors in their respective nations. The European nations had requested that Venezuela submit the issue to arbitration, but Cipriano Castro, the dictator of this nation, refused. Roosevelt was assured by both nations that repayment of the debt, not territory, was the only interest in this intrusion into Latin America. Therefore, he agreed that the Monroe Doctrine was not violated. Roosevelt also agreed that the nations had the right to "spank" Latin American countries that misbehaved.

In December of the same year, Britain and Germany issued an ultimatum to the Castro government and, along with Italy, initiated a blockade of Venezuela, an action which resulted in the capture and sinking of Venezuelan ships. Venezuela then asked President Roosevelt to arbitrate, but the European powers continued the blockade, and Germany twice bombarded Venezuelan territory after this. This continued violence alarmed many Americans, including Roosevelt, who was growing suspicious about European intent, especially of the Germans. And the president demanded that the controversy be settled by arbitration. In February 1903, the blockade was lifted and both sides did submit the dispute to the Permanent Court of Arbitration at The Hague (in Holland). The Hague Court ruled in favor of the European nations in 1904. It is important to note the attention the European powers were paying to the opinions of the United States in this area since the end of the Spanish-American War.

In 1903, the Dominican Republic was also unable to meet financial obligations to several European and American companies, including Germany, Italy, and Spain. President Roosevelt was reluctant to intervene in this affair, but the recent Venezuelan debt crisis had set a precedent for such intervention. In order to forestall military action by the European nations involved, the American and Dominican Republic governments entered into an agreement in late 1904 calling for the United States to take over the operation of all customs houses in the island nation and allocate the funds in a way that would ensure that the country's debts would eventually be paid. When the United States Senate adjourned in March 1905 without acting on the treaty, the administration negotiated an executive agreement the next month that did not require Senate ratification. Roosevelt was well known for his belief that one charged forward if he believed a policy was right, and then one looked for the power to cover the action if necessary.

Roosevelt now believed that a change in policy was warranted to avoid future misunderstandings in foreign affairs in Latin America. Combining his December

1904 annual message to Congress with a statement he made a year later, he gave the world the Roosevelt Corollary to the Monroe Doctrine. Whereas the original Monroe Doctrine (1823) had been only a defensive statement warning European powers to stay out of the western hemisphere, the Roosevelt Corollary turned it upside down by insisting that the United States had the right to interfere in the internal affairs of Latin American nations in order to end "chronic wrongdoing" or the "general loosening of the ties of civilized society." This Roosevelt Corollary became the basis for deeper and almost continuous American involvement in the affairs of Latin American nations in the twentieth century. It is the reason that many, if not most, Latin Americans are still suspicious of American intervention in their region today.

The policy of the "big stick" was expanding. European nations no longer needed to intervene in Latin America because the United States would do it for them. Roosevelt and his successors, Presidents Taft and Wilson, expanded the role of the United States in these areas to bring order to the region, which in turn would increase American prosperity and, indirectly, our security. From 1900 to 1917, the United States intervened in Cuba, Panama, Nicaragua, the Dominican Republic, Mexico, and Haiti.

ARBITRATION, MEDIATION, AND WORLD POLITICS

Theodore Roosevelt believed that the United States had to move away from isolationism and participate with the other Great Powers to settle controversies peacefully. Therefore, the United States took part in the First Hague Conference in 1899 and the Second Hague Conference in 1907, which promoted arbitration between nations of disputes. Both were called by Czar Nicholas II of Russia in order to reduce armaments by international agreement. The conferences did not reduce armaments, but they did bring nations together to confer on peaceful means to end disputes and ironically to formulate laws of war. The 1899 conference of 26 nations established the Permanent Court of Arbitration, formulated laws and customs for war on land, and dealt also with conditions of maritime warfare. The agreements at these conferences were part of the process by which international law was established. The United States Senate, before ratifying the work of the Hague Conference, insisted that situations under the scope of the Monroe Doctrine would not be subject to the Permanent Court of Arbitration. Roosevelt was not president at this time, but he agreed with American participation in the first conference and promoted American participation in the second conference during which he was president. He also worked for bilateral arbitration treaties with other powers in spite of the fact that all excluded areas of certain vital interests from the jurisdiction of arbitration.

As a result of the Alaskan Gold Rush in 1896, in which Americans used the Lynn Canal and the port of Skagway to reach the Klondike River area in Canada, the Canadians insisted that those areas in southern Alaska were really part of British Canada. The dispute lingered for several years until rumors surfaced in 1902 of possible new gold supplies in the disputed area. President Roosevelt then sent 800 additional troops to the area to keep order. Although committed to the idea of arbitration, Roosevelt was afraid that in this case the United States would have to compromise and possibly lose important access to the internal regions of Alaska. But late in 1902, Canada backed off from its earlier demand and told American officials that it would accept a decision which would correspond closely with the American position if the United States would agree to arbitration. The Roosevelt administration agreed in January 1903 to submit the question to arbitration. The question was decided by a commission with three American members and three British members. The British commission was made up of the Lord Chief Justice of England, Lord Alverstone, and two prominent Canadians. Roosevelt let Britain know in no uncertain terms that it would be unfortunate if Lord Alverstone did not agree with the United States in this dispute, and the dispute was settled in favor of the United States.

In 1905, President Roosevelt became involved in mediating a dispute between France and Germany concerning growing French domination of Morocco. Germany insisted that the Moroccan sultan was absolutely independent and sovereign and demanded that Germany be allowed influence to compete with France, but the French refused. The German Kaiser, Wilhelm II, then requested and received Roosevelt's agreement to call a conference to mediate between the disgruntled European nations. The president actually agreed with France, but he felt that Germany must be placated to prevent a possible war. From January to April of 1906, representatives from Germany, France, Britain, and the United States met in Algeciras, Spain to iron out an understanding. In April, the General Act of Algeciras affirmed that Morocco would remain independent and the trade door would be open to all equally, but in reality nothing was agreed upon that stopped France from increasing its interest in Morocco. The Kaiser was reluctant to accept this agreement, but Roosevelt convinced him to accept the agreement in return for public credit for the settlement of the problem.

RELATIONS WITH JAPAN

In 1904 the Open Door Policy toward China was threatened when Japan and Russia went to war over China and Korea. Russian advances into China concerned the Japanese because of the conflict to their own ambitions and security. Japan launched a devastating surpise attack on the Russian fleet at Port Arthur on February 8. Neither side could afford a long war and accepted the offer of President Roosevelt to mediate the affair. The Treaty of Portsmouth signed in Portsmouth, New Hampshire on September 5, 1905 was favorable to the Japanese. Russia recognized Japanese interests in Korea and both powers agreed to leave Manchuria. The Japanese were angry, however, that they did not receive indemnities from Russia.

Roosevelt received the Nobel Peace Prize in 1906 for his contributions in ending the Russo-Japanese War of 1904–1905. That was an interesting award for a man who believed so strongly in the benefits of war. Or to paraphrase the famous Will Rogers, Theodore Roosevelt generally acted like he never met a war he didn't like. For example, Roosevelt had said of the Spanish-American War, "It wasn't much of a war, but it was the best war we had." He also believed that his battle charge in the war was one of his life's finest hours.

Security for the Open Door in China and protection of the Philippines led to further agreements between the United States and Japan. For example, the Taft-Katsura Agreement of July 22, 1905 stated that the United States accepted Japanese domination of Korea, and Japan disavowed any future interest in the Philippines. With the Root-Takahira Agreement of November 30, 1908, both sides agreed to respect each other's possessions and to respect the Open Door Policy in China. Elihu Root was the American Secretary of State at the time.

There were other tensions between the two nations. Americans on the Pacific coast were concerned with the increased Japanese immigration to the area. Many of the Japanese workers were unskilled workers and would work for very cheap wages. Denied the right to exclude immigrants by Congress, cities in California were prepared to isolate the Japanese. In October, 1906, San Francisco passed an ordinance to segregate the Asian students from the city schools. The Japanese government's resentment was great. Japan objected to the ordinance on the grounds that a treaty with the United States gave her nationals the same rights as those enjoyed by the most favored nation. San Francisco amended the school law under pressure from Republican congressmen (called to the White House by Roosevelt and asked to use their influence to overturn the ordinance) and the absence of public support. The Japanese students were allowed to go to school if they were prepared. Roosevelt arranged the "Gentlemen's Agreement" of 1907, under which the Japanese government would not allow Japanese laborers to come to the United States, to prevent future problems of this sort, in return for an American pledge not to exclude all new Japanese immigration.

The president's next move in foreign policy was to attempt to impress the world, particularly the Japanese, with a display of American strength. Roosevelt had not abandoned the benefits of his "big stick" policy. He planned to send the American battle fleet of 16 battleships around the world. Congress at first refused to approve the money for the venture. But Roosevelt threatened that there was enough money to send the fleet to the Pacific, which he would do, and Congress could then worry about getting it back. Backed into a corner, and knowing Roosevelt's tendency to act first and get permission later, Congress then appropriated the rest of the requested funds. America's Great White Fleet conducted an around-the-world tour from 1907–1909. Some nations were duly impressed with the fleet, as hoped, but not the Japanese.

DOLLAR DIPLOMACY

President William Howard Taft, who followed Roosevelt in the White House, supported the Monroe Doctrine and the Roosevelt Corollary in Latin America and the Open Door Policy in China, but instead of wielding a big stick to promote the national interest of the United States, he hoped to accomplish the same goals with American dollars. The policy developed by Taft and his secretary of state, Philander C. Knox, became known as "dollar diplomacy," a nickname given by its critics. The policy was simple. American dollars would advance American foreign policy and, foreign policy would then protect those same American investments. The idea behind the concept was to encourage American investment, especially in Latin America, as a way to promote both economic development and democracy. The government encouraged American companies to invest in plantations, railroads, and mines in the Caribbean. Taft also personally attempted to smooth the way for some American investments in railroads in China. American banks were encouraged to buy up the debts of small Latin American countries to prevent possible European investors from gaining a foothold in areas of strategic importance to the United States.

This type of diplomacy led to economic imperialism in Latin America. In 1910 American bankers took over much of the debt of Haiti's National Bank, and in 1911 American bankers took over the debt of Honduras. Political and economic problems resulted in revolution in some of the countries. Revolutions threatened American investments, and the government was obliged to protect American investments, even to the point of sending troops to support often corrupt and inept but pro-American leaders.

Events in Nicaragua are a clear example of "dollar diplomacy." American dollars helped to support the conservative opponents of the dictator Jose Santos Zelaya to revolt and overthrow their leader in 1909. Zelaya had borrowed large amounts of money from European nations, harassed American business interests, and appeared to be considering the possibility of another inter-ocean canal to be built in Nicaragua. The opportunity to support a revolution to put into place a pro-American government in Nicaragua was not to be ignored by the American business interests, especially in the mining industry. The Taft administration broke off relations with the government of Zelaya and announced it was supporting the revolution when two American citizens were found guilty of attempting to dynamite a government vessel and received the death sentence.

The revolution was a success, but the United States would not have a strong leader to support and to promote American interests until Adolfo Diaz became president in 1911. Diaz had been an official of an American mining firm before the revolution and contributed over half a million dollars to the fight. The money had been given by American business interests. In that same year, New York banks loaned the new Diaz government about $1.5 million, and the Knox-Castrillo Treaty would have given the United States effective economic control in that country, but the United States Senate defeated the treaty. President Diaz himself faced a revolt in 1912 and requested help from the United States. By that time, American banks had increased their loans to Nicaragua to more than $15 million, with the guarantee that the loans were to be secured by customs receipts. Faced with the predictable pressure from powerful bankers and other business interests, President Taft sent 8 warships and 2,000 American troops to assist Diaz, protect the loans, and carry out the treaty that had never been ratified. President Taft was not going to allow forces in Nicaragua to threaten American investments or overall foreign policy. A small contingent of marines remained as an American presence at the embassy compound once the revolution was squelched.

President Taft's foreign policy has received a lot of criticism for its emphasis on promoting American business and then protecting it when it was not always in the best interest of the nation. In his perception, however, it was in the best interest of the nation and would keep the nation out of harm's way more effectively than the "big stick" of Roosevelt. From the Latin American perspective, the economic imperialism of "dollar diplomacy" did not generally result in the raising of their standard of living. American companies were attracted to the region because of low wages, the anti-union climate created by right-wing dictators, and tax-free investments. As a result, such companies usually took out of Latin American countries more than they put in, despite the addition of jobs and benefits to their economies. And that's the major reason that Latin American reformers have often sought to control or take over American companies there. They see that as the only way to control their own resources and destiny.

MISSIONARY DIPLOMACY

Foreign policy was not an issue for President Woodrow Wilson in his presidential campaign in 1912, and it was not mentioned in his first inaugural address. This president was concerned with advancing the Progressive Era domestic concerns of a nation at peace. However, soon after taking the oath of office, foreign policy issues commanded a large portion of the president's attention. And in his second administration, the president had to deal almost exclusively with foreign policy. President Wilson's diplomacy, especially toward Latin America, became known as missionary diplomacy. Explicitly rejecting the imperialistic policies of his two predecessors, Wilson emphasized that the power of the federal government should be used to advance the causes of democracy and peace. In his approach, the United States would apply Christian elements of goodness and justice to other nations. But although he rejected Roosevelt's "big stick" and Taft's "dollar diplomacy," in fact he used both when American interests were at stake. In 1913, he outlined his broad goals for his administration in relations with other nations as being "human rights, national integrity, and opportunity [rather than] material interests . . . the United States will never again seek one additional foot of territory by conquest." Wilson and his Secretary of State, William Jennings Bryan, were sincere in their effort to implement an idealistic foreign policy. But they overlooked the fact that American foreign policy had contained idealism over the decades, but the reality of national interest would and should have to take precedence.

In his first month in office, Wilson withdrew administrative support from a proposed private bank loan to China. It appeared that dollar diplomacy was on its way out, but only for a few weeks. In the Caribbean, his policy was much different. The marines remained in Nicaragua, and the State Department approved a private loan to this nation. A treaty was also negotiated with Nicaragua to lease the Gulf of Fonseca and the Great Corn and Little Corn Islands. This treaty was severely criticized by the Central American Court of Justice for infringing upon the sovereignty of Nicaragua.

The Caribbean

Trouble was brewing in the island nation of Haiti shortly after World War I broke out in Europe in late 1914. Europeans had invested heavily in Haiti, and frequent unrest there since the early years of the new century had made foreign intervention a real possibility. In fact, both Germany and France sent troops there to restore law and order, which really worried the Wilson administration. When the United States attempted to establish control over their customs houses in order to see that Haiti's foreign debts would eventually be paid and to attempt to guarantee that no other power would gain the upper hand there, the Haitian people reacted so violently that in July 1915 President Wilson sent more than 2,000 marines to restore order. Haiti was ruled by an American military government from then until 1934, although customs control remained in effect for an additional 7 years.

About the same time that Haiti was experiencing political turmoil, renewed trouble in the Dominican Republic, which geographically shares the same island with Haiti, led to American efforts to impose a treaty granting the United States even broader powers over its finances than already existed. This effort was rejected by the government there. But in the spring of 1916 the Dominican Republic plunged even deeper into revolution, and President Wilson sent in the marines to establish an American military government. This military occupation lasted for 8 years before it was ended in 1924. The benefits in improvements in education, sanitation, and public works were not paralleled by political benefits, however. After 8 years of American military rule, the Dominican Republic was no closer to democracy or permanent peace. Instead, the United States left a legacy of an American trained Dominican army that would become the new power brokers in that Caribbean nation. One military dictatorship simply led to more military dictatorships.

The Veracruz Invasion of Mexico

Wilson's greatest challenge in this hemisphere came from problems in Mexico. In 1910 and 1911, Mexico was in the throes of a revolution agitated by a small middle class and supported by the peasants hoping to recover their lands. The result of the first phase of the revolution was the overthrow of dictator Porfirio Diaz and the installment of Francisco I. Madero as the president of Mexico in 1911. However, the new president could not keep order, nor was he delivering on his promises of more land for the peasants. Ambassador Henry Lane Wilson (no relation to the president) expressed his own unhappiness with Madero and at least tacit support for General Victoriano Huerta. During a counter-revolution in February 1913, President Madero was assassinated, and Huerta, whom Madero had entrusted with restoring order in Mexico, was installed as the new president. It appeared that both Madero and his vice president were put to death at the orders of Huerta.

President Wilson expressed shock and moral outrage at the assassination, naively acting as if this kind of revolutionary behavior had never happened in world history before. Wilson promptly refused to recognize the presidency of Huerta, regarding his regime as a "government of butchers." Enunciating his refusal to extend diplomatic recognition to the Huerta government, Wilson argued that the

United States would not recognize governments which did not rest on the "consent of the governed." This new American policy became known as the Wilson Doctrine. The Wilson Doctrine represented a radical departure from the Jeffersonian principle of extending official recognition to the de facto government in a nation. The historical American approach had been to recognize the government that is realistically in control of a country, regardless of whether we liked its leaders or not.

Teaching Latin Americans to choose good men and good government was one of Wilson's goals, and Wilson determined to oust Huerta, even if it meant war with neighboring Mexico. The revolution continued in Mexico, and Wilson lifted a previous arms embargo to enable Huerta's enemies to obtain arms. Several European nations and Japan had already recognized the government of Huerta as the legitimate or realistic government of Mexico. Matters came to a dangerous climax on April 9, 1914, when American sailors on shore leave in Tampico became involved in a barroom brawl and were arrested. When local authorities recognized that these arrests, although legitimate, could possibly lead to an international situation, the American sailors were released and escorted back to the *Dolphin*. Using these arrests as an opportunity to oust Huerta, Wilson demanded an apology and a 21-gun salute from the Mexican president. Huerta apologized but would not give the salute unless it was returned. This was not acceptable, and Wilson went to Congress on April 20 for authorization to send the marines into Veracruz. Having learned that a German arms ship was headed for Huerta, the president ordered the marines ashore on the 21st; with its hands tied, Congress gave its consent to use the marines two days after that, on April 23. In the occupation, 17 Americans and more than three hundred Mexicans were killed. When Wilson learned that several civilians had been caught in the crossfire, he again expressed shock and began looking for ways to extricate the American troops from Mexico. Meanwhile, Huerta was overwhelmed by his problems in attempting to hold onto power in Mexico and fled the country in July 1914.

Revolution continued to rage in Mexico with numerous leaders attempting to gain enough power to gain the leadership of the nation. The American government was pressed by American business interests in Mexico to bring some sort of order to the country because more than $1 billion worth of American investments were at stake. The investments were not only endangered by the chaos and violence of the revolutions, but also by the growing sense of nationalism of the patriotic fighters to regain control of many of the resources and businesses that Americans controlled. American companies owned more than half of the mines, oil, rubber plantations, and railroads in Mexico.

At the time of the Veracruz occupation, the so-called ABC powers of Latin America—Argentina, Brazil, and Chile—offered to mediate the problems between Mexico and the United States. Wilson had failed to see the true nature of the civil war in Mexico, based at it was on centuries of economic deprivation. He also underestimated the intensity of Mexican nationalism. Looking for a way to save face, the Wilson administration agreed to accept their help, and the Niagara Falls Conference was held on September 15, 1915, where Uruguay, Bolivia, and Guatemala joined the ABC powers in recommending that the United States recognize the government of Venustiano Carranza, the victor in the latest round of revolution. The United States extended recognition after Carranza agreed to protect American lives and property.

Pancho Villa

For some months the United States had favored Pancho Villa—a bandit and a revolutionary controlling territory in northern Mexico—for the presidency, but Carranza held more power and support from the Mexican people. Villa was resentful of this action and set out to bring American intervention into Mexico to destroy Carranza's presidency. So in January 1916, Villa's followers pulled 16 American engineers from a train in northern Mexico and murdered them. And on March 9, 1916, Villa crossed the border into the United States and led a raid on Columbus, New Mexico, in which 17 Americans were killed. (Some authorities say 19.) Villa received a form of American intervention when General John J. "Black Jack" Pershing was ordered into Mexico to capture Villa either dead or alive. Carranza objected but consented to the expedition because he could not afford to further alienate his powerful northern neighbor.

After 11 months of American troops tramping around northern Mexico and finding nothing, Carranza began demanding that the Americans withdraw. In June 1916, a clash between American and Mexican forces caused Wilson to mobilize the national guard along the Mexican border. Tensions were high between the two nations, and war could have been the outcome. But neither country wanted war, and after a failure to mediate the problems with Mexico and a failure to find Villa, the United States withdrew its forces on February 5, 1917. Wilson could no longer keep his forces in Mexico nor devote his time to the problems of Mexico. American entrance into World War I on the side of the Allies appeared imminent.

The success of Wilson's foreign policy in Mexico was debated. War was avoided, but the enmity of the Mexican people for what they regarded as the interfering bully from the north remained for quite some

Pancho Villa. Credit: The Bettmann Archive.

time. And he was criticized in his own country for not catching Villa. More significant, however, is that the imperialistic policies of the Roosevelt, Taft, and Wilson administrations meant that the United States entered World War I without united Latin American support. The Good Neighbor policy of the Franklin Roosevelt administration in the 1930s would restore much of that lost Latin American support for this country, and when the United States entered World War II in 1941, it did so with almost universal support from Latin America. This would prove that wise foreign policy, one that respects the territorial integrity of other nations, is also in the best national interest of the United States.

In April 1917, the United States declared war on Germany. Once again, Wilson was pulled into a foreign policy he did not want. But his leadership in uniting this country for victory in war far outshone his other areas of foreign policy making. America's expansionism brought rewards and problems. Unresolved tensions created at this time would lead to problems in the future, but immediately after World War I, the United States attempted to return to isolationism toward Europe. The isolationism of the 1920s, however, was not the same as that of the previous periods. The nation had new responsibilities as a Great Power.

ADDITIONAL READINGS

Walter LaFeber, *The New Empire: An Interpretation of American Expansion, 1860–1898* (1963). The best overview of U.S. imperial involvement in the late nineteenth century. Shows how overseas commitments grew out of American leaders' faith in economic expansion and grew continuously, if often chaotically, with the opportunities presented by the crises experienced by the older imperial powers.

Emily S. Rosenberg, *Spreading the American Dream: American Economic and Cultural Expansion, 1890–1945* (1982). Insightfully examines the significance of expansionist ideology. Shows the cultural and social roots of American foreign policy.

William Appleman Williams, *Empire as a Way of Life: An Essay on the Causes and Character of America's Present Predicament* (1982). A lucid general exploration of American views of empire. Shows that Americans allowed the idea of empire and, more generally, economic expansion to dominate their concept of democracy, especially in the last half of the nineteenth century.

CHAPTER EIGHT

World War I

MAJOR EVENTS

1907   Root-Takahira Agreement

1914   First World War begins

1915   Germany declares war zone around Great Britain; German U-boat sinks *Lusitania*

1916   Wilson reelected on pledge to keep U.S. out of war
National Defense Act establishes preparedness program

1917   Germany declares new policy of unrestricted submarine warfare
Zimmerman note
U.S. declares war
Selective Service Act
Espionage Act
Race riot in East St. Louis, Illinois
Bolshevik Revolution begins in Russia

1918   Creation of War Industries Board, National War Labor Board, Food Administration, Fuel Administration, Committee on Public Information
Sedition Act
Eugene Debs imprisoned
U.S. troops in action in France
Armistice ends war
Wilson unveils Fourteen Points

1919   Wilson travels to Paris Peace Conference
Wilson suffers stroke while touring country in support of Versailles treaty
Versailles treaty rejected by Senate

WAR IN EUROPE IS DECLARED

The Archduke Franz Ferdinand, heir to the throne of the Austria-Hungarian Empire, and his wife, the Duchess of Hohenburg, were shot to death in their automobile on the streets of Sarajevo, Bosnia on June 28, 1914. The assassination of the Archduke sparked a war in Europe among the Great Powers to resolve competitions and conflicts that had been simmering for several years. The assassin was Gavrilo Princip, a 19-year-old Serbian student living in Bosnia. Princip was a member of a Serbian nationalist secret society, the Black Hand, which was dedicated to ending Austrian rule of Bosnia. Austria held the neighboring nation of Serbia responsible for the assassination (some members of the Serbian government did have knowledge of the plot against the Archduke) and delivered a list of 10 demands to Serbia on July 23 to be answered in 24 hours or else face the prospects of war. Meanwhile, the empire asked its ally Germany what it would do in case of an attack against the Serbs. Germany's Kaiser Wilhelm sent the famous reply known as the "Blank Check," which told Austria-Hungary that Germany would support it militarily if it chose to attack Serbia. Serbia was in no position to refuse, so it agreed to 8 of the demands and proposed that the Hague Tribunal arbitrate the other two.

Archduke Ferdinand of Austria and Duchess before the Duke's assassination in Sarajevo, 1914. Credit: United Press International, Inc.

But Austria was looking for an excuse to absorb Serbia into its empire, and therefore announced that its demands had not been met. On July 28, 1914, Austria declared war on Serbia. Allies of the two nations joined the conflict until virtually all of Europe was engulfed in the flames of war by August 4, 1914. All believed that the war would be a traditional affair and that the victors would soon march in the streets of the vanquished. They miscalculated, however; the war was 4 years of the most brutal conflict the world had known up to that time. This war was known at the time as the Great War. It would not gain the title of World

War I until the advent of another world war a generation later would put into place a numbering system.

THE UNDERLYING CAUSES OF WORLD WAR I

The assassination of Franz Ferdinand did not cause the war. It simply gave the European powers an excuse to fight a war to solve old rivalries. Most historians agree that there were 4 major underlying causes of the war, along with other smaller problems. These major underlying causes of the Great War were (1) nationalism, (2) imperialism, (3) militarism, and (4) the military alliance systems.

Nationalism is the strong sense of pride in a nation which exalts that nation and its culture above all others. Related to patriotism, nationalism goes well beyond to an arrogant attitude which inevitably leads to an aggressive foreign policy when large numbers of people hold such feelings in a country, or to revolution in the case of those peoples who are being dominated by another power. Particularly in the Austrian-Hungarian Empire, the various ethnic groups wanted the freedom to form their own nations along cultural lines. The Ottoman Turkish Empire had lost its hold on most of southeast Europe in the 1870s, resulting in the creation of several new small, independent nations (such as Romania, Bulgaria, and Serbia). The Austria-Hungarian Empire eventually attempted to fill the vacuum left by the Ottomans by annexing many of these areas into its own empire. But the Serbs especially dreamed of a unified Slavic area, and they looked to Russia for assistance, which it gladly attempted to provide. When Austria-Hungary annexed Bosnia-Herzogovina (on the border of Austria-Hungary and Serbia) in 1908, this caused great alarm in both Serbia and Russia. Bosnian Serbs then wanted to join with the independent nation of Serbia, and terrorism seemed their only weapon against the strong empire. Nationalism also brought to the Great Powers the belief that the culture of their nation was so superior to all others that in war their nation should and would prevail.

During the eighteenth and nineteenth centuries, imperialism had brought the search for overseas possessions, which in turn, had led to conflict among the Great Powers of Europe over the domination of Africa, Asia, and the Pacific. There were also rivalries for areas of Europe itself. Russia, for example, had for some time desired control of the slavs in the Balkan area controlled by Austria-Hungary.

The build-up of armies, navies, and materials of war led to suspicions and tensions on all sides. Especially developing in the late nineteenth and very early twentieth centuries, militarism had turned the continent of Europe into two armed camps before the war actually broke out. Like a powder keg, it was ready to explode.

The Great Powers had formed defensive alliances in the 1880s and 1890s to balance the power structure on the continent. If a member of an alliance were attacked, the others were to come to its aid. Germany, Austria-Hungary, and Italy formed the Triple Alliance, which except for Italy, became known as the Central Powers after the Great War actually broke out. Great Britain, France, and Russia formed the Triple Entente, which became the Allies during the war. These nations also formed other alliances important to the causes of the war in 1914. Serbia was allied to Russia, who had long held ties with the Serbs. Even before Serbia was attacked by Austria-Hungary, the Russian army was given the order to mobilize, that is, to position itself and enter a posture of high military alert. Mobilization is in itself generally considered a warlike act. The alliance systems then proceeded to pull in the other allies on both sides. It was true that the alliances were defensive in nature, and the allies did not have to enter a conflict when their partners committed belligerent acts. Each nation, however, finally believed it to be in their own best interest to support their ally.

Once the war began, the Central Powers consisted of Germany, Austria-Hungary, and later Turkey and Bulgaria. On the opposing side were the major Allied Powers (formerly the Triple Entente), of which the major combatants were Britain, France, Russia, and later, Italy, Japan, and the United States. When the war broke out, Italy initially declared her neutrality and then switched sides in April 1915, claiming that she was not bound by the terms of the Triple Alliance because of the aggressions of Germany and Austria-Hungary. Although that was technically true, the reality was that Italy had been promised certain Austrian territory by the Allies. Japan joined the allies to gain German possessions in Asia and the Pacific. And, of course, much of this chapter tells the story of how and why the United States finally entered the war in 1917.

THE GERMAN INVASION OF BELGIUM

Although the Austrian attack on Serbia was the beginning of military action in World War I, the German march through neutral Belgium in order to attack France is considered the official beginning of the war. All of the major powers had war plans, and in August 1914, the Germans put into place the von Schlieffen plan. This plan was constructed by Count Alfred von Schlieffen in 1905. The core idea of the plan, upon which success in the war depended, was the quick defeat of France by crushing its army between a rapidly advancing force from the north and a fixed force on the eastern border of France. The countryside of Belgium was the closest area with the flat terrain necessary to allow a large force to advance rapidly. When France was defeated, Germany would then send its forces to the Eastern Front and assist the forces of Austria-Hungary in the defeat of Russia.

The German advance was stalled when the Belgians resisted. The German Chancellor von Bethmann-Hollweg notified Belgium on July 27, 1914, that German armies would pass through Belgium soon, but the rights of property and the people would be respected if there was no resistance. However, even just the use of Belgian territory as a means to attack an enemy would be a violation of Belgium's neutral rights according to international law. But the neutrality of Belgium, guaranteed in a treaty by all the powers of Europe, including Germany, was considered by the German chancellor as a "scrap of paper." King Albert of Belgium and his army decided to resist this violation of their neutrality. It is important to note that the invasion of Belgium did bring a declaration of war from Britain on Germany on August 4. The German army, in what became known as "the rape of Belgium," now punished the tiny country for its resistance. But the Belgians were able to hold up the German advance long enough to adversely effect the von Schlieffen plan and allow France time to mobilize her forces and to begin their march north to meet the enemy.

TRENCH WARFARE

The goal for the German army in France was now the city of Paris. The French, with help from British troops, stopped the German advance at the First Battle of the Marne, which began on September 5, 1914. The French were outnumbered, but reserves from Paris were brought to the battle in taxis. Fearing defeat, the German armies retreated to the Aisne River, north of Paris, and there they entrenched themselves in order to regroup and then attack again. This was the beginning of trench warfare for the Western Front of this war. In the efforts to outflank each other, the "race to the sea" began, and the lines of trenches were eventually extended for 500 miles through eastern and northern France from Switzerland to the English Channel and North Sea areas.

The trenches grew into a maze of zigzagging tunnels for both sides. There was usually a front line trench, a support trench a few hundred yards back, sometimes a reserve trench was further back still, and all were connected by communication trenches which were dug from the rear area to the front trench. "No man's land" was the area between the two sides, and wooden stakes and barbed wire were frequently placed in this area to prevent the overrunning of a trench. Both sides went on the offensive at frequent intervals to gain ground or straighten out an awkward angle of the trench line, but then they were back in the trenches with few if any gains. However, small sections of trenches did constantly change hands. In some locations the trenches were very close together, only as far apart as 50 yards.

War is indeed hell, but it often produces bizarre behavior in soldiers. One of the most bizarre episodes of the Great War occurred during a Christmas truce in December 1914 between British and German troops. British soldiers in their trenches heard their German counterparts singing Christmas carols. Suddenly, white flags went up and British and German soldiers got out of their trenches and met in "No Man's Land" between the trenches. There they shook hands, showed pictures of their wives or girl friends, exchanged candy, drinks, and cigarettes, sang Christmas carols together about peace and goodwill toward men (each in their own language, of course), and then went back to their respective trenches, from where they soon began shooting at each other again. Similar stories occurred elsewhere on the lines, but the French did not partake in this sort of fraternization; their historical feelings of hostility toward the Germans prevented even a timeout for civilized relations.

Trench fighting was particularly difficult for the soldiers physically and mentally. Life in the muddy trenches day after day subjected them to damp, cold, filth, vermin, rats, and disease. They were constantly trying to shore up the muddy walls. The tension of constantly facing the enemy and waiting for the order to go "over the top," which often resulted in wholesale slaughter, was excruciating. At the Battle of the Somme in 1916, for example, the British and French sacrificed approximately 600,000 dead and wounded as compared with the Germans' 500,000, all for 125 square miles of territory. Compared with the Second World War a gener-

American Troops in World War I. Credit: National Archives.

ation later, the Great War was definitely more psychologically traumatic for most soldiers.

War on the Western Front developed into a war of attrition because of the trenches, but on the Eastern Front, mobility and offensive strategies characterized the battles. The Russians fought the Austrian-Hungarian and German forces in offensive action. Turkey, another area in the Eastern theater, entered the war on the side of the Central Powers on October 14, 1914, with the bombardment of Russian towns on the Black Sea. A Turkish invasion of Egypt was stopped by the British in February 1915. British troops were also in the Middle East to secure the neutrality of the Arabs, to safeguard the Suez Canal, to protect the oil fields, and to maintain British authority in the area. The war was spreading its tentacles further afield and pulling more nations into the fray.

NEW WEAPONS

New weapons were developed and old weapons were redesigned in this war. Heavier artillery was used to open an avenue for the infantry. The advancing side was faced with machine gun fire, grenades, and trench mortars. In the summer of 1915, the Germans attacked with flame throwers, a new addition to the arsenal. The Germans were usually ahead of the allies in the development and use of new technology in weapons production. Huge guns known as "Big Berthas" could fire upon targets over 75 miles away. The Germans also pioneered the use of poisonous

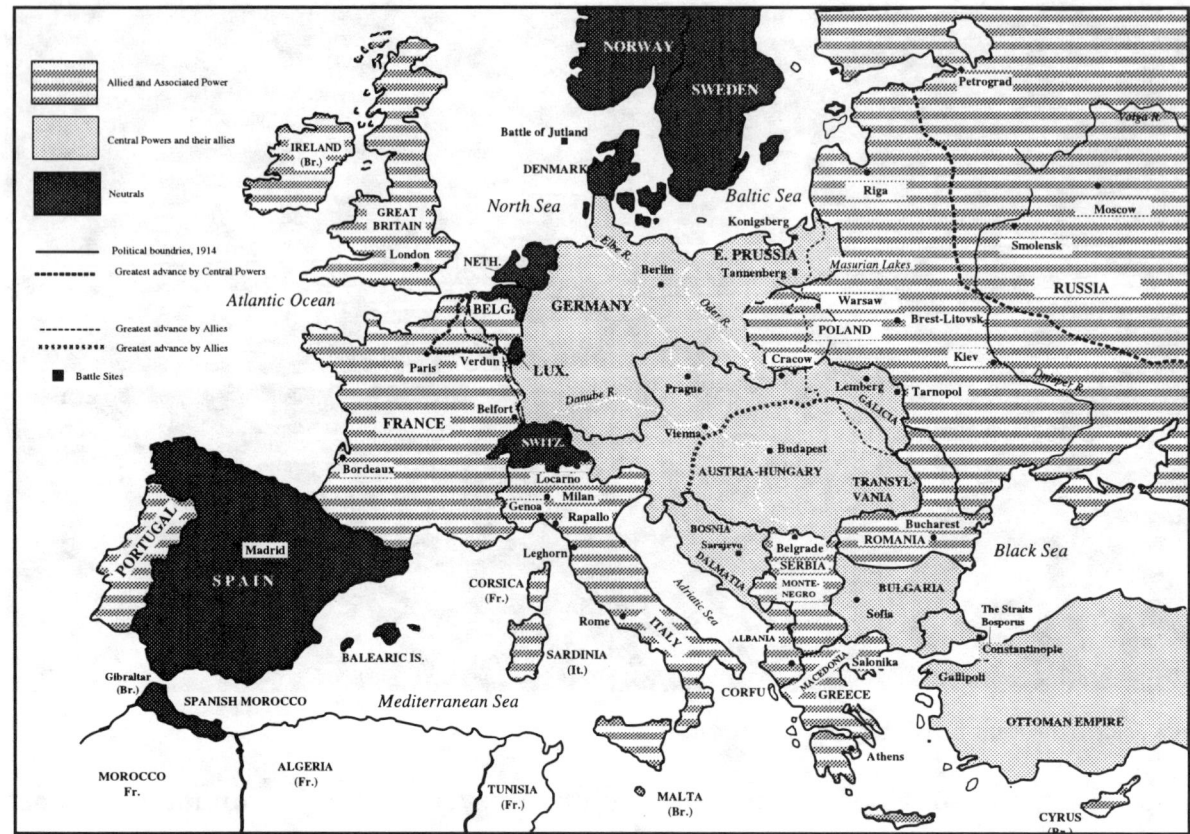

Europe, During World War I (1914-1918)

gas, first against the Russians in January 1915 and then against the French and British in April 1915. Tanks were used for the first time later in the war, although it would be World War II before the tank would be effectively used by both sides.

The Use of Airplanes

The airplane, first flown successfully by the Wright brothers in 1903, became the most dramatic new weapon of the Great War. The Wright brothers had taken their airplane to Europe (by ship) and demonstrated its use in 1908. Aircraft was first used in warfare by the Italians against the Turks in Libya shortly after the European demonstration. By the end of 1913, the year before the Great War began, France, Britain, and Germany had an air corps or service as part of their military establishments. In an age when the military services found it relatively difficult to locate men who could operate motor vehicles, pilots were very scarce, especially during the early days of the war.

At the beginning of the war, the airplane was used to gather information on enemy troop movements. Then, with trench warfare on the Western Front, it was employed to assist the accuracy of artillery units by flying over "No Man's Land"

and sighting how far short or long the shells were falling. There were occasional incidents between planes early in the war, when pilots would carry handguns and shoot at each other from their cockpits. In March 1915, a French pilot by the name of Roland Garros, devised a new method with which to conduct aerial combat with enemy aircraft. Garros mounted a machine gun above the engine at the front of the plane so that he could aim in the direction he was flying. Then he attached steel plating to the propeller blades in order to safely deflect any bullets which didn't get through. With this advantage, Garros had great success for a couple of weeks. But in April 1915, engine trouble forced him down behind the German lines, and the Germans arrived before he had time to burn it.

Anthony Fokker, a Dutchman assisting the Germans with air design, inspected the Garros plane and used it to improve his own design ideas. Instead of using steel plating, which would shorten the life of the propeller, Fokker invented a mechanical device which prevented a machine gun from firing when a propeller blade was in the way. In time, both sides devised such techniques, and real "dogfights" became the standard fare for the pilots of World War I. It was also discovered that small bombs could be dropped with some effectiveness from the airplanes. By later standards, aerial fighting was primitive, but the airplane had gone from a purely reconnaissance tool to a direct weapon of the war.

"Dogfights" became deadly business during the war. Some pilots did not carry parachutes, but often a parachute could not save a pilot anyway. Many, if not most, pilots who were shot down died in a blaze of glory. The major reason for the great number of deadly fires was that the gasoline tank was located as close as possible to the engine. And on most planes, the magnetos were driven directly by the propeller shaft. That meant that even when an engine was hit (and a fuel pipe was usually hit too when that happened), the continued windmilling of the propeller kept the magnetos creating sparks, which inevitably produced a massive fire within seconds. Many inexperienced pilots also died when they lost control of their planes following engine damage which didn't start a fire or damage to one or more surface controls. Planes would often then just spiral out of control toward the earth and crash.

Most of the airplanes in World War I were biplanes, although there were a few triplanes as well. The most famous triplane, the Fokker D.1, was flown by the war's greatest air ace, Manfred von Richthofen. Scarlet-colored, von Richthofen's triplane earned him the nickname of "The Red Baron" on his way to accumulating 80 kills, before the odds finally caught up with him and he was killed late in the war. Other famous aces included the Frenchman Georges Guynemer, the British Mick Mannock, and the American Eddie Rickenbacker. These and other pilots earned their reputations mostly during the heart of the trench warfare on the Western Front, when the goal of reconnaissance was less important than assisting the artillery batteries or clearing one's own side of the lines from enemy planes.

THE UNITED STATES ANNOUNCES ITS NEUTRALITY

When war erupted in Europe, President Woodrow Wilson proclaimed that the United States would maintain a position of neutrality, and he urged Americans to remain neutral "in thought as well as in action." As war raged in Europe, the United States traded with both sides. Most Americans supported the decision of their government. However, neutrality is not the same as impartiality, and Wilson's call for "thought" neutrality had been a futile exercise in excessive morality which even he himself did not abide by. The majority of Americans, like their president, were rooting for the Allies from the beginning of the war. Several reasons were responsible for this attitude. Historical ties to Britain had long left their mark in fundamental areas of American society. Much of our system of law and emphasis on individual rights can be traced to British common law. Economic ties had grown enormously through the years, and by the outbreak of the Great War, the British were our number one trading partner in the world. And, of course, we both possessed a common language. Gratitude to France for her help in the American Revolution had resulted in relatively warm feelings for most of our history up to that time. The French had given us the Statue of Liberty to commemorate those earlier ties. The United States had maintained friendly ties with Russia since the 1820s. And many Americans, Wilson among them, also desired to keep a balance of power in Europe. Toward this end, many nervously viewed Germany as the aggressive power in Europe; it had been united as a nation for the first time in 1871 by Otto von Bismarck through cautious but effective diplomacy and war. And most believed Germany was largely responsible for the Great War as well. Furthermore, the German violation of Belgian neutrality, and the cruel treatment of its civilians, shocked and disillusioned many Americans.

There were, however, three groups of Americans who were hopeful that the Central Powers would secure the victory. German-Americans naturally pulled for their former homeland. Irish-Americans, who resented British rule over Ireland, had for many years supported any nation who fought the British. And Jewish-Americans, many of whom had recently come from Russia, historically the world's most anti-Semitic nation, had reasons to support Germany and her allies.

The propaganda machines of both Britain and Germany attempted to sway public opinion. Britain cut the direct cable from Germany to the United States early in the war, so it was her viewpoint, frequently exaggerated, that more Americans read. Stories of German cruelty and posters of the German "Huns" bayonetting infants were frequently sent to America. The Germans did manage to send reports of the war over wireless and through foreign reporters, but these were so few that they did not influence many Americans.

The Definition of Neutrality

Neutrality is much more than a nation simply staying out of a war. It is a compromise reached between nations, during a war, designed to serve the national interests of all the nations involved in the compromise. This compromise especially concerns international economic trade. Neutral nations would ideally like to continue their trade unrestricted with all nations as if there were no war. And belligerent nations (any nation at war, regardless of which side they are on) would ideally like to prevent its enemies from engaging in any trade whatsoever. But a wise neutral nation is willing to compromise and accept some restrictions on its trade because it wants to remain neutral. And a wise belligerent nation is willing to compromise by allowing some trade to its enemies because it does not want to add to its list of enemies during wartime. Thus, neutrality is a compromise based on common sense. Arms shipments are legal if they are open to both sides in a war. Also, a neutral nation does not have to alter its traditional trading habits in order to conform to some artificial standard of equal trade among both sides in a war.

The Rules of the Game

Various international treaties and conferences have worked out generally accepted rules for the conduct of war and the relationship between neutrals and belligerents during wartime. The Hague Conferences in the early twentieth century and the 1909 Declaration of London, although Britain never signed the latter, formed the basis of what constitutes international law in this area. By such international law, neutral countries during wartime are not permitted to trade, sell, or transfer arms to only one side in the conflict. To intentionally do so is really an act of war and an unofficial declaration that a country has ended its neutral status. They must also do all that they can reasonably do to prevent their waters from being used by belligerents for war purposes; by "reasonable" it is meant that a nation should not allow the action (or invite it, of course) unless it clearly is incapable of preventing some vastly greater military power from forcing its will upon them. And neutral countries are also obligated to do all they can to reasonably prevent their citizens from becoming mercenaries for either side.

The Declaration of London separated contraband items into categories of absolute contraband (items which are only used as war materials), conditional contraband (items which could be used for war or peace and were contraband only if destined for a belligerent country), and non-contraband items (such as food, wood, and certain ores which are essential for civilians). The Declaration also stated that a legal blockade was to be of a specific port and close to the shores of said port so that the blockade represented an actual physical barrier to ships attempting to go in or come out.

In terms of economic trade, there are a number of specific rules for both neutrals and belligerents that govern their behavior on the high seas. A captain of a belligerent ship has the right to stop and inspect any neutral vessel—merchant or passenger liner—for contraband. As a last resort to get the attention of a neutral vessel, the captain of a belligerent ship may fire a shot across its bow. If the neutral vessel (1) refuses to stop, (2) attempts to make a run for it, or (3) attempts to ram the belligerent ship, then it automatically becomes a belligerent ship itself, and in accordance with international law, it may be sunk immediately as any other enemy military ship. If, however, a neutral ship allows itself to be boarded and inspected for contraband, and contraband is discovered on it, then the belligerent vessel has one of two options. Either the contraband may be confiscated and taken aboard its own vessel, or if that is physically impossible, it may sink the neutral ship, provided that the safety of the neutral crew and passengers is guaranteed first. And the safety of the neutral's crew and passengers does not include placing them in life rafts; they must be boarded onto the belligerent vessel and taken back to land in a reasonable period of time, where arrangements for safe passage back to their own country are to be made.

In spite of the sympathies for both sides, American neutrality went forward in harmony with the president's announcement. The United States would trade with both sides, including arms, while accepting some restrictions on its trade in order to maintain its position of neutrality. But both sides, chiefly represented by Britain and Germany, violated American neutrality and international law at various times during more than the first two and one-half years of the Great War. The United States managed to keep out of the war until 1917, but the increasing violations of neutrality by the Germans brought the Americans into the war in April of that year.

BRITISH VIOLATIONS OF AMERICAN NEUTRALITY

The British navy was the most powerful navy in the world at the outset of the war, and they were determined from the beginning to bottle up the German navy (a distant number two in strength) in port and neutralize its effectiveness. Anxious that violations of certain internationally accepted rules of warfare at sea could bring conflict with the United States, on August 6, 1914, Secretary of State William Jennings Bryan called on all belligerent nations to accept the Declaration of London, signed by the major powers in 1909, but never ratified by Britain. The British did not like the restrictions on its navy, which was the focal point of her military strength. The British added items to the contraband list, so that by April 1916 there was no distinction between absolute and conditional contraband. Very early in the war, they announced that they would not accept the definition of a legal blockade, which brought increasingly angry protests from the American government.

On November 3, 1914, the British declared the North Sea a military zone and proceeded to mine the area and later put a blockade in place at its mouth. Britain also instituted the doctrine of continuous voyage, or ultimate destination—that goods could be seized on the way to neutral ports if it could be proved that they were ultimately destined for the enemy. The protest of the American government was met with the British response that since the United States had used the doctrine of the continuous voyage during the Civil War against British shipping, it was acceptable. British ships also violated American neutrality by pulling American ships into British ports to search the cargoes, actions which were reminiscent of the War of 1812 with Britain. The Declaration of London had ruled that neutral ships should be searched at sea, and if no contraband was found, they should be allowed to continue their voyage. But the British claimed that ships could not always be searched at sea because of the threat of German submarines, and besides, some of the cargo must be X-rayed to conduct a thorough search. It was also necessary, the British navy insisted, to pull neutral ships into British ports to pick up a pilot with a map of the mine locations. The final insult was made public in July 1916, when the British published a "blacklist" of more than four hundred firms in neutral countries, including more than 80 in the United States, suspected of having business dealings with the Central Powers. If a firm's name was on the list, it was expected that loyal Britons would cut all business ties immediately. Congress did authorize retaliatory measures after this, but President Wilson did not use them. British violations usually resulted in a loss of time only, and most American monetary losses were reimbursed.

GERMAN VIOLATIONS OF AMERICAN NEUTRALITY

On February 4, 1915, Germany responded to the British actions by issuing an illegal paper blockade of its own with the proclamation that the waters surrounding the British Isles was a "war zone." Enemy merchant ships would be destroyed on sight in the forbidden area without provision for the safety of passengers and crew, which of course violated international law. Neutrals were warned that mistakes in wartime and the misuse of neutral flags could result in the sinking of neutral ships as well. Indeed, the Allies shipped munitions on passenger ships and merchant ships and tried to camouflage warships as passenger ships. Because of the British superiority in surface vessels, Germany resorted to its only weapon of retaliation—the submarine, better known as the U-boat (unterseebot)—by announcing its policy of "unrestricted submarine warfare" at the same time. The one clear advantage the submarine possessed, of course, was the element of surprise. But that very ad-

Sinking of the Luisitania, 1915. Credit: The New York Times.

vantage meant that Germany could and would not abide by international law concerning the safety of non-military and neutral crews and passengers, for if they surfaced, they were almost totally vulnerable and defenseless. The United States quickly sent a sharp protest to Germany in the same month (February 1915), stating that Germany would be held responsible and strictly accountable for any violation of neutral rights at sea. Germany began to fire first and ask questions later as the British blockade became more effective at stopping supplies to Germany.

Germany did not want to provoke the United States into entering the war on the Allies' side. Therefore, early in the war, Wilhelm II, the Kaiser of Germany, informed his navy that submarine war would continue on enemy merchant ships, but the U-boat captains must refrain from attacks on recognized American merchant ships. About the same time, the German ambassador, Count von Bernstorff, urged the American State Department to warn Americans against travel on belligerent ships. President Wilson, however, correctly believed that such actions violated international law, as well as the freedom of the seas that he held so vital a part of American rights. On the practical level, however, American lives were lost at sea as the result; these American citizens were legally right, but they were also "dead" right.

On March 28, 1915, the British liner *Falaba* went down with the loss of one American. A short time later, on May 1, when the *Gulflight*, an American owned tanker, was struck by a torpedo launched in a fight between a submarine and a British naval patrol, two of the crew drowned, but the ship did make it to port. Germany apologized for deaths of the Americans and damage to American property, promised full recompense, and agreed that future attacks on all neutral ships would be avoided. No more American ships were torpedoed until February 1917.

The German government placed notices in American newspapers warning Americans of the risks presented by entering the "war zone" around the British Isles. Many ignored these notices. When the British luxury liner, the *Lusitania*, was struck by a torpedo off the coast of Ireland on May 7, 1915, the ship went down in less than 20 minutes with the loss of 1,198 lives, including 128 Americans. The German U-boat captain initially claimed that he didn't know it was a passenger ship until he read the word "Lusitania" on the side of the ship as it was sinking. Although some fog was present in the area at the time, his statement lacks credibility because every submarine carries an expert in identifying surface ships by their contour, and the *Lusitania* was distinctively large for its day (it had 4 smokestacks).

This event began to turn American public opinion more vehemently anti-German. Wilson sent the first *Lusitania* note demanding that Germany abandon unrestricted submarine warfare and make reparation for the loss of American lives. This note of May 13 insisted once again on the right of Americans to sail on the seas. The German government "apologized" for the American deaths, but claimed that the attack was excused because the ship was armed and carried contraband, and that the Americans had been warned not to travel on it. The liner had left New York City and was headed for Liverpool, England. Of course, that's like arguing that it is all right to violate international law as long as you announce that fact ahead of time. The ship was not armed, but it was later discovered that it was carrying small amounts of munitions. Interestingly, too, the German navy treated its U-boat commander responsible for the attack as a returning hero.

Not satisfied with the German reply, in early June, Wilson prepared another note, explaining to the German government that submarines were not exempt from international laws of the sea and demanding specific pledges that this would not happen again. Secretary Bryan refused to sign this hostile note, fearing it would bring about war between the two nations. Bryan did not recognize the distinction between neutrality and impartiality, and he accused the president of not reacting with the same degree of hostility toward British violations of our neutrality. Of course, the official (and unofficial, for that matter) American reaction to German violations was indeed more hostile most of the time than our reactions to the British violations. But the reason for that was the fact that German violations were killing American civilians and British violations, as far we knew, were not. (Sea mines were laid by both sides, but mines don't pop out of the water and announce what country they belong to before they explode in your face.) As a result of his anger, Bryan resigned on June 8. The new Secretary of State, Robert Lansing, was an Anglophile (very pro-British) and gladly signed the second note, which was dispatched to the German authorities. A third note, sent on July 21, warned that any future acts would be regarded as "deliberately unfriendly." In February 1916, Germany agreed to pay an indemnity for American losses, but President Wilson refused this offer because it did not include a statement of the illegality of the act.

The sinking of the *Lusitania* left many unanswered questions. One of the most puzzling was why the ship sank so quickly. The ship was hit with only one torpedo, and yet survivors clearly reported two distinct explosions, with the second one much louder than the first. In fact, we know that the U-boat commander only had one torpedo left. For years, many people assumed that the munitions had caused the second explosion. But since 1990, an investigation by an American marine salvage expert has combed available data on the explosion, employing cameras and special mini subs to explore the ship up close. Not only were there not sufficient munitions on board the *Lusitania* to cause the ship to sink so quickly, but it was discovered that the hole produced by the torpedo was nowhere near the storage bins that contained the relatively small amounts of munitions. Instead, a new theory has emerged with an enormous amount of credibility. The torpedo had exploded into a nearly empty cargo hold that had held the coal for the ship. Since the liner was nearing home (Liverpool, England), there would have been a huge amount of coal dust present at the time the German torpedo entered the hold. Almost without a doubt, it must have been the ignition of all that coal dust that caused the second explosion and the quick sinking of the ship. Even the U-boat commander must have been surprised, for he did not expect to sink the large luxury liner with just one torpedo; his aim was only to harass it and let the British know that they were still in the area.

For its failure to stop the liner and search its cargo for contraband, the German U-boat was in violation of international law. There might have been a slim chance that, if argued before an impartial tribunal, Britain's standing order to ram surfaced German submarines or to flee made it an offensive weapon and thereby sinkable. But that probably would have been only a slim chance. Morally, the sinking of the luxury liner was no worse than the effects of the British blockade of Germany, which indirectly killed thousands of German civilians before the war was over. But realistically—and nations ought to think in these terms—it was the result of a foolish policy because it led to the death of innocent civilians that brought the Germans nothing but negative publicity and reinforced the British propaganda against the uncivilized and feared "Huns."

The sinking of the *Lusitania* did not, as often believed, bring the United States into the war, for that would not come for almost two full years later. However, it was the biggest civilian disaster on the high seas during the war and the most prominent example of Germany's unrestricted submarine warfare, which later did result in America's entry into World War I.

More American lives were lost and American protest grew stronger. On August 19, 1915, two Americans were killed when the British liner the *Arabic* was sunk. On September 1, the German government made the so-called Arabic Pledge that German submarines would not sink passenger liners without providing for the safety of the passengers and crews. Since U-boats could not provide such safety, this was virtually a promise that no more passenger ships would be sunk. The Germans also agreed to pay an indemnity.

Then on March 24, 1916, the *Sussex*, a French freighter, was sunk while crossing the English Channel, injuring two Americans working for the French merchant fleet. When President Wilson threatened to sever diplomatic relations with Germany, the German government issued its Sussex Pledge on May 4. This pledge promised that Germany would not sink any more unarmed merchant ships without warning and allowing crews and passengers to disembark. (The Allies had begun arming merchant vessels shortly before this incident.) Germany demanded that before this pledge was put into place the United States should also protest British violations of neutral rights. The United States had already protested certain British actions, so in this context, the administration refused to allow Germany to dictate American policy. Because Germany did not offer a follow-up reply, it was assumed that the Sussex Pledge would be kept. And, in fact, relations between the two countries were relatively calm until February 1917. It was relations with Britain that were extremely tense in the latter half of 1916. Inspection of mail to and from the United States that merely happened to be on ships in British or French ports brought a great outcry from the American business world, but Wilson refused to send notes to demand an end to the practice.

GERMAN SABOTAGE IN AMERICA

Early in the war attempts to sabotage the American ability to assist the Allies were directed from the German embassy. German agents sent home information about the quantity of munitions production. They also attempted to prevent the exporting of military supplies or tried to destroy the transport ships. Agents acting as members of the German-American National Alliance tried to persuade Congress to pass measures that would benefit the Central Powers. Some of the incidents attributed to German saboteurs were accidents, but there was proof that some agents were at work in the United States, and their purpose was to damage what they could. For example, the briefcase of Dr. Heinrich Albert, a commercial attache at the German Embassy, was found on a train and confiscated. The case contained documents of German plans to foment strikes and prevent munitions shipments. The British seized the luggage of the journalist James F.J. Archibald, which contained a letter from the Austrian Ambassador Constantin Dumba. The letter named several American munitions companies in which production could be held up for months. The American secret service usually stopped German plots of destruction before they could occur, but the explosion at the Black Tom docks of the Lehigh Valley Railroad in New Jersey on July 30, 1916, was not discovered in time to stop it. Two people were killed and more than $21 million of property damage inflicted. Germany did admit its responsibility later and paid for the damage. The German efforts did not achieve their desired effects. The United States protested these activities and eventually sent diplomats home, but the government was not willing to take more drastic steps until 1917.

THE BUSINESS ASPECT OF NEUTRALITY

As the European powers depleted their stockpiles of industrial goods, munitions, and food, the United States, because of its neutral status, was approached to sell to both sides. British control of the seas fairly well eliminated trade between the Central Powers and the United States. American trade with Germany in 1914 amounted to about $169 million; in 1916 it fell to only about $1 million. This demonstrated the increasing effectiveness of the British navy's illegal paper blockade of Germany on the North Sea. Initially, the Allies purchased American goods with the sale of their American securities, but loans to purchase these goods were soon needed. By October 1914, Wilson began to quietly approve short-term loans, and in 1915 all restrictions were lifted. Germany protested the fact that only the Allies were benefitting from the neutral trade, and they requested that there should at least be an embargo on munitions. The United States refused, stating that an embargo would be an unneutral act and that Germany's inability to receive arms from the United States was due to circumstances beyond its control. This did, in fact, make arms shipments to the Allies technically legal according to international law, but Germany accused the United States of violating the spirit of that law in engaging in what became, in practical terms, a one-sided arms trade.

Actually, before the United States entered the war, investors had advanced the Allies over $2 billion and only $27 million to Germany. But again, this was partly due to the effective British blockade, which prevented most American shipments from being delivered anyway, and partly due to the fact that the United States had historically traded much more with Britain and France than it had with Germany. The advances were used to purchase American goods, which was good for the economy, but it did give many American businesses a strong reason to support an Allied victory. The lopsided loaning of money also brought criticism from the Nye Committee in the 1930s, which investigated American involvement in the Great War. The committee alleged that business interests pressured the Wilson administration into declaring war to protect their investments. There is no evidence to prove this stand. The fact was that Wilson was too interested in moral reasons for fighting to let money influence him. And in reality, many of the nation's business-men would have made more profit if the nation had stayed out of the war.

THE PREPAREDNESS CONTROVERSY AND THE ELECTION OF 1916

Most progressives, farmers, and labor leaders advocated that the United States should maintain a strict neutrality and not sell war material to the belligerents. William Jennings Bryan and Robert LaFollette were leaders of these strict neutral-ists. Others believed that the government and the nation should work for peace be-tween the antagonists. Still others believed that America should ignore all violations of neutrality. And then there were some who asserted that the United States must prepare for war; an increase in American military strength might cause others to think carefully before antagonizing a strong nation.

The National Security League, founded in December 1914, promoted strength-ening national defense. The American Legion organized a military training pro-gram. Approximately 12,000 men voluntarily went to training camps, but the Wilson administration did not support these moves. Both organizations were sup-ported by General Leonard Wood and Theodore Roosevelt. Theodore Roosevelt was probably the most vocal critic of the president's early policies of pacification and non-preparedness. Wilson believed that enlarging and training the army and the navy could interfere with the American role as a peacemaker. By the end of 1915, however, the increasing violation of American neutral rights brought the president to ask for an increase in appropriations for the armed services and increased con-trol over the merchant marines. Citizens, he argued, not large standing armies, should be able to defend their nation. To test the country's views concerning his new stand on preparedness, the president gave a series of speeches and discovered support in most sections of the United States.

In February 1916, the Gore-McLemore Resolution, sponsored by Oklahoma Democratic Senator Thomas P. Gore and Texas Democratic Representative Jeff McLemore, however, was an attempt to embarrass the president. The resolution would have required the government to officially warn American citizens against traveling on any and all belligerent ships, including passenger liners. Many pro-gressives in Congress supported the measure because they feared that America's entrance into the war would end the progressive reforms at home, but President Wilson was finally able to get it tabled on the grounds that it would be giving in to violations of international law.

Despite the opposition of the Bryan Democrats, who came mostly from western states, Congress supported the president's new preparedness stand with the pas-sage of the National Defense Act on June 3, 1916. It provided for an increase of reg-ular army troops from 90,000 to a maximum of 223,000 men and federalization of the National Guard, with an increase up to 440,000 of those troops. Preparedness parades were held across the country. Most of the country, especially outside the West, appeared to approve. Then on August 15, 1916, Congress passed the Naval Construction Act, which appropriated close to $600 million to build at least 5 battle cruisers, together with smaller craft, in a 3-year period. Congress also passed an appropriation to establish the United States Shipping Board (on September 7), with the authority to spend up to $50 million to lease, buy, build, and operate merchant ships through an Emergency Fleet Corporation. By the time the United States did enter the Great War, the American navy was second in strength only to the British.

In 1916, President Wilson and Vice-President Thomas R. Marshall sought re-election. Relations had become increasingly strained with the more liberal progressives in the Democratic Party during 1914 and 1915, and again during the preparedness controversy of 1916, but Wilson's shift to the political left on domestic issues during 1916 enabled him to hold the party together and win renomination. (See Chapter Six for more information.)

Although Theodore Roosevelt wanted the Republican nomination, his independent run for the presidency 4 years earlier really made that impossible. His extremely pro-war rhetoric also scared many voters. When Roosevelt then declined to run as a Progressive, his former third party voted to dissolve itself. In order to attract disenchanted progressive Democrats, the Republicans nominated Charles Evans Hughes, the former progressive governor of New York, who left the United States Supreme Court to accept the nomination and run for president. (In 1930, President Herbert Hoover reappointed Hughes back to the Supreme Court.)

Important to Wilson's campaign was the theme and the slogan "He kept us out of war." Wilson knew that at any moment one incident had the capability of bringing the United States into the war, so he was uncomfortable with the campaign theme. However, that theme had evoked such a positive response at the Democratic convention that year, that Wilson was virtually forced to accept it. During the campaign, Hughes refused to repudiate Roosevelt's pro-war statements. That, along with Wilson's sudden conversion to an aggressive domestic progressive agenda, resulted in many progressive Republicans bolting their party to support Wilson. Even so, the results of the election were close. When Hughes carried most of the East and Midwest, it appeared that he had won the presidency. But returns from the South and the West gave Wilson overwhelming support, with the exception of California, which was so close it took several weeks before the results could be certified as definite. But when the final votes were counted in that state, Wilson had carried it by less than 4,000 votes, and with that margin, he was reelected. The razor-thin margin in California suggests that he may have won the state because of an incident during the campaign. Hughes inadvertantly snubbed the state's popular senator and former governor, Republican Hiram Johnson. As a result, the thin-skinned Johnson gave Hughes only lukewarm support in the election campaign.

The election was almost as close nationally as it had been in California. President Wilson won reelection with 277 electoral votes and 9.1 million popular votes, compared to 254 electoral votes and 8.5 million popular votes for Hughes. Socialist candidate A.L. Benson received about 585,000 votes and Prohibitionist J. Frank Hanly about 221,000 votes, with neither of them receiving any electoral votes.

WILSON ATTEMPTS TO NEGOTIATE PEACE

From the early stages of the war, President Wilson had attempted to negotiate acceptable terms for peace among the major belligerent powers in Europe. The only way to guarantee that the United States would not go to war was if the war were ended. During February, March, and April 1915, Colonel Edward M. House, Wilson's close friend and private adviser, visited as an unofficial and secret emissary the foreign offices on both sides in the conflict. But the talks were not successful. In January and February 1916, Colonel House was in Europe once again to determine if the Allied powers were interested in a just peace, and if they were, Wilson would call a peace conference. In Berlin, House did not find the Germans willing to work toward a proposal that would satisfy the Allies, and the French would not commit to peace proposals. But in London the reception was warm from Prime Minister Grey, and the resulting House-Grey Memorandum promised that Wilson would call a peace conference at a time decided upon by Britain and France. If the Allies agreed to this proposal and Germany did not, the United States would probably enter the war against Germany. And if Germany attended this peace conference and would not accept a reasonable proposal, the United States would probably enter the war against Germany. The peace proposals never came to fruition. Both sides continued to believe that they could prevail on the battlefield and then set their own peace terms.

President Wilson was not ready to stop his mediation efforts. On December 18, 1916, he sent notes to each belligerent government asking for their specific peace terms. The Allies wanted harsh peace terms; the Central Powers were to be blamed for the war, and they had to give up land they had conquered, along with the people they controlled against their will. Germany had spoken in favor of a negotiated peace before receiving the president's note, but now refused to state any peace terms. Wilson now appealed to the people of the warring nations, not their governments, in a message to Congress on January 22, 1917, stating his views to the world on what would constitute a good and lasting peace. A lasting peace must be "a peace without victory. . . . Victory would mean peace forced upon a loser, a victor's peace imposed upon a vanquished. . . . Only a peace between equals can last." A lasting peace must be based on governments chosen by the consent of the people, freedom of the seas, and disarmament. To prevent future wars "peace must be followed by some concert of powers. . . ." The president was establishing the idea of a league of nations after the war. Although the president made a great speech, peace negotiations did not follow.

THE UNITED STATES ENTERS THE GREAT WAR

Germany Resumes the Policy of Unnrestricted Submarine Warfare

On January 31, 1917, Ambassador Bernstorff gave Secretary of State Lansing a note that stated that after February 1 (the next day), Germany would resume its policy of unrestricted submarine warfare in a zone around Britain, France, Italy, and in the Eastern Mediterranean Sea. All ships would be sunk on sight. The United States would be permitted to send one ship, not carrying contraband, to and from Falmouth, England each week. On February 3, Wilson went before a joint session of Congress and announced that he would not accept the German proposal for the ship. He also announced the breaking of diplomatic relations with Germany and his intention to ask Congress for authority to protect American citizens if the

German authorities did carry out their threats. Specifically, the president asked Congress for the authority to arm merchant ships. The bill was defeated in the Senate due to the efforts of southern and western progressives under the leadership of Robert LaFollette. But the president was then informed that he could take this action under executive power, and he did so.

Germany took a great gamble when she broke the Sussex pledge and resumed unrestricted submarine warfare. Most German military and political leaders believed this action would bring the United States into the war. There was conflict among the German high command concerning the advisability of this move. But the admirals convinced most that unrestricted submarine warfare, which would cut off all supplies to the Allies, would bring Britain to the point of surrender before the United States could get soldiers into battle. Time was also running

World War I Campaign Poster. Credit: Library of Congress.

out for the Central Powers to win this war. The British blockade, which illegally stopped food as contraband, was killing German civilians through starvation. By the end of the war, German soldiers were down to about 1,000 calories a day, hardly sufficient for a grown man in any occupation, let alone a combat soldier during wartime. In fact, much more "credit" for Germany's eventual surrender should go to Britain's effective naval blockade than is normally given. The German resumption of its submarine policy was even more of a gamble when historical research a few decades later revealed that the German navy itself estimated it would take 221 U-boats in the North Atlantic at any given moment to make the blockade effective, and the Germans only had a maximum of 21 U-boats in the sea at one time—or only about 10 percent of its own estimate required for success.

More American Lives Lost at Sea

The occurrence of three events in early 1917 finally brought a declaration of war from the United States. Between February 3 and April 1, 8 more American ships were sunk by German U-boats in the North Atlantic. This then made a total of 209 American civilians killed by this means; of course, a majority of them, 128, had been killed in the sinking of the *Lusitania*. Twenty-eight of the American deaths occurred on American vessels, with the remaining number on board various merchant and passenger ships of Allied nations. Incidentally, Norway lost more than 3,000 civilians during the war, yet it maintained its neutrality. Of course, Norway's circumstances were quite different from the United States, the main difference being that Norway was in no position militarily to challenge Germany.

The Zimmerman Telegram

On March 1 the publication of the Zimmermann Telegram (or Note) from the German Foreign Ministry to the German minister in Mexico also hardened Americans' hearts against Germany. The coded message, sent in the middle of January, from the office of German Foreign Minister Arthur Zimmermann, was that if war should commence between the United States and Germany, the minister was to propose an alliance with Mexico. Germany would give Mexico financial support if Mexico would declare war on the United States and attempt to regain territory in New Mexico, Texas, and Arizona that was lost in the Mexican-American War in the late 1840s.

This proposal proved to be one of the most foolish actions taken by the German government, or any other, during World War I. Mexico was not about to commit national suicide by declaring war against the United States, and Germany was certainly in no position geographically or otherwise to assist her in winning back lost territories in the American West. A communications officer in the German Foreign Ministry had forgotten that the British controlled the remaining trans-Atlantic telegraph cable to the western hemisphere. Therefore, British intelligence intercepted this message and turned it over to the appropriate American authorities on February 25, 1917, when relations with Germany were very bad. In what was probably an orchestrated leak to the press, the

World War I Poster for United War Work Campaign.
Credit: Library of Congress.

news of the Zimmerman Telegram became headlines in American newspapers across the country on March 1. The president and the public were outraged at the duplicity of the Germans. Could the United States tolerate Germany activity much longer? The president was indignant that the Germans had plotted this alliance for war when they were continuing to ask him to work for peace. The whole episode was definitely counterproductive to Germany's own national interests because its major significance was to help unite more western Americans behind President Woodrow Wilson.

The Russian Czar Is Overthrown

The overthrow of Czar Nicholas II of Russia and the establishment of a constitutional provisional government in March 1917 was welcome news to the administration and the American public. The United States was the first to recognize the new regime. This event cleared away a great obstacle for Wilson in the decision to go to war. With the end of the autocratic government of Russia, this would now be a war to promote democracy against absolutism. (No one could know, but in the fall of the same year the Bolsheviks would overthrow this provisional government and establish a communist dictatorship under Vladimir Lenin.)

The Declaration of War

On April 2, President Wilson called for a special session of Congress to ask for a declaration of war against Germany and to explain why the United States must enter the war on the Allied side. Believing that Americans would not support a war because of submarine warfare or a proposed alliance between Germany and Mexico, the president had to convince the public, as he was convinced, that this was a crusade for democracy and freedom of the seas. The United States would fight for an ultimate peace and the liberation of the people of the world, including Germany, by making it a safe place for democracy. Woodrow Wilson receives high marks from most historians for his honest attempt to keep the United States out of World War I. But once the United States entered the war, he again reverted to moral and idealistic reasons for a foreign policy action. This was going to be a war to "make the world safe for democracy" and a "war to end all wars." The real reason we went to war was that the United States could not tolerate a major power's attempt to cut us off from all trade with our number one trading partner. That may not be a romantic reason, but it was based on realism. Germany's fateful decision to resume its former policy of unrestricted submarine warfare finally brought the United States into the Great War. On April 4, the Senate vote for war was 82-6. Two days later, on April 6, the House of Representatives voted for war by the margin of 373-50, and Wilson signed the declaration of war the same day. The United States entered the war as an Associate Power on the side of the Allies, and the country was mobilized for war.

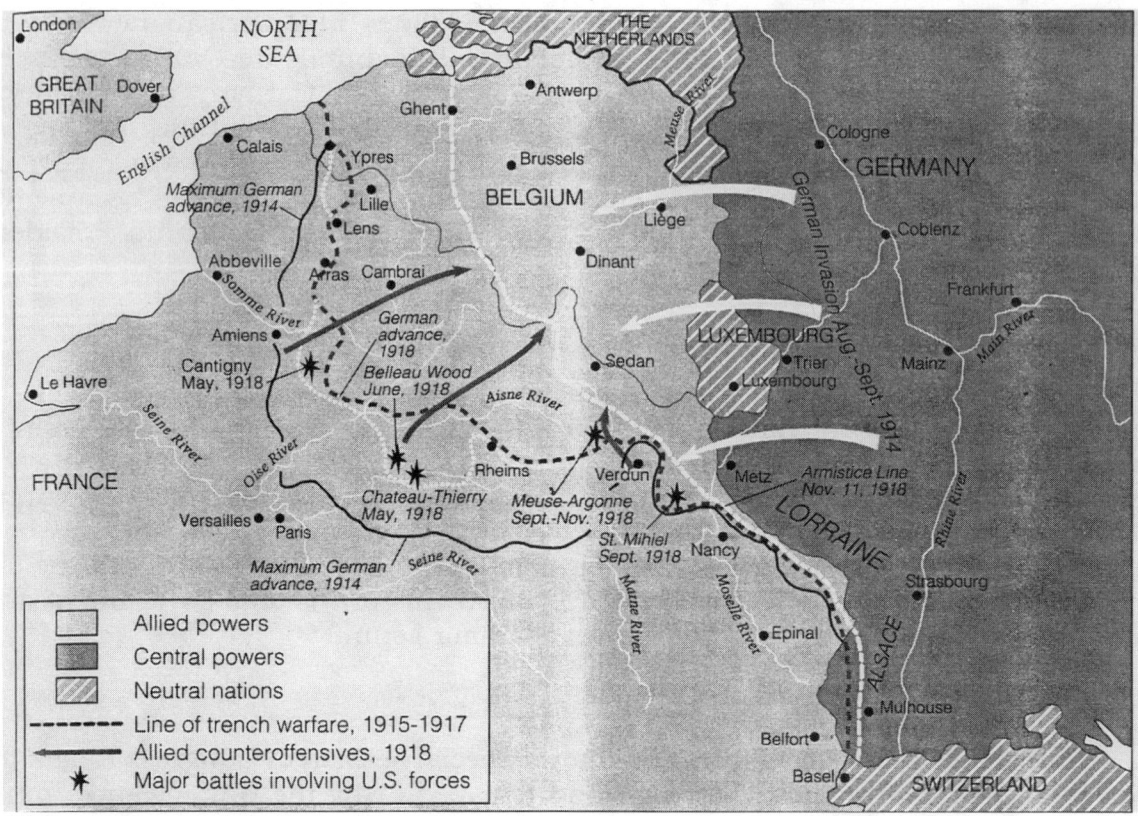

The Western Front. Credit: The United States: Brief Edition, *by Winthrop D. Jordan and Leon F. Litwack, Prentice-Hall, Inc., 1994.*

RAISING AN ARMY

The Selective Service Act was passed on May 18, 1917, requiring all men 21-30 years of age (later from 18–45) to register for the draft. This was only the second time in American history that the United States had established a military draft; the first time was during the Civil War. And there was some fear that draft riots might occur as had happened in the Civil War, but this was not the case. On June 5, over 9 million young men registered and received their serial numbers at 4,557 local draft boards. The soldiers were then called to active duty with a lottery. Secretary of War Newton D. Baker drew the first serial number from a large bowl on July 20. The registrants from each local board with that number were now in the army. Thousands also enlisted in the regular Army, the National Guard, the Navy, or the Marines. Before the declaration of war, 378,619 men were in the armed forces. The number had grown to 4,791,172 when the war ended. Draft dodging stood at about 11 percent. Two million "doughboys" eventually served in Europe. Although there are conflicting stories about the origin of that term, it certainly stuck when the French called the American soldiers by this nickname because, as the fresh, clean soldiers came into France, someone said they looked clean enough to work in a bakery.

Troops returning to New York City after World War I. Credit: Brown Brothers.

The recruits had to be transformed into soldiers. Camps had to be built quickly, and the men needed basic military training and instruction in fighting in a new type of war. Six months of training was necessary. British and French officers came to the training camps as instructors. There was a great need for officers, and special camps were set up to train those selected.

It was important to send at least a small contingent force of American soldiers to Europe as quickly as possible. The morale of the Allied soldiers on the Western Front needed a boost; French troops were deserting in increasing numbers. They had been fighting in the trenches under horrendous conditions for close to 3 syears at this time. General John J. Pershing and approximately 14,000 troops were the first of the American Expeditionary Force (the A.E.F.) to land in France. On July 4, they marched through Paris. The troops were not fully trained, so General Pershing insisted upon further training before they saw combat. A disagreement also developed between the general and other Allied military leaders. Pershing insisted that the Americans would fight together as an army, but the Allies wanted the inexperienced troops disbursed among the veteran French and British units. Pershing eventually prevailed, and American "doughboys" fought in separate American units before the end of the war. In the Spring of 1918, more than a million American soldiers were in France.

MOBILIZING THE NATION FOR WAR

The Council of National Defense, an advisory board established on August 29, 1916, was charged with coordinating industry and resources for national security. The Council consisted of the Secretaries of War, Navy, Interior, Agriculture, Commerce, and Labor. The president appointed an Advisory Commission of business experts to assist the Council, and they did so without compensation. But the Council did not have the authority it needed to carry out its decisions, so they were frequently ignored. As a result, other agencies were developed to fill the various specific needs the war demanded, and these agencies were headed by administrators with the necessary authority to have their demands met, for this was an emergency, and the government has exceptional powers in war.

The Emergency Fleet Corporation

Working under the authority of the War Shipping Board (which had been organized in January 1917), it was the job of the Emergency Fleet Corporation to increase the number of ships available for the war effort through purchases, construction, or requisitioning. When war was declared enemy owned vessels in American ports were turned over to the Shipping Board. The Emergency Fleet Corporation also confiscated ships under construction for neutral countries. Construction of a large number of ships was underway, but because of the time this took, the most effective use of the Shipping Board for about a year was coordinating the effective use of existing vessels. When production methods had been improved, the United States could replace every ship the Germans sank with two ships.

Many other agencies were put in place, but the problem was still the authority needed to carry out their purpose. On August 10, 1917, after a long debate, Congress passed the Lever Act, granting the president the power to establish controls over food, fuel, and fertilizers, along with the machinery and the equipment for producing all of the above. The president was criticized by some for having dictatorial powers, but this country was coordinated into a tremendous war machine. One of the positive aspects of Wilson's presidency was his outstanding leadership in the war.

The Food Administration

In August 1917, the Lever Food and Fuel Control Act established two new agencies, the Food Administration and the Fuel Administration. Herbert Hoover, once the Food Commissioner, now became head of the Food Administration, with legal authority to feed the nation, its soldiers at war, and its allies. The unrestricted submarine warfare policy by Germany brought about a food crisis in much of the rest of Europe. In France, Italy, and England, the survival of the people depended on American food. Hoover had been selected for this job because of his tremendous success in feeding the starving Belgians through the Belgian Relief Commission after Germany's "rape of Belgium." A priority for the Food Administration was to educate the Americans by the use of public signs and posters spread across the country. Americans were encouraged to conserve food, use their leftovers, observe wheatless Mondays and meatless Tuesdays, and plant victory gardens wherever they would grow. Even Mrs. Wilson planted a war garden of easy-to-grow vegetables at the White House. And the president brought in a flock of sheep to graze behind the home of the first family. Farmers were encouraged to plant more wheat by fixing the price at $2.20 a bushel, and a government promise to buy all that was grown. Americans were so successful in their voluntary efforts that exports more than doubled, and the country did not have to resort to formal rationing.

The Fuel Administration

The Fuel Administration was formed to conserve the nation's fuel resources of coal and oil and to stimulate production. It was headed by Harry A. Garfield, the son of the late President James Garfield. The administration fixed a high price on coal to reward the miners for greater efforts. Heatless Mondays, gasless Sundays, and daylight savings time were also part of the effort to save coal and gasoline.

The Railway Administration

When the railroads could not keep goods moving efficiently and quickly for transport to Europe, the government took over their operation in December 1917. Secretary of the Treasury William G. McAdoo, President Wilson's son-in-law, administered the Railway Administration. Surprisingly to most modern Americans, the government proved highly efficient in this endeavor by operating all of the lines as a consolidated system.

The War Industries Board

Production of war material provided a great challenge for the Council of National Defense. Confusion and shortages were caused by the separate purchasing from the various American government agencies. The purchases of the Allies only added to the problems. Therefore, the War Industries Board was established in July 1917 to set up a system of priorities for production and to fix prices on raw materials. But this was not enough to bring about the needed efficiency of production, so in January 1918, Bernard Baruch became the new chairman of the Board and was given almost dictatorial power over American industry. The Board was made an administrative agency reporting directly to the president. Soon all purchases for government bureaus and the Allies began passing through the organization. The Board planned how requests would be met and which ones took priority. Industries were told what they could or could not manufacture and what the price of their goods would be. New industrial development was promoted by the government. For example, the infant chemical industry was given a boost by this effort because the country could no longer rely on the German chemical industry.

More industrial output was needed because goods were not reaching Europe in enough quantity. So in May 1918, the Overman Act gave Wilson the authority to consolidate the agencies for more effectiveness. However, the war was over before

Women Workers in a Philadelphia War Plant During World War I. Credit: National Archives.

American-made artillery was in France. This does not negate the tremendous success of the American industrial machine, however. The Germans were in awe at the speed with which so much was manufactured and sent to the front. The nation's industrial capacity was increased by more than 20 percent by November 1918.

LABOR ON THE HOME FRONT

The war brought prosperity to the American economy, higher wages for workers, and close to full employment for all who wanted to work. Factory workers were in great demand, and large numbers of women replaced their lower paying jobs with the higher pay of a factory job. Approximately 1.5 million African-Americans had migrated from the South by 1920 for the higher pay of factory work. They did find jobs that paid more than sharecropping in the South, but they would also find racism and segregation in the North as well.

Violence broke out in the black community in East St. Louis, Illinois in July 1917. Before order was restored, 40 African-Americans and 8 whites were killed.

Sale of Liberty Bonds. Credit: International Film Service Inc.

African-Americans began to protest for the president to bring a complete democracy to the United States as well as working for the safety of democracy abroad.

Factory workers and union members wanted to share in the war effort by "doing their part." During the war most followed the "no strike" pledge of American Federation of Labor president Samuel Gompers. There were a few groups, however, including the Industrial Workers of the World, that did not follow the "no strike" promise. The National War Labor Board was established in April 1918 to assist with problems that threatened production. It consisted of 5 industry and 5 labor representatives (Gompers was one of these), and two co-chairmen, former President William H. Taft and Frank P. Walsh. Of the two, Walsh was much more sympathetic to organized labor. The board conducted hearings and made recommendations for resolving problems. It recognized union rights, the 8-hour day in some industries, and could and did fix wages. If workers or companies ignored the board, the president could coerce acceptance by simply revoking draft deferments.

FINANCING THE WAR

The United States' cost for the Great War included about $22 billion in direct wartime expenses and about $9 billion in loans to the Allies, or a total of approximately $31 billion. About one-third of the war was paid for with taxes and two-thirds from the sale of Liberty Bonds. Income, inheritance, corporation, and excess profits taxes were increased. New taxes were placed on practically everything else, including transportation, entertainment, insurance, medicine, and jewelry. Most Americans were hit the hardest through these excise taxes, but with the increased support for the war effort and increased prosperity from the war, there was little protest against the tax increases.

There were 4 successful bond drives during the war entitled Liberty Loans and one in May 1919 entitled a Victory Loan. All Americans were encouraged to be a patriot and buy a bond. Hollywood star Mary Pickford gave her support and face to the bond drive. Even children were part of the drive for financial support. They purchased 25 cent "thrift stamps" that could be converted into interest-bearing savings certificates when the proper dollar amount was reached. The annual budget before the war was approximately $750 million; for 1917 and 1918 it stood at $12 billion, representing a 16 times increase.

PROPAGANDA AND PUBLIC OPINION

The Committee on Public Information was created in April 1917. The journalist George Creel was the head of the commission, which was often referred to as the Creel Commission. The agency became a liaison between reporters and the government. Creel did not want to use censorship and hoped that the press would not publish anything that might help the enemy. Creel believed strongly in the ideals of President Wilson, and a major part of his job was to sell those ideals of war to advance a democratic, peaceful world. The commission used patriotic posters, novelists, musicians, speakers (known as "Four Minute Men" because of their short speeches), actors, and motion picture directors to coordinate not only American approval but American enthusiasm for the war. His efforts also sold Liberty Bonds almost as fast as they were issued and urged conservation of food and fuel for the war effort.

Creel also tried to mold the opinions of the German soldiers on the front. Pamphlets were printed in German and dropped from the air to impress the troops with the strength of the American forces and the futility of the fight.

Creel distorted his facts at times and made enemies in Congress, but his accomplishments in mobilizing public opinion for the war were remarkable. A negative aspect of his campaign for the minds of Americans was the development of hostility in some Americans for all things German in America. The Democratic governor of Ohio, James Cox (who became a candidate for president in 1920), persuaded his state to ban the teaching of the German language in the public schools. Other states and localities did the same. German-owned stores were boycotted or attacked. German children were taunted or beaten in school, and many German-Americans changed their names to hide their German heritage; Schmidt became

Smith, for example. And German measles became "liberty measles" and sauerkraut "liberty cabbage."

Not all Americans were won over by Creel's propaganda campaign. There were those who opposed American intervention in the war before it occurred and remained committed to that opposition throughout the war. There were men who registered as conscientious objectors. Some were drafted, but most were assigned to non-combat duties. The Woman's Peace Party was founded in 1915 by Jane Addams, Carrie Chapman Catt, and others. It broke apart, partly because Catt switched to support the war once the United States had entered it in 1917, but Addams stayed an opponent to the war for the duration. Others also kept their anti-war stand, some for religious reasons, like the Quakers or Mennonites, and some for political reasons, like the socialists. Socialists believed that the war was a conflict between capitalists for markets, and therefore not worthy of the support of workers and the masses. For the most part, however, America supported the war effort wholeheartedly.

THE ESPIONAGE AND SEDITION ACTS

Americans became increasingly intolerant of any form of disloyalty to the war and overly concerned with the threat of spy activity. Within this climate, President Wilson proposed that disloyalty should be dealt with in a stern manner. Congress enacted drastic measures to enforce the president's proposal, and the justice system backed both. The Espionage Act passed on June 15, 1917. The law provided for a fine of up to $10,000 and a maximum 20-year prison term for anyone convicted of spying, sabotage, or interfering with the draft or encouraging disloyalty. The Sedition Act, passed on May 16, 1918, provided the same penalty to anyone who obstructed the sale of Liberty Bonds, incited insubordination, discouraged recruiting efforts, verbally or in writing made false statements or used profane language against the government, the Constitution, the flag, or the uniform of the soldiers, or interfered with the production of war goods.

The Sedition Act was mainly enforced against pacifists, socialists, and other radicals opposed to the war, including Victor Berger, a Socialist congressman from Milwaukee, Wisconsin, and the famous Eugene V. Debs, who was pardoned by President Harding in December 1921. German newspapers written by German-Americans in the United States were unconstitutionally weeded out of the mails. The United States Supreme Court, in Schenck v. United States (1919), unanimously upheld the constitutionality of the Sedition Act on the grounds that a "clear and present danger" to national security could make circumvention of the First Amendment necessary. This was a new doctrine in American judicial history, written by Justice Oliver Wendell Holmes, who wrote that no one had the right to scream "Fire!" in a crowded theater. Civil libertarians disagreed that most of those prosecuted under the Sedition Act were guilty of doing that and thereby placing any lives in jeopardy. But, under the normally sound system of judicial review, the Constitution of the United States means what the Supreme Court says it means at any given moment.

A total of 2,168 Americans were actually prosecuted under the law. Of that number, 1,055 were convicted, although only 10 for actual sabotage or spying. That means that 1,045 American citizens became federal convicts primarily because of their political views. Unfortunately, that was not the first or the last time this ever happened in American history. In times of actual or perceived crisis, when the great majority of Americans are very emotionally worked up about an issue, a minority is vulnerable to persecution. On balance, however, compared to other nations, the United States' record on civil liberties is undoubtedly the best in world history.

FIGHTING THE WAR

The Role of the Navy

The United States navy was prepared for action by the time the country entered the war, and within a month American ships were reinforcing the British on the seas. Americans contributed to the anti-submarine warfare through the placement of new anti-submarine mines from the Orkneys to the North Sea (these may have sunk up to 10 percent of the German U-boats) and spotting and destroying U-boats from the air or from the sea with destroyers or Allied submarines. About one-half of the German submarines had been destroyed by the end of the war. The first priority for the American navy was to insure that American troops and supplies reached Europe safely. Although a large percentage of the transport ships were provided by the British, the American navy provided more than 80 percent of the protective cruisers in the convoys organized to protect the transport ships in their Atlantic crossing. Admiral William S. Sims received the credit for getting the British to use the convoy system, which cut tonnage losses from German submarines in half or more. American troops were transported to Europe as quickly as possible, and by the end of 1917 there were approximately 200,000 in France.

African-Americans and Women in the War

It was not only young white males that made up the American Expeditionary Force in Europe. Approximately 260,000 African-Americans volunteered or were drafted, and about 50,000 from this group went to France along with more than 25,000 women. Only a few hundred of the women were in the Army. The African-American soldiers were segregated and usually served in support functions, but there was one all-black division, the ninety-second. Four African-American infantry regiments served under the command of French officers. The experiences of the African-American soldiers in France led to the belief for many that the racism that existed in America before the war could be broken down now that both races had fought for their country. They would discover all too quickly on their return home, however, that they were wrong.

American women served in Europe as nurses with the Red Cross and the armed services hospitals. They were employed by the YWCA, YMCA, and the Salvation Army to cross the Atlantic and help make the soldiers' lives a little more pleasant. Entertainers were also employed for the soldiers. The Signal Corps had female operators, and the Quartermaster Corps had female clerks.

Communist Russia Bows Out and the Allies Intervene

The entrance of America into the war came at a crucial time. In November 1917, the Russian provisional government was overthrown by the Bolsheviks led by Vladimir I. Lenin. The Russian people had suffered greatly during the war. Hunger, insufficient fuel, political chaos, economic problems, and despair over the loss of so many of its sons, opened the door to the communist revolution. Lenin pulled his country out of a war that he believed had been fought for the good of the capitalists and imperialists, not the people who were being sacrificed to fight the battles. Russia and Germany began negotiating the Treaty of Brest-Litovsk in December 1917, and it was signed on March 3, 1918. Germany could now concentrate most of its efforts on the Western Front and the incoming American soldiers.

The Bolshevik Revolution resulted in a period of fighting between anti-communist "White" Russian armies and the "Red" armies of the communists. In an attempt both to protect Allied supplies inside Russia from falling into German hands and support the "White" Russian armies, 14 Allied nations sent forces into Russia through her northern ports. On August 2, 1918, the first American troops arrived in the north, soon followed by more in eastern Siberia. Totalling about 8,000 Americans, these troops remained in Russia until April 1920. The Allied intervention in Russia was a failure as the "White" Russians were eventually defeated. But the Allied intervention there did awaken great hostility toward the West among the Soviet communists. For this reason, some diplomatic historians trace the origins of the later Cold War to this incident.

The 1918 German Offensives Collapse and the Armistice Is Signed

The Germans launched a new spring offensive in March 1918. The Germans now had a numerical advantage on the Western Front, and it had to be used before the Americans could make a difference. The German Commander-in-Chief, General Erich von Ludendorff, had to find new tactics to break the deadlock in the trenches. Instead of a prolonged artillery barrage before the soldiers came out of the trenches to attack, the range of the big guns was determined before they were brought into place. The guns would launch a short but massive bombardment to open up a pathway for newly trained squads of stormtroopers. The infantry would then attack, followed by airplanes that flew in to bomb points of resistance. The Germans had great success in driving back the French and British in the area of the Somme River, breaking through the lines. The drive slowed, however, because of the lack of tanks and transportation, German soldiers stopping to eat whatever they could, and fierce resistance by the British and French. The British and French were using tanks more effectively by 1918. The Germans regretted that they had been so slow to recognize the potential of this new weapon.

Another contributing factor to the success of the German offensive was the Allies' lack of a unified command. On April 14, 1918, the French General, Ferdinand Foch was given overall command of all Allied forces. The Allied armies were threatened by the German advance to separate the French and British armies at Amiens in northwestern France. General Pershing offered American forces to be used wherever needed, but still reminded General Foch that American forces must be grouped into a separate fighting unit. In April, the second German offensive pushed the British back once again. The third offensive in May pushed the French armies back so that Paris was threatened once again. The Americans of the First Division were brought up to repulse the German drive on Montdidier and then assisted in the counterattack for the heights of Cantigny. And the marines were sent to stop the Germans at Chateau-Thierry. On June 5, the American Second Division took the offensive at Belleau Wood, and for three weeks the fighting raged. The fresh young troops were a marvel to behold as they marched toward Belleau Wood, whistling and singing as they advanced. Most were new and inexperienced, but war quickly made veterans of the green soldiers. When they arrived they found no line, only French troops retreating. The Americans formed the line as they marched toward the German machine guns without artillery support or tanks. They finally took the woods, but the price was more than 5,000 out of 8,000 troops killed or wounded. This strategy was later criticized for sending the troops into those battle conditions unsupported. At the time, however, Americans saw it as a test of their mettle and a critical time to stop the Germans. In the future, battle action was planned more carefully. The war was lost for Germany by July after the fourth offensive failed. The fighting continued, but the American forces were too numerous at this time to overcome.

On August 10 the Allied command gave Pershing his separate army. The first task was to straighten out the St. Mihiel salient, which was accomplished in two days. The Americans wanted to press their advantage at this point, but General Foch was preparing for an Allied offensive from Ypres to Verdun. The offensive was to begin on September 25, and the American army's sector was between the Meuse River and the Argonne Woods, a southern sector. The Battle of the Meuse-Argonne lasted for 40 days with more than 1.2 million American soldiers involved. The offensive was a great success; up and down the lines the Germans faced defeat. General Ludendorff informed his government that his men could not hold out, and terms for an armistice should be discussed immediately. The Germans, hoping to court President Wilson as an advocate for a generous peace based on his Fourteen Points, established a parliamentary system of government with Prince Max of Baden forming a liberal group of leaders for the nation. The Kaiser was forced to abdicate his throne. On November 9, he fled to Holland. On November 11, 1918, at the eleventh hour the guns fell silent. America did not win the war for the Allies as many have claimed, but they won the war with the Allies.

MAKING PEACE

In late 1917, President Wilson could not persuade the Allied leaders to state their war aims, so he had taken the task upon himself to draw up his plan for peace. The president asked the advice of very few people when formulating his plan. He did, however, accept the counsel of a group of college professors and experts in the fields of history, geography, and economics, known as the Inquiry. The release of documents by the new Soviet government showing that secret treaties had been made among the Allies for territorial gain at the end of the war made it imperative for the president to state the ideals and aims of the Allies in the war. Italy, Romania, and Greece had been offered territory from the Austria-Hungarian Empire to join the Allies. From the time of his request for a declaration of war, Wilson had stated he did not want territory. He could not now allow his idealistic goals for this war to become tarnished. Therefore, he went before Congress on January 8, 1918, and announced to the world the Fourteen Points for peace in Europe.

Wilson's Fourteen Points was a classical statement of nineteenth century liberalism, as far as international diplomacy was concerned. The most important points, as far as Wilson's philosophy for peace in the future, were: (1) open covenants of peace openly arrived at; (2) freedom of the seas; (3) removal of many trade barriers; (4) reduction of armaments; (5) fair adjustment of colonial claims; and (14) a League of Nations to resolve future conflicts. Article X of the League charter, which was written later, was based on the concept of "collective security"— that an attack on one member-nation would be considered an attack on all, in which case the League Council shall "advise," not coerce, other member-nations how to respond. The other points dealt with the return of conquered territory, forming new nations from the empires, and self-determination for these new countries.

Historically, the British had resisted the idea of the freedom of the seas because that would jeopardize their dominance on the water. France did not agree at first to a peace based on the Fourteen Points, and they did not like the fact that Wilson was negotiating without them. When Colonel House finally threatened a separate peace with the Central Powers, the other Allies capitulated to the Fourteen Points with two exceptions—freedom of the seas would be discussed further, and reparations would be paid by Germany.

THE PARIS PEACE CONFERENCE

Separate meetings in and around Paris took place between the Allies and each Central Power except Germany to construct the formal terms of the peace treaties with them. (Austria-Hungary, Turkey, and Bulgaria) The conference to determine the conditions of peace with Germany were by far the most important. Beginning on January 18, 1919, leaders of the Big Four nations and delegates from the other Allies met at the Palace of Versailles, outside of Paris, to negotiate the treaty for Germany. Originally, 27 nations were represented, but this was found to be too many to deal efficiently with business. So the number was initially reduced to 10 and then 4. Ironically, Germany and several of the Allies, including the Russians, had been excluded from the negotiations from the very beginning. The Big Four consisted of the United States, represented by President Woodrow Wilson; Great Britain, represented by Prime Minister David Lloyd George; France, represented by Premier Georges Clemenceau; and Italy, represented by Premier Vittorio Orlando. Orlando left the conference early when he determined that Italy was not going to receive as much territory as it wanted from Austria-Hungary. That left the Big Three to essentially dictate the terms of the treaty.

"The Big Four" Woodrow Wilson, David Lloyd George, Clemenceau, and Orlando. Credit: AP/Wide World Photos.

When Wilson arrived in Paris in December 1918 and became the first American president to visit Europe while still in office, he was cheered by huge, enthusiastic crowds. The same thing occurred in London and other major cities in Europe during the peace talks, as the people of Europe showered their symbol of idealism with accolades. His position as the leader of the most powerful nation in the world and his popularity with the people of Europe allowed him to influence the negotiations to the extent that he did, but not to the extent he would have liked. Britain and France wanted revenge with a harsh treaty and heavy reparations to pay for the damages and costs they had sustained. Clemenceau had reportedly declared that "God gave us the Ten Commandments and we broke them. Wilson gave us the Fourteen Points—we shall see." Wilson had to compromise repeatedly at Versailles in order to secure his precious League of Nations. He believed the harshness of the treaty that evolved could be worked out later by the League. This was naive, however, because the very same leaders who dominated the peace conference would dominate the future League of Nations.

Wilson made some serious mistakes in his decisions concerning the Paris Peace Conference. He should not have left the country for so long, losing touch with

President Wilson in Paris, 1918. Photo credit: National Archives.

his supporters and not answering his critics. A hostile Paris was a poor choice for the Peace Conference because French Premier Clemenceau was especially bitter toward the Germans. Neutral Switzerland had been discussed, and Wilson should have stayed with this choice. His choice of peace commissioners was another mistake. Henry White, a retired diplomat with no political importance, was the only Republican. It would have been politically wiser if Wilson had chosen more influential Republicans because he had to get any treaty ratified by a Republican dominated Senate. Compounding his problems was the fact that Republicans had won majorities in both houses of Congress in the November elections that year. This was not a vote of confidence for the Democratic president.

THE TREATY OF VERSAILLES

On June 28, 1919, the completed Treaty of Versailles was signed in Versailles' famous Hall of Mirrors. This was not the negotiated, just peace among equals that Wilson had hoped for. The Germans disagreed with much of the treaty but had to sign or face further consequences. The following were the major provisions of the Versailles Treaty:

(1) The Rhineland, the area of Germany west of the Rhine River, was demilitarized as a buffer zone between Germany and France.

Signing of the Peace Treaty in the Hall of Mirrors at Versailles. Copyright: Trustees of the Imperial War Museum.

(2) France regained Alsace-Lorraine, an iron rich area that had been taken by Germany in the Franco-Prussian War during the late 1860s.

(3) The coal-rich Saar valley would be placed under a mandate of the League of Nations for 15 years. At that time, a plebescite (popular vote of the region's inhabitants) would then determine whether the Saar would become part of Germany or France. (The plebescite conducted in 1934 resulted in an overwhelming vote to keep the Saar region in German hands.)

(4) A free, independent Poland was created with a Baltic Corridor cut out of German territory in order to give it access to the Baltic Sea.

(5) The new nations of Czechoslovakia and Yugoslavia were created out of the former Austria-Hungary Empire, which was dissolved.

(6) Article 231, the "war guilt clause," placed the blame entirely upon Germany for beginning the Great War. Historians would later accept that France, Russia, Britain, and Austria-Hungary should have equally shared this blame. This formed the "justification" for the reparations that France and Britain later forced upon Germany.

(7) A League of Nations was created for the collective security of nations, but the United States, in spite of Wilson's determined efforts, would not join.

(8) Germany lost all its overseas colonies, and most were placed under a mandate of the Allied nations.

(9) Limits were placed on the size of the German army and on the type and number of weapons the country could manufacture.

In total, the Versailles Treaty stripped Germany of approximately 10 percent of her population (about 6 million people) and one-eighth of her industrial capacity with the territorial adjustments. War reparations were later set at $33 billion, of which Germany only paid about $9 billion. Britain and France wanted repayment for their losses in the war and to make sure that German strength was destroyed to the point that they would not feel threatened again by this once powerful nation. Instead, however, the harsh and humiliating Treaty of Versailles, along with the Great Depression of the 1930s, would set the stage for Adolf Hitler's rise to power and Germany's revenge in what history would call World War II.

THE TREATY FIGHT IN THE UNITED STATES SENATE

The Divided Senate

The treaty was proposed to the United States Senate for ratification on July 10, 1919. Various groups in that body immediately began to attack one or more aspect of the Versailles Treaty. And when the final vote eventually came in March 1920, the treaty still fell short of the necessary two-thirds vote for ratification.

Four groups in the Senate held different views on the treaty. The "Irreconcilables," led by William Borah of Idaho, Hiram Johnson of California, and Robert M. LaFollette of Wisconsin, were traditional isolationists who opposed the treaty in any form because of the League of Nations. However, this group was probably the smallest faction in the Senate, with about 12–14 senators being so classified. The "Strong Reservationists" were led by Theodore Roosevelt outside the Senate and Henry Cabot Lodge in the Senate. Lodge was the chairman of the powerful Senate Foreign Relations Committee, whose committee had jurisdiction over the treaty. The senators in this group, which numbered about 20, wanted major amendments to the treaty. Most of them were petty amendments, but the major sticky point with the "Strong Reservationists" was the League of Nations. They argued that the League charter (especially Article X) would probably require the use of American forces somewhere in the world in the future, and the United States would lose its sovereignty in foreign affairs. Actually, the League charter called only for the League Council to "advise," and most historians today dispute the objections of Lodge and his followers. The "Mild Reservationists" consisted mostly of internationalist-minded Republicans who wanted only minor amendments; they numbered somewhere just more than a dozen senators. And the last group, the docile Democrats, went along with the president but had no effective leaders in the Senate.

Senator Lodge, as chairman of the Senate Foreign Relations Committee, held public hearings on the Versailles Treaty in 1919. In that process, he used several delaying tactics, including calling a very long list of negative witnesses. When the treaty got to the Senate floor, Lodge insisted that the entire text of the treaty be publicly read word for word. In short, Lodge played an obstructionist role all the way, refusing to compromise with the president.

Wilson's Western Tour

President Wilson, for his part, also refused to compromise, believing he had done enough of that at Versailles. The president grew irritated with Lodge over the matter and at various times called him and his colleagues names. It didn't help that the two men had hated each other for a long time. At one point, Wilson even referred to the "Mild Reservationists" as "men of bungalow minds," a foolish remark since he needed their support to get the treaty ratified. After alienating so many senators, President Wilson appealed directly to the American people on a tour of the West to promote the treaty, beginning on September 3. But after the president left a city, opponents of the treaty would hold a public rally there, following the president everywhere he went and having the last word. At Pueblo, Colorado, on September 25, the exhausted president could not physically complete his speech. His doctor promptly cancelled the remaining portion of the tour. The president suffered a severe stroke on October 2, which left him paralyzed on the left side for the rest of his life.

Despite a partial recovery, Wilson stewed in the White House, becoming cantankerous. During the next few months, he had a falling out with close friend and advisor Colonel Edward House and fired Secretary of State Robert Lansing, accusing the latter of disloyalty. His personal physician, Dr. Cary Grayson, advised the president in January 1920 to resign his office, but Wilson refused. Meanwhile the First Lady, Edith Galt Wilson (his second wife, whom he married in December 1915), kept a close and overly protective eye on the president. With help from Dr. Grayson, she tried to keep his true physical condition a secret. And she jealously guarded his time, even refusing to allow Vice-President Marshall to see him. Her actions alarmed political figures in both parties, but on one occasion, in response to criticism, Mrs. Wilson retorted: "I am not thinking of the country now, I am thinking of my husband." Much later, the Twenty-fifth Amendment to the Constitution (ratified in February 1967) established procedures which provided for the orderly transfer of power to the vice-president in the event that the president is incapacitated for any reason.

The Senate Votes to Defeat the Treaty of Versailles

In this climate of personality conflicts and a physically impaired president, the Treaty of Versailles had to fight its way in the United States Senate. On November 19, 1919, the Democrats and the "Irreconcilables" combined to defeat the treaty with several Lodge reservations attached. The vote was 39 for the treaty and 55 against. Shortly after that, a vote on the treaty with no reservations allowed the "Irreconcilables" and many of both stripes of "Reservationists" to team up and defeat it by a vote of 38 for the treaty and 53 against it.

Support for the treaty among the general public forced a final vote on March 19, 1920, although the president still had refused to compromise. Urging defeat of the treaty with these amendments, the president got his wish. Twenty-one Democrats, however, voted for the treaty along with most of the "Reservationists," but the 49 yeas and the 35 nays still left it 7 votes short of the required two-thirds majority for ratification. The irony is that about 80 percent of the senators had voted for the treaty in one form or another, and yet the failure of leadership on both sides resulted in the United States never ratifying the Treaty of Versailles or joining the League of Nations. Both Senator Lodge and President Wilson must take the lion's share of the blame for this fiasco. But since the president of the United States is **the leader** of the nation, then President Woodrow Wilson probably was more responsible than anyone else for the defeat of the Treaty of Versailles.

On May 20, 1920, when Congress passed a joint resolution declaring the war over, President Wilson vetoed it. It wasn't until after Wilson had left the White House, on July 2, 1921, that Congress passed another joint resolution declaring the war against Germany and Austria-Hungary over, and President Warren G. Harding gladly signed it. Separate peace treaties with Germany, Austria, and Hungary (the latter two nations were split up by the Versailles Treaty) were ratified on October 18, 1921. And the Great War for the United States officially came to an end.

THE RESULTS OF THE WAR

Casualty figures for World War I are not accurate, but it appears that probably 10 million men died as a result of battles. Russia clearly lost the greatest number, suffering somewhere between 1.7 million and more than 2 million casualties. Germany lost nearly as many as Russia did, probably between 1.6 and 2 million men. The French, British, and Austria-Hungarians each lost about one million servicemen. The Italians suffered between 500,000 and 600,000 casulties, and the United States lost only a little more than 50,000 from battle, although another 60,000 or so died from flu or pneumonia. The world was in shock at the extent of the destruction man was now able to commit. American servicemen returning from the war brought the Spanish Flu with them. The flu killed more than 500,000 Americans and more than 22 million people around the world in 1918 and 1919. It is therefore estimated that perhaps the Great War, directly and indirectly, killed as many as 20 million people worldwide.

The map of Europe was redrawn, and independent nations were carved out of the empires of Germany, Austria-Hungary, and Russia. They were Austria, Hungary, Yugoslavia, Czechoslovakia, Poland, Finland, Estonia, Latvia, and Lithuania. Germany and Russia emerged with new systems of government—a representative democracy in Germany and communism in Russia. The world changed rapidly and drastically because of the war. The United States attempted to retreat into its historical policy of isolationism with regard to Europe. But the worldwide developments did not permit a return to a strict isolationist foreign policy.

ADDITIONAL READINGS

Edward M. Coffman, *The War to End All Wars* (1968). A solid overview of the U.S. military during the war.

Robert H. Ferrell, *Woodrow Wilson and World War I* (1985). A close analysis of Wilson's handling of wartime diplomacy and domestic politics.

Maurine Greenwald, *Women War and Work* (1980). The best account of the impact of the war upon working women.

Ellis W. Hawley, *The Great War and the Search for Modern Order* (1979). An important study arguing that World War I was a turning point in the evolution of the managerial institutions and values of modern capitalism.

Friedrich Katz, *The Secret War in Mexico* (1981). A detailed study of the complex relations among the U.S., the European powers, and the Mexican Revolution.

David M. Kennedy, *Over Here: The First World War and American Society* (1980). The best, most comprehensive one-volume analysis of the political and economic impact of the war on the domestic front.

Walter LaFeber, *The American Age* (1989). A fine survey of the history of U.S. foreign policy that includes a good analysis of the pre-World War I era.

N. Gordon Levin, Jr., *Woodrow Wilson and World Politics* (1968). A pathbreaking study of Wilson's response to the Russian Revolution and his role at Versailles.

C. Roland Marchand, *The American Peace and Social Reform, 1898–1918* (1973). A very useful overview of antiwar activists and their connection with prewar reform movements.

Sally M. Miller, *Victor Berger and the Promises of Constructive Socialism* (1973). Includes a detailed account of Berger's fight against the Espionage Act.

Paul L. Murphy, *World War I and the Origin of Civil Liberties* (1979). A good overview of the various civil liberties issues raised by the war and government efforts to suppress dissent.

Joe William Trotter, Jr., ed., *The Great Migration in Historical Perspective* (1991). An excellent collection of essays analyzing the Great Migration, with special attention to issues of class and gender within the African American community.

Neil A. Wynn, *From Progressivism to Prosperity: World War I and American Society* (1986). An illuminating account of the social impact of the war on American life. Effectively connects the war experience both with Progressive era trends and with postwar developments in the 1920s.

CHAPTER NINE

The Roaring Twenties to the Great Depression

MAJOR EVENTS

1919   Race riot in Chicago
Steel strike begins
Red Scare and Palmer raids begin

1920   Prohibition takes effect
Warren Harding elected president
Station KDKA in Pittsburgh goes on the air
Census reports that urban population is greater than rural population
for first time

1921   First immigration quotas established by Congress
Sheppard-Towner Act

1923   Equal Rights Amendment introduced to Congress
Harding dies in office; Calvin Coolidge becomes president

1924   Johnson-Reed Immigration Act tightens quotas established in 1921

1925   Ku Klux Klan at height of its influence
Scopes trial
F. Scott Fitzgerald, *The Great Gatsby*

1926   National Broadcasting Company establishes first national radio network

1927   Warner Brothers produces *The Jazz Singer,* first feature-length motion
picture with sound
Charles Lindbergh makes first solo flight across Atlantic

1928   Herbert Hoover defeats Al Smith for the presidency

1929   Stock market crash

1930   Democrats regain control of House of Representatives

1932   Reconstruction Finance Corporation established
Bonus Army marches on Washington
Franklin D. Roosevelt elected president

THE SOCIAL EFFECTS OF WORLD WAR I

World War I, like a powerful earthquake, sent a number of aftershocks throughout American society in the years to follow. Major changes resulted in the way Americans thought and lived. Although a few of these changes proved temporary, most have left their imprint on a society which has not been the same since.

Effects on Women

American women in urban areas were needed in the war production factories because a significant number of working-age men were drafted into military service. Unlike African-Americans, women were given great credit after the war for having made a major contribution to the Allied victory. The key result was the ratification of the Nineteenth Amendment to the Constitution, granting women the right to vote nationwide. The women's suffrage amendment was officially proposed by a vote of Congress in June 1919, and was ratified in August 1920, just in time for the presidential election that November. Despite increased recognition and the right to vote, many women returned to their families as fulltime homemakers following the war. Some, however, found jobs in the growing service industries, especially in retail sales and in public education.

The Black "Exodus"

African-Americans left the South in the largest exodus to date in order to find work in the Northern factories producing war materials. As was typical, however, they tended to be the last hired and the first to be fired. Therefore, many of them lost their jobs after the war. This black migration to the North, in turn, gave rise to increased racial tensions in that region during the 1920s, as Northern whites took their "opportunity" to prove that they were just as racist as Southerners. This story will be briefly told later in this chapter.

Urban Expansion

The end of the frontier in 1890, the growing industrial and service economy, and the 26 million new immigrants which had come since 1870 all had contributed to a population shift from rural to urban areas. The attraction of wartime jobs during the Great War provided an additional boost to urban expansion. The 1920 census revealed that, for the first time in history, a majority of Americans lived in towns or cities with populations greater than 2,500 persons. This population shift produced a clash of values between those new urban arrivals, who brought their rural values with them, and those multi-generation urban dwellers. Rising friction over such issues as prohibition, entertainment, and sexual mores dominated the rural-urban debate over values during the twenties.

"The Government" Becomes Washington, D.C.

The role of the federal government increased during the Great War. Most of this increase was due to various wartime controls on the economy. The activities of the

War Industries Board, Food Administration, United States Railway Administration, and the National War Labor Board all focused citizens' attentions to the federal government. Even though the wartime controls these agencies administered did fade away after the war, "government" in the minds of most Americans became almost a synonym for Washington, D.C.

Although the word "government" now meant Washington, that did not mean that Americans looked upon government involvement in the economy in a favorable light. Indeed, most Americans had had enough government during the war, with its wartime controls, and this added to the effect of setting back the Progressive movement, which worked for more government involvement, not less. It would be too strong to assert that the war had killed progressivism itself. However, it did end the political domination of progressivism in the country. In other words, the war killed the Progressive Era but not progressivism altogether. There were several notable progressives still active in Congress during the 1920s, such as Robert M. LaFollette of Wisconsin and George W. Norris of Nebraska. But their influence was not what it had been before the war.

Pessimism and Disillusionment

In some ways, perhaps the greatest social effect of World War I on American society was great pessimism and disillusionment. Europeans experienced the same phenomenon. The war had been touted as "the war to end all wars" by President Woodrow Wilson. When the president had outlined his peace aims in his famous Fourteen Points, even Europeans had received them with much enthusiasm. But just months after the armistice was signed, it was all too clear that this war had not been a "war to end all wars" or a "war to make the world safe for democracy." Russia's fall to a communist revolution in the fall of 1917, and its subsequent withdrawal from the war represented a new potential threat to world peace and security. And the Versaille Treaty's punitive measures against Germany, officially blaming her for the entire war and stripping her of much territory, industry, and population, led some intellectuals to believe that the Germans would seek revenge in another world war. The new nations created out of the wake of the old Austria-Hungary Empire seemed fraught with explosive dangers among their differing ethnic and religious heritages. In short, the war had really settled nothing; it seemed that nearly 7 million men had died for no glorious cause.

Rural-Urban Values Clash

Not all Americans shared in this new morality (see Chapter Five), but it certainly intensified the clash of values between rural and urban Americans. It also had profound effects on the literature, music, prohibition attitudes, and sexual mores of the decade that became known as the Jazz Age. Everything, including the politics of the period, can be fully understood and appreciated only by an understanding of the major social effects of World War I.

LITERATURE

H.L. Mencken

Nowhere was the new despair better illustrated than in the literature of the decade following the Great War. A new crop of writers exploded onto the scene to spew forth their cynicism and mockery of traditional values. Henry L. Mencken, the "Bad Boy of Baltimore," used his magazine, *The American Mercury*, to poke fun at nearly every old American value, including patriotism, democracy, and the middle class itself. He accused Americans with traditional values of being Puritans and incorrectly asserted that "Puritans" couldn't stand to see anyone happy. Having founded the magazine in 1924, it quickly became the "Bible" of the decade's intellectuals.

Ernest Hemingway

Perhaps Ernest Hemingway was more affected by the Great War than other authors. Hemingway had actually served as a Red Cross volunteer in Italy during the war. In 1921, while in his early twenties, Hemingway made Paris, France his home. There he caroused with many other intellectuals who were attracted to Paris after the war. In 1926, in *The Sun Also Rises*, Hemingway described disillusioned young people, whose lives had been devastated by the war, wandering aimlessly around Spain. Then in 1929, Hemingway finished *A Farewell to Arms*. Based partly on his own wartime experiences, this novel clearly depicted the futility of the Great War. Hemingway remained very troubled for the rest of his life, which he ended with a shotgun in 1961.

F. Scott Fitzgerald

Then, of course, there was the "Laureate" of the Jazz Age, F. Scott Fitzgerald. After failing a chemistry class at Princeton, Fitzgerald set out on a writing career that eventually took him to New York, Paris, and the Mediterranean. His first novel, *This Side of Paradise*, was published in 1920, when Fitzgerald was only 24 years old. It described the affluent young people of the postwar era. Perhaps his best novel, *The Great Gatsby*, was published in 1925, as a satire on materialistic middle class values. Fitzgerald not only wrote about the Jazz Age; in many ways, he and his wife Zelda personified it.

Lewis, Faulkner, and Eliot

Sinclair Lewis was not a new author, of course, but he did make his contribution to the period. In 1922, in his most famous novel, *Babbitt*, Lewis employed sarcasm against middle class values. In the book, a prosperous, real estate agent named George F. Babbitt was portrayed as being enslaved to his materialism. There was also William Faulkner, a Mississippian who created a fictional story of people in a Southern county in his 1929 novel, *The Sound and the Fury*. Even poetry did not escape the despair of the times. T.S. Eliot, who moved to England and wrote

"The Waste Land" in 1922, probably best captured the sense of a shattered civilization.

PRINT MEDIA, RADIO, SPORTS, AND DRAMA

Newspapers

The newspaper remained the most popular reading material in the decades between the world wars. But competition declined in most cities and towns with populations below 100,000, with only about 20 percent of them having more than one newspaper. In the very large cities, the tabloid newspaper became a popular way of digesting the news on the way to and from work. The *New York Daily News* became the first of these tabloids in 1919, and its style of boiling down the news in easy-to-read paragraphs that didn't require confusing turning of pages really caught on.

Magazines

Among magazine readers, there was more to choose from there too. Mr. and Mrs. DeWitt Wallace began *The Reader's Digest* in 1921, mostly as a collection of important magazine articles which had originally appeared elsewhere. Henry Luce began *Time* magazine in 1923 (and *Life* in 1936). And the Book-of-the-Month Club was organized in 1924.

The Rise of Radio

Ever since the Italian inventor, Guglielmo Marconi, had invented the wireless telegraph in the 1890s, people had been fascinated with the idea of radio. During the Great War, radio had been used for some long-range communications. With the development of voice radio, only a successful commercial venture could open the doors. On November 2, 1920, KDKA, a Pittsburgh, Pennsylvania station, became the first commercial radio station in the world, as it broadcast the results of Warren Harding's landslide presidential election victory. One station in Detroit, Michigan negates the Pittsburgh claim, but historians generally give KDKA the credit since it was the first one to continuously broadcast.

The success of KDKA propelled hundreds of others into the market. By 1922, there were more than five hundred radio stations on the air. During the decade, the three radio networks were organized. The National Broadcasting Company (NBC) was first in 1926. The Columbia Broadcasting System (CBS) was created in 1927, and the American Broadcasting Company (ABC) followed in 1929. In 1927, the Federal Radio Commission was established to regulate the young industry. In 1934, it changed its name to the Federal Communications Commission (FCC).

Radio quickly became for the generation between the world wars what television is for modern Americans. News, sports, weather, music, and entertainment programming was all provided on the airwaves. Soap operas flourished on the radio long before television, so-called because the earliest sponsors were soap manufacturers trying to reach the millions of women listeners who were fulltime homemakers. Other entertainment programming eventually added to the variety on the radio. Radio also contributed to the growth in major sports. For example, radio was there when heavy-weight champion Jack Dempsey knocked out challenger Georges Carpentier. George Herman "Babe" Ruth hit his record-breaking 60th homerun in 1927 before a radio audience as well.

The Movies

Movies had come a long way since the nickelodeon of the very early twentieth century (see Chapter Five). By World War I, southern California's abundant sunshine was making Hollywood the movie capital of the world. The 1920s confirmed the title. This was the beginning of the era of director Cecil B. De-Mille, whose early films included *The Ten Commandments* and *Ben-Hur*; Hollywood did remakes of both of these after World War II. Actors like Mary Pickford, Douglas Fairbanks, Sr., Rudolph Valentino, and Charlie Chaplin dominated the movie entertainment scene. The biggest breakthrough in the industry's history occurred in 1927, when Warner Brothers released *The Jazz Singer*, starring Al Jolson, as the first sound motion picture. Color would have to wait for *The Wonderful Wizard of Oz* in 1939.

Movies became the most popular form of entertainment for most Americans. By 1930, somewhere between 80 and 100 million Americans, out of a population of just under 123 million, were going to the movies on a weekly basis. Of course, many of them were children and others who repeatedly attended.

Babe Ruth. Credit: Baseball Hall of Fame Collection.

Nevertheless, that is an astounding percentage of moviegoers. The effect of such massive attendance was not difficult to see. Attendance at stage theaters fell dramatically, as did attendance at religious services. Movies also helped standardize the American culture because people saw the same movies and idolized the same actors.

ALL THAT JAZZ

Predictably, the music world was also turned upside down by the devil-may-care attitude in the postwar climate. New Orleans and Chicago proved to be the major early centers of jazz, which is characterized by its syncopated rhythms. Jelly Roll Morton and Louis Armstrong were its greatest performers. But jazz music became very popular with young people, both black and white, during the 1920s. And its heavy beat led to such dances as the Charleston. In fact, it was because jazz so epitomized the reckless abandon of the entire decade for many, that the 1920s has come to be called the Jazz Age.

Sexual frankness seemed about as shocking as anything could be during the decade. Before the twenties, in most areas of the country, a kiss had almost been equated to a marriage proposal. The new culture included new dances, jazz music, and "petting" parties in which young women were kissed repeatedly and casually. The woman who participated in such parties and other forms of carefree living became known as a "flapper." The term "flapper" was derived from the practice of such women leaving their rubber boots open and flapping about their ankles. "Flappers" openly smoked and drank, were frequently seen with men, and otherwise partied their lives away. More than any other woman, Zelda Fitzgerald (F. Scott Fitzgerald's wife) seemed to epitomize the consumate "flapper." Zelda spent her final years in a mental institution.

Despite the sexual openness and partying lifestyle of the Jazz Age, it should be remembered that not everyone in America practiced or appreciated the new culture. The revolution in values was fairly well limited to the upper and upper middle classes and young urban Americans. Most Americans were too busy with economic life to follow the latest fad or to wallow in self-pitying cesspools.

PROHIBITION

Prohibition Becomes Law

The Eighteenth Amendment to the Constitution had forbidden the manufacture, sale, and consumption of alcoholic beverages. (See Chapter Five for more information on the prohibition movement.) The era of Prohibition constitutionally went into effect in January 1920, one year after the amendment's ratification. It was left to Congress to define an alcoholic drink, however. And in October 1919, just three months before the Prohibition amendment took effect, Congress passed the Volstead Act over President Woodrow Wilson's veto. The Volstead Act declared .5 percent, or one-half of one percent, to be the maximum legal limit of a beverage's alcohol content. Exceptions were made for medicinal and religious uses, most notably the Roman Catholic mass.

Opposition to Prohibition

In most of the country, Prohibition was well supported. But the larger cities of the East were exceptions to that rule. The corner tavern was replaced by the "speakeasy," so named because one would speak softly through a small window before being admitted into a room that flowed with beer and whiskey. Illegal breweries operated in order to supply the illegal booze to thirsty Americans who resented the government intrusion into their private lives. These illegal operators became known as "bootleggers," a reminder that booze was often smuggled inside a person's boot. Joseph P. Kennedy, father of the later famous Kennedys of Massachussetts, made part of his fortune in the bootlegging business.

Traditionally, Americans have a long history of appreciation of alcohol, beginning with the West Indies' rum trade in the colonial days. Millions of new immigrants who came to this country during the turn of the century and after had been accustomed to drinking in old Europe. Since these immigrants settled in the cities of the East especially, it was there that opposition to Prohibition was particularly centered. The popularity of drinking made it very difficult for politicians to enforce the law. The result was that police departments in major cities usually ignored violations of Prohibition, leaving it up to federal agents to enforce the Volstead Act.

Early Success Fades

Despite the formidable obstacles in parts of the country, Prohibition was generally successful in the early days. By 1921, alcohol consumption was only one-third of its prewar level. However, as time went on, it became increasingly clear that more Americans were ignoring the law. In 1929, alcohol consumption had climbed up to about 70 percent of its prewar level. That statistic makes it difficult to argue with conventional wisdom, which states that Prohibition was a failure.

Yet there were some good reasons to expect failure in this alleged war on alcohol. First, there was the failure of big city police departments to enforce the law, referred to above. This meant that federal agents must do the job. Second, there were never more than 2,800 or so federal agents in the field at any one time. Their top salary was about $3,000 per year, a figure which invited bribery and corruption. That left relatively few federal agents honest enough to enforce the law. Thus, racketeers and other gangsters competed for the illicit alcohol market.

The most famous of these gangsters was "Scarface" Al Capone, who basically controlled the flow of alcohol in Chicago. A rare federal agent, Eliot Ness, hounded Capone for years. But Capone's bribery of police, judges, and witnesses allowed him to escape the clutches of Ness. Ness' group of agents became known as the "Untouchables," however, because they could not be bribed. Ness finally convinced a Treasury agent to infiltrate Capone's inner circle, and in 1931, Capone was convicted of federal income tax evasion. A short time after his release from prison, Al Capone died of syphillis.

The "Noble Experiment" Ends

Despite the fact that the Chicago gangster scene was not typical, events there did convince most Americans that Prohibition had turned ordinary citizens into criminals. In the 1932 presidential election, Democrat Franklin D. Roosevelt vowed to repeal Prohibition because he saw it as a source of revenue and jobs. He kept his promise. What President Herbert Hoover had called the "noble experiment" came to an end when the Twenty-first Amendment repealed the Eighteenth Amendment in December 1933.

THE RED SCARE

Inflation and Labor Troubles

Disillusionment about the war wasn't the only thing that bothered many Americans in 1919. The year was an extraordinarily bad one, economically and socially. Once the war was over, Americans wanted their share of peacetime consumer goods. While industry was retooling for peacetime production, consumer demand produced rampant inflation. The result was a series of labor strikes in an attempt to catch up with rising prices. About 4 million workers participated in about 2,665 strikes during the year. (More on this later in the chapter.) These strikes reminded Americans of the beginnings of communism in Russia, where the Bolshevik Revolution had taken place in the fall of 1917. If communists could take over a large country like Russia, many middle class Americans reasoned, then the same fate was possible for the United States. When a shipyard strike in Seattle led to a 5-day general strike in that city in January 1919, the mayor called for the use of force. The Seattle general strike seemed to awaken these fears, and the Red Scare of 1919–20 was born.

The Palmer Raids

United States Attorney-General A. Mitchell Palmer added fuel to the general hysteria which had broken out in 1919. Palmer wanted to be president and was looking around for an issue which would gain him the Democratic presidential nomination in 1920. The Red Scare became his issue. Bomb threats and explosions around the country assisted Palmer in his endeavors. Palmer had the nickname of "Fighting Quaker" due to his religion and his overwhelming zealousness in going after suspects. When the front porch of his Washington, D.C. home was blown up in June 1919, Palmer formed the General Intelligence Division within the Justice Department (August) to find subversives dedicated to the overthrow of the American political system. This anti-radical division was the forerunner of the later Federal Bureau of Investigation, and it was directed by J. Edgar Hoover. One interesting footnote to the Palmer porch bombing is that Franklin and Eleanor Roosevelt were walking toward Palmer's home for a visit just minutes before the blast occurred. Fortunately, they arrived after the incident and lived to become the future president and First Lady of the United States.

The infamous Palmer raids began on November 7, 1919, and climaxed with the biggest raid on January 2, 1920, in which more than 4,000 alleged communists in 33 cities were rounded up and arrested. Actually, Americans of any leftward political leanings were targeted in the Red Scare. This included labor leaders, progressives, and foreign-born Americans from Russia and eastern Europe. When few charges were filed and most detainees were released, Palmer drew criticism. Finally, afraid that his popularity was waning, Palmer dramatically predicted that on the communist holiday of May Day, May 1, 1920, a coordinated series of violent assaults would begin as part of a communist revolution in the United States. When nothing happened on May 1, Palmer was discredited. He never received the Democratic nomination for president.

Results of the Red Scare

Throughout the Palmer raids, a total of more than 5,000 Americans were arrested and about 600 aliens deported. There was no communist revolution, attempted or otherwise. But one key result of the 1919-20 Red Scare was that the decade of the twenties became the most bigoted decade of the twentieth century, before or since.

THE SACCO-VANZETTI TRIAL

One specific event that illustrates the bigotry of the decade concerned the case of two Italian aliens, Nicola Sacco and Bartolomeo Vanzetti. Residents of Boston, Sacco and Vanzetti were arrested in 1920 for the murder of two men during a robbery of a shoe company. In 1921, they were convicted and sentenced to death by a jury and judge more for their beliefs in atheism and anarchy, and the fact that they were immigrants in a society which was increasingly xenophobic, than by the evidence. Liberals and other progressive minded Americans were shocked at what they considered a travesty of justice. But liberalism was definitely not the "in" thing in the 1920s, and conservative Americans rejoiced in their defense of law and order. The case dragged on for 6 years, until Sacco and Vanzetti were electrocuted in August 1927. Evidence discovered later suggests that Sacco may have been guilty, but Vanzetti was probably innocent.

RACE RELATIONS

The Klan is Revived

The tense times of the twenties called for more scapegoats for the nation's problems. The Red Scare had set the stage. The result was a revival of the Ku Klux Klan. Actually, the Klan had already been reorganized in October 1915 by Colonel William J. Simmons, an Atlanta evangelist and insurance salesman, at a Stone Mountain, Georgia meeting to promote white supremacy. Membership climbed in the climate of the twenties because the Klan expanded its list of enemies. By 1923, there were more than 5 million official members.

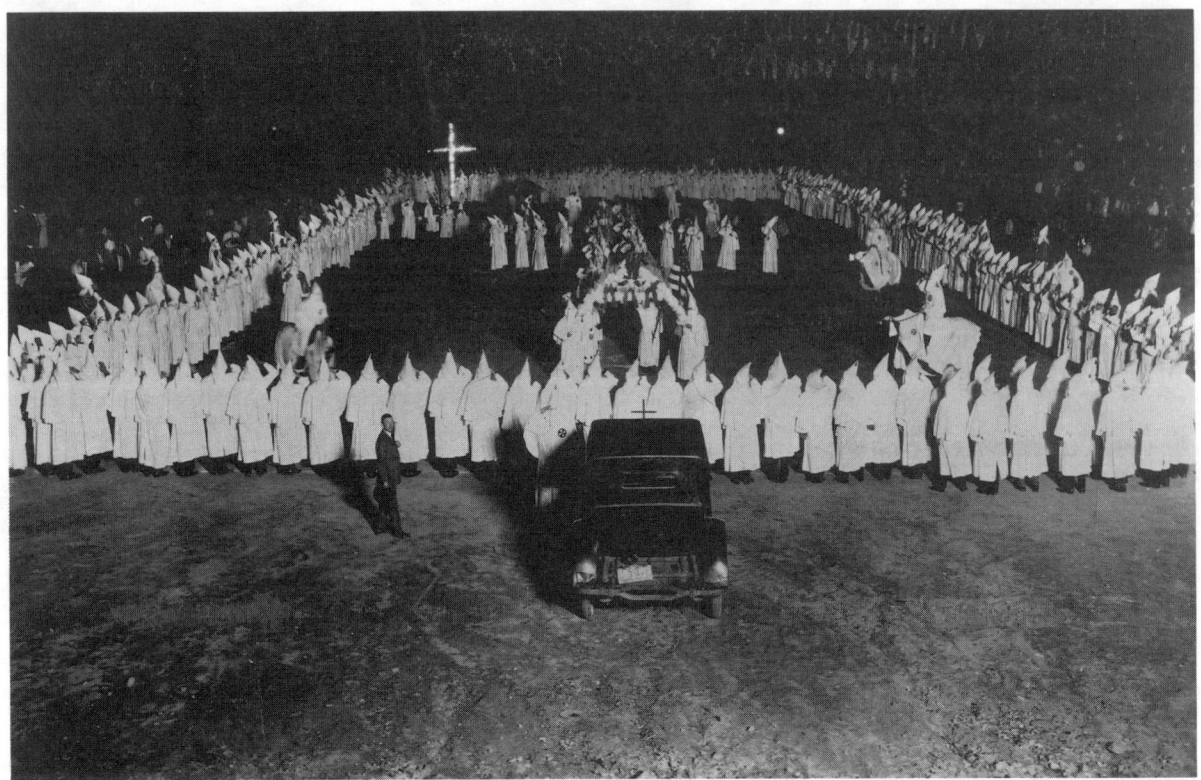

Ku Klux Klan Meeting. Credit: Library of Congress.

Then in 1924, a Texas dentist by the name of Hiram Wesley Evans took over the Ku Klux Klan and shifted its emphasis to less violent, more political tactics. Under Evans' leadership, the Klan grew mighty in political strength, dominating much of the politics of the South, Ohio, Indiana, and California during most of the decade. The Klan became a focal point of Americans' fears against foreigners, Catholics, Jews, blacks, and leftists of all types. Of course, it portrayed itself as the friend of Protestants, Anglo-Saxons, and other white Americans who held to traditional moral and political values. Thus, the Klan had appointed itself as the judge to define what it called "100% Americanism."

The Klan's success turned to failure rather quickly in the face of exposed scandals within its own leadership, and because the highly restrictive immigration laws of the decade gradually diffused the public's fear of allegedly undesirable immigrants. Furthermore, the continuation of incidents with men in white sheets was in itself growing scary to many ordinary Americans. The Klan disappeared during the Great Depression of the next decade, not to be restored until 1946.

Race Riots

The Klan was not the only illustration of racial hostility in the twenties. In the summer of 1919, race riots broke out in about two dozen cities. Chicago was the worst, where 38 people were killed and more than five hundred injured. Several more race riots occurred in the early twenties, in places like Longview, Texas, Tulsa, Oklahoma, Washington, D.C., and Chicago. These riots were instigated by whites who attacked African-Americans, usually in the black communities. Lynchings of young black men also increased during the twenties, an old form of intimidation.

Marcus Garvey and Black Separatism

In the face of open hostility toward Americans of color, some African-Americans developed an exclusive attitude. Marcus Garvey was the most influential of these leaders. Garvey, who had been born in Jamaica, organized the Universal Negro Improvement Association in 1914 to promote a "back to Africa" movement among fellow African-Americans. Garvey was opposed by most black leaders, including W.E.B. DuBois, but perhaps as many as 500,000 joined the UNIA, out of a total of between 11 and 12 million black Americans. The father of Malcolm X was one of Garvey's lieutenants, and he was murdered in the 1920s. Garvey himself was convicted of mail fraud and deported as an undesirable alien in 1923.

BUSINESS AND INDUSTRY

The twenties has sometimes been called the "Dollar Decade," in which the American economy had achieved what President Herbert Hoover mistakenly called the "permanent plateau of prosperity." Consumer demand, recently released by the end of the war, and government tax policies which encouraged investment, among other things, helped fuel the second industrial revolution during the twenties. By this time, assembly-line production techniques had been perfected, and the automobile led the way in this new wave of industrial growth.

Henry Ford and the Automobile Industry

The horseless carriage had first been built by Charles Duryea in 1893. Unreliable and clumsy, the automobile became the toy of the few rich and the butt of everyone else's jokes. But a man named Henry Ford changed all that. Originally an electrical engineer in Detroit's Edison Company, Henry Ford created the Ford Motor Company in 1903. Ford applied mass production techniques to the making of automobiles, and in 1908, he built and sold the first Model T for $950. The Model T was available only in the color black. Ford is reported to have said that Americans could buy a Model T in any color they wanted, as long as it was basic black.

More than anyone else, Henry Ford's application of the assembly line techniques to the manufacturing of automobiles made the automobile affordable to the average American. In 1919, more than one million cars were made in the United States. By the end of the twenties, the auto industry dominated the American economy by accounting for about 9 percent of all wages in manufacturing, and it had stimulated huge industries in steel, rubber, glass, oil, advertising, and highway construction. After stiffer competition in the industry, Ford finally had to offer a few different color options in 1927, when the Model A replaced the Model T in the

First Flight of the Wright Brothers. Credit: Library of Congress.

Charles A. Lindbergh, New York City, 1927. Credit: AP/Wide World Photos

Ford lineup of cars. By 1930, Americans owned more than 26 million automobiles, and Detroit had become the automobile capital of the world.

Aviation

Paralleling the rise of the automobile industry was the development of aviation. Two brothers in the bicycle repair business from Ohio, Orville and Wilbur Wright, built the first "heavier than air" machine that actually flew. On December 17, 1903, in the windy area of Kitty Hawk, North Carolina, Orville Wright flew 120 feet in their machine for about twelve seconds.

The new airplane was perfected on both sides of the Atlantic, and two-winged craft called bi-planes saw limited action in World War I. In the twenties, private companies began offering passenger service and fulfilling airmail contracts with the postal system. In 1920, the first transcontinental airmail service was created between New York and San Francisco.

The appeal of the airplane grew. Adventuresome youth, nicknamed "barn-stormers," engaged in stunt flying and began giving rides to onlookers at local fairs and other public settings. But it was Charles A. Lindbergh who really guaranteed the future of aviation. On May 20, 1927, Lindbergh became the first person to fly solo across the Atlantic Ocean when he piloted his *Spirit of St. Louis* from New York to Paris in 33 hours and 39 minutes. "Lucky Lindy" became everyone's instant hero. And by convincing millions of people that flying was safe, Lindbergh greatly assisted the young commercial aviation industry in getting off the ground.

Electricity and Labor-Saving Products

Other dizzying changes took place in the twenties. The demand for electricity multiplied as hundreds of time and labor-saving devices were invented and marketed for the home. Refrigerators, ranges, washing machines, vacuum cleaners, electric mixers, and other conveniences all needed electricity to work. Thus, by the end of the decade, about 5 of every 6 urban American homes possessed electricity. At the same time, only ten percent of rural homes had electricity since it wasn't very profitable for private utility companies to string electric lines in the country. The federal government would have to get into that business in the 1930s, and it would take a few decades before electricity reached nearly every rural home.

The Advertising Industry

The American economy had certainly perfected production during the twenties. It was necessary to find new methods to advertise the products in order to persuade Americans that they really needed all those goods and services. The advertising business multiplied several times during the decade, and with it, rose the influence of Madison Avenue advertising executives in New York City. Using newspapers, magazines, and radio, ad executives used promises of social success to tell people what they really wanted.

The real founder of Madison Avenue advertising was Bruce Barton, the son of a Protestant minister. In 1925, Barton wrote a book entitled *The Man Nobody Knows*. The book explained that Jesus was the world's first super salesman, whose parables were actually the greatest commercials the world had ever heard. Installment buying plans and the early use of credit cards had their origin in the twenties, as people were encouraged to "buy now, pay later."

Business Heroes

Industrial and other business growth was so rapid during the decade that the business of America was business, according to President Calvin Coolidge. Despite Jack Dempsey and Babe Ruth, for example, the most popular heroes of the day were business heroes. Undoubtedly, Henry Ford was the number one hero of the twenties, but Charles Lindbergh made a strong bid for that title late in the decade. So many dizzying changes took place that, among its other titles, the 1920s has also been called the "Roaring Twenties."

ORGANIZED LABOR

Major Postwar Strikes

Immediately after the end of the Great War, organized labor attempted to catch up with the inflation that was plaguing the country. Also, the "no strike" pledge that was fairly well kept during the war was perceived as no longer binding by unions. An organizing effort by the American Federation of Labor in the steel industry resulted in a major strike against the United States Steel Corporation from September 1919 to January 1920. But state and federal troops were used to prevent picketing, and violence broke out. When it was all over, about 18 strikers had been killed and the union busted.

During the same period, John L. Lewis, president of the United Mine Workers, led a miners' strike in November 1919. In that strike, the federal courts agreed that the Great War was not officially over. Therefore, the "no strike" pledge was still in effect, and the strike was crushed by the government.

But perhaps the most famous strike of 1919 was the Boston Police Strike. A union was seeking official recognition by the city, but the city was not yielding. After the Boston police commissioner fired 19 policemen for union activity on September 8, the Boston Police Strike ensued. This strike turned the public against the labor movement even more. Massachussetts Governor Calvin Coolidge spoke eloquently for the middle class when he publicly declared that there was "no right to strike against the public safety by anyone at any time." He also called out the National Guard to protect Boston. This reaction helped win him the vice-presidential nomination on the Republican ticket in 1920.

Union Membership Declines

These early strikes helped set the tone for public attitudes toward organized labor in the 1920s. Combined with other important factors, union membership declined during the decade, from about 5.1 million in 1920 to about 3.5 million in 1929; by 1932, union membership was down to 2.9 million, although the depression was responsible for the decline since 1929. In fact, the twenties was the first decade in American labor history in which union membership declined during times of general prosperity. Why? Part of the reason lay in the fact that productivity gains had also led to real gains in wages. From 1921 to 1928, the average annual income for non-farm workers rose from $1,171 to $1,408—about a 20 percent increase. Of course, not everyone enjoyed such wage gains. The textile and mining industries suffered an actual decline in wages, which helps explain why those industries had more labor problems than most. But the overall wage increases and a growing job opportunity market did go a long way toward inhibiting the attraction of unions for most American workers.

The Open Shop Campaign

Wage increases alone did not account for the decline in union membership during the twenties. The Red Scare of 1919–20 had created a climate of hostility toward labor leaders, which employers took advantage of during the decade. In 1920, the National Association of Manufacturers (NAM) began a vigorous campaign to keep unions out of the workplace. After a business conference in Chicago in January 1921, a full-blown "open shop" movement emerged to quickly engulf the employment world. The open shop is a workplace in which a worker does not have to join the union in order to keep his job. The NAM hailed the open shop as the "American Plan." The movement caught on as companies delighted in the use of patriotism to keep their workers from joining legitimate labor unions.

Subsequent activity proved the open shop campaign to be hyprocritical. While selling the idea that union membership should be voluntary, not compulsory, employers demonstrated that what they really favored was worker choice only as long as their workers chose against a union. Labor unions countered the open shop argument by declaring that if a union officially represented all the non-supervisory employees in a workplace, then every such employee should share in the costs of that representation. What was more "compulsory" about union membership than the requirement for doctors to belong to the American Medical Association or lawyers to the American Bar Association, they asked. But labor's arguments largely fell on deaf ears.

A Potpourri of Anti-Labor Devices

Company unions, formed and controlled by the company, were frequently offered as evidence that management was already dealing with its employees through a union. Of course, there were no contractual obligations with such "unions," so benefits could be removed as fast as they had been given. Most of the old anti-labor devices were still used during the period as well. Yellow dog contracts, for example, required the signed promise of a worker that he would not strike or join a union for as long as he worked for his employer. Pinkertons were still employed as spies and saboteurs to discredit labor unions and enforce the use of strikebreakers. Other employers stockpiled guns and ammunition in order to threaten union organizers and other "outside agitators." States, the federal government, and courts at all levels were hostile to union activity also. The state of Kansas was the worst. That state banned strikes in any industry which it deemed affected the public interest.

Welfare Capitalism

A new approach was added to the old anti-union weapons during the twenties. Henry Ford, who saw himself as a father figure to his workers, is given the credit for fostering the "carrot" approach called welfare capitalism. Paternalism reigned supreme as corporate managers and owners competed to give their workers just enough benefits to prevent them from joining unions. The two-week paid vacation had first been used by the International Harvester Company in 1919, but it caught on in several industries during the 1920s. An 8-hour day, insurance, company stock bonuses, profit-sharing, and even recreation facilities were awarded to workers to keep them "loyal" to the company. Welfare capitalism proved very effective. Most industries susceptible to unions employed some aspect of welfare capitalism, usually with success.

Conservative Union Leadership

Even labor unions themselves must be partly blamed for the decline in union membership. AFL president Samuel Gompers died in 1924, and was replaced by an even more conservative leader, William Green, of the mineworkers. The AFL opposed minimum wage laws, until about 1929, because it felt that if government gave workers certain advantages, workers would feel no need to join unions. Of course, the Great Depression and subsequent labor history would dramatically change organized labor's attitude toward government protections. Too many labor leaders allowed workers to be content with the gains from welfare capitalism, and did not aggressively seek to organize new workers, especially the unskilled in the growing new industries.

Coal and Textile Industries

Exceptions to the "carrot" approach of welfare capitalism were the coal mine operators and the textile mills. These industries preferred the proverbial "stick" to keep unions out of their companies. And the result was two-way labor-management violence in those industries. West Virginia was the scene of a major organizing drive by the United Mine Workers (UMW) from 1919 to 1922. When the union was met by violent opposition, it formed an army of about 4,000 men by 1921, and went on the offensive throughout the state. The trouble was squelched when President Warren Harding sent about 2,100 federal troops to West Virginia. Early in 1922, UMW president John L. Lewis called for a national coal strike after contract negotiations broke down. Violence broke out in June after two strikers were killed by guards. But the strike was eventually put down.

In the textile industry, many mill owners moved to low-wage areas of the South during the twenties, which led to the mills remaining in New England to slash wages. These measures provoked a series of strikes there. The United Textile Workers then went South to attempt to organize the mills there, but they found a powerful alliance of companies, police, and state governments lined up against them. The key years of conflict in the Southern textile industry were 1929 and 1930, years which ended in virtually total union defeat.

More Sympathetic Labor Action and Legislation

The only notable success for organized labor in the twenties came in the railroad industry. The Esch-Cummins Act (1920) had created the Railway Labor Board as private companies resumed control of the industry after the war. But the Railway Labor Board was ineffective. After a brief nationwide railroad shopmen's strike in 1922, Congress began looking for ways to strengthen the mediation machinery. In 1926, the Railway Labor Act created more effective mediation and arbitration machinery. It also forced railroad companies to deal with real, legitimate unions when it outlawed company unions in the railroad industry.

By the end of the decade, there were signs that more Americans favored a more level playing field for labor. The United States Senate refused to confirm President Hoover's nominee for the Supreme Court in 1930 over labor issues. Circuit Court Judge John J. Parker had upheld the use of injunctions to prohibit union organizers from signing up workers who had already signed yellow dog contracts.

Then, in March of 1932, both political parties kept their 1928 platform promises to restrict the use of federal injunctions in labor disputes. Led by two progressive Republicans, Nebraska Senator George W. Norris and New York Congressman Fiorello LaGuardia, Congress passed the Anti-Injunction Act, sometimes known as the Norris-LaGuardia Act. This federal law made yellow dog contracts illegal and placed significant restrictions on the courts' ability to issue labor injunctions during strikes.

AGRICULTURE

The Golden Age Comes to an End

The period from 1900–1920 is known as the "Golden Age" of agriculture for several fundamental reasons. First, the end of the frontier, reflected in the 1890 census, meant that there were fewer farms. Land prices were rising for the same reason. Second, the urbanization trend in the early twentieth century increased the demand for more farm products by people who no longer farmed. And, third, during the Great War (1914–1918), farm exports increased greatly as American farmers helped feed the Allies. In fact, during the war years, American farmers had the best of both worlds. No matter how much they increased production, Allied demand outstripped the supply and kept farm prices very high.

In order to cash in on the good times during the war, many farmers went deeply into debt to buy more land and the latest tractor or farm implement produced by modern industry. When the war ended and European farmers were harvesting more normal levels of crops again, the bottom fell out of the American agricultural market. Beginning in May 1920, a farm depression hit the United States that did not end until 1941.

Typical Farmers' Problems

Farmers suffer from a variety of problems unique to their business. Overproduction is the key reason that farm prices drop. Beyond that, a host of other problems torment most farmers. For example, farmers have little control over their own productivity, due to weather and pests mostly. They must ordinarily buy supplies at retail prices but sell at wholesale. A number of relatively high fixed costs challenges farmers too, such as taxes, mortgage payments, and fertilizers. To compensate for these high fixed costs, farmers tend to try to produce more, only continuing the cycle of falling farm prices. Diversity of crops is limited by the land, climate, machinery, and experience. Then farmers are traditionally too independent to cooperate very well with each other, especially when they are often competing with different farming interests. And last, but very important, food commodities are not elastic products. You cannot persuade people to eat more when they have more money. With few exceptions, American farmers experienced an economic depression one entire decade before the rest of the country did.

Farmers Organize for Change

Socially, farmers had been the backbone of American democracy since the beginning of the republic. But the Industrial Revolution changed that permanently. By the 1890s, most Americans viewed farmers as relics of the past, simply hicks and hayseeds. Therefore, by the time the farm depression hit the country in 1920, farmers found themselves a political minority. They had lost much political influence at both the state and federal levels of government to corporate America.

The result was an attempt to organize for their own improvement. The American Farm Bureau was created in 1919 to represent the interests of upper class farmers. The Farmers' Union, established back in 1902 in Waco, Texas, became more leftist in its goals, advocating the withholding of products in order to get higher prices. The oldest of the farm organizations, the Grange, founded in 1867, evolved into an insurance company for farmers. Cooperatives, like Sunkist, formed in the twenties as a response to the problems created by buying at retail and selling at wholesale.

These organizations helped create the so-called farm bloc in Congress during the days of the Harding administration, when Henry C. Wallace was the Secretary of Agriculture. The farm bloc consisted of a group of members of Congress who tended to vote as a bloc on agriculture issues. Most of them were Republicans from the Midwest and Middle West, but Democrats from predominantly farm states were part of this Congressional bloc as well. Their earliest leader was Iowa Senator William S. Kenyon. After 1923, Kansas Senator Arthur Capper emerged as the leader of the farm bloc.

The farm bloc had a few successes in Congress, but nothing which turned the agricultural economy around. In August 1921, Congress passed the Packers and Stockyards Act. This law authorized the Secretary of Agriculture to issue cease and desist orders to prevent monopolies in the meatpacking industry. In 1922, the Capper-Volstead Act exempted farmers from some antitrust provisions in order to encourage the development of farm cooperatives. Then, in September 1922, Michigan Congressman Joseph W. Fordney and North Dakota Senator Porter J. McCumber mobilized Congress to pass the Fordney-McCumber Tariff Act. This tariff bill included tariffs on certain farm products for the first time in American history. It also raised the average tariff rate from the Underwood-Simmons Tariff average of about 26 percent to approximately 33 percent.

The most important farm bloc success, however, came with the passage of the Agricultural Credits Act (or Intermediate Credits Act) in March 1923. The Agricultural Credits Act created 12 more farm reserve banks, patterned somewhat after the Federal Reserve System, to provide shortterm farm loans ranging from 6 months to 3 years. This measure enabled farmers of storable crops to withhold farm commodities during a price slump, and then sell them when prices rose. The loan would allow the farmer to pay his bills during the interval.

McNary-Haugenism

The most controversial and important specific farm issue of the decade, which never did become law, was known as McNary-Haugenism. Named for Oregon Senator Charles L. McNary and Iowa Congressman Gilbert Haugen, the idea was really based on a pamphlet published in 1922 by George N. Peek, president of an Illinois plow company, and retired General Hugh S. Johnson, entitled *Equality for Agriculture*. Since the United States did not import many farm products, placing tariffs on farm imports wouldn't help many American farmers. Instead, McNary-Haugenism promised to establish a federal government corporation to buy surplus of certain products, like wheat, at a "fair exchange" price. The corporation would then sell it on the world market for a lower price. American farmers would pay a small equalization fee to help pay for the shipping costs.

This concept would probably keep the prices of participating crops fairly high, and thus, farm incomes also. Its advocates argued for its simplicity and fairness, and also that it was high time the agriculture sector of the economy received support from the federal government rather than only big business. McNary-Haugenism was supported by all the major farm organizations except the very conservative Grange. However, conservative opponents argued that it would encourage farmers to overproduce intentionally and foreign governments to "dump" other exports on the world market in order to lower prices of other American goods in retaliation. Consumer groups worried about higher food prices. And President Calvin Coolidge called McNary-Haugenism socialism and announced his opposition to all special interest legislation, except for big business, of course.

The bill was first defeated in June 1924, when Southern members of Congress refused to support it since cotton prices were pretty good then. After cotton prices fell off in 1926, Southern support for McNary-Haugenism increased in Congress. In February 1927, the bill passed Congress easily, but it was vetoed successfully by President Coolidge. Another attempt was made in May of 1928, but once again, President Coolidge vetoed it as alleged socialistic legislation. McNary-Haugenism haunted the conservative wing of both parties, especially the Republicans, but it never did become law.

PROGRESSIVES IN THE TWENTIES

Progressivism Suffers

As stated earlier in the chapter, the Great War had put an end to the Progressive Era, but it had not really killed progressivism itself. While the war certainly weakened the progressives, other factors also contributed. For example, rural Americans were increasingly coming into conflict with urban citizens over a range of issues. Rural Americans were more inclined toward nativist ideas against foreigners, and they also supported Prohibition to a far greater extent than urban Americans. The deep division between the two demographic groups undercut much rural support for progressive ideas. Also, many intellectual leaders simply left the country in disillusionment to live in France or Britain after the war, leaving a vacuum in that portion of the reform-minded population. The old progressive leaders, men like "Fighting Bob" LaFollette, were perceived as too old in the twenties to offer many new ideas. This lack of leadership to galvanize progressives hurt the movement a great deal. Then, too, the white middle class seemed content with the prosperity and materialism of the decade. There are historians who believe that the middle class had given the nation the Progressive Era in order to regain power lost in the Industrial Revolution, and to humanize it. Then by the 1920s, the same middle class was satisfied with its achievements and settled into a complacent materialism.

Progressive Efforts in Congress

Progressive leaders like Republican Senator Robert LaFollette of Wisconsin, Republican Senator George W. Norris of Nebraska, and Republican Senator Smith W. Burkhard of Iowa still managed to hold the balance of power in the early days of the decade under the Harding administration. Progressives fought hard against regressive, "soak the poor" tax policies and for publicy owned hydroelectric power. In 1920, the Water Power Act had created the Federal Power Commission to regulate electric rates, utility company services and financial operations. However, pro-business appointments to the commission prevented it from being an effective regulatory agency.

The Wilson Dam, being built on the Tennessee River at Muscle Shoals, Alabama, became a symbol of the progressives' struggle to obtain federal hydroelectric power projects. The dam had been begun during the war to provide nitrates for ammunition, but it was still at least 70 percent incomplete after the war had ended. In 1922, Henry Ford and Thomas Edison toured the dam site and offered to lease the dam and provide nitrates for fertilizer for Southern farmers. Progressives sucessfully blocked this effort during the twenties. Senator George Norris, chairman of the Senate Agriculture Committee, wanted the federal government to own and operate Wilson Dam in order to provide cheap electricity to the Tennessee Valley. At the time, nearly 90 percent of the South did not have electricity. In 1928,

Congress approved such a federal project, but President Coolidge vetoed as another example of what he called socialism. Then, in March 1931, the bill passed Congress again, and this time President Hoover vetoed it.

Progressive Efforts in Politics

A former socialist from North Dakota, Arthur Townley, helped found the Non-Partisan League in 1915 with the support of North Dakota wheat farmers. The Non-Partisan League, existing until 1923, favored strict government control of businesses which dealt primarily with farmers. In 1916, the group elected its own governor in North Dakota, and the organization extended itself from Minnesota to Washington State. In Minnesota, it joined with labor unions in a Farmer-Labor movement which played an influential role in that state during most of the century.

This northern movement sparked interest by 1924 in a national progressive party. At the Conference for Progressive Political Action in Chicago, February 1922, that group agreed to campaign for LaFollette to win the Republican nomination for president in 1924, and to go for a third party candidacy if that failed. When President Calvin Coolidge emerged as the big winner at the 1924 Republican convention, the CPPA formed the Progressive Party and nominated Robert M. LaFollette as promised. Of course, LaFollette carried only his home state of Wisconsin that year. Overall, progressives simply were forced to take a back seat to materialism during the "Dollar Decade."

THE 1920 ELECTION

As the 1920 presidential election drew near, it became clearer that the country wanted a change. They were tired of wartime controls and progressive legislation. Inflation and labor strikes in the immediate postwar period added to the voices calling for a return to sanity. The Red Scare had further made the times ripe for a conservative backlash at the polls.

Theodore Roosevelt had mended political fences with the conservative wing of the Republican Party, but his untimely death at the age of 56 from a fever (probably malaria) in January 1919, took him out of the running. Most of his supporters drifted to General Leonard Wood. But Frank Lowden, the moderate governor of Illinois and George Pullman's son-in-law, also wanted the nomination in 1920. Wood and Lowden neutralized each other at the convention that year, which left the nomination to a "dark horse" candidate. Ohio Senator Warren G. Harding, everyone's second choice at the convention, became the Republican nominee. Massachussetts Governor Calvin Coolidge, who had made himself famous in opposing the Boston Police Strike the year before, was selected as Harding's running mate.

President Woodrow Wilson had hinted of an unprecedented third term in order to get the United States into the League of Nations. But in the end, the president decided against another run. However, his waffling confused the Democrats, probably enough to deny the president's son-in-law, William G. McAdoo, the nomination in 1920. Fourteen different Democrats, including Attorney-General A. Mitchell Palmer, vied for the presidential nomination that year in one of the most confusing nominating conventions in history. Finally, on the forty-fourth ballot, the Democrats nominated Ohio Governor James Cox. Governor Cox had convinced the Ohio public schools to ban the teaching of the German language during the war. For Cox's vice-presidential running mate, the convention selected the young Assistant Secretary of the Navy, Franklin Delano Roosevelt, Theodore's fifth cousin. Ironically, Roosevelt and other young Democrats had tried to get Herbert Hoover the nomination since Hoover had not announced a political party preference at the time.

The keynote of the presidential campaign was set by Warren Harding. In a speech in Boston, the Republican nominee called for the country to return to "normalcy." Although an unusual word, "normalcy" was not coined by Harding, as is often thought; he simply made it famous. By "normalcy," of course, Harding and the Republicans meant a return to the good old days before wartime controls and progressive laws. The country was tired of problems and reformers, and it was time to move beyond them. Therefore, the Republicans struck a responsive chord with the "normalcy" theme. By this time, the Wilson administration had alienated nearly everyone, and the voters were ready and eager to put it out of its misery. Harding looked presidential, although he said very few specific things during the campaign.

When the votes were counted in November, Harding had won a landslide victory. He outpolled Cox 16.1 million to 9.1 million in popular votes, and carried thirty-seven of the forty-eight states, for an electoral vote margin of 404 to 127. Labor leader, Eugene V. Debs, received about 920,000 votes while serving prison time under the Sedition Act.

HARDING THE MAN

Warren G. Harding was born at Caledonia, Ohio, in 1865, the year the Civil War ended, the son of a poor family. After returning from college, Harding bought the Marion *Star*, a weekly newspaper which he and a partner turned into a powerful daily. He married Florence, a divorcee and banker's daughter who was 6 years older than he.

Harding used his newspaper to become active in Ohio Republican politics. In 1901, he was elected to the state senate. He lost a gubernatorial race in 1910, and was the keynote speaker at the 1912 Republican convention on behalf of President William Howard Taft. He was elected to the United States Senate in 1914, where he was known for both his pro-business attitudes and absenteeism. Harding soon became embroiled in his two personal weaknesses, alcohol and women. As a senator, Harding had voted for the Prohibition amendment. But he never really felt that it should apply to everyone, certainly not him. This double standard allowed him to

1920	48	WARREN G. HARDING	Republican	16,143,407	404	60.4
		James M. Cox	Democrat	9,130,328	127	34.2
		Eugene V. Debs	Socialist	919,799		3.4
		P. P. Christensen	Farmer-Labor	265,411		1.0

President Warren G. Harding. Photo Credit: AP/Wide World Photos.

utilize the services of his own personal bootlegger, Mort Mortimer, who often delivered Canadian whiskey to the White House in broad daylight.

Harding was also a very promiscuous ladies' man. He had two major affairs during his public life. In his earlier days, there had been Carrie Phillips, his best friend's wife, with whom he had an affair for about 15 years. Mrs. Phillips ended the relationship when Senator Harding voted for the declaration of war against Germany in April 1917, just as she had promised to. (She obviously took her politics seriously!) Then, before Harding was elected president, he began an affair with a 19-year-old doctor's daughter from Marion, Ohio, Nan Britton; Harding was in his fifties at the time. Harding helped get her a job as a secretary in New York City, where she had an illegitimate baby girl in late 1919. As president, Harding continued the affair with Ms. Britton.

THE HARDING CABINET AND OHIO GANG

Harding appointed some brilliant men to his cabinet and some outright crooks. Among his better appointments are included Charles Evans Hughes as Secretary of State, Herbert Hoover as Secretary of Commerce, Henry C. Wallace as Secretary of Agriculture, and Secretary of Treasury Andrew Mellon, the steel magnate. The crooks included Attorney-General Harry M. Daugherty, his campaign manager from Marion, Ohio, Secretary of the Interior Albert B. Fall, and Secretary of the Navy Edwin Danby. Falling into neither category of good or ·bad, some Harding appointments were merely incompetent to handle the positions they were appointed to. One of these was a former Seventh-day Adventist missionary to Burma, Heber H. Votaw, who was named the Superintendent of Prisons; Votaw had married Harding's sister Carolyn back in 1903. Harding's group of official and unofficial advisors that he brought from Ohio to Washington became known as the "Ohio Gang." Many members of the "Ohio Gang" would sit up with the president late at night, playing poker and sipping Canadian whiskey in the White House.

THE HARDING SCANDALS

Except for his drinking and his marital infidelity, there is no evidence suggesting that Warren Harding was personally dishonest. But, like Ulysses Grant before him, Harding surrounded himself with friends and cronies whom he failed to discipline. The many scandals that plagued his administration were not known to the general public until after his death. Even the president himself did not seem to understand what was going on until shortly before his death, and then they probably contributed to his demise.

Harry Daugherty

The leader of the "Ohio Gang" was Attorney-General Harry Daugherty. Jesse Smith and Daugherty operated what was known as the "little green house on K Street" in Washington, D.C. The establishment was part brothel, part "speakeasy," and part business office in which presidential pardons for Prohibition violators were sold. When Jesse Smith committed suicide in Daugherty's apartment on May 23, 1923, press coverage spelled the beginning of the end for the "Ohio Gang."

Daugherty got himself in further trouble with another government official. Thomas W. Miller was the federal custodian for alien property, property confiscated during the war, such as German chemical patents. Miller sold much of this property to American firms for a fee of $50,000, and placed the money in a joint account with Attorney-General Daugherty in Daugherty's brother's bank. In March 1924, Daugherty refused to give testimony to a Senate investigating committee by taking the Fifth Amendment. As a result, President Coolidge was forced to fire Daugherty as Attorney-General. Daugherty was never convicted for his crimes, but Miller went to prison.

The Veterans' Bureau Scandal

Then there was Colonel Charles R. Forbes, head of the Veterans' Bureau, who operated a large swindle costing over $200 million of tax moneys. Forbes sold trainloads of medical supplies intended for veterans' hospitals, which he had first officially declared worthless, at a fraction of the cost to friends in exchange for kickbacks. The Veterans' Bureau then bought them back at higher prices. Forbes resigned in February 1923 and was convicted of 17 counts, including the sale of narcotics. He spent two years in prison and was fined $10,000.

The Teapot Dome Scandal

The biggest scandal in the history of the federal government until Watergate in the early 1970s was the Teapot Dome Scandal. Secretary of the Interior Albert Fall conned President Harding and Navy Secretary Edwin Danby into transferring naval oil lands to the Interior Department in 1921. These oil fields were located in Teapot Dome, Wyoming, and Elk Hills, California. Then Fall leased the fields to friends in the oil industry, Edwin L. Doheny and Harry Sinclair, in 1922. Doheny's son gave Fall about $100,000 in cash, and Sinclair donated about $223,000 worth of liberty bonds to Fall's son-in-law, $80,000 cash to Fall himself, and a herd of cattle for his New Mexico ranch. In late 1923 and early 1924, Montana Democratic Senator Thomas J. Walsh uncovered the bribery scandal with the help of conservationists, who didn't want oil drilling there. Although Fall claimed that the payments were loans, he became the first cabinet member in American history to go to prison for corruption. He was fined $100,000 and spent one year in prison. Fall eventually died broke and lonely.

Harding Dies

President Harding saw the beginning of the scandals being revealed in 1923. In deep personal depression, the president planned an Alaskan vacation for the summer of that year in order to get away from all the bad news. On his way to Alaska, Harding became the first president to visit Seattle, Washington. He returned to Seattle in late July in pain. He then came down with pneumonia in San Francisco, where a stroke killed him on August 2. President Harding's real killers may have been alcoholism and depression. Vice-President Calvin Coolidge was sworn in as the thirtieth president of the United States.

COOLIDGE THE MAN

Calvin Coolidge was a sharp contrast to Warren Harding from a personal perspective. Coolidge had been born in 1872 in Vermont, and exhibited many of the traits of his Puritan ancestors, especially honesty and frugality. He graduated from Amherst in 1895, then studied law, opening a law office in Northampton, Massachusetts. He served as a Republican in the Massachusetts state house, and then was mayor of Northampton for a time. He was elected to the state senate in 1911.

President Calvin Coolidge. Photo Credit: AP/Wide World Photos.

Then he became the lieutenant-governor of Massachusetts in 1915, and governor in 1918. Coolidge rose to national prominence by taking a definite stand against the Boston Police Strike in 1919. This helped win him the place on the Republican ticket with Harding in 1920.

Coolidge was a very popular president, especially with the urban middle class. However, he was probably the most negative and do-nothing president of the twentieth century. He ruled by veto while presiding over inertia. He opposed farm subsidies, reductions in tariffs, a publicly-owned power station at Muscle Shoals, Alabama, and assistance to the League of Nations. His pro-laissez-faire philosophy was matched only by his Hamiltonian view toward industry. Big business was the only special interest group he wholeheartedly supported. "The business of America is business" was his most famous quote. Nicknamed "Silent Cal," President Coolidge often slept 11-hour nights and still managed to take frequent naps during the day. In fact, one can almost say that Coolidge "invented" the long weekend. (No wonder he was so silent!)

LEGISLATIVE ISSUES OF THE HARDING-COOLIDGE ADMINISTRATIONS

While different in personality, Warren Harding and Calvin Coolidge were amazingly similar in political attitudes. So much so that the record of their administrations can be examined together. Some of the issues that these two presidents dealt with were already referred to in earlier sections of this chapter.

The Regulatory System

As conservative Republican presidents, it was Harding's and Coolidge's desire to make federal regulatory agencies as impotent as possible. Progressives still held something of a balance of power in Congress, so rather than launch an all-out assault on government regulation, these two presidents simply appointed other conservatives to these agencies. Because their conservative appointees did not essentially believe these agencies should exist, they certainly saw to it that very little regulation on behalf of the public interest took place during the twenties.

The Tariff Issue

A pro-business attitude made the 1920s similar to the previous Gilded Age. The tariff issue was especially a favorite of business and labor groups. In 1913, under the Democratic Wilson administration, the Underwood-Simmons Tariff Act had reduced the average tariff rate to about 26 percent. In September 1922, the Republicans passed the Fordney-McCumber Tariff Act, which raised the average to about one-third. It also created a Tariff Commission, composed of trade experts, to recommend to the president an increase or decrease of up to 50 percent. Ardent protectionists were appointed to the commission, and in 32 of the 37 recommendations given to Presidents Harding and Coolidge, the tariff rates were raised.

Taxes and the Economy

In May 1921, the Budget and Accounting Act created the Director of the Budget, under the Treasury Department, for the first time in history. It was widely hailed as a good reform measure by both conservatives and progressives. Tax bills did not create such universal agreement, however. Conservatives and progressives battled over Treasury Secretary Andrew Mellon's tax proposals throughout the decade. Progressives lost the battle each time. The Revenue Acts of 1921, 1924, 1926, and 1928 reflected the conservative philosophy that the wealthy deserve their wealth and should pay few taxes in order that they might create jobs through investments. The effect of the tax policies during the twenties was to cut the maximum surtax on high personal incomes down to 20 percent and corporate income taxes to a high of about 11 percent. These tax policies were regressive, the opposite of progressive, in that the more people made, the less social responsibility through taxes they were called upon to provide. Such regressive tax policies, which did stimulate business investment, would have their detrimental effect on the long-range health of the economy.

Immigration Restriction

Since the beginning of the republic, America had pursued an open door policy toward all except Asian immigrants. Such a policy had not been supported by organized labor because of the tendency of newer immigrants to accept lower wages and shun labor unions. But organized labor had never been influential enough to restrict anything but Asian immigration, which racial prejudice had agreed must be restricted. However, because of the Red Scare in 1919–20, business groups in large numbers and for the first time, began pushing for immigration restriction legislation. They still wanted cheap labor, to be sure, but many believed that the very existence of capitalism as they knew it depended on keeping dangerous, leftist radicals out of the United States. Since the very early years of the twentieth century, most new European immigrants had been coming from eastern Europe and Russia. The combination of labor and business groups, supported by bigoted views among large sectors of the population, resulted in the first significant restrictions on non-Asians in our history.

In May 1921, Congress passed the Immigration Act of 1921, sometimes also called the Emergency Quota Act or the Johnson Act, after Congressman Albert Johnson of Washington State. The 1921 law limited European immigrants to 3 percent of a nationality group per year. The 3 percent would be based on the number of Americans in a nationality group as reflected in the 1910 census.

In December 1923, President Calvin Coolidge remarked that "America must be kept American." By that statement, Coolidge implied that true Americans had come from northern or western Europe, and that preferably their ancestors had come to America on the *Mayflower*. It was a kind of statement that would get a president in deep political trouble today, but Coolidge was only reflecting the bigotry and racism of his era. At his request, Congress passed the National Origins Act in May 1924. This new bill proved to be the most restrictive immigration in American history, before or since. It prohibited all new east Asian and African immigration, clearly racist provisions. With regard to European immigrants, it altered the 3 percent figure of the 1921 act by changing it to just 2 percent based on the 1890 census. The census in 1890 was selected because that was the decade that growing percentages of European immigrants were coming from eastern and southern Europe and Russia. Those slavic peoples were the immigrants feared because of their Roman Catholic religion and their non-democratic experiences. A ceiling of 164,000 persons per year was placed on European immigrants, a figure which was reduced in 1927 to 150,000 per year, effective July 1, 1929.

The law did not apply to the western hemisphere at all. Therefore, the 1920s saw huge numbers of immigrants from Mexico and Puerto Rico come to the United States for agricultural and industrial jobs. Mexican immigrants predictably settled in the American Southwest, while most Puerto Rican immigrants settled in the low-rent districts of New York City, called barrios. Japan had already signed a Gentlemen's Agreement with the Roosevelt administration back in 1907, an agreement that prevented any further Japanese from coming to the United States. When they heard of the prohibition of east Asians in the new American law, Japan held a National Humiliation Day to protest the insult.

THE 1924 ELECTION

The Republicans

Although Republican progressives kept their vow to fight for Robert M. LaFollette at the national convention in 1924, that convention was completely dominated by President Coolidge and the conservative wing of the party. Calvin Coolidge was nominated on the first ballot. Frank Lowden, former governor of Illinois was initially nominated as the vice-presidential candidate. Lowden was a friend of agricultural interests and was selected in an attempt to appease the progressives in the party. However, Lowden refused the nomination. The Republicans chose Charles G. Dawes, a Chicago banker, to replace him on the ticket with Coolidge.

The Democrats

The Democrats met in New York's Madison Square Garden to choose their nominees in 1924. As a truly national party, the Democrats were hopelessly divided among its various factions. The rural-urban tensions prevalent in the nation were a large part of the problems the Democrats faced throughout the decade. A resolution condemning the Ku Klux Klan as an un-American and undesirable institution failed to pass the Democratic convention by a single vote in 1924. Aid to farmers was another issue which divided the party. Predictably, then, each demographic wing of the party had its own favorite presidential candidate that year. Urban Democrats favored New York Governor Alfred E. Smith. Rural Democrats, including most Southerners, endorsed former President Woodrow Wilson's Secretary of Treasury and son-in-law, William G. McAdoo, from California. McAdoo probably should have gotten the nomination, but he had once received a retainer from Edwin Doheny to represent him in the Teapot Dome Scandal. Guilt by association tainted McAdoo as a result. Franklin D. Roosevelt made a speech on behalf of Al Smith at the convention.

Real political in-fighting took place during the summer convention, during the days before air conditioning. The stalemate continued through 102 ballots before both McAdoo and Smith finally withdrew from the contest. Humorist Will Rogers remarked during the convention stalemate, "This thing has got to end. New York invited you folks here as guests, not to live." On the 103rd ballot, the Democrats nominated John W. Davis, a conservative corporation lawyer from New York. Davis later was on the plaintiff's side in the famous 1954 *Brown v. Board of Education of Topeka* school desegregation case. Charles W. Bryan, the Nebraska governor and brother of William Jennings Bryan, was given the vice-presidential spot on the ticket.

The Progressives

Republican progressives bolted their party as they had promised to do if LaFollette were not the nominee. The new Progressive Party then proceeded to nominate Robert M. LaFollette of Wisconsin as their standard-bearer. LaFollette's running mate was Burton K. Wheeler of Montana. During the campaign, LaFollette and

Judge and Jury of the Scopes "Monkey" Trial, 1925. Credit: Boston Public Library.

Wheeler ignored the Democrats and campaigned against the Republican ticket. Wheeler invented the "empty chair" debate when the Republican vice-presidential candidate, Charles Dawes, refused to debate him.

The Results

With the Democrats badly divided and the country experiencing a growing prosperity in most circles, a Republican victory seemed certain. There were few fundamental differences between Coolidge and Davis. Nevertheless, Americans did not rally to LaFollette's campaign. "Keep cool with Coolidge" was the successful Republican campaign slogan in 1924. President Calvin Coolidge won a landslide victory, with 382 electoral votes, compared to Davis' 136 and LaFollette's 13. LaFollette disappointedly carried only his home state of Wisconsin.

THE SCOPES TRIAL AND FUNDAMENTALISM

As explained earlier (see Chapter Five), American Christians had undergone dramatic changes since the late nineteenth century. The British naturalist, Charles

1924	48	CALVIN COOLIDGE	Republican	15,718,211	382	54.0
		John W. Davis	Democrat	8,385,283	136	28.8
		Robert M. LaFollette	Progressive	4,831,289	13	16.6

Darwin, had published his earth-shaking theory of biological evolution in his *On the Origin of Species by Natural Selection* in 1859. American Protestantism split over the evolution issue, which led to other movements and other splits.

The Scopes Trial

Liberal Protestants were suspicious of many of the miracles recorded in the Bible, and Higher Criticism was picking and choosing which parts of the Bible they would accept. The conservative reaction to this trend was the fundamentalist movement. Fundamentalists concentrated their energies on the evolution issue in the 1920s. Several states, mostly in the South, passed laws prohibiting the teaching of the theory of evolution in the public schools. When Tennessee passed such a law (the Butler Act) early in 1925, the American Civil Liberties Union (ACLU) offered to defend any teacher willing to openly violate the law. John T. Scopes, a high school science teacher in Dayton, Tennessee, accepted the ACLU challenge and read an explanation of Darwin's theory to his class.

Scopes was arrested, and the trial took place in the summer of 1925. A number of attorneys were brought in by both sides in the case. The most famous attorney for the ACLU, in defense of Scopes, was the criminal lawyer from Chicago, Clarence Darrow. The leader among the attorneys for the prosecution was William Jennings Bryan, the populist and former candidate for president. The "Monkey Trial," as it was quickly dubbed, drew national attention. Newspaper reporters filled the courtroom day after day in the jam-packed, non-air-conditioned environment. (It got so hot and humid that the trial was eventually moved outdoors.) A Chicago radio station, WGN, covered the court proceedings live for its huge Midwest listening audience.

The climax of the trial occurred when William Jennings Bryan took the stand as a self-proclaimed expert in both science and religion. Clarence Darrow made him look foolish to most Americans, as Bryan tenaciously defended the literal meaning of several controversial areas of the Scripture. Included among these was Bryan's stated belief in a literal 6-day Creation week, Eve's origin from a rib belonging to Adam, and Jonah's experience in the great fish.

Fundamentalists won the case, legally and technically, when Scopes was found guilty and fined $100. But in the larger public relations arena, fundamentalism lost in the eyes of most Americans. The Scopes trial was William Jennings Bryan's last hurrah. He died of a heart attack a few days after the end of the trial. Later, the Tennessee Supreme Court overturned Scopes' conviction on technical grounds, and the Tennessee law was never enforced again. For its part, the United States Supreme Court never ruled on the issue until 1968, when it overturned an Arkansas state law that forbid the teaching of evolution in that state's public schools.

Aimee Semple McPherson

While fundamentalism suffered a severe blow in the "Monkey Trial" at Dayton, it was by no means dead. Probably the most famous force for fundamentalism in the decades between the world wars was Aimee Semple McPherson. Head of a large congregation in Los Angeles, California, McPherson was a charismatic evangelist who appealed to other Americans through her radio program. Her fundamentalist theology was accented by a skillful use of theatrical aids. At one service, she actually used an electronic scoreboard to tell the story of the eventual triumph of good over evil. In some ways, then, McPherson was the forerunner of the modern television evangelist. When she died in 1944, McPherson's International Church of the Foursquare Gospel had more than 600 churches in the United States and elsewhere.

THE 1928 ELECTION

The Republicans

Calvin Coolidge took himself out of the presidential race in August of 1927, when he declared, "I do not choose to run in 1928." After that, his Secretary of Commerce, Herbert Hoover, became the Republican frontrunner. Farm groups attempted to nominate former Illinois Governor Frank Lowden, but Lowden withdrew from contention after the Republican convention defeated a platform plank endorsing McNary-Haugenism. Herbert Hoover won the nomination after that. Charles Curtis of Kansas was selected as Hoover's running mate in order to pacify the farm wing of the party.

The Democrats

The Democrats met at Houston in June. The urban wing of the party had finally obtained control by the time of the convention, and the Democratic Party nominated New York Governor Al Smith. Smith had been part of the marathon convention 4 years earlier before being forced to withdraw from the race. A well-respected Arkansas Senator, Joseph T. Robinson, was chosen as the Democratic vice-presidential candidate in 1928. Robinson represented the Protestant, rural, and "dry" wing of the party (on the Prohibition issue).

The Campaign and Results

During the 1928 presidential campaign, Hoover and the Republicans claimed credit for the general prosperity of the times. The Republican platform had also endorsed high tariffs, Prohibition, and the establishment of a Federal Farm Board to establish a farm marketing system designed to stabilize prices through orderly marketing of surplus crops. The Democratic platform had denounced Republican corruption, though it largely stemmed from the Harding years. The Democrats also endorsed lower tariffs and McNary-Haugenism.

Although Al Smith most definitely represented the "wets" on the Prohibition issue, the party platform that year promised an "honest effort" to enforce the law. The farm issue was the most discussed issue in the campaign, with most farm groups endorsing the Democratic ticket because of its support of McNary-Haugenism. However, the Prohibition issue tended to subtract from Smith's rural vote. Perhaps the most important issue in the campaign was Al Smith's religion. Smith had been the first Roman Catholic nominee for president by a major party in American history. In a decade of strong Ku Klux Klan influence, anti-Catholicism revived during the presidential election campaign in 1928. Smith's religion especially hurt him in the traditionally solid Democratic South. Smith was also hurt when the American Federation of Labor voted to remain neutral during the election. Smith's campaign manager, General Motors Chairman John J. Raskob, had influenced Smith to echo the Republicans' pro-business attitude to the degree that the AFL refused to endorse him.

In addition to these built-in disadvantages, Smith was also out campaigned by the Republicans. Herbert Hoover had served presidents of both parties, was a very capable Secretary of Commerce, and looked presidential. Hoover was also a far better

President Herbert Hoover. Credit: AP/Wide World Photos.

radio speaker than Smith. During the campaign, Hoover had promised a chicken in every pot and two cars in every garage.

Hoover carried 40 states and 444 electoral votes, while Al Smith carried only 6 Southern states plus Massachusetts and Rhode Island, for a total of 87 electoral votes. Smith had managed to lose even his home state of New York.

HOOVER'S EARLY EFFORTS

President Herbert Hoover's first concern was the farm crisis. The new president called a special session of Congress and, in June 1929, Congress passed the Agricultural Marketing Act. This bill created the Federal Farm Board in accordance with the Republican Party platform of the preceding year. Headed by Alexander Legge, International Harvester Company president, the Federal Farm Board made loans to agricultural cooperatives to help get them started. The law also established the United States Grain Corporation, a "stabilization corporation" designed to buy and sell grain at sufficient quantities to put and keep grain prices at the Bureau of

1928	48	HERBERT C. HOOVER	Republican	21,391,993	444	58.2
		Alfred E. Smith	Democrat	15,016,169	87	40.9

Agriculture Economics (BAE) level. If prices fell below the BAE price target, the corporation would purchase the commodity until the price reached the acceptable level. If prices rose above the BAE target, then the corporation would sell until the price dropped to the target level. The United States Grain Corporation went into effect the very week of the stock market crash, in October of 1929. After the crash, it kept purchasing wheat, but the price continued to drop until 1932.

THE STOCK MARKET CRASH

Few expected the stock market to crash in late 1929. The market had been riding high since 1927, and prosperity for most Americans indeed seemed to be a lasting affair. National income had increased about 23 percent between 1922 and 1929. The federal debt had been reduced more than 25 percent during the same years. Pro-business Republican administrations had been in power throughout the decade.

But all was not well. Stock prices had been unrealistically high since 1927, at least. In those days, a citizen could purchase stocks with a 90 percent margin. That means that one could buy stocks with only 10 percent cash down; the rest of the purchase was provided by banks on credit. This was only one factor which led to the kind of demand for stocks that raised the prices through the proverbial ceiling. By the late twenties, many stocks cost far more than the assets of the companies they represented, a condition known as "watered stock." It was a paper value that was bound to come down, a fact that many knew would eventually happen, but not when.

Stock prices peaked on September 3, 1929. Later that same month, there was a minor correction when stocks declined from 20 to 50 points. "Black Thursday" came on October 24, as prices took the first major nose dive. That very day, a group of major investors agreed to purchase $240 million worth of stocks, thus setting an example which would restore confidence in the market, stop panic selling, and bring stock prices back up. The market steadied for a few days. But when most of the investors did not follow through with the stock purchase scheme, "Black Tuesday" crushed the stock market on October 29. On that day, more than 16.4 million shares of stock were sold in panic. Brokers and major investors jumped out of windows in despair, although these incidents have been largely exaggerated in number. By mid-November, General Motors stock lost about half its value. By 1932, the average stock had dropped about 75 percent from its 1929 highs, as stockholders had lost about $45 billion.

The stock market crash on Wall Street America triggered a worldwide economic depression, although it did not specifically cause it. It was the worst depression the United States or the world had ever suffered. By 1932, there were some 12 million Americans out of work, roughly a 25 percent unemployment rate. More than 5,000 banks had collapsed by 1932, as millions of ordinary Americans lost their life savings. Private charities and local governments threw up soup and bread lines to feed the starving unemployed. People resorted to selling apples on the street for a nickel, just enough to feed their bellies. Human tragedies dominated statistics as

STOCK PRICES SLUMP $14,000,000,000 IN NATION-WIDE STAMPEDE TO UNLOAD; BANKERS TO SUPPORT MARKET TODAY

Sixteen Leading Issues Down $2,893,520,108;
Tel. & Tel. and Steel Among Heaviest Losers

A shrinkage of $2,893,520,108 in the open market value of the shares of sixteen representative companies resulted from yesterday's sweeping decline on the New York Stock Exchange.

American Telephone and Telegraph was the heaviest loser, $448,905,162 having been lopped off of its total value. United States Steel common, traditional bellwether of the stock market, made its greatest nose-dive in recent years by falling from a high of 202½ to a low of 185. In a feeble last-minute rally it snapped back to 186, at which it closed, showing a net loss of 17½ points. This represented for the 8,131,055 shares of common stock outstanding a total

PREMIER ISSUES HARD HIT

Unexpected Torrent of Liquidation Again Rocks Markets.

DAY'S   SALES   9,212,800

The New York Times *headline on the morning of October 29, 1929. Copyright (c) 1929 by The New York Times Company. Credit:* A History of the United States Since 1861, *by Daniel L. Boorstin and Brooks Mather Kelley, Ginn and Company, 1986.*

nothing seemed to relieve the suffering of otherwise hardworking Americans. This depression became known as the Great Depression. Many Americans have assumed that this was the only economic depression that Americans have experienced. Of course, that is simply not true; there have been at least a half dozen depressions in our history, depending upon one's precise definition. But the depression that lasted through the 1930s can truly be called the Great Depression because it had greater international effects, was deeper than most in some respects, and came suddenly at a time of apparent great prosperity for most Americans.

THE UNDERLYING CAUSES OF THE GREAT DEPRESSION

Most historians and many economists usually list most of the same underlying causes of the Great Depression.

Maldistribution of Wealth

The Secretary of Treasury for all 3 Republican presidents in the twenties, Andrew Mellon, was the chief architect of a tax policy which contributed significantly to the Great Depression. Based on the idea that wealthy individuals create jobs, Mellon's tax policies rewarded the upper class with tax breaks in order to force prosperity to "trickle down" to the rest of society. This "trickle down" economic theory inspired the regressive tax policies that contributed to a growing disparity between rich and poor during the 1920s.

This growing gap between rich and poor is not simply a topic for philosophers to debate the merits of equality versus inequality, as if individual initiative accounted for all of the results in one's socioeconomic status. The growing inequality had two very negative economic consequences in the practical world. First, it eventually reduced consumer demand for goods and services because it left larger numbers of consumers struggling just to pay for the basics of survival. This led, in turn, to an oversupply of goods and services in the marketplace. When businesses realized what was happening, most were forced to lay off workers and make every effort to sell their inventories first.

Second, and more subtle, the growing gap between rich and poor forced banks to increase the percentage of their riskier loans. Basically, this was a no-win situation for many financial institutions. Either they increase the number of risky loans, or they significantly reduce the number of loans they make. In either case, it became much more difficult to make money for such businesses. This contributed to a hidden but growing weakness in the banking industry throughout the decade. The stock market crash largely just revealed the unstable system, and pushed it over the cliff. And when large numbers of banks went bankrupt, the economy was in deep trouble, for financial institutions form the foundation of any economy. When it crumbles, the entire economic house falls down on top of it.

A Poor Banking System

In addition to the effect of the growing economic inequality during the twenties, the Federal Reserve System had not been functioning as it was originally designed in 1913. Instead, the 12 regional banks basically pursued 12 different, certainly uncoordinated, monetary policies. One key result of a poorly regulated banking system was the almost astronomical number of bank scandals, paralleling the speculation prevalent in so many other industries. There was no Federal Deposit Insurance Corporation (FDIC) in those days either, to protect depositors' money. Finally, the banks increased their own instability by unwisely using depositors' money to speculate in the stock market.

The bottom line was the increasing rate of bank failures across the nation in that decade. More than 5,000 banks went under between 1923 and 1928, mostly in rural areas hit hardest by the farm depression. Then, between 1929 and 1932, more than 5,000 additional banks failed, this time more in the urban areas of the nation. And then, from 1933 to 1935, another approximately 5,000 banks either went bankrupt or merged with each other in order to survive.

Poor Corporate Structure

The lack of government regulation of corporations, regressive tax policies, high tariffs, easy availability of credit, and a poor banking system all encouraged extraordinary speculation, the "investing" of moneys in unproductive or highly suspicious ventures. "Get rich quick" schemes outsmarted many individuals right out of their savings. At the corporate level, merger mania swept the nation. Some of these mergers helped increase business productivity, but much of it was simply an unproductive way to boost stock prices and make higher profits for stockholders. Corporate fraud ran rampant as well. All of this constituted an almost invisible instability in the economy. As long as things went well, few people were hurt. But when the stock market crashed, the country's poor corporate structure contributed to the economic chaos and hardships of the Great Depression.

Agricultural Depression in the 1920s

When the Great War ended and European agriculture was finally restored, a sudden decline in demand for American agricultural commodities hit American farmers hard. American farmers had also assumed the largest farm debt in history. This combination of a sudden and sharp drop in European demand and great debt brought such a drop in American farm prices and incomes, that it can only be called a farm depression. During the twenties, farm issues were hotly debated in Congress, but Republican presidents of the period vetoed the most favorable farm legislation. In other words, with the declining numbers and political influence of farmers, politicians could "safely" fail to deal effectively with that crisis. The significance here is that whenever one important segment of the economy is in a depression, it is probable that it will ultimately drag the rest of the economy down with it. And that is exactly what happened by the end of the decade.

International Trade Imbalance

By the end of the war, the United States was the leading creditor nation in the world. Among other things, this meant that it had the most gold, which was acquired from sales of American goods to foreign countries. The United States' trade surplus, partially due to high tariffs, meant that money was available to loan to other nations. Indeed, Americans loaned money to Germany so it could pay its war reparation payments to France and Britain, so that in turn, the British and French could pay on their loans from the United States, taken out during the war in order to purchase large quantities of food. On the other hand, high protective tariffs intensified the international trade imbalance by making it more difficult for foreign countries to sell their products in the United States. This loan cycle and protective tariff policy came crashing down when the American economy crashed in late 1929. This factor probably created a worse worldwide depression than it would otherwise have been.

Poor Economic Theories

To be fair, economics was a relatively new profession, and economists and politicians all had their pet theories, which were often held in dogmatic fashion. Among these were the ideas that the federal government budget must always be balanced, that the gold standard was the only sane and ideal monetary standard, and that high tariffs were needed to protect American industries even during an economic depression. In fact, after the Great Depression had begun, Congress passed the highest tariff in American history at that time, the Hawley-Smoot Tariff Act, in June 1930. This only made the depression worse for us and the Europeans.

HOOVER'S INITIAL RESPONSE TO THE GREAT DEPRESSION

Historically, economic depressions had been treated like violent acts of nature. Nothing could be done but to hang on for the ride. Most government officials echoed this traditional view after the 1929 crash also, including Secretary of the Treasury Andrew Mellon. But President Hoover had a different point of view. Having first been the head of the Belgium relief effort, then the United States Food Administration during World War I, Hoover knew that something could and should be done to bring relief to human suffering, but he was initially hesitant to use the federal government. Therefore, shortly after the stock market crash, the president called major business leaders to a White House conference and urged them to maintain their employment levels, wages, and expansion plans. Although pledges to do so were made at the conference, they were promises that, in most cases, could not be kept for very long.

In October 1930, Hoover created the Emergency Committee for Employment, headed by Colonel Arthur Woods, to coordinate an effort to help people find jobs. When it became apparent that the jobs were simply not there, the President's Organization on Unemployment Relief (POUR) replaced the earlier agency. Headed by American Telephone and Telegraph Chairman Walter Gifford, POUR was handicapped by the same philosophy that President Hoover held—that the character of recipients would be ruined by any kind of federal aid. Meanwhile, during the offyear Congressional elections in November 1930, voters demonstrated their anger by giving the Democrats control of the House of Representatives and several new seats in the Senate as well.

In October 1931, President Hoover took the lead in getting major banks to establish the National Credit Corporation. The idea behind this measure was to pool financial resources with which to make loans to banks that were in dire need. A similar voluntary organization was established for the railroad industry with the creation of the Railroad Credit Association in January 1932. Hoover also took the lead in increasing federal expenditures for road construction and river works, including the Hoover and Grand Coulee Dams out West. This provided a very small economic stimulus, but he negated that action with the Revenue Act of 1932, which increased corporation, excise, and personal income taxes in order to try to keep the federal budget balanced.

All of President Hoover's valiant efforts failed to relieve much suffering or to slow down the negative effects of the depression. By 1932, the unemployment rate was about 25 percent. Despite the president's efforts to keep banks and railroads from going under, relief for individuals was left to private charities and local governments. By 1932, many of these entities simply could not continue these efforts. Many cities went broke that year, as did the Red Cross. Tens of thousands of Americans were homeless. Many of these lived in shanty towns, derisively called "Hoovervilles," consisting of tents and cardboard boxes. Newspapers, dubbed "Hoover blankets," were used to keep warm with at night. Others, especially younger men,

"Shanty Town" 1936. Credit: National Archives.

became vagrants or hobos. Probably 2 million such hobos were traveling the freight cars on trains by the early 1930s, looking for temporary work in order to keep themselves alive.

Although President Hoover made significantly larger efforts than all previous presidents to fight the depression, he was still handicapped by his own philosophy. He was cautious in getting the federal government involved too deeply because of his laissez-faire notions that free enterprise should be allowed to operate with few restraints. He was absolutely adamant that private agencies provide relief to the unemployed because he honestly felt that any kind of federal government assistance would ruin the characters of the recipients. For example, in the summer of 1931, Hoover vetoed a bill to help feed starving farmers, but signed another one which fed the starving cattle of the starving farmers. Hoover was only reflecting what had been a strongly held attitude by most Americans for generations.

But by the early 1930s, the reality of the Great Depression was changing attitudes quickly. While the president demonstrated more flexibility than previous presidents had shown during economic bad times, Herbert Hoover's cautious nature kept him behind the American people's changing attitudes. Later generations would still unfairly blame Hoover for the depression. It is true that his policies continued the conservative tradition of the Harding and Coolidge years. There is little question but that these policies greatly contributed to an "anything goes" attitude in business circles, which fed speculation and fraud on a massive scale. The regressive tax policies had also widened the gap between rich and poor. But most historians believe that Herbert Hoover was the most competent of the 3 presidents during the decade. Certainly, he had already proven that he was a true humanitarian and a capable administrator. For the most part, Herbert Hoover was president at the wrong time in history.

RECONSTRUCTION FINANCE CORPORATION

President Hoover's most significant response to the Great Depression was the Reconstruction Finance Corporation Act, which Congress passed in January 1932. Hoover agreed to this bill only reluctantly, after he had to admit that his National Credit Corporation had been a failure. This new federal law established a government corporation called the Reconstruction Finance Corporation. The RFC was initially given more than $2 billion of federal revenue with which to make loans to large businesses to keep them afloat. As with earlier efforts, banks and railroads were the major recipients of these loans. After July 1932, loans could also be made to state governments to help finance their own relief efforts.

The Reconstruction Finance Corporation was the first time the "general welfare" clause of the Constitution was ever used to prop up the economic system. It was certainly too little too late, but it did lay part of the foundation for Franklin Roosevelt's New Deal. With the RFC, Herbert Hoover became a transition president in that he was the first American president in history to use the authority of the federal government to attempt to do something significant to fight an economic depression.

PROTESTS

Milk Dumping

Led by Milo Reno of Iowa, farmers in the Midwest created the Farmers' Holiday Association in 1931. This radical farm group attempted to force prices up by withholding grain and livestock from the market. Many Wisconsin and Iowan dairy farmers began dumping thousands of gallons of milk on the ground, also in an effort to raise milk prices. The first of these milk dumpings occurred in August of 1932, but several more took place in the next few years. Many Americans shrunk in horror as they heard about the dumping actions of farmers demanding higher prices in the face of human misery. But desperate people often do desperate things.

The Anacostia Flats Incident

But an event outside Washington, D.C. in late July 1932, attracted the most negative attention of all the protests against the Hoover administration. Congress had voted a veterans' bonus annuity back in 1924, over President Coolidge's veto, for all World War I veterans. This annuity was to be paid in 1945. But faced with the misery of economic depression, somewhere between 10,000 and 20,000 World War I veterans marched on Washington to demand the immediate payment of the promised bonus. Many of them brought their families with them. These bonus marchers camped outside the capital on the Anacostia Flats.

From this camp as home base, the veterans went onto Capitol Hill to lobby members of Congress during the day. After the Senate rejected a House-passed bill on June 17, many discouraged veterans went back to their homes. Estimates range anywhere from 2,000 to 10,000 people who remained at Anacostia Flats. Federal Bureau of Investigation Director J. Edgar Hoover and General Douglas McArthur were concerned that communists were the real leaders of the bonus marchers. These two men sought and won permission from President Hoover to use force to move the bonus marchers out of Anacostia Flats. Of course, the charge of communist leadership was entirely false. But on July 28, 1932, a military force of about one thousand men and a few tanks drove the marchers out of Anacostia Flats. The troops burned down the shanty "town" and killed a six-month-old baby, who died from tear gas poisoning. Badly advised, this event made President Hoover look downright callous to the human suffering of the Great Depression. Whatever slim chances the president had of being reelected that November were surely killed by the violence at Anacostia Flats.

THE 1932 ELECTION

The Republicans

The Republican national convention in 1932 had the oppressive air of defeat in it. Since the party could not find another sheep for the slaughter, President Herbert Hoover easily won renomination. Kansas Senator Charles Curtis was selected as Hoover's running mate. The Republican platform praised Hoover for his efforts in fighting the depression, and it endorsed a high, protective tariff and a balanced federal budget. Reluctantly, the Republicans also pledged to end Prohibition, what Hoover himself had once called that "noble experiment."

The Democrats

When the Democrats met in Chicago for their convention that year, the sweet smell of victory was everywhere. Indeed, the Democrats probably could have nominated the devil himself and been confident of victory in 1932. Three major candidates vied for the party's presidential nomination at Chicago. First, there was Al Smith, former governor of New York and the 1928 Democratic candidate. The popular Speaker of the House, Texas Congressman John Nance "Cactus Jack" Garner, hoped for the nomination. Then there was the current governor of New York, Franklin D. Roosevelt, who had been the party's vice-presidential nominee back in 1920.

In the early ballots, Roosevelt held the lead but could not muster the two-thirds majority, which the Democratic Party rules required in those days. Facing the possibility of a deadlocked convention or a "dark horse" candidate emerging, William G. McAdoo, the leader of the California delegation and former presidential aspirant himself, announced that his state's delegates were switching from Garner to Roosevelt. That announcement changed the entire mood of the convention, which then promptly nominated Franklin D. Roosevelt for president. As part of the deal with McAdoo, Roosevelt and the convention accepted John Nance Garner as the vice-presidential nominee.

The Democratic Party platform called for a balanced federal budget and an end to Prohibition. It also appealed to farmers by calling for more federal agricultural programs. Although Roosevelt himself probably did not know the precise direction he wanted to take the country, he did inadvertently name his anti-depression program when he declared in his acceptance speech at the convention, "I pledge myself to a new deal for the American people." The designation New Deal stuck as the term that described his administration's program to fight the Great Depression. The stage was set for a vibrant and vigorous campaign as strains of the song "Happy Days Are Here Again" washed over the audience. And ever since the days of FDR, that song has been identified with the Democrats.

The Campaign and Results

The two presidential campaigns could not have been different in style if they had been night and day. Hoover violated the cardinal rule of politics when he allowed himself to look like the sure loser in the race. He weakly attempted to put the best face on the bad times by making references to the alleged fact that "prosperity is just around the corner." By contrast, Roosevelt campaigned with all the enthusiasm and confidence of a sure winner. Certainly, he had reason to be confident of victory, but it is still true that Roosevelt was optimistic by nature. He would almost surely have campaigned in the same enthusiastic way had the outcome of the race been in doubt. Among other virtues, Franklin D. Roosevelt was a champion campaigner.

When the votes had been counted, 12 years of Republican rule in Washington were coming to an end. Roosevelt won the landslide election victory with 472 electoral votes to Hoover's 59. Although the 1936 election would cement these results, this election victory marked the beginning of the Democratic Party as the nation's majority party. The Great Depression would last throughout the thirties, but the New Deal would change the face of American government for decades to come.

1932	48	FRANKLIN D. ROOSEVELT	Democrat	22,809,638	472	57.4
		Herbert C. Hoover	Republican	15,758,901	59	39.7
		Norman Thomas	Socialist	881,951		2.2

ADDITIONAL READINGS

Alfred D. Chandler, Jr., *The Visible Hand: The Managerial Revolution in American Business* (1977). Includes an excellent analysis of the crucial changes in American business practices after World War I.

Nancy F. Cott, *The Grounding of Modern Feminism* (1987). Includes a sophisticated analysis of the debate among and between feminists during the 1920s. Connects the varies positions of the principal figures with earlier and later feminist movements.

Sara M. Evans, *Born for Liberty: A History of Women in America* (1989). Includes an excellent discussion of the debate over the changing morality of the 1920s.

James J. Flink, *The Car Culture* (1975). The best single volume on the history of the automobile and how it changed American life.

Nathan I. Huggins, *Harlem Renaissance* (1971). The most insightful history of the Harlem Renaissance.

Kenneth Jackson, *Crabgrass Frontier* (1985). The best history of the suburbs. Includes a good survey of suburbanization in the 1920s.

Robert Lynd and Helen Lynd, *Middletown* (1929). A pioneering and still useful sociological analysis, documenting the changes in Muncie, Indiana, between the 1890s and 1920s.

Robert S. McElvaine, *The Great Depression: America 1929–1941* (1984). Includes an excellent analysis of the weaknesses in the American economy in the pre-Depression decade.

Ronald Marchand, *Advertising the American Dream* (1985). A brilliant, beautifully illustrated account of the rise of the advertising industry.

Robert K. Murray, *The Red Scare: A Study in National Hysteria 1919–1920* (1955). A pioneering analysis of the impact of the Bolshevik Revolution on domestic postwar politics.

Gilbert Osofsky, *Harlem: The Making of a Ghetto* (1965). A solid and succinct social history of this key African American community.

Emily S. Rosenberg, *Spreading the American Dream* (1982). An important study of American economic and cultural expansion around the world from 1890 to 1945.

Robert Sklar, *Movie-Made America* (1976). A fine cultural history of the motion picture. Especially strong on the early years of Hollywood.

CHAPTER TEN

Roosevelt and the New Deal

MAJOR EVENTS

1933   Roughly 13 million workers unemployed
First New Deal: National Recovery Administration; Public Works Administration; Agricultural Adjustment Administration; Tennessee Valley Authority; Federal Emergency Relief Administration; Civilian Conservation Corps
Twenty-first Amendment repeals Prohibition (Eighteenth Amendment)

1934   Indian Reorganization Act
Growing popularity of Father Coughlin and Huey Long
General strike in San Francisco

1935   Second Hundred Days: National Labor Relations (Wagner) Act; Social Security Act; Works Progress Administration
Committee for Industrial Organization (CIO) established
Dust Bowl
Boulder Dam completed

1936   Roosevelt defeats Alf Landon in reelection landslide
Sit-down strike begins at Flint

1937   General Motors recognizes United Automobile Workers
"Court-packing" plan
Memorial Day Massacre in Chicago
"Roosevelt recession" begins

1938   CIO unions withdraw from AFL to form Congress of Industrial Organizations
Fair Labor Standards Act

INTRODUCTION

Franklin Delano Roosevelt, the thirty-second president of the United States, brought to the office of the presidency and to the nation a confidence that all problems had solutions. He led the country through two of its most crucial events, the Great Depression of the 1930s and World War II. The confidence he had inspired would gain him the presidency in four unprecedented consecutive elections—1932, 1936, 1940, and 1944.

A BIOGRAPHICAL SKETCH OF FRANKLIN D. ROOSEVELT

Franklin was born into the world of wealth and privilege on January 30, 1882, on his father's Hyde Park, New York estate. Franklin's mother Sara was 26 years younger than her husband, and she would be a dominating force in her son's life. The young Roosevelt was schooled by governesses and private tutors until the age of 14, when he attended Groton Preparatory School. He continued his education at Harvard University, where he joined the Republican Club in honor of his famous cousin Theodore Roosevelt, who was then president of the United States, and graduated with a degree in history in 1904. Following his graduation and an extra year of graduate study, he enrolled in Columbia University Law School. He attended Columbia for 3 years and passed the bar exam in 1907. Meanwhile, in 1905, he married Anna Eleanor Roosevelt, a distant cousin and the daughter of Theodore Roosevelt's older brother Elliot. In fact, because her father was already deceased, President Theodore Roosevelt walked Eleanor up the aisle and gave her away to his fifth cousin Franklin.

It is ironic that much of Franklin's career would parallel his famous cousin's, except as a Democrat. In 1911, he was elected to the state Senate in New York. From 1913–1920 he served as Assistant Secretary of the Navy under President Wilson. He did not resign this position to fight in World War I, however, as Theodore Roosevelt had done to fight in the Spanish-American War. In 1920 he ran, although not successfully, as the Democratic nominee for vice-president on the ticket with Governor James Cox. Then from 1929–1932 he served as the governor of New York, a position he held when his party first nominated him for president in the summer of 1932.

Roosevelt's accomplishments take on an added dimension of fortitude and courage after August 1921. It was at this time that he was stricken with polio, and he would not walk for the rest of his life without the aid of leg braces and crutches or canes. For a while, it seemed that his political career was finished; indeed, most friends and family members urged him to take it easy and enjoy a life of luxury. But with the persuasion of New York Governor Alfred E. Smith and his own wife Eleanor, he eventually continued. His campaigns for governor of New York, and later the presidency, were active and energetic to prove that if elected he could carry out the duties of both offices. At one point in his young career, Eleanor discovered that there was a relationship between her husband and her own personal secretary. For that offense, Eleanor denied him a close physical relationship for the rest of their married lives, although she never left him. His affair, meanwhile, did resume later

Franklin D. Roosevelt. Credit: Keystone-Underwood.

in life, although no one knows whether sex was even possible for him because he suffered from polio.

During his first term as governor of New York, Roosevelt began implementing social reforms and broadening the power of the state government as he stated, "to promote the welfare of the citizens of the state." As the depression in his second term as governor worsened, the programs to assist the people were increased. New York, under the leadership of Roosevelt, was the first state to offer direct unemployment aid of $20 million to its citizens out of work because of the depression. Soon the fate of the unemployed across the nation was his concern, and he expanded the role of the national government to immense proportions to combat the Great Depression.

Roosevelt was a master politician with the uncanny ability to seemingly read the minds and the moods of the people before their thoughts were expressed. He was pragmatic and optimistic in his approach to problems, willing to experiment with policies until he found one that worked. He inspired loyalty to him and to his ideas. Franklin D. Roosevelt, or FDR as he preferred, was the champion political campaigner in American political history. Perhaps only Ronald Reagan, president in the 1980s, was his equal in this respect.

THE INAUGURATION OF FRANKLIN D. ROOSEVELT

Roosevelt took the oath of office on March 4, 1933. He was the last president to hold his inauguration in March. The Twentieth Amendment to the Constitution, ratified in February 1933, moved the inauguration date for all future presidents to January 20, following the November election. His speech on March 4 was extremely important because he was setting the priorites of his administration. On that occasion, he spoke these words:

> First of all, let me assert my firm belief that the only thing we have to fear is fear itself—nameless, unreasoning, unjustified terror which paralyzes needed efforts to convert retreat into advance. In every dark hour of our national life a leadership of frankness and vigor has met with that understanding and support of the people themselves which is essential to victory. I am convinced that you will again give that support to leadership in these critical days. . . . Our greatest primary task is to put people to work . . . .

These words were meant to lay out his plan of action but to also build up the confidence of the American people, one of his greatest assets, that working together they could solve any problem. He inspired a nation to trust him, although he was still not sure of the solutions the New Deal would present to pull this country out of the depression. As he stated in a campaign speech on May 22, 1932, at Oglethorpe University:

> The country needs and, unless I mistake its temper, the country demands bold, persistent experimentation. It is common sense to take a method and try it. If it fails, admit it frankly and try another. But above all, try something. The millions who are in want will not stand by silently forever while the things to satisfy their needs are within easy reach.

He was right, and at the time of his inauguration approximately 25 percent (nearly 13 million people) of the nation's workers were out of work. There were also millions who were out of their homes or farms and living in parks or on the streets, thousands who were out of food and standing in bread lines, and everyone was out of patience with government solutions that did not work.

THE BANKING CRISIS

The president's first order of business was to stabilize the banking system. People had lost confidence in their banks. Runs on banks—citizens withdrawing deposits—and hoarding of currency had caused sound and unsound banks alike to close, eventually jeopardizing the financial system of the nation. From February 1930 to February 1933, approximately 5,500 banks had shut down. In some cities, where banks could not supply cash, employers paid off in IOUs (I Owe You) good at local stores. Other cities resorted to issuing scrip in lieu of dollars. In communities across America, citizens bartered goods and services among themselves. By March 2, every state had closed banks, put them on holidays, or put them under strict state regulation.

President Franklin D. Roosevelt presenting his radio "fireside chat." Credit: AP/Wide World Photos.

On March 5, 1933 (his first full day in office), President Roosevelt, using the dubious authority of the 1917 Trading with the Enemy Act, declared a national bank holiday, which closed all banks, effective the next day, for the next four days—March 6–9. Then on March 9, he called Congress into a special session, and the Emergency Banking Act was passed to confirm the emergency steps the president and the secretary of the treasury had taken since March 4. The president was given broad discretionary powers over all money transactions, including credit, currency, gold and silver, and foreign exchange. Gold hoarding and exporting were forbidden. Sound banks in the Federal Reserve system were allowed to open only with a license from the Treasury Department. The new law authorized federal bank inspectors to examine the books of all the banks to determine if they were viable. Those banks which possessed assets at least equal to their deposits were allowed to reopen.

Then on Sunday evening, March 12, FDR addressed the nation in the first of many so-called radio "fireside chats," because he usually spoke to his radio audience from a position next to the fireplace with his dog Falla at his feet. (FDR did with radio what Ronald Reagan did with television in the 1980s.) Rather than giving a speech, he seemed to be talking to Americans personally, and in his chat he assured the public that the banks allowed to reopen were safe once again and asked citizens to return their deposits. The trust he had inspired in the public, and his use of psychology, worked like a charm. By March 15, half the banks of the country, doing about 90 percent of the banking business, reopened.

Later, on June 16, 1933, Congress passed the Glass-Steagall Banking Act, which created the Federal Deposit Insurance Corporation (FDIC) to federally insure bank deposits. The original maximum amount insured was $2,500, but it was increased to $5,000 in 1935. The June law also separated commercial (deposit) banking from investment banking.

PHILOSOPHY AND THE BRAIN TRUST

The basic philosophy of FDR's New Deal was the recognition that America had arrived at a point that government was required to play a larger role in planning and implementing these plans for a stable economy. Government measures would eventually diminish, and private economic efforts would once again take control of the economy as the depression was dealt with, but certain new responsibilites were accepted permanently by government, such as regulation of the stock market, more coordination of the banking system, and federal development of water power and other resources, to name just a few. Times were so desperate that Roosevelt probably could have brought to the American government more radical measures advocated by socialists, but Roosevelt was dedicated to the capitalist system. He wanted to reform the system so it would work, not overthrow it. More radical groups and ideologies had to be neutralized so as not to appeal to desperate people. Often called revolutionary, his New Deal was actually more evolutionary, building upon many of the concepts of the Progressive Era, which had rejected laissez-faire and promoted social control with more government regulation. World War I and the decade of the 1920s interrupted this progressive agenda, and the New Deal of Roosevelt was to make up for this lost time and more. Countries in northern Europe had already accepted these concepts. Roosevelt's New Deal appeared revolutionary because of the large number and scope of the legislative programs he proposed.

Roosevelt's cabinet and other advisers, known as the "Brain Trust," were responsible for proposing and carrying out the New Deal programs. At least half of the original cabinet members were known as liberal, favorable to the government taking on the task of relief and reform of the economy. Some of the more important posts were filled by Cordell Hull, Secretary of State (until 1944); Henry Morgenthau, Jr., Secretary of the Treasury (from 1934 onward); Henry A. Wallace, Secretary of Agriculture, son of President Warren Harding's Secretary of Agriculture Henry C. Wallace (FDR's Wallace became vice-president in 1941); Frances Perkins, Secretary of Labor, the first female cabinet member in American history (and FDR's state industrial commissioner when he was governor of New York); and Harold L. Ickes, Secretary of the Interior, who was a progressive Chicago Republican who had worked for the Roosevelt campaign in 1932; and Postmaster-General James A. Farley (until 1940), Roosevelt's campaign manager.

The "Brain Trust" was a group of university professors, primarily from Columbia and Harvard, and their proteges, who had advised Roosevelt from his early campaign days. They developed proposals, assembled data, prepared speeches and, when the candidate was in the White House, they prepared legislation; some even held official positions. Roosevelt was a man of many firsts, and this was the first large-scale invasion of academia into government. Raymond Moley, Professor of Public Law at Columbia University, was the most influential of the group, and for a time he was the Assistant Secretary of State and seemed closest to the president. (Moley later broke with FDR and became a critic of the New Deal.) Rexford Tugwell,

Eleanor Roosevelt and Madame Chiang Kai-Shek, 1943. Credit: Library of Congress.

Professor of Economics at Columbia, was an expert in agriculture who was later appointed as Undersecretary of Agriculture. Felix Frankfurter, Professor of Law at Harvard, was a font of ideas and later appointed a Justice of the Supreme Court. Adolf A. Berle was a lawyer and an economist who later became Assistant Secretary of State. Berle had co-authored a book entitled *The Modern Corporation and Private Property* in 1932 that had concluded that it was impossible to recreate the classical society of small competitors; therefore, structural reforms were needed, as in the philosophy of Theodore Roosevelt's New Nationalism. (See Chapter Six for more information on New Nationalism and the various progressive approaches of that time period.)

The two most influential advisors to Roosevelt were probably Harry Hopkins and his own wife Eleanor Roosevelt. Hopkins, a chain-smoking friend of FDR's in his New York state government days, would become the busiest administrator in the New Deal and was appointed as Secretary of Commerce in 1939. Eleanor Roosevelt was well read and had been involved in certain causes for years, and she continued to work for the rights of women and black civil rights as the president's wife. For her efforts to be a politically active First Lady, and her liberal views, Eleanor Roosevelt was severely criticized in her day. But she continued tirelessly to travel and report to her husband the mood of the people she spoke with, and what programs were working and those that did not seem to be. Her travels were so extensive, in fact, that it was news when she was in Washington, D.C. Others advised the president at various times and with varying influence on politics or publicity. This inner circle was often criticized as too radical and for making law rather than executing it as is the job of the executive branch. They were not radicals in the true sense of the word, but they did play an important role in writing legislation. These were times of crisis, and the roles of government and its officials were expanded to meet the emergency. For a while, Congress did give extraordinary power to the executive branch.

THE FIRST ONE HUNDRED DAYS

The special session of Congress called by President Roosevelt on March 9 to deal with the banking crisis remained until June 16, and was later know as the "Hundred Days." This time frame is later looked upon by some historians as the initial phase of the First New Deal, which dealt with relief and recovery from the devastation of the Great Depression. The Second New Deal, if one accepts that there was a separation of the two, began in June–August 1935, and dealt with reform and the problems of the lower classes. During the first few months of the new administration, Congress was desperate for the leadership of the president in solving this crisis. Bills passed quickly without every member even reading them. For example, the Emergency Banking Relief Act was introduced, passed, and approved on the same day. Roosevelt and his people were ready to tackle every task, and the city of Washington was energized by this group of enthusiastic Democrats. The period of the "Hundred Days" (sometimes called the "First Hundred Days") were the busiest, most productive legislative period in American history to date. The following is a chronological list of the legislation of the "Hundred Days":

Emergency Banking Relief Act—March 9
Economy Act—March 20
Beer-Wine Revenue Act—March 22
Civilian Conservation Corps Reforestation Relief Act—March 31
Federal Emergency Relief Act—May 12
Agricultural Adjustment Act—May 12
Tennessee Valley Authority Act—May 18
Federal Securities Act—May 27
Gold Repeal Joint Resolution—June 5
National Employment System Act—June 6
Home Owners Refinancing Act—June 13
Banking Act of 1933 (Glass-Steagall Act)—June 16
Farm Credit Act—June 16
Emergency Railroad Transportation Act—June 16
National Industrial Recovery Act—June 16

The Economy Act and The Beer-Wine Revenue Act were introduced to keep two campaign promises. The Economy Act authorized the president to cut federal government department budgets up to 25 percent and federal salaries up to 15 percent. Roosevelt used this authority to cut about $500 million from federal spending by chopping veterans' benefits and federal employees' wages, all in an effort to balance the budget. (Congress would restore all of these benefits in the near future.) During an economic depression, reducing the federal deficit is the last thing you want to do because it reduces consumer demand for goods and services even further, only serving to aggravate the depressed conditions. The Economy Act, however, reflected the president's fundamental fiscal conservatism, especially early in his administration. He was not the doctrinaire liberal that his reputation now seems to paint him.

Roosevelt had promised in his campaign to push for an end to prohibition, pointing out that a revived liquor industry would provide legitimate jobs and taxes, and that most of the nation was ignoring the prohibition law at this time anyway. The Beer-Wine Revenue Act allowed the sale of beverages with an alcohol content of 3.2 percent. The Twenty-first Amendment, which overturned the Eighteenth Amendment (Prohibition), was considered ratified on December 5, 1933. The Prohibition era was over.

The New Deal laws passed, then and later, and the agencies created to implement those laws, were so numerous that most of them became known by their letters—such as the CCC, WPA, CWA, TVA, NRA, AAA, and others. All were created to fulfill objectives that can be grouped into the three "Rs" of the New Deal—Relief, Recovery, and Reform—to clarify the bewildering array of legislation.

RELIEF

The objective of the legislation under the area of "Relief" was to provide jobs and immediate assistance for the basic necessities of life. The salaries were paid by the federal government. Relief measures were temporary solutions until the economy revived enough for the private sector to once again provide sufficient employment. The Roosevelt administration realized that the cooperation and voluntarism solu-

Civilian Conservation Corps (CCC) workers leaving camp in Lassen National Forest. Credit: U.S. Forest Service.

tions advocated by President Hoover were not able to solve a depression of this magnitude. Massive government assistance was necessary to prevent starvation or perhaps even riots and eventually revolution by a people pushed beyond what they could bear. Roosevelt trusted the American people and democracy, but he was willing to take the country on a new course rather than test their limits.

The Civilian Conservation Corps

The Civilian Conservation Corps (CCC) was established by the Unemployment Relief Act (or the Civilian Conservation Corps Reforestation Relief Act) on March 31, 1933, as the first New Deal relief agency. The CCC provided work for young men, 17–25 years of age. They lived in camps in a quasi-military setting with the youths usually sleeping in tents and eating meals together. Their jobs included planting trees, fighting forest fires, cleaning up national parks, and even building some parks. Most young men in the CCC received $30 a month and free room and board. Twenty-five dollars of their wages was required to be sent to their parents or guardians. Between 2.25 and 2.75 million men were given temporary employment with this agency, which spent a total of about $2 billion during its existence. This was a very popular program, and it received very little criticism.

The Federal Emergency Relief Administration

The Federal Emergency Relief Administration (FERA) was established by an act of Congress on May 12, 1933. Harry Hopkins, a superb manager, was appointed the administrator for the FERA, which now had $500 million dollars appropriated by Congress to advance grants to the states. This action was taken on the grounds that relief was a national problem that the states could simply not handle by themselves. Both the dole, in the form of free butter, cheese, and other over-produced food stuffs, and work relief were features of FERA. This relief administration ended on December 31, 1935, after having spent approximately $3 billion.

The Home Owners Loan Corporation

The Home Owners Loan Corporation (HOLC), begun on June 13, 1933, assisted needy Americans by refinancing their home mortgages at lower interest rates to avoid foreclosure. Eventually during the New Deal, about 20 percent of all home mortgages were refinanced. This government assistance not only allowed more Americans to keep their homes, but it also protected banks and other mortgage companies from more defaults, which damaged their businesses. Three days later, on June 16, the Farm Credit Act created 12 farm credit banks around the country to help farmers refinance their farms and ward off foreclosures.

The Public Works Administration

The Public Works Administration (PWA) was created under Title II of the National Industrial Recovery Act, enacted on June 16, 1933. Administered by Interior Secretary Harold Ickes, its task was to create public works jobs quickly in order to stimulate manufacturing or processing of construction commodites like concrete, steel, lumber, and other materials. The PWA was an example of a new concept in economics labeled pump priming. The government would prime the pump of the economy with money and jobs (as pumps had to be primed with a little water to begin their pumping), and once an economic sector was progressing successfully, the private business sector would step in and take over. Pump priming was based on the theories of government spending "to move the wheels of industry off dead center" of British economist John Maynard Keynes, the father of Keynesian economic theory. Keynes also believed that government deficit spending was a temporary necessity in poor economic times until the employed and profits from industry could rebound and pay it back. This agency spent approximately $3 billion during the course of the New Deal.

The Civil Works Administration

The Civil Works Administration (CWA) was organized in November 1933 after Harry Hopkins persuaded FDR that direct federal relief was necessary to get many Americans through the winter of 1933–34. Almost $1 billion was spent on short-term federal, state and local public works projects. Funds came from FERA, PWA, and local governments. This administration was dissolved in March 1934, and its functions were transferred back to FERA.

The Works Progress Administration

By January 1935, the president shifted the emphasis in relief policy toward providing work relief on a much grander scale than before. Thus, on April 8, 1935, the Emergency Relief Appropriation Act provided $4.88 billion for public works projects and other work relief agencies (such as the Resettlement Administration, the Rural Electrification Administraton, and the Works Progress Administration). The largest relief agency of the New Deal, the Works Progress Administration (WPA), headed by Harry Hopkins, was created in May 1935 to create thousands of short-term work assignments; in 1939 its name was changed to the Work Projects Administration, which allowed it to keep its familiar WPA acronym. Along with the CCC, this was the most famous and popular of all New Deal Agencies. It was criticized by some for waste, inefficiency, and political corruption, but its accomplishments cannot be disputed. At least 85 percent of the funds were spent on salaries, which increased the buying power of the workers. Until its termination on June 30, 1943, it had put about than 8.5 million people to work.

Its primary focus was to put to work manual laborers building highways, building and repairing bridges, improving public buildings, constructing and repairing airport landing strips, and public swimming pools. (The latter helped keep jobless teens out of trouble during the summer months.) Improvement of what we would call the infrastructure today was the primary goal of this program. The program also made provisions for cultural projects. Toward this end, the WPA hired writers, artists, actors, musicians, and historians. For example, the Federal Theatre Project (part of the WPA) hired writers and performers to put together plays on major American history themes. Musicians and performers were paid to tour the United States and conduct plays and concerts. Many historians were employed to research the American past. The analysis of diaries and interviews of former slaves provided new insight into slavery and the Reconstruction Era for the future study of the subjects. The result of WPA historical research was that most historians eventually revised the traditional perspectives on slavery and Reconstruction. (See Chapter One for a discussion of the different schools of thought on Reconstruction among historians.) More than 1.4 million projects were completed with a price tag of $11 billion.

Sign on Site of White Fringed Beetle Project, A Works Progress Administration (WPA) Project. Credit: AP/Wide World Photos.

The National Youth Administration

The National Youth Administration (NYA) was created in June 1935 under provisions of the Emergency Relief Appropriations Act, as was the WPA. Directed by Aubrey Williams, the NYA provided part-time jobs to high school, college, and graduate students to encourage them to remain in school. It also provided work for those who had left school and were between the ages of 18–25. Providing government funded jobs for young people also kept them out of the competition in the private sector for jobs that men with families needed. The work consisted of in-school projects which were typically in the laboratory, library, school administrative offices, or research areas, doing secretarial or janitorial tasks. The out-of-school program built or repaired schools, swimming pools, libraries, bandstands, furniture, and performed other functions around the schools. The pay was $6 per month (high school), $20 per month (college), and $30 per month (graduate school). For the next 7 years following its establishment, the NYA provided part-time employment for more than 4.5 million young men and women at a cost of approximately $325 million.

Some Thoughts on Relief Efforts

Depending on what is precisely counted as relief agencies, and there was enough overlap to make that exact identification difficult, somewhere around $20 billion was spent by the New Deal on relief efforts. The remarkable thing was that there were no major scandals at the national administrative level, although some states and municipalities had some. Conventional wisdom states that these various relief programs greatly lessened human suffering, some even suggesting that perhaps they prevented major riots or even a totalitarian system of government. And certainly, much of the relief work improved the country's natural resources.

RECOVERY

The second "R" dealt with government intervention to recover broad sectors of the economy to their previous level of activitiy, or at least as close as possible. The agricultural and industrial sectors of the economy needed planning and regulation to function efficiently and supply the needs of the nation.

AGRICULTURAL RECOVERY

Agriculture had been in a depression since 1920, and it took many years of government assistance and millions of dollars to create some stability for the farming industry. The success was never as great as was hoped for because there are too many variables in this sector of the economy.

The Agricultural Adjustment Act

The first Agricultural Adjustment Act (AAA) established the Agricultural Adjustment Administration on May 12, 1933, with George Peek, an Illinois Republican as its head. The task of this agency was to restore the purchasing power of agricultural producers by raising farm prices to a parity level that they had experienced from 1909–1914. In other words, the goal was to provide farmers with the same standard of living, with the ability to purchase the same level of goods and services, as they could during the 1909–1914 period.

A basic problem for the farmers was that they had become so efficient at growing food that they grew surpluses which kept crop prices low. The core idea of the first AAA was to eliminate surpluses by paying farmers to produce less farm commodities. To encourage farmers to take part of their acreage out of production, the AAA, on the authority of the secretary of agriculture, paid farmers a direct cash payment for voluntarily signing such allotment plan contracts with it. The funds for these cash payments came from a special tax on food processors. Thus, in two different ways farmers would be helped—by limiting production of farm products, prices would tend to rise; and the cash payments to farmers who agreed to limit their production. Seven products were originally targeted for subsidies—wheat, cotton, field corn, hogs, rice, tobacco, and dairy products. Later, 9 other commodities were added, including beef and sugar.

The growing season was under way by the time the AAA had put into place its plans. It was decided that destruction of crops and hogs was therefore necessary to raise the prices in 1933. Millions of acres of crops were ploughed under and in August, more than 6 million hogs were slaughtered. Mostly little pigs, about 90 percent of their weight was used for fertilizer. The public was outraged that such waste could be allowed, no matter what the reason, when there was hunger in the nation. The AAA took note of the public cry, and in the future special efforts were made to distribute the surpluses. It was ironic that 90 percent of the weight of the slaughtered hogs was used for fertilizer, which was used to increase production, when the goal was to decrease production. With the efforts of the AAA and the droughts in the 1930s, farm prices increased by about 58 percent between 1933 and 1935. This represented 86 percent of the parity that was the original goal, making the first AAA a reasonable success. Many tenant farmers and sharecroppers were actually hurt by the AAA, however, as subsidies went to landlords, who in turn bought tractors and other mechanized equipment that reduced their need to rely on tenant farmers.

In October 1933, the Commodity Credit Corporation was established under the umbrella of the AAA. Its purpose was to loan money to farmers already on the allotment acreage plans in exchange for crops as collateral being stored until the prices rose. If they rose enough, the farmer could then pay off his loan, but if they didn't, then the CCC would absorb the loss. (Don't confuse this CCC with the Civilian Conservation Corps.)

There were critics of the AAA, and on January 6, 1936, the United States Supreme Court agreed with them. In the case of *United States v. Butler*, the AAA was declared unconstitutional by a 6–3 vote. The Court ruled that the contracts to reduce acreage production did not constitute interstate commerce, and the processing tax was not general or uniform in nature.

The Resettlement Administration

The Resettlement Administration (RA) was created by Executive Order on May 1, 1935 and headed by Rexford Tugwell. Its purpose was to relocate farmers from submarginal lands by purchasing those poor lands and moving the families to better farmland. The RA bought about 5 million acres and resettled 4,441 families. The RA also built three so-called "greenbelt" communities, near Washington, D.C., Cincinnati, Ohio, and Milwaukee, Wisconsin, as experiments in suburban planning.

The Farm Security Administration

Conservative opposition to the Resettlement Administration led the president to replace that agency with the Farm Security Administration (FSA) by the authority of the Bankhead-Jones Act, which passed on July 22, 1937. The FSA sought to help tenants become landowners and small farmers to keep their farms with low interest loans (3 percent) over a 40-year payment schedule. This administration was also headed by Rex Tugwell and loaned about $260 million to 41,000 families between 1937 and 1946. It also created about 30 camps for between 12,000 and 15,000 migrant workers' families, although this move brought a storm of protest from southerners and other conservatives. Since August 1946, the FSA has been known as the Farmers' Home Administration.

The Rural Electrification Administration

The Rural Electrification Administration (REA) was organized on May 11, 1935 because it was not profitable for private electric companies to bring electricity to rural areas. So the government stepped in to encourage the adoption of Rural Electric Cooperatives (RECs) to bring electricity to rural America. RECs were loaned money from the REA, either to buy power from existing private power companies or to build their own electric generator system. The REA spurred some private electric companies to enter rural areas in order to compete for consumers. By 1940 approximately 31 percent of rural Americans had electricity in their homes, and by 1955 that figure was 90 percent. Lyndon B. Johnson, a young congressman from a district that included rural areas west of Austin, Texas, was able to attract large amounts of REA money to his district. In this way, Johnson built a long political career from his reputation as the man who turned the lights on. And of course, he later became the thirty-sixth president of the United States.

The Soil Conservation and Domestic Allotment Act

This federal farm law replaced the first AAA in February 1936, about one month after the AAA had been ruled unconstitutional by the Supreme Court. This new farm policy paid out more than $500 million to farmers who would divert part of their farmland from staple crops to soil-building crops in an effort to repair the land damaged by the Dust Bowl. But this policy had little, if any, effect on farm prices.

Dust Bowl, Boise City, Oklahoma, 1935.

The Second Agricultural Adjustment Administration

In February 1938, the second Agricultural Adjustment Act resurrected the Agricultural Adjustment Administration (AAA). It continued the soil conservation and acreage allotment concepts, but the financing was provided from general funds out of the federal Treasury Department and the rules of operation were changed. This act authorized the secretary of agriculture to fix a marketing quota if it was determined that a surplus of any export farm commodity threatened to reduce the price level. A two-thirds vote in a national referendum among specific farmers (such as cotton, tobacco, rice, wheat, and corn growers) was necessary to approve the secretary's decision to establish a marketing quota. Farmers selling more than their quota would be heavily fined. In this more negative way (the first AAA had a positive incentive of cash payments), farmers were still paid not to produce so many crops in order to limit supply and raise farm prices. The second AAA also established the "ever-normal granary," Secretary Henry A. Wallace's brainchild, through which the farmer could receive a loan from the government by storing his surplus crops under government supervision. And the new law established the

Federal Crop Insurance Corporation, providing crop insurance for the first time; initially, crop insurance was made available just to wheat growers. Although it has been amended several times, the second AAA is still the foundation of United States farm policy today.

The Dust Bowl

A series of droughts in the early 1930s turned much of the central plains area into an area that was so devoid of moisture that it became known as the "dust bowl." The dust bowl began in January 1932, when wind storms hit the plains and the Southwest with a fury. The droughts of 1934 and 1936 were the worst the area had known for 75 years. Crop production between the Appalachians and the Rocky Mountains was cut in 1934 by 33 percent. The droughts assisted the federal government in its plans to reduce crop production and raise prices, but at a great price to those who worked the land, especially the tenant farmers. The crops withered, and the winds coming from off the Rocky Mountains blew the topsoil away, sometimes all the way to the Atlantic. The worst dust storm occurred in May 1934, when more than 300 million tons of topsoil was blown 500 miles to the east. The worst year was 1935. On April 14 of that year, a "black blizzard" even hit Washington, D.C. During the dust storms conditions were reported in terms of visibility. "Dust pneumonia" became a serious lung health problem in many of the plains states. People often wore masks outside and put blankets or sheets on the house windows, all in a vain attempt to keep the foul dust out of the human physiological system.

A committee was sent by the Department of Agriculture to determine the causes of the extreme drought damage. The committee reported to Secretary Wallace that most of the problems of the area could be traced to the fact that the system of agriculture developed on the Great Plains was, in fact, more suited to areas where more regular rainfall occurred. The Homestead Act had provided allotments that were too small and required that part of each allotment must be ploughed, which caused overcultivation of the soil. The profits to be made from producing an abundance of crops to feed the Allies during World War I had also enticed the farmers to overcultivate the dry areas. Poor farming methods, such as plowing in too shallow a manner, were the result of pressures from the Food Administration during the war. Everything had been alright during the 1920s because of the normal rainfall which fell in the plains. But the drought conditions of the first half of the 1930s killed microscopic organisms that hold the soil together. The resulting problem is called flocculation. Thus, when the winds blew into the plains under these conditions, large amounts of topsoil were "gone with the wind."

Thousands moved away from the dust bowl areas of western Nebraska, western Kansas, eastern Colorado, the Oklahoma panhandle, the first rows of Oklahoma counties east of the 100th meridian, and the Texas panhandle. These people, who became known collectively as "Okies," moved what they could carry with them to the Pacific Northwest and California. In the 1930s, more than 350,000 moved from the "dust bowl" to California. Landowners in California advertised that there were plenty of jobs available in California. But so many workers came to find work in the fields of California, alongside the other migrant workers, that the Californians turned some away illegally. Those that stayed faced discrimination because they lived in shantytowns, because their wages were so low, or because they could not find work at all. The relief resources of California were stretched even further when the "Okies" could not find work either on the farms or in the cities. The ill treatment suffered by these refugees from the droughts of the Plains was the subject of John Steinbeck's book *The Grapes of Wrath*, published in 1939.

INDUSTRIAL RECOVERY

Former President Herbert Hoover's Reconstruction Finance Corporation was continued during the New Deal. Directed by Jesse H. Jones, a Texas banker, the RFC was broadened in 1934 to make loans to small businesses too. The total amount of RFC loans during its lifetime was about $15 billion.

The National Industrial Recovery Act

The National Industrial Recovery Act (NIRA) of June 16, 1933, created the National Recovery Administration (NRA) as the major instrument for achieving industrial recovery in the nation. Its concept was based on the popular but false premise that too much competition had helped cause the Great Depression. The National Chamber of Commerce, for example, had recommended in 1931 that there be a relaxation of the antitrust laws so a national business council could self-regulate business. Thus, under the New Deal, the NRA's main effort was to (1) end cutthroat competition and (2) raise industrial prices by limiting production to actual needs.

Headed by retired General Hugh S. Johnson, the NRA created hundreds of specialized committees for nearly every kind of business in the economy. For example, there was a steel committee, glass committee, and a rubber committee. These NRA committees, composed of representatives from industry, workers, and consumers, each wrote codes of conduct and set business ethics for its specific industry or business. The final individual codes were submitted to the president or his representative for approval. If the president approved the code, all members of the industry were legally bound by its regulations, even those who had not been involved in its formulation. And any who violated the code could face court injunctions to force compliance. If a committee could not agree on its code of conduct, then the president was authorized to write it himself. Actions under the codes did exempt businesses from the antitrust laws. The goal was to raise prices by limiting production to actual need. Toward this end, the codes usually established production quotas, set prices, limited the number of work hours, and required a minimum wage. Business espionage and bribery were also prohibited. Section 7a of the NIRA, allowing workers "to organize and bargain collectively through representatives of their own choosing," was the first time that a major federal law had encouraged collective bargaining.

As administrator, General Hugh Johnson's task was to bring every industry under a code of fair competition. Using many of the methods he had used as one of Bernard Baruch's lieutenants on the War Industries Board during the Great War,

General Johnson began to mobilize business to fight the depression. There were parades, billboards, and magazine articles to promote the goals of the NRA. It became patriotic to put your industry under a code. The blue eagle was developed as the symbol for all to know who was participating in the program. Companies who signed up under codes were allowed to display the blue eagle and the sign "NRA— We do our part." Americans were encouraged to only buy from those who displayed the blue eagle. By February 1934, only a small segment of American industry remained to be codified.

At first most businesses cooperated because they were desperate for solutions to their failing businesses. But as conditions improved under the NRA, the instances of code violations increased. Criticism of the NRA also increased from old-time progressives (who were trustbusters by nature), from consumers complaining of high prices, and from small businesses who claimed that the codes favored the big businesses. The NRA committees were indeed dominated by big business representatives, and most codes were formulated for those companies which could afford the wage and hours conditions more easily. The result was that many small businesses did not benefit from the protection of the codes and were even hurt by them. The decline of the NRA's popularity was damaging because it depended upon cooperation for its success.

Matters were made even worse when Johnson was replaced by the National Industrial Recovery Board in September 1934. The experiment was in jeopardy, but Roosevelt still asked Congress to extend the NRA for another two years. However, the Supreme Court took the decision of whether or not to extend the legislation out of the control of Congress. In the case of *A.L.A. Schechter Poultry Corporation v. United States*, the Court ruled on May 27, 1935, that the NRA was unconstitutional. The agency had no legal right to punish the Schechter Poultry Corporation for selling alleged sick chickens, because the company was only involved in intrastate commerce, which belonged to the domain of the individual states. The act was also declared unconstitutional because it had delegated legislative power to the president concerning commerce.

After the demise of the NRA, the New Deal began to reverse policy and go after near-monopolies with antitrust suits rather than discourage more competition. World War II would bring this policy shift to an end when big business was needed to supply war equipment. After that, the trend toward a relaxed posture regarding antitrust laws in the United States continued.

REFORM

This third "R" dealt with long-range economic reforms of a more structural nature. Legislation was passed to protect and advance the public's interests through regulation and reform in the areas of natural resource development, the stock market, banking, international trade, old age security, labor laws, and other areas. The reform measures beginning in 1935 were part of Roosevelt's Second New Deal, which began to change the emphasis of the programs toward structural reforms that would make it more difficult for the country to experience another major depression and make it easier to provide more help for the disadvantaged.

The Tennessee Valley Authority

During the Great War the federal government had built a large hydroelectric power plant at Muscle Shoals, Alabama, on the Tennessee River. Attempts to sell the plant to private investors or put it to any other use in the 1920s failed. The Tennessee Valley Authority (TVA) was created on May 18, 1933, as a government corporation to organize and fund a system of dams and hydroelectric power plants on the Tennessee River to provide for flood control, cheap electricity, and to instigate the development of the region. Development of a cheap source of power would further the social and economic development of one of the poorest areas in the country. The states to benefit would be Tennessee, North Carolina, Kentucky, Virginia, Mississippi, Georgia, and Alabama. Headed by David E. Lilienthal, the TVA was a very successful example of federal-regional cooperation and of the ability of the federal government to get the job done when private enterprise is unable or unwilling to do it. The TVA revitalized the entire Tennessee Valley. By 1938 its electricity was being sold to about 40,000 customers, and by 1941, that number was approximately 400,000. During World War II, the TVA provided the power for the manufacture of munitions and for the atom bomb plant at Oak Ridge, Tennessee.

The Securities Exchange Act

The Federal Securities Act (or the Truth in Securities Act), passed on May 27, 1933, had required corporate executives to give the Federal Trade Commission full information on all stocks sold to the public. Hoping to correct unfair practices and severe problems in the securities marketplace, Congress passed the Securities Exchange Act on June 6, 1934, to provide for federal regulation. The Securities and Exchange Commission (SEC), with the authority to license stock exchanges, was established. Full disclosure of information on all securities traded was required. The Federal Reserve Board could also regulate credit used for stock buys with its power to regulate margin requirements. Joseph P. Kennedy, whose son John F. Kennedy would later become the thirty-fifth president of the United States, was the first SEC Chairman. Kennedy himself had been a securities manipulator and was too controversial to remain as chairman for long. He was forced out after serving a little less than one year.

The Public Utility Holding Company Act

The 1920s had witnessed odd octopus-shaped public utility empires across the United States, which had achieved enormous power. On August 28, 1935, the Public Utility Holding Company Act gave the Securities and Exchange Commission full control over financial operations of holding companies and restricted gas and electric companies to operating in one geographical region.

Monetary Reform

One of Roosevelt's first priorities was to stabilize the currency of the nation. The value of the dollar, which was deflated by the depression, had to be inflated in order for prices to rise. On April 5, 1933, FDR issued an Executive Order requiring that all gold was to be taken to local banks, which would then return it to the Federal Reserve banks by May 1. (Coin collectors were exempted by the law.) On June 5, Congress forbade interest payments by government or private bonds to be paid in gold. Later in 1933, FDR reduced the gold content of the gold dollar, and on January 31, 1934, settled on 59.06 percent (or cents) of its previous amount. This was really only a paper percentage because the Gold Standard Act of 1934 (January 30) forbade the new coining of gold; it also mandated that gold stocks were the backing for gold certificates, old greenbacks, and treasury notes, and that Federal Reserve banks must have 40 percent gold reserves behind member bank reserves. All of this represented a modified gold standard, not really a full abandonment of it. (That would come in October 1971, when President Richard Nixon took the nation completely off the gold standard by ordering that dollars could no longer be redeemed in gold.)

The Silver Purchase Act of June 1934 commanded the Treasury Department to purchase silver in order to increase its price, and to issue silver certificates, which were redeemable in silver dollars, into circulation. Western silver interests were elated, for this was the culmination of the old agrarian Bryan Democrats' dream.

All the measures taken by the Roosevelt administration and Congress concerning gold and silver were aimed at a managed currency concept. Specifically, the goals were to (1) increase prices by increasing the money supply, and (2) devalue the dollar on foreign money exchanges so it was cheaper for other countries to buy American products. The actual results of this monetary tinkering did not include a significant increase in prices, but it did increase exports from the United States.

The Banking Act of 1935

The Federal Reserve System, which had been created in December 1913, had never operated as an effective national banking system because the Federal Reserve Board allowed the 12 regional Federal Reserve Banks to pursue 12 different monetary policies. This new legislation, passed in August 1935, strengthened the Federal Reserve System by giving the newly organized Board of Governors direct control over areas such as reserve requirements and interest rates.

The Reciprocal Trade Agreements Act

In June 1934, Congress followed Secretary of State Cordell Hull's recommendations and passed this tariff reform measure. It allowed a president to lower tariffs on individual imports by as much as 50 percent, without Senate approval, in return for reciprocal trade agreements for other nations to accept goods from the United States. The "most-favored nation" trade status originated with this bill also. Technically an amendment to the Hawley-Smoot Tariff Act (June 1930), this new law took most of the tariff battles out of Congress and politics. Twenty-one nations, mostly in Latin America, reached agreements with the United States by 1939.

The Social Security Act

FDR called this law of August 1935 his number one achievement as president. Social Security required compulsory participation in a federally sponsored pension plan, to be funded by taxes on employees' wages and on employers' payrolls. It also created survivors' benefits for victims of industrial accidents, unemployment insurance, aid for dependent mothers and children (ADC), and the blind, to be financed on a federal matching funds basis with the states. It originally excluded farmers, domestic workers, and the self-employed. Much confusion has developed over the years since 1935 concerning the purpose of the system's retirement fund. The clear fact is that Social Security was never intended to constitute the entire retirement plan for senior citizens; it was only a supplemental plan. The significance of the Social Security Act was that it established the principle of federal responsibility for social welfare.

The Revenue Act of 1935

In his June 19, 1935 message to Congress on tax revision, the president declared, "Our revenue laws have operated in many ways to the unfair advantage of the few, and they have done little to prevent an unjust concentration of wealth and economic power." At his request, the Revenue Act of 1935 increased taxes on the wealthy. The surtax rate on income above $50,000 was increased, estate and gift taxes were raised, and the rate on all corporation incomes above $50,000 was raised to 15 percent. But taxes on small corporations were lowered from the uniform 13 percent to 12½ percent. This is sometimes known as the "soak the rich" tax, and it was one indication of changes to come in the New Deal.

The Wagner Act and the Fair Labor Standards Act

The heart of the New Deal's approach to the working class was contained in the Wagner Act and the Fair Labor Standards Act. As these each relate to a larger topic, they are treated elsewhere in this chapter. For a discussion of the Wagner Act, see the section within this chapter entitled "Labor and the New Deal." For information on the Fair Labor Standards Act, see the section entitled "The New Deal Winds Down."

THE SECOND NEW DEAL

The increased Democratic majorities in the Senate and the House in the congressional elections of 1934 strengthened President Roosevelt's position to move the New Deal in the directions that constituents were demanding. Under attack from business on one side and critics who believed the New Deal had not done enough to relieve the problems of the people on the other, Roosevelt pressed for many of the pieces of legislation in 1935 covered in the previous "Reform" section. To maintain political support, and to fulfill the ideals of the New Deal for the country, the Roosevelt administration maintained relief and recovery as needed, but also moved forward with more social legislation to advance the rights of labor, give security to the unemployed and the aged, improve the standard of living for many Americans, and protect the New Deal from the Supreme Court.

CRITICISM FROM THE CONSERVATIVES

Conservative opposition to Roosevelt's New Deal came from Republicans and Democrats who believed that (1) the deficit ($34 billion by 1936) was a disastrous mistake and threatened economic stability; (2) the president's increased power was unconstitutional and actually threatened democracy; and (3) the New Deal's encouragement of labor organizations and other infringements on the authority of business leaders threatened the free enterprise system. The American Liberty League was organized in August 1934 as a right-wing ultraconservative organization to challenge the power and programs of Roosevelt. The DuPonts and other wealthy industrialists financed the activities of the organization. Long-time Democrats like John W. Davis and Alfred E. Smith, the Democratic presidential candidates in the 1924 and 1928 elections respectively, were also vocal members of the Liberty League and two of its original co-founders. FDR had called Alfred Smith the "Happy Warrior" and had nominated him as the Democratic candidate for president in 1928. Smith, a supporter of Roosevelt in 1932, now believed the New Deal was taking the country in the wrong direction.

CRITICISM FROM THE LIBERALS

The liberals, those to the left of center on the political spectrum, were more of a threat to Roosevelt because of their larger followings. They believed that the New Deal fell far short of the types of assistance that ordinary Americans were entitled to. Upton Sinclair, who had written *The Jungle* in 1906 that helped get the Meat Inspection Act passed, was one Roosevelt critic from the left. Sinclair ran for governor of California as a Democrat in 1934 on a platform calling for high state income taxes, an inheritance tax, and a $50 monthly pension to the aged poor (over 60 years of age). He made quite a political impact on the West coast, but he lost the election.

Dr. Francis E. Townsend, a dentist and public health officer from Long Beach, California, advocated something on the same order as Sinclair that became known as the Townsend Plan in the 1930s. It proposed to create an old-age revolving pension fund by giving $200 a month to all retirees over the age of 60, with the stipulation that the money must be spent within thirty days. The funding for the plan was to come from a 2 percent tax on business transactions (something of a national sales tax). The basic premise of the plan was that the spending of this government pension would stimulate the economy with a demand for more goods and services. The plan was not economically feasible, but Townsend Clubs spread across the country in 1935. The excitement generated by Dr. Townsend evaporated when FDR convinced Congress to pass the Social Security Act in August 1935.

Huey P. Long. Credit: AP/Newsfeatures.

Father Charles E. Coughlin was a Roman Catholic priest with his own Sunday afternoon radio program airing from Detroit, Michigan, all over the country on the CBS radio network. Approximately 30 million listeners regularly tuned in to hear what Coughlin had to say in his show's prime. In the early days of the New Deal, Coughlin had been a supporter of the New Deal, calling it "Christ's Deal." But in 1934, Coughlin began to criticize the president and his programs, adding his voice to what became known as the "thunder from the left." He called for a more liberal use of silver in the economy, the nationalization of banks, and finally placed much of the blame for the Great Depression on an international bankers' conspiracy led by Jews. Father Coughlin's admiration for the fascist ideals of Mussolini and Hitler, along with their anti-semitic doctrines would finally bring an order from his superiors in the Catholic Church for his silence. In late 1934, Father Coughlin created the National Union for Social Justice and advocated an economic system similar to Mussolini's fascist corporatism.

The most serious threat from the left came from Louisiana's Democratic Senator, Huey P. Long, who was nicknamed the "Kingfish." Long appealed to the poor, white, uneducated, rural, Protestant and predominantly southern Americans to throw Roosevelt out of the White House in 1936. He formed his own program to fight the depression, the Share our Wealth Society, in February 1934. Long's plan would give every family an estate, or homestead, worth $5,000, and a guaranteed income of $2,500 per year. These benefits would be financed by a 100 percent tax on all incomes over $1 million per year and a complete appropiation of all fortunes over $5 million. By 1935, there were more than 27,000 Share our Wealth Clubs in operation around the country. The plan appealed to more than 7 million Americans, but the reality was that the wealth was not large enough in America to support Long's plan.

Long's ultimate goal was to become president of the United States. Had he lived, he probably could have pulled in several million votes in the 1936 presidential election, which many Democrats feared would give the White House to the Republicans. But his life was cut short as the result of a confrontation with Dr. Carl Weiss, an irate dentist, on September 8, 1935. Weiss pointed a gun at the senator, apparently because he saw Long as a tyrant who had wronged his father-in-law. In response to Weiss' actions, Long's bodyguards began firing indiscriminately in a narrow hall, killing both Weiss and Long. Thirty bullets were fired into Weiss' body. Long was so popular that he virtually ruled Louisiana as a dictator during 1934 and 1935. He even had his own army of private citizens. "I am the law!" he once exclaimed, and in Louisiana that was no exaggeration. Leaders with that kind of power, who also use it arrogantly as Long did, certainly make a number of enemies. From that perspective, it is not surprising that he was finally killed. Reverend Gerald L.K. Smith, a Shreveport minister and close associate of Long, took over the political machine and emphasized the fascist tactics even more; his followers even wore brown shirts like Hitler's supporters in Germany. But Smith did not have the personal charisma that Huey Long had possessed, and the organization quickly crumbled.

THE 1936 ELECTION

The Candidates and the Platforms

In 1936 the Democrats easily and enthusiastically renominated Roosevelt and Vice-President John Nance Garner without any opposition. The platform for the Democrats was the popularity of the president and the numerous achievements of the New Deal.

The Republicans nominated Alfred M. ("Alf") Landon, the governor of Kansas and a former Bull Moose progressive, as their presidential candidate. On an interesting note, the Republicans almost nominated New Hampshire Senator Stiles Bridges as Landon's running mate, but some were afraid that the Democrats would campaign around the country taunting that "Landon's Bridge is falling down!" So Colonel Frank Knox, the publisher of the Chicago *Daily News*, was selected as their vice-presidential candidate instead. Their own slogan was an interesting one, "Off the rocks with Landon and Knox." The governor seemed to have several assets. First, he was an old progressive supporter of Theodore Roosevelt in 1912. Second, he had balanced the state budget in Kansas, and his calm personality might be seen as a pleasant change from the exuberant Roosevelt. He also had the support of the majority of the newspapers across the country. The Republican platform was a promise to keep important aspects of the New Deal, but with more efficient management. For example, the Republicans promised to regulate business, supply benefits to the farmers, guarantee labor the right to organize, and employment or benefits to the unemployed. With all of this, they also promised to balance the budget.

With Huey Long dead, the followers of Townsend, Coughlin, and Smith formed the Union Party in June of that year and nominated Republican Congressman William Lemke of North Dakota. Other third party candidates included Socialist Norman Thomas and Communist Earl Browder.

The Results and the Significance of the Election

The Republican strategy failed miserably to convince Americans that they could manage the New Deal more efficiently than the Democrats. That should not be surprising because the opposition party rarely wins the White House unless it vigorously offers a real alternative to the voters. Franklin Roosevelt won by a landslide, carrying all states except Maine and Vermont, including Landon's home state of Kansas. Roosevelt received 523 electoral votes and 27.8 million popular votes compared to Landon's 8 electoral votes and 16.7 million popular votes. Lemke earned no electoral votes and only about 882,000 popular votes in a disappointing showing. Norman Thomas and Earl Browder received about 200,000 and 80,000 popular votes respectively.

The significance of the 1936 presidential election concerned the support the Democrats received from labor unions and African-American voters. Organized labor, including the AFL and the CIO, gave an unprecedented $1 million and its organizational strength to the Roosevelt campaign and became an integral part of the Democratic Party. And African-Americans cemented the trend begun 4 years earlier by overwhelmingly giving their votes to Roosevelt and most Democratic candi-

FDR's 1937 Courtpacking Scheme ("Nine Old Men"). Credit: Brown Brothers.

1936	48	FRANKLIN D. ROOSEVELT	Democrat	27,752,869	523	60.8
		Alfred M. Landon	Republican	16,674,665	8	36.5
		William Lemke	Union	882,479		1.9

dates, not because FDR pushed civil rights (which he did not), but because the old cliche of "the last to be hired, the first to be fired" gave them an economic incentive to stick with the New Deal. Eleanor Roosevelt's vocal support for black civil rights was also a draw to these voters.

In his second inaugural address, given on January 20, 1937, FDR stated that the country had not reached its goals yet.

> But here is the challenge to our democracy: In this nation I see tens of millions of its citizens—a substantial part of its whole population—who are at this very moment denied the greater part of what the very lowest standards of today call the necessities of life . . . I see one-third of a nation ill-housed, ill clad, ill nourished.

Roosevelt's second administration was to clearly work towards more social justice, but he would also meet more resistance from many areas this second time around, particularly in Congress.

THE COURT-PACKING CONTROVERSY

Due to his growing frustration over the Supreme Court's opposition to New Deal legislation, President Roosevelt proposed the Judiciary Reorganization Bill on February 5, 1937. Between 1935 and 1937 the Supreme Court had declared 7 basic New Deal laws unconstitutional, including the AAA and the NIRA, which the president had considered vital to recovery. Lower courts were also challenging New Deal laws and were included in Roosevelt's plans to change the courts' anti-New Deal stand with the appointment of judges more agreeable to the president's programs. When the president proposed his Reorganization bill, he prefaced the plan by remarking that because of a backlog of work and the elderly ages of so many of the members of the judiciary, it would be wise to appoint new members to help with the work load. Roosevelt proposed that he be allowed to appoint an additional justice to the Supreme Court, up to a maximum of 6, for every justice who failed to retire within 6 months of turning 70 years old. Another important aspect of the bill was the addition of up to 50 judges of all classes to the federal courts.

The plan brought widespread debate and outrage, centering on the Supreme Court membership. Roosevelt was accused by many of attempting to "pack" the Supreme Court with justices who would be expected to uphold his legislative programs. He even outraged many New Deal Democrats, who told the president that this would set a bad precedent that future presidents, including Republican ones, could use to destroy not only judicial independence but the separation of powers built into the Constitution. The bill never made it out of committee, and Roosevelt abandoned it in July.

Although FDR lost the battle over his court-packing scheme, he won the war. Almost immediately the Supreme Court began upholding the constitutionality of New Deal laws that were challenged in the courts. The Court's reversal began in April of that year (1937), when it surprisingly ruled that the National Labor Relations Act was indeed constitutional. In the same year, the Social Security Act and a Washington state minimum-wage law were also upheld.

During his time in office, FDR appointed a total of 9 Supreme Court Justices. Four of them forged a new liberal majority on the High Court for years to come— Hugo Black (1937–1971), Stanley F. Reed (1938–1957), Felix Frankfurter (1939–1962), and William O. Douglas (1939–1975). Ironically, Justice Black, who had been a former member of the Ku Klux Klan, had shifted from one end of the political spectrum to the other by the time he was appointed to the Supreme Court.

THE ROOSEVELT RECESSION

Dubbed the "Roosevelt recession," an economic slump began in August 1937. Although the Great Depression was not over, this slump constituted a recession within a depression because the economy had been slowly improving before this. The major cause for the slump was Roosevelt's decision to dramatically reduce federal relief spending on projects like the PWA and the WPA. He was worried about the increasing amount of deficit spending, for his goal was still to balance the federal budget. Therefore, believing that the country was coming out of the depression, he ordered a cut in government spending in June 1937. At the same time, the Federal Reserve Board tightened credit to stop inflation in the economy. The reduction of government spending, coupled with the Fed's restrictive monetary policies and the withdrawal of Social Security funds from workers' paychecks, reduced the amount of money the public had to spend, which caused the economic recession. Debate raged in the administration as to what caused the recession and what should be done about it. But Roosevelt finally agreed with Harry Hopkins that government spending was still necessary to fight the depression. And on April 14, 1938, he asked Congress to pass new appropriations for the relief programs. The PWA and the WPA received the bulk of the $33 billion voted for public works with their multitude of jobs, and the nation recovered from this recession. Unemployment, however was still a problem for about 10 million workers in 1939, due to the ongoing depression.

The New Deal Winds Down

In the spring of 1938, the New Deal was winding to a close. The aggressive foreign policies of the Italians and the Germans in Europe and of the Japanese in Asia were commanding more of the nation's and the president's attention. The final significant New Deal laws passed were the Wagner-Steagall National Housing Act (1937), which strengthened an earlier effort (the National Housing Act of 1934) to provide funds for housing projects for low-income families; the second Agricultural Adjustment Act (1938), discussed earlier in this chapter; and the Fair Labor Standards Act (1938).

Roosevelt proclaimed the June 1938 Fair Labor Standards Act to be his number two achievement as president. It was also the last major New Deal legislation, as events leading to World War II dominated the national scene shortly after this. This act, applying to most interstate businesses, established the first federal minimum wage law—25 cents per hour at once and gradually raising it to 40 cents an hour (within the bill itself); it was amended to 75 cents an hour on October 26,

1949. The law also set a standard maximum work week of 44 hours at once and provided that it would move down to 40 hours within 3 years, and employers were required to pay time and a half pay for overtime. The Wage and Hour Division was created within the Labor Department to enforce the law. And in an effort to control child labor, the Federal Labor Standards Act prohibited the interstate transportation of goods made by children under the age of 16. This provision was essentially the same as the old Keating-Owen Act of 1916 that the Supreme Court had thrown out in its 1918 *Hammer v. Dagenhart* decision. (See Chapter Six for a discussion of those earlier efforts to control child labor.)

After the *Hammer* decision, social workers and other reformers sought ways to get around the Supreme Court. In 1924 Congress passed the Child Labor Amendment to the Constitution and sent it on to the states for the ratification process. Twenty-eight states had ratified it by early 1937, but that was 8 short of the three-fourths majority required for constitutional amendments. But because the Supreme Court had begun upholding New Deal legislation after the spring of 1935, Congress decided to place child labor restrictions in the Fair Labor Standards Act. This time it stuck, and the nation has not had a major, or serious, child labor problem since.

In his annual message to Congress on January 4, 1939, for the first time since 1933 President Roosevelt did not ask for any new domestic reforms.

LABOR AND THE NEW DEAL

Background and Early New Deal Labor Policies

Labor had suffered during the 1920s, but with the passage of the National Industrial Recovery Act, with its Section 7a guaranteeing collective bargaining, the future looked brighter. This NIRA labor-management honeymoon had resulted in efforts to increase employment, raise wages, reduce hours, and end child and sweatshop labor. And between 1933 and 1935, union membership had increased from about 1 million to approximately 4 million.

President Roosevelt created the National Labor Board by an executive order on August 5, 1933, to serve as a mediation commission designed to cooperate with the NRA. The NLB consisted of labor and management representatives, with New York's Democratic Senator Robert F. Wagner as chairman. The Board attempted to settle many labor disputes with compromise, but opposition to unions mounted as the honeymoon feelings wore off. Because the NLB could only appeal to the NRA and/or federal courts for redress of grievances, and the courts were not sympathetic to labor or the New Deal at this time, the National Labor Board was replaced by the National Labor Relations Board (NLRB) in the spring of 1934. The NLRB was a three-member commission authorized to hold elections to determine the right of a union to represent workers in a given company. But it too was devoid of really effective enforcement machinery, which Senator Wagner had urgently requested. After the Supreme Court ruled the NIRA unconstitutional in May 1935, Senator Wagner led the fight for a comprehensive, effective federal labor law on behalf of organized labor. The result was the National Labor Relations Act, which Congress enacted on July 5, 1935.

The Wagner Act

The National Labor Relations Act is commonly referred to as the Wagner Act in honor of its chief sponsor. The Wagner Act was (and still is today) the most fundamentally pro-union federal labor law in American history. It was based on the philosophy that government support was necessary to put labor on an equal basis with management. Known as labor's Magna Charta ("Great Charter"), the Wagner Act contained the following key provisions: (1) it outlawed all company unions (the 1926 Railway Labor Act had outlawed them in the railroad industry only); (2) it created a new, more effective NLRB, with authority to issue "cease and desist" orders against unfair labor practices engaged in by management; the NLRB also could (and still does) order certification elections, which allow the majority of non-management employees in a given potential bargaining unit to determine if they want a union to represent them or not; decertification elections determine whether a union will continue to represent workers; and (3) it provided a long list of unfair labor practices which an employer cannot engage in—such as interference in union business and refusing to bargain in "good faith."

From July 1935 to April 1937, employers largely ignored the Wagner Act on the advice of business attorneys and others in the anti-union movement, like the American Liberty League. These conservative forces predicted that a test case landing in the United States Supreme Court would result in the Supreme Court declaring the law unconstitutional. This seemed a reasonable possibility, given the growing hostility of the court toward the New Deal.

The AFL and the CIO

During this same basic time period there was conflict within the labor movement itself. A vigorous debate was raging within the American Federation of Labor between craft unionists and industrial unionists. The former wanted to stay the course which opposed much organizing efforts among the unskilled workers, and the latter wanted to organize unskilled workers and bring industry-grouped unions into the AFL along with the craft unions. The industrial unionists were led by United Mine Workers (UMW) president John L. Lewis in a group calling itself the Committee for Industrial Organization (CIO). By the late 1930s there were 10 "dual" unions within the AFL (termed dual because they belonged to both the AFL and the CIO, which originally operated within the AFL). Having already lost ground in the struggle to expand industrial unionism the year before, the AFL Executive Committee ordered the CIO to dissolve in 1936. When it refused to do so, the CIO was removed from the AFL on August 4, 1936. Eventually, in May 1938, the CIO renamed itself the Congress of Industrial Organizations, keeping its same acronym, and put together a new labor federation with John L. Lewis as its first president.

Sit-Down Strikes

The result of the widespread violations of the Wagner Act and the rejection of the CIO by the AFL was a series of sit-down strikes in the mid-thirties to force compliance with the labor law. These strikes were actually spontaneous outbreaks from the rank and file workers, not planned and organized by the CIO. Workers would shut off their machines and simply sit down beside them inside the factories, thereby more effectively preventing management from using strikebreakers to replace them.

The first recorded use of the sit-down strike was in 1933, but the greatest number occurred between late 1935 and early 1937. The most famous and significant of this type of strike was the General Motors Flint Strike, which broke out in Flint, Michigan, and lasted from December 30, 1936 to February 11, 1937. Relatives and friends brought food, newspapers, and radios to the strikers through windows, even using ladders to reach the floors above the first level. Once the strike started, local United Auto Workers (UAW) officials organized committees inside the factories to patrol and prevent strikers from damaging machinery. Destruction of private property was a sure way to turn public opinion against the strike. General Motors appealed to the governor of Michigan, Frank Murphy, to settle the strike because the police force of Flint was far too small to handle the situation. But Governor Murphy was a pro-labor Democrat and refused to intervene, maintaining correctly that National Guard units were unnecessary because there was no general breakdown in law and order. General Motors next appealed to the White House. President Roosevelt believed that the sit-down strike was an illegal tactic (at least trespassing), but he was sympathetic to CIO goals, and he also refused to help General Motors or any corporation ignoring the Wagner Act, especially since it would not be appropriate to go over the state governor's head when no general threat to the public safety existed. With pressure from Governor Murphy, and no assistance from any government quarter, GM agreed to recognize the UAW and negotiate a contract settlement.

The success of the UAW strike at General Motors had at least three significant results at the national level: (1) Walter Reuther came into national prominence as the leader of a strong United Auto Workers Union (he was the national president until his death in 1970); (2) it greatly speeded up union recognition by many industrial leaders, although Henry Ford employed members of his so-called "Service Department" to beat up Reuther and other UAW organizers many times when they tried to break his paternalistic (father figure) hold over his workers; and (3) it probably influenced the United States Supreme Court to uphold the constitutionality of the National Labor Relations Act (the Wagner Act) in the case of *NLRB v. Jones and Laughlin Steel Corporation*, decided on April 12, 1937, a ruling that surprised almost everyone.

Use of the sit-down strike decreased in the second half of the 1930s, and even more so after the Supreme Court declared in the case of *NLRB v. Fansteel Metallurgical Corporation* in 1939 that this type of tactic was illegal.

Industrial Unionism Wins its Fight

Continuing organization drives by the CIO produced violence, however, particularly in the steel industry. It was a surprise to most when the United States Steel Corporation ("Big Steel") formally recognized the Steelworkers' Organizing Committee (forerunner of the United Steelworkers of America) in March 1937. But smaller companies in the industry, led by the Republic Steel Company ("Little Steel") literally fought against the union. On Memorial Day, May 30, 1937, 264 Chicago police officers killed 10 strikers and injured more than 80 others. Senator Robert LaFollette's investigation committee later concluded that the violence had been "clearly avoidable by the police." The "Little Steel" companies were finally forced by the NLRB to recognize the union by 1941.

By 1941, total union membership in the United States was up to approximately 10.5 million workers. This was close to 20 percent of all non-agricultural, non-management employees in the nation. The membership of about 5 million in the CIO-affiliated unions had surpassed the AFL membership of about 4.6 million by then as well. And independent unions claimed close to 900,000 members.

DISCRIMINATION AND GAINS FOR AFRICAN-AMERICANS UNDER THE NEW DEAL

African-Americans were hit especially hard by the depression. By 1932, unemployment in that community was approximately 50 percent; many who held jobs had their wages cut; and even lynchings in the South increased as hardships increased. (Roosevelt still would not support anti-lynching measures before Congress because he believed that was a matter for the states.) Their political clout was nonexistent, and Roosevelt did not address the problems of race relations in his first campaign nor in the early years of the New Deal. If advocates of legislation to guarantee more rights for African-Americans brought up the subject, Roosevelt reminded them that he could not afford to alienate white Democrats in the South and perhaps jeopardize support for his relief and recovery programs. Even without the open support of the president, black voters turned to the Democratic Party and the New Deal in large numbers in the 1934 Congressional elections. At least the New Deal programs were bringing some relief from their problems, small though it was, and the president did attempt to prohibit racial discrimination in some of the federal programs.

In May 1935, Roosevelt issued Executive Order 7046, which banned discrimination on projects of the WPA. Discrimination continued, but the WPA was very important for African-American employment. The PWA was also important in providing jobs for minorities and their fair share in the public housing it built. Roosevelt, ever the politician, began to see the importance of pulling African-American voters more firmly into the Democratic coalition, but he could not be called a strong advocate for African-American rights. In the 1936 elections, Roosevelt won a strong majority of the black vote, and this group of Americans continued to make gains in the New Deal.

The First Lady was more responsible than any other person or factor in changing the attitude of the government and the president toward citizens of color. Mary

McLeod Bethune, the African-American female founder of Bethune-Cookman College in Florida, was appointed the assistant administrator at the National Youth Administration with the sponsorship of Eleanor Roosevelt. In 1939, Eleanor Roosevelt resigned from the Daughters of the American Revolution when they would not allow the African-American opera singer Marian Anderson to give a concert in Constitution Hall. Also in 1937, FDR appointed William Hastie as the first African-American federal judge in American history. And in 1939, the Civil Rights Section in the Justice Department was created. The belief that racial equality would eventually come about was revived during the New Deal.

Although occurring in 1931, before Franklin Roosevelt had been elected president, one incident that demonstrated the racial tensions remaining in the country was the case of the "Scottsboro Boys." These were 8 young African-American men who were convicted and sentenced to death for allegedly raping two white women in a freight car in Scottsboro, Alabama. No persons of color were allowed to sit on the jury, and the young defendants received no legal counsel to defend them at the trial. In 1935, the United States Supreme Court ordered a new trial because of the racial discrimination in the jury selection and the lack of legal representation for the young men. Five of the original 8 were reconvicted in 1936–37 (none were executed), but the entire affair called the nation's attention to racial discrimination in the southern criminal justice system.

DISCRIMINATION AND GAINS FOR WOMEN UNDER THE NEW DEAL

During the depression more women worked outside of the home to maintain their family's standard of living. In 1930, the number of women working was close to 10 million, and by 1940 more than 13 million were counted as paid workers. Married women were especially discriminated against in the job market because it was generally believed that women were taking jobs away from men and married women could rely on their husbands to support them. Actually, women were not usually taking jobs away from men because most of the jobs they applied for were considered "female work," such as clerical positions, teachers, telephone operators, and nurses. It was also true that most women who worked were single and self-supporting.

The New Deal advanced the role of women and placed more women in government because of the pressure of the few prominent female members of the national administration. Eleanor Roosevelt and Frances Perkins, the Secretary of Labor, did not forget others who had worked with them in politics and on social causes. Largely through their influence, Roosevelt appointed the first female federal appeals judge and female ambassadors in American history.

The NRA assisted all workers with maximum hour and minimum wage stipulations while it existed, but pay differentials between male and female workers were allowed, with the salaries of women much lower than that of men even when they performed the same work. The relief agencies hired a much smaller percentage of women than men, and the Civilian Conservation Corps did not hire any women at all. World War II and its need for a large workforce of females, not the New Deal, would do more for the equality of women.

LITERATURE IN THE 1930S

Storytelling was a great mixture of styles and messages during the decade of the thirties. In the early years of the decade, the fiction works were usually more disillusioned and disappointed in society and depicted the materialism and selfish destruction of mankind. Many authors writing in the later part of the decade, however, seemed to point out that all was not hopelessly lost in greed and self-interest. Ernest Hemingway, a very strong critic of humanity in his work in the 1920s, told the story of a young American committed enough to a cause to die for it in his novel *For Whom the Bell Tolls* (1940). John Steinbeck's masterpiece was the novel *The Grapes of Wrath* (1939), a fictionalized account but very true-to-life, of the ordeal of the Joads. They were a family of "Okies" driven from the farm to California by the "dust bowl" conditions only to face discrimination and incredible hardships. This book was a fictional look into a portion of the depression, but it was also an indictment of prejudice and an affirmation of the survival of the positive aspects of the character of people under extremely difficult circumstances. This was a prolific period for Steinbeck with the publication of *Tortilla Flat* (1935), *Cannery Row* (1935), and *Of Mice and Men* (1937), to name only a few.

Among African-American novelists, Richard Wright stood in the forefront. Paid by the Federal Writers' Project, Wright learned his craft well. His masterpiece *Native Son* told the story of Bigger Thomas, a black ghetto dweller who committed murder because of the intolerable conditions that discrimination had forced him to live in. His work exposed what he saw as the true life that African-Americans lived in America and his own rage at the system.

William Faulkner, with *The Sound and the Fury* (1929), *As I Lay Dying* (1930), and *Light in August* (1932) looked at life in the changing South. Thomas Wolfe traced his own youth in

William Faulkner. Photo by Ralph Thompson. Credit: AP/Wide World Photos.

the South, and his later wanderings as the fictional character Eugene Gant in *Look Homeward, Angel* and *Of Time and the River* (1935).

Historical novels were also becoming popular in the 1930s. Many people wanted to escape from the depression of the present. Margaret Mitchell's *Gone With the Wind* (1936), a story of the Civil War and Reconstruction period sold more than 1.5 million copies in a one-year period. The movie version, starring Clark Gable and British actress Vivian Leigh, was released in 1939 and is considered one of most popular of all times. Literature fluorished in the decade and as the nation eventually triumphed over a depression that brought dictatorships to other countries, the creative forces of society acknowledged the accomplishments of the people.

RADIO AND MOVIES ENTERTAIN

Gathering around the radio was the nightly entertainment for many Americans who lived between the world wars. Huey Long claimed that everyone should have a radio, and close to 25 million families did by 1937. Favorite radio shows of the decade included "The Lone Ranger," "Charlie Chan," "Amos and Andy," and "Death Valley Days." Comedians like Jack Benny, and George Burns and Gracie Allen, also found a spot in the hearts of Americans. The afternoon dramas that became known as soap operas (because soap companies usually sponsored them) were listened to faithfully by

Clark Gable and Jean Harlow. Credit: AP/Wide World Photos.

millions of American women. Radio brought entertainment to Americans, but it also brought more standardization of the culture.

The film industry rebounded in 1933. Americans wanted to escape the daily grind of problems, at least in their minds, and during the 1930s as many as 75 million a week escaped in a darkened theater, watching the stars act out their dramas, dance sequences, or comedies. Some of the more important stars of the day were James Cagney, Edward G. Robinson, Mae West, Fred Astaire, Ginger Rogers, Clark

Gable, Shirley Temple (many parents named their daughters after her), Claudette Colbert, and William Powell, to name only a few.

The movies of the 1930s were varied also. The beginning of the decade brought films dealing with social problems of the day, but it was the gangster movies, inspired by the real criminals that became so popular. Movies loosely based on the activities of the FBI's list of "Public Enemies," such as John Dillinger, Pretty Boy Floyd, Baby Face Nelson, and Bonnie and Clyde, played to millions. Until civic groups protested that crime was glorified in these movies, the criminals triumphed in the films. Hollywood, an industry that depends on public opinion, rewrote the scripts so that the police and the G-men (FBI) would become the victors and capture the bad guys. America was fascinated with criminals in the 1930s, particularly the bank robbers mentioned above who made it to Public Enemy #1 on J. Edgar Hoover's most wanted list. Many Americans saw them as romantic and adventurous when compared to their own lives. They had also had unpleasant dealings with bankers and saw this as justice for the cold-hearted bankers. Of course, the money of depositors, not the bankers, was taken.

Above all, the movies offered an escape from reality. A few of the unforgettable ones included *It Happened One Night, Animal Crackers, The Thin Man, King Kong, Little Caesar,* and *The Little Colonel,* not to mention all of the lavish musicals that fluorished during the era.

AN ASSESSMENT OF ROOSEVELT AND THE NEW DEAL

Roosevelt is judged by most historians to have been a great president. His pragmatic approach to the problems of the Great Depression allowed him the flexibility necessary to experiment with solutions and, if they did not work, to try something else. He took this flexible approach primarily because he was skeptical of the new economic theories and the quick-fix mentality of some advisers and the old status quo as well. He did manage to lead this country through one of its most difficult decades with a brilliance of courage and self-confidence that inspired the people to trust him, a larger role for government, and the institutions they had built. Roosevelt has been criticized for not having a more far-reaching, coherent plan for permanent recovery and reform, but he believed strongly in the freedom of capitalism with regulation in the public interest. Roosevelt permanently expanded the power of the presidency, and Congress has looked to the president ever since to present a legislative plan that they can then react to.

The New Deal was a mixture of success and failure. Full employment was not reached by its legislative efforts. The United States was not brought completely out of the depression until the United States entered World War II, although the return of normal rainfall in 1938 did begin to stimulate the agricultural sector. The immense spending on industrial efforts to supply the machines of war brought unemployment down to approximately 1 percent in 1944. There is nothing magical about wartime spending, however, and the New Deal could have ended the Great Depression if Roosevelt had been willing to commit the vast sums necessary to get the job done. Even though the New Deal did not actually end the depression, it did bring this nation through it by relieving much of the human suffering that would have occurred if the massive efforts of government and its money had not intervened. It moved the federal government from the role of a neutral arbiter (as it was becoming in the Progressive Era) to a powerful promoter of society's welfare. And this represented a fundamental change in thinking.

The old Emersonian (Ralph Waldo Emerson) hope of reforming human nature that had been so popular in the nineteenth and very early twentieth centuries was abandoned by the New Deal. In its place, the reform of institutions became the focus of most liberal thinkers and politicians. Even the New Deal relief programs did not provide assistance on the basis of charity to individuals, but it was justified primarily as being necessary to stimulate purchasing power and to stabilize the economy. In all this philosophical shifting, this was another difference with the old Progressives, in that economic reform, rather than simply cleaning out the "bad guys," became the focus of American liberalism.

Certainly, Roosevelt's personal charisma and outstanding communications skills had much to do with his overall psychological contribution to the well-being of the nation. And positive psychology should never be underestimated as an important ingredient in accomplishing great things. FDR was not always a consistent leader in his efforts to lead the country out of the depression; many of his close advisors understood the bigger picture better than he did. But it is virtually undeniable that Franklin Delano Roosevelt's greatest significance to the people of his time, and the secret of his success, was his ability to arouse the country to hope and to action. For this, most Americans have considered him as one of the greatest presidents in American history.

ADDITIONAL READINGS

Irving Bernstein, *Turbulent Years: A History of the American Worker, 1933–1941* (1969). Solid overview of the growth of the American labor movement during the 1930s, with excellent material on the workings of the NLRB.

John Braeman et al., eds., *The New Deal: The State and Local Levels* (1975). A useful collection of essays analyzing the workings of the New Deal in local communities throughout the nation.

Alan Brinkley, *Voices of Protest: Huey Long, Father Coughlin, and the Great Depression* (1982). Offers the best analysis of these two important New Deal critics and the sources of their popular appeal.

Lizabeth Cohen, *Making a New Deal* (1990). A brilliant study of industrial workers in Chicago during the 1920s and 1930s. Demonstrates the transformation of immigrant and African American workers into key actors in the creation of the CIO and in New Deal politics. Includes important material on the complex relationship between ethnic cultures and mass culture.

Paul K. Conkin, *The New Deal* (2nd ed., 1975). A well-written, concise history of the New Deal that emphasizes its limits and nonradical character.

Kenneth S. Davis, *FDR* (3 vols., 1972, 1985, 1986). The most comprehensive biography of FDR.

Melvyn Dubofsky and Warrren Van Tine, *John L. Lewis* (1977). The standard biography of this key labor leader. Excellent on the development of the CIO.

Sidney Fine, *Sit-Down: The General Motors Strike of 1936–37* (1969). The standard account of this epochal strike.

Richard Lowtt, *The New Deal and the West* (1984). A comprehensive study of the New Deal's impact in the West, with special attention to water policy and agriculture.

Robert S. McElvaine, *The Great Depression: America, 1929–1941* (1984). The best one-volume overview of the depression. Especially good on the origins and early years of the worst economic calamity in American history.

Richard Pells, *Radical Visions and American Dreams* (1973). A useful survey of radical culture and social thought during the 1930s.

Lois Scharf, *To Work and to Wed* (1980). Examines female employment and feminism during the Great Depression.

Harvard Sitkoff, *A New Deal for Blacks* (1978). Focuses on the limited gains made by African Americans from New Deal programs, as well as the racism that pervaded most government programs.

William Stott, *Documentary Expression and Thirties America* (1973). An illuminating account of the documentary impulse and its relationship to the political and social upheavals of the 1930s.

Studs Terkel, *Hard Times* (1970). The best oral history of the Great Depression. Includes a very wide range of voices recalling life in the depression era.

Susan Ware, *Beyond Suffrage: Women in the New Deal* (1981). Examines the makeup and influence of the "women's network" within the Roosevelt administration.

CHAPTER ELEVEN

Foreign Policy Between the World Wars

MAJOR EVENTS

1924	Dawes Plan for war reparations
1928	Kellogg-Briand Pact signed
1931	Japan occupies Manchuria
1933	Hitler seizes power in Germany
	U.S. recognizes USSR
	Japan quits League of Nations
1935	Italy invades Ethiopia
1935-37	Neutrality Acts
1937	Japan invades China
	Panay incident
	Roosevelt's quarantine speech
1938	Hitler and Chamberlain meet at Munich
1939	Germany annexes remainder of Czechoslovakia

AMERICAN ISOLATIONISM

The Historical Background

American foreign policy between the world wars was dominated by isolationist Congressional leaders and a public that wanted to isolate the nation from the world because of disillusionment with the Great War, the Versailles Treaty, the League of Nations, and European politics and problems in general. American isolationism of the 1920s and the 1930s was much the same as it had been historically. Its two major characteristics were (1) opposition to American involvement in any international organization or alliance that carried with it a commitment; and (2) opposition to involvement in any European crisis that might explode into a war.

Isolationists defined the word "commitment" in this context to include any agreement that might possibly compel the United States to take any action, especially military, against another nation for alleged violations of international agreements. This had been the core objection by many senators to the Treaty of Versailles, whose League Charter's Article X required the League Council to "advise" all member-nations in case one or more of them were attacked. (See Chapter Eight.) In the minds of isolationists, the language of the League Charter raised the specter of American troops being sent against the will of the American people to some distant land to fight somebody else's battle. Vague international agreements were acceptable, but anything approaching an actual commitment was to be avoided at all costs.

Since the warning in President George Washington's Farewell Address, the United States had avoided all entangling alliances with European nations. Avoiding the most serious European problems did allow for Americans to focus on their own internal population and economic growth, which were enormous. But even concerning economic growth, the isolationists were wrong. Their major assumption was that whatever happens in Europe is of no direct consequence to the United States. That was clearly never the case, however. To a large degree the health of the American economy had always depended upon strong trade ties with Europe. Major events in Europe which threatened those trade relations obviously could have dire consequences for the United States.

Near the end of the nineteenth century, however, the United States took advantage of a weak Spain in the Spanish-American War (1898) to grab territories as far away as the Philippines in the western Pacific. Expediency had temporarily overruled isolationist tradition, although, strictly speaking, the Cuban crisis which had precipitated that war had not really been a European crisis. Then in 1917 the Germans had forced the United States to enter a major European war in order to maintain the integrity of its economic trade with Britain. But the disillusioning effect of the Great War and the Versailles Treaty just seemed to confirm the historical American isolationist attitude toward Europe. (Of course, American isolationism never really applied to Latin America, as events discussed in Chapter Seven and later in this chapter testify.)

General Foreign Policy Direction in the Post-World War I Era

Foreign policy makers from the administration of President Harding through that of President Roosevelt were aware that strict isolationism was not possible. American influence was necessary at times to maintain stability and peace in foreign areas in order to protect our own prosperity and security. Foreign policy changed over the two decades between the two world wars as situations around the globe changed. It became a mixture of isolationism and involvement, depending on the situation and the area of the world involved. However, there were certain constant factors taken into consideration. The American public was not to be pushed into involvements they did not agree with, and any situations that might involve the nation in war were to be avoided. With these limitations, foreign policy focused on disarmament treaties, building friendly relations with neighboring nations, outlawing war, and passing of so-called neutrality laws to prevent American involvement in another war, especially a European one.

President Harding declared his foreign policy to the nation in his inaugural address in March 1921. "We seek no part in directing the destinies of the world," he declared. The public liked the sentiments of Harding because they were tired of former President Wilson's idealism of wanting to make all things right with the world. Americans wanted to focus on concerns at home instead.

On the other hand, Harding's Secretary of State, Charles Evans Hughes (who had been the Republican presidential candidate in 1916), was concerned with an aggressive Japanese foreign agenda. Japan was increasing the size of its navy and securing rights and territory in China and surrounding areas, which was threatening not only the Open Door Policy but the sovereignty of China as well. Hughes was also concerned with the future of American interests in the area because of a formal Anglo-Japanese alliance. His concern was how to protect American interests in the region without bringing isolationist opposition. Secretary Hughes and Senator William Borah of Idaho, a powerful supporter of isolationism, agreed that peace could be promoted with a reduction in the size of the navies of the major powers without a commitment which would compromise the isolationist position. At Senator Borah's urging, the Senate passed a resolution in May 1921 formally asking the president to call a conference among the major powers to discuss reduction of armaments. And President Harding, in agreement with Borah and Secretary Hughes, invited the major world powers to meet in Washington, D.C. in November 1921, to consider naval disarmament and other concerns in the Pacific and the Far East.

THE DISARMAMENT CONFERENCES: DISARMING FOR PEACE

The Washington Conference

The Washington Conference was the first in a series of meetings held in the 1920s and the 1930s designed to keep the peace by placing limits on the size and number of ships built. It was hoped that the limitations would eliminate arms races and the possibilities of conflict which those races evoked. President Harding invited Great Britain, France, Italy, Japan, Belgium, Holland, Portugal, and China to send delegates to the conference. Serving as its chairman, Secretary Hughes opened the conference with a plan for limiting future construction of ships and a proposal to destroy ships previously constructed or presently under construction. Hughes told the surprised delegates that the United States would scrap at least fifteen ships presently under construction as well as fifteen old battleships. He also pointed out to the delegates that, with this plan, competition to build larger and bigger navies would end, and the money once used to compete with each other to build weapons of war could be used to promote the welfare of their citizens.

After considerable discussion, the delegates agreed to fix the tonnage of capital ships (more than 10,000 tons displacement or having guns larger than 8-inch caliber) at a ratio of 5 (United States): 5 (Great Britain): 3 (Japan): 1.75 (France): and 1.75 (Italy) in order to reach parity among the nations. It was also agreed that the nations would maintain a ten-year holiday, or moratorium, during which no new capital ships would be built. Several other treaties resulted from the conference. The United States, Great Britain, France, and Japan agreed in the Four Power Treaty that each would respect the rights of the others over Pacific possessions, and aggressive action would bring all of them together to consult on a response. The Anglo-Japanese alliance was abrogated. All nine nations represented guaranteed, in the Nine Power Treaty, the independence of China and the Open Door Policy. Altogether, nine treaties were drafted and eventually ratified by the United States Senate. The Senate, however, did place a reservation on the treaties that dealt with joint actions with other nations. The reservation was that these were not alliances, and the United States was not bound to join in the defense of any territory.

The Geneva Five-Power Conference

Believing that disarmament must continue to keep the world at peace, President Coolidge called for a five-power conference to be held in Geneva, Switzerland in the summer of 1927. The Geneva Conference was called to increase the limitations agreed to at the Washington Conference on disarmament. In addition to the capital ships, Coolidge wanted to limit the building of cruisers, destroyers, and submarines. France and Italy refused to attend, and the United States, Great Britain and Japan could not agree on a formula for limiting the construction of the smaller crafts. The failure of this conference strained relations between the United States and Great Britain and strengthened the position of the isolationists.

The London Naval Conference

Not willing to give up on limiting the size of the navies as a means to keep the peace, the London Naval Conference met from January 21 to April 22, 1930. Secretary of State Henry L. Stimson represented President Hoover at the conference. Italy and France once again caused problems. Italy demanded to have the right of parity with any European power, and France refused to accept this demand. France wanted defensive military agreements which the other powers would not consider. Both Italy and France refused to sign most of the agreements negotiated at the conference. The United States, Great Britain, and Japan adopted cruiser limitations at a ratio of 10:10:6, respectively. An "escalator" clause did allow the nations to exceed the ratio if the security of any of the nations was threatened by a nation not included in the London agreement, which weakened the intent of the agreement. The London agreement also included a 10:10:6 ratio on other small vessels between the three major sea powers; parity on submarines; and no new capital ships built until 1936 (except those authorized for France and Italy at the Washington Conference). Japan was not happy with its unequal status, but it decided to tolerate it for the time being. The Senate approved the London Treaty on July 21, 1930 by a vote of 58–9, in spite of the warnings from some naval experts that the limitations could hamper the defense of the United States and its possessions.

The World Disarmament Conference

Believing so strongly in the positive aspects of naval limitations, the Hoover administration sent delegates to the World Disarmament Conference, sponsored by the League of Nations, at Geneva, Switzerland in 1932. The United States was not a member of the League but was invited and quickly accepted any opportunity to promote armament reduction. At the conference, the United States proposed the abolition of all offensive armament. When this radical proposal failed, President Hoover proposed that all nations represented reduce their armaments by 30 percent. The proposal was not rejected, but postponed when the delegates agreed to take up the matter again in February 1933. The World Disarmament Conference met again in 1934 and broke up without agreement on limitations. The London Conference, beginning its preliminary meetings in December 1935, was doomed to failure. By this time, the hopes for disarmament alone keeping the peace were fading because nations were rearming in spite of their agreements to the contrary.

THE UNITED STATES AND THE LEAGUE OF NATIONS

At the time of the 1920 presidential election campaign, the possibility of the United States joining the League of Nations was still alive despite the defeat of the Treaty of Versailles earlier in the year. Hoping to win the support of both the internationalists and the isolationists in his Republican Party, Warren G. Harding campaigned in opposition to American participation in President Wilson's bitterly fought-for League while making reference to the possibility of American participation in a "real association of nations." This was not the first time that Harding's political rhetoric made him appear to agree and disagree with an issue at the same time. After his election victory, which Harding believed was a mandate against the League of Nations, his administration distanced itself so far from the League that correspondence from the League to the State Department was not officially acknowledged. (This also kept the Republican "irreconcilables" in his camp.)

It was soon realized, however, that an organization that contained most of the major powers of the world and carried out decisions of this powerful group could not be ignored. In spite of opposition to joining the League of Nations, official observers were sent to sessions sponsored by the League from the beginning. For example, the United States was officially represented at the Second Opium Conference in 1924. And participation in conferences on communications, transportation, and import and export prohibitions was accepted. By 1931, the United States had sent representatives to more than forty such conferences.

The United States also maintained five permanent representatives in Geneva to represent American interests at League meetings in the 1930s. Japanese aggression in 1931–1932 led the United States to support the League's position in opposing such aggression. Cooperation and involvement with the League had grown over time. However, the United States still would not formally commit itself to League activities or controls by becoming an official member. Many would believe later that if the United States had been a member of the League it might have had more effect in stopping the aggressions of the 1930s.

THE WORLD COURT CONTROVERSY

All four American presidents between the two world wars advocated American membership on the Permanent Court of International Justice, known as the World Court, which had been established under Article 14 of the League of Nations charter. Americans had supported the idea of an international tribunal to settle disputes between nations at both the Hague Conferences in 1899 and 1907. However, the isolationists, particularly in the Senate, fought the United States joining the Court. Following Senator Lodge's death in 1924, Senators William Borah, Hiram Johnson, and James Reed continued this opposition because they saw the Court as a tool of the League of Nations, even though it was technically separate from it.

The measure to join the Court finally did make it past the objections of the isolationists of both houses of Congress in early 1926, but the refusal of the members of the Court and its Council in the League to approve all American reservations kept the United States from joining. The reservation that turned into a major stumbling block for Court membership was the American demand that any dispute in which the United States had an interest would not come before the Court without the consent of the United States.

Both President Hoover and President Roosevelt pressed for membership on the World Court bench, but the issue could not get through the Senate because ratification required a two-thirds majority. Even the influence of Charles Evans Hughes and Frank B. Kellogg, former Secretaries of State and World Court judges, could not bring about their nation's membership. (A country did not have to join the Court in order to have any of its distinguished citizens serve as a judge; membership by a nation meant that at least theoretically that nation agreed to adjudicate legal disputes in that body.)

WORLD WAR I DEBTS

Loans to the Allied governments during and following World War I, and to the new nations formed at the end of the war, left the United States with a debt to collect from twenty nations in excess of $10.3 billion. Congress established the World War Foreign Debt Commission to negotiate with all debtors on February 9, 1922. Arrangements for repayment were made with each nation separately. Britain and France approached the United States with a proposal to cancel war debts owed to their governments from other allies if the United States would in turn cancel the debts of Britain and France. Most of Europe was suffering from economic hardships brought on by the necessity of rebuilding after the war, while the United States was prospering following a short recession after the soldiers returned from the war. The debtor nations believed that the prosperity of the United States should be taken into consideration for a cancellation of debts owed. It was also pointed out that the United States had lost a very small number of soldiers compared to the other Allies, and no battles had been fought in the United States. The Allies further argued that the debts should be canceled because they were the contribution of the United States to the war effort before actual involvement. And furthermore, the money from the loans had been primarily used to purchase supplies in the United States, thereby increasing its economic prosperity.

Another problem regarding the repayment of the loans was the fact that the primary means of repaying the debts—through trade with the United States—was made difficult by the high American tariff rates at that time. The debts could not be repaid in gold because what little gold was left in Europe was needed for the stabilization of the nations' currencies. Much of the gold bullion of the nations had been used in the early days of the war for purchases in the United States. Reaching back into history, the French believed their debts should be canceled because they had not demanded repayment when the Americans stopped paying on their loan from France to fight the English in the American Revolution. In spite of the valid arguments of the hard-pressed nations and the bitter feelings that were developing on all sides, Americans held firm in their demand for repayment of the debts. President Coolidge expressed the mood of the nation with his question, "They hired the money, didn't they?"

It became evident that many of the European nations could not repay their debts without some major adjustments. France and Britain were particularly hampered because the German reparation payments they had hoped to use to partially repay their debts were not forthcoming. The United States claimed that there was not a relation between the war debts and reparations, but the European nations maintained that there was a direct relation. In partial acknowledgment of European claims, the United States finally agreed to make concessions for these nations and presented solutions to assist them to achieve economic stability. In 1925, Italy's interest rate was reduced to .4 percent and approximately 80 percent of their debt was canceled. In 1926, the interest rate on the French debt was reduced to 1.6 percent, and approximately 60 percent of the debt was canceled. Finally, there was a reduction of interest rates for all debtors to an average of 2.135 percent and the lengthening of payment schedules to sixty-two years. The reduction of the debts was accepted by Italy, France, and the other nations. But the entire affair brought about more negative feelings toward the United States in Europe and more isolationist feelings in the United States. Isolationists perceived that the Europeans were ungrateful for all that America had done for them.

The new Bolshevik government of the Soviet Union, formerly the Russian Empire, was the one debtor nation not approached by the United States. Following the revolution of 1917, the government of Bolshevik leader Vladimir I. Lenin repudiated all debts contracted by the Russian government. The American loans to assist Russia in the fight against the Central Powers had exceeded $190 million. The refusal to honor previously contracted government debts, the belief that the Bolshevik government was not representative of the wishes of the Russian people, and the concern over the Bolshevik plans for a worldwide revolution of workers led the United States government to a policy of non-recognition of the new government. Thus, under the three Republican presidents of the 1920s, there was no exchange of diplomats between the two countries.

The worldwide depression of the 1930s led President Hoover to declare to the public on June 20, 1931, "the postponement during one year of all payments on intergovernmental debts, reparations and relief payments, both principal and interest." This one-year moratorium eased the international financial crisis. International bankers followed the example set by the governments and placed a similar moratorium on private international debts. It was also hoped that the moratorium on debt payments could save the gold as a standard for currency, as around the world nation after nation was being forced off the gold standard.

The moratorium relieved some of the financial pressures brought about by the depression, but it was not a solution because the debts remained. The United States finally and officially recognized a connection between reparations and war debts. The Dawes and Young Plans and American loans (see next section) had brought Germany sufficient economic stability to meet reparation payments, but the Germans could not meet their obligations because of the Great Depression. Germany's creditors agreed to meet at the Lausanne Conference in June 1932. There it was agreed to cancel more than 90 percent of the original reparations if the United States agreed to decrease the debts of the German creditor nations. Neither the outgoing Hoover administration nor the incoming Roosevelt administration was willing to cancel the war debts. It would certainly have been a political liability for either to have done so. Americans wanted that money repaid to help offset economic problems of their own depression. They were also unwilling to accept the cancellation of debts when the European nations were not willing to cut back on armaments to a degree that would perhaps have allowed them to repay their obligations. When the moratorium ended, the debtors began to default on their loans, either by not repaying their World War I debts at all or only sending partial payments. Only Finland paid off its war debts in full to the United States. This was more ammunition for isolationists, who were confirmed in their conviction that involvement with Europe produced only trouble.

ASSISTING GERMANY IN THE 1920S

The Allied Reparations Commission, established at the Versailles Treaty meetings back in 1919, set the German reparation obligation at about $33 billion on April 27, 1921. The Allies, not including the United States, based many of their plans for economic recovery from World War I upon the reparation payments. But the German economy was devastated following the war. With the value of the German mark at an extremely low point due to inflation, Germany stopped payments to creditors by the end of 1921. On May 21, 1922, the Commission granted Germany a moratorium on its war reparations for the remainder of the year, hoping that German currency would stabilize by that time. In January 1923, Germany remained in default on its debts, so French and Belgian troops began to occupy the German territory of the Ruhr. By September of 1923, German currency was practically worthless, and the currency of France was depreciating also. The economies of the European nations were linked, and it was necessary to assist Germany before all of Europe was in more serious fiscal difficulty. At this point, the United States stepped into the situation.

President Coolidge sent Charles G. Dawes (vice-president from 1925-1929 and head of the Allied Reparations Commission), Henry M. Robinson, and Owen D. Young to investigate German finances in 1923. On April 9, 1924, the commission proposed what became known as the Dawes Plan. The plan called for a reorganization of the German banking system and supervision by representatives of the Allies. German reparation payments would be put on a gradually increasing scale. And American and Allied bankers would loan Germany approximately $200 million in gold to back a new currency issue, which would assist industrial recovery and enable it to make reparation payments again. A small amount of the German payments under the plan went to pay for the costs incurred by the American Army of Occupation and war damages.

The resulting easing of the economic tensions between the European nations lead to the easing of political tensions at a meeting in Locarno, Switzerland in 1925. An important outcome of this meeting was the German agreement to seek admission to the League of Nations, which it received in 1926. Germany also agreed to accept the western boundaries set at Versailles and to seek change of the disputed eastern borders only through peaceful means.

The Dawes Plan had provided for the escalation of payments by Germany, so that annual payments were increased from year to year. After just a few years, Germany was having difficulty in meeting these increasing amounts. Thus, German dissatisfaction with the Dawes Plan led to a new proposal known as the Young Plan in 1929. (Owen D. Young was the American chairman of the Committee on German Reparations.) The new plan reduced the amount due from Germany to slightly more than $8 billion and put into place a payment schedule of $153 million a year for fifty-nine years, with other payments (to nations other than Britain and France, such as Belgium and the United States, whose figures were not included in the war reparations) depending upon the prosperity of the German economy. All foreign control was removed, and Germany was once again responsible for its financial operations. The plan also provided for a reduction of the reparations if the United States reduced inter-Allied debts, which it did not intend to do.

When the Great Depression hit Europe by 1930, the entire issue of war debts began to fall apart. In addition to the economic crisis, the British and French leaders felt some guilt about the overly harsh treatment of Germany levied by the Versailles Treaty. Therefore, at the Lausanne Conference on June 16, 1932, more than 90 percent of Germany's reparations were canceled. All of the bitter feelings and political manuevers had been wasted. Once Hitler came to power in 1933, all remaining reparations were repudiated. And Germany never paid its reparations in full.

THE KELLOGG-BRIAND PACT

On April 6, 1927, Aristide Briand, the French Foreign Minister, proposed in a speech to commemorate the entrance of the United States into World War I that France and the United States should outlaw war between themselves. Outlawing war by treaty was an interesting concept, if not naive, and many wanted to attempt this solution. Secretary of State Frank B. Kellogg was skeptical of the proposal but finally bowed to pressure from the public and leading isolationists and agreed to discuss the proposal if other nations were included. (The Kellogg-Briand Pact was an example of isolationists' willingness to enter into vague, unenforceable international agreements because they did not constitute a real commitment.) Fifteen nations met in Paris in August 1928 and shortly thereafter signed a pact condemning war as a solution for disagreement. By 1935, sixty-two nations were committed to the Kellogg-Briand Pact (Pact of Paris).

The Pact was hailed as a major step toward world peace. The Senate approved the Pact in January 1929 with an eighty-five to one vote. In spite of the high hopes for an end to war, the reservations of the nations and the lack of an enforcement mechanism doomed this idealistic venture from the beginning. Most nations reserved the right to defend themselves with war. And the United States added to her defensive reservations the right to safeguard the Monroe Doctrine. Aggressors in the 1930s—Japan, Germany, Italy, and Russia—had signed the Pact and would use the defensive reservations to cloak their aggression with a false semblance of legality. After all, most nations justify wars with claims of self-defense.

LATIN AMERICAN FOREIGN POLICY IN THE 1920S

Introduction

Immediately following World War I, relations between the United States and her neighbors to the south were cordial. Trade was strong between the neighbors. Seventeen Latin American nations joined the League of Nations, and it was hoped that the United States would follow the premises of the League and President Wilson and that a new spirit of cooperation would begin. The extremely high hopes of the Latin American nations were dampened, however, when it was decided that membership in the League would not free them from the bounds of the Monroe Doctrine of the United States. Neither was the United States going to join the organization.

Trade also diminished as the United States was more interested in selling its products to Latin America than purchasing theirs. The relations among the nations of the western hemisphere could be characterized as a mixture of good and bad policies during the 1920s and the 1930s. But progress was gradually made in moving the United States away from near total domination to the point of Franklin Roosevelt's proclamation of the Good Neighbor Policy.

Relations With Colombia and the Dominican Republic

Relations with Colombia had been strained from the time of American involvement with the Panamanian revolution (1903). The discovery of oil within Colombian boundaries brought pressure from the American oil companies for the normalizing of relations between the two countries. The Wilson administration had tried to persuade Congress to officially apologize to Colombia for the American intervention and to appropriate monies in compensation. But not until Theodore Roosevelt's death (he had been president in 1903) in 1919 did Congress begin to respond. And in 1921 the Thomson-Urrutia Treaty provided that the United States pay Colombia $25 million, which was close to the original demand for the right to build the Panama Canal.

In 1905, in connection with the Roosevelt Corollary, the marines had been sent into the Dominican Republic to establish an American protectorate role there. (Some European nations had threatened the Caribbean nation over debts owed to them.) This situation continued until 1924, when all American marines were ordered to leave the Dominican Republic. The only aspect of American domination remaining on the island was the American collector of customs, kept in place to guarantee that American loans were repaid by the Dominican government.

The Clark Memorandum

American economic interests and the lack of a threat from European nations in the frequently unstable Latin American region slowly changed the policies of the United States from "dollar diplomacy" and the "big stick" to those of conciliation, pan-Americanism, and the "good neighbor." A major turning point for improved relations would not occur until December 17, 1928, when J. Reuben Clark of the State Department submitted the Clark Memorandum (at the request of President Coolidge) to define the scope of the Monroe Doctrine. The Monroe Doctrine had been used repeatedly as an excuse to intervene in Latin American affairs in the early twentieth century. The Clark Memorandum was not published until 1930, during President Hoover's administration. The most important portion of the memorandum clarified that the Monroe Doctrine was "a case of the United States versus Europe, and not the United States versus Latin America." The Roosevelt Corollary (proclaimed in 1904) was repudiated by the memorandum. President Hoover also believed very strongly in American leadership taking the moral high ground in promoting international peace. And his view actually formed the basis for Roosevelt's Good Neighbor Policy.

The Pan-American Conferences in the 1920s

Two Pan-American conferences were held during the 1920s to improve relations among the nations of the western hemisphere. The first conference was held at Santiago, Chile in 1923, and accepted the Gondra Treaty, which supported the establishment of a commission of inquiry to study all conflicts immediately and suggest measures for settling them. The findings of the commission were not binding upon the opponents, but it was hoped that the efforts of such a commission could lead to a peaceful resolution of the problem.

In his desire to continue the building of good relations in the hemisphere, President Coolidge agreed to open the 1928 Pan-American conference in Havana, Cuba. The president urged cooperation from all the nations, including the United States, and stated that all nations represented had equal power at the conference. Secretary of State Hughes did not agree with the president's stated policy, however, as he refused to discuss the issue of nations interfering in the rights of other nations. The proposal that the Governing Board of the Pan American Union should serve as a court of justice for the American republics was also rejected. It was obvious to the South American republics that the United States was still intent on dominating issues in this part of the world. However, economic interests, anti-imperialists, and new foreign policy positions of Presidents Coolidge, Hoover, and Roosevelt did lead to less American coercion. Intervention in Nicaragua, problems in Mexico, and the continued American refusal to share the decision-making power on important issues with the Latin American nations continued as stumbling blocks to true Pan-Americanism.

Problems Between Mexico and the United States

Problems with Mexico primarily concerned the rights of Americans to own minerals, particularly oil, and land in this foreign nation. The Mexican Constitution of 1917 nationalized subsoil minerals, including oil. The government also implemented laws for land reform. Indian village communal lands owned by large private estates were to be restored to the Indian tribes and portions of large landholdings would be expropriated, many of which were owned by Americans. The Harding administration protested these threats to American investments, of which approximately $300 million was in oil, and would not recognize the government of Alvaro Obregon.

Tensions were relaxed in 1923 with the Bucareli Agreement. In this executive agreement (not a treaty) the United States promised to recognize the Obregon government in exchange for his respect of American subsoil rights acquired before 1917. In addition to the Bucareli Agreement, the Mexican Supreme Court ruled that full ownership of Mexican oil resources would apply to those who owned the oil rights before the Constitution of 1917 was enacted if the owners had performed a "positive act" to indicate that the resources were to be developed. Mexican bonds would also be accepted to pay for land owned by Americans and expropriated by the Mexican government. As a result of these changes, the United States recognized the government of President Obregon in August 1923.

Regardless of the agreement, however, nationalization of resources continued, and it was not until 1927, under the diplomacy of President Coolidge's new American ambassador to Mexico, Dwight D. Morrow, that relations were once again put on a more agreeable footing. Morrow's diplomacy, which included disdain for dollar diplomacy and respect for the sovereignty of Mexico, brought about Mexican goodwill and reaffirmation of the 1923 decision that full ownership of the oil rights was confirmed with "positive acts." Morrow was not as successful with American attempts to receive just compensation for Mexican land they owned, however. Litigation in courts and before claims commissions were undertaken by many.

On March 3, 1929, the day before President Hoover was to take office, there was an uprising against the government of Emilio Portes Gil. Hoover demonstrated his desire to improve relations with Latin America and remove their feelings of fear and mistrust when he allowed the Mexican government, but not the rebels, to purchase military supplies. The rebellion was then put down. Hoover had shown his interest in Latin American relations with a tour of the area following his win in the 1928 election. And he continued to improve upon the positive steps President Coolidge had taken by sending J. Reuben Clark as the replacement for Ambassador Morrow. Clark was committed to continuing the spirit of respect and support for Mexico that Morrow had begun. The United States immediately recognized the newly elected Mexican President, Ortiz Rubio, in November 1929. President Rubio visited the United States as an example of his goodwill.

In 1938, President Roosevelt and Secretary of State Cordell Hull had to deal with further appropriations by the Mexican government under the authority of President Lazaro Cardenas. In a departure from traditional American government policy, Hull recognized the right of Mexico to expropriate the American owned mineral rights, but only if fair compensation was paid. A figure for fair compensation of close to $35 million was finally agreed upon for the subsoil rights in April 1942.

American Policy in Nicaragua

American dollar diplomacy, espoused by the Taft administration, had brought extensive intervention into the affairs of Nicaragua. And even though dollar diplomacy fell out of favor as a foreign policy, American involvement continued there. In 1912 President Taft had ordered American marines into Nicaragua to prop up the presidency of Adolfo Diaz, a major supporter of American business policies in his nation. The marines stayed to assure political stability and future governments that favored the interests of the United States through most of the 1920s. One of the major flaws of American attempts to influence politics in this Central American nation was that the conservative leaders the United States supported might agree with American activities in Nicaragua, but they did not have enough national support to remain in power without the presence of American soldiers. This was a mistake the United States would make time and again in Latin America.

The American soldiers were pulled out of Nicaragua in 1925, following the election of Carlos Solorzano as president (a Conservative) and Dr. Juan B. Sacasa as vice president (a Liberal). Then Emiliano Chamorro led a successful revolt against the newly elected executives. Both fled the country, and Chamorro took over the duties of chief executive. But the United States would not recognize Chamorro, and Sacasa returned to instigate a civil war. So American troops returned in June 1926 to bring order to the country once again. New elections were held, and the newly elected President Adolfo Diaz was recognized by the American government. But peace in Nicaragua was threatened once again by revolutionary forces led by former Vice President Sacasa, which brought more American marines into the area in 1927.

The Peace of Tipitapa was signed in 1927, ending the conflict with Sacasa. It was agreed that the rebels would lay down their arms, Diaz would finish his term, the United States would supervise the elections in 1928, and a Nicaraguan national guard, commanded by American officers until it was fully organized, would replace the national army. However, Augusto Sandino, one of the leaders of the Liberal revolutionary army, would not accept the American provisions nor the election of General Jose Moncada, the commander of the Liberal rebels, as the new president. Instead, Sandino carried on a guerrilla war against the American soldiers, whose numbers eventually exceeded 5,000. He became a national hero in his struggle against American interference and corrupt political leaders.

Intervention in Nicaragua was bringing criticism from Americans and from the other Latin American countries. American forces were finally withdrawn by President Franklin Roosevelt in 1933. Meanwhile, Dr. Sacasa had finally won the presidency in 1932 that he had fought for earlier, and Sandino agreed to put down his arms. Shortly after this, Sandino was assassinated on the presidential palace steps following a dinner meeting with Sacasa on February 21, 1934. It is believed that a leader of the national guard, Anastasio Somoza, ordered the death of the popular hero. Sandino would come to symbolize all revolutionary activity from oppressive leaders. The names of Sandino and Somoza would come to importance in American foreign policy again in the future.

THE GOOD NEIGHBOR POLICY

Introduction

In his first inaugural address on March 4, 1933, President Franklin D. Roosevelt announced his philosophy on foreign policy with these words: "In the field of world policy I would dedicate this nation to the policy of the good neighbor—the neighbor who resolutely respects himself and, because he does so, respects the rights of others." Recognition of the government of the Soviet Union on November 16, 1933 applied the president's philosophy to Europe. But a policy to encompass relations with the world quickly focused on relations with Latin America. A primary focus of the good neighbor policy was to increase trade in Latin America. However, to achieve the good relations that would bring this increased trade in a time of worldwide depression, Roosevelt realized that a policy of non-intervention, which had made progress during the Hoover administration, must be firmly established. Building upon the successes of his predecessors, Roosevelt's policies were ably carried out by the formal and informal diplomacy of Secretary of State Cordell Hull and his Under-Secretary Sumner Welles. Welles was named after his great-uncle Charles Sumner, the powerful abolitionist and Radical Republican senator.

At the Pan-American Conference held at Montevideo, Uruguay, in December 1933, Secretary Hull launched the new administration's policy strategies. Hull relied on informal negotiating rather than attempting to dominate the open discussions at the conference. Trade reciprocity was agreed upon, and there were commitments from the nations to outlaw war. A great change in policy for the United States was to approve the statement that "no State has a right to intervene in the internal or external affairs of another." This agreement greatly decreased the tensions and hostile feelings toward the United States.

The Good Neighbor Policy in Haiti and Panama

The Good Neighbor Policy was put into effect toward Haiti. It was agreed that the last of the American marines on the island would withdraw in October 1934. But after a visit to the island, Roosevelt withdrew the marines in August, ahead of schedule. And the Haitian government would also have complete control over the Haitian national guard. Economic control was returned to the Haitians with the right of Haitian President Vincent to appoint a customs collector of his choice, and with the sale of the National City Bank of New York's controlling interest in the National Bank of Haiti to the Haitian government. By the summer of 1935, Haitians once again controlled Haiti. The United States then assisted this nation's economy by agreeing to reduce the Hawley-Smoot Tariff rates on Haitian cocoa, rum, and fruit with reciprocity from Haiti on American machinery.

The Good Neighbor Policy moved on to resolve problems in Panama. The right to intervene in Panama to preserve order and guarantee independence of the nation, given to the United States in the Hay-Bunau-Varilla Treaty of 1903, produced uneasy relations between the two nations because Panama interpreted this clause as a restraint on her sovereignty. Tensions increased when the United States paid the annual rent on the canal in 59-cent dollars rather than the gold which had been agreed upon. Because of the depression the United States had gone off a strict gold standard at this time. Growing strife in other parts of the world brought the United States to work out the problems with Panama for the future protection of the canal. A treaty was written in March of 1936, in which the United States gave up the right to intervene in Panama and the right to obtain additional territory near the terminal points. The canal would be defended by both nations. The United States also agreed to pay the annual rent payment on the old gold exchange rate. Concern that the United States could not protect the canal with the new treaty in place prevented the Senate from ratifying the agreement, even with some changes, until July 1939.

The Good Neighbor Policy in Cuba

During the 1920s the United States did not use military force to intervene in the affairs of this island nation. But political, diplomatic, and economic interference in its affairs did occur. In 1919, General Enoch Crowder was sent to Cuba to revise the electoral codes. For years elections and the resulting governments had been at the mercy of corruption, violence, and threats of revolution. In 1923, Crowder returned as the Ambassador from the United States and effectively controlled the Cuban government. He took control of Cuban finances during the term of President Alfredo Zayas and pressured the government to enact reforms against waste and corruption. With the election of the pro-business candidate Gerardo Machado in 1924, American business increased its capital investment in Cuba.

Corruption and problems in the government were ignored by the United States until President Machado instituted a harsh and brutal dictatorship following his win at the polls in 1928. The United States warned Machado of the possibility of intervention under the conditions of the Platt Amendment but did not intervene directly. Sumner Wells was dispatched as the new American ambassador with the hope that he could force Machado to leave office. Poor economic conditions caused by the depression, a general strike in Cuba, revolutionary activity, and the efforts of Sumner Wells eventually brought down Machado.

Several governments were overthrown before Carlos Mendieta was chosen as the President of Cuba. Mendicta had the support of Fulgencio Batista, the head of the Cuban army, and Jefferson Caffery, the new American Ambassador to Cuba. The United States immediately recognized the government of Mendieta and withdrew several of the ships that had been sent to protect Americans if necessary during the time of turmoil. To counteract the negative criticism of some Latin American neighbors concerning this display of American interference as usual, the Platt Amendment was abrogated in May 1934. The United States did reserve the right to continue its use of the naval base at Guantanamo Bay, Cuba. The Senate quickly approved this treaty.

The United States then took steps to improve trade relations with Cuba. The economic problems of the islands during the latter half of the 1930s were alleviated by the dropping of the import duties on Cuban sugar. Both sides benefitted from increased trade with the Reciprocal Trade Agreements Act of 1934. By 1955 the United States supplied around 73 percent of Cuban imports and was buying close to 69 percent of Cuban exports.

AMERICAN POLICY TOWARD THE PHILIPPINES

The demands from the Philippines for independence were ignored by the Harding and Coolidge administrations, but when the cry was taken up by Americans during President Hoover's term, the government took notice. American farmers during the hard times of the depression did not want competition from the American possession in the areas of cottonseed oil, sugar, and dairy products, which could enter the country duty free. American workers did not want competition from cheap Filipino workers. It was also believed by many in America that the United States could not

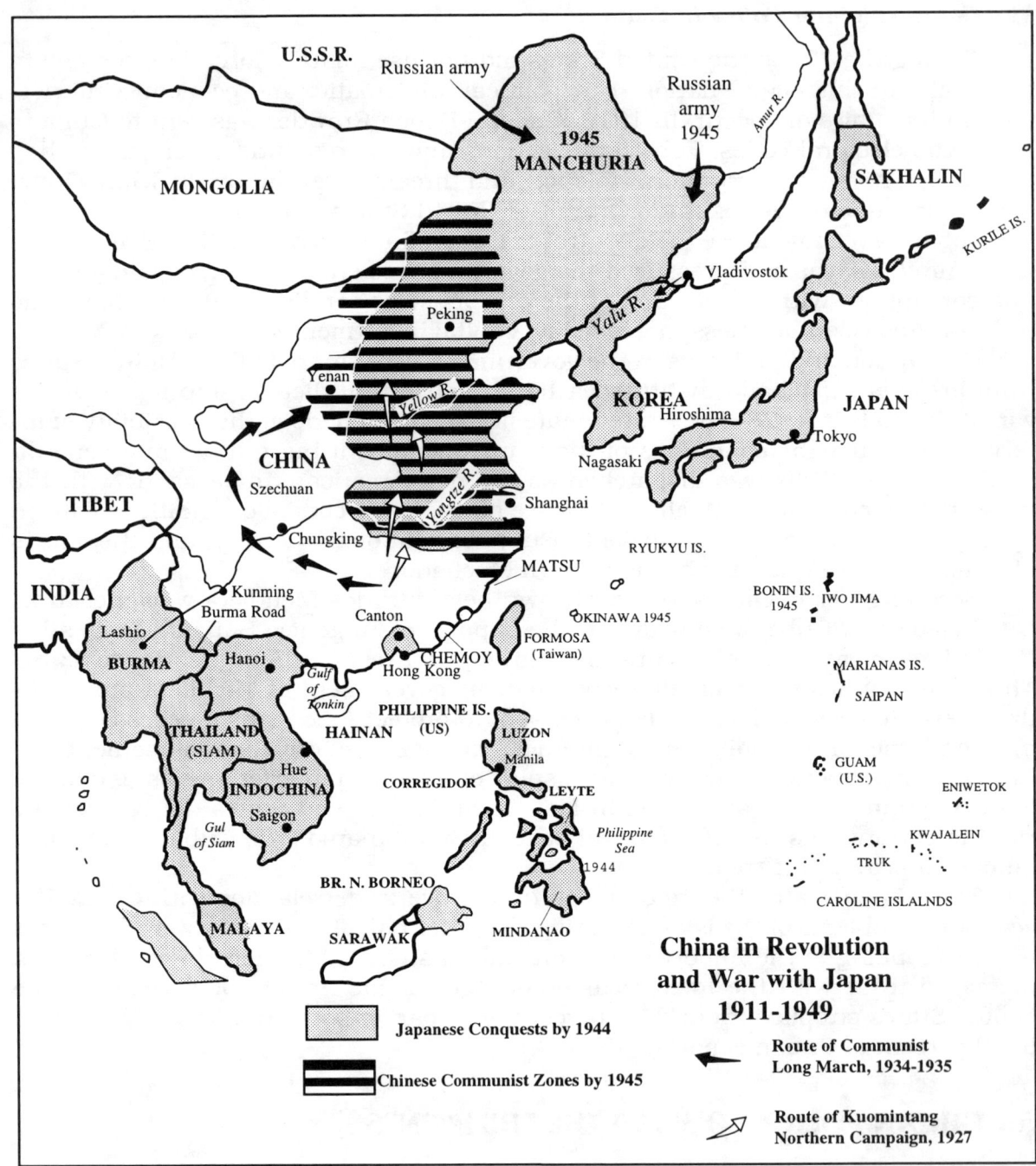

**China in Revolution
and War with Japan
1911-1949**

Japanese Conquests by 1944

Chinese Communist Zones by 1945

Route of Communist
Long March, 1934-1935

Route of Kuomintang
Northern Campaign, 1927

afford to protect the Philippines if Japanese aggression in the Far East included the taking of the islands.

Congress passed the Hawes-Cutting bill over President Hoover's veto in January 1933. The bill contained provisions for a convention in the Philippines to draw up a constitution and submit it to the people along with the question of independence from the United States. If the constitution were approved, a 10-year probationary period would begin. During the probationary period the president of the United States and the Supreme Court would still have jurisdiction over activity on the Philippines. The Philippines would have duties gradually added to her exports to the United States, and certain commodities would have quotas. Immigration to the United States was practically eliminated. The legislature in the Philippines rejected the bill. The conditions eliminating immigration and raising duties on goods exported from the islands were too high a price to pay for an independence that could mean economic ruin.

But the issue of Filipino independence was not dead. The McDuffie-Tydings Act of 1934 was accepted by the Philippine people. The new act retained control of the foreign policy of the islands during the 10-year probationary period, stated that all military forces on the island could be called into American service if danger threatened, increased the immigration quotas to a reasonable number, and established a commission to work out an agreeable tariff arrangement. The Filipinos accepted the new agreement, wrote a constitution, and elected Manuel Queson President of the Commonwealth of the Philippines on November 15, 1935. The Philippines was occupied by the Japanese during the probationary period and did not achieve full independence until July 4, 1946. The domination of a people that began with force in 1899 finally came to a peaceful end.

THE BATTLE FOR CHINA

Introduction

Civil war and revolution raged across China in the 1920s. Foreign nationals in the country lost both property, and in some instances their lives, including citizens from the United States. Some of the nations with trade concerns and holdings in China urged the use of economic sanctions to force an end to the civil war, but when the United States refused to add its voice to this group, the matter was dropped. However, American gunboats were sent to Chinese waters to protect Americans. President Coolidge realized that to attempt any sort of settlement until a single leader emerged from the turmoil was probably futile. By 1928, Chiang Kai-shek, leader of the Nationalists, had defeated most of his opponents except the Communists, who were led by Mao Tse Tung, and the United States (along with other nations) recognized his government. Chiang Kai-shek signed the Kellogg-Briand Pact in August 1928.

The problems were not over for this nation which was economically and physically divided by so many foreign nations and continued internal strife. In 1929 China and the Soviet Union were caught up in a controversy concerning Soviet rights in Manchuria, the northeastern portion of China, centering on the joint control of the Chinese Eastern Railway. The Chinese had taken control of the line, and it appeared that war was imminent. Wanting to protect American interests in China, diplomatic pressure from the United States was placed on both countries to keep their pledge to the Kellogg-Briand Pact. The Soviet Union was particularly indignant that the United States was meddling in the affair because the United

States had not formally recognized the communist nation from its inception. The two nations did finally resort to battle in which the Soviets were victorious. They then forced the Chinese to accept their rights in Northern Manchuria. Without enforcement capabilities, the Kellogg-Briand Pact, along with the diplomatic efforts of Secretary of State Henry Stimson, failed to prevent the violence.

Japan Threatens China

Japanese interests had increased with gains in China at the end of the Russo-Japanese War in 1905 and the presentation in 1915 of the Twenty-one demands to China. The list of demands had been accepted by China and had given Japan a protectorate over the nation. But they were limited by the United States at the Washington Conference in 1922. The Versailles Treaty rewarded Japanese support of the Allies in World War I by furthering Japan's economic privileges in Manchuria and legalizing Japanese claims to Shantung and German Islands in the Pacific.

The onset of the Great Depression in the 1930s strengthened the militaristic and extremist elements of the government, who wanted to expand Japanese territory and find new areas of land to relieve the pressure of an expanding population in a small country, and to provide relief for an increasing unemployment problem. In Japan, as in Italy and Germany, fascist government leaders came into power during a time of economic hardship. The fascists appealed to the spirit of nationalism in each nation and convinced their respective populations of the necessity of expansion through aggressive acts to save their nations.

The Mukden Incident

Manchuria was the initial Japanese target area for expansion because of its abundant resources, its large and sparsely populated areas, and the fact that Japanese soldiers were already in the area to protect their interests. A portion of the Japanese-owned South Manchurian Railroad was blown up near the provincial capital of Mukden on September 18, 1931. The Japanese military in Manchuria blamed the Chinese for the explosion and retaliated with an attack on a small force of Chinese soldiers. The city of Mukden and other strategic locations were soon captured. The Japanese soldiers made their attacks without orders from the civilian government in Tokyo. However, the Japanese government decided to accept capture of Mukden as a *fait accompli* (accomplished fact) and claimed the soldiers were merely acting in self-defense. This Mukden Incident was the spark that began the Japanese aggression in China.

China appealed to the United States and to the League of Nations. Secretary of State Stimson notified the League that the United States would support the League in its efforts to solve the conflict. This represented a change for the United States to unconditionally back the League. The League of Nations, of which China and Japan were members, and the United States, a signatory with Japan of the Nine-Power Treaty guaranteeing the independence of China, urged both to come to terms for peace. Nevertheless, fighting broke out again in October. In spite of the willingness of moderates in the Japanese government to abide by the League's decision, the military was very powerful and determined to control Manchuria as its first step toward the building of an empire. On October 8, Japanese planes bombed the city of Chinchow. And by early January 1932, all of Southern Manchuria was in Japanese hands.

On January 7, 1932, Secretary of State Henry Stimson stated the position toward the conflict in China in what would become known as the Stimson Doctrine. The United States, he said, would not recognize any changes in China which were the result of the use of force. The use of force to effect change would be a violation of the American Open Door Policy and the Kellogg-Briand Pact. Unfortunately, this stand was not enough to force Japan to change her policies, and the United States was not willing to take firmer steps to stop aggression until much later.

More Japanese Aggression

Having met no military challenges to its expansionist policies, Japan suddenly attacked the coastal Chinese city of Shanghai (not in Manchuria) in late January 1932. Thousands of civilians were killed in the attack. Then on February 23, 1932, a letter written by Secretary Stimson to Senator Borah, chairman of the Senate Foreign Relations Committee, was published. The letter stated that the United States would stand by its treaty obligations in the Far East just as all nations should. He also urged that all other nations follow the Stimson Doctrine of nonrecognition. The League of Nations supported the stand of Secretary Stimson, and Japanese troops did withdraw from Shanghai in the face of this worldwide criticism; but they did not withdraw from Manchuria, which they renamed Manchukuo in March 1932.

The weak League of Nations insisted that Japan leave Manchuria, but instead Japan left the League of Nations in February 1933. In the same year Hitler pulled Germany out of the Disarmament Conference in Geneva and the League of Nations. Collective security had not worked, but the nations did not know it yet. The western nations were not willing to become involved in conflict, and their lack of commitment would fuel the growth of aggression in both Asia and Europe.

Japan stated that after 1936 it would not abide by the treaties agreed to at the Washington Naval Conference in 1922. This was another break in the barriers that had been erected to protect the world from war. By 1936 Japan was moving its military machine further into north China. On November 25 of that year, Japan signed the Anti-Comintern Pact with Germany, a move by both countries to prevent the spread of communism in areas that both were interested in. This Pact was the beginning of a friendship that would threaten the world.

The Full-Scale Japanese Invasion of China

On July 7, 1937, Japanese and Chinese forces clashed near the Marco Polo Bridge (in the Peking area), and a full-scale invasion of China ensued. Secretary of State Cordell Hull denounced the use of force and urged the two sides to negotiate their differences and observe international agreements. Japan retaliated with statements then, and in the future, that she had no territorial designs on China, and she had been forced into using aggression in self-defense because the govern-

The Japanese take possession of Chapei in the Battle for Shanghai. Credit: AP/Wide World Photos.

ment of China had refused to adopt a friendly policy toward Japanese interests. This action for self-defense would take the lives of more than two million Chinese.

Because the Japanese did not bother to officially declare war, President Roosevelt refused to declare that a state of war existed in China. Therefore, the Neutrality Laws did not go into effect, which permitted the United States to assist the Chinese. Despite this legal permission, very small amounts of American aid were provided. An American volunteer air group known as the "Flying Tigers" did assist the Chinese in their fierce resistance led by Chiang Kai-shek, based in the more mountainous regions of China. Public opinion in the United States criticized Japanese aggression in China, but there was no call for American intervention. In addition to minimal American assistance, Britain and France were also aiding the Chinese forces.

Antagonism toward the Japanese increased with the sinking of the *U.S.S. Panay*, in which two Americans were killed, on December 12, 1937. The *Panay* was on the Yangtze River assisting American nationals in their attempt to flee from the besieged city of Nanking. The Japanese pilots claimed they did not know the ship was American. This was doubtful, however, because it was a clear day and a large American flag was flying on the ship. The Japanese government quickly apologized for the "accident" and promised that an indemnity would be paid. The Japanese government did not want to bring the United States into the conflict, and American public opinion likewise did not want to intervene militarily. In April 1938 the United States received more than $2 million in compensation for losses. Neither the attack on the *Panay* nor the fall of the city of Nanking moved the United States to assist China further. However, the fall of that city, which became known as the "Rape of Nanking," did shock the world when the victorious Japanese soldiers massacred, looted, and raped the vanquished.

On November 3, 1938, the Japanese premier announced that Japan had established the "New Order in East Asia," which would bring peace. The economics and politics of Manchukuo, China (the portions under Japanese control) and Japan would be coordinated for the benefit of all, and they would stand firm to prevent all encroachment into Asia. The United States responded to the New Order with a warning to Japan not to interfere with the rights of American citizens and economic interests in China. Then in July 1939, President Roosevelt notified Japan that The Treaty of Commerce between the two nations, in place since 1911, would not be renewed when it expired six months later. This was a warning to Japan of an embargo to come if their expansionist policy was not halted. The end of this trade treaty would, in effect, prevent Japan from purchasing gasoline, scrap iron, and other necessary materials for war with China. The president had already received permission from Congress to begin a billion-dollar naval-building program in 1938. Events were escalating to war in spite of continued attempts to negotiate peace.

NEUTRALITY

Introduction

The rise of the totalitarian governments in the Soviet Union, Italy, Japan, and Germany threatened the security of the world in the 1930s. The essence of totalitarianism is the subordination of all individual or social interests to the interests of the state. The threat of the spread of communism from the Soviet Union under the domination of Lenin and later of Joseph Stalin was considered a potential threat to the security of the United States and Europe in the 1920s and early 1930s. But Stalin became a threat to only his own people at this time. It would be the fascist totalitarian leaders, beginning with Benito Mussolini, that would bring the world to war in the 1930s.

Mussolini began totalitarian rule in Italy with his fascist government in 1922. More than a decade later, Adolf Hitler brought totalitarianism to Germany following his appointment as Chancellor in 1933. And Japan borrowed the techniques of the totalitarian states, but not their philosophies, to build their own empire. In all three nations, new leaders exalted power, glorified the state, and appealed to the spirit of nationalism. The nations which accepted the subordination of individual freedoms and regimentation of all activities for the good of the state had been defeated in World War I, lost territory they believed they were entitled to in treaties, or suffered economic and political problems in the post-war years. The promise to their citizens to solve domestic problems, end humiliating international obligations, and bring power and prosperity in the future was very appealing. And for a while their promises were kept.

The Neutrality Laws

As early as 1934 the United States began taking steps to decrease the likelihood of becoming embroiled in problems in Europe that could lead to similar entanglements that had brought American participation in World War I. The Johnson Debt Default Act of April 13, 1934, prohibited loans to any foreign government in default to the United States. The aggression of Japan and Italy, the war between Bolivia and Paraguay, the buildup of land armaments in nation after nation led Congress to take further steps toward ensuring American isolationism. It was believed that stern neutrality laws were the answer. As more nations became involved in aggression in the 1930s, the Neutrality Acts grew in number and scope. These laws went far beyond the legal status of neutrality and really should have been called isolationist laws.

It was a prevalent opinion that American arms sales were a primary reason for American entrance in World War I. The Nye Committee (1934–1937) confirmed for many that the United States had been dragged into the Great War by a conspiracy involving American arms manufacturers and bankers. The Senate committee, chaired by the isolationist Senator Gerald P. Nye (Republican from North Dakota), held hearings and investigated the alleged reasons why the country had entered the Great War in 1917. Its investigation and then final report in early 1937 declared that many business leaders had made great profits from that war and had not paid taxes on those profits, that contracts were obtained through political connections, and that American bankers pushed for war to ensure repayment of their loans to the Allies. The committee could not prove its allegations, but Americans were shocked at the conclusions, and more were converted to isolationism and committed to legislation that would guarantee that position. The public believed World War I had been a mistake. America should never entangle itself in the problems of Europe again. World War I had not made the world safe for democracy, as Wilson had claimed it would. Business seemed to be the only winners in the war. Neutrality, including an embargo on arms sales, appeared to be the solution.

Under the provisions of the Joint Resolution of August 31, 1935, the first Neutrality Act, the president was given the power to decide when a state of war officially existed between nations. And when a state of war did exist, an embargo would be placed on the sale of arms, munitions, and implements of war to the belligerents. Supervision of the sale of munitions was put under the control of the National Munitions Control Board, which consisted of the Secretaries of State, War, Navy, and Commerce. With the presidential declaration that nations were at war, Americans would travel at their own risk on ships owned by belligerents.

President Roosevelt declared that the Neutrality Act would be implemented in the war between Italy and Ethiopia. However, a serious flaw in the legislation was that commodities not on the embargo list could be made into implements of war. Italy, the aggressor in this war, took advantage of this situation. The law also prevented the United States from assisting the innocent victims of aggressor nations, which applied to the Ethiopians, but this was an acceptance of injustice that the country was willing to take to ensure neutrality.

The Neutrality Act of 1936 was passed to continue the measures of the 1935 law and to add amendments to the original legislation. Under this new bill, belligerent nations could not receive loans or credits, although nations in the western hemisphere were exempted from that restriction. Furthermore, the president must extend the embargo measures to other countries that could possibly become belligerents. With the oubreak of civil war in Spain on July 18, 1936, the position of the United States needed to be clarified further because the Neutrality Acts did not apply to civil wars. On January 6, 1937, a Joint Congressional Resolution denied both sides of the conflict American munitions. This measure worked a particular hardship on the Loyalist government in Madrid because the rebels were receiving arms from Italy and Germany.

It was hoped that the Neutrality Act of May 1937 would correct the deficiencies of the other laws. The provisions of the 1936 act were kept, but amendments were added. American ships could not be armed nor carry arms to belligerents. Americans were now forbidden to travel on any ships of nations at war. The status of belligerent could also apply to opposing sides in a civil war. The president could prohibit the use of American ports to ships of belligerents and the selling of American securities to belligerent nations. Non-military goods could be purchased in the United States with cash, but they must be transported on the ships of the purchasers. This last feature made it known as "the cash and carry" law. The new Neutrality Act was applied to the civil war in Spain but not to the hostilities that broke out between Japan and China on July 7, 1937. The president did not want to assist the Japanese in this new act of aggression by denying all assistance to the Chinese, so he used the excuse that the Neutrality Act would not apply because this was not an officially declared war between the two sides.

The Quarantine Speech and the Ludlow Amendment

President Roosevelt was becoming increasingly alarmed by the aggressions of Japan, Italy, and Germany. He expressed his views in a speech in Chicago on October 5, 1937, concerning the course that should be considered in view of the current hostilities around the world: "The peace-loving nations must make a concerted effort to uphold laws and principles on which alone peace can rest secure. . . . When an epidemic of physical disease starts to spread, the community approves and joins in a quarantine in order to protect the health of the community. . . ." This speech, known as the Quarantine Speech, was not well-received by an American public that wanted to stay isolated from the problems they viewed as not their concern. Roosevelt knew he could not push American public opinion faster than it was prepared to go, so he backed off from expressing this view.

Another problem developed for Roosevelt in January 1938, when Indiana Congressman Louis Ludlow proposed a constitutional amendment requiring a national referendum on any American declaration of war unless the nation were directly attacked. Using finely honed tactics, the president persuaded the House of Represen-

Benito Mussolini, 1939. Credit: AP/Wide World Photos.

tatives to defeat the bill. It was a narrow defeat, with 209 against and 188 for the Ludlow Amendment.

Unity in the Western Hemisphere

The rise of dictators and their aggressive actions also brought measures from all of the nations in the western hemisphere to solidify their unity and proclaim their neutrality from the problems outside the region. In 1933 the assembly at the Rio de Janeiro Conference condemned all acts of aggression and refused to recognize the legitimacy of any territory acquired by force. President Roosevelt was so concerned with holding together a united front against aggression in the Americas that he attended the Buenos Aires Conference himself in 1936. At this conference the members again pledged their support to all earlier collective security agreements and promised to consult with the others on peace measures to be taken if any were threatened by war. The final meeting of the regular Pan-American Conference before war erupted took place in Lima, Peru in December 1938. The Declara-

Italian troops march into Addis Ababa, the Ethiopian capitol. Credit: AP/Wide World Photos.

tion of Lima reaffirmed "continental solidarity and their purpose to collaborate in the maintenance of the principles upon which the said solidarity is based."

In spite of all the work that went into keeping the hemisphere safe from war, the decisions to fight or not to fight would be controlled by the actions of the aggressors on the march around the world. But even when the United States did later become embroiled in World War II, there was near unanimity of support from the nations of Latin America. What a contrast that was to the very lukewarm response when the United States had entered World War I. The difference, for the most part, was that American interventionist policies in Latin America, from Theodore Roosevelt to Woodrow Wilson, had left that region hostile to the United States. But the conciliatory policies begun in the late 1920s and which flowered in Roosevelt's Good Neighbor Policy had brought cooperation and unity instead. This was proof that morally right policies can also be very beneficial in the practical world.

THE AGGRESSION OF FASCIST ITALY

Benito Mussolini had organized his fascist movement in Milan, Italy. His organization began to grow when it adopted a policy of nationalism and anticommunism

Joseph Stalin. Credit: Brown Brothers.

with squads of black-shirted ruffians to fight the communist enemies. The Fascist Party was formally organized in 1921 with support from army officers and business leaders. And Mussolini was elected to the Italian parliament in 1921 as a representative of his party. In October 1922, the fascists marched on Rome and seized the government by force. Mussolini came to Rome and was proclaimed Il Duce (the leader) by his followers. He became the head of government with his appointment as premier. Working toward a restoration of the power and prestige once held by the ancient Roman Empire, Mussolini planned to build a new Roman Empire.

He began with an invasion of the African nation of Ehiopia in 1935. Ethiopia lay close to the Italian possessions of Libya and Somaliland. To consolidate all of the area into one possession, and at the same time have access to the reputed raw materials of Ethiopia, seemed a wise move from his perspective. During the winter of 1935–1936, the weakly-defended nation fell. Haile Selassie, the leader of the defeated nation, appealed to the League of Nations for assistance against this blatant act of aggression. Indeed, Italy was denounced and sanctions against the sale of arms, the extension of credit, and imposition of trade embargoes were all invoked to show international displeasure. The exemption of iron, steel, copper, and oil from the trade embargo, however, made the actions useless.

Mussolini was condemned by the League, put under the implementation of neutrality laws by the United States, but applauded by Hitler. In 1936, a pact between Germany and Italy established what Mussolini termed "the Axis." The collaboration of Berlin and Rome to support the Nationalists in the Spanish Civil War (1936–1939) would become "an axis around which all European states . . . may collaborate." The two nations bound many of their foreign policies and goals together. In 1937, Italy joined the Anti-Comintern Pact that had been forged by Germany and Japan in 1936 to fight communism. And when Hitler began to expand into northern Europe, Italy invaded Albania in 1939. The two leaders formed a military alliance in 1939 shortly before World War II officially began.

THE SPANISH CIVIL WAR

In July 1936 an attempt to overthrow the republican government of Spain began when Spanish Army units in Morocco proclaimed they were in revolt against the government in Madrid. General Francisco Franco flew to Spain, and with Spanish army units loyal to him, engineered a coup to overthrow the second Spanish Republic.

The Loyalists in the war were those supporting the legitimate left-wing government which was a coalition of liberals, socialists, and Marxists. Support for the Loyalists came from outside of Spain, including the Soviet Union, and from writers, artists, and intellectuals who sympathized with the Popular Front. Fearing an attack from fascist Germany, the Soviet communist dictator Joseph Stalin called for the world to join in a Popular Front to oppose the fascist leaders, Hitler and Mussolini. There were Americans who supported the Loyalist government with money, clothing, and medical supplies. Some Americans, including those that made up the Abraham Lincoln Brigade, went to Spain to either fight with the Loyalist armed forces or to assist with medical care. They were mistaken in their belief that they were supporting a democracy, but correct that they were allied with the legitimate government.

There were also those in America who supported the opposite side in the conflict, the Nationalists (or fascists), simply because they would not assist any group helped by the Soviet communists. Franco, a fascist, received support from within Spain from monarchists, industrialists, and the Roman Catholic Church. Italy and Germany sent as-

Ruins in Barcelona, Spain during the Spanish Civil War. Credit: AP/Wide World Photos.

sistance to Franco. Mussolini sent air force and infantry units to fight in Spain, but unfortunately they were not highly skilled in warfare. Germany sent the Condor Legion from its new Luftwaffe (air force) and one tank battalion. These forces were highly skilled and of great value to the cause of Franco. The battles in Spain were also considered by the Germans to be valuable training in air and tank battle strategies, perfecting aspects of their later famous blitzkrieg tactics.

The American Neutrality Acts actually aided the forces of Franco and their German and Italian allies in that the United States could not ship arms to the Spanish government. In April 1939, the civil war ended in victory for the rebels, and Franco instituted a fascist dictatorship.

THE AGGRESSION OF GERMANY

Hitler Comes to Power

Adolf Hitler had come to the attention of the people of Germany when his trial for treason against the state was widely publicized in the early 1920s. Hitler and his party, the National Socialist German Workers' party, or Nazis as they became known, attempted to overthrow the government in Munich with a putsch (revolt) in November 1923. Sentenced by a sympathetic judge, Hitler was out of prison in less than a year and rebuilding his party. His speeches denouncing the Allies, Jews, Communists, and German traitors who had caused Germany to lose the war appealed only to a small number in the 1920s.

Soldiers entering Dusseldorf after occupying the demilitarized zone of the Rhineland. Credit: AP/Wide World Photos.

The Nazi Party stagnated until the economic problems beginning in 1930 increased their membership in the German Reichstag (lower house of parliament) from 12 to 107 seats. Germans selected more members of the Nazis because the appeal was growing in a country with political and economic instability. The message from Hitler had broadened over time. His political agenda for Germany was appealing: repudiation of the hated and humiliating Versailles Treaty, which would give Germans respect once again for their nation; an end to war reparations; restoration of German territory lost in the war; an end to political chaos in Germany (Of course, much of this was caused intentionally by the Nazis in order to eliminate political enemies and to secretly provide a chaotic situation which they would be called in to settle.); and the restoration of the

Adolf Hitler, 1938. Credit: AP/Wide World Photos

economy. Hitler began to receive support from some military leaders and industrialists. They believed his strong-arm tactics, which included his own private army of brown-shirted stormtroopers, were the best chance to bring Germany out of its difficulties.

By 1933, the Nazis represented the largest party in the Reichstag. It was not a majority (it never won a majority of the votes in a free election), so it could not pass legislation without a coalition with other party representatives. But it was large enough to block most legislation it did not support. President Paul von Hindenburg requested Hitler to take the position of Chancellor (prime minister) on January 30, 1933. He did not like or trust Hitler, but advisors convinced him that the head of the Nazis could be controlled in that position, and his appointment was necessary for efficient government to begin again.

Shortly after becoming the German Chancellor, a fire burned the Reichstag building. Hitler immediately blamed the fire on the communists, which allowed Hitler to receive dictatorial powers to meet this alleged threat to Germany's security. This emergency measure allowed Hitler to begin to consolidate his power with the slow but measured elimination of all groups who could oppose him. When the beloved President von Hindenburg died in 1934, Hitler combined the offices of chancellor and president with the new title of Führer (leader). His action was ap-

Neville Chamberlain, Edouard Daladier, Adolf Hitler and Benito Mussolini after the signing of the Munich Pact, 1938. Credit: AP/Wide World Photos.

proved by the German people, and he proclaimed his administration of Germany as the "New Order" and the German nation as the "Third Reich" (empire).

The German Reoccupation of the Rhineland

Hitler's march of aggression that would ignite World War II began with the seemingly non-threatening gesture of reoccupying the Rhineland area of Germany west of the Rhine River with German troops in March 1936. The Rhineland had been declared a demilitarized zone in the Treaty of Versailles. Hitler told his generals to immediately retreat to the east side of the river if any military resistance was offered by the French because the German force was too small to put up much of a resistance. Almost miraculously for Hitler, there was no resistance. The British and the French were too caught up in the domestic crises in their nations, brought on by the depression, to do anything about Hitler's move; besides, they had expected this move for a while and apparently had mentally gotten used to it. They also did not perceive Hitler as a threat to peace at this time. The British agreed that he was moving into his own territory. Hitler's little test of the commitment of the European powers to enforcement of the Versailles Treaty encouraged him to move on to the next phase in his plan to dominate Europe, and then move to the east for "lebensraum" (living space) for his Third Reich.

The Anschluss

In March 1938, German soldiers peacefully took control of Austria. This union of Germany and Austria (a Germanic nation and the nation of Hitler's birth) was called the "Anschluss," and had also been prohibited by the Versailles Treaty. The invasion of Austria was preceded with claims to Austrian Chancellor Schuschnigg that he had broken agreements with Germany, and eventually the demand that Schuschnigg, who had attempted to rally the Austrians against a German takeover, resign. Dr. von Seyss-Inquart, the pro-Nazi Minister of the Interior in Austria, took over the duties of the Chancellor and was ordered to request German troops to put down disorder allegedly caused by communists in Austria. Hitler justified his invasions very logically while he was still worried about the opinions of other nations and too weak to make his move toward a general European war.

On March 12, German troops marched through Vienna in what was undoubtedly a popularly supported move in that country. Once again the Western democracies did nothing. Hitler's conviction was growing strong that his plans would not be thwarted for some time. The Soviet Union sent a note to Neville Chamberlain, the British Prime Minister, on March 17, 1938. The note requested a meeting between the American, British, French, and Soviet governments to discuss action against this new aggression. But Chamberlain accepted the Anschluss and would not agree to the proposal to meet. Britain and France believed that Hitler was still adjusting what he believed to be unfair in the Treaty of Versailles. Knowing that that treaty had been grossly unfair and harsh toward Germany, these Allied leaders' guilty consciences prevented them from taking any meaningful steps to stop Hitler—a fact that Hitler used to his advantage.

The Munich (or Sudeten) Crisis

In the summer of 1938, Hitler turned his attention to the Sudetenland, an area in northwest Czechoslovakia that contained about three million Germans. The Versailles Treaty had separated the Sudetenland from Germany to form the western fringe of the new nation of Czechoslovakia after the last major war. One aspect of Hitler's plan for the Third Reich was to rejoin all former German territory into one great empire. Hitler's plan to reclaim this land began with claims to the press that Germans in the Sudetenland were being persecuted. This was not true, but at this time he continued to need to justify to the world his aggression. In this false allegation, Hitler was also making use of his "big lie" theory, which stated that the bigger the lie, and the more often it is repeated with firm conviction, the more likely that people will eventually believe it. The German members of the Nationalist Socialist Party in the Sudetenland were ordered to claim that all Germans in Czechoslovakia were discriminated against as a minority. The Sudeten Germans were then ordered to campaign for privileges that they knew would not be granted because they fell just short of autonomy for the region.

Britain and France were alarmed when Hitler's speeches of concern for the mistreatment of the Germans escalated. The major powers held conferences on the issue, which was finally resolved by the third conference, known as the Munich Conference, held in Munich, Germany from September 29–30, 1938. In spite of agreements from the Czech government in the first week of September to grant virtually all of the German demands in the Sudetenland, Hitler was still demanding that Czechoslovakia allow the return of this area to Germany. The participants in the Munich Conference were called together by Benito Mussolini, Italy's leader. At the meeting British Prime Minister Neville Chamberlain, French Premier Edouard Daladier, German Führer Adolf Hitler, and Mussolini finally signed a document agreeing that the Sudetenland should be ceded to Germany. This became known as the Munich Pact. President Benes of Czechoslovakia wanted to fight rather than give in to the loss of this area which was important for its industry and defensive fortifications, but without the support of the British and the French it was hopeless.

The British and French actions in Munich were an example of the policy of appeasement, which meant that they yielded to Hitler's demands in the expectation that he would not want more. Meanwhile, when Chamberlain got off the plane in England, he took a copy of the Munich Pact out of his pocket, and with a big smile, proudly proclaimed to the crowd and the radio audience that in Munich they had just achieved "peace in our time." Perhaps no world leader in the twentieth century ever spoke less true words. And the world would not have long to wait before Chamberlain was proven wrong because the policy of appeasement did not work.

Instead, Hitler proceeded with his plan to take all of Czechoslovakia. Other minority groups in that country wanting separation were encouraged to pressure the government. When the nation was in chaos, Hitler stated that Germany's security was threatened and ordered President Emil Hacha to Berlin to sign an agreement placing all of Czechoslovakia under German control. On March 15, 1939, German soldiers marched into the capital city of Prague. The attempts of the European powers to appease gave the German leader the confidence to go forward with his plans to not only rejoin all German territory, but to conquer Europe. The appeasement of Hitler can best be described as the result of at least three fundamental attitudes: (1) the memory of the Great War caused such fear and disillusionment that most desired to avoid another general European war at almost any cost; (2) the British and French felt some guilt at the harsh treatment of Germany in the Versailles Treaty; and (3) Hitler was viewed by the leaders of the world as a comical eccentric who could not be taken seriously.

AMERICAN REACTIONS

American reaction to all of the aggressive actions until 1938 was to increase the number and strength of its Neutrality Laws and encourage all sides to negotiate peaceful solutions. President Roosevelt recognized the dangers that were involved if largescale war did break out in Europe or Japan and warned the nation in his State

Four Nazi soldiers picketing Woolworth's (Berlin). They incorrectly assumed the store was owned by a Jewish-American. Credit: AP/Wide World Photos.

of the Union address to Congress on January 3, 1938, that the nation needed to be "adequately strong in self-defense." The nation and the Roosevelt administration continued to focus on the economic problems of the United States, but Roosevelt did ask Congress for a $300 million military appropriation in October 1938, and in November a plan to produce 20,000 planes was announced to the Army Air Corps. Military spending continued to increase beginning with the January 1939 budget.

Americans were aware of the problems of Czechoslovakia, thanks to radio broadcasts on CBS and NBC, and their sympathies were with the Czechs. Opinion was slowly turning against Hitler. In fact, in retrospect, the Munich Crisis proved to be the turning point in American public opinion about Hitler. But despite that, a public opinion poll taken at the time still showed that only a minority of Americans actually disapproved of the Munich Pact.

There can be little doubt, however, about the fact that the crisis had impacted American minds. One month later, on Halloween Eve (October 31, 1938), CBS radio

Jewish shop owner in Berlin clearing broken glass from his shop during Kristallnacht. Credit: AP/Wide World Photos.

broadcast what would become the most famous radio play in the history of that medium. Novelist H.G. Wells' *The War of the Worlds*, broadcast for the first time on radio, caused great hysteria in some areas of the country. The drama was a fictional account of a Martian invasion of Earth, told via a series of on-the-site reporters, with actor Orson Welles as the main narrator of the program. Despite the fact that there were some interruptions in the broadcast to remind listeners that they were only hearing a fictional story, quite a number of Americans grew frightened and panicked. While a few probably thought the Martians had landed, the greater number of those who panicked believed that the reports were telling the story of a German invasion of the United States. This reaction occurred partly because of the "news" format of the show and partly because of the eeriness associated with Halloween. But a major reason for this peculiar reaction was that radio had just one month earlier brought the story of the Munich Crisis into the living rooms of Americans in a dramatic way. Psychologically, then, the radio was still associated with that crisis so that the permission given Germany to invade part of Czeckoslavakia altered the "reality" of *The War of the Worlds*.

Even the plight of the Jews in Germany did not move the country to change in the direction of intervention. Hitler's program for a new Third Reich called for the elimination of the Jews. He believed the Jews were to blame for most of the social and economic problems, not only in Germany, but in the whole world. The campaign to deny the Jews all rights as citizens of Germany, and eventually as human beings, began with the Nuremberg Laws in 1935 and would end with the Holocaust during World War II.

The world was awakened to only a small example of the depths of the hatred of Hitler and many Germans for the Jews (who were Germans themselves) with the events on November 9, 1938—a night known as Kristallnacht (Night of the Broken Glass). On this night across Germany and Austria a well coordinated attack was perpetrated on thousands of Jewish homes, synagogues, businesses, hospitals, and even children's schools by the Nazis. Those Jewish establishments were burned to the ground in plain sight of firemen, who were present only to prevent the fires from spreading to non-Jewish buildings. In response to Kristallnacht, President Roosevelt recalled the American ambassador to Berlin for consultations; he did not return until after World War II had ended. Although few could doubt that persecution of the Jews in Germany was escalating, the United States did not change its immigration quotas to allow more German Jews into this country. The famous or the well educated were welcomed. However, in June 1939, nine hundred Jewish refugees were not allowed to leave their ship to land on the shores of the United States. Instead they were forced to return to Europe and an uncertain destiny.

Following the German takeover of Czechoslovakia in March 1939 and the Italian invasion of Albania the next month, Roosevelt wrote to both Hitler and Mussolini on April 14, requesting a ten-year guarantee for peace in Europe and the Middle East. Neither leader would honor the American president's request. Hitler even publicly ridiculed the proposal in the German Reichstag. By this time, President Roosevelt began adopting what is known as his "Methods Short of War" policy. Its four main components outlined FDR's objectives as follows: (1) increase military preparedness in the event that the Neutrality Laws were modified to permit aid to our allies in Europe and Asia; (2) revise the Neutrality Laws to allow the president more latitude in assisting those nations important to the security of the United States; (3) increase his critical rhetoric against German and Japanese aggression; and (4) when events gave the opportunity the United States would show tangible signs of its displeasure.

President Roosevelt and Secretary of State Cordell Hull widened the gap between the totalitarian states and the United States in July 1939. President Roosevelt asked Congress to repeal the arms embargo through revision of the Neutrality Laws, and the Secretary of State abrogated the trade treaty with the Japanese. The United States was increasingly seen as the only real barrier to the aggressive policies of Japan and Germany.

The war that most of the nations of the world hoped to avoid came with the German invasion of Poland on the morning of September 1, 1939. Britain and France had pledged to come to the aid of Poland if the nation was attacked, and they did so with their declarations of war against Germany on September 3, 1939.

The United States declared its official neutrality on September 5 of that year. Hoping to keep the hemisphere safe from war, the Inter-American Conference proclaimed in the Declaration of Panama that safety zones in the Western Hemisphere were off limits to any naval activity of belligerent powers. The nations at war would ignore this warning. So many treaties signed, so many hours spent in negotiation, so many hopes for a world free from aggression and war were ground in the dust as Germany, Italy, and Japan sent their armies forward. The United States would not remain neutral for long.

ADDITIONAL READINGS

Wayne S. Cole, *Roosevelt and the Isolationists, 1932–45* (1983). Shows the president and his critics sparring over foreign policy. Analyzes the complexities of liberal/conservative division over the war and offers insights into the logic of conservatives who feared the growth of a permanent bureaucratic, militarized state.

Warren Cohen, *Empire Without Tears: American Foreign Relations, 1921–1933* (1988).

R. Dallek, *Franklin D. Roosevelt and American Foreign Policy, 1932–1945* (1979).

Ethan L. Ellis, *Republican Foreign Policy, 1921–1933* (1968).

Robert H. Ferrell, *American Diplomacy in the Great Depression: Hoover-Stimson Foreign Policy, 1929–1933* (1957).

Akira Iriye, *After Imperialism: The Search for a New Order in the Far East, 1921–1931* (1965).

CHAPTER TWELVE

World War II

MAJOR EVENTS

1940   Soviet Union invades Finland
Germany, Italy, and Japan form Axis powers
America First Committee formed
Selective Service and Training Act passed
Franklin Roosevelt elected to unprecedented third term

1941   Lend-Lease Act
A. Phillip Randolph organizes March on Washington movement
Fair Employment Practices Committee formed
Germany invades Soviet Union
Atlantic Charter
Japanese attack Pearl Harbor; U.S declares war on Japan, Italy, and Germany

1942   Internment of Japanese Americans
National War Labor Board, War Production Board, and Supply Priorities and Allocation Board established
Manhattan Project begun
Battles of Coral Sea and Midway in Pacific
U S. invades Egypt; Operation Torch begins in North Africa

1943   Soviet victory over Germans at Stalingrad
German Afrika Korps troops surrender in Tunisia
Coal miners strike
Summer of race riots
Allied invasion of Italy
Casablanca conference

1944   Operation Overlord and liberation of Paris
Roosevelt elected to fourth term

1945 Yalta Conference renews American-Soviet alliance; Roosevelt dies in office; Harry Truman becomes president
Germany surrenders
Decisive Pacific battles; U.S captures Iwo Jima and Okinawa
Potsdam Conference
U.S. bombing of Hiroshima and Nagasaki; Japan surrenders

INTRODUCTION

By the summer of 1939 war had been raging in China for two years in a conflict which the Japanese had not bothered to officially declare war. China's civilian population, especially in the eastern cities, was being devastated by Japanese aggression in which atrocities were commonplace. In Europe, Nazi Germany occupied and controlled Austria and all of Czechoslovakia without arousing any more reaction from the world than hostile but empty threats. Europe was tottering on the brink of another major war before the memories of the last conflagration had faded into oblivion. Would Adolf Hitler, the German Fuhrer, be content with his diplomatic victories or would he force the continent into total war? What would happen next? That was the tense situation in the summer of 1939 when the world was shocked to learn that Hitler's nemesis in the Soviet Union had apparently come to terms with him.

THE NAZI-SOVIET PACT

The mutual hatred and distrust between Hitler and Soviet communist dictator Joseph Stalin was well known. Hitler's right-wing fascist ideology blamed the communists and Jewish conspirators for Germany's problems, and Hitler had used German fears of a communist revolution to propel him to popularity and eventual power. Stalin's communist perspective made him fearful of a fascist leader, especially one which was building up his military forces while also talking aggressively. This context helps explain the shock waves when the two men suddenly announced a non-aggression pact between their two countries in August 1939.

Neither Hitler nor Stalin trusted the other one, but Hitler pursued a pact with Stalin to neutralize the threat from the Soviet Union for his plans to conquer Poland. He knew his armies were not yet powerful enough to challenge the Soviet Union's Red armies. His plans to sieze territory to the east of Germany had been formulated in the mid-1920s, while in prison for his failed coup in the so-called Munich Putsch. While there, Hitler had outlined his grandiose military aims in a book entitled *Mein Kampf* (*My Battle* or *My Struggle*), of which one of his major goals was to seek territory for a new German empire. His main targets had always been to the east. The Slavic peoples, whom he considered inferior, should be obliterated if necessary in order to provide "lebensraum" (living space) for the "master" German race. However, the British and French would have to be knocked out of action first to prevent their hindrance of his aggression in eastern Europe and the Soviet Union. For his part, Stalin was uneasy about such an agreement, but he knew that his own purges of the Red Army had left his military too weak to gamble on a war with the Germans any time soon. Therefore, in what is known as the Nazi-Soviet Pact (or Hitler-Stalin Pact), the two arch enemies signed and announced to the world their agreement not to attack each other.

What the announcement did not mention, however, was that both nations agreed to attack Poland and divide it between them. Portions of western Poland had been part of German soil before the Treaty of Versailles at the end of the Great War. In April Hitler had begun to harrass Poland, charging the government there, as in Czechoslovakia earlier, of persecuting Germans living there. And Russia, long before the communist revolution of 1917, had often used Poland as a "defensive" buffer zone against potential enemies to its west. The Poles have one of the most tragic histories in all of Europe. But this secret agreement was not to be kept secret for long because the militarily weak Poles were easy pickings for the Germans and Soviets.

THE INVASION OF POLAND

At dawn on September 1, 1939, German forces began the invasion of Poland. This event marked the official beginning of World War II because Britain and France honored their commitments to Poland by declaring war on Germany on September 3. Their intervention did nothing to help the Poles, but it did demonstrate their official convictions that the earlier policy of appeasement had not deterred Hitler from his aggressive behavior. The Soviets attacked Poland from the east on September 15, and the country fell easy victim to the military pincer action.

Few Americans favored United States entrance into the armed conflicts on either side of the globe, but the invasion of Poland certainly revived the old sentiments from the last world war in favor of the Allies. The arms embargo, mandated by the Neutrality Laws of the 1930s, was quickly seen by many as penalizing

Warsaw, Poland's capitol, damaged by Nazi troops at the outbreak of World War II, September 1939. Credit: AP/Wide World Photos.

Britain and France, who were now the major European powers opposing Nazi Germany. At the urging of President Franklin Roosevelt, Congress revised the Neutrality Laws to allow private United States arms sales to the Allies on a "cash and carry" basis—the same basis as for non-military supplies going to belligerents. Isolationists in the Senate, led by Republican senators Robert LaFollette, Jr. (son of "Fighting Bob") of Wisconsin, William Borah of Idaho, Gerald P. Nye of North Dakota, and Hiram Johnson of California, argued strenuously that such a revision of the law would only be the first step toward American intervention in the conflict. While that eventually proved to be true, most Americans believed that it was necessary to give the Allies a chance in their fight against Hitler.

In the invasion of Poland, new German military tactics helped produce the swift victory. Known as "blitzkrieg," or lightning war, the German tactics had actually been used in helping Francisco Franco win the Spanish Civil War (1936-1939). Old European military tactics had relied on heavy artillery and slow-moving infantry to attack an enemy. The blitzkrieg, borrowed from British strategists who were ignored by everyone else, depended on speed and timing. While traditional artillery was still employed, much of the "softening" of the enemy was achieved with the use of Stuka dive bombers which, equipped with sirens, screamed as they approached their targets. This added psychological terror to the physical damage inflicted upon civilian populations. After these had done much of their job, fast-moving tanks, used effectively in massive, concentrated numbers, would open up gigantic holes in the enemy lines. Then infantry, riding in motorized vehicles, would race into the interior, more or less to mop up and then set up the military occupation. Of course, the element of surprise was designed to add another dimension favoring victory. There was no effective opposition against the Germans in Poland. However, the blitzkrieg proved to be just as successful in subsequent invasions against other enemies, until the German invasion of the Soviet Union.

NORTHERN AND WESTERN EUROPE FALL TO THE NAZIS

When the attack on Poland precipitated a general European war, Hitler recognized that the time had come to turn west and deal with the French and British. And while he was at it, he would also take over militarily weak countries in order to obtain priority over their natural resources. From September 1939 to the spring of 1940 a threatening military build-up occupied the governments of Germany, Britain, and France, with British troops finally being stationed in France itself. Then the German blitzkrieg was used to perfection, as nation after nation fell easy victims to the Nazi forces in northern and western Europe. Beginning in April 1940, Denmark and then Norway fell into Nazi hands. Holland, Belgium, and Luxembourg each fell in May, in that order.

The big prize in the west was, of course, France. Both sides had bogged down in four long years of trench warfare during the Great War. Between the world wars, France was determined that such a stalemate would not occur on her soil again. So the French built the Maginot Line, a long, impenetrable defensive line of sophisticated underground bunkers, huge cannons fixed toward the east where German invaders would probably initiate an attack, and plenty of stored ammunition. In

Nazi troops in Paris. Credit: National Archives.

other words, the French were still thinking in terms of old traditional warfare. But the German blitzkrieg made the Maginot Line obsolete overnight. Instead of attacking the Maginot Line, the Germans attacked France before the middle of May 1940 from the north, through Belgium, and by-passed it altogether.

By this time, the blitzkrieg had been fine tuned to perfection. Although the French actually had more tanks and better aircraft than the Germans at the time, the German blitzkrieg proved that it's not as much what you have but how you use it that really separates success from failure. France officially fell to the Nazis on June 22, after only about six weeks of fighting. French authorities signed an armistice that gave German control to a large occupation zone along the Atlantic and English Channel areas, including Paris. The southern and much of the eastern portions of the country were left under the control of a government headquartered in Vichy. Led by Marshal Henri Petain, the Vichy government earned the wrath of the French resistance movement and was regarded, with a great deal of truth, as a puppet government of the Nazis.

During the battle for France, British troops north of Paris retreated to the English Channel coast at Dunkirk. From May 28 through June 4 a large group of British naval and civilian ships safely evacuated some 338,000 soldiers, saving them to fight another day against Hitler's armies. Most historians are not certain why Hitler failed to order the Luftwaffe (air force) to wipe out the British at Dunkirk. One standard answer often given is that Hitler wanted to waste no time in moving his troops around the west side of Paris and capturing the French capital. Another likely factor was that Hitler believed at the time that because the English and Germans had closer historical ties than the English and the French, he believed that he might persuade Britain to concede Germany's domination of the continent of Europe in exchange for Germany not challenging the British domination of the high seas. Thus, Hitler did not want to alienate the British any further by massacring tens of thousands of more or less helpless British soldiers on the beaches of Dunkirk.

AMERICAN REACTION TO THE FALL OF FRANCE

American reaction to the fall of France was mixed, but there was little doubt that the trend of public opinion was shifting toward helping the British, who now represented the lone obstacle to Nazi aggression. The progressive journalist William Allen White chaired the Committee to Defend America by Aiding the Allies. It organized letter-writing campaigns, bought newspaper advertising space and radio air time, and otherwise pressed Congress to increase its assistance to Britain. The alternative, said the committee, was for the United States to enter the war directly. In May 1940, polls indicated that only 35 percent of Americans supported aid to Britain at the risk of United States involvement in the war; by September, 60 percent supported such aid.

The American isolationist spirit toward Europe was still relatively strong. The chief organization representing isolationist sentiment in the country was the Committee to Defend America First, created in July 1940, and headed by Chicago businessman Robert E. Wood. Better known as the America First Committee, it was financed by prominent Americans like Henry Ford and former President Herbert Hoover. Its chief spokesman, however, was aviation hero Charles A. Lindbergh, who himself had toured Nazi Germany and expressed admiration for Hitler's achievements. Lindbergh also harbored some anti-semitism in his own thinking, once accusing the Jews as having too much influence in the government, movies, and media. He traveled the nation, warning against President Roosevelt's alleged attempts to drag us into the war. The America First Committee proclaimed the "Fortress America" concept—that the United States could stand alone against Hitler if necessary, so there was no need to assist Britain.

THE DESTROYERS FOR BASES DEAL

With France out of the way, the German Luftwaffe began bombing raids on military and civilian targets in Britain in August 1940, hoping to persuade the British to make a deal or surrender. British Prime Minister Winston Churchill, who had replaced Neville Chamberlain after the war had broken out, beseeched the United States to assist his country. Roosevelt, never an isolationist, pushed Congress for more aid. In the meantime, in early September 1940, the United States and Britain concluded an agreement that would give the British 50 old World War I destroyers in exchange for 99-year leases on 8 naval and air bases in the western hemisphere.

The idea to bypass a reluctant Congress by negotiating an executive agreement between the two leaders was urged by White and other interventionists. Such an agreement could be portrayed as a move to strengthen American security rather than as help for Britain, and there was historical precedent for such a move. In point of fact, the Destroyers for Bases Deal probably did benefit the United States more than Britain. But the symbolic message it sent the British was that America was moving in her direction, and that was a message that was welcomed by the

British people. The agreement was indeed made without Congressional approval, but it was immediately made public by the president; there was nothing clandestine, or covert, about it. And by the time it was announced, there was relatively little negative reaction to the deal.

OTHER STEPS IN SEPTEMBER 1940

On September 16, 1940, Congress had swung in behind the president as far as military preparedness was concerned and, at his urging, it passed the Selective Training and Service Act (also called the Burke-Wadsworth Act). This law created the first peacetime military draft in American history. Prior to this, the only military draft laws, one in the Civil War and one for World War I, had been instituted only after the nation was at war. The 1940 conscription law provided for one year's service for all able-bodied men between the ages of 21 to 35. In December of 1941, after the attack on Pearl Harbor, it was amended to mandate draft registration of men between the ages of 20 and 44.

Altogether in World War II, about 9.8 million American men were drafted and more than 5 million others voluntarily enlisted in the various armed services, for a total of between 15 and 16 million persons. Almost 350,000 of the volunteers were women, who served in the Women's Army Corps (WACs) or the Women Accepted for Voluntary Emergency Service (WAVES) in the navy. American service personnel were nicknamed GIs, which stood for Government Issue. Of the more than 15 million GIs who served in World War II, about 4.7 million actually got combat experience in the war.

On September 27, 1940, Japan officially joined Germany and Italy in a military alliance called the Tripartite Pact. This cementing of a growing relationship among the three aggressor nations increased tensions in the United States since Japan had been building a powerful navy during the 1920s and 1930s. As events unfolded, it became clear how Japan was to fit in with the overall Axis strategy. While Germany and Italy consolidated its grip on Europe and North Africa, Japan's goal was to move south and east beyond China and toward India and the Persian Gulf region of the world. In the meantime, the Germans and Italians would gain control of much of the Middle East and the two forces would meet somewhere between India and the Persian Gulf area. In this way, the entire eastern hemisphere would ultimately come under Axis control.

THE 1940 ELECTION

During the tense and sensitive events of late 1940, the American people were faced with a presidential election. Roosevelt kept the nation and his party guessing as to whether he would buck the traditional limit of two terms and seek a third one for his presidency. In the end, he believed that it was not prudent for the country to change national leaders in the midst of the deteriorating world situation. His close advisors persuaded the Democratic Convention to "draft" him at the convention so that it would not appear that he was personally eager to seek a third term. The convention did so and nominated Secretary of Agriculture Henry A. Wallace for the vice-presidency.

All the likely hopefuls in the Republican Party were passed by, largely because most of them were well-known, staunch isolationists. Foremost among these possible candidates was Ohio Senator Robert A. Taft. Instead, the Republicans chose a relatively unknown candidate to head their party's ticket in 1940, Wendell L. Willkie, an Indiana attorney and utility company president who had never held any elective office in his life. Oregon Senator Charles L. McNary, a noted supporter of farm legislation and co-author of McNary-Haugenism in the 1920s, was selected as Willkie's running mate.

The campaign was not an overly exciting one. Willkie did not directly attack the New Deal as such, but only decried what he called waste and inefficiency in its implementation. He promised that his administration would run the New Deal more efficiently than the Democrats had done. On foreign policy issues, Willkie represented the internationalist wing of his party and did not significantly differ with Roosevelt on questions of assisting Britain and strengthening the nation's national defense. Late in the campaign, with his candidacy fading in the polls, Willkie did charge the Roosevelt administration with secretly planning to drag the country into the war. But he later apologized for the comment as something said in the heat of the campaign. By November of 1940, however, the war issue actually helped Roosevelt because most Americans worried that the nation might get into the war, and polls indicated they wanted an experienced president in the White House should that occur. The result was the election of Franklin Delano Roosevelt to an unprecedented third term by an electoral margin of 449 to 82.

THE BATTLE OF BRITAIN

In Europe, Hitler was realizing that America was slowly waking out of its slumber. Knowing that Britain was the only site from which the Americans could ever hope to successfully invade western Europe, Hitler began an attempt to soften up the British people in August 1940 by ordering his Luftwaffe to batter Britain in a series of bombing raids on its cities. For the next few months, the British people would endure hardship and danger from the air in the Battle of Britain. Initially, the German strategy was to eliminate the Royal Air Force (RAF). In retaliation, the RAF dropped bombs on Berlin, which accidentally missed their military targets and instead, damaged civilian areas. After that, the German strategy was to aim at primarily civilian targets to terrorize the British people into demanding that their government reach an agreement with Hitler. Parts of London and other cities, including the entire city of Coventry, were reduced to ashes.

Hitler's strategy backfired, however, as he had grossly underestimated the British people in an obvious lack of knowledge about their long history. The Battle of Britain only stiffened their will to resist the Nazis to the death. Although out-

1940	48	FRANKLIN D. ROOSEVELT	Democrat	27,307,819	449	54.8
		Wendell L. Wilkie	Republican	22,321,018	82	44.8

London after Nazi bombing, 1940. Credit: British-Combine.

numbered by German aircraft, the Royal Air Force put up a stubborn resistance with their Hurricane and Spitfire fighters and the technological superiority of radar. During the German air blitz, Winston Churchill (nicknamed "Winnie") used radio and his personal charm as well as Roosevelt had done in his fireside chats. "We shall never surrender," boomed Churchill in typical British stubbornness. The German Luftwaffe suffered heavy aircraft losses in the Battle of Britain and failed to budge the British. Hitler tasted his first military setback of the war as he abandoned his plans for an invasion of Britain and ordered the temporary end to the air blitz before that winter.

The temporary abandonment of the effort to knock Britain out of the war was a serious strategic mistake. The next summer, when Hitler ordered the invasion of the Soviet Union with Britain still surviving in the west, it seemed certain that if and when the United States entered the war, Britain would serve as the staging area for an eventual invasion of western Europe. These factors would seal Germany's fate in World War II.

THE LEND-LEASE ACT

Despite the apparent end of the Battle of Britain, no one knew in very late 1940 whether it would resume or not, and when. Also, German submarines were still attacking British ships in the north Atlantic. This submarine warfare, in addition to the fact that Britain was running out of cash, threatened to make the "cash and carry" arms sales from the United States a useless provision. Therefore, Churchill kept asking for more American assistance from Roosevelt. In December, President Roosevelt urged greater support for the British war effort. In a December 29 radio fireside chat, the president proposed to the American people what would become known as Lend-Lease. The idea was compared to a man lending his water hose to a neighbor whose house is on fire. If he doesn't put it out, it could spread to your own house. Roosevelt argued that if Britain fell victim to the Nazis, the United States might be forced into the war. Therefore, he urged, the United States must become the "great arsenal of democracy" by loaning, leasing, or otherwise transferring war materials to any nation the president deemed necessary to the defense of the United States.

In early January 1941, Lend-Lease legislation was introduced in Congress. In the House of Representatives it was patriotically labeled House Bill 1776. Debate raged on in Congress, where isolationist members held the bill up from a floor vote as long as they could. One senator even charged that the measure would "plow under every fourth American boy," which brought an angry retort from Roosevelt. Other critics said the concept was something like loaning your used chewing gum to someone else; you don't want it back later. But opinion polls showed that 80 percent of Americans now supported the increased aid to Britain as a way to stay out of the war. It passed the House by a vote of 317 to 71 and the Senate by a lopsided vote as well, as the Lend-Lease Act was passed into law on March 11, 1941. The bill appropriated an initial $7 billion for arms transfers to nations the president deemed vital to United States security. Dozens of nations received American arms via the Lend-

Winston Churchill. Credit: Internal War Museum.

Lease Act, including the Soviet Union, with a total price tag of more than $50 billion. The immediate significance of the new measure, however, was that it represented the point of no return. America's entrance into World War II was virtually assured after March 1941.

THE BATTLE OF THE ATLANTIC

In order to protect Lend-Lease military supplies headed for Britain, the American navy began helping the British track German submarines in the Atlantic in April 1941. During that same month, the United States signed an agreement with the Danish ambassador in Washington, in which we promised to defend the Danish possession of Greenland in exchange for the right to build an American military base there. In July of the same year, the United States established a base in Iceland with its permission in order to protect it from German invasion. Iceland had declared its independence from Denmark after the latter's defeat the year before. Such actions fortified the Atlantic against German domination and later provided assistance for the safe transportation of American troops to Britain in anticipation of the Allied invasion of western Europe.

Additional steps were taken during the summer of 1941. The United States froze all German and Italian assets under American control. Thus, bank accounts, stocks, bonds, and real estate holdings became unavailable to the European Axis powers. During the summer the American navy increased its role in convoying British Lend-Lease supplies from the United States to Britain. All these actions led to an undeclared shooting war on the north Atlantic between German submarines and American destroyers, known as the Battle of the Atlantic. Neither side was willing or ready to actually declare war on the other, but for all practical purposes the two nations were conducting a limited war against each other. This war escalated in September, when President Roosevelt ordered all naval commanders to "shoot on sight" any German submarine approaching the western hemisphere after a German submarine fired a torpedo at the destroyer the *Greer*. (No one was killed in the attempt.) In October, a German submarine attacked and sank the American destroyer the *Reuben James* near Iceland, killing seventy-six of its crew members. In November, Congress passed a bill that authorized the arming of American merchant ships and allowed those merchant vessels to carry supplies directly to Allied ports.

THE ATLANTIC CHARTER

While the Battle of the Atlantic was heating up, Roosevelt and Churchill met secretly aboard ship in Argentia Bay off the coast of Newfoundland in August 1941. The two leaders took this opportunity to get better acquainted with each other and to issue a pronouncement of their goals following the defeat of the Axis powers. Although formally not at war, the resulting Atlantic Charter sounded very much like a statement of war aims—to explain why Nazi aggression must be stopped in its tracks. The Atlantic Charter declared British and American disinterest in acquiring new territories; reaffirmed their support of self-determination for all peoples; proclaimed support for freedom of the seas; advocated a peace in which people could live in freedom from fear and want; and maintained that aggressor nations must be disarmed after the war. Privately, and what remained unpublished, was Roosevelt's assurance that he would do all he could to help Britain defeat the Nazi threat, which he was certain would provide an "incident" to draw America further into alliance with Britain.

THE GERMAN INVASION OF THE SOVIET UNION

Hitler's patience was running thin by mid-1941. And although the United States had already begun helping the British track German submarines in the north Atlantic and the agreement to build an American base on Greenland had been secured, Hitler left the growing Anglo-American alliance and turned on his "ally," the Soviet Union. On June 22, 1941, exactly one year after the defeat of France, Hitler ordered the invasion of the Soviet Union in violation of the Nazi-Soviet Pact. In April he had already invaded and defeated Yugoslavia and Greece; other nations in eastern Europe voluntarily offered Nazi occupation in order to avoid the destruction of war. Many of these eastern European countries supplied troops to assist in the German attack on the Soviet Union.

The German invasion of the Soviet Union was code-named Operation Barbarossa, after a 12th century Teutonic emperor famed for his military aggressiveness. The assault on the Soviets included approximately three million troops in a three-pronged drive into Soviet territory. The targets were Leningrad, Moscow, and Stalingrad, along with the precious and abundant oil fields of the Caucasus Mountains region that provided roughly 90 percent of the Soviet's oil supply.

For about two weeks after the first assault, Joseph Stalin remained unconvinced that German armies had actually invaded his country. The Soviets were as initially unprepared militarily as they were psychologically. The initial attacks on the Soviet Union produced a series of easy victories for the German armies. By October 20 the Germans were within forty miles of the Soviet capital. But the autumn rains produced enough mud to slow the German advance to a snail's pace. Despite the mud and stiff Soviet resistance, German forces managed to get within twenty-five miles of Moscow by the first week of December. But before the Germans could completely recover from the mud and take the city, heavy winter snows and sub-zero temperatures succeeded in completely halting the German advance on December 5. Hitler's early successes with the blitzkrieg had blinded him into thinking that his armies could take the huge Soviet Union just as easily and quickly, long before the Russian winter. Thus, he had ordered that no winter coats, blankets, or antifreeze for the vehicles be taken on the invasion. Hitler's cockiness was finally catching up with him.

Then on December 6, 1941, a surprise Soviet counter-offensive, led by General Georgi K. Zhukov, began pushing the Germans back. This was the first time that German armies had been pushed back in the war, and it would prove to the world that Hitler's "master race" army was not invincible after all. The battle for the Soviet Union would be a very long one indeed.

German soldiers in a snowstorm in Russia. Credit: Press Association, Inc.

REPEAL OF THE NEUTRALITY LAWS

With American entrance into World War II all but certain, and the American people overwhelmingly anxious to prevent a German victory, the bulk of the restrictions remaining under the Neutrality Laws were repealed in November 1941. The House of Representatives voted 212 to 194 and the Senate 50 to 37 for the repeal. This relatively close vote even at this late date indicates that many Americans, probably most, were still hopeful of avoiding direct involvement in the war. But the surprise Japanese raid on Pearl Harbor, less than one month later, would change everything.

PEARL HARBOR

Military and Diplomatic Background

In growing numbers, Americans were becoming concerned about Japan's war against China as it continued into 1939. Therefore, in the summer of 1939, Roosevelt reacted by announcing that a 1911 trade treaty with Japan would not be renewed when it expired six months later in January 1940.

In the spring of 1940 the Japanese were moving toward Southeast Asia outside of China. The oil, rubber, and tin resources of that region of the world would prove invaluable to Japan as its relations with the United States were deteriorating. Japan obtained about 90 percent of its oil from the United States and roughly half of other staple raw materials, such as scrap iron and steel. With its relations with the United States strained, Japan needed to find new sources for these materials in order to continue to wage war. Wanting to avoid war but express American displeasure with the Japanese at the same time, President Roosevelt ordered the navy's Pacific Fleet moved from its home port in San Diego to Pearl Harbor, Hawaii in April of that year. This was a symbolic way to declare that Americans were watching Japanese actions and were not happy about them.

In August the Japanese expanded its New Order, first proclaimed in November 1938, announcing the Greater East Asia Co-Prosperity Sphere, which it so "graciously" chose to lead. In that same month, Japan demanded from the Vichy government in France that it be allowed to build military bases in Indochina. With the oil-rich Dutch East Indies the apparent next target of Japanese aggression, the United States slapped an embargo on scrap iron and aviation fuel against Japan in late September, reserving the more drastic total oil embargo as a last resort in economic coercion.

The Japanese government, under Prime Minister Prince Fumimaro Kenoye, was not ready to go to war against the United States. Thus, beginning in early 1941, negotiations began that would drag on into early December of the same year. Secretary of State Cordell Hull and the Japanese ambassador to the United States, Kichisaburo Nomura, were the main players in the early months of these negotiations. The major American demand repeated over and over was that Japan must give up on its imperial plans, including the conquest of China, before the flow of raw materials would resume to Japan. This the Japanese government would not do. And when Japan announced on the 25th of July that she was assuming the role of protectorate for all of French Indochina, President Roosevelt ordered the freezing of all Japanese assets in the United States the next day. This action meant that all stocks, bonds, bank accounts, and real estate holdings held by the Japanese in this country were no longer available for withdrawal or any type of control by them. By September there was a complete oil embargo imposed on Japan. The significance of these events was that all trade with Japan came to a halt. It was hoped that the absence of any American oil would mean no expansion of the war in Asia, but that proved to be a futile hope. Instead, the American action represented the point of no return. Unless there were a major break in the negotiations, war between the two countries was now inevitable.

The Japanese military, which held the real balance of power in that country, decided in late summer (1941) that if no agreement were reached with the United States by October, they would strike at the Dutch East Indies. No settlement came, and in mid-October Prince Kenoye resigned as prime minister and was replaced by Hideki Tojo, leader of the military expansionists. The militarists were now in complete charge of the government, relegating Emperor Hirohito to an insignificant role.

The Tojo government then made the decision to delay the assault on the Dutch East Indies until the end of November, to give negotiations several more weeks to reach an agreement which would restore trade relations between the two nations. And in mid-November, an experienced diplomat, Saburo Kurusu, was sent to Washington, D.C. to assist Japanese Ambassador Nomura. But the negotiations went nowhere, and on November 25 a large Japanese naval fleet left the Kuril Islands headed toward the north Pacific in complete radio silence, following a pre-arranged path east and then south toward Hawaii. With radio silence, November 25 was Japan's point of no return; the attack on Pearl Harbor was now inevitably less than two weeks away. The diplomatic plan was for Nomura and Kurusu to read a long document to Secretary Hull on December 7 in Washington, D.C., ending with what amounted to a declaration of war. Then just minutes after that meeting was to end, the attack on Pearl Harbor was to begin. As it turned out, delays in Washington meant that the air raid at Hawaii was actually begun while the two Japanese diplomats were waiting to meet with Hull.

The Yamamoto Plan

Admiral Isoroku Yamamoto, supreme commander of the Japanese navy, had spent some time in the United States and knew that Japan could not win a long war with the United States. Therefore, he argued, Japan's only hope in a war with the Americans was to knock out their Pacific Fleet in a surprise attack. This would give Japan at least six months of opportunity to conquer other islands in the Pacific and so heavily fortify them that the price Americans would be forced to pay in blood would be so high that the United States would agree to a negotiated settlement favorable to Japan. That was Japan's only hope; the longer a war with the United States lasted, the more certain a Japanese defeat would be. Historians now know that the Japanese accepted the basic plan and began planning the military details as early as January 1941, just in case negotiations proved futile.

The Attack on Hawaii

It was decided that an early Sunday morning attack would have the best chance for success because of sailors' reputation for drinking parties on Saturday nights. At 7:53 a.m. Hawaiian time, on Sunday, December 7, 1941, flight commander Mitsuo Fuchida flew over Barber's Point and yelled "Tora! Tora! Tora!" ("Tiger! Tiger! Tiger!"), signalling that they had taken the Americans by surprise. About two minutes later, the first wave of aircraft began dropping their bombs on the Pacific Fleet in Pearl Harbor and on American airplanes parked at nearby Hickam and Wheeler Fields.

A second wave of Japanese followed, making a total of about 360 Japanese planes involved in the raid. Within two hours the Japanese destroyed or severely damaged eight battleships in the harbor. Six were eventually repaired before the war was over, but the U.S.S. *Arizona* and the U.S.S. *Oklahoma* were completely destroyed. Three cruisers and other miscellaneous ships were damaged, making a total of 19 warships knocked out of commission. The army planes at Hickam and Wheeler Fields, there to protect the navy's fleet, were also hit from the air, with 188

Destruction of Pearl Harbor. Credit: U.S. Navy Photos.

of them completely destroyed and more than 100 others damaged but repairable. A total of 2,403 Americans were killed in the attack, and an additional 1,178 others were injured.

As bad as the attack had been, there was some "good" news, relatively speaking. All three American aircraft carriers—the *Yorktown*, the *Enterprise*, and the *Hornet*—were out to sea on maneuvers, so none of them was hit. Had they been at Pearl Harbor at the time of the air raid, their destruction probably would have set the American military back by well more than six months. Furthermore, the Japanese mysteriously missed the fuel depot and repair facilities in the confusion. And the Japanese also erred in not following up with yet another attack wave, which certainly would have corrected the earlier omissions. Apparently they were so astonished at the ease of their victory that these things were overlooked. A few American fighters managed to get into the air and engage the enemy. American fighters and anti-aircraft guns on the ground did manage to shoot down 29 Japanese airplanes. The Japanese also lost six midget submarines in the attack. (They used midget submarines to try to block the harbor because it was too shallow for regular submarines.) A total of 129 Japanese lost their lives in the surprise raid.

When Admiral Yamamoto heard the report about the attack, and the fact that all three American aircraft carriers had not been there, he prophetically sighed that he believed all they had done was to awaken a sleeping giant. Unfortunately, he would not live to see the full truth of those prophetic words.

Later on the same day (December 8 in the western Pacific, across the International Date Line) the Japanese also struck at the following American and British territories: the Philippines (specifically at Clark Field); Guam; Wake Island; Midway; Hong Kong; Malaya; and Thailand (called Siam at the time).

The Aftermath of Pearl Harbor

On December 8, 1941, President Franklin D. Roosevelt addressed a joint session of Congress. Referring to the events of the previous day, the president declared that December 7 was "a date which will live in infamy." Knowing the nation was completely united now, Roosevelt asked for a declaration of war against Japan. The House of Representatives voted 388 to 1, and the Senate vote was unanimous. The lone "no" vote in Congress was cast by Montana Congresswoman Jeanette Rankin, giving her the distinction of being the only member of Congress to have voted against United States participation in both World War I and World War II.

On December 11, Hitler declared war on the United States against the advice of many of his advisors. German troops were just experiencing their first setback of the war on the Russian front, and the prospect of a two-front war was not a smart move for him to make. Italy declared war later the same day. Then before the day was out, the United States Congress returned the "favors" by officially declaring war on Germany and Italy. Obviously, the greatest significance of the Japanese raid on Pearl Harbor was that it got the United States directly involved in World War II.

The "Back Door to War" Conspiracy Theory

There have been a number of different conspiracy theories regarding the attack on Pearl Harbor. What they all have in common is the allegation that President Roosevelt knew sometime in advance that the Japanese would strike at Pearl Harbor and that he deliberately did not alert American forces there. This, so the theories go, was his way of dragging the United States into the war, through the so-called "back door." With only a few exceptions, these conspiracy theories are discredited by trained historians for a number of reasons.

It is true that intelligence authorities had a great deal of information which conspiracy theorists would later use. In reality, the information specialists had too much information—some of it conflicting—and too few experts to sift through it all and properly analyze it. That's not nearly as exciting, or sensational, as a conspiracy theory, but it is much more like real life. American code-breakers had broken the Japanese diplomatic code before Pearl Harbor in an intelligence operation code-named "Magic." Conspiracy theorists point to certain references to Pearl Harbor in our intelligence data as documented "proof" that American officials knew all along about the planned raid. The problem with that kind of evidence, however, is that other places in the Pacific and East Asia were identified as main targets as well. No one expected the Japanese to hit them all at once, so the question remained, "Which one or few would be the main target?"

Hawaii was also the last place almost anyone expected the Japanese to attack first because that was where the Americans were the strongest. We know now, of course, long after the fact, that that was precisely why they hit Pearl Harbor. But the pervasive assumption appeared reasonable at the time. This assumption, by the way, was made by just about every informed citizen in the country, not just by the president and his political and military advisors and officials. The most common assumption was that the first strike would come at the Philippines.

The commanders at Pearl Harbor were indeed warned on November 27, 1941, along with all other American bases in the Pacific, of a possible impending surprise Japanese attack. Even though the November 27 message did not specifically mention Hawaii as a probable target, a November 30 "War Warning" from Washington was also sent to Pearl Harbor. Admiral Husband Kimmel was in charge of the Pacific Fleet, and General Walter Short was in charge of protecting that fleet and the airplanes. These men were warned to prepare for a possible attack. But between them they made three serious mistakes. First, there were too few planes available for reconnaisance, and the aircraft they had were flying in the wrong areas. None of them were flying north of the Hawaiian Islands, which was the most isolated part of the ocean and therefore the more likely direction from which a Japanese attack would come. Second, the radar operators "watching" the skies for enemy aircraft were inexperienced. Therefore, when some of them reported a large formation of aircraft coming from the north, they were not believed. And third, General Short prepared for sabotage instead of an air raid, which meant that he ordered the planes bunched close together so that guards would have less space to cover against saboteurs cutting through fences and planting explosives.

In January 1942 an official inquiry into the military actions of Admiral Kimmel and General Short, headed by Chief Justice Owen Roberts, concluded that the two commanders at Pearl Harbor were guilty of dereliction of duty. And Kimmel and Short were forced into retirement from the service. Those who insist that Roosevelt and others conspired to get us into the war claim that Kimmel and Short were simply subordinates who took the fall.

United States intelligence had monitored the diplomatic exchanges between Tokyo and the Japanese embassy in Washington, D.C. Within hours before the attack, this source of information told American officials that an attack somewhere in the Pacific was imminent. Colonel Rufus Bratton tried to reach Chief of Staff George C. Marshall since Bratton expected the attack to be aimed at the Philippines. But Marshall was out horseback riding that Sunday morning, and it was two and one-half hours before he was contacted. The result was that a new alert went out to San Francisco, the Panama Canal Zone, the Philippines, and Pearl Harbor. However, atmospheric conditions over Hawaii interfered with the Army Message Center's transmissions to Pearl Harbor. Finally, the message was sent by Western Union telegraph, but it arrived well after the attack on Pearl Harbor.

All of the mistakes and mix-ups pointed to varying degrees of incompetence, and not to a conspiracy theory. Besides, President Roosevelt was already focused on helping the British defeat Germany. This "Hitler first" strategy was part of his understanding with Churchill. The Battle of the Atlantic had already been going on before Pearl Harbor. If Roosevelt had really wanted an excuse to drag the American people into the war, he might well have focused on American casualties suffered in that on-going undeclared conflict.

THE HOME FRONT

The War Bureaucracy

After the fall of France in June 1940, the United States began an effort to strengthen its national defense and, of course, to assist the British. But two factors delayed the effort. First, American industrial leaders were fearful that the war would not last much longer. After all, Britain was the only significant power still left on Germany's enemy list as of the summer of 1940. And if major factories retooled for war production, and the war in Europe ended, there would be insufficient demand for war materials. Retooling to peacetime consumer goods once again would be a costly affair for businesses to bear. Second, although President Roosevelt perceived the threat to world security early on, he was a little hesitant to push the country's industrialists too fast lest he be labeled a warmonger. Thus, by the time of Pearl Harbor, all the military services combined had only about 1.6 million men, and war production accounted for only about 15 percent of the total industrial output of the nation.

The Japanese raid on Pearl Harbor, however, changed all that. The country was then united as isolationism faded into oblivion. Within one week of the Hawaiian disaster, Congress passed the War Powers Act, giving the president more emergency authority than any previous president had ever held. Roosevelt used that new authority to create dozens of wartime agencies to coordinate the war effort at home.

Recognizing the truly worldwide scope of this war, Roosevelt knew the country needed a massive military establishment and more officials to coordinate its complex structure. Therefore, he created the Joint Chiefs of Staff, initially headed by Admiral William D. Leahy. The Joint Chiefs of Staff proceeded to expand the army air force. They also established the Office of Strategic Services (OSS) to engage in spying and other forms of intelligence gathering. The OSS became the model for the Central Intelligence Agency (CIA), which was created during the Cold War years after World War II. To house the military bureaucracy needed to coordinate the military war effort, the Pentagon was opened in 1942 just outside of Washington, D.C. It was the world's largest building in terms of square feet, providing a place to work for some 35,000 military personnel.

To help boost the war effort by building new war plants and converting many others from peacetime to wartime production, the War Production Board was established. Its nine members included Donald Nelson as chairman. The WPB had the authority to allocate materials according to military priority, limit or stop peacetime production, and give government contracts to various industrial companies in order to increase war production. While the WPB was directly involved with moving industry toward more wartime production, the nine-member War Manpower Commission, chaired by Paul V. McNutt, helped mobilize the manpower needed to work in those war factories. Approximately 50 million men and 20 million women were employed on the home front in supplying the materials used by American servicemen and other Allies.

In October 1942 the president persuaded Justice James F. Byrnes to resign his seat on the Supreme Court in order to become a federal czar in charge of improving overall cooperation and coordination of federal agencies and private industry. Then in May 1943 he became head of the new Office of War Mobilization (OWM), which operated with awesome power over the economy, much as Bernard Baruch's War Industries Board had done during the Great War. As Roosevelt put it in 1943, "Dr. New Deal" was replaced by "Dr. Win the War." The nation was already making gigantic strides in this direction even before the president had created the OWM. Auto makers were among the first industrialists to retool, making tanks and airplanes instead of cars. Other industries followed suit, and by the end of 1942, war production had more than doubled to 33 percent of the nation's industrial output.

New industries were created as part of the war effort. Some 50 synthetic rubber factories were built because 97 percent of rubber imported to the United States was lost when the Japanese took over and dominated almost all of the world's rubber plantation regions in southeast Asia. By the end of World War II, the United States had gone from being the world's largest importer of crude rubber to being the world's largest exporter of synthetic rubber.

The National Defense Research Committee had been created before the United States entered the Second World War. This organization coordinated an effort to utilize the knowledge and skills of scientists to develop new weapons and to perfect other technologies useful to the prosecution of the war. In 1941, President Roosevelt established the Office of Scientific Research and Development (OSRD) as a federal agency to funnel federal monies to private arms and medical contractors.

Major OSRD accomplishments included vast improvements in radar and sonar technologies, amphibious tanks, flamethrowers, and high-altitude bombsights. In the medical area, OSRD-funded research resulted in penicillin and other drugs that saved thousands of lives during the war. Of course, the most notable success was the successful development of the atomic bomb, which was used to shorten the war in 1945.

By the end of World War II, the United States had produced more war materials than all the Axis powers combined. This wartime production included about 300,000 airplanes, 86,000 tanks, 372,000 artillery pieces, 2.6 million machine guns, and 6 million tons of aircraft bombs. And the War Shipping Board supervised the building of more than 5,000 merchant ships and 86,000 warships during the war.

The president was concerned about inflation and created the Office of Price Administration (OPA) to fight that threat. The basic problem was that increased war production was creating too much consumer demand for fewer goods and services because most of the new goods were used up in the war overseas and some normal consumer items were no longer available or were in short supply. In 1942 prices rose about 2 percent per month, which was an annual rate over 20 percent. So at the end of that year Congress gave the president, through the OPA, the authority to freeze wages, prices, and rents. This economic freeze was successful in ending the disastrous price spiral. In fact, the increase in the cost of living from 1940 to 1945 was limited to 28 percent, which was markedly better than the 62 percent jump in prices from 1914 to 1918 in the Great War. The OPA also rationed certain products to fight inflation and conserve scarce resources under the slogan of "Use it up, wear it out, make it do or do without." Items such as sugar, coffee, meat, butter, cheese, gasoline, and tires were available only through the use of ration coupons.

The Food Administration sponsored "meatless Tuesdays" as a means of conserving meat for the armed forces, which consumed about 30 percent of the nation's meat supply. Most Americans adjusted to wartime controls and dietary restrictions out of a sense of patriotic duty to help loved ones in the service. As usual, of course, there were black market operations in which one could obtain some restricted items illegally for a high price. But overall, Americans made use of car pooling, participated in collection drives to recycle rubber, scrap metal, and paper, and planted victory gardens as practical ways for civilians to contribute to the war cause.

Organized Labor and the War

Within a month after Pearl Harbor, the National War Labor Board (NWLB) was established with twelve members to help settle labor-management disputes through mediation and arbitration rather than strikes and lockouts. Union membership climbed from about 9 million in 1940 to 14.8 million by 1945. This membership growth meant that 35 percent of the non-agricultural workforce belonged to labor unions by the end of the war. Part of this growth was the natural result of organized labor's drive to organize the unskilled workers in major industries, an effort begun in earnest in the 1930s. Of course, the rapid expansion of factory jobs also assisted the labor movement in this effort. The NWLB contributed to the union membership increases itself by ruling that all current union members would have to maintain their membership during the life of their labor contract.

When the NWLB attempted to sharply limit wage increases, unions sought to add and/or strengthen fringe benefits in their contracts. Unions made major gains in areas like health insurance, pensions, and paid vacations during the war in lieu of significant wage gains. As requested by the administration, all mainstream labor leaders gave a "no strike" pledge after Pearl Harbor in order to prevent any major halt in war production. The "no strike" pledge was generally kept by union leaders, although there was minimal trouble from some short-lived "wildcat" strikes—strikes called at the local level without the national union authorization.

The major exception to the faithfulness of the labor leaders' "no strike" pledge was the United Mine Workers. Its president, John L. Lewis, conducted three separate walkouts in two months during the spring of 1943. Congress responded by passing, over President Roosevelt's veto, the Smith-Connally War Labor Disputes Act in June (1943). This federal law limited the right to strike in any workplace deemed essential to the war effort by the president and authorized the president to take over and operate (with federal troops) any struck war plant. The significance of the War Labor Disputes Act was that this bill paved the way for an increase in anti-union laws at the state and federal level after the war.

The Cost of the War

World War II cost American taxpayers between $315 and $320 billion dollars from 1941 to 1945, ten times the cost of World War I and almost twice the total federal expenditures since the ratification of the Constitution. Wartime needs increased the federal budget from $9 billion per year in 1940 to $98 billion in 1945. The national debt went from about $47 billion to $247 billion during the same time period. And the number of federal civilian workers rose from 1.1 million to 3.8 million. About 50 percent of financing the war came from the sale of war bonds and the other half from taxes. Roosevelt wanted to rely more heavily upon tax increases because of his natural aversion to debt. But he received less than he requested, and income tax rates were also less progressive than he wanted. However, the top personal income tax rate did climb from 60 percent to 90 percent under the Revenue Act of 1942. The bill also quadrupled the number of Americans who were required to file an income tax return. In 1943 a payroll-deduction system was enacted to withhold taxes from wages and salaries. Thus, it was World War II that really made the federal income tax a part of the lives of most Americans.

Corporate profits also rose sharply during the war, partly due to a system of government contracts guaranteeing company costs plus a fixed fee for those doing business for the war effort. Larger tax write-offs and the willful neglect of the antitrust laws also contributed to the rise in corporate profits, all in an effort to get industry to enthusiastically convert and produce war materials in abundance. Of course, the largest corporations benefited the most, with two-thirds of the war contracts going to the 100 largest companies; the 10 largest companies received about 30 percent of the war contracts. All this led to the movement toward the concentration of economic power that continued long after the war had ended. After-tax corporate profits rose by 70 percent, and real wages (adjusted for inflation) of industrial workers rose by 50 percent, helped along by the creation of 17 million new industrial jobs because of the war. The jobs and tax policies also resulted in a significant income shift. The share of income of the wealthiest 5 percent decreased from 26 percent to 20 percent. The bottom 40 percent of Americans increased their share of income from 13 percent to 16 percent, while the earnings of the lowest 20 percent rose by 68 percent. And the size of the middle class doubled.

Minorities and the War

More than 6 million women entered the workforce during World War II as a result of wartime production needs and government pressure to hire them. This swelled the total number of employed women to approximately 19 million. As a percentage of the total workforce, women went from just under 25 percent in 1940 to about 35 percent in 1945. Seventy-five percent of the female workers were married, and 60 percent were over 35 years of age. "Rosie the Riveter," dressed in cap and overalls on posters everywhere, became the symbol of working women, who performed virtually every job previously held only by men. Such tasks included, but were not limited to, welding, operating cranes and lathes, and working in steel mills and shipyards. Although federal regulations mandated equal pay for equal work, women still earned an average of about 65 percent of what men who did the same work earned.

Despite government pressure, there was still much resistance to the idea of women working outside the home. Opinion polls at the end of the war showed that the great majority of Americans, both men and women, disapproved of women working fulltime. Even government propaganda insisted that it was only a temporary policy to fill the emergency needs in the war industries. And government assistance in the area of child care reflected this bias against women in the workforce. Less than 10 percent of defense workers' children were helped by federal child-care centers because the perception was that the worst mother was better than the best nursery. Fulltime working wives and mothers noticed the strain on their families too. Juvenile delinquency increased five times during the war, and the divorce rate rose from 16 per 100 marriages in 1940 to 27 per 100 in 1944.

During World War I, W.E.B. DuBois had urged African-Americans to "close ranks" behind the war effort and lay aside the campaign for civil rights until the war was over. It was a far different story during the Second World War. Black leaders realized that the United States government needed national unity, and under the leadership of the NAACP, they urged other African-Americans to demand an end to racial discrimination as the price for that unity. The NAACP coined the slogan "democracy in our time" to characterize its aims. With the United States fighting a war at least partly against Nazi racism abroad, these leaders called for a "Double V" campaign to include a fight against racism at home.

The African-American community responded with high expectations, and the NAACP membership increased ten times, to 500,000 members by 1945. It worked tirelessly to get federal legislation to prohibit poll taxes, lynchings, and racial discrimination in hiring practices in the defense industries as well as the armed forces. In 1944 the civil rights movement scored a partial victory on the voting

American woman working in a war factory. Credit: Official OWI Photo by Palmer.

rights front when the Supreme Court, in *Smith v. Allwright*, ruled in a Texas case that all-white primary elections were unconstitutional. Although this invalidated the primary election procedures for eight southern states, other ways were found to deny African-Americans equitable voting representation.

In 1942 the Congress of Racial Equality (CORE) was founded as another black civil rights organization to fight racial injustices in the country. The leaders of CORE adopted the methods used by Mahatma (Mohandas) Gandhi to lead India out of the British colonial empire and into self-rule. Gandhi's passive, nonviolent resistance relied on political, economic, and social boycott, and a willingness to suffer the legal consequences of civil disobedience. In the same year of its founding (1942), CORE staged a sit-in at a Chicago restaurant that had refused to serve African-Americans. Following success there, the organization went on to cities like Detroit and Denver, successfully opening places of public accomodation to people of all races.

In the jobs sphere, a peaceful threat of another kind proved effective in getting at least some federal action. In 1941 A. Philip Randolph, the president of the Brotherhood of Sleeping Car Porters (a black union), threatened a "thundering march" of

100,000 African-Americans on Washington, D.C. "to wake up and shock white America as it has never been shocked before." This strategy was aimed at persuading President Roosevelt to take action to end hiring discrimination in the defense industries, the federal government, and the armed services. Roosevelt was not a liberal champion of black civil rights, but he was basically a fair man who was willing to listen. Among those who pressed him on this issue was his wife Eleanor. The First Lady, more liberal in general than the president, was indeed a woman far ahead of her time on civil rights as well as on other issues. For her outspokenness, she was often criticized and even vilified; it was long after her days in the White House that she became universally praised.

Randolph's promised march threatened to upset the tenuous New Deal coalition of workers, African-Americans, and white southerners in the Democratic Party. It was to avoid losing white southern support that Roosevelt had not pushed for federal legislation on lynchings or voting rights. But now his refusal to act on behalf of black rights would cause political damage from another element of the coalition that kept re-electing him. Faced with this dilemma, and pressed by the First Lady, the president issued Executive Order 8802, the first such federal action on racial matters since the end of Reconstruction. The president's action was sufficient to have Randolph call off the threatened march on Washington. (In the famous 1963 March on Washington, Randolph would be a key organizer in an attempt to force a reluctant Congress to pass a major civil rights law.) Roosevelt's order prohibited racially discriminating hiring practices by the federal government and by companies in the defense industry. It also created the Fair Employment Practices Commission (FEPC) to enforce the order. The FEPC was given relatively weak enforcement power, but wartime production needs resulted in tripling the number of African-American workers in war factories, to over 2 million. Black union membership doubled during World War II to 1,250,000 members. Job skills improved dramatically, and average wages increased by a factor of between three and four times, compared to just over two times for white workers.

Success for African-American workers brought resentment and anger from parts of the white community. In 1943 dozens of American cities experienced racial rioting, including Harlem (in New York City), Mobile, Alabama, Beaumont, Texas, and Detroit, Michigan. African-American leaders reacted to these events by attempting to calm the situation and to urge a "go slow" approach to demands for greater opportunities, which was generally accepted.

Approximately 1 million African-American men and women served in the armed forces during the war. Most of them served in segregated units commanded by white officers. The all-black 99th Pursuit Squadron earned 80 Distinguished Flying Crosses for their service against the German Luftwaffe in Europe. But despite a war record of duty and heroism equal to that of white soldiers, African-Americans in the military services faced humiliating treatment. Even the Red Cross segregated blood banks despite the fact that an African-American doctor, Charles Drew, had invented the process of safely storing blood plasma. Base commanders and other military officers generally failed to protect black servicemen off the post as well as on. The result was racially motivated violent incidents on nearly every military base in the South and many abroad, with at least fifty African-Americans dying in those riots.

Occasionally, a black serviceman stood his ground. The most notable example of this was Lieutenant Jackie Robinson, who refused to sit at the back of a segregated army bus. Robinson was court-martialed but won his case before the military court. (In 1947 Robinson became the first African-American baseball player to play in the major leagues when he joined the Brooklyn Dodgers.)

In the beginning, the navy limited African-American sailors to the menial tasks such as serving in the mess hall. The army likewise restricted the black soldiers' duties to noncombatant areas. And the marine corps and the coast guard excluded African-Americans from their services altogether. The practical demands of war finally brought change to some of the branches of service. The army and navy began an experiment with partial integration of personnel in 1944. But racially integrated units were the exception rather than the rule.

The migration of more than 700,000 African-Americans out of the South to work in northern war factories added to the racial mix of northern society and forced many whites in that region to think about matters of race and public policy. The success of black workers and servicemen, and the growing awareness of the horrible effects of Nazi racism, all combined to begin to undermine racism at home and laid the foundation for the modern civil rights movement that would come in the postwar era.

Propaganda and the Japanese-American Internment Policy

In the days following the Japanese raid at Pearl Harbor in December 1941, fear of security leaks and a strong desire to intensify public reaction against the Axis powers led President Roosevelt to establish the Office of Censorship that same month. More than 14,000 people were employed at its peak. The Office of Censorship examined all mail going overseas in order to maintain the secrecy of vital military information. The agency also won cooperation from publishers and radio broadcasters in limiting graphic or other negative facts about American defeats. Not until 1943 were any pictures of dead Americans on the battlefield published, and they were limited in number even after that. And details about damage and casualties at Pearl Harbor were not revealed until a year after that tragedy.

In June 1942 Roosevelt created the Office of War Information, headed by Elmer Davis, a well-respected radio news commentator. This agency was reminiscent of the old Committee on Public Information—the Creel Commission—which operated as the major federal agency of propaganda during World War I. Its chairman, George Creel, had been a popular journalist. The OWI employed more than 4,000 writers and artists, who were used chiefly to focus public opinion on the cruelty of the Axis nations. The OWI philosophy and regulations were summed up with the key question they asked themselves: "Will this help win the war?"

Unlike their treatment on the home front during World War I, German-Americans, along with Italian-Americans, were treated fairly well during the Second World War. However, the same could not be said concerning Japanese-Americans living on the west coast. Beginning in February 1942, more than 112,000—two-thirds were native-born United States citizens—were picked up by authorities, forced to sell

Japanese-American children awaiting evacuation bus, 1942. Credit: War Relocation Authority.

their homes almost overnight, and placed in ten internment, or relocation, camps scattered in the West. Many well-to-do Americans, including some leading politicians who also benefited politically from bashing Japanese-Americans, saw this time of hysteria as a great opportunity to buy up Japanese-American real estate quite cheaply. Army General John L. DeWitt, head of the Western Defense Command, was placed in charge of implementing this policy.

The internment policy did not affect Japanese-Americans living anywhere else in the United States, including the large numbers in Hawaii. Only those living on the West Coast were taken to the relocation camps. The factors were many, but the fundamental reason was simple. Right after the Japanese attacked American installations in Hawaii, panic broke out on the West Coast of the United States. Californians were especially fearful that an attack, or even full-scale Japanese invasion of the West Coast, was likely to be attempted and soon. Fear blinded tens of thousands of otherwise civil liberties-conscious Americans. Of the many thousands of Japanese-Americans living there, many reasoned, surely a significant number would assist their Japanese brothers in the coordination of such an invasion. American propaganda fueled this suspicion by constantly referring to the Japanese as representing the "Yellow Peril." Communication links and coordinated acts of sabotage were expected and feared. Despite this overwhelming fear, absolutely no evidence was ever uncovered to link a single Japanese-American with any spy ring or sabotage group.

The Japanese-Americans affected by this evacuation and relocation campaign lost, on average, about 50 percent of their wealth. Most were given little time—some just days or even hours—to dispose of their property. Not only were they forced to sell their homes and farms at drastically reduced prices, but they were only allowed to bring what they could wear and carry to the internment camps. Meanwhile, the irony was that about 17,600 Japanese-Americans served the American cause bravely in the United States armed forces in the European theater of the war. In fact, one Japanese-American regimental combat team was the most highly decorated unit in World War II in the American army.

Once the likelihood of a Japanese assault on the West Coast of the United States was nil, the internment policy was ended. The first releases from the camps occurred in mid-1942. Although those Japanese-Americans interned were eventually released before the end of the war, the United States Supreme Court ruled in a suit brought by Fred Korematsu in 1944. In that decision, *Korematsu v. United States*, the Supreme Court declared that the evacuations and internments had indeed been constitutional.

The Commission on Wartime Relocation and Internment studied the policy of Japanese-American internment during World War II. The completed report, released in 1982, officially blamed the experience on "race prejudice, war hysteria, and a failure of political leadership." And it extended an official apology to the Japanese-American community. Then in 1988, Congress appropriated $20,000 for each survivor of the camps as a token compensation. (About 60,000, more than half of the detainees, were still living in 1988.) The entire experience demonstrates that even in the United States of America, with its First Amendment guarantees, personal civil liberties can be taken away from those who find themselves in a distinct minority when the majority are in panic and looking for scapegoats.

ALLIED GOALS AND STRATEGIES TO WIN THE WAR

Even before the United States entered the war, there had been a general agreement that the Allies should concentrate on defeating Germany (and Italy) as their first priority. This "Hitler first" goal was based on a number of sound reasons. From the American point of view, the Nazis posed a greater threat to the entire western hemisphere. The geography of the Atlantic Ocean, including the distance across it, gave the Germans a far greater chance to dominate it and then use Atlantic bases to attack the hemisphere than the Japanese had of using the Pacific in a similar manner. In addition to the United States, the continent of Europe was the most industrially developed region in the world. An Axis victory there would severely handicap other nations, including a likely devastation of the American economy. For the same reason, Germany was more likely than Japan to develop some new weapon of mass destruction by which it could win the war. Therefore, if Hitler and Mussolini could be defeated first, then Japan would be militarily isolated and face almost certain defeat.

Shortly after the Japanese attack on Pearl Harbor, British Prime Minister Winston Churchill traveled to Washington, D.C. for a series of important talks with President Franklin Roosevelt. During these discussions, the two leaders confirmed the "Hitler first" strategy, hoping the Americans could, in the meantime, hold off the Japanese from any further major acts of aggression toward British and American possessions in the Pacific. The two men also agreed to establish several joint military boards to coordinate their war effort. Among the most important of these joint boards was the British-American Combined Chiefs of Staff, to which the supreme Allied commanders in the various theaters of the war would answer. The Soviets, forced into the Allied camp by Hitler's invasion of the Soviet Union in late June 1941, were not included in these early talks among the Allies. This was largely due to the fact that it was a communist-run government and that neither leader trusted Joseph Stalin, who had already demonstrated his ruthlessness with his own people. Stalin would later be included in the major Allied conferences. But in the meantime, the Soviet war effort against the Nazis proceeded on a mostly independent basis.

Although the Allies agreed that the Axis powers in Europe and North Africa should be defeated first, there was great disagreement on precisely where to hit the enemy. The Soviets urged the Americans and British to launch an invasion of France, thus forcing Hitler into fighting a two-front land war in Europe. American military leaders agreed and pushed for such an invasion before the end of 1942. However, Churchill vigorously opposed such an early assault across the English Channel. Remembering the bloody trench warfare of the last European war and the near British disaster at Dunkirk in the spring of 1940, the British prime minister argued for a more thorough build-up of Allied forces in England before engaging the enemy in France. Instead, Churchill suggested an attack on the so-called "soft underbelly" of Europe, in Italy, after first defeating the Axis in North Africa. When Roosevelt agreed, the Soviets were outvoted. The first Allied offensive would occur in North Africa.

THE WAR IN NORTH AFRICA AND EUROPE

North Africa

From its colonial base in Lybia, Italy had begun an attack on Ethiopia in 1935, winning a war of tanks and planes against warriors on horseback with spears and little else. After the fall of France in late June 1940, the puppet Vichy government in France "gave" the Germans and Italians the three French colonies in North Africa to use in their war effort—French Morocco, Algeria, and Tunisia. In September 1940, the Italians began an offensive against the British in Egypt, who ruled that possession. The major Axis goal in this part of the world was to secure not only the Mediterranean Sea but also the Suez Canal, which connected the Mediterranean with the Indian Ocean via the Red Sea. The Suez Canal was a crucial part of the Axis strategy to unite with Japanese forces coming from Asia. Thus, the three Axis powers could then dominate the entire eastern hemisphere of the world.

The British army maintained a strong defensive position at the Suez Canal and operated a naval base at Alexandria on the Mediterranean coast. The Italians could not push the British out of Egypt. Instead, a see-saw series of battles across the sands of North Africa ensued. To help his Italian allies, Hitler sent one of his best generals, Field Marshal General Erwin Rommel, to North Africa in February 1941. Rommel used his Afrika Korps and its resources masterfully, earning himself the nickname of the "desert fox." Nevertheless, Rommel could not take Alexandria or the Suez Canal either.

Then in late October 1942, General Sir Bernard Montgomery, commander of the British Eighth Army, launched a counter-offensive against Rommel at El-Alamein in northern Egypt. In coordination with Montgomery's effort, combined British and American forces landed in Casablanca (Morocco), Oran (Algeria), and Algiers (Algeria) on November 8, 1942, in what was code-named Operation Torch. This three-pronged invasion was under the command of the American General Dwight D. Eisenhower. By coincidence, Admiral Jean-Francois Darlan, second in command to Marshal Petain in the Vichy French government (which collaborated with the Nazis), was visiting the city of Algiers at the time of the Allied landings. The Allies hoped that Darlan would cooperate with them against the Nazis, but Darlan hated Charles de Gaulle (the recognized leader of the Free French who had escaped France and was living in exile in England) and insisted upon seeking permission from Petain in Vichy. This resulted in British and American troops fighting the French in North Africa for a short time.

Unwittingly, however, the Germans played into the Allied hands by ordering the Nazi military occupation of the rest of France (upon learning of the Allied landings) over the objections of Petain. At this point, Darlan agreed to order a cease-fire on November 11 in return for his being named the chief of state in French North Africa. Although the agreement with Darlan undoubtedly saved thousands of British and American lives (as well as French), it was widely denounced as a cruel act of expediency. Fortunately for Allied unity, Darlan was assassinated soon after the deal was made, and General Henri Giraud, who had not collaborated with the Nazis (he had even escaped a Nazi prison camp), took his place.

With Operation Torch, the German and Italian armies were caught in a two-front war between the British in the east and a combination of British and Americans in the west. This was to spell the defeat of the Axis in North Africa. Early in 1943 Montgomery's Eighth Army again took the offensive against Rommel and pushed him back across Lybia. Meanwhile, less experienced American troops were having a difficult time against the more seasoned Germans, who defeated an American force at Kasserine Pass in Tunisia. However, outnumbered and outmaneuvered, time was running out for the Axis. On May 7, the Americans took Bizerte and the British took Tunis, both in northern Tunisia. The remaining German armies made a last ditch effort at Cape Bon, but the end came on May 13, 1943, when between 250,000 and 275,000 Axis troops surrendered on the Mediterranean coast. (Rommel himself escaped and would remain to fight another day on the continent of Europe.) All of North Africa had promptly fallen into the Allied hands.

While the war for North Africa was still being waged, Roosevelt and Churchill met in Casablanca in January 1943. Stalin refused their invitation to meet there because of the situation with the Germans in his own country. However, he sent word that he still wanted a second front opened in France as soon as possible in order to force Hitler to divert troops from the eastern front to meet the new threat in western Europe. Nevertheless, Churchill maintained his opposition to this for the time being, and the two Allied leaders agreed to carry out plans for the invasion of Italy. The Casablanca Conference also produced a statement that the war would continue until the "unconditional surrender" of the Axis nations.

The Italian Campaign

On July 10, 1943, having secured North Africa, about 250,000 British and American troops invaded Sicily in the Mediterranean, considered too dangerous to ignore before launching an assault on Italy proper. The Sicilian operation, code-named Operation Husky, was under the overall command of General Dwight D. Eisenhower. With some assistance from powerful Mafia families, the island was under Allied control by August 17, although at least 40,000 Germans fled to Italy proper. Meanwhile, on July 25, King Victor Emmanuel III dismissed Benito Mussolini, and a new military government headed by Marshal Pietro Badoglio placed him in jail. The Italians had never had much enthusiasm for the war or for their German ally. The new government offered not only to surrender, but to join the Allies against German forces in their country. However, any such agreement was delayed because of the shock of such an offer and the suspicion that it might not be genuine.

On September 3 (1943), the very day that Allied troops first landed on the Italian peninsula, Premier Badoglio signed a truce; it was not announced publicly until the 8th of that same month. Hitler would not allow his Italian allies to surrender, however, and ordered tens of thousands of German soldiers from the north into Italy. As they did so, the Germans also rescued Mussolini from jail on September 12. After that, Mussolini was little more than a figurehead, with the Germans making the most important decisions. Meanwhile, the rival Italian government declared war on Germany on September 13. Most Italian army units were forced into an alliance with the Germans, but many others joined Allied forces while some worked behind the German lines with the civilian resistance movement. In other words, it was really left to the Germans to continue the bulk of the war in Italy. Rommel entrenched his armies in northern Italy while Field Marshal Albert Kesselring quickly occupied central and southern Italy. About the same time, the Germans evacuated Sardinia and Corsica—the other two major Mediterranean islands—between September 18 and October 3.

The "soft underbelly" of Europe proved to be anything but soft. The struggle for Italy became a very bloody campaign, with every inch being paid for in many lives. In less than two weeks, however, several beachheads had been secured, and by October 1, the Allies had captured Naples, an important southern port city. The rest of the Italian campaign would prove extremely costly.

By the time of a stalemate in mid-January 1944 along the Gustav Line (which ran all the way across Italy about halfway between Rome and Naples), both Montgomery (December 30, 1943) and Eisenhower (January 1944) had left Italy for England to coordinate the invasion of France, which Churchill conceded should occur sometime in 1944. However, the liberation of Rome was considered an important objective before that second front was opened. Toward that goal, an Allied force of about 50,000 made an end-run along the Mediterranean Sea and landed on the beaches of Anzio, north of the Gustav Line and south of Rome, on January 22, 1944. German troops from Rome quickly moved south and surrounded the beach-head there. The Allies suffered some 30,000 casulties in repeated efforts to break out over the next four months.

To the south, the Allies finally broke through west of the city of Cassino near the Gustav Line in the middle of May. Shortly afterwards, on May 23, 1944, the Allies broke out of their encirclement at Anzio. When those two Allied armies joined forces two days later (May 25), they marched toward Rome. On June 4, 1944, Rome was liberated without firing a shot because the Germans had already abandoned it and moved further north of the city to reinforce other German positions. Fighting in the more mountainous regions of northern Italy would continue until the very end of the war in Europe, but the world's attention sooned turned to the beaches of northern France. Just two days after the liberation of Rome, the long-awaited D-Day opened the second front in western Europe.

The Battle of the Atlantic and the Air War over Europe

During the campaign to take Italy, the Battle of the Atlantic (begun in the summer of 1941) was being won by the Allies. More specifically, superior American technological advances in radar, sonar, and depth charges were ensuring the safety of American men and supplies on their way to England to assist her and to prepare for the eventual invasion of France.

Round-the-clock air raids began bombing numerous key German cities in January 1943. The Americans bombed by day, and the British bombed by night throughout the rest of the war in Europe. Long before D-Day, the Allies controlled the skies over England, the English Channel, and much of northern and western Europe. In typical American humor, someone remarked that the Allies had dropped everything on the Germans but the kitchen sink. Whereupon an American bomber literally dropped a kitchen sink on a German city before the end of the war.

It would be difficult to over-estimate the importance of Allied control of the Atlantic and the skies over much of Europe by 1944. The survival of England depended on control of both of those arenas. And any chance at all for a second front invasion of France was dependent upon using England as a base from which to launch the assault. It is doubtful at best whether Hitler could have been defeated without this control. One might argue that the eventual Soviet push of the German armies, coupled with the Italians out of the war for all practical purposes, spelled Hitler's doom even without D-Day. But there can be no doubt that it shortened the war in Europe and made Hitler's defeat a sure thing. When D-Day came in June 1944, General Dwight Eisenhower could confidently tell the troops, "If you see fighting aircraft over you, they will be ours."

The Allied Conferences in Late 1943

By the middle of 1943, Allied gains in the Atlantic and in the air war with Germany finally persuaded Churchill that an invasion of France should be planned for sometime in 1944. The result was a scheduled conference among the "Big Three" of World War II—Roosevelt, Churchill, and Stalin—in late November of 1943. In a preliminary meeting, Secretary of State Cordell Hull, British Foreign Secretary Anthony Eden, and Soviet Foreign Minister Vyacheslav M. Molotov met in Moscow in late October. The Soviets agreed to enter the war against Japan after the defeat of Germany when they learned that an invasion of France would occur in 1944. In the Moscow Declaration, these Allies announced that a new world organization to promote peace would be established after the war. They also created the European Advisory Commission, with headquarters in London, to develop plans for the occupation of Germany after the war.

Then from November 22 to 26, Roosevelt, Churchill, and Stalin met in Cairo, Egypt with Chiang Kai-shek, leader of the nationalist forces fighting the Japanese inside China. The Declaration of Cairo confirmed the earlier Allied resolve to bring Japan to an unconditional surrender. It also declared that all territories acquired by Japan since the late nineteenth century would be taken away from her. Among other things, that meant that all areas taken from China would be restored to China, and that Korea would eventually be restored to an independent status.

Just two days after the Cairo Conference ended, the Big Three Allied leaders met in Teheran, Iran; the meetings lasted from November 28 to December 1. The Teheran Conference proved to be the most important Allied conference to that time. The major purpose of the meeting was to plan the invasion of France, which the Soviets agreed to support with a near simultaneous counter offensive on the eastern front. Stalin also reaffirmed his earlier commitment to declare war on Japan once the German threat was over. And the leaders issued a statement supporting the agreement at the Moscow Conference to establish an international peace-promoting organization after the war. The final sentence in their declaration noted that "We leave here, friends in fact, in spirit, and in purpose." Subsequent events after the end of the war would prove these words to be overly optimistic, if not downright false. But during times of crisis, even strained allies feel compelled to make grand statements about their unity.

The Russian Front

After being repulsed from Moscow in early December 1941 (see "The German Invasion of the Soviet Union" in this chapter), Hitler foolishly announced on December 19 that he was taking personal command of the German army. The Soviet Red Army continued to push the Germans back, however, and Hitler agreed to withdraw further from Moscow on February 15, 1942. By the end of that month, German troops ranged from 75 to 200 miles from the city.

The German failure to take Moscow before the first winter altered Hitler's strategy. Having suffered more than 1 million casualties thus far (more than one-third of the original invasion force), Hitler realized that his armies did not have sufficient strength for another assault on Moscow in 1942. Therefore, he turned his full attention toward the southern flank, aimed at acquiring the Caucasian oil fields in an effort to shut down the Soviet war machine as well as supply Axis forces with huge new oil reserves to continue and even expand the war.

The plan involved a number of different maneuvers in order to cut off Soviet railroad access to the Caucasus region. In the meantime, the German Sixth Army would surround Stalingrad and cut it off from the outside world. By late August, part of the German army was in the foothills of the Caucasus Mountains. There, however, they encountered strong Soviet resistance, and the delay caused serious supply problems. These problems caused Hitler to become more preoccupied with actually capturing Stalingrad. The city, which lay on the banks of the Volga River, was an important industrial center with a population of about 500,000 persons. On August 23, 1942, the Germans bombed the city mercilessly, reducing much of it to rubble. The next day German artillery bombarded it further. Meanwhile, General Friedrich Paulus was closing in on the city.

The Soviets, under the command of General Vasily Chuikov, built a supply line access route with ferries and foot bridges across the Volga. Chuikov divided his army into "storm groups" and scattered them in dozens of strategic positions inside the city. The bombing raids and heavy artillery barrage had created too much rubble for the Germans to use tanks. Therefore, when the Germans entered the main portion of Stalingrad in mid-September, the result was hand-to-hand combat fighting throughout the city. At night, Soviet snipers would use the city sewer system and underground tunnels to relocate to new positions for the next day's fighting. Casualties ran as high as 60 percent for both sides during the Battle of Stalingrad.

Then on November 19, the Soviets launched a well-coordinated counter-offensive with about 1 million troops that completely surprised the Germans. At the same time, other Soviet armies were engaging the enemy in counter-offensive measures elsewhere to keep Paulus from being reinforced. By November 23, the Germans inside Stalingrad were surrounded and cut off from outside ground help. Only the day before, Paulus had asked Hitler to authorize an orderly withdrawal from the city because of the difficulty of getting supplies to his troops. Hitler had refused, stating that Field Marshal Hermann Goering had promised his Luftwaffe (air force) could airlift the necessary 600 tons of supplies needed every day at Stalingrad. The reality was that the Luftwaffe only managed to deliver an average of 70 tons per day. (The Germans still controlled both airports in the city.)

After both airports had been retaken by the Soviets by January 24, 1943, the Germans knew that surrender was imminent. Now a Field Marshal, General Paulus requested permission to surrender, but Hitler forbade him to surrender. Totally exhausted, and with nowhere to turn, Paulus surrendered to the Red Army anyway on January 31, 1943. The Soviets took the remaining 91,000 troops of the German Sixth Army prisoner. Stalingrad was the second defeat of the German military during World War II. (Moscow had been the first.) The defeat of Stalingrad, however, was a decisive one. Having failed to seize the rich oil fields of the southern Soviet Union, and demoralized by enormous losses from unexpectedly strong Soviet counter-offensives, the Battle of Stalingrad represented a turning point in the war, although fighting would continue for more than two years.

By the spring of 1943, Soviet factories had been torn apart, loaded onto railroad freight cars, shipped far to the east of Moscow, reassembled, and were in full war production. This amazing feat, unheralded in the West because it occurred under a communist system, was made almost unbelievable by that fact. Nevertheless, it was an astounding accomplishment and a major factor which contributed to the ultimate defeat of Nazi Germany. By the end of 1943, the Soviets outnumbered the Germans by about 3 million troops, 6,100 tanks, and 12,000 heavy guns.

In the meantime, the largest tank battle in history proved to be another major setback for Nazi armies on the eastern front. In the summer of 1943, Hitler ordered an offensive near the city of Kursk, which in his words, "would shine like a beacon around the world." Kursk lay south of Moscow and to the east-north-east of Kiev. Code-named Operation Citadel, the German panzer (tank) divisions took the offensive in early July. But Hitler was forced to suspend the offensive on the 13th in order to transfer troops to Italy. (The Allied invasion of Sicily had begun on July 10.) Despite this interruption, the Germans nearly won the Battle of Kursk. But by the end of July, the Soviets had regained the offensive and had secured the city of Kursk. The central and southern flanks of the German invaders were pushed backwards toward the west after Kursk. On November 6 the Soviets recaptured the city of Kiev. After that, Hitler ordered a "scorched earth" policy, in which retreating Germans would destroy everything of military value in order to prevent the Soviets from using it against them.

The siege of Leningrad, which had begun by September 1941, would last until January 1944. Because Lake Ladoga (northeast of the city) froze in the winters, the Germans essentially ignored it. But the Soviets built a road over the frozen lake, keeping a narrow snow path relatively clear. Although inadequate for the large city, some supplies were trucked into Leningrad during the long siege. Very few civilians in the city took advantage of the rare opportunities to leave it via the lake "road," for this city built by Peter the Great (and originally named St. Petersburg after Peter), had developed a very proud tradition. Conditions in the city were horrible, with most citizens forced to eat rats, shoe leather, and whatever else they could find just to survive. The Germans were forced to abandon their siege of Leningrad on January 19, 1944, after their supply lines had deteriorated as a result of the Battle of Kursk. From that point onward, the Germans were in full, although orderly, retreat.

The Russian front had been costly for both major countries. It is estimated that the Soviets lost more than 20 million people in World War II, both military and civilian deaths. But as bad as it was for the Soviets, the Russian front was a total strategic disaster for the Third Reich.

D-Day

Stalin had been demanding for a long time that the other Allies should open the so-called second front, the nickname given to an invasion of France. Churchill had been afraid of another "Dunkirk" and was reticent until the summer of 1943. Confirmed at the Teheran Conference in late 1943, the second front would be opened sometime the following year. During discussions between Churchill and Roosevelt in Cairo just after the Teheran Conference (on December 4-6), the two

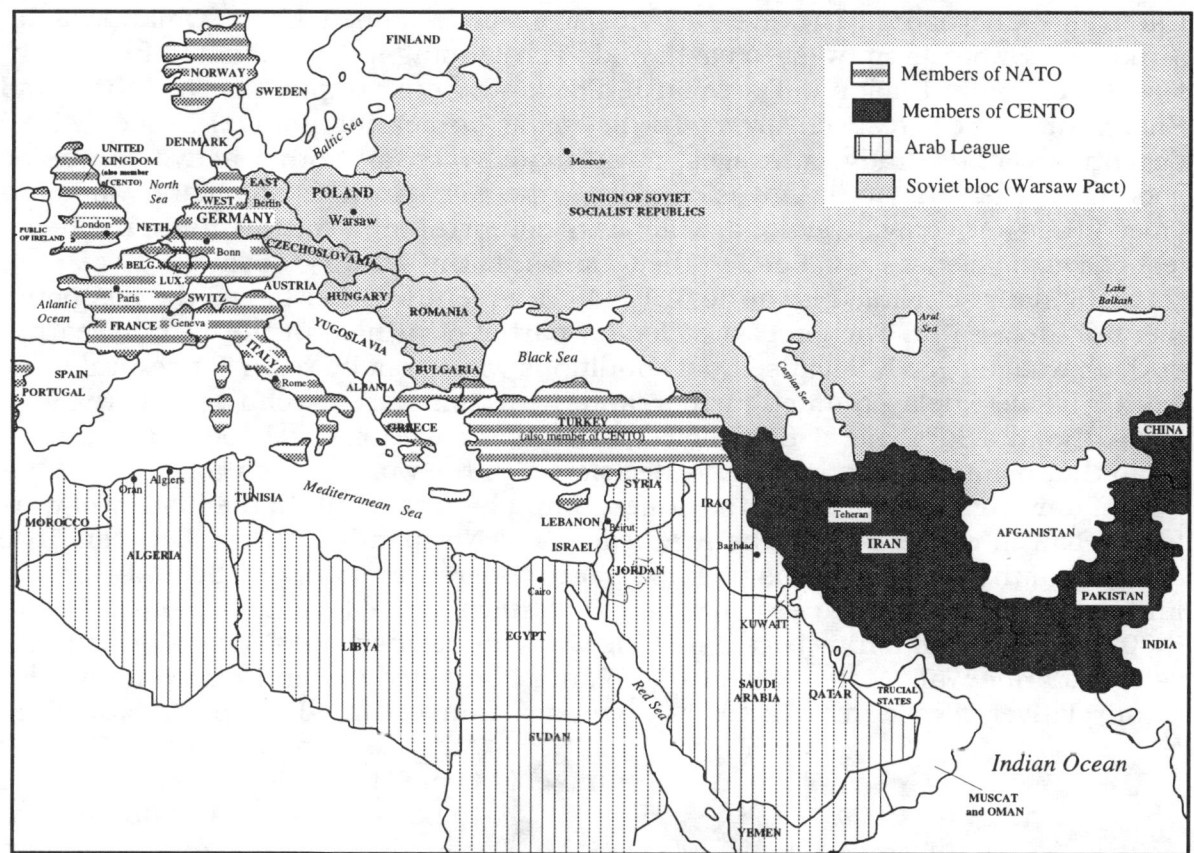

Post-World War II map of Europe, North Africa, and the Middle East

leaders agreed to place General Dwight Eisenhower in charge of planning such an invasion. American forces had been gathering in England for many months, assembling with other Allies the men, ships, weapons, and other supplies needed to make the invasion a success. But plans were kicked into high gear when General Eisenhower arrived in England in mid-January 1944 to assume the role of the Supreme Allied Commander from D-Day to the end of the war in Europe. The headquarters for the invasion planning in London was called the Supreme Headquarters, Allied Expeditionary Forces (SHAEF).

The second front invasion was known as D-Day, which stood for Disembarkation Day (as when the troops disembarked from the landing craft), but its military code name was Operation Overlord. The highly secret invasion plans called for the Allies to land where the Germans would not really expect them to land. Hitler and most of his German army staff believed that the attack would almost surely have to come at or near Calais because that was where the English Channel was the narrowest. The English Channel was known for its rough seas, and an assault across its wider parts could jeopardize the entire Allied operation. Eisenhower counted on that German reaction and therefore planned for a series of five major initial landings along a sixty-mile stretch in the Normandy region of northern France, between

Caen and Cherbourg. The five beaches were code-named Utah, Omaha, Gold, Juno, and Sword (from west to east), and each landing force originated from a different location in England. (Dartmouth, Portland, Southampton, Portsmouth, and Shoreham-by-Sea, respectively, were the major originating points.) In fact, Allied deception via false radio messages, naval maneuvers, and other activities was so good that when the actual invasion began, the German high command was convinced they were only diversionary tactics. And, fortunately for the Allies, the heaviest German defenses remained in the Calais area until it was too late.

Originally scheduled for June 5, 1944, inclement weather forced the postponement of the assault. The forecast called for partial clearing, but the overall weather outlook was not good. Because tidal conditions would not be ready for several more weeks if it were delayed much further, and the troops were psychologically ready to begin the attack, General Eisenhower solemnly looked around the headquarters room that night and announced his decision with the words, "Let's go!"

At dawn on June 6, 1944, the largest amphibious assault in the history of warfare began in earnest along the five beaches of Normandy. Earlier, between 1:00 and 2:00 a.m., three divisions of Allied paratroopers were dropped behind German lines to secure the two flanks (eastern and western) of the beaches. And just before 6:00 a.m., Allied warships began shelling German defensive positions along the so-called Atlantic Wall. More than 11,000 planes blanketed the entire area to prevent what relatively few German bombers there were from getting through. At 6:30 a.m., American troops under General Omar N. Bradley began hitting the beaches at Utah and Omaha, and less than an hour later, British and Canadian forces commanded by General Miles Dempsey landed at Gold, Juno, and Sword.

Not only were the Germans not expecting the attack in this general area, but the bad weather had lulled them into thinking that it would not come when it did. Rommel, for example, who commanded three armored divisions, was in Germany when the invasion began, and it was nearly dark on the 6th of June before he had returned to Normandy. In less than 24 hours, more than 150,000 Allied troops had disembarked from about 4,000 landing craft. Although most experienced stiff German resistance, the Americans at Omaha Beach had

General Dwight D. Eisenhower. Credit: European Picture Service.

D-Day Landing, June 6, 1944. Credit: Acme Photo.

it the worst. Unusually heavy seas had battered the landing craft and left the troops scattered in the water and on the beach. The German defenses above Omaha Beach were also especially heavy. Despite the obstacles, in less than three weeks, 9,000 ships had ferried more than 1 million men and more than 170,000 vehicles, supported by 702 warships, nearly 1,400 transport planes, 867 gliders, and over 200 minesweepers. The largest sea-to-land invasion in history had been successful thus far in securing a second front.

Sensing that the war was lost, several leading German military personnel conspired to kill Hitler in order to negotiate a quick end to the war. On July 20, Hitler was injured in a bomb blast which killed other military leaders. Hundreds of conspirators, as well as dozens of innocent people, were murdered without trial across Germany in retaliation. General Erwin Rommel himself had hoped to see Hitler assassinated. When the Gestapo (secret German police) arrested him, he was given the option of a humiliating trial and firing squad or voluntarily taking a cyanide capsule. He chose the latter and committed suicide in order to save his family any worse humiliation and embarrassment.

Although more men and equipment were piling onto the beaches of Normandy, the Allies were mostly penned up for several weeks. On July 25, however, American

General George S. Patton's Third Army broke through German lines near Caen, and the Germans began to actually retreat in large numbers. Once the major roads in northern France were secured, the Allies marched toward Paris. In coordination with the French resistance movement, the Germans were forced to withdraw from the French capital, and Paris was officially liberated on August 25, 1944. Charles de Gaulle marched down Paris as the national hero he had become.

Meanwhile, a joint French-American force, under the command of American General Jacob L. Devers, landed in southern France between Cannes and Toulon. German troops there proceeded to withdraw in an orderly fashion, and by September 11 the two Allied invasion forces had joined together. Germany was now facing the dreaded two-front squeeze and its troops were retreating in both the eastern and western theaters of the war.

The German Rocket Attacks

When the end had become obvious in late 1918, Kaiser Wihelm had abdicated and fled Germany. But Hitler was not a mentally stable person, and he grew more and more irritable and unreasonable as the end drew near. Refusing to yield to reality, the German Fuhrer now clung to the vain hope that one of his super weapons projects would yet bring the Allies to their knees. On June 14, Hitler ordered the first pilotless "buzz bombers" to raid London. These V-1 rockets, however, were too slow and relatively easy to shoot down. Then in early September, the V-2 rockets were available from secret German factories and began bombing London. These first ballistic missles were indeed capable of completely destroying entire cities and armies. Fortunately for the Allies, their secret launching sites were discovered and taken before Hitler could bring utter catastrophe upon England.

German scientists had also been working on developing an atomic bomb based on nuclear fission of uranium atoms. Secret laboratories and factories making heavy water necessary for the production of nuclear weapons materials in Germany and Norway were also destroyed late in the war. There is no doubt but that if Hitler had developed the atomic bomb first, the outcome of World War II would have been entirely different.

The Election of 1944

The war did not end politics in the United States, of course. With the war still continuing, Franklin D. Roosevelt asked and received the Democratic nomination for a fourth consecutive time. But the end of the New Deal because of the war had strengthened the southern conservative wing of his party, and they demanded the removal of Vice-President Henry Wallace, who was indeed quite liberal. Instead, the Democrats nominated Missouri Senator Harry S. Truman, a Kansas City machine Democrat who was best known nationally for uncovering corruption in the military supply procurement system, for the number two place on the ticket in 1944. The Republicans nominated Thomas E. Dewey, the popular governor of New York. They then named Ohio Governor John Bricker on the ticket as his running mate.

The campaign did not turn on the issues for there were no major areas of dispute between Roosevelt and Dewey, domestically or internationally. Instead, Dewey campaigned on the theme that it was time to retire the "tired old men" who had run the White House for the last twelve years. When the electoral votes were cast, Roosevelt had carried thirty-six states with 432 electoral votes compared with Dewey's 99 electoral votes among twelve states. President Franklin Roosevelt had set yet another record, winning his fourth consecutive term of office for the presidency.

The Battle of the Bulge

The Allies' push toward Germany proceeded too quickly in the late summer of 1944. British General Montgomery (nicknamed "Monty") took Antwerp, Belgium on September 4. He and Patton tried to persuade Eisenhower that their armies were ready to move straight for Berlin with all deliberate speed. Eisenhower, however, correctly perceived that his armies were running out of gasoline and other supplies needed to take them to Berlin. Their supply lines were simply stretched too thin. He therefore took the more cautious approach of weeding out pockets of stubborn German resistance that threatened that supply line instead of proceeding too quickly. As it was, a daring attempt to take the key bridges across the Meuse, Waal, and Rhine Rivers in Holland in mid-September was only partially successful. Code-named Market Garden, the bridges across the Meuse and Waal Rivers were secured, but the attempt to control the Rhine River bridges failed. By early October the Allies were getting bogged down.

Meanwhile, Hitler had been trying to pull out all the stops to rally his forces one last time. With Allied supply lines still in some trouble, Hitler reasoned that by concentrating large numbers of tanks and using massive numbers of troops, he might be able to break through the Allied line. By this strategy he hoped to cut off tens of thousands of such troops from all help and use them as bargaining chips in forcing the Americans and the British to negotiate an end to the war that might leave him in power, or at least alive. With good reason, Hitler feared being taken by the Soviets.

Rumors swept through the American lines that the war was almost over, and perhaps many of the men would be on their way home for Christmas. But this was wishful thinking. German forces were secretly assembled, and they launched their last offensive of the war in what history records as the Battle of the Bulge, beginning at dawn on December 16, 1944. The strike came along a fifty-mile front in Belgium and Luxembourg under the cover of thick clouds that prevented air reconnaisance. Moving toward Antwerp, the German forces bogged down at Bastogne. Just before the city was surrounded by Germans, reinforcements arrived, although not enough to hold out for long. When the Germans demanded the surrender of Bastogne, American General Anthony McAuliffe replied on December 22, "Nuts!" Not understanding the reply, the German officer was informed by an American courier that it meant "Go to hell." The next day the cloud cover lifted, and Allied airplanes attacked the Germans and dropped in more supplies to their com-

1944	48	FRANKLIN D. ROOSEVELT	Democrat	25,606,585	432	53.5
		Thomas E. Dewey	Republican	22,014,745	99	46.0

rades in the town. The siege of Bastogne ended on December 26. Before the end of January, the Battle of the Bulge had failed to achieve its goals, and the Germans were in full retreat on both fronts.

The Yalta Conference

The most significant and controversial Allied conference was the Yalta Conference in February 1945, held just after the Battle of the Bulge had ended in German failure. At the Soviet port of Yalta, on the Black Sea, Roosevelt, Churchill, and Stalin met for the last time as the Big Three Allied leaders. Roosevelt was ill and looked it, but he had decided to attend the conference anyway. Agreements were reached on a variety of subjects dealing with the postwar world. Among them was the agreement to call a special conference of all Allied nations in April at San Francisco, California for the purpose of drafting a charter for what became known as the United Nations.

Germany was to be divided into American, British, French, and Soviet occupation zones for the purpose of supervising the restoration of eventual self-government. An adjustment of Poland's border favorable to Poland and the Soviet Union at the expense of Germany was also agreed to. The Soviets also agreed specifically to free elections in Poland and to allow for the timely restoration of democratic governments in all liberated European countries. In return for reaffirming its commitment to enter the war against Japan after Germany's defeat, Roosevelt and Churchill promised to restore the Soviet sphere of influence in Manchuria, which it had held before the Russo-Japanese War of 1904–05. The Soviets would also receive an occupation zone in the Korean penninsula upon the ouster of the Japanese there.

After Yalta, but before the official end of the war in Europe, President Franklin Delano Roosevelt died of a cerebral hemorrage on April 12, 1945. At the time of his death, Roosevelt was resting in his second home in Warm Springs, Georgia. His death came while he was working on a Jefferson Day speech. The last words he wrote in that speech were: "The only limit to our realization of tomorrow will be our doubts of today. Let us move forward with strong and active faith." The end of a political era and dynasty had come to an end.

The End of the War in Europe

Because of the time-consuming Battle of the Bulge and the decision made at Yalta that placed Berlin in the Soviet occupation zone, Eisenhower decided to save more American lives and not race the Soviets to Berlin. Thus, the Soviets reached the German capital first, entering the outskirts of Berlin in April. Hitler knew that if the Soviets captured him alive, they would probably display him as a caged animal or torture him, at least, before executing him. For this reason, he clearly hoped the Americans would have reached Berlin first. But when that hope also faded, Hitler and his longtime girlfriend Eva Braun, whom he had married in the closing days of his stay in the underground bunker, committed suicide on April 30, 1945.

Meanwhile, Italy's Fascist dictator Mussolini was captured by fellow Italians while attempting to flee to Switzerland on April 28, 1945. He and his mistress were murdered, and their bodies were publicly displayed. On May 7, Hitler's successor (named in his will), Admiral Karl Doenitz, signed an unconditional surrender. The next day, May 8, 1945, the German surrender was formally announced, and that day became V-E Day (Victory in Europe Day).

THE WAR IN THE PACIFIC

Introduction

World War II was truly a global war, with theaters in Europe and the Pacific area. As far as the Allies were concerned, the Pacific theater began on December 7, 1941, when the Japanese attacked Guam, Wake Island, Midway Island, the Philippines, Hong Kong, Malaya, and Thailand (Siam), nearly simultaneous with the raid at Pearl Harbor. These attacks produced a series of Japanese victories that month. Guam was conquered and occupied by the 10th, Wake Island by the 23rd, and British Hong Kong by Christmas Day (the 25th). The airfield and other targets on Midway were left in shambles, but the Japanese did not attempt to occupy that distant island at the time. The American bombers at Clark Field, near the capital city of Manila, were left lined up in close proximity on the ground despite receiving a ten hours' notice of the air raid on Pearl Harbor, and most of them were destroyed. Japanese military invasions were well under way in the Philippines and Thailand, and the Gilbert Islands were under their control by the end of December.

1942: More Bad News Before the Turning Point

Thailand discreetly chose to surrender in very early 1942 rather than receive the full brunt of the Japanese wrath. That country was then used as a base of operations from which to move down the Malay Peninsula (British territory). Malaya's capital of Singapore fell on February 15.

The assault on the Philippines had forced American General Douglas MacArthur to abandon Manila on December 27 (1941). And by January 7, 1942, his American and Filipino troops were pushed onto the Bataan Peninsula and the island fortress of Corregidor, nicknamed "The Rock." With insufficient forces to counter-attack the enemy, MacArthur was evacuated on March 12 after declaring to the Filipinos, "I shall return." MacArthur was secreted off to Australia to take command of all Allied forces in the southwest Pacific. As supplies were running low, the Allied troops MacArthur had been ordered to leave earlier surrendered on Bataan on April 9. And on May 6, the troops on Corregidor did the same.

Meanwhile Rabaul, in New Britain, fell into Japanese hands in January. And by February 1942 Borneo, Java (the capital of the Dutch East Indies), and other Dutch colonies in the south Pacific were being overrun by the Japanese. To defend Java, an Allied naval fleet was sent to the area late that month (February). In the ensuing Battle of the Java Sea, February 27–March 1, the Japanese almost completely destroyed the Allied force. Thus, on March 9, the Dutch colonial authorities officially surrendered. Other Japanese forces landed in New Guinea and the Solomon Islands and established military bases there. By July the Japanese were occupying Rabaul, the northern segment of New Guinea, and the more northern Solomon Islands.

On the same day the Dutch colonies surrendered to Japan (March 9), Rangoon, Burma was captured. The Burma Road had been used since 1938 to transport supplies from British India to the nationalist Chinese forces, whose government was headquartered in Chungking, China. The defeat of Burma meant that the Burma Road was now cut off. To compensate for that important loss, the Allies began airlifting needed supplies to the Chinese across some 500 miles over the Himalayan "hump" (some of the tallest mountain peaks in the world), and construction on a new road from Ledo, India to Chungking was begun.

By the spring of 1942, the Japanese had exceeded even their own expectations. In a matter of a few short months, Japan had managed to carve out an empire of southeast Asia that ran to the gates of India and extended eastward and southward to control most of the western Pacific north of Australia. At this point, what some later called "victory disease" swept through the Japanese military command, and the overall strategy was altered. The original plan had called for heavy fortifications to be built up on newly acquired areas. This was to make it virtually impossible for the Americans and their allies to retake those possessions, and the Allies would be forced to negotiate a settlement favorable to Japan. But new confidence in their military capability led the Japanese to attempt to extend still further eastward in the Pacific in the hope of completely isolating Australia. Then Hawaii would be hit again in order to complete the destruction of the American Pacific Fleet that had begun on December 7 of the year before.

This eventually proved to be a fatal mistake in change of policy because the Japanese simply over-extended themselves. All three American aircraft carriers had survived Pearl Harbor because they had not been there at the time of the attack. These were now used to launch raids on Japanese forces on their extended edge, especially against targets in the Gilbert Islands and Marshall Islands. On April 18, American B-25 bombers led by Colonel James Doolittle from the carrier *Hornet*, even made a daring raid on Tokyo, Japan. Since they were incapable of landing on the carrier, the pilots hit Tokyo and flew on to a remote part of China. The air raid was not significant from a military point of view, but it certainly did boost American morale. It also added impetus to the new Japanese strategy in order to push their defensive arc outside of American bomber range.

Once committed to the new strategy, in early May the Japanese sent a large convoy of troop and supply ships toward Port Moresby on the south coast of New Guinea. The purpose of this movement was to use the area as a base of operations for an assault on Australia. The Americans met them in the region, and the resulting Battle of the Coral Sea (May 7-8) became the first naval battle conducted entirely with airpower. Americans suffered worse losses than the Japanese, although both sides lost one aircraft carrier (the Americans lost the carrier *Lexington* in the battle) in what was called a military draw. Strategically, however, it was an American victory because Port Moresby remained in Allied hands, and the Japanese advance toward Australia was thwarted.

Less than a full month later the Americans would deal the Japanese a hard blow that would later be called the turning point of the war in the Pacific. In order to set themselves up to strike more safely at Hawaii, the Japanese sent a large naval force to Midway to actually take the island this time. (Midway lay a little more than 1,000 miles west-north-west of Hawaii.) Revenge for Doolittle's raid on Tokyo a couple of weeks earlier provided an extra incentive to finish off this stepping stone to Hawaii. By this time, however, the Americans had broken the Japanese naval code in Operation Magic, and they learned that an island with the initials of "AF" was going to be attacked. Guessing that it might be Midway, but not knowing for certain, the Americans sent a decoy message that Midway had run out of drinking water. Soon after the American message had been sent, a Japanese transmission was intercepted that declared the island of "AF" had no drinking water. Thus, the Americans knew in advance that Midway was the next major target. And Admiral Chester Nimitz moved a large carrier force near the island to meet the coming assault. In this sense, the Americans were able to do to the Japanese what the latter had done to them at Pearl Harbor; the element of surprise was on the Americans' side this time.

On June 4 Japanese planes lifted off carriers and hit Midway, but in that first attack they lost about one-third of their aircraft. Then American planes first spotted the enemy fleet, including three of the four carriers involved in the operation. But the American torpedo bombers that attacked the enemy were too slow-moving, and most of them were shot down. Early in the Battle of Midway (May 4–8), both sides experienced rather severe losses. However, the Americans redeemed the situation with waves of dive bombers, which did manage to find their targets. The Japanese lost all four of their carriers, while the Americans lost one carrier and one destroyer. The Japanese defeat at Midway was devastating. This turning point in the war in the Pacific was almost exactly six months after the humiliating American defeat at Pearl Harbor, proving Yamamoto correct in his prediction that the Americans would be generally set back about six months after the original blow to their Pacific fleet.

When the Aleutian islands of Attu and Kiska, off the main body of Alaska in the north Pacific, were taken by the Japanese during the summer of 1942, they proved to be hollow victories. Without Midway Island, the Japanese would find it difficult to defend the Aleutians whenever the Americans made a move to retake them.

After their defeat at Midway, Japanese forces began building an air base on the island of Guadalcanal in the southern Solomon Islands. It was hoped that this base would support bombers whose mission would be to attack Allied transport convoys headed for Australia. On August 7, 1942, the American marines landed and began the costly effort to take Guadalcanal. Although the airstrip and the port of Tulagi were quickly captured, the remainder of the campaign turned extremely bitter and bloody as it continued into the early portion of the next year. In response to the early American successes there, the Japanese initiated a vicious naval effort that resulted in a series of confusing battles which neither side really won. So horrible were these naval engagements that Savo Island Sound was nicknamed "Iron Bottom Bay." The real significance of these battles, however, was that they put the Japanese on the defensive for the rest of the war.

1943: Americans Take the Offensive

The Battle of Guadalcanal lasted from August 7, 1942 until American victory was achieved on February 9, 1943. Meanwhile, MacArthur's command of American and Australian troops was shoving the Japanese off New Guinea, where they had been entrenched on the north side. By the end of January 1943, the eastern end was under Allied control.

Then on March 2–3, an air battle just off the northeast coast of New Guinea allowed the Americans to pursue a different strategy in the war. In this Battle of the Bismarck Sea, the American planes sank 18 Japanese ships bringing reinforcements and supplies to parts of northern New Guinea where Japanese troops still remained. This Japanese catastrophe meant that no longer could they risk resupplying outlying posts. The new American strategy to take advantage of this situation became known as leapfrogging" (or "island hopping"). Leapfrogging tactics called for the use of air and sea power to neutralize some of the stronger Japanese-held islands, cutting them off from resupply opportunities, and thus allowing them to "die on the vine." In this way, the war could proceed at a faster pace, with fewer American casualties. This new Pacific strategy continued for the rest of the war. Premier Tojo himself later admitted that this "leapfrogging" strategy was largely responsible for the military retreats and the ultimate defeat of Japan.

In the spring of 1943, the Combined Chiefs of Staff agreed to separate proposals made by General Douglas MacArthur and Admiral Chester W. Nimitz. Each of these men envisioned a different geographical approach to winning the war against Japan, although the new "leapfrogging" strategy was able to blend with both of the plans. MacArthur proposed to move west along the north coast of New Guinea, liberate the Philippines, and then prepare for a major strike on the home islands of Japan itself, culminating in Tokyo. Nimitz, on the other hand, proposed to move his naval forces through the central Pacific, aiming for China. When both proposals were accepted, the naval operations acted to provide protection for MacArthur's north flank.

Just before the American offensive commenced in mid-April, United States code breakers discovered the exact location of Japanese Admiral Yamamoto. American pilots stationed on Guadalcanal intercepted and shot down Yamamoto's plane, which was headed for Bougainville in the northern Solomons. Thus, the architect of the Japanese attack on Pearl Harbor died before he could see the end of World War II. However, by the time of his death, he must have recognized the fact that his worst fears about losing a long war with the United States were coming to pass. His death marked a new low in Japanese morale. Meanwhile, in the north Pacific, the Aleutian Islands of Attu and Kiska were retaken by American forces in May and July of 1943, respectively.

Beginning the major American offensive, the first goal was to isolate Rabaul (on the north end of New Britain) by securing the northern Solomon Islands. This would protect MacArthur's troop movements across northern New Guinea. Rabaul was isolated before the end of December. By the end of the year, Makin and Tarawa, both in the Gilbert Islands chain, had been liberated from the Japanese. The offensive that was to begin in the Gilberts and run through the Marshall, Caroline, and Mariana Island chains was under way as the year 1943 came to a close.

1944: More American Victories

The campaign for the Marshall Islands began in earnest on January 31, 1944, with the quick fall of Kwajalein and Eniwetok. About the same time, carrier-based planes conducted a massive air raid on Truk, an island in the Caroline Islands which had been dubbed the "Japanese Pearl Harbor" because it was the hub of Japanese activity in the Pacific. After enemy ships and planes had been severely damaged, Truk was by-passed like Rabaul had been earlier. The assault on Japanese-held fortifications in the Mariana Islands was launched with an attack on Saipan, which was taken by the Americans on June 15. The capture of Saipan placed B-29 bombers based there within reach of targets located on the home islands of Japan.

The numerous Japanese defeats in the island chains of the Pacific during the first half of the year (1944) resulted in Japan daringly employing its navy in a desperate attempt to stop the American offensive. One of the major naval battles of the year occurred on June 19–20 and was called the Battle of the Philippine Sea. Nicknamed the "Marianas Turkey Shoot," the Battle of the Philippine Sea consisted mostly of aerial combat. The Japanese lost four more aircraft carriers and almost 400 airplanes, while the Americans lost only 17 aircraft. The significance of this battle lay in its plural effects. First, it placed the entire Mariana Islands under American control. Second, by doing this, the door was now open for MacArthur to keep his promise to return and liberate the Philippines. And third, it also convinced Premier Tojo that the war was lost, and he and his entire cabinet resigned on July 18. General Kunikai Koiso replaced Tojo as the new Japanese premier.

President Roosevelt, General MacArthur, and Admiral Nimitz met in Honolulu on July 27–28, 1944 to set the final strategy for further moves toward Japan. South China had been the original jumping off position for that attack. But a Japanese offensive in April of that year had recaptured most of the airfields in southern China which the Allies needed to use. MacArthur, who had made his famous promise to the Philippines, won his argument to take and then use them for the final push against Japan.

Before the American assault could begin, the island of Guam, to the south end of the Mariana Islands, was retaken by August 10. Admiral Nimitz's offensive, begun in late November of 1943 against Japanese positions in the Gilbert, Marshall, Caroline, and Mariana Islands had now achieved total success by August 1944.

On October 20, 1944, a force of about 200,000 men invaded the island of Leyte in the central portion of the Philippine Islands. After the Americans had safely secured a beachhead, General Douglas MacArthur waded ashore and announced that he had returned. The Japanese defenders were caught ill-prepared because they expected an attack on Mindanao, the major island in the southern Philippines, instead. But realizing that the loss of the Philippines would cut off their supplies of oil and other vital resources from southeast Asia, what was left of the Japanese navy moved in from three different directions to challenge the American naval forces. In separate engagements that became known collectively as the Battle of Leyte Gulf (October 23–25), the largest naval battle in history took place. Japanese sea power was absolutely crushed.

The battle also saw the first significant use of the infamous suicide raids by young and inexperienced "Kamikaze" pilots, named after the so-called "Divine Wind" that had saved Japan from a Mongol invasion several centuries before. The Japanese culture worshipped the emperor (Hirohito) as a god. To die in battle for the emperor was to ensure for oneself a position of high honor in the after-life. That is why surrender was considered a dishonorable action. And that is a major reason why relatively few Japanese surrendered during the entire war, which in turn, made American liberation efforts more difficult and time-consuming. Used late in the war in desperation to defeat the Allies, the "Kamikaze" pilots aimed their bomb-laden planes for the decks of American ships. (Not relying on the bravery of the pilots alone, the military attempted to guarantee success by providing only enough fuel to reach their targets.) Although they did great damage at times, the youthful inexperience of these pilots led many to crash in the sea, and the overall impact of the suicide missions was minimal.

1945: The War Winds Down

The success of the American invasion of the Philippines was assured by the Battle of Leyte Gulf in late October of 1944. Leyte was secured in January 1945, and the American troops proceeded northward into the main northern island of Luzon. There the capital city of Manila was liberated on March 4 despite stubborn Japanese resistance. In fact, fighting in Luzon continued until the end of the war. In terms of the Philippines as a whole, which consisted of dozens of mostly small islands, some Japanese soldiers in isolated areas did not learn of their government's surrender until years after the war had ended. Many of them joined guerilla bands that opposed the Filipino government, apparently thinking that in doing so, they were actually fighting the American war effort. The last Japanese soldier to surrender officially did not do so until March 1974. Army Lieutenant Hiroo Onoda, age 52, put down his rifle on the island of Lubang after his last military superior officer flew down from Japan and personally read to him the 29-year-old Imperial order to surrender.

Pushing toward Japan and needing a base for fighter planes that could escort bombers on bombing missions inside Japan (and for crippled bombers to make emergency landings), the marines landed on Iwo Jima, a small five-square-mile volcanic island about 750 miles from Japan, on February 19, 1945. In about six weeks of fighting exceptionally tough resistance, the island was secured by mid-March. The loss of 20,000 marines made the battle for Iwo Jima the bloodiest single battle in the history of the American marines. After the island was taken, a small group of marines hoisted the American flag on a hilltop. The picture taken of that placing of the flag became one of the most famous photographs of World War II.

Okinawa, a 65-mile long island north of the Philippines, and about 350 miles south of Japan, was the prime site from which to launch a land invasion of Japan. Therefore, 50,000 military personnel hit the beaches of Okinawa on Easter Sunday, April 1, 1945. Altogether, some 300,000 troops were involved in this largest of amphibious landings in the Pacific theater of the war. A ragtag group of ten Japanese ships left southern Japan with supplies and just enough fuel for a one-way trip. These included the battleship *Yamato*. But American air attacks sank the *Yamato* and damaged the rest of the fleet, stopping it in its tracks. This spelled the very end of the Japanese navy during the war. Hundreds of Kamikaze pilots were used in the naval engagement here, sinking 24 American ships in a single day.

However, fighting on the island of Okinawa lasted until June and proved to be the last major battle of World War II. Americans experienced almost 50,000 casualties, including the death of the popular war correspondent Ernie Pyle. The Japanese lost more than 110,000 killed and between 7,000 and 10,000 taken as prisoners of war. The major significance of the American victory at Okinawa was the fact that it wore down the Japanese forces. And its location relatively close to the southern edge of Japan also meant that a Japanese defeat there reduced them to their home islands.

The Atomic Bombs: Japan Surrenders

The theoretical possibility of an atomic fission bomb was known as far back as 1905, when the Jewish-German scientist Albert Einstein first proposed his theory of relativity, including the famous equation of $E=mc^2$. In the early 1930s, atomic research was being done in England under the supervision of Ernest Rutherford. In early 1939, just before World War II erupted in Europe, a German scientific journal reported that uranium isotope U-238 had been split in Berlin, resulting in a chain reaction. This announcement led many research scientists to theorize that nuclear fission—the splitting of atoms—might produce sufficient heat and pressure to trigger nuclear fusion, the forced combining of atoms.

When war broke out in Europe, a number of scientists expressed great concern that Nazi Germany might be successful in developing the first atomic bomb. Such a weapon, although its effects were not then known, would surely give the user a great advantage in warfare. Niels Bohr, a Danish physicist who was smuggled out of Copenhagen (Denmark) in 1942, was a great help in assisting nuclear researchers in England. Meanwhile, President Roosevelt created an advisory board on uranium research after Einstein warned him in August 1939 that Germany was working on such a project. (Einstein had been lecturing in the United States in 1933 and wisely elected to remain there because he was Jewish, and Hitler had just come to power in Germany.)

It was Leo Szilard, a Polish scientist living outside the Nazi reach, who was the one-man promoter of the idea that England and the United States should pool their respective research results and jointly develop an atomic bomb (called an A-bomb). Therefore, he approached Enrico Fermi, an Italian scientist who had come to the United States because his wife was Jewish. At Szilard's request, he, Fermi, and Einstein wrote a joint letter to President Roosevelt in October 1939, urging the president to provide the federal funds necessary to complete their nuclear research before Germany got an A-bomb. Roosevelt legally, but secretly, diverted a $5,000 initial grant from army and navy funds in 1940. After Pearl Harbor, nuclear research was better funded.

The secret Manhattan Project to develop an atomic bomb was organized on August 13, 1942. General Leslie R. Groves was named to head the program. The entire project employed more than 120,000 persons and cost about $2 billion during its lifetime, all of which was begun without Congressional knowledge. On December 2, 1942, at the University of Chicago, Enrico Fermi and other associates achieved controlled atomic fission in a laboratory. This confirmed the feasibility of an atomic bomb and provided renewed energy for the Manhattan Project to expand. Factories were then built to provide the raw nuclear material for the bomb. A complex built in Oak Ridge, Tennessee provided U-238, and another in Hanford, Washington provided plutonium.

General Groves appointed Dr. J. Robert Oppenheimer, from Berkeley, California, to manage the actual designing and building of the structure of the bomb. This work was carried on in Los Alamos, New Mexico. Although security was tight, a spy for the Russians named Klaus Fuchs did work there and apparently helped pass on secrets to the Soviet Union. During the research conducted at Los Alamos, scientists there discovered that plutonium, a by-product of the fission of U-238, was actually a more fissionable element than uranium. However, the uranium bomb was developed first. And such an atomic bomb was successfully exploded in the New Mexico desert on July 16, 1945. The nuclear age had been born.

After President Franklin Roosevelt's death on April 12, 1945, Vice-President Harry S. Truman assumed the American presidency. By July of that year, the war in Europe had been over for two months, and the war against Japan had all but officially ended. Allied leaders were anxious to end the war in the Pacific and were concerned about postwar issues as well. Thus, the heads of the major Allies met for their last World War II conference outside Berlin in the town of Potsdam, Germany from July 17 into early August. In addition to Truman, Churchill, and Stalin, Clement R. Attlee, who replaced Churchill as the new British prime minister during the Potsdam Conference, also attended. The Potsdam Declaration was issued on July 26, demanding that Japan surrender unconditionally or face "prompt and utter destruction." This was issued by Truman and Attlee since Stalin did not officially know about the existence of the atomic bomb; we now know, however, that he did know from spies about its existence even while he was attending the conference. The Soviets renewed their pledge to declare war on Japan in order to build more pressure for an unconditional surrender. The conferees also agreed on a plan for the occupation of Europe, although relations were deteriorating between Stalin and the Western leaders; the latter had never really trusted the communist dictator but had needed him to defeat Hitler.

In the meantime, President Truman and his advisors, led by Secretary of War Henry Stimson, were aware of the secret development and successful test of the A-bomb. These American leaders had begun discussions on the best way to force Japan to surrender. One option was to invade its home islands, but that was rejected because it was believed that too many casualties would be suffered by both Allied military personnel and Japanese civilians. One official estimate stated that an invasion of Japan would result in the loss of at least 1 million lives. Another option considered by the policymakers in Washington was to invite certain Japanese leaders to a remote Pacific island and explode an atomic bomb in order to demonstrate its great destructive power. The idea was that this might deter Japan from holding out any longer as they saw what a weapon like that could do to any of its cities. But the Americans had only two such bombs at the time. Furthermore, this

Hiroshima, after the Atomic Bomb, August 6, 1945. Credit: AP/Wide World Photos.

option was rejected on the grounds that they would look very foolish if the test happened to be a failure. Such an occurrence would surely result in prolonging the war. A third option would have been to impose a complete blockade around Japan and wait for it to run out of food and oil. But that was rejected largely because no one knew how long that would take, and there was fear that the Soviets might insist on a piece of occupation territory in Japan if the surrender was postponed for very long. Besides, the war was over in Europe, and Americans have never been very patient in foreign affairs. Therefore, the only other option readily available was to use the dreaded atomic bomb on one or more Japanese cities. The Truman administration adopted this latter option primarily on the grounds that it would shorten the war and save more lives than it would take.

On July 25, the day before the Potsdam Declaration demanded the unconditional surrender of Japan, President Truman ordered the atomic bomb used if Japan did not surrender before August 3. American air crews on Tinian Island in the Marianas had been getting ready for such a mission for weeks. Colonel Paul W. Tibbetts commanded the operation and had named his B-29 bomber the *Enola Gay* after his mother. When Japan had failed to surrender by the deadline, the word came that August 6 was to be the date for the dropping of the atomic bomb. The *Enola Gay*, along with an instrument plane and a plane equipped with cameras, took off from Tinian Island and headed for southern Japan at the appointed time. Three separate possible targets had already been selected—Hiroshima, Nagasaki, and Kokura—and the one with the best weather conditions early that morning would be the actual target. Thus, three weather planes had proceeded toward their separate destinations well ahead of the fateful B-29 and its two support aircraft.

When Colonel Tibbetts received the word that the skies over Hiroshima were clear, he headed for that city. About 8:15 a.m. on August 6, 1945, the *Enola Gay* dropped the atomic bomb on Hiroshima, a major industrial city in southern Japan. The bomb dropped on Hiroshima was as powerful as about 16,000 tons of TNT. Although estimates vary widely, somewhere between 60,000 and 80,000 people were killed in the blast. A blinding flash of light and a huge mushroom-shaped cloud combined to create a spectacular but deadly site. The force of the explosion created extremely hot winds which swept through the city with incredible speed and intensity. Many victims literally vaporized into nothingness, giving the eery feeling that this was something out of a science fiction story. Many survivors roamed the streets with skin peeling off their bodies. And many of those "fortunate" to survive all those effects began experiencing nausea and other similar symptons of a strange disease. Although scientists had not anticipated it, these people were suffering with radiation sickness, which took the lives of several thousand additional civilians over the next several years. Perhaps as many as 125,000–130,000 people altogether were killed as a result of the atomic bomb dropped on the city of Hiroshima.

The next day President Truman gave the appropriate military leaders the authority to drop another atomic weapon in the event that Japan did not surrender shortly. On August 9, the Soviet Union kept its pledge and declared war on Japan, moving troops across the border into Mongolia and Manchuria. The Japanese government still refused to surrender. Actually, her communications system had been demolished by conventional bombing by this time, and there had not been time enough to assess what had happened at Hiroshima. Nevertheless, a second atomic bomb (this one was a plutonium A-bomb) was dropped on the port city of Nagasaki in the late morning hours of August 9, the same day the Soviets declared war on Japan. This plutonium bomb had the equivalent potency of at least 20,000 tons of TNT, and it killed approximately 60,000 people.

In the days that followed the Nagasaki bomb, negotiations between representatives of Emperor Hirohito and President Truman occurred over the treatment of the emperor and his family. Sensing that a small degree of continuity might make the task of an occupation government easier, Truman agreed not to depose Hirohito or prosecute him or any members of his family. Hirohito was to remain the Japanese emperor, but only with the title; even he would be subject to the Allied Supreme Commander in Japan, Douglas MacArthur. Secretary of State James F. Byrnes vehemently objected to the agreement on the grounds that Hirohito had been partly responsible for the atrocities committed by Japanese troops in China and elsewhere and for the cruel treatment afforded American prisoners of war in Japanese prison camps. But the president overruled Byrnes, and the agreement was finalized. Emperor Hirohito addressed his nation by radio on August 14 and announced the Japanese surrender.

The formal surrender ceremony occurred on board the *U.S.S. Missouri* in Tokyo Bay on September 2. General Douglas MacArthur personally accepted the surrender. Therefore, September 2, 1945 became known as V-J Day (Victory over Japan Day). And World War II was officially over.

AFTERMATH OF THE WAR

The Holocaust

The single greatest tragedy of World War II was the intentional mass slaughter of several million civilians by Nazi Germany. Hitler and his henchmen were filled with hate toward those groups that did not conform to their racial theories. Influenced by a new strain of racism that had developed in Europe in the late nineteenth century (See Chapter Five for more information on this new racism), Hitler's Nazis placed the so-called Aryan race, representing Germanic peoples, at the top of the racial hierarchy. These northern and western European peoples were considered by Hitler to be the "master race," which deserved to dominate all others on the planet.

The Nazi goal was to perfect the "master race" through controlled breeding. It did so by attempting to use forced sterilization of "undesirables" and by using SS officers to impregnate hundreds of women in the search for a purer Aryan race. Women selected for this purpose were treated as baby factories whose children were then raised by the state.

Nazi philosophy and propaganda placed the Jews on the bottom of the racial hierarchy. The Jews, Hitler said, had been responsible for just about all of Europe's major problems; thus the Jews were the world's scapegoats. Feeding on the historical anti-semitic feelings all over Europe (Russia has the worst record of anti-semitism), Hitler determined that the Jews must be exterminated as one would exterminate vermin. This annihilation of the Jewish race represented his "final solution." Hitler didn't view the Slavic peoples of eastern Europe and Russia as much better than the Jews. And even Germans with physical defects (such as hearing loss, blindness, and other maladies) became targets of the Third Reich. Many were executed while others were sent to forced labor camps. But it was the Jewish people for whom Nazi racial policies reserved their greatest wrath.

The first reports of Nazi extermination camps circulated outside the Third Reich in early 1942, shortly after the United States had entered the war. But many Americans remembered that western propaganda during the Great War had been infamous for exaggerating stories about German atrocities. In addition to this, anti-semitism was quite strong in the United States as well. Furthermore, these reports were simply too horrible for most people to believe. Thus, there was no significant outbreak of concern in the United States or elsewhere.

It was late November 1942 before the State Department officially admitted that stories about Nazi concentration camps were true. By that time, Hitler's "final solution" had carried out the execution of approximately 2.5 million Jews. Still the American reaction was woefully inadequate. Finally, in early 1944 President Roosevelt created the War Refugee Board to help in the rescue and relocation of condemned Jews and others. But the British government pressured the American policymakers to delay the full implementation of this board's activities in order to appease their Arab allies, who did not want European Jews relocated to Palestine.

Jewish prisoners in a Nazi concentration camp. Credit: U.S. Army.

Also, Americans did not want large numbers of Jews coming to the United States. Even most American Jewish leaders were strangely quiet because they wanted to avoid stirring things up and creating a backlash wave of anti-semitism. Nevertheless, the War Refugee Board did manage to save about 200,000 Jews and 20,000 others from Nazi atrocities.

Even late in the war, the Allies declined to bomb the rail lines going into Auschwitz (Poland), the largest of all the Nazi death camps. They calculated that more civilian lives could be saved in the long run by bombing strictly military and industrial targets and thus shortening the war. After the war, and the extent of Nazi horrors had been revealed, many people criticized this decision. Although estimates vary widely, it is generally recognized that approximately 6 million Jews and anywhere from 1–4 million others were murdered by SS firing squads and concentration camp gas chambers during the reign of Nazi terror.

Allied Military Occupations

About a month after the surrender of Germany, it was divided among the major Allies into four occupation zones. The American zone lay in the southern part of the country; the French occupied the southwestern region; the British zone of occupation lay in the northwestern area; and the eastern part of the country made up the Soviet zone. As earlier agreed by the Allies, the historic capital of Berlin was also divided into four occupation zones, with the Soviets in the eastern portion and the other powers in the western part of the city. Thus, the Soviet zone there became known as East Berlin, and the other zones combined made up West Berlin. The purposes of the Allied occupation of Germany were to ensure the demilitarization of that nation, maintain law and order, and provide for a smooth transition to civilian government. General Lucius D. Clay served as the military governor of the American zone.

While the Soviets increased their control over the eastern zone of the country, the American, British, and French officials slowly allowed for an increasing role by the Germans themselves in their respective zones. Finally, the three western zones were combined to create the Federal Republic of Germany in 1949, with Bonn as its national capital. The Soviets eventually established the German Democratic Republic, with East Berlin serving as its capital. The two separate nations became better known as West Germany and East Germany, respectively. In order to protect West Berlin, the Americans, British, and French maintained the military occupation of that city throughout the remainder of the Cold War.

The Allies also occupied Italy and the former Nazi-dominated Axis nations in eastern Europe. The occupation in most of these areas did not last long, however, because peace treaties were signed with them in 1947, although the Soviets then refused to leave. (There was no such problem in Italy.) There was no official peace treaty with Germany because events led to the separation of that country into two different nations. Austria was divided into the same four occupation zones that Germany was after the war. But in 1955 the four major Allies signed a peace treaty with Austria, granting it complete independence but forbidding political union with Germany (just as the Treaty of Versailles had done after World War I).

In Japan's case the Allies had created a commission, headquartered in Washington, D.C., consisting of representatives from thirteen Allied nations, including the United States, Britain, France, and the Soviet Union. This commission was charged with directing the military occupation of Japan. Because the war against Japan ended before the Soviets could effectively enter the war on that front the United States was able to exclude Soviet troops from the occupation forces, and Japan was not divided into various Allied zones. With General Douglas MacArthur as the military and political ruler of Japan, the great majority of Allied occupation troops were American. (Several British Commonwealth nations sent a minimal number of forces.) As with Germany, the major goals of occupation included the demilitarization of the country and the transition to democracy in Japan.

In 1951 a peace treaty between Japan and forty-nine Allied nations was signed in San Francisco, California. The treaty ended military occupation there, although a later treaty did provide for the long term maintenance of American forces and bases. The Soviets were unhappy with certain elements of the 1951 treaty and therefore refused to sign it. Five years later, in 1956, the Soviet Union signed a separate peace treaty with Japan.

Casualty Statistics

The devastation of war is more than the sum total of the numbers of people killed and wounded. It is the story of human beings, with hopes and dreams, whose lives are shattered and changed forever. And World War II, fought on a truly global scale, affected more ordinary lives than any other war has done before or since. The Second World War was clearly the most devastating military conflict in human history.

On the other hand, casualty numbers can at least provide some picture of the extent of the disaster. Perhaps just having the mind jolted with huge numbers can pierce the human consciousness and tell something about the bloody tragedy. The following table gives estimates of those numbers of military personnel killed and wounded on both sides of the war (only major powers are included):

Allied Nations	Deaths	Wounded	Total Casualties
China	1.3 million	1.75 million	3.1 million
France	213,000	400,000	613,000
Great Britain	265,000	277,000	542,000
Soviet Union	11 million	Unknown	more than 11 million
United States	294,000	672,000	966,000

Axis Nations	Deaths	Wounded	Total Casualties
Germany	3.5 million	5 million	8.5 million
Italy	242,000	66,000	308,000
Japan	1.3 million	4 million	5.3 million

When the statistics from all of the nations involved in the war are added together, approximately 19 million military personnel and more than 20 million civilians were killed. The total number of war-related deaths during World War II, therefore, is close to 40 million. The war was truly a global catastrophe.

ADDITIONAL READINGS

Stephen E Ambros, *The Supreme Commander: The War Years of General Dwight D. Eisenhower* (1970). A popular account of the future president as military coordinator. Analyzes Eisenhower himself and the key decisions he made in coordinating the Allied forces and establishing a framework for world peace.

Allan Berube, *Coming Out Under Fire: The History of Gay Men and Women in World War Two* (1991). A study of government policy toward homosexuals during the war and the formation of a gay community in the military. Offers many insights into the new opportunities offered homosexuals through travel and varied companionship, and the effects of sanctions against them.

John Morton Blum, *V Was for Victory: Politics and American Culture during World War II* (1976). A colorful narration of American society and culture during wartime. Seeks to recreate the patriotic spirit that quelled potential conflict among diverse groups.

Paul Boyer, *By the Bomb's Early Light: American Thought and Culture at the Dawn of the Atomic Age* (1985). An analysis of the intellectual and cultural assumptions underlying the development of atomic weaponry. Examines the development in President Truman and others of a political logic that made use of atomic weapons against the Japanese inevitable.

Richard M. Dalfiume, *Desegregation of the U.S. Armed Forces: Fighting on Two Fronts, 1939–1953* (1969). Analyzes wartime race relations in the military. By examining both the official mechanisms for ending discrimination in the armed forces and the patterns of racism that remained, Dalfiume reveals how changing attitudes from the top ran up against old assumptions among enlisted men and women.

Roger Daniels, *Concentration Camps USA: Japanese Americans and World War II* (1981). Perhaps the best account of Japanese American internment. Details the government internment programs, the experiences of detention and camp life, and the many long-run consequences of lost liberty.

Sherna Berger Gluck, *Rosie the Riveter Revisited: Women, the War, and Social Change* (1987). An oral history-based study of women workers during World War II. The subjects reveal the diverse experiences and attitudes of women workers, but also their common feelings of accomplishment.

Akira Iriye, *Power and Culture: The Japanese-American War, 1941–1945* (1981). Depicts the Pacific War from U. S. and Japanese perspectives. By showing the logic of both sides and analyzing a war rarely understood by the public, Iriye clarifies the military and political differences between the contesting powers.

Richard Polenberg, *War and Society: The United States; 1941–1945* (1972). An overview of the home front. A useful survey of many issues, from government labor policies to cramped consumerism to domestic political controversies.

Gordon Wright, *The Ordeal of Total War, 1939–1945* (1968). A standard account of the military mobilization. Gives a sense of the battles behind the war, the creation of firepower and supplies, and the vast casualties of actual warfare.

David S. Wyman, *The Abandonment of the Jews: America and the Holocaust 1941–1945* (1984). A detailed examiniation of U S. immigration policy and the American response to Hitler's program of genocide. Shows both the indifference of the Roosevelt administration to appeals for Allied protection of Jews, and the inclinations of leading American Jewish organizations to stress the future formation of a Jewish state above the protection of European Jewry.

CHAPTER THIRTEEN

The Cold War:
Korea and Vietnam

MAJOR EVENTS

1945   Yalta Conference
Vietnam declares independence from France

1946   Kennan's Containment policy recommendation
Churchill's "Iron Curtain" Speech

1947   The Truman Doctrine
The Marshall Plan

1948   Berlin Blockade and Airlift begins

1949   Creation of North Atlantic Treaty Organization (NATO)
Communists win Chinese Civil War
Soviet Union explodes its first atomic bomb

1950   Korean War begins
NSC #68 is adopted
U.S. begins support of France in Vietnam

1951   Truman fires MacArthur
Armistice talks begin in Korean War

1953   Armistice ends fighting in Korea

1954   French defeated at Dien Bien Phu
Geneva Accords signed
Creation of South East Asia Treaty Organization (SEATO)

1955   Republic of Vietnam created in the South

1956   Vietnam Elections Cancelled

1957   Vietcong begin guerrilla attacks in South Vietnam

1959   Ho Chi Minh Trail begins operating

1963   President Diem is assassinated in South Vietnam

1964   Tonkin Gulf Incident and Resolution

1965   Vietcong attack at Pleiku
Operation Rolling Thunder begins

1966   Declaration of Hawaii announced

1968   The Tet Offensive
The My Lai Massacre
Peace Talks begin in Paris to end Vietnam War

1969   The March Against Death anti-Vietnam War rally

1970   The Kent State University Tragedy

1973   Truce Ends U.S. Role in Vietnam

1975   Communists win the Vietnam War
Saigon is renamed Ho Chi Minh City

INTRODUCTION

The international crises that gripped the United States and the world soon after the end of World War II ushered in a new era that would dominate world politics for the next 45 years. It came to be called the Cold War, a term first made popular by American journalist Walter Lippman, because the two antagonists, the United States and the Soviet Union, fought no direct major military battles with each other. Instead, proxy troops, supported by the Soviets or the Central Intelligence Agency (CIA), were often used in attempts to take or defend a third party's territory. And although there were times when conflict between the two sides threatened direct military confrontation, the lack of a direct battle confrontation made the term Cold War a fairly accurate one. In addition, the United States Congress specifically authorized the use of American troops in the Korean and Vietnam wars.

The Cold War was not just a conflict of interest between two superpowers—the United States and the Soviet Union. It was an ideological conflict over the deeply philosophical issues of right versus wrong, good versus evil, and who possessed universal truth, from at least 1946 to 1991. (At the end of 1991 the Soviet Union officially ceased to exist.) The root word of "ideological" is "idea," which emphasizes the fact that philosophical perspectives were at the heart of the conflict. Because both sides in this ideological conflict pretended to answer life's ultimate questions, the Cold War can actually be referred to as a holy war. Communists would despise that term because they are officially atheistic, but communism is, in effect, a religion—a man-centered religion which proclaims mankind's eventual perfectability and a future millennium of peace and prosperity on earth. Thus, for many Americans, especially in the 1950s and 1960s, the Cold War represented a conflict between Christian America (and the West in general) and "godless communism."

ORIGINS OF THE COLD WAR

The Legacy of World War II

When World War II ended in Europe in May 1945, the Soviets had about 10 million troops occupying eastern Europe, in places such as Poland, eastern Germany (including Berlin), Czechoslovakia, Hungary, Romania, and Bulgaria; independent communist governments took over almost immediately in Yugoslavia and Albania.

One of the most important Allied conferences of the war occurred in February 1945 at Yalta, a resort city on the Black Sea in the Soviet Union. In the Yalta Conference, the Big Three—Roosevelt, Churchill, and Stalin—agreed, among other things, that the Soviets would give a reasonable time to end the chaos in eastern Europe; then they would allow for free elections and withdraw their occupation forces.

By the end of 1945, however, it was clear that the Soviets were not going to keep their Yalta agreements. Late in that year they forbade free elections in Poland, and Stalin called Poland "not only a question of honor for Russia, but one of life and death." President Harry S. Truman (FDR had died of a cerebral hemorrage on April 12, 1945) reacted quickly and harshly to the cancellation of elections in

"The Big Three" Roosevelt, Stalin, Churchill at the Yalta Conference, 1945. Credit: Franklin D. Roosevelt Library.

Poland, partly because of principle and partly because he knew there were about 6 million Polish-American voters in the United States.

Meanwhile, the Soviets began confiscating raw materials from occupied areas of eastern Europe and gradually forcing those countries to close their doors to the trade and influence of the West. Many Republicans charged Presidents Roosevelt and Truman with giving away Poland and the entire eastern portion of Europe, first at Yalta and then after the war. That, of course, was simply not true. The Soviet Union had been our ally in World War II. Indeed, without its struggle against Nazi forces on the eastern front, D-Day almost certainly would never have been successful. British Prime Minister Winston Churchill and American President Franklin D. Roosevelt both believed that they had made a pact with the devil when the Soviets became our ally, but they recognized that it was Hitler's invasion of the Soviet Union in 1941 which forced it into the war as an ally. Furthermore, they knew they had to have the Soviets in order to defeat Germany. With that reality, it was an obvious fact of geography that the Soviets were going to occupy eastern Europe as they pushed the Germans back toward Germany. The only hope was to get a realistic agreement, which most historians believe they did at Yalta, and then hope that world opinion would force the Soviets to keep it after the war.

By 1946 it was certainly clear that the Soviets were not going to keep the Yalta Agreement, and the Truman administration found itself in the uncomfortable position of choosing from three less-than-ideal policy choices. One option was for the United States to engage in a conventional war in eastern Europe in order to force the Soviets out. But several million battle-experienced troops would make that effort very doubtful. Perhaps the Soviets might even take all of Europe; or even a relative draw would solve nothing except the deaths of hundreds of thousands of more men on both sides. Besides, the American people have always been impatient about war. They had just won World War II, so Americans simply wanted to bring the boys home, and they would not have tolerated any renewal of fighting which was not entirely defensive in nature.

A second option called for the United States to drop one or more atomic bombs on Soviet cities because it still had a monopoly of the A-bomb. But that was rejected also. First, it was not perceived as a moral necessity to knock out an enemy by killing thousands of civilians, as had been done against Japan in 1945. And second, it was feared that the use of atomic weapons under these circumstances might be a terrible propaganda blunder which would make the Soviet Union look like the good guys and America like the bad guys, especially in the undeclared parts of the world (later to be called the Third World).

Third, the United States could vigorously protest and have a better-than-even chance of winning any propaganda war against the Soviets. Although the United Nations had been organized in the latter part of the war (its Charter had been signed in June 1945), it was powerless because the Soviet Union was a permanent member of the Security Council (of the UN) and could veto any action. Therefore, from a realist's perspective, the Truman administration probably did the only practical thing it could do when it accepted an unsatisfactory situation while protesting it in the court of world opinion. Like the famous Serenity Prayer, American policymakers were in a position of having to accept some things that it likely could not change.

Stalin's Tough Speech

In February 1946, Soviet communist dictator Joseph Stalin delivered a speech aimed at the West. In it Stalin asserted the incompatability of capitalism and communism and predicted the eventual downfall of capitalism. Of course, we now know that Stalin was not a prophet. He was right about the two systems being incompatible, but wrong about which one would triumph. But in early 1946, this tough speech continued the process of both sides hardening their positions in the developing Cold War.

Kennan's Containment Policy Recommendation

George Frost Kennan was a State Department officer who was also a student of Russian history and who had spent much of the war inside the Soviet Union. In late February 1946, shortly after Stalin's antagonistic speech toward the West,

George F. Kennan. Credit: Harris & Ewing.

Kennan sent a 16-page, 8,000-word policy recommendation paper to his superiors in Washington, D.C. In it he outlined a policy designed to contain the Soviets where they were in eastern Europe and to prevent further Soviet expansion toward the west. Kennan's recommendation included the employment of large numbers of Allied troops in western Europe as a deterrent. This was to be the vanguard of the containment policy. Such a recommendation ran counter to the prevailing mood of the American people, who viewed the war as over and were anxious to get back to civilian life and ways of thinking.

Although he made the term "containment policy" famous, Kennan's containment ideas were more limited in scope than the later American containment policy proved to be. Kennan declared that Russian history, not communist ideology, was the decisive factor in the Soviet betrayal of its Yalta agreements. Russia has had a long, bitter history of invasions by various enemies. Centuries ago this had led Czarist Russia to develop a foreign policy strategy of conquering neighboring lands along its borders and using them as buffer zones against enemy invasions. The communists, said Kennan, were simply continuing the policies of the Czars in this matter. And like the Czars, the Soviets viewed their aggression as essentially defensive in nature. His analysis of this postwar Soviet action did not attempt to justify it, but only to explain why they were refusing to leave eastern Europe.

Because Kennan's recommendation was based on Russian history rather than on communist ideology, it was limited to containing the Soviets in Europe; it was not a recommendation to embark on a global anti-communist crusade. The Kennan containment policy recommendation did eventually form the basis for American support of the North Atlantic Treaty Organization (NATO), the Allied military alliance that implemented such a containment policy in Europe.

The "Iron Curtain" Speech

The refusal of the Soviets to leave eastern Europe and allow democracy to be built or restored there was increasing tensions among administration personnel and other careful observers. Many anxious late nights were spent in policymaking rooms all over the nation's capital, with advice and counsel coming from all directions. One of those whose voice was more widely respected than most was Winston Churchill. Surprisingly, British Prime Minister Churchill had been turned out of office almost as soon as World War II had ended. Thus it was that as a private British citizen, Winston Churchill addressed the Soviet-West tensions in a speech at Westminster College in Fulton, Missouri, in early March 1946.

In an address that came to be called the "Iron Curtain" speech, the former British Prime Minister described the growing frustration of the West at Soviet intransigence. In the most famous line of his speech, Churchill declared that " . . . an iron curtain has descended across the continent." His reference to an "iron curtain" was a metaphor which represented the division of Europe into a communist eastern half and a democratic western half. He warned that this circumstance constituted a significant danger to the stability of Europe, a danger that warranted large peacetime military establishments that would deter further Soviet aggression. Churchill especially called for the United States, as the undisputed leader of the West, to re-arm itself in the light of this Soviet threat in Europe.

The Truman Doctrine

American Cold War policy developed gradually in the period after World War II. In 1947 the policy was beginning to take shape with the announcement by the president of the so-called Truman Doctrine. This new foreign policy pronouncement came in reaction to two specific crises, one in Greece and the other in Turkey.

Because of its strong navy, the British had been the chief force in driving out the Germans from Greece at the end of the war. During British occupation of that country, the British helped establish a new monarchy, who was naturally pro-British in its orientation. But the new conservative Greek monarchy angered many Greeks, who also objected to what they referred to as a British-imposed government. As a result, by 1947 a civil war had broken out which pitted conservative supporters of the monarchy against Greek partisans who opposed it. Most, but not all, of the partisans were Marxist in their political leanings. The Soviets were happy to provide military arms to assist the partisan rebels because they wanted access to the Mediterranean Sea and the Suez Canal, and Greece occupied a geographic

President Harry S. Truman speaking to the United Nations Conference in San Francisco, 1945. Credit: AP/Wide World Photos.

position which was vital to such access. Therefore, if the Soviets could help a Marxist revolt obtain political power there, they would undoubtedly gain the access so long desired.

The Second World War had almost completely ruined the economic and financial means of Britain, and by early 1947 it could no longer financially afford to stay in Greece and prop up the government. Therefore, in late February (1947), the British government appealed to the United States to assume the financial role that it could no longer continue.

The crisis in Turkey, meanwhile, was precipitated by Stalin's demand for control of the Bosporous Straits. Located near the Turkish city of Istanbul, the straits allowed for access to the Aegean Sea and thus, to the Mediterranean. In other words, both crises in Greece and Turkey were directly related to the Soviet desire to gain access to the Mediterranean Sea and ultimately the Suez Canal. But in late 1946 Stalin had backed down from his demand for control of the Bosporous Straits, and the severity of the Turkish crisis subsided somewhat.

After weighing the circumstances, President Harry S. Truman addressed the Congress on March 12, 1947, and requested $400 million in aid for Greece and Turkey combined. It was in his defense of the request that the president proclaimed his Truman Doctrine, which was that the United States should support democratic governments against external attack and internal subversion. Although it was not entirely clear how far this new foreign policy principle would be applied, events in subsequent years demonstrated that the new policy would be applied globally against communist threats. In other words, it was the Truman Doctrine which opened the proverbial can of worms by drawing the United States into involvement in the political turmoil, including civil wars, of several non-aligned nations around the world.

The reasons for this involved at least two assumptions implicitly made by the Truman administration. One was the idea that if a nation in a given region of the world fell to the communists, then ultimately most, if not all, the nations in that region would eventually fall under the communist umbrella as well. This concept was later given the name "domino theory" by the Eisenhower administration in the early 1950s. A second important assumption was that communists everywhere in the world were being directed by the Soviet communists in Moscow. This monolithic communist conspiracy thesis was erroneous, largely because the Chinese communists (who took over there in 1949) consistently failed to get along with the Soviets during the Cold War. Nevertheless, the assumptions were made and the dye was cast.

Congress agreed in essence with Truman's new foreign policy perspective, and in May it voted the requested aid. The Greek partisans were defeated shortly thereafter, although the more important factor in their defeat was undoubtedly the result of a falling out between Stalin and Yugoslavia's communist dictator Marshall Tito. Tito had made it clear to Moscow that he would be following an independent foreign policy and would not be tied to Soviet policies.

THE MARSHALL PLAN

The acceptance of the Truman Doctrine made it clear that the Cold War was definitely under way by 1947. While most of the American efforts to wage that war involved diplomacy and military strategies, a new proposal to counter potential communist growth in western Europe was unveiled in June 1947 by Secretary of State George C. Marshall. Known officially as the European Recovery Program (ERP), the Marshall Plan was a scheme to consolidate piecemeal relief measures for Europe into a comprehensive aid program which would help Europeans rebuild their war-torn economies, and thus reduce the appeal of communism there.

The Second World War had left much of the continent of Europe devastated. Many manufacturing plants had been targeted by Allied bombing raids, so there were relatively few jobs available. In some key cities, such as Hamburg and Dresden (both in Germany), there was little left of once thriving metropolitan centers. Water mains and damaged sewage systems rendered thousands of homes and other buildings unusable in wide areas of the continent. Tens of thousands of Europeans were left homeless, many of whom wandered from place to place, frantically looking for loved ones who had been displaced by the war. As a result of conditions, starvation and disease became rampant in some places. And, of course, morale was fairly low for countless people.

War Destruction in London. Credit: British-Combine.

Under these conditions, Marshall argued that communism might find itself attractive to desperate people, who are eager for immediate assistance with the necessities of life. He knew that very desperate people are more likely to believe a lie than those who are living in reasonable comfort. In this way, a potential danger existed that communism might win at the ballot box what it could not take by military force in western Europe. Therefore, the secretary of state called in non-ideological terms for a war to fight "hunger, disease, and chaos." Helping Europeans rebuild their infrastructure (bridges, public buildings, factories, water and sewage systems, roads, railroads, etc.) would help them rebuild their economies. And in this way the United States could greatly reduce the appeal of communism there and thus fight the Cold War partly through peaceful, humanitarian means.

More specifically, the United States government invited all nations in Europe to join the Marshall Plan by determining their infrastructure and industrial needs. Each participating nation would then negotiate with the United States over the details of its "wish list." When agreement was reached as to the raw materials needed, the United States government would purchase those raw materials from American suppliers and provide them at no cost to the participating nation. The stipulation agreed to was that all participating countries would use these construction materials to actually rebuild their own infrastructure and economy. In other words, the United States would provide the raw materials, but the Europeans would do the actual work of rebuilding. Credit was extended to participants in the plan to purchase American goods. The United States also provided cash grants in order to encourage more trade among the European nations.

While proposed in 1947, the Marshall Plan actually went into operation the next year (1948). Sixteen nations accepted the American offer and received materials worth approximately $17 billion over the next five years. By 1952, the industrial output of western European countries had returned to its 1939 pre-war levels. Although some Americans objected to taxpayers' dollars being used in a so-called "give-away" program, there is no question that the Marshall Plan was a great success. First, it helped stimulate our own economy and provide jobs for Americans who produced these basic materials for the federal government to purchase. And second, supporters of the program generally realized that a healthy European economy had always been a prerequisite to a healthy American economy. And in the long run, by helping Europe to rebuild more quickly, Americans reaped those indirect economic benefits sooner as well.

In addition to the economic benefits of the Marshall Plan, there were other important advantages also. By offering Marshall Plan assistance to any nation in Europe, including communist and others under the Soviet umbrella, the United States put itself in a "no-lose" diplomatic situation. If the Soviet Union allowed its satellite countries in eastern Europe to participate in the program, that would be a virtual admission that communism could not do the job itself. On the other hand, if the Soviets forbade its satellite countries there to participate in the aid program, then the Americans would appear to the rest of the world as the good guys who were offering their generosity even to their emerging diplomatic enemy. Either way the United States would win this round in the propaganda war for world public opinion. The Soviets opted to deny participation to the countries under their domination in eastern Europe, and the Americans indeed won broad support and respect in world opinion.

THE BERLIN BLOCKADE AND AIRLIFT

As agreed upon at the Yalta Conference near the end of World War II, the Allies had divided Germany into four occupation zones after the war (see Chapter Twelve). But the emerging Cold War had compelled the Americans, British, and French to gradually unite their occupation zones in the face of potential Soviet threats to western Europe. In February 1948 the Americans and British united their two zones in what became known as "Bizonia." And by June of that same year, the French added their zone to what then was called "Trizonia." This was quickly followed by the organizing of state governments within this "Trizonia" and the beginning of the election of delegates to a constitutional convention for the purpose of creating an independent West German government.

It had also been agreed at Yalta that the city of Berlin itself would be divided into four occupation zones after the war. What made the Berlin occupation especially sticky was that the city lay entirely within the Soviet zone in the eastern part of Germany. This meant that the American, British, and French had to be given access to West Berlin, where their occupation zones were located.

Both the Marshall Plan and the movement toward an independent government in West Germany made the Soviets quite nervous. An additional crisis finally precipitated a Soviet reaction that history would record as the Berlin Blockade. The crisis that tipped things over the edge concerned occupation currency, the money used inside Germany. All four Allied nations had agreed on the design of paper money in Germany during the postwar transition, and each had its own set of plates from which that money could be printed. But the Soviets used their plates to print too much money, and then went into the other zones to make large purchases of western goods which were either unavailable or of poor quality in the communist nations. This action threatened to ruin the entire German economy with runaway inflation.

The Berlin Blockade

When the Soviets refused to curtail this practice, the other Allies issued a new kind of occupation currency in April 1948 and announced limits on spending in each other's zones. When the Soviets refused to take the new money plates, the western Allies carried out their new currency plans unilaterally, which meant that the Soviets could buy nothing in the western zones. At this point, the Soviets issued their own occupation currency in the east, but unlike the western Allies, they also introduced it in their sector of Berlin. This led the western Allies to include West Berlin in their new currency. Before the month of April had ended, the Soviet Union reacted by restricting Allied access to West Berlin. Then, after the western Allies announced their intentions in early June to continue with the process of creating a West German government, the Soviets closed all access to West Berlin late that month. Road, railroad, and canal usage was completely cut off from western Germany into West Berlin. The purpose of this Berlin Blockade was to force the western Allies to either abandon the city of Berlin or their plans to create a separate country in western Germany.

The Berlin Airlift

The Truman administration was not willing to give up either Berlin or plans to establish a West Germany. Military options were discussed but rejected as potentially risking another major war in Europe. Instead, plans were drawn up that called for the resupplying of West Berlin by aircraft. Thus was born the Berlin Airlift. Beginning in late June (1948), American C-47 and C-54 cargo planes landed, one about every three minutes round the clock, until the end of the airlift in mid-May 1949—about 10 1/2 months. These planes shipped almost 5,000 tons of food, coal, and other supplies each day, or about 1.5 million total tons of supplies to assist the 2.2 million people living in West Berlin. So much of it was food that the entire Berlin Airlift became known as "Operation Vittles."

The Soviets were no more willing to risk war than the West, so they did not attempt to destroy any of the cargo planes. However, Soviet planes did harass American pilots by flying close to them. There were a number of plane crashes due to pilot fatigue, but no incident occurred to inflame the tensions into actual war.

In an interesting "aside," the American military commander in West Berlin managed to harass the Soviet commander in East Berlin by shutting off the gas line that ran through the American zone to the Soviet's own house. Then, when the Soviet commander attempted to move to another location, his furniture was confiscated as it passed through the American zone.

As suddenly as the Soviet shut-down had begun, the Berlin Blockade ended on May 12, 1949, after lengthy negotiations finally provided them with a face-saving way to end the blockade. Primarily, the Soviets agreed to end the blockade and re-

Berlin Airlift (1948–1949). Credit: U.S. Air Force Photo, Washington D.C.

open western access to West Berlin in exchange for the meeting of the foreign ministers in Paris to formally discuss the entire German situation, including the future of Berlin. That Paris meeting later proved ineffectual, but by then, of course, the Berlin Blockade had already ended. The Berlin Airlift had been an enormous success and had also demonstrated that the Soviets were willing to use civilians as pawns in its Cold War struggle with the West, a tactic which was used by the other side as well.

AFTERMATH OF THE BERLIN BLOCKADE CRISIS

Two German Nations Emerge

The Cold War had been heating up in recent months, and the Berlin Blockade itself had contributed to widespread fears in the west that the Soviet Union was a real threat to security and stability in western Europe. One result of this was to speed up the momentum for the creation of a separate West German government because of its location in central Europe.

The Signing of the North Atlantic Treaty, 1949. Credit: North Atlantic Treaty Organization.

Therefore, in May 1949, the same month that the Berlin Blockade was lifted, the western zones of Germany formally ratified a new constitution, and by the end of the year, the new Federal Republic of Germany (West Germany) was functioning as a nation. The Soviets retaliated at the end of May with the announcement of the German Democratic Republic (East Germany) in the Soviet occupation zone. Thus, two separate German countries existed until their reunification in October 1990 near the end of the Cold War.

North Atlantic Treaty Organization

Another result of the heating up of the Cold War in the late 1940s was the creation of the North Atlantic Treaty Organization (NATO) in April 1949. The Brussels Pact, signed in March 1948, had committed Britain, France, Belgium, Luxembourg, and the Netherlands (Holland) to a 50-year economic and diplomatic alliance. This agreement turned out to be a forerunner of an even more important alliance. The five nations of the Brussels Pact, along with seven others, signed the North Atlantic Treaty on April 4, 1949. The twelve original nations which signed this treaty were the five Brussels Pact countries, the United States, Canada, Iceland, Denmark, Norway, Italy, and Portugal. Greece and Turkey joined the Atlantic alliance in 1952, West Germany in 1955, and Spain in 1982. The Soviet Union eventually responded to NATO by creating its own eastern bloc military alliance known as the Warsaw Pact in 1955.

The North Atlantic Treaty provided that an attack on any member of NATO would be considered an attack on all member nations. Thus, it was a defensive military alliance. In September 1950 this alliance took steps to form a large defensive military force, of which American General Dwight D. Eisenhower was later selected to be its first military commander. And it was NATO forces that enforced the American containment policy in Europe that had been proposed by George F. Kennan earlier.

When the United States Senate ratified this treaty in July 1949, it was the first time in American history that the United States had entered into a peacetime military alliance with any European powers. This illustrated that traditional American attitudes of isolationism toward Europe had really come to an end, although a few Republicans led by Ohio Senator Robert A. Taft produced thirteen votes against the treaty.

OTHER COLD WAR CRISES IN 1949–1950

The Chinese Civil War

During much of the nineteenth century, China was dominated by European countries which had carved out large spheres of influence for themselves. Finally, the ineffective Manchu dynasty collapsed in 1911 from civil war. It was followed by a long series of equally ineffective governments in Peking (Beijing). In this power vacuum, a Nationalist People's Party government emerged under the leadership of Sun Yat-sen. He promised extensive reforms and modernization of his country. But the United States and other western nations refused to offer him any economic assistance. Thus, he turned to the relatively new communist regime in the Soviet Union, which sent advisors to help strengthen the Nationalist Party.

Sun Yat-sen died suddenly in 1925, and General Chiang Kai-shek emerged as the new Nationalist leader in China. In the 1926–1927 period, he ordered all the Soviet advisors to leave China and began the purging of his party from communist elements. During this time, the communist leader, Mao Tse-tung, broke away from the Nationalist Party and ruled a rebel government in the southern portion of China.

Chiang Kai-shek and Mao Tse-tung formed an alliance to fight the Japanese in World War II, but when the war ended, civil war was renewed. The United States initially tried to mediate between the two sides, but the emerging Cold War caused the Truman administration to abandon that policy in favor of open aid to Chiang Kai-shek. Between 1945 and 1949, the United States provided almost $3 billion in aid to Chiang's forces in the hope of preventing a communist victory in China. But American financial aid could not prop up an increasingly unpopular government. The Nationalist government was openly corrupt, and much of the aid money wound up in the pockets of Chiang, his wife, and other supporters. In some key respects,

Mao Tse-Tung. Credit: Thomas from SYGMA.

Chiang Kai-Shek. Credit: Black Star.

Chiang represented the old ways of imperial China. No amount of American insistence could get him to institute badly needed reforms in the part of China which he controlled. Life in the cities was deteriorating, and the peasants in the countryside and small villages were in desperate need of food and land reform to help them produce it.

Meanwhile, Mao Tse-tung appealed primarily to the rural peasants, which represented the majority of the Chinese population. He promised land reform, which indeed he did institute in areas under his control. Mao also dressed like his soldiers, ate with them, and slept in similar quarters. All these actions brought him greater popularity among the peasants. And it was certainly true in China that whoever won the hearts of the peasants would win control of China.

As the Communist forces in the late 1940s moved further south toward Nationalist areas, many of Chiang's troops mutinied and surrendered with little resistance. By the end of 1949, what was left of Chiang Kai-shek's army fled to the island of Formosa (Taiwan) off the coast of China. There he began a government in exile, later to be known as Nationalist China.

News of the communist victory in China in late 1949 was devastating to American policymakers and observers alike. The world's most populated nation had just fallen to communism. The relatively successful Cold War policies in Europe were not enough to comfort the Truman administration. Americans living in the western part of the United States were especially irritated because westerners had long argued that America's future lay in trade and diplomacy with China. Now those dreams seemed shattered. Many Republican leaders accused President Truman of giving China away to the communists. However, Mao won the Chinese Civil War because he appealed to the peasants, and Chiang Kai-shek had not. No amount of American aid, including military force, could have changed the outcome of that conflict. The communist victory in China only added to the president's political woes at home.

The Soviets Enter the Nuclear Age

About the same time that the communists were winning the Chinese civil war, President Truman announced in September (1949) that the Soviet Union had successfully exploded its first atomic bomb. This news, coupled with the defeat of the Nationalists in China, sent Americans reeling with disbelief. Anti-communist hysteria began to spread, especially as unfolding events proved that the Soviets had obtained some key nuclear information from spies who had worked in the Manhatten Project in New Mexico during the war. (See Chapter Fifteen for a discussion of this anti-communist hysteria.)

The news about the Soviet testing of the atomic bomb also forced President Truman to order the Atomic Energy Commission in January 1950 to embark full steam ahead toward the development of a hydrogen bomb, based on nuclear fission instead of fusion. There had been much debate in the scientific community about the viability and morality of building such an H-bomb. But the political climate, both at home and abroad, ended the debate. And in November 1952, the United States exploded its first H-bomb in the Marshall Islands of the Pacific Ocean. The explosion created a mile-long and 175-feet deep canyon on the ocean floor and sent a radioactive cloud about twenty-five miles into the atmosphere. Nine months later, in August 1953, the Soviet Union had successfully exploded its own first hydrogen bomb. The world had definitely entered the nuclear age in the post-World War II era.

NSC #68

President Truman's reputation had been so damaged by world events that he was politically compelled to make decisions that would escalate the Cold War tensions. In addition to the order to develop the hydrogen bomb, the president accepted a foreign policy recommendation in 1950 which would have far-reaching consequences for the next forty years. In early 1950 a thorough review of national defense policies was undertaken by a special blue-ribbon committee consisting of several top officials from both the Defense and State Departments. Written by Paul Nitze, National Security Council Study #68 (NSC #68) recommended to the president that the containment policy of George Kennan, based in Europe against the Soviets, be widened into a global containment policy to show resistance whenever and wherever communism was perceived as a threat. This proposal was based on the communist doctrine of a worldwide revolution and on the notion that communists everywhere took their orders from Moscow. Therefore, the study concluded further that the United States would have to maintain a large standing military force and levy higher federal taxes in order to increase its defense expenditures by about 400 percent.

The National Security Council accepted the proposals in April, but the administration was very nervous over the tax increases that would be necessary to implement it. The defense spending slated for 1950 was about $13 billion. But NSC #68 would mean huge tax increases in order to approach $40-$45 billion annually after that. These political doubts were ended by the necessity of having to respond militarily to the North Korean invasion of South Korea in late June 1950. Therefore, President Truman ordered the implementation of NSC #68 in 1950 because of the Korean War. The longrange significance of NSC #68 was that it formed part of the foundation for later American actions during the Cold War, including numerous interventions in the internal affairs and civil wars of other nations.

THE KOREAN WAR

Historical Background

Most of Korea is located on a peninsula that juts off the northeast coast of China (attached to Manchuria, more precisely). Because of its location, Korea has a long history of invasion by both the Chinese and the Japanese peoples especially. As a result of the Sino-Japanese War of 1894–1895, Japan gained control of Korea. Korea was officially annexed by Japan in 1911. A ruthless Japan ruled Korea until after World War II. In the middle of that war, Nationalist Chinese leader Chiang Kai-shek was invited to meet with American President Franklin D. Roosevelt and British Prime Minister Winston Churchill. The three leaders met in Cairo, Egypt in November 1943 and issued the Cairo Declaration, which among other things, promised a "free and independent" Korea in "due course" following an Allied victory in the war.

As the Second World War was winding down in August 1945, the United States proposed to the Soviets a temporary division of Korea into two occupation zones divided at the 38th parallel. American policymakers were afraid that Korea's close proximity to the far eastern regions of the Soviet Union might make it an easy victim of Soviet aggression on their way to joining the war against Japan. In what some American officials thought was a vain, if hopeful, attempt to prevent a Soviet domination of Korea, the proposal to the Soviet Union was quickly made. And to the surprise of many of these American officials, the Soviets accepted the proposal. Therefore, north of the 38th parallel became the Soviet zone of occupation, while the Americans occupied the peninsula south of that parallel.

After the war, of course, the developing Cold War made it abundantly clear that unification of the two occupation zones in order to create a "free and independent" Korea was not to be expected. Rhetoric on both sides intensified, and the United States and the Soviet Union could not agree on procedures designed to reunite Korea under one government. The Americans then referred the matter to the United Nations General Assembly, which established a commission in November 1947 to administer free elections in all of Korea sometime the next year. The Soviets refused to allow UN officials north of the 38th parallel, however, so elections were conducted only in the south (May 1948), where American-educated Syngman Rhee (age 73) was declared the winner in the presidential contest. In September 1948, Kim Il-sung was announced as the president of the People's Republic of

Korea (North Korea). Before the end of 1948 there were two separate governments on the Korean peninsula, and Soviet occupation troops had left the region. American occupation forces left in June 1949.

In January 1950 both General Douglas MacArthur and Secretary of State Dean Acheson made statements that led others to believe that both Korea and Taiwan were no longer part of the American defense perimeter in the western Pacific. Coupled with the fact that North Korea had developed a much stronger military force than the South Koreans, the inadvertant omission of Korea from the American defense perimeter seemed to encourage North Korean leaders to believe they could unite all Korea under their rule.

The Korean War Begins

On June 25, 1950 (June 24 in Washington, D.C.), the North Koreans suddenly, and without warning, crossed south of the 38th parallel and began a full-scale invasion of South Korea. President Truman responded to the news of the invasion by declaring that "Korea is the Greece of the Far East." By this he meant that the Soviet Union was behind the effort to destabilize the Korean peninsula just as it had earlier helped destabilize Greece. In another parallel, Korea was the first real shooting war of the Cold War in East Asia just as Greece had been the first real hot spot of the Cold War on the continent of Europe. Despite the president's strong feelings, the Soviets appeared to be as surprised as everyone else at events in Korea.

The "Munich syndrome" now dominated American foreign policy thinking. This was the fear that a policy of not challenging aggression was an appeasement policy which would prove just as disastrous for world peace as did British and French appeasement of Hitler at Munich in September 1938. And, of course, President Truman could not afford politically to do anything other than respond quickly and furiously to the crisis in Korea. Red China had been intolerable to most Americans; prospects of a Red Korea only added to the anguish. Therefore, Truman declared that failure to stop this aggression would only encourage efforts by communists "to override nations closer to our own shores."

Bypassing Congress, the Truman administration immediately asked the United Nations Security Council to become involved. The afternoon after the attack—June 25 (Washington time)—the UN Security Council voted unanimously to demand that North Korea end its "breach of peace" and withdraw to the north of the 38th parallel. Under UN Security Council rules, any one of the five permanent member nations there can veto a resolution and prevent it from going into effect. The Soviets certainly would have defended its ally, but ironically they were boycotting the Security Council to protest the failure of the United Nations to replace Nationalist China with Red China as one of the five permanent members on that body. Then when Yugoslavia abstained, the Security Council resolution passed 9-0.

After the North Koreans ignored the first Security Council resolution, the Council met again on June 27 and passed another resolution (Soviets still boycotting), this time authorizing the use of force by UN member nations to "repel the armed attack and to restore international peace and security in the area." President Truman immediately ordered American ground, naval, and air forces to Korea, with General Douglas MacArthur in command of the operation. Later, the

United Nations confirmed Truman's selection of MacArthur to take charge of the UN "police action." (The use of the term "police action" complied with UN language; Truman's use of the expression was therefore technically correct, although most Americans tended to scoff at him for this, for indeed it really was a war.)

A total of fourteen nations sent military units to Korea, and five others sent medical units only. During the Korean War, approximately 48 percent of all troops were Americans, about 43 percent were South Koreans, and the other approximate 9 percent were composed of troops from a dozen other countries. The predominance of American troops in a UN action, including the highest ranking military commander, with the American president acting as civilian commander-in-chief, set a precedent for later UN actions. It also left many Americans resentful of playing the lead role within the framework of what purported to be a world organization. And it also led to frequent American participation in wars in which Congress was never even asked to officially declare war, thereby tilting the balance of power since World War II even more to the presidency.

The First Phase of the War

Caught by surprise, the South Korean armed forces were repelled by the northern invasion. Despite American forces arriving early on after the invasion began, the combined forces were driven south to the port city of Pusan on the southeast coast of South Korea within a couple of months. Then in a surprise move on September 15 (1950), General MacArthur commanded a UN counterattack by sea, landing them on shore at Inchon, a port city near Seoul, South Korea (its capital). This Inchon Landing, as it was called, showed a flash of brilliance in Douglas MacArthur's military genius, for at the same time, UN forces broke out of Pusan and began pushing northward. This surprise combination move forced the North Koreans to quickly reevaluate their situation. Now they were in danger of having the bulk of their armies trapped in a large circle. The North Koreans began fleeing north and were even pushed north of the 38th parallel.

The Korean War might have ended in the fall of 1950. However, the quick success of the UN, and prospects of totally defeating the North Koreans and fulfilling the promise to unify all of Korea, led the Truman administration to change the rules in the middle of the contest. Therefore, on September 27, President Truman yielded to MacArthur's request and granted him permission to chase North Korean soldiers across the 38th parallel and toward the Yalu River, which formed the border between North Korea and Red China. (George Kennan objected strenuously, by the way, to an action that would widen the war.) MacArthur's troops crossed the 38th parallel by October 1; six days later, on October 7, the United States won UN General Assembly approval for this change in UN policy. (The Soviets had ended their boycott and vetoed such an attempt in the Security Council; that's why the Americans took the matter to the General Assembly, where no one nation could exercise a veto power.)

Meanwhile, the Red Chinese government of Mao Tse-tung threatened intervention on North Korea's behalf. Historically, they had rarely been on good terms with the Koreans, and that included the short history of the North Korean government. And his long experience in the Chinese Civil War had taught Mao that it was not a good idea to challenge a superior military force. However, the UN movement toward the Chinese border threatened to endanger his own credibility as the leader of the most populated nation on earth. Furthermore, this was an opportunity, albeit perhaps too soon after the communist victory in China, in which to establish Chinese dominance and stature in the Far East. And thus, the Chinese government was warning that it could not "stand idly by" and watch its border threatened. As a result of comments like this, President Truman flew to Wake Island in the Pacific for a conference with MacArthur on October 15. At the conference, MacArthur assured Truman that the Chinese would not intervene, but even if they did, "there would be the greatest slaughter."

On October 26, several thousand "Chinese volunteers" crossed the Yalu River and attacked the UN forces, halting their advance and driving them back. Then about one week later the Chinese troops disappeared back across the Chinese border. This action was meant to send a loud and clear message: keep the war confined to South Korea. But MacArthur ignored the message, and on November 24 he declared confidently that the UN troops would be "home by Christmas" as soon as they saw the Yalu River. Not only did this cause great anger among our allies in western Europe, but it absolutely infuriated the Chinese. Meanwhile, MacArthur divided his forces not far from the Chinese border among the mountains there, contrary to protests from several subordinate officers. Then on November 25, one day after MacArthur's statement about Christmas and the Yalu River, massive numbers of Red Chinese crossed the border in an invasion which totalled about 300,000 men. MacArthur's divided forces were caught off guard and were nearly wiped out. A remarkable fighting withdrawal prevented any UN military equipment from falling into the hands of the North Koreans or the Red Chinese. Nevertheless, the communists recaptured Seoul on January 4, 1951. Thanks in large measure to American General Matthew B. Ridgway, whose command of the Eighth Army resulted in a general regrouping of all UN forces just south of Seoul, by March 1951 the Korean War had been reduced to a slower pace, even almost to a stalemate situation.

"An Entirely New War"

The introduction of Chinese troops into the war brought about "an entirely new war," according to MacArthur. It certainly did that, as the war eventually settled down to a series of losing and retaking the same hills or mountains, for the most part. However, MacArthur had something else altogether in mind. He began insinuating that the failure of his own offensive inside North Korea was really the responsibility of the Truman administration. In some ways perhaps it was, for in retrospect, Truman certainly erred in agreeing to change the purpose for which the war was being fought. The difference between Truman and MacArthur, however, was that the president learned the lesson of his mistake and MacArthur did not. Instead, MacArthur not only publicly blamed the administration for his failure, but in declaring that it was "an entirely new war," the general urged that he be allowed to bomb Red Chinese bases in Manchuria (the Chinese province which bordered North Korea). He further argued for permission to blockade the entire Chinese coast, use Nationalist Chinese forces in Korea, encourage and support a National-

Korean War.

ist Chinese attack on the mainland of China, and forever separate Korea from Manchuria by placing large quantities of radioactive waste (the by-products of the atomic fission process) along the Chinese-Korean border. (Although not revealed until a few days after his death in 1964, we now know that privately MacArthur had requested the use of atomic bombs in North Korea.)

President Truman and several administration spokesmen countered that actions against Red China proper might push the Soviet Union into open military support in compliance with its defensive agreements with China. Furthermore, they argued, Nationalist Chinese forces under Chiang Kai-shek had already proven themselves ineffective, so encouraging them to attack the mainland would be the same as inviting the Nationalists to commit national suicide. The bottom line, said the president, was that the United States should not take such bold and foolish steps which would threaten to unleash another world war. Thus, President Truman rejected MacArthur's proposals, although that did not stop MacArthur from continuing to criticize the president publicly and repeatedly.

Instead of adopting MacArthur's tactics, Truman proposed a cease-fire in March 1951 in order to negotiate an end to the conflict. MacArthur wrecked all chance of a cease-fire at that time by crossing the 38th parallel again and demanding that the Chinese surrender unconditionally. At that point, Truman knew that MacArthur would have to be replaced. No American president could tolerate repeated and public criticism from a military commander. The Constitution had given ultimate control of the military to civilian authority when it had made the president the commander-in-chief of the nation's armed forces. Truman had been patient long enough. On April 5, while the president was waiting for advisors to finish gathering written documentation about MacArthur's public statements, House Minority Leader Congressman Joseph Martin (Massachusetts Republican) read a letter from MacArthur on the floor of the House. In it MacArthur once again criticized the president and declared that "there is no substitute for victory." After obtaining all the evidence and the unanimous support of the Joint Chiefs of Staff, President Harry S. Truman fired General Douglas MacArthur on April 11, 1951, and replaced him with General Matthew B. Ridgway.

The firing of Douglas MacArthur ignited a firestorm in the United States. Most Americans clearly sided with MacArthur and blamed Truman for the bad state of affairs in Korea. When the general returned to the United States that spring, for the first time since he had left in 1937, he came back to a hero's welcome. Addressing a joint session of Congress, MacArthur referred to himself when he repeated a line from an old song, " . . . old soldiers never die; they just fade away." And although he was seventy-one years of age at the time, MacArthur had no intention of simply fading away. He proceeded to receive ticker-tape parades and other accolades from prominent American cities and people. He even let it be known that he would like to have the Republican nomination for president in 1952. As some of his critics would say, "If that's fading away, let me fade away like that!"

The Truce Talks

In late June 1951 the Soviet ambassador to the United Nations proposed a cease-fire in Korea because indeed the war had been reduced to what some called a "meat-grinder" in the way it produced casualties, especially among the Chinese and North Koreans. So truce talks began on July 10, 1951 at Panmunjom, near the border between the two Koreas. But these talks bogged down over issues of prisoner exchanges and the insistence of the South Koreans on uniting all of Korea. Meanwhile the fighting continued.

During the 1952 presidential election campaign, Republican candidate Dwight D. Eisenhower, the World War II hero and former commander of UN forces in Europe, promised to go to Korea if he were elected. The implication was that he would energize the peace talks going on there. After his election victory (see Chapter Fifteen), Eisenhower did go to South Korea that December, where he fraternized with UN soldiers. And before his inauguration, Eisenhower had used private channels to warn the North Koreans and Red Chinese that if they did not agree to an immediate cease-fire, the United States might use some new means to force a peace. Was this a veiled reference to the use of atomic bombs? At least that appears to have been what Eisenhower wanted the enemy think he meant. Then in his Inauguration Address, the new president chose his words carefully and implied that Chiang Kai-shek was "unleashed" to attack Red China. Although this latter statement unnerved some allies in Europe, Secretary of State John Foster Dulles was sent there to calm their fears.

Then Joseph Stalin died in the Soviet Union in March 1953. His immediate successor, Georgi Malenkov, was a more moderate leader who was interested more

General Douglas MacArthur addresses Congress, 1951. Credit: Acme Photo.

in domestic problems than in foreign crises. This change in communist leadership in the Soviet Union probably accounts more for the success of peace talks that year than the blustering of the Eisenhower administration. In any event, peace talks got down to serious negotiating in July 1953, and on July 27 a truce was agreed to and the fighting in Korea ended. At that point, the UN line was generally just north of the 38th parallel. The terms of the truce included a demilitarized zone of about 2.5 miles along the border between the two sides and the creation of a neutral commission to supervise the voluntary return of prisoners of war. Most prisoners of war released by the UN forces simply vanished into South Korean society because they did not want to return to communist rule.

The Cost and Significance of the Korean War

There never was a peace treaty to officially end the Korean War; a more or less permanent truce existed throughout and even beyond the Cold War. And Korea, like Germany, remained divided during the same period also. The Korean War cost the United States about $15 billion and almost 138,000 casualties, which included

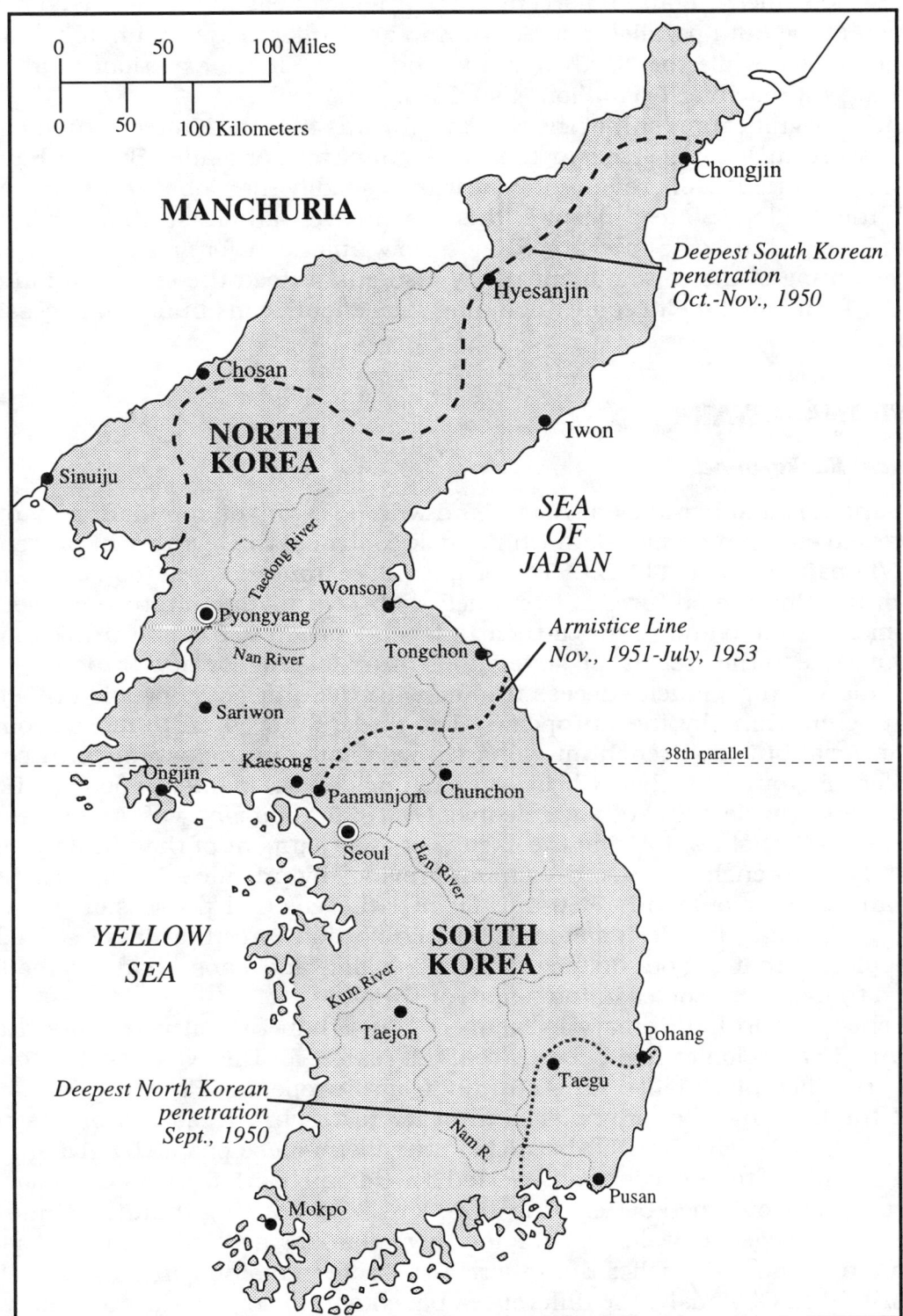

Map of the Korean War

about 34,000 killed. About 80 percent of the American casualties occurred in fighting north of the 38th parallel. The South Koreans suffered approximately 1 million total casualties, while the North Koreans and Red Chinese experienced a total of something approaching 1.5 million casualties.

A more significant result of the Korean War was that the United Nations gained some stature in lending itself to the anti-communist crusade. But perhaps the most significant effect of the Korean War was to solidify the global containment policy of the United States, despite the Eisenhower administration rhetoric of brinkmanship that some interpreted as a new American foreign policy direction. This cementing of the containment policy also guaranteed the continuation of the Cold War for a long time to come, including the general arms build-up necessary to wage it.

THE VIETNAM WAR

Historical Background

Vietnam is another ancient Asian land with a history of domination by others, and wars to end that domination. China took control of the territory of present-day North Vietnam in about 111 B.C. The people in the annexed area took on many aspects of the Chinese culture, but retained their own distinct culture as well. The Vietnamese revolted and regained their independence in 939 A.D. Europeans from Portugal came to the area in the sixteenth century looking for new trade areas. The traders did not have much success trading with the unfriendly people of Vietnam, called Cochin China by the Europeans. The traders moved on to more promising areas in Asia, but the French missionaries who came in the seventeenth century found fertile ground for their Christian teachings and remained, opening the way for the French traders and others to come. By 1800, thousands of Vietnamese had converted to Catholicism. Using the excuse of mistreatment of the missionaries, in the 1850s the French conquered Vietnam province by province. Neighboring Cambodia and Laos, along with Vietnam, formed the colonial possession known as French Indochina. (The designation of "Indochina" indicates that it is believed that the peoples of that region—in Vietnam, Cambodia, and Laos—had originally descended from either peoples in India and/or China.)

French rule in Indochina was far more cruel than British rule of its thirteen North American colonies had been. Part of the reason for this was that the Indochinese were different racially and culturally from Europeans. French rule often included the burning of entire villages in order to teach a lesson to others not to resist colonialism. The French also divided the Vietnamese people by giving preferential treatment to those who converted to Roman Catholicism. Catholic Vietnamese usually obtained better education, jobs, and housing than the Buddhists, and other privileges as well. Probably no more than 10 percent of the Vietnamese population became Catholic; the other 90 percent remained in their traditional Buddhist faith. Obviously, the differences based on religion produced deep resentments between the two groups. Resistance to this colonial domination was sporadic and on a small scale, but the Vietnamese had eventually overthrown the

Chinese and would overthrow the French as well. Americans should have paid attention to this history.

In the early years of 1900, the spirit of nationalism grew. In 1911, a young nationalist, known later as Ho Chi Minh, left his homeland for a trip to foreign lands that would impact heavily on the future of Vietnam. In 1920 Ho Chi Minh was one of the charter members of the French Communist Party. He continued his dedication to the independence of Vietnam, but he believed the economic and political aspects of communism were appealing ideas for government. He increased his knowledge of communism by going to the Soviet Union and working in the party. He would later accompany Soviets on a trip to visit with the communist party developing in China.

World War II and Vietnam

Following the bombing of Pearl Harbor, Japanese forces occupied all of Indochina and administered the colony through the offices of the French Vichy officials. The Vietminh, a nationalist-communist coalition, was organized in May 1941 by Ho Chi Minh to fight Japanese occupation and end French domination. Ho Chi Minh fought with the Allies, which included the French, because his limited knowledge of American history told him that they had been thirteen colonies of an imperial power and would understand his people's desire for independence. Ho Chi Minh also believed the Allies would win the war and that his assistance would help gain independence for Vietnam. What was most misunderstood about Ho Chi Minh by American policy makers was that he was always a nationalist first, and then a communist.

Small forces of Vietminh commandos led by Vo Nguyen Giap (later a commander in the North Vietnamese Army), and based in China, crossed into Vietnam and conducted raids against the Japanese. Because of action against the Japanese, the Vietminh received support from the American Office of Strategic Services (O.S.S.). In return, the Vietminh rescued downed American pilots and passed along intelligence concerning Japanese troop movements to the O.S.S. The expectations for the end of French rule at the conclusion of World War II were strengthened by the words in President Roosevelt's Atlantic Charter that spoke of the right of self-determination of all people, the broadcasts of the United State Office of War Information stating the American commitment to freedom for colonial people, and the support of the O.S.S. members in Vietnam.

Resisting the French

Not realizing that forces were at work behind the scenes for the French to regain power following the occupation of Indochina, Ho Chi Minh proceeded with the business of establishing an independent Vietnam. On September 2, 1945, the very day that the Japanese were formally surrendering to Douglas MacArthur in Tokyo Bay, Ho proclaimed the new Democratic Republic of Vietnam to be in existence with the words borrowed from Thomas Jefferson, "We hold these truths to be self-evident, that all men are created equal." American officers watched the celebrations, and American planes flew overhead. Believing the United States supported

President Ho Chi Minh. Credit: North Vietnamese Embassy.

the new nation, Ho asked for, but did not receive, aid for his struggling nation. The United States was not going to support an independent Vietnam and risk a rift in relations with France. In May 1945, Secretary of State Edward R. Stettinius reassured the French of American support for their goals in Indochina. Friendly relations with the French were necessary to fight the growing numbers of communists in western Europe. As the Cold War increased in intensity, the support of the communist Ho Chi Minh was unthinkable.

The forces of Ho Chi Minh held the northern part of Vietnam, but the French were steadily gaining control in the south. In 1946, an agreement was reached recognizing Vietnam as a "free state" within the French Union. But conflict developed when the French did not keep their agreement and began establishing a new regime in the south. French warships bombarded Haiphong Harbor, close to Hanoi, in November 1946. The Vietminh retaliated with attacks on French garrisons in Hanoi, and then withdrew to the outlying areas to begin the war to oust the French once and for all.

Truman and Eisenhower Support the French Against the Communists

The war in Vietnam grew more significant to the United States with the fall of China to communism in 1949 and then the attack from communist North Korea on South Korea in 1950. It appeared that the Cold War had come to Asia, and with it, the containment policy. The United States began to assist the French in their war with Ho Chi Minh to prevent a communist takeover. The war was no longer perceived as a local conflict with anticolonial or pro-national goals as so many conflicts around the globe were perceived, but an area of importance in the Cold War.

The United States recognized the government of Emperor Bao Dai, who had been reinstated by the French in June 1949, as the legitimate government of Vietnam. Anticipating the international recognition of Bao Dai, Ho Chi Minh requested recognition from China and the Soviet Union and received it in January 1950. These ties to communists was more proof to the American government of the Cold War implications of the war in Vietnam, and American vital interests. Ho Chi Minh was not the puppet of the Soviets and the Chinese, as Americans claimed. He merely used their support to fight his enemies. In May 1950, the Truman administration sent its first significant financial aid to support the French effort in Vietnam. Then on June 27 of the same year, just after the outbreak of the Korean War, thirty-five American military advisors were sent to assist the French forces in Vietnam. By the end of that year, the United States had sent close to $150 million to assist the French efforts. A condition of the aid was an agreement for more autonomy for Vietnam. American leaders did not ideologically support the colonial system, but attempts to send the aid to the government of Emperor Bao Dai to support that autonomy were thwarted by the French.

President Eisenhower increased assistance to the French to more than $1 billion by the end of 1954. This amounted to paying for close to 80 percent of the war and about one-third of all American foreign aid. The money was allocated for the direct support of French troops, to provide military equipment, and to provide economic and technical assistance. At a press conference in 1954, President Eisenhower added a new dimension to the struggle in Vietnam with his "Domino Theory." He compared the nations in Southeast Asia to a row of dominos. If one fell, the others would eventually topple one after another.

The Vietminh were winning the war by 1954, when the French asked the United States for troops to fight with them. Eisenhower rejected the request after consulting with Britain on the possibility of a joint venture to assist France and being turned down. Eisenhower also decided it was not a wise move to entangle the nation in another land war in Asia.

The Geneva Accords End the French Phase of the War in Vietnam

In spite of American military technology, the French controlled very small areas of Vietnam by 1953. The last major battle before the surrender of the French occurred on May 7, 1954, at the Battle of Dienbienphu (or Dien Bien Phu). The French hoped to lure the forces of Ho Chi Minh into the valley at Dienbienphu with the building of a fortress and defeat them with superior weapons. The Vietminh, under the command of General Giap came, but with much more sophisticated ar-

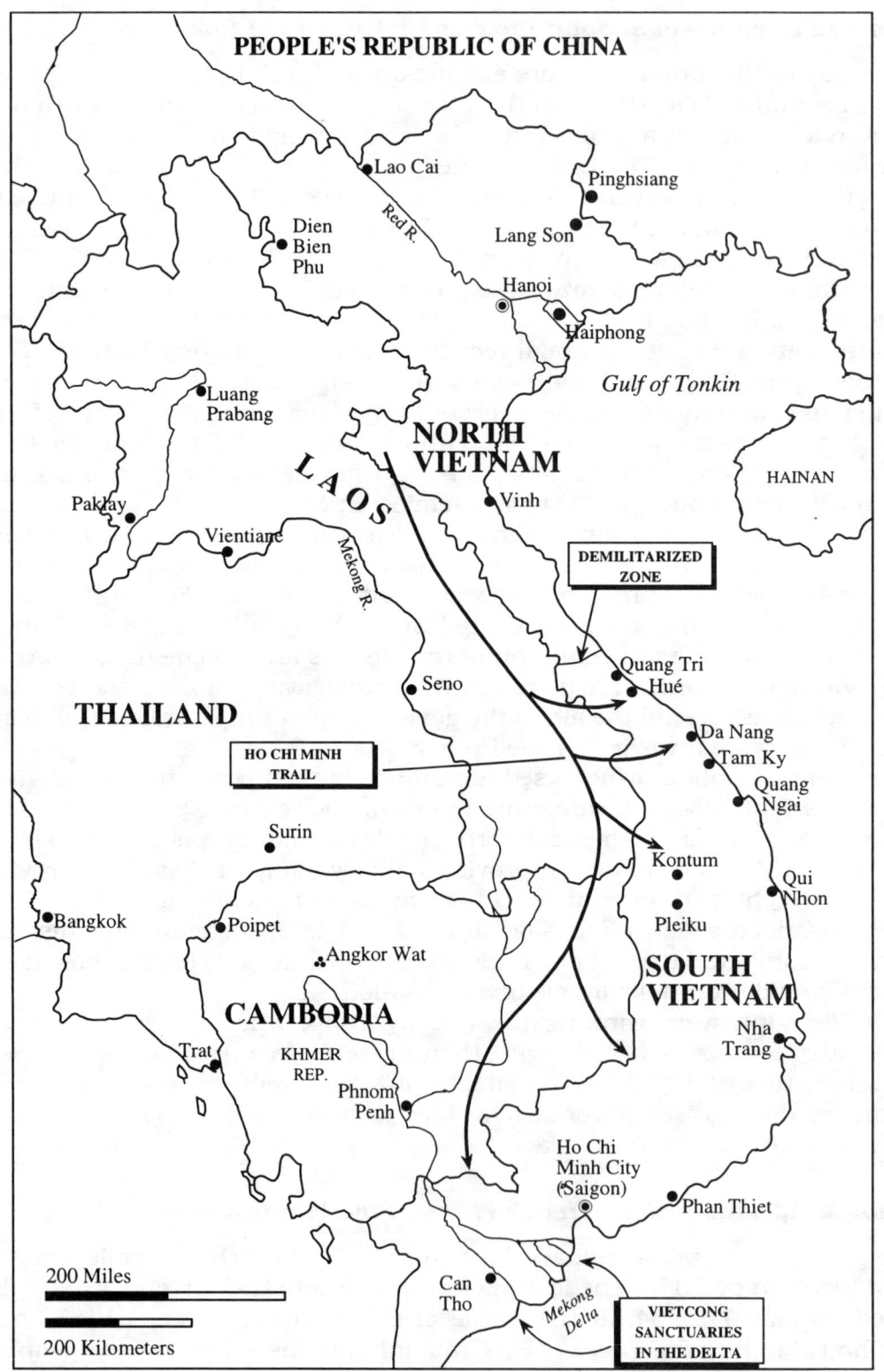

Map of the Vietnam War

tillery than expected and pounded the French into submission. Following this humiliating defeat, the French spent about six more weeks in the field.

Consideration of the conditions for peace took place at the Geneva Conference on May 8, 1954. The Final Declaration of the Geneva Accords (known also as the Geneva Agreement), negotiated that summer in Geneva, Switzerland, called for a truce in the fighting and declared Vietnam an independent nation to be temporarily divided at the 17th parallel into a northern zone and a southern zone until elections could be held in the summer of 1956 to determine the political future of a reunited Vietnam. A demilitarized zone of five kilometers would separate the two halves. The Vietminh would remove troops to the north of the parallel and the French to the south. The citizens could freely choose the area they wished to call home. This would give any Vietnamese allies of the French the opportunity to move south and be evacuated when the French troops finally left Vietnam altogether. Laos and Cambodia were declared neutral states. The United States sent representatives to Geneva but declined to sign the final agreement while promising to abide by the terms. The government of Bao Dai did not sign the agreement either.

The Creation of South Vietnam

On June 16, 1954, Bao Dai selected Ngo Dinh Diem as the premier of South Vietnam. (Actually, the French chose Diem following a suggestion from the Americans.) Diem had been living in the United States and was well known in certain political circles as very pro-American. Diem was Roman Catholic and welcomed the several hundred thousand Catholics coming to the south to escape a communist government. The United States navy assisted the migration south. Eisenhower sent a special envoy to Saigon with the promise of $100 million in aid for the new government in the south. The United States had now established its commitment to help build a new nation strong enough to resist the spread of communism from China and the Soviet Union through the actions of North Vietnam. The American commitment seemed to grow apace with the economic assistance. Between 1954 and 1959, the aid to this small but strategic interest in Asia was close to $2.3 billion. The United States would provide military equipment, the CIA, and American military advisors to train the Army of the Republic of Vietnam (ARVN) and its police forces. By the end of the Eisenhower administration in early 1961, there were approximately 700 military advisors in South Vietnam. Reforms were also suggested within South Vietnam to win the support of the people and build a democracy, although these American requests went largely unheeded.

In 1955, Diem quickly consolidated his power and called for presidential elections to be held. Widespread fraud at the polls gave Diem a 92.8 percent landslide victory and ended Bao Dai's administration. The new president proclaimed the existence of the Republic of Vietnam on October 26, 1955. With the approval of the United States, Diem refused to hold the 1956 elections guaranteed in the Geneva Accords. Neither country had signed the Accords, although it had been made clear that no interested nation would interfere with its implementation either. It was made very clear to President Eisenhower that in any fair election held in 1956, Ho Chi Minh would defeat any opponent (such as Bao Dai) and win an election with at least 80 percent of the vote. Even though the United States had historically de-

South Vietnamese President Ngo Dinh Diem.
Credit: AP/Wide World Photos.

clared itself in favor of the principle of self-determination for all peoples, such self-determination in this case would certainly have meant the election of a communist. For this reason, the Eisenhower administration, along with the South Vietnamese government, helped cancel the elections.

Diem promised political and economic reforms for his fellow countrymen after the United States urged him to give the people a reason to shun communism and support a government that improved their circumstances. However, promises for land reform, a priority for the Vietnamese peasant farmers, went mostly unfulfilled. Instead, Diem attempted to eliminate opposition in the various religious sects, and placed political opponents in reeducation camps. Buddhists faced increasing discrimination and repression of their religion. Long-standing local village governments were abolished, and some villages moved by order of the government to prevent their opposition of the policies of the government. Moving the villagers away from the graves of their ancestors was a cruel blow because many worshipped at the gravesites as part of their religion. Corruption and lavish spending was also part of the Diem government.

In 1957, dismayed by the actions of President Diem, guerrilla groups with communist and non-communist members formed and began attacking government forces in the beginnings of a civil war to overturn the Diem government. The guerrillas were soon known as the Vietcong. The Vietcong recruited soldiers for their cause with coercion and persuasion, and their numbers grew rapidly. They armed themselves with weapons captured from the government troops and obtained money through tribute payments forced upon villages they controlled, charging tolls on roadways, and selling guarantees from harm to merchants. By 1960 the Vietcong had organized a political unit known as the National Liberation Front to coordinate the efforts to overthrow the South Vietnamese government. The United States continued to support Diem, especially with this new communist threat, but it was also known that the support of the South Vietnamese was vital to the continuation of the government of Diem. The United States poured more money into South Vietnam, hoping to make the nation stronger.

The actions of the Vietcong caught North Vietnam by surprise. North Vietnam planned to unify all of Vietnam in compliance with the spirit of the Geneva Accords, but time was needed to build up the strength of their military and economy in order to carry out a new war. The success of the Vietcong, however, opened an early opportunity for defeating the South Vietnamese government. Ho Chi Minh began sending arms and military advisers down the Ho Chi Minh Trail in Laos to aid the Vietcong with their civil war in 1959.

Laos

Communist activity in Southeast Asia increased during the Kennedy administration. President Kennedy believed, as did those before him, that this was an area of confrontation in the global Cold War battle between democracy and communism. Kennedy had to face communist expansionism in Laos and Vietnam, as well as threats to Thailand from Laotian communist troops. An international conference meeting in Geneva agreed that peace in Laos stood a chance with a government of three leaders representing the positions previously supported in war by the United States, the Soviet Union, and the neutralists. Another Geneva Accord, signed by fourteen nations, guaranteed Laotian neutrality. But the factions were not satisfied with the leadership, and fighting broke out again in the summer of 1963.

President Kennedy and Vietnam

The number of North Vietnamese troops coming into the south to assist the Vietcong increased, while the determination of the South to resist diminished. Kennedy refused to abandon Diem, but he was pressuring the South Vietnamese government to institute political reform and land redistribution to win the people away from the communists while he was evaluating the form American assistance should take. In May 1961, Vice-President Lyndon Johnson was sent to South Vietnam on a fact-finding mission. Johnson recommended that American aid should continue in order to prevent the fall of the dominoes in Southeast Asia, but that American combat troops were not necessary. In Johnson's public pronouncements, he praised President Diem as the "Winston Churchill of Southeast Asia," but he was privately concerned with the leadership abilities of Diem. White House aide Walt Rostow and General Maxwell Taylor were sent to South Vietnam to reassess the situation in the summer following Johnson's visit. Their recommendation was to commit several thousand American combat troops to the South Vietnamese military.

President Kennedy was not willing to send in Americans as combat troops, but he was determined that the South Vietnamese should fight for the security of their country with indirect American assistance. Kennedy had been accused, along with other liberal Democrats, of being soft on communism. The accusation was never true about Kennedy, but its political implications led the young president to set about proving that they were not true. Thus, during the first eighteen months of his presidency, Kennedy increased the number of military advisors in South Vietnam to more than 16,000. Of course, the United States also provided military equipment, and other forms of assistance to South Vietnam. With so many American military advisers in such a small country, it became increasingly difficult, at the practical level, to tell where the line was between "advisors" and combat "troops." For example, eventually American advisors began accompanying ARVN units into battle, and American helicopter pilots were flying troops into battle. In 1963 alone, 489 American advisors were killed in combat situations. Kennedy also sent the Rangers to organize the mountain tribes to resist the communists, and supported the organization of Special Forces known as the Green Berets to fight in the guerilla wars that were increasing around the world.

In addition to military solutions to defeat the communists, the government began the "strategic hamlet" program. Villagers were moved to new fortified villages complete with barbed wire to protect the members of the villages from the Vietcong and to cut off the support of the villagers for the Vietcong. Secretary of State Dean Rusk supported Kennedy's commitment to containment in Asia. Secretary of Defense Robert S. McNamara also agreed with Kennedy and built up the military for the job.

President Diem is Assassinated

By 1963, what little support Diem had was eroding quickly. The Vietcong were gaining strength in their fight to overthrow the government with promises to the peasants of land, lower taxes, an end to the corruption in Vietnamese government with the elimination of Diem and his American friends, along with the threat of violence for not cooperating. There was criticism from all elements of society concerning the corruption in the government in the South. The Buddhists were protesting the repression of the government. When the government cracked down harder on the vocal Buddhist monks, some sat down on the sidewalks of Saigon and set themselves on fire. The situation was out of control in the South, and Diem seemed incapable of holding his country together to win the war. The United States had more than 16,000 advisors in the country at this time, and although reports to the American public claimed the communists were being successfully resisted, this was not the truth.

By this time, Kennedy agreed with others who believed Diem must be removed. The American ambassador, Henry Cabot Lodge, was advised that the American government would not oppose a change in leadership. Clandestine meetings between CIA agents and enemies of Diem within the military resulted in a coup on November 1, 1963. Diem and his brother Ngo Dinh Nhu, his cohort in power and corruption, were caught hiding in a Catholic church and shot shortly after their capture. With Diem out of the way, it was hoped that a new government, with the assistance of the United States, could once and for all end the civil war.

Within three weeks of Diem's assassination, Kennedy would be dead, and the war would be in the hands of President Lyndon Johnson. Many believed that Kennedy was pulling out of Vietnam because of his orders to bring home 1,000 thousand advisors by December 1963. However, his commitment seemed to remain strong to the new nation, as indicated by his words spoken on September 2, 1963: "In the final analysis, it is their war. . . . All we can do is help, and we are making it very clear. But I don't agree with those who say we should withdraw. That would be a great mistake." But it cannot be predicted with certainty what the president

Buddhist Monk setting himself afire to protest alleged persecution of Buddhists by the Vietnamese government, Saigon 1963. Credit: AP/Wide World Photos.

would have done in Vietnam had he lived beyond the year. However, Kennedy's Secretary of Defense Robert S. McNamara, in his 1995 book *In Retrospect: The Tragedy and Lessons of Vietnam*, stated his belief that "had President Kennedy lived, he would have pulled us out of Vietnam."

President Johnson Acquires the War in South Vietnam

With regard to Vietnam, President Johnson continued the policies of his slain predecessor in 1963 and 1964. But without the knowledge and understanding of international affairs that Kennedy had, the new president tended to have policies in Vietnam that were not realistic. The situation in South Vietnam was not considered any more important at this time to Johnson than many other foreign policy matters, but the commitment to keep the new nation free from communism remained firm. The same advisors and cabinet members continued to formulate foreign policy. A series of new leaders in South Vietnam was not able to stop the guerilla activity, so Johnson increased the number of advisors and other non-combat personnel to around 22,000. Johnson brought his own prejudices and perspectives to the war. To Johnson the aggression of Ho Chi Minh was comparable to that of Hitler, and thus it could not be appeased. Appeasement would result in further aggression which would be a threat to the United States. Johnson also personalized the war, which Kennedy had not done. Losing would reflect on the president's personal courage as a male, and he strongly rejected the concept that he would be the first president to lose a war.

The Gulf of Tonkin Incident and Resolution

A war fought thousands of miles away was not a major issue to the American public until Barry Goldwater, the Republican presidential candidate in 1964, brought it into the spotlight. During the campaign, Goldwater criticized the Johnson administration for not winning in Vietnam. Defense Secretary Robert McNamara and others had prepared plans for the bombing of industrial targets in the North, and other targets, to force Ho Chi Minh to stop supplying the Vietcong, which it was believed would put an end to the conflict. In an election year, however, the president was not going to allow this escalation which could be politically damaging. While campaigning as the peace candidate who was "not going to send American boys nine or ten thousand miles away from home to do what Asian boys ought to be doing for themselves," Johnson was considering new options to bring to a successful conclusion the American presence in South Vietnam. Barry Goldwater was perceived as the war candidate with his references to increasing the military role and vague references suggesting that he might support the use of nuclear weapons.

Claiming to be the peace candidate, and yet smarting under the attacks of Goldwater that he might be weak when it came to fighting, Johnson increased his reputation as a strong and decisive leader in August 1964. On August 2, North Vietnamese torpedo boats appeared to be in pursuit of the American destroyer *Maddox*, sailing in the Gulf of Tonkin off the coast of North Vietnam. The *Maddox* fired on the boats, which retaliated with torpedoes that missed. Johnson warned North Vietnam that the United States would not tolerate their ships menacing American ships in international waters. What the president did not explain to the public was that the American ships sometimes went into North Vietnamese territorial waters, that the ships were frequently on electronic eavesdropping missions, and that the ships followed South Vietnamese ships en route to some of their attacks on the shores of the North that had been planned by American advisors. The *C. Turner Joy* was ordered to join the *Maddox* on patrol, and on the night of August 4, the ships believed they were both under attack, so they began firing into the night at the enemy.

In retaliation, Johnson ordered bombing raids in the North against ships and oil storage tanks, although some reports almost immediately after the raid claimed there had probably not been an attack by North Vietnamese vessels. (Two planes were shot down on the bombing raid. One of the pilots, Everett Alvarez, was captured and became the first American prisoner of war, or POW, in the Vietnam War.) The blips on the radar could not be explained with certainty, and there was no evidence the next day of wreckage from battle or hits on the American ships from the alleged battle. Johnson heard the reports of uncertainty, but there were still others who believed there had been an attack. For all Johnson knew he said, "the sailors could have been shooting at flying fish." Although National Security advisor Mc-George Bundy now claims that he urged the president to wait for confirmation as to what had happened in the gulf, Johnson was in no mood to wait. As far as he was concerned, the American vessels had been fired on by the North Vietnamese, and this is what he told Congress and the American people.

On August 7, Congress received a message from the president requesting the power "to take all necessary steps, including the use of armed force" to protect South Vietnam and American forces in any threatening situation. Congress passed the Gulf of Tonkin Resolution with overwhelming support. While the House of Representatives passed it unanimously, only two senators, Wayne Morse of Oregon and Ernest Gruening of Alaska, voted no. President Johnson now had a "blank check" to fight the war when the conditions were right. Johnson won the 1964 election, only partly because the American public admired the resolve of the president who used a show of strength in a situation where it appeared the United States was being pushed around by a negligible adversary. It would not be long until the provocation necessary to put into place plans for American bombing raids and combat troops would come. It was discovered later that the plans for the bombing raids and the resolution were drawn up before the incident in the Gulf of Tonkin, bringing later charges of deceit by the Johnson administration toward the people. McNamara later testified before committee hearings on the war that the public had been misled.

Johnson Escalates the War into an American Conflict

In December 1964, two Americans were killed and fifty-eight injured when a car bomb exploded close to the Brinks Hotel in Saigon. This hotel housed American military advisers. Senior military officials in Saigon called for retaliation against North Vietnam, but President Johnson was not prepared to take this step yet. By the end of January 1965, Johnson had decided that the bombing of North Vietnam was necessary. First he agreed to meet with the Soviet Premier Alexei Kosygin in an attempt to neutralize hostile feelings that would be directed toward the United States when action was taken against North Vietnam, a nation receiving assistance from the Soviets and Communist China.

Meanwhile, McGeorge Bundy, Special Assistant for National Security Affairs, was sent to South Vietnam in February to assess the situation. He notified the president that the political situation was grim. The very influential Buddhists were considering a policy of neutrality for South Vietnam and negotiations with the communists, and the government was unstable as usual. Then on February 7 (1965), the Vietcong attacked the American barracks at Pleiku. Eight Americans were killed and 126 were wounded. This was the provocation that President Johnson had awaited before pursuing stronger military action. American bombs fell on North Vietnam in retaliation. President Johnson claimed the United states wanted "no wider war," but in the next week other raids were carried out.

The efforts of Secretary General U Thant of the United Nations, the Soviets, and the French to organize meetings to negotiate an end to the hostilities were turned down by the United States, even with indications from North Vietnam of a willingness to discuss peace. President Johnson believed the South was too weak to negotiate for independence, and he would accept nothing less. In March, the president ordered bombing raids on targets to stop the flow of supplies from the North. This "Operation Rolling Thunder" developed into the sustained bombing of targets in North and South Vietnam until 1968, with very few gaps in the missions, to break the will of the North Vietnamese to fight and to bring them to the bargaining table.

In March 1965, marines were ordered to Da Nang to guard the American air base. And by May, the marines were on military "search and destroy" missions as combat troops. General William Westmoreland, the American commander in Vietnam, requested and received more troops. Close to 190,000 regular ground troops were in South Vietnam by the end of 1965, and then 380,000 by the end of 1966. Escalation of the war was under way. American troops were not the only foreign forces assisting South Vietnam. Troops were also sent from Australia, New Zealand, and South Korea.

The President did not ask Congress for a declaration of war because that would have meant the loss of funds to his Great Society (see Chapter Sixteen.) So he hid the costs of the war in the budget of the Defense Department, increased the number of young soldiers in Vietnam, and was not completely honest with the American public concerning the depth of commitment to stop the spread of communism. With the publication of *The Pentagon Papers* in June 1971 (see Chapter Seventeen), the public would have a clearer picture of all the facts of the decision-making process.

The Nature of the War

None of the American presidents who presided over the Vietnam War understood the will of the Vietcong and the North Vietnamese to fight to victory. Before 1965, Ho Chi Minh had warned his troops of the coming war with the United States. "It will be a war between an elephant and a tiger," he declared, "but the tiger will not stand still. He will leap upon the back of the elephant, tearing huge chunks from his side, and then he will leap back into the dark jungle. Slowly the elephant will bleed to death." Ho Chi Minh also declared that his side was willing to suffer ten times the number of enemy casulties in order to win the struggle for a united, independent Vietnam. And that is just about what they ended up doing by the time the war had ended.

The United States was not fighting a conventional war, for this was a guerilla war of hit-and-run tactics, hidden mines, booby traps, networks of underground tunnels for the enemy to travel through and hide in, not always knowing who the enemy was, and secret supply routes. Traditional bombing attacks would not close down the supply lines along the Ho Chi Minh Trail or hurt the Vietcong or North Vietnam enough to force a surrender. There were very few large-scale battles for the technologically superior American forces to use their weaponry and wipe out the enemy. Attrition of soldiers and weapons was also no more effective than it had been for the French. Pacification of rural areas was another tactic that was used and failed. The villages would be pacified, but when the American troops moved out, the Vietcong simply moved back in. Body count of the enemy dead became the method of determining success in this war. Therefore, despite the fact that by Feb-

Vietnam War. Credit: AP/Wide World Photos.

ruary 1969 the number of American troops reached the peak of 542,000, superior firepower and advanced military technology simply could not win this war.

Peacemaking

Along with the military efforts to successfully conclude the conflict, the administration continued offers for peace. In April 1965, President Johnson offered $1 billion in aid for Southeast Asia when South Vietnamese independence was recognized and the war was over. In January 1966, the president explained the American commitment to this small nation so far away by declaring that "a just nation cannot leave to the cruelties of its enemies a people who have staked their lives and independence on our solemn pledge." The bottom line was that containment had come to Asia. The president met with Premier Nguyen Ky of South Vietnam in February 1966 on the Hawaiian Islands, and both agreed to the "Declaration of Hawaii." The governments of both nations were dedicated to the defeat of the Vietcong, the end of social injustice in Vietnam, and the establishment of democracy. In response to American proposals for negotiation, the North refused to meet until the bombing ceased. Johnson's strategy of bombing the enemy into submission

Vinh Long, a city in South Vietnam, was destroyed during the Tet Offensive, 1968. Credit: AP/Wide World Photos.

was not working. By the end of 1967 the military estimated that close to 65 percent of South Vietnam was controlled by the South Vietnamese government. And in the same time period, the American public was told that victory was near.

The Tet Offensive

During the celebration of Tet, the Vietnamese New Year, the traditional cease-fire usually was observed. But on January 31, 1968, the first day of the new year, the cease-fire was broken, and for ten days approximately 80,000 North Vietnamese and Vietcong soldiers engaged in a series of coordinated attacks on cities and towns across South Vietnam, hitting American bases, and even managing to penetrate the American Embassy compound in Saigon. The Vietcong was prevented from entering the building, but the fact that an attack on the grounds was successful at all compromised the truth of the "we are winning" statements of the military and the administration. The enemy suffered heavy casualties when their offensive was pushed back within a few weeks, and the Tet Offensive had definitely ended in a military failure for the Vietcong and their allies.

But while the Tet Offensive had been a military defeat for the Vietcong, it soon became a political victory. The story of the Tet Offensive, and the American reaction to it, dominated fifteen to twenty minutes of the half-hour evening newscasts on all the major networks for a few weeks. As a result of this coverage, most Americans realized that there was no place in Vietnam which was beyond the reach of the enemy. Not only then was the war not close to a victorious conclusion, but most Americans came to believe that the war in Vietnam was not winnable. Thus, the Tet Offensive represented a turning point in American public opinion, and therefore, a turning point in the war. Even Walter Cronkite, the CBS news reporter and anchorman, and one of the most trusted men in America, now turned from the belief that the United States could and should fight until victory to the acceptance that the war would probably end in a stalemate.

President Johnson had some difficult decisions to make shortly after the Tet Offensive. General Westmoreland requested an additional 200,000 troops, but others in the administration were advising turning the war over to the South Vietnamese and getting American soldiers out of Vietnam. Secretary of Defense Robert McNamara had resigned because he did not think the war could be won at an acceptable cost, and Clark Clifford assumed his office. Polls were indicating that a majority of Americans did not necessarily oppose the war in principle, but most did want to get out in some manner and not lose. A growing segment of the population began researching the origins of our involvement in Vietnam, decided we should never have been there, and demanded an immediate withdrawal. Although this viewpoint was clearly not representative of the majority in the country, it increasingly became a vocal and highly organized group. Still other Americans were undecided about the war. It was also an election year, and the president was damaged by poll results showing a decline of his popularity down to a 35 percent approval rating.

Meanwhile, protestors of the war were increasing in number and intensity. Early in the year, Minnesota Democratic Senator Eugene "Clean Gene" McCarthy challenged President Johnson for his party's nomination because of his opposition to the war and his demand for an immediate withdrawal. In the New Hampshire Democratic primary in March, the president pulled 48 percent of the vote compared to 42 percent for McCarthy, although the manner of selecting delegates allowed McCarthy to win twenty out of twenty-four. This unexpectedly strong showing by McCarthy, which was followed by a challenge from Senator Robert Kennedy, brought a somewhat surprising announcement from President Johnson in a March 31, 1968 television address: "I shall not seek, and I will not accept, the nomination of my party for another term as your president." In the same speech, the president also offered to stop the bombing north of the twentieth parallel in North Vietnam in exchange for the start of peace negotiations.

On May 10, 1968, peace talks did begin in Paris, and they would continue for five years. Interestingly, it took the negotiators several weeks of arguing about the shape of the table before they finally got down to the business of discussing peace. The Democratic candidate for president, Vice-President Hubert Humphrey, was too closely tied to the Johnson's Vietnam policies, and with talks moving slowly in Paris, lost to Richard Nixon. (See Chapter Sixteen for a more complete discussion of the 1968 election.)

Protesting the War

In the early days of the Americanization of the war, anti-war protests were fairly well confined to the academic community, students, and small numbers of pacifists and intellectuals. The first "teach in," a seminar discussing the war and American involvement, was held at the University of Michigan in March of 1965. In 1966 the protestors increased in numbers and participated in peace marches in cities across America, picketed the White House, and burned draft cards in public. The involvement of the college students in the anti-war efforts were natural because it was a war fought by very young men, but at the same time, confusing to many because college students in good standing until close to the end of the war received college deferments, and those drafted with college credits tended not to be placed in combat units. Thousands of those opposed to the war fled to Canada or were jailed for refusing to register or show up when drafted.

There was also a decrease in support from Congress. Senate Majority Leader Mike Mansfield spoke out against the bombings in 1966, and in 1967 a small group of Congressmen asked the president to stop the bombings. Hearings on the war were held by the Senate Foreign Relations Committee, chaired by William J. Fullbright, who quickly became a critic of American policy in Southeast Asia. By 1968, Johnson was reluctant to leave the grounds of the White House because of the constantly critical remarks. He could not, however, shut out the cries of demonstrators in front of the White House chanting, "Hey, hey, LBJ, how many kids did you kill today?"

The student protests had increased in violence as the war continued. At Columbia University, in June 1968, and at San Francisco State College in December 1968, the schools were closed because of rioting and destruction of property by anti-war students. Recruiters from the armed services were routinely picketed or assaulted. Most student demonstrations were peaceful, but the violence did escalate and, of course, stood out in the minds of most Americans.

President Nixon and Vietnam

The longer the war lasted, the more divided the nation became, until it seemed like a domestic war between the "hawks" and the "doves." When Nixon took office, American troop strength in South Vietnam was approximately 542,000, with the death rate at 30,000 and the cost of the war at more than $2 billion per month. The internal divisions at home were destroying the soldiers' will to wage war. With negotiations under way, it appeared certain that the war would not be a military victory, so soldiers were not wanting to take unnecessary risks. Racial tensions were high between black and white soldiers. The use of drugs was also a serious problem among the fighting units. And the "fragging" of officers, killing them (usually with grenades) by enlisted men, increased.

Talks continued in Paris, with National Security Advisor Henry Kissinger now a major negotiating agent for the United States. At the same time, Nixon instituted his program known as Vietnamization, turning the war over to the South Vietnamese while withdrawing American troops. It appeared that Nixon was keeping his campaign promise to bring "peace with honor." However, with his refusal (like

Anti-war protest. Credit: Tania D'Avignon.

Johnson's) to become the first president to lose a war, Nixon secretly widened the war so he could negotiate from a stronger military position and call it a victory. So in 1969 he widened the American war when he began secretly bombing communist bases and supply lines in neighboring neutral Cambodia. He even kept it secret from Congress until 1970. The communists had been fleeing across the border to escape the American soldiers, knowing they could not follow. A limited "incursion" into Cambodia by American and ARVN ground forces was authorized in April 1970, with the same purpose as the bombing missions. When the president notified the nation of the bombings and invasions of Cambodia, demonstrations erupted across the nation because many felt betrayed by the actions in Cambodia.

Protest of the War Continued

In the fall of 1969, protests across the nation were organized to pressure the Nixon administration to end the war. The "March Against Death," held in Washington, D.C. in November that year, was perhaps the most poignant of the messages to the nation about the brutality of the war. Almost 300,000 protestors walked through the streets of Washington to the Capitol Building with plaques bearing the

National Guard arriving at Kent State University during anti-war riots, 1970. Credit: UPI.

names of soldiers who had died in Vietnam. But President Nixon would not validate the concerns of the protestors, choosing to ignore them whenever he could.

Giving validity to the protestors' condemnation of the inhumanity of the war, and America's immorality in the slaughter, was the release of a story on November 13, 1969, of the murder of approximately 350 men, women, and children in the small village of My Lai. The My Lai Massacre was perpetrated by American soldiers on March 16, 1968, but the army had covered up the attack. But in November 1969, newspaper stories told about 100 American soldiers, who were not fired upon or in immediate danger from this village, beating old men, raping the women, and shooting babies in the head. Then, after massacring people, the soldiers killed the farm animals and burned the village and its crops. The army had pictures of the atrocities, so they charged twenty-five soldiers and officers with the murders and the attempt to cover it up. Only Lieutenant William Calley Jr. was convicted of any crime in connection with the massacre when in March 1971, he was convicted of premeditated murder and sentenced to life in prison. However, President Nixon personally intervened by reducing his sentence. As a result, Calley only spent three years under house arrest. In explanation of what it was like for soldiers in Vietnam, Calley related that it was all about "body count" of the enemy. Not being able to tell friend from foe, facing the deaths of friends from an enemy that hit and then ran away, many of the soldiers did not care if the body count was the enemy or the civilians they were there to protect from the communists. (For their part, the Vietcong and the North Vietnamese regularly committed atrocities to prevent cooperation with the South Vietnamese government.)

The revelation of the President on April 30, 1970, of a new area of war in Southeast Asia sparked off a new round of protests. As typical in the anti-war movement, college students led the way with protests which closed hundreds of classes on university campuses across the nation over the next few days. At Kent State University, in Ohio, the National Guard was called out to break up the student protests. A few of the students had gone so far as to fire-bomb the Reserve Officer Training Corps (ROTC) building. The young troops advancing on the taunting and stone-throwing students suddenly opened fire. Eleven students were wounded and four were killed. None of those killed were considered radicals, but had been caught in the wrong place at the wrong time; two were on their way to lunch. The soldiers apparently just panicked, but their actions were condemned by most in the anti-war movement. However, most Americans seemed to support the guardsmen in putting down unlawful and disorderly conduct and condemned the actions of the demonstrators instead.

The War Comes to an End

Peace talks continued, but in February 1970 Kissinger and the representative from North Vietnam, Le Duc Tho, moved to a secret meeting place to talk without the pressures from the press or the United States State Department. With the peace talks stalled and 120,000 North Vietnamese troops crossing the Demilitarized Zone on March 30, 1972, President Nixon had to face more tough strategy choices. If he did not assist the South Vietnamese, they might face complete defeat, for they were already retreating under the onslaught. Nixon had been pulling out American ground forces, so the assistance would have to come in the form of bombing raids, if at all. On the other hand, if the war escalated, a proposed summit with the Soviets might be threatened. In May, Nixon risked damaging relations with the Soviets and ordered a resumption of bombing attacks in the North. This decision also fit in with his concept that convincing the North Vietnamese that he was capable of anything, might produce a faster peace agreement. Toward this end, Nixon hoped to become known as the "mad bomber."

The bombing campaign, known as Linebacker I, targeted air bases, power stations, and railroad lines, sometimes close to Hanoi (the capital of North Vietnam). The government usually banned Hanoi as a target in an attempt to cut down on civilian casualties. Haiphong and other harbors in the North would be sewn with mines to prevent the delivery of supplies, including those from the Soviets. The North Vietnamese Army would have to stop its advance if their supplies were cut off. The Soviets did not cancel the summit to discuss the SALT treaty. (See Chapter Seventeen.) The new friendly relations between the United States and the Chinese were also threatening to the balance of power protecting Soviet interests. The troops from the North pulled back, and the peace talks went forward again.

Progress in the war was important to President Nixon's run for the presidency in 1972. Kissinger's announcement that "peace was at hand" in Vietnam on October 26 was a boost to the president's chances, which were already considered excellent. This statement was forced prematurely from Kissinger by North Vietnam going public with the terms of the peace arrangement and blaming the Americans for the delay. A problem with the peace agreement was the fact that President Thieu of South Vietnam refused to sign an agreement that left North Vietnamese troops in the South with the implementation of the cease-fire. Then the North began to back away from the October Agreements altogether. President Nixon assured Thieu that if Hanoi did not live up to the agreement, the United States would take action. His message to the North fell from the skies in the form of the Christmas bombing campaign from December 18 to 30, except for Christmas Day. There were around 120 B-52 strikes a day against military targets. It was important to prevent civilian casualties in order to quiet the protests back home that would arise from this action.

Finally, the North Vietnamese and President Thieu gave in to the pressure of Nixon, and on January 23, 1973, Nixon announced that a truce had been agreed upon in Paris. Four days later, on January 27, the settlement to end the war was signed by representatives from South Vietnam, the United States, North Vietnam, and the Vietcong. For their efforts, Kissinger and Le Duc Tho received the Nobel Peace Prize in 1973. Ironically, when President Nixon first announced to the world that a truce agreement had been reached (on January 23), former President Lyndon B. Johnson died of a heart attack on his Texas ranch. The Vietnam War had killed the former president politically, and his own physical death had coincided with its end.

The Peace Accords and the Communist Takeover

The terms of the peace agreement included the following major points: (1) a cease-fire (or truce) with all forces to remain in their same places and enforced by an international commission; (2) the removal of American military advisors and troops within 60 days (of which there were only about 27,000 left in the country); (3) the cessation of all military actions in Laos and Cambodia; (4) the return of approximately 500 American prisoners of war; and (5) a National Council of National Reconciliation and Concord, consisting of representatives from both sides, to meet in the future and coordinate national elections. To calm the fears of the South Vietnamese government, military and economic aid was guaranteed by the United States.

Fighting between the Vietnamese commenced soon after the peace was put into place, and the war dragged on for about two additional years. By April 1975, Saigon was close to defeat. The final picture of South Vietnam in the minds of many was of American helicopters loaded with Americans and South Vietnamese lifting off the rooftop of the American Embassy on April 30, 1975. America did not keep Nixon's promise to come to the aid of the South if the North threatened their independence again. In 1976, Vietnam was officially declared a united, independent nation, and Saigon was renamed Ho Chi Minh City, in honor of the nationalist-communist who had died in September 1969 without seeing his dream come true. Two decades after this ignoble end to America's longest war, Americans are back in Vietnam today, but this time as business investors and tourists rather than soldiers.

Results and Legacies of the War

The scars of this war ran deep among Americans. Close to three million Americans had participated in active service to keep South Vietnam free from communism, and yet it fell to communism. Many wondered what they had fought for. More

Last minute evacuation of authorized personnel and civilians from the U.S. Embassy. Credit: AP/Wide World Photos.

than 58,000 died from battle wounds, more than 300,000 were wounded in action, and around 2,500 were missing in action. The direct costs of the war for the United States was above $150 billion, and perhaps as high as $250 billion if all financial factors were included.

Soldiers returned with drug addictions and psychological troubles that would take years to resolve. About 700,000 documented cases of mental breakdowns occurred because of this war; that compared to about 500,000 document cases for World War II. The Vietnam veterans were not well-received when they returned home, and this added to the emotional scars among those young men and women. (The average age of the soldiers was about nineteen.) After all, they had only followed the orders of their government and put their lives on the line. The Vietnam veterans became the first group of veterans who would have to pressure for a monument to their war themselves. The American public wanted to put the long and divisive war behind them, and monuments were reminders of what many considered a mistake and an immoral war.

In Southeast Asia, the invasions into Cambodia destabilized the government further. Assistance from North Vietnam to the communists there, known as the Khmer Rouge, resulted in another victory for communism. In the efforts of the Khmer Rouge to dominate Cambodia, close to three million Cambodias died. Because of the attempted genocide by the victors there, Cambodia became known as the "killing fields." Then in 1979, the Vietnamese communists drove the Khmer Rouge from power.

The Vietnam War resulted in a loss of prestige for the United States, as allies wondered whether we would keep our commitments in the future, and third-world nations viewed us with even more suspicion because we had opposed Vietnam's independence and seemed to care very little about the number of human casualties. Right-wing anti-communist dictators also worried that the United States might not continue to support them as a result of the war in Vietnam.

The war produced a credibility gap between American citizens and their own government because of the lies and misinformation given by the Johnson and Nixon administrations. The presidency itself was weakened, and along with it, growing numbers of Americans became cynical about democratic institutions and their ability to govern themselves. This cynicism, and the massive opposition to the war, had played into Richard Nixon's own personality defects and encouraged him to take a siege mentality in the White House. This played a role in the Watergate scandal, the worst national scandal in American history, which in turn led to a serious crisis of confidence. Not all of this can be blamed on the Vietnam War, of course, but there is little doubt that the war played an important role in depressing the confidence and mood of the American people over the next several years.

The war also had a lasting affect on future foreign policy decisions. For most Americans, the lessons are split down ideological lines. For those in the liberal (or realist) school of thought, the country should not fight in future wars unless there is a clear threat to American security or some other vital national interest. Conservatives who supported the war do not believe the United States should enter wars unless a military victory is the goal (the nationalist school of thought). Many blamed the defeat on politicians limiting military commanders in what they could do to prosecute the war. It must be kept in mind, however, that the government had to consider the reaction of the Soviet Union, China, and other allies in its decisions to limit the military targets, as well as the level of acceptable destruction for the public. Furthermore, the nature of the war, which was contrary to American experiences, made it difficult for many to understand why an increased use of superior military force and technology could not defeat the enemy in such a small country. Some historians maintain that the United States really did not lose the Vietnam War because it did not often face the enemy in open combat. On the other hand, there are historians who maintain that because the enemy was not defeated, the United States lost the war.

The future presidents and Congress would be extremely reluctant to use American military power under any circumstances because of the fear of another Vietnam. As a direct consequence of the Vietnam War, Congress has passed one hundred fifty restrictions on the power of the president to send troops, weapons, and military support to foreign nations. Finally, there is close to unanimous concurrence by all groups that a lengthy war cannot be waged without the support of the American public. And while the war, and its lessons, are still argued to this day, perhaps billionare H. Ross Perot summed up the feeling of most citizens when he declared, "We must commit the nation before we commit the troops."

ADDITIONAL READINGS

Loren Baritz, *Backfire: A History of How American Culture Led Us Into Vietnam and Made Us Fight the Way We Did* (1985). A keen study of U.S. military policies and dissent within the military during the Vietnam War. Shows how decisions for aggressive military policies in Vietnam divided poorer young men from their middle- and upper-class counterparts by sending to war those who did not or could not manage deferments. Analyzes the increasing bitterness toward the government and the military by the men who fought the war.

Lloyd C. Gardner, *Architects of Illusion: Men and Ideas in American Foreign Policy, 1941–1949* (1970). Biographical vignettes with critical interpretation of the major figures of U.S. international policy. Faults their efforts to control world policy making for drawing the country into an arms race and a mutually destructive Cold War.

George C. Herring, *America's Longest War: The United States and Vietnam, 1950–1975* (2d ed., 1986). A narrative account, including a chapter on the legacy of the war. Attempts to demonstrate that diplomatic policy was based on flawed assumptions that made the war unwinnable at a moral or material cost most Americans could accept.

Joyce and Gabriel Kolko, *The Limits of Power: The World and United States Foreign Policy, 1945–1954* (1972). A detailed commentary on U.S. efforts to dictate world conditions. Shows that the complexities of world politics, especially the rise of colonized nations toward independence, placed control outside American hands.

Neil Sheehan, *A Bright Shining Lie: John Paul Vann and America in Vietnam* (1988). A study of U.S. government deception of the public, perpetrated with greater and greater intensity as the Vietnam War grew worse. Emphasizes the ways in which prowar messages played upon false images of a noble and committed South Vietnamese government and a military force always on the verge of defeating an unpopular enemy.

Daniel Yergin, *Shattered Peace: The Origins of the Cold War and the National Security State* (1977). Lucidly interprets the motives of the Americans and the Soviets that led to a full-scale arms race. Shows that each side misinterpreted the motives of the other and thereby lost the opportunity to attain world peace.

Marilyn B. Young, *The Vietnam Wars, 1945–1990* (1991). An excellent overview of French and American military and diplomatic involvement in Vietnam from the 1910s to 1975, and of the various movements against them. Highlights the nationalism of the Vietnamese as ultimately more powerful than the troops and weaponry of their opponents.

CHAPTER FOURTEEN

Social History: 1945–1970

MAJOR EVENTS

1946   Television sets become available to general public
The Common Sense Book of Baby and Child Care published (Dr. Benjamin Spock)

1947   Jackie Robinson joins the Brooklyn Dodgers

1948   *Shelly* v. *Kraemer* Supreme Court decision
Sexual Behavior in the Human Male published (Kinsey)

1952   *The Power of Positive Thinking* is published (Norman Vincent Peale)
TV Guide begins publication

1953   *Sexual Behavior in the Human Female* is published (Kinsey)

1954   *Brown* v. *Board of Education* Supreme Court decision
Sports Illustrated begins publication

1955   Montgomery Bus Boycott begins

1956   "Heartbreak Hotel" is released by Elvis Presley

1957   Southern Christian Leadership Conference (SCLC) is founded
On the Road is published (Jack Kerouac)
The Little Rock Incident at Central High

1960   Greensboro Sit-In
Student Non-Violent Coordinating Committee (SNCC) is created
The Birth Control Pill becomes available

1961   The Freedom Rides in the South

1962   Students for a Democratic Society (SDS) is founded
The Battle of Oxford in Mississippi
Second Vatican Council (Vatican II) begins

1963   The Birmingham Demonstrations
The Civil Rights March on Washington
The Feminine Mystique is published (Betty Friedan)

1964   The Civil Rights Act of 1964
The Mississippi Summer Project establishes Freedom Schools
The Beatles "invade" the U.S.

1965   Malcolm X is assassinated
The Selma, Alabama Demonstrations
The Voting Rights Act of 1965
The Watts Riots
"Free Speech" Movement at Berkeley

1966   *Human Sexual Response* is published (Masters and Johnson)
The Black Panther Party is founded
The National Organization for Women (NOW) is created

1968   The Kerner Commission Report is issued
Martin Luther King, Jr. is assassinated in Memphis
The American Indian Movement (AIM) is formed
The Columbia University Strike
A Rating System first adopted by the Motion Picture Association

1969   The Woodstock Music Festival
American Indian occupation of Alcatraz Island

1970   *Human Sexual Inadequacy* is published (Masters and Johnson)
The Women's Strike for Equality March in New York City

INTRODUCTION

Americans witnessed a great number of changes in society during the 25 years after the end of World War II. These changes affected the way that millions of Americans worked, worshipped, thought, and spent their leisure time. The changes were so fundamental that the best way to describe them is revolutionary. The economy, the growth of suburbs, the political awakening of several minority groups, and the entire youth culture were among the major components of society that would never be the same again.

THE POSTWAR ECONOMIC BOOM

Although not everyone shared in the prosperity in the postwar era, these years represented a period of rising living standards for most Americans. While the decade after the end of the First World War (the Great War) had also been a time of economic advancement, there were differences. By 1945 the United States was ready to assume a large share of responsibility in the world community. The United Nations also would be more active than the old League of Nations had been, so there would be more efforts made to increase international cooperation. This, in turn, led to increased world trade, which especially benefited the United States because many other countries were forced to rebuild after the war.

The prosperity of the post-World War II era was based on a stronger foundation. The factors contributing to this economic period increased the purchasing power of ordinary Americans, thus creating a larger middle class, and led to an economy obsessed with consumption of goods and services. When these factors are viewed in the context of the Great Depression of the 1930s, when few had dollars to purchase, and the wartime shortages and rationing of the Second World War, it is easy to see why Americans were so anxious to purchase as many goods and services as they could. The gross national product (GNP), which is the total value of goods and services produced (now called the gross domestic product, or GDP), saw a steady increase during the postwar period. Before the end of this era, Americans were consuming at a disproportionate rate compared to their population. By the middle of the 1960s, in fact, the United States represented about 5 percent of the world's population, but Americans were producing and consuming more than one-third of the world's total goods and services.

Consumer Confidence and Demand

Victory brought the United States the status of superpower and confidence in the future of the nation, both politically and economically. Now that America had so substantially contributed to the winning of World War II, Americans themselves emerged with all of the confidence and pride expected of a world superpower. This confidence in American world leadership translated into confidence in the economy. And confidence in the economy always translates into consumers' willingness to spend money. When you feel good about the economic future, people naturally are more willing to loosen their financial belts because they know they can always find a good job. Therefore, pent-up consumer demand was released following the war, providing incentives for industry to increase its production and hire more workers. And although this spurt in consumer demand initially caused great inflation and related problems (see Chapter Fifteen), the longterm rise in consumer demand was a very important element in the postwar economic boom. An explosion of consumer credit helped fuel this consumer spending spree. In 1946 American consumers borrowed $8 billion to finance major purchases; in 1970 the figure was up to $127 billion.

The Baby Boom

Consumer demand was not the only thing pent-up during the war. As service personnel returned home, the pervasive optimism and confidence was also reflected in the largest baby boom period in American history. From 1946 to 1964, 75.9 million births occurred in the United States. The peak year of this baby boom was 1957, when 4.3 million babies were born in this country. In the 1930s, by contrast, the number of births in a single year never exceeded 2.6 million. And from 1929 to 1945, a total of only 44.4 million babies were born.

The baby boom contributed to the postwar economic boom in a variety of ways. Babies are consumers too. From their first year in diapers through their school years, the goods they consume increase. As more children reached school age, more schools and teachers were required to meet the demands of the rapid growth in the youth population. This postwar boom in births then led to a construction boom, as some families added on to their existing house and many others bought new homes, and as public school districts were forced to construct more school buildings. Government assistance in the form of low-interest loans to war veterans and Federal Housing Administration mortgage insurance helped families expand or purchase housing. In 1946, new housing starts topped 1 million homes, an annual figure which continued even well after the baby boom had ended.

Automobile Production

American families needed to replace their automobiles because of an inability to purchase new ones during the depression and the war. But it was more than the age of cars that fueled the desire to replace them with new models. During the 1920s, Americans had fallen in love with the automobile, and it had come to symbolize the freedom and independence associated with the American spirit. Furthermore, the construction boom in new housing after the war was focused primarily outside the cities themselves, in the rapidly growing suburbs. (See the next section for more information on population shifts and suburbia.) Because most people who moved to the suburbs still worked in the cities, it was essential that they have reliable transportation to get to and from the workplace. The result was a boom in automobile sales and production. The automobile industry has a significant multiplier effect on the entire economy. That is because demand for cars automatically creates a demand for steel, glass, rubber, and other basic industrial products which are required to make cars.

The Buick Super Riviera leads the automobile industry, 1950. Credit: AP/Wide World Photos.

The Cold War

The emergence of the Cold War soon after the end of World War II resulted in unprecedented levels of defense expenditures during peacetime. The Department of Defense was created in 1949, but the breakout of the Korean War the next year really provided the impetus for vastly increased military spending. In 1949, the defense budget was just over $13 billion per year. In 1951, it was more than $22 billion, and by 1953, it had surpassed the $50 billion mark annually. In other words, the Cold War had created what President Dwight D. Eisenhower called the "military-industrial complex," in which many large private industrial contractors came to do most of their business with the defense sector of the federal government, producing everything from missles to tanks, jets, and other sophisticated weapons systems.

The defense establishment, along with the space program, stimulated several industries, including the electronics field. For example, the transistor was developed in 1948 as a replacement for the more cumbersome vacuum tubes, thus beginning an electronics and, eventually, a computer revolution. This, in turn, greatly increased productivity and produced higher quality radios, stereos, televisions, and other consumer goods. In addition to promulgating new technologies, the existence of the Cold War also provided new government jobs as well as those in the private defense contracting companies. With more people working, and confident of always having a decent job, consumers were willing to spend money which, in turn, kept the cycle of economic production in a healthy state. Whatever the defects of the "military-industrial complex," there is no doubt that it greatly assisted in making the postwar period one of growing economic prosperity for most Americans.

The GI Bill

In a relatively rare moment in American history, political leaders thought about the peace before the war had ended. There was concern that dumping all the World War II veterans into the civilian job market at once might return the nation to the Great Depression. The passage of the Servicemen's Readjustment Act of 1944 prevented a glut of returning veterans into the economy. This act of Congress quickly became known as the GI Bill of Rights, or simply the GI Bill. It provided federal dollars for college tuition and living allowances to help encourage veterans to go to college after the war. There was also some aid given for those who wished to start a small business instead, but the primary emphasis was on education.

During the 1946–1947 academic year, almost half of all college students in the United States were World War II veterans. In a cultural note, this fact certainly forced college administrators to rethink many of their traditional college rules. Grown men—and all those who returned from the Second World War were indeed men—could not be expected to adhere to strict curfews, dress standards, or dating rules. Fortunately for higher education, college and university administrators quickly learned to adapt in order to compete favorably for student enrollment.

Another significance of the GI Bill lies in the fact that it gave a psychological boost to veterans. The federal government was saying that it cared about ordinary people and wanted to help those who had made victory in the war possible to prosper in civilian life. Beyond the psychological factor, which should never be underestimated in the story of human achievement, the GI Bill vastly improved the general education level of society, which was recognized as absolutely vital if longterm economic growth were to be sustained.

The Marshall Plan

As discussed in the last chapter, the Marshall Plan was a brilliant success in helping western Europe to rebuild its infrastructure and economy after the end of the war. Although some balked at the amount of federal dollars going for assistance outside the country, supporters accurately knew that a healthy and rising European economy was necessary for a healthy American economy in the long run. Indeed, it had always been true.

POPULATION SHIFTS AND THE GROWTH OF THE SUBURBS

One of the most significant social changes that occurred early in the postwar era was the growth of the suburbs, which both reflected and caused a realignment of the population. The population census of 1920 was the first to show that the majority of Americans were then living in towns and cities. A wave of new immigrants, changes on the farm, and an internal migration toward the cities (which was intensified during World War I) were all factors resulting in that fact.

The Second World War had a similar effect in that millions of Americans migrated into the cities in order to work in the prosperous war factories. But after the war, congestion and crime in the big cities and the need for more space to accomodate the baby boom, led many urban dwellers to move to newly created housing neighborhoods in what became known as the suburbs. Racial factors also played an important role among many whites because, as in the previous world war, African-American and Hispanic Americans had moved in even greater numbers into the cities for wartime jobs. Because minority groups usually were paid less, and with racial discrimination rampant in the home mortgage industry, blacks and Hispanics were almost entirely kept out of the new suburbs. Thus, the exodus to suburbia was overwhelmingly an affluent white phenomena. This so-called "white flight" from the cities was also encouraged by the federal highway program of the Eisenhower administration in the 1950s, because the interstate system that linked major cities by road also made access into the cities from outlying areas more convenient.

From 1945 to 1960, the population of the suburbs increased from approximately 36 million to about 68 million persons. During the same time, the numbers of Americans living in the inner cities still increased from approximately 52 million to about 58 million, which represented about a 12 percent increase. The big loser, in terms of numbers, was rural America, whose population declined from about 59 million to about 54 million persons. This shifting of the population increased the concentration of black Americans in the inner cities. By 1960, African-Americans accounted for about 20 percent of the population of the largest two hundred cities in the nation, although they represented only about 12 percent of the total national population. And by 1970, the black population in about a dozen major cities represented more than 40 percent of the persons living there.

Levittowns

No person or organization contributed more to the growth of suburbia than Abraham Levitt and his sons Alfred and William. Shortly after World War II, Levitt and Sons accurately perceived a severe housing shortage and bought over twelve hundred acres of farmland on Long Island, New York. Then, using standardization techniques, they initially built 2,000 homes on the site, which they rented out. By 1951, Levitt and Sons had built more than 17,000 ranch-style homes there and had begun selling them. Then, using their profits as a source of further investment, Levitt and Sons eventually built Levittowns, as they were soon nicknamed, in Bucks County, Pennsylvania, and Willingboro, New Jersey. The standardization used in the construction of Levittown homes meant that they used several different

New Post-World War II Suburb. Credit: AP/Wide World Photos.

crews, each trained in one specific task, to build them. This less expensive way to build a home has led some social historians to conclude that the Levitts did for housing construction what Henry Ford had done for automobiles.

By today's standards, the houses were far too small and uniform. Each Levittown house was only 720 square feet, with two bedrooms, one bath, a kitchen equipped with a refrigerator, range, and washing machine, and a living room with a picture window, a fireplace, and a built-in television set. Legally, homeowners in Levittown were required to have door chimes, not buzzers, and to mow their lawn on a regular basis; and picket fences were prohibited. Trees were planted exactly every twenty-eight feet. Nevertheless, young families used to cramped quarters in city apartments or with in-laws, flocked to buy them. Compared to their previous experiences, Levittown homes represented their American dream.

Afraid of great financial losses if "white flight" ever afflicted Levittowns, the company intentionally refused to sell to African- Americans. But in the mid 1960s, after blacks had sued on grounds of racial discrimination, Levitt and Sons began selling to persons of color. Despite that breakthrough, however, unofficial discrimination continued in the housing industry. And by 1970, 95 percent of the population living in the suburbs was white.

Other developers soon followed the profitable example of Levitt and Sons, and suburbs with look-alike houses sprang up almost overnight near Chicago, Los Angeles, San Francisco, and other major cities. One such development, Daly City, California (near San Francisco) inspired a popular song of the day, called "Little Boxes." As suggested above, this rapid trend toward suburban living was made possible by government assistance by means of low-interest loans to veterans and FHA mortgage insurance, as well as massive new highway construction. And American cities have never been the same.

NEGATIVE FACTORS IN THE POSTWAR ECONOMY

The Corporate Merger Movement

During World War II, the federal government largely ignored antitrust laws in order to encourage a fast and massive armaments build-up. Having become accustomed to this policy, it continued in the postwar period as well. Combined with strong economic growth, the relaxation in the enforcement of antitrust laws resulted in a new wave of postwar company mergers. Unlike the merger movements of the 1890s and the 1920s, however, which consisted of big companies buying up smaller ones in the same or similar industries, the postwar merger mania included a heavy dose of corporations swallowing up companies in totally unrelated fields. This diversification occurred in order to spread corporate assets, which would limit damage during future recessions. Such multi-faceted corporations came to be called conglomerates.

The concentration of economic power resulting from increased mergers was reflected in a Federal Trade Commission report in 1968, which stated that the nation's 200 largest corporations possessed the same percentage of total manufacturing assets as the largest 1,000 companies had in 1941. And by the time of that report, the ten largest companies were in automobiles, oil, electronics, and communications.

While some political economists argue that larger corporations use their greater financial resources to make products more efficiently and cheaply, others perceive grave dangers instead. The trend among most American historians is to emphasize the negative factors more than the positive ones. For example, while it is obviously true that bigger companies have greater financial resources, it has not always followed that they have used those resources in order to reduce prices or maintain price stability. Instead, many have become bloated bureaucracies which do not respond efficiently to consumer needs. The concentration of economic power, particularly in a specific industry, more often has simply allowed companies to raise prices, and otherwise become less responsive to consumer needs, by reducing competition. Furthermore, many historians, partially echoing Thomas Jefferson and others from the early days of the republic, raise questions about how the concentration of economic power in the hands of a relatively few endangers democracy itself. In the adage of the British Lord Acton, "Power corrupts, and absolute power corrupts absolutely."

A Decline in Family Farms

A number of factors in the postwar era resulted in a significant decline in family operated farms, which had once been the backbone of both the American economy and its political democracy. In order to remain competitive in the postwar years, farmers needed to make greater investments in new machines, fertilizers, and pesticides. New agricultural technologies did greatly improve agricultural productivity, but their ever-increasing cost made it difficult for many families to continue farming. At the same time, these factors attracted large investors, who often were willing to buy the family farm for a fair price. Even coporations got into the agri-business as a way to make good profit in those states that allowed corporate farming. In turn, these big investors' demand for land increased the value of good farmland, making it more difficult for the struggling family farmer to resist the pressure to sell.

An additional reason for selling the family farm was the attitude of many farmers' children, especially sons, who were most often expected to inherit it. As younger people, they often possessed less of a commitment to run the farm in the face of rapidly rising costs. And, of course, there was also the lure of big city life, with its entertainment, education, and relatively plentiful jobs to attract them. The result was that agriculture was increasingly becoming a big business, and many small family farmers were being squeezed out. From 1945 to 1970, the percentage of Americans engaged in farming fell from 17.5 percent to 4.8 percent.

The Persistence of Poverty

Not all Americans shared in the postwar economic boom. In fact, probably the greatest irony of the era was the persistence of poverty on a fairly large scale in the midst of a prosperous economy. During the recession of 1950, nearly 36 percent of all Americans were classified as poor. But even during the prosperity of the non-recession early 1960s, the poverty rate stood at almost 25 percent. The greatest geographical, or demographic, pockets of poverty were among whites in the poor Appalachian Mountain region; among blacks in the inner cities of the North; among Mexican-Americans in the Southwest; among Native Americans on the reservations of the West; and within the Puerto Rican population of New York City. Among all those classified as poor, more than 50 percent were either over the age of 65 or under the age of 18. Twenty percent were almost evenly divided between African-Americans and Native Americans, and 25 percent lived in households headed by a single woman.

The causes for this persistence of poverty were many and complex. Certainly one of the factors that aggravated the situation was the revolution taking place on the farms. Not only were ordinary people being squeezed out of farm ownership, but the trend toward increasing mechanization on the farms significantly reduced the need for farm laborers. This caused people who were already marginal in economic terms to flee to the big cities to look for factory work. Furthermore, the social legislation of the New Deal had basically aided major industrial workers rather than agricultural laborers; Social Security and minimum wage laws did not cover

Poverty in a rural southern setting: Mrs. Everett Canada poses with three of her seven children in front of their shack in Kentucky. Credit: AP/Wide World Photos.

migrant farm workers, restaurant employees, and many other service workers in those days.

Many inhabitants of the cities, among both those already there and those displaced persons who had migrated to them to look for jobs, often met discrimination that kept them unemployed or under-employed. Job discrimination was especially aimed at racial minorities and women (including single mothers), who lost their war jobs when preferential treatment was given to veterans. And the saying which accurately reflected the employment practices of many employers toward racial minorities was "the last to be hired; the first to be fired." Of course, a lack of education also hampered many poor Americans and made it difficult, if not impossible, for them to escape their poverty.

The agricultural revolution, racial discrimination, poor education, and the lack of social legislation for certain economic groups all combined to create a cycle of poverty. This cycle of poverty, with its pervasive feeling of hopelessness and despair, is passed down from generation to generation. A pyschological barrier is erected which is extremely difficult to overcome.

Suburbs attracted businesses along with people. Over the years, this trend of moving to the suburbs has reduced the tax base for the cities at the very time that more city services were needed. Public education was especially hurt by this movement because most states based most of their financial support for education upon property taxes. With fewer property owners, and poorer ones, the cities could not adequately fund education. The cities began deteriorating, and all this only added to the feelings of hopelessness on the part of the urban poor.

Poverty was invisible to most Americans, who did not live in close proximity to it. But many gradually became more aware of it through the efforts of reformer Michael Harrington, whose book, *The Other America* (1962), influenced both Presidents Kennedy and Johnson, and inspired Johnson's so-called war on poverty in the mid to late 1960s. (See Chapter Sixteen.)

THE MODERN CIVIL RIGHTS MOVEMENT

The modern civil rights movement is usually dated from the famous Supreme Court decision in 1954 declaring racial segregation in the nation's public schools to be unconstitutional. (Please see Chapters Twelve and Fifteen for the roots of the movement.) Some historians have called the 1940s the forgotten decade as far as the civil rights movement is concerned. Those years, both during and after the war, witnessed minimal results, but organizations like CORE (the Congress of Racial Equality) and men like A. Philip Randolph had laid the foundation for what followed in the 1950s and 1960s. Presidents Roosevelt and Truman had used the presidential authority of an executive order to achieve some early results. Even the Supreme Court had begun to think differently about civil rights, with its 1946 *Morgan v. Virginia* decision outlawing segregation on interstate buses and its 1948 decision, in *Shelley v. Kraemer*, to forbid racially closed real estate contracts. And on the personal front, Jackie Robinson had become a symbol of racial change when he became the first black baseball player to play in the major leagues, joining the Brooklyn Dodgers in 1947. With the important foundation having been laid in the 1940s, the first full decade after the war would produce the beginning of a mostly peaceful revolution in an attempt to make that American ideal of the Declaration of Independence a reality for everyone, when it stated that "All men are created equal."

Brown v. Board of Education of Topeka

Ever since the Supreme Court had ruled in *Plessy v. Ferguson* in 1896 that "separate but equal" facilities for whites and blacks on railroad cars was constitutional, that judicial doctrine had been used to justify racial segregation throughout society. In the North, racial segregation was based primarily on social custom, while in the South, it was required by state laws. Such segregation of the races included public schools nearly everywhere in the country. As of the early 1950s, it was specifically mandated by law in seventeen states, most but not all, in the South. And although the Supreme Court had prohibited segregation by race on interstate buses back in 1946 (see above section), the fundamental doctrine of "separate but equal" remained judicially intact until 1954, fifty-eight years after the *Plessy* decision.

In 1954 the United States Supreme Court handed down a landmark ruling on school segregation in *Brown v. Board of Education of Topeka*. The *Brown* case involved a lawsuit filed back in 1951 by a black NAACP attorney named Thurgood Marshall against the racially segregated public school system of Topeka, Kansas. To support their suit, Marshall and the other NAACP lawyers used current psychological and sociological research data provided by Kenneth Clark, a black psychologist. That research indicated that separating black school children from white children damaged the black children psychologically, thereby creating an inherently unequal educational environment for them.

When the case finally reached the Supreme Court, Marshall was one of the lawyers who personally argued the case before the justices. And thirteen years later, in 1967, President Lyndon Johnson appointed Marshall as the first African-American justice ever appointed to the Supreme Court. On May 17, 1954, the Supreme Court unanimously agreed with the plaintiffs in the case by declaring the old "separate but equal" doctrine unconstitutional for the country's public school systems. Writing for the Court, Chief Justice Earl Warren stated that separating school children by race "generates a feeling of inferiority as to their status in a community that may affect their hearts and minds in a way unlikely ever to be undone." The written opinion also added that "in the field of public education the doctrine of 'separate but equal' has no place." A year later, the Court ordered that public school desegregation should proceed "with all deliberate speed."

The movement toward desegregation of the nation's public schools proceeded fairly smoothly in the border states of the Upper South, in places like Maryland, Delaware, West Virginia, Kentucky, Oklahoma, and the District of Columbia. In the Deep South, however, it was a much different story. Not only token compliance was lacking, but every year more open defiance characterized southern reaction. Supported by newly formed White Citizens' Councils and the old Ku Klux Klan, leaders in the Deep South were typified by Virginia Senator Harry F. Byrd, whose rallying cry was "Massive Resistance." Southern states passed laws to assign students to schools in an effort to evade the Supreme Court's order. And in March 1956, a Southern Manifesto appeared with the names of 101 southern members of Congress signed to it, denouncing the *Brown* decision for allegedly being "a clear abuse of judicial power." President Eisenhower himself may have added fuel to the southern fire by his far less than enthusiastic reaction to the Supreme Court ruling. Eisenhower refused to take a leadership role in persuading southerners to accept it. And privately, the president said that "the Supreme Court decision set back progress in the South at least fifteen years. The fellow who tries to tell me you can do these things by force is just plain nuts."

Meanwhile, during the next few years after the *Brown* decision, some serious clashes between white mobs and black students and supporters occurred. When Autherine Lucy, a 26-year-old African-American woman, attempted to enroll at the University of Alabama in 1956, school officials denied her application, and mobs attacked her both verbally and with rocks. And in Clinton, Tennessee, riots involving about 1,000 white citizens broke out after a court ordered the enrollment of 12 black students in the high school. Only the National Guard was able to finally restore order in the small town. By the end of 1956, there were six southern states in which not a single black student attended a public school with white students.

The Montgomery Bus Boycott

Although the Supreme Court's landmark 1954 ruling had specifically applied only to racial segregation in public schools, it had laid the foundation for the argument that "separate but equal" must be eliminated as a rule of life everywhere in the nation. Of course, that idea had been tested by the Congress of Racial Equality (CORE) in the 1940s, when restaurants and other places of public accomodation in Detroit and Chicago were desegregated by means of peaceful sit-ins. (See Chapter Twelve.) But the use of direct, peaceful action by ordinary black citizens to end racial segregation was begun in earnest by an unlikely heroine in late 1955. It was also begun in one of the most unlikely places in the country, Montgomery, Alabama, the "Cradle of the Confederacy." (The old Confederacy had been created by a special convention there in early 1861.)

On December 1, 1955, an African-American seamstress named Rosa Parks was taking a city bus home from work. A city ordinance in Montgomery, as in many other southern cities, allowed blacks to sit anywhere on a city bus until a bus was being filled up with passengers. Then black passengers were required to move to the back of the bus. But on this particular day, Mrs. Parks was especially tired. So when a white man asked for her seat, she refused him. This prompted her arrest—an arrest which was destined to spark the modern civil rights movement into high gear—and a ten-dollar fine.

That very night African-American community leaders met in the Dexter Avenue Baptist Church to discuss how they should respond to the situation. The young pastor, Dr. Martin Luther King, Jr., was elected as the president of the newly formed Montgomery Improvement Association and asked to lead a nonviolent boycott of the city bus system in order to force the city to desegregate the buses. King, the grandson of a slave and the son of a minister, had earned a seminary degree at Crosier Theological Seminary in Pennsylvania and a Ph.D. in philosophy at Boston University in Massachusetts. Soon after receiving his doctorate, he had accepted the position as pastor of this black Baptist congregation in Montgomery, Alabama. He was just 26 years old at the time. Dr. King's academic studies had drawn him to accept the nonviolence of Mahatma Ghandi, the rebel leader who opposed British colonial rule in India. As a civil rights leader, King would soon adopt Ghandi's theory of civil disobedience—use nonviolent methods to move the consciences of people, and peacefully accept the consequences of that disobedience. (King had also been influenced in this direction through the study of the nineteenth century American, Henry David Thoreau.) King encouraged his community to "use the weapon of love." And he added, "We must realize so many people are taught to hate us that they are not totally responsible for their hate."

The Montgomery Bus Boycott proved to be more valuable in demonstrating the ability of the black community to maintain solidarity than it did in actually deseg-

Rosa Parks touched off the bus boycott in Montgomery, Alabama by refusing to move to the back of a bus. She is being fingerprinted by Deputy Sheriff D.H. Lackey. Credit: AP/Wide World Photos.

regating the city buses. For one year, African-Americans used car pools or walked to work and other places. But although the bus company urged the city to change its statute, the city fathers tenaciously refused to budge. Moreover, during that year, several boycott leaders' houses were bombed, including King's home, and several black churches were burned. And when hotheads in the community wanted to riot, King persuaded them that such action was not only wrong, but it would be counterproductive to their cause. Meanwhile, the boycotters had filed a lawsuit in federal court challenging the constitutionality of the city ordinance that required blacks to move to the back of the buses. For more than a year, the case lingered in the judicial system. After a federal judge ruled against the city, Montgomery officials appealed it all the way to the United States Supreme Court. Finally, on December 20, 1956, the Supreme Court upheld the lower court's decision to desegregate the city buses. "Separate but equal" could no longer be used as a guiding principle, even within a state's jurisdiction. The Supreme Court had assisted the civil rights movement again.

The Montgomery Bus Boycott proved to white Americans that African-Americans did not prefer segregation, as alleged by some southern leaders. It also proved that they could take direct, peaceful action that was awakening at least some white consciences. The boycott also made Martin Luther King, Jr. the leading spokesman for the civil rights movement until his death in 1968. Early in 1957, King and other black ministers organized the Southern Christian Leadership Conference (SCLC). This was King's organization which he took to cities all over the South in peaceful attempts to end racial segregation and win voting rights for black Americans. Among his top aides were Bayard Rustin, Ralph Abernathy, Fred Shuttlesworth, Ella Baker, and Andrew Young.

The Little Rock Incident

The *Brown* decision had resulted in only token desegregation in public schools anywhere, but not even that in the Deep South. President Dwight Eisenhower was reluctant to push the issue, declaring that "you cannot change the hearts of people by law." But an incident in Little Rock, Arkansas forced him to take action in 1957.

Choosing to move slowly toward complying with the Supreme Court ruling so as to keep the city calm, the Little Rock Board of Education had asked the local NAACP to carefully select nine black students to attend Little Rock Central High School in September 1957. The students selected were all bright, well-behaved students, who were considered unlikely to arouse hostility. The governor of Arkansas at the time, Orval E. Faubus, had been considered a moderate Democrat. But sensing the mood of the people, and wanting to be reelected governor, Faubus embarked on a belligerent course of action by announcing that he would prevent violence by preventing the enrollment of the nine students at the high school. On the day the school year opened, Arkansas National Guardsmen were stationed outside the building and refused to allow the nine black students to enter, thus defying a court order to admit the students.

When this situation continued for several days, television reports made it clear to President Eisenhower that he could not permit a state to defy federal authority even if he personally disagreed with the decision of that authority. Thus, a meeting was arranged between the president and Governor Faubus at the White House. The meeting ended with Eisenhower thinking that Faubus was going to withdraw the National Guard and allow the students admission to the school. But when that soon proved not to be the case, the president became frustrated. Then when another federal court ordered Faubus to withdraw the National Guard, the governor complied by finally directing their removal. However, at that point, a mob of about 1,000 whites, composed of parents and other white supporters, showed up outside Central High and shouted insults every day as the nine black students entered the school. By this time, the television network news coverage showed pictures each evening across the nation. Most Americans clearly saw that the hostility and rudeness of the mob sharply contrasted with the calm behavior of the students, who did not retaliate against their accusers.

This television coverage not only created widespread sympathy among white citizens outside the South, but it forced President Eisenhower to take decisive ac-

Chaos outside Little Rock Central High School in September 1957. Credit: AP/Wide World Photos.

tion. So the president placed the Arkansas National Guard under federal control and sent about 1,000 paratroopers from the 101st Airborne Division to Little Rock in order to protect the black students. This was the first time since Reconstruction that federal troops had been used to defend civil rights in the South. The soldiers remained on duty throughout the entire 1957–58 school year, escorting the black students everywhere they went and standing outside classroom and bathroom doors when the students were in those places. In the beginning, white bigots would taunt the students as they went into the building each day with jeers of "Two, four, six, eight, we ain't gonna integrate!" However, things calmed down within a few weeks. Inside Central High, most white students eventually accepted their black colleagues, while some actually grew into adulthood as strong supporters of the civil rights movement because of their experience.

Governor Orval Faubus, however, did not accept the federally mandated integration of Central High. The soldiers were withdrawn at the end of the school year, and Faubus closed all Little Rock high schools during the next school year in order to prevent the continuation of racial integration in the system. Once again challenged in federal court, a 1959 court order finally forced the reopening of the high schools in that year.

After the Little Rock Incident, few other public school districts in the South remained quite so defiant. Outside the South, housing patterns delayed implementation of the *Brown* decision. When housing patterns did not exclude all black children from attending predominantly white schools, more affluent white parents sometimes placed their children in established or newly formed private schools in order to avoid having them go to school with black children. Even by the early 1960s, less than one-half of one percent of the black students in the South were in integrated public schools. Nevertheless, the principle had been established at the federal level that racial segregation was unconstitutional. There would be other attempts to enforce that principle.

The Civil Rights Acts of 1957 and 1960

Although President Eisenhower was not a strong advocate for civil rights, he did support the right to vote for all adult American citizens, regardless of race. Furthermore, he hoped to cause further divisions between northern and southern Democrats on the civil rights front, and perhaps win back some black voters for his Republican Party, by proposing in 1956 a federal law to guarantee black voting rights. Southern opposition in the Senate delayed a final vote on the bill by that body by use of the filibuster rule. But Majority Leader Senator Lyndon Johnson finally won approval for the bill after stricter language was removed from it. Thus, Congress passed the Civil Rights Act of 1957 in September of that year.

The new law created the Civil Rights Commission for a two-year period with powers to investigate alleged denials of voting rights and equal protection of the laws for reasons of color, race, religion, or national origin. It also established a Civil Rights Division within the Department of Justice, with authority to seek federal court injunctions against any state or local officials who were violating anyone's right to vote. In 1959 the life of the Civil Rights Commission was extended for two more years. The enforcement power in the Civil Rights Act of 1957 was weak, but its greatest significance is that it represented the first federal civil rights law since the Civil Rights Act of 1875, some 82 years earlier.

The Civil Rights Commission reported to President Eisenhower that the Civil Rights Act of 1957 was ineffective in protecting the right to vote for black citizens. As a result, the Civil Rights Act of 1960 was passed during Eisenhower's last year in office. The new law empowered federal courts to appoint special "referees" to register black voters whenever a court determined that a clear pattern of discrimination existed. It also made it a federal crime to cross a state line to bomb a building, or to escape prosecution after having bombed a building. This latter provision was a response to a wave of bombings of churches and schools frequented by African-Americans.

The Sit-in Movement

Borrowing a tactic first used by industrial workers in the famous sit-down strikes of the 1930s, and which was being used by Martin Luther King, African-American college students began using the sit-in technique to desegregate restaurants and other public places in the South in 1960. Four black male students from the North Carolina Agricultural and Technical College at Greensboro sat down at the "whites only" lunch counter of a local Woolworth store on February 1, 1960, and asked to be served a cup of coffee. The refusal to serve them made heroes out of Joseph McNeil, Franklin McCain, Billy Smith, and Clarence Henderson, who brought other students with them for the next several days. Popular support from other students, both black and white, all over the country, provided funds to help organize boycotts of Woolworth and other five-and-ten cent store chains whose southern branches refused to serve southern black students. And the idea of the sit-in spread all over the South within a few weeks, with financial and moral support from the NAACP (under Roy Wilkins), King's SCLC, and the Congress of Racial Equality (CORE), led by James Farmer.

That same spring, Ella Baker of the SCLC called for a meeting to better coordinate the sit-in movement, which had begun spontaneously. In April, at Shaw University in Raleigh, North Carolina, student leaders formed the Student Nonviolent Coordinating Committee (SNCC). A national SNCC office was soon established in connection with the SCLC office in Atlanta, Georgia.

During the 1960–1961 school year, dozens of eating establishments were racially integrated all over the South by use of the SNCC sit-ins. The sit-in tactic was also transformed into kneel-ins at churches, read-ins at libraries, and even wade-ins at segregated public swimming pools. By the end of 1961, approximately 75,000 black and white college students had participated in the sit-in movement, which had proven to be a very effective strategy.

The Freedom Rides

In May 1961, CORE organized a Freedom Ride to force bus terminals in the South to comply with the 1960 Supreme Court ruling in *Boynton v. Virginia*, which had prohibited racial segregation at all bus terminals and train stations. The buses traveled from Washington, D.C. to New Orleans, Louisiana, with the black and white passengers refusing to honor segregated restrooms and insisting on service in the coffee shops at the terminals.

White southern reaction grew more hostile as the Freedom Riders continued their journey. At Rock Hill, South Carolina, a mob beat up John Lewis, a Nashville SCLC member, and Albert Bigelow, a white rider, when they attempted to enter the bus waiting room. The worst violence awaited the Freedom Riders in Alabama. In Anniston (in May), Ku Klux Klan members beat the riders on one bus and burned a second bus. Savage beatings also were given to the civil rights volunteers in Birmingham and Montgomery. When the bus drivers refused to continue for fear of their own lives, the original Freedom Riders were forced to complete their trip to New Orleans by air. However, more Freedom Riders left on new buses to make the journey.

A freedom rider bus went up in flames when a fire bomb was tossed through a window near Anniston, Alabama. Credit: AP/Wide World Photos.

Meanwhile, President John F. Kennedy, who had been sworn into office four months earlier, in January, found himself in a difficult political situation. Although Kennedy was not enthusiastic about the civil rights cause, he was moderately sympathetic. In any case, he knew that he needed to keep the black voters who had helped elect him the year before. On the other hand, the president wanted to maintain white southern Democratic support as well. So during the Freedom Ride, he called for a cooling off period by both sides. This greatly offended the civil rights activists, who believed that African-Americans had remained cool enough for the last few centuries. Thus, Kennedy's proposal was ignored. While the president was agonizing over his political predicament, his brother Robert, who was the nation's new attorney-general, had contacted both the governor of Alabama and Mississippi to urge them to guarantee the safety of the Freedom Riders. Both governors refused to make any promises and failed to provide adequate protection.

Sympathy and support were growing all over the nation for these courageous Americans who risked their lives and limbs for equal protection under the law. Finally, after the vicious assault on the riders at Montgomery, President Kennedy allowed the attorney-general to send hundreds of federal marshals to stop the violence. But it was not until the local arrests of hundreds of more Freedom Riders that the president pressured the Interstate Commerce Commission to order bus companies to comply with the Supreme Court decision. The ICC did so on September 22, 1961, and the Freedom Rides came to a halt. Soon afterwards, the railroad and airline companies voluntarily opened their facilities to all races.

The Desegregation of Public Universities

Before World War II, African-American college students in the South had no choice but to attend one of a handful of all-black institutions of higher education. Beginning in the 1950s, however, a few were permitted to enroll in some white colleges and universities in the region, but only in token numbers. James H. Meredith, a black air force veteran, decided to challenge the virtually all-segregated higher education establishments of the South when he obtained a federal court order allowing him to register at the University of Mississippi at Oxford in September 1962. On several attempts to enroll, however, Meredith was met and stopped by white mobs; on two of those occasions, Mississippi Governor Ross Barnett personally barred the door in defiance of the court order. Barnett was a racist who believed that God had made the black man "different to punish him."

At that point, Attorney-General Robert F. Kennedy sent a few hundred federal marshals to escort Meredith. But when the marshals were attacked by segregationists, they used tear gas and other measures to defend themselves. When this so-called Battle of Oxford had ended, two persons lay dead and several hundred injured. Then President Kennedy was forced to send in federal troops to restore order and protect Meredith's right to enroll at "Ole Miss." Meredith did so, and soldiers remained with him throughout the academic year until his graduation the next spring.

Even after the federal government had used its power to guarantee the admission of James Meredith to a major university, another state governor challenged the admission of African-American students less than one year later. When two such students tried to enroll at the University of Alabama for the summer session in June 1963, Governor George C. Wallace personally stood in the doorway and refused to let them inside. Fearing a repeat of the violence at "Ole Miss," President Kennedy quickly nationalized the Alabama National Guard and sent them to assure that the black students could register for school. The defiant governor backed down, and the university was integrated peacefully.

Police Violence in Birmingham

In the spring of 1963, African-Americans stepped up their efforts to end racial segregation in public facilities. In city after city in the South, black and white civil rights activists continued the winning tactics of nonviolent demonstrations and sit-ins to achieve their goals. The consciences of more and more white Americans were becoming awakened to the injustices and hostilities that black Americans had faced for centuries. The decisive battle that would finally persuade President Kennedy to go all out for the civil rights cause in Washington occurred in Birmingham, Alabama in April and May of that year.

*Firemen turn their hoses on a jeering crowd during a protest demonstration, May 1963.
Credit: AP/Wide World Photos.*

Dr. Martin Luther King, Jr. had chosen Birmingham as a test. If that largest city of Alabama could be integrated, then the rest of the South would fall in line sooner than most people realized. Not only was Birmingham an important southern city, but King had chosen it as the site of the next battleground because he was aware of the city police commissioner's reputation. Commissioner Eugene "Bull" Connor was known for his hardball tactics, and these might just be sufficient enough to win overwhelming popular sympathy for the integration struggle and force President Kennedy to propose tough new federal civil rights legislation.

A series of peaceful demonstrations and sit-ins began on Good Friday in April. As the days passed, and more protestors were arrested, Commissioner Connor boasted that he had just about beaten King by declaring that the latter had almost "run out of niggers" (a totally unacceptable expression today). But when more women and school children swelled the ranks of the demonstrators, Connor grew frustrated, and his reaction turned nasty. In May, police began using attack dogs, water hoses, and even electric cattle prods against the protestors, and hundreds were arrested.

King himself was among the many demonstrators arrested during the demonstrations in Birmingham. While in jail, King eloquently defended his tactics in an open letter to America called "Letter from Birmingham City Jail." In it, the civil rights leader defended the strategy of civil disobedience when he wrote that "one who breaks an unjust law must do so openly, lovingly, and with a willingness to accept the penalty." The letter became a classic of the American civil rights movement.

Meanwhile, millions of Americans were viewing the events in Birmingham every evening on the network television news. King's strategy was proving successful because "Bull" Connor had played right into his hand. Widespread sympathy and support for the demonstrators was generated, and even President Kennedy had grown exasperated and "sick" of the hostile and violent treatment of peaceful citizens. Recognizing that Connor had inadvertantly created sympathy for the movement, the president remarked that "the civil rights movement should thank God for Bull Connor. He's helped it as much as Abraham Lincoln." And indeed he had. The president worked behind the scenes to calm the situation, and on May 10, a settlement was reached that ended the demonstrations in return for an end to segregation in the city's libraries and parks and an agreement from the department stores to hire more minority employees.

The 1963 March on Washington

The Birmingham crisis had ended in victory for the advocates of racial change, but the war had not yet been won. In scores of other cities across the nation in the spring and early summer of 1963, a movement for "Freedom Now" rang out in the form of nonviolent protests. There were more than 750 demonstrations during those months; nearly 14,000 persons were arrested in the South alone.

Prodded both by events and his brother Robert, President Kennedy moved forward with plans to ask Congress to pass a major, comprehensive civil rights act. On June 11, 1963, he addressed the nation on television and proclaimed that Americans faced "a moral crisis as a country and as a people." He explained the need for federal legislation to advance the cause of equal justice for all. "If an American, because his skin is black, cannot enjoy the full and free life which all of us want," he said, "then who among us would be content to have the color of his skin changed and stand in his place? Who among us would be content with the counsels of patience and delay?" As if to answer back in defiance, a sniper murdered Medgar Evers, the head of the NAACP in Mississippi, later that very night.

Eight days after his nationwide speech, the president sent a major civil rights bill to Congress for their action. It proposed to prohibit racial discrimination in restaurants, hotels, stores, theaters, ballparks, and stadiums, and it would authorize the attorney-general to initiate lawsuits to promote desegregation in public schools. Many civil rights leaders wanted tough sanctions to enforce prohibitions against job discrimination, but they decided to support the bill as the best the president could probably get from the current Congress. Liberals in the House of Representatives managed to strengthen certain provisions of the bill, but the old conservative coalition of southern Democrats and many Republicans fought it in the Senate. Specifically, Mississippi Democratic Senator James O. Eastland, chairman of the Senate Judiciary Committee, held up the bill in his committee.

In order to pressure Congress to end its delay and pass the president's measure, civil rights leaders organized a massive March on Washington, set for August

The August 1963 March on Washington. Credit: AP/Wide World Photos.

28, 1963. On that date, close to 250,000 people assembled on the Mall between the Lincoln Memorial and the Washington Monument, the largest civil rights demonstration in American history. Included in the events were the singing of civil rights songs, like "We Shall Overcome," folksingers Joan Baez and Bob Dylan, and at least a dozen speakers preaching solidarity and urging Congress to act. Among the speakers was A. Philip Randolph, the African-American president of the Brotherhood of Sleeping Car Porters, who had once threatened Franklin Roosevelt with a massive march on Washington. Walter Reuther, president of the United Auto Workers, was probably the most famous white speaker at the demonstration.

But the highlight of this momentous occasion was the famous "I Have a Dream" speech delivered by Dr. Martin Luther King, Jr. In a rousing, inspirational address, King repeatedly used the phrase, "I have a dream" to enunciate his racial goals for American society. "I have a dream," he spoke, that someday his four children would "not be judged by the color of their skin but by the content of their character." He closed in a resounding crescendo with these words: "I have a dream that . . . all of God's children, black men and white men, Jews and Gentiles, Protestants and Catholics, will be able to join hands and sing in the words of that old Negro spiritual 'Free at last! Free at last! Thank God almighty, we are free at last!'"

Those who saw and heard King's speech, whether in person or on television, knew they had witnessed an historic event and one of the greatest speeches in the history of the republic. Unfortunately for his cause, it did not win everyone. Just a little more than two weeks after the March on Washington, a black church in Birmingham, Alabama was bombed, killing four girls who had arrived early to attend a Sunday school class. And still the president's bill languished in the Senate. Senator Eastland had bottled it up in his Judiciary Committee until it was too late for the full Senate to take action before adjourning. And the assassination of President Kennedy on November 22, 1963 would mean that he would never live to see his bill enacted into law.

The Civil Rights Act of 1964

After the assassination of President Kennedy, Vice-President Lyndon B. Johnson assumed the presidency. Johnson, a southern Democrat who had shown some support for civil rights as Majority Leader in the Senate, proved to be a passionate defender of the civil rights movement. Using his considerable leadership skills that he had fine tuned during his years in Congress, President Johnson set out to twist arms and otherwise persuade Capitol Hill to pass a major civil rights bill in honor of the late President Kennedy. In February 1964, the House of Representatives passed a tougher bill than Kennedy had originally proposed, but a southern filibuster in the Senate prevented a vote on the bill for fifty-seven days. Johnson, along with liberal and moderate supporters in the Senate, kept up a relentless pressure to end the filibuster. Finally, the Senate voted to end the debate on June 10, the first cloture vote on a civil rights measure in its entire history. About a week later, the bill passed easily by a vote of 76 to 18, and the president signed it into law on July 2.

The 1964 Civil Rights Act, the most significant and far-reaching federal civil rights law since the Civil Rights Act of 1875, contained the following major provisions: It (1) outlawed racial segregation in places of public accomodation, such as restaurants, theaters, hotels, and public swimming pools; (2) required the withholding of federal grants or contracts from any businesses or other institutions which discriminated against nonwhites; (3) authorized the attorney-general to file suits against any public school district in the country in order to desegregate it; (4) made a sixth-grade education the standard for literacy in an attempt to get states to end literacy tests altogether; (5) created the Community Relations Service to help resolve local racial disputes; (6) prohibited discrimination by race, gender, national origin, or religion in most places of employment; and (7) created the Equal Employment Opportunity Commission (EEOC) to enforce the employment anti-discrimination provisions of the law.

606 / The American Journey: 1865 to the Present

The Grassroots Efforts to Guarantee Voting Rights

The Civil Rights Act of 1964 had marked an important milestone in the struggle for equal rights in American history. But its relatively mild provisions on the voting rights issue failed to persuade many that minority citizens would be guaranteed an opportunity to exercise their constitutional right to vote. The Twenty-fourth Amendment, first passed by Congress in 1962 and then ratified in late January 1964, had outlawed the use of poll taxes in federal elections. But the continued use of literacy tests and other measures to prevent black registration left major obstacles in the way toward full black suffrage.

Younger black activists especially saw the enfranchising of their community as an important key element in establishing real political power that could maintain the gains of the movement and broaden the influence of African-Americans. Therefore, in the summer of 1964, representatives of the SNCC and CORE organized the Mississippi Summer Project to galvanize action in that very hostile state. College students from all over the nation, many of them white, volunteered to help register black voters there. And "Freedom Schools" were established to teach black history to African-American children and encourage activism to achieve full equality. These young people were met with violent resistance from the Ku Klux Klan and local law enforcement officials. Nearly 100 were beaten, many others were shot at, and hundreds were arrested on one phony charge or another. In August, the bodies of three activists—two white and one black—who had been missing since earlier in the year, were discovered buried in an earthen dam.

Although the effort in Mississippi resulted in very few new black registered voters (perhaps 1,200), the volunteers did organize the Mississippi Freedom Democratic Party and signed up almost 60,000 black members in it. At the Democratic National Convention that August, the MFDP delegation unsuccessfully challenged the all-white Mississippi delegation in an attempt to replace them as voting members on the floor. Lyndon Johnson was seeking the nomination and re-election that year, and he was afraid of a massive southern walkout if the MFDP were seated in place of the regular party delegation. Therefore, he engineered a compromise in which two MFDP members were seated as at-large delegates in return for a resolution denying seats to any future convention delegation which came from states that denied voting rights to minorities. Not everyone was satisfied with the compromise, but it did succeed in preventing a walkout by southern delegates at the convention that year.

Trouble at Selma

Armed with the Nobel Peace Prize, which he had received in October 1964, Martin Luther King, Jr. marshaled his Southern Christian Leadership Conference for an all-out assault on the denial of black voting rights in the South. King's purpose was to pressure the federal government to enact a tough new law that would ensure the constitutional right to vote for all citizens. He chose Selma, Alabama as the site for his peaceful demonstrations, partly because Selma was located in a county in which only 1 percent of the potential black voters were registered, and partly because county sheriff Jim Clark had a reputation like "Bull" Connor in Birmingham.

The campaign in Selma began in January 1965, but after two months, only 50 new black registered voters had been added. So in early March, King decided to stage a march from Selma to the state capital of Montgomery, just fifty miles away. The march began on March 7, and it was promptly stopped by Sheriff Jim Clark's men and state troopers, who used tear gas, billy clubs, and cattle prods to viciously attack the demonstrators at a bridge. Two white participants from the North were killed a short time later; one was a housewife from Detroit, and the other was a young minister. The television networks all carried pictures of the attack on the bridge, which produced anger and more support for a strong federal voting rights bill.

Meanwhile, a federal judge issued an order to Alabama Governor George C. Wallace, demanding that he allow the march from Selma to Montgomery to continue and that he guarantee the personal safety of the participants. When Wallace replied that he could not do this, President Johnson nationalized the state's National Guard and ordered it to protect the demonstrators. The march resumed from Selma on March 21, and on the 25th of the same month, a rally of some 25,000 to 35,000 people was held on the steps of the state capital to conclude it. The irony, of course, was that Montgomery had been the first capital of the old Confederacy back in early 1861.

The Voting Rights Act of 1965

On March 15, while the Selma crisis was continuing, President Johnson addressed the nation, deploring the violence at Selma and urging members of Congress to support a tough new voting rights bill which he outlined. The president concluded his television speech with an already-famous civil rights statement of solidarity and commitment: "We **shall** overcome!"

That summer Congress responded to public pressure and passed the Voting Rights Act of 1965 (sometimes called the Civil Rights Act of 1965), and the president signed it into law in early August. The new law dispensed with the old approach of reacting to each formal complaint one at a time, and authorized federal examiners to go into the South to supervise the voter registration process and to directly register eligible voters whenever they believed that local officials were not cooperating. It also banned literacy tests as a requirement for voting where less than half of the potential minority voters were registered, thus effectively throwing out their use to deny voting rights.

The results of the new law were nothing less than astounding. By the end of 1965 alone, approximately 250,000 new black voters had been registered. From the presidential election of 1964 to the election in 1968, the number of black registered voters more than tripled, from about 1 million to 3.1 million. In Alabama, the number of registered black voters rose from 24 percent of those eligible in 1964 to 57 percent in 1968. The jump in Mississippi was even more dramatic, with the percentages leaping from 7 percent in 1964 to 59 percent in 1968. Not since Reconstruction had African-Americans been able to vote in such large numbers.

The vast increases in black voter registration had a profound effect on southern politics within a few short years. More moderate white leaders gradually replaced the defiant die-hard segregationists, whose strident voices and thundering opposition to racial equality had dominated southern politics for decades. As predominantly Democratic voters since the New Deal days, the larger number of African-American voters also began to moderate their party from within. As this transformation of the southern Democratic Party took place, the threat of walkouts by white southern delegations at future national party conventions seemed to disappear. By 1972, more than 1,000 African-Americans had been elected to state and local offices in the South, as compared to about 100 in 1966. And in more irony, Charles Evers, the brother of the slain civil rights leader Medgar Evers, became the mayor of Fayette, Mississippi. Soon there was talk about the more moderate New South.

The Summer Race Riots

Suddenly, and without warning to many civil rights leaders and most other Americans, black communities in major cities outside the South began to explode in a series of summer rioting. In late July 1964, violence had broken out in several northern cities, but after order had been restored no one really expected any further outbursts. But on August 11, 1965, less than a full week after the Voting Rights Act of 1965 had been signed into law, rioting erupted in Watts, a black urban area in south Los Angeles, after a confrontation between a white police officer and a young black motorist. Emotions ran so high during the rioting and looting that the cry of "Burn, baby, burn!" became an unofficial slogan of those caught up in the mayhem. National Guard troops were sent to the area to assist local police and protect fire fighters. After six days of rioting and looting by several thousand persons, 34 people lay dead (28 of them were African-American), about 900 injured, and at least $35 million worth of property was destroyed. It was the worst race riot since the end of World War II. But unlike the race riots of the 1920s and earlier, in which white mobs had attacked black communities, the Watts Riot had been born of frustration and represented primarily black-on-black violence. Similar outbursts in the black neighborhoods of Chicago and Springfield, Massachusetts soon followed that summer.

Much of the racial violence of the 1960s was begun by black youth who were out of school for the summer season and unemployed as well. The same was true in the summer of 1966, when riots rocked more than 40 cities, the worst being in Chicago and Cleveland. The summer of 1967 was the worst summer of all, with rioting in 128 cities. Newark, New Jersey, and Detroit were the hardest hit. In Newark, 25 African-Americans were killed by police after violence was sparked by the arrest of a black taxi driver. And then Detroit experienced the bloodiest racial violence of the decade when 43 people were killed (33 of them were African-American), more than 1,000 others injured, and approximately $50 million worth of property destroyed. To end the violence, army tanks and soldiers from the 101st Airborne Division had to be called in to the city. Many older observers compared the scene in Detroit to that of Berlin in 1945. Including the rioting which broke out after the assassination of Martin Luther King, Jr. in 1968, racial rioting from 1964 through 1968 resulted in the deaths of about 200 persons, injuries to some 7,000 people, and property damage in the range of $200 million.

Although the nation experienced shock and disbelief, it is not difficult, in ret-rospect, to understand why the violence was so prevalent and forceful. African-Americans had been coming to the cities in search of jobs for decades. By the mid 1960s, just about 70 percent of the black population in the nation lived in urban areas. Many well-to-do whites had promptly left the cities for the greater comfort of the suburbs. Even so, the population of the major cities was expanding, but unfor-tunately most of the expansion was among poorer citizens. Those factors had led to a decline in urban property values, which further speeded the decline in the tax base just at the time that there was a greater demand for city services. The result was general structural decay and a lack of decent job opportunities in many inner cities.

In addition to the demographic and financial conditions of the big cities, African-Americans still had to contend with de facto segregation. The successful struggle to end legally imposed segregation ("de jure" segregation, ie., segregation imposed "by law") had been one thing, but segregation which naturally occurred because of housing patterns (segregation as a simple fact of life, ie., "de facto") was quite another matter. And the nonviolent methods employed by the SCLC and other civil rights organizations were not capable of ending this form of segregation and discrimination. Then too, the long, successful battle to end segregation and other forms of discrimination by law had resulted in excessively rising expectations in large parts of the black community. And the continuation of these injustices in the face of that victory seemed too much for many younger, less patient African-Americans to take. The environment of frustration, coupled with the hot summer months, had proven too explosive to handle safely, and the entire nation suffered the pain and anguish in the ghetto fires of the mid and late 1960s.

President Johnson appointed a special commission, chaired by former Illinois Governor Otto Kerner, to investigate the causes of the violent outbreaks in the cities. In March 1968, the National Advisory Commission on Civil Disorders (more commonly called the Kerner Commission) made its analysis and recommendations public. It concluded that racism and poverty were the main causes of the riots and warned that "our nation is moving toward two societies, one black and one white—separate and unequal." Its recommendations called on the federal government to increase its expenditures for more jobs, public housing, and a "national system of income supplementation." At the same time, the Kerner Commission also urged more help for local law enforcement officers and better training in riot-control tech-niques.

By this time, however, many moderate whites who had previously supported the civil rights movement had begun to think that the nation had gone too far. Just as television coverage of the crises in Little Rock (1957), Birmingham (1963), Selma (1965), and other places had brought sympathy and support for the black struggle for equal rights from many whites, so television coverage of the riots in Watts, Chicago, Newark, and Detroit had created a huge white backlash against the same civil rights movement. Even President Johnson, loaded down with the stress of the Vietnam War (see Chapter Thirteen), and realizing the radically changed political reality, ignored the Kerner Commission's call for more social spending. Congress did pay some attention to its other recommendations, which were far more politically acceptable, and voted to increase funding to help strengthen local police departments and provide better training for National Guardsmen.

Black Power

Racism and poverty were hardly new in American society. The explosions during the long, hot summer months of the late sixties had not occurred in a vacuum. The frustration and impatience felt by many young African-Americans in urban America had been the result of a number of factors, some more recent and others more distant. And by the middle of the 1960s, a number of circumstances had come together to create a serious division within the African-American community. This division often separated the older, more experienced civil rights leaders from younger, more radical ones. The new movement used the expression "Black Power," a broad term that came to represent black pride, militancy, and separatism, depending upon who was using the term.

The roots of the Black Power movement went back at least as far as the 1920s, when Marcus Garvey had preached black separatism and encouraged black Americans to return to Africa. Then in 1931, Elijah Poole (who took the Muslim name Elijah Muhammad) organized the Nation of Islam in Detroit. This Black Muslim movement viewed Christianity as the white man's religion and preached black superiority and separatism as the means to protect themselves from "blue-eyed devils," a term Muhammad used for whites.

In the 1950s, a young black street hustler named Malcolm Little was converted to Islam while serving time in prison. Calling his last name a "Christian slave name," he changed it to Malcolm X, with the "X" representing his lost African name. By the early sixties, Malcolm X had become Elijah Muhammad's right-arm man and the most eloquent spokesman for the Nation of Islam. He urged black Americans to study their African roots and be proud of their heritage. Self-respect and self-discipline, he said, were necessary in order for the black community to survive in a white world. Separatism and independence, rather than racial integration, should be the goal. Referring to every caucasian as a "white devil," Malcolm X proclaimed the gospel of black superiority and urged blacks to defend themselves "by any means necessary." It was his inflammatory language and talk of active self-defense which aroused fear among both white and black moderates. When repeatedly pressed to specify exactly what he meant by the phrase "by any means necessary," he never seemed to answer the question clearly and forthrightly.

Just as W.E.B. DuBois had opposed Marcus Garvey four decades before, so moderate black leaders viewed Malcolm X as a demagogue and a racist. Martin Luther King, Jr. especially sought to avoid being identified with the Black Muslim leader for fear of losing white liberal support, which had been so important for his coalition's success. Of course, the two men also espoused opposite goals and philosophies. While King preached nonviolence and advocated racial integration as his goal, Malcolm X advocated black separatism, enunciated black superiority, and at least hinted at violence as one means of defending themselves. The two leaders met on just two informal occasions and exchanged only brief comments as they passed each other.

Before the middle of the decade, however, Malcolm X made a journey to Mecca (the pilgrimage of Muslims to their holy site in Saudi Arabia) in search of a better understanding of his Islamic heritage. It was there that he noticed Muslims of all colors from all over the world worshipping harmoniously together. This experience apparently affected him deeply, for shortly after his return to the United States, his views began to show some signs of moderation. In 1964 he left the Nation of Islam over disagreement and disappointment with Elijah Muhammad, and formed his own Organization of Afro-American Unity. Although he continued to emphasize black pride and African-American culture, Malcolm X tentatively began to forge an alliance with white liberals. Unfortunately, he did not

The Reverend Martin Luther King, Jr. and Malcolm X smile for photographers at the Capitol. Credit: AP/Wide World Photos.

have sufficient time to fully develop or demonstrate his changing attitudes, for he was assassinated in February 1965 in Harlem, New York, allegedly by rival forces within the Nation of Islam. Nevertheless, his book entitled *The Autobiography of Malcolm X*, published about the time of his death, kept his name and ideas alive and became a classic Black Power text.

Young, non-violent civil rights workers in the South had repeatedly met violence, which began to change their ideas. More radically oriented activists eventually took over the SNCC, and in May 1966, named Stokley Carmichael, a young graduate of Howard University, as the head of that organization. In a Mississippi rally that same summer, Carmichael gave the more radical wing of the civil rights movement the slogan "Black Power" when he cried, "We been saying freedom for six years and we ain't got nothin'. What we gonna start saying now is Black Power!" Older leaders of the movement abhorred the slogan as wrong and counterproductive, and agreed with NAACP leader Roy Wilkins when he called Black Power "the father of hatred and the mother of violence." But they were ignored as shortly thereafter both the SNCC and CORE began expelling white members from their organizations. H. Rap Brown, who succeeded Carmichael as head of the SNCC in 1967, was even more explicit in his use of violent language when he told supporters to get guns and "kill the honkies" (a totally unacceptable expression today).

Two college students from Oakland, California, Bobby Seale and Huey Newton, founded the Black Panther Party for Self Defense in 1966 in order to raise the self-esteem of black ghetto youth and intimidate police officials into fairer treatment of urban blacks. They soon dropped the latter part of their name and became simply the Black Panther Party. Black Panther members patrolled the ghetto streets in several major cities, wearing paramilitary clothing and armed with guns. As a result of a famous shootout with police in Oakland, Huey Newton was convicted of killing a police officer and was sent to prison. The Black Panthers preached a curious mix of militant black nationalism and Marxist ideology. Eldridge Cleaver, who later became the so-called "minister of information" for the party, wrote the book *Soul on Ice*, which terrified most whites and moderate blacks with its highly inflammatory language and advocacy of violence against the white establishment.

According to public opinion polls taken among African-Americans near the end of the decade, most members of that community still revered Martin Luther King as the most honored leader of the civil rights movement. Most also rejected the separatism of the new militants, still believing that the full integration into society should be the ultimate goal of the movement. And instead of withdrawing into a shell or turning to violence, most seemed to favor the use of "affirmative action" methods to eliminate de facto segregation and discrimination. Although "affirmative action" soon came to be viewed by many whites as a racial quota system to hire and promote minorities, the term (apparently first used by President Kennedy earlier in the decade, and supported by President Johnson) really denotes a broad spectrum of programs which essentially boils down to companies and other institutions taking the initiative to seek out and encourage minorities to become an integral part of the establishment. But while most African-Americans rejected the more militant political goals and methods of the Black Power movement, they gave much greater support to the more cultural elements of that movement. Thus, in the late sixties and into the seventies, Afro hairstyles, soul music, soul food, and black studies programs at major universities enjoyed fairly wide support among African-Americans, especially from the young.

Martin Luther King Changes Focus and is Assassinated

With the success of the civil rights movement to end de jure ("by law") segregation and discrimination, Martin Luther King, Jr. turned his focus toward the North and launched a campaign against the de facto discrimination there. Early in 1966, King established his new headquarters in Chicago and initially made better housing and open access to housing his top priorities. He organized peaceful demonstrations in white neighborhoods to demand open housing for all, but most of the white ethnic groups resented any calls for government assistance in housing because their ancestors had had to go it alone when they came to America and faced discrimination. King and his supporters were often the victims of rocks and glass bottles that were thrown at them on these marches. Chicago Mayor Richard J. Daley, the last of the old Democratic Party machine mayors, also resisted King's movement as representing outsiders having come to his city to stir up trouble.

Meanwhile, by August 1965 King had also become an active protester of the Vietnam War, which he saw as disproportionately killing poor black young men and as draining financial resources from the Great Society programs which would have benefitted minorities and other poor Americans. This political break with the Johnson administration infuriated the president, who gave his blessing to FBI Director J. Edgar Hoover's campaign to discredit King. Hoover had already been trying to do just that since 1962 because he had suspected that communist elements had infiltrated King's inner circle. Therefore, he had been wiretapping and recording the civil rights leader's phone conversations. But even after Hoover could find no evidence of communist presence or influence, he continued the surveillance. Discovering that King had engaged in sexual affairs with other women (he was a married man) and sometimes drank too much, Hoover leaked such information to various journalists and religious leaders in order to destroy his reputation and thus his movement. Once Hoover had an FBI agent send King an anonymous audio tape which proved he was having an affair, with the suggestion that he commit suicide. But after King had openly broken with the president over the Vietnam War, Johnson himself approved of Hoover's illegal and unconstitutional efforts.

In December 1967, King announced another new direction for the SCLC. A "Poor People's Campaign" was begun to pressure the federal government to provide housing, education, and jobs for all the poor, regardless of their race. The high American standard of living must be more equitably shared in society. This direction steered King into the economic realm and caused him to support unionization efforts among the working poor. It was to support striking sanitation workers in Memphis, Tennessee, that King had gone to that city in the early spring of 1968. On April 4, 1968, he was shot to death by a sniper while standing on the balcony outside his Memphis hotel room. Shortly afterwards, James Earl Ray was arrested for the murder and was sent to prison after his conviction, although some believe that he was set up by some white racist group or even by the FBI.

News of King's assassination sent shock waves throughout America, and resulted in racial rioting in the ghettos of several big cities, including Chicago, Detroit, Baltimore, and Washington, D.C. Forty-six people were killed and more than 3,000 injured before some 55,000 federal troops finally restored order. The nation's most respected civil rights leader was dead, and the movement which he had helped lead since the mid 1950s would never be the same again. Ralph Abernathy, an African-American minister and close advisor to King, inherited the reins of leadership within the SCLC and tried to pursue the Poor People's Campaign. But a large group of protesters on the Mall in Washington, D.C. that summer quickly splintered due to internal disputes and a lack of effective self-discipline. Nicknamed "Resurrection City," the protest was a complete failure, and by June it had been abandoned.

The Civil Rights Act of 1968

After the death of Martin Luther King, President Johnson urged Congress to attempt to end racial discrimination in housing by federal legislation. The president had vigorously sought open housing legislation before, but it had been defeated in 1966 and again in 1967. But in memory of the slain civil rights leader, the president and Congressional supporters overcame a filibuster in the Senate this time, and the Civil Rights Act of 1968 was passed. The new law prohibited racial discrimination in the advertising, financing, sale, or rental of most public and private housing in the nation, and also required the executive branch of government to "affirmatively" pursue the goal of racially integraged housing in the United States. In areas unrelated to the housing issue, the bill also outlawed racial discrimination in the selection of juries, extended legislative federal protection for civil rights workers, and provided stiff penalties for interfering with certain personal rights, such as attendance at school or work. In a thinly veiled concession to South Carolina Senator J. Strom Thurmond, and other conservative members of the Senate, the so-called "Rap Brown" section was added that made it a federal crime to use any interstate commerce facility to organize, promote, assist, or particpate in any act of rioting. This provision made it easier to stop the organizing efforts of radicals.

A Brief Assessment of the Civil Rights Movement

The modern civil rights movement of the postwar era had accomplished many of its goals within a decade or so of the *Brown* decision of 1954. Racial discrimination and segregation was prohibited by law, the voting rights of black citizens had fairly well been secured, and the New South was beginning to emerge in the wake of these changes. African-Americans were also discovering their African roots and developing a greater self-respect and confidence in what they could achieve as individuals. But the breakdown of the movement due to the rise of the more militant Black Power leaders, and the riotous explosions in the big cities each summer from 1964 through 1968, had created an enormous white backlash that would make further progress extremely difficult. And the nature of de facto discrimination and segregation proved to be a much greater problem to overcome, even in the best of political environments. The civil rights movement had come a long way in a very short time, but the next leg of its journey would prove tough indeed. (see Chapters Seventeen and Eighteen.)

NATIVE AMERICANS

Native Americans had experienced very rough times ever since Europeans had first come to the New World. Disease, encroachment on lands they had occupied for centuries, broken promises and treaties, and wars had reduced most Native Americans to an existence of poverty. Gradually, they had been squeezed into smaller areas until they were given only the least desirable lands for reservations to live on. Then, beginning in the Gilded Age period of United States history, the Dawes Act (1887), and then the Burke Act (1906), had attempted to "Americanize" the Native Americans by encouraging individuals to leave the reservations and become integrated into white man's society. This had not worked well, partly because Native American culture did not view land as something belonging to individuals and partly because of severe discrimination by whites. Thus it was that Native American policies of the 1930s and 1940s, based on the Wheeler-Howard Act (1934), reversed the so-called "Americanization" approach and instead fostered tribal efforts to preserve their own culture and traditions. Individuals could still choose to leave the reservations, but official policy encouraged cultural preservation and development on the reservations instead. (See Chapter Two for a brief discussion of these points.)

The Relocation and Termination Policies of the 1950s

Many Native Americans had voluntarily left the reservations in order to seek jobs in the cities during World War II. In the early 1950s, the Eisenhower administration reversed Native American policy once again by encouraging the breakup of the reservations in favor of the trend toward urbanization. In 1952, for example, the Voluntary Relocation Program (later changed to the Employment Assistance Program) was established with offices in ten cities. To lure individuals off the reservations, the VRP paid the moving expenses for those who moved to one of those cities, and then a living allowance was also provided until they could find jobs. By the early 1960s, about one out of eight Native Americans, more than 60,000, had fled the reservations for life in one of these urban areas.

Even more radical than the relocation program was the termination policy approved by Congress in 1953 under House Concurrent Resolution 108. This new policy resulted from great pressures exerted by the lumber, mining, and agricultural interests who wanted the remaining Indian lands in order develop them and increase their personal profits. The new policy provided for the eventual termination of the Native Americans' status as wards of the federal government with the complete extinction of the reservations being the ultimate goal. In other words, as tribes gradually came under the new policy, all benefits resulting from the special relationship with the federal government were ended. By 1968 more than one hundred tribes had been so terminated.

The relocation and termination policies had devastating effects on Native Americans. More than 500,000 acres of Indian land was transferred to non-Indians under the termination policy. This land transfer especially hurt those tribes who had occupied valuable timberland, thus adding to the spread of poverty. Individuals who moved off reservations and into the cities often found the transition extremely difficult. The supporters of the new policies had expressed confidence that they would ultimately save federal tax dollars, but that proved not to be the case. Few Native Americans supported the new policies, and with protests mounting, the Eisenhower administration finally conceded that it would not attempt to enforce it against the will of any tribe.

A Revised Policy and Red Power

During the 1960s, Indian policy was revised to help provide new economic opportunities on the reservations rather than to completely abandon them. For example, in 1966 the Bureau of Indian Affairs (within the Department of the Interior) began granting tribal councils more independent authority over the affairs of their respective reservations. Various business ventures were also undertaken in the decade, including oil production, small manufacturing, and tourism. By the end of the decade, the Bureau of Indian Affairs estimated that about 35 percent of all the Native Americans who had relocated to the cities had returned to the reservations. Experts indicated that perhaps as many as 75 percent would have done so if there had been more economic opportunities available there. Nevertheless, by 1970 nearly two-thirds of all Native Americans were living on the nation's 260 reservations.

The African-American struggle for equality in the 1950s and 1960s eventually inspired a movement among Native Americans for greater respect and more economic and political control over their lives on the reservations. In 1961 representatives from 67 tribes met in Chicago and adopted a Declaration of Purposes. And when President Lyndon Johnson announced his war on poverty in 1964, several hundred Native Americans besieged the national capitol to demand that his proposals include assistance for them as well. Indeed, Native Americans experienced the worst poverty, education, housing, and disease and death rates of any group in the nation. The president responded the next year by creating the National Council on Indian Opportunity to funnel anti-poverty funds into health services, job training, and other community needs.

By the late 1960s, the demand for Red Power by some Indian activists had begun. The successes of the black civil rights movement and the nearly desperate conditions among Native Americans had encouraged this new political force. Among Native Americans, for example, the life expectancy (at 47 years) was twenty years lower than the national average; the per capita income was 60 percent less than that of whites; and the unemployment rate was 10 times higher than the national average. In 1968, Native Americans confronted state officials in Washington State and demanded that treaties granting them fishing rights in the Columbia River and the Puget Sound be honored. Then in November 1969, militants took over and began an occupation of Alcatraz Island in San Francisco Bay, declaring it theirs "by right of discovery" and offering to buy it for $24 worth of cloth and beads—which, allegedly, was what the Dutch had paid the Indians for Manhattan Island in 1626. They apparently chose Alcatraz Island because its undrinkable water, poor sanitation, and unsuitable buildings resembled conditions which prevailed on most Indian reservations. The Red Power movement exhibited even more militancy after Chippewas in Minnesota played the leading role in organizing the American Indian Movement (AIM) in 1968. Like the Black Panthers, AIM formed armed patrols on several reservations in order to "protect" their communities from police harassment. (See Chapter Seventeen for more information.)

HISPANIC-AMERICANS

Hispanic-Americans—those of Spanish-speaking heritage—grew into the second largest minority group in the country by 1970. Most of that growth occurred in the 1960s. In 1960, there were a little more than 3 million Hispanics in the United

United Farm Worker leader Cesar Chavez, pictured with sign, leads protesters in front of a Safeway Supermarket. Credit: AP/Wide World Photos.

States, but by 1970 their numbers had increased to almost 9 million. The largest Hispanic group in the country was Mexican-Americans, who primarily occupied southern California and the Southwest region in general. Puerto Ricans became the second largest Hispanic group, who, in keeping with earlier tradition, predominantly settled in the New York City area. In fact, by 1970, Puerto Ricans represented approximately 16 percent of the population of New York City. And because of Fidel Castro's rise to power in Cuba, and the resulting hardships there, Cuban refugees poured into southern Florida during the sixties. By 1970, Cubans accounted for close to two-thirds of the population of the city of Miami.

Among these various Hispanic groups, the Cuban-Americans seemed to be more successful on average, and therefore, more widely accepted than Puerto Ricans and Mexican-Americans. The language barrier hampered educational advances, however, and led to increasing calls for bilingual education in Hispanic areas of the country. Cultural prejudice also ran high among many caucasians, with the stereotype of the "lazy" Hispanic dominating the mainstream cultural thinking. These problems translated into widespread discrimination in employment and housing, which only served to perpetuate the high poverty rates among those communities.

Except for the anti-Castro activities of Cuban-Americans, the Mexican-American community was the most politically active in challenging white domination of American society by demanding greater respect and economic clout. Their most effective spokesman was Cesar Chavez, who formed the United Farm Workers' Union in the sixties in order to improve the pay and working conditions of migrant farm laborers, especially among California's rich agricultural valleys. Chavez won widespread support for a national consumer boycott of table grapes in the late sixties; the boycott was a major part of an effort to win union recognition and end a grape pickers' strike which had begun in 1965. By 1970 the United Farm Workers had won union recognition and established a collective bargaining relationship which eventually spread to other agricultural sectors during the next decade, although a lettuce boycott in the late sixties did not prove as successful as the grape boycott had been. Clearly, however, Cesar Chavez was to the Mexican-American community what Martin Luther King, Jr. had been to African-Americans.

Younger Mexican-American activists, like many of their African-American counterparts, were less patient and more inclined toward radical demands and strategies. Also influenced by the black civil rights movement, these younger activists demanded that they be called Chicanos, a term probably derived from "Mejicano," the Spanish word for "Mexican." Chicano Power began to echo the demands among black militants for Black Power, calling for Chicano studies in leading universities, bilingual education, and control over their own destinies. Various organizations sprang up to demand different sections of the Chicano Power agenda, including the Crusade for Justice in Colorado, the Alianza in New Mexico, La Raza Unida in Texas, and the Brown Berets in California. The latter group was essentially modeled after the Black Panthers. The activists of the movement, like those within the African-American and Native American movements, did not maintain a high profile of visibility for very long after the sixties, but its major contribution apparently was to awaken a greater sense of identity and cultural pride among Hispanic-Americans.

THE MODERN WOMEN'S MOVEMENT

The origin of the women's movement in America can be traced at least as far back as the 1840s, when women like Lucy Stone, Lucretia Mott, and Elizabeth Cady Stanton had begun the crusade for women's property rights, equal education, and the right to vote. Others took up the cause for feminine justice in the late nineteenth and early twentieth centuries, notably Susan B. Anthony, Margaret Sanger, and Alice Paul. But the limited victories in property rights and education within the individual states had seemed to satisfy most women. And when the Nineteenth Amendment to the Constitution, granting women the right to vote nationwide, was ratified in 1920, the women's movement virtually died from lack of support. Individual leaders, like Alice Paul, continued to promote the idea of an equal-rights amendment to the Constitution, but the steam was already out of the movement as a whole; success had killed it.

Early Developments in the 1960s

By the late fifties and early sixties, however, the social climate in the country was changing rapidly. The legal victories of the black civil rights movement in that era had begun to make many women believe that they too should be liberated from the old stereotypes and discrimination which they too often faced in society. Pressured by several prominent women in his own party (Democratic), President John F. Kennedy appointed the President's Commission on the Status of Women in late 1961. Chaired by former First Lady Eleanor Roosevelt, the Commission issued its report in 1963. The report documented sexual discrimination in the workplace, such as the fact that while women constituted 51 percent of the population, traditional professions like doctors and lawyers were represented by less than 10 percent female participation. It called for an end to job discrimination against women, government assistance for day-care centers, and paid maternity leave for married working women. The report was hardly a radical document, however, because of its insistence that the "fundamental responsibility" of women was to be mothers and housewives and its opposition to an equal-rights amendment.

Largely as a result of the President's Commission on the Status of Women, the Equal Pay Act was adopted the same year. That act attempted to legally prohibit the pervasive reality of paying women significantly less for doing the same work as men, although it fell far short of accomplishing that goal. Then a year later, the Civil Rights Act of 1964 included a provision making job discrimination on the basis of gender illegal. Ironically, the gender provision had been inserted by southern Democrats who believed that its inclusion might kill the entire bill. But they underestimated the growing clout of the women's rights movement, and the provision remained in the new federal law.

Betty Friedan and NOW

Another factor which both reflected and contributed to the development of the modern women's movement was the publication of Betty Friedan's book, *The Feminine Mystique*, in 1963. Ms. Friedan had graduated from Smith College in 1947, married, and raised three children in suburban New York. As a free lance writer, Friedan interviewed her former classmates several years later to ask them how they felt about their lives. Most of them were living the stereotypical roles of mother and homemaker that social custom had dictated. But similar to her own experience, Friedan found that many women were unhappy and frustrated in their attempts to fulfill what she called the "feminine mystique." Instead of feeling fulfilled and glamorous, many were downright miserable about the narrow roles they felt restricted to, and then guilty about their hidden desires to "find themselves" in careers and other activities outside the home circle. Those interviews resulted in Friedan writing *The Feminine Mystique*, which struck a responsive chord among American women and quickly became a best-seller. Raising the consciousness of other women, the book proclaimed that women should not feel confined to domestic roles, but should find their own identity through careers and in the accomplishment of other meaningful goals.

Betty Friedman, key figure in the Women's Liberation Movement, speaks at New York's Central Park. Credit: AP/Wide World Photos.

Friedan took the lead among other feminist leaders in the formation of the National Organization for Women (NOW) in October 1966. The immediate catalyst for its creation was the slow speed and feeble efforts of the Equal Employment Opportunity Commission to investigate and enforce the ban on sex discrimination in the workplace. (The EEOC had been created two years earlier by the 1964 Civil Rights Act.) NOW campaigned for equal rights for women, including the Equal Rights Amendment (ERA), filed lawsuits in support of women who felt discriminated against on the job, advocated the right to a legal abortion and subsidized day-care for the children of working women, and otherwise preached the gospel of women's rights. The organization described its ultimate purpose as the incorporation of women into "full participation in the mainstream of American society NOW." The National Organization for Women soon became the most effective group fighting for female rights in the nation, attracting some 15,000 members by the end of the 1960s, and coming to represent women in much the same way that the NAACP represented the rights of African-Americans.

The Challenge of the Women's Liberation Movement

While NOW represented the mainstream of the women's rights movement, a more radical element did emerge in the late sixties. Like the more radical participants in the black civil rights movement, these so-called women's "liberationists" ("libbers" for short) were usually younger than the well-educated middle class followers of Friedan. These new leaders adopted the tactics of the Black Power and radical student movements because most of them, in fact, had gained experience in organizations like the SNCC and SDS. But even within those radical organizations, the female participants had been relegated to clerical and other more invisible duties. This treatment at the hand of even radical males convinced most "libbers" that a separate feminist movement must exist and fight to end "sexism" in all its forms.

The more radical "liberationist" feminists also began to reevaluate the entire role of women in society, which led to a tendency to minimize all differences between the sexes. Most of them came to believe that nearly all differences observed between males and females were the result of early training and education rather than inheritance and natural inclination. Some even argued that marriage and the traditional family were major instruments in keeping women in a subordinate role in society. Beginning about 1968, a technique called "consciousness-raising" was catching on across the country. Used as both therapy for women and the recruitment of new females into the movement, "consciousness-raising" involved small circles of females talking about their grievances and frustrations. This technique led many participants to conclude that sexism was the cause of most of their problems, and that it was so rampant that only political action could bring individual women true happiness.

The tactics of the women's lib movement to achieve their goals were as radical as some of its ideas. For example, in September 1968, radical feminists picketed the Miss America contest in Atlantic City and crowned a live sheep "Miss America" in order to dramatize their opinion that beauty contests are sexist and degrading to women. Other tactics designed to publicize the cause included the use of so-called "freedom trash cans," into which women threw their curlers, high-heeled shoes, and bras. In another kind of public display, women burned their bras. In fact, the public burning of bras by women activists became about as popular as the burning of draft cards by young men to protest the Vietnam War. Using more conventional means, women's "libbers" also helped establish day-care centers and demonstrated against advertisements and commercials that reinforced the image of women as sex objects.

The End of the Decade

As the decade of the sixties was closing, a rift was becoming increasingly visible between the moderate reformers in NOW and the more radical women's "libbers" in organizations such as Redstocking and Radical Feminists. The moderates viewed the radicals as counterproductive in that they tended to turn many other women, and men, against the entire struggle for equal rights. The truth is that most reform movements seem to attract radical fringe elements who often become an embarrassment to the cause at-large. However painful the tensions between these internal groups, both moderates and radicals usually play an important role in placing attention upon significant social problems and in rallying very different parts of the national community to join the struggle for change. Radical elements may possibly delay much action, but when the cause is just, Americans as a whole eventually seem to see that and to effect at least some necessary reforms. The same was true for the women's rights movement, although much still remained to be done as the decade came to a close.

The sixth decade of the twentieth century did come to a close on a positive note of cooperation between the moderates and the radicals within the women's movement. Despite their differences, organizations from both spectrums of the struggle for gender equality joined forces to celebrate the fiftieth anniversary of the women's suffrage amendment (the Nineteenth) in August 1970. Under the name of the Women's Strike for Equality, about 50,000 women demonstrated in New York City for an end to gender discrimination in the workplace and the legal right to an abortion. The decade of the seventies would see the legalization of abortion and a controversial struggle to win approval for an Equal Rights Amendment to the Constitution. But regardless of the outcomes of future debates, the women's movement in the 1960s had awakened the consciousness of many American women, and men, and made them more sensitive to the way in which the two sexes were treated differently.

GROWING STUDENT DISCONTENT

During the postwar era, the number of college and university students in the United States was steadily increasing. By 1960 there were about 4 million students, a number which would double by the end of that decade. Three primary reasons accounted for the vast increase in the student population attending institutions of higher education: (1) the baby boomers born after the war were reaching college age; (2) a college degree was perceived to be an essential ingredient for a successful career; and (3) federal aid was becoming increasingly available to large numbers of college students, making the attraction of a degree affordable to millions of young people for whose parents it had been out of reach.

The Emergence of the New Left and the SDS

But not all students were seeking a lucrative career. Many were resentful of their parents' placid conformity to the social conventions of the fifties, in which upward mobility and material possessions with life in the boring suburbs seemed the end-all of their existence. By the early sixties there was a kind of spiritual hunger affecting an important sector of the baby boomers. Life, they reasoned, must have more meaning than just the acquisition of material goods. This growing discontent with the lifestyle of their parents was typically experienced by white, middle class students who came from homes which had experienced the prosperity of the postwar economic boom. These college students tended to take all the social science and humanities courses that they could because these disciplines emphasized the quality of life and its human relationships more than math, business, and the hard sciences did.

Many of the more socially minded students were children of parents who had been politically active in the pro-Soviet cause of the 1930s before disillusionment with communism had set in. These so-called "red-diaper babies" were not dogmatic or ideological, however. While influenced by the political liberalism of the Democratic Party, and John F. Kennedy's enthusiasm in particular, they were also skeptical of mainstream liberalism. In their view, the American working class had "sold out" to the corporate establishment and were no longer capable of spearheading the drive for social justice. These radical students began to view themselves as the only reliable agents of social change. Therefore, they became involved in the emerging civil rights movement and then the anti-Vietnam War protests of the sixties. But they were also prime candidates for a new movement of student radicalism, referred to as the New Left, which became part of the scene on many large, well-known university campuses.

The most important radical organization that reflected the frustrations of the more affluent white college students was the Students for a Democratic Society. Better known simply as the SDS, it was founded by several University of Michigan students in 1962 as the student affiliate of an old anti-communist socialist group called the League for Industrial Democracy. In June of that year, students Tom Hayden and Al Haber took the lead in forming SDS and issuing its manifesto, called the Port Huron Statement. Written primarily by Hayden, who was the former editor of the student newspaper at the University of Michigan, the statement called for a "participatory democracy" in order to end the feeling of powerlessness in society. Although vague in its details, SDS leaders envisioned a system in which citizens would more directly control the decisions which affected their lives. To effect this change in the current establishment required not only direct, nonviolent student action (such as sit-ins and demonstrations), but an informed and politically active working class, which students would lead back into the movement for social justice. Ironically, student radicals who did not fully trust working class people were assisted by a small part of the organized labor movement when the United Auto Workers provided a modest grant to encourage SDS efforts to get more blue collar workers registered to vote.

By the middle of the sixties the SDS had chapters on more than two hundred campuses and had clearly become the focal point for student radicalism and the political New Left. In opposition to the League for Industrial Democracy's insistence on excluding communists from membership, the SDS shed its affiliation with that parent organization and opened its doors to communists of all persuasions. Although the SDS focused most of its energies in the late sixties on opposition to the Vietnam War, its increasingly radical tone helped create a backlash against it. At its national convention in June 1969, with its old leaders out of power, the SDS split apart from factional fighting between those favoring more independent student radical action and those who adhered to hard-line Marxist dogma. What was left of the organization survived in a weakened condition until it faded from the scene altogether in the mid-seventies.

The Free Speech Movement

Although the SDS had been organized in 1962, it was a series of events on the campus of the University of California at Berkeley in 1964 that swelled the ranks of student radicalism. Student activists from the civil rights movement were rallying and recruiting other students for involvement in that cause, while others were protesting the racially discriminatory hiring practices of the conservative owner of the *Oakland Tribune*. Under political pressure from the *Tribune* and other conservatives in the area, on September 14 the university administration suddenly shut down the area near the campus gate which they had traditionally allowed students to use to advertise political causes. This university action prompted students to organize the Free Speech Movement to protest the decision and to demand that the First Amendment be protected on the campus. When police arrested a civil rights student activist (Jack Weinberg) for defying the ban and setting up a table on October 1 of that year, student protest took the form of direct action. Mario Savio, an Italian-American philosophy major, suddenly jumped to the top of the police car into which Weinberg had been placed, and began speaking to the crowd of students who gathered. Soon about 2,000 students had gathered around and were staging a sit-in, which prevented the police vehicle from moving. For thirty-two long hours, no one left the squad car. Finally, after negotiations with leaders of the Free Speech Movement, in which university administrators promised to drop the charges against Weinberg and eight other students, the demonstrators dispersed.

Then in December, after new charges were brought against several students for conduct during the October demonstration, Mario Savio delivered an emotional speech on the steps of the administration building and called for students to "put your bodies upon the gears and upon the wheels, upon the levers, upon all the apparatus and . . . make it stop." Immediately after his speech several hundred students marched into the building and began a sit-in, which was dispersed the next morning with the arrest of approximately 500 students for trespassing. For several weeks the Berkeley campus was rocked by more sit-ins, public rallies, and a strike which was honored by some 70 percent of the student body. By early 1965 the university authorities reversed their earlier ban and allowed political activity once again. But by then the student revolt had already spread to other major campuses, where student demonstrations and sit-ins were staged to protest the Vietnam War, mandatory ROTC programs (Reserve Officers' Training Corps), racism in higher education, student dress codes, curfews, and other matters.

The Columbia University Strike

The most famous of these student demonstrations in the late sixties occurred at Columbia University in New York City in April 1968. The university administration had announced plans to expand into a black Harlem neighborhood in order to build a new gymnasium, and this had galvanized student opposition. In late April, led by Mark Rudd, leader of the local chapter of the SDS, radical students began entering and occupying several buildings on campus, including the president's office; a college dean was even held against his will. Offices were ransacked, and administrators were forced to cancel classes. When school officials finally called in local police to remove the demonstrators, their excessive force which injured several innocent by-standers led the majority of students on campus to initiate a general boycott of the university. With no alternative in sight, university officials were forced to cancel classes for the remainder of the semester.

During most of the late sixties, the radical student movement employed most of its energies in organizing massive protests against the Vietnam War. (See Chapter Thirteen.)

AN EMERGING COUNTERCULTURE

The violence frequently associated with student radicalism and its failure to radically alter the social structure of American society led other young people to abandon political activity altogether and revolt in more cultural ways. This cultural revolution, known as the counterculture (a term popularized by historian Theodore Roszak), featured the so-called Hippies, much experimentation with consciousness-altering drugs, and a sexual revolution. The sixties came to be known as the "flower generation" to those who sought to express their contempt for white, middle class values by growing long hair, wearing old tattered clothing, finding "peace" through psychedelic drugs, and making love, not war. Ironically, young people from affluent, middle class background tended to join the counterculture, or at least to exhibit certain of its main features, because they felt extreme alienation from their parents' generation. Although the thesis is controversial, some developmental psychologists and others believe that the more permissive parenting in the immediate postwar period contributed to the decline in traditional values among significant elements in the next generation. Dr. Benjamin Spock, a pediatrician who wrote the widely read book *The Common Sense Book of Baby and Child Care* in 1946, is often blamed for encouraging this trend toward more permissive parenting. However, a careful reading of his book does not substantiate the indictment against him, a fact which was confirmed by Spock's own testimony criticizing the misinterpretation of his advice.

The Beat Generation

The forerunners of the hippies were the Beats (or beatniks) of the 1950s. The Beats were a group of noncomformist writers who ridiculed the materialism and conformism of their decade which they most often identified with white middle class suburbanites. Rejecting their generation's values, Beat writers often met in coffee houses to publicly read their essays and poems. Attracted to the message of the Beats, many young people gathered in those places, rubbed shoulders with budding authors, and "applauded" the reading performances by rapidly snapping their fingers. Jack Kerouac's *On the Road*, published in 1957, is considered the best representative of the Beat literature. It was a novel that glorifed the free and easy life of hitchhiking through the country, enjoying drugs, promiscuous sex, and Eastern religious mysticism (especially Zen Buddhism). Kerouac and other Beat writers bitterly satirized middle class values and advocated the kind of life which was described in *On the Road*. Kerouac scorned his generation by describing their existence as "rows of well-to-do houses with lawns and television sets in each living

Hippies form a parade protesting the Vietnam War on San Francisco's Market Street, April 15, 1967. Credit: AP/Wide World Photos.

room with everybody looking at the same thing and thinking the same thing at the same time." They promoted Eastern mysticism, with its emphasis on meditation techniques, as that which would produce a total acceptance of one's being, or beatitude; the terms "Beats" and "Beat generation" were derived from the word "beatitude." In the political world of the fifties, the Beats protested the work of the House Un-American Activities Committee and the nuclear arms race. Their philosophical approach to life influenced the young readers of the Beats, many of whom became the hippies of the next decade.

The Hippie Movement

The word "hippie" is derived from the expression "to be hip," associated with jazz music vocabulary and meaning to be aware of the latest popular trends and fads. Hippies espoused a carefree lifestyle of "doing your own thing" to spite the "establishment" (the conventional norms), which usually consisted of dressing in worn-out clothing, wearing long hair, "tripping" on psychedelic drugs, using obscene language, and engaging in promiscuous sexual relations (called "free love"). Hippies, like most of the youthful political radicals of their day, usually came from white middle class homes. But unlike typical SDS activists, hippies usually skipped higher education and flocked to major cities to join others in communal living arrangements, where they hoped to enjoy their rebellious lifestyle in relative peace. But these communes rarely lasted very long because the hippie disdain for the work ethic led to internal strife about such mundane things as who would get the food, make the meals, and clean the dishes. Eager to be free of parental and institutional restraints, the hippies soon discovered that they lacked the self-discipline necessary for the creation of their utopian life. And many came to depend on panhandling or food stamps in order to meet the basic necessities of survival.

In January 1967, the hippie movement staged a so-called "Human Be-in" at the San Francisco Golden Gate Park. This event was meant to celebrate the coming of a new age by the liberated people of the counterculture, but what it really did was to put the hippie movement on the proverbial map by drawing attention to its major West Coast center, the Haight-Ashbury district in San Francisco. The publicity soon attracted large numbers of "turned off" youth to the San Francisco hippie community, while others traveled to the East Village neighborhood in New York City. During that summer (1967), thousands of young people flocked to those hippie centers to celebrate the Summer of Love. They hung out together, smoked dope and took LSD, and listened to "acid rock" music. Many discovered a down side to the experience, however, as rape, disease, and bad drugs took their toll; several hippies were murdered before the summer had ended. Because of the trouble, 1967 proved to be the last "Summer of Love" held by the hippie movement.

One of the characteristics of the hippie movement was its heavy involvement in a drug culture. While the Beats had smoked marijuana and peyote to increase their writing creativity, the hippies used these and other drugs simply as an "easy" way to alter their state of consciousness, or in other words, to get "high." LSD—lysergic acid diethylamide—quickly became the psychedelic drug of choice because of the very potent hallucinogenic effect that it produced. Hippies loved to talk about their LSD "trips" and encouraged others to join them in a journey which often took the participants into a world of striking color and wonderful sensations. Of course, what many did not know at the time was that LSD damages the genetic structure and can lead to mental instability and even psychosis. One of the gurus of the drug culture was Harvard University professor of psychology, Timothy Leary, who was fired in 1963 for urging students to "tune in, turn on, drop out" through the use of LSD.

Another guru of LSD and an indirect founder of "acid rock" music was Ken Kesey, a novelist living on the West Coast. Kesey and his followers, called the Merry Pranksters, promoted the use of LSD in the 1960s by freely distributing tablets of the acid in orange juice. In San Francisco, they also pioneered the use of psychedelic paints on dancers who moved wildly to the beat of electrified rock music and strobe lights. Heavily promoted by bands like the Grateful Dead, Jefferson Airplane, and Country Joe and the Fish, "acid rock" stormed its way into the music world of youthful America by the second half of the sixties.

The Woodstock Music Festival

As music increasingly mirrored, and encouraged, the drug culture of the hippie movement, large rock music concerts became fashionable. The largest, and most memorable, of these concerts occurred on Max Yasgur's 600-acre farm near Woodstock, New York in August 1969. Nearly 400,000 young people poured onto

Joe Cocker performs at the Woodstock music festival near Bethel, New York in August 1969. Credit: AP/Wide World Photos.

the farm to hear such musicians as Joan Baez, Jimi Hendrix, Joe Cocker, Santana, and dozens of other rock singers. Marijuana was cheap and plentiful, and the sex was free. For three days, concert goers listened to rock music, smoked plenty of dope, and engaged in full sexual intercourse in broad daylight. Sanitation was extremely poor, and people defecated anywhere they pleased and as openly as they had had sex. The Woodstock Music Festival became the most famous symbol of the counterculture.

Music promoters organized another huge rock concert in December 1969 at Altamont, California. There the Rolling Stones rock group hired the Hell's Angels motorcycle gang to provide security for the event. But while lead singer Mick Jagger sang "Sympathy for the Devil," some drunk Hell's Angels "security" members beat a black man to death in front of the stage. Three others died at the concert, and the days of the wild rock concerts were never quite the same after that.

The Yippies

A different type of hippie emerged in the sixties when Abbie Hoffman and Jerry Rubin created the Youth International Party (YIP). Calling themselves Yippies, these two leaders sought fame through media attention of their bizarre antics. The idea was that a revolution of theatrical demonstrations aimed at the establishment would cause materialism and its allies to crumble. One of their most famous episodes occurred when Yippies entered the New York Stock Exchange and threw paper money at brokers who were busily trying to buy and sell paper securities. Such radical, but nonsensical, behavior that Yippies engaged in did nothing to effect political change in society. But it did transform Hoffman and Rubin into household names in the late sixties, as the media paid more attention to them than serious radicals ever did.

The Sexual Revolution

One of the most pervasive and long-lasting elements of the postwar counterculture was the so-called sexual revolution. Although the sexual revolution burst upon the American scene in the 1960s, many factors had been pushing it along since the end of World War II. In 1948, Indiana University zoology professor Alfred C. Kinsey wrote *Sexual Behavior in the Human Male*, which was followed in 1953 by *Sexual Behavior in the Human Female*. These controversial books were based on scientific research and purported to show that sexual relations before marriage (premarital) and outside of marriage (extramarital) were fairly common even though people did not openly talk about such behavior. Many Americans chose not to believe Dr. Kinsey's reports, but when Hugh Hefner published his first monthly edition of *Playboy* magazine in December 1953, it quickly became a popular seller among men. Calling his magazine "entertainment for men," Hefner featured pictures of attractive, unclothed women and espoused a philosophy of sexual liberation through expressions of physical intimacy with a variety of partners. Some social historians believe that the success of *Playboy* magazine was due to widespread male frustration with a society which expected the husband to earn the family income and the wife to supervise its spending. Thus, grown men were encouraged to act out their boyish sexual fantasies.

Popular psychology added an intellectual rationale for promiscuous sexual behavior in the postwar era as well. Although Sigmund Freud's works had become available in the English language during the Roaring Twenties, most Americans had not actually read them for themselves. As with Charles Darwin, more people received their information about his teachings from more popular, less scholarly authors. Freud had indirectly affected American society during the twenties with his view that repressed inhibitions were unhealthy and must be openly expressed. (See Chapter Five.) However, it was the paperback revolution, begun just before World War II, that resulted in the widespread publication and reading of so-called "pop psychology" books which really made Freudian and pseudo-Freudian theories popular. Authors like Herbert Marcuse, Norman O. Brown, and Wilhelm Reich told American readers that many, if not most, social problems were being caused by the repression of "normal" desires. In other words, it was the repression of the desires which society labeled as wrong or sinful, not the desires themselves, which were actually wrong and unhealthy. Therefore, the road to improved mental health could only be traveled by throwing off one's inhibitions and doing whatever felt natural. And although many authors cautioned that ethical behavior never hurt someone else, that distinction was often lost among those who were hearing the "experts" tell them to "do their own thing."

Other factors significantly contributed to the sexual revolution of the sixties as well. For example, many serious thinkers believe that the development of rock 'n' roll music in the postwar era helped push society toward such a revolution in morals because its lyrics often trivialized love, and its beat often led to behavior which tended to break down the inhibitions. Also, the trend toward permissive parenting in the postwar era, along with the tremendous increase in television viewing, led to a generation of young people which had less parental guidance and which was therefore ready to absorb more of what the growing counterculture was teaching them. Then, in the context of all these cultural factors, two medical technology breakthroughs made it increasingly possible for sexual permissive partners to avoid the most serious physical risks. First, the availability of mass produced antibiotics after the war greatly reduced the danger of the social diseases of syphilis and gonorrhea. Second, the birth control pill, which was highly effective (although not 100 percent) in preventing pregnancy, became available in 1960. And by 1970, at least 12 million American women were using "the pill" to avoid becoming pregnant.

All the major factors had come together so that at least by the middle of the sixties the sexual revolution had clearly arrived. Influenced by the cultural forces referred to above, and freed from the high risks of disease and pregnancy by the easy access to antibiotics and "the pill," many men and women began exploring their sexuality earlier, more often, and more openly. Many younger couples, fearing the "trap" of marriage, began "living together" before deciding whether or not to get married. Even some married couples engaged in a new trend of "swinging," the practice of exchanging sexual partners among two or more married couples. Sex researchers William H. Masters and Virginia E. Johnson seemed to reinforce the sexual revolution by challenging many traditional beliefs about masturbation, homosexuality, and other social taboos in their two books, *Human Sexual Response* (1966) and *Human Sexual Inadequacy* (1970). The decade of the sixties also saw thousands of homosexual men and women, who had kept their sexual orientation secret before, use this new "freedom" to openly come out of the proverbial closet and declare themselves to be "gay," a term which increasingly was used to describe homosexual men and lesbian women. Homosexuals then organized the Gay Liberation Front in New York City in 1970 to publicly fight job and housing discrimination on the basis of sexual orientation.

Literature and the movies increasingly reflected the new sexual morality, especially by the 1960s. Many novelists did not hesitate to use sexually explicit language to describe steamy scenes in their books. Moreover, the so-called love stories and other genres using such titillating language generally sold in very high numbers among the public. Movies also got on the new cultural bandwagon by portraying intimate bedroom scenes and other acts of a sexual nature. Parental and religious groups protested so vigorously against the rising tide of the "new morality" that the Motion Picture Association voluntarily adopted a rating system in 1968 in order to provide some type of help for parents to use in supervising the viewing habits of their children. Movies with the "G" rating, for "General" audiences, were considered the safest for all members of the family. On the other end of the spectrum, "R" movies ("Restricted") and "X" movies featured "adult" entertainment, with very explicit nudity, sexuality, and profanity. Even television yielded to the new morality in the sixties by relaxing its standards on language and nudity, although more tradition would be abandoned in the seventies and eighties, especially when cable television and video recorders brought increased competition with the major networks and their movie suppliers.

In 1939, the hit movie *Gone With the Wind* had shocked movie-goers by becoming the first film to use any swear words when Clark Gable had told Vivian Leigh's character, "Frankly, my dear, I don't give a damn!" The movies, including television, had come a long way by 1970, until more personally conservative Americans wondered if there were any taboos left in their culture anymore. Shocked by the sexual, student, and women's revolutions, and by the outbreaks of summer riots in many of the nation's major cities in the late sixties, millions of voters yearned for political leadership that could take the country back to more traditional values. The resulting conservative backlash blamed political liberalism for the perceived decline in morality, which helped propel the United States into a protracted period of conservative political domination in the next decades.

Concluding Comments

By the end of the sixties, the hippie movement, and much of the counterculture, had run out of steam. (Most scholars view the sexual revolution as continuing full steam until about the mid-eighties, when the graying of the sixties generation and the AIDS scare seemed to reduce promiscuity, except among teenagers.) Even Timothy Leary complained that "it was good for a time; then we went so far that we lost it." But perhaps the best line used to describe the demise of much of the counterculture was sung by John Lennon after the breakup of the Beatles in 1970: "The dream is over. What can I say?"

RELIGIOUS TRENDS AND LEADERS

Secular Religion

Organized religion was making a come-back in the United States in the 1940s, but the emerging Cold War late in that decade quickened the revival. The Cold War brought the elements of patriotism and belief in a Supreme Being together, as increasingly it was characterized by religious and political leaders as a struggle between "godless communism" and "Christian America." J. Edgar Hoover, the Director of the FBI, summed up the religious overtones of the Cold War when he announced that "since communists are anti-God, encourage your child to be active in the church." Even Hollywood got into the act by producing popular religious films like *The Robe*, *Ben-Hur*, and *The Ten Commandments* during the era. In the early fifties, the American Legion organized a "Back to God" movement, which was successful in getting Congress to insert the words "under God" into the Pledge of Allegiance in 1954 and "In God We Trust" onto all currency, as the national motto, in 1955. President Dwight Eisenhower reflected this mood when he declared that "recognition of the Supreme Being is the first, the most basic, expression of Americanism." Although he had never officially joined a church until he was president in 1953, Eisenhower considered himself a very religious man. The president further encouraged religious belief by stating that "everybody should have a religious faith, and I don't care what it is."

Many Americans also felt the strains of a loss of community during the fifties, as corporate expansion and maneuvering played a major role in frequently moving people to new locations. An average of at least 20 percent of Americans moved their residences each year during that decade. The joke went around that IBM, a major employer in the postwar era, actually stood for "I've Been Moved." The resulting fluid situation created an environment in which many middle class Americans longed for stability and a greater sense of community. Although long known for being joiners, these Americans joined all kinds of voluntary organizations in record numbers, including churches, synagogues, civic clubs, bridge clubs, and garden clubs. In 1940, about 48 percent of Americans belonged to an organized religious group. By 1960, that figure was at least 65 percent, a percentage that held fairly steady during the sixties.

Church or synagogue affiliation does not in itself measure the depth of religious convictions. Indeed, most social historians of American religion in that period emphasize the shallowness of many believers, and point out that secular religion (the union of patriotism and religion) generally does much more to cement religious believers to their country's policies than to a strong religious faith. And in the process, there is a strong tendency to blindly overlook any serious flaws within society or in the nation's relations with other countries. "My country, right or wrong" is a statement that defines the patriotism of many religious believers who are under the influence of secular religion. In a real sense, then, there is evidence to suggest that secular religion does not do either the church or the state much real good. That is to say nothing about the increased possibility of closer ties between church and state that secular religion sometimes engenders, ties which have historically resulted in the persecution of those religious minorities who do not conform to the prevailing religious dogma. (See Chapter Five for a discussion of the Sunday law movement of the late nineteenth century.)

Influential Religious Leaders

The most prominent religious leaders during the postwar period included Protestant evangelist Billy Graham, *Guideposts* founder Norman Vincent Peale, Roman Catholic Bishop Fulton J. Sheen, and Jewish Rabbi Joshua Liebman. Bishop Sheen used his weekly television program, "Life is Worth Living," to gain a large following, while the others held people spellbound with their preaching and writing. Billy Graham, a Southern Baptist by upbringing, became the most widely known and successful of all Protestant evangelists of postwar society. Graham preached to huge audiences in convention halls and outdoor ampitheaters, emphasizing the basic sinful condition of man and the grace of God through Christ which permits those who accept it by faith to receive salvation and peace of mind.

A Trend Toward Psychology in Religion

Billy Graham was viewed as partly an exception, however, to the prevailing religious trend of the day. Most preachers and other religious leaders tended to avoid the old "fire and brimstone" approach to evangelism and instead placed an emphasis on more comfortable messages in order reassure people that their nation and their personal lives were in harmony with God's desires. Thus, the concepts of sin and personal responsibility to a God of judgment were minimized because these aspects of religion tended to make people nervous and unsettled. The most influential leader of this new direction in American religion, at least among Protestant Christians, was Norman Vincent Peale, who had founded *Guideposts*, a monthly religious magazine, in 1945. In 1952 Peale published his controversial book entitled *The Power of Positive Thinking*. In this and subsequent books and lectures, Peale identified faith as positive thinking, and urged believers to relieve their insecurities and solve their problems by flushing out "depressing, negative, and tired thoughts" and "start thinking faith, enthusiasm, and joy." Throughout his ministry, Peale's significance was to attempt to bring the elements of popular psychology and Christianity together in a harmonious marriage.

When *The Power of Positive Thinking* was published (1952), it brought sharp criticism from many quarters. Christian and Jewish intellectuals attacked Peale's theology for essentially reducing faith to an inward search for self-esteem and self-improvement rather than directing believers to a divine Power outside of themselves. Faith should result in more positive thinking, they said, but true faith is not the same thing as positive thinking. And fusing them together was likely to reduce religion to a psychological process of learning to feel good about oneself, a charge the critics said was contrary to the Judeo-Christian tradition. Furthermore, critics alleged that Peale's views amounted to a formula that selfishly promised prosperity and good fortune to those who conquered their personal weaknesses; this would later be called the "gospel of wealth." Will Herberg, a professor of Judaic Studies at Drew University, criticized the Peale theology in a 1955 book entitled *Protestant—Catholic—Jew*, calling it an empty "religiousness without religion." Opposition to Peale's ideas slowly dissipated over the years, however, until they eventually became quite popular and an important part of American religion.

Evangelist Billy Graham in San Francisco to address the Southern Baptist Convention, June 22, 1951. Credit: AP/Wide World Photos.

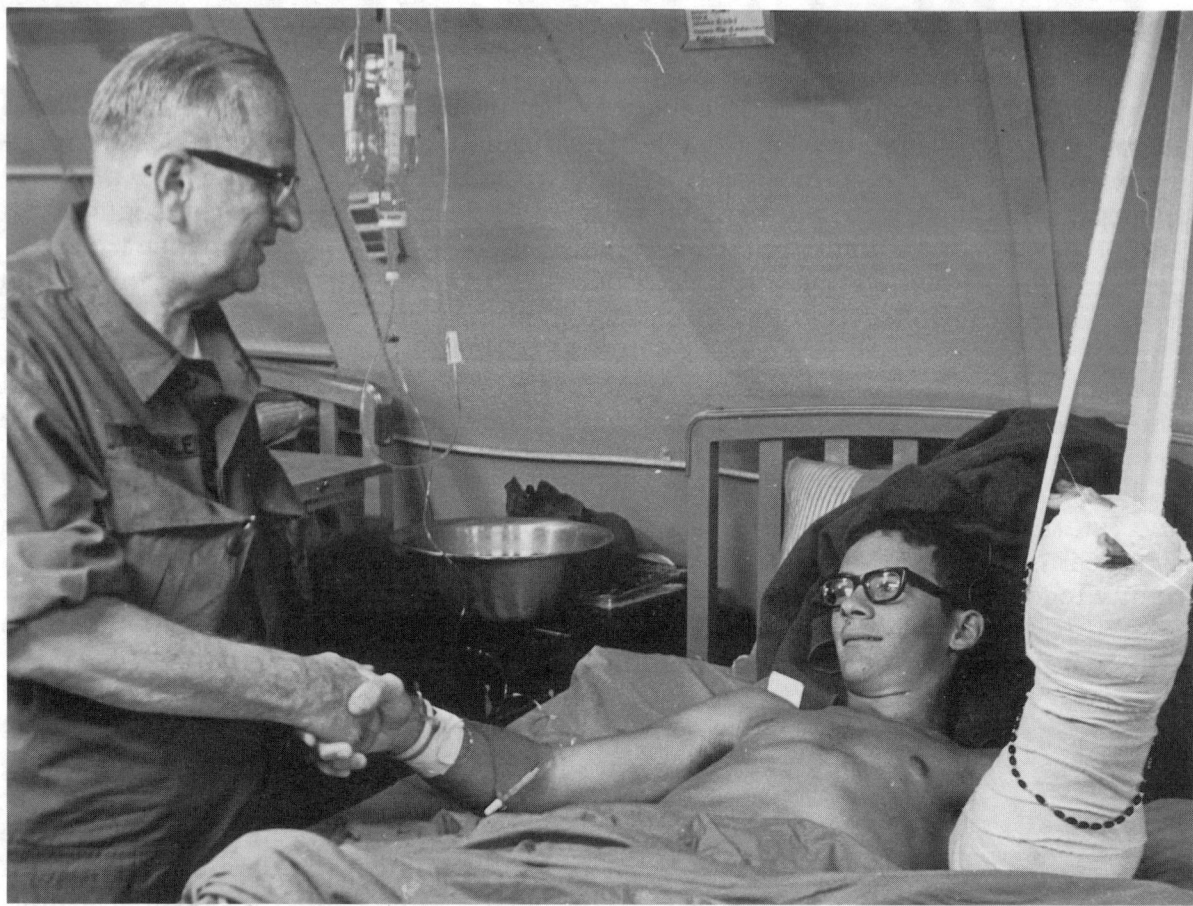

Dr. Norman Vincent Peale, in Vietnam, shakes hands with Marine Lance Corporal Mark Bird at an evacuation hospital in Danang. Credit: AP/Wide World Photos.

The Neo-Orthodoxy Movement

Herberg and other Jewish and Christian theologians, who became known as proponents of "neo-orthodoxy," also were angry because they saw the cultural snobbishness of a religious trend which labeled anything American as superior being used as a justification for the materialistic status quo in society. The most important representative for the "neo-orthodox" movement was Reinhold Niebuhr, a professor at Union Theological Seminary in New York who died in 1970. Niebuhr was a politically liberal theologian who believed that democracy was the most viable form of human government. However, unlike many liberal American Protestants of the past, who had held optimistic views of human nature and believed in the perfectibility of both mankind and human society, Niebuhr believed in the traditional Christian doctrine of original sin. Accordingly, he taught that man was inherently sinful and would never perfect his basic nature or create the millennium on earth because of what he called the "irreducible irrationality of human nature." In this theological perspective, Niebuhr also condemned the psychological emphasis of Peale and others by declaring that its focus on the need to develop self-love lay at the very heart of the definition of sin.

The Spirit of Unity and the Ecumenical Movement

Two of the most significant trends in the postwar era which affected some of the organizational structures of American Christianity were the trend toward consolidation and unity among various Protestant churches and the trend toward ecumenicism. Several Protestant denominations after World War II merged together so as to partially reduce sectarianism (absolute belief in one's denomination) and to increase unity. Cooperation among Protestants was also enhanced by the establishment of the National Council of the Churches of Christ in the United States in 1950. At its founding, this new body consisted of twenty-six Protestant denominations and four different Eastern Orthodox churches. The Council of Churches, as it is commonly called, helps coordinate relief work among the poor at home, as well as to draft joint policy statements on various social-political issues, usually from a more liberal perspective than most fundamentalist churches represent.

The trend toward ecumenicism—the promotion of unity among all Christian groups—was partly a by-product of the growing popularity of a more generic Christianity among Protestants (the "feel good" emphasis referred to above and the increased cooperation among themselves). But it was greatly assisted by revolutionary changes within the Roman Catholic Church in the 1960s. Pope John XXIII called the Second Vatican Council into session in Rome (1962–1965) in order to deal with the growing challenge to church authority among modern Catholics, especially in the United States, and to maintain and increase the relevance and viability of the church. Vatican II, as it was more popularly called, surprised many within and without the Roman Catholic Church by its recommendations for large, and even radical, changes. Among the changes adopted as a result of Vatican II were to replace the centuries-old tradtional Latin with the common language of the people during Catholic services, an increase in the participation of lay members in those services, and the modernization of the lifestyles of priests and nuns. Official statements adopted at Vatican II also called for an ecumenical spirit of attempting to bring Roman Catholic, Eastern Orthodox, and Protestant Christians together into one unified Christian body eventually. Before Vatican II, the Roman Catholic Church had always referred to non-Catholics as "heretics." Afterwards, however, the church has fairly consistently referred to them merely as "separated brethern," a term as radically different as it is conciliatory. Complete organizational unity within Christianity was not achieved by the end of the decade, but the goal had been set, and talks among various groups would continue into the next decades.

American Judaism

Because of the problems in gaining acceptance into American society, many Jewish immigrants of the late nineteenth and early twentieth centuries tended to separate themselves from more traditional religious practices which set them apart from other citizens even more. But after World War II, largely as the result of the Holocaust's attempt to exterminate the Jewish people, American Jews in large numbers returned to more traditional rituals and ceremonies in order to find their identity as a separate people again.

Orthodox Jews did not have to make any significant changes in order to facilitate an understanding of their distinctive identity because they had never really left that behind. For that reason, Orthodox Judaism experienced a resurgence of influence within the Jewish community. But the Conservative and Reform branches of Judaism underwent major changes, especially during the 1960s, both to reestablish their identity as Jews and to counter the expanding influence of the Orthodox branch. Conservative Jewish congregations increasingly permitted women to participate in the synagogue services and even to hold lay offices there. Parts of the Reform branch of Judaism went even further and allowed women to serve as ordained rabbis. Reform Judaism also reestablished many of the old rituals which they had especially abandoned in the earlier decades of their American experience.

Concluding Comments

The fifties and sixties were exciting times for American religion, as many trends, new thinking, and organizational patterns broke sharply with many of the long-held traditions of the past. Almost every religious person in the country was affected by the nearly dizzying changes. And whatever a person thought about those changes, many of them were significant enough to affect the face of the American religious communities for a very long time to come. (For a brief discussion of the two major Supreme Court decisions on religion in the sixties—the *Engel* decision and *Abington v. Schempp*—see Chapter Sixteen, under "The Warren Court.")

THE LITERATURE OF POSTWAR AMERICA

The Beats

Much of the serious literature of postwar society aimed its social criticisms at the conformist, materialistic lifestyle of the middle class. The Beats, like Jack Kerouac in *On the Road* (1957), were especially sarcastic and bitter in their denunciations of their generation in the fifties, so much so that they encouraged a free-swinging lifestyle that rejected the work ethic, used psychedelic drugs, and practiced Eastern meditation. As such, they were the forerunners of the hippie movement. (See "The Beat Generation" earlier in this chapter.) Allen Ginsberg, the foremost Beat poet, wrote *Howl* in 1956 as an assault on American society whose gods, he alleged, were machines. While Kerouac and Ginsberg were the most influential of the Beats, other well-known Beats included William Burroughs, Gregory Corso, and Gary Snyder. Burroughs, for example, was a bizarre character whose own personal experiences sadly seemed to reflect a bright person completely out of control. Although he had studied medicine in Vienna, Austria, and graduated from Harvard University in the 1930s, Burroughs held a variety of odd jobs, including detective, bartender, advertising copywriter, and a pest exterminator. In 1959 he wrote a novel entitled *Naked Lunch*, in which he rejected all authority as something which only and always leads to more control over people's lives. He seemed to live his own philosophy too, demonstrating a tendency to live dangerously. Once he cut off one of his own fingers after contemplating the artist Van Gogh. Tragically, he eventually became a heroin addict and killed his wife while attempting to shoot an apple off her head. Whether they were writers, musicians, or artists, the Beats all possessed an angry contempt for most of the social norms of their day. In this way, they set the stage for the growing counterculture in the 1960s.

Other Social Critics

Other serious authors, who did not experience the radical personal lifestyles of the Beats, also emerged in the fifties to criticize what they deemed as a decline in middle class values. Among these writers was David Riesman, whose book *The Lonely Crowd* (1950) argued that the personality of mainstream Americans was undergoing a radical change from what he called the traditional "inner-directed" personality to the "other-directed" type. In Riesman's thesis, Americans had historically been dominated by people who had internalized a strong set of values given them by their parents and others, values which bestowed upon them the virtues of hard work and a spirit of individualism. But the huge bureaucratic modern corporation had altered the dominant American culture and turned "inner-directed" people into "other-directed" ones who were constantly adjusting to new corporate demands in order to make the boss, or the "system," happy. According to Riesman, the change of personality type had robbed Americans of many of their ethical standards by forcing them to comply with whatever was demanded at the moment. Agreement with Riesman came from sociologist C. Wright Mills, whose *White Collar Society*, published in 1956, accused the new corporate culture of producing employees who not only resented the conformity to its bureaucracy, but who were also forced to repress those resentments as well. And William A. Whyte, Jr., the editor of *Fortune* magazine, painted essentially the same picture of conditions in the corporate offices when he published *The Organization Man* in the same year.

In other serious literature of the period, *The Crack in the Picture Window* (1956) portrayed John Keats' social critique of the monotonous sameness of suburban life, in which he charged that the Levittowns and similarly planned suburbs had been "conceived in error" and "nurtured in greed." (For a description of the Levittown movement, see the section labeled "Levittowns" earlier in this chapter.) In his 1958 book *The Affluent Society*, economist John Kenneth Galbraith challenged the majority view of his day that nearly all of the nation's social problems could be solved by a long period of sustained economic growth. In a sense, his work inspired Michael Harrington to write *The Other America* (1962), which inspired President Lyndon Johnson to launch his so-called war on poverty in the sixties. (See Chapter Sixteen for a discussion of Johnson's Great Society programs.)

The Novelists of the Period

William Faulkner and Ernest Hemingway were two of the literary giants still active during the decade or so after World War II. Faulkner, for example, continued his regional story of Yoknapatawpha County, Mississippi, in *The Town* (1957) and *The Mansion* (1960). But other literary stars emerged to capture the attention of

Ralph Ellison (far left) wins the National Book Award for his first novel Invisible Man, *1953.*
Credit: AP/Wide World Photos.

American readers in the late forties, the fifties, and the sixties. These included such
authors as Norman Mailer, J.D. (Jerome David) Salinger, James Jones, Truman
Capote, Saul Bellow, John Updike, Ralph Ellison, and Philip Roth. Mailer's first
book, *The Naked and the Dead*, published in 1948, was a war novel which pitted
the good guys against the fascist bad guys. But perhaps James Jones' *From Here to
Eternity*, published in 1951, became the most widely read World War II novel. *The
Catcher in the Rye* (1951), written by J.D. Salinger, captured readers with its story
of a young man who is expelled from school, cannot get along with the hypocrisy he
witnesses among adults, and finally suffers a nervous breakdown. Truman
Capote's *Other Voices, Other Rooms* (1948) is a depressing account of a fantasy
world. Saul Bellow portrayed the difficult effort of people to find meaning for their
lives in such works as *Herzog* (1964) and *Mr. Sammler's Planet* (1970). In Bellow's
Seize the Day (1956), his main character finds himself lonely in a world which is indifferent to him at best. In *Rabbit, Run*, John Updike's "Rabbit" Angstrom struggles
with an alchoholic wife and a job that is dull and boring. And like so much of the
postwar literature, the character Angstrom fails to find peace or make sense out of
his frustrated world. Serious American literature during those years, as in the
twenties and thirties, was not characterized by upbeat stories of happy endings.

Among the African-American and Jewish authors of the period, Ralph Ellison is renown for his *Invisible Man*. Published in 1952, Ellison's novel depicts the alienation that most African-Americans felt in a white-dominated society. Another black author, James Baldwin, chronicled the trials of the African-Americans who migrated out of the South to the cities of the North in *Go Tell it on the Mountain* (1953). In 1959, Philip Roth examined the life of middle class American Jews living amid the prosperous postwar economy in *Goodby Columbus*, although his more popular novel was *Portnoy's Complaint*, published in 1969.

The Rise of the Paperbacks

The most significant development affecting the publishing industry in the entire twentieth century was the printing of softcover books, commonly called paperbacks. Robert D. de Graff is given the major credit in introducing this revolutionary concept when Simon and Schuster first offered a set of ten classic books reprinted in paperback editions in 1939. Softcover books could be printed at a greatly reduced cost to the consumer. As a result, the idea quickly gained widespread support among the general public, and sales quickly took off. The paperback revolution had begun with the beginning of World War II. And by 1960, there were nearly 350 million paperbacks being sold annually in the United States.

Magazines and Newspapers

During the 1930s, the trend among magazine publishers was to move away from more narrowly focused magazines that attracted specific readers such as sportsmen, women, or specific hobbyists. Instead, publishers began to produce more magazines of a general interest that would attract wider readership. However, this trend was reversed in the fifties, when some very successful specific interest magazines began publication. For example, in 1952 *TV Guide* made its appearance to take advantage of the growing popularity of television by providing viewers with listings, brief explanations, and short articles about programs and actors. In that same year, Hugh Hefner introduced *Playboy*, a monthly periodical which featured nearly-nude centerfold photographs of beautiful young women. Then in a successful attempt to attract sports enthusiasts, the publishing firm created by Henry R. Luce (of *Time* and *Life* fame) debuted the monthly *Sports Illustrated* in 1954.

By the early 1960s, rising production costs and competition from suburban papers and television were forcing many urban newspapers to merge with other papers or go out of business. Before the end of the decade, most big cities had only one or two newspapers left in operation.

HOLLYWOOD AND THE GOLDEN AGE OF TELEVISION

The Movies

The 1920s through the end of World War II has been called the golden age of Hollywood's movie industry, with studios like Twentieth Century Fox, MGM, Paramount, and Warner Brothers dominating the period, dictating who would work and

Marilyn Monroe. Credit: AP/Wide World Photos.

become stars and who would not. Part of the reason for the huge profits which these major studios earned was the fact that most of them owned national theater chains that "block booked" the entire line of a specific studio's films. When federal courts declared this practice to be a violation of the federal antitrust laws in 1948, the huge, dominating studios began a sharp decline in their own movie production. Instead of producing as many of their own films, the big studios began leasing their facilities to smaller, independent producers who made films with their own production staffs. This increased competition in the movie industry, and a greater variety of movies were made in the fifties and sixties.

At the same time, competition from television resulted in a sharp decline in theater attendance. After all, why go to the movies when you can sit in your favorite chair in your comfortable home and watch shows free of charge on the television set? By 1960, weekly movie attendance had fallen from its postwar high of 90 million to 40–45 million; by the end of the sixties, the figure had fallen still further to below 20 million. One significant effect of this was that since television programs generally appealed to family audiences, the movies could afford to attract certain people by relaxing the standards on language, nudity, and sexual scenes. Therefore, the movie industry itself began phasing out its own self-censorship program in the fifties. And when states began attempting to fill in the gap, the Supreme

Court ruled in 1961 that the First Amendment protected film content as free speech, thus forbidding state licensing efforts. It was not until pressure from religious and parental organizations that the industry instituted its rating system in 1968.

The steady decline in movie attendance did not apply to the drive-in theaters, however. These outdoor theaters featured a very large screen and individual speakers by which each car parked. The drive-ins especially appealed to young people, who loved the independence which the car gave them. It must be admitted, however, that a number of these movie-goers were not always interested in watching the movie. Teenage attendance at the movies, whether in the drive-in or the traditional theater, became the salvation of the movie industry in the postwar era. In fact, 72 percent of all movie-goers in the 1950s were people under the age of 30. As the baby boomers grew into adolescence by the late fifties and early sixties, this trend continued. One effect of this trend was the production of movies aimed specifically at younger audiences. *Rebel Without a Cause*, starring young actor James Dean, and released in 1955, was perhaps the most famous of these youth cult films.

Among the new movie stars who emerged in the fifties were Elizabeth Taylor, Marlon Brando, and Marilyn Monroe. Monroe usually played the stereotyped "dumb" blonde, and her natural charm and physical beauty made her the major Hollywood sex symbol of her day until she died in 1962. Some of her most notable films included *Gentlemen Prefer Blondes* (1953), *River of No Return* (1954), *Bus Stop* (1956), and *Some Like it Hot* (1959).

The Golden Age of Television

Even during the heyday of radio in the 1920s, electronics experts were attempting to develop a system which would transmit pictures over the airwaves. Although quite primitive by modern standards, a radio network—the National Broadcasting Company (NBC)—opened an experimental television station in New York City in 1930. Near the end of the decade, in 1939, Franklin D. Roosevelt became the first American president to be seen on television when he officially opened the New York World's Fair that year. However, only a few selected people had access to sets which could pick up the signal. Many of the technical difficulties had been overcome by then, but the outbreak of World War II diverted resources elsewhere, and the growth of television would have to wait until the end of the war.

In 1946, the year after the war ended, black-and-white television sets became available to the general public for the very first time, and by the end of the year, about 8,000 families owned one. The idea of having a mini-theater in the home was a captivating one that appealed to nearly everyone, and the growth in the number of households with televisions multiplied at an incredible rate. By 1950, the number of households with televisions had increased to about 4 million, and television had eclipsed radio as the nation's favorite medium. That number climbed to 46 million by 1960 and reached 61 million in 1970.

By the early fifties, all three radio networks had expanded into the television network business and were offering programs like "Texaco Star Theater," hosted by Milton Berle, who has since become known as "Mr. Television." While there were network news shows as early as the fall of 1947, entertainment was clearly television's most important commodity. Situation comedies and westerns dominated the evening airwaves in the fifties and into the sixties. Lucille Ball starred as the zany housewife in "I Love Lucy," which was nearly everyone's favorite comedy. Another favorite comedy was "The Honeymooners," featuring Jackie Gleason and Art Carney. More traditional family comedies included "Leave it to Beaver," "Ozzie and Harriet," "Father Knows Best," "The Donna Reed Show," and "My Three Sons." Americans had long viewed the mythical West with fondness, and westerns like "The Lone Ranger," "Bonanza," "Gunsmoke," "The Virginian," and "Maverick" delighted viewers with the simple, although sometimes violent, justice of the good guys triumphing over the bad guys. Lawyer, police, and detective shows became an important part of the

Jerry Mathers, star of the "Leave it to Beaver" television show. Credit: AP/Wide World Photos.

evening line-up on television beginning in the late fifties (and extending throughout the sixties), with such popular programs as "Perry Mason," "The Fugitive," and "Mannix."

Just as advertising had made it possible for commercial radio to succeed, so it also became the source of profits for stations and the networks. Corporate America paid $171 million for the airing of commercials in 1950. That annual figure for advertising costs rose to $1.6 billion by 1960 and soared to $3.6 billion by 1970. This tremendous rise in the costs of television advertising occurred because Americans became TV addicts. In 1950, the average amount of television watched per household was four hours and thirty-six minutes. That number rose to five hours and six minutes by 1960 and extended to five hours and fifty-four minutes by 1970.

The quality of the programming on television was questioned by many from almost the very beginning of its history, with some calling it the "idiot box" and others the "one-eyed monster." Indeed, many observers believed that the networks intentionally produced programs of mediocre value in order to attract a wider viewing audience. Even the commercials have historically been written for a sixth or seventh grade level. Comedian Fred Allen had the poor quality of television in mind when he humorously commented: "They call television a medium because it's rare when it is well done."

ART

Painting

With the coming of the post-World War II era, major changes among American painters broke new ground. First, during the depression years of the thirties, American painting had been dominated by a group of artists who emphasized the hardships of ordinary life. This period of social realism featured such painters as Jack Levine, William Gropper, and Isabel Bishop. And second, American painters had generally followed the lead of European artistic styles, such as French impressionism or cubism, even though the content was varied, of course. But a new style of painting dominated the postwar years until the sixties. Known as abstract expressionism (sometimes called action painting or the New York School), it represented the first significant move away from the imitation of any European style of painting. Instead of the realism of the past, artists like Jackson Pollock, Robert Motherwell, Mark Rothko, and Joan Mitchell focused on the utilization of space and complex patterns of mixed colors. In this way, they intentionally abandoned the traditional use of real objects or scenes, such as still life or the human body, as subjects for painting. Pollock himself invented the "drip" technique, in which paint is slowly applied to a large canvas. His "Autumn Rhythm," painted in 1950, is representative of this new way of painting. The break with European painting tradition was so successful that the painting capital of the world shifted from Paris, France to New York City.

Artistic realism did not disappear from the scene, however, as the popularity of Andrew Wyeth testified. And magazine covers often featured painted illustrations of realistic scenes, with Norman Rockwell becoming the most famous illustrator of his day. And by the late fifties, a backlash had developed among many painters who felt that the abstract expressionists had come to represent a kind of elitism. Therefore, a new movement known as "pop" art (popular art) was clearly challenging the painting establishment by the decade of the sixties. "Pop" art depicted realistic representations of common objects and scenes that the masses of people could understand. Andy Warhol, the best-known "pop" artist of the decade, used the new style of painting to especially mock what many considered to be the monotonous consumerism of American materialism. In 1962, Warhol's "100 Cans," showing row after row of cans of soup on supermarket shelves, was a superb example of this new trend among "pop" artists.

Sculpture

In the 1950s, Alexander Calder challenged the tradition of realism in sculpture by creating abstract "objects" from metal. These pieces of art included mobiles, which hang from the ceiling, and stabiles, which are made to stand on the floor. Based on the pioneering work of David Smith, sculpturing in the next decade was dominated by the creation of huge abstract metal "objects."

Fans turn out to see Elvis Presley perform at the Mississippi-Alabama state fair. Credit: AP/Wide World Photos.

THE MUSIC WORLD ROCKS TO A DIFFERENT BEAT

Music in the Fifties

Even music was not immune from the enormous social changes sweeping the country in the years following the Second World War. A new form of popular music called rock 'n' roll emerged in the mid-fifties as a blend of a rather large dose of black rhythm-and-blues music with elements of country-and-western and jazz thrown in for good measure. Two radio disc jockeys played important roles in making the new sound popular among white listeners. First, Alan Freed, a Cleveland, Ohio disc jockey who played classical music introduced a new radio program called "Moondog's Rock and Roll Party" in 1952 after he observed white teenagers listening and dancing to rhythm-and-blues music in a record store. Thus, Freed coined the term "rock 'n' roll" to describe the new music. His program was a smashing success with young people, so he took advantage of the opportunity to move to WINS in New York City, where he helped propel rock 'n' roll into the most popular form of music among the youth. Then in 1954, Bill Haley, a white Philadelphia disc jockey, adapted black musician Ike Turner's song "Shake, Rattle, and Roll" with his band the Comets, and "Rock Around the Clock" became the first big rock 'n' roll hit.

Rock 'n' roll music's strong beat and loud volume relied heavily on the guitar and drums to provide its distinctive style. While the tunes exuded high energy levels, the lyrics most often spoke of love and made frequent sexual innuendos. Black and white musicians rushed to the new musical expression, and Buddy Holly, Chubby Checkers, Chuck Berry, Jerry Lee Lewis, and "Little Richard" Penniman became well-loved celebrities to the youth of America. Assisting the rise of rock 'n' roll was a big push from the record companies, whose cheap 45 r.p.m. records (revolutions per minute) flooded the market with hit music in much the same way that the paperback revolution filled the bookstores with cheap paperbacks. Sales of records tripled from 1954 to 1960, aided by radio stations and television programs like *American Bandstand*, hosted by Dick Clark and making its nationwide debut in 1957.

But it was a young white Mississippian by the name of Elvis Presley who really launched rock 'n' roll music to its lofty heights of popularity. Born in Tupelo, Mississippi, Elvis Aron Presley was a young truck driver in the mid-fifties who loved to sing. On the spur of a moment, Presley recorded two songs at a Memphis studio in 1954. Two years later, in January 1956, "Heartbreak Hotel" was released and became his first big hit. When he then appeared on *The Ed Sullivan Show* on television, Elvis Presley shocked adults with the hip gyrations that accompanied his singing, and he quickly was dubbed by critics as "Elvis the Pelvis." Parents and other adults complained that he was leading the youth of the nation to moral ruin. But the more parents condemned Presley's music, the more popular he became among the young.

Music in the Sixties

Rock 'n' roll underwent some significant changes in the 1960s. Electric guitars and other instruments which electronically amplified the sounds gave the music an even louder beat. And influenced by British musical groups, rock 'n' roll began emphasizing more of the black rhythm-and-blues at the expense of the country music influence. In addition, the abbreviated term "rock" gradually became accepted as the new designation for the young people's music. Chief among the British practitioners of rock music who influenced its new image were the Beatles, which featured four young men from Liverpool, England—John Lennon, Paul McCartney, George Harrison, and Ringo Starr. The Beatles invaded the United States in 1964, and were welcomed with such young female screaming and other hoopla that a new term had to be coined to describe it—Beatlemania. Two of their earliest hits in America were "She Loves You" and "I Wanna Hold Your Hand." The Beatles paved the way for other British groups, like the Rolling Stones, with lead singer Mick Jagger, which became known for its vulgarity. Among the home-grown rock groups in

The Beatles. Credit: AP/Wide World Photos.

the United States, the Beach Boys arose in the sixties with their distinctive happy, upbeat music and lyrics, derived largely from the California beach scene. Beach Boys' classics include "Good Vibrations," "California Girls," and "Surfin' USA."

Another form of rock music made its appearance in the sixties as well. Blending folk-style music with rock, composer and singer Bob Dylan created folk rock music as a vehicle to protest the Vietnam War and to express other socially conscious messages. Joan Baez and the group known as Peter, Paul, and Mary were two of the most popular folk rock performers.

SPORTS

Socially speaking, the most important development in professional sports during the postwar era was the breaking of the color barrier. And the biggest change occurred in major league baseball, which had historically been the most segregated sport in the country. A few black players had played with whites in the early days of organized baseball. But the rise of state laws requiring racial segregation in the South in the 1880s, and the accompanying social custom outside that region, all led to the expulsion of blacks from what became known as the white leagues. By the 1920s, black players had formed the Negro Leagues in order to play some kind of professional baseball, but they were never as prestigious as the all-white National and American Leagues.

Realizing that a lot of valuable talent had been kept out of the major leagues, Brooklyn Dodger president and general manager Branch Rickey made the decision to buck the system and introduce black players to the major leagues. In order for this revolution to be successful, Rickey knew that he must find and carefully prepare not only a talented player,

Mickey Mantle, New York Yankee outfielder. Credit: AP/Wide World Photos.

but also one who would willingly suffer the abuse he was certain to receive. Rickey found just such a player in Jackie Robinson, and in 1947, Robinson became the first African-American baseball player to play in the major leagues when he put on a Brooklyn Dodger uniform.

Despite the fact that Robinson played superb baseball and won the National League Rookie-of-the-Year Award in his first season, many white fans still refused to accept him. For two years, Robinson kept his promise to suffer abuse without

Jackie Robinson in a Brooklyn Dodgers uniform.
Credit: Los Angeles Dodgers.

comment, as he became the recipient of jeers, insults, hate mail, and even death threats. But eventually Robinson's outstanding play on the field compelled fans to accept the reality that major league baseball could be greatly enhanced by the admission of black players. His courageous stand also opened the door for black players to enter other sports, like basketball and football, on a much larger scale. In his own way, Jackie Robinson paved the way for Americans to eventually see that the "separate but equal" racial policies of the past no longer belonged in an enlightened society. He retired in 1957 and later entered the Baseball Hall of Fame in Cooperstown, New York.

MODERN MEDICINE

One of the benefits of the postwar economic boom was that most Americans could afford to utilize the latest medical treatments being developed. High on the list were a series of so-called "wonder drugs" called antibiotics. The origin of modern antibiotics is traced to the discovery of penicillin in 1928 by the British scientist Alexander Fleming. By the 1940s, penicillin was being effectively used to treat a large variety of diseases, including most types of pneumonia, syphilis, gonorrhea, and scarlet fever. Other antibiotics developed in the forties included streptomycin (1945) and aureomycin (1948), which were quite effective in treating influenza, whooping cough, stomach infections, and other maladies. One of the greatest medical breakthroughs of all time was the development of the polio vaccine by Dr. Jonas Salk. The head of a viral research laboratory at the University of Pittsburgh, Dr. Salk began testing a new vaccine for the dreaded disease in 1954. The next year the Food and Drug Administration formally approved its effectiveness and use, and the number of cases of infantile paralysis (polio) declined some 97 percent by 1962.

With the dreaded epidemic diseases all but gone, the infant mortality rate dropped dramatically from 34 deaths per 1,000 live births in 1945 to 20 deaths per 1,000 in 1970. This sharp decline in the infant mortality rate accounted for most of the increase in the average life span, which rose from about 67 years of age in 1946 to approximately 71 years of age in 1970. On the downside, however, racial differences between whites and blacks continued to prevail. For example, the infant mortality rate for whites in 1970 was about 18 deaths per 1,000 live births, compared to nearly 31 deaths per 1,000 live births among African-Americans. And as of 1970, white men still outlived black men an average of 6.5 years, while white women lived an average of 6 years longer than black women. Economic resources and education still made a difference in how much one shared in the benefits of new medical advances.

CONCLUDING STATEMENT

Americans both witnessed and experienced innumerable changes in their society during the first twenty-five years following the Second World War. Great social movements involving African-Americans, women, student activists, and others brought millions more into the political and economic system. The baby boomers grew up and had a profound effect on society, as did the growth of television and other new technologies over those same years. Those changes did not end with the 1960s, however, for they would continue to have major ripple effects across the social spectrum in the decades to come.

ADDITIONAL READINGS

Erik Barnouw, *Tube of Plenty* (1982). The best one-volume history of television, with excellent material on the new medium's impact upon cultural and political life.

Michael R. Belknap, *Federal Law and Southern Order: Racial Violence and Constitutional Conflict in the Post-Brown South* (1987). The best overview of the evolution of federal policy toward controlling anti-civil rights violence.

Taylor Branch, *Parting the Waters: America in the King Years,* (1988). A deeply researched and monumental narrative history of the Southern civil rights movement organized around the life and influence of Rev. Martin Luther King, Jr.

Clayborne Carson, *In Struggle: SNCC and the Black Awakening of the 1960s* (1981). The most comprehensive history of the Student Nonviolent Coordinating Committee, arguably the most important civil rights organization. Carson stresses the evolution of SNCC's radicalism during the course of the decade.

William Chafe, *Civilities and Civil Rights: Greensboro, North Carolina and the Black Struggle for Equality* (1980). Examines the community of Greensboro from 1945–1975. Chafe focuses on the "etiquette of civility" and its complex relationship with the promise of racial justice, along with black protest movements and relations between the city's blacks and whites.

Sara Evans, *Personal Politics: The Roots of Women's Liberation in the Civil Rights Movement and the New Left* (1979). A pathbreaking study showing the important connections between the struggle for black rights and the rebirth of feminism.

Herbert Gans, *The Levittowners* (1967). A classic study of postwar suburban life, arguing that suburban communities were far more diverse and less conformist than pictured in popular accounts of the 1950s.

David J. Garrow, *Bearing the Cross: Martin Luther King, Jr. and the Southern Christian Leadership Conference* (1986). An exhaustively researched biography of King that effectively ties together King's student days, his understanding of Gandhi, and his economic views. Garrow makes excellent use of FBI files and other government documents.

James B. Gilbert, *A Cycle of Outrage* (1986). An insightful analysis of juvenile delinquency and its treatment by social scientists and the mass media during the 1950s.

Charlie Gillett, *The Sound of the City* (rev. ed., 1983). A detailed, pioneering history of rock 'n' roll, with special emphasis on its urban roots.

Kenneth T. Jackson, *Crabgrass Frontier* (1985). The most comprehensive overview of the history of American suburbs. Provides a broad historical context for understanding postwar suburbanization, and offers an excellent analysis of the impact of government agencies, such as the Federal Housing Administration.

Richard Kluger, *Simple Justice* (1977). Explores the politics of civil rights at the national level through a close examination of the landmark *Brown* v. *Board of Education* ruling.

George Lipsitz, *Time Passages* (1990). An illuminating set of essays charting developments in American popular culture. Especially strong analysis of music and early television.

Greil Marcus, *Mystery Train* (1976). A provocative set of essays on rock 'n' roll and its connections with older forms of American culture. Includes a brilliant analysis of Elvis Presley's career and impact.

Douglas T. Miller and Marion Novak, *The Fifties: The Way We Really Were* (1977). A very useful critical appraisal of the decade's cultural life and social trends.

Aldon D. Morris, *The Origins of the Civil Rights Movement: Black Communities Organizing for Change* (1984). An important study combining history and social theory. Morris emphasizes the key role of ordinary black people, acting through their churches and other community organizations before 1960.

Gerald Nicosia, *Memory Babe: A Critical Biography of Jack Kerouac* (1983). Both the best biography of this key Beat writer and the best analysis of the Beat Generation.

Richard Polenberg, *One Nation Divisible* (1980). A concise overview of American society from World War II to the 1970s, with special attention to the persistence of class, racial, and ethnic divisions.

Howell Raines, *My Soul is Rested: Movement Days in the Deep South Remembered* (1977). The best oral history of the Movement, drawing from a wide range of participants and points of view. It is brilliantly edited by Raines, who covered the events as a journalist.

Jo Ann Gibson Robinson, *The Montgomery Bus Boycott and the Women Who Started It,* ed. David J. Garrow (1987). An important memoir by one of the key behind-the-scenes players in the Montgomery bus boycott. Robinson stresses the role of middle and working-class black women in the struggle.

Harvard Sitkoff, *The Struggle for Black Equality, 1954–1980* (1981). A brief, well-researched, narrative history of the Movement, with good material on the complex relationship between racial justice and economic issues.

Robert Weisbrot, *Freedom Bound: A History of America's Civil Rights Movement* (1990). Offers one of the best single volume syntheses of the Movement. Weisbrot is especially strong on the often turbulent relations between black activists and white liberals, and the relationship between civil rights and broader currents of American reform.

CHAPTER FIFTEEN

The Critical Era: 1945–1960

MAJOR EVENTS

1945   Harry S. Truman is sworn in as President
The United Nations Conference held in San Francisco

1946   Truman Seizes Coal Mines

1947   The Taft-Hartley Act
The National Security Act
Truman Issues Loyalty Order

1948   Truman's "Miracle" Election Victory
The Organization of American States (OAS) is created
The modern nation of Israel is established

1950   Senator Joseph McCarthy begins Anti-Communist Crusade
Alger Hiss is convicted

1952   The first hydrogen bomb is exploded by U.S.
Dwight D. Eisenhower is elected president

1953   The Soviets exploded their first hydrogen bomb
The Rosenbergs are executed as spies

1954   The U.S. Intervenes in Guatemala

1955   The Warsaw Pact is formed in eastern Europe
The AFL and CIO united to form the AFL-CIO

1956   The Highway Act begins interstate highway system
The Suez Crisis
The Hungarian Revolt
Eisenhower is re-elected president

1957   *Sputnik* is launched into space by the Soviets
The Eisenhower Doctrine is announced

1958   The National Aeronautics and Space Administration (NASA) is founded
The National Defense Education Act

1959   The Landrum-Griffin Act

1960   An American U-2 Spy Plane is shot down over Soviet Union
John F. Kennedy is elected president

INTRODUCTION TO THE TRUMAN ADMINISTRATION

At 7:09 p.m. on April 12, 1945, Harry S. Truman was administered the oath of office for the presidency of the United States. The sudden death of President Franklin Roosevelt had the nation and the former vice-president reeling with the shock. The day after he took office Truman told reporters, "I don't know whether you fellows ever had a load of hay fall on you, but when they told me what had happened, I felt like the moon, the stars, and all the planets had fallen on me." Truman had been chosen as President Roosevelt's running mate in the 1944 elections because he was a good compromise candidate. He was an experienced politician, a supporter of the New Deal, a reliable member of the Democratic Party, and had gained influence in the Senate without making many enemies. However, few even considered the remote possibility of his becoming the president.

Truman's career in politics began in 1922, with his election as judge to the Jackson County Court in Jackson County, Missouri. This was an administrative position that compared to the positions of county commissioner or county supervisor in other states. His support in this election by Kansas City political boss Tom Pendergast would have people wondering for years whether or not Truman was actually part of the corrupt Pendergast machine. Truman had come to Pendergast's attention through his friendship with the boss's brother. Not allowing his association with a political machine to compromise his integrity in carrying out his duties in any way, Truman advanced up the political ladder through hard work, reliability, and honesty, not by selling favors to anyone.

In 1934, and again in 1940, he was elected to the United States Senate. His influence in Washington and national recognition peaked with his selection during World War II as chairman of the Committee to Investigate the National Defense Program (the Truman Committee). The committee was put together to oversee the efficient and economical spending of the nation's defense budget to produce weapons of war. Recommendations made by the committee saved the government approximately $15 billion. His next step in service to his country was to accept the Democratic National Convention's offer to become the candidate for vice-president in 1944, after Vice-President Henry A. Wallace had alienated many party officials with his more radical leftist views.

After just 82 days as vice president, Harry S. Truman became the nation's thirty-third president. The problems he faced were immense, and his task was made even more difficult by the fact that President Roosevelt had not briefed him on the details of the crises the nation faced. He had not been kept informed by President Roosevelt concerning strategies to win the Second World War, the diplomatic negotiations with the other allies, nor the plans for reconversion of the nation once the war was won. Doubting his own abilities to steer the nation safely through the next few years, the new president went to work with great energy and an emerging decisiveness that was to characterize his administrations.

With the surrender of Japan, the war was suddenly over, but then came the awesome task of making a successful peace. A new organization for world peace, the United Nations, must be successfully launched; the areas controlled by the former Axis nations must be occupied; the criminals of World War II must be brought to justice; the developing Cold War with the Soviet Union must be dealt with (see

Chapter Thirteen); the American economy must be converted back to a peacetime economy without bringing back the depression; and Truman must determine his own program for the future direction of the nation.

ORGANIZING THE UNITED NATIONS

Background

On January 1, 1942, 26 of the Allies at war with the Axis powers had signed the Declaration of the United Nations, which reaffirmed the principles of the Atlantic Charter for the nations of the world to join together to prevent wars. Nations continued to believe that in spite of the failure of the League of Nations to prevent the outbreak of World War II, an organization for collective security was the most promising hope for world peace. Delegates from 46 nations met in San Francisco from April 25 to June 26, 1945, at the United Nations Conference on International Organization to formalize a charter for the new organization. President Truman opened the Conference and pledged American support for the ideals of this organization. Although many nations joined the United Nations, all agreed that the future peace of the world would be determined by the cooperation of the five great powers—the United States, the Soviet Union, Great Britain, France, and China. The first General Assembly of the United Nations met in London on January 10, 1946, with 51 charter nations represented. A donation from John D. Rockefeller, Jr., of $8.5 million bought land on New York City's East River to bring the organization to its permanent location, which is considered international territory.

The General Assembly and the Security Council

The major goals of the United Nations, according to its charter, included the following: maintaining international peace and security, becoming a center for international cooperation to solve international problems, and promoting human rights and fundamental freedoms. Trygvie Lie, the former Foreign Minister of Norway, served as the first Secretary General until 1952. The Secretary General is the chief administrative officer for the organization. This position is not only administrative; the Secretary General has also been authorized on occasion to mediate in serious disputes between nations. The delegates of member nations make up the General Assembly. Each nation has one vote on issues, and all are considered equal. The United Nations does not have the authority to order members to take specific actions, except in cases when the Security Council calls for an enforcement action against aggression.

It is the primary responsibility of the Security Council to assure peace and security around the world. Today the Council consists of five permanent members (the United States, the United Kingdom, France, Russia, and China), and 10 non-permanent members that rotate every two years. Any one of the five permanent members of the Security Council may veto a Security Council proposal. The veto can be a powerful weapon and, unlike an American president's veto, it cannot be overridden. The veto had been used by the Soviet Union 21 times by the spring of

1948 in order to block action that the other permanent members hoped to take. The United Nations became another arena of conflict for the United States and the Soviet Union. Because of the power of the Security Council and its veto, the United Nations has become frequently more of an organization of debate rather than an active problem solver.

The Work of the UN

Most of the work to carry out the goals of the charter in solving international problems, other than military, have come from the multitude of advisory committees, councils, and an International Court of Justice. The United Nation's International Trade Organization was particularly useful during the Truman terms in facilitating world trade. The International Atomic Energy Agency was formed to advance the peaceful use of atomic energy. The dangerous possibilities of the uses of atomic energy, even though the United States was the only nation capable of producing atomic bombs at this time, prompted the United States Congress to increase the control of atomic energy through passage of the McMahan Act on August 1, 1946, establishing the Atomic Energy Commission for the United States. The act allowed the army and navy to produce atomic weapons and prohibited the distribution of fissionable materials or information on atomic energy.

All presidents from Truman onward have supported American involvement in the actions of the United Nations, frequently instigating the actions. The organization has not prevented war, as President Woodrow Wilson so fervently wished when he was laying the groundwork for the first collective security organization, but the wars that have occurred since its inception have been localized. The United Nations has been involved in attempts to settle disputes in Iran, Greece, Indonesia, Israel, and Korea with a mixed record of success.

WAR TRIALS

The Allies decided to seek justice for the victims of the Axis powers in World War II. Thus, a charter was adopted in London in August 1945, to bring German and Japanese civilian and military officials to trial for their crimes against humanity. Thousands were tried in courts established by the Allies in occupied Europe and Japan. Bringing the perpetrators of war to court presented many problems. First, many of the worst offenders were dead, most notably Adolf Hitler. Second, there were some criticisms of applying codes of law retroactively. And third, many believed it was revenge rather than justice to have the accusers sit in judgment of the defendants. Nevertheless, 23 nations signed the charter designating that certain acts during war were punishable offenses.

The Nuremberg Trials

The most important of the war trials conducted by the International Military Tribunal was at Nuremberg, Germany. The trial of top Nazi officials began on November 20, 1945. The trials not only set precedents in international law for the fu-

Nazi defendants in the Nuremburg War Crimes Trials, November 22, 1945. Credit: AP/Wide World Photos.

ture, but brought to light the extent of the inhuman activity of Hitler's Nazi regime. Twenty-two defendants were put on trial at Nuremberg. The charges were grouped into four categories: (1) Creating a conspiracy to seize power in Germany and then using that power in acts of aggression; (2) Crimes against peace; (3) War crimes in occupied territory and on the high seas; and (4) Crimes against humanity. One judge and an alternate sat on the bench from the United States, Great Britain, France, and the Soviet Union. Each nation also had its own prosecuting staff. At the end of the Nuremberg Trials, twelve defendants were sentenced to death. The most prominent of these was Reichsmarschall Hermann Goering, second in power to Hitler during most of the Nazi regime. Goering, however, cheated the executioner by swallowing poison.

Japanese War Crimes Trials

Japanese war leaders were tried by the International Military Tribunal for the Far East. Former Premier Hideki Tojo and six generals were hanged in Tokyo on December 23, 1948. Because Emperor Hirohito had survived the war and the surrender of Japan, it was necessary to decide what his fate should be. A trial and punishment for his role in the war was considered, but General Douglas MacArthur convinced Washington that the fairly smooth occupation of Japan and its conversion into a strong ally in the Pacific would be severely threatened if the Emperor did not stay as the nominal head of Japan. Despite strong objections by other advisors, President Truman accepted MacArthur's recommendation. By the end of 1949, however, 720 officers in the Japanese army and navy had been executed.

DOMESTIC ISSUES UNDER TRUMAN

Demobilizing the Military

Following the unexpected collapse of Japan in August 1945, the concern was how to demobilize a military organization of 12 million men and women back into civilian life without creating a crisis for the economy. A high unemployment rate could bring back the depression that participation in the war had finally brought to an end. The administration determined that the release of close to 5 million military personnel within one year would be a reasonable number to reintroduce to the work force while the nation was reconverting to a peacetime economy. The public, however, pressured the government to bring the men home more quickly and in much larger numbers. In December of 1945, President Truman received thousands of postcards asking him to "Bring the boys home by Christmas."

By January 1946, Truman was concerned that the massive demobilization he had agreed to under pressure was compromising the occupation commitments of the nation in former Axis-controlled countries. The overseas bases garrisoned with American soldiers were also in jeopardy, so he slowed down the process. Congress was bombarded with letters and delegations pleading to bring the soldiers home. American soldiers overseas also demonstrated to express their displeasure with the slow demobilization. The soldiers and the country calmed when General Dwight Eisenhower explained the necessity of American troops overseas for national security and the occupation of defeated territories. In spite of decreasing the releases, the army would have a shortage of men by the winter of 1946. Therefore, Congress reluctantly agreed to extend the draft until March 31, 1947.

The GI Bill of Rights

The implementation of the Servicemen's Readjustment Act (the GI Bill of Rights) assisted in keeping unemployment rates lower than expected from the quick release of members of the armed services. President Roosevelt had signed the bill into law on June 22, 1944. Foreseeing the problems that the release of so many soldiers would create, and to assist the returning soldiers to a grateful nation, the president asked Congress for money to allow the soldiers to readjust to civilian life. The bill provided funds for 52 weeks of unemployment, partial guarantees on loans for houses or businesses, expansion of the United States Employment Service, and college expenses.

RECONVERSION OF THE ECONOMY

Converting the economy from wartime to peacetime production was a situation that caused great anxiety for the new president. There was considerable doubt that production could be stimulated sufficiently to avoid an economic depression such as had preceded World War II. In August 1945, there was not a well coordinated plan for a peacetime economy in place. The Office of War Mobilization and Reconversion, which had been established in 1944, was the coordinating agency for the government's reconversion plans. On August 9, the president ordered the War Production Board to ensure that civilian production was facilitated by removing most production controls and allowing the distribution of materials that had been set aside for the war effort. Before Congress met to consider Truman's reconversion plans, the executive agencies were informed through Executive Order 9599 of the president's expectations during the transition phase. He expected the agencies to give every assistance possible to the manufacturing of goods, to continue controls only to stabilize the economy and remove them when they were no longer necessary, to allow wage and salary increases if prices did not rise along with the salaries (except in salary disputes in which the salaries had been extremely unfair), and to consider labor disputes that interfered with military production or reconversion to a peaceful economy as contrary to the national interest.

Not waiting for Congress to act, the administration worked on the problem of reconversion. By the end of 1945, the only government contracts that businesses held were for essential military goods. Rationing continued only on tires, meats, fats, oils, sugar, and shoes. The War Production Board had removed close to two-thirds of the production control regulations. The Office of Price Administration, fearing inflation, lifted price controls on only a few nonessential goods, such as furs, for example.

Companies returned to the production of consumer goods, and the peacetime economy surged. A combination of factors prevented a depression after the war. Wartime savings of about $140 million, and citizens purchasing long-denied products, created such a large consumer demand that manufacturing could not keep up. Inflation, not depression, was the problem for the country. The GI Bill stimulated economic growth and reduced unemployment. A 1945 tax cut, and profits from the war, encouraged businesses to invest in new factories. International trade was increased while other nations were recovering from the effects of the war. International trade and finance was easier for the United States and other nations because of new institutions put in place in 1944 under the Bretton Woods Agreement, which created the International Monetary Fund, the General Agreement of Tariffs and Trade (GATT), the World Bank, and valued foreign currencies in relation to the dollar. New technologies and new synthetic materials developed during the war made improvements in established industries and created new industries.

LABOR PROBLEMS FOR TRUMAN

Pressure for Wage Increases

For a time, labor unrest and strikes hampered the ability of the government to implement its reconversion policies. By August 1945, there was a proposal for a conference to resolve the problems between government, labor, and management officials that were slowing production, which in turn affected employment. On September 11, the United Steelworkers demanded a wage increase, which opened the floodgates for other unions to demand increases of about 30 percent. Workers had almost doubled their wages during the war with overtime and production bonuses, and they wanted new wage increases to compensate for those lost wages, especially in the face of growing inflation. Union membership was close to 14.5 million by 1945, and their formidable size gave the workers and their unions leverage to back their demands.

The national government became involved in the problems between management and labor in the auto industry, coal mining, steel production, and railroads. Strikes and unrest were effecting the prosperity of the nation. The problem of inflation would become worse if wage increases caused further increases in prices. Truman urged collective bargaining to resolve the disputes between the two sides and also let it be known that he would not accept strikes in industries that were crucial to the well being of the nation. On October 4, he acted on his resolve when he ordered the seizure of 26 petroleum plants on the grounds that the loss of their product constituted a national security risk. He called upon representatives at the Labor-Management Conference on November 5, to handle their own problems, but let all know that he would not tolerate any actions which threatened to prevent the economy from reaching full production. The conference adjourned without significant recommendations as to how to avoid the work stoppages that had increased as the representatives met.

The General Motors Strike

General Motors workers walked off the job in 20 states on November 21, 1945. Walter Reuther, vice-president of the United Auto Workers union, justified the strike with an explanation that the workers were entitled to raises, and the company could afford the raises and would still realize a sizable profit without raising the price of the product. The strike was calm on both sides. Reuther made sure that the strike did not alarm or alienate the general public with violence as had sometimes been the case with labor unrest in the past. The company refused the demands of the workers, especially the demand to open its books to determine if the pay raise would necessarily warrant an increase in product price, and countered with an offer of a 10 percent raise and more work hours. President Truman appointed a commission to study the position of both sides. General Motors refused the commission's recommendation of a raise of close to 17 percent. Settlement was finally reached in March 1946, with an 18.5 cent pay increase and a vacation allowance. The General Motors settlement set the pattern for Ford and Chrysler, which reached similar agreements with their workers without strikes.

The Steel Strike

Of more importance to the nation was an impending steel strike, because such a strike would affect many other industries. The United Steel Workers union called for its workers to strike on January 18, 1946, after management in the industry turned down Truman's recommendation of a wage increase of 18.5 cents per hour. The owners of the plants wanted the government to allow a per ton price increase before they would consider giving the workers a raise. In February, the steel companies accepted the government's offer to increase the prices to $5 a ton, and the strike was soon over. February was a real trial for the president, with close to 2 million workers engaged in various labor strikes.

Truman Seizes Coal Mines

In March, the number of ongoing strikes lessened and industrial production rose. In April, however, United Mine Workers Union President John L. Lewis called his members to walk out of the bituminous coal mines. Lewis realized that the government might seize the mines, but he be-

John L. Lewis, United Mine Workers Chief, addresses the joint meeting of coal operators and mine workers at the Shoreham Hotel in Washington. Credit: AP/Wide World Photos.

lieved that instead of seizure, the government would agree to union demands for a health-and-welfare fund, pay increases, and an increase in other benefits. Because the strike caused other industries to curtail their production, however, President Truman ordered the seizure of the bituminous mines, effective May 22, under wartime authority. (A few days later, the president asked Congress to authorize the military drafting of workers engaged in illegal strikes and the confiscation of profits from any industry to the federal government, but Congress refused.) Angered, Lewis expanded the strike to the anthracite coal mines. But by June 8, negotiations with the Department of the Interior were brought to a successful conclusion. However, the unwillingness of many of the mine owners to accept this settlement led to continued nominal control of the bituminous mines by the federal government.

A Railroad Strike

On May 23, the Locomotive Engineers union and the Railway Trainmen union called a strike against the railways. This strike would shut down most of the country's industry which was dependent on the rails for transportation of raw materials and finished products to market. Truman demanded that the workers return to work by 4 p.m. on May 25. The president also announced that he would address Congress on the serious problem that the strikes were causing for industrial recovery and prosperity. President Truman accepted the idea that the army should run the trains until a settlement was reached. Thus, Truman went before Congress to ask for the authority to send in troops to run the trains and requested legislation to stop strikes against the government and to deal with labor leaders who violated this law. In his anger and frustration with an issue that he seemed unable to control, the president again asked for the power to draft workers on strike against the government into the armed forces. While speaking, the president was given a message that informed him the strike had ended on terms he had proposed. The president accepted the end of the strike, but asked Congress to pass a new labor law that would protect workers, management, and the public. After Truman's message to Congress, labor and management handled their disputes more carefully.

The Labor Movement is Hurt by Too Many Strikes

The year 1946 would stand out in history as the time when more than four million workers had gone out on strike, the worst year for strikes the nation had experienced. In spite of the work of the unions and the strikers, labor suffered in 1946. Hourly wages increased, but weekly wages decreased. Inflation also took its toll on wages, with labor back to the same purchasing power level of 1942. The unions also suffered a loss of political support from the public as a result of the turmoil of 1945–1946. So in 1947, Congress passed the Taft-Hartley Act, which further curtailed the power of the unions. The unions continued to fight into the 1950s asking for second, third, and fourth rounds of higher wages and better working conditions.

TRUMAN AND THE CONGRESS

In 1945 and 1946, Congress passed few of the Truman administration's requests for converting to a peacetime economy. Coming to power because of the death of Roosevelt denied Truman a constituency of his own from which would have come more influence and power. Adding to that difficulty was the fact that Congress had begun asserting its independence from Roosevelt while he was president, and Truman simply did not have the resources to persuade his former colleagues on Capitol Hill to endorse much of his legislative program, which in domestic areas was a continuation of the New Deal. The American weariness of rule from Washington added to the president's lack of support.

On September 6, 1945, the president outlined his program for postwar America in a message to Congress. Truman's 21 points were considered liberal and continued many New Deal programs. His program to carry the country into peace and prosperity included (1) improving unemployment compensation; (2) improving the disposal of surplus property; (3) continuing the use of his wartime authority of economic controls; (4) increasing the minimum wage; (5) legislating full employment; (6) improving collective bargaining; (7) increasing security for farmers; (8) reducing taxes; (9) increasing public works programs; (10) providing adequate medical care for all Americans via a national health insurance system; (11) improving education and housing; (12) assisting nations damaged in war; (13) regulating atomic energy; and (14) providing for universal military training. Central to his program was increased production to the point of full employment.

Congress denied most of his programs, although his efforts to cut federal expenditures and reduce taxes were supported enthusiastically. Taxes were cut by $6 billion rather than the $5 billion that the administration had asked for. Authority was given to reorganize the executive branch, mostly to eliminate the wartime agencies. The president's war powers, including price-control authority, was renewed for only six months; he had asked for one year. Another success was the passage of the Employment Act on February 20, 1946, which declared it was a responsibility of the federal government to plan for and utilize resources toward maximum employment and production, which would in turn increase purchasing power. This legislation represented a political compromise for Truman, who had hoped for a guarantee from Congress that all resources of the government would be utilized to bring about full employment for American workers. The bill also created the Council of Economic Advisors to assist the president in recommending programs to carry out the purpose of the act and prepare an annual national economic report.

THE MID-TERM CONGRESSIONAL ELECTIONS OF 1946

"Had enough? Vote Republican." This campaign slogan for the Republican candidates in November 1946, also reflected the views of the American voters. A Republican majority of 246 to 188 was elected to the House of Representatives, while election results produced a 51 to 45 split in the Senate, in favor of the Republicans. The Republican Party had been gaining strength since 1938, and with the blame for the postwar difficulties being placed on the heads of the Democratic Congress and the Democratic president, their victory was almost assured. The Democrats were blamed for the continued shortage in housing and consumer goods, an unbalanced federal budget, a heavy tax burden, communist activity, and the labor problems.

The president accepted the elections as a mandate from the people that all remaining wartime regulations were unacceptable. And within a week of the elections, Truman ordered all controls on prices and wages dropped except on rent and the rationing of sugar and rice. By the end of December 1946, the $10,000 sales ceiling for the construction of new homes and the $80 maximum limit on rentals was eliminated. The ceiling price for new houses had been an attempt to force builders to construct less expensive homes that the veterans could afford. Congress continued to enforce rent control, but an agreement could be reached between landlords and tenants to pay 15 percent higher than the $80. The public's demands for government to return to a hands-off policy toward the economy led to a dramatic increase of the inflation that the Truman administration had fought against with its price controls. By the summer of 1947, wholesale prices had increased by 31 percent. This brought new demands from labor for increased wages in 1947 and 1948, which in turn led to higher prices. President Truman had been correct in his warnings, but the public would not be denied.

THE TAFT-HARTLEY ACT

It was hoped that the new Republican Congress could find some solution to the continuing labor problems. Since late May, the Interior Department had nominal control over the bituminous mines (see above). In November, John L. Lewis, head of the United Mine Workers, demanded that the labor contract signed in early June be reopened. But when the government refused to do so, Lewis defied federal control of the mines as well as an injunction against strikes in the mines when he called for the miners to walk out on strike shortly after the November elections. Lewis and the United Mine Workers Union were found guilty in a federal district court of contempt of court for calling a strike. Lewis was fined $10,000 and the union $3.5 million. Economic activity around the nation slowed down even to the point that "brown outs" were necessary in some communities to conserve energy. The case went to the Supreme Court for review, but Lewis ordered the miners back to work on December 7, 1946, while the Court was still considering the case. The Court upheld the injunction of the lower court, but did reduce the fine against the union to $700,000, with the stipulation that the full fine would be reinstated if the union defied the injunction further.

Unions were now the target of Congress for more severe regulation. The perception was that labor leaders had grown too powerful, and it was not acceptable that the decisions of a few union leaders could shut down the production of the nation. The Taft-Hartley Labor-Management Relations Bill (the Taft-Hartley Act), passed in June 1947, was the Congressional answer to the perceived threat of the unions to the nation's economic security. The bill banned the closed shop, in which non-union workers could not be hired. It allowed the union shop, in which workers were required to join a union within so many days after being hired in order to keep their job, if this practice was allowed by the state. However, section 14(b) allowed states to enact so-called "right to work" laws, which would ban the union shop within a given state. Several "unfair labor practices" prohibiting certain union activities were included in the bill. These included a ban on secondary boycotts, "featherbedding" (pay for work not done), and refusing to bargain in good faith. Employers and injured third parties were empowered by the law to file lawsuits against labor unions. In addition, labor unions were required to publish financial statements and could not make direct contributions to political parties or candidates.

(Unions were allowed to keep their political action committees—PACs—but they could only function on a voluntary basis.) Union officers were also required by the Taft-Hartley Act to take oaths that they were not communist and did not support any organization that advocated the overthrow of the government. Federal employees were forbidden to strike, and a cooling-off period of eighty days could be enforced by the president on any strike that he believed would be harmful to the national health and safety.

President Truman vetoed the bill and declared that it "would reverse the basic direction of our national labor policy, inject the Government into private economic affairs on an unprecedented scale. . . . Its provisions would cause more strikes, not fewer. . . ." On June 20, the same day that the president vetoed the bill, Congress overrode the veto and passed the bill with overwhelming Republican support and considerable Democratic support as well. The unions called the Taft-Hartley Act a "slave-labor act," and Truman's veto brought many workers and their unions back to Truman and the Democratic Party. The law was obeyed in spite of the unions' anxiety that the law would weaken future leverage in bargaining, and the names of the Congressional supporters were remembered in the next elections. By 1954 some fifteen states, mostly in the South, had adopted "right to work" laws prohibiting the union shop. Arguments still persist today as to whether the labor movement is weaker in "right to work" states because of those anti-union laws or whether they were already weak in those states and that is the reason the "right to work" laws were passed there. The truth is that probably it is a combination of both a cause and effect relationship between those facts.

THE "MIRACLE" ELECTION OF 1948

The Candidates and Party Platforms

The Republican Party approached the 1948 elections with great confidence. Republican gains in the House and the Senate in the 1946 midterm elections seemed to indicate the country was responding to Republican solutions to problems. Republicans charged the administration with taking the internal communist threat too lightly. There were also numerous accusations of corruption against government officials. Within the Democratic ranks, Henry Wallace on the political left and southern conservatives on the right were threatening to split the party if Truman were the nominee for the presidency.

The Republicans nominated Thomas E. Dewey, governor of New York, as their presidential candidate and Earl Warren, governor of California, as their vice-presidential candidate. Support from the voters of these two heavily populated states would certainly aid their success. The party platform included a reduction of government spending and taxes, support for the United Nations, and the commitment to eliminate the threat of communism to the United States. But overall, the Republican platform and candidates did not radically differ from the New Deal traditions of Harry Truman.

President Truman won the Democratic nomination and Alben W. Barkley, a senator from Kentucky, was the party's choice for vice-president. There were many in the party who worked for other choices as the nominee, but when Dwight Eisenhower could not be persuaded to run as a Democrat, it was decided that the controversial incumbent president was the only hope for a Democratic victory. The platform finally adopted at the convention, particularly in the areas of civil rights and foreign policy, would split the party and bring about two new parties from those who could not support the party's positions.

Hoping to keep the southern Democrats in the party, the platform committee officially recommended a watered down civil rights plank to the convention delegates. President Truman and Hubert H. Humphrey, mayor of Minneapolis, Minnesota, both pushed for a stronger Democratic civil rights plank instead. Standing before the Democratic National Convention at Philadelphia on July 14, 1948, Humphrey stated, "There are those who say to you, 'We are rushing this issue of civil rights.' I say we are 172 years late. There are those who say this issue of civil rights is an infringement on states' rights. The time has arrived for the Democratic Party to get out of the shadow of states' rights and walk forthrightly into the bright sunshine of human rights." When a strong civil rights plank was adopted, 35 delegates from Mississippi and Alabama walked out of the convention. The platform also called for continued support for the president's foreign policy and the implementation of his Fair Deal. These positions would send other Democrats from the party.

On July 17, the southerners who could not tolerate the civil rights stand of their own party or the thought of ending segregation of African-Americans formed the States' Rights Democratic Party (nicknamed the Dixiecrats) at a convention at Birmingham, Alabama. Governor J. Strom Thurmond, of South Carolina, was their presidential nominee, and Governor Fielding Wright, of Mississippi, was the nominee for vice-president.

Some of Truman's more liberal critics within the Democratic Party, led by Henry Wallace (Vice-President from 1941–1945 and Secretary of Commerce from 1945–1946), also pulled away from the party and formed a new Progressive party. Truman had asked for Wallace's resignation when he began to openly criticize American foreign policy, bringing threats of resignation from Secretary of State James Byrnes. Wallace had told Truman that he believed that the Soviet fear of American policy was justified. He also gave a speech on September 12, 1946, criticizing American foreign policy as confrontational and only adding to the Soviet fears. When President Truman admitted to the press that the statements in the Wallace speech were a correct representation of his foreign policy, Byrnes and others were highly incensed. Then on September 14, Truman recanted this statement, saying that he agreed with the right of Wallace to make the speech, but not the contents. He then asked for the resignation of the Secretary of Commerce Wallace because he certainly did not want to risk losing Secretary of State Byrnes. After this, Wallace became the rallying point for many to the political far left. And he was selected as the presidential candidate of the new Progressive Party, with Senator Glen Taylor (D-Idaho) being named as the vice-presidential candidate. The party platform included peace with the Soviet Union, the abolition of atomic bombs, and a broad program of domestic reforms, along with the nationalization of oil compa-

President Harry Truman holds up a copy of a newspaper with the headline "Dewey Defeats Truman," 1948. Credit: AP/Wide World Photos.

nies, railroads, and other basic industries that were of great concern to the public interest.

The Campaign and Results

The Republicans, along with most political analysts and pollsters, believed that the splintering of the Democrats was the final step in guaranteeing a Republican victory in 1948. Relying on these assumptions, Dewey ran a very low-key campaign and avoided issues that could be controversial.

The Republicans underestimated the president, who was not about to give up without a fight. To illustrate that the Republican stands on the issues were contrary to the best interest of the people, Truman called the Republican dominated Eightieth Congress back into session to confront the issues of inflation, housing, and civil rights. Congress did pass weak supports for farmers, but that was all. After challenging the Republicans in Congress, Truman took his campaign to the people. He traveled more than 30,000 miles and gave dozens of speeches from the ends of railroad cars or from station platforms. "Give 'em Hell Harry" was shouted by a listener in the crowd and stuck with the scrappy campaigner until election day. Nearly everywhere he went, the president condemned the Republican-dominated Congress for being the "do-nothing Congress."

Analysts were predicting a Republican victory as the votes were being counted. The headline in the Chicago *Daily Tribune* even announced "DEWEY DEFEATS TRUMAN" before all the votes were in. But when they all had been counted, President Harry S. Truman had pulled off the biggest upset election victory in United States history. And a beaming Truman held up the Chicago *Daily Tribune* headline triumphantly. He was re-elected with 303 electoral votes. Dewey received 189 electoral votes, Thurmond won 39 electoral votes, and Wallace won none. The Democrats had also won back the House of Representatives with 262 seats to 171 for the Republicans and the Senate, with 53 seats to 43 for the Republicans. Among the new Democrats in the Senate were Hubert Humphrey of Minnesota and Lyndon B. Johnson of Texas.

Numerous factors contributed to the Republican loss. Many Republicans had not bothered to vote because they falsely believed that Truman could not win re-election. Republicans lost some of the agricultural states because farmers believed that more government assistance would come from the Democratic Party. Communist support for Wallace damaged his ability to siphon votes from Truman. The brilliant and fearless campaign waged by Harry S. Truman, however, cannot be overestimated in any final analysis of the reasons for the seemingly "miracle" election of 1948. And finally, credit must be given to presidential advisor Clark Clifford's suggestions (and Truman's agreement) that the New Deal coalition put together by Franklin Roosevelt must be strengthened by more movement to the "left" on most domestic issues. Truman needed the labor and black votes in urban areas; therefore, he addressed their concerns. Certainly, his veto of the Taft-Hartley Act, though unsuccessful, won him widespread support from organized labor, as did his strong push for a tough pro-civil rights plank in the Democratic platform that year help him with African-American voters. Truman also needed the support from midwestern and western farmers, which he did largely receive in the election.

However, Clifford partially miscalculated when he predicted that the South would stay solidly Democrat no matter what. Strom Thurmond's showing in parts of the deep South began a long, slow trend of southern defection from the Democratic Party. For the time being, however, most southern Democrats were not willing to bolt their historical party. As one Virginia Democratic politician put it, "The only sane and constructive course to follow is to remain in the house of our fathers—even though the roof leaks, and there be bats in the belfry, rats in the pantry, a cockroach in the kitchen and skunks in the parlor."

1948	48	HARRY S. TRUMAN	Democrat	24,105,812	303	49.5
		Thomas E. Dewey	Republican	21,970,065	189	45.1
		J. Strom Thurmond	States' Rights	1,169,063	39	2.4
		Jenry A. Wallace	Progressive	1,157,172		2.4

THE FAIR DEAL

The new administration was committed to continuing the programs set in motion previously. Domestically, President Truman was committed to economic growth and reform in government to promote efficiency. In his State of the Union message given on January 5, 1949, the President labeled his program the Fair Deal when he stated that "every segment of our population and every individual has a right to expect from our government a fair deal. . . ." In his Inaugural Address given on January 20, 1949, (the first telecast address) the president reaffirmed the deep philosophical differences between the United States and the Soviet Union that had led to a foreign policy of containing the spread of Soviet-backed communism around the world. He stated that ". . . the United States and other like-minded nations find themselves directly opposed by a regime with contrary aims and a totally different concept of life. . . . Democracy is based on the conviction that man has the moral and intellectual capacity, as well as the inalienable right, to govern himself with reason and justice. . . ." The president also outlined his Fair Deal legislative program. The program called for a national commitment to civil rights, federal assistance for housing and education, new labor laws, and compulsory national health insurance.

The Eighty-first Congress, elected in 1948, stymied most of the president's Fair Deal proposals. The Democrats held a majority, but conservative Southern Democrats consistently sided with conservative Republicans. The president was unsuccessful in repealing the Taft-Hartley Act, which he strongly opposed, and he could not garner enough support in Congress to enact a national health insurance program.

President Truman did not meet disappointment on all issues before Congress. In October 1949, the Fair Labor Standards Act was amended to raise minimum wages from forty to seventy-five cents an hour. It also increased the number of employees eligible for the minimum wage, and increased the regulations against child labor abuses. In August 1950, Congress acted upon prodding from the president to pass Social Security Amendments to increase assistance by doubling old-age and survivors benefits and including 10 million more Americans in the program. On July 15, 1949, Truman signed the Housing Act into law. This law was to continue New Deal legislation, which used federal funds to clear slums and then rebuild the areas with low-cost public-housing units, mostly apartments.

REORGANIZING A GOVERNMENT

The National Security Act

A goal of Truman's throughout both of his administrations was to reorganize certain areas of the executive branch to provide for greater efficiency and to save taxpayer money while, at the same time, meeting the expanded foreign policy goals of the country. President Truman and Congress agreed that the armed services needed reform at the highest levels of control to carry out their missions in a more unified manner than had been the case in World War II. Therefore, in July 1947, the National Security Act created the National Military Establishment, which was renamed the Department of Defense in 1949, to coordinate the armed services. The Chief of Staff from the Army and Air Force, the Chief of Naval Operations, and the Chief of Staff assigned to the president made up the new Joint Chiefs of Staff to integrate defense plans in order to better advise the president. In August 1949, Congress added a non-voting chairman for the Joint Chiefs of Staff to break discussion deadlocks. The first to hold the position of Chairman of the Joint Chiefs was the World War II General, Omar Bradley. The National Security Act had also established the National Security Council, which was to coordinate details of domestic, foreign, and military affairs as they related to national security. And the Central Intelligence Agency was established under the new National Security Act also, in an effort to gather intelligence information about foreign countries more efficiently.

The Hoover Commission

Further study and recommendations for reorganization were supplied by the non-partisan Commission on Organization of the Executive Branch. The Commission, headed by former President Herbert Hoover, recommended a reduction of government departments and agencies, taking the Post Office out of the influence of politics and running it as a business, implementing a uniform accounting system throughout the national government, and placing government agencies involved in foreign policy under the authority of the State Department. The Commission sent eighteen reports to Congress with recommendations which would have saved an estimated $3 billion if implemented. Congress passed the Reorganization Act of June 20, 1949, which allowed the president to further reorganize the Executive Branch.

The Presidential Succession Act

In another area of federal government management, the president and others were uncomfortable with the line of succession if something should happen to the president and the vice-president because the presidency would then not pass to an elected official. Following the law of 1886, the Secretary of State would step into the presidency if the vice-president was struck down with or after the president. To remedy this situation, the Presidential Succession Act passed on July 18, 1947. It provided that the Speaker of the House would be first in line if something happened to both the president and the vice-president, followed by the president pro tempore of the Senate.

The Twenty-Second Amendment

Another measure that could impact on the future of the presidency was the Twenty-second Amendment to the Constitution. In 1947 the Republican controlled Congress sent this amendment, which limited a president to two terms, to the state legislatures. Regarded by most as a rebuke of the power of Franklin Roosevelt, who had been elected to four consecutive terms as president, the amendment was ratified and went into effect in February 1951. Supported by the Republicans in the beginning, it was the Democrats in the South that actually brought about final ratification. Although Truman was exempted from the restrictions of the amendment,

Hearing of the House Un-American Activities Committee in August, 1948. Credit: AP/Wide World Photos.

it was widely believed that it would have a negative impact on his chances if he should decide to run for a third term.

PROMOTING LOYALTY AND BATTLING COMMUNISM AT HOME

Background

The evolving Cold War between the United States and the Soviet Union led the nation into another anticommunist frenzy at home that became known as the second Red Scare. The fear of communist subversive activity leading to the downfall of the American government had died down after World War I, but it had not completely vanished. (See Chapter Nine.) In 1938 the House Committee to Investigate Unamerican Activities (later relabelled the House Unamerican Activities Committee, or HUAC) was established to investigate Nazi, Fascist, Communist and other organizations considered "un-American" and their danger to the nation. There were even those who saw the New Deal as part of a communist plot to turn the United States into a socialist nation.

Security within the United States became a concern when relations with the Soviet Union, a communist nation railing against the capitalism and proclaiming a world-wide revolution of workers as the true path to freedom for all, were beginning to break down in 1945. There had been a communist party of an estimated 80,000 members during World War II that was now seen as a threat. Events led the government and the nation to take measures to locate all alleged disloyal and dangerous citizens and neutralize their threat.

Truman's Loyalty Oath Program and HUAC

In 1945, confirmation for many that there was communist activity in the United States came from several sources. For example, in the offices of *Amerasia*, a small magazine with sympathies for the Chinese communists, some classified documents from the United States government were found. In 1946, Canada reported that there was a Soviet spy ring operating within its borders, and Canadians had participated in the sending of information on atomic weapons to the Soviet Union. Reacting to the rising fear of the population, the investigating of communist activity by Congress through HUAC, and allegations from Republicans that Democrats were not only soft on communism but that many were communists themselves, President Truman ordered measures taken to probe disloyalty among federal government employees. In 1946, the president established the Temporary Commission on Employee Loyalty, and then on March 22, 1947, the Loyalty Order (an Executive Order) authorized investigations of all employees in the executive branch. By March 1952, around 380 federal employees were fired and more than 2,500 others were forced to resign. The increasing fear of internal subversion by communists would be the danger to individual rights that Truman believed it would, but it was also used by the administration to increase the public and Congressional support for the containment policy of communism overseas.

HUAC became more active in its investigations across the country, and a variety of groups came under suspicion in the late 1940s and early 1950s. The committee distributed millions of copies of the pamphlets "One Hundred Things You Should Know About Communism" and "Where Can Communists be Found? Everywhere." Truman criticized the tactics of the committee, but the House continued to fund it. Hollywood was a favorite target. A group of directors and writers were sent to federal prison for failing to cooperate with investigations. The lesson was learned, and all who even seemed radical were blacklisted from the movie industry. Hollywood could not afford the public's ill will. Not wanting to come to the attention of HUAC, labor unions expelled communist members and stayed away from causes that would even appear to be pro-communist.

The Supreme Court Adds to the Fear

The successful testing of an atomic bomb in the Soviet Union in 1949, and the fall of China to the communist forces of Mao Tse-tung in the same year, increased the public's hysteria and the efforts to stamp out communist activity in America. It

Alger Hiss, former State Department official, convicted of perjury, sits in a prison van. Credit: AP/Wide World Photos.

was doubtful to many Americans that these events could have been successful without support from disloyal Americans. Eleven of the top leaders of the Communist party in the United States were convicted on October 17, 1949, for violation of the Smith Act of 1940. The Smith Act (Alien Registration Act) made it a crime to advocate the overthrow of the United States government by force or violence or to join any organization with the same philosophy. In 1951, in *Dennis v. United States*, the Supreme Court upheld the convictions of the 11, declaring that the Smith Act was constitutional and did not violate free speech because of the "clear and present danger" to America's national security. In other words, any American citizen who supported certain radical views could be convicted as a dangerous felon even without having committed any overt dangerous act.

This second Red Scare certainly tested the viability of the First Amendment and proved once again that its value is only as good as the commitment to maintain it.

The Alger Hiss Case

Especially damaging to the administration was the case of Alger Hiss, a former State Department employee and, at the time, president of the Carnegie Endowment for International Peace. Hiss was convicted and sentenced to five years in prison in January 1950, on the charge of committing perjury before a grand jury when he had stated that he had not been involved in espionage against the United States. This conviction came after a first jury had deadlocked. (The statute of limitations on espionage had expired, so that's why he was charged with perjury.) The charges against Hiss stemmed from the accusations made on August 3, 1948, by Whittaker Chambers, a former communist courier (and then currently a senior editor at *Time* magazine) testifying before HUAC, that Hiss had been a communist in the 1930s and had given him classified documents. Hiss denied the charges and sued Chambers for libel.

Ethel and Julius Rosenberg wait to board a prison van. Credit: AP/Wide World Photos.

President Truman and Secretary of State Dean Acheson declared they believed in Hiss's innocence. Truman even called the charges a "red herring" that the Republicans were using to divert attention from their legislative failures. Congressman Richard Nixon, a member of HUAC, pressed the investigation of Hiss to its conclusion. In fact, it was his role on HUAC that promoted Richard Nixon to national prominence. Chambers finally presented evidence of memos typed on a typewriter from the model that Hiss had owned, letters in Hiss's handwriting, and microfilm of State Department documents.

The McCarran Act

The situation escalated again in 1950. Communist-supported North Korea attacked South Korea in June. (See Chapter Thirteen for information about the Korean War.) This was perceived as another example of a monolithic communist movement engineered from Moscow to spread the tentacles of communism around the world. One result of the outbreak of that war was the Internal Security Act of

Senator Joseph McCarthy during a nationwide telecast. Credit: AP/Wide World Photos.

1950. Known as the McCarran Act, the law made it unlawful to assist in establishing a totalitarian dictatorship, prohibited the entry into the United States of anyone who had been a member of a totalitarian organization, and called for the registration of members of communist-front organizations to register with the government.

Klaus Fuchs and the Rosenbergs

It was also discovered from the arrest of Klaus Fuchs in Britain in January 1950 that there was a spy ring operating in Britain and the United States, selling secrets of the development of the atomic bomb to the Soviets. Fuchs was a German nuclear scientist who had worked on the Manhattan Project during World War II. The arrest of Fuchs in turn led to the arrest of Julius and Ethel Rosenberg (accused by their sister-in-law and brother-in-law, who had been a machinist at Los Alamos during the Manhatten Project), two Americans who allegedly had participated in the espionage ring. The Rosenbergs were both children of Jewish immigrants, had lived in New York City, and often spoke Yiddish. They were found guilty of conspiracy to commit espionage in March 1951, more on the fact that they were different from most Americans than on hard evidence. Then on June 13, 1953, the

Rosenbergs were executed for their role in the affair, although both went to the electric chair claiming their innocence.

McCarthyism

Senator Joseph McCarthy, the Republican Senator from Wisconsin, used Americans' fear of internal communist activity to become one of the most powerful figures in Washington, D.C. McCarthy was looking for a political issue which would resurrect his failing career and guarantee him re-election to the Senate in 1952. In the growing fear over alleged communist threats to the nation, McCarthy found his issue. Addressing a Republican women's group in Wheeling, West Virginia on February 9, 1950, McCarthy claimed to have a list with 205 known communists in the State Department. He also claimed that the most dangerous person in the State Department was Dean Acheson, the Secretary of State. As he repeated his claims over the next few weeks, the numbers on his list changed, but it did not matter to the public. Here was the nation's savior. Here was the man who knew who the communists were and would expose and eliminate the threat.

McCarthy was using this issue to promote his own failing political career, and it worked. He became so powerful that many were afraid to challenge him for fear that they would be labeled a communist and have their own careers ruined. The reasons why McCarthy was not challenged early on are varied. For one thing, conservative Republicans had grown very tired of New Deal liberalism and were also fearful of the growing Soviet nuclear threat. Republicans were also tired of being out of the White House; Herbert Hoover had been the last Republican president, but he had left office on March 4, 1933, at the inauguration of Franklin D. Roosevelt. Although most Republican members of Congress did not particularly like McCarthy's tactics, they were, in fact, producing more Republican voters in the country. Democrats left the senator alone because they too feared that he would turn on some of them and ruin their careers. Thus, nearly everyone kept relatively silent for several years. Even when President Eisenhower took office, he did not want to challenge the senator overtly.

In 1953, McCarthy forced the firing of several hundred State Department employees because he opposed their views, despite no evidence of subversiveness. He criticized the United States Information Agency libraries for carrying "controversial" books—books written by great American writers such as Ralph Waldo Emerson, Henry David Thoreau, and Mark Twain. McCarthy's downfall finally came after he attacked the United States Army for allegedly protecting and promoting communists. When army spokesmen retorted that the senator had used his influence on behalf of a staff member who had been drafted, Congress voted to hold televised hearings. The hearings began on April 22, 1954. Because of radio and television, ordinary Americans were able to witness McCarthy's unethical slandering of people, berating them sarcastically and without evidence. Finally, army attorney Joseph Welch had had enough of the senator's rudeness and asked him in a pleading voice, "Have you no sense of decency, sir? At long last, have you no sense of decency?" Those words seemed to break McCarthy's spell on America. And in December 1954, the United States Senate voted 67 to 22 to formally censure the Wisconsin Republican; that was only the third time in American history that the Senate had censured one of its own members. He kept his seat as a senator until his death in 1957, but his power had been broken. Thereafter, fellow senators walked out on him, and the media largely ignored him.

In all his ranting and raving over the years, he had not uncovered a single communist agent or plot. However, his name has been ever after associated with the tactics of making wild accusations without a shred of proof; such activity is called McCarthyism.

THE FAIR DEAL AND CIVIL RIGHTS

Congress Stalls on Civil Rights

President Truman believed that equal rights for Americans should be legislatively guaranteed, and he pushed for civil rights legislation during both of his administrations. Following World War II, tensions existed between white Americans and minority groups, including African-Americans, Native-Americans, Jews, Mexican-Americans, and Japanese-Americans. But it was the violent assaults on African-Americans that brought to the foreground the need for equality of all Americans guaranteed by the federal government. Truman met strong opposition and achieved only small gains for civil rights from Congress. The conservative Democrats and Republicans in the Senate, especially southern Democrats, blocked most proposals with the use of the filibuster.

Truman did make some progress, however, using other powers at his disposal. In 1946, he approved the formation of the Indian Claims Commission to investigate the financial claims of Native-Americans, and he also approved the appointment of a Puerto Rican as governor of Puerto Rico. The President's Committee on Civil Rights was established to find ways to protect the rights of minorities. The Committee recommended legislation to protect all minorities from violence, discrimination, and segregation, and to extend to them full and equal rights of citizenship regardless of race, color, or creed. In 1947, Congress did nothing with the report of the committee, except to allow the citizens of Puerto Rico the right to choose their president at the ballot box.

Truman Uses Executive Orders to Further the Civil Rights Cause

In February 1948, the president sent his message to Congress outlining his specific proposals that civil rights should be extended to all Americans, not only because "all men are created equal" but also to set forth an example to the rest of the world that the United States supported freedom for all. The outrage was so strong in Congress that Truman did agree to put the issue of civil rights on the back burner for the time the current Congress was in session. He did, however, move forward to end discrimination in federal employment and the armed services. Executive Order 9980 established the Fair Employment Board in 1948 to give minorities an equal chance in gaining employment within the federal government. Once again the results were minimal for minorities. Executive Order 9981 established the President's Committee on Equality of Treatment and Opportunity in the Armed

Services, which was charged with the duty of integrating the military services. The army, which contained the largest number of minority troops, was the most reluctant of all of the services to integrate. By 1950, the army was coming around to the idea of integration, but the beginning of the Korean War in June 1950 would force the implementation of integration of the fighting troops for the sake of efficiency, if nothing else. By 1953, integration in the armed services was progressing as the president had hoped.

Minimal Progress

The second administration of President Truman began with invitations to African-Americans to important social events in connection with the inauguration, signalling that the president's goals for equal treatment of all Americans continued. Efforts were increased to place more African-Americans in public housing and to stop the Housing and Home Finance Administration and the Veterans Administration from supporting restrictive segregated neighborhoods. Using his power of appointment, African-Americans were appointed to important government positions, but by 1953 the number was still small at 94.

Ralph Johnson Bunche was an exception to the rule that kept minorities out of powerful positions. He was an African-American who rose to importance in the State Department and was instrumental in organizing the United Nations in 1945. Bunche was also awarded the Nobel Peace Prize in 1950 for his role in mediating an end to the Arab-Israeli war of 1948–1949. President Truman had not been a successful champion for civil rights, but he did crack some of the barriers and gave minority groups the confidence to become better organized and more vocal for the fight ahead. The fight would continue and increase in dimension and size during President Eisenhower's terms. The federal courts became the major arena for success in the opening rounds of the modern civil rights movement, when the Congress would not aid the cause with legislation. (See Chapter Fourteen for a discussion of the modern civil rights movement up through 1968.)

FOREIGN AFFAIRS UNDER TRUMAN

Latin America Policy

Containing the expansion of communism in Europe dominated the foreign policy of Truman's first administration. Containing the expansion of communism around the world would occupy center stage in his second administration. For example, the United States went to war in 1950 to prevent South Korea from falling to communism. (See Chapter Thirteen.) In other areas around the globe, other methods would be used to advance the fight. Alliance systems, financial aid, and support for pro-American governments were important weapons in the fight for democracy.

The Rio Pact

In August 1947, the Rio Treaty (or Rio Pact) was signed by the United States and 18 of the other American republics in an effort to strengthen ties on the continent. The treaty was a permanent defensive alliance. The attack of any member nation, whether from within or outside the continent, would bring the assistance of the other countries to repel the attack. Assistance would also be forthcoming if any situation, other than armed aggression, endangered the peace of the continent. In 1948, the American republics represented in the alliance system became the legal entity of the Organization of American States (OAS).

Foreign Aid and Point Four

Latin American nations asked for financial aid, but in 1948, Truman only asked Congress to increase the lending authority of the Export-Import Bank by $500 million. Priorities had to be established for the spending of American dollars, and Latin America was not in grave danger from communism.

On January 20, 1949, in his inaugural address Truman added a new dimension to his foreign policy with "Point Four." Along with other methods to prevent the spread of communism, the United States would begin, "a bold new program for making the benefits of our scientific advances and industrial progress available for the improvement and growth of underdeveloped areas." On June 5, 1950, Congress committed $25 million to friendly Third World Nations. It would not be enough then, or later, for the troubled area. Revolutions and social upheaval came to be commonplace in an area that was so poor. In some instances the United States would back military dictators who seemed to be able to bring order and an end to the social discontent that could be the beginnings of communism in those areas. Most of the presidents following Truman would have to deal with trouble in Latin America.

Assassination Attempt on Truman

As if President Truman did not have more than enough to contend with, there was an assassination attempt on his life. The president was temporarily staying at Blair House, which is across the street from the White House, while the White House was undergoing renovations. While there, two Puerto Rican nationalists (who favored independence for Puerto Rico) attempted to enter and kill the president on November 1, 1950. One of the assassins was killed, along with a White House guard. The other assassin was captured, convicted, and sentenced to life in prison. Puerto Rico was given commonwealth status in 1952, but not independence.

MIDDLE EAST POLICY

The Creation of Israel

The Nazi holocaust had created widespread support for a Jewish homeland in the Middle East. In November 1947 the United Nations General Assembly voted in favor of the partition of Palestine, the ancient homeland of the Jews which, since World War I, had been a British protectorate, into separate Jewish and Arab states. Britain announced that it would end the protectorate status of Palestine on May 15, 1948. Officials in the Departments of State and Defense believed that the United States should not support the partition, which was sure to antagonize the oil-rich Arab states of the area. A split within the administration became public when the United States ambassador to the United Nations, Warren R. Austin, announced, without prior discussion with Truman, that American policy in Palestine was to form a temporary trusteeship by Britain, France, and the United States. To avoid the charge that he was not in control of foreign policy, President Truman announced that the United States was in favor of the partition, but the trusteeship would go into place until the details were worked out.

Jewish Zionists did not wait for the other powers to give them a homeland, however. A Jewish state was proclaimed in Palestine on May 14, 1948. The United States became the first nation to officially recognize the state of Israel when President Truman did so only 10 minutes after the proclamation. The administration believed it was necessary to forge an immediate alliance with the new state of Israel in order to block any moves the Soviet Union might make to create ties with the new nation. On May 15, Arab forces invaded Israel. Truman promised to work for aid to the new nation, but a truce negotiated by the United Nations brought a temporary end to the hostilities on May 11, 1949. At that time, Israel was also admitted into membership in the United Nations.

The Middle East was an unstable area at this time. New Arab nations were being established in the area, with many nations vying for influence over the nations with oil. The United States could not back away from the trouble spot and allow the Soviet Union influence that could affect the oil connections in the Middle East, nor allow Israel to fall to its enemies. Although at times the alliance was strained, the United States and Israel became strong allies, and relations with Arab nations of the area definitely suffered as a result. The United States worked diligently for a peaceful settlement of the discord between these traditional enemies with little success until the presidency of Jimmy Carter. (See Chapter Seventeen.) Hoping to win favor with all groups, Congress granted aid to Israel, Arab states, and the Palestinian refugees leaving their nation in 1949 and 1950.

Iran

In Iran, the support of the government of the shah, Mohammed Reza Pahlavi, was believed to be the best defense against Soviet intervention in this nation. The shah came to the throne on September 16, 1941, following the abdication of his father, Reza Khan Pahlavi. The young shah allowed the parliamentary system to function without interference, and he sponsored social and economic reforms that had Western influences. The rise of power of Premier Mohammed Mossadegh, however, was seen as a threat to English and American interests in Iran. The premier nationalized the oil industry and accepted the support of Communist Iranian party members.

ASIAN POLICY

Following World War II, the United States had hoped that the Chinese Communist forces following Mao Tse-tung and the Chinese Nationalist forces of Chiang Kai-shek would work out a truce to end their bitter struggle. The United States had a long standing trade interest in China. Therefore, General George C. Marshall, who had resigned as chief of staff of the United States Army in November 1945 and became Truman's Secretary of State in 1947, was sent to negotiate with Chiang Kai-shek to end the hostilities. Marshall reported to the president that Chiang Kai-shek was not interested in reforms that could bring peace. He also reported that the Chinese leader was not in a position to broaden his own political strength in China, so intervention by the United States on his behalf would be useless. On December 8, 1949, the Nationalist Chinese forces and their leader were pushed onto the island of Taiwan (or Formosa), where they would stay and develop a new Chinese nation which the United States government would aid and support in the future. (See Chapter Thirteen for a discussion of the Chinese Civil War.)

Congressional Republican supporters of Chiang Kai-shek, known as the China Lobby, were extremely critical of the administration's so-called loss of China to communism. The victory of communism in China would eventually bring the American policy of containment to Asia.

THE HOMEFRONT DURING THE KOREAN WAR

Fighting Inflation

In 1950 the country had to mobilize for war once again when American troops were sent to Korea. The Office of Defense Mobilization directed the efforts of the nation. Prosperity increased, but the problem of inflation increased as well. The price of food was the most inflated. To compensate for the high price of meat, horse meat became quite popular in Portland, Oregon. President Truman was reluctant to impose price and wage controls with the power given to him in the Defense Production Act, September 1950. Instead, he encouraged Americans to practice voluntary controls. The nation was weary of hardships caused by war and the price and wage controls of World War II and the postwar period. The nation would not support the necessary home front measures wholeheartedly. Korea did not seem to threaten the security of the United States as other military conflicts had. And as the war proceeded, American involvement became less popular with the people.

But voluntary controls did not work, and some mandatory government controls were used once again. On January 26, 1951, price ceilings were placed at the highest level charged between December 19, 1950 and January 25, 1951. Wages were to remain at their January 25, 1951 level unless the Wage Stabilization Board authorized an increase. Truman asked for more authority from Congress to fight the problem of inflation, but the measures they passed were so watered down with exceptions as to be mostly useless. The Office of Price Stabilization did fix prices on beef on May 3, 1951.

Labor Problems

The administration continued to have problems with labor during the Korean War. On February 8, 1951, nationwide rail service was restored when striking workers won their pay raise. To avoid a steel strike, Truman ordered that the federal government would take control of the steel mills in Youngstown, Ohio in April 1952 because steel was considered a necessary material to support the war. However, on June 2 of the same year, the United States Supreme Court ruled the president's actions unconstitutional in the case of *Youngstown Sheet and Tube v. Sawyer*. The ruling limited the power of the president. Strikes in the industry shut down the mills for weeks until a wage and price increase was settled on July 24, 1952. There was no end in sight for the Korean conflict nor the problems of the president. Therefore, Truman chose not to run for reelection in 1952. He would leave the nation's problems, both domestic and foreign, to his successor.

The McCarran-Walter Act

One of the last battles President Truman lost with Congress was the passage of the McCarran-Walter Act over his veto, which occurred when the Senate voted to override 57 to 26 on June 25, 1952. Congress had passed several acts during Truman's terms concerning the immigration problem. In 1948 Congress had enacted a bill which amended the immigration laws to permit 205,000 European refugees from World War II to enter the United States without reference to the quotas based on national origin. Then in June 1950, the Displaced Persons Act liberalized the 1948 law to allow a total of 415,000 refugees into the United States. The McCarran-Walter Immigration and Nationality Act incorporated all of the existing laws. Countries were limited to a quota of one-sixth of one percent of its share of the population reflected in the United States census in 1920. Asians with as little as one half Asian ancestry were linked to the country of their ancestors regardless of their birthplace. The new law also kept out security risks and other undesirables. American presidents were allowed to admit persons in emergencies, but Truman still believed it was discriminatory to certain nationalities.

THE 1952 ELECTION

The Democratic Ticket and Platform

Although he was exempted from the new Twenty-second Amendment, because of low approval ratings, President Truman announced his decision not to run again on March 30, 1952. With the field open in the Democratic Party, Tennessee Senator Estes Kefauver was the early frontrunner for the nomination. Kefauver had earned a reputation for his investigation of corruption in a Senate committee he chaired. But in earning that same reputation, he had irritated the big city Democratic machine organizations. In addition, President Truman made it clear that he preferred Illinois Governor Adlai E. Stevenson. Stevenson, a popular reform-minded governor of an important state, was the grandson of Grover Cleveland's second vice-president (in the 1890s), who had the same name. And although Stevenson really

Dwight D. Eisenhower (second from right) receiving the Republican Party's vote as candidate in the 1952 Presidential Election. Credit: AP/Wide World Photos.

wanted another term as governor, he was drafted by the Democratic National Convention on the third ballot that summer. The convention also selected Alabama Senator John Sparkman as its vice-presidential candidate.

During World War II, Adlai Stevenson had worked in the office of the Secretary of the Navy. He was also an advisor to the American delegates at the United Nations Conference in 1945, and in 1948 he was elected governor of Illinois. His background, his moderate political position, and his strong anti-communist stand garnered the nomination for him. The Democratic platform promised assistance to farmers and small businessmen, repeal of the Taft-Hartley Act, and continuation of the successful New Deal and Fair Deal policies of the last two Democratic presidents.

The Republican Ticket

Before either of the party's national conventions in 1952, both parties had courted General Dwight D. Eisenhower. But early in the year, Ike remained uncommitted, although his family roots were Republican. Meanwhile, many Republicans began organizing Citizens for Eisenhower clubs around the nation and placing his name on primary ballots. In early April, Eisenhower retired from his position as the head of NATO's military forces in Europe, and in early June, he officially entered the race for the Republican nomination for president. Most conservative Republicans, including strong supporters of Douglas MacArthur, favored Ohio Senator Robert A. Taft, the son of former President William Howard Taft. Taft also represented the more isolationist wing of his party; thus, his nomination was bound to alienate millions of voters. The tide turned when public opinion polls showed Ike would probably win easily. Therefore, Dwight D. Eisenhower was indeed nominated at the Republican National Convention on the first ballot. As a general, Eisenhower had often relied on subordinate officers to make personnel recommendations. Therefore, Eisenhower asked others to name his running mate. Thomas Dewey, who had been the Republican presidential candidate in 1948, selected California Senator Richard M. Nixon, who was promptly nominated for the vice-presidency. Nixon had made himself famous by his earlier crusade against Alger Hiss.

The Campaign and Results

The Republicans campaigned on the three issues of Korea, Communism, and Corruption (K1, C2). Eisenhower was winning voters with his own personal popularity (one of the campaign slogans was "I like Ike") and by constantly reminding Americans of the Democrats' failure to solve the major problems of the nation. He was an ineffective speaker, but his war-hero status and his grandfatherly image were enormous political assets. Ike also scored points with voters when he stated that he would travel to Korea if elected, in order to end the Korean War. Nixon was used to attack the Democrats for being soft on communism and putting an end to the large government of the New Deal. This 1952 presidential election was the first one to see television commercials for candidates, Eisenhower being the first presidential candidate in American history to use that media for political campaign purposes.

Obstacles for Stevenson to overcome in the campaign included charges from the Republicans that the Democratic Party in Washington was riddled with corruption, and that the Democrats were soft on communism and could not successfully conclude the Korean War. Stevenson was also attacked as the candidate for liberals and "eggheads" (a new unflattering label for intellectuals). Stevenson was a gifted speaker; indeed, he may have been too good. He attacked the Republicans with such witty and intellectually inspiring speeches in person and on television that many Americans were uncomfortable with this candidate. Historically strong anti-intellectualism among the American people proved to be a strong negative in the campaign for the Democratic candidates.

Republican charges that there was corruption in the administrations of Truman were true. President Truman was embarrassed during both of his terms by the unethical, and in some instances, illegal activities of officials in or close to his administration. The president consistently refused to disavow these officials, fueling the increasing number of charges from the Republicans that the administration accepted and even covered up corruption. In August and September 1949, an inquiry was led by Senator Clyde R. Hoey, Democrat of North Carolina, into charges that officials who were close to the White House were selling their influence on government contracts and loans. These men were known as 5 percenters because they often charged 5 percent of the cost of government contracts to those private business interests desiring their influence. Truman's military aid, Brigadier General Harry H. Vaughn, was criticized by the Hoey committee for connections with those involved in selling influence. Vaughn was also criticized for accepting freezers as gifts for himself, Mrs. Truman (Bess), and four others in the administration. John Maragon, who had connections to Vaughn, was sent to prison for perjury by the same committee. Truman did not publicly criticize Vaughn, and the latter remained at his post in the White House until Truman left. The Reconstruction Finance Corporation and the Internal Revenue Bureau (Internal Revenue Service) were also targets of successful influence peddlers. It was revealed that agents in the Bureau had accepted money and gifts to stop tax fraud investigations and prosecutions for tax fraud. When the president ordered the Bureau to clean up the mess, close to 200 resigned from the agency. The executive branch was not the only target for Republicans who wanted to use the corruption of the Democrats as a campaign issue. The Senate Special Crime Investigation Committee, chaired by Tennessee Democratic Senator Estes Kefauver, revealed there were ties between organized crime and politicians in large cities under Democratic control.

The Republican campaign was going very well until the allegations of scandal hit. On September 18, 1952, the *New York Post* ran a full-page headline, SECRET NIXON FUND. The *Post* claimed that millionaire acquaintances of Richard Nixon in California had collected $18,000 for the comfort of the vice-presidential candidate. The trustee of the so-called secret "slush fund" maintained that the money had been raised for Nixon's campaign against communism as a senator. As a result, many Republican leaders called for Nixon to withdraw from the campaign. Eisenhower then declared that he would have to investigate the matter himself before making a decision with regard to what Nixon should do. This appearance of corruption was especially disturbing to the Republicans who were using corruption in Truman's administration as a reason to throw the Democrats out of the White House. Thomas Dewey finally persuaded Nixon to hit the attack head on via national television. The idea was that if his speech bombed, he would then withdraw from the campaign, but if it were received well, he would remain in the race.

For thirty minutes on national television on September 23, 1952, Senator Nixon told approximately 55 million Americans that he had not used any of the money for personal benefit. He told the audience about his ordinary life with his wife Pat and his two daughters Julia and Trisha. They were not a wealthy family, but had debts like all Americans; his wife wore a respectable Republican cloth coat. With tears in his eyes, he told about a little black and white cocker spaniel that a supporter had sent to the Nixons named "Checkers," and no matter what, he was not giving back the dog that six-year-old Trisha loved so much. In spite of not giving answers to all of the accusations from the Democrats, an overwhelming positive response to the speech left no doubt as to what Nixon should do, so he stayed in the race as the Republican vice-presidential candidate.

Eisenhower won with 442 electoral votes to 89 for Stevenson. The popular vote was around 89 million for Eisenhower and 27 million for Stevenson. Republicans also won a very slim majority in both houses of Congress. In the House it was 221 Republicans to 213 Democrats, and in the Senate it was 48 Republicans to 47 Democrats. The elections were more of an endorsement of Eisenhower personally than his party. Eisenhower would work with a Republican majority in Congress only for the first two years of his administration.

DOMESTIC ISSUES UNDER EISENHOWER

Dynamic Conservatism Begins

Eisenhower labeled his plan for governing the nation "Dynamic Conservatism," also known as "Modern Republicanism." Under this banner, Ike supported conservative monetary policies in an effort to balance the budget, which he accomplished in 1954 and 1960. He also worked on reducing the size of the federal government and the military. In areas of social welfare, on the other hand, he supported an expansion of programs from the federal government. He had to work with a Democratic Congress to accomplish his goals, except for his first two years as president. Eisenhower frustrated the Democrats to the left of center on the political spectrum and the Republican right, but he pleased the majority of Americans. They approved of this middle-of-the-road president for 8 years. He was also often assisted by the Democratic leadership in the House and Senate, especially Speaker of the House Sam Rayburn of Texas. He put together a cabinet that he leaned upon more heavily than most presidents for advice. Most members were drawn from large commercial or manufacturing organizations.

The poor young man from Abilene, Kansas had traveled a long road to Washington. He had graduated from West Point in 1915, and worked his way up to commanding general of United States forces in Europe in World War II. He was chosen Supreme Commander of Allied Expeditionary Forces in Europe in 1943. At the end of the war, he was chief of staff of the United States Army. He was then chosen the head of Columbia University from 1948–1950. His country called upon him once again in 1951, to lead the NATO forces in Europe as the Supreme Commander. Finally he was chosen by the nation to fulfill his most difficult leadership role as president of the United States.

SOCIAL WELFARE

In April 1953, Congress created a Department of Health, Education and Welfare to better coordinate and promote federal assistance to Americans in need. Then in August 1954, the Social Security Act was broadened to include farmers, state and local government workers, and clergymen. This action expanded Social Security coverage to about 7.5 million new Americans. In 1956, the age for women to become eligible for Social Security was lowered to 62, and for disabled workers to 50.

1952	48	DWIGHT D. EISENHOWER	Republican	33,936,234	442	55.1
		Adlai E. Stevenson	Democrat	27,314,992	89	44.4

Congress once again increased the numbers of those eligible by bringing in more farmers, doctors, some self-employed professionals, and those in the armed services.

In order to improve the standard of living for many disadvantaged Americans, Eisenhower recommended that Congress continue Truman's commitment for government assistance in providing low cost housing. Congress was asked to increase public housing units by 140,000 in his first administration. He met opposition in Congress for such a large outlay of public funds, so instead he took the middle course and accepted a commitment for 35,000 units from 1953–1954. The Housing Act of 1954 stimulated homebuilding to provide more housing for Americans, which in turn, increased business activity. Down payments for FHA (Federal Housing Administration) guaranteed loans were reduced, loan periods were lengthened, and the FHA was allowed to insure loans for the renovation of older buildings.

THE HIGHWAY ACT OF 1956

Gaining support for road construction from Democrats and Republicans was easier than for many of his other programs. Most agreed that the neglect of the highway systems during the depression and war must be remedied in order to service the rapidly expanding automobile traffic. The trend of moving to the suburbs also increased the need for more roads. Therefore, in June 1956, Congress passed the Highway Act of 1956, which authorized $33.5 billion dollars to construct close to 41,000 miles of modern, four-lane limited-access highways over the next 16 years. The states would build the highways with the federal government providing 90 percent of the cost. Increased federal taxes on gasoline and tires would provide the funds.

The Highway Act of 1956, in other words, began the creation of the interstate highway system that we know and use today. And it was probably the most significant accomplishment of the entire Eisenhower administration, domestically speaking. It helped reduce transportation costs, improve highway safety, and stimulate the automobile, trucking, and tourist industries. On the negative side of the ledger, the interstate highway system had really begun to hurt the railroad industry by the 1960s. And it also encouraged white flight from major cities by making it easier to live in the suburbs and still work in the cities.

FARMERS AND LABORERS

Farmers continued to suffer from falling prices on agricultural products, which in turn lowered the income of the nation's farmers. Secretary of Agriculture, Ezra Taft Benson, believed that the government policy of government price supports at 90 percent of parity in 1954 was adding to the underlying cause of the farmer's problems, which was overproduction. Benson persuaded President Eisenhower to change his position from the full parity that he had favored in the 1952 campaign to a flexible parity. The Agricultural Act of 1954 implemented flexible parity on the basic crops of corn, cotton, peanuts, rice, and wheat. The goal was to force the farmers to stop planting unprofitable crops, bring down surpluses, and allow the laws of supply and demand a chance to operate. The law continued some price support for milk, tobacco, and other commodities.

In 1956 Eisenhower vetoed an attempt by the Democratic controlled Congress to restore 90 percent price supports. Congress and the president did agree in the Agricultural Act of 1956 to a plan to lower the amount of surplus crops by paying the farmers to take acres out of production and making a deposit of those acres into a "soil bank." The government would pay farmers to take land used for planting staple crops and plant pasturage or forest instead. The Agricultural Trade and Development Act of 1954 had taken care of some of the surpluses stored by the government by allowing the farm products to be used for school lunches and the feeding of victims in disaster areas.

Blue collar workers were having more success in improving their situations at this time than the farmers. Organized labor was more unified, and this helped increase their bargaining power. In 1955 Ford Motor Company accepted the United Auto Workers proposal of a guaranteed annual salary. Other companies would soon follow. The power of labor was increased in December 1955, when the American Federation of Labor and the Congress of Industrial Organizations merged to become the AFL-CIO. The combined membership was approximately 15 million. Congress assisted workers across America by raising the minimum wage to one dollar an hour with a revision to the Fair Labor Standards Act.

THE 1956 ELECTION

The Candidates and Platforms

Adlai Stevenson was once again the nominee from the Democratic National Convention in the summer of 1956, after a tough primary campaign against Estes Kefauver. He was considered a moderate who could represent the various interests of the party and hold those interests together long enough to gain a victory. During the primary campaign season, Stevenson had gathered a considerable number of convention delegates, and he was nominated on the first ballot. Then he allowed the convention to choose his vice-presidential running mate. The choice was Senator Estes Kefauver from Tennessee, Stevenson's primary campaign opponent, who just edged out the young Senator John F. Kennedy of Massachusetts. The platform advocated higher parity supports for farmers, took a fairly conservative position on civil rights, and criticized Eisenhower's foreign policy as vacillating and his domestic policies as catering to the interests of big business while giving away national resources.

That summer the Republicans met in San Francisco. Eisenhower was still personally popular and despite a couple of recent bouts of illness, he was easily renominated. There was some opposition to the nomination of Nixon again for vice-president, but with the support of Eisenhower and most party leaders, Nixon was the candidate again. The Republican platform cheered the peace and prosperity of the first administration of Eisenhower and claimed acceptance of the Supreme Court decision that segregation was to be eliminated.

The Campaign and Results

Stevenson put together a vigorous campaign against the incumbent popular president, although he gave more attention to Vice-President Nixon than usual, calling him a "man of many masks." Stevenson supported the idea that further tests of hydrogen bombs should be banned with an international agreement. Scientists were divided on the dangers of radioactive fallout, so voters could not be expected to have informed opinions on the issue. The president's health was another issue that Stevenson attempted to exploit, but there was a lot of criticism of Stevenson for attempting to take advantage of Eisenhower's illnesses. Eisenhower had suffered a "moderately severe" heart attack on September 24, 1955 while vacationing in Denver, but following a convalescence of about three months, he was fully recovered. His doctors reported that the damage had been minimal, and he could probably continue an active life for five to ten more years. Then in June 1956, President Eisenhower was in the hospital once again. He underwent emergency surgery to remove an intestinal obstruction caused by ileitis. He recovered quickly and staged such a vigorous campaign that few Americans doubted his physical ability to govern the nation. He would suffer from illness once again for a brief time following a mild stroke in November 1957. When Israel, Britain, and France invaded Egypt shortly before the election, Stevenson thought he had a good case for the failure of the president's foreign policy. It appeared that a serious war could possibly break out from this Middle East crisis. But once again the Democratic candidate was disappointed. The crisis produced more votes for Eisenhower because voters believed he could ensure peace for the nation.

Eisenhower was even more successful in the 1956 election than he had been four years earlier. His popular vote was 35.3 million to Stevenson's 25.8 million. The electoral vote was 457 to 73. By carrying the southern states of Louisiana, Texas, and Florida, Eisenhower became the first Republican presidential candidate to carry a Deep South state since Reconstruction. Stevenson carried only seven states, none of which included either his home state of Illinois or his running mate's home state of Tennessee. The Republican Party as a whole was once again not included in the sweeping victory of their presidential candidate. In fact, the Democrats actually increased their majorities slightly in Congress. In the Senate the Democrats maintained 49 seats to the Republicans' 47; in the House the Democrats won 235 seats to 200 for the Republicans. This was the first time since President Zachary Taylor's successful election in 1848 that the winner had failed to gain a majority for his party in either house of Congress.

| 1956 | 48 | DWIGHT D. ESIENHOWER | Republican | 35,590,472 | 457† | 57.6 | |
| | | Adlai E. Stevenson | Democrat | 26,022,752 | 73 | | 42.1 |

†Walter B. Jones received 1 electoral vote.

THE BUDGET BATTLE

In January 1957, the administration sent a $72 billion budget for the 1958 fiscal year to Congress for approval. This represented an increase of $3 billion over the previous year and was the largest peacetime budget in American history. Foreign aid, defense, atomic energy, public housing, and education were all increased. There was apparent confusion in the White House because Eisenhower expressed surprise at the size of his own budget, and his Treasury Secretary Robert B. Anderson told reporters on the same day the administration's budget was sent to Congress that "there are a lot of places in this budget that can be cut." Anderson also warned that an economic depression might result unless the tax burden was relieved. By this time, however, the president had no time to cut it back. So it was left to Congress to take the proverbial axe to the budget. Both liberals and conservatives in Congress, from both parties, managed to cut some $4 billion from the president's proposed budget, including cuts in foreign aid and defense. Then an economic recession hit the economy in August, although there did not seem to be any connection between that and the budget cuts. Nevertheless, an April 1958 $1.8 billion road construction bill was passed to fight the recession, which did not last long.

SOCIAL WELFARE MEASURES CONTINUE

In a series of public housing bills in 1957, 1958, and 1959, Congress agreed to increase appropriations for public housing to help subsidize housing for the poor. In 1958 old age and retirement benefits were increased by close to 7 percent. The president objected to the government paying for more benefits, so Congress increased the payroll taxes.

ADDRESSING THE PROBLEMS OF FARMERS

Farmers continued to have many of the same problems and government the same solutions after the 1956 elections. Prices on agricultural goods were up some, but not enough. Agricultural Secretary Benson pushed for farmers to accept strict acreage planting restrictions on staples before they could receive price supports. No one was happy with this solution, but during the recession of 1957–1958, farm income was up by 10 percent while the rest of the nation suffered economically. Of course Secretary Benson claimed his plan was the reason for the increase, but a poor year for agriculture in 1957 and more exports were probably the more important of the reasons for the upturn. Congress continued to use both price supports and acreage restrictions as the problems of surpluses continued. Diminishing numbers of farmers would decrease the number of voters, and the problems of farmers would receive less attention from Congress.

THE SHERMAN ADAMS SCANDAL AND
THE MID-TERM ELECTIONS OF 1958

The White House Chief of Staff for President Eisenhower was Sherman Adams, a former governor of New Hampshire. Adams ran such a tight ship coordinating communications and screening Ike's visitors that he earned the nicknames of "Sherm the Firm" and the "Abominable No-Man." During Eisenhower's second term, it was discovered that Adams had used his connections to open some doors to the Securities and Exchange Commission and the Federal Trade Commission for a Boston industrialist named Bernard Goldfine. In return, Adams had apparently accepted a fur coat and an Oriental rug. Adams had been an efficient Chief of Staff for the president, but the public clamor forced him to accept Adams' resignation reluctantly in September 1958.

The Sherman Adams scandal could not have come at a worse time for the Republicans in Washington. The appearance of corruption, along with a mild economic recession, combined to give the Democrats large gains in Congress in the midterm elections of November 1958. The results gave the Democrats nearly two to one margins in both the House and the Senate.

THE LANDRUM-GRIFFIN ACT

The American people appeared ready to further restrict the activities of labor unions, especially after Senate investigations linking the Teamsters' Union (and its president, Jimmy Hoffa) to organized crime. President Eisenhower, whose cabinet had really been a "who's who" in corporate America, and a coalition of Republicans and conservative southern Democrats in Congress, also pushed for a major strengthening of the 1947 Taft-Hartley Act. Senator John F. Kennedy, who had chaired a Senate committee looking into union corruption in the late 1950s, offered several moderate amendments to Taft-Hartley. But conservatives turned these into a very anti-union bill, which passed Congress in 1959 as the Landrum-Griffin Act. This bill required unions to report their membership and finances, outlawed secondary boycotts and organizational picketing, provided for federal controls over union elections, and excluded anyone from union office who had been convicted of certain crimes.

REMAINING ISSUES

In remaining domestic business late in the Eisenhower presidency, Alaska was admitted as the forty-ninth state on January 3, 1959, and Hawaii as the fiftieth state on August 21, 1959.

THE SUPREME COURT DURING THE EISENHOWER ADMINISTRATIONS

Eisenhower nominated Earl Warren (in 1953) as the Chief Justice to the Supreme Court along with three other justices to sit on the bench. The Court, particularly the influential Warren, moved to a more liberal interpretation of the Constitution in the 1950s. The Court took the liberal position of advancing civil rights, expanding the rights of the accused, and protecting the rights of Americans to express unpopular views. Right-wing conservatives would become frustrated with the Court to the point of putting up signs to "Impeach Earl Warren." Eisenhower later revealed that appointing Warren had been one of the biggest mistakes of his presidency. The case that would bring the most criticism for the court and problems for the president was *Brown v. Board of Education of Topeka* in 1954. This case declared segregation in schools to be unconstitutional and brought resistance from the South to its implementation. Eisenhower had to step into a political maelstrom that he had not created and did not want to deal with. (See Chapter Fourteen.)

In the case of *Jencks v. United States* (1957) the Court expanded the rights of the accused to inspect government documents that the prosecution had used as evidence against them. And in the case of *Yates v. United States* (1957) the Court overturned the convictions of Communist party officials found guilty under the Smith Act. The Court stated that there was a distinction protected by the Constitution between advocating unlawful acts and teaching general revolutionary philosophy. The Court continued along a more liberal path increasing the protection of the rights of the individual. (See Chapter Sixteen.)

FOREIGN AFFAIRS UNDER EISENHOWER

Eisenhower and Dulles Formulate Foreign Policy

The importance that foreign policy would play in the two administrations of President Eisenhower was established in his first inaugural address. Most of the address focused on his plans for a foreign policy that continued international commitments, supported cooperation among countries to "remove causes of mutual fear," and denounced appeasement of aggressors. The Republicans had criticized the foreign policy of the Democrats during the Truman administration as weak and unproductive, but they soon discovered that the wisest course to pursue was a continuation of Truman's policies.

Eisenhower's Secretary of State

Eisenhower selected as his Secretary of State, John Foster Dulles. The new Secretary of State was an international lawyer and, at times, a diplomat. He had counseled American delegates at the Versailles Conference in 1919 and had negotiated the peace treaty with Japan. He was the son of a minister, and his own policies would frequently take on an almost religious crusading zeal of good against evil, with little compromise in between. Ike chose Dulles for his intelligence and his experience, but he also chose him because he represented the strong views of those in Congress and around the nation who wanted to "rollback" communism, not merely contain it. Dulles called for the "liberation" of those under communist domination in Europe, but when the Soviet Union put down riots of East German workers in 1953 and crushed a revolt in Hungary in 1956, the United States did nothing. Although Dulles maintained that the Eisenhower administration would pursue a much more vigorous course in maintaining security and promoting American interests around the globe, foreign policy differences between the Truman and Eisenhower administrations were mostly in rhetoric rather than in actions. Dulles continued to counter the Soviet Union's attempts to dominate nations around the world by granting aid to those nations resisting communism and building alliances with others.

The CIA would play an increasingly important role in foreign policy making and implementation with Allen Dulles as its director. It is interesting that John and Allen Dulles were brothers controlling the overt and covert activities of foreign affairs. Many believed that the rigid and righteous Dulles (John) controlled the president in foreign affairs decisions. Eisenhower did allow Dulles a lot more authority in making policy than he allowed many other close advisors, and he did stay in the background on many of the day-to-day mechanics of leading the nation. But studies of his administration after he had left office showed that Eisenhower really was in charge of the policy making in the executive branch.

The "New Look"

In order to cut back defense spending, which was important to balancing the budget, and yet maintain a defense strong enough to protect the nation, President Eisenhower, Secretary Dulles, and the Joint Chiefs of Staff took a "New Look" at the American defense establishment. The "New Look" enlarged the dependence upon nuclear weapons even in limited-war situations and substantially reduced the conventional forces and weapons of the army and the navy. Depending more heavily on nuclear weapons would bring "more bang for the buck." It was also believed that increasing nuclear capability would not only deter Soviet aggression because of the possible actions of the United States, but also deter the actions of those who did not have nuclear weapons in their arsenal.

Brinkmanship and Massive Retaliation

The "New Look" prompted Secretary Dulles to add the policy of "brinksmanship" to his arsenal of cold war weapons. In 1956 Dulles declared that with a policy of confrontation of communism, the United States must be willing to "go to the brink" of war. This policy of brinkmanship was based on the idea of "massive retaliation" against an enemy with the use of nuclear weapons. Dulles claimed it was an "art" looking over the edge into the absolute possibility of war without bringing on that war. To use this policy as a deterrent to conflict other nations must be aware of your commitment and the destruction which could be unleashed. One example of willingness to go to the "brink" were the maneuvers of Eisenhower and Dulles to warn Red China of the consequences if the stalemate in Korea were not broken in 1953.

SOVIET-AMERICAN RELATIONS

The Growing Arms Race

President Eisenhower worked for disarmament to reduce the tensions between the United States and the Soviet Union, which were partially caused by the arms race between the two nations. The United States had successfully exploded its first hydrogen bomb (the H-bomb) in November 1952, based on nuclear fusion rather than fission. When the Soviets developed their own H-bombs about 9 months later, the stakes in the nuclear game had been raised considerably. Throughout the 1950s, much emphasis was placed on refining the H-bomb and various delivery systems, such as the intercontinental ballistic missles (ICBMs). Along with the H-bomb came the construction of nuclear shelters in public buildings and homes and nuclear attack drills in schools. "Better dead than red" was a popular saying during the decade.

This arms race was a drain on the economies of both nations, and the potential for total destruction was increasing. On December 8, 1953, Eisenhower addressed the United Nations with his "atoms for peace plan." The plan called for nations to stockpile atomic materials under the oversight of the United Nations, controlled destruction of atomic weapons, and unlimited monitoring of nations with atomic capability. The Soviets countered with a proposal that all nuclear weapons should be banned and that there would be no inspections. An accord was not reached, but both nations joined eighty other nations in approving the creation of the International Atomic Energy Agency by 1957, to which the United States had donated fissionable material and technical knowledge for power projects.

NATO Versus the Warsaw Pact

Steps were taken to strengthen the North Atlantic Treaty Organization (NATO) after the October 1954 Paris Agreement gave West Germany full sovereignty and allowed it into NATO membership with about 500,000 troops. In response to the strenghtened NATO, the Soviet Union took the lead in establishing the Warsaw Pact in 1955. The Warsaw Pact became the Soviet Union's own defensive alliance system in eastern Europe, and included all of the communist nations of eastern Europe as well as the Soviet Union.

Khrushchev Takes Power

On March 5, 1953, Joseph Stalin, the communist dictator of the Soviet Union, died. This bolstered the hope within foreign policy circles in the United States that Cold War tensions could be reduced between the two superpowers. Of course, it would depend on the goals of the new Soviet leaders. Georgi Malenkov moved into the position of Premier of the Soviet Union, and Nikita Khrushchev was selected as the first secretary of the Communist party. By 1956 Malenkov was forced to resign, Nikolai Bulganin replaced him as Premier, and Bulganin and Khrushchev were ruling the Soviet Union. It was soon apparent that Khrushchev was the true head of the Communist party and the Soviet government.

At first Khrushchev appeared genial and sincere in his goals to follow a course of peace. He spoke of peaceful coexistence with the United States and other nations, summit meetings were held, talk of disarmament expanded, and Khrushchev even visited the United States and extended an invitation to Eisenhower to visit the Soviet Union. However, the promising beginning for the reduction of Cold War tensions deteriorated over the years to a point that the two nations came close to war (See Chapter Sixteen for a discussion of the Cuban Missile Crisis).

The Geneva Summit Conference and the Open Skies Proposal

In July 1955, however, hopes were high when the leaders of the United States, the Soviet Union, Britain, and France came together at a summit meeting in Geneva to discuss reducing international tensions. The Summit Conference had been proposed by President Eisenhower. One of the thorny issues creating tensions was the Soviet insistence that any united Germany be free of all foreign troops. That issue was never resolved. But the representatives of the nations, including Khrushchev and Bulganin, listened to the proposals of Eisenhower for the foundations for a secure world. Eisenhower proposed that the United States and the Soviet Union, as the two nations with nuclear power, work toward a program of disarmament.

To show that the United States was sincere, they offered to exchange blueprints of military establishments with the Soviets and proposed that both nations have an "open skies" policy to the other for aerial surveillance to determine if each nation was carrying through with their promises. The Soviet leaders claimed publicly to support the ideal of lowering tensions then and later, but nothing concrete ever came out of the Geneva Summit Conference. Privately, however, Khrushchev related to Eisenhower that he believed that the plan was just a ploy to spy on the Soviet Union. The "spirit of Geneva" led to future attempts to reach an accord between the two superpowers with little success, but it did open up the way for future exchanges between the nations.

The Hungarian Revolt

Soviet-American relations were temporarily damaged by the cruel Soviet crushing of a popular uprising in Hungary in October and November 1956 that became known as the Hungarian Revolt. In January 1953, Secretary of State John Foster Dulles had given a radio speech aimed at eastern Europeans. In the address, Dulles referred to them as "captive peoples" who could "count" on United States support against the Soviets, thus encouraging them to rebel. Then in February, his own written resolution introduced in Congress denounced the Soviet occupation of the "captive nations" of eastern Europe. More than three and a half years later, "freedom fighters" in Hungary revolted against Soviet control. But Soviet tanks quickly crushed the Hungarian Revolt while the United States did nothing. Nor in reality, could the United States have really done anything meaningful. This event produced justified criticism of Secretary Dulles for agitating the eastern Europeans to revolt when he knew all along that the American government could not and would not take any military steps to assist them.

Street fighting during the Hungarian Revolt in 1956. Credit: AP/Wide World Photos.

More Soviet Antics

Khrushchev again raised American hopes that he was a man of peace when he denounced Stalin at the 1956 Communist Party Congress for crimes against the Soviet Union and misrule. In 1958, Khrushchev became premier while remaining head of the party. He called for another summit of the major powers. In March 1958, the Soviet Union declared that it was suspending testing nuclear weapons, and the United States had to follow suit. This unwritten suspension remained in effect until Eisenhower left office. The Soviets, however, continued to avoid serious negotiations on the elements of a disarmament program. A Soviet exhibition was held in New York City, American symphony orchestras were heard in the Soviet Union, Soviet ballet companies toured in the United States, and in July 1959, Khrushchev guided Vice-President Nixon through an exhibition of American products in Moscow. Standing in front of American stoves and refrigerators, the two leaders argued the positive and negative aspects of their respective nations in what became known as the famous "kitchen debate."

Khrushchev Visits the United States

Khrushchev had called West Berlin a bone in his throat. That was because it was a showplace of Western prosperity and an easy place for East Germans, and other citizens of communist nations, to escape communism. So in November 1958, Khrushchev gave a six-month deadline to the other three Allied powers (United States, France, and Britain) to reach agreement with the Soviets on the question of Berlin, or they would sign a separate peace treaty officially ending World War II with East Germany and force the West to deal with the East German government. The idea behind that was to force the other Allies out of West Berlin. The United States and the other NATO nations could not accept this ultimatum. Eisenhower tried to ignore the issue and deadline altogether, so Khrushchev finally gave the word to British Prime Minister Harold Macmillan that the main point was to get negotiations going, not the May 1959 deadline. Shortly after that, the foreign ministers of the four Allied nations met, but without success. And, indeed, the Soviet deadline came and went with no Soviet action.

After the foreign ministers' talks ended unsuccessfully, Khrushchev accepted Eisenhower's invitation in September to visit the United States. Therefore, on September 15, 1959, Khrushchev began a visit to the United States. On a tour across the country, he was exposed to a sample of life in America. He visited farms, factories, supermarkets, and even Disneyland. Then just before leaving the country, the Soviet leader met with President Eisenhower in September 1959, at the president's retreat at Camp David, Maryland. Both leaders agreed to continue to work for peaceful solutions to problems and to consider another summit of the four major powers. A new summit meeting was planned for Paris in May 1960.

The U-2 Spy Plane Incident

Any chance for success in Paris was eliminated when an American U-2 reconaissance plane was shot down inside Soviet territory east of the Ural Mountains on May 1, 1960. The Soviets revealed that they had shot down such a spy plane on May 5, but at that time they said nothing about capturing the pilot. The administration at first denied that any spy planes ever operated over the Soviet Union, although the president knew that such flights had been going on for the previous three and a half years. The American government even suggested that it must have been a weather plane. Efforts to cover up the spy mission of the aircraft were revealed as lies when the Soviets released the information that they had the pilot, Francis Gary Powers. They also announced that Powers had confessed the nature of his mission, and that the cameras had been recovered with film of Soviet military installations. Finally, Eisenhower admitted on May 11 that he was personally responsible for the spy missions, which he justified for security reasons. He did not apologize and state that they would cease, but he did, in fact, cancel future flights.

The Big Four met in Paris on May 16, but Khrushchev used it to demand that Eisenhower apologize for the incident and to "pass severe judgment on those responsible." When Eisenhower refused, Khrushchev stormed out of the meeting, and the talks on Berlin collapsed. The invitation for Eisenhower to visit the Soviet Union was also canceled. Khrushchev and others blamed the U-2 incident for the failure of the conference, but later proof indicates that the Soviets had used this as an excuse to sabotage the meeting in Paris. The Soviets had known about the spy missions since 1956 and could have revealed the information at any time. Powers was sentenced to 10 years in a Soviet prison, but he was exchanged in early 1962 for a Soviet spy captured in the United States.

Khruschev was not finished with denouncing the actions of the United States. In September 1960, he spoke to the United Nations General Assembly in New York City. In an outburst of childish behavior, the Soviet leader announced that he would ignore the United States as long as Eisenhower was president. He also warned the world that the missile gap favored the Soviet Union, and he denounced Secretary General Dag Hammarskjold while hammering on a table with his shoe. His display at the UN was a definite repudiation of accommodation with the United States. American policy with the Soviets had clearly not been very successful.

THE RACE FOR SPACE

Sputnik

Fear for American security was dramatically increased when the Soviet Union successfully launched the first man-made satellite into orbit around the earth on October 4, 1957. The satellite, called *Sputnik* (which means "fellow traveler of earth"), weighed only 194 pounds. It was followed by the placing of a dog in another orbiting *Sputnik* early the next month (November). The *Sputnik* satellites themselves were not a threat, but the ability of the Soviets to launch and sustain the satellites in space was a blow to American beliefs of superiority in all areas. The Soviets' ability to launch artificial satellites sent a clear message that intercontinental ballistic missiles (ICBMs) could reach targets in the United States. Therefore, there were calls for remedying the so-called "missile gap" between the Soviet Union and the United States. President Eisenhower knew that there really was no such missile gap, but he could not clearly state that fact because it had been revealed from photographs taken by secret U-2 spy planes flying over Soviet territory.

The Reaction of NATO

The Soviets were making rapid developments in armament, but the West still had the power of massive retaliation and bases in England, western Europe, and North Africa to deliver the destruction. A meeting of NATO was called on November 25, 1957 to discuss deterring the Soviets with bases in Europe supplied with intermediate range ballistic missiles (IRBMs). But the Soviets threatened any nation that built bases to contain missiles that had an anti-Soviet mission. The United States did not then back off from its position, but did emphasize to its allies that it would offer the weapons only if a nation really wanted to build the bases.

Explorer I and the Creation of NASA

The United States began its own program to challenge the Soviets in the race for space. On January 31, 1958, the United States launched *Explorer I*. Then in

July of the same year, Congress created the National Aeronautics and Space Administration (NASA) to coordinate all research and promote the technology that would lead America into exploration of space. By the end of the year, NASA had devised a plan to put a manned craft into orbit. During the last three years of Eisenhower's administration, American satellites travelled in space. In 1959, a Soviet satellite sent back pictures of the dark side of the moon. And on May 5, 1961, Alan Shepard, Jr. became the first American to orbit the earth. The challenge of exploring space would be left for President Kennedy to take up in his "New Frontier."

The National Defense Education Act

In further response to the Soviet space program, Congress passed the National Defense Education Act in September 1958. Many Americans had pointed to studies that supported the claim that students in the United States lagged behind Soviet students in science and the technologies, and that this could account for the Soviets jumping ahead of the United States into space. The National Defense Education Act answered that challenge by establishing nearly $300 million for student loans and fellowships at the college and graduate levels of education. Money was also appropriated for federal grants for laboratories in public schools and more textbooks to improve the teaching of math, science, and modern languages at all levels of education.

LATIN AMERICAN POLICY

General Attitude Toward the Region

The long standing regional interest of the United States in Latin America to present a united hemispheric front for trade and security was relegated to a lower priority under the Eisenhower administration. Problems of communist activity in Europe and Asia were the most important foreign policy considerations, and Latin America received the most attention only when the danger of communism moved to that area. Latin America needed economic assistance from the Eisenhower administration to solve internal social and economic problems that were leading to revolution and the growth of internal communist groups. But the United States, while willing to give military and technical assistance to fight the spread of communism in the area, was more inclined to reduce economic assistance and to support dictatorships that denounced communism.

The president's brother, Milton S. Eisenhower, led a fact finding mission to Latin America to determine ways to reduce Latin American discontent. Dr. Eisenhower's report indicated that better economic cooperation was of vital importance to better relations, but that the Latin American nations themselves and private business should bear most of the burden of economic assistance, not the United States government. The United States gave $317 million worth of military assistance to 12 nations in the region, but large-scale economic assistance was slow to come. Fighting communism in the area took priority. Two problem areas for Eisenhower, Guatemala and Cuba, would also bring the CIA (Central Intelligence Agency) into the Cold War battle. The CIA put together covert actions to undermine or topple regimes believed to be hostile to the United States. The success of the CIA in its clandestine operations led to close to 80 percent of its budget being used for subversion of foreign governments, bribing foreign government officials, and secretly giving money to newspapers and labor unions that were pro-American.

The 1954 Guatemalan Intervention

In Eisenhower's first term, the Central American country of Guatemala became a focal point of the administration's Latin American policy. Guatemala was a small nation that had been undergoing revolutionary reform pushed by leftist leaning political groups which included socialists, communists, and nationalists. One of the driving forces for this change was the fact that only about 2 percent of Guatemala's population owned roughly 70 percent of its land. The political leader who made the first major attempt to remedy the severe problems in his country was Colonel Jacobo Arbenz Guzman, who was first elected president of Guatemala in 1946. Arbenz himself was a nationalist who believed in democracy, but his coalition government did include communist party members, whom he leaned on for support to enact his programs of social reform.

Arbenz's reforms included an income tax, expanded public works, and a 1952 land reform measure. Under the land reform program, the government expropriated uncultivated landholdings for redistribution among the peasants, paying the landowners for it. The largest landowner in Guatemala was the American-owned United Fruit Company, which intentionally bought land it did not intend to use in order to reduce competition. In the early 1950s, about 85 percent of its land was uncultivated. In 1953, the Guatemalan government offered about $600,000 for that unused land, but the company considered that a woefully inadequate amount for compensation.

In concert with United States Ambassador John Peurifoy, the United Fruit Company began pressuring the State Department and Congress to use their influence to help them keep all of their land. It found willing listeners in Secretary of State John Foster Dulles and his brother Allan (the CIA director), who had both come from a law firm with close ties to the United Fruit Company. American officials began painting Arbenz as a communist, or as Ambassador Peurifoy asserted, "if not actually one, [Arbenz] would do until one came along." Pressure to receive just payments for seized property, concern for communist elements within the Guatemalan government, and the Cold War context in general, persuaded President Eisenhower that Arbenz was a bad influence who must be forced out of office. Therefore, in the summer of 1953, Eisenhower authorized the CIA to begin training a military force in Honduras and on an island off Nicaragua, which could be used to topple the Arbenz regime. An exiled Guatemalan army colonel, Carlos Castillo Armas, was endorsed by the CIA as the replacement for Arbenz. Meanwhile, the administration tried a series of diplomatic moves designed to oust the Guatemalan president. During this diplomatic struggle, the Arbenz government appealed to the United Nations Security Council for assistance, but of course, the United States blocked any such request. As a result, Arbenz turned to the Soviet Union for help. This, of course, simply permitted Eisenhower and Dulles to adopt an "I told you he was a communist" attitude.

On May 17, 1954, Secretary of State Dulles revealed that the Arbenz government had just received a shipment of small arms from Czechoslovakia via a Swedish ship. The American response was to secretly airlift close to fifty tons of rifles, machine guns, and ammunition to a site near United Fruit Company property inside Guatemala on May 23. At the same time, weapons were sent to Honduras and Nicaragua in the event that they had to protect themselves from Guatemala. In June 1954, CIA-trained mercenary forces under Armas began an invasion of Guatemala while CIA pilots began bombing government targets in Guatemala City (the capital). Arbenz made a last-minute appeal to the Organization of American States (OAS), and then the UN Security Council. But when these appeals proved unsuccessful, his army personnel began deserting. On June 27, President Arbenz was forced to resign and flee the country.

Colonel Armas took the reins of power in Guatemala and quickly became a military dictator. The United Fruit Company got all of its land back, and the Eisenhower administration was pleased that it had (allegedly) defeated communism there. The truth was that United States policy had pushed a democratic, reform-minded president into closer ties with the Soviets, and then helped replace his government with an undemocratic, ruthless dictatorship which had little interest in social reform. American action in Guatemala also represented a radical departure from the Good Neighbor Policy of the Franklin Roosevelt presidency of the 1930s and 1940s. And the result was a series of anti-American demonstrations across Latin America protesting the role of the United States in the overthrow. Clearly in Latin America, the fear of American intervention to prevent the spread of communism became much more intense than the threat of communism itself.

Hostility on Nixon's Goodwill Tour

Feelings toward the United States were so negative by 1958, that Vice-President Richard Nixon, on an 8-nation goodwill tour of South America, was met with a mixture of friendly welcome and great hostility. While attempting to speak at the University of San Marcos in Lima, Peru (the oldest institution of learning in the western hemisphere), spit, stones, and rocks flew at Nixon, forcing him to leave the university. A hostile crowd was waiting next at the airport in Caracas, Venezuela. There Vice-President and Mrs. Nixon walked through a storm of saliva and jeers before reaching their car. The motorcade taking Nixon and other dignitaries, including Venezuelan officials, was met by crowds that stopped the processional. Rocks and bodies were pounding on the cars. A path was finally opened, and the destination was changed to the United States embassy. It was obvious at this point that American policy toward Latin America must be changed. Measures were taken to assist the economic development of the area, which was at the root of most of the hostility.

The Emerging Cuban Crisis

Cuba emerged near the end of the decade as a source of concern for the Eisenhower administration, and later for President Kennedy as well. Ever since the overthrow of Spanish colonial rule there in the Spanish-American War (1898), Cuba had been heavily dominated by American policy and private American economic investments. Its impoverished economy had been made worse by the oppressive regime under Fulgencio Batista since the early 1950s, and Cuba was ripe for revolution. A young middle class law school graduate named Fidel Castro had begun using a mountainous headquarters to lead hit-and-run attacks on the Batista government in 1956. Finally, on January 1, 1959, the Batista regime was forced into exile, and Castro proclaimed himself the new Cuban leader. The Eisenhower administration, which had earlier begun to distance itself from the unpopular Batista, officially recognized the new Castro government within one week of his ascendancy to power.

Castro was not a communist, and this was not a communist revolution. Yet it was difficult to describe the philosophy of this new Cuban leader. He certainly was a radical who favored a state-managed economy as a way to achieve economic and social reforms. And he distrusted parliamentary democracy as a vehicle to accomplish these radical goals. He had flirted with fascism, whose central tenet is the glorification of the state under a dictatorial leader. And while the term fascist may arguably be the best political label applicable to him, basically, Castro was non-ideological. His major concern seems to have been to use any means necessary to seize and then hold on to political power. Circumstances developed, however, that would push Cuba into the Soviet orbit of influence.

Once in power, Castro decided that there would be drastic political and social reform. Those Americans who had hoped the revolution would begin a democracy in Cuba were quickly disappointed. Castro's infamous "war courts" tried and executed Cuban political opponents with little regard for legal procedures. Programs of land reform and the nationalization of foreign-owned property without compensation added to the American outcry against the new leader. By 1960, his government had seized approximately $1 billion of American property in Cuba without paying a dime for any of it. Opposition from upper and middle class Cubans forced Castro to turn to Cuban communists in order to carry out his reforms. The Eisenhower administration still hoped to influence the future government of Cuba, so the earliest responses to Castro's actions were not retaliatory.

In February 1960, Castro negotiated a five-year trade agreement with the Soviet Union that permitted the Soviets to trade oil, machinery, and arms in exchange for Cuban sugar. The deal also included a $100 million loan to the Cuban government, charged at only 2 percent interest. Then in June the Soviets began to assist in the build-up of the Cuban military capability. During that same month, Castro seized a Texaco Oil Company refining plant after the company refused to process Soviet crude oil. In reaction to Castro's June actions, in July 1960 the United States retaliated by suspending Cuban sugar imports. This American action dealt a serious blow to the Cuban economy and escalated the tensions between the two countries. The Cubans responded by bartering Cuban sugar to Red China and other communist countries in exchange for goods, but such activities did not prove very prosperous for the Cuban people. Therefore, in October 1960, Castro accused the United States of "economic aggression." And Soviet communist dictator Nikita Khrushchev announced that his nation would protect Cuba from any foreign intervention. Soviet arms and technicians soon began arriving in Cuba in large amounts.

Before the end of the year, the United States cut off all trade with Cuba except for exports of food and medical supplies, and appealed to the Organization of American States to support them in an attempt to stop the Soviet infiltration into Cuba. The Latin American nations refused to become involved in the problems between the United States and Cuba, except to condemn outside interference in the area. Continued American resistance to the Cuban government resulted in Castro being seen as a hero to many Latin Americans because he was challenging the United States and winning. Now firmly in the communist camp, the Cuban dictator represented a potentially greater threat to the region. President Eisenhower then (in 1960) approved a plan for the CIA to train and equip Cuban exiles in Guatemala and Nicaragua for the eventual purpose of invading the island nation and overthrowing Castro. This CIA operation was approved in theory by President-Elect John F. Kennedy as well. In January 1961, just before Eisenhower left office, the Cuban government ordered a reduction in the staff at the American Embassy in Havana that would leave only 11 staff members. At that point, President Eisenhower cut off all diplomatic relations with Cuba instead.

MIDDLE EAST POLICY

American policy in the Middle East under the Eisenhower administration had mixed goals, some of which were in conflict with each other at times. These goals included the containment of communism, which was always a priority. There was also concern that the oil resources of the nations in that region be kept free from the domination of the Soviet Union. And while the independence of Israel had to be maintained, friendships with the Arab nations had to be cultivated in order for the other goals to be successful. The strategies to achieve these goals included another set of alliances for the area, supporting or putting into place pro-American governments, and military and economic aid.

The CIA Coup in Iran

In the early 1950s, Iran was a problem for both the United States and Britain. A left-wing, pro-Soviet leader of Iran, Mohammed Mossadegh, had taken over the government of Shah (King) Mohammed Reza Pahlavi in 1949. Premier Mohammed Mossadegh was also an extreme nationalist who abhorred the idea of foreign control of any area of Iranian life. Thus, in 1951, he nationalized the oil industry by taking over control of the Anglo Iranian Oil Company, under which American and British oil companies operated their oil business in that country. Mossadegh's program also called for the eradication of Western influences, and he was assisted in this effort by Iran's Communist party. As part of this process, the Iranian parliament granted Mussadegh dictatorial powers in August 1952.

The next year, Shah Mohammed Reza Pahlavi was forced to leave the country. The Shah supported Western influence as a way to improve the economy of his nation; thus, he could be a threat to Mossadegh's dictatorial powers. The CIA contacted the exiled Shah in Rome with plans to return him to power. The Shah's secret police, who were still loyal, were ordered to arrange street demonstrations against Premier Mossadegh. The CIA provided approximately $1 million to the organizers of the demonstrations. Soldiers loyal to the Shah were stirred to overthrow Mossadegh. And in August 1953, the Shah was brought back from his short exile to resume his authority on the throne. A new premier arranged for the British and the Americans to each receive 40 percent of Iran's exported oil. The United States would also have a strong pro-American ally in the area. Close ties between Iran and the United States would continue until the Shah was permanently forced out of power in the late 1970s.

The Baghdad Pact

An attempt to stop communist infiltration into the Middle East region was the motivation for the American sponsorship of another alliance system. Created in 1955, the Middle East Treaty Organization (METO), commonly known as the Baghdad Pact, consisted of Britain, Turkey, Iraq, Iran, and Pakistan. Dulles eventually hoped to surround the Soviet Union with alliances dedicated to the United States policy of containment. The organization was not representative of the Arab nations, and resistance to Western domination in the region made it ineffective from the start.

The Suez Crisis

The most troublesome nation in the region for the Eisenhower administration proved to be Egypt. In 1956, a crisis over the Suez Canal brought about the most dangerous situation in the Middle East. The Suez Canal had been built in the nineteenth century as a joint British-French venture, and completed in 1869. But after the British government bought the largest share of stock in 1875, the canal became a British-controlled entity. And since 1882 British armed forces protected it as a cheaper, more direct link with its Asian colonies via the Mediterranean and Red Seas, thus avoiding having to go around the continent of Africa.

In 1952, General Gamal Abdel Nasser overthrew King Farouk. Nasser was a bitter enemy of Israel who authorized Egyptian raids across the Egyptian-Israeli border along the Sinai Peninsula. He was also an extreme nationalist who wanted complete control of his country, including the Suez Canal, and he was willing to trade with the Soviet Union to achieve his objectives. Hoping to build a friendship with Nasser which would freeze out the Soviets, the United States offered to help finance a dam at Aswan on the Nile river. Nasser wanted the dam to provide hydroelectric power to his country. It would also irrigate more than 2 million acres of land, thus alleviating some of the poverty that was a fertile ground for communist doctrine. And when Nasser began demanding that the British withdraw its military forces from the Suez Canal, the Eisenhower administration supported him. The result was the Anglo-Egyptian Treaty of 1954, in which the British promised to complete such a withdrawal within 20 months.

But on July 19, 1956, Secretary of State Dulles canceled the American offer to guarantee loans to build the dam. Dulles was convinced that Nasser was courting the United States to squeeze aid only and to give no allegiance in return. And

Dulles would not give American aid to neutral nations who acted against the interests of the United States. What convinced Dulles of this attitude were several recent actions that Nasser took. Among these was the purchase of weapons from the Czechoslovakians, although the agreements were with the Soviet Union. He was also pushing the United States to increase the size of their offer for building the Aswan Dam with comments of what the Soviets were willing to do. And approximately 1,000 Soviet military technicians and military officers were in Egypt by 1956. In addition to these actions, Nasser had recently given official diplomatic recognition to Red China.

Nasser was furious, and the British and French were to bear the brunt of his anger. In July (1956) he suddenly declared that he was nationalizing the British and French-owned Suez Canal and that he would build his own Aswan Dam from the fees the ships were charged for passing through the canal. He also announced that the canal was closed to all Israeli shipping and that he was mobilizing the Egyptian military.

The British and French governments were unexpectedly threatened with loss of control of the Suez Canal, so they initiated a series of negotiations with Nasser to get him to change his mind. When the negotiations dragged through the summer and into the fall of the year, Israeli forces finally invaded the Egyptian Sinai peninsula and the Gaza Strip on October 29, 1956, and headed for the Suez Canal. The next day the British and French called for a cease-fire that asked for Israelis and Egyptians to withdraw 10 miles from the canal. Nasser rejected this call because it was a violation of the Tripartite Declaration of 1950, in which Britain, France, and the United States had promised to guarantee that there would be no border violations of either Israel or any of the Arab nations. Then Nasser promptly closed the canal by sinking ships in the passageway. Meanwhile, militant Arabs assisted Nasser's goal by sending oil from those ships up the canal from the Persian Gulf to the Mediterranean Sea. This caused such an oil shortage in Europe that rationing was necessary on that continent. So on October 31, a joint British-French attack began, which included the bombing of Egyptian air fields and dropping paratroopers in to take control of Port Said, at the north end of the canal. Port Said was under British-French control by November 3. Later reports confirmed that Britain, France, and Israel had each coordinated their assaults on Egypt.

Moscow threatened retaliation on the side of the Egyptians against this imperialistic aggression and offered to send Russian volunteers. There was even a hint from Moscow that England and France might face nuclear weapons if the invasion was not halted. Some believed World War III was in the making. Eisenhower was furious at Britain and France for not consulting with the United States before an invasion; he was especially irritated because their actions came right in the middle of a presidential election campaign in which he was seeking re-election. The president was also truly concerned with what the Soviets would do. Therefore, Eisenhower could not support his NATO allies. He also disagreed with the military force used by Britain and France, colonial powers who had created much of the animosity of the area toward the Western powers in the first place. So in a strange scenario, the United States found itself joining a Soviet move to push the United Nations to condemn the aggression. The United States also threatened the three invading nations with embargoes. They had no choice but to agree to a cease-fire, which began on November 6. The UN General Assembly voted to establish an Emergency Force for Palestine, and by the end of the year, UN forces were occupying the Sinai region in a peacekeeping role. War did not occur from the crisis, but the prestige and ideas of Nasser rose sharply all across the Middle East, spreading nationalism, turmoil, revolution, and anti-Western feelings.

The Eisenhower Doctrine

In the aftermath of the Suez Crisis, President Eisenhower was very concerned about stemming the growing influence of the Soviet Union in the Middle East. Therefore, in January 1957, the president urged Congress to grant him authority to declare that the United States would defend any Middle East nation against external attack. After a long debate, Congress approved what became known as the Eisenhower Doctrine in March of that year. The Eisenhower Doctrine declared that the independence and integrity of Middle East nations was vital to the security of the United States, and armed force would be considered to assist any nation requesting assistance to resist "armed aggression from any nation controlled by international Communism." Financial aid was also promised as part of this new American policy. Although under a different name, the Eisenhower Doctrine certainly widened the scope of the American containment policy, even though internal subversion was the more likely danger facing most Middle East nations.

The Eisenhower Doctrine was first applied in Jordan. In April 1957, Jordanian officials discovered a plot to depose and possibly assassinate the king. The leftist group planning the coup had support from both Egypt and Syria. The king had opposed the leaning of his government toward communism and the influence of Nasser. So King Hussein officially dismissed his government, an action which led to riots and demonstrations in the streets. The United States came to the aid of King Hussein. The Sixth Fleet was dispatched to the area, and Jordan received $10 million to build up the economy and the military. In 1958 more unrest followed in Jordan, when assistance came from British paratroopers ordered to the area.

Crisis in Lebanon

Nasser's increased prestige led him to pursue a greater leadership role in the Middle East. Thus, in February 1958, he took the lead in establishing the United Arab Republic with the nations of Syria and Yemen, with Nasser as its president. But not all leaders in the region viewed Nasser as their saviour. When Nasser helped found the U.A.R., Jordan and Iraq countered with the formation of the Arab Union.

Then in July 1958, a military coup in Iraq deposed and killed the pro-American King Faisal and others. The new government quickly moved the country closer to the Soviet Union. Western powers, including the United States, assumed that Nasser and his U.A.R. were behind the Iraqi coup, although this conclusion later proved false. There was general unrest in Lebanon as well, a country badly divided along religious lines, between Christians and Muslims. Most of the Muslims in Lebanon favored closer ties with Nasser and the United Arab Republic. Its Christian, pro-American president, Camille Chamoun, requested help under the Eisenhower Doctrine in 1958.

Beginning in July 1958, President Eisenhower agreed to the Lebanese request and sent 14,000 troops to Lebanon. They were limited to the capital city of Beirut and its airport because Ike wanted to see if the government there really had popular support. After an internal compromise among the factions, American troops were withdrawn in October of the same year. The area calmed down for a while, but peace in the Middle East in the forseeable future would be defined as brief periods of calm between a tremendous amount of turmoil.

ASIAN POLICY

Background

The fall of China to communism, the Korean War, and the defeat in Indochina of the French by the communist forces of Ho Chi Minh, set the stage for the Eisenhower and Dulles policies in Asia. On April 7, 1954, the president advanced his "domino theory" that compared communist success in Asia to a row of dominoes. When dominoes are lined up just right, and the first one falls, the others quickly follow. Eisenhower seemed to favor more assistance to the French in their final days of battle in Vietnam, but Congress did not. The "domino theory," however, would be part of the policies of his successors in the fight to contain communism in Asia. (See Chapter Thirteen for a thorough treatment of the entire Vietnam War.)

Dulles believed that another mutual defense organization was needed in Southeast Asia to warn communists of American interest in holding the line against, or containing, communism in this area of the world. A ring was now pretty much drawn around the communist nations. The Southeast Asia Treaty Organization (SEATO), also known as the Manila Pact, was organized in September 1954 in response to the Geneva Agreement following the French defeat in Vietnam. Actually, there were only three Asian members in SEATO—the Philippines, Thailand, and Pakistan. A special protocol added Indochina. The other original members were Britain, France, Australia, New Zealand, and the United States. Neither India or Indonesia joined. The members of SEATO agreed to consult each other when members were threatened or in danger from acts of subversion. An attack on one member was considered a threat to all, but each member would act according to their "constitutional practices" with regard to retaliation. The United States qualified their treaty obligations by maintaining it was communist aggression that would involve the interest of this nation.

Quemoy and Matsu

Mainland Communist China was threatening Formosa in the summer of 1954. In September, the communists began shelling the islands of Quemoy and Matsu (and Tachen too), held by the Nationalist Chinese on Taiwan (once known as Formosa). Their ultimate intention was to take the Nationalist island, but they claimed they were merely defending the mainland approaches that the islands threatened. In December 1954, the United States and the Nationalist Chinese signed a Treaty of Mutual Defense. The United States guaranteed the security of Taiwan and its nearby Pescadore islands. The Nationalists pledged they would not attack mainland China or reinforce offshore locations. Quemoy, Matsu, and Tachen were not specifically mentioned, but Eisenhower gave his guarantee to Chiang Kai-shek (the Nationalist leader) that they would be protected. Tachen was abandoned by the Nationalists because it was too far to defend, but Dulles was determined that the other two islands must be defended or the communists would take it as another sign of weakness and expand throughout Southeast Asia. The Red Chinese government backed down after the Eisenhower administration "leaked" word, through comments to journalists by the chief of naval operations, that the United States was considering a plan "to destroy Red China's military potential and thus end its expansionist tendencies."

But in August 1958, the Chinese communists renewed shelling the islands of Quemoy and Matsu. Eisenhower declared that he would avoid a "Western Pacific 'Munich.'" As a result, the American Seventh Fleet began escorting Nationalist Chinese supply ships through the dangerous waters in September. The Americans supplied and trained Nationalist Air Force, equipped with American air-to-air missiles, gained control of the skies, and howitzers capable of firing nuclear shells were turned over to the Nationalists, even though the nuclear shells themselves were not turned over to them. The American response worked to diffuse the tensions, and Taiwan was not invaded. On October 1, Ike suggested a cease-fire and negotiations, and the Red Chinese accepted the proposal and began the cease-fire on the 6th of the same month. The worst of the crisis was over. Once again Asia was stabilized in Korea, Taiwan, and Vietnam, but it would not remain so for very long in Vietnam. (See Chapter Thirteen.)

Trouble in Laos

Problems in Laos brought support from the Eisenhower administration for its pro-Western supporters. The geographical position of Laos made this nation important to the United States. It was a gateway for communism to spread southward in Southeast Asia, particularly into South Vietnam. In the 1954 Geneva Agreement, Laos was to maintain a neutral position. But from the beginning, there was a struggle for control of the country among the neutralists, led by Prince Souvanna Phouma, the pro-communist Pathet Lao, a guerilla group with power in the northeastern provinces, and the anti-Communists, led by General Phoumi Nosavan. The United States sent economic aid, military supplies, and a training mission for the Royal Laotian Army when the anti-communists finally gained control of the government.

But in August 1960, there was a coup which overthrew the pro-Western government. In an attempt to stop the killing of the various factions around the country, Prince Phouma was restored to the throne to form another coalition government. The prince was too dependent on the support of the Pathet Lao and too friendly to the Soviet Union and Red China to satisfy the anti-communist forces, so the anti-communist faction was once again intent on taking control of Laos. Most of the Royal Laotian Army followed General Nosavan as he marched against the government with American support. By January 1961, the United States had pledged its support to the new anti-communist government of Prince Boun Oum. After that, the problem of Laos then fell into the lap of President Kennedy.

THE 1960 ELECTION

The Candidates and Platforms

Three main contenders for the Democratic presidential nomination emerged in 1960. All three were members of the United States Senate—John F. Kennedy of Massachusetts, who had nearly won the vice-presidential nomination in 1956; Hubert H. Humphrey, the former mayor of Minneapolis who had delivered the fiery pro-civil rights speech that had resulted in a partial southern walkout at the 1948 national convention; and Senate Majority Leader, Lyndon B. Johnson of Texas. Senator Humphrey had strong support from organized labor and civil rights organizations, but could not match Kennedy's charisma or money. And Senate Majority Leader Johnson had the reputation of a wheeler-dealer, although he probably was one of the most effective leaders in Congress since the days of House Speaker Henry Clay in the first half of the nineteenth century.

Senator John F. Kennedy was born into a life of luxury that his self-made wealthy father, Joseph P. Kennedy, had created for his family. The grandson of poor Irish-Catholic immigrants, Joseph Kennedy made his millions in real estate, in the stock market and in bootlegging during the 1920s, and in the movie-making industry in the 1930s. Joseph Kennedy also wanted to work within the seat of power, the government. President Franklin Roosevelt appointed him as the first chairman of the Securities and Exchange Commission in 1934, a position from which FDR had to request his resignation because of his controversial personality. In 1937, he was chairman of the Maritime Commission. And he finally persuaded President Roosevelt to name him ambassador to Britain from 1937–1940. Joseph Kennedy had decided that one of his sons should become president of the United States. When his oldest son, Joseph Kennedy, Jr., was killed in World War II, the dream fell to John Kennedy, the next in line. In all his endeavors, one of the primary motivations seemed to be an intense desire to vindicate the family name as being of successful Irish-Catholic immigrant stock in stuffy old Puritan Boston.

During World War II, John Kennedy served as a skipper of a torpedo boat in the Pacific. After his *PT 109* was hit and sunk by a Japanese warship in the South Pacific, young Kennedy displayed great courage in rescuing several of his crew. This action earned him the distinction of a war hero, which greatly assisted him later in his political career.

After the war, young John Kennedy dutifully followed the path that his somewhat tyrannical father had laid out for his life. In January 1947, at the age of just 29, Kennedy took his seat in the United States House of Representatives from the 11th Congressional District of Massachusetts. He was reelected in 1948 and 1950. Then in 1952, Kennedy's tireless energy, witty charm, and family money helped him win a surprising upset victory for the Senate over the powerful and popular Republican Senator Henry Cabot Lodge, Jr. Lodge had held office since 1936, except for a brief period when he served in World War II. Kennedy was re-elected to the Senate in 1958, after he nearly won the vice-presidential nomination at the

1956 Democratic National Convention. In the Senate, Kennedy had tolerated Joseph McCarthy, held hearings on corruption within the Teamsters Union, and failed to support civil rights strongly. In 1956, he had written a book, *Profiles in Courage*, about Americans who had taken courageous stands in times of trouble. But his own public career had not matched the profiles of the heroes in his book. Despite an undistinguished record in Congress, however, Kennedy became an increasingly popular man, and talk increased of the senator running for president in 1960.

Kennedy began the race for president with the enthusiastic support of his powerful and energetic family. Robert Kennedy, his brother, was his campaign manager. Many of the leaders of the party did not believe that Kennedy could win the Democratic nomination in 1960. They felt that, at the age of 43, he was too young and inexperienced. Moreover, he was a Roman Catholic. And the only other Catholic who had run for president on a major party ticket had been Al Smith, and he had been soundly defeated back in 1928. Did he stand a chance against experienced opponents such as Senators Hubert Humphrey of Minnesota and Senator Lyndon Johnson of Texas? Kennedy proved the experts wrong when he won all 7 states in which he entered the primaries. The biggest surprise was probably his 61 percent victory margin in winning West Virginia, a very heavily Protestant state, where many voters had traditionally been quite hostile to Catholics. That victory proved to be a crucial turning point as well, because Senator Humphrey withdrew from the race after losing that state. By the time the Democratic National Convention met at Los Angeles in July, more than 600 delegates were pledged to Kennedy. To capture the southerners, Kennedy shrewdly selected Senate Majority Leader Lyndon Johnson as his vice-presidential running mate. Johnson had arrived at Los Angeles with the second largest group of committed delegates. Kennedy won the nomination on the first ballot.

In his acceptance speech, the Massachusetts senator proclaimed that the United States was poised at a "New Frontier—the frontier of the 1960s—a frontier of unknown opportunities and perils—a frontier of unfilled hopes and threats." The Democratic platform pledged to work for justice and dignity for all; the restoration of military, political, and economic strength; a 5 percent per year rate of economic growth; extending social security, which would include medical care for the elderly; ending segregation in schools because of color; ending poll taxes and literacy tests, which prevented African-Americans from voting; and allowing African-Americans to demonstrate peacefully for change. This strong civil rights stand would alienate many southerners.

Among the Republicans, the only possible serious threat to Vice-President Richard Nixon's chances for the nomination could come from the liberal governor of New York, Nelson Rockefeller. But Rockefeller was more involved in trying to influence the party platform than winning the nomination. So the Republicans easily selected Vice-President Richard M. Nixon as their candidate, and Henry Cabot Lodge, Jr., the United States ambassador to the United Nations, as his vice-presidential running mate. Henry Cabot Lodge, Jr. was the grandson of the famous former statesman and senator, Henry Cabot Lodge. (The famous Lodge had denied President Woodrow Wilson ratification of the Versailles Treaty after World War I.) Of

Senator John Kennedy of Massachusetts and Vice President Richard Nixon during a nationally televised debate for the 1960 presidential election. Credit: AP/Wide World Photos.

course, Nixon was well known and would run on his years of experience as vice-president and the successes of the Eisenhower years. The Republican platform was forced into some positions on issues by the stand of the Democrats. The platform included a defense of the civil rights of minorities to protest peacefully against discrimination in all walks of life; a strengthening of the nation's defenses, especially in the missile program; and the need for responsible leaders for the nation.

The Campaign and Results

In the campaign, Kennedy's greatest weaknesses were his inexperience, a playboy image, and his Catholicism. Against these were Nixon's greater political experience, big business money, and the fact that he was the heir to Ike. But the young Kennedy learned to blunt criticism of him by use of his major assets—money, good looks, charm, youthful energy, and honest candor. Nixon's political experience did not help him with all voters, for long ago he had earned the nickname of "Tricky Dick" because of shady campaign activities. And although Eisenhower supported Nixon in the campaign, not until late in the campaign did he show much enthusiasm. And once during the campaign, the president responded to a reporter's question asking him to name one idea that Nixon had ever given the administration, by replying in rather typical bumbling fashion, "If you give me a week, I might think of one. I can't remember."

One of the most important underlying issues of the campaign was Kennedy's religion. Although to his credit, Nixon never personally attacked his opponent over his Catholicism, many other Republicans did not hesitate to do so. Knowing that he must deal with the issue, Kennedy addressed the Houston Ministerial Association, a Protestant group of clergy, in September. There he unequivocally confirmed his belief in a separation of church and state. "I believe in an America," he announced, "where the separation of church and state is absolute—where no Catholic prelate would tell the president—should he be Catholic—how to act, and no Protestant minister would tell his parishoners for whom to vote." As president, he would make his decisions on issues in the interest of the nation "and without regard to outside pressure or dictate." Experts disagree as to how effective that speech was, but evidence does seem to indicate that Kennedy still lost a lot of votes in the South and the rural Midwest because of his religion. However, most of those anti-Catholic Democratic voters who refused to vote for Kennedy were scattered in states where it did not do very much political damage.

On the civil rights front, Democrats knew that Kennedy's Catholicism and mediocre support for civil rights would hurt him among African-American voters. Yet those voters were still loyal Democrats from the days of the New Deal and the Democratic commitment to civil rights. So Kennedy knew he must go all out to win their support. Two events proved very beneficial to Kennedy in this area. One was a Republican mistake. During the campaign, the Republican vice-presidential candidate, Lodge, promised that at least one African-American cabinet member would appear in the Nixon administration if he won. But when Nixon heard about his running mate's promise, he disavowed it. Then when Martin Luther King, Jr. was sentenced to four months of hard labor on a trespassing charge for a peaceful sit-in at Atlanta on October 19, Kennedy called Mrs. Coretta Scott King to ask what he could do for her. Then the candidate's brother and campaign manager, Bobby Kennedy, personally called the judge, who was a close friend of the Democratic governor of Georgia, and requested that the charge be reduced to a lesser offense and that King be let out of jail on bail by sundown if he were a decent American. The judge did, and the story of Bobby Kennedy's personal intervention won millions of African-American votes for John Kennedy that November.

One of the events that probably put Kennedy over the top that November election day had occurred back on September 25. As the underdog in the race, Kennedy challenged Nixon to a series of four televised debates. Nixon broke one of the cardinal rules of politics when, as the much better known and favored candidate in the race, he accepted the challenge. Nixon believed he would destroy Kennedy's chances of winning with his brilliant knowledge of the issues and how to run a government. But that proved to be a fatal mistake. In the first debate, held on September 25, Nixon was still recovering from a recent surgery (his knee was infected), and he looked tired and drawn. He was fidgety and uncomfortable, his clothes did not fit well, and he had a five o'clock shadow. Even his selection of a shirt, white in color, proved to be a poor choice for television cameras. And he seemed to hesitate too frequently while speaking. By contrast, Kennedy was suave, comfortable, and seemed surprisingly knowledgeable on the issues. To those Americans who only heard the debates on the radio, Nixon was perceived as the winner. But the television audience gave Kennedy higher marks for success in this first debate. In the other three encounters, Nixon's performance was much improved, but that first debate benefitted Kennedy by making him appear to be a viable presidential figure.

Both candidates carried their appeals to the voters. Kennedy hammered on the theme that the nation had stalled and needed to get going again. He also argued that the United States had fallen behind the Soviets in a so-called missile gap. Nixon vigorously defended the policies of the Eisenhower years and promised even greater things for the future. On November 8, 1960, Kennedy won with 303 electoral votes to Nixon's 219. A committed segregationist, Virginia Democratic Senator Harry F. Byrd, had won a total of 15 electoral votes as an independent candidate by carrying all 8 from Mississippi, 6 of the 11 from Alabama, and 1 from Oklahoma. The popular vote was much closer than the electoral vote indicated, with Kennedy receiving about 34.2 million votes to Nixon's 34.1 million; Nixon even carried a majority of the states. Byrd received just over 500,000 popular votes. Alleged fraud in the ballot counting in Chicago, Illinois, and Texas may have helped give Kennedy the victory. But Nixon refused to challenge the election results because he feared that respect for the process would be diminished. By just over 100,000 votes, or about one vote for every precinct in the nation, Democrat John F. Kennedy was elected as the thirty-fifth president of the United States.

| 1960 | 50 | JOHN F. KENNEDY | Democrat | 34,227,096 | 303† | 49.9 |
| | | Richard M. Nixon | Republican | 34,108,546 | 219 | 49.6 |

†Harry F. Byrd received 15 electoral votes.

ADDITIONAL READINGS

Charles C. Alexander, *Holding the Line: The Eisenhower Era, 1951–1961* (1975). A good overview of the Eisenhower years.

Stephen Ambrose, *Eisenhower* (2 vols., 1983, 1984). The most comprehensive scholarly biography of the general and president.

Archibald Cox, *The Warren Court: constitutional Decision as an Instrument of Reform* (1968). An attorney's view of the liberal Warren Court.

Martin Bauml Duberman, *Paul Robeson* (1988). A biography of the renowned African-American singer and actor who was driven from the stage for political reasons. Shows Robeson as a great artist but also a self-conscious representative of black rights who felt compelled to oppose U.S. foreign policy and suddenly lost his public career.

Elaine Tyler May, *Homeward Bound: American Families in the Cold War* (1988). A thoughtful social history linking family life of the 1950s with the political shadow of the Cold War.

David G. McCullough, *Truman* (1992). An uncritical rendition of Truman's personal life and political career. Through personal correspondence and other documents, details Truman's view of himself and the generally favorable view of him by supporters of Cold War liberalism.

Victor S. Navasky, *Naming Names* (1980). A fascinating account of government informants, McCarthyism, and the blacklist. Especially interesting treatments of academic life, where blacklisting made only a slight impact, and Hollywood, where McCarthyism changed American popular culture.

David M. Oshinsky, *A Conspiracy So Immense: The World of Joe McCarthy* (1983). A study of McCarthyism and the driving personality within it. Presents a keen view of McCarthy as a product of his background and the political conditions of the time, a clever politician who found widespread support in the Republican Party.

Walter and Miriam Schneir, *Invitation to an Inquest: A New Look at the Rosenberg-Sobell Case* (1983 ed.). An account of the "atom spy" case. Convinced of the defendants' innocence, the Schneirs examine the evidence, the questionable (perhaps illegal) methods used to gain conviction, and the significance of the death sentence that was handed down.

G. Edward White, *Earl Warren: A Public Life* (1982). An excellent biographical look at Warren the public figure.

CHAPTER SIXTEEN

The Tumultuous Sixties

MAJOR EVENTS

1961 The American-Soviet Race to the Moon begins
Alan B. Shepard becomes first American in Space
The Peace Corps is established
The Bay of Pigs Fiasco
The Alliance for Progress is announced
The Berlin Wall is begun

1962 The Trade Expansion Act
Silent Spring is published (Rachel Carson)
The Other America is published (Michacl Harrington)
The Cuban Missile Crisis
Baker v. *Carr* Supreme Court decision
Engel v. *Vitale* Supreme Court decision

1963 The Clean Air Act
Project Gemini replaces the Mercury program
Jacobellis v. *Ohio* Supreme Court decision
Gideon v. *Wainwright* Supreme Court decision
Kennedy is assassinated in Dallas, Texas

1964 The Economic Opportunity Act
Lyndon B. Johnson is elected president

1965 The Appalachian Regional Development Act
The Elementary and Secondary Education Act
The Medical Care Act (Medicare)
The Housing and Urban Development Act
The Immigration Act of 1965
American Marines invade the Dominican Republic

1966 *Miranda* v. *Arizona* Supreme Court decision

1967   The Six-Day War in the Middle East

1968   The *U.S.S. Pueblo* Incident
The Czech Revolt
Richard M. Nixon is elected president

INTRODUCTION TO THE KENNEDY ADMINISTRATION

The New Frontier

When John Fitzgerald Kennedy was sworn into office as the thirty-fifth president of the United States on January 20, 1961, he was the youngest person ever elected to the highest office in the land. He brought with him all of the energy and optimism that one might expect from someone of his age. At the Democratic National Convention the summer before, the young Kennedy had challenged the country to advance with him toward "the frontier of unknown opportunities and perils." Thus, his administration theme would be known as the New Frontier. Displaying the famous Kennedy charm and excellent rhetorical skills, the new president used his Inaugural Address to call Americans to bring new energy to the struggle to remember and advance the American traditions. "Let the word go forth from this time and place, to friend and foe alike," he declared, "that the torch has been passed to a new generation of Americans—born in this century, tempered by war, disciplined by a hard and bitter peace, proud of our ancient heritage." To the world he proclaimed, "Let every nation know, whether it wishes us well or ill, that we shall pay any price, bear any burden, meet any hardship, support any friend, oppose any foe, to assure the survival and success of liberty." Loud applause was the response to these most famous of all the lines ever delivered by President Kennedy: "The energy, the faith, the devotion which we bring to this endeavor will light our country and all who serve it—and the glow from that fire can truly light the world. And so, my fellow Americans, ask not what your country can do for you; ask what you can do for your country."

Defining the Man

Although Kennedy's wife, Jacqueline, once called him "an idealist without illusions," Kennedy seems better described as an ambitious, hard-headed realist. This probably explains why his congressional record revealed a cautious politician who had not distinguished himself in the political arena. As an avid Cold War warrior, Kennedy had been associated with Joseph R. McCarthy's anti-communist crusade in the 1950s (See Chapter Fifteen). His voting record was only moderately liberal, and he had been no great champion of the black civil rights movement. Nevertheless, as president, John F. Kennedy would become convinced that he must act on his conviction that all men and women, regardless of race, must be given equal access to the opportunities that enabled them to pursue happiness. As a result, he would propose a strong civil rights bill to Congress in 1963, although he could not muster enough votes to get it passed (See Chapter Fourteen). And the young president would also attempt the beginning of a federal war on poverty, again with limited success.

Even what he proposed as president fell short of what most liberals in his party wanted him to do. Therefore, Kennedy can only accurately be called a moderately liberal president. Many have speculated that a second term might have brought him more success, and with that new success, he may have moved more to the political left. However, only one thing is certain. President Kennedy's charm and rhetorical skills endeared him to his generation like no president ever has before or since. It was his charismatic style, youthful energy, and calls to service that Americans remember and love about the man they said turned Washington, D.C. into "Camelot." (Camelot was the mythical place where King Arthur and the Knights of the Roundtable lived in Alfred Lord Tennyson's *Idylls of the King*, a classic of English literature.)

The Kennedy Cabinet

Consistent with his own youthful energy and practical realism, President Kennedy selected the so-called "best and brightest" individuals to serve in his cabinet. Although more liberal Democrats had pushed for two-time party candidate for president Adlai E. Stevenson to become the next Secretary of State, Kennedy named Dean Rusk, a career diplomat who was president of the Rockefeller Foundation at the time. Stevenson was appointed as the United States ambassador to the United Nations instead. In another surprise move, aimed at reassuring the business community, Kennedy chose C. Douglas Dillon, a New York banker and a Republican who had been Eisenhower's undersecretary of state, to be his Secretary of the Treasury. Another Republican, Ford Motor Company president Robert S. McNamara, was named as the new Secretary of Defense. Other appointments to the cabinet included former Connecticut Governor Abraham Ribicoff as Secretary of Health, Education, and Welfare and Arthur J. Goldberg, a well-known labor lawyer, as Secretary of Labor. When the president named his younger brother, Robert F. Kennedy, as the Attorney-General, critics charged that the thirty-five-year-old Bobby was too inexperienced to occupy the top legal position in the country. At such criticism, the president humorously replied, "I don't see what's wrong with giving Bobby a little experience before he goes into law practice." McGeorge Bundy was appointed as special assistant to the president for national security affairs; Kennedy once called Bundy "the second smartest man I know."

The primary emphasis in Kennedy's cabinet positions and other high-level federal appointments was to fill these jobs with vigorous, hardworking, pragmatists. It was a federal government dominated by policymakers who were confident of their ability to shape the country and the world into their dream. The New Frontier awaited them.

DOMESTIC ISSUES UNDER KENNEDY

The Conservative Coalition in Congress

President Kennedy had high hopes for domestic change, and public opinion polls taken immediately after the inauguration showed that about 75 percent of the people approved of the new president. But despite his charm and increasing popularity, most of Kennedy's reform proposals were either defeated outright or moderated even further by the same conservative coalition of Republicans and southern Democrats that had hampered Truman's Fair Deal programs in the late 1940s. Southern Democrats, nicknamed Dixiecrats by their critics, especially irritated the president and his supporters because they were members of the same party. Nevertheless, since 1938 this same conservative coalition had been blocking or diluting progressive legislation in Congress. While Kennedy could usually count on the Senate to pass his measures, the conservative coalition in the House of Representatives (which included between 50 and 75 southern Democratic representatives) frustrated his efforts.

Early Major Domestic Defeat

Most notable of the outright defeats suffered by the president early in his administration was the demise of his proposed federal aid-to-education bill. The bill would have provided for a three-year federal grant of approximately $3.2 billion to be given to the states for both teachers' salaries and the construction of new schools. It also included a provision to provide $3.3 billion over five years for aid to colleges and universities and for federal scholarships to students. After it passed the Senate in May 1961, Roman Catholic Church leaders demanded equal assistance for parochial schools. President Kennedy rejected their demand, clinging to his campaign pledge that he would not support measures weakening the separation of church and state. As a result, the bill was never passed by the House.

Some Partial Victories

The president did score some partial victories early in his administration, but even there the conservative coalition watered down what he had originally asked from Congress. The Housing Act of 1961 allocated almost $5 billion for major urban renewal projects over a four-year period. These funds helped clear some of the slums and replace them with new housing for the poor, but it was a pitifully small amount to do anything more than just scratch the surface of the slum problem. In September 1961 the Minimum Wage Act raised the minimum wage from $1 an hour to $1.25 an hour for almost 25 million workers already covered under the federal law (i.e., Fair Labor Standards Act of 1938; see Chapter Ten). In addition, the new law expanded federal minimum wage coverage to more than 3.5 million workers not already covered, mostly in the service and retail sectors of the economy. And in May 1961, Congress passed Kennedy's proposed Area Redevelopment Act, which made almost $400 million of federal grants and loans available to those regions in the country plagued by excessively low economic growth and high unemployment. The money was to be used for training workers and other redevelopment programs.

NATIONAL DEFENSE MEASURES

An economic recession had begun in 1960, the last year of the Eisenhower administration. Kennedy had hoped that his domestic reform proposals would provide much of the stimulus to get the country moving again. But because he was obtaining from Congress relatively little of what he had hoped for, the president turned his attention in 1961 to military spending as a means of stimulating the economy. In this area of national defense, he received little opposition from the conservative coalition.

Specifically, Kennedy persuaded Congress to increase the defense budget by almost 20 percent in 1961. Some of the extra allocations went to obtain more intercontinental ballistic missles (ICBMs)—five times more than President Eisenhower had believed the country needed. (In the 1960 presidential election campaign, Kennedy had accused the Eisenhower administration of permitting a "missile gap" to develop between the Soviets and the United States.) More medium-range missiles and nuclear submarines equipped with Polaris missiles were also added to the American arsenal of weapons. To undo the Eisenhower administration reduction in conventional forces in the 1950s, the Kennedy Administration added new divisions to the army and air force, and created the so-called "Green Berets," which were Special Forces units especially trained in counter-guerrilla warfare. (The Green Berets distinguished themselves in the Vietnam War.) These measures, said the president, were designed to strengthen our conventional forces and thus to offer a "wider choice than humiliation or all-out nuclear action."

THE SPACE PROGRAM TAKES OFF FOR THE MOON

Partly to demonstrate American pride and ingenuity and partly to stimulate the economy, President Kennedy addressed a joint session of Congress on May 25, 1961, and called for a crash program to land a man on the moon by the end of the decade. The overwhelming positive response from the American people and Congress meant that such a specific space achievement goal was adopted quickly. This proposal soon led to a decade-long race to the moon between the United States and the Soviet Union.

Previous to the beginning of the moon project, the space program had been hampered by both military and financial concerns. The nuclear age, begun with the dropping of the two atomic bombs near the end of World War II, had escalated in the early 1950s with the development of the hydrogen bomb (the H-bomb) by both the Americans and the Soviets. Under Secretary of State John Foster Dulles' influence, the Eisenhower administration had made the decision to dominate the Soviets with its nuclear arsenal. Therefore, the military priority of developing missiles that could deliver nuclear weapons to the Soviet Union took precedence over any civilian space program. Then too, the Eisenhower administration had been concerned about the financial wisdom of investing so heavily in a program which might not gain much for the country.

The reticence to develop any kind of civilian space program was altered, however, by the success of the first Soviet space capsule, the *Sputnik*, which was placed in orbit in October 1957. The United States quickly followed by placing its first space craft, the *Explorer I*, in orbit, and by creating the National Aeronautics and Space Administration (NASA), both in 1958. (For a discussion of these matters, see Chapter Fifteen.)

NASA had begun the American manned space program with Project Mercury in November 1958. Two notable successes were achieved within three and a half years. On May 5, 1961, Alan B. Shepard, Jr. became the first American in space. And John H. Glenn, Jr. became the first American to actually orbit the earth in a Mercury space capsule about one year later. (Soviet astronauts Yuri A. Gagarin and Gherman S. Titov had achieved those same goals in April and August 1961, respectively.)

While acknowledging these early American pioneers of the space program and their contributions to future manned flights, the civilian space program really did not get fully off the ground until NASA began its long task of preparing to land a man on the moon. President Kennedy's bold challenge had given the space program a major boost. The American space program of the 1960s enjoyed the highest levels of popular and political support than perhaps it ever would again. Congress responded almost immediately to the president's challenge by increasing the NASA budget by 61 percent. And under the Kennedy administration, its budget would climb from less than $1 billion to more than $5 billion; NASA's employees increased ten-fold, from about 6,000 to about 60,000 during the same time period; and the total number of employees working on the civilian space program (both in NASA and among private contractors) surpassed 410,000.

After the last Mercury mission in May 1963, Project Gemini began the practice of placing more than one astronaut in space at a time. There were "spacewalks," and frequently two different space craft would rendezvous, or dock, with each other, so that astronauts could maneuver from one craft to the other. This Gemini program was just beginning by the time of President Kennedy's death in late 1963. (See Chapter Seventeen for the Apollo Project.)

MORE ADMINISTRATION SETBACKS

The New Frontier had not fared very well in 1961. And with only a couple of exceptions, the next two years of the Kennedy administration saw even more setbacks. One of the more significant reasons for this was the death of the Speaker of the House, Sam Rayburn, Democrat from Texas. Rayburn had assisted the administration several times by using his enormous political clout as Speaker. But he died in November 1961, after a bout with cancer. The new Speaker was less influential in exerting party discipline, and the southern Democratic chairman of the powerful House Rules Committee was able to keep several bills from coming to the floor of the House of Representatives for a vote.

Congress did pass the Revenue Act of 1962, but it was not the bill that President Kennedy really wanted. It granted businesses and corporations approximately $1 billion a year in new tax credits in order to encourage investment in new machinery and other equipment. However, the law did not contain either of Kennedy's requests for an income tax on corporate dividends and interest or limits on what could be deducted on business expense accounts. In the same year Congress gave the president authority to allocate $900 million into regions experiencing high unemployment rates, but it refused to give him discretionary authority to spend an additional $2 billion for the same purpose.

Other Kennedy proposals were defeated outright. Among them was a bill to provide a government-based health insurance to the elderly through the Social Security system. This so-called Medicare proposal was narrowly defeated in the Senate in July 1962, largely because the American Medical Association had vigorously attacked the bill by calling it "socialized medicine." Medicare would have to wait for President Lyndon Johnson's political muscle; it would pass three years later. Other legislation was killed by the House Rules Committe and never made it to the floor of the House of Representatives for a vote. In this category was a bill to provide jobs for unemployed youth and federal funding to assist cities in building mass transit systems in order to reduce automobile congestion and pollution. And, of course, Kennedy's proposed new civil rights bill to end racial segregation was stalled in committee and was not passed until the Johnson administration was in the White House.

THE TRADE EXPANSION ACT

Probably the most important piece of legislation passed during the Kennedy administration was the Trade Expansion Act in September 1962. This act gave the president a great deal of flexible authority in negotiating with nations in the European Common Market—a group of several western European countries which had formed an economic union in order to stimulate economic growth and higher employment within their economies. Specifically, the Trade Expansion Act authorized the president to reduce tariffs placed on Common Market nations' goods by up to 50 percent over a five-year period and to abolish tariffs altogether on any items in which both the Common Market nations and the United States together made up at least 80 percent of the world trade. It also created a program of "trade adjustment assistance" to assist American workers and companies negatively impacted by lower tariff rates. The key effect of this law was to eventually reduce average tariff rates by 35 percent between the United States and the European Common Market countries.

THE CLEAN AIR ACT OF 1963

The conservation movement of the late nineteenth and early twentieth centuries had placed a focus on preserving America's natural resources, such as timber, coal, water, and even certain wildlife. Although a close cousin to this conservation movement, the modern environmental movement added a new emphasis. A larger number of Americans had begun to notice that, especially in some heavily populated areas, the smokestacks of industry and the carbon monoxide fumes of automobiles and trucks had taken their toll on the quality of life. The atomic age had given Americans great concern for the highly dangerous radiation of nuclear fallout. And then in 1962, marine biologist Rachel Carson published a book entitled *Silent Spring*. In that book, Carson documented the dangers of DDT and other pesticides that were being widely used on American farms and other places. And just as Upton Sinclair's expose of the meat-packing industry, *The Jungle* (1906), had ignited President Theodore Roosevelt to action (See Chapter Six), so Carson's book led President Kennedy to appoint a special task force to further study pesticides with a view to recommending federal regulations concerning their use. Although not directly related to pesticides, the earliest congressional response was the passage of the Clean Air Act of 1963, which regulated automobile and industrial emissions for the first time in our history. The Clean Air Act of 1963 was the beginning of additional federal laws that regulated air and water supplies in the nation.

KENNEDY REACTS TO STEEL PRICE HIKES

In order to keep price inflation to a minimum, President Kennedy had called for corporations and unions to keep their price and wage increases to a minimum. In this way, prices could be kept low enough that neither management nor labor could justify huge price or wage increases in order to keep up with inflation. This presidential request was put to the test in the spring of 1962. In March of that year, contract negotiations had broken down between United States Steel Corporation and the United Steelworkers of America. At that point, President Kennedy and Labor Secretary Arthur Goldberg intervened by pressuring the union to settle for a minimal, non-inflationary wage increase. The union agreed, and a labor contract was signed on March 31. The president immediately congratulated both labor and management for their "industrial statesmanship," but his applause was premature. Within a couple of weeks, United States Steel announced a price hike of $6 a ton for their steel; five other major steel companies then announced the same price increase the very next day.

At a press conference that month (April), President Kennedy angrily denounced the steel price hikes and accused the steel executives of betraying him and the "interest of 185 million Americans." He then promptly ordered the Federal Trade Commission to look into the possibility of illegal price fixing among the steel companies. At the same time, the Department of Justice declared that it was investigating the matter to see if any antitrust laws had been violated, while a spokesman for the Defense Department suggested that it might boycott those companies and purchase their steel from those smaller steel manufacturers which had not raised their prices. The six steel companies quickly revoked their price increases, giving the president an apparent victory of national interest over greed and private profit.

Despite the apparent victory for the president, general reaction from the business community to the administration forced him to back down also. And when the steel companies raised prices twice within one year, Kennedy ignored them.

THE INCOME TAX CUT PROPOSAL

The steel price hike crisis had more significant consequences than merely forcing Kennedy to back away from publicly criticizing their price decisions. By greatly cooling relations between the business community and the White House, the crisis also forced Kennedy to mend the fences by not proposing any new major social legislation. In effect, the New Frontier was dead. Instead, the administration turned its attention to tax reduction as a way to stimulate economic production, consumption, and employment. He was determined to maintain a steady growth rate for the economy, and tax cuts would be more preferable to the business community than increased social spending.

As a result, Kennedy announced his tax cut plan to Congress in January 1963. He asked Congress to reduce federal income tax burdens by $11 billion for individuals and $2.6 billion for corporations—thus, a total federal income tax cut of $13.6 billion, which was a huge sum in the early 1960s. Opposition to the proposal came from both organized labor and business groups. The former complained that the tax cuts did not help the lower income groups as much as they should, and

Peace Corps volunteer Kimery Anne Campbell is a forestry volunteer in Korsimoro. Credit: AP/Wide World Photos.

most business groups argued that middle income taxpayers would not benefit as much as they deserved in the president's plan. In addition, many members of Congress wondered about the wisdom of major tax cuts at a time when the federal budget was projected to show an $8.3 billion deficit. Despite opposition, in September (1963) the House of Representatives did finally pass a version of the bill which closely resembled the president's plan. But the Senate adjourned late that year without acting on the bill, and the president did not get his income tax reduction plan enacted into law.

FOREIGN AFFAIRS UNDER KENNEDY

The Peace Corps

Although President Kennedy took steps to increase the military's "flexible response" to new Cold War crises, he also sought various foreign aid programs in an effort to reduce the appeal of communism in Latin America, Africa, and Asia. His most celebrated and popular program of this kind was the Peace Corps, which the president created by Executive Order in March 1961. The idea was to train thousands of volunteers to serve as teachers, agricultural specialists, health workers, and other technicians in order to help raise the standard of living in the so-called Third World. These trained Americans would live abroad for two years and receive a modest living allowance for their services.

Congress endorsed the Peace Corps and made it permanent in September of the same year. R. Sargent Shriver, Jr., the president's brother-in-law, was appointed as the first director of the Peace Corps. The program attracted hundreds of idealistic young people, who responded to the president's call with enthusiasm. By 1963 approximately 5,000 volunteers were helping people help themselves in more than 40 Third World countries. While it was a symbol of the youthful Kennedy's optimism, the Peace Corps could not hope to conquer poverty in poor nations by itself. And as American economic woes increased in the next decade, the agency was never funded in the way its most ardent defenders had hoped.

KENNEDY'S LATIN AMERICAN POLICY

The Bay of Pigs Fiasco

As a result of Fidel Castro's actions in Cuba since his ascendancy to power on January 1, 1959, the Eisenhower administration had ordered the Central Intelligence Agency (CIA) to secretly train volunteers for an invasion of Cuba. (See Chapter Fifteen.) Such training began in Guatemala in 1960, and the United States Joint Chiefs of Staff had approved the invasion plans. The idea was that invasion of the island nation would result in a massive popular uprising against Castro by the Cubans themselves, an uprising that would topple the Castro government. In training operations, however, the CIA promoted former pro-Batista men to the forefront, thus alienating the Cuban volunteers who really wanted to see democracy there and hurting morale among the invasion forces. During the 1960 presidential campaign, Kennedy had criticized the Eisenhower-Nixon administration for not being tough enough against Castro. Thus, when he was briefed on the invasion plans during the campaign, Kennedy approved them. However, he did so only on a "contingency" basis, partly because he knew that such bold interventionism would result in widespread condemnation. Therefore, if elected president, Kennedy would only order such an invasion on the condition of no direct American military assistance.

In preparation for the invasion, Cuban airfields were bombed by unmarked B-26 bombers on the morning of April 15, 1961. The United States initially claimed that this action had been taken by defecting Cuban air force pilots, although some of them actually were flown by American pilots. Later, however, it was revealed that the bombers had taken off from a base in Central America. Then just two days later, on April 17, a force of about 1,500 exiles landed at the Bay of Pigs on the southeast coast of the island. But at the last minute, President Kennedy's doubts about the viability of the entire operation caused him to cancel air strikes scheduled to provide cover for the landing. The CIA base in Guatemala had long been an open secret. And specifically, Castro's agents among the exiles had forewarned him of an attack. The result was that the Cuban military was ready for the invasion force, and within three days, the invaders were pinned down on the beaches.

The entire operation was a total disaster which resulted in about 300 exiles killed and approximately 1,100 others captured. There was no popular revolt among the Cuban people either. In fact, no contact was even made with the anti-Castro underground because the men never got off the beaches. Before the survivors were forced to surrender on the beaches, Kennedy authorized an air expedition to rescue them. Typical of the entire operation, this rescue mission failed because no one remembered to take the change in time zones into account when planning the rendezvous pick-ups. Most of the men were released after two years, but only after an embarrassed United States paid a ransom of over $50 million in food and medicine to the Cuban government.

President Kennedy accepted full blame for the Bay of Pigs fiasco and undoubtedly won some political respect with Americans because of his candid admission of error. In the court of world opinion, however, reaction was quite different. Soviet communist leader Khrushchev lectured the young American president on international law. And most Latin American nations, while showing little sympathy for Castro, nevertheless expressed fear that the United States still behaved as if it had the right to intervene in the internal affairs of their nations. In Cuba, the American disaster only served to strengthen Castro, who was able to portray himself as a heroic "victim" of American imperialism. Castro then formally declared Cuba a socialist country, and he took further steps to strengthen his ties to the Soviet Union.

Speaking in the context of the Bay of Pigs disaster, President Kennedy sighed that "victory has a thousand fathers, but defeat is an orphan." Indeed, the United States had looked foolish and incompetent. Humiliated by the stinging defeat, Kennedy then ordered the CIA to organize a secret war against Castro. Called Operation MONGOOSE, it was headed by Bobby Kennedy and had its own independent navy and air force. This particular operation got nowhere. But apart from MONGOOSE, the CIA did engineer at least eight attempts on Castro's life by the end of 1965, all without success.

Alliance for Progress

In March 1961 President Kennedy proposed a "vast cooperative effort" to modernize the societies of Latin America in order to reduce the appeal of revolutionary nationalists like Fidel Castro in the region. Believing that sustained economic growth was the key to providing Latin Americans a more moderate alternative to radical leaders, Kennedy envisioned his proposed Alliance for Progress as becoming for Latin America what the Marshall Plan had once been for Europe.

The American proposal gained momentum after the Cuban crisis the following month. And the Alliance for Progress was officially organized in August 1961 in a meeting of representatives from 20 Latin American countries in Uruguay. These participating nations agreed to promote greater democratic reforms, extensive land and tax reforms, and to wipe out illiteracy and other serious obstacles to greater prosperity and stability. For its part, the United States committed at least $20 billion in financial loans over the next decade to help these nations achieve their goals.

Economically, the Alliance for Progress was disappointing. Economic growth in Latin America did increase during the 1960s, but it was well below the anticipated goal of 2.5 percent per year. The most important factor for the disappointing results was that private investment did not materialize on a massive scale. And all had agreed that everything the various governments would do under the Alliance was designed to encourage such private investment. But traditional political instability continued to undermine movements toward greater democracy and investor confidence.

By far the greatest effect of the Alliance for Progress program was its generating of enormous amounts of goodwill among Latin Americans for the United States. Not since Franklin D. Roosevelt, architect of the Good Neighbor policy, had an American president been so loved by Latin Americans. It appeared to be a repudiation of Cold War interventionism in the hemisphere and specifically of the Bay of Pigs fiasco. Unfortunately, that optimism was not fully warranted, especially after the death of Kennedy. American presidents would continue to view regions south of the United States border as their own backyard.

The Cuban Missile Crisis

The Bay of Pigs crisis had helped convince Soviet communist dictator Nikita Khrushchev that Kennedy was a weak president. (That, in turn, had played a role in the building of the Berlin Wall during the second half of 1961. See "The Berlin Wall" below.) It had led to the Castro regime bringing Cuba into a closer relationship with the Soviet Union. In the year and a half since the Bay of Pigs, Cuba had become a Soviet satellite nation and a veritable military base for the Soviets. Especially during the summer of 1962, large numbers of Soviet arms and technicians poured onto the island, including offensive missiles aimed at the United States.

Khrushchev's reasons for testing the American will by placing offensive nuclear missiles in Cuba, less than 100 miles off the coast of Florida, were varied. Khrushchev's recent calls for "peaceful coexistence" had worried hardliners within his own party. Many of them believed that such talk was allowing Red China to take the leadership role in world communism. Thus, he needed to shore up his political support by moving in a more aggressive manner against the United States. Cuba was a new ally, and certainly, the Soviets were under pressure to demonstrate their reliability to their allies. Moreover, the placing of missiles in Cuba could ensure that there would be no further American invasions of that island. The Americans had missiles in Turkey that were aimed at the Soviet Union, so if Khrushchev could place his own in Cuba, then he could gain a psychological stalemate.

On October 14, 1962, American U-2 spy plane photographs revealed the existence of at least 40 Soviet light bombers, the same number of medium and intermediate range missiles, and 9 missile sites under construction inside Cuba. The American government was concerned that Soviet missiles launched from Cuba might arrive too quickly for effective warning to be possible. And, of course, the psychological effect of just knowing that they are that close to the United States (they could hit most areas in the continental United States, including Washington, D.C.) also made their existence there unacceptable. Just a year and a half before, Kennedy had been hu-

Department of Defense picture showing the medium range missile base at Sagua La Grande in Cuba , November 3, 1962. Credit: AP/Wide World Photos.

miliated in the Bay of Pigs disaster. Then the Berlin Wall had been erected under the watchful eye of the West. And now the United States was facing off-year Congressional elections. There was simply no way the president could allow those missiles to remain in Cuba.

President Kennedy's goals were to force the Soviets to remove the missiles and to avoid nuclear war at the same time. He had just read *The Guns of August*, which made it clear that the First World War had come because nations had miscalculated in ignorance. Therefore, Kennedy was determined but cautious. On October 18, he raised the issue of Soviet war materials going into Cuba with the Soviet Foreign Minister Andrei Gromyko and Soviet Ambassador to the United States, Anatoly Dobrynin. They told Kennedy that such materials were for defensive purposes only. Although Kennedy knew they were lying, he decided not to confront them with the photographic evidence until he had decided how to proceed.

Kennedy wanted the very best advice he could get about how to handle this crisis, so he appointed an Executive Committee of the National Security Council ("Ex Comm"), chaired by Secretary of State Dean Rusk. Some of the other members of Ex Comm included Defense Secretary Robert S. McNamara, Attorney-General Robert F. Kennedy, presidential advisor McGeorge Bundy, former Secretary of State Dean

Acheson, General Maxwell Taylor (presiding officer of the Joint Chiefs of Staff), and occasionally the United States Ambassador to the United Nations, Adlai E. Stevenson. President Kennedy himself did not attend many of their meetings because he wanted to encourage a free-wheeling exchange of ideas, and he could not afford to have anyone intimidated by his presence.

Ex Comm narrowed the options to just two: (1) a surgical air strike to knock out the missiles, and (2) a naval blockade of Cuba in order to force the Soviets to withdraw the missiles. The surgical air strike option was favored by General Maxwell Taylor and former Secretary of State Dean Acheson. But Bobby Kennedy and Secretary of Defense McNamara argued for a naval blockade instead, declaring that an air strike might fail to do the job completely, or that even if it did, Khrushchev might be angered into launching a nuclear World War III. Bobby Kennedy proved to be most influential in getting Ex Comm to advise the president to order a blockade of Cuba. Because international law views a blockade as an act of war, the word "quarantine" was used instead. Mindful of the need to maintain good relations with our Latin American neighbors, the administration refused to invoke the Monroe Doctrine to act alone. Instead, Kennedy kept the Organization of American States (OAS) informed, which resulted in those nations rallying around the United States in this crisis.

On Monday, October 22, President Kennedy briefed members of Congress, and then the American people, about the offensive missiles and launch sites in Cuba, labeling their presence as a "clandestine, reckless, and provocative threat to world peace." He further defined the entire situation as an "unjustified change in the status quo which cannot be accepted by this country, if our courage and our commitments are ever to be trusted again by friend or foe." At the same time, he also announced a "quarantine" of that island and issued an ultimatum that the Soviets dismantle and remove their missiles and launching pads in Cuba or the United States would do so. After the president's television address, the Soviets publicly denied the allegations, so Ambassador Adlai Stevenson dramatically revealed the photographic evidence to the United Nations, proving that the Soviets had lied.

Khrushchev then accused Kennedy of pushing mankind "to the abyss of a world missile-nuclear war" and defiantly proclaimed that Soviet ships would ignore the quarantine. The world waited as mankind tottered on the brink of nuclear war. The United States put 180 ships in the Caribbean area to enforce its "quarantine." An increased level of military alert placed more American B-52s loaded with nuclear weapons in the air during much of the crisis, and almost 250,000 troops were sent to Florida for possible use in an invasion of Cuba. Then on October 24, several Soviet ships headed for Cuba were ordered to turn around by Moscow just before they reached the quarantine line. Upon hearing the news, Secretary Rusk said to McGeorge Bundy, "We're eyeball to eyeball and I think the other fellow just blinked."

Although the Soviets had decided, at least for the moment, to heed the quarantine, the crisis was not over. On October 26, an agent of the Soviet embassy in Washington met ABC television news correspondent John Scali and offered to withdraw the missiles from Cuba in exchange for an American promise never to attempt another invasion of Cuba. Scali relayed the unofficial offer to the White House and the response that the United States was interested, all on that same day. But that night proved to be a very strange one at the White House. First, a letter arrived by teletype from Khrushchev, officially making the same offer that had been unofficially given earlier in the day. Then, while Ex Comm members were discussing the offer, a second message arrived. This one demanded that the United States remove all NATO missiles stationed in Turkey as a precondition for the Soviet dismantling of their missiles in Cuba. The president had already privately ordered the missiles in Turkey to be removed because they were obsolete and unnecessary. However, he would not have it appear that he was backing down in the face of a Soviet demand.

The debate raged late into the night, and an air strike and invasion of Cuba seemed likely after news reached the White House that an American U-2 plane had just been shot down over Cuba. However, Bobby Kennedy, who had essentially been the real leader of Ex Comm, suddenly proposed a solution. President Kennedy should respond favorably to the first letter and ignore the second message altogether, on the grounds that the second one reflected a division of opinion among the Soviet advisors to Khrushchev (which, in fact, it did). So Kennedy accepted the first Soviet offer and agreed to promise that the United States would never again attempt an invasion of Cuba in exchange for the Soviets pulling their missiles out of Cuba. Finally, on October 28, Khrushchev accepted the agreement to halt more missiles going into Cuba, remove those already there, and permit international inspection to prove that they would keep their promise.

The Cuban missile crisis proved to be the most dangerous crisis of the Cold War. It was clearly the closest the world ever came to nuclear war. And while President Kennedy certainly gets deserved credit for standing tall and walking the line between war and humiliation ever so delicately, it was his brother Bobby whose influence was so vital in the successful conclusion of the crisis. Some have questioned if there would have been a Cuban missile crisis had there been no Bay of Pigs fiasco a year and a half before. Both superpowers agreed to install a "hot line" in order to provide for personal, direct, and speedy communications between them during any future crises. Surplus American wheat was sold to the Soviet Union; the NATO missiles were eventually removed from Turkey; and the Nuclear Test Ban Treaty, banning atomic testing in the earth's atmosphere, was signed between the United States and the Soviet Union in August 1963.

FOREIGN POLICY IN EUROPE: THE BERLIN WALL

The existence of democratic West Berlin in the midst of the communist Soviet occupation zone in East Germany had been a source of irritation to the Soviets ever since the end of World War II. West Berlin was a showcase of Western prosperity and freedom, and an embarrassing reminder that communism could not satisfy the material desires of its people. (See Chapter Fifteen for a discussion of the previous Berlin crisis.) With a new American president in the White House, Khrushchev once again brought up the Berlin issue.

In June 1961, Kennedy and Khrushchev met in Vienna, Austria, to exchange views on Berlin and a possible nuclear test ban treaty. The Bay of Pigs fiasco had apparently convinced the Soviets that Kennedy was weak and easily intimidated. Therefore, at the Vienna meeting, Khrushchev once again threatened that if the Allies could not agree on and sign a peace treaty with Germany (officially ending World War II), the Soviet Union would sign one with East Germany by the end of the year. Then he threatened to demilitarize the city of Berlin, thus forcing the three Western Allies out of West Berlin. His lecture of the young American president had been rather one-sided, but Kennedy went home determined not to yield to Soviet pressure.

Back in Washington, President Kennedy publicly asserted the Western Allies' right to West Berlin, called up reserve and National Guard units, sent about 45,000 more troops to Europe, and asked Congress for another $3.2 billion in defense appropriations. Meanwhile, citizens of East Germany and other eastern European communist nations were continuing to escape communist tyranny by way of West Berlin at a rate of about 1,000 per day, including some of the best minds east of the Iron Curtain.

Berlin Wall being erected in 1961. Credit: AP/Wide World Photos.

In August 1961, in view of this mass exodus and in response to Kennedy's actions, the Soviets allowed the East Germans to string barbed wire between East and West Berlin. Immediately thereafter, the East Germans began constructing a 28-mile cinder block wall across the city to more permanently keep East Germans and others from escaping into West Berlin. (The communists were able to easily control and cut off other access routes into West Berlin; it was only where the two halves of the city lay adjacent to each other that the wall proved necessary.) In October of that year, the Soviets announced that a separate peace treaty with East Germany was indefinitely postponed, and the latest Berlin crisis had finally come to an end. The erection of the Berlin Wall had been the alternative chosen by the Soviets in order to avoid possible nuclear war. It certainly did drastically stem the

President John F. Kennedy at Dallas Airport, November 22, 1963. Credit: AP/Wide World Photos.

tide of escapees from communism, but it also became a physical symbol of the communist denial of freedom. And it would remain as that symbol for the next 28 years.

OTHER ISSUES

For information about the modern civil rights movement in the early 1960s at the time of Kennedy see Chapter Fourteen. And for information about the role of Kennedy in the Vietnam War, see Chapter Thirteen.

THE KENNEDY ASSASSINATION

Despite a mediocre record of accomplishment, President Kennedy was growing in popularity among the general public and had decided to run for re-election. But there were serious political problems in Texas, the home of Vice-President Lyndon

Johnson and an important electoral state. Texas Democrats were split between a liberal wing led by Senator Ralph W. Yarborough and a conservative wing led by Governor John B. Connally. In addition to the party split, Kennedy had alienated many traditional Texas Democratic voters with his fight, albeit unsuccessful, to get Congress to enact a major civil rights bill. Thus, in late November 1963, the president began a quick tour of that important state. First Lady Jacqueline, Lyndon and Lady Bird Johnson, and Governor and Mrs. Connally accompanied him on the tour. The president was warmly received in visits to Houston, San Antonio, and Fort Worth, before arriving at Dallas' Love Field on Friday, November 22.

The president was scheduled to speak at the Dallas Trade Mart around noon that day. Thus, a motorcade was to move slowly from the airport through downtown before arriving at the speaking appointment. The Kennedys rode in the backseat of an open Lincoln convertible, with the Connallys in the front seat of the same car. It was a beautiful day in Dallas, and all along the streets enthusiastic crowds greeted the president. The people were so friendly that Kennedy actually stopped the motorcade on two occasions to more personally greet the crowds. Then as the motorcade turned onto Elm Street, shots rang out, apparently from a sixth floor window of the Texas School Book Depository building. President Kennedy was hit in the head and neck, while Governor Connally was hit in the back, left thigh, and right wrist, where a bullet shattered several bones. The presidential car sped for Parkland Memorial Hospital, where President John F. Kennedy was pronounced dead about 1:00 p.m.

Vice-President Lyndon Johnson was sworn in as the thirty-sixth president of the United States later that same day on board Air Force One in an effort to reassure Americans and the rest of the world that the republic had not died with the president. Jacqueline Kennedy, still in clothes blood-stained by her husband's wounds, stood in shock beside the new president while he took the oath of office.

Meanwhile, a radical loner by the name of Lee Harvey Oswald was arrested later that afternoon in a theater after allegedly shooting and killing a Dallas policeman. Oswald, who worked in the Texas School Book Depository, was charged also with the assassination of the president, although he proclaimed his innocence. Two days later (Sunday, November 24), while being transferred from one jail to another, Dallas nightclub owner Jack Ruby, known to have had connections with the mob and the police department, shot and killed Oswald inside the police station in front of a live national television audience.

President Johnson appointed a panel to investigate the assassination and to close the books on the tragic events. Headed by Chief Justice Earl Warren, the Warren Commission produced 26 volumes of evidence and concluded that there was no reasonable doubt about the fact that Lee Harvey Oswald had indeed killed the president and, in doing so, had acted alone. Nevertheless, serious questions have persisted about the findings of the Warren Commission. Most prominent among these has been the denial of belief by many Americans, including some prominent ballistics experts, of the alleged maneuvers of the so-called "magic bullet"—a bullet that critics have charged would have had to change directions more than once in order to have accounted for all of the wounds attributed to it. This "magic bullet" was then allegedly found on a hospital cot in nearly pristine condition at Parkland Memorial shortly after the president was taken there.

There have been other questions about the amount of time necessary to fire the rifle from the sixth floor window. Actually, there have been no end to the questions and theories raised about who killed President Kennedy. A later investigation by a House committee in the 1970s concluded that probably more than one person was involved in a conspiracy to assassinate the president. Then in the early 1990s, new high technology photographic evidence seemed to suggest that one killer was firing from behind the picket fence on the grassy knoll. (This evidence, if genuine, would support the reactions of many citizens and even police who, at the time of the shootings, thought that some shots had been fired from that direction.) Although many documents have been released for public access, most opinion polls suggest that many Americans do not believe the Warren Commission Report, and nor do they believe that we will ever know what really happened that fateful day in late November of 1963.

What we do know for certain is that the assassination of President John F. Kennedy gripped this nation's emotions in ways reminiscent of Abraham Lincoln's assassination and the Japanese surprise attack on Pearl Harbor. Few Americans alive at the time will ever forget the images embedded into their memory banks. On Sunday, November 24, Kennedy's body was placed in the rotunda of the Capitol on the same catafalque which had contained Abraham Lincoln's body almost 100 years before. There, more than 250,000 persons paid their last respects. The funeral ceremony the next day began with a procession witnessed in person by about 1 million people and by millions more on national television. The old Kennedy family friend, Cardinal Richard Cushing (archbishop of Boston), said the funeral mass. And there was little John Kennedy, Jr., who movingly saluted his father outside the church in Washington. Finally, the thirty-fifth president of the United States was laid to rest in Arlington National Cemetery just outside the nation's capital.

INTRODUCTION TO THE JOHNSON ADMINISTRATION

A Brief Biographical Sketch

Lyndon Baines Johnson was a far different man and president from what John Kennedy had been. Born in Texas in 1908, Johnson grew up in poverty and then experienced the Great Depression as a young adult. Although he earned a teaching degree and taught school for one year, Johnson left the classroom to enter his one true love—politics. He went to Washington, D.C. in 1932 as the personal secretary of a Texas member of the House of Representatives. Shortly after this, he was appointed to head the National Youth Administration program in his home state. Then beginning in the late 1930s, Johnson served as a representative in Congress for a little more than one decade. It was while a member of the House of Representatives that Lyndon Johnson used his growing political influence to bring electricity to his rural Texas district. His voters back home remained loyal to him throughout the years, often calling him "the man who turned the lights on." In 1948, Johnson was elected to the United States Senate after a razor-thin Democratic primary victory. It was in the Senate that Lyndon Johnson began to exercise real political clout. His leadership skills were quickly recognized, and he was picked by his own party to be the Senate Minority Leader in 1953. Then after the Democrats had regained control of the Senate in the off-year congressional elections of 1954, Johnson became the Senate Majority Leader. This was the position which propelled him into becoming a Democratic presidential contender in 1960, when he was defeated by the young senator from Massachusetts, John F. Kennedy, who then selected him as his running mate in the general election that fall.

On a personal level, Johnson was a compulsive, hard-working man who exhibited the energy and determination of several men. Even his best friends privately acknowledged that he was insecure and therefore needed frequent praise to stroke his large ego. Johnson also was often intolerant and abusive to those who worked with him, demonstrating a problem with a fiery temper. And for his critics, he left few words of profanity unspoken in personally denouncing them. With an intelligent use of his personality traits, however, Johnson the politician had fine tuned the art of political intimidation and deal-making. Many historians rate him as one of the most effective leaders in Congress since Henry Clay, the powerful early nineteenth century Speaker of the House. These leadership skills he also would use effectively in the early years of his presidency.

The Cabinet and Philosophy

President Lyndon Johnson assumed the presidency with the Kennedy cabinet in place. But within two years, Attorney-General Robert Kennedy and Treasury Secretary C. Douglas Dillon had resigned to further their career goals. Dean Rusk and Stewart Udall, among others, remained throughout the Johnson years as Secretary of State and Secretary of the Interior, respectively. Philosophically, Lyndon Johnson was a child of the New Deal. He admired Franklin D. Roosevelt so much, in fact, that he preferred to be called LBJ (just as Roosevelt had been known by his initials, FDR). And like Roosevelt, Johnson believed that government must do for the poor and downtrodden what they cannot do for themselves. It would be the Johnson administration that truly inherited the legacy of the New Deal tradition.

DOMESTIC ISSUES UNDER JOHNSON

Early Legislative Successes

President Johnson was not only a shrewd politician who pushed hard for concensus, but he also knew that the assassination of President Kennedy would give him an almost unprecedented window of opportunity to accomplish things. Sympathy for the fallen president could be used to push some of the Kennedy agenda through the Congress. And that's what happened in early 1964. In February, Congress finally passed the federal income tax cut which the late president had proposed earlier. It reduced income taxes by about $10 billion, and encouraged economic growth by increasing consumer spending and thereby reducing unemployment. But the most significant Johnson legislative victory in early 1964 was the passage of a major civil rights bill in June. This Civil Rights Act of 1964 was essentially the same as the bill that Kennedy had proposed one year earlier. (For a complete discussion of this act and the entire modern civil rights movement, see Chapter Fourteen.)

THE GREAT SOCIETY BEGINS

In 1963 President Kennedy had read a book by Michael Harrington entitled *The Other America* (released in 1962) that would have far-reaching consequences. In his book, Harrington documented the fact that between 20 percent and 25 percent of all Americans were living in poverty. Although most Americans were not even aware of it, somewhere around 40 million people lived in substandard housing, received poor nutrition, and did not have the same educational and employment opportunities as the rest of the nation. These included mining families in the Appalachian region, the elderly, migrant agricultural workers, ghetto dwellers, and families headed by a single mother. As a result of reading the book, President Kennedy asked advisors to look into the entire question of poverty in America.

The Economic Opportunity Act

Although Kennedy had died before his advisors finished their report, President Johnson picked up the idea and championed the anti-poverty cause. In January 1964, during the new president's first address to Congress, Johnson declared an "unconditional war on poverty in America." Shortly after this announcement, he sent Congress a series of proposals for legislation. In late August 1964, Congress passed the Economic Opportunity Act, which established the Office of Economic Opportunity (OEO) to coordinate a new array of social programs. This act was the centerpiece of the Great Society's war on poverty. Johnson named former Peace Corps Director R. Sargent Shriver, Jr. as the first head of the OEO. With an initial budget of close to $1 billion, the OEO was authorized to fund (1) a Job Corps to train young people, aged 16 to 21, in marketable job skills; (2) a Neighborhood Youth Corps to provide work experience for youth in the inner cities; (3) the Volunteers in Service to America (VISTA), a type of domestic Peace Corps; and (4) the Community Action Programs (CAP) to help encourage "maximum feasible participation" by the poor themselves.

The CAPs were the most controversial part of the Economic Opportunity Act because federal dollars were directly placed into the hands of local leaders who emerged within the poor communities of the nation. This angered many local politicians, who wanted some voice in how federal funds were spent in their municipalities; the law was later amended to give city officials some input into the allocation of federal resources. It was various CAPs that initiated Head Start, a program of preschool education for deprived youngsters, legal aid for the poor, family planning services, and other innovative projects. The Economic Opportunity Act also provided for the creation of adult literacy programs and work-study programs that would allow some poor youths to go to college. In a separate action, Congress confirmed the late President Kennedy's executive order creating a limited Food Stamp plan, and gave it the force of legislative law in 1964.

In May 1964 President Johnson gave his domestic anti-poverty agenda the name of Great Society during a graduation address at the University of Michigan in Ann Arbor. "The Great Society," declared the president, "demands an end to poverty and racial injustice, to which we are fully committed in our time." The war on poverty had begun and would continue in full swing after the presidential election later that fall.

THE 1964 ELECTION

The Candidates

As 1964 rolled around, it was clear that President Johnson would have no difficulty winning the Democratic nomination to seek election in his own right. And indeed, the Democratic National Convention nominated him in August at Atlantic City, New Jersey. Although some had favored Robert Kennedy for the vice-presidential spot on the ticket, Johnson chose Minnesota Senator Hubert H. Humphrey. Humphrey, an ardent supporter of the civil rights movement, had made the rousing pro-civil rights speech at the 1948 convention which had resulted in some southern delegates walking out and running Strom Thurmond of South Carolina as a third party candidate.

Few Republicans tested the political waters in 1964 because the incumbent president looked hard to beat. The narrower field of candidates allowed the conservative wing of the party to make a strong bid for control and to nominate one of their own. For years the more conservative Republicans had complained that their party had been nominating "me too" candidates for president, men who simply claimed they could administer the New Deal government programs more efficiently than the Democrats. And since the death of Ohio Senator Robert A. Taft in 1953, this conservative wing had not really had a towering national leader. This would change in 1964.

Two prominent Republicans emerged to compete for their party's nomination. New York Governor Nelson Rockefeller represented the more moderate, almost liberal, wing of the party. A recent divorce and remarriage had hurt Rockefeller with many voters in general, and his more liberal views had angered many Republican voters in particular. The conservative voice in the fight for the Republican nomination was Arizona Senator Barry Goldwater. His family owned a very successful department store in Phoenix, which had provided Goldwater with quite a personal fortune. He had been in politics for a number of years by then, and in 1960 he had written *The Conscience of a Conservative* outlining his conservative political philosophy. When Goldwater won the California Republican primary late in the season, he was all but assured of victory at the convention. And despite a last-minute "Stop Goldwater" effort at the Republican National Convention in July at San Francisco, Barry Goldwater won the Republican nomination on the first ballot. Then, instead of attempting to heal political wounds, the senator picked William Miller, an equally conservative upstate New York Congressman, to be his running mate. In his acceptance speech, Goldwater proclaimed proudly that "extremism in the defense of liberty is no vice . . . And let me remind you also," he continued, "that moderation in the pursuit of justice is no virtue." He was determined that his candidacy would give voters "A Choice, Not An Echo." It certainly did.

The Campaign

The presidential campaign that year offered voters a clear choice between a liberal Democrat and a very conservative Republican. One of Johnson's advantages was that Goldwater's statements, both in the past and during the campaign, allowed the Democrat to appear as the moderate candidate in the race. As one observer put it, Goldwater had a talent for scaring voters. For example, the Republican senator defended his votes against the censure of Joseph McCarthy in the 1950s and against the Civil Rights Act which had passed Congress just a few months before the election. He advocated that the federal government sell the Tennessee Valley Authority, one of the New Deal's most successful ventures, for one dollar. During the campaign he also spoke negatively about the "compulsory" nature of the Social Security system, but then protested when he was accused of wanting to abolish it. He had once stated his conviction that NATO commanders in Europe should have the right to employ nuclear weapons without presidential permission. His statements also seemed to suggest that he would be happy to see the abolition of the graduated federal income tax. And he urged wholesale bombing of North Vietnam after he accused the Johnson administration of engaging in a "no-win" war. That last remark allowed President Johnson to sound moderate: "We are not about to send American boys nine or ten thousand miles from home to do what Asian boys ought to be doing for themselves."

The campaign did produce some interesting symbols and slogans, and one of the most memorable commercials of all time—whether political or not. The Republicans issued some bumper stickers with the chemical symbols for "gold" and "water"—Au H_2O. When the Republicans campaigned with the slogan, "In your heart, you know he's right," the Democrats responded with, "In your guts, you know he's nuts." The Democrats aired a very negative campaign commercial, known later as the "Daisy Girl" commercial, which was then taken off the air after only one broadcast because of the strong reaction from both the Republicans and the general public. This commercial featured an innocent little girl in a field of flowers counting petals, when suddenly the camera focused on one of her pupils, which then reflected an atomic explosion. The implication was that the Republican candidate would use nuclear weapons and destroy world peace.

The Results

Before the November 3 balloting, it was clear to all objective observers that President Johnson would be re-elected. The only question left was the margin of victory. The voters answered that important question with a resounding "huge." The president won an impressive landslide victory with 486 electoral votes to Goldwater's 52. The popular vote was equally lopsided as the president polled about 43.1 million votes across the country, compared to about 27.2 million votes for Goldwater. The Democrats also gained 38 seats in the House of Representatives and 2 seats in the Senate. This gave them a 295 to 140 margin in the House and a 68 to 32 margin in the Senate. It was a sweeping Democratic victory and a clear repudiation of what most Americans felt were extreme views represented by the Goldwater wing of the Republican Party. Clearly, the Great Society would continue to march on for the next few years at least.

THE APPALACHIAN REGIONAL DEVELOPMENT ACT

The first major Great Society legislation to pass Congress after the 1964 presidential election was the Appalachian Regional Development Act in March 1965. The Appalachian region stretched from parts of Pennsylvania in the north to northern Alabama in the south, encompassing 11 states altogether. Within the region, the unemployment rate was approximately 50 percent higher than the national average and per capita income about 40 percent lower. The new law created a joint federal-state agency, called the Appalachian Regional Commission, to approve and administer $1.1 billion for construction of highways, operation of health centers, and the development of other resources. Under the plan, each state would ascertain its own special needs and then carry them out after the commission approved them.

THE ELEMENTARY AND SECONDARY EDUCATION ACT

President Johnson considered education the single most important part of his Great Society program because without good educational opportunity Americans in poverty would have little hope of ever getting out. President Kennedy had felt the same way and had proposed a major federal aid-to-education bill early in his first year in office, but Congress had refused to pass it.

Then in April 1965, the Elementary and Secondary Education Act became the first major federal aid-to-education law in United States history. The law appropriated $1.3 billion in the form of grants and loans to elementary and secondary schools for their purchase of textbooks, library books, and special education programs. Using grant and loan moneys in these ways only indirectly benefited students and teachers, so most objections on church and state grounds were dropped. Obviously, Catholic leaders were pleased that the nation's parochial schools could receive at least some federal assistance through this bill.

THE HIGHER EDUCATION ACT

After precedence for federal aid to education had been set in the Elementary and Secondary Education Act, the education agenda naturally focused on aid to colleges and universities and their students. Therefore, in October 1965, Congress passed the Higher Education Act at the urgent request of the president. It appropriated approximately $650 million for scholarships and low-interest loans to needy

1964	50	LYNDON B. JOHNSON	Democrat	42,676,220	486	61.3
		Barry M. Goldwater	Republican	28,860,314	52	38.5

President Lyndon Johnson signing the Medicare Bill of 1965. Credit: AP/Wide World Photos.

college and university students. Some of the federal dollars also helped institutions of higher education improve their libraries and other research facilities. In addition, the bill established the National Teachers Corps to help find good teachers for economically depressed areas of the country.

THE MEDICAL CARE ACT (MEDICARE)

President Harry S. Truman had proposed a comprehensive federally funded health insurance program for the elderly in 1945. But for the next 20 years, the American Medical Association had blocked passage of any such bill, labeling it un-American and "socialized medicine." The last attempt had come from President Kennedy in 1962. But the results of the congressional elections in November 1964 meant that Lyndon Johnson probably had the votes to get just such a program enacted into law.

While the president's supporters in Congress were working on federal health insurance legislation for the elderly, others attached provisions for a program to assist the poor as well. The original idea had been for the government to pay part of hospital costs. But when the American Medical Association (AMA), an organization representing the interests of physicians, realized that the Medicare concept would

The Tumultuous Sixties / 743

become law, it lobbied for provisions to have the government pay a portion of doctors' bills also. It was added to the bill, which Congress passed in July 1965 as the Medical Care Act. (It is popularly called the Medicare Act, but that is misleading because the same law created the Medicaid as well as the Medicare system.) In honor of former President Harry Truman, President Johnson signed the bill into law on July 30, 1965 in Independence, Missouri, with Truman personally watching him.

The Medical Care Act of 1965 established Medicare, which provided a federal health insurance system for those 65 years of age or older, or those who are disabled. (Basically, anyone receiving Social Security benefits is eligible for Medicare.) It is administered by the Social Security Administration, through payroll taxes on incomes, which means it is entirely a federal program. While hospital insurance is mandatory under the act, recipients may voluntarily choose to pay a minimal monthly fee which entitles them to federal insurance that pays for most doctors' bills and drug costs. The second part of the Medical Care Act was the establishment of the Medicaid system. Medicaid pays the medical expenses of those poor who are covered under AFDC (Aid to Families with Dependent Children). Since creation of the Supplemental Security Income program—SSI—in 1972, recipients of SSI payments are also eligible for Medicaid coverage. The Medicaid program is administered by the states, with the funding for it divided between the federal government and the states on a matching basis.

Both Medicare and Medicaid recipients are completely free to choose the doctor and hospital from which they receive medical services. The chief weakness in the two programs is that because the only role the federal government plays is in payment of medical bills, there is no real cost control measures to help contain medical costs. The result was that the Medicare and Medicaid programs have cost taxpayers a lot more than anyone imagined in 1965.

THE HOUSING AND URBAN DEVELOPMENT ACT

In order to improve the nation's housing, especially in the big cities, Congress passed the Housing and Urban Development Act in late summer 1965. It provided funds for the construction of 240,000 public housing units for low-income Americans and authorized $2.9 billion in federal grants over the next four years to municipalities for use in urban renewal projects. A controversial provision to pay direct federal subsidies for rent supplements to low-income families was not funded until the next year. The Department of Housing and Urban Development (HUD) was also created, and the next January, President Johnson named Robert C. Weaver to head the cabinet-level agency. In assuming the position of Secretary of Housing and Urban Development, Weaver became the first African-American member of a presidential cabinet.

THE IMMIGRATION ACT OF 1965

Another major piece of legislation that emerged from Congress during the Johnson administration was the Immigration Act of 1965. Since 1924, under the National Origins Act, American immigration policy had discriminated against peoples from eastern and southern Europe in a quota system and denied access to East Asians and Africans altogether. (See Chapter Nine for details.) Senator John F. Kennedy, with support from the Anti-Defamation League, had written a booklet entitled *A Nation of Immigrants* in 1958. It had celebrated the positive role that immigrants had played in American history and called for a major overhaul of the nation's immigration laws. When president, Kennedy had pressed Congress to enact immigration reform in 1963, but it was among the several bills still bottled up in committee at the time that Kennedy was assassinated.

In his State of the Union address in early 1964, President Johnson had mentioned immigration reform as something he wanted Congress to enact. There was so little opposition to the old Kennedy bill that it passed with little change in October 1965. The Immigration Act of 1965 replaced the old quota system for each nationality with a system of maximum numbers of people per hemisphere and per country each year. Immigration from outside the western hemisphere was limited to 170,000 persons per year, while 120,000 immigrants per year were allowed from the western hemisphere. The law also limited to no more than 20,000 immigrants from any one specific country each year. Exceptions allowing more than the limit in any category were written into the law as well. Close relatives of those already living in the United States topped the list of exceptions. Such persons could come regardless of their numbers. Other relatives of American residents, skilled workers, and those classified as refugees were next given priority for annual visas.

No one really expected immigration patterns to the United States to change significantly, but a number of factors did, in fact, lead to a major shift. First, the economies of northern and western Europe generally were prosperous during the 1960s. And, of course, eastern Europeans living under communist rule could not come. Therefore, relatively few Europeans emigrated to the United States during the rest of the decade. That left Latin Americans and many Asians who could come and who had economic incentives to do so. And second, as these immigrants multiplied, they used the family preference system under the new law to send for other family members. The Vietnam War also added to the flood of refugees from southeast Asia. All of these factors resulted in Latin American and Asian immigrants coming to dominate the face of American immigration since 1965.

REMAINING ISSUES

A broad range of other laws were enacted during the Great Society for the purpose of enhancing the quality of life for more Americans. For example, the Land and Water Conservation Act and the National Wilderness Preservation Act, both passed in 1964, represented concern about the effect of spreading civilization on natural surroundings. Worry about the effects of civilization upon the quality of life now and in the future were reflected in the Water Quality Act and the Air Quality Act, both of which were enacted in October 1965. Lady Bird Johnson (the First Lady) pushed for passage of the Highway Beautification Act (October 1965), which allocated federal funds to the states for eliminating billboards and other objects that distracted from the natural beauty of the landscape along the nation's highways. In the Demonstration Cities and Metropolitan Area Redevelopment Act of 1966, Congress authorized $1.4 billion to help finance most of the cost of slum clearance in several selected "model cities." Special housing, mass transit, and welfare subsidies also went to those metropolitan areas. Federal safety standards were established for the automobile industry in the Motor Vehicle Safety Act (1966).

To promote more appreciation for the arts and literature, the Johnson administration persuaded Congress to establish the National Foundation of the Arts and Humanities (September 1965) and the Corporation for Public Broadcasting. The latter created the Public Broadcasting System of radio and television stations (PBS) via the Public Broadcasting Act of November 1967. Of course, a major accomplishment of the Johnson administration was the Voting Rights Act of 1965, which attempted to guarantee black voting rights, especially in the South (See Chapter Fourteen). With regard to consumer protection, the Truth in Packaging Act (1966) and the Truth in Lending Act (May 1968) expanded federal labeling standards for food, drugs, and other products, and required lenders to disclose full information on the total cost of credit purchases, respectively.

In the area of government reorganization, the Department of Transportation was created in 1966 to develop and coordinate the various federal programs in the transportation sector of the economy. And the Twenty-fifth Amendment to the Constitution, having passed Congress in 1965, was ratified in early 1967. This amendment resolved growing concerns about how a disabled president could be replaced and what to do in cases where there was no vice-president to succeed the president. President Eisenhower had had more than one serious illness, and the nation had not had a vice-president for more than a year after Kennedy's death. (Of course, similar situations had existed earlier in our history also.) Therefore, the Twenty-fifth Amendment provided for procedures to allow the vice-president to assume the powers of the presidency in case the president were to become incapacitated and to allow a recovered president to resume his authority. It also authorized the president to appoint a vice-president whenever that office became vacant, subject to confirmation of a majority in both houses of Congress.

Congress failed to take action on only two matters submitted by President Johnson: (1) his recommendation to repeal section 14b of the Taft-Hartley Act, which permits states to enact so-called "right to work" laws prohibiting union shops (this repeal effort was enthusiastically supported by the AFL-CIO); and (2) his recommendation that the District of Columbia be granted home rule.

AN EVALUATION OF THE GREAT SOCIETY

Lyndon Johnson had idolized Franklin Roosevelt and had always wanted to achieve a significant legislative record comparable to his. There is no question but that his administration did that because of the sheer volume of domestic legislation and major changes in society which those laws effected. Some of the Great Society programs were based on New Deal objectives which had never been met fully, as in the case of Medicare's expansion of the Social Security system. But the Great Society also moved into areas never dreamed of by most New Dealers. Examples of such areas included federal aid to education, the arts and humanities, and the creation of a public broadcasting system.

But the most controversial part of the Great Society, and that which clearly defined it, was Johnson's war on poverty. The centerpiece of that war was, of course, the Economic Opportunity Act of 1964. It is ironic that this legislation, based primarily on the principle that government should assist the poor through job train-ing, education, and the development of local community projects by the poor them-selves, would quickly become the symbol of federal bureaucratic interference to politically conservative Americans.

Was the Great Society successful in its war on poverty? That will depend partly upon whom is asked. Conservatives believe that not only did the war on poverty prove to be a failure, they insist that its federal programs created a class of poor who were dependent upon the federal government much like a junkie depends on his drugs. Furthermore, by robbing people of their initiative, they argue, it was also robbing them of their freedom. And by diverting large sums of dollars to the war on poverty, conservatives maintain that private investment was reduced and inflation increased. Furthermore, opponents made the argument that any reduction in the poverty rate during the 1960s was the result of economic growth, not Great Society programs.

Liberal supporters of the Great Society respond by asserting that poverty was reduced in the 1960s from close to 25 percent to about 13 percent, and that the war on poverty certainly was responsible for some of that effect. Besides, they argue that relatively little money was spent on the actual anti-poverty programs, and that the escalation of the Vietnam War deprived the nation of the resources which would have been necessary to get the job done completely. As to the allega-tion that the Great Society created a huge dependent class of poor, liberals counter that the cycle of poverty, often called generational poverty, already existed and was well documented before the Great Society was begun. Beyond that, liberals regard most of the anti-poverty programs to be a matter of simple justice in the American tradition of opening access to economic opportunity to more of its citizens.

Clearly, the Great Society left us a mixed legacy. Even most conservative Re-publicans do not object to the Head Start program, nor have they attempted to eliminate the Medicare system or federal aid to education. Certainly nearly every-one agrees that millions of students were able to attend college who would not have otherwise. And all agree that the roots of the cycle of poverty among the inner cities and in depressed rural areas were not pulled out. Michael Harrington, whose book entitled *The Other America* had inspired the war on poverty, later complained that "what was supposed to be a social war turned out to be a skirmish and, in any case, poverty won." Despite a lot of good which was done, the Great Society cer-tainly did not succeed in any phenomenal way. And with its creation of Medicare and Medicaid, along with other factors, the federal deficit would soar in the decades following the sixties. One scholar has remarked that as far as the Great Society is concerned, "it is a story about the good, the bad, and the ugly."

THE WARREN COURT

The Great Society was not the only thing that conservative Americans were com-plaining about in the 1960s. The United States Supreme Court handed down a number of decisions in the late 1950s and in the 1960s which greatly aroused their anger. President Eisenhower had appointed former Republican governor of California Earl Warren as Chief Justice in 1953. It soon became surprisingly apparent that Warren was taking the court in a decidedly liberal direction, especially in its avid defense of the First Amendment. This prompted Eisenhower to later declare that the Warren appointment was "the biggest damn fool mistake I ever made." (See Chapter Fourteen for a discussion of the famous *Brown v. Board of Education* decision, and Chapter Fifteen for references to the *Jencks* and *Yates* decisions, all handed down in the 1950s.)

Even before the election of John F. Kennedy in 1960, the John Birch Society had erected billboards all across the country calling for the impeachment of Chief Justice Earl Warren. (The John Birch Society had been founded by Robert Welch, a New England candy manufacturer, and had accused persons such as Eisenhower and John Foster Dulles of being communists.) Then after President Kennedy appointed two liberals to the Supreme Court in 1962, Byron White and Arthur Goldberg, and Johnson named Abe Fortas (1965) and Thurgood Marshall (1967), the Warren Court proved to be even more liberal.

The following is a listing of some of the more significant decisions of the Warren Court in the 1960s:

Baker v. Carr—In March 1962, the Supreme Court ruled in a Tennessee case that the "one man, one vote" principle must apply in national and state elections. This meant that legislative districts for both national and state governments must be drawn up based on population, not on land area or other factors. This gave urban minorities more opportunities to elect candidates and thereby increase their political representation and voice. It also meant that rural, more conservative, areas would lose some representation as a natural consequence.

Engel v. Vitale—Also in 1962, the Supreme Court prohibited public prescribed prayer in the nation's public schools on the grounds that such practices violated the establishment clause of the First Amendment. Millions of Americans since the *Engel* decision have incorrectly believed that the Supreme Court forbids all prayer in public schools, but that is simply not the case. There is no legislative or case law that denies the right of a child (or teacher) to say a silent prayer over his or her lunch or just before an exam is taken.

Abington v. Schempp—Following the *Engel* decision, the Supreme Court ruled in 1963 that public Bible reading in the nation's public schools also violated the First Amendment.

Jacobellis v. Ohio—In 1963 the Supreme Court moved to protect even sexually explicit material if it has any "literary or scientific or artistic value." This decision angered many Americans, who saw it as the federal government advocating pornographic material. This reflects the classical difference in emphasis between conservatives and liberals over First Amendment issues. Conservatives place their emphasis on community standards whenever individual behavior runs counter to the community. Liberals, on the other hand, place their emphasis upon individual choice whenever there is a conflict with the community. To First Amendment liberals, the acid test of a free society is its willingness to protect the private behavior of even its most obnoxious citizens.

Gideon v. Wainwright—In this 1963 decision, the Supreme Court used a Florida case to rule that a state must provide an attorney at public expense for those defendants in felony cases who could not afford one.

Miranda v. Arizona—In this very controversial 1966 case, the Supreme Court declared that the police must inform a person of his right to remain silent and to have counsel present during questioning at the time of his arrest. This *Miranda* ruling is the basis for the police statement to arrested persons which nearly every television viewer can probably recite from memory: "You have the right to remain silent. If you give up the right to remain silent, anything you say may be held against you in a court of law. You have the right to an attorney; if you cannot afford one, an attorney will be provided for you." Law enforcement officials complain that this decision hampers their ability to arrest criminals, but defenders of the decision simply view it as providing a basic constitutional right and as a small price to pay in order to avoid living in a police state.

The liberal-conservative debate over the interpretation of the First Amendment continues and undoubtedly always will. In any case, Chief Justice Earl Warren never was impeached or forcibly removed from his position. However, he did resign in 1969, and Supreme Court appointments in the next couple of decades definitely moved the court more to the moderate center on some issues, even though the most controversial Warren Court decisions were not overturned.

FOREIGN AFFAIRS UNDER JOHNSON
RELATIONS WITH LATIN AMERICA

The Panamanian Dispute

The Hay-Bunau-Varilla Treaty of 1903 had given the United States the right to build and control the Panama Canal, which connected the Atlantic and Pacific Oceans by water across the small Central American country of Panama. It had been negotiated under shady circumstances. (See Chapter Seven.) American control of this canal had been a source of irritation to the Panamanians for a long time. Then an incident in early 1964 produced a crisis which threatened to end the long-time relationship between the two nations.

By January 1964 a dispute had developed concerning the flying of the Panamanian and American flags on the Canal Zone's American high school grounds. That same month American high school students took down the Panamanian flag and desecrated it. When a mob of angry Panamanians burst into the Canal Zone, American troops battled them. The result was that 23 Panamanians and 3 Americans lay dead. The crisis escalated when the government of Panama then ended diplomatic relations with the United States to protest the killings. And it quickly sought help to mediate the dispute from the United Nations and the Organization of American States (OAS). When it became clear that Panama wanted to renegotiate the original treaty with the United States so that Panama would have control of the canal, the Johnson administration refused. After Johnson won a landslide re-election in November, he announced to the world that the United States was thinking about building a new canal either across Panama, Nicaragua, or Colombia because the present one was not easily defended, and neither did it accomodate large aircraft carriers. The matter remained unresolved until 1977, when the Carter administration completed negotiations that had begun earlier under the Nixon White House. (See Chapter Seventeen for more details.)

Intervention in the Dominican Republic

The Good Neighbor policy of the Franklin Roosevelt years, in which the United States specifically repudiated any previous claims of the right to intervene in the internal affairs of Latin American nations, had been violated in spirit during the 1954 Guatemalan crisis. But no American troops had specifically and overtly intervened in the region since Roosevelt had announced his policy in the 1930s. That policy would be seriously tested in a crisis in the Dominican Republic during the height of the Cold War in the mid-1960s. Thirty years of dictatorial rule by Rafael Trujillo were ended with his assassinaton in 1961. President Kennedy had viewed this small Caribbean island country as a good place to showcase his Alliance for Progress. Encouraged by the election of Juan Bosch to the presidency of the Dominican Republic in December 1962, the Kennedy administration continued to send economic aid there. However, Bosch's political failure to make significant headway against the economic poverty there led to a military coup the next September. President Kennedy responded to the coup by canceling all economic aid and refusing to officially recognize the new military government.

When Lyndon Johnson assumed the presidency, he restored diplomatic relations with the island nation. Although Bosch remained in exile, his supporters staged a revolt against the army in April 1965 that resulted in civil war there. The Johnson administration had taken Fidel Castro's proclamation of a western hemispheric revolution seriously and decided that a number of Castro agents were an integral part of the Dominican Republic civil war. Therefore, on April 28, President Johnson ordered an invasion of some 20,000 American marines. Having labeled the civil war as a Castro-led communist revolution, Johnson appealed to the OAS for support. At the same time (May), the president issued what many have since called the Johnson Doctrine: "American nations cannot, must not, and will not permit the establishment of another Communist government in the Western Hemisphere." Specifically, he asked them to organize an Inter-American Peace Force so that his actions would not appear as American aggression. Reluctantly, the OAS approved Johnson's request the same month, which allowed many of the American troops to withdraw from the island. Finally, elections were held in June 1966, and a moderate conservative candidate, Joaquin Balaguer, defeated a returned Juan Bosch in a surprising upset. That September the remaining American troops left the Dominican Republic.

Ironically, the Roosevelt Corollary justifying United States intervention in Latin America had been issued by President Theodore Roosevelt in late 1904 because of a crisis in the Dominican Republic. Now, after more than 30 years of American repudiation of the Roosevelt Corollary, it was a crisis in the Dominican Republic which precipitated another long stretch of American intervention south of the border.

THE MIDDLE EAST

The Six-Day War

The tentative peace in the Middle East established after the Suez Crisis of 1956 convinced no one of its permanent nature. The United States continued to supply arms to both Israelis and Arabs after that, and Egyptian President Nasser continued his relationship with the Soviets as well. Along with other Arab nations, Egypt had created the Palestine Liberation Organization (PLO) in 1964 to build pressure on Israel to recognize a new Palestinian nation. And Nasser also demanded that the UN peacekeeping force along the Israeli-Egyptian border be removed. Not long after the UN did, in fact, pull its peacekeeping force out (May 1967), Egyptian forces moved into the Sinai Peninsula and seized the strategic location of Sharm el-Sheikh, which overlooked the Gulf of Aqaba. As a result, Israel was denied access to its only port. In coordination with these Egyptian movements, Palestinian raids inside Israel were stepped up, and Syrian and Jordanian troops gathered along Israel's borders. All indications seemed to point to an imminent general Arab attack on Israel.

The world watched intently to see what would happen next. They did not have long to wait. Seizing the element of surprise, Israel launched a preemptive strike against its Arab enemies. On the morning of June 5, 1967, Israeli jets avoided Egyptian radar by flying low and coming in from over the Mediterranean Sea and destroyed the bulk of the Egyptian air force while it was on the ground. The same tactic was used against the military planes of Syria, Jordan, and Iraq. Israeli ground forces proceeded to enter the Sinai Peninsula, where they routed the Egyptian army, retook Sharm el-Sheikh, and blocked the Egyptian entrance to the Suez Canal. After six days of fighting, the Israelis occupied the old city of Jerusalem, the West Bank along the Jordan River, and the Golan Heights near the border with Syria.

Neither the United States nor the Soviet Union intervened militarily in the Six-Day War, as it came to be called. Use of the "hotline" probably prevented the kind of miscalculation that could have led to a widespread all-out clash between the two superpowers. Israel's astonishing and quick victory forced the Arab nations to accept a cease-fire on June 10. In late November of the same year, a UN-sponsored truce was agreed to on the basis of UN Security Council Resolution 242. The resolution called for an Israeli withdrawal from all newly occupied territories in exchange for guarantees of secure borders and free access to the major waterways in the region. It also called for a "just settlement of the refugee problem," which was interpreted by the Arabs to be the eventual establishment of an independent Palestinian state. Demilitarized zones would guarantee the peace. However, despite Israel's brilliant military performance, the war really settled nothing. The Soviets rearmed Nasser, terrorist attacks on Israel continued, and both the Soviets and the Americans reaffirmed their commitments to Middle Eastern allies. For its part, Israel refused to give up any territory conquered in the war, and the terms of the UN resolution were never implemented. The only positive thing that can be said about the Six-Day War is that the United States and the Soviet Union avoided a major military clash.

ASIA

The USS Pueblo Incident

By the end of 1967, prospects for a thaw in Soviet-American relations appeared promising. In June of that year, President Johnson and Soviet Premier Alexei Kosygin had met on a college campus in New Jersey to discuss the war in Vietnam and the current Middle East crisis. While the two men had not resolved either of those thorny issues, the talks had been amicable. Then in September, with public opinion polls showing that most Americans believed our participation in the Vietnam War had been a mistake, Johnson softened his stand on what the United States would require before engaging in peace talks to end that war.

But several events in early 1968 ruined any chance for peace in southeast Asia. Senator Eugene McCarthy challenged the president in the Democratic primaries over the issue of the Vietnam War, and an American B-52 loaded with four H-bombs suddenly disappeared over Greenland. But the most serious crisis of all was the taking of an American intelligence ship by the North Koreans. The *U.S.S. Pueblo* was an American intelligence ship loaded with sensitive intelligence-gathering devices. While operating in the Sea of Japan, North Korean forces captured the ship on January 23, with all 82 members of the crew. They accused the *Pueblo* of having invaded North Korean territorial waters and engaged in illegal spying activities.

Public opinion in the United States clearly wanted immediate military retaliation against the North Koreans, but President Johnson refused to take such action because he did not want a war with North Korea while already engaged in Vietnam. Instead, he continued to negotiate for the release of the ship and crew. After almost an entire year in captivity, and obviously under duress, the American crew members signed a statement admitting their ship had violated North Korean waters and apologizing for their activities. In a bizarre move, the American commander was allowed to denounce the statement both before and after it was signed. The crew members then were released, although the North Koreans kept the ship. The incident damaged United States credibility in the world and demonstrated that there were limits to the abilities of even superpower countries.

Stoldiers and civilians in Prague during the Czech Revolt in 1968. Credit: AP/Wide World Photos.

SOVIET-AMERICAN RELATIONS

The Czech Revolt

Signs of growing discontent behind the Iron Curtain were reemerging in the late 1960s. Czechoslavakia had been among the last of the eastern European nations brought forcibly under Soviet political domination in the late 1940s. Now under the leadership of its own communist party head, Alexander Dubcek, modest reforms were being instituted which threatened to undermine Soviet-style communism there. The Soviets realized the danger of what was happening in Czechoslavakia, and they warned Dubcek to stay the course laid out by the Soviet Union. When the Dubcek government failed to respond to their pressure, the Soviet leaders recognized that they must set an example promptly, before reforms spread to other eastern European nations. They also knew that President Johnson was a weak, lame-duck president, which would make Soviet intervention easier. Therefore, on the night of August 20–21, 1968, Soviet tanks and soldiers marched into Prague and quickly crushed the rebellion. The Soviet Union defended its actions by announcing the Brezhnev Doctrine, named after General Secretary Leonid Brezhnev. Essentially, the Brezhnev Doctrine proclaimed the Soviet right to intervene in any allied nation

Senator Robert F. Kennedy addresses supporters in Los Angeles. Credit: AP/Wide World Photos.

in order to defend its interests and the interest of the worldwide communist revolution.

President Johnson protested the crushing of the Czech Revolt just as Eisenhower had done when the Soviets had crushed a similar revolt in Hungary in 1956. But American involvement in the Vietnam War and its intervention in the Dominican Republic both seemed to undermine and weaken the president's protest. Less hypocritical were the protests of most Europeans, including some prominent individuals within eastern Europe and the Soviet Union itself. The real results of the incident included a hardening of relations between the two superpowers, a rapid increase in the arms race, and a boost for Richard Nixon's election chances that fall.

The Czech Crisis also threatened to derail the Nuclear Non-proliferation Treaty, which 61 nations had signed in July 1968 (including the United States) in an effort to prevent the spread of nuclear weapons in the world. Although the United States Senate did delay any action on the treaty after the Soviet intervention in Czechoslavakia, it finally did ratify it in March 1969, shortly after Nixon had been inaugurated president.

As demonstrators are placed into police vans, center, Chicago police form a battle line against thousands of others. The street rioting is near the headquarters for the 1968 Democratic National Convention. Credit: AP/Wide World Photos.

THE 1968 ELECTION

The Candidates

Events during the second half of the Johnson presidency spelled political trouble for the Texas Democrat. The Vietnam War's escalation in 1965 had drained resources from the Great Society programs, and turmoil resulting from rising expectations in the African-American community had produced a conservative, white backlash. When television news showed pictures of the Tet Offensive in early 1968, most Americans had been convinced that the war was probably unwinnable. Johnson had few strong political allies left, and prospects for his reelection were growing dimmer by the week.

Then in November 1967, Minnesota Democratic Senator Eugene McCarthy announced that he would challenge the incumbent president and make opposition to the Vietnam War his major issue in the Democratic primaries that coming spring.

Most political experts knew that Johnson was weak, but few expected that he could be denied the nomination by his own party in 1968. Then in the March 1968 Democratic primary in New Hampshire, McCarthy took the president by surprise. Even in that conservative state, "Clean Gene" McCarthy captured 42 percent of the popular vote and 20 of the 24 delegates.

McCarthy's success in New Hampshire convinced other Democrats that Johnson was indeed beatable. Thus, on March 16, New York Senator Robert F. Kennedy announced that he was a candidate for president. Kennedy too promised to challenge Johnson on the Vietnam War issue. Johnson knew that Kennedy represented the greater threat because he could appeal to each of the traditional Democratic constituencies. As a result, President Johnson addressed the American people on national television on March 31 and withdrew his name from the race with the following words: "I have concluded that I should not permit the presidency to become involved in the partisan divisions that are developing in this political year. Accordingly, I shall not seek, and I will not accept the nomination of my party for another term as your president."

With Lyndon Johnson out of the race, Vice-President Hubert Humphrey cast his hat into the ring on April 27. Thus, it became a three-man race between McCarthy, Kennedy, and Humphrey. While Humphrey could count on "organization" Democrats for delegate support and strength at the convention that summer, he entered the race too late to be officially entered in the primaries. He would have to count on voters writing his name on the ballot. This hurt his own chances and allowed McCarthy and Kennedy to battle it out in primary state after state. Kennedy won most of those contests, including a narrow victory in California in early June, at the end of the primary season. Although he did not have enough delegates pledged to him to assure his nomination on the first ballot, Kennedy was clearly perceived to be the frontrunner. But that status was short-lived because Sirhan B. Sirhan shot the senator (who died the next day) in a Los Angeles hotel during a victory celebration on June 5. (He was apparently unhappy with Kennedy's pro-Israel position.)

The assassination of Kennedy left Humphrey as the frontrunner because he had gathered more delegates among regular party officials than McCarthy had in his primary victories. South Dakota Senator George McGovern, also a critic of the war, then entered the race at the last minute. The Democrats met for their convention in Chicago that August. And while the "peace" Democrats put up a tough but losing floor fight in support of an anti-war plank in the party platform, other critics of the war were demonstrating in the streets outside the convention. Chicago Mayor Richard J. Daley, a supporter of Humphrey, ordered his police department to use whatever means necessary to rid the streets of hippies and other Vietnam War protesters. While it now appears that both sides wanted a confrontation, an investigating committee later described the roughing up of protesters and other innocent bystanders a "police riot." In any case, Humphrey won the nomination on the first ballot and promptly named Maine Senator Edmund S. Muskie as his running mate. The chaotic events outside the convention hall convinced many Americans that the Democrats were not the party of "law and order." In short, the chances of the Republicans to regain control of the White House appeared very good indeed.

Richard Nixon and Spiro Agnew triumphantly accept the 1968 Republican nomination at the Republican National Convention. Credit: AP/Wide World Photos.

The Republicans met for their convention in Miami Beach, Florida in August. Former Vice-President Richard M. Nixon had been the frontrunner throughout the Republican primaries, although there were others seeking the nomination. Among the other candidates were Nelson Rockefeller, Hollywood actor Ronald Reagan, and Michigan Governor George Romney. Most Republicans seemed happy with Nixon and wanted to see if he could redeem himself after his very close loss to John Kennedy in 1960. So Richard Nixon won an easy nomination on the first ballot. He then surprisingly selected Maryland Governor Spiro T. Agnew as his choice for the vice-presidential nominee. Ironically, just six years earlier, after Nixon had lost the race for governor of California, he had told the press that "you won't have Nixon to kick around anymore, because, gentlemen, this is my last press conference." What a difference just six years can make.

Many Democrats and independents were disenchanted with the two party choices in 1968, so they rallied around Alabama Governor George C. Wallace, who ran with the American Independent Party label. Wallace was an avid segregationist who became a rallying point for those Americans who believed that the civil rights movement had gone too far. Wallace chose retired air force general Curtis LeMay, who had earlier expressed a desire to bomb North Vietnam back to the "stone age," earning him the nickname "bombs away LeMay."

The Campaign and Results

Early in the campaign the situation went from bad to worse for the Democrats. Believing that the vice-president was a certain loser, many of the regular contributers to Democratic candidates refused to donate to his campaign. And George Wallace was appealing to large numbers of blue collar and ethnic Democrats in the northern and midwestern big cities. After Humphrey finally put some distance between himself and President Johnson by announcing on September 30 that as president he would halt the bombing of North Vietnam in exchange for their promise to stop sending more troops into the South, Humphrey's campaign picked up momentum. Even Eugene McCarthy endorsed Humphrey late in October, declaring that the vice-president could be "relied on to tell the difference between the pale horse of death and the white horse of victory. I am not sure Nixon can make that distinction."

Nixon campaigned on the twin themes of "law and order" and "peace with honor." The first was a more subtle appeal than Wallace's to the white backlash against the violence in the black communities over the last few summers and the perceived excesses of the welfare system. The second slogan referred to his view that the Vietnam War should be gradually brought to an end through negotiations. Although the media picked up on his Vietnam views and reported that Nixon claimed to have a "secret plan" to end the war in Vietnam, it is unclear whether he ever used those words. Clearly, however, even on Vietnam, Nixon portrayed himself as the moderate candidate in the race, distancing himself from Humphrey, whom he identified with Johnson, and from the more extreme statements of Wallace and LeMay.

The longer the campaign continued the more that traditional Democrats were coming home to the Democratic Party. The electoral system had always made it more difficult for third party candidates. Thus, over time the anger of white ethnic Democrats who liked Wallace was replaced with realism. And given the record, few self-described Democratic voters would ever dare vote for Richard Nixon. Labor unions were influential also in informing their members that Wallace's labor record was hostile to unions and collective bargaining. So as the campaign neared its end, the Humphrey-Muskie ticket was fast closing the gap with Nixon. Most political experts later said that if the trend had continued and the election held just a couple of weeks later, Humphrey would have pulled off an upset victory. But that was not to be.

When the votes were counted in November, Richard Nixon had been elected the thirty-seventh president of the United States with about 31.8 million popular votes and 301 electoral votes. Humphrey finished a close second with 31.3 million popular votes and 191 electoral votes. George Wallace, although fading in the last few weeks of the campaign, managed to carry five deep South states and 46 electoral votes. In the final analysis, his nearly 10 million popular votes nationwide did take away just enough normally Democratic votes in certain key northern industrial states to deliver them into the electoral column for Nixon. It appears probable that without Wallace in the race, Hubert H. Humphrey would have been elected president of the United States.

1968	50	RICHARD M. NIXON	Republican	31,785,480	301	43.4
		Hubert H. Humphrey	Democrat	31,275,165	191	42.7
		George C. Wallace	American Independent	9,906,473	46	13.5

ADDITIONAL READINGS

Robert A. Divine, ed., *Exploring the Johnson Years* (1981). Includes several good essays on the War on Poverty and its relationship to the civil rights movement.

Todd Gitlin, *The Sixties: Years of Hope, Days of Rage* (1987). A political view of the protest movements. Outlines the sharp difference between the peaceful antiwar movement of the middle 1960s and the destructive turn of the student movements at the end of that decade.

Michael B. Katz, *In the Shadow of the Poorhouse: A Social History of Welfare in America* (1986). Offers an important historical perspective on the expansion of public assistance in the 1960s and 1970s. Katz is especially good on demonstrating how the great increase in federal entitlement spending went largely to the middle class, not the poor.

Joe McGinnis, *The Selling of the President* (1969). A look at the 1968 presidential election.

Doris Kearns, *Lyndon Johnson and the American Dream* (1976). A realistic look at the Johnson presidency.

Allen J. Matusow, *The Unraveling of America: A History of Liberalism in the 1960s* (1984). Offers a useful overview of the promises and failures of the Great Society.

James T. Patterson, *America's Struggle Against Poverty, 1900–1985* (1986). Provides a critical analysis of the War on Poverty in the historical context of other 20th century efforts to end poverty.

Arthur M. Schlesinger, Jr., *Robert Kennedy and His Times* (1978). A good examination of the president's brother.

Arthur M. Schlesinger, Jr., *A Thousand Days: John F. Kennedy in the White House* (1965). A favorable treatment of the Kennedy presidency.

CHAPTER SEVENTEEN

A Decade of Crises: The 1970s

MAJOR EVENTS

1969   Neil Armstrong becomes first man to walk on the moon
The Environmental Quality Policy Act

1970   The first Earth Day celebrated

1971   The 26th Amendment is ratified
Swann v. Charlotte-Mecklenburg Board of Education Supreme Court decision
Phases I and II of Nixon's Economic Policies

1972   *Ms.* magazine begins publication
Nixon becomes first President to visit Communist China
SALT I (Strategic Arms Limitation Talks) is signed
The Watergate Break-in
Nixon is re-elected president

1973   Incident at Wounded Knee, South Dakota
The War Powers Act
Roe v. Wade Supreme Court decision
Televised Watergate Hearings begin
"The Saturday Night Massacre"
Vice-President Spiro T. Agnew resigns in disgrace
Gerald R. Ford becomes vice-president under the 25th Amendment
The Yom Kippur War

1974   President Nixon resigns under impeachment threat
President Ford pardons Nixon

1975   The *Mayaguez* Incident

1976   Jimmy Carter is elected president

1977   The Department of Energy is created

1978   The Panama Canal Treaties are ratified
The Camp David Accords are signed by Egypt and Israel

1979   Nuclear accident at Three Mile Island in Pennsylvania
The Soviets invade Afghanistan
The Iranian Hostage Crisis begins

1980   Ronald Reagan is elected president

INTRODUCTION TO THE NIXON ADMINISTRATION

Richard Nixon, the thirty-seventh president of the United States, gave his inaugural address on January 20, 1969. He told the American people that they had to come together and resolve the problems that were dividing the nation—the Vietnam War, civil rights, and a disregard for law and order. He stated, "To go forward at all is to go forward together." He also put the nation on notice that foreign policy matters would be an important part of his presidency. "I have taken an oath today in the presence of God and my conscience: To uphold and defend the Constitution of the United States. And to that oath, I now add this sacred commitment: I shall consecrate my office, my energies and all the wisdom I can summon, to the cause of peace among nations." Americans remained divided on the issues, but the country was pleased enough with the president's handling of his office that he was re-elected in 1972. His administration scored some important successes, particularly in the area of foreign policy. But lies, cover-ups, and other illegal activities cut his second term short, and he became the first president in American history to resign.

Richard Nixon had been a success-oriented person for most of his life. Born on January 9, 1913, on a farm in Yorba Linda, California, the future president and his four brothers were raised by their mother as peace-loving members of the Quaker faith. Nixon was always a dedicated student, and in secondary school he excelled as a debater, a skill that remained with him and served him well in his political career. He was active in clubs and school politics in high school and in his college years. Popular enough to be elected president of his senior class at Whittier College (in California), Nixon had never really felt accepted by those in fraternities and by the wealthier students at the college. In reaction to this, he and a few others formed their own club, the Orthogonians, a club for students with limited financial resources and those who were not part of the "in" crowd. This feeling of non-acceptance haunted his public life and formed the basis for some of the actions as president that would prove to be his undoing. After graduating from Whittier College, Nixon pursued a law degree at the Duke University law school on a tuition scholarship. Once again he worked hard, both in the classroom for his grades and outside the classroom for his living expenses. He lived in an old farmhouse without running water or electricity because he could not afford better accomodations. His research job at the law library paid thirty-five cents an hour. In his final year at Duke, he was elected president of his graduating class.

Regardless of his third-place ranking in his graduating class, Nixon was not offered a position at a top firm. Once again it seemed to him as if his poor background worked against his chances for success and would continue in the future in law, politics, and social situations. In spite of his Quaker beliefs (Quakers are generally pacifists), he applied for, and was commissioned, as a lieutenant (junior grade) during World War II. After the war, he entered politics and was elected to the House of Representatives in 1946 and 1948. His performance on the House Un-American Activities Committee brought the young congressman national attention with his commitment to protect the United States from communism internally as well as externally. In his campaign for the Senate in 1950, Nixon attacked his Democratic opponent, Congresswoman Helen Gahagan Douglas, with the claim that she supported policies that were communistic. Nixon referred to Mrs. Douglas as the Pink Lady. Before and after his campaign for senator, he was known for his ruthless campaign style which had very few restraints on what he would do.

His firm stand against communism and his willingness to annihilate opponents were two of the reasons he was chosen by President Eisenhower as a running mate in both the 1952 and 1956 presidential elections. Following his eight years as vice-president, Nixon lost a very close contest for the presidency in 1960 and then the office of governor of California in 1962. He laid partial blame for his defeat in the gubernatorial race on what he called unfair coverage of the media. Showing bitterness toward the media right after that defeat, Nixon made the following remarks to them in a press conference: "But as I leave you I want you to know—just think how much you're going to be missing. You won't have Nixon to kick around any more, because, gentlemen, this is my last press conference . . . Thank you gentlemen and good day." It was not his last press conference, and enmity for the press and feelings of persecution by the media increased when he became president.

Most believed that Nixon's career in politics had come to an end in 1962, but this did not prove to be the case. In his televised speech to answer charges that he had a secret fund during the 1952 election for vice-president, he had stated, "I don't believe I ought to quit because I am not a quitter." Then, finally, in 1968, he was the voters' choice. Ending the war in Vietnam was the priority on his agenda. "Peace with honor" was necessary so the president could turn his attention to other foreign policy goals. Indeed, foreign policy was Nixon's passion, but he did not ignore domestic issues of the nation either. He had more success in foreign policy because he did not usually have to battle with Congress in this area as he did in domestic policy making. Partly to blame for his problems with Congress was the fact that he was the first president since 1849 to begin his administration with both the House and the Senate controlled by majorities of the opposite party. In his first year, Congress rejected 38 out of the president's 40 proposals. He had to work with Democratic majorities throughout his presidency, but for the most part, he learned to adapt.

DOMESTIC ISSUES UNDER NIXON

Social Welfare Programs

In 1968, Nixon had campaigned against the massive welfare programs of the Great Society and the large size of the federal government. He stated that he was against "pouring billions of dollars into programs that have failed." He was not against all social reform, but he did want to reduce the number of programs and support those that he believed would bring independence to the individual. In 1969 he proposed to Congress the Family Assistance Plan put together by Daniel Patrick Moynihan, head of the Council on Urban Affairs, and a Democrat. The plan would give $1,600 in annual income, along with food stamps worth $800, to a family of four on welfare. To qualify, heads of families had to register for job training and accept work if it was suitable. The bill was soon embroiled in political controversy, especially in the Senate, as conservatives argued that it was too much federal support for welfare, and liberals argued that it was a confusing package that did not go far enough to help the poor. However, a new federal food stamp program was implemented in 1970, which increased the allotment and decreased the price of the stamps.

Congress and the president agreed to a twenty percent increase in Social Security benefits in the summer of 1972. On October 30, 1972, an amendment to the Social Security Act increased benefits for the elderly by more than $5 billion and extended benefits to disabled Americans under the age of 65. Under the Nixon administration, the nation actually increased spending on social programs rather than reducing it as the president had planned.

NIXONOMICS

Stagflation: the Impossible Possibility

From 1947 to 1967 the American economy had prospered as the Gross National Product (GNP) increased annually. Productivity per man-hour grew at an average annual rate of close to 3 percent, and unemployment was below 4 percent, which was a good sign of a healthy economy. American exports had increased from close to $4 billion in 1945 to approximately $180 billion by the beginning of the 1970s. However, in spite of a consistently good economy, an increase in income, and a high standard of living, there were major flaws in the economy, flaws which few people registered until the country was feeling the consequences. The economy entered an extremely unusual state that later became known as "stagflation." It was based on two words, "stagnant" and "inflation," with the first referring to stagnant, or declining, production, and the second referring to rapidly rising prices. It had been previously considered impossible for high unemployment and high inflation to exist simultaneously, but the experts accepted that it was indeed happening in the seventies. Unemployment rose from a little over 3 percent in 1969 to close to 6 percent in 1970. In 1971, the inflation rate was at 4.5 percent, which was the highest level since World War II. By early 1973, the inflation rate stood at 8 percent. Nixon, basically a conservative in economics (he believed in a balanced budget and less federal government intervention in the economy), would have to use a combination of interventionist and more liberal measures in his attempt to bring back a strong economy in both of his terms.

Reasons for Economic Stagnation

By the late 1960s, the United States was faced with strong international competition for markets from other industrial countries, particularly Japan and West Germany, which had finally recovered from the economic devastation of World War II. By the early seventies, West Germany and Japan had replaced the United States as the number one exporters of the highest quality steel. Those same two nations also surged ahead in the marketing of high technology electronic products, such as televisions, radios, cameras, and computers. And Japanese automobiles imported into the United States were also threatening American industry. Adding to the problem of competition was the naive supposition that America would always be economically superior to all other nations, and many industrial leaders were slow to utilize new technologies and adopt new ways of producing their products. For the first time since 1893, American imports exceeded exports in 1971, a condition which has prevailed in each subsequent year. This fundamental problem helped increase unemployment, as many of the better, high-paying jobs were lost to our competitors. Adding to the pressure toward more unemployment was the fact that baby boomers had reached the age where they were looking for fulltime work. And at the same time, more women, influenced by the modern women's movement, also began entering the job market.

Reasons for High Inflation

President Johnson's acceptance of large deficits, which included simply printing more money, in order to fight the war in Vietnam and continue the spending for his Great Society without a corresponding tax increase contributed to the economic problems of the 1970s. Increased consumer demand for goods and services compelled suppliers to raise prices. This occurred partly because productivity per manhour had declined to the point that supply could not keep up with demand. Therefore, inflation began to threaten the economy. And trouble in the Middle East in the seventies would bring retaliation from the Organization of Petroleum Exporting Countries (OPEC), which would suddenly and massively raise the price of crude oil and send American inflation rates through the ceiling. Once that inflation danger had risen sharply, then unions demanded higher wages to keep up with inflation, which were then reflected in still higher prices, creating what economists call a wage-price spiral.

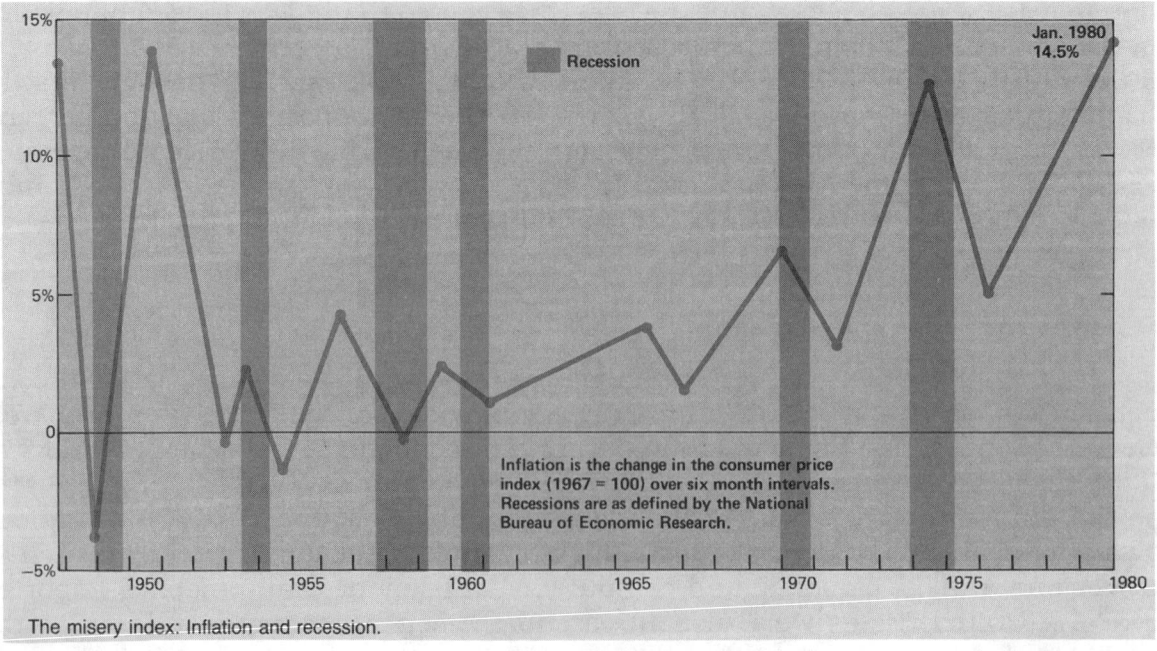

The misery index: Inflation and recession.

Inflation and Recession. Credit: The United States: Combined Edition, *by Winthrop D. Jordan and Leon F. Litwack, Prentice-Hall, Inc., 1991.*

Nixon's Early Reaction

To fight inflation, Nixon managed to balance the federal budget in 1969 through significant spending cuts. After 1969, however, the Democratic controlled Congress rejected such efforts. The Federal Reserve Board also followed Nixon's suggestion to increase interest rates in order to reduce consumer spending, and thereby inflation. But these measures did not work, and by 1971, the economy was in its first recession since 1960. Clearly, it was time for a change in policy. In early 1971, the president who believed in balanced budgets announced, "I am now a Keynesian." Keynesian economists, followers of British economist John Maynard Keynes, whose ideas had been promulgated during the Great Depression, proposed that it was acceptable for governments to stimulate economies with deficit spending. Politically, Nixon could not afford a recession, so he accepted deficit government spending in order to fight a recession. He still refused to consider controls on prices and wages as he had when asked if he would consider controls in 1969. Nixon had worked as a lawyer for the Office of Price Administration (OPA) during World War II, and from that experience he believed that government-imposed price controls should not be used.

Phase I

Suddenly, on August 15, 1971, Nixon changed his stand and included government enforced price and wage controls in what he called Phase I of his "New Economic Policy." First, the problem of the imbalance of trade was addressed when Nixon stated the United States would no longer convert dollars into gold for foreign banks. Without the foundation of converting American dollars to gold at $35 an ounce, foreign currencies were forced to "float" against each other to set their value. This step officially took the United States off the gold standard, cheapened the price of the American dollar, and led to a reduction in the price of American goods sold abroad. A 10 percent surcharge on imports was added to make the price of American goods at home more competitive. Working toward assistance for Americans, businesses could earn a 10 percent tax credit for investments in new plants and equipment. Finally, Nixon placed a 90-day freeze on wages, prices, and rents as a means to slow inflation. This plan, motivated in part by politics, boosted Nixon's popularity in preparation for the 1972 elections. Phase I measures, along with Federal Reserve Board Chairman Arthur Burns' decision to increase the money supply by lowering the discount rate, greatly increased inflation, which was more acceptable than recession. Nixonomics had some measure of success in the short term, but unemployment and inflation rose again in 1973.

Using government resources to stimulate the economy, Congress passed the Public Service Act in July 1971 with $2.5 billion to create from 150,000 to 200,000 new jobs. The following month the public works program was given $2.5 billion for public building projects.

Along with fiscal and monetary policies to bring economic stability, Nixon implemented a new direction for economic relations between the federal government and the states known as "New Federalism," which was also one of the labels for his domestic program. The Revenue Sharing Act, passed in October 1972, sent federal dollars to the states, with fewer strings attached on how the money was to be spent. Nixon believed that state and local governments could administer more programs more efficiently and cost effectively.

Phase II

On November 14, 1971, the second phase of Nixon's economic plan called for flexible guidelines for wage and price increases, but a ceiling was placed on the increases. Increases would be allowed if they were offset by improvements that would make a company more productive. A Cost of Living Council was organized to make sure the guidelines for Phase II were followed.

A POTPOURRI OF NEW LAWS AND OTHER CHANGES

The Environment

In his State of the Union Message in January 1970, President Nixon urged Americans to "begin to make reparations for the damage we have done to our air, to our land and to our waters." Ceremonies and gatherings across the nation for the first national Earth Day on April 22, 1970 signaled that protection of the environment had been added to the public agenda. Nixon was certainly not an environmentalist, but he realized that some protection of the environment was necessary, and he also realized that this issue was gaining in importance to the nation and it would be politically advantageous to push for quick government action.

The Environmental Quality Policy Act, passed in 1969, required every new federal program to file an environmental impact statement before commencing operation. However, more legislation would be needed to control, if not eliminate, pollution. The Environmental Protection Agency (EPA) was established in July 1970 by executive order and activated in December as the agency that would enforce the nation's environmental agenda. Recycling was encouraged by the Resource Recovery Act of 1970. On December 31, 1970, Nixon signed the National Air Quality Standards Act, which increased the standards for cleaner air and demanded that pollution from automobile exhaust decrease by 1975.

The Water Pollution Control Act was passed by Congress on October 12, 1972, but this law had to be enacted over the president's veto. More stringent restrictions were set in the various industries for the dumping of waste into waterways; the federal government would also provide funds for waste treatment plants. Fear of the extra costs that would be added to goods because of the expense of complying with the Water Pollution Control Act had resulted in the president's veto. Liberals and active environmentalists believed he was not pressing for enough legislation, but he was going to take a somewhat middle-of-the-road attitude on the issue. Then on December 31, 1972, the EPA declared a ban on the use of DDT pesticides, a full decade after Rachel Carson's exposé (*Silent Spring*) had been published.

Earth Day Celebrations in Philadelphia on April 22, 1970. Credit: AP/Wide World Photos.

Governmental Changes

Representation of the District of Columbia in the national Congress was signed into law on September 22, 1970. A non-voting delegate would sit in the House of Representatives, allowing limited representation for the first time since 1875.

Problems and a lack of efficiency in the United States Postal System led Congress, with President Nixon's support, to transfer the Post Office from a cabinet position to an independent agency on August 12, 1970.

Safety in the workplace, a concern of workers since the Industrial Age, and pushed for by organized labor, was assisted in 1970 with the creation of the Occupational Health and Safety Administration (OSHA). The purpose of OSHA was to develop and enforce standards for the various and sometimes hazardous work environments.

New Voters and Campaign Laws

In 1970, the Democrats in Congress passed a federal law which gave the right to vote to 18-year-old citizens in national elections. Then Congress passed the Twenty-sixth Amendment to the Constitution in March 1971, which was ratified three months later, giving 18-year-olds the right to vote in all elections. It had not seemed fair to ask young men to die for their country and yet not have a say in the government of their nation. Approximately 11 million new voters between the ages of 18 and 21 were eligible to vote by the end of the year. It was believed that the 18-year-old vote would be of great benefit to Democratic Senator George McGovern, who opposed American involvement in the Vietnam War and ran against Nixon in the 1972 presidential election, but that did not prove to be the case.

The War Powers Act

In response to Nixon's almost limitless use of power to wage war in South Vietnam, Congress passed the War Powers Act in November 1973, but again only over the president's veto. The law required the president to consult with Congress before committing troops to combat overseas and to withdraw the troops at the end of 60 days if Congress refused to extend approval to the commitment.

LAW AND ORDER AND THE SUPREME COURT

Federal Anti-Crime Legislation

Restoration of "law and order" had been a major theme during Nixon's campaign for the presidency in 1968. And as president, he pressured Congress for stronger legislation to fight crime, and he appointed more conservative justices to the Supreme Court. On October 15, 1970, Nixon declared war on organized crime by signing the Organized Crime Control Act. With this law, penalties for "dangerous special offenders" would be more severe. The Drug Abuse Control Act of 1970 was enacted as part of the plan to reduce the growing drug abuse problem in the nation. Penalties were reduced for those who possessed drugs, but penalties were increased for selling drugs. The controversial "no-knock" provision of the new law allowed law enforcement agents to break into any area in which they believed illegal drugs were present without announcing their presence or obtaining a search warrant. While civil libertarians expressed concern for possible weakening of the First Amendment, most Americans believed that the "no-knock" policy was necessary to prevent the destruction of the evidence on the site.

The Supreme Court

The opportunity to take the Supreme Court in a more conservative direction began with the swearing in of Warren Burger as the new Chief Justice of the Supreme Court on June 23, 1969. Nixon was intent on placing justices with more strict constructionist and traditional views concerning the interpretation of the Constitution on the bench of the nation's highest court, and he wanted southern justices on the bench to assist his political career through the so-called "Southern strategy." It was hoped that more conservative constructionist justices would reverse the liberal judicial activism of the Warren Court with regard to desegregation in the public schools and the rights of the accused. Nixon filled three other vacancies on the Court, beginning with Harry Blackmun. Burger and Blackmun were nicknamed the "Minnesota twins" because of their friendship in their hometown of St. Paul, Minnesota, and their similar judicial views. Lewis F. Powell, Jr., a southerner from Virginia, and William Rehnquinst from Arizona, were the other confirmed candidates.

Nixon had hoped to give the South more representation on the Court to gain supporters from this region and because the South was under-represented in top federal appointments, but his first two southern nominations were not confirmed. Clement Haynsworth, a Fourth Circuit Appeals Judge from South Carolina, was denied the nomination by the Senate in 1969. Claims that Haynsworth was both racist and anti-labor, along with charges that he had sat on a case in which he had a small financial interest in the company involved, finally caused the Senate to vote "no" on his confirmation. After that, Nixon followed Haynsworth's rejection with another selection from the South, G. Harrold Carswell of Florida, a judge on the bench of the Fifth Circuit Court of Appeals. The Senate rejected Carswell, who had admitted to beliefs in white supremacy in his early political career, and whose decisions were frequently overturned by superior courts. In both the Haynsworth and Carswell nominations, civil rights organizations and the AFL-CIO had lobbied strenuously and successfully for their defeat. Nixon's failure to place his early choices on the bench was a failure for his influence on Congress, but his persistent efforts for a southern justice did garner support for him in the South.

The court did move in a more conservative direction, but not all its decisions reflected President Nixon's positions. For example, Nixon believed that the Supreme Court decisions to end segregation in the nation's public schools should be implemented, but he also believed that this change should be made more slowly so that the violence and the disruption to education that sometimes resulted from this policy were minimized. In 1969, the Court decided that segregation must come to a quick end with its decision in *Alexander v. Holmes County Board of Education.* Then in April 1971, in *Swann v. Charlotte-Mecklenburg Board of Education*, the Court ruled that the busing of students from different sections of a city could be used to integrate schools. Busing was opposed by citizens in the South as well as in the North and brought division, and sometimes violence, to prevent busing in many cities in which it was ordered by the federal courts. In 1972, Nixon signed a bill that barred the implementation of busing orders from federal courts until all appeals had been exhausted. Nixon's stand brought criticism from the NAACP and from lawyers in the Justice Department, but desegregation under Nixon proceeded in a less confrontational manner to white Americans, whose political support the president wanted. By 1972, close to 90 percent of African-American students attended integrated schools in the South.

In *Furman v. Georgia* (1972), the Supreme Court ruled that the death penalty laws of the states were unfair because the death penalty was falling disporportionately on the poor and minorities, with too much discretion for juries on sentencing;

therefore, they must be rewritten. Conservatives decried the decision because of their tendency to support the death penalty as a deterrent to crime, but liberals agreed that if society was going to impose the death penalty, that it must do so in an even-handed manner. Then on June 19, 1972, the Supreme Court ruled, in *United States v. U.S. District Court, Eastern Michigan*, that the government did not have the right to tap the phones of alleged subversives or domestic radicals without a court order.

Attacks on Protestors and the Media

Protestors of the Vietnam War, radicals, and the press were perceived as enemies of not only Nixon but the nation. Nixon believed that he stood for what was right and good in America, so to dispute his opinions and programs was un-American. Following the Kent State shootings in May 1970, the student protest movement began to slowly dissipate. (See Chapter Thirteen.) Vice-President Spiro Agnew was the spokesman for the administration's verbal attacks against the protestors and the press. Agnew labeled those who protested the war as "anarchists and ideological eunuchs." The news media was considered liberal and "nattering nabobs of negativism."

MAN REACHES THE MOON AND CONTINUES SPACE EXPLORATION

Following the Gemini Project (See Chapter Sixteen), Project Apollo began in late 1966 as the program to land a man on the moon. The new phase got off to a tragic start in January 1967 when astronauts Virgil Grissom, Edward White, and Roger Chaffee were killed in a fire aboard *Apollo I* while still on the ground at Cape Kennedy, Florida. Although this delayed the first Apollo mission until October 1968, three astronauts on board *Apollo 8* did succeed in orbiting the moon on Christmas Day 1968. Other practice missions in early 1969 perfected the procedures, and NASA seemed ready to launch its mission of an actual moon landing by that summer.

On July 20, 1969, the dream began in the term of President Kennedy, and the culmination of thousands of hours of work on previous missions and millions of dollars, was realized. Millions of Americans watched on television as Neil Armstrong stepped from the *Eagle*, a lunar landing module from the *Apollo 11* spacecraft, into his place in history as the first man to step on the moon. Armstrong transmitted the first words spoken from the moon as he stepped onto its surface: "That's one small step for man, one giant leap for mankind." Before returning to their spacecraft, Armstrong and his fellow astronaut Colonel Edwin "Buzz" Aldrin (Lieutenant Colonel Michael Collins was left in control of the *Columbia*, which was orbiting the moon) placed an American flag, a lunar capsule, and a plaque on the cold dark surface. The plaque declared, "Here men from the planet Earth first set foot upon the moon July, 1969, AD. We came in peace for all mankind."

The landing on the moon was a great moment in exploration of the space frontier, and an American victory over the Russians, but the work did not stop there. In November 1969, astronauts Charles Conrad, Jr. and Alan Bean, from the *Apollo*

The Historic Apollo II Lunar Landing Mission, 1969. Credit: AP/Wide World Photos

12, spent close to thirty-two hours on the moon's surface. In other space news, the *Mariner 7* transmitted pictures of the planet Mars to earth in August 1969. In a continuation of a manned space program, NASA undertook the launching of *Skylab* in 1973, with the idea that it would become a permanent orbiting space station around the earth. Trouble with its solar panels resulted in a gradual loss of electric power to *Skylab,* and for the next several years it began to lose its orbit. Finally, *Skylab* lost orbit altogether and crashed to the earth in July 1979. The Space Transportation Service (STS), or shuttle, was developed in the seventies as the major new direction for manned space flight. The idea of the shuttle was to devise a craft which would be lifted off by rocket but be able to land as a jet airplane. This would save NASA large amounts of money because the shuttle could be reused. It would not be until 1981 that a shuttle craft would be successfully launched and landed.

THE 1972 ELECTION

The Candidates and Platforms

In the early Democratic primaries, Senator Edmund Muskie of Maine, Senator George McGovern of South Dakota, and Senator Hubert Humphrey of Minnesota were the front runners. Muskie was out of the race, although he still claimed he was a candidate, when shortly after his win in the New Hampshire primary, he was brought to tears by slurs repeated by the media. If name-calling and dirty tricks in a campaign could bring Muskie to tears, many Americans wondered how he would react to the criticism of Congress and the public that was frequently aimed at the president.

President Nixon was more concerned with the candidacy of George Wallace than George McGovern. If Wallace put together a successful campaign as a Democratic candidate in 1972, he would most likely receive many votes from conservatives in the Sun Belt states and "law and order" conservatives from other areas that Nixon was confident would vote Republican otherwise. But Wallace had to withdraw his candidacy when he was shot while campaigning at a shopping center during the Maryland Democratic primary. The attempted assassination permanently paralyzed him from the waist down.

When Humphrey dropped out of the campaign after his loss to McGovern in the California primary, McGovern's nomination was ensured. Indeed, George McGovern was chosen on the first ballot by the Democratic National Convention in July 1972. Senator Henry M. "Scoop" Jackson of Washington State was a distant second choice, winning the votes of those delegates at the convention who were pro-organized labor. The Democratic platform called for an immediate withdrawal of American troops from Southeast Asia, a reduction in defense spending, desegregation with busing if necessary, tax reform, an end to the death penalty, a ban on handguns, and more participation from Congress on the decisions that affected war and peace.

The McGovern campaign was in serious trouble almost immediately after the convention had ended, when it was revealed by the press that his running mate, Senator Thomas F. Eagleton of Missouri, had previously undergone electric shock therapy for depression. At first, McGovern stated he stood behind his choice for vice-president "1,000 percent," but he quickly changed his mind and chose F. Sargent Shriver to replace the politically negative Eagleton. Shriver was a Kennedy brother-in-law and a former director of the Peace Corps.

President Nixon was the overwhelmingly popular choice of the Republican convention for "Four More Years." Nixon's strategy to win in 1972 was to appeal to the conservative coalition he had been focusing most of his programs on since the 1968 election and during his first administration. In the 1968 election, Kevin Phillips, an assistant to campaign manager John Mitchell, revealed his theory that the time was ripe to build a new conservative majority with conservative Republicans and conservative Democrats disillusioned with the liberal direction of the Democratic Party and domination by the intellectual elite and liberal media of the Northeast. According to Phillips' "Southern Strategy," a new alliance should be formed, consisting of socially conservative Roman Catholic blue collar workers, white southerners, those living in the suburbs of the Sun Belt states of California, New Mexico, Arizona, Texas, and Oklahoma, and the average white middle class American. Nixon labeled middle class Americans the "silent majority" in a speech in 1969. It was obvious from the success of third party candidate George Wallace, a conservative Democrat who had run as an independent in 1968, that there were a great many Democrats who disagreed with their party. In 1972 Nixon focused much of his efforts toward winning the supporters of George Wallace. The "Southern Strategy" included a slower paced plan for desegregation in the South, more autonomy for the citizens of the southern states on the methods of desegregation, opposition to the idea of busing students, and placing more Southerners on the Supreme Court. He appealed to all supporters with plans for law and order and by appealing to the work ethic and patriotism of many Americans.

The Republican platform opposed busing to bring about integration, national health insurance, and withdrawing completely from Vietnam without the release of all prisoners of war. The platform supported a volunteer army, full employment, and an end to the arms race.

The Campaign and Results

The Republicans painted McGovern as a radical liberal who would stain the national honor by withdrawing from Vietnam without negotiating a successful peace accord, spend too much money on welfare programs, and protect the criminals more than the public. McGovern criticized the dirty tricks and lies of the Nixon campaign, but few wanted to listen even when it was discovered that there had been a break-in at the Democratic National Headquarters in the Watergate complex in Washington, D.C. on June 17, 1972. The five intruders were caught trying to place wiretaps on the phones and install hidden video recording equipment. It was quickly discovered that the five burglars had been paid by the Committee to Reelect the President to gather information on the Democratic campaign. The official message from the White House regarding the incident was that the president and his staff had no knowledge of the affair. The public believed the statement, and the incident was ignored by most at the time. As more information came to light from trials and more intensive investigations, the White House and the president were brought into the affair.

During the campaign, Nixon was able to point to his foreign policy successes of arms limitations with the Soviet Union, opening relations between the United States and the People's Republic of China, and withdrawing thousands of troops from the war in Vietnam. It was a boost to his campaign when a few weeks before the elections, Henry A. Kissinger, Nixon's National Security Advisor, announced that "peace was at hand" in the Paris peace talks with North Vietnam. The economy was also on an upswing in the spring and summer of 1972. Along with accentuating the positive aspects of Nixon, the campaign was fortunate that the Democrats were so divided at the time, that McGovern's ideas were believed to be radical, and that the Watergate affair was not given more attention once the president denied any knowledge by the White House of the burglary. Further investigations of Watergate would destroy this great victory.

Nixon won a landslide victory with 61 percent of the popular vote and 521 electoral votes to McGovern's 17, but once again a Democratic majority was sent to Congress. Like the victories of the Eisenhower-Nixon team in the 1950s, the results in 1972 gave Nixon a personal victory but not a party victory. The president would have to continue working with the opposition party during his second term.

NIXONOMICS IN THE SECOND TERM

Phase III

In January 1973, President Nixon put into place Phase III of his economic plan. Mandatory wage and price controls were dropped, except for food, health, and housing. In all other areas of pricing decisions, the administration hoped that businesses would voluntarily follow anti-inflation guidelines and keep prices level. But when prices continued to climb, the president tightened price controls again in May, imposing restrictions on six hundred companies to give thirty days' notice of any price increases that could raise average prices more than 1.5 percent above the January level.

The president disagreed with Congress on the amount of money spent on federal programs during a time of economic difficulty and rising deficits. During his second term, he began to impound (refuse to spend) money appropriated for federal programs in order to curb government spending.

Phase IV

On June 13, 1973, President Nixon froze all retail prices once again for sixty days. A new system of economic controls would be prepared when the sixty days ended, controls which focused on stabilizing the prices of food and gasoline.

THE WOMEN'S MOVEMENT DURING THE NIXON ADMINISTRATION

Women advocates continued to work for occupational, social, legislative, and economic equality in the 1970s, building upon the gains made in the 1960s to change the status of women. The women's movement was diverse in its supporters and the goals of those supporters, but nonetheless, the unfair treatment of women in American society was revealed, and attempts to remedy the situation came in many forms. The consciousness level of women was raised by joining small groups, joining more organized and larger groups, or merely watching and listening as more information became available. Activist Gloria Steinem began publication of *Ms.*

1972	50	RICHARD M. NIXON*	Republican	47,165,234	520	60.6
		George S. McGovern	Democrat	29,168,110	17	37.5

*Resigned August 9, 1974: Vice President Gerald R. Ford became President.

magazine in 1972, and NOW membership climbed to about 50,000 in 1975. School textbooks were revised to eliminate many of the sexual sterotypes, and colleges were putting women's studies progams into the curriculum. There were opponents to the movement to change the role and status of women. Working class and African-American women had little use for the feminists. Stay-at-home wives and mothers believed that the radicals in the movement belittled women who chose not to go into the workforce as somehow useless and not living up to their potential. The feminists won more support from men and women in the 1970s when more moderate voices were heard in the movement.

Legislation in the seventies advanced the equal treatment of women. Title IX of the Education Amendments Act of 1972 prohibited discrimination on account of sex in education programs receiving federal funds. The Revenue Act of 1972 provided tax credits for child care expenses. An earlier disappointment for working women, who had hoped for good day care facilities organized by the federal government, came when President Nixon vetoed a 1971 bill for a national system of day care facilities. Nixon believed that bringing government into the child care process was too much interference in the family's child rearing responsibility. The affirmative action policies of the government, which were designed to reverse the effects of the long years of discrimination through the recruitment of minorities by federal contractors, was another method used to bring equality to women.

The Equal Rights Amendment

Because all of the laws passed could be negated by the federal courts, or by other laws, for years an amendment to the Constitution had been the goal to guarantee equality. An Equal Rights Amendment (ERA) to the Constitution, first proposed in 1923 by Alice Paul and endorsed by the National Organization for Women (NOW), was passed by Congress in 1972 and sent on to the states for ratification. The proposed amendment simply stated, "Equality of rights under the law shall not be denied or abridged by the United States or any state on account of sex." It was believed that these simple words would guarantee equal treatment for women. The ERA was approved by 33 of the 38 states necessary for passage by 1974.

In the meantime, conservative groups organized to "Stop-ERA" because of a perceived threat to the role of the American woman and family values. Phyllis Schlafly, a Roman Catholic lay person and lawyer, was a prominent leader in the fight to stop the amendment, constantly professing that the role of wife and mother would be threatened if the amendment passed. Conservative opponents often argued that the adoption of the ERA would bring an end to separate restroom facilities in public places, the drafting of women into the military, and the complete integration of women into the armed services, including combat units. Many others opposed the amendment because they believed it would mostly benefit the feminists, who were considered as too radical in their views and demands. The amendment did not pass even after Congress, in 1979, granted a time extension for ratification to 1982. Although the ERA did not pass, that did not mean that women or the government stopped working toward equality in all areas. Congress passed the Equal

Credit Opportunity Act in 1974, which forced banks to treat men and women equally with regard to loans and the obtaining of credit cards.

The Supreme Court Aids the Women's Movement

The Supreme Court added to the success of the women's movement with protection for the rights of women against governmental interference. In the case of *Reed v. Reed* (1971), the Supreme Court ruled that any restrictions against women on the basis of gender "must be rational, not arbitrary." In 1973, in *Roe v. Wade*, the Court ruled that the states could not infringe on a woman's right to privacy with laws that prohibited abortions in the first trimester. Only in the final trimester could the states absolutely deny abortions. The Court ruling was heralded as a major victory by feminists, but a "right to life" movement resulted from the Court's decision that would grow into another divisive and highly emotional issue for years to come.

AMERICAN INDIANS PUSH FOR CHANGES IN POLICIES

Government policy toward the American Indian has been a mixture of intervention and neglect, depending on the philosophy at the time of what was best for white society. In the 1950s, the federal government decided the best place for most Native Americans was off the reservations and assimilated into white uban society. Thus, the termination of the reservations was the goal. The termination policy was a disaster, however, as most of those who left their reservations faced poverty and discrimination, and without the support of other tribal members, life was more miserable than on the rundown reservations. In the 1960s, Native Americans joined other minority groups to work for their own place in American society. A call for "red power" was the opening of the attempts to regain territory, rights, dignity, and control of their own destiny. (See Chapter Fourteen for a discussion of Native American policies in the fifties and sixties.)

Then in the 1970s, tribes began suing states for the return of territory that had been illegally seized, and won their cases in Oklahoma, New Mexico, and Washington. Burial grounds and some fishing and timber rights were returned to the tribes. Presidents Kennedy and Johnson agreed that the policy of termination was unacceptable and that the tribes should have more control over the decisions governing their reservations. Native Americans encouraged each other to preserve their individual cultures. In 1974, Congress passed the Indian Self-Determination and Cultural Assistance Act. The act increased the control of the tribes over federal programs on the reservations, including the schools.

In the attempts to bring about change, there were those who used confrontational methods. In 1968 the American Indian Movement (AIM) was organized. Members of the Chippewa tribe in Minnesota formed the organization to protest the treatment of tribal members by the Minneapolis, Minnesota police department and demand equal justice. In late 1969, a small group of activists had landed on the unoccupied Alcatraz Island, the famous prison known as "the Rock;" the occupation did not end until 1971. AIM members also organized a march on Washington in 1971, called the "Trail of Broken Treaties." The members of the march took over the offices of the Bureau of Indian Affairs for a short time, but failed to accomplish anything meaningful.

Incident at Wounded Knee

On February 27, 1973, Wounded Knee, South Dakota was the site of another confrontation between American Indians and the United States government. Wounded Knee was the site of a massacre of Sioux by soldiers in December 1890. (See Chapter Two.) About 200 armed members of AIM and local supporters seized the small town of Wounded Knee on the Oglala Sioux Reservation to bring the government to the bargaining table on issues of concern. The protesters took local hostages and demanded a review of the rights of the tribes in 371 treaties and an investigation of the Bureau of Indian Affairs. There were also charges of corruption and mismanagement of funds against the federal government and tribal officials on the reservation. The small town was quickly surrounded by the FBI, federal marshals, and police of the Bureau of Indian Affairs. During the siege, two of the protestors were killed after gunfire between the two sides commenced. Efforts from outside sources to assist the protestors with food, clothing, and medical supplies were not allowed. The siege ended after 71 days when the government agreed to investigate Indian affairs and examine the 1868 treaty establishing the rights of the Sioux in South Dakota, but 120 of the protestors were arrested.

The 1868 treaty was declared valid, but the rule of "eminent domain" gave the government the authority to take land set aside by treaties. The second battle at Wounded Knee exposed the bleak existence of the residents on the reservations. Studies conducted by magazines and newspapers revealed that of the $8,000 average annual federal appropriation for Oglala families, only $1,900 made it into the hands of those it was intended for; payments for administration took most of the money. The high school dropout rate on the reservations was around 80 percent, the unemployment rate was running close to 50 percent, and alcoholism was a serious problem. After the incident at Wounded Knee, the movement settled into bringing about change by focusing on the pride of the old cultures and the desire to succeed in spite of the barriers of white society.

AFRICAN-AMERICANS AND THE POLITICAL SYSTEM

In the 1970s, African-Americans began to work for change to a greater degree within the political system. On March 10, 1972, approximately 3,000 delegates attended the first National Black Political Convention in Gary, Indiana. The delegates came from a variety of sources, including civil rights groups, the Nixon administration, the Black Panthers, the business community, elected officials, organized labor, and others. The major focus of the group was to unify African-Americans across the nation to gain political power to implement the changes still needed. It was decided that the convention would meet every four years before the regular party conventions, although that goal was not implemented for very long.

The civil rights struggle in the seventies concentrated its efforts on voter registration in order to elect more African-Americans to public office. And although they did not draw much media attention, African-Americans were elected at all levels of government in record numbers, from the mayor's office in several cities to state legislatures and the United States Congress.

FOREIGN AFFAIRS UNDER NIXON
RELATIONS WITH THE SOVIET UNION

Nixon's Philosophy and Strategy

President Nixon and his National Security Advisor Henry Kissinger, a political science professor from Harvard and a foreign policy advisor to Kennedy and Johnson, formulated the foreign policy directions for the country. Secretary of State William Rogers and Secretary of Defense Melvin Laird frequently were left out of the secret machinations of Nixon and Kissinger. Foreign policy was an area of longstanding interest for the president, and he intended to act as his own Secretary of State and leave his mark on history. For Nixon, ending American involvement in Vietnam with a peace of honor was at the top of his agenda. (See Chapter Thirteen.) To bring security to the world, he would also work towards arms reduction in the United States and other nations (he knew Congress did not want to support a continuing arms race). Finally, his foreign policy hopes were detente with the Soviet Union and normalizing relations with the People's Republic of China (Communist China, or Red China). Detente is a French word used in foreign policy to refer to the thawing of tensions between two or more nations. Good relations with the Soviets and the Communist Chinese would allow the United States to urge these two nations to stop supporting the North Vietnamese war efforts, and to use their influence on the North Vietnamese to come to agreeable peace terms to end the war.

Nixon also believed that the timing was good for the United States to become friendlier with these two communist superpowers in order to form a triangular balance of power by using America as the leverage against either nation if there were a threat to American or world security from the actions of the other. In the 1960s, skirmishes on the Sino-Soviet border had seriously damaged the good relations between Communist China and the Soviet Union, and the split was used by Nixon to the advantage of the United States. Nixon's negotiating with the communist nations brought very little criticism from Americans because of his longtime hard line stand against communism.

Detente and the SALT Talks

The United States and the Soviet Union sent representatives to Helsinki, Finland on November 17, 1969, to begin the preliminaries for further Strategic Arms Limitation Talks (SALT). During the talks, the two nations signed the United Nations Nuclear Nonproliferation Treaty. This treaty was an agreement for those nations who had the knowledge to closely guard that technical knowledge of how to make and launch nuclear weapons and to not release the material for others to engage in nuclear weapons production. On April 16, 1970, SALT negotiations continued in Vienna, Austria.

There were still areas of tensions between the two nations that Nixon hoped to ease before traveling to Moscow and furthering detente personally. In September 1971, the Soviets guaranteed that the nations of the West would have open access to West Berlin, an area of conflict since the end of World War II. The United States reciprocated with the guarantee that West Germany would not incorporate West Berlin, which was in East Germany. Another sign of good will was the announcement that the United States would sell close to $136 million in grain to the Soviet Union.

President Nixon arrived in Moscow to sign the Strategic Arms Limitation Treaty (SALT I) with Soviet leader Leonid Brezhnev on May 26, 1972. Actually, two agreements were signed. One limited the number of intercontinental ballistic missiles (ICBMs) to those under construction or those in place at that time. The number of ICBMs on submarines were also frozen at current levels. The second limited the construction of antiballistic missile sites, which were defensive systems, to two for each nation. With no limitations put on new weapons systems and no on-site inspections, SALT I still managed to produce a beginning for detente by bringing a rough balance of power between the two nations with arms control rather than disarmament. The treaty was beneficial to the Soviets as well as the United States, but it was not an end to weapons build-ups and suspicions from both sides. But the Soviets could reduce military spending, which would allow more attention to be paid to their sagging economy, and the new trade agreements brought in greatly needed shipments of American grains. This was a great coup for Nixon, especially in an election year.

Brezhnev visited the United States in June 1973 for another summit. Brezhnev and Nixon agreed to continue talks on limiting strategic offensive weapons, to work to avoid nuclear conflict, to restrain using or threatening to use force against each other, and to open dialogue if dangerous situations appeared to be developing. SALT negotiations continued during the terms of the next presidents.

LATIN AMERICAN RELATIONS

In Latin American policy, the Nixon administration had two major priorities. One was to keep Cuba isolated and the other was to destabilize or eliminate governments that contained communist elements when it was possible to use covert operations. The latter objective was contrary to Franklin Roosevelt's Good Neighbor policy (See Chapter Eleven), but it was the Cold War application of Theodore Roosevelt's Corollary to the Monroe Doctrine, in which the United States claimed the right to act as the policeman for Latin America.

With the election of the Marxist candidate Salvador Allende in Chile in 1970, nationalization of much of the nation's resources, industry, and land impacted negatively upon American investments in that country, along with those of upper and middle class Chileans. Nixon and Kissinger worked in secret with the CIA to rid the hemisphere of this Marxist regime. The Chilean economy was in shambles, and the United States was using its influence to keep it that way while the CIA was giving money to opposition groups and courting army officials who wanted a change in the government. In September 1973, the army overthrew Allende, and he was killed when the presidential palace was stormed. The official report from Chile was that Allende committed suicide. General Augusto Pinochet replaced Allende. President Nixon and Kissinger, who had been named Secretary of State for Nixon's second term, congratulated themselves on their ability to still control the internal events in Latin American nations. What they had actually done was to put into place a brutal military regime responsible for murdering, in some estimations, up to 2,000 Chileans for their political beliefs in the first month after the death of Allende. American and Chilean critics accused the administration of plotting the overthrow of Allende, but Nixon and Kissinger declared that they had no involvement in the overthrow. That was later proved to be false.

MIDDLE EAST POLICY

The Yom Kippur War

American support for the young nation of Israel since its creation in 1948 was consistent over the years. Support for Israel in peace and war brought the United States into conflict with the oil-rich Arab nations dedicated to the destruction of Israel. It became obvious to the United States that policies in the Middle East that had backed Israel unconditionally had to undergo modification in order to secure oil imports, stop Soviet attempts to build alliances with Arab nations, and yet continue to support Israel's right to exist.

In October 1973, Egypt and Syria suddenly attacked Israel to avenge the Israeli victory in the Six-Day War. The Six-Day War had been fought in June 1967, and resulted in the Israelis taking territory from Egypt, Syria, and Jordan. Following the 1967 defeat, Soviet aid had enabled the Egyptian and Syrian armies to build up to the point that they were ready to regain the lost territory. They attacked on October 6, 1973, which was the day of Yom Kippur, the holiest of days for the Jews. The United States quickly sent military aid to Israel to counter Soviet aid to the Arab nations. The United Nations called for a cease-fire with the approval of the United States and the Soviet Union. Egypt and Israel agreed to the cease fire, but maintained the military positions they held on October 25 when shots were still being exchanged. Syria had agreed to a cease fire on October 24.

OPEC and the PLO

OPEC (members of the Organization of Petroleum Exporting Countries) decided at this time to begin using its oil resources to force the United States and other nations to change their policies in the Middle East to favor the Arab nations. OPEC announced an immediate 400 percent increase in the price of its crude oil. Furthermore, production was reduced until Israel gave back territory gained in 1967, and the rights of the Palestinian refugees from Israel were recognized. Oil exports to the United States were stopped from October 1973 to March 1974. The oil embargo, and subsequent higher prices for gasoline and home heating fuel, sent shock waves across the industrialized nations, although the United States was among the worst victims because of its long and careless reliance on cheap foreign oil to help fuel prosperity. Specifically, the OPEC actions caused fuel shortages and greatly increased the problem of inflation in this country, thus contributing to the stagflation of the 1970s.

The fighting had ceased, but Henry Kissinger was determined to bring stability to the Middle East with his "shuttle diplomacy." For two years he flew to the capitals of Israel and its Arab neighbors. The increasing terrorist acts of the PLO (The Palestinian Liberation Organization was formed in 1964 by Palestinian refugees to support guerilla activity to recover their homeland). presented problems for the United States for which there were few solutions. The PLO demanded recognition of their rights in Israel and called for the destruction of the Jewish state. The right to a homeland for the Palestinians was supported by the Arab nations and disputed by Israel. Extremist groups within the PLO turned to highjacking planes from Western nations, hit and run raids on Israel, and even murdering eleven Israeli athletes at the 1972 Olympic Games in Munich, Germany to force Israel and the Western nations to accept their goals. There were moderate factions in the PLO who believed the terrorism was going too far, but there were many who were committed to violence to regain their homeland. Israel retaliated against the PLO with assassinations and attacks on training bases and refugee camps that harbored the terrorists, especially in Lebanon, and the problem escalated through the 1980s.

ASIAN RELATIONS

Altering American responsibilities in Asia were necessary to realign American foreign policy goals. President Nixon announced that American troops would be pulled out of Vietnam, and the war would be turned over to the South Vietnamese Army in the process known as Vietnamization. In reality, Nixon continued to widen the war and use military intimidation to bring a "peace with honor" if a victory were not possible. Countries fighting commumism would have to bear more of the military burdens of fighting for their independence with American political, economic, and military support from the sea and the air but not on the ground. Finally, Nixon wanted to begin the process of normalizing relations with Communist China.

Communist China would be the linchpin in foreign policy with regard to the Soviet Union. Friendly relations between the United States and Communist China would balance the threat of a too-powerful Soviet Union. The Soviets and the Chinese, both communist nations, had maintained friendly relations for some time, but tensions had developed between the two nations. In 1969 the Soviets placed more than 1 million soldiers on the border between the two nations, and there were three clashes along the border that same year. The United States and Communist China had not had diplomatic relations since 1949, when all of China but the island of Formosa (Taiwan) fell to the forces of Mao Tse-Tung. The United States had supported Taiwan as the legitimate China, but that support was now being put aside.

President Nixon (center with light coat) at the Great Wall of China near Peking. Credit: AP/Wide World Photos.

Nixon Visits Communist China

In 1969, at a gathering of ambassadors, a few comments were exchanged between the ambassador from the United States and the ambassador from the People's Republic of China that there might be interest on both sides to open a dialogue. Secret communications between the two nations were passed through diplomatic channels in Romania and Pakistan for a future meeting of high level officials. An example of Communist China's thaw towards the United States was an invitation to the American ping pong team to play in Beijing, the capital. President Nixon showed his goodwill with the end of a 21-year trade embargo against Communist China. On July 15, 1971, President Nixon announced his acceptance of the invitation of Premier Chou En-lai to visit Communist China. An important signal to the world of the acceptance of Communist China and its government was the support from the United States for it to replace Taiwan as the Chinese representative in the United Nations.

Nixon's trip to China in February 1972 was a public relations, as well as a foreign policy, success. Public attention was averted from the disappointments in Vietnam, and the television coverage of areas not seen in decades by the Western world was riveting for Americans. On his first day in China, the president was met at the airport by Premier Chou En-Lai, met in secret with Chairman Mao, and attended a banquet in the Great Hall of the People. In the days following, talks were interspersed with sightseeing to the Great Wall and the Forbidden City (250 acres of palaces and temples once occupied by the Chinese emperors), watching exhibitions of gymnastics and table tennis, and the acceptance of two giant panda bears as gifts to the Americans.

Relations between the two nations did not change dramatically immediately following the trip, largely because the United States had not formally recognized Communist China. There were promises to increase contact between the nations in science, technology, culture, sports, journalism, and perhaps most importantly, trade. It was also an important change to foreign policy that anti-communism seemed to no longer be the paramount factor in policy making.

THE WATERGATE SCANDAL RESULTS IN THE RESIGNATION OF NIXON

A History of Suspicion and Questionable Activities

The "us" (the President and his closest advisors) against the "them" (the press, the eastern establishment, disloyal government employees, and disloyal Americans) atmosphere of the inner circle of the White House from the early days of the Nixon presidency brought the president and his team to accept the escalation of illegal and unethical methods of dealing with their problems. Within a few months of taking office, President Nixon was reading stories in the *New York Times* and the *Washington Post* containing information from classified national security files, which disturbed him and caused him to take action. A list of stories was sent to the president from the CIA, stories that could be damaging to national security. From 1969 to 1971, Nixon ordered wiretaps placed on the telephones of a few government officials and reporters considered anti-Nixon to discover the sources of the leaks. The president approved a plan (the Huston Plan) for further surveillance of his perceived enemies, but FBI Director J. Edgar Hoover and Attorney-General John Mitchell prevented its adoption. Hoover did not want a rival surveillance network. The Nixon White House had taken on a siege, or fortress, mentality.

With the rejection of the Huston Plan, the White House resorted to forming its own undercover team in 1971. The group became known as the "plumbers" because it was their job to find the source of leaks to the press and stop them. The "plumbers" conducted one of their most infamous operations attempting to find information to discredit Daniel Ellsberg by breaking into his psychiatrist's office. Ellsberg, a former Defense Department official, had been added to the list of enemies and leaks when he decided the American public had a right to know information in a secret government report entitled *The History of the U.S. Decision Making Process in Vietnam* and gave the report to the *New York Times*, which began publishing the report in June 1971. Commissioned by Secretary of State Robert McNamara, it was a detailed account of American decision making and contingency planning up to 1965 in Vietnam. The lies, half truths, and plans of the former administrations were exposed. The Nixon administration appealed to the Supreme Court to stop the *Times* and the *Washington Post* from publishing the so-called *Pentagon Papers*, which the government claimed would endanger national security and keep the United States in the war longer. On June 30, the Supreme Court voted 6–3 to allow the publication of the papers. Ellsberg went to trial for his role in stealing government documents, but the charges against him were dropped on May 11, 1973, after an investigation into the Watergate affair uncovered the fact that E. Howard Hunt and G. Gordon Liddy, defendants in the Watergate burglary, had also burglarized the psychiatrist's office.

In 1972 John Mitchell resigned as Attorney-General and began organizing Nixon's re-election campaign. Millions of dollars were collected from supporters of Nixon, and a great deal of that money was used to finance "dirty tricks," which is not unusual in campaigns. But this campaign was dirtier than most because it included spying, spreading false stories about leading Democrats, and paying for burglaries to gather information about enemies or the opposition in the campaign. The campaign organization became known as CREEP (the Committee to Re-Elect the President).

The Break-In and the Cover-Up

In the early morning of June 17, 1972, five burglars were discovered by a security guard attempting to bug the offices of the Democratic National Committee headquarters in the Watergate apartment-office complex in Washington, D.C. The men were arrested with bugging devices and bundles of $100 bills in their possession. The bills were traced to CREEP, and the arrest of G. Gordon Liddy (counsel for CREEP and a member of the "plumbers") and E. Howard Hunt (former CIA agent and currently employed in the White House and a member of the "plumbers") soon followed.

The president denied that anyone in the White House was involved with the burglary. The story did not receive much attention in spite of the claims of George McGovern and Democratic National Committee Chairman Lawrence F. O'Brien that this was another of Nixon's dirty campaign tactics. Evidence later supported the idea that Nixon was aware after the burglary was exposed of the involvement of members of CREEP, and began to cover up the connection with the White House to save his chances for re-election. H.R. Haldeman, Nixon's Chief of Staff, was ordered to stop the FBI investigation of the situation, but he could not. The CIA was then ordered to stop the FBI's investigation on the grounds that national security was once again at stake. Private donations totaling about $400,000 were raised as hush money to keep Liddy, Hunt, and the other burglars quiet; hints of presidential pardons were also used for the same purpose.

The Investigation Broadens

In January 1973, all seven men arrested in connection with the Watergate break-in were convicted of conspiracy, burglary, and electronic eavesdropping. All seven had pleaded guilty and said nothing about who planned the break-in, but Judge John J. Sirica was not satisfied that the burglars were the leaders of the break-in scheme, so he pressured them to reveal everyone involved or face sentences of up to 40 years. Finally, in March, one of the men, James W. McCord (who was a former CIA employee and the security chief for CREEP), informed Sirica in a letter that there were others from the highest level of government involved in the scheme, there had been an attempted cover-up, and money had been given to the seven to "plead guilty and remain silent." Specifically, McCord claimed that John Mitchell, chairman of CREEP, was ultimately responsible for the authorization of the Watergate affair.

Meanwhile, Bob Woodward and Carl Bernstein, two *Washington Post* reporters, began in early 1973 to work to uncover any information leading to the White House. Their stories of the connection between the Watergate break-in and CREEP's "dirty tricks" campaign, illegal contributions, and other sordid activities, made the front page frequently. A great deal of their information allegedly came from an unnamed White House source known as "Deep Throat." (There was also a pornographic movie entitled "Deep Throat" that was popular in some circles at the time.)

With Woodward's and Bernstein's stories beginning to appear, public pressure mounted for Congress to begin its own investigation of the Watergate break-in and allegedly related "dirty tricks" and other campaign irregularities. On February 7, 1973, the Senate unanimously formed the Select Committee on Presidential Campaign Activities, chaired by Democratic Senator Sam J. Ervin of North Carolina, to investigate Watergate and other areas of wrongdoing in the president's campaign. The witty and plain-speaking senator became a folk-hero to many Americans. Having stated he was "just a plain country lawyer," this expert on constitutional law oversaw the uncovering of a variety of illegal activities perpetrated by members of the Nixon administration.

Before the televised meetings of the Select Committee began, resignations of some key figures were announced. The first to go was John W. Dean III, Nixon's own counsel, who was fired by the president because Dean was cooperating with the Select Committee. On March 22, Dean had ominously warned the Select Committee that the Watergate scandal had become "a cancer growing on the presidency." Then in April (1973), L. Patrick Gray, Acting FBI Director (since the death of J. Edgar Hoover in 1972) admitted to destroying evidence before his resignation. And on April 30, President Nixon announced the resignations of Chief of Staff H.R. Haldeman and domestic affairs assistant John Ehrlichman, Nixon's top two aides. Attorney-General Richard G. Kleindienst also resigned on the same day; Kleindienst had taken John Mitchell's place when the latter had resigned to head CREEP in 1972. At the time of these announcements, President Nixon promised the country that he would get to the bottom of things.

Defense Secretary Elliot Richardson was appointed to the position of attorney-general and ordered to appoint a special prosecutor with broad investigative and subpoena powers to carry out a systematic inquiry into the Watergate scandal. The

Senate Select Committee had been pressing Nixon to name someone to just such a position. Richardson selected Harvard Law Professor Archibald Cox, who was also a Democrat. Nixon, still clinging to his position that he was not involved, reiterated his innocence to the American public on television in early May, by emphatically declaring "Well, I am not a crook."

Televised Senate Hearings

The questioning of witnesses during the televised Senate hearings began on May 17, 1973, and lasted until August of the same year. Over the course of the hearings, it would be revealed that the Nixon White House had an "enemies list," that favors were traded for illegal campaign contributions, and that orders for harassment and illegal wiretaps of political opponents had been issued to the IRS, FBI, and other federal agencies from members of the White House staff. In June, John Dean testified that Nixon had approved a cover-up of the break-in, but he had not ordered the break-in. However, Haldeman, Ehrlichman, and Mitchell had testified that Nixon knew nothing of the cover-up. Throughout the hearings, Senator Howard Baker, Republican from Tennessee, repeatedly asked witnesses, "What did the President know and when did he know it?" This question that brought fame to Senator Baker became the driving force behind deeper probing by many; it became the crucial question of the Watergate investigation.

Former presidential aide Alexander Butterfield gave the committee information on July 16 that stunned both the committee and the nation. He revealed that the president had secretly recorded conversations in the Oval Office since early 1971. This bombshell meant that tapes of conversations could prove whether Dean or the other Nixon aides were telling the truth. Therefore, obtaining those tapes relevant to the Watergate investigation became a top priority for all parties. On July 23, Cox issued a subpoena for nine White House tapes of President Nixon's conversations. About the same time, the Senate Select Committee subpoenaed five tapes and other materials. And the battle for the tapes had begun.

The "Saturday Night Massacre"

President Nixon refused to turn over the tapes to Cox and the Select Committee, claiming "executive privilege," a risk to national security from the information on the tapes, and exemption of the presidency from subpoenas from Congress. He claimed the subpoena from Congress violated the principle of the separation of powers inherent in the Constitution. He did offer to turn over a typed summary of the tapes, but Cox refused the offer.

In late August, federal district court Judge John J. Sirica rejected Nixon's arguments and ordered that he turn over the requested tapes. Nixon still refused. Then in October, prosecutor Cox went to the federal Court of Appeals, which upheld Sirica's ruling and gave the president a deadline of October 19 to hand over the tapes. President Nixon still refused to obey the court order. Instead, on Saturday evening, October 20, he ordered Attorney-General Elliot Richardson to fire Special Prosecutor Cox, who had refused Nixon's offer to turn over a written synopsis of the material on the tapes. But Richardson, a man of convictions, resigned in

John Dean, former White House aide, before the Senate Select Committee hearings on the Watergate Scandal. Credit: AP/Wide World Photos.

protest rather than fire Cox. Then when Nixon ordered Richardson's next in command, Deputy Attorney-General William Ruckelshaus, to fire Cox, he too resigned ·in protest. Finally, Solicitor General Robert Bork, third in line at the Justice Department, fired Archibald Cox. Thus, the night of October 20, 1973, became known as the "Saturday Night Massacre."

Criticism resulting from the "Saturday Night Massacre" was quick and furious, including from many Republicans. This criticism forced Nixon to appoint Leon Jaworski, a lawyer from Texas, as the new special prosecutor. Seven of the tapes were then turned over to Judge Sirica. Nixon claimed that two of the tapes did not exist. When the tapes were played, Judge Sirica revealed in late November that there was an 18½ minute gap of silence on one. Nixon's secretary, Rosemary Woods, testified later that she might have accidentally caused the erasure when she was copying the tapes. However, tests performed by electronics experts confirmed that the erasure was definitely intentional.

Vice-President Agnew Resigns

Acts of corruption and unethical behavior were multiplying in the Nixon administration. On October 10, 1973, Vice-President Spiro Agnew resigned after entering a plea of "no contest" to a single charge of tax evasion. The charge stemmed from other allegations that he had accepted bribes from contractors in exchange for favors while he was governor of Maryland and later during his vice-presidency. Thoses bribery charges were dropped in a deal which resulted in Agnew's resignation. Following his plea, Agnew was sentenced to three years of probation and fined $10,000. Agnew became just the second vice-president in American history to resign; Vice-President John C. Calhoun had resigned from the administration of Andrew Jackson in the early nineteenth century.

Invoking the authority of the Twenty-fifth Amendment for the first time, Nixon nominated, and Congress confirmed, House Minority Leader, Gerald R. Ford of Michigan, as the new vice-president. Ford was sworn in on December 6. Nixon chose Ford as the new vice-president because of his experience in the House of Representatives, his reputation for honesty, and the fact that he was well-liked. He was not well known around the country, but he was well known in Washington. He had served in the House of Representatives from 1949–1973, and as the House Minority Leader from 1965–1973. Ford was one of the two House members on the Warren Commission, which was put together by President Johson to study the assassination of President Kennedy. As a conservative Republican member of the House, he was not a strong supporter of civil rights; he opposed Medicare; and he lambasted President Johnson from the floor of the House in 1967 to either use the military to win in Vietnam or pull out. President Johnson had commented when selecting Ford to serve on the Warren Commission that "Ford was a nice guy, but he had played college football too often without a helmet." The sentiment of that comment would resurface when Ford was president.

The Battle for the Tapes Continues

President Nixon notified the Senate Select Committee on January 4, 1974, that he would not turn over the approximately five hundred tapes and documents which had been subpoenaed by then on the grounds once again of "executive privilege." The public was not appeased, so the House of Representatives authorized the House Judiciary Committee, chaired by Democratic Congressman Peter W. Rodino, Jr. of New Jersey, to subpoena tapes to aid into their investigation for possible impeachment charges against the president. In late February 1974, that House committee had subpoenaed many additional White House tapes.

Then in March, Special Prosecutor Jaworski convened a federal grand jury that brought indictments against seven presidential aides and named Nixon as an "unindicted co-conspirator." That same month, Jaworski also subpoenaed additional tapes from Nixon. Still resisting, on April 30 Nixon gave them edited transcripts full of gaps and "expletives deleted" instead. Both Jaworski and the House Judiciary Committee went after the original tapes, and on July 24, the Supreme Court, in the case of *U.S.A. v. Richard Nixon*, ruled that the president could not withhold evidence in a criminal case, and ordered that the tapes be sent to the Special Prosecutor. Ironically, it was Nixon-appointee Chief Justice Warren Burger who wrote the court's opinion.

Meanwhile, in July, articles of impeachment were approved by the Judiciary Committee. On July 27, the first article of impeachment passed the House Judiciary Committee, charging the president with obstruction of justice. The vote was 27 to 11, with all 21 Democrats and 6 of the 17 Republicans voting in favor of the

President Nixon says goodbye outside the White House after his resignation in August 1974. Credit: AP/Wide World Photos.

article. Two days later, on July 29, the second article of impeachment was voted by the committee, charging Nixon with abuse of power, especially regarding his use of the FBI and IRS to harass opponents. The vote was 28 to 10, with all 21 Democrats and 7 of the 17 Republicans voting in favor. Then on July 30, the committee adopted a third article of impeachment, which alleged that Nixon had unconstitutionally refused to obey a Congressional subpoena to release the tapes. The vote this time was 21 to 17 along strict party lines.

President Nixon Resigns

With time on releasing the remainder of the tapes running out, on August 5, 1974, President Nixon admitted to the American public via a television address that he had known about the cover-up from the beginning and had tried to get the FBI to stop its investigation. On the same day, he released the tapes as ordered by the Supreme Court. The tapes indeed revealed that Nixon had encouraged a cover-up. Specifically, a conversation between Nixon and Haldeman on June 23, 1972, just six days after the break-in, Nixon told Haldeman to direct the CIA to use a phony national security story to stop the FBI investigation. At this turn of events, even Nixon's strongest allies on the House Judiciary Committee publicly took back their "no" votes on his impeachment.

On August 7, Republican Congressional leaders personally told Nixon that he was dead politically. With impeachment by the House certain, and conviction by the Senate probable, the next evening, August 8, President Nixon addressed a national television audience and announced that he was resigning the presidency, effective noon (eastern time) the next day. In his television speech, Nixon admitted no wrongdoing or guilt of any kind—only mistakes in judgment, which he thought at the time were in the nation's best interest. He was resigning, he said incredibly, because of the lack of political support necessary to govern. Thus, at noon on August 9, 1974, President Richard Milhouse Nixon became the first president in American history to resign.

The Aftermath of Watergate

Nixon's resignation left Vice-President Gerald R. Ford to be sworn in as the nation's only unelected president in our history. (That is, he had not even been elected as vice-president.)

In January 1975, Haldeman, Ehrlichman, and Mitchell were all convicted, bringing the total to 17 the number of persons found guilty in court of various charges in connection with the Watergate scandal.

The legacy of Watergate was to breed suspicion and cynicism of government. And the American people, in many ways, have not completely recovered from the constitutional shockwaves that rocked the nation in the early 1970s.

INTRODUCTION TO THE FORD ADMINISTRATION

"Our Constitution works; our great Republic is a government of laws and not of men." This was the truth as spoken by Gerald Ford following his swearing in as president by Chief Justice Warren Burger just minutes after the official resignation of President Nixon at 12:00 noon Washington, D.C. time, on August 9, 1974. In a footnote to history, Gerald Ford became the first president not elected to the presidency or the vice-presidency, and yet, he was accepted according to the provisions of the Twenty-fifth Amendment to the Constitution.

President Ford then used the Twenty-fifth Amendment to nominate Nelson A. Rockefeller for the vacancy in the vice-presidency. Rockefeller was the grandson of the wealthy industrialist John D. Rockefeller. At the time of his confirmation hearings, he revealed that his personal worth, not adding in all of his assets, which were mostly in trusts, was close to $62 million. Rockefeller had been active for years in politics. He had served for a while as Undersecretary of Health, Education, and Welfare during the Eisenhower years. He was a member of the liberal wing of the Republican party and had thrown his hat in the ring for the Republican nomination for president in 1960, 1964, and 1968. While he was active in national politics, he also served for four terms as governor of New York. He was more liberal on most issues than most Republicans, but on the issue of law and order he generally stood with the conservatives. Rockefeller was easily confirmed and then sworn into office in December 1974.

Ford Pardons Nixon

On August 9, 1974, President Ford stated that "Our long national nightmare is over," but he was not entirely correct. The aftershocks from the resignation of a president, and the criminal activity within the highest level of government, would last for years. One of the greatest shocks was the announcement on September 8, 1974 that President Ford had granted former President Nixon "a full, free, and absolute pardon . . . for all offenses against the United States which he . . . has committed or may have committed or taken part in" while serving as president. The outcry was immediate and loud from the country and those serving in government. Many believed there had been a deal between Ford and Nixon to exchange a pardon for the vice-presidency, but Ford insisted that there was no such deal. He argued that Nixon's resignation was fair and just punishment for the president, and that it was time for the nation to leave Watergate behind.

Gerald Ford makes a point during a debate with Jimmy Carter in Philadelphia. Credit: AP/Wide World Photos.

DEALING WITH CONTINUING STAGFLATION

The Democratic controlled Congress and the Republican president soon squared off because of differences concerning how to stimulate economic growth and deal with the problems of inflation, recession, and deficits caused by government spending more than it received. Most Democrats believed that the federal government had to maintain deficit spending in order to alleviate the problems of the growing recession. Ford believed that economic stability could be achieved only by reducing government spending, raising interest rates, and reducing taxes for businesses. For a president who wanted to get along with Congress, Ford was not having much success. He vetoed 39 pieces of legislation in a single year.

President Ford turned to the public for support of his policies and to fight inflation with a campaign known as "Whip Inflation Now." WIN buttons were passed out and worn by supporters. But the recession deepened, and Ford was forced to drop the unsuccessful WIN campaign, which had been little more than psychological wishful thinking. By 1975, inflation was at 11 percent and unemployment close to 9 percent. None of the old solutions to these two conditions were working. Normally, high unemployment rates reduced inflation of prices, but not this time.

The economies of the states and cities were suffering from economic troubles along with the national government. New York City was facing bankruptcy in 1975 and approached the federal government for assistance. Ford was originally opposed to loaning federal money to the troubled city and threatened to veto any legislation. However, in November the president reversed his stand when Congress agreed that the government would guarantee loans, and it was evident that the city government was working on the problem with higher taxes and reduced spending.

REMAINING ISSUES

Ford's time in the White House was short, and he was not assessed as a very effective president. There were, however, important changes. In the search for ways to bring down the cost of energy, including oil, Ford signed a bill to create the Energy Research and Development Administration. Hoping to cut back on overseas oil imports, which were putting the United States in a dependent position on Middle Eastern oil exporting countries, duties on imported oil were increased and deregulation of the prices in the domestic oil industry were slowly implemented.

The discovery during the Watergate trials of illegal campaign contributions to Nixon's campaign brought about new regulations from Congress. Several major corporations, including Goodyear, Braniff Airlines, and American Airlines admitted in November 1973 to giving illegal contributions. The Federal Election Campaign Act, passed in 1974, created the Federal Election Committee to enforce the new law, provided public financing for presidential primaries and general elections from the $1 checkoff on federal income tax forms, and limited the contributions of individuals and groups.

To bring more Americans into the electoral process, President Ford agreed to include voters who spoke Spanish and other minorities who did not speak fluent English in the provisions of the 1965 Voting Rights Act. So in late July 1975, the Voting Rights Act was extended for seven years to prolong the guarantees it provided. The law eliminated registration tests that were discriminatory and brought the authority of the federal government into any area that discriminated against the registration of particular groups.

Continuing to react to information on government activity revealed by Watergate, Congress amended the Freedom of Information Act to allow the public more access to information gathered on individuals by government agencies. Ford vetoed the measure, claiming the possibility of endangering national security, but Congress overrode the veto.

ATTEMPTS TO KILL THE PRESIDENT

Ford was perceived as a likeable, honest, and yet somewhat bumbling president. He tripped on steps, hit his head going through the doorway into his helicopter, and could not seem to solve the pressing problems of the nation. The press revived an earlier comment made by President Johnson in his assessment of Gerald Ford, that "he had played too much football without his helmet." In all fairness, he encountered problems that were not solvable with quick action by one president. The economy and the energy crisis were encountered by Nixon, Ford, Carter, and Reagan, and each of them had his limits on what he could accomplish.

There were some, however, who did not believe that President Ford should continue to lead the nation. In two separate incidents, assassins attempted to take his life in September 1975. Ironically, just before Ford was to deliver a speech on crime in Sacramento, California on September 5, Lynette "Squeaky" Fromme, a follower of Charles Manson, accused and convicted for masterminding the murder of seven people, reached out to shake the president's hand with pistol drawn. The gun was loaded, but it did not fire, and the Secret Service quickly disarmed Fromme. She was found guilty and sentenced to life in prison. At her trial, Fromme's lawyer presented the viewpoint that she was not a murderer, but just someone attempting to gain attention for lost causes, especially the imprisonment of Manson. The president had testified on videotape at the request of the defense, which was attempting to show that Fromme was very nervous and unstable. This was the first time in history that a president, while in office, gave sworn testimony in a trial. After that incident, Ford wore a bullet proof vest at certain times when in public. Then on September 22, Sara Jane Moore fired at the president when he was leaving a hotel in San Francisco. Luckily for Ford, a bystander saw Moore take aim and spoiled the shot when he hit her arm. She was also convicted and sentenced to life in prison.

FOREIGN AFFAIRS UNDER FORD

Soviet-American Relations

Ford continued the foreign policy strategies of President Nixon, depending heavily on the experience of Henry Kissinger, whom he kept on as Secretary of State and National Security Advisor. Kissinger continued to promote detente with the Soviet Union. Ford met with Soviet Premier Leonid Brezhnev in Vladivostok in November 1974 to continue talks on arms limitation. Both sides agreed that further reductions of strategic weapons was desirable. Then the two leaders met again in Helsinki, Finland in August 1975, along with representatives from 33 other nations, at the Conference on Security and Cooperation in Europe, to discuss ways to alleviate East-West tensions. The West recognized the current boundaries of the Eastern European nations and agreed to refrain from interfering in the internal affairs of those communist nations. The Eastern nations promised to improve communications and relax the travel restrictions both within and from their nations. Communist violations of the Helsinki Agreements brought criticism from supporters and critics of the agreement, and, as a result, Ford cooled considerably toward detente with the Soviet Union. Also in 1975, Congress passed the Jackson-Vanik Amendment, tying future trade agreements with the Soviet Union to the relaxation of Jewish immigration from that country.

MIDDLE EASTERN POLICY

Kissinger continued his "shuttle diplomacy" in the Middle East to bring peaceful relations to Israel and Egypt, but by March of 1975 the negotiations had stalled. Talks continued in the summer, however, with the United States exerting pressure on Israel and promising aid to both sides to reach an agreement. The Sinai Agreement was finally reached in September of 1975. Premier Yitzhak Rabin signed the agreement for Israel. Territory captured in the Yom Kippur War in the Sinai Peninsula would be returned to Egypt, and Israeli troops would be withdrawn from the Mitla and Gidi Passes. Both Israel and Egypt agreed to solve problems with each other through peaceful means, to keep a UN-patrolled buffer zone, and to limit the size of military forces close to the buffer zone. President Anwar Sadat signed the agreement for Egypt. Israel would be allowed to ship or receive non-military goods through the Suez Canal carried on ships of other nations. The United States assisted the peace process by extending more than $2 billion in aid to Israel and close to $500 million to other Middle Eastern nations. The agreement also provided that the United States send 200 Americans to monitor a surveillance system in the returned passes that would alert either side of the movement of forces other than UN troops.

This was not a peace treaty, as Sadat pointed out to his critics in the other Arab nations. Sadat agreed with the other nations that a peace treaty was unlikely until other problems, such as a homeland for the Palestinians and ending Israeli occupation of the Syrian Golan Heights, were satisfactorily resolved. Egypt needed peace and American assistance to build up an ailing nation. Kissinger flew to Saudi Arabia, Jordan, and Syria to assure those nations that the United States would continue its efforts until peace was brought to the area. The problems of the area would get worse, however, before real gains toward peace were made. Attacks on Israel by Arab guerillas, frequently members of the PLO, and counterattacks by Israel on Palestinian camps and other attacking Arab nations kept the area destabilized.

FOREIGN POLICY IN ASIA

In 1975, communist forces gained important victories in Southeast Asia. Thousands of American lives had once been given to stop the fall of South Vietnam and other nearby nations to communism, but now the United States would not intervene to stop this new round of communist aggression. In April, the communist Pathet Lao took control of the government in Laos; the communist Khmer Rouge took control of Cambodia; and Saigon was taken by the communist forces in Vietnam (the latter on April 30).

The Mayaguez Incident

The taking of the American merchant ship the *Mayaguez* in May 1975 by Cambodian gunboats in the Gulf of Siam, allegedly for violating Cambodia's national waters, did bring American action. Without waiting for an investigation or a Cambodian government response, President Ford was anxious to demonstrate American military credibility. Therefore, he ordered marines to islands off the coast of Cambodia, while warships sank three Cambodian ships and aircraft destroyed an air base and oil storage facility inside Cambodia. Meanwhile, the president did not know that the crew of the *Mayaguez* had already been set free, and he ordered an operation to obtain their freedom. Ford then announced that the 39 crew members had been rescued by military force. This little fiasco resulted in the death of 41 Americans who had engaged in the "rescue."

The End of the War in Vietnam

In South Vietnam, the first units fell to the communist North Vietnamese troops in January 1975. From that point on, it was a steady advance for the North Vietnamese troops to Saigon. President Ford, Secretary of State Kissinger, and Secretary of Defense James Schlesinger placed much of the blame for the failure of the South Vietnamese to fight back on the decision of Congress to reduce military aid to South Vietnam from $1.2 billion in 1974 to $700 million in 1975. The cut-back did result in some shortages in fuel, ammunition, and spare parts. However, poor leadership and not enough commitment on the part of the South Vietnamese, played an extremely important role in its defeat. This lack of dedication was also a problem when Americans were involved in the war. By April 27, Saigon was under rocket attack. President Thieu had resigned on April 21 and fled to Taiwan. Thieu claimed that the United States betrayed South Vietnam by not coming to its aid as Nixon had promised as a condition for Thieu's signature on the cease-fire of 1973. Letters were later made public that appeared to give Thieu's claim credibility. South Vietnam surrendered unconditionally on April 30, 1975, and the Vietnam War had finally come to an end. Close to 45,000 Americans and South Vietnamese were evacuated from the country in airplanes and, at the last minute, by helicopter. The final evacuees fled by helicopter from the rooftop of the American Embassy in Saigon. Thousands who had left the country were picked up by American ships.

Refugees fleeing the communists went to Thailand, the Philippines, Singapore, Hong Kong, other areas in Asia, and the United States. The United States relaxed immigration quotas to allow at least 132,000 refugees from the Indochina region into the country. On May 16, Congress appropriated $405 million to resettle those who had lost their homes and their country. These people were not welcomed by all Americans, however. Fear that they would take away jobs in a time of recession was a major concern. By 1976, the two Vietnams were united into the Socialist Republic of Vietnam, and Saigon was renamed Ho Chi Minh City in honor of the Vietnamese nationalist and communist who had died back in September 1969. So much had been sacrificed by the South Vietnamese and the Americans to prevent the fall of this small Southeast Asian country to communism, and yet in the end, the communists prevailed.

THE 1976 ELECTION

The results of the 1974 midterm Congressional elections indicated that Republicans could expect to fight a tough race for the presidency in 1976. Close to 60 percent of the votes cast had gone to Democrats. The Republicans lost 48 seats in the House of Representatives. Even President Ford's old seat in the House went to a Democrat for the first time since 1910.

The Candidates and the Platforms

In the Democratic presidential primaries, Jimmy Carter (James Earl Carter), the former governor of Georgia and a virtually unknown political figure, campaigned vigorously, winning in primary after primary until he had enough delegates to overwhelm his opposition for the party's nomination at the Democratic National Convention in New York City. He chose Senator Walter F. Mondale of Minnesota as his running mate. Carter began his acceptance speech as he had begun most of his previous speeches, "My name is Jimmy Carter and I'm running for President." Name recognition had been a major problem for Carter when he had begun his early effort in 1975, but the fact that he was not a longterm, well recognized political face would work to his advantage in the primaries as well as the general election. Many Americans wanted a political outsider after the Watergate debacle, and Carter stressed that he was an outsider to the Washington arena of politics.

Carter's campaign promises included a reduction in the size and an increase in the efficiency of the federal bureaucracy, a restoration of honesty and simplicity to government and politics, an end to racial and economic discrimination, and a voice in government for the powerless. Another major issue in the Carter campaign was the fact that he was a deeply religious "born again" Christian who practiced his faith. Many Americans believed that his religious convictions would lead the country to the correct path once again, but others wondered if his religious convictions would negatively influence his position as president. The official Democratic platform included a pledge to reduce unemployment, to oppose an anti-abortion amendment, and to fight for tax reform, national health insurance, a smaller defense budget, gun control, and busing school children as a last resort to achieve racial integration.

President Ford was the Republican choice after defeating the strong challenge of former California Governor Ronald Reagan. The Republican platform opposed most of the Democratic platform. Ford and his running mate, Senator Robert Dole from Kansas, endorsed tax cuts for business, constitutional amendments that would end busing and abortion, no national health insurance or gun control, and a larger budget for defense.

The Campaign and Results

Early in the campaign, Carter damaged his chances by giving an interview to *Playboy* magazine. This seemed a strange move for a deeply religious man, but Carter was trying to appeal to a variety of Americans, including those who did not have strong religious convictions or religious convictions that were the same as his. He wanted the American people to believe that he had the same problems and weaknesses they did. The comment that caused concern for his chances was his confession that he had "looked upon a lot of women with lust. I've committed adultery in my heart many times," he frankly admitted.

Early on, Ford was behind Carter in the polls, so he became the first incumbent president to challenge an opponent to debate the issues. The candidates debated on three separate occasions. The first debate was considered a win for Ford, but the second debate was a decisive victory for Carter when Ford claimed that

Eastern Europe was not under the domination of the Soviet Union. This was patently an untrue statement, and it did great damage to Ford's credibility. Most experts believed that Ford's pardon of Richard Nixon had also hurt his chances for reelection, a pardon which Carter reminded voters of during the campaign.

For the first time in history, the vice-presidential candidates also debated before national television audiences. Dole did some damage to the Republicans when he fixed the blame on the Democrats for all the wars in the twentieth century. By election day, Carter had lost his immense lead over Ford, and the candidates were close in the polls. Carter won with about 50 percent of the popular vote to Ford's 48 percent. The electoral vote was 297 for Carter and 240 for Ford. Carter managed to pull together many Democrats who had gone over to the Republican side in the last two elections. He was supported across the South, among labor union members, especially in the industrialized areas of the North, and among African-Americans and white ethnic groups. And despite the fact that the nation was celebrating its bicentennial—200 hundred years of independence—an incumbent president lost the White House.

INTRODUCTION TO THE CARTER ADMINISTRATION

President Carter's inauguration on January 20, 1977 was an example to the nation in that he hoped Americans perceived him as an ordinary person with the same problems and goals as most of them had. He took the oath of office on an old family Bible while dressed in his inexpensive three-piece suit. It was customary for presidents to take the oath in formal attire. Then President Carter, First Lady Roslynn, and their daughter Amy broke tradition again when they walked down Pennsylvania Avenue to the White House following the inauguration. (Thomas Jefferson had walked the route in 1801.) Hopes of both the nation and the new president were high in January 1977, but the Carter administration was soon in trouble. The president had campaigned as an outsider and aligned himself with the American people against those powerful men and women in Congress who were considered a stumbling block rather than aids in solving problems. Carter forgot that he would have to win support for his programs from that same Congress that he had purposefully separated himself from. Partly as a result of that outsider image, he failed to work well with both houses, and therefore did not accomplish what he hoped to even though he had a Democratic Congress to work with. Another major reason for Carter's ineffectiveness as president was his style of leadership. The president simply involved himself in too many of the details which should have been delegated to subordinates. This hampered his ability to accurately see the big picture and to understand what the American people were really thinking about a given problem.

On his first day on the job, the president pardoned the remaining 10,000 Americans who had broken the law by evading the draft during the Vietnam War. The Veterans of Foreign Wars condemned the pardoning of these young men who

1976	50	JIMMY CARTER	Democrat	40,828,929	297	50.1
		Gerald R. Ford	Republican	39,148,940	240	47.9
		Eugene McCarthy	Independent	739,256		

refused to serve their nation in time of need, but Carter did not extend the pardon to deserters in the war.

Following up on another campaign promise, President Carter increased the number of women, African-Americans, and members of other minority groups into government positions. Among these was the appointment of Andrew Young, an African-American civil rights activist, as the ambassador to the United Nations.

THE ENERGY CRISIS GROWS

With the conclusion of the embargo on oil from the Middle East, Americans were quick to forget the seriousness of the problem, or even admit that there was one, once gasoline was easy to purchase again. President Carter was concerned, however, about the increasing shortage in energy resources and the increasing dependency on foreign nations for oil. America relied on overseas oil for about 50 percent of the nation's supply, and this dependency made the nation too vulnerable to those foreign nations. In February, and again in April of 1977, the president spoke to the nation in his campaign to convince the public and Congress that measures, most importantly conservation, must be taken immediately to counteract a problem that had become a permanent feature of the future. Carter told Americans they were headed toward a "national catastrophe . . . the moral equivalent of war."

During the 1976–77 winter, the most severe in this century to that time, schools and factories had to shut down in the Northeast because they could not get sufficient oil or natural gas, and Congress had to pass emergency legislation to allow the president to raise the price ceiling on interstate natural gas prices. In April, he outlined his National Energy Plan to meet the crisis before a joint session of Congress. The program was a mixture of restraints and incentives to conserve oil and gas in order to reduce American dependence on outside sources. He proposed new taxes on domestic crude oil, on automobiles that did not meet fuel efficiency guidelines, and on businesses and utilities that refused to convert to other fuel sources. A standby tax on gasoline would be implemented if consumption exceeded the government's target levels. The president also contended that the price of American oil should be deregulated by the government. Oil prices should be able to rise to the international level in order to give companies an incentive to increase production of oil and gas. A windfall profits tax was proposed to allay criticism of the excessive profits that would result from deregulation. Federal price controls on natural gas would continue.

Carter had promised to deregulate newly discovered natural gas, so controls were a surprise to members of the industry. Congress would not pass the energy bill until October of 1978, and even then it fell short of what the president had requested. Carter failed to build a coalition in Congress which would have given him everything he wanted. The bill passed by Congress did not include the extra taxes, except a small penalty for cars that used a lot of gas. Congress decided to encourage competition with fewer limitations rather than encourage conservation, but the president was willing to sign the bill as a sign that Washington was doing something to solve the problem.

The Hope of Nuclear Power Diminishes

Nuclear power was viewed by many as the future hope of a cheap source of energy to replace the diminishing supplies of fossil fuels. By 1979, there were 72 nuclear reactors operating, with 91 more under construction to generate electricity. An accident at the Three Mile Island, Pennsylvania, nuclear power plant on March 28, 1979, brought protests from thousands of Americans and damaged the future of nuclear energy. A problem with the cooling system caused one of the reactors to overheat, threatening a meltdown of the uranium fuel core, which would have sent radioactive material into the surrounding community. Because of the threat from the radioactive emissions, pregnant women and preschoolers within five miles of the plant were advised to leave the area. Evacuation plans were made for a ten to twenty-mile radius. Fortunately, the reactor was stabilized by April 1. But protestors marched on Washington D.C. and picketed various plants to protest the danger the government was willing to pass on to the people for cheaper electricity. The commission appointed by Carter to assess the status of nuclear power plants around the nation recommended that more stringent safety standards should be implemented before more plants were constructed.

More Trouble From OPEC

In 1979, Americans faced gasoline shortages again. A revolution in Iran, beginning in January 1979, resulted in the overthrow of the Shah and a 69-day moratorium on oil production. Iran provided approximately 20 percent of the oil in the OPEC organization, which in turn, provided close to 50 percent of the world's oil supply. Even with the return of Iran, OPEC nations decided to produce less and charge more for their oil. By April, some areas of the United States had gasoline shortages caused by the machinations of OPEC. Motorists waited in line to fill their gas tanks, and in some instances, had to drive around to find a station without the sign "Sorry, out of gas." The president asked Congress for the power to ration gas if necessary, but the House voted "no" by 246–159. To meet the shortage, Carter then announced price controls on domestic oil would be gradually eliminated, resulting in further deregulation of the oil industry. It was believed that decontrol would stimulate domestic exploration and production, thereby alleviating the shortage. Prices on gasoline rose, as predicted, from 70 cents per gallon in 1977, to $1.30 per gallon in 1980. Prices on heating oil increased from 40 cents per gallon in 1977, to $1.00 per gallon in 1980. Carter hoped higher prices would force Americans to conserve energy.

President Carter addressed the nation on July 15, 1979, and outlined his energy proposal. He called for an all-out effort to produce alternative sources of energy, including new synthetic fuels. He then went on to speak with the nation concerning the "crisis of confidence" that was presenting a "fundamental threat to American democracy." He believed the nation was undergoing a problem with "malaise" and that it was time to pull together and solve the dangerous problems facing the nation. In early July, the OPEC nations announced their most recent price increase. Prices between January and July 1979 had been raised by approxi-

Long Gasoline Lines in Fort Lauderdale, Florida During the Oil Crisis in the 1970s.

mately 50 percent. Drastic measures were needed to wrench control away of this important resource from the OPEC nations.

Between October and December 1979, Congress passed most of the president's energy plan, including measures they had denied earlier. A standby rationing plan was authorized if a shortage in gasoline warrented such an action, and money was authorized to develop and produce synthetic fuels. A windfall profit tax on the oil industry was also approved, with the stipulation that money received from the tax would finance the synthetic fuel development, an expanded mass transit system, and the purchase of heating fuel for those in poverty. Tax credits would also be allowed for homeowners and businesses respectively for measures taken to reduce energy consumption and converting to alternative sources of energy.

A SOCIAL SECURITY CRISIS

The Social Security system was rapidly approaching a dangerous low point in funds. Inflation and the increasing numbers of Americans on social security had increased the amount paid out of the fund, while the revenue coming into the system had diminished. On December 20, 1977, President Carter signed a bill that tripled payroll taxes for the next ten years to put the system on more solid ground for the future. This increase, that could prove to be the largest peacetime tax increase in history, shook the confidence of the business community. The president had promised in his campaign that he would not raise payroll taxes. He hoped to offset this raise in taxes with a reduction in income taxes, but that was not done. For business men, the fear was a cycle of higher taxes, more inflation, larger government deficits, and finally, an economic recession. The Dow-Jones average, reacting to these concerns, dropped to its lowest level in almost two years.

ECONOMIC POLICIES AND ADMINISTRATION REORGANIZATION

Rising inflation and unemployment continued to plague the nation in the second half of the seventies. Inflation rose from 6 percent in 1977 to close to 13 percent by the end of 1980. Interest rates increased partly because of the wage-price spiral and partly because of the increasing price of oil. In 1980, the Federal Reserve Board raised the rediscount rate charged to banks, hoping to check price increases and shrink consumer demand. Interest rates were about 20 percent by the end of 1980. One result of higher interest rates was a decrease in home sales, which depressed that entire basic industry. As a result, the unemployment rate was up to 8 percent by the end of 1980. Carter's economic policies were confused and as ineffective as his predecessors had been. He decided to work on the problem of unemployment first. Congress agreed to cut taxes and increase spending in the federal government. When inflation began skyrocketing, he switched fiscal policy from fighting unemployment to fighting inflation, for which the tools were to raise taxes and reduce federal spending. But the recession only deepened.

A major portion of Carter's problems in economic policy making along with other areas of his agenda was his failure to convince the Congress or the public to follow his lead. He began his term with a lot of energy and attempted to tackle every problem immediately with personal input from anyone involved with the issue. This was soon discovered to be a confusing and exhausting way to run the executive branch. Therefore, the president reorganized his staff and appointed Hamilton Jordan as Chief of Staff. He had allowed too much access to him personally in order to avoid the pyramid type of organization Nixon had used, with Haldeman and Ehrlichman having an excessive amount of control over the information that reached the president. As far as his ability to persuade a Democratic controlled Congess to pass his programs, he had sold himself as a political outsider, and he continued that philosophy to his detriment while in the White House.

REFORMS IN GOVERNMENT

One way to cut government expenditures was to cut the size of government. Working toward reduction and efficiency in the federal bureaucracy, President Carter began cleaning house with a 28 percent cut in his own house. The Civil Service Reform Act, signed on October 13, 1978, brought the first major changes for employees of the federal government since the days of President Arthur. The Civil Service

Commission was eliminated, and a Senior Executive Service was implemented in its place. Promotions and higher salaries were tied to job performance, and supervisors were allowed to terminate workers if they had just cause. Presidents since Carter have tried to reform and reduce government bureaucracy, but they have not had much more success with their measures than he did.

The Department of Energy was established as a cabinet-level department on October 1, 1977. The Department was given an annual budget of approximately $7 billion, along with 21,000 employees to work on this most serious of problems for a nation that had a constantly growing need for energy sources. Another cabinet-level department was established when the Department of Education was separated from Health and Welfare.

Releasing the federal government from the task of regulating some areas of business and transportation was another method of streamlining the federal bureaucracy and spending fewer taxpayer dollars. Deregulation would also benefit consumers with the decrease in prices because competition should reduce prices for consumers. It was estimated that the cost for government to regulate this activity was as high as $100 billion annually. In 1977 there were 90 separate regulatory agencies issuing thousands of new rules each year. Legislation would deregulate commercial airlines in 1978, natural gas in 1978, and trucking in 1980.

FOREIGN AFFAIRS UNDER CARTER
SOVIET-AMERICAN RELATIONS

Carter's Human Rights Cornerstone

In his 1977 Inaugural Address, President Carter stated, "Because we are free we can never be indifferent to the fate of freedom elsewhere." Carter was announcing his commitment to the advancement of human rights around the world as a cornerstone of his foreign policy goals. Secretary of State Cyrus Vance defined human rights to mean political and civil liberties as well as economic and social rights. Committees met every two or three weeks to decide which nation would or would not receive restrictions on aid from the United States, according to their human rights activities. Criticism came from foreign nations and from Americans when it was apparent that countries of important strategic or economic interest were allowed violations of the policy, but countries of limited or no interest to the United States were punished.

Carter's public criticism of the human rights violations in the Soviet Union came close to ending another major foreign policy goal, eliminating nuclear weapons. In the beginning of his attempts to persuade Soviet President Leonid Brezhnev to participate in further talks, Carter had been clumsy to the point of offending Brezhnev. Carter criticized the Soviet Union for violating the human rights of Soviet citizens, and when Secretary of State Cyrus Vance arrived in Moscow in March 1977 with new proposals from the president, the Soviet government was not receptive. The Soviets demanded that President Carter remain silent on the internal affairs of their nation, but Carter refused to alter his commitment to advance the cause of human rights in all nations with which the United States had foreign relations. In spite of the strain on the relation, the Soviets agreed to talks concerning a new strategic arms limitation agreement because SALT I would expire in October 1977.

The SALT II Agreement

Secretary of State Vance and the Soviet foreign minister Andrei Gromyko met in Geneva to resume SALT negotiations. The agreement reduced the number of strategic missiles and bombers on both sides, but the number was small and new systems were exempted. While negotiations continued in Geneva, members of Congress and other government agencies were concerned about the advance of communism from the Soviet Union and its allies. Cuban troops appeared alongside Soviet advisors in Angola, Ethiopia, and other African nations to support left-wing revolutionary groups challenge the authority of regimes in power. The Soviet Union was also supplying weapons to terrorists and other nations in the Middle East and Central America. Critics of the new SALT treaty pointed to the increased activity of the hard-line communist nations and concessions to the Soviets in the treaty as a danger to American security because the Soviets were allegedly allowed military advantages. The negotiations continued, however, and Carter and Brezhnev signed the SALT II treaty on June 18, 1979. The treaty was under consideration of the Senate Foreign Relations Committee when it was discovered that the Soviets had placed approximately two thousand troops in Cuba. The Soviets would not call the troops home in spite of a demand from the Carter administration and threats from many senators that they would not vote to ratify the treaty under those conditions.

Results of the Afghanistan Invasion

Then on Christmas Day, 1979, the Soviets surprised the United States by invading Afghanistan. Attempting to keep the pro-communist regime in power in this small backward country would cost the Soviets dearly in the end, and resistance fighters would eventually drive the Soviets out of their nation. President Carter reacted on January 4, 1980, when he placed an embargo on all sales of grain and high tech equipment to the Soviet Union. The president also notified the Soviets that the American athletes would not attend the 1980 Summer Olympics to be held in Moscow unless a withdrawal from Afghanistan was forthcoming. Many athletes and non-athletes believed that the Olympics should be free from politics, but the United States Olympic Committee voted to support the boycott. Then President Carter convinced 67 other nations to join the Americans in the boycott. Of course, many of these nations would not have sent representatives to the games anyway. A total of 80 nations were represented in Moscow the following summer. The United Nations Security Council could do nothing about the problem in Afghanistan because the Soviets vetoed a proposal to condemn the invasion. President Carter then asked Senate Majority Leader Robert Byrd to keep the SALT II treaty off the floor of the Senate because it probably would be defeated.

LATIN AMERICAN RELATIONS

The Panama Canal Treaties

A trouble spot for the United States in Latin America since the 1960s was the Panama Canal. From the time the Panama Canal was built with the Canal Zone under the control of the United States, there had been protests at times from Panamanians who did not believe the United States should control the canal. In January 1964, rioting broke out and American soldiers were killed along with Panamanians. At that point, the government of Panama demanded a discussion to revise the treaties with the United States to prevent more bloodshed.

Presidents Johnson, Nixon, Ford, and Carter agreed that new treaties should be negotiated with Panama, but opposition to turning over the canal zone was strong in Congress and around the country. In September 1977, the United States and Panama concluded negotiations on two separate treaties, known collectively as the Panama Canal Treaties. The first treaty proposed joint American and Panamanian operation of the canal until the end of 1999, at which time Panama would receive total control of operations. The second treaty declared that the canal would remain permanently neutral, and the United States would still have the right to defend the canal's neutrality by force, if necessary.

The treaties faced stiff opposition in the Senate, where a two-thirds majority was needed for ratification. Conservatives joined together from both parties to fight the "give away" of the canal. The Republican National Committee stated the treaties would endanger national security. Ronald Reagan completely ignored the history of the canal when he declared that the Canal Zone was sovereign American territory purchased from Panama. Actually, the 1903 treaty with Panama stated that the Canal Zone belonged to Panama, but the United States was given the right to operate it as if it were the owner (like a renter of someone else's house; see Chapter Seven for the story of the Panama Canal). During the debate, one senator asked an emphatic but rhetorical question, "We stole it fair and square, so why can't we keep it?" (He was closer to the truth than he probably realized, for Theodore Roosevelt's actions had been shady at best.)

Hoping to gather support for the treaty, President Carter brought influential Americans from across the nation to the White House to explain his position on the canal issue. Officials in the cabinet and employees from the State and Defense Departments traveled across the nation to explain the treaties to Americans on a more personal level. The message they gave was that Latin American resentment against admittedly imperialistic actions of the United States had limited our ability to control the region, whether we liked it or not. Therefore, the Panama Canal Treaties were essential steps in showing respect for the region and improving relations in Latin America. Surprisingly, actor John Wayne, who usually supported military actions, actually came out in support of the treaties. However, it was support for the treaties by Senator Robert Byrd, the Democratic Majority Leader, and Senator Howard Baker, the Republican Senate Minority Leader, that began to change the position of a majority of the Senate. The first treaty was finally ratified by the Senate in March 1978, and the second one was ratified on April 18 of the same year, both by votes of 68 to 32. When President Carter visited Venezuela and Brazil later in the month (April), he was received as a popular hero, proving once again that good foreign policy usually also brings the benefits of respect.

Revolution in Nicaragua

Since 1936 the United States had supported the anti-communist dictatorship of the Somoza dynasty in Nicaragua. Especially during the Cold War, American administrations had ignored the regime's cruel treatment of its citizens and had sold arms to it. The poverty in that Latin American country fostered a spirit of rebellion against a repressive dictatorship that served the needs of a few. In 1978, the Sandinista National Liberation Front (FSLN) began a civil war to remove President Anastasio Somoza. (They took their name from Cesar Augusto Sandino, who had led rebels against American forces in Nicaragua in the twenties and thirties.) The Sandinistas soon won widespread support among the people, including businessmen, despite their leftist political leanings. Due to a crackdown by Somoza on opponents attempting to force him out of office, American military ties were ended and economic support reduced from 1977 to 1979. Carter hoped to force Somoza to rein in his National Guard, stop the killing of innocent Nicaraguans, and negotiate some type of agreement with the Sandinistas to end the abuses. But the United States could not influence either Somoza or the Sandinistas to negotiate an end to the discord. The Carter administration could not support the Sandinistas because of their Marxist and socialist views, although they refused to align themselves with the Soviet Union and opposed the pro-Soviet Communist party in Nicaragua. In 1979, Somoza was ovethrown by the Sandinistas and fled the country. (He was later assassinated in Paraguay.) President Reagan would have to deal with this new government and the problems they represented to the United States. (See Chapter Eighteen.)

ASIAN POLICIES

President Carter announced that full diplomatic relations with Communist China would resume on January 1, 1979. The two countries had ended formal diplomatic relations in 1949, when Mao Tse-tung's communists had won the civil war in China. Nixon had opened the door for a new relationship with China in 1972, but full diplomatic recognition was not extended at the time. Formal diplomatic relations were postponed by the Chinese until President Carter was willing to accept their terms to end military and diplomatic relations with Taiwan. The 1954 American defense agreement with Taiwan would end in 1979, but other agreements, such as commercial relations, would remain in place. The normalization of relations would open up possibilities of trade with a nation containing close to one billion people. There was heavy criticism from the government in Taiwan and the United States for this seeming betrayal of a nation guaranteed the protection and support of the United States government. Realpolitics, however, demanded that a nation of the size and strength of Communist China could not be ignored.

Egyptian President Anwar Sadat, Israeli Prime Minister Meanchem Begin and U.S. President Jimmy Carter at the signing ceremony of the Camp David Accords. Credit: AP/Wide World Photos.

MIDDLE EAST POLICIES

The Camp David Accords and Egypt-Israeli Peace

Peace in the Middle East was the goal of Presidents Nixon, Ford, and Carter. Caught in the middle between a commitment to Israel and needing the oil of the Arab states committed to the destruction of this American ally, the only solution was to bring peace to these enemies. In 1977, President Carter became the first American president to publicly call for a Palestinian homeland. Hopes were raised when President Anwar Sadat of Egypt offered to go to Israel and explore new avenues for peace between the two nations. Israeli Prime Minister Manachem Begin issued an invitation for Sadat to express Egypt's position for a future peace before the Knesset (the Israeli parliament) in Jerusalem. And President Carter offered encouragement to both leaders in their mission. As a result, Egyptian President Sadat went to Jerusalem in November 1977 and addressed the Israeli Parliament, declaring to a worldwide television audience that "Israel has become an established fact." But by August 1978, the dialogue had not only stalled, but relations were even more strained. Israel refused to discuss autonomy for Palestinians in the West Bank area and refused to surrender captured territory in the Sinai Peninsula.

In order to move the dialogue forward, Carter invited Sadat and Begin to meet at Camp David, the retreat for presidents in Maryland, and continue talks with mediation. Both leaders agreed, and with help from the Carter administration, Begin and Sadat signed two documents before television audiences on September 17, 1978. It was a high point for the Carter presidency when the first peace accords between Israel and an Arab nation were signed. This was not a peace treaty, but a preliminary step on the way to one. Technically, the agreements were called the "Framework for Peace in the Middle East" and a "Framework for the Conclusion of a Peace Treaty between Egypt and Israel," but they were better known simply by the collective title of the Camp David Accords.

The signing of the final treaty was delayed when Begin announced plans to expand Jewish settlements in the West Bank area, which was to be an area for Palestinian autonomy that had been a point of contention in the early stages of negotiations. But American shuttle diplomacy between Cairo and Jerusalem finally brought forth a peace treaty, which was signed at the White House on March 26, 1979. The issue of Palestinian autonomy was not completely settled, but the treaty was signed in which Israeli-occupied Sinai territory would return to Egypt in stages, with the final stage to be completed by April 1982.

Unfortunately, a peace treaty between Israel and Egypt did not result in peace for the area in spite of American attempts to add other Arab nations to the peace process. Arab nations and the Palestinian Liberation Organization severed diplomatic and economic ties with Egypt, labeling Sadat a traitor to the Islamic and Palestinian causes. And government officials in Syria, Libya, and Iraq even stated that Sadat should be assassinated. (Sadat was in fact assassinated in October 1981, and was succeeded by Hosni Mubarek.) Relations were also strained between the United States and Israel. Jews in the United States resented criticisms of Israeli activities and the fact that the United States government had pressured Israel to make concessions to Egypt for peace. When Carter criticized Israel for raids perpetrated against PLO strongholds in Lebanon, the Israelis feared the United States was beginning to favor the Palestinian side.

The Iranian Hostage Crisis

Instability in the area increased with the overthrow of the government of the pro-Western Shah of Iran, Shah Reza Pahlavi, on February 11, 1979. Opposition to the Shah had grown to the point that abdication was his only option. The Shah was one of the few allies the United States had in the Middle East. The leader of the new regime, the Ayatollah Khomeini, was an Islamic fundamentalist with strong anti-American sentiments. He quickly overturned the Western-style laws and customs the Shah had put in place, and declared that Iran was now an Islamic republic ruled by Islamic law.

Violence toward Americans and other Westerners prompted the government to advise all Americans who could to leave Iran. The Iranians were hostile to any country that had supported the oppressive government of the Shah, but particularly the actively supportive American government. On October 22, President

Carter, over the protests of several advisors, allowed the Shah to enter the United States to obtain medical treatment for lymphatic cancer. In retaliation for American sanctuary to the Shah, on November 4, 1979, young militants stormed the American embassy in Teheran (the capital of Iran) and took 63 hostages. Their demands for the release of the Americans were simple: return the Shah to Iran to stand trial. The Ayatollah ordered the captors to release most of the women, the African-American hostages, and one ill captive. But the remaining 52 Americans were held captive for 444 days.

President Carter used every means at his disposal short of war to secure the release of the hostages. But this crisis was difficult for the president to resolve, as later events would prove that the Iranians were intentionally seeking to hurt the Carter administration. Carter must secure the release of the hostages, but at the same time not allow the United States to appear weak by acceding to the demands of the Iranian kidnappers. Faced with a no-win situation, Carter would appear weak by the time the

Rioters burning the American flag at the U.S. Embassy in Tehran, Iran, 1979. Credit: AP/Wide World Photos.

hostages were returned at the end of his presidency. Nothing the president tried was successful. Oil imports from Iran were stopped, Iranian assets were frozen, economic sanctions were imposed, the UN Security Council demanded the release of the hostages, even a military rescue operation was authorized but was aborted when problems developed while the raid was underway.

Then in November 1980, the hostages were turned over to the Iranian government. Khomeini made many demands on the United States for the return of the hostages, but he agreed to drop all demands and release the Americans for the return of Iranian assets frozen in the United States. In his last act as president, Carter released several billion dollars of Iranian assets under American control. The hostages left Iran on January 20, 1981, as Ronald Reagan began his term as the new president of the United States. And Jimmy Carter flew to an American base in Wiesbaden, West Germany, to meet the released American hostages as President Reagan's personal representative.

THE 1980 ELECTION

The Democrats

President Carter was running very poorly in the polls during 1979. High inflation and interest rates, coupled with the Iranian hostage crisis, seemed to doom his chances for reelection if he could even manage to win his party's nomination to run again. Many Democratic Party leaders urged Massachusetts Senator Edward M. "Ted" Kennedy to challenge Carter in the primaries. With Kennedy's numbers in the polls showing him ahead of the incumbent president, Kennedy entered the race for the nomination. But once Kennedy actually became a candidate, his lead in the polls shrank rather dramatically.

Haunting Ted Kennedy's candidacy was the tragic and controversial Chappaquiddick Affair. Kennedy had been considered a possible Democratic candidate for president ever since his last brother, Bobby, had been assassinated in 1968. But in July 1969, Kennedy's car had fallen from a narrow wooden bridge on Martha's Vineyard, Massachusetts, resulting in the drowning of a 28-year- old secretary by the name of Mary Jo Kopechne. Kennedy's failure to report the accident for ten hours, and apparent inconsistencies in his story of exactly what happened, led Kennedy to offer his resignation from the United States Senate. While pressure from loyal constituents changed his mind, it ruined his presidential chances for the forseeable future at least. As it turned out, the general public had a long memory as far as Chappaquiddick is concerned, and the incident appeared to hurt him in many of the primaries in the spring of 1980.

Kennedy suffered a series of defeats in the Iowa caucuses, the New Hampshire primary, and in Southern primaries in early 1980. In April, a major victory in the New York primary, which Carter had failed to win in 1976 as well, seemed to revive Kennedy's campaign. The result was a string of victories in the important states of Pennsylvania, Michigan, and California. But they were too little too late for a Kennedy nomination victory. Although Carter entered the Democratic National Convention in August with about 300 delegates more than he needed to ensure his nomination, Kennedy refused to withdraw from the race. Instead, he used the convention to give a rousing speech that sounded more like an acceptance speech than anything else. And the Democrats entered the official campaign badly divided with Jimmy Carter at the head of their ticket.

The Republicans

Ronald Reagan, representative of the views of the very conservative, right wing of the Republican Party, was the Republican choice for the presidential nomination at the convention after easily defeating George Bush in the primaries. Bush had been a former Texas congressman, director of the CIA, and chairman of the Republican National Committee. And at Reagan's request, the Republicans nominated George Bush, representative of the center of the party, as the vice-presidential running mate on the ticket. Reagan was a former movie actor, who, as his career declined, turned to politics. If one believes politics involves acting, this was a good career choice for Reagan. Certainly he made good use of his ease in front of cameras and his ability to communicate orally. In 1966, Reagan was elected governor of

President Ronald Reagan and Vice President George Bush wave to the cheering delegates at the Republican National Convention in Dallas, 1984. Credit: AP/Wide World Photos.

California with promises to cut taxes and fight student militancy, which was an affront to order. In 1980 he represented a choice for Americans who wanted a candidate who was strongly anti-communist, concerned for the traditional family and Christian values of this country, opposed abortion and radical feminists, and was committed to a foreign policy of strength and determination of purpose once again. Fundamentalist religious leaders such as Jerry Falwell and Pat Robertson supported the candidacy of Reagan and pulled together their followers and others under the blanket designation of the "Moral Majority."

Ironically, Reagan had begun his political thinking as a New Deal Democrat in Dixon, Illinois. His father headed up the relief effort in Dixon during the Great Depression. After his graduation from Eureka College in 1932, Reagan began a career as a sportscaster on the radio. In 1937, he went west with the Chicago Cubs' spring training camp, but ended up getting a screen test and becoming an actor instead. Then he became the host of "General Electric Theater" from 1954 to 1962, when he switched to hosting "Death Valley Days" until 1965. Politically, Reagan supported Democrat Helen Gahagan Douglas in her 1950 bid to unseat California Republican Senator Richard Nixon. But his support was actually played down by Douglas because Reagan was considered too liberal. Precisely why it happened we might never fully understand, but Reagan supported Nixon in the 1960 presidential election and became a registered Republican in 1962. Within one decade, Ronald Reagan had gone from liberal New Deal Democrat to arch-conservative Republican. And by 1980, Reagan was seen as the most obvious choice to head the Republican ticket because conservatism appeared ready for widespread acceptance, particularly if an articulate spokesman were advocating those ideas.

The Campaign and Results

During the 1980 presidential campaign, Carter tried to narrow Reagan's large lead in the polls by accusing Reagan of introducing "racism" into the race. But that strategy backfired, and support for Reagan grew even more impressive. Liberal Illinois Republican Congressman John B. Anderson had entered the race as an independent candidate. And when the League of Women Voters insisted that any presidential debate should include Anderson, Carter was placed in a no-win situation. He needed a debate in order to try to narrow the gap between himself and the frontrunner, but Anderson threatened to take more Democratic votes away than traditional, conservative Republican votes. Therefore, Carter refused all offers to debate, and Reagan was able to score more points for his willingness to debate with both Carter and Anderson.

In October, as the campaign started to get really serious, a number of voters began having second thoughts about Reagan's bumbling speeches in which he frequently quoted lines from old Hollywood movies. At the same time, Anderson's support began to fade in the tradition of third-party candidates in American history, and President Carter was the beneficiary of these developments. Then, independently of the League of Women Voters, Carter challenged Reagan to a debate between the two of them. But the debate, conducted on October 28, one week from the election, seemed to clinch the election for Reagan, as his easy and charming style contrasted with a relatively stiff President Carter.

On November 4, the first anniversary of the beginning of the Iranian hostage crisis, Ronald Reagan won a landslide victory over the incumbent president, whether voters really agreed with the very conservative Republican platform or merely disagreed with the way Carter had handled the presidency. Reagan won with 43.9 million popular votes to Carter's 35.5 million. The electoral college victory was even more decisive, with 489 electoral votes for Reagan and 49 for Carter. Independent John Anderson won 5.7 million popular votes, but won no electoral votes. Ronald Reagan had been elected the fortieth president of the United States.

1980	50	RONALD REAGAN	Republican	43,201,220	489	50.9
		Jimmy Carter	Democrat	34,913,332	49	41.2
		John B. Anderson	Independent	5,581,379		

ADDITIONAL READINGS

Peter Carroll, *It Seemed Like Nothing Happened* (1983). A delightful collection of anecdotes about the 1970s. Captures the everyday lives of Americans, especially their frustrations to achieve according to their expectations. Finds a bitter comedy in the blunders of the era's mediocre political leaders.

Daniel F. Ford, *Three Mile Island: Thirty Minutes to Meltdown* (1982). A journalistic account of the crisis at the time of the nuclear accident.

Susan Hartmann, *From Margin to Mainstream: American Women and Politics Since 1960* (1989). An interpretation of women's growing role in American politics. Analyzes the important developments of the 1970s, most pointedly women's influence on the Democratic party. Also looks at the forces that pushed the Equal Rights Amendment through Congress but failed to see it ratified in the states.

Jerome L. Himmelstein, *To the Right: The Transformation of American Conservatism* (1990). The story of the decline of "Old Right" fiscal conservatives, isolationists, and Republican "centrists" during the 1970s and the rise of the "New Right" based in evangelical Protestantism. Analyzes the New Right's ability to rally support for Cold War foreign policy and the rollback of social welfare programs at both federal and state levels of government.

John P. Hoerr, *And the Wolf Finally Came: The Decline of the American Steel Industry* (1988). A personal and journalistic view of Pittsburgh's eclipse as a steel-producing center. Details the decline in productivity since the complacently prosperous years of the 1950s and the failure of plant managers, as well as unions, to adjust to the more competitive methods of steel production abroad.

William Quandt, *Camp David* (1986). An insider's story of Jimmy Carter's greatest triumph. Analyzes the Middle Eastern diplomacy as the centerpiece of Carter's otherwise unsuccessful program of world peace through negotiations and better understanding.

Arthur M. Schlesinger, Jr., *The Imperial Presidency* (1973). It examines the growing power of the White House to conduct foreign policy as part of the reason for the Watergate scandal.

Edwin Schur, *The Awareness Trap: Self Absorption Instead of Social Change* (1976). A description of the various contemporary "awareness" movements. Schur gives detailed examples of how programs of self-improvement and religious mysticism appealed to people disoriented by social change and willing to pay money to find "meaning" in their lives.

James I. Sundquist, *The Decline and Resurgence of Congress* (1981). A close political study of changing relations between two key branches of government. Sundquist underlines the revival of congressional strength after President Johnson's successful broadening of executive powers, and the bipartisan tug of war that took place between Congress and its 1970s counterparts: the often haughty Nixon, the congressional-style "weak" president Gerald Ford, and the distant Jimmy Carter

Tad Szulc, *The Illusion of Power: Foreign Policy in the Nixon Years* (1978). This book looks at the manner in which Nixon engaged in foreign affairs.

Ronald Taylor, *Chavez and the Farm Workers* (1975). This book focuses on Cesar Chavez's organizing work on behalf of Hispanic agricultural workers.

Cyrus Vance, *Hard Choices* (1983). A former secretary of state's day-to-day recollections of his time in office during the Carter years. Vance, a career diplomat, reviewed the crucial policy decisions concerning Afghanistan and the Middle East, as well as the factors that caused him to resign from the Carter administration.

Robert Woodward and Carl Bernstein, *All the President's Men* (1974). This book records the uncovering of the Watergate scandal by the two *Washington Post* reporters who exposed it in the first place.

CHAPTER EIGHTEEN

The Eighties and Beyond

MAJOR EVENTS

1981   The Economic Recovery Tax Act
The Air Traffic Controllers Strike is squashed
Acquired Immune Deficiency Syndrome (AIDS) first appears in U.S.

1982   Equal Rights Amendment (ERA) fails in the states

1983   Interior Secretary James Watt is forced to resign
241 Marines killed in Beirut bombing
The U.S. invades Grenada

1984   The Strategic Defense Initiative (SDI, or Star Wars) is proposed by Reagan
Reagan is re-elected president

1985   The Gramm-Rudman-Hollings Act

1986   The *Challenger* space shuttle disaster
The Tax Reform Act
The Immigration Reform and Control Act
The Iran-Contra Scandal becomes public

1988   George Bush is elected president

1989   The Tiananmen Square Massacre in Beijing, China
The Berlin Wall is torn down
Panamanian leader Noriega is kidnapped by U.S. troops

1990   The American Disabilities Act

1991   The Persian Gulf War
The Clarence Thomas Supreme Court Nomination fight

1992   The Rodney King beating and the Los Angeles Riots
Bill Clinton is elected president

1993   The Family and Medical Leave Act
The Waco Tragedy
The North American Free Trade Agreement (NAFTA) is ratified
The Brady Bill is enacted

1994   Republicans win big in off-year elections

1995   The Alfred P. Murrah Federal Building in Oklahoma City is bombed

INTRODUCTION TO THE REAGAN ADMINISTRATION

Pomp and pageantry were back in the White House with the inauguration of the oldest president in United States history. Ronald Reagan, the fortieth president, took the oath of office in his formal attire on January 20, 1981. Four years before, Jimmy Carter had worn a three-piece suit. For the first time, a president was sworn in from the West Front of the Capitol, with the impressive monuments of Washington in sight. The message to the nation concerning the problems and their solutions was clear, "It is time to reawaken this industrial giant, to get government back within its means and to lighten our punitive tax burden . . . ." Reagan also stated that "government is not the solution to our problems; government **is** the problem." Along with a stronger military defensive position and increased prestige for the office of the presidency, these were his priorities. The highlight of the inauguration ceremonies was the announcement that the American hostages were flying out of Iran. The long Iranian hostage ordeal finally was coming to an end.

DOMESTIC ISSUES UNDER REAGAN
REAGANOMICS

Early Economic Efforts

Inflation, unemployment, and government deficits had to come down. The president proposed to cut taxes and government spending, except for the defense budget, in order to get the economy moving again. Along with federal income tax cuts, fewer government regulations on businesses were proposed to allow businesses larger profits as motivation for growth and new investments. He believed that revenue flowing into the government coffers would increase, in spite of tax cuts, because the economy would be moving forward once again with incentives to businessmen. Many had doubts concerning the proposition that reduced taxes and increased military spending could work without creating dangerously high deficits. Before George Bush was Reagan's running mate, he had called candidate Reagan's plan "voodoo economics." And John Anderson, the independent candidate in the 1980 election, believed that the only way Reagan's policy would work was to use "blue smoke and mirrors."

The annual inflation rate stood at about 13.2 percent in 1981, and it was the most pressing problem for the new administration. The policies of Nixon, Ford, and Carter, which had focused on the demand side of the economic curve, had not been successful at bringing the rate down to a level that would get the economy moving. Therefore, Reagan was ready for new solutions. Unemployment would be allowed to increase without government intervention, allowing the recession to continue until inflation was down. Reagan was a convert to "supply-side" economic theories, which stated that the economic problems causing inflation and unemployment were caused by a reduced supply of goods. The president began to put into place his new economic policies quickly. He issued an executive order to end government price controls on oil. On April 24, 1981, he lifted the grain embargo on the Soviet Union, increasing markets for American farmers. The Federal Reserve Board kept interest rates up to contract the money supply and reduce inflation.

The Economic Recovery Tax Act

Congress gave President Reagan most of what he asked for in his economic policy proposals. On August 4, 1981, the Economic Recovery Tax Act was signed, putting into place a three-year tax (33 months, to be precise) reduction plan of 25 percent federal income tax reduction rather than the 30 percent Reagan had requested. In the first year, there was an across-the-board cut of 5 percent in personal income taxes and 10 percent for the next two years. There were tax breaks for businesses; the capital gains tax was reduced from 28 percent maximum to 20 percent. And the maximum tax rate was decreased from 70 percent to 50 percent. The public cheered the new tax cuts, but it would be the wealthiest Americans who would directly benefit the most. Instead of the "new beginning" that Reagan had promised, this was similar to the "trickle down" theory of Secretary of the Treasury Andrew Mellon during the 1920s.

Attempts to Reduce the National Debt Failed

Next on the agenda was to decrease the deficit with cuts in government programs. Reagan was particularly critical of the large amounts of tax dollars allocated to President Johnson's Great Society welfare programs. Welfare programs had increased steadily since the New Deal, and conservatives believed government should be smaller and individuals should take more responsibility for themselves. Congress cut approximately $40 billion in the 1981 budget from education, food stamps, the National Endowments for the Arts and the Humanities, Aid for Families with Dependent Children, health block grants, urban mass transit systems, job training programs, and the Corporation for Public Broadcasting, to name a few. Among the programs eliminated entirely was former President Carter's synthetic fuels project, an effort to further research in alternative sources of energy in order to reduce American reliance on foreign oil. Limits were also put into place on unemployment insurance and the cost of Medicare and Medicaid health insurance.

For fiscal year 1982, the Reagan budget cuts amounted to about $35.2 billion. Meanwhile, the president asked for major increases in military spending, which Congress authorized to the tune of $12.3 billion (in increase) for the same fiscal year. In other words, the spending cuts were almost three times larger than the increased military spending. Logic would dictate that this would result in a net spending reduction, but apparent logic often does not apply to economics in the real world. The vast spending cuts in the non-entitlement, non-military areas actually drove significantly larger numbers of Americans into the ranks of poverty, where they then qualified for the various entitlement programs lumped together by many Americans by the word "welfare." Although President Reagan said he wanted to return government assistance to helping only the "truly needy," which he believed were those who could not work, his economic approach to the budget created a larger percentage of Americans below the poverty line while, at the same time, putting more money into the pockets of the middle and upper classes with his tax cuts. Thus, the gap between rich and poor was at least partially assisted by these fiscal measures. By 1983, about 15.3 percent of the population was below the poverty line. The net effect on the deficit was to double it to approximately $110.6

billion in fiscal year 1982. And for the first time in American history, the national debt was more than $1 trillion.

The Recession of 1982–1983

In 1982, the recession that was lingering from the Carter presidency worsened. The high interest rates used by the Federal Reserve Board (and approved by the Reagan administration) to fight inflation reduced consumer spending, which caused businesses to lay off employees. In addition to that, the rising public debt created fears of even higher interest rates, which helped propel the stock market into a slump in 1982, with unemployment rising with the market's decline. Reagan insisted that his policies would work, but time was needed. The decline in American exports, which would triple between 1981 and 1984 because of the increase in the value of the American dollar in comparison to foreign currencies, was another cause for the American recession. Millions of Americans lost their jobs in the steel mills and factories because of the lack of demand for American-made products. Farmers were hurt as well by the drop in exports.

Because of the strain of the recession, Reagan was willing to accept a small reduction in military spending and smaller cuts than he wanted in social programs, along with an emergency job program. Fear of the growing budget deficit persuaded the president to work with Congress to raise revenues (they were called "revenue enhancements," not tax increases). In September 1982, Reagan signed the Tax Equity and Fiscal Responsibility Act, to be effective on January 1, 1983, after the off-year Congressional elections were safely over. The bill raised approximately $98.3 billion by closing some of the tax loopholes in the federal tax system, and by raising the excise taxes on airline tickets, telephone service, and cigarettes. Other measures taken for the same purpose during Reagan's first term in office included an April 1983 Social Security Amendment, which made social security income taxable for the first time. And in July 1984, Reagan signed the Deficit Reduction Act of 1984, which raised about $50 billion in invisible areas, despite the president's promises not to raise taxes.

By 1984, the economy was definitely in recovery, and consumer confidence resulted in consumer spending on a larger scale. The federal income tax cuts, and an inflation rate down to 4 percent, gave Americans the confidence and the ability to buy once again. The tight money policies of the Federal Reserve Board, supported by the administration, helped to check inflation, although most of the credit should probably go to the Iran-Iraq War, which badly divided the Arab oil-rich nations in the 1980s and rendered OPEC ineffective as an instrument of retaliation against the Western economies. This war resulted in plummeting oil prices worldwide, greatly reducing the inflation rate in the United States. Finally, unemployment dropped slightly. Consumer spending increased business activity, which led to a "bull" market on the stock exchange. Prosperity apparently was coming back again.

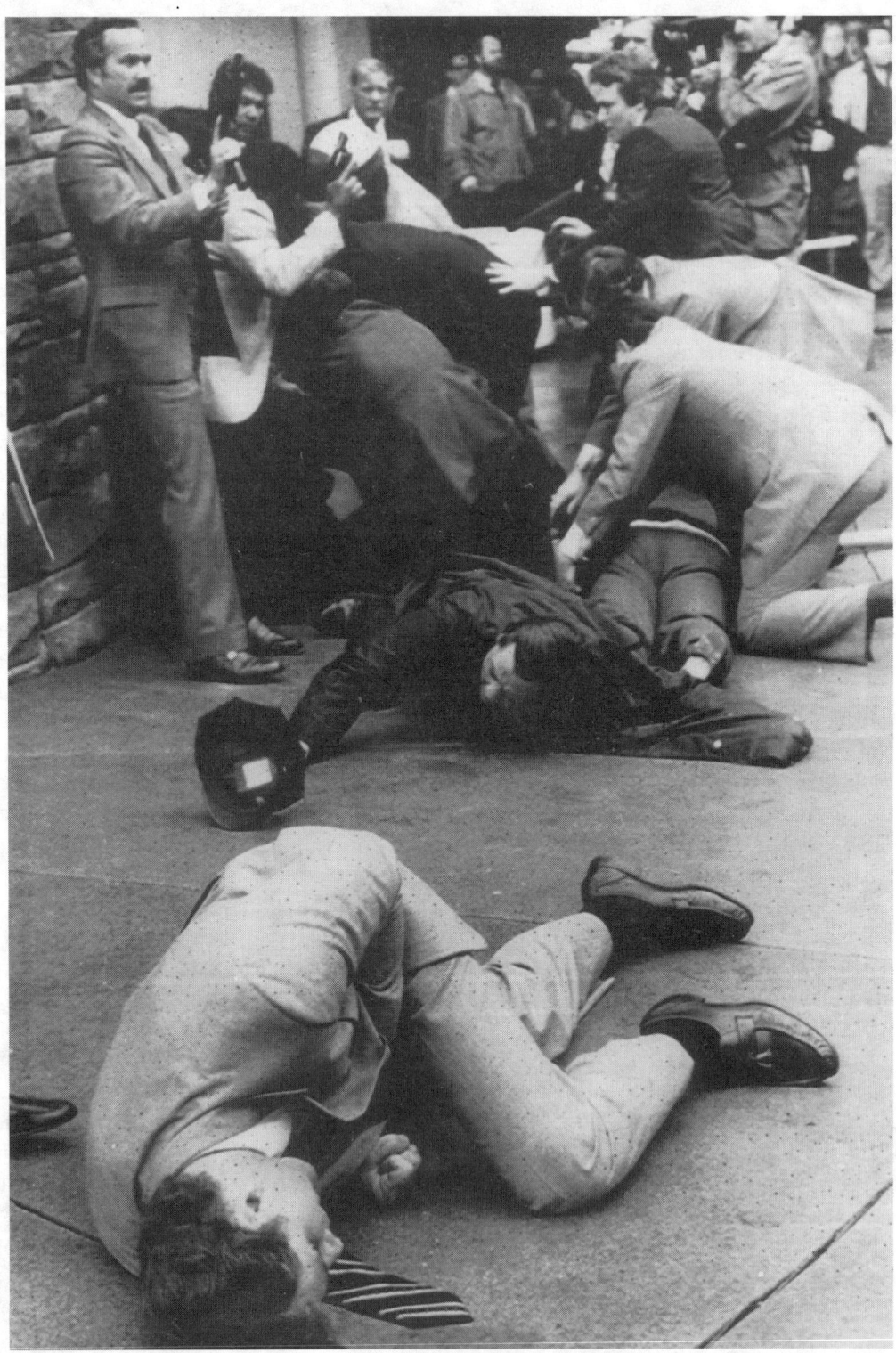

Assassination attempt on President Ronald Reagan in Washington, D.C., March 1981.
Credit: AP/Wide World Photos.

AN ASSASSINATION ATTEMPT

On March 30, 1981, President Reagan had been shot while getting into his limousine after delivering a speech at the Washington Hilton Hotel in Washington, D.C. The would-be assassin, John Hinckley, Jr., shot the president, it was discovered later, to impress the actress Jodie Foster, with whom Hinckley was obsessed. Three other men were shot, including the president's press secretary, James Brady, but all survived. Brady was shot in the forehead, with extensive damage done to his brain; he would be confined to a wheelchair following surgery and extensive physical therapy. The Brady Bill would eventually pass through Congress (under the Clinton administration) due to the efforts of Brady and his wife Sarah to limit access to handguns; Hinckley had bought a small handgun to kill the president without any type of background check.

President Reagan had been hit in the back and underwent surgery soon after the shooting. The president was known for his wit, but the nation was impressed with the courage he showed with his joking manner before and after the surgery. His wife Nancy was greeted with the comment "Honey, I forgot to duck." He also told his surgeons, "I hope you're all Republicans." Hinckley was found mentally incompetent and sent to a mental hospital rather than prison.

The president and his wife Nancy were extremely close. Following the attempt on her husband's life, it was discovered that Ms. Reagan consulted with an astrologer and had done so since his campaign for the presidency. The influence of astrological information on Mrs. Reagan was strong, and her influence on the president was also. Donald Regan, the president's Chief of Staff, later said that in his view, the influence of astrology on policy was real.

ORGANIZED LABOR

Following the rejection of the government's new contract, some 13,000 members, representing 70 percent of the Professional Air Traffic Controllers Organization (PATCO), walked out on strike on August 3, 1981. President Reagan warned the strikers that those not back on the job by August 5 would be fired. Reagan said he sympathized with the workers in this very stressful occupation and their needs for higher salaries, but the government could not afford the $700 million the controllers wanted in the increasingly tough economic times, nor could he allow government workers to strike. He was the first president to have ever headed a union; he had served for six terms as the president of the Screen Actors Guild and had led the first strike in that union's history. But this strike was illegal and would create a national emergency. Thousands of Americans would be endangered on the daily flights around the country. Congress had passed a law forbidding government employees to strike, and the members of PATCO had signed agreements not to strike. Reagan differentiated between workers striking in private industry and government positions in much the same way that President Calvin Coolidge had as governor of Massachusetts when the police in Boston had gone out on strike in 1919. Coolidge maintained that "There is no right to strike against the public safety by anyone at anytime."

The decision was up to the controllers, and those who did not return to work on August 5 were terminated. The number of flights were reduced, and supervisors and non-striking controllers, along with military controllers, were placed in the radar towers until replacements could be trained. Ironically, PATCO was one of only a handful of labor unions to have endorsed Reagan in the 1980 presidential election.

Reagan may have been the head of a union at one time, but his appointments to the National Labor Relations Board were definitely not pro-union. (He had also been a New Deal liberal Democrat at one time.) The federal courts also were consistently nonsupportive of organized labor. The government slant in favor of business owners and the diminishing industrial strongholds for organized labor (such as steel, manufacturing, and coal mining) reduced the numbers of union members across the nation. By the early 1990s, union membership was down to about 15 percent of the total job force. Part of the reason for this decline was that the areas of the labor market that were growing were in the service industries, which were low-paying and not unionized. Ironically, although President Reagan's firing of the air traffic controllers in 1981 set the tone for the anti-union environment in the decade and beyond, local, state, and federal employees experienced much greater success in unionization efforts since the early eighties than workers in the private sector.

CONSERVATIVES UNITE

Support for Ronald Reagan and other conservative Republicans was strong within the traditional conservative groups and the so-called "New Right," made up of a large number of evangelical Christian groups. (They are also commonly referred to as the Religious Right.) To the conservatives of the 1980s, the liberal attitudes of government and society in the 1960s had promoted big government with increased welfare spending and an irreverent attitude toward the traditional values that most Americans held. It was believed that the traditional values must be regained or the society would not last. These conservatives were concentrated in the Sunbelt area of the South and Southwest and from the large numbers of fundamentalist Protestants, traditional Catholics, Orthodox Jews, and other more conservative groups. The television ministries of fundamentalist evangelical preachers such as Jerry Falwell with his "Old Time Gospel Hour," Jim Bakker's "PTL" program (Praise the Lord Club), and Jimmy Swaggart, added the support of their millions of viewers to conservative politicians.

Ronald Reagan mirrored many of the conservative views of these Americans despite the fact that he was the first divorced president in the White House, had trouble controlling his own children (his daughter Patti was such an outspoken critic that she was eventually not welcome in the White House), and admitted he did not attend church regularly. He did, however, espouse the traditional values of the necessity of keeping families together, moral lifestyles that denounced sexual promiscuity and drugs, individual effort to get ahead, a strong military to keep America safe, and less federal government intervention into the lives of American citizens.

The New Right saw many problems in the nation that illustrated a need to return to the old values, not only of society but also of government. It was believed that the removal of school-sponsored prayer and the teaching of morality was greatly responsible for the increase among the young of discipline problems, crime, drug use, and sexual promiscuity. In 1962 in *Engel v. Vitale*, the Supreme Court had declared it unconstitutional for public officials to write or sanction official prayers in school. This was only one of the so-called liberal rulings of the Supreme Court that many claimed had brought on the immorality of the 1980s. It was believed that sex education classes in the schools promoted promiscuity and were largely responsible for the increase in teenage pregnancies. Objections to textbooks that taught secular humanism rather than a belief in a higher being were also raised.

Schools were not the only areas of concern. The lax laws on pornography were determined to add to the deterioration of society. Feminism and its views on the equality of American women were believed by the New Right to be especially responsible for bringing about an end to the traditional role of wife and mother in society and threatening the family unit itself. Feminism also was believed to promote the cause of abortion, in spite of public opinion polls that indicated that the majority of Americans, not only feminists, believed that women had the right to choose abortion as an option to end unwanted pregnancies. The growing number of homosexual rallies and demands for their rights was another concern for conservatives that society was deteriorating.

The most significant organization to come out of this religious New Right movement as the eighties gave way to the 1990s was the Christian Coalition. Television evangelist and sometimes presidential candidate Pat Robertson, and most other fundamentalist leaders, provided support and leadership to this organization, which essentially became the successor to Jerry Falwell's Moral Majority of the 1970s. The Christian Coalition strategy is to work at the local level of politics, electing school board members and city council people all over the country, until it is ready to dominate the national political scene. While it is officially non-partisan, the Christian Coalition is essentially a very powerful arm of the Republican Party in many areas of the country. According to opinion polls in the early nineties, its agenda for turning the United States into what it calls a "Christian nation" is troubling to most Americans, and has many concerned that its cures for what ails the country may be worse than the disease itself.

IMMIGRATION FROM NEW AREAS OF THE WORLD INCREASES

The number of immigrants coming from Europe had greatly decreased by the 1980s and was being replaced by immigrants predominantly from countries in the Western Hemisphere and Asia. Between 1981 and 1990, close to 7.3 million immigrants came into the country legally, with estimates running into the millions of those entering the country illegally. Undocumented aliens from Mexico were a problem for many of the states close to the Mexican-American border. The Immigration Act of 1965 is to be blamed or credited for the new groups of immigrants and their large numbers. The act ended the national origins quotas and established a total quota of 290,000 immigrants allowed in annually, with preferences determined by a seven-category system. (See Chapter Sixteen.) The reuniting of families and creating safe havens for those fleeing from armed conflicts or communist regimes were priorities for legal immigration. The immigrants were a mixture of skilled professionals, hard working former middle-class merchants, and unskilled laborers.

Americans began to pressure Congress to put more restrictions on the number of immigrants. Upper- and middle-class citizens tended to believe the immigrants were a burden on all public resources in the larger cities. Other Americans, particularly in the low-income categories, believed the immigrants were taking away jobs or government assistance. Although there were grounds for the concern toward the large number of immigrants, there was also evidence of the positive aspects of immigration. A large number of Asian-American students were excelling in academics, which contributed to the well-being of the nation. The skilled immigrants had not taken anything from the American taxpayer, and even the unskilled purchased goods and contributed taxes that could equal or exceed the drain on government resources. Employers also pointed out that without the willingness of immigrants to work in the low-paying service industries and the fields of the farmers, they would not have any workers. Whichever side one was on, there was general agreement that immigration had to be controlled or the nation would suffer hardships from the influx of newcomers, especially from illegals.

Congress decided to approach the problem from a different direction with the 1986 Immigration Reform and Control Act, which made it illegal to hire immigrants who were in the country illegally. It also provided amnesty to those who had entered the country illegally before January 1, 1982 and could prove it. The law did not solve the problem of illegal entry from Mexico and other Latin American nations, however. The government continued to search for solutions, with remedies ranging from more border patrol guards to helping the economies of the nations from which they flee so they would have good reason to stay home. A majority of Americans into the 1990s continued to favor limits on immigration.

WOMEN IN THE 1980S

After Congress gave three more years to the time limit for the ratification of the Equal Rights Amendment (ERA) in 1979, supporters failed to obtain the necessary three-fourths of the states. Thus, in 1982, the ERA was declared dead. This was a blow to the feminists and other women who believed that this was their only chance at complete equality. In 1983 more than 50 percent of the American female population worked outside of the home. However, with the increase in divorces and more out-of-wedlock mothers, the "feminization of poverty" was under way. Close to 80 percent of the jobs taken by women were in low-paying industries.

The defeat of the ERA was a victory for conservative activists, including Phyllis Schlafley, a leader in the movement against the ERA who invested much time and effort in its defeat. And with the election of Ronald Reagan to the presidency in 1980, the conservative backlash against the ERA had a powerful political ally. In fact, Reagan was not seen as a friend by a majority of women. He had cut many of the social programs, including AFDC, which had assisted many. Politically, there was a real gender gap in the approval of the president, with the percentage of women being much smaller than that of men.

AFRICAN-AMERICANS IN THE 1980S

Living the American dream had become a reality for many African-Americans by the 1980s. There were no legal restrictions on voting or public accommodations on account of race. The number of black students attending college had more than tripled from the numbers in 1965. By 1990, close to 46 percent would hold white-collar jobs. African-Americans were voting and running for public office in unprecedented numbers. Large metropolitan areas were run by black mayors across the nation.

All was not fair, equal, and good, however. Private prejudice continued in all areas of society, and the number of groups that hated because of the color of a person's skin increased. The Aryan Nation, the Ku Klux Klan, and the neo-Nazi "skinheads" (young people with shaved heads who attacked people of African and Asian descent) actively were promoting their views on the dangers to white society of the empowerment of any non-white groups, and the need to fight against non-whites. On college campuses, hate crimes against Jews, blacks, and homosexuals increased. By 1986 there were close to 300 documented attacks a year across the nation motivated by hatred of a race.

Although Reagan claimed to vigorously support civil rights, the actions of the Justice Department were supported by the president, and it was not actively promoting a strong civil rights policy. Busing and affirmative action were opposed, and attempts were made to cut back on the powers of the Civil Rights Commission. The Commission investigated civil rights violations, including situations that seemed to indicate that African-Americans were being restricted in their rights to vote. When first approached, Reagan had even opposed the extension of the 1965 Voting Rights Act, which allowed the Attorney-General to send federal supervisors into areas to investigate voter registration where fewer than half of an eligible minority was registered.

Congressional action to cut back on social programs affected the black urban communities particularly hard. The black middle class had expanded, but so had the number in poverty. In 1980 the poverty rate for the United States overall was at about 13 percent, but in the black community the poverty rate was at about 33 percent. African-American children were hard hit by the poverty. They were more likely to live in poverty, drop out of school, and face unemployment than white children.

Reagan and the Justice Department opposed most affirmative action programs and racial quotas, believing that individual merit, not preferential treatment, should be the primary consideration in obtaining jobs and entrance to higher education facilities. In *Bakke v. Board of Regents of California* (1978), the Supreme Court had restricted the use of racial quotas in higher education. There were drastic cuts in social programs that a large number of Americans needed. One of the by-products of this trend toward increased poverty was homelessness, which increased drastically in the 1980s among white Americans as well.

GOVERNMENT IN REAGAN'S FIRST ADMINISTRATION

Reagan promoted the idea of reducing government, but would soon discover that this was no small feat. Although he cut very little from the size of the federal bureaucracy, he did convince Congress to cut the budget for several agencies, bureaus, and commissions, and to continue the federal deregulation of industries. The Consumer Product Safety Commission was reduced, and the Environmental Protection Agency was also cut back.

Reagan and some of his appointees, including Interior Secretary James Watt, believed that economic growth and productivity could not be stifled at the cost of onerous environmental legislation. Watt set about his task of creating a more favorable climate for business by transferring some federal timber, mineral, and water rights to private businesses, an action which brought heavy criticism from environmental groups, but were praised by local economic interests. Watt was a leader in the Sagebrush Rebellion and maintained that, rather than the traditional conservationist viewpoint that the federal government should protect most of the national resources, this was the responsibility of the local communities instead. Watt's motives for his anti-environmental stance, while most of the typical ones seemed to be present, also included an unusual one. He used his personal religious belief in the soon Second Coming of Christ as another reason why it didn't really matter a great deal if the environment were spoiled; it would all be destroyed soon anyway. (In fairness to other Christians who hold to this religious belief, most of them do not seem to use it as an excuse to spoil the environment or plunder national resources.)

Insensitive remarks made by Watt created enemies for him in many sectors of American society, until groups began calling for his resignation in 1983. In January 1983, for example, he stated in an interview that reservations were "an example of the failure of socialism." The National Congress of American Indians immediately called for his resignation. Responding to criticisms that his new coal advisory board did not represent the nation, Watt defended his board with the statement "I have a black, a woman, two Jews, and a cripple." Not many government officials have the capacity to offend so many people in such a short period of time. Watt could not stand up to the public's outrage, he was forced to resign on October 9 of that year.

In his own appointments to government positions, President Reagan was criticized for appointing white males from the country club set. Indeed, only 8 percent of his high-level appointees were women and only 4 percent were black. It was certainly a step back from President Carter's record of 12 percent women and 12 percent black. Furthermore, scandals and problems with ethics affected more than 100 Reagan appointees during his administration.

THE 1984 ELECTION

The Candidates

By March of 1984, former Vice-President Walter Mondale and Senator Gary Hart of Colorado were the front runners for the Democratic nomination for presi-

Walter Mondale and Geraldine Ferraro at the Democratic National Convention in 1984. Credit: AP/Wide World Photos.

dent. The Reverend Jesse Jackson, formerly a close associate of Dr. Martin Luther King, was still in the race, but was not considered to have a strong chance for the nomination. In November 1983, Jesse Jackson had announced his candidacy with the hopes of putting together a "rainbow coalition" of African-Americans, Hispanics, women, and other minorities who had been neglected by the policies of the Reagan administration. At the Democratic National Convention in San Francisco in July, Jackson spoke of the "desperate, the damned, the disinherited, the disrespected and the despised." Despite his inspiring speech, Jackson was perceived as a candidate incapable of winning back the White House. Instead, the convention nominated Walter Mondale for president and New York Representative Geraldine Ferraro for vice-president. Ferraro became the first female candidate for this second highest position by a major political party in American history. However, she would soon face trouble when hearings were held looking into her husband's financial affairs.

During his acceptance speech at the convention, Mondale took a bold gamble when he announced that the fast-rising national debt could not be obliterated without tax increases. He attacked President Reagan for being dishonest about this fact and declared that whichever candidate were elected, taxes would have to be raised. "Mr. Reagan will raise taxes, and so will I," he told the delegates. "He won't tell you. I just did." That proved to be his biggest mistake of the campaign. Voters do not like to hear the words "raise" and "taxes" in the same sentence, no matter what. In retrospect, Mondale should have focused on the fact that Reagan had indeed raised taxes in 1982, 1983, and in 1984, despite promises that he would never do that.

The Republicans easily and quickly renominated President Ronald Reagan and Vice-President George Bush without opposition. Despite the growing national debt, Reagan was still a very popular president.

The Campaign and Results

During the campaign, Mondale and the Democrats attacked Reagan for his cuts in social programs, such as the proposal he had made to cut social security, and his increased "taxes" and deficits. Despite the record, Reagan continued to declare that he would not approve Congressional tax increases, and he would continue to work toward less government and more private business enterprise to increase the strength of the economy. The president declared that he had success to offer the American people if they gave him the honor of another term. In spite of the national debt problem, the economy gave Reagan a boost during the election campaign. Inflation had been reduced by the tight money policies of the Federal Reserve Board and the foreign policy "luck" of the Iran-Iraq War. The unemployment rate was down to 7.4 percent, which Americans were gradually accepting as a positive development (although that rate was about 7.5 percent in 1980), and most people perceived that the recession of 1982 and 1983 was coming to an end.

In addition to improved economic news, Ronald Reagan's personal charisma was always a political asset to him. Regardless of scandals or embarrassments within his administration, nothing seemed to "stick" to him personally. Even when Americans disagreed with his policies, most did not hold him responsible for their effects. Thus, Reagan went down in history as the so-called "teflon" president, a nickname given him by Colorado Democratic Representative Patricia Schroeder.

When the votes were counted in early November, President Ronald Reagan was easily re-elected with 58.4 percent of the popular vote and 525 electoral votes. He lost the electoral votes of only Minnesota and the District of Columbia, whose combined 13 electoral votes went to Mondale. Despite the reaffirmation of Ronald Reagan's personal popularity, the Democrats kept their majority in the House of Representatives and the Republicans in the Senate.

ECONOMICS IN THE SECOND TERM

The 1986 Tax Reform Act

Calling for "a Second American Revolution of hope and opportunity," President Reagan challenged Congress to raise taxes over his veto. Using the line from a Clint Eastwood movie (Reagan frequently quoted from old movies), the president told Congress to "Go ahead and make my day" with regard to ignoring his stand. Tax re-

| 1984 | 50 | RONALD REAGAN | Republican | 53,428,357 | 525 | 59.0 |
| | | Walter F. Mondale | Democrat | 36,930,923 | 13 | 41.0 |

forms to simplify the process for paying taxes and eliminating loopholes was the focus in the beginning of his second term. Finally, Congress passed and the president signed the Tax Reform Act in September 1986. The new act reduced the number of tax brackets from 14 to 2 by 1988 and the maximum tax rates from 50 percent to 15 and 28 percent. The number of tax shelters that the wealthy could use to keep from paying taxes were also reduced. It had been the tax shelters that had allowed those in the upper income brackets to circumvent the purpose behind a progressive income tax—the wealthier paying a greater proportion in taxes. Millions of low income Americans would not have to pay taxes at all as a result of the new law. The efforts to simplify the tax system via the Tax Reform Act were not as successful. Many, in fact, believed that tax system was even harder to understand than the previous system, and every bit as long.

The Gramm-Rudman-Hollings Act

The nation's increasing deficit was a concern of a Congress that did not want to lose the support of constituents with tax hikes or reductions in spending. But deficits were at record levels, and most believed that something must be done about them. So in 1985, Congress passed the Gramm-Rudman-Hollings Act (sometimes shortened to the Gramm-Rudman Act). This bill, which easily passed both houses of Congress, mandated automatic across-the-board spending cuts of $11.7 billion per year until a balanced budget was achieved in fiscal year 1991, if Congress could not prioritize the cuts on its own. The automatic cuts prevented the public from putting the blame on any individual members of Congress. The economy seemed strong with inflation at 1.1 percent and unemployment down, but the debt of the nation and the personal debt of Americans was growing, which meant that interest payments on the borrowed money was another payment for both consumers and the federal government.

However, there were simply too many ways to get around the Gramm-Rudman-Hollings Act. Excise taxes on various goods were levied, such as increasing the taxes on cigarettes and alcohol (so-called "sin" taxes). More social programs were simply passed onto the states to fund (which most could not do adequately). The length of time to balance the budget was increased, and more items were taken "off budget" so that they would not count toward the deficit. All of this reflected the lack of political courage by members of Congress in both parties. And the federal debt kept rising; it had tripled by the end of Reagan's second term in office.

THE STOCK MARKET WOES

"Black Monday"

Throughout the mid-1980s, the stock market had increased in value. On October 19, 1987, known as "Black Monday," panic selling dropped the Dow Jones 508 points, which was 22.6 percent of its total. This was almost twice the amount of the drop in the infamous stock market crash of October 28, 1929 (which had been 12.8 percent). The fall on the New York Stock Exchange affected the markets in Tokyo, London, Paris, and Toronto. The cause of the crash was argued by economists and politicians of all philosophies. Many believed that the computerized trading programs had distorted the trades on the market and caused panic. Most agreed that the bottom line of the problem was that the United States was continuing to import more goods than it exported and paying for those goods with borrowed dollars that had fallen in value compared to Japanese and European currencies.

President Reagan reassured the nation that the "underlying economy remains sound." These were a distant echo of the words that President Herbert Hoover had uttered as the nation was moving into its worst depression in 1929 and 1930. However, the economic circumstances in the 1980s were not entirely the same. The economic reforms put in place by Roosevelt's New Deal probably prevented this stock market crash from spiraling into a depression.

Junk Bonds and Insider Trading

Greed seemed to be the operative word to describe the economic climate of the 1980s, so much so that some historians have referred to it as a new gilded age. "Get rich quick" schemes and other shady investment dealings epitomized the decade, creating the largest boom in millionaires in more than a half-century. In the process, however, people and businesses were gobbled up and thrown away like so much trash left over from a ball game. Corporate merger mania and other buy-outs hit the country as it had in the 1920s. The difference, though, was that a new technique had been developed by the middle of the decade to take over a corporation in order to make money. The term to describe the innovation was "leveraged buyouts" (LBOs).

In a leveraged buyout situation, a group of corporate "raiders" would use borrowed money to purchase a controlling interest in the shares of stock of its intended corporate victim. The idea was that the borrowed money would be repaid from the profits of the company which had just been taken over. After doing so, the schemers would then use the company's value to underwrite so-called "junk bonds," which were highly speculative bonds that attracted investors looking for an easy, quick profit. The net result was that the increased number of investors drove up the price of the stock to enormous, artificial highs. This meant that the new stockholders could sell their shares and make huge profits, while the company was saddled with the extra burden of debt. Often, to further add to their profits, the corporate "raiders" would break up the company and sell it piece by piece because its parts were worth more than the whole. In 1988, the largest leveraged buyout occurred when an investment firm took over the R.J. Reynolds-Nabisco Company for $24.9 billion.

The trend toward leveraged buyouts was fueled by a political climate which told investors and business that government was not in a regulating mood. Human nature took over, and by the end of the decade (1980s), approximately 25 percent of American corporations' cash flow was being paid on corporate debt. Most of this new debt was the direct result of leveraged buyout situations, although some companies intentionally increased their debt in order to make them less attractive to LBO schemers; this was called swallowing the "poison pill." This rise of corporate debt was proportionately worse than the federal government debt.

Greed escalated during the second half of the eighties, with yet another trend spinning off the leveraged buyout movement. "Risk arbitrage," which was not new, involved a matter of buying shares of stock that were low on one market and selling it higher on another market; computers were used to make the change quickly so as to reduce the risk. But the new form of risk arbitrage which arose in the eighties was to buy stock in the hope that its value would rise sharply due to a corporate takeover. The problem was that it was extremely risky because one could never be certain that a threatened takeover would actually succeed—unless an investor had inside information. Receiving and trading on inside information is illegal, but that did not prevent such insider trading from taking off in a major way.

With tips that insider trading was occurring in record numbers, the Securities and Exchange Commission (SEC) increased its investigations. In November 1986, Ivan Boesky, a risk arbitrageur, was arrested on charges of insider trading. The year before his arrest, Boesky had told students at the University of California at Berkeley that "Greed is healthy." After his arrest, Boesky decided that it would be better to reduce his fine and prison sentence by cooperating with federal authorities. The biggest "fish" fingered by Boesky turned out to be Michael Milken. Nicknamed the "junk king," Milken was indicted on 96 charges, including fraud and conspiracy, in 1989. After pleading guilty to six of the charges, Milken was sentenced to ten years in prison, three additional years of probation, and 5,400 hours of community service in November 1990.

THE SUPREME COURT DURING REAGAN'S TERMS

One method used by American presidents to advance their political philosophies is through appointments to the Supreme Court, appointments which are for life. For his first appointment, Reagan wanted a conservative and a woman because of his campaign promise. So he nominated Sandra Day O'Connor, who was confirmed by the Senate on September 21, 1981. The nominee had sidestepped revealing her opinions on abortion and the Equal Rights Amendment, but she did reveal that she was opposed to judicial "activism," which meant that she believed that federal courts should more strictly interpret the Constitution rather than make policy, as the Warren Court had done in the 1950s and 1960s. Then in 1986, Reagan nominated Supreme Court Justice William Rehnquist to move into the Chief Justice chair vacated by retiring Warren Burger. Antonin Scalia then was confirmed to fill the vacancy on the Court.

In 1987, with the retirement of Justice Lewis Powell, President Reagan was able to nominate another conservative to the Supreme Court and truly stop the moderates and liberals on the bench. He nominated federal appeals court Judge Robert Bork. The Bork nomination began a battle in Congress. Liberal institutions, like the NAACP, the AFL-CIO, and NOW, accused Bork of disregarding the right to privacy (especially on the abortion issue), of not being pro-civil rights, and of being too conservative in his belief that the Supreme Court should be guided by the "original intent" philosophy of the founding fathers when ruling on Congressional actions. (Bork was the Solicitor-General who obeyed Nixon's order to fire Special Prosecutor Archibald Cox in 1973; see Chapter Seventeen.) With mounting pressure, Bork lost the nomination by a wide margin in what became one of Reagan's worst repudiations by Congress. Reagan's next nominee, Douglas Ginsburg, withdrew his name from the process when the Senate Judiciary Committee questioned him about drug use, and he admitted that he had smoked marijuana while teaching in law school. Judge Anthony Kennedy was confirmed quickly by the Senate in 1988.

TECHNOLOGICAL ADVANCES

Medicine

The medical advances of the 1980s opened up startling new possibilities to improve the quality and quantity of human life. A mechanical heart was implanted in place of the biological organ of Barney Clark, and kept Clark alive for 112 days in 1983. A 15-day-old infant known as Baby Fae, born with a defective heart, was kept alive for three more weeks with a heart transplanted from a baboon at the Loma Linda Medical Center in southern California. Although medical ethicists debated the merits of using animal organs in humans, most Americans seemed to be in awe of the accomplishment even though it did not prove to be a permanent success.

Medical reports were released showing that there was a definite cause-and-effect relationship between high levels of cholesterol and heart attacks. Exercise was linked to longevity, sparking a craze in the late 1980s and early 1990s for exercise equipment and exercise videos from favorite stars.

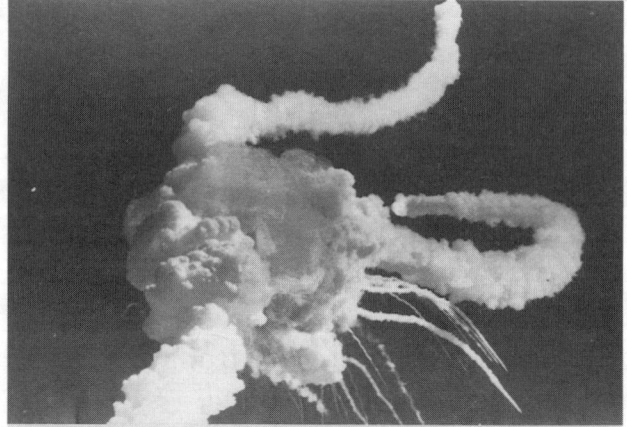
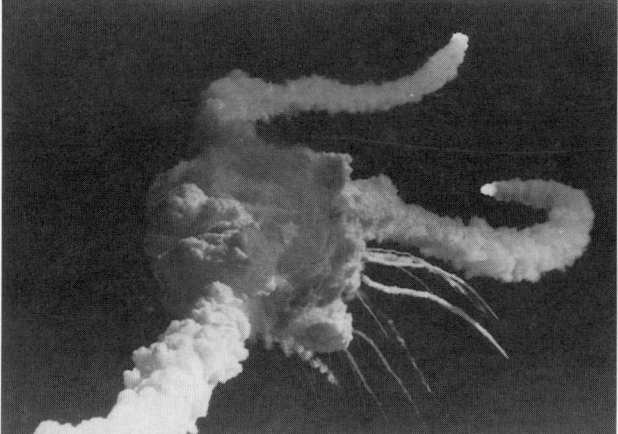
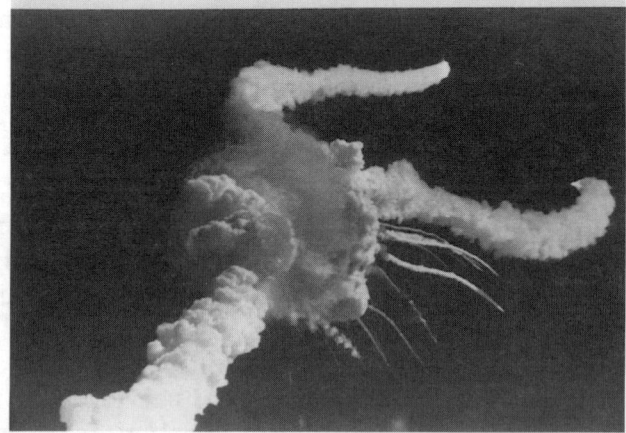

The Space Shuttle Challenger Explosion in Mid-Air, January 1986. Credit: AP/Wide World Photos.

Space

The United States had enjoyed great success with the space program almost from its very beginnings in the late fifties. But disaster hit on January 28, 1986, when the space shuttle *Challenger* exploded one minute after take-off because of the technical failure of an O-ring. All seven crew members were killed instantly in the plain sight of national television viewers. Among the dead was Christa McAuliffe, a social studies teacher, and the first teacher ever on a space mission. The disaster brought back the debate on whether so much should be invested in the space program. Congressional investigations uncovered mismanagement at NASA, and government investment in the space program suffered. The program did continue, however, with eventual inclusion of a commercial benefit by launching satellites or retrieving them.

THE THREAT OF DRUGS AND AIDS

First Lady Nancy Reagan launched a new education program for the rising problem of illegal drug consumption in the nation, called "just say no" to drugs. This was too simplistic an approach, however, as the drug-related problems in the inner city were increasing as were new drugs on the scene. One of the most popular of the new drugs was called "crack," a more potent and deadly form of cocaine.

Medical advances were successfully challenging life-threatening conditions, but at the same time a new disease appeared that was incurable and a deadly threat to the world. AIDS (Acquired Immune Deficiency Syndrome) originally appeared in the United States in 1981 in the male homosexual community. AIDS is a virus that renders the body's immune system inoperative, thereby allowing the infected person to pick up illnesses that it would otherwise fight off. Eventually, the patient becomes so sick and weak from a body racked by illness that he dies. Originally, very little attention or money for research to determine its cause or to find a cure was forthcoming because of the minority community it was attacking and the belief from many, particularly the New Right conservatives in the religious and other communities, that AIDS was a divine punishment for the gay lifestyle.

Nevertheless, gay and lesbian activists kept pressure on the government to put money into research and medical assistance to alleviate the pain of those suffering from this disease that ravaged the body before it killed. The disease began to claim famous Americans, such as actor Rock Hudson, and even victims in the heterosexual communities. The World Health Organization estimates that by the year 2000, 40 million people worldwide will have been infected with the disease.

FOREIGN AFFAIRS UNDER REAGAN
FOREIGN POLICY AND THE SOVIET UNION

American Arms Build-up and the "Evil Empire"

The priority in Reagan's foreign policy was the buildup of American military strength to counter the expansionism and threat which the Soviets presented. The defense budget increased from $171 billion in 1981 to $300 billion by 1985. Reagan was convinced that the detente of the 1970s, along with the SALT treaties (even though SALT II had not been ratified), had allowed the Soviets to surpass the strength of America's traditional and nuclear weapons arsenals. There were those who attempted to point out the misconceptions of the missile gap to the president, but Reagan was committed to superiority in strength and numbers, particularly in missiles. He was willing to cut back in other areas of government spending, but in defense he would vastly increase the expenditures. Defense Secretary Caspar Weinberger oversaw the build-up of American military weaponry. The B-1 bomber was on the assembly line again, even though doubt as to its effectiveness had stopped production in the Carter administration. The MX missiles also were manufactured again. In the president's view, the United States was going to resume its role as the undisputed leader of the free world.

In the first administration, relations with the Soviets were allowed to slip back into the traditional cold war mode. In the president's first news conference, he referred to the Soviet leaders as liars and cheaters. Speaking before the British Parliament on June 8, 1982, he criticized Soviet expansion and called upon Europeans and Americans to mount a "crusade for freedom." Then in a speech given on March 8, 1983, to the National Association of Evangelicals, Reagan labeled the Soviet Union the "evil empire."

Soviet actions seemed to underline Reagan's assessment and brought support for his big defense budgets and a continuation of the worldwide containment policy which had begun under the Truman administration. Communist takeovers and revolutions around the world were believed to be supported and led by the Soviets. Afghanistan, Kampuchea (formerly Cambodia), Nicaragua, and Angola were nations involved in revolutions which contained communist elements. In Poland, labor strikes and the formation of the anti-communist and anti-Soviet labor union Solidarity, under the leadership of Lech Walesa, brought a few concessions from the Polish government. However, when the demands from the people grew to include more democratic reforms, such as official recognition of an independent labor movement's right to exist and bargain collectively, the government declared martial law and imprisoned Walesa and other labor leaders. The United States retaliated with mild economic sanctions against Poland and the Soviet Union. The struggle in Poland for freedom continued amid martial law and numerous trials of political activists. As a result of this agitation for democracy, Lech Walesa received the Nobel Peace Prize in October 1983.

Soviet-American Arms Talks

In the early eighties, the United States convinced the NATO allies to deploy Pershing II and cruise missiles in Europe to counter the increase in Soviet missiles. This set off protests across Europe from citizens who wanted a freeze on nuclear weapons. The idea of a nuclear freeze also had advocates in the United States. The Reagan administration, and other conservatives, opposed the nuclear freeze idea. Nevertheless, Reagan did open up new talks labeled START (Strategic Arms Reduction Talks), but these negotiations, he argued, would only benefit the United States if they were conducted from a position of strength. Then in 1984, Reagan proposed a new defense system titled SDI (Strategic Defense Initiative) and frequently called

"Star Wars," after the successful movie trilogy in the late seventies. SDI was an electronic shield in space that was supposed to eliminate incoming missiles with lasers. There was enormous controversy over the probable cost of such a system and if it could be put into place and be used with any reliability. Congress did fund the research effort, which had mixed scientific results. However, the proposal did bring the Soviets to the negotiating table on arms control.

In his second term, the president approached the new leader of the Soviet Union, Mikhail S. Gorbachev, to visit the United States to discuss arms limitations. Gorbachev was younger and more open to change than the other Soviet leaders during the 1980s, Leonid Brezhnev, Andropov, and Konstantin Chernenko. Gorbachev had come to power in 1985 and quickly realized that the Soviet economy was near collapse. Gorbachev made it his mission to correct the downward slide inside the Soviet Union. The government also was grossly inefficient under the one-party dictatorship, and the expense of maintaining an arms race and a large military force was a crushing weight on the nation. An agreement with the United States to reduce arms might assist Gorbachev with some of his problems.

The leaders of the two superpowers first met in Geneva in November 1985. There were no agreements from the meeting, but both men agreed to another summit. Reagan was very critical of Soviet policies concerning human rights abuses, Soviet troops in Afghanistan, and aid to communists in wars in Angola and Ethiopia. Gorbachev was critical of the arms build-up of the United States, especially SDI. But President Reagan was convinced that the threat of SDI more than anything else would bring Gorbachev to eventually accept American conditions on arms control.

Perestroika and Glastnost

Before the next summit meeting, Gorbachev was already initiating changes in the Soviet Union. The economy and the bureaucracy was reorganized under the policy known as perestroika (loosely translated as "restructuring"). More open market capitalism was allowed to motivate Soviets to increase production. Gorbachev also realized that, in order to encourage a more effective restructuring, Soviet citizens must be willing to speak new ideas openly. Therefore, a policy of glasnost ("openness") was also implemented. Under glasnost, the press and the public were allowed more freedom of expression. Gorbachev soon discovered, however, that freedom of expression, once encouraged, could not be confined simply to economic topics. Eventually, the forces of perestroika and glastnost, begun with the desire to make the communist system more efficient, proved to be the undoing of the communists in the Soviet Union. In foreign policy, Gorbachev repudiated the Breshnev Doctrine, which had justified Soviet intervention in the internal affairs of other communist nations. As proof of this radical change in Soviet foreign policy, Gorbachev began the withdrawal of Soviet troops from Afghanistan in 1988–1989. (Many have compared the Soviet quagmire in that country with the American debacle in Vietnam.)

Soviet Secretary General Mikhail Gorbachev. Credit: AP/Wide World Photos.

Some Success in the Arms Talks

In the context of these major changes, Gorbachev and Reagan met in Reykjavik, Iceland in October 1986 to discuss arms reductions once again. Some surprising offers were put on the table. Gorbachev agreed to reduce strategic weapons by 50 percent if the United States would agree to delay the deployment of SDI for ten years. Reagan countered that the two nations should eliminate all of their strategic missiles but allow SDI to be developed. In fact, Reagan had in mind to give to other nations the technological blueprint for SDI. No agreement was reached, but the mood was very positive.

Gorbachev visited Washington in December 1987, and the two leaders signed the Intermediate Nuclear Force Treaty. Negotiators had reached an agreement to eliminate all Soviet and American intermediate range missiles from Europe and allow on-site verification inspections. This affected only about 5 percent of the nuclear weapons of both sides, but it was a definite positive step in the relaxing of the cold war. With the beginning of the Soviet withdrawal from Afghanistan and the modest success in arms reduction talks, President Reagan accepted an invitation from Gorbachev and visited Moscow in May 1988.

Rescue workers carry the body of a U.S. Marine killed in the bombing of the Marine Operations Center in Beirut, Lebanon, October 1983. Credit: AP/Wide World Photos.

MIDDLE EAST POLICY

Unrest continued in the Middle East during the 1980s. Relations between Israel and Egypt were peaceful, but other Arab states and the PLO (Palestinian Liberation Organization) continued to desire the elimination of Israel, which was an American ally, and the establishment of a homeland for the Palestinian refugees. Yassir Arafat was the leader of the PLO and would not compromise the fight for a return of self-rule for the Palestinians in the former Palestine. Communist aggression was not the problem as far as American interest was concerned; however, Soviet assistance in any conflict produced concern on the part of the United States, and Reagan believed that the Soviets were sponsoring terrorist actions. Protecting both Israel and the flow of oil in the region remained concerns of American policymakers.

Lebanon

The Palestinians were training commandos in Lebanon to carry out hit-and-run attacks against Israel and to organize terrorist operations against supporters of the Jewish nation. Israel invaded Lebanon in 1982 to destroy the Palestinian strongholds. There was a civil war raging at the time between Lebanese Christians and Lebanese Muslims. Israeli troops were attacked by the Muslim faction which had ties to Syria and assistance from the Soviet Union.

An agreement was reached in August 1983 for Israel to withdraw and for American troops to be added to an international force to keep the peace in Lebanon during the withdrawal. American forces were withdrawn in September, but they were sent back in October to attempt to bring some sort of stability to Beirut (the capital city) following the assassination of Lebanon's president. On October 23, a truck loaded with explosives was driven into the United States Marine compound in Beirut and the explosives were ignited. This terrorist bombing killed 241 American troops. As a result, Americans began to criticize the administration's policies in Lebanon that were meant to bring peace to the Middle Eastern nation and yet ended with dead Americans and no peace. So Reagan pulled the troops out in April 1984, without reaching his goal of ending Syrian dominance and bringing peace to Lebanon. Syria was especially hostile to the state of Israel. American intervention allied the United States too closely with Israeli policy in the Middle East and, according to the PLO and other Arab states, this made the United States an enemy and a target.

Terrorism

The Palestinians and other militant Islamic groups did not have the capability of fighting a traditional war to gain their goals, so a war of terrorism was the answer for many. Planes and ships were highjacked in the Mediterranean region, Americans and Europeans were kidnapped, and airports and other public facilities were bombed. One of the first hijackings was perpetrated against Trans World Airlines flight 847 on June 14, 1985. The plane was traveling from Athens to Rome when Shiite Muslim extremists from the group known as the Hzbollah forced the plane to land in Beirut, Lebanon, and later to fly to Algiers. There were 40 Americans on the plane, one of whom was killed before the incident was over, his body thrown onto the runway.

Terrorists also hijacked an Italian cruise ship, the *Achille Lauro*, killing an American man who was confined to a wheelchair. The terrorists then attempted to fly to Tunis after leaving the ship, but their plane was forced to land in Italy by American jets. The hijackers were arrested and stood trial in West Germany. President Reagan's message to terrorists was "you can run, but you can't hide." Between 1981 and 1985, seven Americans were captured and held hostage in Beirut. One hostage from the American embassy, William Buckley, was tortured and killed, but the other Americans remained hostages.

The bombing of a disco in West Berlin frequented by American soldiers was linked to Muslim terrorists. One American was killed and 60 wounded in the blast on April 5, 1986. The terrorists were connected to Moamar Qaddafi, the anti-American ruler of Libya. Qaddafi was called "the mad dog of the Middle East" by Reagan and was seen as a real threat to American interests and peace in the area. He sponsored terrorism by the PLO and other groups, and was thought to be manufacturing internationally outlawed chemical weapons. A few days after the bombing, President Reagan retaliated against Qaddafi by ordering air strikes on targets in Libya. Americans cheered the strong message the president sent to terrorists, but not much else came from the strike. In December 1988, the explosion of a Pan American plane over Lockerbie, Scotland killed more than 250 people. It was discovered that a terrorist's bomb was responsible for the explosion, and once again there was a connection to Qaddafi.

FOREIGN AFFAIRS IN CENTRAL AMERICA AND THE CARIBBEAN

In the 1980s, attempts to bring change through revolutions which had some communist elements or philosophies in Central America and the Caribbean were looked upon by the Reagan administration as Soviet-sponsored moves that required American intervention. Reagan would not allow the countries south of the borders of the United States to fall like dominoes to communism. The president's rhetoric about events south of the border made many Americans anxious because it was so reminiscent of the talk of previous administrations concerning the Vietnam War. The public, and then Congress, refused to accept an extensive commitment to address the problems of the region.

El Salvador

Concern for the continuing civil war in El Salvador against the government of President Jose Napoleon Duarte led President Reagan to increase military aid and the number of American advisors to the small Central American nation. A military solution, rather than pressures for reform, seemed more feasible to stop what the government considered a Soviet-backed revolution. Duarte had been supported by Carter and Reagan with both economic and military aid because of his anti-communist stand, although the government of Duarte was brutal and repressive via "death squads" sent out by the military to eliminate rebels or those opposed to the policies of Duarte. Duarte was the first civilian president in nearly 50 years.

There was criticism of Reagan's policies from government officials and the public. Americans were determined to prevent a reoccurrence of another Vietnam, this nation's longest war. But Reagan continued his commitment to support the government in El Salvador. In 1984, Duarte won the presidency again under American supervised elections. During his next term, the activities of the death squad decreased, the military was more receptive to the more moderate policies and reforms proposed by Duarte, and the president met with the rebels to explore a peaceful end to the war.

Grenada

In March 1979 a leftist group organized the overthrow of the anti-communist government on Grenada, a small island in the Caribbean Sea. The new government established by Maurice Bishop accepted Soviet arms and ammunition delivered on a Cuban ship soon after the overthrow. Bishop also accepted the offer of Castro to build an internationanal airport, signed a treaty to allow Moscow to land military planes, and received offers of financial assistance from Moscow. Reagan believed this to be a dangerous move into the hemisphere by the Soviets, and he was determined to stop it. An attempt by Grenadians to overthrow the Bishop government gave Reagan the excuse he needed to invade the island and eliminate a potentially threatening situation. He ordered the invasion of Grenada on October 25, 1983, ostensibly to protect close to 700 American citizens, many in medical school on the island. The fighting was scattered and brief, with the strongest resistance coming from the Cuban workers and soldiers at the airstrip. There were 18 American soldiers killed and 116 wounded.

There was criticism of the invasion from United Nations' members, including Britain, but President Reagan was given accolades by the American public. The use of military force indicated an end to the "Vietnam Syndrome," the fear of using American troops to achieve a goal.

Nicaragua

Reagan rejected Carter's policy of assisting the Sandinista government in Nicaragua and cut off their economic aid in 1981. He considered them tools for the Soviets and Cubans to spread their philosophy in Central America and, therefore, dangerous. The Sandinistas also were assisting the pro-communist revolutionaries attempting to overthrow the government in El Salvador. William Casey, the Director of the CIA, was ordered to train and fund resistance fighters. The CIA gathered about 10,000 anti-Sandinistas, known as the Contra freedom fighters, together in bases of operation in Honduras and Costa Rica. Reagan called the Contras "the moral equivalent of the Founding Fathers," a statement which many Americans scoffed at while others believed.

Thus assisted by the CIA, the Contras carried on a guerilla war to oust the Sandinistas. The media uncovered covert aid to the Contras, including the mining of Nicaraguan harbors by the CIA in 1984 and their direct role in the carrying out of the guerilla war. (In fact, Nicaragua won a judgment against the United States in the World Court for America's illegal mining.) Public pressure and a Congress that remembered the long and twisting path into the Vietnam conflict resulted in the Boland Amendment, passed by Congress in late 1984, that allowed only humanitarian aid to be sent to the Contras. Reagan repeatedly tried to get Congress to change its mind, especially after Daniel Ortega, Nicaragua's president, was photographed with Gorbachev in Moscow, but Congress refused to budge.

The Iran-Contra Affair

Then in 1986, the media broke the story that arms had been sold to Iran in a secret deal in exchange for Iranian assistance in the release of American hostages in Lebanon and for money to buy arms to illegally assist the Contras. National Security advisors Robert McFarlane and John Poindexter, along with their aide Lieutenant Colonel Oliver North, broke the law with the secret operation assisted by the CIA. Congress had put a trade embargo on Iran and forbidden military assistance to the Contras. A special commission led by former Texas Senator John Tower, and a joint House-Senate investigative committee chaired by Democratic Senator Daniel Inouye of Hawaii, investigated the covert operation with a great deal of the testimony of the witnesses nationally televised during the summer of 1987. Poindexter and North were convicted later of lying to Congress to keep the opera-

Oliver North objects to a comment from the House panel during the Iran-Contra hearings on Capitol Hill in 1987. Credit: AP/ Wide World Photos.

tion secret and breaking numerous other federal laws. But their convictions were set aside in 1991 on appeal.

The investigations did not prove that the president had known about the illegal operation, but both Reagan and Bush would have to answer questions of what they knew then and in the future. This scandal, which became known as the Iran-Contra Scandal (or Irangate, in memory of the Watergate affair) was damaging to the Reagan image.

THE 1988 ELECTION

The Candidates

The Democrats nominated Massachusetts Governor Michael Dukakis at its national convention in the summer of 1988. Dukakis offered few new policies or programs in his campaign. But he had brought renewed economic stability to Massachusetts, and promised to bring the same economic stability to the nation. In foreign policy matters, he advocated a continuation of a tough stand for American national interests and the relaxing of cold war tensions. In an attempt to attract southern Democrats, the party nominated highly respected Texas Senator Lloyd Bentsen as Dukakis' running mate.

Vice-President George Bush was the choice of the Republicans in 1988. Bush was the most logical choice. His experience in government was vast in both domestic and foreign service. He had served as a member of the House of Representatives from Texas, Ambassador to the United Nations, Chairman of the Republican National Committee, Chief Liaison Officer to Mainland China, Director of the CIA, and then Vice-President from 1981 to 1988. His choice of J. Danforth "Dan" Quayle, a little-known senator from Indiana, brought a lot of criticism from Republicans at the convention and around the country because of Quayle's inexperience. But Bush had picked Quayle to appeal to the young people of the nation and because his conservative votes in the Senate would appeal to the conservative wing of the party. Criticism for Quayle increased during the campaign, however, because it was learned that his family had called friends to secure him a place in the Indiana National Guard in order to avoid serving in the regular army during the Vietnam War. Bush himself had been one of the youngest pilots in the Naval Air Force during World War II, and was awarded the Distinguished Flying Cross when his plane was shot down during a bombing raid in the Pacific. Bush stood firm on Quayle as his running mate.

Bush's acceptance speech was the high point of the Republican convention. He declared his support for the death penalty, the right to own firearms, the Pledge of Allegiance, prayer in public schools, and the advances that President Reagan had made in domestic and foreign policy. He celebrated the differences of Americans with his statement that there was "a brilliant diversity spread like stars, like a thousand points of light in a broad and peaceful sky." These "thousand points of light" were his metaphor for the American spirit of volunteerism and a mild repudiation of government intervention. He also called for a "kinder, gentler America." Bush wanted the conservatives who had supported Reagan to know that the so-called conservative revolution would continue. Toward that goal, he uttered what became his most famous line of the speech when he boldly declared, "read my lips; no new taxes!"

The Campaign and Results

The campaign between Bush and Dukakis is known as one of the most negative in recent times, with Bush jumping out to an early lead. The Bush campaign used television advertising to its fullest potential. Dukakis was portrayed as the candidate who would raise taxes, was soft on crime, and was the representative of special interest groups. In television ads, Dukakis was usually shown in dark light and not smiling. Bush was usually in light that illuminated his presence. A political commercial that was very damaging to Dukakis concerned the Massachusetts furlough program for convicts serving time. An African-American convict on furlough named Willie Horton committed a sexual assault. In spite of the statistics that showed the success of the furlough program, Americans were too concerned about rising crime rates to accept a candidate who appeared to have too much concern for the criminal. Although many others viewed the Willie Horton ad as a subtle racist statement that labeled black men as criminals, most white Americans responded to the emotional button that had cleverly reminded them of the crime issue.

In contrast to the Republicans, the Dukakis campaign seemed poorly organized, and it never connected with sufficient numbers of the public. For example, George Bush hammered away at Dukakis' lack of experience in foreign affairs. In response, Dukakis tried to look like a commander-in-chief by donning an army helmet and riding in a tank, but polls showed that most voters thought he looked rather foolish instead. The Democratic candidate was only somewhat more effective when he focused on the economy. His home state of Massachusetts had attracted a large number of high tech companies in the recent past, which had given the state's economy a boost. As its former governor, Dukakis took credit for the prosperity that he called the Massachusetts "miracle," and he promised to do for the nation what he had done in Massachusetts. This gave the Republicans the opportunity to argue that whatever prosperity Massachusetts was experiencing, it was in spite of Dukakis' policies of high taxes and financial mismanagement. Bush reminded voters that the nickname for the state was "Taxachusetts." Indeed, two years after the election, financial difficulties put the state in extremely bad economic shape.

In a series of debates between both the presidential and vice-presidential candidates of both parties, the most memorable moment occurred when Democrat Lloyd Bentsen responded to Dan Quayle's attempt to liken himself to the young John F. Kennedy. "You are no Jack Kennedy!" declared Bentsen emphatically.

When election night was over, Bush won the presidency with 426 electoral votes to 112 for Dukakis, which made him the first incumbent vice-president elected president since Democrat Martin Van Buren in 1836. Americans wanted to build upon the positive aspects of Reagan's policies, and Bush was content to keep the status quo in most policies. In doing so, however, he would be criticized for not leading the nation in its struggle to deal with domestic problems.

DOMESTIC ISSUES UNDER BUSH

Economic Problems

Congress and the president would have to deal with problems that had their beginnings in the Reagan era. It was soon discovered that much of the prosperity of the late eighties was built on borrowed money and faulty economic assumptions that created severe underlying economic problems.

The Savings and Loan Crisis

Of immediate and particular concern was the horrible condition of the Savings and Loan industry (S&Ls). In various forms, the industry had been operating for decades. In 1934, the Franklin Roosevelt administration got Congress to create the Federal Savings and Loan Insurance Corporation (FSLIC), a government corporation which insured depositors and regulated the industry in a similar manner as the FDIC did for banks. The creation of the FSLIC was intended to encourage home

| 1988 | 50 | GEORGE BUSH | Republican | 48,901,046 | 426 | 53.4 |
| | | Michael Dukakis | Democrat | 41,809,030 | 111 | 45.6 |

ownership, which in turn helped boost the construction industry. By the late seventies, with double-digit inflation a major problem, the S&Ls began offering higher interest rates to their depositors in order to remain compatible with regular banks. The federal income tax cuts of the early eighties also indirectly encouraged more depositors in the S&Ls. Unfortunately, however, most of the assets of these institutions were tied up in long-term mortgages whose interest rates were usually fixed. This put a financial bind on the S&Ls, who urged the Reagan administration and Congress to loosen regulations in order to get themselves out of this predicament. About that same time, Congress raised the limit of insured deposits from $40,000 to $100,000 per deposit.

Then in 1982, Congress took the additional step of allowing S&Ls to invest as much as 40 percent of their assets in non-residential real estate. The result was a boom in the construction of high-rise office buildings everywhere. Shortly after that, California became the first state in the union to allow state-chartered thrift organizations (state S&Ls, in effect) to invest up to 100 percent of their assets in virtually any economic scheme it chose to. Other states followed suit, with the result being that the industry became almost completely intoxicated with greed and oblivious to the dangers of high-risk speculative investments.

Late in the decade, the proverbial house of cards was beginning to come down. Nearly 600 S&Ls went out of business between 1988 and 1990. Because the S&Ls were insured by the federal government, it had to repay depositors. To do so, the FSLIC was forced to sell off millions of dollars of real estate owned by the bankrupt S&Ls, usually below market value. In effect, the American taxpayers had to finance the bailout, which was estimated as high as $400 billion. And even with that price tag, many Americans never recovered their life savings.

The Keating Five

Personal greed and corrupt investment practices dominated the industry. The most notorious of these S&L managers was Charles Keating, who headed the Lincoln Savings and Loan Association in Irvine, California. Keating illegally paid himself $3.2 million a year, and his family members received at least $34 million. But it was his illegal campaign contributions to a group of five senators that put him in the spotlight and exposed his personal empire. The senators, collectively known as the "Keating Five" (four of them were Democrats), were officially scolded by the Senate Ethics Committee for failing to avoid the appearance of evil. The arrest and conviction of Charles Keating himself sent shockwaves across the nation, and it earned him a place among the scoundrels of the greedy eighties.

Economic Recession and the Growing National Debt

The Savings and Loan bailout increased the amount of the national debt, and the country went into a recession in the summer of 1990. Retail sales were down, new housing starts declined, and unemployment was up again. To make up for the increasing deficits, Congress put political pressure on President Bush to agree to new taxes. In June 1990, Bush agreed in principle to "tax revenue increases" as an unavoidable step in order to reduce the deficit. In the fall of 1990, after long, and sometimes bitter, negotiations between the White House and the Democrats in Congress, both sides finally agreed to a five-year package of major spending cuts and tax increases to fight the deficit. By this action, President Bush had gone back on his campaign promise ("read my lips; no new taxes!"), although he believed he had not really done so because he said that the revenue increases were not new taxes; he also assumed the public soon would forget it. The Gross National Product (GNP) had fallen to an annual rate of 1.2 percent in July 1990. But the economy showed some signs of recovering in 1991, but it was a weak recovery, and unemployment remained a problem well into 1992. By 1992 the national debt was more than $3 trillion.

THE SUPREME COURT UNDER BUSH

President George Bush was able to leave his mark on the Supreme Court because of retirements from the High Court. On September 11, 1990, the Senate confirmed David Souter with little controversy. Souter was expected to be another fairly conservative justice for the Supreme Court. Then in 1991, President Bush nominated Clarence Thomas to replace the retiring Thurgood Marshall on the High Court. The Thomas nomination proved to be very controversial. Thomas was an African-American federal appeals judge who had served on the bench for a short period of time. He was conservative and did not believe in affirmative action, which he thought had brought promotion by government, not individual effort. Criticism was levelled against the new nominee because of his inexperience on the bench, his conservative ideology, and his selection, many believed, because of his race. (The retiring Marshall had been the first African-American justice to ever serve on the Court.) Civil rights groups, women's groups, and labor organizations worked hard to defeat the nomination.

The political and judicial criticisms paled, however, compared with the charges of the University of Oklahoma law professor Anita Hill that Clarence Thomas had repeatedly harrassed her sexually. Hill had worked with Thomas at the EEOC (Equal Employment Opportunity Commission), and they investigated charges of this nature from others. The Senate Judiciary Committee held televised hearings of the allegations against Thomas. While the country was divided between Thomas and Hill, public opinion polls suggested that more Americans thought Hill was lying than Thomas. Some liberals complained that the Anita Hill allegations only served to obscure the issues of Thomas' inexperience and hostile attitudes toward many civil rights measures. In any case, Clarence Thomas was confirmed by the Senate by a very close vote of 52-48.

As expected, the Supreme Court did move in a more conservative direction, but more by restricting rather than overturning previous decisions. The Court upheld the right of Missouri and Pennsylvania to place restrictions on the right to abortion. A woman still had a constitutional right to an abortion, however, so the famous 1973 *Roe v. Wade* decision was not overturned. The rights of arrested persons also were restricted, and civil rights laws were narrowly interpreted.

Supreme Court Justice nominee Clarence Thomas and his wife Virginia listen during his nomination hearing before the Senate Judiciary Committee on Capitol Hill. Credit: AP/Wide World Photos.

THE SELF-PROCLAIMED ENVIRONMENTAL AND EDUCATION PRESIDENT

The world celebrated the 20th anniversary of Earth Day on April 22, 1990. Festivals, concerts, exhibits, and "teach ins" were held to remind the world of the environment and the future of the planet. The ecology movement of the 1970s had moved into new realms by the 1990s. Recycling of aluminum cans, bottles, tin cans, or styrofoam boxes was only one of the approaches to the problem of limited resources and pollution of the environment. Scientists were concerned with a hole in the ozone layer of the earth, global warming, and America's appetite for resources and energy. Containing only 4 percent of the population of the world, the United States used up to 30 percent of all resources and energy. Strategies such as driving more fuel efficient cars or using more efficient light bulbs were positive measures, but most scientists agreed that there would come a time that use of resources would have to be sharply curtailed. On November 15, 1990, a new Clean

Air Act was signed by President Bush. Businesses were required to control emissions of sulfur dioxide and nitrogen oxides. The environmental goals were stymied, however, by the relaxing of government regulations.

President Bush had campaigned that American students would improve their standing in the world to first place in science and math by the year 2000. This commitment would take dedication and dollars. Failing to put federal money where his mouth was, Bush asked for $3 billion less than Reagan had for education. The high school dropout rate increased, and even more of the work force was functionally illiterate. Bush did push for vouchers for parents to send their children to public or private schools. The students at private schools usually had higher test scores. This so-called "school choice" movement was vigorously advocated by a coalition of concerned parents, conservative politicians, and an odd mix of religious groups such as the Christian Coalition and the Roman Catholic bishops. (The Catholic Church operates a vast education network for young people of all ages.)

However, "school choice," especially when it included private, parochial schools, was vigorously opposed by traditional advocates of public education, such as the National Education Association and the American Federation of Teachers, and by religious organizations opposed to tax support for private, religious schools. The latter coalition included the Americans United for the Separation of Church and State and the Seventh-day Adventist Church, which operates one of the largest Protestant education networks in the world.

THE STATUS OF MINORITIES

The American Disabilities Act of 1990

Protection from discrimination was extended to Americans with physical and mental disabilities with the passage of the Americans with Disabilities Act, which was signed into law on July 26, 1990. The law requires that major employers, schools, and government institutions provide for the needs of citizens with various disabilities, whether they be physical or mental. Conservative opponents complain that it forces businesses and others into spending money which will benefit too few people to be cost effective. But advocates of disabled persons championed the new law as long overdue to ensure that such citizens receive access to the same kind of services as others have always enjoyed.

Other Civil Rights Matters

The Civil Rights Act of 1990 was vetoed by President Bush because he claimed it would lead to quotas for minorities in hiring and promotion. Nevertheless, he signed a new bill in 1991 that was very similar to the one he had vetoed.

While President Bush's record of government appointees was not rated high by civil rights organizations, he did appoint General Colin Powell as the first African-American to serve as Chairman of the Joint Chiefs of Staff. That proved to be one of his most popular appointments because General Powell enjoyed widespread respect and support from Americans of all colors and races.

Rodney King and the Los Angeles Riots

A major race riot in South Central Los Angeles in April 1992 was an example that racial tensions, and the anger of the poor and disadvantaged, still existed and was close to the surface. The spark for the riot was the acquittal of four white police officers who were on trial for severely beating Rodney King, an African-American, following an automobile chase on March 3, 1991. The beating was captured on videotape by a witness to the event. The video confirmed for many that the Los Angeles Police Department was racist and predisposed to violence against African-Americans. The police officers maintained that they had to use an extreme level of force because King was violent and would not stay down as ordered. But the videotape suggested to most Americans in clear terms that the beating he received was not necessary to subdue King. The trial of the police officers was moved to the white, upper middle class area in Simi Valley, California. And when the all white jury there acquitted the officers, it confirmed for many that minorities did not receive justice in this nation.

For three days rioters burned buildings, looted stores in South Central and Koreatown, and injured and killed fellow citizens. The rioting was not only black versus white but also damage and violence upon and between Koreans and Latinos. More than 12,000 persons were arrested, 51 people lost their lives, and over $750 million worth of property was destroyed. This was worse than the Watts riot of 1965. The riot exposed the problems of the inner cities and poverty that, if not eliminated, could erupt into violence again.

FOREIGN AFFAIRS UNDER BUSH
FOREIGN POLICY AND THE SOVIET UNION

The End of the Cold War

The Soviet Union was undergoing pivotal changes in 1988 and 1989. Meeting President Bush on Malta in December 1989, Gorbachev declared that the Cold War was at an end. Bush, too cautious to quickly accept such a startling fact, stated that the two nations were working toward a lasting peace. The end of the Cold War would alter a situation that had existed since 1946. Change that brought an end to communist governments already had begun in Soviet-dominated Eastern Europe following the statement by Gorbachev that "Freedom of Choice was a universal principle." In 1989, Poland, led by Lech Walesa's Solidarity labor union (which had begun in Gdansk, the old German city of Danzig), was the first nation to overturn its communist government. Then one by one, like dominoes acting in the reverse of the old domino theory of the Cold War era, several nations in Eastern Europe ousted their communist rulers. After Poland came Hungary, then Czechoslovakia, Bulgaria, and Romania. The year 1989 became known as the year of the peaceful revolution. In Romania, however, the brutal dictator Nicolae Ceausescu and his wife were executed by gunshots to the head at close range on Christmas Day 1989.

In East Germany, the Berlin Wall came down as if it had been scripted by a Hollywood writer. With the fate of the East German communist dictator all but certain, both East and West Germany announced on November 9, 1989, that all bor-

Post-Cold War Europe. Credit: The United States: Brief Edition, *by Winthrop D. Jordan and Leon F. Litwack, Prentice-Hall, Inc., 1994*

der crossings between them were opened. Then two days later, on the 11th, and without warning, West Berliners suddenly appeared at the Berlin War and began chipping away at it with hammers and chisels. East German border guards on the other side just watched as hundreds, then thousands, of West Berliners appeared at the Wall and began tearing it down. The communist government was ousted and reunification plans with West Germany went forward. On October 3, 1990, the five states of East Germany were reunited with the West; Germany was reunified for the first time since the end of World War II in 1945. The new Germany remained in NATO.

There were problems within the newly freed nations, particularly with their switch to free market capitalism, but the excitement kept the worries at bay for a while. By the end of 1990, Latvia, Estonia, and Lithuania led the separation of the Soviet states into a federation.

Soviet leader Mikhail Gorbachev met with President Bush in Washington, D.C. from May 30 to June 3, 1990. Agreements were signed to reduce long-

The Berlin Wall coming down in 1989. Credit: AP/Wide World Photos.

range nuclear weapons and increase trade. The official end of the Soviet Union came at midnight on December 31, 1991. It was incredible that the end had come so quickly; the final movements certainly were rapid ones. Just before the end, Gorbachev resigned on December 25, 1991. Bush was not sure what new foreign policy problems would replace the Cold War, but there would be problems. There were still nuclear weapons in some of the republics, and the new nations were suffering from severe economic problems.

The Former Yugoslavia

Most changes from communism to non-communist governments were peaceful, but the end of Yugoslavia in 1991 provoked a long, bloody conflict. Ethnic groups divided the old Yugoslavia into individual republics. Disputes between the ethnic groups over the areas of the republics and autonomous regions broke out in Bosnia-Herzegovina. Christian Serbs attacked and besieged Bosnian Muslims, and ethnic cleansing—the systematic murder of an ethnic group—was being perpetrated by the Serbs against the Bosnian Muslims in the early nineties. NATO, the

United Nations, and efforts by individual nations could not stop the fighting. The United States, along with several other nations, sent both humanitarian aid and UN peacekeepers to Bosnia, but the European nations were all hesitant to intervene in the situation. The Bush administration, ever mindful of the Vietnam syndrome, in which Americans feared being drawn into a Vietnam-like quagmire, sought to keep its European allies in harmony with each other and the United States. Therefore, American policymakers perceived NATO and the UN as the principal players in the regional conflict within the previous Yugoslavian nation.

ASIAN FOREIGN POLICY

The events in the Soviet Union and in Eastern Europe could not be hidden even from the traditionally isolated Chinese. By the late eighties, protests had begun in China for a democratic system of government. Young intellectuals, students of the Chinese universities, organized rallies and meetings to propose the end of the authoritarian communist government of Deng Xiaoping. The students brought their protest to Tiananmen Square in the capital city of Beijing. A statue resembling the Statue of Liberty, but named the "Goddess of Liberty," was brought to the Square and set up in plain view. After several days of demonstrations, the authorities cleared Tiananmen Square on June 4, 1989, killing anywhere from 400 to 800 young people and arresting many others. All across China, a wave of terror struck among intellectuals and other free thinkers, as thousands of dissidents were arrested, imprisoned, and executed. President Bush condemned the brutality of the Chinese government and praised the efforts of the students, but he would not order economic sanctions as a reprisal. China was moving to a free market society, and Bush did not want to end good relations between the two nations for any reason.

MIDDLE EAST POLICY

Trouble in the Persian Gulf

Saddam Hussein, the dictatorial leader of Iraq, stunned the world when he ordered the invasion of Kuwait on August 2, 1990. Actually, trouble had been brewing for at least two years. In early August 1988, just one day after the UN-arranged cease-fire effectively ended the Iran-Iraq War, Kuwait began increasing its oil production in opposition to the Organization of Petroleum Exporting Countries (OPEC) policy. This action resulted in the decline of oil prices on the world market, which angered Saddam Hussein, whose country was saddled with heavy debts as a result of its recent war against Iran. Iraq's primary source of revenue was its own oil, whose price had gone down in the world marketplace as a natural by-product of Kuwait's decision. Thus, Saddam Hussein accused Kuwait of "economic aggression" and demanded that the Kuwait government reduce its oil production. In addition to this demand, he also insisted that Kuwait and Saudi Arabia cancel Iraq's combined debts of $30 million which it owed to the two nations. He also revived an old dispute concerning the legitimacy of Kuwait's independence, which had been separated from Iraq by the British in 1921.

As tensions in the Persian Gulf region mounted, United States ambassador to Iraq, April Glaspie, met with Saddam Hussein on July 25, 1990. The meeting resolved nothing; in fact, the two participants could not even agree on the content of Ambassador Glaspie's message. Iraq released a supposed text of the meeting which indicated that Glaspie was timid and that she had assured Saddam that the United States would not interfere in a fight between two Arab nations. Glaspie later testified before Congress that she told the Iraqi leader the United States would "defend our vital interests, . . . [and] support our friends in the Gulf . . ." Whichever version of the meeting was more accurate, the fact was that Iraq invaded and occupied Kuwait rather easily on August 2, 1990.

World Reaction to the Iraqi Invasion of Kuwait

The world reacted in almost total unanimity to condemn the Iraqi invasion of Kuwait. The UN Security Council almost immediately met and passed a resolution condemning the action and demanding an immediate withdrawal by a 14 to 0 vote. A few days later, on August 6, the Security Council passed Resolution 661, calling for a complete trade embargo against Iraq, by a vote of 13 to 0; Yemen and Cuba abstained. President Bush reacted on the day of the invasion by denouncing it as "naked aggression," and the very next day, a joint American-Soviet statement by Secretary of State James Baker and Soviet Foreign Minister Edouard Shevardnadze also condemned the Iraqi move. The world also recognized that Iraqi troops also were amassed along its border with Saudi Arabia, which was friendly to Kuwait. President Bush quickly perceived the invasion of Kuwait and the threatened invasion of Saudi Arabia as a direct threat to the economic security of the United States and its industrialized allies worldwide. The United States could not sit idly by and allow Iraq to grab possession of more oil production. Such increased power could be used by Iraq to blackmail and humble the West at Saddam's slightest whim. Vital American national interest was at stake.

Therefore, Operation "Desert Shield" to protect the oil rich nation of Saudi Arabia from attack by Iraq began with the deployment of American troops to Saudi Arabia on August 7, 1990. British troops soon joined the American forces, as did Arab soldiers from Egypt, Qatar, Oman, and the United Arab Emirates. In September, after a meeting with Gorbachev in Helsinki, Finland, President Bush declared a "New World Order" in which "the strong respect the rights of the weak." On October 1, both houses of Congress overwhelmingly approved the preliminary actions of the president up to that point in time. And in early November, just after the Congressional elections, Bush announced that the United States would double its troop strength in Saudi Arabia from 200,000 to 400,000. Meanwhile, diplomacy to prevent war continued while troops were gathering in Saudi Arabia to fight if necessary. Bush had promised President Mubarek of Egypt and King Hussein of Jordan to exhaust diplomacy so as not to turn the Arab states against the American action.

The Debate Over the Use of Force

On November 29, the UN Security Council passed Resolution 678, which authorized the use of force to end the Iraqi control of Kuwait if the forces of Saddam Hussein were not out of that country by January 15, 1991. Debate within the United States and in the Congress began to pick up in intensity, especially on January 10, 1991, when Congress officially began debating a resolution authorizing the use of force if the president deemed it necessary. Many Democrats argued that the country should wait to determine if the worldwide economic sanctions against Iraq would force Saddam Hussein to withdraw from Kuwait without the need for war. Some expressed concern about a possible parallel with the Tonkin Gulf Resolution, which in 1964, had given President Johnson a blank check to involve American troops in the Vietnam War. But others, mostly but not entirely Republicans, argued that the world did not have time to wait; in any case, the country should unite behind their president in this time of crisis. The debate over the "use of force" resolution will probably go down in history as one of the greatest debates in the history of the Senate, both because it was focused entirely on the serious issue (rather than name-calling) and so many senators argued so eloquently for their position. On January 12, the House of Representatives passed the resolution by a vote of 250 to 183, and the Senate did so by the narrow margin of 52 to 47.

The Persian Gulf War

The UN deadline of January 15 passed with no evacuation of Kuwait. By this time, some 28 nations were part of the UN force in the Middle East, 16 of which had sent actual ground troops. On January 16, 1991, at approximately 6:45 p.m. Eastern Time, American and allied planes began to bomb Iraqi targets as Operation Desert Storm began. Approximately 1,000 sorties were flown against communications systems, chemical weapons plants, weapons depots, and facilities with the possibility of housing nuclear weapons. CNN (Cable News Network) reporters in Baghdad (the capital of Iraq) reported the bombing of that city firsthand. In fact, the military of the United States and Iraq received information on the war from the CNN broadcasts. This was even more of a living room war than the Vietnam war had been. What Saddam Hussein had arrogantly boasted would be the "mother of all battles" proved to be a relatively brief and easy victory for UN forces under the military command of American General H. Norman Schwarzkopf, who was known as "Stormin' Norman."

On February 15, Saddam Hussein agreed to leave Kuwait if certain conditions, such as the end to economic sanctions and no reparations exacted for war damages, were met. Bush rejected the offer. Then on February 23, 1991 (Washington time), General Schwarzkopf sent 200,000 soldiers against the Iraqi army in Kuwait as the ground war officially began. The Iraqi army was reported to be a strong, well-trained, well-armed force. But it was outflanked and pushed back into Iraq following about 100 hours of hostilities. There were 148 American battle deaths during the Persian Gulf War, of which 11 were women and 35 were victims of "friendly fire," and more than 450 were wounded in the fighting. Conservative estimates of Iraqis killed in action put the total at 100,000, but the real figure was probably

Devastation Following the End of the Persian War. Credit: AP/Wide World Photos.

higher than that. The war was clearly a total disaster for Iraq, so when President Bush proposed a cease-fire on February 28, Saddam Hussein accepted. The war was over only six weeks after it had started.

Bush's approval ratings went through the roof as a result of the success of the Persian Gulf War, but those opinion poll numbers ironically did not last very long. The military had performed well, and demonstration of the high tech weaponry was impressive. Perhaps most significant was the perception that the United States had regained the prestige it had lost after the Vietnam War.

But the negative aspects of the war soon were exposed. The retreating Iraqis had set fire to the oil wells in Kuwait, which was an environmental concern with smoke blackening the skies for miles. Saddam Hussein was still in power and took out his anger on Kurds and Shiite Muslims who had revolted, slaughtering them by the hundreds. The public also was made aware that the United States had sent foreign aid and sophisticated American technology to Iraq to counter the power of Iran during the Iran-Iraq War of the 1980s. Many wondered at the wisdom of building up one tyrant against another, especially when circumstances led to battle with a previous "ally." Other critics of administration policy warned against the dangers of personalizing the war by making Saddam Hussein himself the personal enemy. If that had not been done, it was argued, then Saddam's personal survival would not be a sign of defiance, or even victory, as Saddam tried to make it after the war. Furthermore, there would not be cries of only a partial American victory because of a failure to kill or capture Saddam, as some of the more conservative critics of the administration were saying. Finally, on the financial side, the costly war took money away from domestic programs. All these appeared to be the main reasons that the victory in the Persian Gulf War did not translate into a more permanent mantle of support for the president.

LATIN AMERICAN POLICY

Bush decided that less direct intervention and more diplomacy should be used to bring about foreign policy goals in Latin America. He supported political leaders in Central America using their influence, and as a result, free elections were held in Nicaragua in 1990. Debts owed to American banks, and the increased drug trade in the region, were ongoing problems for the United States. The United States military organized small operations to try to stop the flow of drugs from Colombia, Bolivia, and Peru. This was a major theater in Bush's overall war on drugs. The president also created a new Office of National Drug Control Policy with William J. Bennett the new head, or "drug czar."

Panama

In February 1988, federal grand juries in Florida indicted General Manuel Noriega, the leader of Panama, on drug trafficking charges as part of the American war on drugs. American intelligence agencies had known of Noriega's involvement in the illegal drug trade and money laundering for drug cartels, but had looked the other way because he had supplied the CIA with information on Central America and South America for years. Enemies of Noriega in Panama, hoping to have him removed from power, made information on his involvement in the drug trade, with Cuba, with the CIA, and as part of the administration's schemes for the Contras available to the American media.

When the National Assembly of Panama supported the leadership of Noriega, the United States decided to take action to force Panama to get rid of the general. President Bush viewed Noriega as an evil influence who must go. In March 1988, Panamanian assets in American banks were frozen in an effort to push Noriega out of power. As the dispute continued during the year, Noriega grew more vocal in his verbal assaults on the American government's effort to remove him from power. Then on December 15, 1989, the National Assembly of Panama declared General Manuel Noriega to be the official head of the government and declared that a state of war existed with the United States. And on December 16, an off-duty American Marine was killed in Panama.

At that point, President Bush ordered the military to invade Panama and bring Noriega to justice in Operation Just Cause. Shortly before Christmas, on December 20, 1989, 12,000 American soldiers joined the 12,000 soldiers already in Panama as the invasion began. Resistance virtually ended when Noriega took refuge in the Vatican Embassy on December 24. Twenty-three Americans died and 322 were wounded in the brief invasion, with Panamanian casualties reported to be about 4,000. Noriega was brought back to the United States to stand trial. Many observers believed that the media seemed to lose its objectivity and became virtual cheerleaders for the American military action. There were some critics of the administration's action who believed that kidnapping a head-of-state was a violation of international law, as well as something that the United States would never toler-

U.S. Invasion of Panama. Credit: AP/Wide World Photos.

ate if it happened to its own president. But public opinion polls showed a huge and enthusiastic support for the president's actions in Panama.

Nicaragua

President Bush deviated from the Reagan administration's policy toward the civil war in Nicaragua. While the Reagan policy had sought ways to get around the Boland Amendment (1984), which had prohibited all but humanitarian aid to the Contras, President Bush reduced even the humanitarian aid and used diplomatic measures to encourage the two sides to negotiate an end to the conflict. In 1987, a coalition of five Central American nations had negotiated the Contadora Plan as a way to bring peace to Nicaragua. The Bush administration endorsed the proposal, which finally resulted in the Contra rebels ending their military operations in return for political reforms begun by the Sandinista regime of Daniel Ortega. These reforms led to free elections in February 1990, when opposition candidate Mrs. Violeta de Chamorro defeated Ortega for the presidency of the country. Although some confrontations continued sporadically, the change of government generally was peaceful. The nearly decade-long civil war had come to an end.

Bill Clinton and Al Gore wave to a cheering crowd. Credit: AP/Wide World Photos.

Haiti

In 1991, the popularly elected leader of Haiti, Jean-Bertrand Aristide, was overthrown by the Haitian military. Aristide came to the United States, and the American government put economic sanctions on the new government of Haiti, which it refused to recognize. Thousands of Haitians followed Aristide in their leaky boats, claiming they were political refugees fleeing from the harsh treatment of the new government. Most were sent back because it was believed they really were fleeing the poverty of the island instead. Critics of the Bush administration claimed they were not allowed into the country because they were black.

THE 1992 ELECTION

The Candidates

Initially perceiving that George Bush would be virtually impossible to unseat, leading Democrats like New York Governor Mario Cuomo stayed out of the race for the Democratic nomination in 1992. After the dust had settled from the Persian Gulf War, and Americans began to focus on the current economic recession, other Democrats did enter the race, among them former Massachusetts Senator Paul

Tsongas, Iowa Senator Tom Harkin, civil rights activist Jesse Jackson, and House Majority Leader Richard Gephardt of Missouri. However, Arkansas Governor William Jefferson "Bill" Clinton had gotten off to an early, fast start, and with his youthful energy and articulate, and sometimes, inspiring rhetoric, he could not be overtaken in the primaries. At the Democratic National Convention that summer, Bill Clinton was nominated on the first ballot.

He was a young candidate, only 46, and the first candidate of a major party from the "baby boom" generation (which is to say that he had been born after World War II). To capitalize on his "baby boom" generation status and to court the young vote during the campaign, Clinton appeared on "The Arsenio Hall Show," where he wore dark glasses while playing the saxophone. He also appeared before an MTV (Music Television) audience to answer questions posed by young people. Clinton had been a Rhodes Scholar at Oxford University in Britain and a graduate of Yale Law School. His political experience consisted of serving as the attorney-general and then the governor of Arkansas for several terms. After his nomination, Clinton then chose popular Tennessee Senator Albert "Al" Gore to be his running mate. Gore was considered a moderate Democrat and an active environmentalist. His book, *Earth in the Balance: Healing the Global Environment*, was released in 1992. It also was important that Gore had served in Vietnam because Clinton had not, a fact which led to much criticism of the Democratic presidential candidate, especially from veterans.

President George Bush was challenged within his own Republican Party by conservative television commentator Patrick "Pat" Buchanan. Buchanan represented the more extreme conservative elements within the party who were disappointed with Bush's commitment or action on behalf of the Religious Right and what they called "family values." Although the president defeated Buchanan in every primary election that spring, Bush did permit the ultra-conservative wing of the party to dominate the rhetoric at the national convention that summer. At the convention, Buchanan, and several others, declared a religious or cultural war against social liberalism in the country, attacking the pro-choice movement, homosexuals, and affirmative action. Although George Bush easily won renomination, many observers of politics later believed that the tone at the Republican convention contributed to his defeat in the fall elections because of perceptions that it was mean-spirited and negative. After the president was renominated, he asked the convention to renominate Vice-President Dan Quayle as his running mate, a request with which the delegates complied.

Texas billionaire and businessman H. Ross Perot caught the attention of many who believed a political outsider was necessary to get the government back on track of serving the people. Perot had made his fortune in the computer industry, and a popular belief was that if he could run an economically successful business, then he also could run an economically successful nation. Perot reflected the frustration of millions of Americans who had lost faith in their government and wanted a new kind of leadership. Millions approved of his plain-language explanations, his personal success, and his independence from any special interest groups. Perot poured millions of dollars of his own money into his campaign. In late March, Perot named retired Vice-Admiral James B. "Bond" Stockdale as his running mate.

Stockdale was a former navy combat pilot who had spent seven years as a prisoner of war (POW) in North Vietnam. The entrance of the Perot-Stockdale ticket into the campaign made it a three-way race. Such a race among candidates with strong support turned the election into a closer race than had been predicted.

The Campaign

Bush attempted to hold the Republican voting block amassed by Nixon and later, Reagan, together. Since 1968 the Republican Party had won the presidency in five of the six elections with a coalition of diverse voters. Reagan had merged together economic and political conservatives, many blue-collar Democrats, white voters in the South who disliked the Democrats' stand on civil rights, young Americans between 18 and 30 who were prospering (often called "yuppies"), and voters in the suburbs. Bush ran into trouble, however, because the issues that had held the coalition together were no longer in place. The economy was sluggish, the Cold War was over and no longer an issue to get votes, and Bush did not have the appeal of Reagan, the "great communicator."

The issues which the president could use for his advantage were few. He promised to safeguard the traditional conservative "family values," and it was fairly obvious that even those to the political right of Bush would probably not vote for anyone else in large numbers. He took credit for the end of the Cold War and victory in the Persian Gulf War. The Bush-Quayle campaign strategy also focused on painting Clinton as a person with low character and morals. Clinton had avoided the draft during the Vietnam war, smoked marijuana (although, during the campaign, Clinton offered that he had not "inhaled"), and was reported to have had several extramarital affairs. Bush maintained that a major difference between Clinton and himself was "trust." Could the voters especially trust Clinton with foreign policy problems because he had no experience in that area?

In spite of his own experience and accomplishments, President Bush did not give the public a clear vision for the future or specific remedies for the nation's problems, particularly the economy. He was also at a disadvantage because the mood of the country was anti-incumbent at the time. The number of Americans who saw the government as the problem had increased. Members of Congress, and government officials who had served for a long time, were seen as contributing to gridlock between the executive and legislative branches and nothing was changing. States were passing term limits for their congressmen and senators. And President Bush was not only an incumbent president, but he had been part of the Washington establishment for many years.

Bill Clinton ran on the promise that he was a "new Democrat." This meant that Clinton wanted to move the Democratic Party to a more moderate stand on some issues to attract businessmen and white suburban voters, many of whom had been dubbed "Reagan Democrats" because of their support for Ronald Reagan in the 1980s. Clinton maintained that private business was the force behind economic progress and that government should assist the businessman to achieve success. Welfare should be reformed so that people would not stay on the system for years, and more police officers on the streets were necessary to reduce crime. The concern with high crime rates was an issue for all Americans in this campaign.

In other areas the Democratic candidate advocated more liberal policies. For example, he advocated that more federal money should be invested in public education and job training programs. The nation's infrastructure of roads and bridges, he believed, were badly in need of repair, which he argued should be paid for with smaller defense budgets. He made it clear that he was "pro-choice" on abortion, an issue which did tend to help him with women vis-à-vis Bush. And in one of his major election campaign themes, Clinton hammered away in support of the idea that Americans had the right to affordable health care. The details would come later, but the Democratic candidate promised to use his power as president to get the country to adopt some form of national health insurance, an idea which had been favored by progressive Democrats since the days of President Harry Truman. Above all else, Clinton kept stressing to voters that he was the candidate for "change."

During the campaign, Ross Perot became famous for his poster-size charts explaining what the growing national debt was doing to the health of the economy. In fact, the national debt was his most frequent subject. Some voters who identified with his frank talk were less thrilled with his specific solutions, especially with his proposal for a 50-cents per gallon federal tax increase on gasoline to help eliminate the debt. Perot also hit the idea of career politicians every opportunity he got, endorsing the concept of term limits for members of Congress. There was enormous support for this rhetoric and for term limits, and Perot scored well in the opinion polls among those voters who listed "incumbency" of politicians as the most important issue. However, Perot lost support when he returned to the race in October after having dropped out on July 16, the last day of the Democratic National Convention. At the time of his withdrawal in July, Perot had cited a "revitalized" Democratic Party as one of the major reasons for his surprise decision. In late October, however, after he had reentered the race, Perot accused the Republican Party of having plotted to disrupt his business interests and his daughter's wedding, and declared that this had been the real reason for his earlier withdrawal from the race.

The Results

The voter turnout of 55 percent was the largest since 1976. Many believed that the candidacy of Ross Perot added more excitement and interest in the election. Although voter polling suggested that Perot's votes would have been evenly divided between Bush and Clinton if Perot had not been in the race, there was a general consensus after the election that the votes cast for Perot hurt Bush more than Clinton. This was because Perot votes in certain key states enabled Clinton to win a plurality of the popular votes, and thus all of those states' electoral votes. The Clinton-Gore ticket performed well in the strong Republican areas of the suburbs, the Sunbelt, high-tech strong business areas, and areas with high concentrations of retired Americans. The Democratic ticket won 43 percent of the popular vote and 370 electoral votes; the Republican ticket won 37 percent of the popular vote and 168 electoral votes; the independent ticket of Ross Perot and James Stockdale won 19 percent of the popular vote but not a single electoral vote. Such a strong popular vote showing by the independent candidates was an indication to the two major parties that a larger percentage of Americans were dissatisfied with the job performance of both parties.

The Democrats retained control of both houses of Congress, but their composition changed. The new members were younger, and representation was a closer reflection of American society, but still not truly representative. Four more women were added to the Senate and 19 to the House. And there were more black and Hispanic representatives as well.

Before leaving the presidency, one of the last acts of Bush was to pardon former Secretary of Defense Caspar Weinberger and other officials from indictments in the Iran-Contra affair. The charges were lying to Congress and obstructing the congressional investigation into the scandal.

INTRODUCTION TO THE CLINTON ADMINISTRATION

Bill Clinton entered the White House on January 20, 1993 with the most ambitious agenda since the presidency of Lyndon Johnson. Not only had this self-proclaimed "new Democrat" promised to establish some form of national health insurance, overhaul the welfare system, strengthen federal anti-crime efforts, and improve public education and the environment, he did so in the context of pledging to shrink the size of government in general, and the national debt in particular.

Most observers of the first half of his presidency generally gave him mixed results on his domestic agenda at best. Part of the reason for his lack of great success seems to be that in his virtually inexhaustible supply of personal energy and his unusual ability to grasp complex issues rather quickly, President Clinton often left the American people behind. He moved too fast and proposed too many complex solutions to social problems that many found themselves in shock or bewilderment. Of course, that condition also allowed Clinton's critics to slow down the presidential agenda.

Clinton's leadership style, evident during the first half of his presidency, also contributed to his limited success. Clinton probably allowed too many administration officials open access to him, thus tending to bog him down in too many day-to-day decisions that could have been more efficiently left to competent subordinates. And Clinton himself seemed intent on getting answers on every aspect of a complex matter before presenting his detailed proposals to Congress. Therefore, while he introduced numerous programs in principle to the American people, there seemed to be an inordinate time delay before the details actually were provided to Congress and the country. This seemed to create unnecessary impatience among voters, which also played into the hands of congressional critics and other opponents.

Then too, many voters, even among those who had voted for him, did not really trust the man whose critics had labeled "Slick Willy." There were too many rumors about his alleged affairs with other women. And investigations about the Clintons'

1992	50	BILL CLINTON	Democrat	43,728,275	370	43.2
		George Bush	Republican	38,167,416	168	37.7
		H. Ross Perot	United We Stand, America	19,237,247		19.0

land investments made years before the presidential election continued to haunt him. Congressional opponents were successful in getting an independent counsel to investigate this Whitewater deal (which involved a savings and loan institution that later went bankrupt).

Key Clinton Cabinet and Supreme Court Appointments

President Clinton generally received high marks for his cabinet-level and Supreme Court appointments. Not only were most chosen for their qualifications, but also to better represent the various groups of Americans. He purposely considered gender, race, and ethnicity in his screening process. Lloyd Bentsen was named as the Secretary of the Treasury, a white man who was well-respected by Democrats and Republicans alike. His cabinet also included Ron Brown, the first African-American to head the Commerce Department, Mike Espy, the African-American Secretary of Agriculture, and the former Hispanic mayor of San Antonio, Henry Cisneros, as Secretary of Housing and Urban Development. (Brown, Espy, and Cisneros were each clouded by allegations of impropriety after their confirmations.) Janet Reno became the first woman to head the Department of Justice, as the Attorney-General, and Hazel O'Leary became the first female Secretary of Energy.

Two retirements from the Supreme Court during Clinton's first 18 months in office allowed him to name the first justices appointed by a Democratic president since Lyndon Johnson appointed Thurgood Marshall in 1967. When Justice Byron R. White announced his retirement, President Clinton nominated Ruth Bader Ginsburg to replace him. Ginsburg had specialized as an attorney working on gender equality cases for the American Civil Liberties Union before the 1980s. In 1980, President Jimmy Carter had appointed her to the Federal Court of Appeals for the District of Columbia. Despite her earlier work for the ACLU, Ginsburg was considered a moderate, and the United States Senate overwhelmingly confirmed her in early August 1993. She became only the second woman ever named to the Supreme Court in American history.

In May 1993, Clinton nominated another Carter-appointed federal Court of Appeals judge (also in 1980) when Justice Harry A. Blackmun announced his retirement that spring. Known as a consensus builder, Stephen G. Breyer was confirmed easily by the Senate in late July of the same year.

DOMESTIC ISSUES UNDER CLINTON

The Issue of Gays in the Military

During the presidential election campaign, Bill Clinton had pledged to strike down the ban on gays in the United States armed services. The Clinton White House announced in late January 1993 that the president was suspending enforcement of the current ban on gays in the military. However, the same announcement stated that the president would delay for six months before deciding to make the suspension permanent, pending negotiations over the details. This six-month delay was forced because of a huge furor over his campaign promise, which had not been particularly heavy during the campaign, but which suddenly intensified after the inauguration. Meanwhile, on January 28, a federal court ruled that the Pentagon's ban on gays in the military was unconstitutional.

The issue partially eclipsed other important matters, and it generally was regarded as a strategic error for the president to begin his administration on this highly controversial matter. The president received relatively little support for an outright abolition of the ban on gays in the military, and negotiations involving the White House, Congress, and the Pentagon continued, partly behind the scenes and partly in public view. Military officials worried about morale among soldiers and sailors should the ban be revoked, while still others appeared motivated by their personal views of morality.

In late May, with his proposal in serious jeopardy, President Clinton said he would support a policy whereby the military would not ask about a person's sexual orientation, and the service member would not volunteer such information. This position became known as the "don't ask, don't tell" policy. To satisfy moderates of both parties in Congress, the president finally accepted a compromise crafted by Georgia Democratic Senator Sam Nunn, the influential and respected chairman of the Senate Armed Services Committee. Essentially, the compromise included the "don't ask, don't tell" feature, but it also prohibited service personnel from engaging in homosexual acts when on duty or off duty. This policy was codified into law as part of a defense appropriations bill in November 1993. Many conservatives vowed to fight the new policy and overturn it.

THE FAMILY AND MEDICAL LEAVE ACT

The increasing number of working women in the country, coupled with renewed interest in and discussion of family values, led to a growing movement for federal legislation permitting parents and other working adults to take time off from work for certain good causes and still be assured that their jobs would be protected. Public opinion polls in the early nineties showed that most Americans believed that the birth, or adoption, of a child and the serious illness of an employee or an immediate family member were of sufficient value to merit job protection. Women's rights groups and organized labor (especially the AFL-CIO) spearheaded the drive to persuade Congress to pass such legislation. In fact, Congress did so on two different occasions in the early nineties, but each time the bills were vetoed by President Bush.

Calling it a high priority for his administration, President Clinton made it clear that he supported such legislation and would sign it into law. With Clinton's backing, both houses of Congress passed the Family and Medical Leave Act in early February 1993, and the president signed it into law the next day. The new law, effective in August of the same year, applied to most employees of government, non-profit organizations, and private companies which employed 50 or more people. It required such employers to give up to twelve weeks of unpaid leave during any 12-month period in order to deal with the birth or adoption of a child, or a serious illness to the employee or to an immediate family member. Employers would have to continue their workers' health insurance benefits during the leave and to guarantee the same or equivalent job upon their return to work. It was President Clinton's first significant legislative victory of his administration.

THE CLINTON ECONOMIC PLAN

The growing national debt had been a major issue in the 1992 presidential election campaign, and President Clinton was anxious to move the country in the direction of deficit reduction. In February 1993, Clinton proposed to Congress a comprehensive economic plan which he estimated would provide about $500 billion in net deficit reduction over the next five years, through 1998. On the tax side of the package, the president proposed to raise the personal federal income taxe rate for the highest income group, with a 10 percent surtax on family incomes of more than $250,000 a year. That would raise the top rate to an effective 39.6 percent. Corporate income taxes on profits greater than $10 million a year would rise marginally, and deductions for business meals and entertainment would be cut from 80 percent to 50 percent. Clinton also proposed a complicated energy tax, based on the output as measured by British thermal units (BTUs), which the administration estimated would raise the average family's total energy bills by $100 to $150 per year. The energy taxes would be partially offset by an expansion of the earned income tax credit for low-income families to include those families earning up to $30,000 a year. Some investment tax credits for new equipment would also be restored to businesses.

On the spending side of the ledger, the Clinton economic program called for the elimination of 100,000 federal jobs through attrition over four years. The defense budget would be significantly reduced through reductions in troop levels and slower pay raises. Agricultural subsidies also would be cut. And government streamlining measures would be taken to reduce the size and increase the efficiency of the federal government. (President Clinton named Vice-President Al Gore to head a commission charged with "reinventing government," which would recommend major changes in the way government did business.) Believing that the nation's infrastructure, environment, and education were important prerequisites for long-term economic growth, the Clinton plan included some spending increases for mass transit, public education, and the environment.

In order to speed up the slow economic recovery from the previous recession, Clinton's economic plan included a short-term stimulus package worth about $30 billion through 1997. This consisted of $16.2 billion in highway construction, public works projects, and summer youth jobs programs, and approximately $14 billion in short-term investment tax credits and other tax incentives for private business.

The Clinton economic plan initially won widespread support from a diverse cross section of the American public. For example, both the AFL-CIO and conservative Federal Reserve Board Chairman Alan Greenspan endorsed the plan. The most controversial part of the package was the short-term economic stimulus proposal, with conservative Republicans criticizing it as unnecessary government spending, and liberal Democrats criticizing it for being too small. But as the debate continued, partisan politics took its toll on the total budget plan, with most Republicans quarreling over numerous details, and most Democrats getting on the president's bandwagon.

Changes were made in both houses of Congress, especially in the Senate, and both chambers had passed different versions of a budget bill by the first of April 1993. The president's economic stimulus portion of the total package became a casualty of the legislative process, however. The House had passed the stimulus package in March, in a vote mostly along party lines, Democrats favoring it and Republicans voting against it. But in the Senate, a three-week Republican filibuster forced the Democrats to abandon it in late April, although both houses did pass an extension of unemployment benefits.

The final version of the Omnibus Budget Reconciliation Bill of 1993 passed both houses of Congress in early August and was signed by the president. The bill passed the House of Representatives by a very narrow margin along party lines. And in the Senate, Vice-President Gore had to break a 50-50 tie to obtain passage in that body. The bill, which provided for $496 billion in net deficit reduction over the next five years (through 1998), substantially resembled the president's original proposal despite numerous changes. Not all of Clinton's proposals were included in the final version, however. In addition to the economic stimulus part of the proposal (which already had been defeated), the other major part of the Clinton plan that met defeat was his proposed energy, or BTU, tax. In place of that complex idea, the final version of the bill levied a 4.3 cent-per-gallon excise tax hike on all transportation fuels. It was a badly needed victory for President Clinton from a political point of view, but it was by the narrowest of margins.

THE NORTH AMERICAN FREE TRADE AGREEMENT (NAFTA)

The globalization of the world's economy by the 1980s had forced nations to rethink their trade policies and how they conducted business in general. Multinational corporations, companies which operated freely around the world, were taking advantage of cheaper wage rates and less restrictive environmental laws in order to maximize profits. In a truly global marketplace, legal trade barriers seemed out of date. With pressure to relieve such barriers, some nations grouped geographically together began to form or strengthen existing blocs to increase their economic power in the world marketplace. Within these trading blocs, many tariffs were greatly reduced while others were eliminated altogether.

In order to take advantage of the new trend toward larger trading blocs, the Bush administration negotiated the North American Free Trade Agreement (NAFTA) with Mexico and Canada. Signed by representatives of all three countries in December 1992, the agreement eliminated most tariffs and other trade barriers between Canada, the United States, and Mexico over a 15-year period. It would be made effective January 1, 1994, pending ratification by the national legislatures in all three countries.

Bill Clinton had campaigned in favor of NAFTA during the 1992 presidential campaign, but opposition by the AFL-CIO and certain environmental organizations did force him to agree that certain labor and environmental protections for Mexican workers would have to be renegotiated by all three countries. Most union leaders

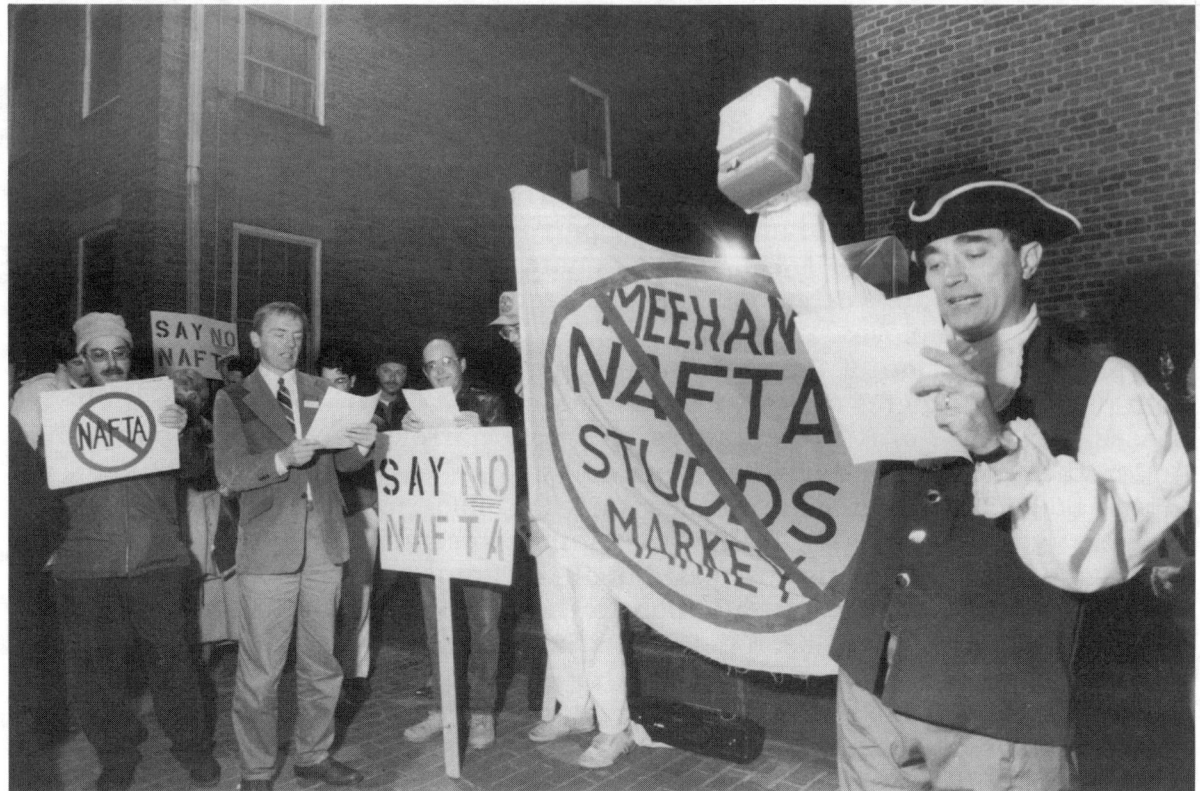

Anti-NAFTA rally in Boston, Massachusetts, 1993. Credit: AP/Wide World Photos.

made the argument that for the free trade agreement to constitute "fair trade," Mexican workers' wages would have to be significantly raised and their right to bargain collectively guaranteed. Otherwise, they alleged that NAFTA would only give official sanction to American companies moving operations there in order to exploit workers. And, in the long run, Mexican consumers would not be able to purchase large amounts of American products, thus producing a trade deficit with Mexico which would further erode American jobs. (Both the American and Mexican labor movements agreed on these principles.) For their part, environmental opposition focused on the relative lack of enforcement of environmental standards in Mexico, and the pollution left by American companies, many of whom operated along the Mexican border with the United States.

Predictably, most business groups staunchly supported the NAFTA agreement, arguing that America would have to keep up with the changing world market if it were to compete effectively in it. President Clinton was philosophically inclined to support the goals of free trade, so after some labor and environmental stipulations were added to NAFTA or promised by the Mexican government in 1993, the president announced his intention to ask Congress to ratify the agreement. But the new so-called "side" agreements that had been renegotiated were unacceptable to most of the groups who had earlier opposed NAFTA (including the AFL-CIO), largely because they were allegedly difficult or impossible to enforce. Ross Perot also weighed into the debate on the side of the opposition, declaring that if NAFTA were passed, Americans would soon hear the swishing sound of jobs leaving for Mexico. In early November 1993, Perot engaged in an unofficial debate on CNN's "Larry King Live" television show with Vice-President Al Gore. Nearly everyone who saw the debate thought that Gore had won it easily, and it turned out to be an important boost to its chances of passing Congress. Ironically, it was Republican votes which ensured the ratification of NAFTA, with most Democrats (especially in the House) voting against the president. The North American Free Trade Agreement was ratified by both houses of Congress that same November.

THE GENERAL AGREEMENT ON TARIFFS AND TRADE (GATT)

In another aspect of the world trade issue, the so-called Uruguay Round of the General Agreement on Tariffs and Trade (GATT) were concluded in December 1993 and formally signed in April of the next year. GATT was both an agreement and an organization, which consisted of 117 nations around the world. Made effective in July 1995, GATT cut tariffs on most imports by at least one-third, eliminated many others, scheduled quotas and other import limits on textiles and clothing to be phased out over the next ten years, and took other action generally designed to increase world trade. One of the most controversial provisions of the agreement was the creation of the World Trade Organization (WTO), which was given the authority to mediate trade disputes among nations.

GATT, like the NAFTA agreement, had been negotiated by the Bush administration and was supported by President Clinton. Most interest groups in the United States also supported the new agreement, although organized labor tried to lead the opposition on the grounds that GATT was essentially a measure designed to assist multinational corporations at the expense of working people. Some of the more conservative members of Congress also opposed GATT, alleging that the proposed World Trade Organization would mean the potential surrender of American control over their own economy. But the opposition to GATT never really got off the ground, and Congress ratified it by overwhelming majorities by the first of December, after the congressional elections the month before.

THE CLINTON HEALTH CARE PLAN FAILS TO PASS

One of the top priorities of the Clinton presidency was the major overhaul of the nation's health care system. At least since the days of Harry Truman, liberal Democrats had supported some kind of national health insurance system to replace the fragmented and poorly distributed health delivery systems in the nation. The closest they had come was the institution of the Medicare and Medicaid programs in the mid-sixties. Although the Medicare program was considered successful, neither of those programs had done an effective job of controlling health care costs because they applied only to the elderly and the poor. Of course, neither did they address the problem of working people losing their health insurance when they became unemployed or changed jobs. Candidate Bill Clinton had focused the nation's attention on the health care issue, and at the time of his election, there was widespread support for his general ideas.

Shortly after his inauguration, the president appointed his wife, Hillary Rodham Clinton, to head a commission to draft a plan that would provide health care for all Americans. The First Lady faced criticism, and even downright hostility, in a manner not unlike that which Eleanor Roosevelt had received during the days of Franklin Roosevelt's presidency. Hillary Clinton was a Yale Law School graduate with a successful law practice and a strong personal political agenda. She had long been a powerful advocate for the rights of children. Many people believed that she exercised too much influence over her husband's policies, and declared that she had not been elected to anything. The president saw her as a bright and capable citizen and advisor, whose talents should not be wasted. After all, the president could appoint study commissions as he chose because they could not legislate anything, but only recommend legislation or other actions.

Hillary Clinton's study commission unveiled its final recommendations in late 1993. One of the major criticisms levied at the proposed plan was that it was too complex, which was about the only perception which was shared by both liberals and conservatives. For example, its major structural format involved the establishment of large private organizations that would compete with each other for health subscribers in what was called "managed competition." Conservative opponents of the plan charged that these highly regulated health organizations would replace the doctor-patient relationship in terms of making important medical decisions. For their part, more liberal critics accused the plan of merely replacing the already confusing health care system with another confusing one. Instead, many liberals argued for a single-payer system that, like the successful Medicare program, would make the government the sole payer of medical expenses.

On the financing aspect of the Clinton proposal, employers would be required to provide basic coverage for their employees. Higher taxes on cigarettes, and other miscellaneous sources of revenue, would also help pay for the new system. The National Chamber of Commerce, the National Association of Manufacturers, and other representatives of small businesses opposed the Clinton plan on the grounds that many small businesses could not afford to comply with its requirements and would thus be forced out of business, costing Americans thousands of jobs in the long run. President Clinton countered with various tax credits to help small businesses meet their obligations. He also reminded the country that most businesses already provided health insurance for their employees, and that without a national health insurance system, businesses which refused to provide health coverage would remain in a competitive advantage over those who did cover their employees.

The entire country debated national health insurance during the year 1994. But the longer the debate continued, the more complex the president's plan seemed to be, and the more the opposition to it grew. The health insurance industry lobbied strenuously against the Clinton plan, using paid television ads to drive home its message that Americans would end up with poor medical service and government intrusion into their personal lives. Other opponents labeled the Clinton health plan as socialized medicine, a term which has always struck fear into most Americans. In an irony of American politics, both the American Medical Association and the AFL-CIO endorsed the package. But in the controversial atmosphere, the plan was slowly torn apart piece by piece, until it seemed that some opponents organized their opposition around the fact that Hillary Clinton had headed the commission. Assailed by well-financed opponents, and not enthusiastically supported by many liberals either, Clinton's health care plan was politically dead before the end of the year. (Following the failure to get the health plan through Congress, Hillary Rodham Clinton reduced her public role.)

FEDERAL ANTI-CRIME EFFORTS

In August 1993, President Clinton unveiled a major federal anti-crime plan which he asked Congress to enact. The major areas of concern were to tighten federal gun control laws and provide funds to put at least 50,000 new police officers on American streets. While Congress debated the crime package, perhaps the most controversial crime legislation discussed that year was the so-called Brady Bill. This bill was named after James S. Brady, ex-President Reagan's press secretary, who was badly injured during the assassination attempt on Reagan's life in March 1981. The Brady Bill provided for a five-day waiting period before anyone in the country could purchase a handgun. During those five days, local law enforcement authorities would be required to do background checks on handgun applicants. Convicted felons, minors, drug abusers, and illegal aliens were forbidden to buy a handgun. The bill also authorized about $200 million per year over several years to help states develop a computerized system for checking backgrounds instantaneously.

James Brady and his wife Sarah personally lobbied members of Congress for several months, arguing that the tragedy of the Reagan assassination attempt had changed their minds about the gun control issue. Sarah Brady, pushing her husband in his wheelchair along the corridors of the Capitol, produced a very emotional impact on Congress and the nation. Nevertheless, the National Rifle Association (NRA), and its conservative allies in Congress, lobbied vigorously against the Brady Bill, declaring that it was in opposition to the Second Amendment's right to bear arms, and that a computerized system to do quick background checks would be completed anyway in a few years and thus make the bill unnecessary. But public opinion polls showed support for the bill, and the NRA's reputation as one of the most powerful lobbies in Washington was damaged somewhat when Congress passed the Brady Handgun Violence Prevention Act (Brady Bill) in November 1993, making it effective the next March.

Meanwhile, Congress continued to debate the president's overall anti-crime package as both sides jockeyed to claim credit for being tougher on crime than the other side. Public pressure, political negotiations, and White House lobbying finally produced a bill that was acceptable to the president. The final version of the crime bill, passed in late August 1994 and signed into law in September, included $8.8 billion to help states and communities hire 100,000 new police officers over the next six years, and additional funding for the construction of new prisons. It also banned the manufacture, sale, and possession of 19 types of assault weapons and so-called "copycat" versions, although 650 types of semi-automatic weapons were exempted. Gun owners were allowed to keep the banned guns which they already possessed. In addition, the crime bill provided for stricter sentencing measures, including the extension of the death penalty to more than 50 federal crimes. The ban on assault weapons was the most controversial part of the Clinton-backed bill, with the NRA working hard to keep it out. Opinion polls, however, showed popular support for the assault weapons ban, and although it became part of the new law, several leading Republicans in Congress vowed to repeal it the first chance they got.

ANGER IN AMERICA

The Waco Tragedy

About 100 officers from the Bureau of Alcohol, Tobacco, and Firearms (BATF, or often simply ATF) launched a raid on the Branch Davidian compound near Waco, Texas on February 28, 1993. Vernon Howell, who called himself David Koresh, was the leader of the religious cult, which had spun off another sect years before. The federal agents sought to arrest Koresh, a self-proclaimed messiah figure (he sometimes claimed he was Jesus Christ), on charges of illegal possession and stockpiling of fully automatic firearms and explosives. There also were concerns about numerous reports of child abuse and allegations that Koresh had several wives.

Koresh was tipped off shortly before the raid, and four government agents were killed and more than one dozen injured in a gun battle while attempting to get inside the compound's main building. The Federal Bureau of Investigation (FBI) soon took charge of the scene after the initial attempt to arrest Koresh had failed. The incident quickly bogged down into a siege that lasted 51 days. During that time, the FBI tried to obtain the release of the cult members who were in the building, but the cult leader became unpredictable, first announcing the time he would release everyone, and then declaring that God had told him to wait further. Nevertheless, during the 51-day siege at Waco, 37 people did leave the building at different times, including 21 children. On April 19, after Koresh repeatedly had broken promises about when he would surrender, armored vehicles began battering the walls and launching tear gas into the building. The building soon erupted into flames and burned to the ground. At least 86 persons were killed in the tragedy.

Controversy about the raid almost immediately divided the nation. Why had federal agents simply not arrested Koresh during one of his visits to town? Who started the fire that killed all those people? Federal authorities admitted that mistakes had been made, and President Clinton and Attorney General Janet Reno each accepted full responsibility for the decision to end the siege. Right-wing political groups and some leading Republicans called for congressional investigations into the Waco tragedy. When official inquiries were not as thorough as critics of the BATF and FBI had hoped for, charges of a government conspiracy against unpopular religious groups and a cover-up were heard throughout the land. The Waco tragedy became a celebrated symbol of anti-government sentiment, as demonstrated by the rising popularity of right-wing radio talk shows hosted by Rush Limbaugh, G. Gordon Liddy (of Watergate fame), and others. In the summer of 1995, Congressional hearings began investigating the federal agencies' handling of the Waco tragedy.

Terrorism in the Heartland

The Waco tragedy had come on the heels of the terrorist bombing of the World Trade Center in New York City on February 26, 1993. Six people had been killed in that incident, and more than 1,000 others injured, most of them treated for smoke inhalation and released. A bomb had been placed in a Ryder rental van which was then parked in a garage below the World Trade Center. Investigations led the authorities to link the incident with radical elements within the Middle Eastern Muslim community, and several persons were later arrested and convicted of the crime.

Then tragedy struck the nation in unprecedented dimensions when the Alfred P. Murrah Federal Building in Oklahoma City, Oklahoma was blown up on April 19, 1995. The death toll was 169 men, women, and children, many of whom were not removed from the building for a week or more. It was a total shock because most could not believe that such an act of terrorism could take place in the very heartland of America. While a Middle Eastern connection had not been ruled out, authorities first arrested an American, Timothy McVeigh.

For a time, at least, the nation seemed to come together in a spirit of unity to assist the victims and their families pick up the pieces and move on with their lives. But would it last? Perhaps a new world had come to America, bringing many of the same problems that others have faced for decades. The Oklahoma City bombing soon escalated the anti-government rhetoric on the more conservative radio talk shows. Much talk was devoted to the alleged excessive power of government agencies like the BATF and the FBI. And several people pointed out that the Oklahoma City bombing had occurred precisely on the second anniversary of the Waco incident, implying that perhaps the bombing had been a way to draw attention to the alleged injustices committed by the feds at Waco. Most Americans also became aware of the existence of private militia organizations in several states. Generally speaking, these groups stockpile guns and other weapons in the fear that at some point in the future, it might become necessary to take up arms against the United States government or to prevent a United Nations takeover of the world, including the United States. Their leaders publish pamphlets and tapes in which they claim to be the true defenders of the Constitution. What the future holds for the United States is awaited by millions of Americans.

THE 1994 CONGRESSIONAL ELECTIONS

President Clinton's shaky start left him and his Democratic Party vulnerable as the country faced the congressional and statewide elections in November of 1994. Attacking Clinton for allegedly failing to be the "new Democrat" that he had promised, and promising a "Contract With America," the Republicans swept into political dominance as a result of the off-year elections in November. Several leading Democrats were defeated in their bid for re-election, notably including Speaker of the House Tom Foley of Washington State. Despite the anti-incumbent mood that was reflected in the opinion polls, not one single Republican incumbent running for re-election was defeated across the nation. The GOP (Grand Old Party, ie., Republicans) picked up a net gain of 11 governorships in state elections. And for the first time in 40 years, the Republicans took control of both the House of Representatives and the Senate.

More polarization in the political arena was expected because several moderate Democrats had been defeated and replaced with strong conservatives in Congress. In other words, as a result of the elections, stronger conservatives (among Republicans) and stronger liberals (among Democrats) were left to represent both major parties in Congress. Only time will really answer the question about how this will affect the ability of our national leaders to engage in the kind of compromise which is the engine of our political democracy.

Among the new congressional leaders, none rose to greater heights of prestige and power than the new Republican Speaker of the House, Congressman Newt Gingrich of Georgia. It was Gingrich who had supervised the writing of, and orchestrated his party's public campaign on behalf of, the Republican "Contract With America." In this contract, the Republican Party pledged at least a vote in Congress on each of its major goals. These goals included support for a balanced budget amendment to the Constitution, term limits for members of Congress, a stronger anti-crime bill, certain business incentives (such as a capital-gains tax cut), so-called "loser pays" laws and limits on punitive damages in civil suits, and major welfare reform.

The Trial of the Century

Among the tragic and memorable events of the 1990s, the murders of Nicole Brown Simpson and Ronald Goldman, and the subsequent trial of O.J. Simpson, will probably stand out for many years. On the night of June 12, 1994, Goldman had gone to Ms. Simpson's home in Brentwood, California to return her mother's pair of eyeglasses. During the very early hours of the next day, their bodies were discovered with multiple knife wounds outside the house; Ms. Simpson, O.J.'s white ex-wife, was nearly decapitated. It was revealed that O.J. Simpson, former professional football star turned sportscaster and actor, previously had a stormy relationship with his ex-wife. And when a bloody glove was allegedly discovered behind a guesthouse on his estate, this confirmed him as the number one suspect. He was soon arrested with the double murder.

The trial began in January 1995 with Judge Lance Ito allowing the proceedings to be televised. This reflected a growing trend to satisfy viewer demands to watch reality-based entertainment. Americans, and millions of others around the globe, became fascinated with what was quickly dubbed "the trial of the century." Simpson's wealth allowed him to hire some of the best criminal defense attorneys in the country. His team, including Robert Shapiro, Johnnie Cochran, Jr., F. Lee Bailey, and Barry Scheck, became known as the "Dream Team." Lawyers representing both sides often fought furiously in hearings held outside the presence of the jury to determine what evidence should be admissible in the case. Judge Ito was severely criticized by media commentators for a failure to control the lawyers and get the case completed in a timely fashion.

During the trial, the prosecution attempted to portray O.J. Simpson as a man obsessed with Nicole, who had murdered her in the ultimate escalation of his spousal abuse. Lead prosecution attorneys Marcia Clark and Christopher Darden spoke about "a mountain of evidence" against the defendant. The defense team, on the other hand, pointed to alleged police misconduct as sufficient reason to distrust the evidence against their client. The peak of the trial came when witnesses and excerpts from audiotapes proved that Detective Mark Fuhrman had lied about using racial epithets about and against African-Americans. Because Fuhrman had been the officer who allegedly found the bloody glove, the defense argued that he had actually planted it to frame Simpson. When the defense later recalled him to the stand in order to confront him with his statements, Fuhrman took the Fifth Amendment and refused to answer any questions.

After nearly nine months in sequestration, the jury of 9 African-Americans, 2 whites, and 1 Hispanic took less than three hours of deliberation to reach its verdicts of "not guilty" on both counts. According to public opinion polls, most white Americans believed that Simpson was guilty and had gotten away with murder. However, most African-Americans believed he was not guilty and were satisfied with the verdicts. There was talk of reforming the criminal justice system, including calls for verdicts in criminal cases to be decided by majority vote rather than a unanimous vote by the jury. Only time will tell how badly race relations were damaged by the trial; but the early signs were not encouraging. Perhaps the most positive legacy of the O.J. Simpson case will be the public awareness of spousal abuse and other domestic violence. Denise Brown, the sister of Nicole, has said that she will devote her life to this cause. Whatever the ultimate outcome for the nation, the riveting attention paid to the case surely warrants the label, "the trial of the century."

FOREIGN AFFAIRS UNDER CLINTON
FOREIGN POLICY IN AFRICA

Somalia

Somalia, an East African country located on the horn of that continent, was thrown into a famine in 1992 as the result of a long drought and a civil war. Global communications made possible by satellite and computer technologies had "shrunk" the world in a way that people all over the planet could know the awful details of the situation in Somalia. Television pictures especially brought the news of the disaster there and created great sympathy among Americans for the plight of the starving Africans. Many later concluded that perhaps television was the most important factor that led to world intervention. In any case, the Bush administration had sent 20,000 American troops, under UN auspices, to Somalia in December 1992 in order to assist in distributing food to the people. President-elect Bill Clinton voiced support for President Bush's actions and pledged cooperation with the United Nations under his presidency.

However, the matter was complicated by the fact that during the interval between Bush's intervention and Clinton's inauguration, the UN mission underwent a change. In addition to the continuation of humanitarian aid, the new policy also was to attempt to establish the necessary political stability that would result in a settlement of the civil war there. During the first year of the new Clinton adminstration, the situation in Somalia grew more complicated. Rival factions continued their warfare in areas not controlled by the United Nations, which represented a sizable portion of the country. President Clinton knew that the food distribution would not totally be successful (some of it was stolen from rival factions after it had been distributed), and that the famine itself would not end as long as the civil war continued.

But as the situation grew more tense, American soldiers found themselves in more frequent fire-fights with belligerent Somalians. In October 1993, 17 American troops were killed in fighting. This event caused Americans to fear that we might get bogged down in a protracted conflict similar to the Vietnam War, and leading Republicans and Democrats began calling for the United States to withdraw from Somalia. Clinton reluctantly agreed that there was no alternative, and American withdrawal was completed by April 1994.

South Africa

South African blacks officially had been segregated and discriminated against by the white South African government for decades in a system known as apartheid. The African National Congress (ANC), created in 1912, had become the chief protest group among the black majority by the 1960s, a time when the Kennedy administration had sought to encourage the growth of democracy on the African continent. The ANC leader, Nelson Mandella, was arrested and sentenced to life imprisonment in the early sixties for sabotage, but the movement did not die.

With support from the American civil rights movement, talk of using economic sanctions against the South African government surfaced in the 1980s. President Ronald Reagan's opposition to imposing sanctions prevented them from being passed by Congress until 1988. In that year, the government in South Africa used a great deal of brutality in putting down black demonstrations there. In reaction to that event, Congress passed a bill imposing certain economic sanctions against South Africa over Reagan's veto.

Unlike his predecessor, President Bush gave his support to the policy of sanctions. At the same time, Bush encouraged the new South African president, F.W. de Klerk, to negotiate an end to apartheid and open the elections process to all citizens of South Africa. Despite some fierce opposition from the right-wing, de Klerk released Nelson Mandella from jail in the early nineties. Mandella, who had been a symbol of oppression even in jail, became an instant hero and leader of most of the black majority in his country. Somewhat mellowed from his experience in jail, Mandella accepted the idea of negotiations, and he and de Klerk began a dialogue to end apartheid and allow for eventual majority rule. The two leaders eventually did reach such an agreement, for which they each received the Nobel Peace Prize in 1993. In April 1994, in South Africa's first free, multi-racial elections, Nelson Mandella was elected as the first black president of South Africa.

CONFLICTS IN BOSNIA AND HAITI CONTINUED

Bosnia

The problems in Bosnia-Herzogovina, begun during the Bush administration, continued, and by 1994, more than 100,000 people had died in the former Yugoslavia. (See "The Former Yugoslavia," earlier in this chapter, for background information.) President Clinton suggested that air strikes be used against the attacking Bosnian Serbs in order to force negotiations between the warring factions. But in the beginning, NATO allies were reluctant to become involved in any military capacity. However, by the spring of 1994, the fear that the conflict might spread beyond Bosnia-Herzogovina caused NATO countries to begin a limited and occasional use of air strikes.

Haiti

Since the overthrow of the popularly elected Aristide government in 1991, conditions in Haiti had grown steadily worse. (See "Haiti" under "Foreign Affairs Under Bush" earlier in this chapter for background information.) Although Clinton had criticized President Bush during the 1992 election campaign for refusing to allow Haitian boat people to enter the United States, President Clinton soon realized that he too faced the same dilemma, and after allowing Haitian refugees access, he later reversed himself and denied it. This action only produced cries of inconsistency from both Republicans and more liberal Democrats (especially members of the Black Caucus in Congress).

In 1994, Clinton believed the only way out for the United States was to restore Aristide to power, even if American troops had to use force to accomplish it. However, just before a Clinton-imposed deadline to invade Haiti, former President Jimmy Carter negotiated the resignation of the military rulers. Then in September, Clinton ordered American troops to Haiti as a police force to help assure the success of the electoral process. Although the use of American soldiers in Haiti was criticized by most Republican leaders, the mission seemed to be successful.

The various crises since the end of the Cold War illustrate that despite its end, the world remains a dangerous place. The United States will need an active and wise foreign policy and a watchful eye as it steers its course in the post-Cold War era. Many of the crisis situations introduced in this chapter have not been fully resolved, and only time will determine what the next chapter of the American journey will be.

ADDITIONAL READINGS

Donald Barlett and James B. Steele, *America: What Went Wrong* (1992). An expansion of the authors' series in the *Philadelphia Inquirer,* this book offers a mass of interesting data documenting the declining fortunes of the American middle class in the 1980s.

Larry Bluestone and Bennett Harrison, *The Deindustrialization of America* (1982). A path-breaking analysis showing how corporate strategy and government policy combined to weaken America's industrial base after the late 1960s.

Sidney Blumenthal and Thomas B. Edsall, eds., *The Reagan Legacy* (1988). A collection of critical essays assessing the impact of Reagan's presidency on American society and culture.

Barbara Ehrenreich, *Fear of Falling* (1989). A thoughtful and well-argued book that examines the cultural and economic insecurities of the American middle class in recent years.

Haynes Johnson, *Sleepingwalking through History* (1991). A readable, journalistic narrative of the Reagan presidency.

Michael T. Klare and Peter Kornbluh, eds., *Low Intensity Warfare* (1988). A valuable set of essays offering case studies of counterinsurgency and antiterrorist tactics during the 1980s.

Robert Lekachman, *Visions and Nightmares* (1987). An economist's view of Reagan's legacy, emphasizing the long-range impact of military spending, tax cuts, and the shrinking of social programs.

Michael Mandlebaum, *Reagan and Gorbachev* (1987). Solid overview of the two superpower leaders and what they accomplished in arms control.

Nicolaus Mills, *Culture in an Age of Money* (1990). An acerbic account of the impact of corporate power and big money on the cultural life of the nation during the 1980s.

Kevin Phillips, *The Politics of Rich and Poor* (1900). A fascinating, superbly documented, and often brilliant analysis of the growth in economic inequality that characterized the 1980s. Phillips, a prominent Republican strategist, makes historical comparisons with the 1920s and the late nineteenth century to bolster his argument.

Everett M. Rogers and Judith K. Larsen, *Silicon Valley Fever* (1984). Useful account of the rise of the computer industry in Silicon Valley with special emphasis on the development of Apple and Hewlett-Packard.

Randy Shilts, *And the Band Played On* (1986). The best history of the AIDS epidemic and the politics surrounding AIDS research and treatment.

William Serrin, *Homestead* (1991). A study of Homestead, Pennsylvania, and the decline of the American steel industry.

Micah L. Sifry and Christopher Cerf, eds., *The Gulf War Reader* (1991). An excellent collection of historical essays, government documents, and political addresses that provides a comprehensive overview of the Persian Gulf War.

James B. Stewart, *Den of Thieves* (1991). A well-documented inside look at the people and events at the center of Wall Street's insider trader scandal. Offers a detailed account of the shady financial practices of the 1980s.

Garry Wills, *Reagan's America* (1987). A thoughtful meditation that analyzes Reagan's popularity largely as a function of the nation's nostalgia for a more "innocent" time.

APPENDIX

THE DECLARATION OF INDEPENDENCE

When in the course of human events it becomes necessary for one people to dissolve the political bands which have connected them with another and to assume, among the powers of the earth, the separate and equal station to which the laws of nature and of nature's God entitle them, a decent respect to the opinions of mankind requires that they should declare the causes which impel them to the separation.

We hold these truths to be self-evident, that all men are created equal; that they are endowed by their Creator with certain unalienable rights; that among these are life, liberty, and the pursuit of happiness. That, to secure these rights, governments are instituted among men, deriving their just powers from the consent of the governed; that, whenever any form of government becomes destructive of these ends, it is the right of the people to alter or to abolish it, and to institute a new government, laying its foundation on such principles, and organizing its powers in such form, as to them shall seem most likely to effect their safety and happiness. Prudence, indeed, will dictate that governments long established should not be changed for light and transient causes; and accordingly, all experience hath shown that mankind are more disposed to suffer, while evils are sufferable, than to right themselves by abolishing the forms to which they are accustomed. But when a long train of abuses and usurpations, pursuing invariably the same object, evinces a design to reduce them under absolute despotism, it is their right, it is their duty, to throw off such government and to provide new guards for their future security. Such has been the patient sufferance of these colonies, and such is now the necessity which constrains them to alter their former systems of government. The history of the present King of Great Britain is a history of repeated injuries and usurpations, all having, in direct object, the establishment of an absolute tyranny over these States. To prove this, let facts be submitted to a candid world.

He has refused his assent to laws the most wholesome and necessary for the public good.

He has forbidden his governors to pass laws of immediate and pressing importance, unless suspended in their operation till his assent should be obtained; and, when so suspended, he has utterly neglected to attend to them.

He has refused to pass other laws for the accommodation of large districts of people, unless those people would relinquish the right of representation in the legislature; a right inestimable to them and formidable to tyrants only.

He has called together legislative bodies at places unusual, uncomfortable, and distant from the depository of their public records, for the sole purpose of fatiguing them into compliance with his measures.

He has dissolved representative houses, repeatedly for opposing, with manly firmness, his invasions on the rights of the people.

He has refused, for a long time after such dissolutions, to cause others to be elected; whereby the legislative powers, incapable of annihilation, have returned to the people at large for their exercise; the state remaining, in the meantime, exposed to all the danger of invasion from without and convulsions within.

He has endeavored to prevent the population of these States; for that purpose, obstructing the laws for naturalization of foreigners, refusing to pass others to encourage their migration hither, and raising the conditions of new appropriations of lands.

He has obstructed the administration of justice by refusing his assent to laws for establishing judiciary powers.

He has made judges dependent on his will alone for the tenure of their offices and the amount and payment of their salaries.

He has erected a multitude of new offices and sent hither swarms of officers to harass our people and eat out their substance.

He has kept among us, in time of peace, standing armies, without the consent of our legislatures.

He has affected to render the military independent of, and superior to, the civil power.

He has combined with others to subject us to a jurisdiction foreign to our Constitution and unacknowledged by our laws, giving his assent to their acts of pretended legislation—

For quartering large bodies of armed troops among us;

For protecting them by a mock trial from punishment for any murders which they should commit on the inhabitants of these States;

For cutting off our trade with all parts of the world;

For imposing taxes on us without our consent;

For depriving us, in many cases, of the benefit of trial by jury;

For transporting us beyond seas to be tried for pretended offenses;

For abolishing the free system of English laws in a neighboring province, establishing therein an arbitrary government, and enlarging its boundaries, so as to render it at once an example and fit instrument for introducing the same absolute rule into these colonies;

For taking away our charters, abolishing our most valuable laws, and altering, fundamentally, the powers of our governments;

For suspending our own legislatures and declaring themselves invested with power to legislate for us in all cases whatsoever.

He has abdicated government here by declaring us out of his protection and waging war against us.

He has plundered our seas, ravaged our coasts, burnt our towns, and destroyed the lives of our people.

He is, at this time, transporting large armies of foreign mercenaries to complete the works of death, desolation, and tyranny already begun with circumstances of cruelty and perfidy scarcely paralleled in the most barbarous ages, and totally unworthy the head of a civilized nation.

He has constrained our fellow citizens, taken captive on the high seas, to bear arms against their country, to become the executioners of their friends and brethren, or to fall themselves by their hands.

He has excited domestic insurrections amongst us and has endeavored to bring on the inhabitants of our frontiers, the merciless Indian savages, whose known rule of warfare is an undistinguished destruction of all ages, sexes, and conditions.

In every stage of these oppressions, we have petitioned for redress in the most humble terms; our repeated petitions have been answered only by repeated injury. A prince whose character is thus marked by every act which may define a tyrant is unfit to be the ruler of a free people.

Nor have we been wanting in attention to our British brethren. We have warned them, from time to time, of attempts made by their legislature to extend an unwarrantable jurisdiction over us. We have reminded them of the circumstances of our emigration and settlement here. We have appealed to their native justice and magnanimity, and we have conjured them, by the ties of our common kindred, to disavow these usurpations, which would inevitably interrupt our connections and correspondence. They, too, have been deaf to the voice of justice and consanguinity. We must, therefore, acquiesce in the necessity which denounces our separation, and hold them, as we hold the rest of mankind, enemies in war, in peace, friends.

We, therefore, the representatives of the United States of America, in general Congress assembled, appealing to the Supreme Judge of the world for the rectitude of our intentions, do, in the name and by the authority of the good people of these colonies, solemnly publish and declare, that these united colonies are, and of right out to be, free and independent states: that they are absolved from all allegiance to the British Crown, and that all political connection between them and the state of Great Britain is, and ought to be, totally dissolved; and that, as free and independent states, they have full power to levy war, conclude peace, contract alliances, establish commerce, and to do all other acts and things which independent states may of right do. And, for the support of this declaration, with a firm reliance on the protection of Divine Providence, we mutually pledge to each other our lives, our fortunes, and our sacred honor.

THE CONSTITUTION OF THE UNITED STATES OF AMERICA

We the people of the United States, in order to form a more perfect union, establish justice, insure domestic tranquillity, provide for the common defense, promote the general welfare, and secure the blessings of liberty to ourselves and our posterity, do ordain and establish this Constitution for the United States of America.

Article 1

SECTION 1.   All legislative powers herein granted shall be vested in a Congress of the United States, which shall consist of a Senate and House of Representatives.

SECTION 2.   1.   The House of Representatives shall be composed of members chosen every second year by the people of the several States, and the electors in each State shall have the qualifications requisite for electors of the most numerous branch of the State legislature.

2.   No person shall be a representative who shall not have attained to the age of twenty-five years, and been seven years a citizen of the United States, and who shall not, when elected, be an inhabitant of that State in which he shall be chosen.

3.   Representatives and direct taxes[1] shall be apportioned among the several States which may be included within this Union, according to their respective numbers, which shall be determined by adding to the whole number of free persons, including those bound to service for a term of years, and excluding Indians not taxed, three fifths of all other persons.[2] The actual enumeration shall be made within three years after the first meeting of the Congress of the United States, and within every subsequent term of ten years, in such manner as they shall by law direct. The number of representatives shall not exceed one for every thirty thousand, but each State shall have at least one representative; and until such enumeration shall be made, the State of New Hampshire shall be entitled to choose three, Massachusetts eight, Rhode Island and Providence Plantations one, Connecticut five, New York six, New Jersey four, Pennsylvania eight, Delaware one, Maryland six, Virginia ten, North Carolina five, South Carolina five, and Georgia three.

4.   When vacancies happen in the representation from any State, the executive authority thereof shall issue writs of election to fill such vacancies.

5.   The House of Representatives shall choose their speaker and other officers; and shall have the sole power of impeachment.

SECTION 3.   1.   The Senate of the United States shall be composed of two senators from each State, chosen by the legislature thereof,[3] for six years; and each senator shall have one vote.

2.   Immediately after they shall be assembled in consequence of the first election, they shall be divided as equally as may be into three classes. The seats of the senators of the first class shall be vacated at the expiration of the second year, of the second class at the expiration of the fourth year, and of the third class at the expiration of the sixth year, so that one third may be chosen every second year; and

[1]See the Sixteenth Amendment.
[2]See the Fourteenth Amendment.
[3]See the Seventeenth Amendment.

if vacancies happen by resignation, or otherwise, during the recess of the legislature of any State, the executive thereof may make temporary appointments until the next meeting of the legislature, which shall then fill such vacancies.[4]

3. No person shall be a senator who shall not have attained to the age of thirty years, and been nine years a citizen of the United States, and who shall not, when elected, be an inhabitant of that State for which he shall be chosen.

4. The Vice President of the United States shall be President of the Senate, but shall have no vote, unless they be equally divided.

5. The Senate shall choose their other officers, and also a president pro tempore, in the absence of the Vice President, or when he shall exercise the office of the President of the United States.

6. The Senate shall have the sole power to try all impeachments. When sitting for that purpose, they shall be on oath or affirmation. When the President of the United States is tried, the chief justice shall preside: and no person shall be convicted without the concurrence of two thirds of the members present.

7. Judgment in cases of impeachments shall not extend further than to removal from office, and disqualification to hold and enjoy any office of honor, trust or profit under the United States: but the party convicted shall nevertheless be liable and subject to indictment, trial, judgment and punishment, according to law.

SECTION 4. 1. The times, places, and manner of holding elections for senators and representatives, shall be prescribed in each State by the legislature thereof; but the Congress may at any time by law make or alter such regulations, except as to the places of choosing senators.

2. The Congress shall assemble at least once in every year, and such meeting shall be on the first Monday in December, unless they shall by law appoint a different day.

SECTION 5. 1. Each House shall be the judge of the elections, returns and qualifications of its own members, and a majority of each shall constitute a quorum to do business; but a smaller number may adjourn from day to day, and may be authorized to compel the attendance of absent members, in such manner, and under such penalties as each House may provide.

2. Each House may determine the rules of its proceedings, punish its members for disorderly behavior, and, with the concurrence of two thirds, expel a member.

3. Each House shall keep a journal of its proceedings, and from time to time publish the same, excepting such parts as may in their judgment require secrecy; and the yeas and nays of the members of either House on any question shall, at the desire of one fifth of those present, be entered on the journal.

4. Neither House, during the session of Congress, shall, without the consent of the other, adjourn for more than three days, nor to any other place than that in which the two Houses shall be sitting.

SECTION 6. 1. The senators and representatives shall receive a compensation for their services, to be ascertained by law, and paid out of the Treasury of the United States. They shall in all cases, except treason, felony, and breach of the peace, be privileged from arrest during their attendance at the session of their re-

[4]See the Seventeenth Amendment.

spective Houses, and in going to and returning from the same; and for any speech or debate in either House, they shall not be questioned in any other place.

2.   No senator or representative shall, during the time for which he was elected, be appointed to any civil office under the authority of the United States, which shall have been created, or the emoluments whereof shall have been increased, during such time; and no person holding any office under the United States shall be a member of either House during his continuance in office.

SECTION 7.   1.   All bills for raising revenue shall originate in the House of Representatives; but the Senate may propose or concur with amendments as on other bills.

2.   Every bill which shall have passed the House of Representatives and the Senate, shall, before it become a law, be presented to the President of the United States; If he approves he shall sign it, but if not he shall return it, with his objections, to that House in which it shall have originated, who shall enter the objections at large on their journal, and proceed to reconsider it. If after such reconsideration two thirds of that House shall agree to pass the bill, it shall be sent, together with the objections, to the other House, by which it shall likewise be reconsidered, and if approved by two thirds of that House, it shall become a law. But in all such cases the votes of both Houses shall be determined by yeas and nays, and the names of the persons voting for and against the bill shall be entered on the journal of each House respectively. If any bill shall not be returned by the President within ten days (Sundays excepted) after it shall have been presented to him, the same shall be a law, in like manner as if he had signed it, unless the Congress by their adjournment prevent its return, in which case it shall not be a law.

3.   Every order, resolution, or vote to which the concurrence of the Senate and the House of Representatives may be necessary (except on a question of adjournment) shall be presented to the President of the United States; and before the same shall take effect, shall be approved by him, or being disapproved by him, shall be repassed by two thirds of the Senate and House of Representatives, according to the rules and limitations prescribed in the case of a bill.

SECTION 8.   The Congress shall have the power

1.   To lay and collect taxes, duties, imposts, and excises, to pay the debts and provide for the common defense and general welfare of the United States; but all duties, imposts, and excises shall be uniform throughout the United States;

2.   To borrow money on the credit of the United States;

3.   To regulate commerce with foreign nations, and among the several States, and with the Indian tribes;

4.   To establish a uniform rule of naturalization, and uniform laws on the subject of bankruptcies throughout the United States;

5.   To coin money, regulate the value thereof, and of foreign coin, and fix the standard of weights and measures;

6.   To provide for the punishment of counterfeiting the securities and current coin of the United States;

7.   To establish post offices and post roads;

8. To promote the progress of science and useful arts, by securing for limited times to authors and inventors the exclusive right to their respective writings and discoveries;

9. To constitute tribunals inferior to the Supreme Court;

10. To define and punish piracies and felonies committed on the high seas, and offenses against the law of nations;

11. To declare war, grant letters of marque and reprisal, and make rules concerning captures on land and water;

12. To raise and support armies, but no appropriation of money to that use shall be for a longer term than two years;

13. To provide and maintain a navy;

14. To make rules for the government and regulation of the land and naval forces;

15. To provide for calling forth the militia to execute the laws of the Union, suppress insurrections and repel invasions;

16. To provide for organizing, arming, and disciplining the militia, and for governing such part of them as may be employed in the service of the United States, reserving to the States respectively, the appointment of the officers, and the authority of training the militia according to the discipline prescribed by Congress;

17. To exercise exclusive legislation in all cases whatsoever, over such district (not exceeding ten miles square) as may, by cession of particular States, and the acceptance of Congress, become the seat of the government of the United States, and to exercise like authority over all places purchased by the consent of the legislature of the State in which the same shall be, for the erection of forts, magazines, arsenals, dockyards, and other needful buildings; and

18. To make all laws which shall be necessary and proper for carrying into execution the foregoing powers, and all other powers vested by this Constitution in the government of the United States, or any department or officer thereof.

SECTION 9. 1. The migration or importation of such persons as any of the States now existing shall think proper to admit, shall not be prohibited by the Congress prior to the year one thousand eight hundred and eight, but a tax or duty may be imposed on such importation, not exceeding ten dollars for each person.

2. The privilege of the writ of habeas corpus shall not be suspended, unless when in cases of rebellion or invasion the public safety may require it.

3. No bill of attainder or ex post facto law shall be passed.

4. No capitation, or other direct, tax shall be laid, unless in proportion to the census or enumeration hereinbefore directed to be taken.[5]

5. No tax or duty shall be laid on articles exported from any State.

6. No preference shall be given by any regulation of commerce or revenue to the ports of one State over those of another: nor shall vessels bound to, or from, one State be obliged to enter, clear, or pay duties in another.

7. No money shall be drawn from the treasury, but in consequence of appropriations made by law; and a regular statement and account of the receipts and expenditures of all public money shall be published from time to time.

[5]See the Sixteenth Amendment.

8.   No title of nobility shall be granted by the United States: and no person holding any office of profit or trust under them, shall, without the consent of the Congress, accept of any present, emolument, office, or title, of any kind whatever, from any king, prince, or foreign State.

SECTION 10.   1.   No State shall enter into any treaty, alliance, or confederation; grant letters of marque and reprisal; coin money; emit bills of credit; make any thing but gold and silver coin a tender in payment of debts; pass any bill of attainder, ex post facto law, or law impairing the obligation of contracts, or grant any title of nobility.

2.   No State shall, without the consent of the Congress, lay any imposts or duties on imports or exports, except what may be absolutely necessary for executing its inspection laws: and the net produce of all duties and imposts laid by any State on imports or exports, shall be for the use of the treasury of the United States; and all such laws shall be subject to the revision and control of the Congress.

3.   No State shall, without the consent of the Congress, lay any duty of tonnage, keep troops, or ships of war in time of peace, enter into any agreement or compact with another State, or with a foreign power, or engage in war, unless actually invaded, or in such imminent danger as will not admit of delay.

Article II

SECTION 1.   1.   The executive power shall be vested in a President of the United States of America. He shall hold his office during the term of four years, and, together with the Vice President, chosen for the same term, be elected, as follows:

2.   Each State shall appoint, in such manner as the legislature thereof may direct, a number of electors, equal to the whole number of senators and representatives to which the State may be entitled in the Congress: but no senator or representative, or person holding any office of trust or profit under the United States, shall be appointed an elector.

The electors shall meet in their respective States, and vote by ballot for two persons, of whom one at least shall not be an inhabitant of the same State with themselves. And they shall make a list of all the persons voted for, and of the number of votes for each; which list they shall sign and certify, and transmit sealed to the seat of the government of the United States, directed to the president of the Senate. The president of the Senate shall, in the presence of the Senate and House of Representatives, open all the certificates, and the votes shall then be counted. The person having the greatest number of votes shall be the President, if such number be a majority of the whole number of electors appointed; and if there be more than one who have such majority, and have an equal number of votes, then the House of Representatives shall immediately choose by ballot one of them for President; and if no person have a majority, then from the five highest on the list the said House shall in like manner choose the President. But in choosing the President, the votes shall be taken by States, the representation from each State having one vote; a quorum for this purpose shall consist of a member or members from two thirds of the States, and a majority of all the States shall be necessary to a choice. In every case after the choice of the President, the person having the greatest number of votes of the electors shall be the Vice President. But if there should remain two or more who have equal votes, the Senate shall chose from them by ballot the Vice President.[6]

3.   The Congress may determine the time of choosing the electors, and the day on which they shall give their votes; which day shall be the same throughout the United States.

4.   No person except a natural born citizen, or a citizen of the United States, at the time of the adoption of this Constitution, shall be eligible to the office of President; neither shall any person be eligible to the office who shall not have attained to the age of thirty-five years, and been fourteen years a resident within the United States.

5.   In case of the removal of the President from office, or of his death, resignation, or inability to discharge the powers and duties of the said office, the same shall devolve on the Vice President, and the Congress may by law provide for the case of removal, death, resignation or inability, both of the President and Vice President, declaring what officer shall then act as President, and such officer shall act accordingly until the disability be removed, or a President shall be elected.

6.   The President shall, at stated times, receive for his services a compensation which shall neither be increased nor diminished during the period for which he shall have been elected, and he shall not receive within that period any other emolument from the United States, or any of them.

7.   Before he enter on the execution of his office, he shall take the following oath or affirmation:—"I do solemnly swear (or affirm) that I will faithfully execute the office of President of the United States, and will to the best of my ability, preserve, protect and defend the Constitution of the United States."

SECTION 2.   1.   The President shall be commander in chief of the army and navy of the United States, and of the militia of the several States, when called into the actual service of the United States; he may require the opinion in writing, of the principal officer in each of the executive departments, upon any subject relating to the duties of their respective offices, and he shall have power to grant reprieves and pardons for offenses against the United States, except in cases of impeachment.

2.   He shall have power, by and with the advice and consent of the Senate, to make treaties, provided two thirds of the senators present concur; and he shall nominate, and by and with the advice and consent of the Senate, shall appoint ambassadors, other public ministers and consuls, judges of the Supreme Court, and all other officers of the United States, whose appointments are not herein otherwise provided for, and which shall be established by law; but the Congress may by law vest the appointment of such inferior officers, as they think proper, in the President alone, in the courts of laws, or in the heads of departments.

3.   The President shall have power to fill up all vacancies that may happen during the recess of the Senate, by granting commissions which shall expire at the end of their next session.

[6]Superseded by the Twelfth Amendment.

SECTION 3. He shall from time to time give to the Congress information of the state of the Union, and recommend to their consideration such measures as he shall judge necessary and expedient; he may, on extraordinary occasions, convene both Houses, or either of them, and in case of disagreement between them with respect to the time of adjournment, he may adjourn them to such time as he shall think proper; he shall receive ambassadors and other public ministers; he shall take care that the laws be faithfully executed, and shall commission all the officers of the United States.

SECTION 4. The President, Vice President, and all civil officers of the United States, shall be removed from office on impeachment for, and conviction of, treason, bribery, or other high crimes and misdemeanors.

Article III

SECTION 1. The judicial power of the United States shall be vested in one Supreme Court, and in such inferior courts as the Congress may from time to time ordain and establish. The judges, both of the Supreme and inferior courts, shall hold their offices during good behavior, and shall, at stated times, receive for their services, a compensation, which shall not be diminished during their continuance in office.

SECTION 2. 1. The judicial power shall extend to all cases, in law and equity, arising under the Constitution, the laws of the United States, and treaties made, or which shall be made, under their authority;—to all cases affecting ambassadors, other public ministers and consuls;—to all cases of admiralty and maritime jurisdiction;—to controversies to which the United States shall be a party;[7]—to controversies between two or more States;—between a State and citizens of another State;—between citizens of different States;—between citizens of the same State claiming lands under grants of different States, and between a State, or the citizens thereof, and foreign States, citizens or subjects.

2. In all cases affecting ambassadors, other public ministers and consuls, and those in which a State shall be party, the Supreme Court shall have original jurisdiction. In all the other cases before mentioned, the Supreme Court shall have appellate jurisdiction, both as to law and fact, with such exceptions, and under such regulations as the Congress shall make.

3. The trial of all crimes, except in cases of impeachment, shall be by jury; and such trial shall be held in the State where the said crimes shall have been committed; but when not committed within any State, the trial shall be at such place or places as the Congress may by law have directed.

SECTION 3. 1. Treason against the United States shall consist only in levying war against them, or in adhering to their enemies, giving them aid and comfort. No person shall be convicted of treason unless on the testimony of two witnesses to the same overt act, or on confession in open court.

[7]See the Eleventh Amendment.

2.   The Congress shall have power to declare the punishment of treason, but no attainder of treason shall work corruption of blood, or forfeiture except during the life of the person attainted.

Article IV

SECTION 1.   Full faith and credit shall be given in each State to the public acts, records, and judicial proceedings of every other State. And the Congress may by general laws prescribe the manner in which such acts, records and proceedings shall be proved, and the effect thereof.

SECTION 2.   1.   The citizens of each State shall be entitled to all privileges and immunities of citizens in the several States.[8]

2.   A person charged in any State with treason, felony, or other crime, who shall flee from justice, and be found in another State, shall on demand of the executive authority of the State from which he fled, be delivered up to be removed to the State having jurisdiction of the crime.

3.   No person held to service or labor in one State under the laws thereof, escaping into another, shall, in consequence of any law or regulation therein, be discharged from such service or labor, but shall be delivered up on claim of the party to whom such service or labor may be due.[9]

SECTION 3.   1.   New States may be admitted by the Congress into this Union; but no new State shall be formed or erected within the jurisdiction of any other State; nor any State be formed by the junction of two or more States, or parts of States, without the consent of the legislatures of the States concerned as well as of the Congress.

2.   The Congress shall have power to dispose of and make all needful rules and regulations respecting the territory of other property belonging to the United States; and nothing in this Constitution shall be so construed as to prejudice any claims of the United States, or of any particular State.

SECTION 4.   The United States shall guarantee to every State in this Union a republican form of government, and shall protect each of them against invasion; and on application of the legislature, or of the executive (when the legislature cannot be convened) against domestic violence.

Article V

The Congress, whenever two thirds of both Houses shall deem it necessary, shall propose amendments to this Constitution, or, on the application of the legislatures of two thirds of the several States, shall call a convention for proposing amendments, which in either case, shall be valid to all intents and purposes, as part of this Constitution, when ratified by the legislatures of three fourths of the several States, or by conventions in three fourths thereof, as the one or the other mode of ratification may be proposed by the Congress; Provided that no amendment which may be made prior to the year one thousand eight hundred and eight

[8]See the Fourteenth Amendment, Sec. 1.
[9]See the Thirteenth Amendment.

shall in any manner affect the first and fourth clauses in the ninth section of the first articled; and that no State, without its consent, shall be deprived of its equal suffrage in the Senate.

Article VI

1.   All debts contracted and engagements entered into, before the adoption of this Constitution, shall be as valid against the United States under this Constitution, as under the Confederation.[10]

2.   This Constitution, and the laws of the United States which shall be made in pursuance thereof; and all treaties made, or which shall be made, under the authority of the United States, shall be the supreme law of the land; and the judges in every State shall be bound thereby, any thing in the Constitution or laws of any State to the contrary notwithstanding.

3.   The senators and representatives before mentioned, and the members of the several State legislatures, and all executive and judicial officers, both of the United States and of the several States, shall be bound by oath or affirmation to support this Constitution; but no religious test shall ever be required as a qualification to any office or public trust under the United States.

Article VII

The ratification of the conventions of nine States shall be sufficient for the establishment of this Constitution between the States so ratifying the same.

Done in Convention by the unanimous consent of the States present the seventeenth day of September in the year of our Lord one thousand seven hundred and eighty-seven, and of the independence of the United States of America the twelfth. In witness whereof we have hereunto subscribed our names.

[Names omitted]

* * *

Articles in addition to, and amendment of, the Constitution of the United States of America, proposed by Congress, and ratified by the legislatures of the several States, pursuant to the fifth article of the original Constitution.

Amendment I [First ten amendments ratified December 15, 1791]

Congress shall make no law respecting an establishment of religion, or prohibiting the free exercise thereof; or abridging the freedom of speech, or of the press; or the right of the people peaceably to assemble, and to petition the government for a redress of grievances.

Amendment II

A well regulated militia, being necessary to the security of a free State, the right of the people to keep and bear arms, shall not be infringed.

[10]See the Fourteenth Amendment, Sec. 4.

Amendment III

No soldier shall, in time of peace be quartered in any house, without the consent of the owner, nor in time of war, but in a manner to be prescribed by law.

Amendment IV

The right of the people to be secure in their persons, houses, papers, and effects, against unreasonable searches and seizures, shall not be violated, and no warrants shall issue, but upon probable cause, supported by oath or affirmation, and particularly describing the place to be searched, and the persons or things to be seized.

Amendment V

No person shall be held to answer for a capital or otherwise infamous crime, unless on a presentment or indictment of a grand jury, except in cases arising in the land or naval forces, or in the militia, when in actual service in time of war or public danger; nor shall any person be subject for the same offense to be twice put in jeopardy of life or limb; nor shall be compelled in any criminal case to be a witness against himself, nor be deprived of life, liberty, or property, without due process of law; nor shall private property be taken for public use, without just compensation.

Amendment VI

In all criminal prosecutions, the accused shall enjoy the right to a speedy and public trial, by an impartial jury of the State and districts wherein the crime shall have been committed, which district shall have been previously ascertained by law, and to be informed of the nature and cause of the accusation; to be confronted with the witnesses against him; to have compulsory process for obtaining witnesses in his favor, and to have the assistance of counsel for his defense.

Amendment VII

In suits at common law, where the value in controversy shall exceed twenty dollars, the right of trial by jury shall be preserved, and no fact tried by a jury shall be otherwise reexamined in any court of the United States, than according to the rules of the common law.

Amendment VIII

Excessive bail shall not be required, nor excessive fines imposed, nor cruel and unusual punishments inflicted.

Amendment IX

The enumeration in the Constitution of certain rights shall not be construed to deny or disparage others retained by the people.

Amendment X

The powers not delegated to the United States by the Constitution, nor prohibited by it to the States, are reserved to the States respectively, or to the people.

Amendment XI [January 8, 1798]

The judicial power of the United States shall not be construed to extend to any suit in law or equity, commenced or prosecuted against one of the United States by citizens of another State, or by citizens or subjects of any foreign State.

Amendment XII [September 25, 1804]

The electors shall meet in their respective States, and vote by ballot for President and Vice President, one of whom, at least, shall not be an inhabitant of the same State with themselves; they shall name in their ballots the person voted for as President, and in distinct ballots, the person voted for as Vice President, and they shall make distinct lists of all persons voted for as President and of all persons voted for as Vice President, and of the number of votes for each, which lists they shall sign and certify, and transmit sealed to the seat of the government of the United States, directed to the President of the Senate;—The President of the Senate shall, in the presence of the Senate and House of Representatives, open all the certificates and the votes shall then be counted;—The person having the greatest number of votes for President, shall be the President, if such a number be a majority of the whole number of electors appointed; and if no person have such majority, then from the persons having the highest numbers not exceeding three on the list of those voted for as President, the House of Representatives shall choose immediately, by ballot, the President. But in choosing the President, the votes shall be taken by States, the representation from each State having one vote; a quorum for this purpose shall consist of a member or members from two thirds of the States, and a majority of all the States shall be necessary to a choice. And if the House of Representatives shall not choose a President whenever the right of choice shall devolve upon them, before the fourth day of March next following, then the Vice President shall act as President, as in the case of the death or other constitutional disability of the President. The person having the greatest number of votes as Vice President shall be the Vice President, if such number be a majority of the whole number of electors appointed, and if no person have a majority, then from the two highest numbers on the list, the Senate shall choose the Vice President; a quorum for the purpose shall consist of two thirds of the whole number of Senators, and a majority of the whole number shall be necessary to a choice. But no person constitutionally ineligible to the office of President shall be eligible to that of Vice President of the United States.

Amendment XIII [December 18, 1865]

SECTION 1.   Neither slavery nor involuntary servitude, except as a punishment for crime whereof the party shall have been duly convicted, shall exist within the United States, or any place subject to their jurisdiction.

SECTION 2.   Congress shall have power to enforce this article by appropriate legislation.

Amendment XIV [July 28, 1868]

SECTION 1.   All persons born or naturalized in the United States, and subject to the jurisdiction thereof, are citizens of the United States and of the State wherein they reside. No State shall make or enforce any law which shall abridge the privileges or immunities of citizens of the United States; nor shall any State deprive any person of life, liberty, or property, without due process of law; nor deny to any person within its jurisdiction the equal protection of the laws.

SECTION 2.   Representatives shall be apportioned among the several States according to their respective numbers, counting the whole number of persons in each State, excluding Indians not taxed. But when the right to vote at any election for the choice of electors for President and Vice President of the United States, representatives in Congress, the executive and judicial officers of a State, or the members of the legislature thereof, is denied to any of the male inhabitants of such State, being twenty-one years of age, and citizens of the United States, or in any way abridged, except for participating in rebellion, or other crime, the basis of representation therein shall be reduced in the proportion which the number of such male citizens shall bear to the whole number of male citizens twenty-one years of age in such State.

SECTION 3.   No person shall be a senator or representative in Congress, or elector of President and Vice President, or hold any office, civil or military, under the United States, or under any State, who having previously taken an oath, as a member of Congress, or of any State legislature, or as an executive or judicial officer of any State, to support the Constitution of the United States, shall have engaged in insurrection or rebellion against the same, or given aid or comfort to the enemies thereof. But Congress may by a vote of two thirds of each House, remove such disability.

SECTION 4.   The validity of the public debt of the United States, authorized by law, including debts incurred for payment of pensions and bounties for services in suppressing insurrection or rebellion; shall not be questioned. But neither the United States nor any State shall assume or pay any debt or obligation incurred in aid of insurrection or rebellion against the United States, or any claim for the loss or emancipation of any slave; but all such debts, obligations, and claims shall be held illegal and void.

SECTION 5.   The Congress shall have the power to enforce, by appropriate legislation, the provisions of this article.

Amendment XV [March 30, 1870]

SECTION 1.   The right of citizens of the United States to vote shall not be denied or abridged by the United States or by any State on account of race, color, or previous condition of servitude.

SECTION 2.   The Congress shall have power to enforce this article by appropriate legislation.

Amendment XVI [February 25, 1913]

The Congress shall have power to lay and collect taxes on incomes, from whatever source derived, without apportionment among the several States, and without regard to any census or enumeration.

Amendment XVII [May 31, 1913]

The Senate of the United States shall be composed of two senators from each State, elected by the people thereof, for six years; and each senator shall have one vote. The electors in each State shall have the qualifications requisite for electors of the most numerous branch of the State legislature.

When vacancies happen in the representation of any State in the Senate, the executive authority of such State shall issue writs of election to fill such vacancies: *Provided*, That the legislature of any State may empower the executive thereof to make temporary appointments until the people fill the vacancies by election as the legislature may direct.

This amendment shall not be so construed as to affect the election or term of any senator chosen before it becomes valid as part of the Constitution.

Amendment XVIII[11] [January 29, 1919]

After one year from the ratification of this article, the manufacture, sale, or transportation of intoxicating liquors within, the importation thereof into, or the exportation thereof from the United States and all territory subject to the jurisdiction thereof for beverage purposes is thereby prohibited.

The Congress and the several States shall have concurrent power to enforce this article by appropriate legislation.

This article shall be inoperative unless it shall have been ratified as an amendment to the Constitution by the legislatures of the several States, as provided in the Constitution, within seven years from the date of the submission hereof to the States by Congress.

Amendment XIX [August 26, 1920]

The right of citizens of the United States to vote shall not be denied or abridged by the United States or by any State on account of sex.

Congress shall have the power to enforce this article by appropriate legislation.

Amendment XX [January 23, 1933]

SECTION 1.   The terms of the President and Vice President shall end at noon on the 20th day of January and the terms of Senators and Representatives at noon on the 3d day of January, of the years in which such terms would have ended if this article had not been ratified; and the terms of their successors shall then begin.

---

[11]Repealed by the Twenty-first Amendment.

SECTION 2.   The Congress shall assemble at least once in every year, and such meeting shall begin at noon on the 3d day of January, unless they shall by law appoint a different day.

SECTION 3.   If, at the time fixed for the beginning of the term of President, the President-elect shall have died, the Vice President-elect shall become President. If a President shall not have been chosen before the time fixed for the beginning of his term, or if the President-elect shall have failed to qualify, then the Vice President-elect shall act as President until a President shall have qualified; and the Congress may by law provide for the case wherein neither a President-elect nor a Vice President-elect shall have qualified, declaring who shall then act as President, or the manner in which one who is to act shall be selected, and such person shall act accordingly until a President or Vice President shall have qualified.

SECTION 4.   The Congress may by law provide for the case of the death of any of the persons from whom the House of Representatives may choose a President whenever the right of choice shall have devolved upon them, and for the case of the death of any of the persons from whom the Senate may choose a Vice President whenever the right of choice shall have devolved upon them.

SECTION 5.   Sections 1 and 2 shall take effect on the 15th day of October following the ratification of this article.

SECTION 6.   This article shall be inoperative unless it shall have been ratified as an amendment to the Constitution by the legislatures of three-fourths of the several States within seven years from the date of its submission.

Amendment XXI [December 5, 1933]

SECTION 1.   The Eighteenth Article of amendment to the Constitution of the United States is hereby repealed.

SECTION 2.   The transportation or importation into any State, Territory, or possession of the United States for delivery or use therein of intoxicating liquors in violation of the laws thereof, is hereby prohibited.

SECTION 3.   This article shall be inoperative unless it shall have been ratified as an amendment to the Constitution by conventions in the several States, as provided in the Constitution, within seven years from the date of the submission thereof to the States by the Congress.

Amendment XXII [March 1, 1951]

No person shall be elected to the office of the President more than twice, and no person who has held the office of President, or acted as President, for more than two years of a term to which some other person was elected President shall be elected to the office of the President more than once.

But this article shall not apply to any person holding the office of President when this article was proposed by the Congress, and shall not prevent any person who may be holding the office of President, or acting as President, during the term within which this article becomes operative from holding the office of President or acting as president during the remainder of such term.

This article shall be inoperative unless it shall have been ratified as an amendment to the Constitution by the legislatures of three-fourths of the several States within seven years from the date of its submission to the States by the Congress.

Amendment XXIII [March 29, 1961]

SECTION 1.   The District constituting the seat of Government of the United States shall appoint in such manner as the Congress may direct.

A number of electors of President and Vice President equal to the whole number of Senators and Representatives in Congress to which the District would be entitled if it were a State, but in no event more than the least populous State; they shall be in addition to those appointed by the States, but they shall be considered, for the purposes of the election of President and Vice President, to be electors appointed by a State; and they shall meet in the District and perform such duties as provided by the twelfth article of amendment.

SECTION 2.   The Congress shall have power to enforce this article by appropriate legislation.

Amendment XXIV [January 23, 1964]

SECTION 1.   The right of citizens of the United States to vote in any primary or other election for President or Vice President, for electors for President or Vice President, or for Senator or Representative in Congress, shall not be denied or abridged by the United States or any State by reason of failure to pay any poll tax or other tax.

SECTION 2.   The Congress shall have power to enforce this article by appropriate legislation.

Amendment XXV [February 10, 1967]

SECTION 1.   In case of the removal of the President from office or of his death or resignation, the Vice President shall become President.

SECTION 2.   Whenever there is a vacancy in the office of the Vice President, the President shall nominate a Vice President who shall take office upon confirmation by a majority of both Houses of Congress.

SECTION 3.   Whenever the President transmits to the President pro tempore of the Senate and the Speaker of the House of Representatives his written declaration that he is unable to discharge the powers and duties of his office, and until he transmits to them a written declaration to the contrary, such powers and duties shall be discharged by the Vice President as Acting President.

SECTION 4.   Whenever the Vice President and a majority of either the principal officers of the executive departments or of such other body as Congress may by law provide, transmit to the President pro tempore of the Senate and the Speaker of the House of Representatives their written declaration that the President is unable to discharge the powers and duties of his office, the Vice President shall immediately assume the powers and duties of the office as Acting President.

Thereafter, when the President transmits to the President pro tempore of the Senate and the Speaker of the House of Representatives his written declaration that no inability exists, he shall resume the powers and duties of his office unless the Vice President and a majority of either the principal officers of the executive departments or of such other body as Congress may by law provide, transmit within four days to the President pro tempore of the Senate and the Speaker of the House of Representatives their written declaration that the President is unable to discharge the powers and duties of his office. Thereupon Congress shall decide the issue, assembling within forty-eight hours for that purpose if not in session. If the Congress, within twenty-one days after receipt of the latter written declaration, or, if Congress is not in session, within twenty-one days after Congress is required to assemble, determines by two-thirds vote of both Houses that the President is unable to discharge the powers and duties of his office, the Vice President shall continue to discharge the same as Acting President; otherwise, the President shall resume the powers and duties of his office.

Amendment XXVI [June 30, 1971]

SECTION 1. The right of citizens of the United States who are eighteen years of age or older to vote shall not be denied or abridged by the United States or by any State on account of age.

SECTION 2. The Congress shall have power to enforce this article by appropriate legislation.

Amendment XXVII* [Adopted 1992]

No law, varying the compensation for services of the Senators and Representativees, shall take effect, until an election of Representatives shall have intervened.

PRESIDENTS, VICE PRESIDENTS, AND CABINET MEMBERS

PRESIDENT AND VICE PRESIDENT	SECRETARY OF STATE	SECRETARY OF TREASURY	SECRETARY OF WAR	SECRETARY OF NAVY	POSTMASTER GENERAL	ATTORNEY GENERAL	SECRETARY OF INTERIOR
1. George Washington (1789) John Adams (1789)	Thomas Jefferson (1789) Edmund Randolph (1794) Timothy Pickering (1795)	Alexander Hamilton (1789) Oliver Wolcott (1795)	Henry Knox (1789) Timothy Pickering (1795) James McHenry (1796)		Samuel Osgood (1789) Timothy Pickering (1791) Joseph Habersham (1795)	Edmund Randolph (1789) William Bradford (1794) Charles Lee (1795)	
2. John Adams (1797) Thomas Jefferson (1797)	Timothy Pickering (1797) John Marshall (1800)	Oliver Wolcott (1797) Samuel Dexter (1801)	James McHenry (1797) John Marshall (1800) Samuel Dexter (1800) Roger Griswold (1801)	Benjamin Stoddert (1798)	Joseph Habersham (1797)	Charles Lee (1797) Theophilus Parsons (1801)	
3. Thomas Jefferson (1801) Aaron Burr (1801) George Clinton (1805)	James Madison (1801)	Samuel Dexter (1801) Albert Gallatin (1801)	Henry Dearborn (1801)	Benjamin Stoddert (1801) Robert Smith (1801) J. Crowninshield (1805)	Joseph Habersham (1801) Gideon Granger (1801)	Levi Lincoln (1801) Robert Smith (1805) John Breckinridge (1805) Caesar Rodney (1807)	
4. James Madison (1809) George Clinton (1809) Elbridge Gerry (1813)	Robert Smith (1809) James Monroe (1811)	Albert Gallatin (1809) George Campbell (1814) Alexander Dallas (1814) William Crawford (1816)	William Eustis (1809) John Armstrong (1813) James Monroe (1814) William Crawford (1815)	Paul Hamilton (1809) William Jones (1813) Benjamin Crowninshield (1814)	Gideon Granger (1809) Return Meigs (1814)	Caesar Rodney (1809) William Pinckney (1811) Richard Rush (1814)	
5. James Monroe (1817) Daniel D. Tompkins (1817)	John Quincy Adams (1817)	William Crawford (1817)	Isaac Shelby (1817) George Graham (1817) John C. Calhoun (1817)	Benjamin Crowninshield (1817) Smith Thompson (1818) Samuel Southard (1823)	Return Meigs (1817) John McLean (1823)	Richard Rush (1817) William Wirt (1817)	
6. John Quincy Adams (1825) John C. Calhoun (1825)	Henry Clay (1825)	Richard Rush (1825)	James Barbour (1825) Peter B. Porter (1828)	Samuel Southard (1825)	John McLean (1825)	William Wirt (1825)	

Courtesy: U.S. Immigration and Naturalization Service

PRESIDENT AND VICE PRESIDENT	SECRETARY OF STATE	SECRETARY OF TREASURY	SECRETARY OF WAR	SECRETARY OF NAVY	POSTMASTER GENERAL	ATTORNEY GENERAL	SECRETARY OF INTERIOR
7. Andrew Jackson (1829) John C. Calhoun (1829) Martin Van Buren (1833)	Martin Van Buren (1829) Edward Livingston (1831) Louis McLane (1833) John Forsyth (1834)	Samuel Ingham (1829) Louis McLane (1831) William Duane (1833) Roger B. Taney (1833) Levi Woodbury (1834)	John H. Eaton (1829) Lewis Cass (1831) Benjamin Butler (1837)	John Branch (1829) Levi Woodbury (1831) Mahlon Dickerson (1834)	William Barry (1829) Amos Kendall (1835)	John M. Berrien (1829) Roger B. Taney (1831) Benjamin Butler (1833)	
8. Martin Van Buren (1837) Richard M. Johnson (1837)	John Forsyth (1837)	Levi Woodbury (1837)	Joel R. Poinsett (1837)	Mahlon Dickerson (1837) James K. Paulding (1838)	Amos Kendall (1837) John M. Niles (1840)	Benjamin Butler (1837) Felix Grundy (1838) Henry D. Gilpin (1840)	
9. William H. Harrison (1841) John Tyler (1841)	Daniel Webster (1841)	Thomas Ewing (1841)	John Bell (1841)	George E. Badger (1841)	Francis Granger (1841)	John J. Crittenden (1841)	
10. John Tyler (1841)	Daniel Webster (1841) Hugh S. Legaré (1843) Abel P. Upshur (1843) John C. Calhoun (1844)	Thomas Ewing (1841) Walter Forward (1841) John C. Spencer (1843) George M. Bibb (1844)	John Bell (1841) John McLean (1841) John C. Spencer (1841) James M. Porter (1843) William Wilkins (1844)	George E. Badger (1841) Abel P. Upshur (1841) David Henshaw (1843) Thomas Gilmer (1844) John Y. Mason (1844)	Francis Granger (1841) Charles A. Wickliffe (1841)	John J. Crittenden (1841) Hugh S. Legaré (1841) John Nelson (1843)	
11. James K. Polk (1845) George M. Dallas (1845)	James Buchanan (1845)	Robert J. Walker (1845)	William L. Marcy (1845)	George Bancroft (1845) John Y. Mason (1846)	Cave Johnson (1845)	John Y. Mason (1845) Nathan Clifford (1846) Isaac Toucey (1848)	
12. Zachary Taylor (1849) Millard Fillmore (1849)	John M. Clayton (1849)	William M. Meredith (1849)	George W. Crawford (1849)	William B. Preston (1849)	Jacob Collamer (1849)	Reverdy Johnson (1849)	Thomas Ewing (1849)
13. Millard Fillmore (1850)	Daniel Webster (1850) Edward Everett (1852)	Thomas Corwin (1850)	Charles M. Conrad (1850)	William A. Graham (1850) John P. Kennedy (1852)	Nathan K. Hall (1850) Sam D. Hubbard (1852)	John J. Crittenden (1850)	Thomas McKennan (1850) A. H. H. Stuart (1850)
14. Franklin Pierce (1853) William R. King (1853)	William L. Marcy (1853)	James Guthrie (1853)	Jefferson Davis (1853)	James C. Dobbin (1853)	James Campbell (1853)	Caleb Cushing (1853)	Robert McClelland (1853)

PRESIDENT AND VICE PRESIDENT	SECRETARY OF STATE	SECRETARY OF TREASURY	SECRETARY OF WAR	SECRETARY OF NAVY	POSTMASTER GENERAL	ATTORNEY GENERAL	SECRETARY OF INTERIOR
15. James Buchanan (1857) John C. Breckinridge (1857)	Lewis Cass (1857) Jeremiah S. Black (1860)	Howell Cobb (1857) Philip F. Thomas (1860) John A. Dix (1861)	John B. Floyd (1857) Joseph Holt (1861)	Isaac Toucey (1857)	Aaron V. Brown (1857) Joseph Holt (1859)	Jeremiah S. Black (1857) Edwin M. Stanton (1860)	Jacob Thompson (1857)
16. Abraham Lincoln (1861) Hannibal Hamlin (1861) Andrew Johnson (1865)	William H. Seward (1861)	Salmon P. Chase (1861) William P. Fessenden (1864) Hugh McCulloch (1865)	Simon Cameron (1861) Edwin M. Stanton (1862)	Gideon Welles (1861)	Horatio King (1861) Montgomery Blair (1861) William Dennison (1864)	Edward Bates (1861) Titian J. Coffey (1863) James Speed (1864)	Caleb B. Smith (1861) John P. Usher (1863)
17. Andrew Johnson (1865)	William H. Seward (1865)	Hugh McCulloch (1865)	Edwin M. Stanton (1865) Ulysses S. Grant (1867) Lorenzo Thomas (1868) John M. Schofield (1868)	Gideon Welles (1865)	William Dennison (1865) Alexander Randall (1866)	James Speed (1865) Henry Stanbery (1866) William M. Evarts (1868)	John P. Usher (1865) James Harlan (1865) O. H. Browning (1866)
18. Ulysses S. Grant (1869) Schuyler Colfax (1869) Henry Wilson (1873)	Elihu B. Washburne (1869) Hamilton Fish (1869)	George S. Boutwell (1869) William A. Richardson (1873) Benjamin H. Bristow (1874) Lot M. Morrill (1876)	John A. Rawlins (1869) William T. Sherman (1869) William W. Belknap (1869) Alphonso Taft (1876) James Cameron (1876)	Adolph E. Borie (1869) George M. Robeson (1869)	John A. J. Creswell (1869) James W. Marshall (1874) Marshall Jewell (1874) James N. Tyner (1876)	Ebenezer R. Hoar (1869) Amos T. Akerman (1870) G. H. Williams (1871) Edwards Pierrepont (1875) Alphonso Taft (1876)	Jacob D. Cox (1869) Columbus Delano (1870) Zachariah Chandler (1875)
19. Rutherford B. Hayes (1877) William A. Wheeler (1877)	William M. Evarts (1877)	John Sherman (1877)	George W. McCrary (1877) Alexander Ramsey (1879)	R. W. Thompson (1877) Nathan Golf, Jr. (1881)	David M. Key (1877) Horace Maynard (1880)	Charles Devens (1877)	Carl Schurz (1877)
20. James A. Garfield (1881) Chester A. Arthur (1881)	James G. Blaine (1881)	William Windom (1881)	Robert T. Lincoln (1881)	William H. Hunt (1881)	Thomas I. James (1881)	Wayne MacVeagh (1881)	S. I. Kirkwood (1881)
21. Chester A. Arthur (1881)	F. T. Frelinghuysen (1881)	Charles J. Folger (1881) Walter Q. Gresham (1884) Hugh McCulloch (1884)	Robert T. Lincoln (1881)	William E. Chandler (1881)	Timothy O. Howe (1881) Walter Q. Gresham (1883) Frank Hatton (1884)	B. H. Brewster (1881)	Henry M. Teller (1881)
22. Grover Cleveland (1885) T. A. Hendricks (1885)	Thomas F. Bayard (1885)	Daniel Manning (1885) Charles S. Fairchild (1887)	William C. Endicott (1885)	William C. Whitney (1885)	William F. Vilas (1885) Don M. Dickinson (1888)	A. H. Garland (1885)	L. Q. C. Lamar (1885) William F. Vilas (1888)

PRESIDENT AND VICE PRESIDENT	SECRETARY OF STATE	SECRETARY OF TREASURY	SECRETARY OF WAR	SECRETARY OF NAVY	POSTMASTER GENERAL	ATTORNEY GENERAL	SECRETARY OF INTERIOR
23. Benjamin Harrison (1889) Levi P. Morgan (1889)	James G. Blaine (1889) John W. Foster (1892)	William Windom (1889) Charles Foster (1891)	Redfield Procter (1889) Stephen B. Elkins (1891)	Benjamin F. Tracy (1889)	John Wanamaker (1889)	W. H. H. Miller (1889)	Jon W. Noble (1889)
24. Grover Cleveland (1893) Adlai E. Stevenson (1893)	Walter Q. Gresham (1893) Richard Olney (1895)	John G. Carlisle (1893)	Daniel S. Lamont (1893)	Hilary A. Herbert (1853)	Wilson S. Bissel (1893) William L. Wilson (1895)	Richard Olney (1893) Judson Harmon (1895)	Hoke Smith (1893) David R. Francis (1896)
25. William McKinley (1897) Garret A. Hobart (1897) Theodore Roosevelt (1901)	John Sherman (1897) William R. Day (1897) John Hay (1898)	Lyman J. Gage (1897)	Russell A. Alger (1897) Elihu Root (1899)	John D. Long (1897)	James A. Gary (1897) Charles E. Smith (1898)	Joseph McKenna (1897) John W. Griggs (1897) Philander C. Knox (1901)	Cornelius N. Bliss (1897) E. A. Hitchcock (1899)
26. Theodore Roosevelt (1901) Charles Fairbanks (1905)	John Hay (1901) Elihu Root (1905) Robert Bacon (1909)	Lyman J. Gage (1901) Leslie M. Shaw (1902) George B. Cortelyou (1907)	Elihu Root (1901) William H. Taft (1904) Luke E. Wright (1908)	John D. Long (1901) William H. Moody (1902) Paul Morton (1904) Charles J. Bonaparte (1905) V. H. Metcalf (1906) T. H. Newberry (1908)	Charles E. Smith (1901) Henry Payne (1902) Robert J. Wynne (1904) George B. Cortelyou (1905) George von L. Meyer (1907)	Philander C. Knox (1901) William H. Moody (1904) Charles J. Bonaparte (1907)	E. A. Hitchcock (1901) James R. Garfield (1907)
27. William H. Taft (1909) James S. Sherman (1909)	Philander C. Knox (1909)	Franklin MacVeagh (1909)	Jacob M. Dickinson (1909) Henry Stimson (1911)	George von L. Meyer (1905)	Frank H Hitchcock (1909)	G. W. Wickersham (1909)	R. A. Ballinger (1909) Walter L. Fisher (1911)
28. Woodrow Wilson (1913) Thomas R. Marshall (1913)	William J. Bryan (1913) Robert Lansing (1915) Bainbridge Colby (1920)	William G. McAdoo (1913) Carter Glass (1918) David F. Houston (1920)	Lindley M. Garrison (1913) Newton D. Baker (1916)	Josephus Daniels (1913)	Albert S. Burleson (1913)	J. C. McReynolds (1913) T. W. Gregory (1914) A. Mitchell Palmer (1919)	Franklin K. Lane (1913) John B. Payne (1920)
29. Warren G. Harding (1921) Calvin Coolidge (1921)	Charles E. Hughes (1912)	Andrew W. Mellon (1921)	John W. Weeks (1921)	Edwin Denby (1921)	Will H. Hays (1921) Hubert Work (1922) Harry S. New (1923)	H. M. Daugherty (1921)	Albert B. Fall (1921) Hubert Work (1923)
30. Calvin Coolidge (1923) Charles G. Dawes (1925)	Charles E. Hughes (1923) Frank B. Kellogg (1925)	Andrew W. Mellon (1923)	John W. Weeks (1923) Dwight F. Davis (1925)	Edwin Denby (1923) Curtis D. Wilbur (1924)	Harry S. New (1923)	H. M. Daugherty (1923) Harlan F. Stone (1924) John G. Sargent (1925)	Hubert Work (1923) Roy O. West (1928)

PRESIDENT AND VICE PRESIDENT	SECRETARY OF STATE	SECRETARY OF TREASURY	SECRETARY OF WAR	SECRETARY OF NAVY	POSTMASTER GENERAL	ATTORNEY GENERAL	SECRETARY OF INTERIOR
31. Herbert C. Hoover (1929) Charles Curtis (1929)	Henry L. Stimson (1929)	Andrew W. Mellon (1929) Ogden L. Mills (1932)	James W. Good (1929) Patrick J. Hurley (1929)	Charles F. Adams (1929)	Walter F. Brown (1929)	W. D. Mitchell (1929)	Ray L. Wilbur (1929)
32. Franklin D. Roosevelt (1933) John Nance Garner (1933) Henry A. Wallace (1941) Harry S. Truman (1945)	Cordell Hull (1933) E. R. Stettinius, Jr. (1944)	William H. Woodin (1933) Henry Morgenthau, Jr. (1934)	George H. Dern (1933) Harry H. Woodring (1936) Henry L. Stimson (1940)	Claude A. Swanson (1933) Charles Edison (1940) Frank Knox (1940) James V. Forrestal (1944)	James A. Farley (1933) Frank C. Walker (1940)	H. S. Cummings (1933) Frank Murphy (1939) Robert Jackson (1940) Francis Biddle (1941)	Harold L. Ickes (1933)
33. Harry S. Truman (1945) Alben W. Barkley (1949)	James F. Byrnes (1945) George C. Marshall (1947) Dean G. Acheson (1949)	Fred M. Vinson (1945) John W. Snyder (1946)	Robert P. Patterson (1945) Kenneth C. Royal (1947)	James V. Forrestal (1945)	R. E. Hannegan (1945) Jesse M. Donaldson (1947)	Tom C. Clark (1945) J. H. McGrath (1949) James P. McGranery (1952)	Harold L. Ickes (1945) Julis A. Krug (1946) Oscar L. Chapman (1949)
34. Dwight D. Eisenhower (1953) Richard M. Nixon (1953)	John Foster Dulles (1953) Christian A. Herter (1959)	George M. Humphrey (1953) Robert B. Anderson (1957)	*Secretary of Defense* James V. Forrestal (1947) Louis A. Johnson (1949) George C. Marshall (1950) Robert A. Lovett (1951) Charles E. Wilson (1953) Neil H. McElroy (1957) Thomas S. Gates (1959)		A. E. Summerfield (1953)	H. Brownell, Jr. (1953) William P. Rogers (1957)	Douglas McKay (1953) Fred Seaton (1956)
35. John F. Kennedy (1961) Lyndon B. Johnson (1961)	Dean Rusk (1961)	C. Douglas Dillon (1961)	Robert S. McNamara (1961)		J. Edward Day (1961) John A. Gronouski (1963)	Robert F. Kennedy (1961)	Stewart L. Udall (1961)
36. Lyndon B. Johnson (1963) Hubert H. Humphrey (1965)	Dean Rusk (1963)	C. Douglas Dillor (1963) Henry H. Fowler (1965) Joseph W. Barr (1968)	Robert S. McNamara (1963) Clark M. Clifford (1968)		John A. Gronouski (1963) Lawrence F. O'Brien (1965) W. Marvin Watson (1968)	Robert F. Kennedy (1963) N. deB. Katzenbach (1965) Ramsey Clark (1967)	Stewart L. Udall (1963)
37. Richard M. Nixon (1969) Spiro T. Agnew (1969) Gerald R. Ford (1973)	William P. Rogers (1969) Henry A. Kissinger (1973)	David M. Kennedy (1969) John B. Connally (1970) George P. Schultz (1972) William E. Simon (1974)	Melvin R. Laird (1969) Elliot L. Richardson (1973) James R. Schlesinger (1973)		Winton M. Blount (1969)	John M. Mitchell (1969) Richard G. Kleindienst (1972) Elliot L. Richardson (1973) William B. Saxbe (1974)	Walter J. Hickel (1969) Rogers C. B. Morton (1971)

PRESIDENT AND VICE PRESIDENT	SECRETARY OF STATE	SECRETARY OF TREASURY	SECRETARY OF DEFENSE	SECRETARY OF NAVY	POSTMASTER GENERAL	ATTORNEY GENERAL	SECRETARY OF INTERIOR
38. Gerald R. Ford (1974) Nelson A. Rockefeller (1974)	Henry A. Kissinger (1974)	William E. Simon (1974)	James R. Schlesinger (1974) Donald H. Runsfeld (1975)			William B. Saxbe (1974) Edward H. Levi (1975)	Rogers C. B. Morton (1974) Stanley K. Hathaway (1975) Thomas D. Kleppe (1975)
39. James E. Carter, Jr. (1977) Walter F. Mondale (1977)	Cyrus R. Vance (1977) Edmund S. Muskie (1980)	W. Michael Blumenthal (1977) G. William Miller (1979)	Harold Brown (1977)			Griffin B. Bell (1977) Benjamin R. Civiletti (1979)	Cecil D. Andrus (1977)
40. Ronald W. Reagan (1981) George H. Bush (1981)	Alexander M. Haig, Jr. (1981) George P. Schultz (1982)	Donald T. Regan (1981)	Caspar W. Weinberger (1981)			William French Smith (1981)	James G. Watt (1981) William Clark (1983) Donald P. Hodel (1985)
41. Ronald W. Reagan (1985) George H. Bush (1985)	George P. Schultz (1985)	James A. Baker III (1985)	Caspar W. Weinberger (1985)			Edwin Meese III (1985)	
42. George H. Bush (1989) James D. Quayle III (1989)	James A. Baker III (1989)	Nicholas Brady (1989)	Richard B. Cheney (1989)			Richard L. Thornburgh (1989)	Manuel Lujan, Jr. (1989)
43. William J. B. Clinton (1993) Albert Gore (1993)	Warren Christopher (1993)	Lloyd Bentsen (1993)	Les Aspin (1993)			Janet Reno (1993)	Bruce Babbit (1993)

Presidential Elections

YEAR	NUMBER OF STATES	CANDIDATES	PARTY	POPULAR VOTE*	ELEC-TORAL VOTE†	PERCENT-AGE OF POPULAR VOTE
1789	11	GEORGE WASHINGTON	No party designations		69	
		John Adams			34	
		Other Candidates			35	
1792	15	GEORGE WASHINGTON	No party designations		132	
		John Adams			77	
		George Clinton			50	
		Other Candidates			5	
1796	16	JOHN ADAMS	Federalist		71	
		Thomas Jefferson	Democratic-Republican		68	
		Thomas Pinckney	Federalist		59	
		Aaron Burr	Democratic-Republican		30	
		Other Candidates			48	
1800	16	THOMAS JEFFERSON	Democratic-Republican		73	
		Aaron Burr	Democratic-Republican		73	
		John Adams	Federalist		65	
		Charles C. Pinckney	Federalist		64	
		John Jay	Federalist		1	
1804	17	THOMAS JEFFERSON	Democratic-Republican		162	
		Charles C. Pinckney	Federalist		14	
1808	17	JAMES MADISON	Democratic-Republican		122	
		Charles C. Pinckney	Federalist		47	
		George Clinton	Democratic-Republican		6	
1812	18	JAMES MADISON	Democratic-Republican		128	
		DeWitt Clinton	Federalist		89	
1816	19	JAMES MONROE	Democratic-Republican		183	
		Rufus King	Federalist		34	
1820	24	JAMES MONROE	Democratic-Republican		231	
		John Quincy Adams	Independent Republican		1	
1824	24	JOHN QUINCY ADAMS		108,740	84	30.5
		Andrew Jackson		153,544	99	43.1
		William H. Crawford		46,618	41	13.1
		Henry Clay		47,136	37	13.2
1828	24	ANDREW JACKSON	Democrat	647,286	178	56.0
		John Quincy Adams	National Republican	508,064	83	44.0
1832	24	ANDREW JACKSON	Democrat	687,502	219	55.0
		Henry Clay	National Republican	530,189	49	42.4
		William Wirt	Anti-Masonic	33,108	7	2.6
		John Floyd	National Republican		11	
1836	26	MARTIN VAN BUREN	Democrat	765,483	170	50.9
		William H. Harrison	Whig		73	
		Hugh L. White	Whig	739,795	26	49.1
		Daniel Webster	Whig		14	
		W. P. Mangum	Whig		11	
1840	26	WILLIAM H. HARRISON	Whig	1,274,624	234	53.1
		Martin Van Buren	Democrat	1,127,781	60	46.9
1844	26	JAMES K. POLK	Democrat	1,338,464	170	49.6
		Henry Clay	Whig	1,300,097	105	48.1
		James G. Birney	Liberty	62,300		2.3
1848	30	ZACHARY TAYLOR	Whig	1,360,967	163	47.4
		Lewis Cass	Democrat	1,222,342	127	42.5
		Martin Van Buren	Free Soil	291,263		10.1
1852	31	FRANKLIN PIERCE	Democrat	1,601,117	254	50.9
		Winfield Scott	Whig	1,385,453	42	44.1
		John P. Hale	Free Soil	155,825		5.0
1856	31	JAMES BUCHANAN	Democrat	1,832,955	174	45.3
		John C. Frémont	Republican	1,339,932	114	33.1
		Millard Fillmore	American	871,731	8	21.6

*Percentage of popular vote given for any election year may not total 100 percent because candidates receiving less than 1 percent of the popular vote have been omitted.

†Prior to the passage of the Twelfth Amendment in 1904, the electoral college voted for two presidential candidates; the runner-up became Vice-President. Data from *Historical Statistics of the United States, Colonial Times to 1957* (1961), pp. 682–683, and *The World Almanac*.

Courtesy: U.S. Immigration and Naturalization Service

Presidential Elections (*continued*)

YEAR	NUMBER OF STATES	CANDIDATES	PARTY	POPULAR VOTE*	ELEC-TORAL VOTE†	PERCENT-AGE OF POPULAR VOTE
1860	33	ABRAHAM LINCOLN	Republican	1,865,593	180	39.8
		Stephen A. Douglas	Democrat	1,382,713	12	29.5
		John C. Breckinridge	Democrat	848,356	72	18.1
		John Bell	Constitutional Union	592,906	39	12.6
1864	36	ABRAHAM LINCOLN	Republican	2,206,938	212	55.0
		George B. McClellan	Democrat	1,803,787	21	45.0
1868	37	ULYSSES S. GRANT	Republican	3,013,421	214	52.7
		Horatio Seymour	Democrat	2,706,829	80	47.3
1872	37	ULYSSES S. GRANT	Republican	3,596,745	286	55.6
		Horace Greeley	Democrat	2,843,446	*	43.9
1876	38	RUTHERFORD B. HAYES	Republican	4,036,572	185	48.0
		Samuel J. Tilden	Democrat	4,284,020	184	51.0
1880	38	JAMES A. GARFIELD	Republican	4,453,295	214	48.5
		Winfield S. Hancock	Democrat	4,414,082	155	48.1
		James B. Weaver	Greenback-Labor	308,578		3.4
1884	38	GROVER CLEVELAND	Democrat	4,879,507	219	48.5
		James G. Blaine	Republican	4,850,293	182	48.2
		Benjamin F. Butler	Greenback-Labor	175,370		1.8
		John P. St. John	Prohibition	150,369		1.5
1888	38	BENJAMIN HARRISON	Republican	5,447,129	233	47.9
		Grover Cleveland	Democrat	5,537,857	168	48.6
		Clinton B. Fisk	Prohibition	249,506		2.2
		Anson J. Streeter	Union Labor	146,935		1.3
1892	44	GROVER CLEVELAND	Democrat	5,555,426	277	46.1
		Benjamin Harrison	Republican	5,182,690	145	43.0
		James B. Weaver	People's	1,029,846	22	8.5
		John Bidwell	Prohibition	264,133		2.2
1896	45	WILLIAM MCKINLEY	Republican	7,102,246	271	51.1
		William J. Bryan	Democrat	6,492,559	176	47.7
1900	45	WILLIAM MCKINLEY	Republican	7,218,491	292	51.7
		William J. Bryan	Democrat; Populist	6,356,734	155	45.5
		John C. Woolley	Prohibition	208,914		1.5
1904	45	THEODORE ROOSEVELT	Republican	7,628,461	336	57.4
		Alton B. Parker	Democrat	5,084,223	140	37.6
		Eugene V. Debs	Socialist	402,283		3.0
		Silas C. Swallow	Prohibition	258,536		1.9
1908	46	WILLIAM H. TAFT	Republican	7,675,320	321	51.6
		William J. Bryan	Democrat	6,412,294	162	43.1
		Eugene V. Debs	Socialist	420,793		2.8
		Eugene W. Chafin	Prohibition	253,840		1.7
1912	48	WOODROW WILSON	Democrat	6,296,547	435	41.9
		Theodore Roosevelt	Progressive	4,118,571	88	27.4
		William H. Taft	Republican	3,486,720	8	23.2
		Eugene V. Debs	Socialist	900,672		6.0
		Eugene W. Chafin	Prohibition	206,275		1.4
1916	48	WOODROW WILSON	Democrat	9,127,695	277	49.4
		Charles E. Hughes	Republican	8,533,507	254	46.2
		A. L. Benson	Socialist	585,113		3.2
		J. Frank Hanly	Prohibition	220,506		1.2
1920	48	WARREN G. HARDING	Republican	16,143,407	404	60.4
		James M. Cox	Democrat	9,130,328	127	34.2
		Eugene V. Debs	Socialist	919,799		3.4
		P. P. Christensen	Farmer-Labor	265,411		1.0

*Because of the death of Greeley, Democratic electors scattered their votes.

Presidential Elections (continued)

YEAR	NUMBER OF STATES	CANDIDATES	PARTY	POPULAR VOTE*	ELEC- TORAL VOTE†	PERCENT- AGE OF POPULAR VOTE
1924	48	CALVIN COOLIDGE	Republican	15,718,211	382	54.0
		John W. Davis	Democrat	8,385,283	136	28.8
		Robert M. La Follette	Progressive	4,831,289	13	16.6
1928	48	HERBERT C. HOOVER	Republican	21,391,993	444	58.2
		Alfred E. Smith	Democrat	15,016,169	87	40.9
1932	48	FRANKLIN D. ROOSEVELT	Democrat	22,809,638	472	57.4
		Herbert C. Hoover	Republican	15,758,901	59	39.7
		Norman Thomas	Socialist	881,951		2.2
1936	48	FRANKLIN D. ROOSEVELT	Democrat	27,752,869	523	60.8
		Alfred M. Landon	Republican	16,674,665	8	36.5
		William Lemke	Union	882,479		1.9
1940	48	FRANKLIN D. ROOSEVELT	Democrat	27,307,819	449	54.8
		Wendell L. Willkie	Republican	22,321,018	82	44.8
1944	48	FRANKLIN D. ROOSEVELT	Democrat	25,606,585	432	53.5
		Thomas E. Dewey	Republican	22,014,745	99	46.0
1948	48	HARRY S. TRUMAN	Democrat	24,105,812	303	49.5
		Thomas E. Dewey	Republican	21,970,065	189	45.1
		J. Strom Thurmond	States' Rights	1,169,063	39	2.4
		Henry A. Wallace	Progressive	1,157,172		2.4
1952	48	DWIGHT D. EISENHOWER	Republican	33,936,234	442	55.1
		Adlai E. Stevenson	Democrat	27,314,992	89	44.4
1956	48	DWIGHT D. EISENHOWER	Republican	35,590,472	457†	57.6
		Adlai E. Stevenson	Democrat	26,022,752	73	42.1
1960	50	JOHN F. KENNEDY	Democrat	34,227,096	303‡	49.9
		Richard M. Nixon	Republican	34,108,546	219	49.6
1964	50	LYNDON B. JOHNSON	Democrat	42,676,220	486	61.3
		Barry M. Goldwater	Republican	26,860,314	52	38.5
1968	50	RICHARD M. NIXON	Republican	31,785,480	301	43.4
		Hubert H. Humphrey	Democrat	31,275,165	191	42.7
		George C. Wallace	American Independent	9,906,473	46	13.5
1972	50	RICHARD M. NIXON*	Republican	47,165,234	520	60.6
		George S. McGovern	Democrat	29,168,110	17	37.5
1976	50	JIMMY CARTER	Democrat	40,828,929	297	50.1
		Gerald R. Ford	Republican	39,148,940	240	47.9
		Eugene McCarthy	Independent	739,256		
1980	50	RONALD REAGAN	Republican	43,201,220	489	50.9
		Jimmy Carter	Democrat	34,913,332	49	41.2
		John B. Anderson	Independent	5,581,379		
1984	50	RONALD REAGAN	Republican	53,428,357	525	59.0
		Walter F. Mondale	Democrat	36,930,923	13	41.0
1988	50	GEORGE BUSH	Republican	48,901,046	426	53.4
		Michael Dukakis	Democrat	41,809,030	111	45.6
1992	50	BILL CLINTON	Democrat	43,728,275	370	43.2
		George Bush	Republican	38,167,416	168	37.7
		H. Ross Perot	United We Stand, America	19,237,247		19.0

†Walter B. Jones received 1 electoral vote.‡ Harry F. Byrd received 15 electoral votes.
*Resigned August 9, 1974: Vice President Gerald R. Ford became President.

Supreme Court Justices

Name	Service	Appointed by
John Jay	1789–1795	Washington
James Wilson	1789–1798	Washington
John Blair	1789–1796	Washington
John Rutledge	1790–1791	Washington
William Cushing	1790–1810	Washington
James Iredell	1790–1799	Washington
Thomas Johnson	1791–1793	Washington
William Paterson	1793–1806	Washington
John Rutledge*	1795	Washington
Samuel Chase	1796–1811	Washington
Oliver Ellsworth	1796–1799	Washington
Bushrod Washington	1798–1829	J. Adams
Alfred Moore	1799–1804	J. Adams
John Marshall	1801–1835	J. Adams
William Johnson	1804–1834	Jefferson
Henry B. Livingston	1806–1823	Jefferson
Thomas Todd	1807–1826	Jefferson
Gabriel Duval	1811–1836	Madison
Joseph Story	1811–1845	Madison
Smith Thompson	1823–1843	Monroe
Robert Trimble	1826–1828	J. Q. Adams
John McLean	1829–1861	Jackson
Henry Baldwin	1830–1844	Jackson
James M. Wayne	1835–1867	Jackson
Roger B. Taney	1836–1864	Jackson
Philip P. Barbour	1836–1841	Jackson
John Catron	1837–1865	Van Buren
John McKinley	1837–1852	Van Buren
Peter V. Daniel	1841–1860	Van Buren
Samuel Nelson	1845–1872	Tyler
Levi Woodbury	1845–1851	Polk
Robert C. Grier	1846–1870	Polk
Benjamin R. Curtis	1851–1857	Fillmore
John A. Campbell	1853–1861	Pierce
Nathan Clifford	1858–1881	Buchanan
Noah H. Swayne	1862–1881	Lincoln
Samuel F. Miller	1862–1890	Lincoln
David Davis	1862–1877	Lincoln
Stephen J. Field	1863–1897	Lincoln
Salmon P. Chase	1864–1873	Lincoln
William Strong	1870–1880	Grant
Joseph P. Bradley	1870–1892	Grant
Ward Hunt	1873–1882	Grant
Morrison R. Waite	1874–1888	Grant
John M. Harlan	1877–1911	Hayes
William B. Woods	1880–1887	Hayes
Stanley Matthews	1881–1889	Garfield
Horace Gray	1882–1902	Arthur
Samuel Blatchford	1882–1893	Arthur
Lucius Q. C. Lamar	1888–1893	Cleveland
Melville W. Fuller	1888–1910	Cleveland
David J. Brewer	1889–1910	B. Harrison
Henry B. Brown	1890–1906	B. Harrison
George Shiras	1892–1903	B. Harrison
Howell E. Jackson	1893–1895	B. Harrison
Edward D. White	1894–1910	Cleveland
Rufus W. Peckham	1896–1909	Cleveland
Joseph McKenna	1898–1925	McKinley
Oliver W. Holmes	1902–1932	T. Roosevelt
William R. Day	1903–1922	T. Roosevelt
William H. Moody	1906–1910	T. Roosevelt
Horace H. Lurton	1910–1914	Taft
Charles E. Hughes	1910–1916	Taft
Willis Van Devanter	1910–1937	Taft
Joseph R. Lamar	1911–1916	Taft
Edward D. White	1910–1921	Taft
Mahlon Pitney	1912–1922	Taft
James C. McReynolds	1914–1941	Wilson
Louis D. Brandeis	1916–1939	Wilson
John H. Clarke	1916–1922	Wilson
William H. Taft	1921–1930	Harding
George Sutherland	1922–1938	Harding
Pierce Butler	1923–1939	Harding
Edward T. Sanford	1923–1930	Harding
Harlan F. Stone	1925–1941	Coolidge
Charles E. Hughes	1930–1941	Hoover
Owen J. Roberts	1930–1945	Hoover
Benjamin N. Cardozo	1932–1938	Hoover
Hugo L. Black	1937–1971	F. Roosevelt
Stanley F. Reed	1938–1957	F. Roosevelt
Felix Frankfurter	1939–1962	F. Roosevelt
William O. Douglas	1939–1975	F. Roosevelt
Frank Murphy	1940–1949	F. Roosevelt
Harlan F. Stone	1941–1946	F. Roosevelt
James F. Byrnes	1941–1942	F. Roosevelt
Robert H. Jackson	1941–1954	F. Roosevelt
Wiley B. Rutledge	1943–1949	F. Roosevelt
Harold H. Burton	1945–1958	Truman
Frederick M. Vinson	1946–1953	Truman
Tom C. Clark	1949–1967	Truman
Sherman Minton	1949–1956	Truman
Earl Warren	1953–1969	Eisenhower
John Marshall Harlan	1955–1971	Eisenhower
William J. Brennan, Jr.	1956–	Eisenhower
Charles E. Whittaker	1957–1962	Eisenhower
Potter Stewart	1958–1981	Eisenhower
Byron R. White	1962–1993	Kennedy
Arthur J. Goldberg	1962–1965	Kennedy
Abe Fortas	1965–1969	Johnson
Thurgood Marshall	1967–1991	Johnson
Warren E. Burger	1969–1986	Nixon
Harry A. Blackmun	1970–	Nixon
Lewis F. Powell, Jr.	1972–1988	Nixon
William H. Rehnquist	1972–1986	Nixon
John Paul Stevens	1975–	Ford
Sandra Day O'Connor	1981–	Reagan
William H. Rehnquist	1986–	Reagan
Antonin Scalia	1986–	Reagan
Anthony Kennedy	1988–	Reagan
David Souter	1990–	Bush
Clarence Thomas	1991–	Bush
Ruth Bader Ginsburg	1993–	Clinton

Note: **Chief Justices appear in bold type.**
*Acting Chief Justice; Senate refused to confirm appointment.

Admission of States into the Union

State	Date of Admission	State	Date of Admission
1. Delaware	December 7, 1787	26. Michigan	January 26, 1837
2. Pennsylvania	December 12, 1787	27. Florida	March 3, 1845
3. New Jersey	December 18, 1787	28. Texas	December 29, 1845
4. Georgia	January 2, 1788	29. Iowa	December 28, 1846
5. Connecticut	January 9, 1788	30. Wisconsin	May 29, 1848
6. Massachusetts	February 6, 1788	31. California	September 9, 1850
7. Maryland	April 28, 1788	32. Minnesota	May 11, 1858
8. South Carolina	May 23, 1788	33. Oregon	February 14, 1859
9. New Hampshire	June 21, 1788	34. Kansas	January 29, 1861
10. Virginia	June 25, 1788	35. West Virginia	June 20, 1863
11. New York	July 26, 1788	36. Nevada	October 31, 1864
12. North Carolina	November 21, 1789	37. Nebraska	March 1, 1867
13. Rhode Island	May 29, 1790	38. Colorado	August 1, 1876
14. Vermont	March 4, 1791	39. North Dakota	November 2, 1889
15. Kentucky	June 1, 1792	40. South Dakota	November 2, 1889
16. Tennessee	June 1, 1796	41. Montana	November 8, 1889
17. Ohio	March 1, 1803	42. Washington	November 11, 1889
18. Louisiana	April 30, 1812	43. Idaho	July 3, 1890
19. Indiana	December 11, 1816	44. Wyoming	July 10, 1890
20. Mississippi	December 10, 1817	45. Utah	January 4, 1896
21. Illinois	December 3, 1818	46. Oklahoma	November 16, 1907
22. Alabama	December 14, 1819	47. New Mexico	January 6, 1912
23. Maine	March 15, 1820	48. Arizona	February 14, 1912
24. Missouri	August 10, 1821	49. Alaska	January 3, 1959
25. Arkansas	June 15, 1836	50. Hawaii	August 21, 1959

TERRITORIAL EXPANSION OF THE UNITED STATES

Territory	Year	Method of Acquisition
Original states and territories	1783	Treaty with Great Britain
Louisiana Purchase	1803	Purchase from France
Florida	1819	Treaty with Spain
Texas	1845	Anexation of independent nation
Oregon	1846	Treaty with Great Britain
Mexican Cession	1848	Conquest from Mexico
Gadsden Purchase	1853	Purchase from Mexico
Alaska	1867	Purchase from Russia
Hawaii	1898	Annexation of independent nation
Puerto Rico	1899	Conquest from Spain
Guam	1899	Conquest from Spain
The Philippines	1899	Conquest from Spain (granted independence in 1946)
American Samoa	1900	Treaty with Great Britain and Germany
Panama Canal Zone	1904	Treaty with Panama (returned to Panama by treaty in 1978)
Corn Islands	1916	Treaty with Nicaragua (returned to Nicaragua by treaty in 1971)
Virgin Islands	1917	Purchase from Denmark
Pacific Islands Trust	1947	Trusteeship under United Nations (some granted independence)

Others (Midway, Wake, and other islands)

Courtesy: D.C. Heath and Company

IMMIGRATION TO THE UNITED STATES, FISCAL YEARS 1820–1990

Year	Number	Year	Number	Year	Number	Year	Number
1820–1989	55,457,531	1871–80	2,812,191	1921–30	4,107,209	1971–80	4,493,314
		1871	321,350	1921	805,228	1971	370,478
1820	8,385	1872	404,806	1922	309,556	1972	384,685
		1873	459,803	1923	522,919	1973	400,063
1821–30	143,439	1874	313,339	1924	706,896	1974	394,861
1821	9,127	1875	227,498	1925	294,314	1975	386,194
1822	6,911	1876	169,986	1926	304,488	1976	398,613
1823	6,354	1877	141,857	1927	335,175	1976, TQ	103,676
1824	7,912	1878	138,469	1928	307,255	1977	462,315
1825	10,199	1879	177,826	1929	279,678	1978	601,442
1826	10,837	1880	457,257	1930	241,700	1979	460,348
1827	18,875					1980	530,639
1828	27,382	1881–90	5,246,613	1931–40	528,431		
1829	22,520	1881	669,431	1931	97,139	1981–90	7,338,062
1830	23,322	1882	788,992	1932	35,576	1981	596,600
		1883	603,322	1933	23,068	1982	594,131
1831–40	599,125	1884	518,592	1934	29,470	1983	559,763
1831	22,633	1885	395,346	1935	34,956	1984	543,903
1832	60,482	1886	334,203	1936	36,329	1985	570,009
1833	58,640	1887	490,109	1937	50,244	1986	601,708
1834	65,365	1888	546,889	1938	67,895	1987	601,516
1835	45,374	1889	444,427	1939	82,998	1988	643,025
1836	76,242	1890	455,302	1940	70,756	1989	1,090,924
1837	79,340					1990	1,536,483
1838	38,914	1891–1900	3,687,564	1941–50	1,035,039		
1839	68,069	1891	560,319	1941	51,776		
1840	84,066	1892	579,663	1942	28,781		
		1893	439,730	1943	23,725		
1841–50	1,713,251	1894	285,631	1944	28,551		
1841	80,289	1895	258,536	1945	38,119		
1842	104,565	1896	343,267	1946	108,721		
1843	52,496	1897	230,832	1947	147,292		
1844	78,615	1898	229,299	1948	170,570		
1845	114,371	1899	311,715	1949	188,317		
1846	154,416	1900	448,572	1950	249,187		
1847	234,968						
1848	226,527	1901–10	8,795,386	1951–60	2,515,479		
1849	297,024	1901	487,918	1951	205,717		
1850	369,980	1902	648,743	1952	265,520		
		1903	857,046	1953	170,434		
1851–60	2,598,214	1904	812,870	1954	208,177		
1851	379,466	1905	1,026,499	1955	237,790		
1852	371,603	1906	1,100,735	1956	321,625		
1853	368,645	1907	1,285,349	1957	326,867		
1854	427,833	1908	782,870	1958	253,265		
1855	200,877	1909	751,786	1959	260,686		
1856	200,436	1910	1,041,570	1960	265,398		
1857	251,306						
1858	123,126	1911–20	5,735,811	1961–70	3,321,677		
1859	121,282	1911	878,587	1961	271,344		
1860	153,640	1912	838,172	1962	283,763		
		1913	1,197,892	1963	306,260		
1861–70	2,314,824	1914	1,218,480	1964	292,248		
1861	91,918	1915	326,700	1965	296,697		
1862	91,985	1916	298,826	1966	323,040		
1863	176,282	1917	295,403	1967	361,972		
1864	193,418	1918	110,618	1968	454,448		
1865	248,120	1919	141,132	1969	358,579		
1866	318,568	1920	430,001	1970	373,326		
1867	315,722						
1868	138,840						
1869	352,768						
1870	387,203						

Source: U.S. Immigration and Naturalization Service, 1991.

IMMIGRATION BY REGION AND SELECTED COUNTRY OF LAST RESIDENCE, FISCAL YEARS 1820–1989

Region and Country of Last Residence[1]	1820	1821–30	1831–40	1841–50	1851–60	1861–70	1871–80	1881–90
All countries	8,385	143,439	599,125	1,713,251	2,598,214	2,314,824	2,812,191	5,246,613
Europe	7,690	98,797	495,681	1,597,442	2,452,577	2,065,141	2,271,925	4,735,484
Austria-Hungary	—[2]	—[2]	—[2]	—[2]	—[2]	7,800	72,969	353,719
Austria	—[2]	—[2]	—[2]	—[2]	—[2]	[3]7,124	63,009	226,038
Hungary	—[2]	—[2]	—[2]	—[2]	—[2]	[3]484	9,960	127,681
Belgium	1	27	22	5,074	4,738	6,734	7,221	20,177
Czechoslovakia	—[4]	—[4]	—[4]	—[4]	—[4]	—[4]	—[4]	—[4]
Denmark	20	169	1,063	539	3,749	17,094	31,771	88,132
France	371	8,497	45,575	77,262	76,358	35,986	72,206	50,464
Germany	968	6,761	152,454	434,626	951,667	787,468	718,182	1,452,970
Greece	—	20	49	16	31	72	210	2,308
Ireland[5]	3,614	50,724	207,381	780,719	914,119	435,778	436,871	655,482
Italy	30	409	2,253	1,870	9,231	11,725	55,759	307,309
Netherlands	49	1,078	1,412	8,251	10,789	9,102	16,541	53,701
Norway-Sweden	3	91	1,201	13,903	20,931	109,298	211,245	568,362
Norway	—[6]	—[6]	—[6]	—[6]	—[6]	—[6]	95,323	176,586
Sweden	—[6]	—[6]	—[6]	—[6]	—[6]	—[6]	115,922	391,776
Poland	5	16	369	105	1,164	2,027	12,970	51,806
Portugal	35	145	829	550	1,055	2,658	14,082	16,978
Romania	—[7]	—[7]	—[7]	—[7]	—[7]	—[7]	11	6,348
Soviet Union	14	75	277	551	457	2,512	39,284	213,282
Spain	139	2,477	2,125	2,209	9,298	6,697	5,266	4,419
Switzerland	31	3,226	4,821	4,644	25,011	23,286	28,293	81,988
United Kingdom[5,8]	2,410	25,079	75,810	267,044	423,974	606,896	548,043	807,357
Yugoslavia	—[9]	—[9]	—[9]	—[9]	—[9]	—[9]	—[9]	—[9]
Other Europe	—	3	40	79	5	8	1,001	682
Asia	6	30	55	141	41,538	64,759	124,160	69,942
China[10]	1	2	8	35	41,397	64,301	123,201	61,711
Hong Kong	—[11]	—[11]	—[11]	—[11]	—[11]	—[11]	—[11]	—[11]
India	1	8	39	36	43	69	163	269
Iran	—[12]	—[12]	—[12]	—[12]	—[12]	—[12]	—[12]	—[12]
Israel	—[13]	—[13]	—[13]	—[13]	—[13]	—[13]	—[13]	—[13]
Japan	—[14]	—[14]	—[14]	—[14]	—[14]	186	149	2,270
Korea	—[15]	—[15]	—[15]	—[15]	—[15]	—[15]	—[15]	—[15]
Philippines	—[16]	—[16]	—[16]	—[16]	—[16]	—[16]	—[16]	—[16]
Turkey	1	20	7	59	83	131	404	3,782
Vietnam	—[11]	—[11]	—[11]	—[11]	—[11]	—[11]	—[11]	—[11]
Other Asia	3	—	1	11	15	72	243	1,910
America	387	11,564	33,424	62,469	74,720	166,607	404,044	426,967
Canada & Newfoundland[17,18]	209	2,277	13,624	41,723	59,309	153,878	383,640	393,304
Mexico[18]	1	4,817	6,599	3,271	3,078	2,191	5,162	1,913[19]
Caribbean	164	3,834	12,301	13,528	10,660	9,046	13,957	29,042
Cuba	—[12]	—[12]	—[12]	—[12]	—[12]	—[12]	—[12]	—[12]
Dominican Republic	—[20]	—[20]	—[20]	—[20]	—[20]	—[20]	—[20]	—[20]
Haiti	—[20]	—[20]	—[20]	—[20]	—[20]	—[20]	—[20]	—[20]
Jamaica	—[21]	—[21]	—[21]	—[21]	—[21]	—[21]	—[21]	—[21]
Other Caribbean	164	3,834	12,301	13,528	10,660	9,046	13,957	29,042
Central America	2	105	44	368	449	95	157	404
El Salvador	—[20]	—[20]	—[20]	—[20]	—[20]	—[20]	—[20]	—[20]
Other Central America	2	105	44	368	449	95	157	404
South America	11	531	856	3,579	1,224	1,397	1,128	2,304
Argentina	—[20]	—[20]	—[20]	—[20]	—[20]	—[20]	—[20]	—[20]
Colombia	—[20]	—[20]	—[20]	—[20]	—[20]	—[20]	—[20]	—[20]
Ecuador	—[20]	—[20]	—[20]	—[20]	—[20]	—[20]	—[20]	—[20]
Other South America	11	531	856	3,579	1,224	1,397	1,128	2,304
Other America	—[22]	—[22]	—[22]	—[22]	—[22]	—[22]	—[22]	—[22]
Africa	1	16	54	55	210	312	358	857
Oceania	1	2	9	29	158	214	10,914	12,574
Not specified[22]	300	33,030	69,902	53,115	29,011	17,791	790	789

Source: U.S. Immigration and Naturalization Service, 1991.

Region and Country of Last Residence[1]	1891–1900	1901–10	1911–20	1921–30	1931–40	1941–50	1951–60	1961–70
All countries	3,687,564	8,795,386	5,735,811	4,107,209	528,431	1,035,039	2,515,479	3,321,677
Europe	3,555,352	8,056,040	4,321,887	2,463,194	347,566	621,147	1,325,727	1,123,492
Austria-Hungary	592,707[23]	2,145,266[23]	896,342[23]	63,548	11,424	28,329	103,743	26,022
Austria	234,081[3]	668,209[3]	453,649	32,868	3,563[24]	24,860[24]	67,106	20,621
Hungary	181,288[3]	808,511[3]	442,693	30,680	7,861	3,469	36,637	5,401
Belgium	18,167	41,635	33,746	15,846	4,817	12,189	18,575	9,192
Czechoslovakia	—[4]	—[4]	3,426[4]	102,194	14,393	8,347	918	3,273
Denmark	50,231	65,285	41,983	32,430	2,559	5,393	10,984	9,201
France	30,770	73,379	61,897	49,610	12,623	38,809	51,121	45,237
Germany	505,152[23]	341,498[23]	143,945[23]	412,202	114,058[24]	226,578[24]	477,765	190,796
Greece	15,979	167,519	184,201	51,084	9,119	8,973	47,608	85,969
Ireland[5]	388,416	339,065	146,181	211,234	10,973	19,789	48,362	32,966
Italy	651,893	2,045,877	1,109,524	455,315	68,028	57,661	185,491	214,111
Netherlands	26,758	48,262	43,718	26,948	7,150	14,860	52,277	30,606
Norway-Sweden	321,281	440,039	161,469	165,780	8,700	20,765	44,632	32,600
Norway	95,015	190,505	66,395	68,531	4,740	10,100	22,935	15,484
Sweden	226,266	249,534	95,074	97,249	3,960	10,665	21,697	17,116
Poland	96,720[23]	—[23]	4,813[23]	227,734	17,026	7,571	9,985	53,539
Portugal	27,508	69,149	89,732	29,994	3,329	7,423	19,588	76,065
Romania	12,750	53,008	13,311	67,646	3,871	1,076	1,039	2,531
Soviet Union	505,290[23]	1,597,306[23]	921,201[23]	61,742	1,370	571	671	2,465
Spain	8,731	27,935	68,611	28,958	3,258	2,898	7,894	44,659
Switzerland	31,179	34,922	23,091	29,676	5,512	10,547	17,675	18,453
United Kingdom[5,8]	271,538	525,950	341,408	339,570	31,572	139,306	202,824	213,822
Yugoslavia	—[9]	—[9]	1,888[9]	49,064	5,835	1,576	8,225	20,381
Other Europe	282	39,945	31,400	42,619	11,949	8,486	16,350	11,604
Asia	74,862	323,543	247,236	112,059	16,595	37,028	153,249	427,642
China[10]	14,799	20,605	21,278	29,907	4,928	16,709	9,657	34,764
Hong Kong	—[11]	—[11]	—[11]	—[11]	—[11]	—[11]	15,541[11]	75,007
India	68	4,713	2,082	1,886	496	1,761	1,973	27,189
Iran	—[12]	—[12]	—[12]	241[12]	195	1,380	3,388	10,339
Israel	—[13]	—[13]	—[13]	—[13]	—[13]	476[13]	25,476	29,602
Japan	25,942	129,797	83,837	33,462	1,948	1,555	46,250	39,988
Korea	—[15]	—[15]	—[15]	—[15]	—[15]	107[15]	6,231	34,526
Philippines	—[16]	—[16]	—[16]	—[16]	528[16]	4,691	19,307	98,376
Turkey	30,425	157,369	134,066	33,824	1,065	798	3,519	10,142
Vietnam	—[11]	—[11]	—[11]	—[11]	—[11]	—[11]	335[11]	4,340
Other Asia	3,628	11,059	5,973	12,739	7,435	9,551	21,572	63,369
America	38,972	361,888	1,143,671	1,516,716	160,037	354,804	996,944	1,716,374
Canada & Newfoundland[17,18]	3,311	179,226	742,185	924,515	108,527	171,718	377,952	413,310
Mexico[18]	971[19]	49,642	219,004	459,287	22,319	60,589	299,811	453,937
Caribbean	33,066	107,548	123,424	74,899	15,502	49,725	123,091	470,213
Cuba	—[12]	—[12]	—[12]	15,901[12]	9,571	26,313	78,948	208,536
Dominican Republic	—[20]	—[20]	—[20]	—[20]	1,150[20]	5,627	9,897	93,292
Haiti	—[20]	—[20]	—[20]	—[20]	191[20]	911	4,442	34,499
Jamaica	—[21]	—[21]	—[21]	—[21]	—[21]	—[21]	8,869[21]	74,906
Other Caribbean	33,066	107,548	123,424	58,998	4,590	16,874	20,935[21]	58,980
Central America	549	8,192	17,159	15,769	5,861	21,665	44,751	101,330
El Salvador	—[20]	—[20]	—[20]	—[20]	673[20]	5,132	5,895	14,992
Other Central America	549	8,192	17,159	15,769	5,188	16,533	38,856	86,338
South America	1,075	17,280	41,899	42,215	7,803	21,831	91,628	257,954
Argentina	—[20]	—[20]	—[20]	—[20]	1,349[20]	3,338	19,486	49,721
Colombia	—[20]	—[20]	—[20]	—[20]	1,223[20]	3,858	18,048	72,028
Ecuador	—[20]	—[20]	—[20]	—[20]	337[20]	2,417	9,841	36,780
Other South America	1,075	17,280	41,899	42,215	4,894	12,218	44,253	99,425
Other America	—[21]	—[21]	—[21]	31[21]	25	29,276	59,711	19,630
Africa	350	7,368	8,443	6,286	1,750	7,367	14,092	28,954
Oceania	3,965	13,024	13,427	8,726	2,483	14,551	12,976	25,122
Not specified[22]	14,063	33,523[23]	1,147	228	—	142	12,491	93

Region and Country of Last Residence[1]	1971–80	1981–89	1984	1985	1986	1987	1988	1989	Total 170 Years 1820–1989
All countries	4,493,314	5,801,579	543,903	570,009	601,708	601,516	643,025	1,090,924	55,457,531
Europe	800,368	637,524	69,879	69,526	69,224	67,967	71,854	94,338	36,977,034
Austria-Hungary	16,028	20,152	2,846	2,521	2,604	2,401	3,200	3,586	4,338,049
Austria	9,478	14,566	2,351	1,930	2,039	1,769	2,493	2,845	1,825,172[2]
Hungary	6,550	5,586	495	591	565	632	707	741	1,666,801[2]
Belgium	5,329	6,239	787	775	843	859	706	705	209,729
Czechoslovakia	6,023	6,649	693	684	588	715	744	526	145,223
Denmark	4,439	4,696	512	465	544	515	561	617	369,738
France	25,069	28,088	3,335	3,530	3,876	3,809	3,637	4,101	783,322
Germany	74,414	79,809	9,375	10,028	9,853	9,923	9,748	10,419	7,071,313
Greece	92,369	34,490	3,311	3,487	3,497	4,087	4,690	4,588	700,017
Ireland[5]	11,490	22,229	1,096	1,288	1,757	3,032	5,121	6,983	4,715,393
Italy	129,368	51,008	6,328	6,351	5,711	4,666	5,332	11,089	5,356,862
Netherlands	10,492	10,723	1,313	1,235	1,263	1,303	1,152	1,253	372,717
Norway-Sweden	10,472	13,252	1,455	1,557	1,564	1,540	1,669	1,809	2,144,024
Norway	3,941	3,612	403	386	367	372	446	556	800,672[6]
Sweden	6,531	9,640	1,052	1,171	1,197	1,168	1,223	1,253	1,283,097[6]
Poland	37,234	64,888	7,229	7,409	6,540	5,818	7,298	13,279	587,972
Portugal	101,710	36,365	3,800	3,811	3,804	4,009	3,290	3,861	497,195
Romania	12,393	27,361	2,956	3,764	3,809	2,741	2,915	3,535	201,345
Soviet Union	38,961	42,898	3,349	1,532	1,001	1,139	1,408	4,570	3,428,927
Spain	39,141	17,689	2,168	2,278	2,232	2,056	1,972	2,179	282,404
Switzerland	8,235	7,561	795	980	923	964	920	1,072	358,151
United Kingdom[5,8]	137,374	140,119	16,516	15,591	16,129	15,889	14,667	16,961	5,100,096
Yugoslavia	30,540	15,984	1,404	1,521	1,915	1,793	2,039	2,464	133,493
Other Europe	9,287	7,324	611	719	771	708	785	741	181,064
Asia	1,588,178	2,416,278	247,775	255,164	258,546	248,293	254,745	296,420	5,697,301
China[10]	124,326	306,108	29,109	33,095	32,389	32,669	34,300	39,284	873,737
Hong Kong	113,467	83,848	12,290	10,795	9,930	8,785	11,817	15,257	287,863[11]
India	164,134	221,977	23,617	24,536	24,808	26,394	25,312	28,599	426,907
Iran	45,136	101,287	11,131	12,327	12,031	10,323	9,846	13,027	161,946[12]
Israel	37,713	38,367	4,136	4,279	5,124	4,753	4,444	5,494	131,634[13]
Japan	49,775	40,654	4,517	4,552	4,444	4,711	5,085	5,454	455,813[14]
Korea	267,638	302,782	32,537	34,791	35,164	35,397	34,151	33,016	611,284[15]
Philippines	354,987	477,485	46,985	53,137	61,492	58,315	61,019	66,119	955,374[16]
Turkey	13,399	20,028	1,652	1,690	1,975	2,080	2,200	2,538	409,122
Vietnam	172,820	266,027	25,803	20,367	15,010	13,073	12,856	13,174	443,522[11]
Other Asia	244,783	557,735	55,998	55,595	56,179	51,793	53,717	74,458	940,099
America	1,982,735	2,564,698	208,111	225,519	254,078	265,026	294,906	672,639	12,017,021
Canada & Newfoundland[17,18]	169,939	132,296	15,659	16,354	16,060	16,741	15,821	18,294	4,270,943
Mexico[18]	640,294	975,657	57,820	61,290	66,753	72,511	95,170	405,660	3,208,543
Caribbean	741,126	759,416	68,368	79,374	98,527	100,615	110,949	87,597	2,590,542
Cuba	264,863	135,142	5,699	17,115	30,787	27,363	16,610	9,523	739,274[19]
Dominican Republic	148,135	209,899	23,207	23,861	26,216	24,947	27,195	26,744	468,000[20]
Haiti	56,335	118,510	9,554	9,872	12,356	14,643	34,858	13,341	214,888[20]
Jamaica	137,577	184,481	18,997	18,277	18,916	22,430	20,474	23,572	405,833[21]
Other Caribbean	134,216	111,384	10,911	10,249	10,252	11,232	11,812	14,417	762,547
Central America	134,640	321,845	27,626	28,447	30,086	30,366	31,311	101,273	673,385
El Salvador	34,436	133,938	8,753	10,093	10,881	10,627	12,043	57,628	195,066[20]
Other Central America	100,204	187,907	18,873	18,354	19,205	19,739	19,268	43,645	478,319
South America	295,741	375,026	38,636	40,052	42,650	44,782	41,646	59,812	1,163,482
Argentina	29,897	21,374	2,287	1,925	2,318	2,192	2,556	3,766	125,165[20]
Colombia	77,347	99,066	10,897	11,802	11,213	11,482	10,153	14,918	271,570[20]
Ecuador	50,077	43,841	4,244	4,601	4,518	4,656	4,736	7,587	143,293[20]
Other South America	138,420	210,745	21,208	21,724	24,601	26,452	24,201	33,541	623,454
Other America	995	458	2	2	2	11	9	3	110,126
Africa	80,779	144,096	13,594	15,236	15,500	15,730	17,124	22,485	301,348
Oceania	41,242	38,401	4,249	4,552	4,352	4,437	4,324	4,956	197,818
Not specified[22]	12	582	295	12	8	63	72	86	267,009

[1]Data for years prior to 1906 relate to country whence alien came; data from 1906–79 and 1984–89 are for country of last permanent residence; and data for 1980–83 refer to country of birth. Because of changes in boundaries, changes in lists of countries, and lack of data for specified countries for various periods, data for certain countries, especially for the total period 1820–1989, are not comparable throughout. Data for specified countries are included with countries to which they belonged prior to World War I.

[2]Data for Austria and Hungary not reported until 1861.

[3]Data for Austria and Hungary not reported separately for all years during the period.

[4]No data available for Czechoslovakia until 1920.

[5]Prior to 1926, data for Northern Ireland included in Ireland.

[6]Data for Norway and Sweden not reported separately until 1871.

[7]No data available for Romania until 1880.

[8]Since 1925, data for United Kingdom refer to England, Scotland, Wales, and Northern Ireland.

[9]In 1920, a separate enumeration was made for the Kingdom of Serbs, Croats, and Slovenes. Since 1922, the Serb, Croat, and Slovene Kingdom recorded as Yugoslavia.

[10]Beginning in 1957, China includes Taiwan.

[11]Data not reported separately until 1952.

[12]Data not reported separately until 1925.

[13]Data not reported separately until 1949.

[14]No data available for Japan until 1861.

[15]Data not reported separately until 1948.

[16]Prior to 1934, Philippines recorded as insular travel.

[17]Prior to 1920, Canada and Newfoundland recorded as British North America. From 1820 to 1898, figures include all British North America possessions.

[18]Land arrivals not completely enumerated until 1908.

[19]No data available for Mexico from 1886 to 1893.

[20]Data not reported separately until 1932.

[21]Data for Jamaica not collected until 1953. In prior years, consolidated under British West Indies, which is included in "Other Caribbean."

[22]Included in countries "Not specified" until 1925.

[23]From 1899 to 1919, data for Poland included in Austria-Hungary, Germany, and the Soviet Union.

[24]From 1938 to 1945, data for Austria included in Germany.

[25]Includes 32,897 persons returning in 1906 to their homes in the United States.

—represents zero.

NOTE: From 1820 to 1867, figures represent alien passengers arrived at seaports; from 1868 to 1891 and 1895 to 1897, immigrant aliens arrived; from 1892 to 1894 and 1898 to 1989, immigrant aliens admitted for permanent residence. From 1892 to 1903, aliens entering by cabin class were not counted as immigrants. Land arrivals were not completely enumerated until 1908. For this table, fiscal year 1843 covers 9 months ending September 1843; fiscal years 1832 and 1850 cover 15 months ending December 31 of the respective years; and fiscal year 1868 covers 6 months ending June 30, 1868.

Growth of U.S. Population and Area

Census	Population	Percentage of Increase over Preceding Census	Land Area, Square Miles	Population per Square Mile
1790	3,929,214		867,980	4.5
1800	5,308,483	35.1	867,980	6.1
1810	7,239,881	36.4	1,685,865	4.3
1820	9,638,453	33.1	1,753,588	5.5
1830	12,866,020	33.5	1,753,588	7.3
1840	17,069,453	32.7	1,753,588	9.7
1850	23,191,876	35.9	2,944,337	7.9
1860	31,443,321	35.6	2,973,965	10.6
1870	39,818,449	26.6	2,973,965	13.4
1880	50,155,783	26.0	2,973,965	16.9
1890	62,947,714	25.5	2,973,965	21.2
1900	75,994,575	20.7	2,974,159	25.6
1910	91,972,266	21.0	2,973,890	30.9
1920	105,710,620	14.9	2,973,776	35.5
1930	122,775,046	16.1	2,977,128	41.2
1940	131,669,275	7.2	2,977,128	44.2
1950	150,697,361	14.5	2,974,726*	50.7
†1960	178,464,236	18.4	2,974,726	59.9
1970	204,765,770	14.7	2,974,726	68.8
1980	226,504,825	10.6	2,974,726	76.1
1990	248,709,873	9.8	2,974,726	83.6

*As remeasured in 1940.
†Not including Alaska (pop. 226, 167) and Hawaii (632,772).
‡As of July 1, 1987.

The Enduring Vision, Volume 1, Second edition, D.C. Heath and Company, 1993, Page xx, ISBN: 0-669-29794-1

POPULATIONS OF UNITED STATES COLONIES AND STATES, 1650-1990

STATES	1650	1700	1750	1770	1790	1800	1820	1840
Alabama							127,901	590,756
Alaska								
Arizona								
Arkansas							14,273	97,574
California								
Colorado								
Connecticut	4,139	25,970	111,280	183,881	237,946	251,002	275,248	309,978
Delaware	185	2,470	28,704	35,496	59,096	64,273	72,749	78,085
District of Columbia						8,144	23,336	33,745
Florida								54,477
Georgia			5,200	23,375	82,548	162,686	340,989	691,392
Hawaii								
Idaho								
Illinois							55,211	476,183
Indiana						5,641	147,178	685,866
Iowa								43,112
Kansas								
Kentucky				15,700	73,677	220,955	564,317	779,828
Louisiana							153,407	352,411
Maine[4]				31,257	96,540	151,719	298,335	501,793
Maryland	4,504	29,604	141,073	202,599	319,728	341,548	407,350	470,019
Massachusetts[4]	16,603	55,941	188,000	235,308	378,787	422,845	523,287	737,699
Michigan							8,896	212,267
Minnesota								
Mississippi						8,850	75,448	375,651
Missouri							66,586	383,702
Montana								
Nebraska								
Nevada								
New Hampshire	1,305	4,958	27,505	62,396	141,885	183,858	244,161	284,574
New Jersey		14,010	71,393	117,431	184,139	211,149	277,575	373,306
New Mexico								
New York	4,116	19,107	76,696	162,920	340,120	589,051	1,372,812	2,428,921
North Carolina		10,720	72,984	197,200	393,751	478,103	638,829	753,419
North Dakota[3]								
Ohio						45,365	581,434	1,519,467
Oklahoma[5]								
Oregon								
Pennsylvania		17,950	119,666	240,057	434,373	602,365	1,049,458	1,724,033
Rhode Island	785	5,894	33,226	58,196	68,825	69,122	83,059	108,830
South Carolina		5,704	64,000	124,244	249,073	345,591	502,741	594,398
South Dakota[3]								
Tennessee				1,000	35,691	105,602	422,823	829,210
Texas								
Utah								
Vermont				10,000	85,425	154,465	235,981	291,948
Virginia[6]	18,731	58,560	231,033	447,016	691,737	807,557	938,261	1,025,227
Washington								
West Virginia[6]					55,873	78,592	136,808	224,537
Wisconsin								30,945
Wyoming								
Total[1]	50,368	250,888	1,170,760	2,148,076	3,929,214	5,308,483	9,638,453	17,069,453[2]

[1]All figures prior to 1890 exclude Indians unaffected by the pioneer movement. Figures for 1650 through 1770 include only the British colonies that later became the United States. No areas are included prior to their annexation to the United States. However, many of the figures refer to territories prior to their admission as States. U.S. total includes Alaska from 1880 through 1970 and Hawaii from 1900 through 1970.
[2]U.S. total for 1840 includes 6,100 persons on public ships in service of the United States, not credited to any State.
[3]South Dakota figure for 1860 represents entire Dakota Territory. North and South Dakota figures for 1880 are for the parts of Dakota Territory which later constituted the respective States.

Populations of United States Colonies and States, 1650-1990

1860	1880	1900	1920	1940	1950	1960	1970	1980	1990
964,201	1,262,505	1,828,697	2,348,174	2,832,961	3,061,743	3,266,740	3,444,165	3,893,888	4,062,608
	33,426	63,592	55,036	72,524	128,643	226,167	302,173	401,851	551,947
	40,440	122,931	334,162	499,261	749,587	1,302,161	1,772,482	2,718,425	3,677,985
435,450	802,525	1,311,564	1,752,204	1,949,387	1,909,511	1,786,272	1,923,295	2,286,435	2,362,239
379,994	864,694	1,485,053	3,426,861	6,907,387	10,586,223	15,717,204	19,953,134	23,667,565	29,839,250
34,277	194,327	539,700	939,629	1,123,296	1,325,089	1,753,947	2,207,259	2,889,735	3,307,912
460,147	622,700	908,420	1,380,631	1,709,242	2,007,280	2,535,234	3,032,217	3,107,576	3,295,669
112,216	146,608	184,735	223,003	266,505	318,085	446,292	548,104	594,317	668,696
75,080	177,624	278,718	437,571	663,091	802,178	763,956	756,510	638,432	609,909
140,424	269,493	528,542	968,470	1,897,414	2,771,305	4,951,560	6,789,443	9,746,342	13,003,362
1,057,286	1,542,180	2,216,331	2,895,832	3,123,723	3,444,578	3,943,116	4,589,575	5,463,105	6,508,419
		154,001	255,881	422,770	499,794	632,772	769,913	964,691	1,115,274
	32,610	161,772	431,866	524,873	588,637	667,191	713,008	944,038	1,011,986
1,711,951	3,077,871	4,821,550	6,485,280	7,897,241	8,712,176	10,081,158	11,113,976	11,426,596	11,466,682
1,350,428	1,978,301	2,516,462	2,930,390	3,427,796	3,934,224	4,662,498	5,193,669	5,490,260	5,564,228
674,913	1,624,615	2,231,853	2,404,021	2,538,268	2,621,073	2,757,537	2,825,041	2,913,808	2,787,424
107,206	996,096	1,470,495	1,769,257	1,801,028	1,905,299	2,178,611	2,249,071	2,364,236	2,485,600
1,155,684	1,648,690	2,147,174	2,416,630	2,845,627	2,944,806	3,038,156	3,219,311	3,660,257	3,698,969
708,002	939,946	1,381,625	1,798,509	2,363,880	2,683,516	3,257,022	3,643,180	4,206,312	4,238,216
628,279	648,936	694,466	768,014	847,226	913,774	969,265	993,663	1,125,027	1,233,223
687,049	934,943	1,188,044	1,449,661	1,821,244	2,343,001	3,100,689	3,922,399	4,216,975	4,798,622
1,231,066	1,783,085	2,805,346	3,852,356	4,316,721	4,690,514	5,148,578	5,689,170	5,737,037	6,029,051
749,113	1,636,937	2,420,982	3,668,412	5,256,106	6,371,766	7,823,194	8,875,083	9,262,078	9,328,704
172,023	780,773	1,751,394	2,387,125	2,792,300	2,982,483	3,413,864	3,805,069	4,075,970	4,387,029
791,305	1,131,597	1,551,270	1,790,618	2,183,796	2,178,914	2,178,141	2,216,912	2,520,638	2,586,443
1,182,012	2,168,380	3,106,665	3,404,055	3,784,664	3,954,653	4,319,813	4,677,399	4,916,759	5,137,804
	39,159	243,329	548,889	559,456	591,024	674,767	694,409	786,690	803,655
28,841	452,402	1,066,300	1,296,372	1,315,834	1,325,510	1,411,330	1,483,791	1,569,825	1,584,617
6,857	62,266	42,335	77,407	110,247	160,083	285,278	488,738	800,493	1,206,152
326,073	346,991	411,588	443,083	491,524	533,242	606,921	737,681	920,610	1,113,915
672,035	1,131,116	1,883,669	3,155,900	4,160,165	4,835,329	6,066,782	7,168,164	7,364,823	7,748,634
93,516	119,565	195,310	360,350	531,818	681,187	951,023	1,016,000	1,302,981	1,521,779
3,880,735	5,082,871	7,268,894	10,385,227	13,479,142	14,830,192	16,782,304	18,241,266	17,558,072	18,044,505
992,622	1,399,750	1,893,810	2,559,123	3,571,623	4,061,929	4,556,155	5,082,059	5,881,813	6,657,630
	36,909	319,146	646,872	641,935	619,636	632,446	617,761	652,717	641,364
2,339,511	3,198,062	4,157,545	5,759,394	6,907,612	7,946,627	9,706,397	10,652,017	10,797,624	10,887,325
		790,391	2,028,283	2,336,434	2,233,351	2,328,284	2,559,253	3,025,290	3,157,604
52,465	174,768	413,536	783,389	1,089,684	1,521,341	1,768,687	2,091,385	2,633,149	2,853,733
2,906,215	4,282,891	6,302,115	8,720,017	9,900,180	10,498,012	11,319,366	11,793,909	11,863,895	11,924,710
174,620	276,531	428,556	604,397	713,346	791,896	859,488	949,723	947,154	1,005,984
703,708	995,577	1,340,316	1,683,724	1,899,804	2,117,027	2,382,594	2,590,516	3,121,833	3,505,707
4,837	98,268	401,570	636,547	642,961	652,740	680,514	666,257	690,768	699,999
1,109,801	1,542,359	2,020,616	2,337,885	2,915,841	3,291,718	3,567,089	3,924,164	4,591,120	4,896,641
604,215	1,591,749	3,048,710	4,663,228	6,414,824	7,711,194	9,579,677	11,196,730	14,229,288	17,059,805
40,273	143,963	276,749	449,396	550,310	688,862	890,627	1,059,273	1,461,037	1,727,784
315,098	332,286	343,641	352,428	359,231	377,747	389,881	444,732	511,456	564,964
1,219,630	1,512,565	1,854,184	2,309,187	2,677,773	3,318,680	3,966,949	4,648,494	5,346,818	6,216,568
11,594	75,116	518,103	1,356,621	1,736,191	2,378,963	2,853,214	3,409,169	4,132,180	4,887,941
376,688	618,457	958,800	1,463,701	1,901,974	2,005,552	1,860,421	1,744,237	1,950,279	1,801,625
775,881	1,315,497	2,069,042	2,632,067	3,137,587	3,434,575	3,951,777	4,417,933	4,705,521	4,906,745
	20,789	92,531	194,402	250,742	290,529	330,066	332,416	469,557	455,975
31,443,321	50,189,209	76,212,168	106,021,537	132,164,569	151,325,798	179,323,175	203,235,298	226,547,346	249,632,692

[4] Maine figures for 1770 through 1800 are for that area of Massachusetts which became the State of Maine in 1820. Massachusetts figures exclude Maine from 1770 through 1800, but include it from 1650 through 1750. Massachusetts figure for 1650 also includes population of Plymouth (1,566), a separate colony until 1691.

[5] Oklahoma figure for 1900 includes population of Indian Territory (392,060).

[6] West Virginia figures for 1790 through 1860 are for that area of Virginia which became West Virginia in 1863. These figures are excluded from the figures for Virginia from 1790 through 1860.

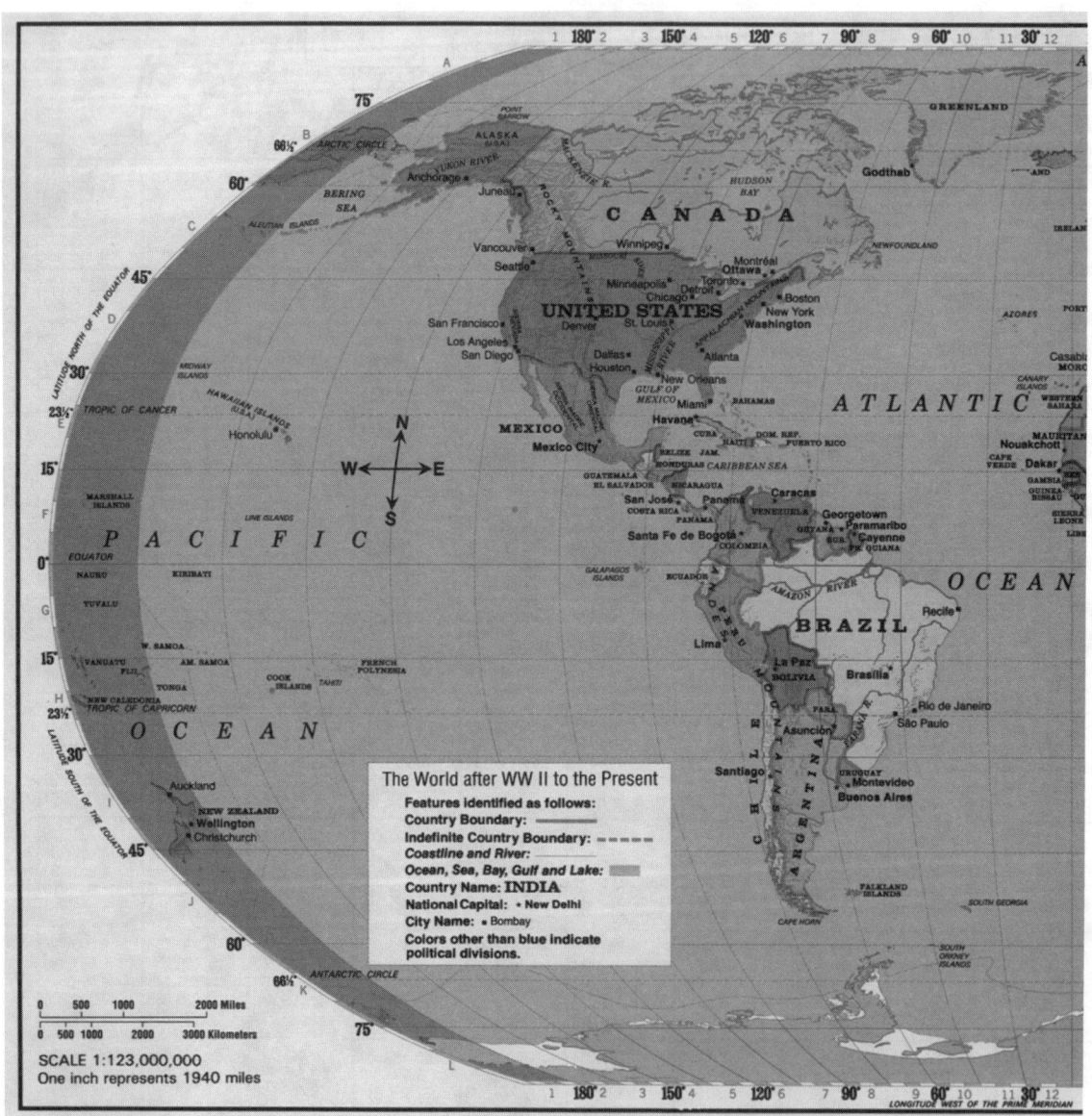

Post World War II

| 1946 Cold War begins | 1947 Marshall Plan proposed | 1949 NATO is formed | 1950 Korean War begins | 1953 Eisenhower becomes president | 1954 Supreme Court decision on school segregation | 1961 John F. Kennedy becomes president | 1962 First U.S. manned space orbit | 1963 J.F.K. assassinated | 1964 Civil Rights Act passed | 1968 Martin Luther King assassinated | 1969 U.S. astronauts land on the moon |

Taft-Hartley Act passed

1945 1947 1949 1951 1953 1955 1957 1959 1961 1963 1965 1967 1969

Europe after WW II to 1994

0   100   200   300 miles

44

Map (c) by Rand McNally, R.L. 95-S-266.

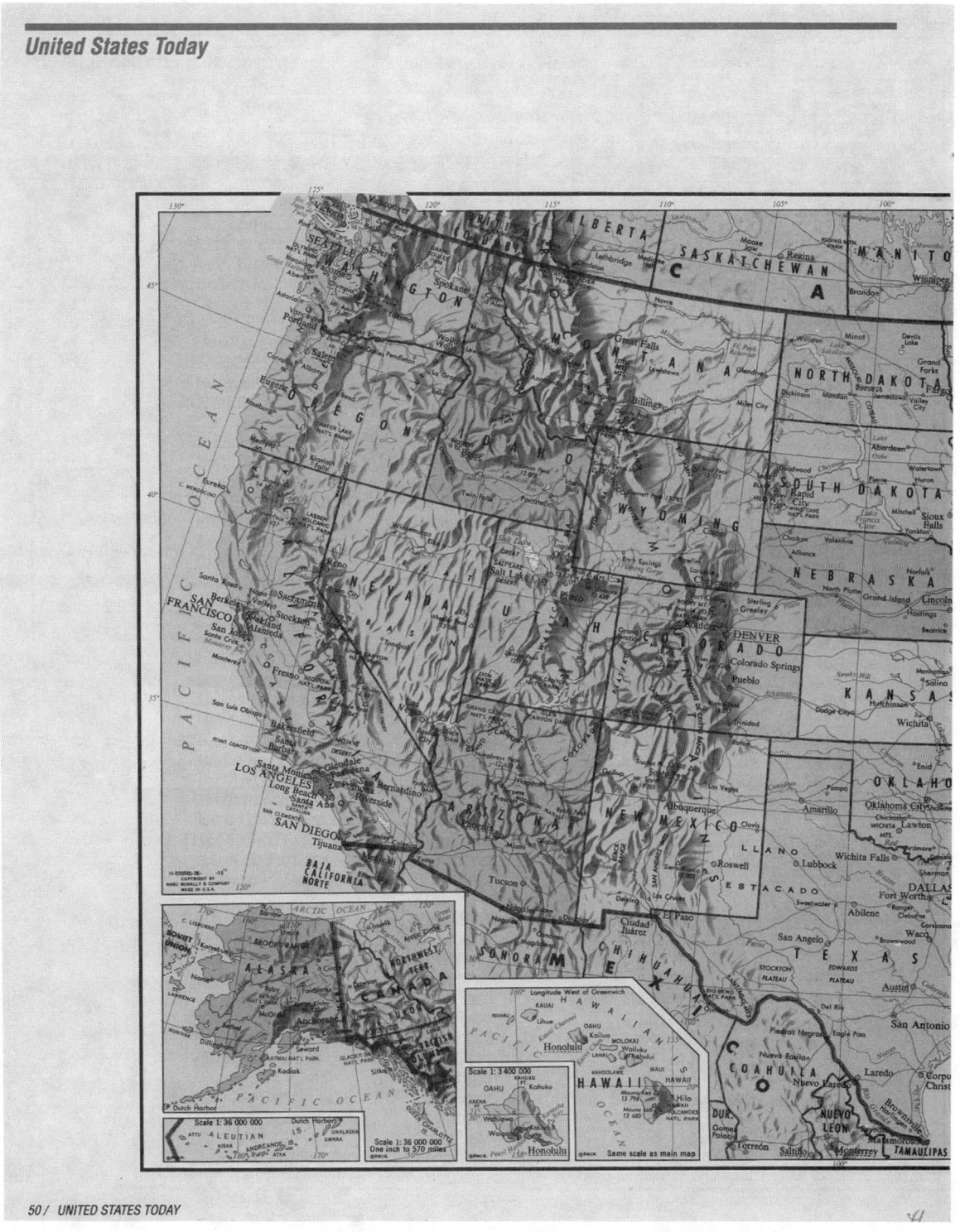

Map (c) by Rand McNally, R.L. 95-S-266.

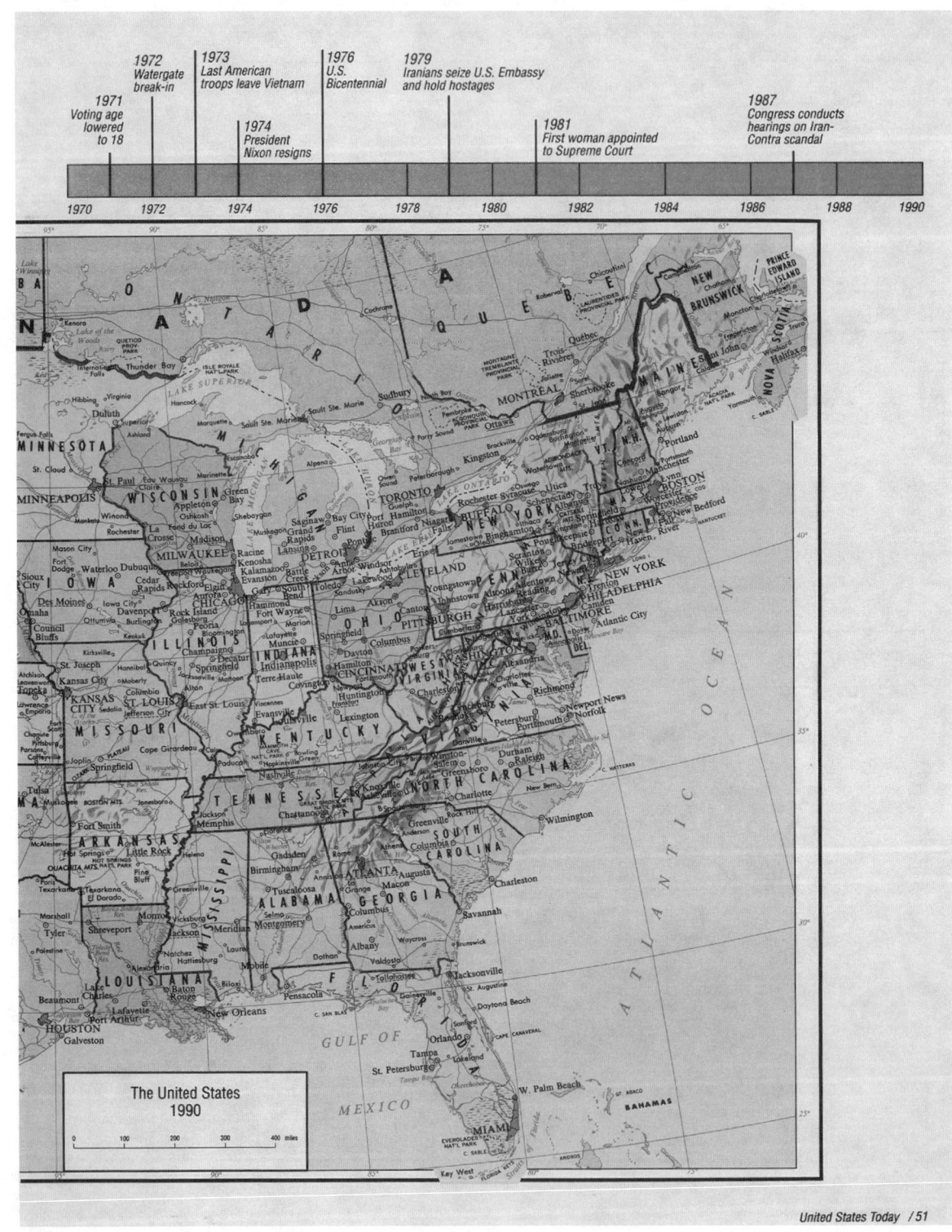

1971
Voting age
lowered
to 18

1972
Watergate
break-in

1973
Last American
troops leave Vietnam

1974
President
Nixon resigns

1976
U.S.
Bicentennial

1979
Iranians seize U.S. Embassy
and hold hostages

1981
First woman appointed
to Supreme Court

1987
Congress conducts
hearings on Iran-
Contra scandal

1970   1972   1974   1976   1978   1980   1982   1984   1986   1988   1990

The United States
1990

0   100   200   300   400 miles

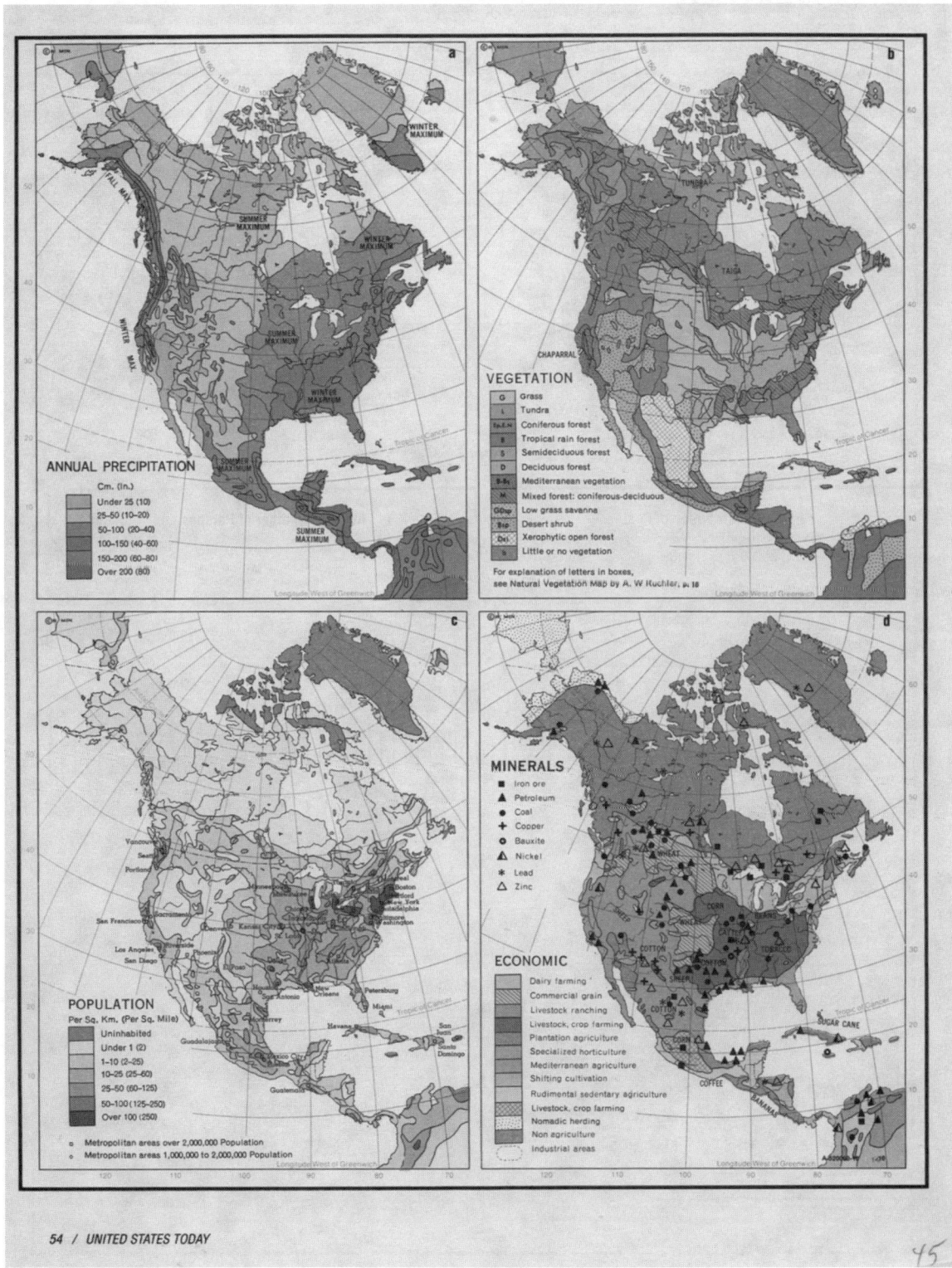

Map (c) by Rand McNally, R.L. 95-S-266.

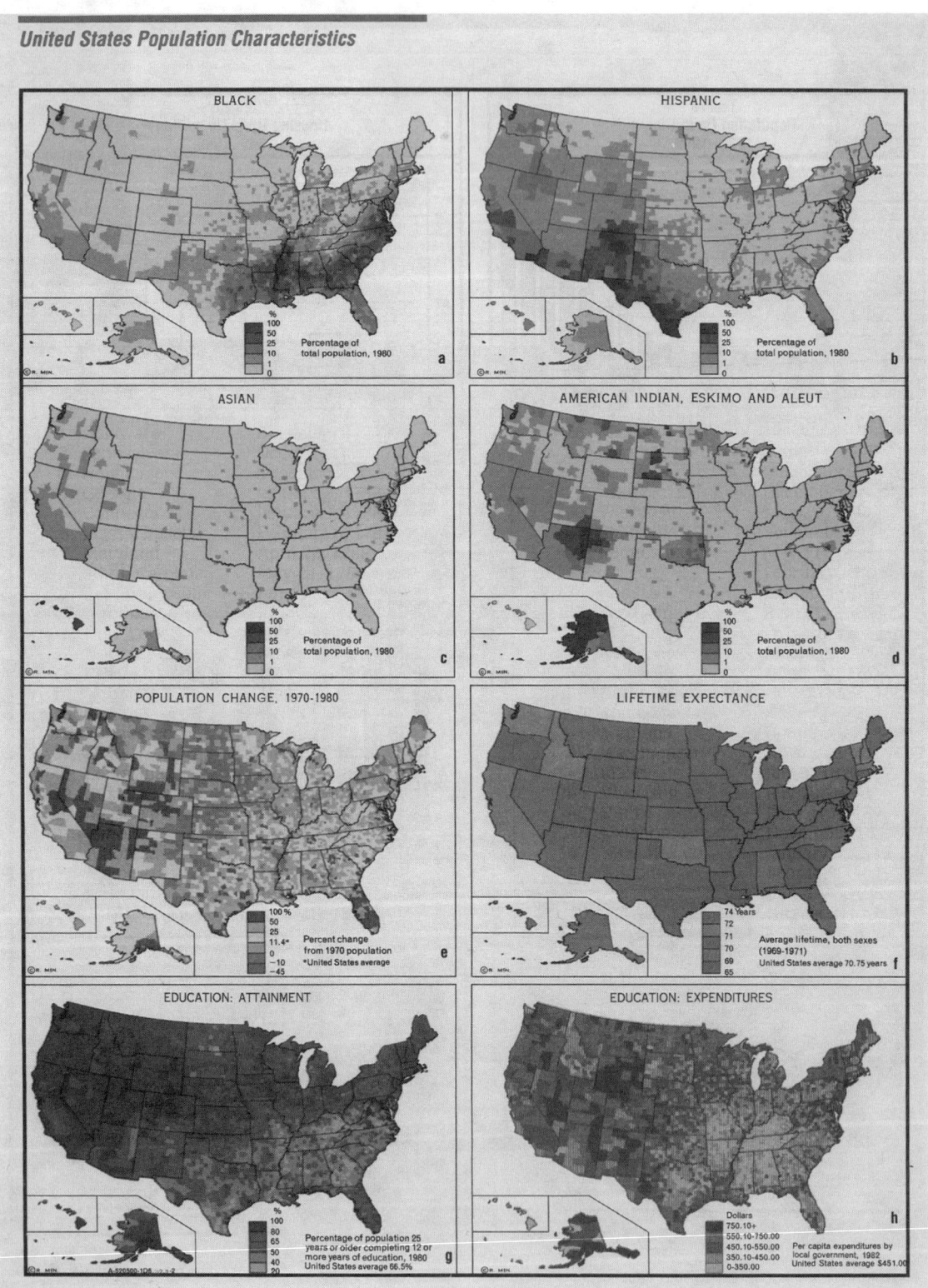

Map (c) by Rand McNally, R.L. 95-S-266.

INDEX